October 10, 1973: Agnew resigns and pleads 'no contest' to tax evasion charge.

October 12, 1973: Appeals court orders Nixon to surrender tapes.

October 19, 1973: Nixon proposes 'Stennis compromise' on tapes. Cox rejects Nixon order forbidding an appeal.

October 20, 1973: Nixon fires Cox; Richardson quits; Ruckelshaus fired.

October 23, 1973: Nixon reverses position, promises tapes to Sirica, after protest telegrams flood Congress.

October 30, 1973: House begins impeachment inquiry.

October 31, 1973: White House lawyers tell court two key tapes never existed.

November 1, 1973: Saxbe named attorney general; Jaworski appointed as new special prosecutor.

November 21, 1973: Erasure of subpoenaed tape of Nixon-Haldeman conversation disclosed.

December 8, 1973: Nixon discloses data on personal finances.

Jan. 4, 1974: Nixon tells the Senate Watergate Committee he will not comply with its subpoenas for tapes and documents.

Jan. 15, 1974: Panel of experts examining the tapes surrendered by Nixon reports that an 18-minute gap in one of the tapes was caused by at least five separate erasing and re-recording operations, and not by a single, accidental erasure.

Jan. 24, 1974: Egil Krogh Jr. sentenced to six months in prison.

Feb. 6, 1974: The House approves 401–4 Judiciary Committee's impeachment investigation and grants the panel broad subpoena power to compel testimony or production of documents from any source, including the President.

Feb. 8, 1974: Gesell dismisses Senate Watergate Committee's suit.

Feb. 14, 1974: Jaworski writes to Sen. Eastland that he and the White House have reached an impasse on release of tapes.

Feb. 21, 1974: House Judiciary Committee's staff report states that violation of criminal law need not be a requisite for impeachment.

Feb. 25, 1974: Nixon asserts at a televised news conference that he does not expect to be impeached.

March 1, 1974: Watergate grand jury indicts Haldeman, Ehrlichman, Colson, Strachan, Mitchell, Mardian and Parkinson on charges of covering up the Watergate break-in.

March 7, 1974: St. Clair writes Rodino that Nixon would provide the House Judiciary Committee with the same materials already given to Jaworski, but would not comply with requests for further materials. Watergate grand jury indicts Ehrlichman, Colson, Liddy, Barker, Martinez and DeDiego for 1971 break-in at Ellsberg's psychiatrist's office.

March 18, 1974: Sirica rules that the grand jury report on Nixon's role in Watergate case should be sent to the House Judiciary Committee. Decision upheld by the U.S. Court of Appeals March 21.

March 19, 1974: Sen. James L. Buckley (Cons-Rep, N.Y.) urges Nixon to resign because he had lost his 1972 election mandate to carry out his proclaimed goals.

April 3, 1974: White House announces Nixon will pay $465,000 in back taxes plus interest on the basis of a report from the IRS.

April 5, 1974: Chapin convicted of perjury.

April 8, 1974: Sen. Lowell P. Weicker Jr. (R, Conn.) accuses the IRS of politically motivated tax audits of individuals and organizations opposed to the President.

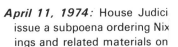

April 11, 1974: House Judici[ary] issue a subpoena ordering Nix[on to turn over tapes of conversat]ings and related materials on [...]

April 18, 1974: Sirica issues a new subpoena for tapes of 64 presidential conversations from June 20, 1972 to June 4, 1973.

April 28, 1974: Mitchell and Stans acquitted of all charges.

April 29, 1974: Nixon announces on national television that he will turn over 1,200 pages of edited transcripts of his conversations.

May 9, 1974: House Judiciary Committee opens hearings with a brief public session, and then goes into closed session to hear a presentation of events leading to the break-in.

May 16, 1974: Kleindienst pleads guilty to a misdemeanor charge of incomplete testimony before a Congressional committee.

May 21, 1974: Magruder sentenced to 10 months–4 years in prison.

May 22, 1974: Nixon informs House Committee he will not comply with May 15 subpoenas or any future subpoenas "allegedly dealing with Watergate."

May 30, 1974: House Judiciary Committee notifies Nixon that his refusal to comply with subpoenas "might constitute a ground for impeachment."

June 3, 1974: Colson pleads guilty to felony charge of obstruction in Ellsberg trial.

June 6, 1974: White House acknowledges that the Watergate grand jury in February named Nixon as an unindicted co-conspirator in Watergate cover-up.

June 7, 1974: Kleindienst receives a suspended sentence.

June 11, 1974: Kissinger threatens to resign unless charges that he participated in wiretapping and had prior knowledge of formation of 'plumbers' are cleared up.

June 14, 1974: Gesell orders Ehrlichman to stand trial June 26 with three other defendants for 1971 Fielding break-in.

July 8, 1974: St. Clair and Jaworski argue executive privilege before Supreme Court.

July 11, 1974: Committee releases 4,133-page record of evidence assembled by staff about Watergate break-in and aftermath.

July 12, 1974: Ehrlichman, Liddy, Barker, and Martinez found guilty of violating civil rights of Dr. Lewis J. Fielding, Ellsberg's psychiatrist.

July 13, 1974: Senate Watergate Committee issues final report, focusing on campaign abuses.

July 24, 1974: The Supreme Court rules 8–0 that Nixon must provide 64 tapes subpoenaed by Jaworski.

July 30, 1974: House Judiciary Committee recesses after approving three articles of impeachment, charging Nixon with obstruction of justice in connection with Watergate scandal, abuse of presidential powers and attempting to impede the impeachment process by defying committee subpoenas for evidence. The White House turns over to Sirica 20 Watergate-related tapes.

July 31, 1974: Ehrlichman is sentenced to 20 months–5 years in prison.

Aug. 5, 1974: Nixon issues statement admitting he tried to obstruct the investigation of the Watergate break-in in June 1972. Earlier in the day, Sen. Robert P. Griffin (Mich.), assistant Senate Republican leader, called for Nixon's resignation.

Aug. 6, 1974: Nixon tells the Cabinet he will not resign.

Aug. 8, 1974: Nixon announces his resignation.

Aug. 9, 1974: Gerald Ford sworn in as President.

WATERGATE
AND THE WHITE HOUSE

January/September 1974

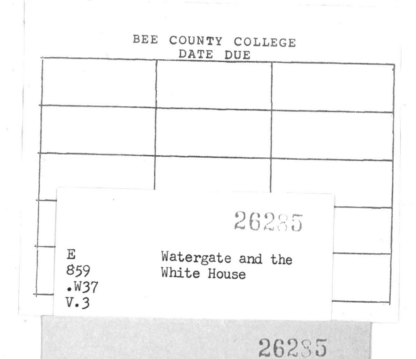

BEE COUNTY COLLEGE
DATE DUE

26285

E
859
.W37
V.3

Watergate and the
White House

26285

E
859
.W37
V.3

Watergate and the White
House

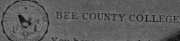
Volume 3

WATERGATE
AND THE WHITE HOUSE

January/September 1974

Editors: Edward W. Knappman and Evan Drossman

Contributing Writers: Judith Buncher, Mary Elizabeth
Clifford, Joseph Fickes, Christopher Hunt,
Stephen Orlofsky, Gerald Satterwhite, Henry H.
Schulte, Jr.

Volume 3

Facts On File, Inc. / 119 West 57th Street / New York City, New York   10019

WATERGATE
AND THE WHITE HOUSE
January/September 1974

Volume 3

Copyright 1974, by Facts On File, Inc.

Library of Congress Catalog Card No. 73-83049.

ISBN 0-87196-354-X

9 8 7 6 5 4 3 2 1

PRINTED IN THE UNITED STATES OF AMERICA

(Cover photo: U.S. Library of Congress)

Preface

This third and final volume of Watergate and the White House *records the resignation and pardon of Richard Nixon and the developments that led up to these dramatic events. It covers from January through September 1974, the period when the three branches of the federal government moved inexorably toward a confrontation over fundamental Constitutional issues. The first section of Volume Three traces developments from the experts' report on the mysterious tape gap through President Ford's decision to pardon Richard Nixon for all crimes he committed or may have committed during his tenure as President. Written by the editors of the* Facts On File Weekly News Digest, *this section reports every important event, statement and court decision—clearly, concisely and objectively.*

The second half of the volume consists of full-text editorials from some 120 major newspapers commenting on the principal Watergate developments between January and September. Carefully selected by the editors of Editorials On File, *these 300 editorials represent a true cross-section of American opinion on every important aspect of the Watergate Affair.*

Edward W. Knappman
October 1, 1974

Contents

WATERGATE DEVELOPMENTS JANUARY–SEPTEMBER 1974

EDITORIAL REACTION TO THE WATERGATE AFFAIR

Biographical Sketches

ABPLANALP, Robert H.: Personal friend of President Nixon whose income tax returns were subpoenaed by Watergate prosecution in connection with Howard Hughes' $100,000 gift.

BARKER, Bernard L.: Former CIA agent arrested at Watergate break-in, pleaded guilty at trial, sentenced, later changed plea to not guilty. Convicted of violating civil rights of Daniel Ellsberg's psychiatrist.

BITTMAN, William O.: Howard Hunt's attorney, cited as contact for pay off of Hunt.

BUCHANAN, Patrick J.: Nixon speechwriter, testified at Senate Watergate hearings that Democrats were guilty of similar campaign activities as those allegedly committed by GOP.

BURCH, Dean: Former chairman of the FCC who became counselor to the President with cabinet rank in Feb. 1974.

CASEY, William J.: Chairman of the SEC in 1972 when Robert Vesco contributed to the Nixon re-election campaign. Testified in Mitchell-Stans trial.

CHAPIN, Dwight L.: Haldeman's former chief aide and appointments secretary to President Nixon, sentenced to a prison term of 10–30 months in May 1974 for lying to a grand jury about his involvement in political sabotage operations during the 1972 campaign.

COLSON, Charles W.: Former special counsel to the President, sentenced to 1–3 years in prison and fined $5,000 in June 1974. Colson pleaded guilty to a charge that he obstructed justice by disseminating derogatory information in 1971 about Daniel Ellsberg.

CONNALLY Jr., John B.: Indicted for receiving payoffs by Associated Milk Producers, Inc., former Secretary of the Treasury.

COOK, G. Bradford: Former SEC chairman who resigned because of his involvement in the Mitchell-Stans case. Testified that Mitchell and Stans had attempted to block an SEC investigation of Robert Vesco in exchange for a contribution to Nixon's 1972 campaign.

COX, Archibald: Former Harvard law professor, appointed special Watergate prosecutor by Attorney General Richardson, fired at President Nixon's order following disagreement over Watergate tapes.

DANNER, Richard G.: Aide to Howard Hughes.

DEAN 3rd, John W.: Former counsel to the President, forced to resign, admitted helping to coordinate Watergate cover-up and implicated President Nixon in Senate testimony, pleaded guilty to one count of conspiracy while agreeing to be a witness for federal prosecution. Sentenced to 1–4 years in prison.

DOAR, John M.: Chief counsel of the House Judiciary Committee.

EHRLICHMAN, John D.: Former advisor to the President on domestic affairs, found guilty July 1974 of conspiring to violate the civil rights of Dr. Lewis J. Fielding, Daniel Ellsberg's psychiatrist. He was also found guilty of three of four counts of making false statements. Sentenced to 20 months–5 years in prison.

ELLSBERG, Daniel: Defendant in Pentagon Papers trial, freed when the case was dismissed following disclosure of the White House 'plumbers' group's break-in at his psychiatrist's office.

FIELDING, Fred F.: Former aide to White House counsel John W. Dean 3rd, resigned January 1974 as deputy White House counsel.

FORD, Gerald R.: Former House minority leader, nominated and confirmed to succeed Agnew as vice president. Became President August 1974, upon Nixon's resignation.

GESELL, Judge Gerhard A.: U.S. District Court judge, presiding in 'plumbers' trial, sentenced Colson and Ehrlichman.

GURNEY, Sen. Edward J.: Republican member of Senate Watergate committee, indicted by Federal grand jury for bribery and perjury.

HAIG Jr., Gen. Alexander M.: Former Army vice chief of staff, named permanent chief of White House staff to replace Haldeman.

HALDEMAN, H. R.: Former White House chief of staff, indicted in Watergate cover-up, accused of organizing GOP espionage operations, resigned from office in April 1973.

HUGHES, Howard R.: Billionaire industrialist, gave campaign gift to Nixon friend Rebozo, which allegedly was returned 3 years later.

HUNT Jr., E. Howard: Former White House consultant, convicted Watergate conspirator, sentenced to 30 months–8 years in prison and fined $10,000.

HUTCHINSON, Rep. Edward: Ranking Republican representative on House Judiciary Committee.

JACOBSEN, Jake: Former Associated Milk Producers attorney indicted for having made a false declaration before the Watergate grand jury in connection with dairy industry political contributions, indictment dismissed for poorly-worded questioning of Jacobsen by Watergate prosecutors, re-indicted in connection with Connally case.

JAWORSKI, Leon: Houston lawyer who replaced Cox as Watergate special prosecutor.

KALMBACH, Herbert W.: President Nixon's personal attorney, pleaded guilty to two violations of the Federal Corrupt Practices Act and sentenced to 6–18 months in prison and a $10,000 fine.

KISSINGER, Henry A.: Secretary of State, denied instigating the 1969–1971 wiretapping of people with access to sensitive information and denied having prior knowledge of the creation of the 'plumbers', threatened to resign if charges were not cleared up.

KLEINDIENST, Richard G.: Former U.S. Attorney General, pleaded guilty to a misdemeanor charge of failing to testify 'accurately' before a Senate hearing, received suspended sentence.

KROGH Jr., Egil: Former White House aide, transportation undersecretary, once headed 'plumbers', sentenced to 6 months in prison for break-in at Ellsberg's psychiatrist's office.

LIDDY, G. Gordon: Former presidential assistant and counsel to Finance Committee to Re-Elect the President, convicted for Watergate break-in. Sentenced to 6–20 years in prison.

MAGRUDER, Jeb Stuart: Former deputy director of Committee to Re-Elect the President, sentenced to 10 months–4 years in prison for role in plotting the Watergate break-in and cover-up.

MARDIAN, Robert C.: Former assistant attorney general, indicted on charges of covering up Watergate break-in, pleaded innocent.

MARTINEZ, Eugenio: Associate of Bernard Baker, arrested at Watergate break-in, sentenced to prison and paroled, convicted for Dr. Fielding's office burglary.

McCLORY, Rep. Robert: House Judiciary Committee's second ranking Republican, voted for impeachment.

McCORD Jr., James W.: Former CIA agent, convicted Watergate conspirator, appealed conviction charging that Nixon had 'deliberately concealed and suppressed' evidence of improper government conduct in the case. Sentenced to 1–5 years in prison.

MITCHELL, John N.: Former U.S. attorney general, director of the Committee to Re-Elect the President, acquitted of all charges stemming from a secret cash campaign contribution from Robert Vesco, indicted for conspiracy, obstruction of justice, perjury, and false statements to the FBI, pleaded not guilty.

O'BRIEN, Paul L.: Attorney for Committee to Re-Elect the President, alleged to have been told by Hunt that he wanted $120,000 to make no further disclosures.

PARKINSON, Kenneth W.: Former CREP attorney, indicted in Watergate cover-up, pleaded not guilty.

REBOZO, Charles G. (Bebe): Personal friend of President Nixon, reported to have kept $100,000 political contribution from Howard Hughes to Nixon fund for three years before returning it, alleged to have been financial banker in Nixon purchase of San Clemente estate.

REINECKE, Ed: Lieutenant Governor of California, convicted of perjury before a Senate committee investigating the political implications of antitrust settlements involving the International Telephone & Telegraph Corp.

RODINO Jr., Rep. Peter W.: Chairman of House Judiciary Committee.

ST. CLAIR, James D.: Boston lawyer named special presidential counsel in charge of Watergate matters, January 1974, replacing Fred Buzhardt, Jr.

SEARS, Harry L.: Former New Jersey State Senator (R), head of Nixon campaign in New Jersey, scheduled for separate trial in Vesco case.

SILBERT, Earl J.: Headed the original Watergate prosecution team while an assistant US attorney, nominated by President Nixon to be U.S. attorney for the District of Columbia January 1974, criticized at Senate hearings on nomination for mishandling Watergate investigation.

SIRICA, Judge John J.: Watergate conspiracy trial judge, charged that prosecution had failed to develop all the facts behind break-in, handed down long prison terms credited with forcing conspirators to talk, ruled in favor of grand jury access to secret White House tapes.

STANS, Maurice H.: Former chief GOP fund raiser and chairman of the Finance Committee to Re-Elect the President, accused of conspiracy, obstruction of justice and perjury for attempting to block SEC investigation of Vesco contribution, acquitted in April 1974 trial.

STRACHAN, Gordon C.: Former presidential aide, indicted in Watergate cover-up, pleaded not guilty.

STURGIS, Frank A.: Convicted of burglary, wiretapping and conspiracy in connection with Watergate break-in, sentenced to prison, paroled, and resentenced to prison for transporting stolen cars.

VESCO, Robert L.: Financier under Federal indictment on charges stemming from a secret $200,000 contribution made to the President's re-election campaign in an alleged attempt to influence an investigation by the SEC.

WALTERS, Vernon A.: Deputy CIA director, disclosed in Senate testimony that White House aides had attempted to enlist agency's aid for 'plumbers' operations.

WEICKER Jr., Sen. Lowell P.: Republican member of Senate Watergate committee, outspoken in criticism of Nixon Watergate positions.

WIGGINS, Rep. Charles E.: Republican member of House Judiciary Committee, outspoken defender of the President during impeachment debate.

YOUNG Jr., David R.: Former National Security Council member, granted immunity from prosecution of Los Angeles break-in charges in return for testimony.

Tape Struggle
& Impeachment Pressures

Nixon rejects committee subpoenas. President Richard M. Nixon informed the Senate Watergate Committee Jan. 4 that he would not comply with its wide-ranging subpoenas for tapes and documents, but later comments by White House aides and committee sources indicated that a compromise might be in the making.

In a letter to Committee Chairman Sam J. Ervin Jr. (D, N.C.), Nixon called the three subpoenas "an overt attempt to intrude into the executive to a degree that constitutes an unconstitutional usurpation of power." Compliance with the subpoenas, Nixon said, would "destroy any vestige of confidentiality of presidential communications."

Nixon noted that the subpoenas had listed, "with widely varying precision," broad categories of presidential material, sometimes identified by participants and time spans measured in months and years. Prominent among these, Nixon added, was the request for his daily diary for almost four years.

"Neither the judiciary nor the Congress," Nixon said, "could survive a similar power asserted by the executive branch to rummage through their files and confidential processes."

Nixon also told Ervin that "disclosures to you, and through you to the public" could "seriously impair" the work of the special prosecutor and the Watergate grand juries in their effort to prosecute criminal cases "which may arise." "Incurring these adverse consequences," Nixon continued, would "serve no legislative purpose which I can discern."

Nixon said that "in the current environment" there might be "some attempt to distort my position as only an effort to withhold information," but concluded that he must "protect the office of the President."

In a statement released later Jan. 4, Ervin replied that the committee had "no desire to gain access to any confidential communications" relating to the President's performance of "constitutional or legal duties," but only evidence relating to political activities by Nixon, his aides and re-election committees, and "information in the possession of the President of criminal violations on the part of his aides."

Ervin said the committee "necessarily had to subpoena tapes and materials believing that the White House would not obey" and that the subpoenas might lead to a judicial determination of what materials might be relevant.

Samuel Dash, chief committee counsel, said no action to enforce the subpoenas would be taken until after a new ruling on the enforcement of its subpoena for five tapes served in July 1973. [See below] Acknowledging that the latest subpoenas covered "quite a bit," Dash said they could be cut down to "high priority items" before the issue was taken to court. However, Dash said every new tape and document requested had been carefully selected as relevant to the Senate investigation.

In an appearance on the National Broadcasting Co.'s "Meet the Press" program Jan. 6, Vice President Gerald R. Ford supported Nixon's refusal to comply with subpoenas which Ford called "far too broad, far too much of a fishing expedition." But, Ford continued, if the committee was "willing to make some refinements in the demand, cutting it down to things that are more relevant," then there "may be—and I underline 'may be'—an area of compromise."

Deputy White House Press Secretary Gerald L. Warren said Ford had been "speaking as vice president" and that "nothing has changed since the President's letter [to Ervin]." Warren denied there was any split between Nixon and Ford, adding that if the committee "sent something new down we'd have to evaluate it based upon the attitude reflected in the request."

News reports Jan. 9 quoted White House officials and Ervin as hinting at compromise. The presidential aides said Nixon might be willing to release some material on a limited, voluntary basis but would not yield to subpoenas. And Ervin suggested that the committee's main concern was the tapes covered in its first subpoena.

Panel asks enforcement of first subpoena—The Senate Watergate Committee petitioned the federal district court Jan. 7 to enforce its original subpoena for presidential tapes and documents, a request which had earlier been dismissed for lack of jurisdiction by Judge John J. Sirica. The U.S. Court of Appeals had returned the case to Sirica for a ruling under a new law on jurisdiction.

The purpose of the litigation, the committee said in a memorandum to the court, was to definitively establish the right to have its subpoenas enforced. Events which had occurred since Sirica's dismissal of the case in October 1973 supported that right, the committee argued. Among them were the new jurisdiction law and the fact that Nixon had released material to the special Watergate prosecutor—including four of the five conversations sought by the committee.

The committee contended that, unlike the special prosecutor, it had an "informing function" which demanded "public revelation of all Watergate facts" to "deter repetition in the future of wrongdoing by government officials." To permit the President to "pick and choose among evidence . . .withholding the best," would represent "a serious disservice to the legislature, the public . . . and the investigatory process," the memo said.

The committee also stressed the legislative purpose of its investigation, noting that it had been considering wide-ranging political reforms to prevent future scandals. Among these, the memo said, were a constitutional amendment limiting presidential tenure to one term, "drastically" curtailing a President's participation in the campaign to choose his successor, and severely limiting the amount of private money contributed to campaigns.

Sirica, as chief judge, reassigned the case to Judge Gerhard A. Gesell. Nixon was given 10 days to reply.

White House legal team revamped. Boston lawyer James D. St. Clair was named special presidential counsel in charge of Watergate matters, replacing J. Fred Buzhardt Jr., the White House announced Jan. 4.

Buzhardt was named counsel to the President—technically a promotion, but widely seen as a reflection of presidential

C

D

E

F

G

dissatisfaction with his handling of the tapes issue.

Leonard Garment, who as acting counsel was prominent in Watergate legal matters, was named assistant to the President, primarily in domestic affairs, the White House said.

St. Clair, a partner in the firm of Hale and Dorr and Harvard Law School lecturer, had worked with the late Joseph N. Welch as Army counsel during the late Sen. Joseph R. McCarthy's 1954 investigation.

The White House announced Jan. 8 that Charles Alan Wright would return as a legal consultant to handle executive privilege issues involved in the Senate Watergate Committee's subpoenas.

Saxbe becomes attorney general. William B. Saxbe was sworn in Jan. 4 as attorney general. In remarks at the Justice Department ceremony, Saxbe called himself a "law and order man" predicated on his belief in "a society operated in a manner to give each individual the opportunity to express himself without the fear of Big Brother taking over [or] interfering in his personal life . . . in the name of protection or in the name of defense."

In a UPI interview Jan. 3, Saxbe said he had accepted President Nixon's nomination to the post in 1973 with only one condition—"that I'll be able to talk with him when I need to."

On the special federal Watergate prosecution being conducted by Leon Jaworski, Saxbe affirmed the probe's independence. "He has his operation and I have mine," Saxbe said. "I don't know of any place I'd get involved unless he wants me to."

He also offered some opinions on the Senate Watergate committee's probe—that its subpoena of more than 400 White House tapes and documents was a "fishing expedition" motivated "to keep [the committee] in business" and that the committee's action would "come to a point where the President has to decide whether there is any privacy in his office."

Saxbe said he favored "vigorous enforcement of the antitrust laws," saying "conglomerates have hurt more people than they've helped." He said he supported a Justice Department probe of whether the big oil corporations had acted deliberately in some instances to contribute to the fuel shortage.

Saxbe, who had announced he would not seek re-election in 1974, resigned from the Senate Jan. 3.

Metzenbaum gets Senate seat. Howard M. Metzenbaum (D), 56, was sworn in to replace William B. Saxbe (R) in the Senate Jan. 4. Metzenbaum was appointed to the year remaining in the term by Ohio Gov. John J. Gilligan (D) Dec. 19, 1973.

Metzenbaum commented on Watergate in the ceremony Jan. 4 when he became the Senate's 58th Democrat. Metzenbaum said President Nixon had been "less than frank with the American people" in the Watergate scandals and should obey subpoenas from the Senate Watergate committee for the more than 400 White House tapes and documents, unless the courts barred the subpoenas.

Nixon popularity rating 29%. President Nixon's final popularity rating for 1973, as measured by the Gallup Poll, was 29%. Those disapproving of the way he was handling his job as president totaled 60% (11% held no opinion).

The rating, published Jan. 6 from a Dec. 7–10, 1973 sampling, represented a 39-point decline since January 1973, when a record 68% approved of Nixon's performance in office, the steepest decline since the popularity rating was first surveyed in the presidency of Franklin D. Roosevelt.

A key factor in the decline was the Watergate scandal, according to the Gallup analysis, which pointed out that in surveys since June 1973, 75% of the public had held the view that Nixon was "at least to some extent involved in the scandal." The analysis cited inflation as another major factor in the popularity loss.

Nixon's average popularity rating for the year 1973 was 42% (47% disapproval), compared with his ratings of 62% for 1969, 57% for 1970, 50% for 1971 and 51% for 1972.

'Thin hold on office'—A Roper survey to test public reaction to talk of possible impeachment of President Nixon showed that 79% of respondents queried in depth believed one or more of the most serious charges against Nixon were justified. The survey, published Jan. 6, reported a one-point majority against impeachment—45%–44%, but only 11% of those opposed based their stand on belief that the charges were unjustified. The interpretation was that the opposition to impeachment arose not from belief in Nixon's innocence but from fear of the unsettling effect of an impeachment.

According to the Roper analysis, "the President would seem to have a thin hold indeed on his office in the court of public opinion." The interviewing for the survey was conducted in early November 1973 before disclosure of the 18-minute gap in a key White House tape sought by the federal Watergate prosecution.

Of those persons polled who believed that at least one or more of 13 serious charges against Nixon were justified, more than 50% believed the charge that he was involved in covering up the Watergate break-in and that he was withholding evidence from investigators.

"Acceptance of both the seriousness of the charges and the President's responsibility for them was widespread throughout all segments of the population," according to the analysis. The most critical groups, it found, were "young people, those in the highest income category, those living in the West, the college-educated, single people, union members, those moderately active socially and politically, and Democrats." Two-thirds of the Republicans accepted one or more of the charges against Nixon, it said.

Among those expressing the least concern about the charges were those 60 years and older, those in the lowest income brackets, those living in sparsely populated rural areas and those with a grade-school education or less.

3 Watergate burglars granted parole. The U.S. Parole Board announced Jan. 7 that it had granted parole, effective March 7, to Eugenio R. Martinez, Frank A. Sturgis and Virgilio R. Gonzalez, all of whom had pleaded guilty to charges of burglary, wiretapping and conspiracy in connection with the Watergate break-in June 17, 1972. (Sturgis was sentenced to nine months in jail Jan. 9 after being convicted in federal court in Miami Nov. 30, 1973 of transporting stolen cars to Mexico. He was to begin serving his term March 7.)

Bail for Watergate conspirator James W. McCord Jr., who had not been imprisoned, was reduced from $50,000 to $5,000 by U.S. District Court Judge John J. Sirica Jan. 8.

Barker: plumbers bugged Soviet embassy—Convicted Watergate burglar Bernard L. Barker told the Miami Herald Jan. 6 the White House "plumbers" had intercepted and taped communications from the Soviet embassy in Washington that showed it had access to the Pentagon Papers. Barker declined to say whether he had heard the tapes, but he insisted they existed.

(The plumbers were created in 1971 to stem news leaks that were thought to threaten national security.)

Impeachment panel studies probe. Chairman Peter W. Rodino Jr. (D, N.J.) of the House Judiciary Committee, which was considering the question of impeachment proceedings against President Nixon, said Jan. 7 the panel's staff "is now dealing with a consideration of the areas in which the inquiry should go, and has yet to reach any conclusions on the questions of what is an impeachable offense and what sort of evidence should be gathered." Rodino said a full report would "hopefully be ready" to be presented to the House by late April.

According to the committee's chief counsel John Doar Jan. 7, the committee had taken soundings on its access to material gathered by the Senate Watergate committee and the special Watergate prosecution and the latter wanted assurance on the security of the information to be made accessible. Doar said an agreement had not yet been reached on this point.

The committee did gain assurance Jan. 7 in another area of concern—a bipartisan approach to its inquiry. Chicago trial lawyer Albert E. Jenner, 66, was named chief legal adviser to the panel's Republican minority, and he immediately praised Doar, his counterpart on the Democratic side. Jenner told reporters, "This is a joint effort. There is no controversy on the professional staff."

Jenner had been senior counsel to the Warren Commission probe of the assassination of President Kennedy. One of his specialities was the field of evidence in federal legal cases.

Nixon issues ITT, milk fund statements. President Nixon Jan. 8 released two white papers detailing his involvement in two controversial decisions made by the Administration in 1971 related to an increase in the federal price support for milk and an antitrust suit against the International Telephone & Telegraph Corp. (ITT). [For further details, see p. 35E1]

Nixon in seclusion at San Clemente. President Nixon celebrated his 61st birthday Jan. 9 in his office at San Clemente, Calif. "He is approaching this year in a positive way," one of his spokesmen, Gerald L. Warren, told reporters.

The President had been in semi-seclusion inside his compound at San Clemente since his arrival in California Dec. 26, 1973. His rare public appearances were essentially private—a wedding in La Jolla Dec. 28, 1973, an excursion drawing hostile protest; church services in San Clemente Jan. 6, his first churchgoing since Easter 1973 (not counting White House worship services); a stop at a McDonald's restaurant Jan. 9 on a 100-mile drive to Palm Springs for a private visit.

The President reportedly was conferring primarily with his chief of staff, Gen. Alexander M. Haig Jr., and press secretary, Ronald L. Ziegler.

Secretary of State Henry A. Kissinger held a series of meetings with the President. At the conclusion, Kissinger held a news conference Jan. 3 to stress that Nixon could function effectively in foreign affairs despite his domestic difficulties, chiefly the threat of impeachment, a question brought up three times at the session. "I have no reason to assume that there will be an impeachment," Kissinger said, and reports that he and not the President was actually in control of American foreign policy were "totally incorrect."

Jaworski withdraws from 4 cases. Special Watergate prosecutor Leon Jaworski had withdrawn from personal involvement in four cases because of possible conflict of interest, it was reported Jan. 9. The cases involved connections with Jaworski's former law firm—Fulbright, Crooker and Jaworski of Houston. [For further details, see p. 37G1]

Fielding resigns. Fred F. Fielding, a former aide to ousted White House counsel John W. Dean 3rd, resigned Jan. 11 as deputy White House counsel. Dean had testified that Fielding had acted as an innocent messenger in delivering cash to H. R. Haldeman, then White House chief of staff, ostensibly for use in "polling" purposes.

Jaworski bars data to House probe. Special Watergate prosecutor Leon Jaworski said Jan. 12 he would resist, unless the courts ruled otherwise, sharing with the House impeachment inquiry any presidential tapes, documents or other information furnished him by the White House. Jaworski said his requests to the White House for information in connection with his federal probe were related to the grand jury procedures and "we have no right to access to that information otherwise. Because of that, we are bound by the rules of secrecy attached to that information."

Jaworski said he considered it improper for him even to supply the House probe with a list of material deemed pertinent to its inquiry.

Asked whether he would give priority to an indictment or an impeachment proceeding against a president, assuming the evidence existed, Jaworski indicated he was inclined to remain within his grand jury preserve although the issue was still unresolved.

Regarding information obtained from the White House, Jaworski said nothing had been volunteered and nothing refused although he had had to threaten to subpoena requested material. Since mid-December 1973, he said, the White House had been cooperating and the information received was "not only substantial but I think meaningful and so far as I know, all of it is relevant." He still had outstanding requests for material that may, he said, have been misfiled or "may not exist."

Jaworski said it was possible that a need for testimony from President Nixon might arise in order to shed more light on his taped conversations.

Saxbe's views—According to Attorney General William B. Saxbe, the House impeachment investigation could "be dragged out" indefinitely if the issue of executive privilege were invoked anew by the President in refusing to turn over tapes or other material. Use of the privilege during an impeachment investigation, he said Jan. 13, "is new ground that has never been explored before and I would guess it's finally going to be decided by the Supreme Court." "The President is certainly entitled to some privilege," Saxbe said. "How much has to be determined."

Saxbe said "there is a serious question whether a president can be indicted" by a federal grand jury and that this might also be taken up by the court.

At his first news conference as attorney general Jan. 11, Saxbe took an opposite view from Jaworski on the matter of sup-

plying information to the impeachment inquiry. He said he expected the special Watergate prosecutor to "cooperate" with the House inquiry as far as he could legally by providing it with information that might arise on criminal activity by the President.

An impeachment itself, Saxbe said, should be based only on "indictable offenses." If it consisted of criminal charges, Saxbe saw a neutral role for the Justice Department in the House and Senate proceedings. He said the department would not help President Nixon fight impeachment by the House unless the House were proceeding on "obviously political grounds" and not on "criminal charges." If the impeachment went to the Senate for trial, he said, the department would have "no role."

In such cases, the President's defense "obviously would be in the hands of his personal attorneys," Saxbe said.

Question of Nixon responsibility. The view that President Nixon should be held responsible for actions of his aides that would be impeachable offenses if committed by the President was expressed on a Chicago television program Jan. 13 by Albert E. Jenner Jr., chief Republican counsel for the House Judiciary Committee's impeachment probe. "Certainly within some areas," he said, "the President should be responsible for the actions of aides even if he didn't know, for example, that an aide was doing something that would be regarded as an impeachable offense if the President himself did it." The President, he said, "can only act through his aides . . . He appoints them and has to be responsible for them."

Judiciary Committee member Charles E. Wiggins (R, Calif.) objected to the remark Jan. 14. He said a staff member should not be "making pronouncements" on the impeachment inquiry.

Saxbe, commenting on the responsibility issue Jan. 15, said he thought it "a rather bizarre theory of American law. We've never been able to impute the illegal activities of the servant to the master," he said. "You have to show collusion . . . or a tie-in."

(Saxbe also disclosed that he had authorized three national security wiretaps during his first week as attorney general.)

Nixon returns to Washington. President Nixon returned to Washington Jan. 13 after an 18-day stay in California. The return flight was on a small Air Force jet departing from Palm Springs. A commercial flight was not used, as it was on the flight to California, because of security considerations.

The President underwent a brief physical examination Jan. 14 and received a good report. A look of weariness at times was attributed to lack of sleep, his physician said. A complete physical scheduled for Dec. 22, 1973 had been postponed. Since his last regular complete check-up a year earlier Nixon had undergone a thorough examination in July 1973 when he was hospitalized with viral pneumonia.

Ford scores drive to 'crush' Nixon. Vice President Gerald R. Ford warned Jan. 15 that President Nixon's critics were waging "an all-out attack" in an attempt to "crush" him and his policies.

Addressing members of the American Farm Bureau Federation in Atlantic City, N.J., Ford identified the President's antagonists as "a few extreme partisans" and as a "relatively small group of political activists." He specifically cited the American Federation of Labor and Congress of Industrial Organizations (AFL-CIO) and Americans for Democratic Action. These and other "powerful pressure organizations," he said, were waging the "massive propaganda campaign against the President of the United States."

"Their aim," Ford said, "is total victory for themselves and the total defeat not only of President Nixon but of the policies for which he stands. If they can crush the President and his philosophy, they are convinced that they can then dominate the Congress and, through it, the nation."

They were attempting "to stretch out the ordeal," he said, "to cripple the President by dragging out the preliminaries to impeachment for as long as they can, and to use the whole affair for maximum political advantage."

If they were successful, the vice president said, "with the super-welfare staters in control of the Congress, and the White House neutralized as a balancing force, we can expect an avalanche of fresh government intervention in our economy, massive new government spending, higher taxes and a more rampant inflation."

Ford said "the majority of responsible, thinking Americans must not let it happen, and I don't believe they will."

Ford reaffirmed his belief that there were no valid grounds for impeachment of Nixon. He said he thought a majority of the House committee inquiring into the issue would reach the same conclusion. "But whatever their feelings," he added, "they owe it to all of us to do their job promptly and responsibly. They have no right to leave America hanging, when so much that is important remains to be done."

(A text of Ford's speech was released by the White House but presidential spokesman Gerald L. Warren assured reporters, while he had "no quarrel" with the speech, President Nixon had not ordered it. A Ford aide similarly assured Ford's independence. "This is the vice president's speech; he meant every word of it." But Warren and Ford both acknowledged Jan. 16 that the speech had been drafted by White House speech writers. Ford said he had provided the ideas.)

Later Jan. 15, the Americans for Democratic Action issued a statement by

its national director, Leon Shull, saying, "No amount of rhetoric by Vice President Ford can obscure the fact that ADA's call for the impeachment of President Nixon is based on solid evidence."

Grant programs politically aimed. Frederic V. Malek, deputy director of the Office of Management and Budget, acknowledged responsibility Jan. 15 for a secret project in 1972, when he was a special assistant to the President, of redirecting federal grants to reap political gain for President Nixon. The acknowledgement followed reports published that day about the secret project and based on memorandums in possession of the Senate Watergate Committee. [For further details, see p. 37C3]

Goldwater blames liberal Democrats. Sen. Barry Goldwater (R, Ariz.) Jan. 15 assailed what he called an "impeachment lobby" to remove President Nixon from office. "This matter has dragged on and on for an insufferable period of time," he said, "for what appears to be no better reasons than to gain political advantage for the liberal Democrats or to make unbearable the life of the President."

Goldwater said he did not think Nixon "will ever resign as President and I don't believe the liberal Democrats have what it takes, either in evidence or guts, to push through an impeachment in the House and a subsequent trial in the Senate."

Goldwater made the remarks in a speech at a Baltimore Republican fund-raising dinner.

Interviewed Jan. 13, on NBC's "Meet the Press," Goldwater was asked about the possibility, which had been subject to speculation, that he might be called upon to be the bearer of the Republican Party's message to Nixon to resign.

"I don't think I would because I don't think it's the prerogative of one man to put himself above 46 or 47 million Americans who voted for Mr. Nixon or the 23 or 24 per cent of the American people who still believe he should be the President."

In his estimation, Nixon had "started a recovery" of his leadership status and was "better off now" than two months ago when he, Goldwater, had considered Nixon's credibility at an "all-time low."

"We have much greater problems in this country and in this world than Watergate," Goldwater said, "and I think the American people are taking that attitude—let's get these other things solved. And unless there's something more unusual about the President in Watergate than what's come out, let's get off his back."

Experts report multiple tape erasures. The panel of technical experts examining the Watergate tape recordings surrendered by President Nixon reported Jan. 15 that an 18½-minute gap in one of the tapes had been caused by at least five separate erasing and rerecording opera-

tions, and not by a single, accidental erasure as the White House had contended.

While the experts declined to characterize the erasures as either accidental or deliberate, the report raised new questions of Nixon's personal credibility and—according to some members of Congress—weakened his position on the issue of impeachment.

The tape in question was of a June 20, 1972 conversation between Nixon and H. R. Haldeman, then his chief of staff. According to Haldeman's notes already in evidence, the conversation had dealt with the Watergate break-in.

In their written report to U.S. District Court Judge John J. Sirica, the experts said "magnetic signatures" measured directly on the tape showed that "buzzing sounds were put on the tape in the process of erasing and rerecording at least five, and perhaps as many as nine, separate and contiguous segments." The erasures involved separate manual operation of keyboard controls on the recorder in making each segment, whether or not a foot control pedal was used.

(Rose Mary Woods, Nixon's personal secretary, had testified in November 1973 that she had accidentally pressed the "record" button on the machine and had kept her foot on the recorder pedal—a combination of actions resulting in erasure—while talking on the phone for about five minutes. White House Chief of Staff Alexander M. Haig Jr. suggested later that Miss Woods might have been on the phone longer than she thought.)

The magnetic "signatures" cited by the panel were put on the tape by the on-and-off operation of the "erase" and "record" heads of the machine. During the series of operations, the report said, the erase head had missed fragments of "speech-like sound" at three places on the tape, each lasting less than one second. The panel said it was impossible to determine what was said in these fragments. Nor would recovery of the portions totally obscured by the buzzing be possible "under any methods known to us."

The buzzing sound itself, the report stated, originated in noise picked up from the electrical power line to which the recorder was connected. Variations in the strength of the buzz "probably arose from several causes," including changes in the noise from the power line, erratic functioning of the recorder, and changes in the position of the operator's hand.

The panel concluded further that the erasing operations had been done directly on the tape in evidence, which was an original, and that the "signatures" were "almost certainly" those of the Uher 5000 recorder already in evidence as the one used by Miss Woods. The panel also said they had found no evidence of "physical splices" on the entire length of the tape.

Questioning members of the panel after the release of the report, assistant special prosecutor Richard Ben-Veniste tried—over the repeated objections of presidential counsel James D. St. Clair—to elicit an opinion as to whether the tape had been erased deliberately.

Thomas G. Stockham Jr., one of six panel members, said they had "no idea when it occurred or who was responsible," but that the pattern of variations on the tape was "thoroughly consistent" with a deliberate start-and-stop process of erasing. Panel member Richard H. Bolt agreed with Ben-Veniste's contention that if it had been an accident, "it would have to be an accident that was repeated at least five times."

Judge Sirica asked Stockham at one point to explain the significance of the magnetic markings. The witness replied that the record head was released each time, "which can only be done by pressing one of the buttons."

"With the hand?" Sirica asked.

"With a hand, or with a stick," Stockham replied to laughter in the courtroom, "but not with a foot pedal."

St. Clair centered his questioning of the panelists on the possibility that defects in the recorder had caused the markings. After Mark R. Weiss said a part on the machine had to be repaired during their testing, St. Clair asked if the defect might have caused the buzz as well as the markings. Possibly the buzzing noise, the witness replied, but not the magnetic signatures.

Under questioning by St. Clair, Bolt stressed that "just how the buzz started" was "not really relevant." What mattered, Bolt said, was the distinct series of "starts and stops" during the gap.

After the hearing, St. Clair remarked to Bolt, "I think I'm going to talk to my own experts."

"I thought we were your experts," Bolt replied. (The panel had been chosen jointly by White House counsel and the special prosecutor's office.)

Asked about the incident by reporters Jan. 16, Deputy White House Press Secretary Gerald L. Warren said he knew of no other experts "in the employ" of the White House.

Testimony before Judge Sirica Jan. 16 tended to narrow the time span during which the erasure could have occurred and at some points contradicted Miss Woods' testimony in November 1973.

Secret Service agent Louis B. Sims said he had arranged purchase of the Uher machine around mid-day Oct. 1, 1973, at the request of presidential assistant Stephen B. Bull, because Miss Woods wanted a machine with a foot-pedal device, unlike the recorder she had been using to make transcriptions. Sims said the recorder was delivered to Bull at 1:15 p.m., then to Miss Woods.

Ben-Veniste noted that Miss Woods had testified she listened to the recording for about 2½ hours before making her "terrible mistake" and immediately informing Nixon of it. Miss Woods had not mentioned using any machine other than the Uher that day, the prosecutor said, and Nixon's logs showed her arriving at his Executive Office Building office at 2:08 p.m. (Miss Woods had also testified that

she had rushed to tell Nixon of the erasure in his White House Oval Office.)

With Bull as witness, Ben-Veniste focused on the question of access to the tape. Bull said he had access, along with Miss Woods and presidential assistant John C. Bennett, custodian of the tape collection. "Beyond that," Bull said, "I would be guessing."

Who had he "heard" to have access? Ben-Veniste asked.

"Mr. Buzhardt delivered the tape to the court, did he not?" Bull replied, "So add him on your list."

(White House counsel J. Fred Buzhardt Jr. had been replaced by St. Clair as special Watergate counsel Jan. 4.)

Bull added that Nixon had access to the tape Sept. 29, 1973 when he visited Miss Woods as she was listening to the tape—and before she received the Uher recorder.

Two Secret Service agents provided insight Jan. 17 into concern within the White House over the taping system and how it might be used regarding the Watergate scandal—long before the system's existence was publicly revealed.

Sims testified that shortly after John W. Dean 3rd, then presidential counsel, warned publicly in April 1973 that he would not let himself be the "scapegoat" in the Watergate case, Bull asked Sims if anyone in the Secret Service had told Dean about the taping system. Sims said he told Bull that the Secret Service had not informed Dean, but that he "could not speak for" the few others who knew about the system.

Under questioning by Ben-Veniste, agent Raymond C. Zumwalt acknowledged that a Secret Service project to improve the taping system—begun in mid-1971—was set aside after the exposure of the Watergate burglary and never completed.

Zumwalt also disclosed that although the automatic taping had been discontinued in July 1973, shortly after the system became publicly known, the microphones remained in their original positions in Nixon's offices. The wires were not cut, Zumwalt said, until "early November [1973]." This was finally done because it was "just not very good policy to have a hot microphone" which might be used again without the Secret Service's knowledge.

Two Democratic members of the Senate Watergate Committee called the disclosure a major blow to Nixon. Daniel K. Inouye (Hawaii) said he was "saddened" because he had been hoping the report would show the erasure to be "the result of some legitimate accident." Joseph M. Montoya (N.M.) said the report "clearly confirms the already prevalent opinion of the nation as to the credibility of the President."

FBI enters probe—A spokesman for the Federal Bureau of Investigation (FBI) said Jan. 16 that, at the request of special Watergate prosecutor Leon Jaworski, the

FBI was beginning an investigation into the tape erasure and would report directly to Jaworski. According to the Justice Department, the special prosecutor had the authority to order an FBI probe without permission from the attorney general.

Deputy White House Press Secretary Gerald L. Warren said Jan. 17 that the White House would "cooperate totally" with the investigation.

White House reaction—Deputy Press Secretary Warren said Jan. 16 that President Nixon had not deliberately or accidentally erased the segment of his conversation with Haldeman. Asked how he knew Nixon was not involved, Warren said there had been "many discussions about this matter with the President."

Warren refused to answer most other questions, referring to the statement released the previous day by special counsel St. Clair, who said that any "premature comment would only contribute further to existing public confusion surrounding the tapes."

"It would be altogether incorrect and improper," St. Clair said, "for premature judgments or conclusions to be reached" in the absence of immediate White House comment and while the judicial process "is still under way."

In separate interviews Jan. 15–16, presidential assistants Stephen B. Bull and John C. Bennett—both of whom had access to the disputed tape—denied having had any part in the erasure.

Congressional reaction—Members of both parties in Congress said Jan. 15 that the technical experts' report on the possibility of tampering with one of the key Watergate tapes would cause a further erosion in public confidence in President Nixon and would provide added impetus to a House committee's consideration of impeachment proceedings.

Sen. Howard H. Baker Jr. (R, Tenn.), vice chairman of the Senate Watergate Committee, called the incident "another in an unfortunate, bizarre set of circumstances," and "potentially damaging to Nixon."

Tennessee's other Republican senator, William E. Brock 3rd, said the disclosures were like waiting for another shoe to drop, adding "we keep getting hit with new shoes . . . I feel like I've been dealing with a centipede this last year." Brock said he was "depressed and concerned" that his party had been "wounded severely."

In the House, Republican leaders John J. Rhodes (Ariz.) and John B. Anderson (Ill.) said the report could be harmful, but Rhodes cautioned that there was "no evidence to connect the President with the erasure." However, Anderson called it another "link in the chain of evidence that has steadily been forged to show that there has been a conscious, deliberate effort to obstruct justice. One has the feeling of approaching the final denouement in this drama."

Sen. William L. Scott (R, Va.), defended Nixon, saying that if he [Scott] were President and had found anything incriminating on the tapes, "I'd have burnt the durn things up long ago."

Among Democrats, House Majority Leader Thomas P. O'Neill (Mass.) said he would not be surprised if Vice President Gerald Ford became the next president—"and I don't mean elected president."

Rep. Jerome Waldie (Calif.), a member of the Judiciary Committee, suggested that the matter could itself become grounds for impeachment.

Cole named domestic affairs aide. Kenneth R. Cole Jr., 36, was appointed by President Nixon Jan. 16 as his special assistant for domestic affairs. He would retain his post as executive director of the Domestic Council. Nixon's former chief adviser on domestic affairs, John D. Ehrlichman, had resigned in April 1973. Cole joined the White House staff in 1969 from an advertising agency in New York.

Nixon sought Hughes gift. Richard G. Danner, an official in President Nixon's 1968 campaign and currently an employee of billionaire industrialist Howard Hughes was reported Jan. 16 to have told the Senate Watergate Committee that he attended a meeting in 1968 with Nixon and Charles G. Rebozo, a friend of Nixon, during which a campaign gift was solicited from Hughes. [For further details, see p. 38A1]

Nixon popularity at record low. President Nixon's popularity dropped to record lows in two major polls in January.

His standing in a Harris Survey (published Jan. 17) was 30%, an all-time low for the poll and a seven-point drop from the previous survey in November 1973. The interviewing was conducted Jan. 7–10.

The Harris Survey reported at the same time a 47%–42% plurality of the American people in agreement with the statement that Nixon had reached the point "where he no longer can be an effective President and should resign for the good of the country." In November 1973, the finding was a 45%–44% plurality that did not feel Nixon should resign.

On the tapes issue, Harris found that a plurality, 48%–40%, thought Nixon should be impeached if the court were to decide that he was "negligent in the care he took of the Watergate tapes."

A Gallup Poll published Jan. 20 reported Nixon's popularity rating had again plunged to 27%, the low point reached in October 1973 after the firing of the first Watergate special prosecutor.

Other Gallup results from the same survey period, Jan. 4–7: the public was split 46%–46% on the question of whether Nixon should resign; on impeachment, 53% were opposed, 37% in favor.

Nixon election data subpoenaed. President Nixon was subpoenaed Jan. 17 by Common Cause for "all documents, memoranda and other writings" on contributions and expenses in Nixon's 1972 re-election campaign. [For further details, see p. 38D2]

Nixon asks dismissal of committee suit. Attorneys for President Nixon Jan. 17 urged U.S. District Court Judge Gerhard A. Gesell to reject the Senate Watergate Committee's attempt to gain access to five presidential tapes subpoenaed in 1973, arguing that the issue was "a classic example of a political question" and "clearly inappropriate for judicial resolution."

The White House brief stated that there were "serious doubts" about the constitutionality of the recently-enacted law authorizing court jurisdiction in the suit. Even if the law were assumed to be proper, the brief argued, the judiciary should not become "embroiled" in a confrontation between the two other branches of government.

Citing the President's "power to withhold information from Congress" in the "public interest," the White House said Nixon had responded to the committee's "political decision" to seek the tapes with a "political determination" that compliance would not be in the public interest. In that context, the brief contended, there was no place for the court to insert its "political judgment" as a "referee."

Resignation talk in Congress. Rep. Wilbur D. Mills (D, Ark.) said Jan. 18 his advice to President Nixon would be to "resign in the near future." He told reporters during an informal news conference: "Under existing circumstances, we would be better off with [Vice President] Jerry Ford as president."

Mills expressed doubt that there was enough proof on the public record of Nixon's participation in the "high crimes and misdemeanors" set by the Constitution as grounds for impeachment. But he said if the House Judiciary Committee recommended impeachment, then "it would be much better for the President to consider resigning rather than put the country into the greatest schism since the Civil War."

"If it takes legislation granting him immunity from criminal prosecution after leaving office for him to resign," Mills said, "I would be willing to sponsor it."

Mills was chairman of the House Ways and Means Committee and the Congressional Joint Committee on Internal Revenue Taxation, which was investigating Nixon's tax returns.

As Congress reconvened Jan. 21, a recommendation that Nixon resign came from House Democratic Leader Thomas P. O'Neill Jr. (Mass.) Nixon had "lost the credibility of the nation," he said, resignation "would be in the best interest of the nation economically" and "we'd be better off" with Ford in the White House.

Several other Democrats also called for Nixon's resignation—Reps. B. F. Sisk (Calif.), Wayne Hays (Ohio) and Jack Brooks (Tex.).

But House Speaker Carl Albert (D, Okla.) said he would "have to think a long time before I'd recommend to the President that he resign." Several other House leaders—Democratic Whip John J. McFall (Calif.) and Republican Leader John J. Rhodes (Ariz.)—considered resignation suggestions "premature."

Rep. John B. Anderson (Ill.), chairman of the House Republican Conference, said some were "wistfully" talking of resignation, which he opposed. The Constitutional course for removal or exculpation was impeachment, he noted. And "it's a Republican problem and we can't turn aside from it."

In the Senate, many returning members reported that constituents were more concerned about the economy and the energy crisis than about the Watergate scandal, although Watergate and the President's conduct were in the public mind, and unresolved.

Sen. Barry Goldwater (R, Ariz.), who had blamed the "impeachment lobby" on "liberal Democrats" the previous week, said Jan. 22 that unless some "magic" redeemed the Nixon presidency soon, "it's going to be god-damned tough for any Republican to get re-elected." Watergate would cost Republican candidates a "disastrous" 10% of the total vote, he said, and "I can sense a strong feeling right here on the Hill—and you're going to see it more and more as weeks go on—that many Republican members of Congress would like to run this year without Mr. Nixon."

If he were running for the first time, Goldwater told the Washington Star-News, he probably "wouldn't associate myself at all with the President."

In another interview the same day, Goldwater told the Associated Press, "We have a good man in the vice president and there would be no transition problem at all." Ford, he said, was "Mr. Clean," an "All-American boy. Everybody likes him."

Other impeachment comments—Impeachment talk also was raised outside Congress. The National Committee for an Effective Congress predicted Jan. 19 that Nixon would be impeached because of developing legal and political problems. While many members of Congress "seek to make themselves innocuous and indispensable parts of the political architecture, a function performed previously by the hat racks," it said in a statement, by spring, "for most congressmen it will take more courage to vote against impeachment than for impeachment." According to the statement, Republicans could more easily explain impeachment to Nixon loyalists as a chance for exoneration before the Senate than justify a vote against impeachment to Nixon critics. Both Democrats and Republicans, it said, faced the risk that a vote against impeachment could be construed by challengers as "trying to suppress the facts."

Former Attorney General Elliot L. Richardson also believed a House vote for impeachment would be "easier" to cast than a vote against it. Meeting with reporters Jan. 22, Richardson said, "A congressman can say, 'All I did was say there are grounds to justify a charge—that the whole thing should be aired.' "

Richardson thought "the tragic flaw" of the Nixon presidency was "a set of attitudes" toward the presidency and the political process, that it was "an adversarial process" that condoned "tactics that would be used against an enemy."

Richardson opposed resignation as a resolution, favoring the impeachment process for "a Congressional and public verdict."

The Committee for Economic Development expressed "deep concern" Jan. 20 about the "dizzying revelation of scandal, corruption and wrongdoing in very high places." "Public cynicism concerning the conduct of the presidency," it said, "is at an all-time high."

It urged the President to make full disclosure of his 1972 campaign funding and "to increase accountability in his Administration through a more open government."

A nonprofit, nonpolitical research group of 200 corporate and university executives, the committee noted that "business has a major responsibility to help remedy the abuses of the election process, yet remarkably few corporations are advocating and supporting election reforms."

Grand jury to probe tape gaps. U.S. District Court Judge John J. Sirica recommended Jan. 18 that a grand jury investigate "the possibility of unlawful destruction of evidence and any related offenses" regarding an 18½-minute gap in one Watergate tape recording surrendered by President Nixon and the nonexistence of two other tapes subpoenaed by the special prosecutor.

Special prosecutor Leon Jaworski said in a statement released later in the day that his office, along with the Federal Bureau of Investigation, would "conduct an exhaustive investigation into all phases of the matter and any relevant information will be referred to the grand jury."

The White House responded with a statement cautioning that Sirica's decision to refer the matter to a grand jury "is not a conviction of any individual, nor is it even an indictment." It would be wrong to conclude, the statement continued, "that any individual in the White House is guilty of impropriety or wrongdoing in the handling of the Watergate case."

"The American people should bear in mind," the White House said, "that the focus of the investigation . . . is primarily how the tape may have been erased, not what the tape contained."

The statement maintained that the content of the tape had been "forgotten in the rhetoric about the lost 18 minutes." Hand-written notes of the June 20, 1972 conversation by H. R. Haldeman, then Nixon's chief of staff, "clearly indicate that presidential conversation and concern in the 18-minute segment were directed solely to the negative public relations impact of the Watergate break-in on the campaign of 1972."

Other gaps revealed—With his recommendation for grand jury action, Judge Sirica suspended the hearings, which began Oct. 31, 1973, into whether there had been unlawful attempts to resist the special prosecutor's subpoena of presidential tapes and documents.

Noting that while the subpoena had been ruled "valid and binding on the President," Sirica said there were "three instances known to the court" of failure to comply: the allegedly nonexistent tape of a June 20, 1972 telephone conversation with former Attorney General John N. Mitchell, the likewise nonexistent tape of an April 15, 1973 conversation with John W. Dean 3rd, then Nixon's counsel, and the disputed erasure in the conversation with Haldeman.

"Substantial questions" of responsibility and justification remained unanswered, Sirica said, and should be sent to the "uniquely equipped" grand jury to determine whether indictments were appropriate.

Sirica warned that his statements "cannot be construed as identifying any particular wrongdoer or unlawful act," nor did they mean he had concluded that any illegal conduct had occurred. But, he continued, the "possibility of unlawful tampering with or suppressing of evidence is sufficiently strong to merit grand jury scrutiny."

Sirica noted that the panel of technical experts would continue to examine the material released by the White House. And—during the hearings Jan. 18—two new gaps were revealed for the experts to analyze.

The gaps—both in Nixon's dictated "recollections" of conversations with Mitchell and Dean—were disclosed as assistant special prosecutor Richard Ben-Veniste questioned presidential counsel J. Fred Buzhardt Jr.

Ben-Veniste said the dictation belt concerning the June 20, 1972 phone conversation with Mitchell began with 23 seconds of Nixon's remarks, followed by a 38-second blank space, after which Nixon began speaking again in mid-sentence on another subject. Buzhardt said he could not explain the gap.

The second gap was in the cassette recording of Nixon's remarks about his March 21, 1973 meeting with Dean (during which, according to Dean's testimony before the Senate Watergate committee, he had warned Nixon of "the cancer growing on the presidency.")

Ben-Veniste noted a 57-second gap in the dictation followed by remarks beginning in mid-sentence. Buzhardt said the explanation was simple: Nixon would "frequently" record his thoughts, stop the machine, then "start talking again before he pushed the button down." Buzhardt insisted that the gap could not have been caused by an erasure.

Buzhardt was then questioned by Charles S. Rhyne, attorney for Nixon's personal secretary Rose Mary Woods. Rhyne contended that White House lawyers had, in effect, "pleaded her guilty" for the 18½-minute gap in the Haldeman tape by suggesting to Judge Sirica during a private meeting that Miss Woods was responsible for an improper, rather than an accidental erasure in the tape.

With Sirica's permission, Rhyne read the transcript of a Nov. 21, 1973 meeting between White House lawyers and Sirica during which Buzhardt had said there was no innocent explanation for the gap and suggested that the matter be referred to a grand jury.

(Rhyne had said outside court Jan. 17 that Miss Woods had not been questioned "in the slightest" by Nixon or presidential lawyers after the full length of the tape gap was discovered. According to Rhyne, Nixon had personally told Miss Woods "there wasn't a four or five minute gap but 18 minutes." That, said Rhyne, "was the sum and substance of the conversation . . . it was left hanging." Shortly afterwards, Rhyne recalled, Miss Woods was told by White House Chief of Staff Alexander M. Haig Jr. to "get yourself a lawyer.")

In other testimony Jan. 18, Ben-Veniste questioned presidential assistant Stephen B. Bull about events in Key Biscayne, Fla. during the weekend of Oct. 4–7, 1973, when several reels of tape and the recorder reported by the experts to have caused the gap were taken there for Miss Woods to work on transcriptions.

Ben-Veniste noted that, according to Secret Service logs, the disputed Haldeman tape was among those taken to Key Biscayne and stored in a safe in Miss Woods' quarters. (Miss Woods had testified that Oct. 1—when her "terrible mistake" was made—was the last time she had worked with the Haldeman tape.)

Bull said he had done little during the weekend but take tapes out of the safe for Miss Woods' use. The safe was under 24-hour Secret Service guard, Bull said, but he was the only person who knew how to open it. However, Bull insisted that he could not recall the dates of the tapes he had removed.

Reading from Secret Service logs, Ben-Veniste noted that the safe had been opened and closed twice during a 15-minute period around 2 a.m. Oct. 5. Bull explained that he had been summoned by Miss Woods, but he could not recall whether it was to deposit something in the safe or take something out.

Ben-Veniste asked if Bull had ever taken anything from the safe out of Miss Woods' quarters. Bull said he remembered taking "an envelope containing a memorandum or something of that nature" to Nixon's study. The envelope might have come from the safe, Bull said, and he might have taken it to Nixon's study around the time of the early-morning summons from Miss Woods. In any case, Bull said, Nixon was not present when the delivery was made.

Bull said the envelope was sealed, but that he was "reasonably certain" it did not contain a tape, only sheets of paper. Bull said he never saw the envelope again.

Nixon support at record low in 1973. Congressional support for Administration-backed legislation in 1973 was at an all-time low, according to the Congressional Quarterly Jan. 19. Nixon won 50.6% of the 310 votes where a clear presidential position was assumed, the lowest rating any president received in the 20 years the magazine had been measuring support.

Nixon's 1972 record was 66%, his 1971 record was 77%. The previous low was 52% in 1959 during the Eisenhower Administration.

In the Senate, Nixon was backed 52% of the time, in the House 48%, compared with his 1972 backing of 54% in the Senate and 81% in the House.

Senate Democrats voted against Nixon 51% of the time (41% in 1972) and supported Nixon 37% (44% in 1972). In the House, Democrats supported the President 35% of the time (47% in 1972) and opposed him 55% (37% in 1972).

Republican support for Nixon was 61% in the Senate and 62% in the House, down 5% and 2%, respectively, from 1972. Opposition votes from Republicans were cast 27% of the time in the Senate and 30% in the House, an increase from the year before of 7% in the Senate and 8% in the House.

The decline in presidential support was apparently not attributable to the Watergate scandal since Congress backed the President only 43% of the time in the first seven months of the session. During that period there was anti-Vietnam war antagonism in Congress as well as opposition to Nixon's drive against long-standing social programs.

Second session convenes. The second session of the 93rd Congress convened Jan. 21. The political line-up in the Senate: 58 Democrats and 42 Republicans, with one Conservative-Republican aligned with the Republicans and one Independent-Democrat aligned with the Democrats. There were 243 Democrats, 188 Republicans and four vacancies in the House.

Ford, Scott say data clears Nixon. Vice President Gerald R. Ford and Senate Republican Leader Hugh Scott (Pa.) asserted that the White House possessed information that could clear President Nixon of wrongdoing in the Watergate affair.

Ford told reporters Jan. 22 that the information "will exonerate the President" and "will totally undercut" testimony of former presidential counsel John W. Dean 3rd that Nixon had knowledge of the cover-up prior to March 21, 1973, when Nixon said he learned of it.

"I spent time talking to the President about Watergate yesterday," Ford asserted, "and I know from our conversation that the President had no prior knowledge of the Watergate break-in or had any part of the cover-up."

"I haven't had time to read the information," Ford said, but said the President had volunteered to show it to him. "There's some question in my mind whether I should see it," he said later. "It's an open question with me."

Asked why the data had not been made public, Ford said he understood the material had been turned over to the special Watergate prosecutor and "it would be improper for the White House to release it now."

Ford assured the reporters Nixon had had nothing to do with the 18½-minute erasure of the key Watergate tape. "I know that the President was not involved," he said.

Ford said he believed it would be "very unwise" for Nixon to resign and assured reporters that Nixon "is not going to resign." "Having spent an hour and 45 minutes with him just yesterday," he said, "I can say he is in good health, mentally and physically."

Scott, interviewed by CBS Jan. 20, was asked if he had information "which gives you the feeling that the President can establish his complete innocence" on Watergate. Scott's reply: "I have the feeling, and information available to me—and I wouldn't want you to misinterpret how complete that is—which would indicate that on specific items the President would be exculpated entirely, yes."

Scott added later he had "some information which is not yet public—which is enormously frustrating to me, because it seems to me to exculpate the President—but I cannot break through the shell down there of all of his advisers, who feel differently about it, who feel that the President no longer needs to make some of these replies. I think it would help if he did. I have found nothing that indicates any guilt on the part of the President of a nature that would be impeachable, but I think they'd help themselves if they told the public some of the things that I know."

Scott said he had advised Nixon "to let it all hang out" and release the information.

Later Jan. 20 an Associated Press story, from "an informed source," linked the information to White House transcripts of presidential tapes said to pinpoint the date of the President's first knowledge of the cover-up to the March 21 meeting with Dean.

AP reports Jan. 22 said the special prosecutor's office had not found evidence to contradict Dean's testimony. CBS Television News reported that the transcripts had been the ones prepared for verification by Sen. John C. Stennis (D, Miss.) in October 1973 in a plan, later discarded, for the Senate Watergate committee to have access to the material.

In a court memorandum filed Jan. 23, the Watergate special prosecutor defended his intention to call Dean as a witness in one of its cases. Observers noted the action was an apparent vote of confidence in his word.

McGovern: 'Mysterious contentions'— Sen. George McGovern (S.D.), the 1972 Democratic candidate for president, commented Jan. 20 on "these mysterious contentions" from Scott and others that "if the President would just tell us what he has told them we might be less inclined to indict him." McGovern said, "Well, all of that could presumably come out, whatever it is, ... but an impeachment trial is a fair system."

McGovern thought there were "ample grounds" to vote a bill of impeachment in the House. "I'd like to see that supported by a good many Republicans," he added, pointing out that this did not mean conviction but merely a trial in the Senate.

Nixon intends to stay, Ziegler says. President Nixon's determination to serve out his term and not be "consumed another year by the Watergate matter" was relayed to reporters Jan. 22 by his press secretary, Ronald L. Ziegler. The President, he said, "is not entertaining at all the subject of resignation. He feels there are a number of programs and a number of initiatives that remain to be done in the next three years in both the foreign and domestic areas, and that is his attitude. That is how he feels, and that is what he is doing."

Ziegler said Nixon had been "under massive attacks" and been "substantially maligned" over the past year but he [Nixon] knew he had "not been involved in any wrongdoing." Ziegler said the President believed that "we have had almost a year of extensive investigation of Watergate ... and that it's time to wrap this matter up and conclude it."

Ziegler attributed Nixon's low poll standing largely to the impact of "unsupported charges" against him. "The mistakes of Watergate" had an impact, he said, "but I think this other element [unsupported charges] has had even a more substantial impact."

The "way to see those [poll] figures go up," Ziegler said, "is to be not constantly devoted to proving the negative ... and constantly being on the defensive."

As for the 18½-minute gap in the presidential tape currently at issue in the special federal Watergate probe, Ziegler said "the President does not feel it [the erasure] was deliberate, whatever happened." Referring to the court proceedings, Ziegler said "we attempted to find out how it took place" but "we don't know how it happened and if we did we would say so."

Ziegler, an infrequent spokesman at the regular White House press briefings for six months, said he would conduct the briefings "more often" in the future. The practice had largely been turned over to Deputy Press Secretary Gerald L. Warren.

Ziegler defended a new White House requirement that presidential aides report all press contacts to him. Reporters feared an inhibiting effect from the practice. It would produce more comment on the record, Ziegler said, and less for background. "Source stories have been getting somewhat out of hand," he said, referring to stories attributed to "sources" and not individuals. Warren, confirming the requirement Jan. 21, said it had been adopted about 10 days previously.

Nixon to 'fight like hell.' Nixon was quoted Jan. 23 as having told a group of Republican congressmen he would "fight like hell" against impeachment. Nixon told them, according to Rep. Peter H. B. Frelinghuysen (R, N.J.): "There is a time to be timid. There is a time to be conciliatory. There is a time, even, to fly and there is a time to fight. And I'm going to fight like hell."

Nixon met with the 18 House members Jan. 22. Frelinghuysen, who had taken notes, said Nixon had authorized release of the quotes.

Krogh sentenced, denies Nixon role. Egil Krogh Jr., the former White House aide who once headed the special investigative unit known as the "plumbers," was sentenced to six months in prison Jan. 24 in connection with the 1971 break-in at the office of the psychiatrist who had treated Pentagon Papers defendant Daniel Ellsberg. Krogh had pleaded guilty Nov. 30, 1973 to a charge of conspiring to violate the civil rights of Dr. Lewis J. Fielding.

Although there had been widespread speculation that Krogh would implicate President Nixon in illegal activities by the plumbers, Krogh said in a statement released after the sentencing that he had "received no specific instruction or authority whatsoever regarding the break-in from the President, directly or indirectly."

Regarding other prosecutions, Krogh had said—and reiterated in his statement—that he would cooperate with the special Watergate prosecutor, but had deferred giving information until after sentencing.

In his appearance before U.S. District Court Judge Gerhard A. Gesell in Washington, Krogh said he accepted sole responsibility for "repulsive conduct" in the violation of individual rights in the guise of "national security." Judge Gesell said he was convinced that Krogh was not involved in other plumbers' activities still under investigation. Nonetheless, Gesell said, "any penalty short of jail would, in the court's view, be inadequate." "A wholly improper, illegal task was assigned to you by higher authority, which you carried out," Gesell said.

Gesell sentenced Krogh to a term of 2-6 years, but suspended all but six months. Krogh would also be subject to two years' unsupervised probation. Other federal and state charges had been dropped in return for the guilty plea.

In his statement, Krogh detailed how his role had begun on July 15 or 16, 1971, when John D. Ehrlichman, then Nixon's domestic affairs adviser, told him he was to "perform an urgent assignment in response to the unauthorized disclosure of the Pentagon Papers." The "entire resources of the executive branch" were to be used to determine responsibility for the leaks, and to assess Ellsberg's motives and "his potential for further disclosures." Krogh added that Ehrlichman later told him the unit's activities "were to be impressed with the highest classification and kept secret even within the White House staff."

The plumbers' mandate was expanded, Krogh continued, after his July 24, 1971 meeting with Nixon and Ehrlichman. The meeting followed the leak of the U.S. "fallback position" at the Strategic Arms Limitation Talks (SALT). Nixon called the leak "intolerable," Krogh said, and directed the "extensive" use of polygraph tests, emphasizing that "protection of national security information must outweigh any individual reluctance to be polygraphed."

The unit's work on the SALT leak, the Ellsberg case and "some other unauthorized disclosures" was completely "fired up and overshadowed" by the "intensity of the national security concern expressed by the President."

It was in this context, Krogh said, that the "Fielding incident" took place. Krogh suggested that this "deep concern" explained why John W. Dean 3rd, Nixon's former counsel, had testified that Krogh had described the authority for the Fielding burglary as coming directly from "the oval office."

Krogh said he had "just listened" to the tape of the July 24, 1971 meeting, and "Ellsberg's name did not appear to be mentioned." (The tape had been voluntarily turned over to the special prosecutor.)

That meeting, Krogh said, was the "only direct contact I had with the President on the work of the unit." As for the instructions to gather data on Ellsberg, they must have been "relayed to me by Ehrlichman."

Krogh contended that, "to [his] knowledge, the break-in netted nothing." He concluded that a mistake had been made and recommended to Ehrlichman that "no further actions of that sort be undertaken." Ehrlichman agreed "and stated that he considered the operation to have been in excess of his authorization."

Krogh related that his activity in the unit then diminished, ending "for all intents and purposes" in November 1971. He was called back briefly the following month in connection with the "India-Pakistan conflict leak," and was asked to authorize a wiretap concerning a "highly sensitive aspect of that leak." Krogh said he refused and was "removed from the unit the same day." He had since learned that the tap was carried out—along with another in the same investigation—after his removal. Krogh contended that these were the only wiretaps by the unit "of which I am aware."

Krogh said that during 1971 the goals of the Ellsberg investigation—including the "potential use of the information in discrediting Dr. Ellsberg as an antiwar spokesman" seemed "dictated by the national security interest as I then understood it." This "strained interpretation" of security needs had led to his false statements in a sworn deposition about the travels to California by the burglary team.

Since then, Krogh continued, he had become convinced that the entire operation was a mistake, a crime and—especially the intention to discredit Ellsberg—a "repulsive and inconceivable national security goal." But in the atmosphere of 1971 it seemed "presumptuous if not unpatriotic" to question those purposes. "Freedom of the President to pursue his planned goals," Krogh said, "was the ultimate national security objective."

House panel seeks subpoena power. Leaders of the House Judiciary Committee decided Jan. 24 to seek subpoena power from the House in order to obtain information and documents relevant to its impeachment inquiry. Chairman Peter W. Rodino (N.J.) said the committee leadership was in agreement that the subpoena power would be shared by the Democrats and Republicans. Differences between Rodino and Rep. Edward Hutchinson (R, Mich.), who would be the minority's voice on the matter, would be taken before the full committee. Hutchinson was senior Republican on the committee.

House Republican Leader John J. Rhodes (Ariz.) had pledged to support the subpoena resolution, Rodino said.

The resolution being sought by the committee would encompass specific authorization from the House for the committee to make the impeachment inquiry concerning President Nixon's conduct in office.

Up to this point, the committee's inquiry was merely a request by House leaders to study impeachment resolutions submitted to the House in 1973.

The committee was still studying the matter of procedures for obtaining data collected by the special Watergate prosecutor, who saw legal restrictions confining the material to the grand jury.

Rodino had warned Jan. 22 that if the committee had no access to the data and had to duplicate it by its own effort, the committee's inquiry would be delayed by a year beyond the April target date. He said the committee was going to go to great lengths "to show we can handle it [the grand jury data]" without allowing it to leak into general circulation.

Another question pending before the committee was whether to hold public hearings to get expert testimony on a definition of an impeachable offense, whether it was an indictable one in the criminal canon.

Court seeks explanation of privilege claim. U.S. District Court Judge Gerhard A. Gesell Jan. 25 requested that President Nixon file a personal statement explaining why he was withholding five subpoenaed White House tapes from the Senate Watergate Committee.

Gesell said if Nixon wished to invoke executive privilege, he should submit to the court "the factual ground or grounds for his determination that disclosure to the select committee would not be in the public interest." Gesell said Nixon could submit the statement through his attorneys but that it "must be signed by the President, for only he can invoke the privilege at issue." Earlier privilege claims, Gesell added, were "too general" and outdated in relation to the current litigation.

Gesell also asked for a report from special prosecutor Leon Jaworski on what effect release of the tapes to the Senate committee might have on the prosecution's efforts.

Another subpoena served by the committee in July 1973 was quashed on the ground that it was "too vague" and "wholly inappropriate for a case involving claims of executive privilege." The subpoena had requested all records concerning "any alleged criminal acts" by 25 White House aides and 1972 campaign officials.

Nixon-Hughes aide meetings reported; one confirmed. Richard G. Danner, an employe of industrialist Howard R. Hughes, told a closed session of the Senate Watergate Committee that he had met with President Nixon on two occasions in 1970 and 1973, it was reported Jan. 25. Both meetings, Danner reportedly said, came shortly after his own transactions with Charles G. Rebozo, a friend of Nixon, on the disputed $100,000 campaign contribution from Hughes.

Danner told the committee, however, that money had not been discussed during either of the meetings with Nixon. [For further details, see p. 38B3]

Conservatives hold parley. A conservative political action conference was held in Washington Jan. 25-26 under the joint sponsorship of the American Conservative Union (ACU) and the Young Americans for Freedom (YAF). Dissatisfaction with President Nixon's national leadership was a recurring theme but the group did not resolve the issue of whether to support the President in his Watergate problems. Nixon was seen as having violated conservative principles in his domestic and foreign policies after having traditionally drawn conservative support and being identified in the public mind as conducting a conservative administration. Many speakers sounded dire warnings of coming defeat of conservative candidates under existing conditions.

YAF President Ronald F. Docksai told the gathering Jan. 25 Nixon should either make a complete explanation to Congress of his role in Watergate or quit the presidency. ACU Chairman M. Stanton Evans Jan. 26 opposed impeachment or resignation. Gov. Ronald Reagan (R, Calif.), a favorite of the conservatives, addressed a banquet Jan. 25 after a rousing welcome, but he was circumspect on the issue. As he was saying in a series of speeches in the South and New England the previous week, those guilty of Water-

gate wrongdoing should accept the consequences while America got on with the business of government.

Presidential aide Patrick J. Buchanan told the group Jan. 26 that Nixon "may not be a card-carrying member of the conservative movement" but he had been for 25 years "and remains, a conservative sympathizer and fellow traveler." He urged them not to be "stampeded" into "doing the liberals' dirty work" by impeaching the President without due cause and thus "discrediting the political verdict of November 1972."

But Rep. John Ashbrook (R, Ohio), a conservative challenger to Nixon in the 1972 primaries, warned Jan. 25 that personal loyalty to Nixon was "the worst possible trap we can fall into." "I don't happen to belong to that branch of the sheep family that follows a bellwether over the precipice," he said. Citing the conflict between Nixon pledges and actions on inflation, economic controls, detente with the Soviet Union and China and "ethics and honesty in office," Ashbrook urged conservatives to stake out their policy differences with Nixon in the current Congressional session.

Senate panel postpones hearings. Sen. Sam J. Ervin Jr. (D, N.C.), chairman of the Watergate Committee, announced Jan. 26 that public hearings on contributions to President Nixon's 1972 re-election campaign would be postponed indefinitely. [For further details, see p. 38G3]

New York City bar report. A broad definition of an impeachable offense was supported in a report filed with the House committee Jan. 26 by the Association of the Bar of the City of New York. Investigating the general question of impeachment, the report concluded that Congress had the sole power to impeach and remove a president for a "gross breach of public trust or serious abuse of power" whether or not the conduct was also a crime. Without mentioning Nixon, the report stated that the impeachment process was not subject to court review and was significantly different from conventional criminal litigation. It cited the fact that the process encompassed only removal from office, that the power contained no other penalty, such as fine or imprisonment, and was no barrier to subsequent criminal prosecution.

In assessing the constitutional basis for impeachment, the phrase "treason, bribery or other high crimes and misdemeanors," the report concluded that the phrase referred to "acts which, like treason and bribery, undermine the integrity of government." The term "high misdemeanor," it said, deriving from English impeachment law, was "a catch-all term covering serious political abuses."

The report provided several warnings: Congress should exercise its own "firm sense of constitutional restraint" in any impeachment proceeding; Congress

should not impeach a particular president "except for conduct for which it would be prepared to impeach and remove any president;" and "impeachment was not intended as a method by which a president could be turned out of office because Congress dislikes his policies." Differences on "purely political" grounds, it noted, could be resolved by periodic elections.

The report rejected two recent pragmatic views of impeachment—Gerald R. Ford's in 1970 that an impeachable offense "is whatever a majority of the House of Representatives considers it to be" and two-thirds of the Senate agreed; Richard G. Kleindienst's in 1973 (then attorney general) that to impeach a president "you don't need facts, you don't need evidence . . . all you need is votes."

"These statements," the New York bar report said, "bear no resemblance to the considered judgments of the Founding Fathers," who were committed "to a government of constitutional principle."

In support of its position, the report cited some views of the framers of the Constitution: Benjamin Franklin said "that impeachment was necessary to prevent the drastic remedy of assassination where a president 'has rendered himself obnoxious' "; James Madison said a president was subject to impeachment for failure to prevent the excesses of subordinates as well as for personal misconduct; Alexander Hamilton said impeachment dealt with "the misconduct of public men, or, in other words, from the abuse or violation of some public trust," that impeachments were "of a nature which may with peculiar propriety be denominated political, as they relate chiefly to injuries done immediately to the society itself."

Porter pleads guilty. Herbert L. Porter, former scheduling director for the Committee to Re-elect the President, pleaded guilty in Washington Jan. 28 to a charge of making false statements to the Federal Bureau of Investigation (FBI) during its investigation of the Watergate break-in.

During his testimony before the Senate Watergate committee June 7, 1973, Porter had admitted lying to the FBI as part of a concocted story to cover the fact that funds for campaign "dirty tricks" had been given to G. Gordon Liddy, who was later convicted in connection with the Watergate burglary. Porter had said that he and Jeb Stuart Magruder, another campaign official, decided to tell the FBI that the money had been used to pay college-age students for infiltrating radical groups. Magruder had since pleaded guilty to plotting the burglary.

Assistant special prosecutor Richard Ben-Veniste told the court Jan. 28 that Porter had cooperated fully with the prosecution.

Porter faced a maximum of five years in prison and a $10,000 fine. U.S. District Court Judge William B. Bryant delayed sentencing pending a probation investigation.

Nixon to be called in 'plumbers' trial. A California state judge said in Los Angeles Jan. 29 that he would summon President Nixon as a witness for the defense in the trial of three former White House aides charged in the burglary of the office of Dr. Lewis J. Fielding, the psychiatrist who had treated Pentagon Papers defendant Daniel Ellsberg.

Charged with burglary and conspiracy were Nixon's former domestic adviser John D. Ehrlichman, and G. Gordon Liddy and David R. Young Jr., both members of the special "plumbers" investigative unit. Ehrlichman was also charged with perjury for his statements to a grand jury. State charges against a fourth defendant, Egil Krogh Jr., had been dropped in return for his guilty plea on a federal count of lying to the Federal Bureau of Investigation.

Acting at the request of the defense, Judge Gordon Ringer said he was "persuaded" that Nixon was a "material witness" and that he would issue a "properly prepared certificate commanding . . . Nixon to testify before this court" on Feb. 25 for a pretrial hearing and on April 15 for the trial. Under procedural rules, the certificate would be forwarded to a District of Columbia court, which would then issue a subpoena.

The Feb. 25 hearing had been set for argument on a motion for dismissal based on a claim that the defendants had acted in "good faith" as federal officers. According to defense attorneys, the state prosecution was "discriminatory," since law enforcement officers in California were not customarily charged with crimes for actions taken in the performance of assigned duties.

Deputy White House Press Secretary Gerald L. Warren said in Washington Jan. 30 that Nixon's lawyers would recommend that he "respectfully decline to appear" on constitutional grounds. Asked whether Nixon might respond to questions in writing, Warren said that "other requests" would be dealt with "as they arise."

Clawson appointed. Kenneth W. Clawson, 37, a White House aide, was appointed Jan. 30 White House director of communications, a post formerly held by Herbert G. Klein. Clawson would report to Ronald Ziegler, President Nixon's press secretary.

Nixon's State of the Union Message. President Nixon delivered a State of the Union Message in person before a joint session of Congress Jan. 30. In his nationally televised prime-time address, he pledged there would be no recession, inflation would be checked and the back of the energy crisis broken. He declared major new initiatives for a national health-care insurance plan, welfare reform and mass transit. He stressed his "overriding" and persistent attempt to build a structure of lasting world peace.

Before he began his address, Nixon handed a longer 22,000 word message to Congressional officials. Since Nov. 17,

1973, Nixon's public appearances had been essentially private affairs. He had not personally delivered his State of the Union message to Congress in 1973.

At the conclusion of his address, Nixon added "a personal word" on "the so-called Watergate affair:"

Mr. Speaker, and Mr. President and my distinguished colleagues and our guests, I would like to add a personal word with regard to an issue that has been of great concern to all Americans over the past year.

I refer, of course, to the investigations of the so-called Watergate affair.

As you know, I have provided to the special prosecutor voluntarily a great deal of material. I believe that I have provided all the material that he needs to conclude his investigations and to proceed to prosecute the guilty and to clear the innocent.

I believe the time has come to bring that investigation and the other investigations of this matter to an end. One year of Watergate is enough.

And the time has come, my colleagues, for not only the executive, the President, but the members of Congress, for all of us to join together in devoting our full energies to these great issues that I have discussed tonight which involve the welfare of all the American people in so many different ways as well as the peace of the world.

I recognize that the House Judiciary Committee has a special responsibility in this area, and I want to indicate on this occasion that I will cooperate with the Judiciary Committee in its investigation. I will cooperate so that it can conclude its investigation, make its decision and I will cooperate in any way that I consider consistent with my responsibilities for the office of the Presidency of the United States.

There is only one limitation: I will follow the precedent that has been followed by and defended by every President from George Washington to Lyndon B. Johnson of never doing anything that weakens the office of the President of the United States or impairs the ability of the President of the future to make the great decisions that are so essential to this nation and the world.

Another point I should like to make very briefly. Like every member of the House and Senate assembled here tonight, I was elected to the office that I hold. And like every member of the House and Senate, when I was elected to that office I knew that I was elected for the purpose of doing a job, and doing it as well as I can possibly can.

And I want you to know that I have no intention whatever of ever walking away from the job that the people elected me to do for the people of the United States.

Now needless to say, it would be understatement if I were not to admit that the year 1973 was not a very easy year for me personally or for my family. And as I've already indicated, the year 1974 presents very great and serious problems as very great and serious opportunities are also presented.

But my colleagues, this I believe: With the help of God who has blessed this land so richly, with the cooperation of the Congress and with the support of the American people, we can and we will make the year 1974 a year of unprecedented progress toward our goal of building a structure of lasting peace in the world and a new prosperity without war in the United States of America.

The President's affirmation that he would not resign drew standing applause from Nixon partisans in Congress and the gallery, where his family was assembled.

The President drew several such ovations, one from his hope to leave a legacy of world peace "for the eight years of my Presidency." At one point he also bid for cooperation from Congress "in these final three years of my Administration." A more general applause was accorded his appearance and departure from the chamber. As he moved into his speech, the applause at various remarks was more notably partisan from the Republican side of the aisle; many Democrats remained

seated and silent. At the end, when he qualified his promise of cooperation with the House impeachment inquiry, there were some hisses and boos from the Democratic side.

On the right of personal privacy, where the President wanted to "erect new safeguards," he specifically identified the culprits as modern information systems, data banks, credit records, mailing list abuses, electronic snooping, "the collection of personal data for one purpose that may be used for another."

House panel united on subpoena power. The House Judiciary Committee voted unanimously Jan. 31 to seek House approval for broad subpoena power in its impeachment inquiry.

The resolution it sought would authorize the panel "to investigate fully and completely whether sufficient grounds exist for the House of Representatives to exercise its constitutional power to impeach Richard M. Nixon, President of the United States of America." It would authorize the committee to subpoena "any person" or "such things" it deemed necessary to its inquiry.

Committee Chairman Peter Rodino (D, N.J.) stressed that the committee's authority for the impeachment probe, deriving directly from the Constitution, was "full, original and unqualified" and did not "depend on any statutory provisions or require judicial enforcement."

The panel's chief counsel, John Doar, and its minority counsel, Albert Jenner, were in agreement that presidential defiance of a committee subpoena could lead either to a House contempt citation, which would be subject to judicial review, or impeachment, which would not be subject to judicial review.

The suggested subpoena power being sought by the committee would be shared by Rodino and the panel's senior Republican, Rep. Edward Hutchinson (Mich.), who could issue them together or separately. Any differences between them on the matter would be submitted to the full panel for resolution.

Several Republican proposals were rejected by the committee Jan. 31, but none on straight party-line votes. One called for an April 30 deadline for the committee's inquiry. It failed, 23–14, with two Republicans joining the Democratic majority. Rodino conceded public impatience over the issue but said it was more important to "do it right" than quickly.

The Republicans sought the right to issue subpoenas over the objections of the Democratic majority, in the interest of "fairness" since the Democrats had the right. This failed, 21–16, with three Republicans joining the majority vote, and three Democrats voting on the other side.

Hutchinson said Jan. 29 that in his opinion the House impeachment authority prevailed over executive privilege to withhold information. If the White House asked his advice, he said, "I would tell them that executive privilege, in the face of an impeachment inquiry, must fail."

Jenner agreed. He said presidential definance of a subpoena could be part of "the consideration of whether articles of impeachment should be brought."

Hutchinson reported Jan. 28 that the Republican members of the committee were in general consensus that the President could not be impeached for criminal acts of subordinates without evidence of his specific knowledge or authorization of the acts. Their position was made known after Jenner met with the committee minority and clarified an earlier view attributed to him that the President could be held accountable for acts of his aides.

Judiciary Committee member Jerome R. Waldie (D, Calif.) Jan. 16 asserted his intention to demand an immediate vote on impeachment, first in the committee and then on the House floor, if the President impeded the committee's inquiry and defied it by withholding requested information. Impeachment was an issue that was not restricted by House rules to preliminary committee action; it could be brought to the floor by any member at any time for an immediate vote.

House Speaker Carl Albert (D, Okla.) said Jan. 28 he believed the full House would be called upon to vote whatever recommendation the committee presented—to impeach or not to do so.

A White House spokesman said Jan. 25 that the legal staff had "under study," on whether it was a valid policy precedent, a 1970 letter by President Nixon declaring the executive was "clearly obligated" to supply information to an impeachment inquiry. The letter, applying to the unsuccessful attempt to impeach Supreme Court Justice William O. Douglas, made accessible Administration documents, including tax returns and Justice Department files, to that inquiry.

Prosecution backs Dean. An assistant on the staff of special Watergate prosecutor Leon Jaworski said in federal district court Jan. 31 that the prosecutors had "no basis to believe" that former presidential counsel John W. Dean 3rd had made false statements "in any proceeding." The statement followed assertions to newsmen during the previous week by Vice President Gerald R. Ford and Senate Republican Leader Hugh Scott (Pa.) that Dean might have lied in his testimony before the Senate Watergate Committee about President Nixon's knowledge of the Watergate cover-up.

Assistant prosecutor Richard J. Davis told Judge Gerhard A. Gesell that "based on the evidence accumulated so far" there were no grounds for a perjury charge against Dean, either for his committee testimony or for subsequent statements to a grand jury.

Davis' statement came in a pretrial hearing in the case of former White House aide Dwight L. Chapin, who was charged with perjury in his grand jury testimony on campaign "dirty tricks."

Chapin's attorney had argued that the defense was entitled to any evidence the government might have that Dean—who was scheduled to appear as a prosecution witness—had lied, even in matters extraneous to the Chapin case.

Chapin's attorney also contended that Dean should be excluded as a witness because of an attorney-client relationship between Dean and Chapin while they were on the White House staff. Judge Gesell set another hearing for arguments on that issue.

Gesell denied a defense motion for a change of venue, calling it "an affront to the jury system" for the defense to argue that a District of Columbia jury would be biased against a white Republican.

Scott, Ford, Krogh on Dean evidence— Asked about the prosecution statement in the Chapin hearing, Sen. Scott said Feb. 1 that he was not "backtracking one single inch" on his charge that Dean had lied about Nixon's role in the cover-up. Scott then added to conflicting reports as to whether special prosecutor Jaworski already had the evidence, saying that he hoped the prosecutor "would have available to him ultimately all the material that's been made available to me."

Regarding the White House tape transcript summaries allegedly refuting Dean, Scott had said January 30 that "if the rug is pulled out from under me I will have something to say later. I'll be goddamned if I'll be a patsy for anyone."

Scott also told reporters that he had urged the White House to make public any still-secret tapes of Nixon's conversations on Watergate with Dean and other aides.

Vice President Ford said Jan. 25 that "on reflection" he had decided—at least for the present—not to "personally see what Senator Scott says exonerates the President." Ford explained that if he did read the summaries, "all my good friends in the press corps will be asking me for the details. I don't want to be in the position of disclosing such evidence."

Ford said he was certain the summaries would exonerate Nixon because "I am relying on the faith and trust of Senator Hugh Scott, who I think is a man of great integrity. I am relying on the President, who also in my opinion is a man of faith and high integrity."

In a television interview Jan. 27, former White House aide Egil Krogh Jr. described his meeting with Dean on March 20, 1973, when they discussed "a lot of things that John [Dean] had been working on which I learned about for the first time." According to Krogh, Dean said concerning the Watergate cover-up that "the President is being badly served. He just doesn't know what's been going on." Krogh asserted that Dean gave Nixon the details of the cover-up the following day.

Krogh's attorney Stephen N. Shulman said Jan. 28 that Krogh's television re-marks did not necessarily contradict Dean's testimony that Nixon knew of the cover-up long before the March 21 meeting. Shulman contended that Dean "may have an entirely different, more complete scope of knowledge." The meaning of Dean's remarks to Krogh, Shulman said, was that Nixon did not understand everything that was happening. Nixon "could have known something," Shulman added, "but Krogh and Dean didn't discuss that."

CIA destroyed its Watergate tapes. The Central Intelligence Agency (CIA) destroyed tape recordings related to the Watergate break-in one day after it had acknowledged receipt of a letter from Senate Majority Leader Mike Mansfield (D, Mont.) asking the CIA to save any Watergate evidence it might have, National Broadcasting Co. (NBC) News reported Jan. 31.

William E. Colby, director of the CIA, Jan. 29 had admitted the destruction of all but one of its tapes from the Watergate period. A tape recording of the June 22, 1971 conversation between E. Howard Hunt Jr., then a White House investigator, and Marine Gen. Robert B. Cushman Jr., then deputy director of the CIA, had "survived normal procedures of destruction because it was put into a separate drawer somehow," Colby said.

All other tapes had been destroyed periodically "when the storage space got too full," Colby added.

According to NBC, Mansfield had sent requests to various federal agencies asking them to save any material pertinent to Watergate. A receipt in Mansfield's office files showed that a high-ranking CIA official had signed for the letter Jan. 17, 1973. CIA tapes were destroyed the following day, NBC reported.

A spokesman for the Senate Watergate Committee said Jan. 31 that the committee would seek to determine if the destruction of the tapes had been a deliberate attempt to conceal the CIA's role in the Watergate affair.

Mansfield responds to Nixon's message. Senate Democratic Leader Mike Mansfield (Mont.) said Feb. 1 that the "crimes of Watergate" could not "be put to rest by Congress, nor can any words of the President's or from me mitigate them." Delivering his party's nationally-televised response to President Nixon's State of the Union address, Mansfield said he raised the Watergate issue "reluctantly," but felt compelled to answer Nixon's call to end the investigations.

Speaking from his office, Mansfield said the President's address was "welcomed by the Congress" and would receive "full and cooperative consideration." "Whatever the legal difficulties which confront the Administration, the regular business of the nation must come first."

Nevertheless, Mansfield said, the question of impeachment and the Senate Watergate Committee's hearings had created "onerous" but "inescapable" responsibilities for Congress which "have had to be assumed in order to cleanse the political processes of the nation. The members of the Congressional committees which are pursuing them—members of both parties—deserve every support in these endeavors."

Mansfield emphasized that both proceedings were valid constitutional functions of Congress and were being handled properly. He said he expected both to be completed in the current session.

As for the crimes of Watergate, Mansfield said their disposition was a function of the Justice Department and the courts. Both—including special prosecutor Leon Jaworski—Mansfield added, were doing their job, and "there the matter must rest for however long may be necessary. Whether it is months or years, there are no judicial shortcuts."

Mansfield accepted Nixon's strong statement against resignation: as far as Congress was concerned, the matter was closed.

The remedies for scandals like Watergate, Mansfield said, would come with a "new system of open elections openly paid for." "The people have a right to an electoral system free of shenanigans, capable of yielding honest, responsible and responsive government." This could be achieved when "we are prepared to pay for the public business of elections with public funds."

Nixon activities. President Nixon increased his visibility on the Washington scene Jan. 31–Feb. 12. Among his activities:

Prayer breakfast—Some 2,500 government officials, diplomats, clergymen and laymen from across the counry attended the 22nd annual National Prayer Breakfast, held in a Washington hotel Jan. 31. The President gave a 15-minute talk recalling his Quaker heritage and urging the nation to pray. "Too often we are a little too arrogant," he said in reference to prayer. "We try to talk and tell Him what we want. What all of us need to do, and what this nation needs to do, is to pray in silence and listen to God to find out what He wants us to do."

Republican club meeting—Nixon was host at a breakfast meeting Feb. 6 of the Chowder and Marching Society, a Republican Congressional club. He said he thought the party would do better than predicted in the November elections and named four Republicans he considered to be in good position to succeed him in 1976: Vice President Gerald R. Ford, Gov. Ronald Reagan (Calif.), and former Govs. Nelson A. Rockefeller (N.Y.) and John B. Connally Jr. (Tex.).

Lincoln Memorial visit—Several hundred persons had gathered Feb. 12 for the annual Lincoln Day ceremony at the Washington memorial when the presidential limousine and entourage arrived, unannounced. Nixon ascended the steps and gave a brief speech on "the Lincoln heritage"—that the nation use its strength and wealth to build world peace. He also remarked on Lincoln's strength of character. "No President in history has been more vilified or was more vilified during the time he was President," he said, "than Lincoln. Those who knew him, his secretaries, have written that he was very deeply hurt by what was said about him and drawn about him, but on the other hand, Lincoln had the great strength of character never to display it, always to stand tall and strong and firm no matter how harsh or unfair the criticism might be."

Longworth birthday party—Nixon visited the 90th birthday celebration Feb. 12 for Alice Roosevelt Longworth, a daughter of Theodore Roosevelt. Later, he attributed her longevity to "not being obsessed by the Washington scene." "If she had spent all of her time reading the [Washington] Post or the [Washington] Star [-News] she would have been dead by now," he told reporters. "Mrs. Longworth keeps young by not being obsessed with the miserable political things that all of us unfortunately think about in Washington, by thinking about those great issues that will affect the future of the world, which the Post, unfortunately seldom writes about in a responsible way."

Physical exam report: excellent—The President went to the naval medical hospital in Bethesda, Md. for his annual physical examination Feb. 13. The report was he was in "excellent" condition and showed "no evidence whatsoever of any emotional strain." Nixon's physician said he would like to see him "get more sunshine."

Nixon and members of his staff left shortly afterwards for a visit to his home in Key Biscayne, Fla.

Nixon reliance on ex-aides reported. The Washington Post reported Feb. 1 that President Nixon had continued to maintain a close association with three of his former key aides who were targets of Watergate investigations: former domestic affairs adviser John D. Ehrlichman, former chief of staff H. R. Haldeman and former counsel Charles W. Colson.

The Post report was based on interviews with John K. Andrews Jr., a presidential speechwriter who resigned in December 1973, and with present White House sources. Quoting the present sources, the Post said Nixon had been building his public and legal defenses on Watergate problems "in concert" with

the three former aides, and had also often sought the advice of two close friends, businessmen Charles G. Rebozo and Robert H. Abplanalp.

According to the Post, Secretary of State Henry A. Kissinger and White House Chief of Staff Alexander M. Haig Jr. had repeatedly—and unsuccessfully—urged Nixon to end the association with Ehrlichman, Haldeman and Colson. Andrews said, however, that both Haig and Kissinger had tended to tread lightly on the issue, since they were aware of Nixon's feelings of personal loyalty to the former aides.

Kissinger was "pragmatic" about it, Andrews added, and did not want to know "how much the President is involved in Watergate." According to Andrews, Kissinger considered Nixon's resignation or removal from office "as events that would be cataclysmic to world order."

The other White House sources said that Haig had already "used up about all his good will" with Nixon by urging compliance with a court order to release Watergate tapes in October 1973.

Questioned about the Post report, White House Press Secretary Ronald L. Ziegler said he was "not going to respond to a story which was generated in that way and contains a mixture of supposed discussions, many of them out of context."

(Ziegler said at the same news briefing that the new White House press policy would be to turn aside questions on Watergate and concentrate on "the business of government." The only exceptions, Ziegler said, would be when a formal statement was necessary or when White House lawyers wished to "provide relevant answers.")

John J. Wilson, an attorney for both Haldeman and Ehrlichman, said Feb. 4 that recent contact between his two clients and the White House had been only "sporadic." But Wilson dismissed speculation that Ehrlichman's attempt to have Nixon subpoenaed as a witness in the California "plumbers" trial signaled a "break" between the two.

Popularity at a new low—26%. President Nixon's popularity rating on a national poll, a Gallup Poll conducted Jan. 18–21, was at the lowest point of his term, with 26% of the respondents approving of the way he was handling his job as President (64% disapproving, 10% undecided). Results were published Feb. 3.

Another Gallup survey published Feb. 4 showed a plurality (46%) preferring Vice President Ford over Nixon (32%) as chief executive for the remaining three years of Nixon's term.

Surveillance of Nixon's brother. Investigators for the Senate Watergate Committee said the Secret Service was ordered during President Nixon's first term to keep the President's brother, F. Donald

Nixon, under physical surveillance, the New York Times reported Feb. 4. [For further details, see p. 39G2]

Dean evidence dispute continues. The dispute over the reliability of former presidential counsel John W. Dean 3rd as a Watergate witness continued Feb. 3–7 as special prosecutor Leon Jaworski, on one side, and—on the other—White House lawyers, Vice President Gerald R. Ford and Senate Minority Leader Hugh Scott (R, Pa.), traded opinions and occasional accusations of improper public comment.

In a television interview Feb. 3, Jaworski stood behind earlier courtroom statements by his staff: "If we believed John Dean's veracity was subject to question, we would not use him as a witness." Jaworski maintained that he had found no basis for perjury charges against Dean.

The White House responded Feb. 4 with a statement by special counsel James D. St. Clair, who criticized Jaworski and his staff for having "seen fit to discuss in public their view regarding John Dean's veracity."

St. Clair continued that he could state "categorically" that "the tapes and other evidence furnished to the special prosecutor—at least as far as the President is concerned—do not support sworn statements before the Senate select committee made by Mr. Dean as to what the President knew about Watergate, and especially when he knew it."

St. Clair said he should not discuss "the technical legal issues of perjury;" the time and place for such matters, he said, "is in court, or perhaps before the House Judiciary Committee."

Spokesmen for Jaworski's office said later that their first public references to the Dean evidence were made properly in court as necessary responses to defense efforts to have Dean excluded as a witness. The prosecutor's office noted that the dispute had begun with public statements against Dean by Scott and Ford by way of the White House.

According to Congressional sources and aides to Sen. Scott, the St. Clair statement was issued at Scott's insistence, after the minority leader had made it clear to Nixon's chief of staff Alexander Haig that he felt vulnerable to criticism without additional public support from a high-level White House legal spokesman such as St. Clair.

Vice President Ford told a news conference Feb. 7 that Nixon had assured him that public release of evidence exonerating the President was "being actively considered." It was "a matter of timing," Ford said, but he had no information "as to the time."

Ford added that both he and Scott had urged Nixon to release the material, "the quicker the better."

Ford again said he had not examined the evidence. In explanation, he posed a hypothetical situation: "Supposing, let's speculate for a minute, I did examine it. Assume, which isn't the case, I might wish to use that evidence for my own personal benefit, to undercut the President. I think it would be very inappropriate with that possibility existing for me to examine the evidence, the tapes in this case, when I might if I were so inclined use it for my own benefit."

Asked if there might be material damaging to Nixon, Ford replied, "Not at all, because I still have faith in Sen. Scott's interpretation of those transcripts . . ."

Democrat elected to GOP House seat. State Rep. John P. Murtha (D), 41, won a 229-vote victory over Harry Fox (R), 49, in a special election in Pennsylvania's 12th Congressional District Feb. 5. More than 120,000 votes were cast. The seat had been held for the last 24 years by John P. Saylor (R), who died in October 1973, although Democrats held a slight lead in voter registrations.

The election had been watched for possible political fallout from the Watergate scandal, but the close decision negated clear-cut interpretation. Both candidates avoided the issue during the campaign.

Murtha, who would become the first Vietnam veteran to enter the House, received help from organized labor, which had long supported Saylor. Fox, Saylor's long-time aide, announced Feb. 6 he would demand a recount and blamed the national news media for interfering with the election by injecting the Watergate issue. Vice President Gerald R. Ford had visited the district to help Fox's campaign.

Nixon explains tape privilege claim. President Nixon said in a letter to U.S. District Court Judge Gerhard A. Gesell Feb. 6 that release of five tape recordings subpoenaed by the Senate Watergate Committee would infringe upon the confidentiality of the presidency and could be harmful to criminal prosecutions. Nixon was responding to Gesell's request that he personally explain why the tapes were being withheld.

Nixon said he was responding "out of respect for the court," but reiterated that the issue was essentially political and "inappropriate for resolution by the judicial branch."

Nixon gave two reasons:

"First, the Senate select committee has made known its intention to make these materials public. Unlike the secret use of four out of five of these conversations before the grand jury, the publication of all of these tapes to the world at large would seriously infringe upon the principle of confidentiality, which is vital to the performance of my constitutional responsibilities as President.

"Second, it is incumbent upon me to be sensitive to the possible adverse effects upon ongoing and forthcoming criminal proceedings should the contents of these subpoenaed conversations be made public at an inappropriate time. The dangers connected with excessive pretrial publicity are as well known to this court as they are to me. Consequently, my constitutional mandate to see that the laws are faithfully executed requires my prohibiting the disclosure of any of these materials at this time and in this forum."

Special prosecutor Leon Jaworski, who had also been asked for comment on the advisability of releasing the tapes, said the four tapes currently held by the grand jury contained "important and material evidence" for future criminal trials, but that he would take no position on whether the court should consider that danger of pretrial publicity was a decisive factor if the subpoena were found "otherwise enforceable."

Jaworski said public release of information would "add only marginally to other publicity," but suggested that the committee use the tapes with "restraint."

The committee filed its reply to Nixon's letter Feb. 7, arguing that the President's claims were still too vague to upset the subpoena. Committee lawyers contended that they were now entitled to a favorable judgment since Nixon had failed to provide the "particularized statement" Gesell had requested.

Nixon's citation of the public interest, the committee said, was "highly suspect," and the "fears of pretrial publicity were both belated and unconvincing." The panel said Nixon himself had already commented publicly on the contents of some of the conversations and had allowed Senate Minority Leader Hugh Scott (R, Pa.) to examine "purported transcripts."

Dean disbarred. Former presidential counsel John W. Dean 3rd, who had pleaded guilty to conspiracy charges in connection with the Watergate cover-up, was disbarred in Virginia Feb. 6 by a three-judge state court.

The disbarment action had been filed by the Virginia State Bar, which charged Dean with unprofessional conduct by withholding evidence, inducing a witness to commit perjury, authorizing payoffs to the Watergate burglars and diverting money to his own use.

Dean's attorney asked for a reprimand or suspension from practice, arguing that when the "full information in the final chapter of Watergate" came out it would be "largely mitigating" for Dean.

House backs committee powers. By a vote of 410–4 Feb. 6, the House approved a resolution ratifying the Judiciary Committee's impeachment investigation and granting the panel broad subpoena power to compel testimony or production of documents from any source, including the President.

In two developments the next day, Committee Chairman Peter W. Rodino Jr. (D, N.J.) announced that, on President Nixon's initiative, White House counsel James D. St. Clair and committee counsel would meet "promptly" to discuss the extent of Nixon's cooperation with the inquiry, and the Senate Watergate Committee voted unanimously to give the House panel access to its investigative files.

In the final House vote, the four members voting against the resolution—all Republicans—were Ben B. Blackburn (Ga.), Earl F. Landgrebe (Ind.), Carlos J. Moorhead (Calif.) and David C. Treen (La.).

The resolution was approved after the House rejected, 342–70, an attempt to open the resolution to various amendments, including an April 30 deadline for the investigation, Republican power to issue subpoenas over the objection of Democrats and a formal restriction to "relevant" information on the panel's subpoenas.

Republican support for the amendments dwindled after Minority Leader John J. Rhodes (Ariz.) said Rodino's pledge to conduct the inquiry fairly and to try to conclude it by April 30 was "good with me." The investigation so far, Rhodes added, had been "fair and highly professional."

Rodino told the House that the panel must "now proceed with such care and decency and thoroughness and honor" that the public would be convinced "this was the right course. There was no other way."

Asked repeatedly during the debate whether he intended to subpoena Nixon, Rodino replied that such action would be taken "only if it becomes necessary to complete the inquiry and assure a fair judgment."

According to a group of House Republicans who had attended a breakfast meeting with Nixon Feb. 6, Rep. Louis C. Wyman (N.H.) had urged the President to testify voluntarily. Nixon had replied that he was considering "all viable alternatives."

Senate panel delays report. The Senate Watergate Committee voted unanimously Feb. 7 to delay issuing a report on its investigation until May 28. Further hearings on campaign fund issues had already been postponed, but the panel had reportedly been considering preparation of at least an interim report by Feb. 28. [For further details, see p. 39D3]

Senate panel's tape suit dismissed. U.S. District Court Judge Gerhard A. Gesell Feb. 8 dismissed the Senate Watergate Committee's suit to enforce its subpoena of five presidential tape recordings on the ground that publicity surrounding the panel's hearings might be harmful to criminal prosecutions.

Weighing the competing assertions of

the "public interest," Gesell said the committee had not demonstrated a "pressing need" for the tapes or that hearings on their content would "at this time" serve the public interest.

But, Gesell said, he also rejected President Nixon's contention "that the public interest is best served by a blanket, unreviewable claim of confidentiality over all presidential communications." Gesell added that his rejection of Nixon's claim was also based on the President's unwillingness to submit the tapes for the court's private inspection "or in any other fashion to particularize his claim of executive privilege."

The "critical factor" in the present case, Gesell continued, was the "mutual and concurrent obligation" of the President, Congress and the courts to "preserve the integrity of the criminal trials arising out of Watergate." Nixon was "quite properly concerned with the dangers inherent in excessive pretrial publicity."

"That the President himself may be under suspicion does not alter this fact," Gesell said, "for he no less than any other citizen is entitled to fair treatment and the presumption of innocence." Therefore, the public interest did not require that Nixon provide evidence to a Senate committee "in order to furnish fuel for further hearings which cannot, by their very nature, provide the procedural safeguards and adversary format essential to fact finding in the criminal justice system."

But other Congressional demands for tapes "in furtherance of the more juridical constitutional process of impeachment would present wholly different considerations," Gesell said.

Gesell commended the committee for having "ably served" its function for the past several months, but said the time had come "to question whether it is in the public interest for the criminal investigative aspects of its work to go forward in the blazing atmosphere" of publicity on issues related to pending criminal proceedings.

Tape tests approved. In a memorandum made public Feb. 8, U.S. District Court Judge John J. Sirica overruled the objections of presidential lawyers and approved the examination of untested Watergate tape recordings by a panel of technical experts. Sirica said the panel should examine all the tapes surrendered by President Nixon to the prosecution while compiling backup data for its earlier report of erasures on one of the tapes—a June 20, 1972 conversation between Nixon and John W. Dean 3rd.

Nixon lawyers had asked that the panel not be allowed to test other tapes for possible tampering until they had completely documented the conclusions in their first report.

Presidential bid explored. An exploratory bid for the 1976 presidential nomination was announced Jan. 17 by Sen. Walter F. Mondale (D, Minn.). Mondale established a fund-raising committee to finance the effort.

Sen. Charles H. Percy (R, Ill.), who had set up a similar committee in 1973, scorned the customary early "non-candidate tango" and reaffirmed Feb. 8 he "would like to be a candidate for president in 1976." His position on the Watergate issue: "We must not put ourselves in the position of even seeming to condone or gloss over the misdeeds of Watergate. In no way, shape or form is Watergate what the Republican Party is all about, and we'd better make damn sure the American people understand it or our party will be paying for that 'third-rate burglary' for decades to come."

Truck strike ends. Most of the nation's independent truckers returned to the highways Feb. 11, indicating their acceptance of a strike pact negotiated with the aid of Pennsylvania Gov. Milton J. Shapp (D) with Administration officials. There were pockets of resistance to the agreement in New Jersey and areas of the Midwest, government officials said, but truck traffic was reported at near normal levels across the rest of the country.

The government reportedly was divided in negotiating strategy, with several officials taking a law and order position favoring use of federal troops to restore order on the highways. The White House also resented Shapp's leading role as mediator in the talks and he in turn accused President Nixon of being indecisive on the issue because of his preoccupation with Watergate-related matters.

Nixon makes Southern appearances. President Nixon spoke at a hospital dedication in Miami Feb. 14 and at an "Honor America Day" rally in Huntsville, Ala. Feb. 18. His Miami appearance was marked by distracting heckling. The Huntsville audience of more than 20,000 was generally friendly, with the few anti-Nixon slogans outnumbered by pro-Nixon ones.

The President's appearance in Miami to dedicate the Cedars of Lebanon Hospital Center drew a crowd of about 3,000 persons, most of them friendly. But picketing protestors on the outskirts of the crowd chanted "Impeach Nixon Now" during his speech and punctuated it with heckling.

A
B
C
D
E
F
G

The President attended the Huntsville rally Feb. 18 with Gov. George C. Wallace (D, Ala.), who introduced him with warmth: "God bless you, Mr. President, and I submit to you that you are among friends." Joining Nixon and Wallace at the rally were Govs. William Waller (D, Miss.) and Winfield Dunn (R, Tenn.)

At the conclusion of his "what's right with America" speech, the President added a "personal note" disparaging news reporting in Washington. There was a tendency there, he said, "for partisanship to take over from statesmanship, . . . a tendency in the reporting of news—I do not say this critically, it's simply a fact of life —that bad news is news and good news is not news." As a result, he continued, "those of us who work there and try to develop the policies of the nation may get a distorted view of what is America and what it is really like. It is there that you hear more than any other place in America that America is sick, that there is something wrong with America that cannot be corrected."

He thanked his audience "for reminding all of America that here in the heart of Dixie we find that the heart of America is good, the character of America is strong and we are going to continue to be a great nation."

While the country was strong and rich, he said, "there is so much more work left to be done here at home to build better opportunities for our children for education and health, and all the other areas that we want for them."

There were problems, Nixon said, but they were "problems of peace and they are problems we can solve."

White House, prosecution in evidence dispute. Questions involving the availability of White House evidence to special prosecutor Leon Jaworski, and the integrity of evidence already released, occupied the White House, the prosecutor and the courts Feb. 14–19.

After Jaworski revealed Feb. 14 that President Nixon had refused to turn over a number of tapes and documents, a presidential lawyer made it clear that Nixon stood by the statement in his Jan. 30 State of the Union message: the prosecutor had been given "all the material that he needs."

Regarding the disputed gaps or erasures in tapes under investigation by a grand jury, U.S. District Court Judge John J. Sirica told White House lawyers and the prosecution Feb. 19 that "continued public comment" on the tapes by anyone connected with the investigation was inappropriate. Sirica acted after a weekend rash of speculation on whether an 18½-minute gap on one tape might have been caused accidentally and whether two other tapes were re-recordings rather than the subpoenaed originals.

Similar action was taken Feb. 15 by District Court Judge Gerhard A. Gesell,

who scolded Jaworski for public comments on the reliability of former presidential counsel John W. Dean 3rd as a witness. Gesell suggested that, in the interest of fair trials for other Watergate defendants, all public debate about Dean be shut off.

In a footnote to the events, the Senate committee which had directly or indirectly brought most of the Watergate issues to public attention, decided Feb. 19 to cancel further public hearings, partly to avoid interfering with the prosecution and the House impeachment inquiry, and—according to panel member Herman E. Talmadge (D, Ga.)—because "the train has already passed our station."

Nixon refuses to release evidence—Special prosecutor Jaworski said Feb. 14 that he and the White House had reached an impasse on release of presidential tapes and documents and that it was "clear that evidence I deem material to our investigations will not be forthcoming."

In a letter to Senate Judiciary Committee Chairman James O. Eastland (D, Miss.)—to whom Jaworski had promised to report on the progress of his dealings with the White House—the prosecutor said he had been informed by special presidential counsel James D. St. Clair that release of the material would be "inconsistent with the public interest and the constitutional integrity of the Presidency."

After a series of meetings and exchanges of letters with St. Clair, Jaworski continued, he was finally told Feb. 13 that Nixon had refused to reconsider his earlier decision "to terminate his cooperation with this investigation, at least with regard to producing any tape recordings of presidential conversations." Jaworski noted that in response to Nixon's concern about "an endless stream of requests," he had assured the White House there would be no further demands for evidence relating specifically to the Watergate break-in and cover-up—if the outstanding requests were granted.

The outstanding requests concerning the break-in and cover-up included 27 recordings of conversations Jaworski said he had requested in January, telling the White House that "each of the conversations is material to a particular facet of our investigation." Jaworski emphasized to Eastland that he had never asked for evidence irrelevant to his operations, and that Nixon's latest refusals had not been based on claims of irrelevance or "particularized privilege."

Jaworski conceded that the grand jury would be able to return indictments without the requested material, but maintained that the tapes were "important to a complete and thorough investigation and may contain evidence necessary for any future trials."

Jaworski listed other major areas in which White House cooperation had been limited at best. Regarding campaign contributions by the dairy industry, Ja-

worski said the investigation was "far from complete" and would be seriously hampered by White House refusal to produce requested material. Jaworski said his office had been told that Nixon would consider "a request narrower in scope."

(Jaworski noted that he had disqualified himself from the milk fund probe and that his report was based on advice from his deputy, Henry Ruth.)

In his investigation of the special "plumbers" unit, Jaworski said, the White House had provided one tape and "a number of documents" and had permitted a review of the unit's files. But, Jaworski added, the White House had refused to allow a review of the files of two unnamed former staff members in connection with the "plumbers" probe, noting that one review was first requested in August 1973.

Finally, Jaworski said, there were six requests—dating back to the last five months of 1973—for documents relating to unnamed "distinct areas of investigation still pending." Some documents had been released in response to two of these requests, and presidential counsel J. Fred Buzhardt Jr. had reported in regard to a third that a "limited search" had found no material. But, Jaworski concluded, "we have reason to believe that there are additional documents somewhere in the White House files."

St. Clair and Press Secretary Ronald L. Ziegler defended the White House position Feb. 15, and said meetings with Jaworski would continue.

In a written statement, St. Clair said Nixon had "fully cooperated" with the prosecutor "to the extent consistent with the constitutional responsibilities" of the presidency. "Conversations and papers voluntarily have been produced in a volume unprecedented in our history."

As for the additional requests, St. Clair said compliance "would have the necessary result of further delaying grand jury deliberations many months." A "careful review" of the request had led to the conclusion that this new material "was at best only corroborative of or cumulative to evidence already before the grand jury and therefore not essential to its deliberations."

Under these circumstances, St. Clair said, Nixon had decided that "continued and seemingly unending incursions into the confidentiality of presidential communications was unwarranted."

Questioned by reporters about St. Clair's "careful review" of the prosecutor's request, Ziegler said this did not mean that St. Clair, the President or anyone else at the White House had listened to the tapes or read the documents. Rather, Ziegler said, the decision was based on the principle of separation of powers, on "how far we have gone up to this point on a voluntary basis," and on St. Clair's discussions with Jaworski on the possible relevancy of the material.

Asked about Jaworski's status in view of the impasse, Ziegler said there was no desire "to move to a point of confrontation" with the prosecutor, nor had there been any discussion of dismissing him or ordering him to stop requesting additional material.

Tape copying, erasure debated—Citing White House and prosecution sources, the Washington Post reported Feb. 17 that the court-appointed panel of technical experts examining the Watergate tapes had found "technical indications" that two of the tapes might be re-recordings rather than the originals said to have been surrendered by the White House.

The Post said the White House and special prosecutor Jaworski's office had been informed of the panel's suspicions.

Told in advance of the story's content, presidential aides Alexander M. Haig Jr. and J. Fred Buzhardt Jr. disagreed with its implications. Buzhardt said he was "dead sure" all the tapes were originals, although he had heard that the panel had begun to question their authenticity. Haig said it would be "blasphemous speculation" and a "gross intrusion on grand jury proceedings" to imply that there had been any doctoring of tapes.

In a statement Feb. 17, special presidential counsel James D. St. Clair said that although the White House was aware of an "opinion" by one member of the technical panel that two tapes might have been re-recorded, no report by the panel, "tentative or otherwise," had been filed with the court to support the suggestion.

St. Clair said that because of this "opinion," an independent, White House-sponsored "technical investigation" had been conducted. The findings, which he said were being made available to the court-appointed panel, "do not indicate a re-recording was made."

St. Clair attacked the "inaccuracy and innuendo" of the Post report and said he would ask for a Justice Department investigation into the "person or persons who may have violated legal restraints" in referring to matters before the grand jury.

According to St. Clair, the White House technical study had also concluded that the disputed 18½-minute gap and erasure marks in the tape of a Nixon conversation with H. R. Haldeman "could well have been and probably were caused by the admittedly defective recording machine" used by Rose Mary Woods, Nixon's personal secretary. St. Clair did not identify the White House experts.

The possibility of an accidental erasure on the Haldeman tape was offered again Feb. 18 by another independent investigator who said he had volunteered his services to Charles S. Rhyne, Miss Woods' attorney.

Allan D. Bell Jr., president of Dektor Counterintelligence and Security Inc. of Springfield, Va., said his firm had found that a defective part in the recorder (which had been found by the court-appointed panel), or any variations in the recorder's electric power could have caused the machine's erase and record heads to make the reported marks on the tape.

Bell said his study had been made with a copy of the gap section of the tape and a rented recorder similar to the one used by Miss Woods. "Certain of our findings," Bell said, "completely support those of the panel." But, "based upon the information available to us, we cannot accept the conclusion that manual manipulation of the keyboard controls was required to produce the erase-head-stop signatures."

Rhyne said he considered the Bell study "so important" that he had sent copies to the court, the White House and Jaworski. Bell noted that "we are involved" and "probably the source" of some of St. Clair's comments about a White House investigation, but Press Secretary Ziegler denied the next day that St. Clair had been referring to the Bell report.

Disturbed by the heightened public debate on the tapes, Judge John J. Sirica met with lawyers for all sides Feb. 19 and said later that certain "precautionary measures" had been agreed upon to "prevent the disclosure of matters which ought, for the time being at least, to remain confidential." Sirica said the lawyers and the technical panel would refrain from further public statements, and the grand jury had been instructed to disregard press reports and "all statements not properly submitted."

Court orders Dean debate curbed—U.S. District Court Judge Gerhard A. Gesell took steps Feb. 15 to cut off public comment on the truthfulness of former presidential counsel John W. Dean 3rd.

During a pretrial hearing in the perjury case of former White House aide Dwight L. Chapin, Gesell called special prosecutor Jaworski to the bench to warn against any further comments supporting Dean's veracity such as Jaworski had made on a television program Feb. 3. Gesell said that another "lapse would have very serious consequences. It seems to me your good sense should keep you off talk shows." Jaworski promised "the greatest of care" in the future.

Gesell denied a defense motion to have Dean barred as a witness and instructed Chapin's attorney, Jacob A. Stein, to do his part in stopping "all this public debate."

Gesell noted that he could not direct President Nixon, Vice President Gerald R. Ford or Senate Republican leader Hugh Scott (Pa.) to "cease doing what they are doing." Gesell added, however, that in view of Nixon's expressed concern about pretrial publicity, "every effort" should be made by "appropriate authorities to stop discussing matters before this court."

Ford told a news conference in Omaha, Neb. later that day that he had urged Nixon to make public a recording bearing on the Dean evidence. Ford said he was "absolutely convinced it would prove the President is innocent and Mr. John W. Dean is a liar."

Senate panel cancels hearings—The

Senate Watergate Committee voted Feb. 19 to hold no further public hearings but decided to continue its investigation—behind closed doors—of possible campaign fund irregularities involving industrialist Howard Hughes, President Nixon's friend Charles G. Rebozo, and the dairy industry, and links between the Central Intelligence Agency and the Watergate break-in.

Chairman Sam J. Ervin Jr. (D, N.C.) said after the closed meeting that his committee believed "it should be careful not to interfere unduly" with the impeachment process of the House Judiciary Committee or the criminal cases being handled by the special prosecutor "on which the attention of the country appears now to be focused."

All seven members had voted to end the public hearings, but Edward J. Gurney (R, Fla.) had opposed the decision to continue investigations.

(Later in the day, the Senate approved, by voice vote, an extension of the committee's mandate to May 28. The authorization had been scheduled to expire Feb. 28.)

Ervin said the cancellation might be reversed "should special circumstances develop." A committee source said such circumstances would include a favorable ruling on an appeal of the dismissal of the panel's suit to obtain five White House tapes. The committee had voted during the same meeting to authorize its staff to proceed with an appeal.

Milk funds reported 'laundered.' The Senate Watergate Committee was investigating allegations that at least $200,000 in contributions from the dairy lobby was donated to two Republican Congressional campaign committees in 1972 in a scheme to conceal and "launder" money actually intended for President Nixon's re-election campaign, the New York Times reported Feb. 15 [For further details, see p. 40C8]

Burch joins White House staff. The White House announced Feb. 15 that Dean Burch would leave his post as chairman of the Federal Communications Commission (FCC) to become counselor to the President with cabinet rank. Burch had been with the FCC since November 1969.

Press Secretary Ronald Ziegler said Burch would engage in special projects. He specified that the appointment was not a replacement for Melvin R. Laird, who left the White House Feb. 1 as counselor to the President to become a Reader's Digest executive.

GOP retirements in House continue. The number of Republican members of Congress planning to retire after the current session increased to 17 by mid-February. The record for such announcements in a session was 17, set in 1972 by election time. House Republican Leader

John Rhodes (Ariz.) expressed concern Feb. 1 about the Republican exodus rate and the increasing "polarization" in Congress between the two major political parties.

The number of Democrats who had announced they would not seek re-election was 10. In the Senate, three from each party had made similar announcements.

The latest announcements were made Jan. 28 by Rep. Charles S. Gubser (R, Calif.), 57, 11 terms; Jan. 29 by Rep. Howard W. Robison (R, N.Y.), 59, nine terms; Feb. 15 by Reps. Henry P. Smith (R, N.Y.), 62, five terms, and Wendell Wyatt (R, Ore.), 56, five terms.

Robison, dean of the New York Congressional delegation, told reporters Jan. 29 "it truly isn't much fun any more, particularly under the circumstances." He felt that Watergate should be put in the past, but it was "unclear to me what I should do, this year, to help resolve it."

Democrats rebut Nixon speech. House Democratic Whip John J. McFall (Calif.) and Pennsylvania Gov. Milton J. Shapp (D) gave their party's reply Feb. 16 to President Nixon's Feb. 9 radio address on transportation.

Shapp, who had helped negotiate a settlement, said that neither Nixon nor his top aides had been fully aware of the true dimensions of the strike, "nor was it apparent that they were willing to take the bold action needed to bring the strike to an end." The problems, Shapp said, had been the Administration's "isolation, inaccessibility and an unwillingness on the part of the President to come to grips with reality."

Poll reports. Public approval of the way President Nixon was handling his job rose two points to 28% in early February, according to the Gallup Poll Feb. 17. The survey, taken Feb. 1–4, showed 28% approval, 59% disapproval (13% no opinion). The previous rating figures were 26%, 64%, 10% respectively. The Republican Party was the only major population group in the survey giving majority approval for the President (59%), who received his strongest regional support from the South (35%).

A Gallup Poll published Feb. 18 (same survey period) found that 49% of the respondents opposed Nixon's resignation (42% favored) and 51% opposed his removal from office (38% favored). Another finding: more than 70% of those surveyed believed that Nixon either planned (9%), tolerated (28%) or tried to cover up (34%) the Watergate burglary.

A Louis Harris poll published Feb. 12 showed that the public's rating of the job Congress was doing was 69% negative to 29% positive, the lowest recorded by the polling group and lower than Nixon's negative standing of 68% to 30%, also its lowest point.

Democrat wins Ford's seat. Richard F. VanderVeen (D) was elected to Congress Feb. 18 from Michigan's 5th District, a seat held by Republicans since 1910 and for the past 25 years by Gerald R. Ford, who vacated it in 1973 to become vice president.

VanderVeen, 51, a corporation lawyer, based his campaign on the Watergate issue, calling for President Nixon's resignation. He defeated Robert VanderLaan (R), 43, State Senate majority leader, 53,-008–46,159. The total turnout of 104,186 was considered a "moderate" voter participation. Two minor party condidates divided the difference.

VanderVeen billed his campaign as a "referendum on Richard Nixon." "Our President must stand beyond the shadow of a doubt," his ads said. "Our President must be Gerald Ford."

In Washington Feb. 21, prior to being sworn in, VanderVeen told reporters, "The silent majority has spoken and its message is clear: Richard Nixon has failed us, Richard Nixon cannot lead us."

The loss of the "safe" GOP district in the party's Midwest heartland—the district included Grand Rapids—was a surprise. Vice President Ford, saying he was "very disappointed by the results," spoke of the effect of the "deteriorating economic situation" but he conceded another element, a "general skepticism" about politics that "certainly would include Watergate." The next day he admitted he was a little "frightened" by the outcome. GOP National Chairman George Bush said he was "concerned" since "this man injected Watergate and made the President an issue." Michigan Republican Chairman William McLaughlin was more blunt: "Watergate killed us," he said.

Republican concern was matched by Democratic confidence. House Speaker Carl Albert (Okla.) summarized it: "Can anyone pick a district in the United States that the Republicans are sure to win this fall?" he asked.

AFL-CIO reaffirms impeachment call. The AFL-CIO reaffirmed its call for impeachment of President Nixon Feb. 18. At its October 1973 convention, the federation had called for Nixon's resignation and for impeachment if he did not.

The latest demand was issued in Bal Harbour, Fla. by the organization's Executive Council, which approved an impeachment resolution with only one dissent, by Paul Hall, president of the Seafarers International Union. Hall had been the sole dissenter in the council's previous impeachment resolution.

The new resolution stated that "no President in history had been so widely distrusted by his fellow citizens" and an impeachment trial by the Senate was "the only way for the President to get his day in court" and "the only way the American people can get at the truth."

In an economic statement Feb. 21, the council denounced the "Nixon Administration's so-called stabilization program" as a "failure" and "a fraud." "Economic justice would dictate that workers' wages reflect at least increases in the cost of living plus the rise in productivity," it said.

AFL-CIO President George Meany specified that for wages to catch up with the cost of living increases of at least 10% were required.

At a news conference Feb. 18, Meany said he did not expect any "explosion of wage demands" in upcoming contract negotiations, but he was pessimistic about the economy. "We've already reached the recession point in my book," he said, and he expected the jobless rate to "go over 6%, maybe to 6.5%" in 1974.

Discounting as "ridiculous" charges that the federation was prolonging a campaign of harassment against the President, Meany said, "We're not the ones who are dragging it out. He is. We're not the ones who have hired new lawyers or tape experts or specialists on erasure."

Meany cited a poll by the International Association of Machinists (IAM) showing that 72% of its membership would like to see the President out of the White House, 49% favoring resignation and 23% impeachment. "I'm sure that this 72% reflects the thinking of our whole membership, not just the machinists," Meany said.

In announcing the findings of the poll, based on about 5,000 replies to a questionnaire, IAM President Floyd Smith said Feb. 17 the membership was "becoming convinced that their government is rigged for the benefit of the big corporations and the richest families" and such disenchantment from the middle class "could become dangerous."

At a meeting of the federation's political arm, the Committee on Political Education (COPE) Feb. 20, a goal was set to gain "a veto-proof Congress" by electing in November 25 more representatives and seven more senators friendly to labor.

Gov. George C. Wallace (D, Ala.) came to the Florida site to meet with Meany Feb. 15, the first time the two had met. Meany said Wallace had requested the meeting. At his news conference Feb. 18, Meany was asked whether he still considered Wallace a racist. His reply: "the fellow has mellowed." They had not discussed politics, Meany said, but taxes, pensions and Social Security, issues on which he found himself largely "in the same ball park" with Wallace.

Aides say House need not allege crime. In a study on the nature of presidential impeachment, counsel for the House Judiciary Committee concluded that violation of criminal law need not be a requisite for impeachment. The study, released by the committee Feb. 21, was prepared by the panel's special counsel John M. Doar and its Republican counsel Albert E. Jenner Jr. and their staff.

Committee Chairman Peter W. Rodino Jr. (D, N.J.) affirmed his agreement with the study's conclusion that grounds for impeachment "don't necessarily have to arise out of criminal conduct."

The committee's ranking Republican, Rep. Edward Hutchinson (Mich.), disagreed. "There should be criminality involved," he said. Hutchinson emphasized that the study was a staff report and that "it speaks to the committee, not for the committee." The second-ranking GOP member, Rep. Robert McClory (Ill.), said he and Hutchinson were "very close together" on the issue but in his own view "it may be that certain offenses that don't fit any definition of a crime might be regarded as impeachable."

The staff report stressed that impeachable offenses "cannot be defined in detail in advance of full investigation of the facts." It said "no fixed standards for determining whether grounds for impeachment exist" were being offered in the report, and, in fact, the framers "did not write a fixed standard" into the Constitution but had adopted from English history "a standard sufficiently general and flexible to meet future circumstances."

The study found that this standard for presidential impeachment could include commission of "constitutional wrongs that subvert the structure of government, or undermine the integrity of office and even the Constitution itself." It found that a president's "entire course of conduct in office" could be considered in as much as, "in particular situations, it may be a course of conduct more than individual acts that has a tendency to subvert constitutional government." It found that, flowing from the Constitutional requirement that a president faithfully execute the laws, he was responsible "for the overall conduct of the executive branch."

The study concluded that impeachment was "a constitutional remedy addressed to serious offenses against the system of government," that in the American experience of 13 impeachments criminality may or may not have been charged, and that "the emphasis has been on the significant effects of the conduct—undermining the integrity of office, disregard of constitutional duties and oath of office, abrogation of power, abuse of the governmental process, adverse impact on the system of government."

It noted the three major presidential duties explicitly stated in the Constitution—to "take care that the laws be faithfully executed," to faithfully execute the office and to preserve, protect and defend the Constitution. It also noted that

these embraced an affirmative duty involving "the responsibility of a president for the overall conduct of the executive branch" and an affirmative duty "not to abuse his powers or transgress their limits—not to violate the rights of citizens . . . and not to act in derogation of powers vested elsewhere by the Constitution."

The study stressed one further requirement for impeachment, a finding of "substantiality," that "the facts must be considered as a whole in the context of the office, not in terms of separate or isolated events." Impeachment was "a grave step," it cautioned, and "it is to be predicated only upon conduct seriously incompatible with either the constitutional form and principles of our government or the proper performance of constitutional duties of the presidential office."

In its arguments that legal criminality was not a requisite for impeachment, the counsel report said impeachment and the criminal law "serve fundamentally different purposes," that the former was remedial—for removal from office and possible disqualification from future office—and its purpose not personal punishment but "primarily to maintain constitutional government." It pointed out that the Constitution itself provided that impeachment was no substitute for criminal law since it did not immunize the officer from criminal liability later.

"To confine impeachable conduct to indictable offenses," the report said, "may well be to set a standard so restrictive as not to reach conduct that might adversely affect the system of government. Some of the most grievous offenses against our constitutional form of government may not entail violations of the criminal law."

Earlier developments. Release of the brief superseded a public hearing scheduled by the committee for that day on the issue. Rodino said Feb. 20 the brief should "speak for itself" and individual members of the committee would have to reach their own conclusions on what constituted impeachable misconduct. His view was consonant with the committee's Republican minority, which had decided at a caucus Feb. 15 to seek to delay or cancel the public hearing. Ranking GOP member Edward Hutchinson (Mich.) said afterwards that "I don't know why there is any need for a hearing" and that "every member will assess the question as he sees fit and utilize it [the staff brief] in any way he feels necessary."

Meeting with Nixon counsel—Doar and Jenner had reported to the committee members Feb. 14 on their Feb. 12 meeting with James D. St. Clair, special counsel to the President. Both described the meeting as "cordial." Jenner said there had been "no element of noncooperation whatsoever." But there was an obvious conflict on the nature of the inquiry, they reported.

St. Clair had presented the White House view that it constituted an adversary legal proceeding in which the White House should have the right to file counterbriefs on legal points and the right to cross-examine witnesses. The committee attorneys rejected this, contending the inquiry was a search for truth, not a lawsuit, and Congress was supreme in the impeachment area.

St. Clair also reportedly had expressed the President's concern about how the committee would control any documents made available to it. The committee was developing procedures for this. Rodino made clear Feb. 14 that the procedures would not be subject to White House approval or disapproval. "We are not saying to Mr. St. Clair that these are the rules we adopted," he told reporters. "We are saying, we have rules and it is now necessary to move forward and we will make our requests for information."

Rodino's position reportedly was endorsed by the panel's Democratic majority at a caucus Feb. 20, when they reportedly also decided to present to the White House formal requests for specific items of Watergate evidence in order to discover the extent of the President's willingness to cooperate. Rep. Robert F. Drinan (Mass.) said after attending the caucus there was some expectation of encountering "dilatory tactics" from the President's counsel and that a confrontation was "inevitable." In Drinan's view it was incumbent on the committee to "demonstrate we're not going to be delayed, we're not going to be pushed around."

The primacy of the House on the impeachment area was stressed by Rodino during an appearance on the ABC "Issues and Answers" broadcast Feb. 10. "The House is vested with tremendous power here," he said. "It is our inescapable responsibility to do this job, to settle this question, to assure the American people that we will discharge our duty under the Constitution once and for all."

The right to inquire under the power of impeachment, he said, "is such that it can go as far as the secret recesses of the presidency, as President [James K.] Polk once said, and we hope there is going to be this kind of cooperation."

Referring to the recent House vote ratifying the committee's impeachment investigation, Rodino said the House had given his committee the authority to investigate "impeachment in totality."

He said the authority, which included broad subpoena power, covered a summoning, if necessary, of President Nixon for testimony and access to material obtained by the Watergate special prosecutor. The subpoena power, he specified, "goes wherever it must and therefore executive privilege, I think, cannot be asserted."

Probe covers personal finances—The committee's probe extended into the area of President Nixon's personal finances.

Committee members reported Feb. 14 that Doar had informed them that two staff investigators were in California for that purpose and staffers had been assigned as liaison with the joint Congressional panel investigating Nixon's tax returns.

The other areas of investigation by the committee (reported by Newsweek magazine Feb. 18) included the Watergate break-in and cover-up, campaign intelligence activities (espionage and "dirty tricks"), domestic surveillance activities ("plumbers" group in this category), efforts to use federal agencies for political purposes and other areas, such as the secret bombing of Cambodia and impounding of Congressionally mandated funds.

White House reception for backers. President Nixon held a reception at the White House Feb. 22 for the approximately 400 supporters who attended a $100-a-plate hotel luncheon earlier that day in Washington sponsored by the National Citizens' Committee for Fairness to the Presidency. "It's not me that you honor," he told them "it's for the presidency and peace in the world." "At the cost of personal criticism against me and my family, even more than the man Nixon I am considering the office of the presidency and the country," he said.

Vice President Gerald R. Ford and Sen. Strom Thurmond (R, S.C.) were among the speakers at the luncheon. Thurmond told the group "no president has stood more for individual freedom of the citizen than Richard Nixon."

Ford, expressing concern that Nixon's popularity rating had dropped so low "under the hammering of hostile critics," endorsed the group's efforts to stimulate fairness in the presidential controversy. But he urged a broadening of the effort to include all of the institutions of government. "Do we not also need fairness to Congress?" he asked. "Do we not also need fairness to the courts—as we expect fairness from the courts?"

Ford aids Cincinnati candidate—At a rally in Cincinnati Feb. 20 for the Republican Congressional candidate in a scheduled special election, Ford warned that "labor outsiders" were moving in to influence the outcome as they had in recent GOP Congressional losses in Michigan and Pennsylvania. He called on local Republicans "to turn the tide and to stop this stampede."

Privacy panel announced. President Nixon announced in a radio address Feb. 23 that he was creating a "top-priority" Cabinet-level committee to recommend measures to protect individual privacy against computerized data banks and other developments of "advanced technology" used by both government and private institutions. [For further details, see p. 160G3]

Nixon barred charges in NSC spying case. Sources close to the inquiry by the special White House investigative unit, the "plumbers," said Feb. 23 that President Nixon had personally ordered his former domestic affairs adviser John D. Ehrlichman, also nominal head of the "plumbers," not to seek prosecution of any of the military personnel suspected of passing top secret documents from the National Security Council (NSC) to the office of Adm. Thomas H. Moorer, chairman of the Joint Chiefs of Staff (JCS). [For further details on this and other revelations related to the NSC spying case, see chapter on domestic spying]

Nixon handling of spying probed—The New York Times reported Feb. 26 that the office of special Watergate prosecutor Leon Jaworski had begun an investigation of President Nixon's handling of military spying in the NSC in 1971. Investigators for Jaworski's office were allowed to see the classified report on the snooping prepared by David R. Young Jr., a member of the plumbers, the Times reported.

White House news conference. President Nixon asserted at a televised news conference Feb. 25 that he did not expect to be impeached. He said his interpretation of the Constitution required a criminal offense by a president for impeachment.

At the news conference, the first at the White House since Oct. 26, 1973, the President also disclosed that he had declined, on constitutional grounds, a request from the special prosecutor to testify before the federal grand jury investigating the Watergate case.

The impeachment issue—The President said the Constitution was "very precise" in defining an impeachable offense and it was "the opinion of White House counsel and a number of other constitutional lawyers . . . that a criminal offense on the part of the President is the requirement for impeachment." He said his counsel was preparing a brief on the matter for presentation to the House Judiciary Committee, whose counsel had recently prepared a study favoring a broader interpretation of the impeachment requisites, that a finding of legal criminality was not one of them.

The President was asked if it would not be in his best interest and that of the country "to have this matter finally resolved in a proper judicial form, that is, a full impeachment trial in the Senate?"

Nixon replied that a full impeachment trial in the Senate "comes only when the House determines that there is an impeachable offense. It is my belief that the House, after it conducts its inquiry, will not reach that determination. I do not expect to be impeached."

Nixon reaffirmed his position, as stated in his State of the Union message, that he was "prepared to cooperate with the [Ju-

diciary] committee in any way consistent with my constitutional responsibility to defend the office of the presidency against any action which would weaken that office and the ability of future presidents to carry out the great responsibilities that any president will have."

Nixon said his counsel and the counsel for the committee were conducting negotiations on the matter and the decision on extent of cooperation "will be made based on what arrangements are developed between the two [counsel] for the confidentiality of those particular items where they must remain confidential and also based on whether or not turning over to the committee will in any way jeopardize the rights of defendants or impair the ability of the prosecution to carry on its proper functions in the cases that may develop."

Election issue—The political question was raised about the Republican loss of Vice President Gerald R. Ford's former House seat to a Democrat who campaigned for Nixon's removal from office. "What advice would you give Republican candidates this year to counter that argument?" a newsman asked.

Nixon recalled the 1948 campaign when Republicans "confidently expected to gain in the House" and when Sen. J. W. Fulbright (D, Ark.) "called for President Truman's resignation in the spring because the economy was in a slump and President Truman had other problems, and we proceeded to campaign against Mr. Truman. He was the issue. And we took a bad licking in the Congress in 1948."

Nixon's advice to candidates: "It is that nine months before an election no one can predict what can happen in this country. What will affect the election this year, 1974, is what always affects elections—peace and prosperity. On the peace front we're doing well and I think we'll continue to do well." And on prosperity, "I think that this economy is going to be moving up" and "it will be a good year for those candidates who stand for the Administration."

Later, the President was asked if he would reconsider his resolve not to resign if "it became evident that your party was going to suffer a disastrous defeat in this year's election." "No," Nixon responded, "I want my party to succeed, but more important I want the presidency to survive" and it was "vitally important" that the presidency "not be hostage to what happens to the popularity of a president at one time or another."

"The stability of this office," he continued, "the ability of the President to continue to govern, the ability, for example, of this President to continue the great initiatives which have led to a more peaceful world than we have had for a generation, and to move on the domestic front in the many areas that I have described—all of these things, these goals, are yet before us. We have a lot of work left to do, more than three years left to do, and I'm going to stay here till I get it done."

His tax deductions—Nixon was asked if he intended to pay state or local income taxes on his 1973 returns and whether he "had any second thoughts about your claimed deductions for the gift of the vice presidential papers?" He said he would pay any state taxes "the law requires." He referred to a recent California ruling that he was apparently not required to pay that state's taxes. (The state's Franchise Tax Board had ruled Feb. 1 that Nixon was not a California resident for state income tax purposes. The ruling did not resolve the question of whether a nonresident could be taxed on California source income, such as Nixon's income from a resale of land in California.) "I would be glad to pay those taxes," Nixon continued, "and of course deduct that from my federal income tax liability as others can do if they desire to do so."

As for the gift of the papers, Nixon said "there's no question about my intent" to make the gift. All of his vice presidential papers were delivered to the Archives four months before the deadline, he said. "The paper work on it apparently was not concluded until after that time. This raises a legal question as to whether or not the deduction therefore is proper." He cited his request that Congress look into the matter and said, "If it was not a proper one [deduction] I will of course be glad to pay the tax."

Later, he was asked if he thought he had paid his "fair share of taxes." The questioner noted that the notary date of the deed of the papers to the government was the same date of his tax reform message deploring special preferences in the law permitting "far too many Americans to pay less than their fair share of taxes."

Nixon said he had not written the law, that others had taken such deductions and he had taken them on the advice of the late President Lyndon Johnson. Nixon mentioned others who he said had taken such deductions: Sen. Hubert Humphrey (D, Minn.), who had in 1973 disclosed that he had taken a tax deduction of $199,153 for donating his vice presidential papers to the Historical Society in his home state of Minnesota; Jerome B. Wiesner, president of the Massachusetts Institute of Technology and former science adviser to Presidents Kennedy and Johnson; and John Kenneth Galbraith, who had been Kennedy's ambassador to India.

(Wiesner disputed Nixon's statement Feb. 25, asserting that he had donated his official papers to the National Archives but had claimed no tax deduction. "I never placed a monetary value on the papers, nor have I ever taken an income tax deduction for them," Wiesner said. "I don't know why the President thinks I did." The White House acknowledged Feb. 26 that Nixon had erred in citing Wiesner's tax deductions. Deputy Press Secretary Gerald Warren said the President "certainly regrets the mention of Wiesner." Warren said the comment was

based on press reports.)

(Galbraith said Feb. 25 that he had taken a tax deduction of $4,500 but it was for a gift of private papers, none of which were written in his government role. "It was 100 times less than the President's and no juggling of dates was required," he said.)

Agnew's resignation—The President was asked whether he believed Agnew had "brought dishonor upon his office, this Administration and the country." Nixon responded:

"It would be very easy for me to jump on the vice president when he's down. I could only say that in his period of service that he rendered dedicated service on all of the assignments that I gave to him. He went through, along with his family, a terribly difficult situation and he resigned as I think he thought he should, because of the embarrassment that he knew that would cause to the Administration and also because he felt that in view of the criminal offense that was charged that he should not stay in office. Now at this point I am not going to join anybody else in kicking him when he's down."

Kalmbach pleads guilty. Herbert W. Kalmbach, President Nixon's personal attorney and one of his chief fund raisers, pleaded guilty Feb. 25 to two violations of the federal law governing campaign funds. He admitted raising $3.9 million for a secret Congressional campaign committee in 1970 and also promising an ambassador a better diplomatic post in return for a $100,000 campaign contribution. [For further details, see p. 41C2]

House panel asks Nixon for data. The House Judiciary Committee sent a request to the White House Feb. 25 for specific information for its impeachment inquiry. The request was in a letter from special counsel John Doar to presidential counsel James D. St. Clair.

The committee had received from special Watergate prosecutor Leon Jaworski Feb. 21 a list of 700 pages of documents and 17 tapes that his office had received from the White House for its grand jury investigations. The committee's request to the White House for specific items reportedly was based on this list. Jaworski had turned the list, not the items themselves, over to the Judiciary panel after assurance the committee was intent upon rules to protect the confidentiality of its sensitive material. The rules, adopted unanimously Feb. 22, restricted open access to such material to the committee's chairman and senior Republican member and their two top staff members; other committee members could examine the material at certain times in a secure place without making copies; none of the material could be made public except by a vote of the committee.

Doar advised the committee at a briefing Feb. 22 that White House compliance with the request for data should take no more than "a day or two." "The public is looking for expeditious action," chairman Peter W. Rodino Jr. (D, N.J.) said. "Congress has asked us to act promptly. Any delay will not be forthcoming from our side."

Panel members dispute Nixon—Four senior Republicans on the House Judiciary Committee Feb. 26 disputed Nixon's news conference assertion that a criminal offense was a requirement for impeachment.

Tom Railsback (Ill.) said it was "incumbent on us to find evidence of a very serious offense, but not necessarily a crime." Charles E. Wiggins (Calif.) agreed, but cautioned that "we should exercise our power narrowly" in dealing with a President elected to a fixed term.

A similar view was expressed by Robert McClory (Ill.), who praised the committee staff's finding that noncriminal grounds might be sufficient, but added that he questioned its applicability "at this time." Charles W. Sandman Jr. (N.J.) said a proper standard would be any offense "of a highly serious nature affecting the conduct of the nation's business."

Two Democrats on the panel were less cautious: Robert W. Kastenmeier (Wis.) said that since Nixon was "personally involved," his views would "have to be biased in the extreme. It seems pretty self-serving to suggest so narrow an interpretation." Jerome R. Waldie (Calif.) contended that "most people who have read the Constitution" would disagree with Nixon's interpretation.

Ex-aide urges impeachment. Former White House speechwriter John K. Andrews Jr. called for Nixon's impeachment Feb. 25, becoming the first present or former presidential aide to do so publicly.

In an interview broadcast on public television, Andrews said he did not believe Nixon was criminally involved in acts connected with the Watergate scandal. But, Andrews said, from approval of a domestic intelligence plan in 1970 through the Watergate cover-up, Nixon "was not exerting the kind of leadership, was not monitoring the acts of his subordinates as he is obligated to do under his oath of office and his constitutional duties."

Andrews said Nixon's consistent attempts to "minimize the exposure, to fight ditch by ditch against giving out evidence" compounded the President's responsibility.

Impeachment, Andrews said, might "ultimately be interpreted as a conservative action" preserving the "essence of our liberties and our democracy to bring to account a leader who has abused his trust, and I'm afraid the President has."

Senate panel appeals tape ruling. The Senate Watergate Committee filed an appeal Feb. 25 of U.S. District Court Gerhard A. Gesell's dismissal of its suit to obtain five presidential tape recordings. Gesell had ruled against the committee on the ground that publicity about the tapes might be harmful to criminal prosecutions.

The committee's brief argued that Gesell's ruling was apparently based on a questionable conclusion that a "legislative need for relevant evidence may be subjugated to the court's view" of the need to prevent pretrial publicity. The ruling was contrary to what the committee called the "well-established principles" prohibiting a court from overturning a Congressional action "simply because it disagrees with the legislative wisdom or policy behind that measure."

The committee said that in addition to its legislative function of possible election law reforms, it had an "informing function" to be aided by access to the tapes. In the event that criminal cases ended in guilty pleas or tapes were not allowed into evidence in trials, committee access "would ensure that the tapes are in the public domain and will not be forever hidden under a cloak of secrecy." The panel said, however, that it would accept a protective order keeping the tapes secret while criminal actions were proceeding.

The brief noted that the special prosecutor had taken no position on what action the court should have taken, and that President Nixon had "allowed many of his aides to testify fully as to the contents of the tapes, an action obviously inconsistent with the claim of prejudicial pretrial publicity" he had raised in connection with the committee's suit.

Nixon rejected request to testify. President Nixon disclosed Feb. 25 that he had rejected a request that he testify before a Watergate grand jury.

Asked at his news conference whether he had been asked for testimony "in any form," and if so whether he would comply, Nixon said, "I believe it's a matter of record that the special prosecutor transmitted a request that I testify before the grand jury, and on constitutional grounds, I respectfully declined to do so."

Nixon added that he had offered to "respond to any interrogatories that the special prosecutor might want to submit or to meet with him personally and answer questions, but he indicated he did not want to proceed in that way."

(White House sources said later that Nixon answered the news conference question under the mistaken impression that the request was a matter of public record, while it was, in fact, a tightly-guarded secret among Nixon's closest aides.)

Special prosecutor Leon Jaworski said Feb. 26 that the testimony request had not come from him directly, but from Vladimir N. Pregelj, the foreman of the original Watergate grand jury. Jaworski said Pregelj's Jan. 30 letter to Nixon had stated that written answers would not be sufficient. The request was rejected Jan. 31 in a reply by special presidential counsel James D. St. Clair, citing the need to preserve the independence of the presidency.

Sources in Jaworski's office said the prosecutor had decided not to try to enforce the request by subpoenaing the President.

Nixon bars role in Ehrlichman trial. Lawyers for President Nixon Feb. 26 rejected a California state judge's order that he appear as a witness in the burglary and conspiracy trial of John D. Ehrlichman, his former domestic affairs adviser, and two members of the special "plumbers" investigative unit.

The White House also said Nixon would decline to appear at a District of Columbia court hearing on the merits of the California order. D.C. Superior Court Chief Judge Harold H. Greene had scheduled a hearing for March 15 under interstate legal compacts relating to out-of-state witnesses.

In a brief and letter to Judge Greene, the White House said "to accede to the compulsory processes of a state court would not only unduly interfere with the grave responsibility of a President to make the decisions which affect the continued security of the nation but would open the door for unfettered and wholesale imposition upon the office of the President by the courts in each of the 50 states."

The White House said Nixon had been advised to "follow the precedents established by his predecessors" in declining both appearances, citing the 1807 case in which President Thomas Jefferson had refused to "abandon superior duties" to respond personally to a subpoena.

(The White House documents did not mention whether Nixon might respond in writing, as Jefferson had done.)

The President's constitutional responsibility to "perform his official duties" could not be overcome by an inferior state jurisdiction, Nixon's lawyers argued; the language of Article 6 of the Constitution was "unmistakably clear": "The Constitution, and the laws of the United States . . . shall be the supreme law of the land; and the judges of every state shall be bound thereby. . . ."

White House tape consultant revealed. The White House hired the Stanford Research Institute of Menlo Park, Calif. (SRI) to study the Watergate tapes already under examination by a court-appointed panel of technical experts, it was reported Feb. 27. Previous White House references to an independent "technical investigation" had not identified the investigators.

A spokesman for SRI, a nonprofit research center not connected with Stanford University, said the institute had been retained Jan. 20 for "experimental work" and for "providing technical cooperation to the White House." Michael Hecker, a specialist in hearing and speech sciences, was the principal consultant.

The Washington Post reported Feb. 28 that Hecker was concentrating on the disputed 18½-minute gap in one of the tapes, but that no tapes had been taken to SRI headquarters.

Nixon appeals to young Republicans. President Nixon, in an address to the Young Republican Leadership Conference in Washington Feb. 28, told the group, "You learn from your defeats, and then you go on, fight again, never quit, never quit. Always go on and fight for those things you believe in."

Cheered by the 500 delegates who at one point chanted "three more years," the President said, "You never win even when you win big and just assume that now the job is done, because the battle always goes on."

He added: "When the battle looks toughest, get in there and fight for the cause. Keep your faith. Keep your confidence."

Nixon aides described his speech as part of a new "positive response" to the problems of Watergate.

In urging Republicans not to become disillusioned by special election defeats, Nixon said GOP candidates should not assume that the only time to run for office was "when it is a sure thing."

"Show me a candidate who is not a hungry candidate, show me a candidate who isn't willing to take a risk and risk all, even risk losing, and I will show you a lousy candidate," Nixon said.

He said a Republican will be in the White House "for the next three years and for eight years after that."

During his address, Nixon again said he would veto the energy bill pending in Congress and said flatly that the country was not going to have gas rationing.

Sen. Barry Goldwater (R, Ariz.), addressing the group Feb. 28, criticized the President's recent $304 billion budget, which he said "I cannot live with."

"If you think our party is in trouble at this point," Goldwater said, "I suggest that you take a shot at predicting what kind of shape it will be in if the inflationary dynamite of a $304 billion budget is laid at our doorstep."

White House says crime finding vital. The White House presented its legal position on the nature of presidential impeachment Feb. 28. According to its 61-page analysis, "a president may only be impeached for indictable crimes" and those crimes must be of "a very serious nature" and "committed in one's governmental capacity."* President Nixon had said at his Feb. 25 news conference that he interpreted the Constitution as requiring a criminal offense by a president for impeachment.

Nixon's attorneys, under the direction of James D. St. Clair, submitted the analysis of constitutional standards for impeachment to the House Judiciary Committee. That panel's impeachment inquiry staff had reached the opposite conclusion, that criminality was not essential to impeachment, which it said was a remedy against serious offenses against the system of government.

The White House analysis said the words of the Constitution "inherently require a criminal offense" for justification of impeachment and that such offense be serious and committed in an official capacity. It said "the use of a predetermined criminal standard for the impeachment of a president is also supported by history, logic, legal precedent and a sound and sensible public policy which demands stability in our form of government."

Among its other arguments:

■ The impeachment clause was drafted in the context of the English precedents, which hewed to two distinct types of impeachment—a criminal process "for reaching great offenses committed against the government by men of high station," and a criminal process for "the political purpose of achieving the absolute political supremacy of Parliament over the executive." The framers of the U.S. Constitution rejected the political impeachments.

■ The enabling phrase, "high crimes and misdemeanors," meant to the framers "such criminal conduct as justified the removal of an officeholder from office." And, "in light of English and American history and usage," there was "no evidence to attribute anything but a criminal meaning" to the phrase.

■ The framers had "emphatically rejected 'maladministration' as a standard for impeachment" and their debates "clearly indicate a purely criminal meaning for 'other high crimes and misdemeanors.' "

These words, along with "treason" and "bribery," the other part of the enabling phrase, then and now "mean what they clearly connote—criminal offenses."

■ A study of American impeachment precedents revealed that the House "has supported different standards for the im-

*According to Article II, Section 4 of the Constitution: "The President, Vice President and all civil Officers of the United States, shall be removed from Office on Impeachment for, and Conviction of, Treason, Bribery, or other High Crimes and Misdemeanors."

peachment of judges and a president since 1804." A president was subject to elections, a judge was not, therefore the Constitution had a "good behavior" clause applying to judges that "must be construed together" with the impeachment clause. "Thus, consistent with House precedent, a judge who holds office for a life tenure may be impeached for less than an indictable offense. Even here, however, Senatorial precedents have demonstrated a reluctance to convict a judge in the absence of criminal conduct."

■ A review of the one American precedent of presidential impeachment (President Andrew Johnson in 1868) "indicates that the predicate for such action was a bitter political struggle between the executive and legislative branches of government." The first attempt to impeach then "failed because 'no specific crime was alleged to have been committed.' " The acquittal by the Senate "strongly indicates that the Senate has refused to adopt a broad view of 'other high crimes and misdemeanors' as a basis for impeaching a president. This conclusion is further substantiated by the virtual lack of factual issues in the proceeding. The most salient lesson to be learned from the widely criticized Johnson trial is that impeachment of a president should be resorted to only for cases of the gravest kind—the commission of a crime named in the Constitution or a criminal offense against the laws of the United States."

■ ". . . The Constitutional proscription against ex post facto laws, the requirement of due process, and the separation of powers . . . preclude the use of any standard other than 'criminal' for the removal of a president by impeachment."

Justice Department study—A Justice Department study of the nature of impeachment indicated the viability of both interpretations concerning the necessity of a finding of criminality in a presidential impeachment. The study was released in two phases Feb. 22 and 27. In issuing the first, Assistant Attorney General Robert G. Dixon stressed that the study was an "overview" that did not "reach conclusions or propose solutions" or address itself to any current charges.

The study issued Feb. 22 said "one can make a strong argument, based on the text of the Constitution alone, that impeachment can only be predicated on a 'high' criminal offense." The words, it said, "suggest the need for a criminal offense, although, of course, they do not expressly forbid an additional noncriminal penumbra."

But, it said, "as soon as one turns to the background of the impeachment clause [See footnote] and the precedents set under it, the matter becomes far more complicated. There are historical pre-

cedents and writing showing a broad definition" of the impeachable ingredient. The study cited the first American impeachment in 1798 involving a senator, stating that it was a political process "not so much designed to punish an offender as to secure the State." "Under this hypothesis," it continued, "one can conceive of serious abuses of power which have not been made crimes" as grounds for impeachment.

The study put forward the view it ascribed to "many citizens and many members of Congress" that "impeachment of a president is, if anything, more serious than an ordinary criminal trial . . . and that strict standards should be applied."

According to the section of the study issued Feb. 27, the framers of the Constitution intended the phrase "high crimes and misdemeanors" to have a "rather limited technical meaning." There was "no clear intent to adopt wholesale English practice and precedent on impeachment," which, it said, imparted a broader definition that extended to abuse of office.

But it also appraised the Federalist papers and the record of state ratification conventions as "lend[ing] support to the view that impeachment may be based upon certain types of non-criminal conduct."

The report supported the view that the impeachment process was not within the purview of court review. This in turn, it pointed out, favored the position that impeachment may be based on political, instead of criminal acts, but it also pointed out that the broader basing "rests upon the view that the underlying purpose of the impeachment process is not to punish the individual but to protect the public against gross abuse of power."

The Justice Department analysis said there was no precedent for a president to withhold information in the impeachment process under a claim of executive privilege. If such a situation persisted, it warned, "a constitutional confrontation of the highest magnitude would ensue."

Democrats' civil suit settled. Robert S. Strauss, chairman of the Democratic National Committee, said Feb. 28 that agreement had been reached to settle out of court for $775,000 its civil damage suit against the Committee to Re-elect the President. The Democrats had sued for $6.4 million over the break-in at the party's Watergate headquarters.

Co-defendants in the suit were former Nixon campaign officials and Cabinet members John N. Mitchell and Maurice H. Stans, convicted conspirators G. Gordon Liddy and E. Howard Hunt Jr., and former re-election committee treasurer Hugh W. Sloan Jr.

The settlement accord included commitments by the Republicans to drop countersuits against the Democrats.

ITT, Milk Fund
& other Campaign Fund Abuses

Nixon said 'tied' by oil firms. Rep. Les Aspin (D, Wis.) charged Jan. 1 that 413 directors, senior officials and stockholders of 178 oil and gas companies had contributed $4.98 million to President Nixon's re-election campaign. Because of these donations, nearly 10% of Nixon's total campaign receipts, Aspin said, "President Nixon's hands are tied, preventing him from dealing effectively with the current energy crisis. After their massive contributions, there is little he can do to control them."

The list, which did not include large gifts from the Rockefeller family (Exxon stockholders), was compiled from public information on file with the General Accounting Office and from a secret donors list obtained after a court fight by Common Cause, the public interest lobby.

The largest group of these contributions, $1.17 million worth, came from Richard M. Scaife and others associated with the Gulf Oil Co.

Nixon issues ITT, milk fund statements. President Nixon Jan. 8 released two white papers detailing his involvement in two controversial decisions made by the Administration in 1971 related to an increase in the federal price support for milk and an antitrust suit against the International Telephone & Telegraph Corp. (ITT).

In the latest steps taken to recapture his plummeting personal credibility with the public, Nixon branded as "utterly false" charges that presidential actions were offered in the matters as a quid pro quo "either in return for political contributions or the promise of such contributions."

(Nixon's statements on the milk fund and ITT constituted an end to the Administration's Operation Candor. Bryce N. Harlow, counselor to the President, said Jan. 9 that the operation had "just about run its course. The President can't indefinitely keep this kind of thing up and he shouldn't," Harlow said.)

Nixon had promised Nov. 17, 1973 to "put out all the facts" on the milk fund and ITT cases but no tapes or documents were issued with the statement denying wrongdoing. However, according to the White House release, supporting material had been provided the Watergate special prosecutor. It "should be clear that the accounts published today are consistent with the basic facts contained in these documents and tapes," the Nixon statement added.

The milk fund—In a 17-page statement, Nixon defended as "totally proper" his decision to reverse an Agriculture Department ruling and allow an increase in the federal price support of milk, although he admitted for the first time that before he ordered the increase he was aware that the dairy industry had pledged at least $2 re-election campaign. [For further details, see p. 38D2]

However, the statement continued, "he at no time discussed the contributions with the dairy industry and the subject was not mentioned in his meeting of March 23, 1971" with dairy representatives. The statement added, "It is also worth noting that the ultimate contributions by the dairy industry to the President's re-election effort (1) were far less than the industry leaders had hoped to raise; (2) were far less than the dairy industry gave to other candidates for the House and Senate, including many prominent Democrats; and (3) represented less than 1% of the total contributions to President Nixon's re-election campaign."

Nixon said his decision to raise the price support was based on three factors:

■ "Intensive Congressional pressure"

■ "The economic merits of the case itself, as presented by the industry leaders in the meeting with the President, and as weighed by the President's advisers [in a meeting later that day]"

■ "Traditional political considerations relating to needs of the farm states."

According to Nixon, dairy lobbyists had mobilized 29 senators and more than 100 congressmen in an effort to raise price supports to levels that were 85%–90% of parity. To bring this about, legislation had been introduced that appeared certain of passage, according to Nixon, and any presidential veto also appeared certain to be overridden.

"Moreover," the statement continued, "if the President were to try to force his will in this matter (i.e., to push parity down to 80%) it could be politically disastrous in some of the Midwestern states, and, in the light of known Congressional intentions, would be both foolish and futile."

It was this "overwhelming" Congressional "pressure," Nixon said, that he referred to as the "gun to our head" in his press conference Nov. 17, 1973.

During the conference with advisers March 23, 1971, "the political power of the dairy industry lobby was also brought to the President's attention," according to the statement. Treasury "Secretary [John B.] Connally [Jr.] said that their votes would be important in several Midwestern states and he noted that the industry had political funds which would be distributed among House and Senate candidates in the coming election year—although neither the secretary nor anyone else discussed possible contributions to the President's campaign," the statement continued.

"The fundamental themes running through this March 23 meeting were two: (1) the unique and very heavy pressures being placed upon the President by the Democratic majority leadership in the Congress and (2) the political advantages and disadvantages of making a decision regarding a vital political constituency.

"The President himself concluded that the final decision came down to the fact that the Congress was going to pass the higher support legislation, and he could not veto it without alienating the farmers—an essential part of his political constituency."

In claiming that the "economic consequences of the decision [to raise milk price supports] have been beneficial to the entire country," Nixon cited four "results" of his action: the smallest increase in cost of milk to consumers from 1971–72 when compared with previous years; (a .9¢ boost in the average retail cost of a half gallon of milk compared with a 1.5¢ a half gallon increase from 1970–71); a drop in taxpayers' costs of the milk support program (down to $116.6 million in fiscal 1972 from $174.2 million in 1971); an end to the

C

D

E

F

G

downward trend in milk production; and a decline in government supplies of surplus milk.

Nixon said the dairy industry's lobbying and contribution activities "followed a separate track" and to emphasize this fact, the statement discussed fund-raising and other money matters in a separate context from its justification of the price support increase.

The paper acknowledged that Charles W. Colson, then a White House special counsel, had sent a memo to the President in September 1970 informing him of Associated Milk Producers Inc.'s (AMPI) pledge of $2 million for the re-election campaign; that a letter had been sent in December 1970 to Nixon confirming the pledge, but the President claimed not to have seen it; that AMPI's first Nixon contribution had been given to Herbert Kalmbach, Nixon's personal attorney and chief fund-raiser, in August 1969 (money which Nixon said he knew nothing of although it was deposited by Kalmbach in a trustee bank account used for money left over from the 1968 presidential campaign); that $232,500 in dairy funds had been recorded on a list of secret campaign contributors kept by Rose Mary Woods, Nixon's personal secretary, as "House Account" money. No effort was made to explain why the Administration and the dairy industry took such extraordinary precautions to conceal the source of the campaign donations.

The ITT case—Nixon claimed that his order to Deputy Attorney General Richard Kleindienst to drop a pending appeal with the Supreme Court on one of the government's antitrust suits against ITT was based entirely on Nixon's personal philosophy that corporations should not be challenged on grounds of "bigness per se." Further, Nixon said in his eight-page statement, he was unaware of ITT's campaign pledge to fund the Republican National Convention when he personally intervened in the case in April 1971.

Nixon limited his role in the case to the phone call to Kleindienst April 19, 1971 and a subsequent call April 21, 1971 reversing his earlier instruction. The order to halt a court appeal of one of three suits pending against ITT was withdrawn, Nixon said, because he feared that Solicitor General Erwin Griswold would resign if the Supreme Court were prevented from considering the case. This warning came from Attorney General John Mitchell who said Nixon's decision to halt court proceedings was "inadvisable," the President said. (In earlier testimony, Kleindienst claimed that it was his threat to resign which prompted Nixon's turnaround.) Nixon also claimed that Mitchell feared unspecified "legislative repercussions" if the case were dropped.

According to the statement, Nixon's intercession resulted from his "irritation" with Richard McLaren, head of the Justice Department's antitrust division, who refused to follow Administration policy on

the case as it was set down by John Ehrlichman, Nixon's domestic policy adviser.

The ITT case eventually was filed for appeal with the high court but a settlement was reached before arguments were heard. Nixon said he did not "direct the settlement or participate in the settlement negotiations directly or indirectly."

ITT President Harold Geneen tried to discuss the case with Nixon during the summer of 1969, Nixon disclosed, but the meeting was never held because Administration aides considered it "inappropriate." However, other White House aides did discuss the case with ITT representatives, the statement added without further detail.

According to the statement, ITT did not make its offer to underwrite the Republican National Convention in San Diego until June 1971. "Apparently," its pledge totaled $200,000, of which $100,000 was returned when the site was moved from San Diego to Miami Beach. In any case, the site-selection process was "separate and unrelated" to considerations in the federal antitrust case against ITT, Nixon stated.

Reaction to Nixon's milk fund, ITT papers. President Nixon's release of two statements justifying his actions in the milk fund and International Telephone & Telegraph Corp. (ITT) cases prompted comparison with previous remarks on the issues by Nixon and others.

At his press conference Oct. 26, 1973, Nixon had declared that throughout his public life he had refused to personally accept campaign contributions, that he had "refused to have any discussion of contributions" and that prior to the 1972 presidential campaign, he had issued orders "that he did not want to have any information from anybody with regard to campaign contributions."

That statement conflicted with Nixon's admission Jan. 8 that an aide, Charles W. Colson, had sent him a written memo detailing a dairy group's pledge of $2 million.

A White House press spokesman said there was no contradiction in the two remarks. "Occasionally people break rules," the official said, referring to Colson's apparent violation of the President's order about campaign gifts.

Nixon's white paper account also appeared to contradict former Agriculture Secretary Clifford Hardin's sworn testimony that the decision to raise federal milk price supports was based solely "on the basis of statutory criteria," i.e., supply, costs and farm income. President Nixon admitted that "traditional political considerations" in farm states also played a major role in his decision to increase milk supports.

In his official statement, Nixon stated that he had been forced to act because of Congressional pressure in support of the dairy lobby. Sen. William Proxmire (D, Wis.), a supporter of the increase, said Jan. 9 that Nixon's argument was "ridiculous." He and other proponents of higher prices "were consistently unable to persuade our colleagues to enact such legislation over the past 15 years. In any event, it would have been impossible for Congress to override a presidential veto," Proxmire added.

Sen. Edmund S. Muskie (D, Me.), another supporter of the increase, said Jan. 9 that despite his support of the water pollution bill, Nixon had not been deterred from vetoing it. "There is nothing in the President's record to indicate that he is sensitive to the Congress' point of view," Muskie declared.

Lawyers for Ralph Nader introduced into evidence Jan. 11 an extract from a tape recording of Nixon's meeting March 23, 1971 with dairy industry leaders. According to the brief, Nixon's remarks contradicted his assertions in the white paper that campaign contributions were not mentioned.

According to the tape, Nixon told the group:

"I first want to say that I am very grateful for the support that we have had [inaudible word] from this group. I know that in American agriculture you're widely recognized; that it cuts across all the farmer organizations, is represented in all the states.

"I know, too, that you are a group that are politically very conscious, not in any party sense, but you realize that what happens in Washington not only affects your business success but affects the economy; our foreign policy [inaudible word] affects you.

"And you are willing to do something about it. And I must say a lot of businessmen and others I get around this table, they yammer and talk a lot but they don't do anything about it. But you do and I appreciate that. I don't need to spell it out. Friends talk and others keep me posted as to what you do."

Nader's lawyers also contended that a memo prepared for the President by his staff prior to the March 1971 meeting reminded Nixon of the campaign pledge. The memo "briefly noted that the dairy lobby—like organized labor—had decided to spend political money," according to the testimony of a Nixon aide, David Wilson. The lawyers asked the White House to produce the entire memo.

Former Solicitor General Erwin Griswold said Jan. 9 that he disagreed with part of Nixon's statement claiming that on April 19, 1971, he had "authorized the Justice Department to proceed with the [ITT] case in accordance with its own determination." Griswold claimed that he had not received authorization from the White House to file for appeal with the Supreme Court until "about May 15, 16, or 17, 1971."

Observers also noted that in limiting his own involvement in the case to two telephone calls, Nixon failed to mention specifically that ITT officials had met numerous times with key Administration officials.

Nixon also failed to disclose that lawyers for ITT suggested that Deputy Attorney General Richard Kleindienst seek a delay in filing the appeal (a delay that was granted) because the firm feared an adverse Supreme Court ruling and sought time to negotiate an out-of-court settlement with Justice Department officials (a strategy that was successful).

In another major contradiction with previous sworn testimony, Nixon's assertion that he had discussed the case with John Mitchell, then attorney general, and Kleindienst, then deputy attorney general, conflicted with their statements at Senate hearings considering Kleindienst's nomination as attorney general.

According to the Washington Post Jan. 10, officials in the Justice Department's antitrust division "never heard of" a "proposal for creating a central clearing house for information about government anti-trust policy within the White House," a plan that Nixon said in his statement had been "authorized."

Other milk fund, ITT developments—David L. Parr and Keifer L. Howard, former officials of Associated Milk Producers Inc.'s (AMPI) Arkansas division, pleaded guilty Jan. 11 to charges that they had conspired to donate $22,000 in corporate funds to the 1968 Democratic presidential campaign.

The Arkansas Electric Cooperative Association, its general manager and 15 of its member co-ops had pleaded guilty in September 1973 to charges that they had conspired to funnel AMPI's money to the Democrats.

A federal district court judge in Hartford, Conn. Jan. 14 denied Ralph Nader's request that the court appoint a special master to investigate whether President Nixon or other members of his Administration had intervened for political reasons in the ITT settlement.

"The judiciary has neither the power nor the facilities to initiate and conduct investigations into the conduct of members of the executive branch of government," the court ruled.

Jaworski withdraws from 4 cases. Special Watergate prosecutor Leon Jaworski had withdrawn from personal involvement in four cases because of possible conflict of interest, it was reported Jan. 9. The cases involved connections with Jaworski's former law firm—Fulbright, Crooker and Jaworski of Houston.

The case involving illegal campaign contributions by Ashland Oil Inc. had already been prepared when Jaworski took office.

A spokesman for Jaworski said he would not be involved in the investigation of campaign contributions by the dairy industry until a separate civil action involving Associated Milk Producers Inc. (AMPI) was concluded. Marketing Assistance Plan, a farm group represented by Jaworski's former firm, had accused AMPI of taking away members.

The other two cases were not made public because of the secrecy of the grand jury investigation, the spokesman said.

Agnew disbarment recommended. A special three-judge panel Jan. 14 unanimously recommended disbarment of former Vice President Spiro T. Agnew "to protect the public from one who has demonstrated his unworthiness to continue the practice of law." The recommendation was made to the Maryland Court of Appeals on a move by the Maryland State Bar Association for disciplinary action against Agnew. Agnew had pleaded "no contest" to a charge of income tax evasion after resigning as vice president.

The special panel—Shirley P. Jones of the Supreme Bench of Baltimore City, presiding judge, Ridgely P. Melvin Jr. of the Anne Arundel Circuit Court, and William H. McCullogh of the Circuit Court of Prince Georges County—was appointed by the Court of Appeals to recommend on the disciplinary issue. It found that Agnew's "conduct, characterized as it must be as deceitful and dishonest, strikes at the heart of the basic object of the legal profession, and constitutes conduct prejudicial to the administration of justice."

"The proper administration of justice, the proper respect of the court for itself and a proper regard for the integrity of the profession," it said, "compel us to conclude that the respondent is unfit to continue as a member of the bar of this state."

The panel saw "no extenuating circumstances allowing a lesser sanction."

"The uncontroverted evidence," it said, was that Agnew "deliberately failed to report on his 1967 federal income tax return nearly $30,000 of taxable income which he knew the law required him to report and pay taxes on." Further, Agnew "participated in a contrived scheme to cheat the federal government of taxes through the simple expedient of claiming the 'contributions' or 'payments' he received to be nontaxable political contributions, when in reality they were, as he then knew, taxable income."

The panel specified that in its deliberation it considered only the one charge to which Agnew had pleaded "no contest." It pointed out that the charge was a felony and "one which involves moral turpitude."

It said there was "lack of a clear pattern insofar as sanctions for the errant lawyer are concerned," but there was "no difficulty in discerning precedents for and stability of the basic tenets of conduct and behavior expected of lawyers." It noted that the canons of ethics of the American Bar Association and the Maryland courts called for "high standards of moral and ethical conduct" by lawyers.

It concluded: "We believe that any lawyer, whether in public office or not, owes a general duty to the public at large, as well as to other members of the bar, to adhere unfalteringly to the high ethical standards peculiar to his chosen profession. To fail to do so in any arena demonstrates an unworthiness to continue the practice of law."

Grant programs politically aimed. Frederic V. Malek, deputy director of the Office of Management and Budget, acknowledged responsibility Jan. 15 for a secret project in 1972, when he was a special assistant to the President, of redirecting federal grants to reap political gain for President Nixon. The acknowledgement followed reports published that day about the secret project and based on memorandums in possession of the Senate Watergate Committee.

Malek confirmed the "responsiveness" project but denied it was an attempt to buy votes or had brought improper political influence on federal agencies. He said the project had been "fluffed up a little bit" in his memos to please H. R. Haldeman, then Nixon's chief of staff.

According to the memos, every Cabinet agency except the State Department was urged to make Nixon's re-election a priority factor in award of government contracts and grants. "The political priorities would be spelled out in terms of key states and major voting bloc groups upon which departmental action could have an impact," Malek wrote. "The departments would be updated as needed as the political priorities evolve."

Malek spoke of "improving departmental responsiveness in support of the President's re-election." He cited examples—a grant for migrant workers in Texas was switched from an anti-Administration group to a pro-Nixon group; a federal antidiscrimination suit against the University of Texas, which might have "a serious negative impact in a key state," was quashed; a federal probe of a Philadelphia local of the Dock and Wharf Builders Union was dropped, a move considered "very helpful to the Administration in impacting on the blue-collar vote."

Malek made it clear that, "naturally," steps would be taken to insure that information about the program would not be leaked and to "keep the President and the White House disassociated with the program in the event of a leak."

Hughes official: gift sought from Hughes. Richard G. Danner, an official in President Nixon's 1968 campaign and currently an employe of billionaire industrialist Howard R. Hughes, told the Senate Watergate Committee that he attended a meeting in 1968 with Nixon and Charles G. Rebozo, a friend of Nixon, during which a campaign gift was solicited from Hughes. (Danner had introduced Nixon and Rebozo to each other in 1948.)

"We have denied that the President discussed a possible contribution of any amount from Hughes," a White House spokesman said Jan. 16.

The New York Times reported the testimony Jan. 16, the Washington Post Jan. 17.

The Times reported Danner told committee investigators that Nixon personally suggested he attempt to solicit a campaign contribution from Hughes. The Post reported that Nixon was present at the meeting when the request was made.

According to the accounts:

Danner subsequently raised the issue of a gift with Edward P. Morgan, a lawyer for Hughes, who then relayed the request to Hughes aide Robert Maheu.

According to Morgan, Maheu said Hughes would be favorably disposed to make a contribution, provided that Nixon personally—but privately—acknowledge the gift. A few weeks later, Morgan met with Danner and Rebozo in Rebozo's Washington hotel suite to discuss Nixon's acknowledgement of the gift, a meeting, Morgan said, he left "not adequately satisfied" that the condition would be met.

In a sworn deposition by Danner in a suit filed by Maheu against Hughes, Danner said Rebozo at one point had almost decided that the gift would best be forgotten, as he had been told that Hughes aide John Meier and Nixon's brother, F. Donald Nixon, would be involved in delivering the gift.

A few months later, Danner said in his deposition, Maheu, accompanied by Paul Laxalt, a former Nevada governor, attempted to deliver a $50,000 cash contribution to President Nixon, who was staying at the Palm Springs, Calif. home of Walter Annenberg, later named U.S. ambassador to Great Britain. The two couriers were turned away with the explanation that Nixon was too busy to see them.

Danner, hired by the Hughes organization in February 1969, finally delivered a $50,000 cash payment to Rebozo in July 1970 and followed it with another $50,000 cash contribution in August of that year.

Maheu testified in a deposition given in his suit against Hughes that the first $50,000 was intended for Nixon's 1968 campaign. The second $50,000, Maheu said, related to an antitrust problem Hughes was having concerning his attempts to acquire a Las Vegas, Nev. hotel. After the second gift was received, Maheu testified, John N. Mitchell, then attorney general,

granted Hughes an antitrust exemption over objections of the Justice Department's antitrust division. However, the transaction was never consummated, Maheu said.

Hughes blank checks to campaign—Hughes, acting through an agent, gave signed blank checks to President Nixon's 1972 re-election campaign, it was reported Jan. 9.

According to sworn testimony she gave in connection with civil suits stemming from the Watergate break-in, Sally Harmony, former secretary to convicted Watergate conspirator G. Gordon Liddy, said she had filled in amounts payable on the blank checks at the direction of Liddy.

Harmony named Robert F. Bennett, a publicist for Hughes, as signer of the checks. She noted that they had been received only a few days before a new federal campaign finance disclosure law went into effect April 7, 1972. Meanwhile, Bennett confirmed reports that the gift had totaled $50,000, but he asserted that the amount had been fixed in advance and the use of blank checks was only a clerical matter.

Nixon election data subpoenaed. President Nixon was subpoenaed Jan. 17 by Common Cause for "all documents, memoranda and other writings" on contributions and expenses in Nixon's 1972 re-election campaign. The action was authorized under a court ruling won by Common Cause July 24, 1973 requiring disclosure of the Nixon campaign financial records. The ruling authorized an ascertaining by Common Cause that Nixon's accounting was complete.

The subpoena to the President, the fourth in the Watergate scandals, was based on Nixon's statement that he had personal custody of some of the material sought, such as tapes. The President had been named previously in two subpoenas issued by the Senate Watergate Committee and one by the Watergate special prosecutor.

Convention funding studied. Both major parties were jointly considering new ways to finance their national conventions. At a joint meeting Jan. 22, of a committee selected by the Republican and Democratic National Committees, dissatisfaction was expressed with the past funding method—from corporate sources solicited for advertisements in convention programs—and acknowledgement made that such a method might not be productive in the current climate of scandal in political fund-raising. Alternative methods were suggested at the meeting, such as a joint national telethon, lotteries by each state party, and mini-conventions by each state party that would be linked by closed-circuit television to a central convention where each state party would be represented by two delegates.

In 1972, when a full-page advertisement sold for $10,000, the convention program method raised $1.7 million for the Republicans and $980,000 for the Democrats.

Nixon-Hughes aide meetings reported; one confirmed. Richard G. Danner, an employe of industrialist Howard R. Hughes, told a closed session of the Senate Watergate Committee that he had met with President Nixon on two occasions in 1970 and 1973, it was reported Jan. 25. Both meetings, Danner reportedly said, came shortly after his own transactions with Charles G. Rebozo, a friend of Nixon, on the disputed $100,000 campaign contribution from Hughes.

Danner told the committee, however, that money had not been discussed during either of the meetings with Nixon.

Deputy White House Press Secretary Gerald L. Warren confirmed Jan. 25 that Nixon had met with Danner at Camp David, Md. in May 1973. Warren called the meeting a "courtesy visit" lasting five or ten minutes and said the "mood of the people in the West" had been discussed, not money.

According to committee sources, Danner testified that during May 1973 Rebozo summoned him from Las Vegas, Nev. to Washington. At Rebozo's suggestion, they and Robert H. Abplanalp, another friend of Nixon, flew in Abplanalp's private plane to an undisclosed location in upstate New York for lunch. During the trip, Danner said, Rebozo asked him to take back the $100,000 cash contribution. Danner refused, and—after their return to Washington—was told by Rebozo that Nixon wanted to see him.

Danner recalled that he went to Camp David the following day and met with Nixon for about two hours, during which their conversation was limited to the mood of the people over the Watergate scandals.

(According to other committee testimony, the money was returned to another Hughes aide in June 1973.)

Regarding the 1970 meeting, Danner testified that he had delivered $50,000 in cash to Rebozo at San Clemente, Calif. Shortly afterwards, Rebozo took him to Nixon's office, where, Danner said, they discussed the difficulty of booking "clean" shows in Las Vegas hotels.

Senate panel postpones hearings. Sen. Sam J. Ervin Jr. (D, N.C.), chairman of the Watergate Committee, announced Jan. 26 that public hearings on contributions to President Nixon's 1972 re-election campaign would be postponed indefinitely. The two items remaining on the committee's schedule were the $100,000 payment from industrialist Howard R. Hughes to Nixon's friend Charles G. Rebozo, and contributions by the dairy industry.

Ervin said the delay had been decided upon to avoid prejudicing the trial of former Attorney General John N. Mitchell and former Commerce Secretary Maurice H. Stans on charges of perjury and obstruction of justice, scheduled to begin Feb. 19 in New York City.

The Mitchell-Stans trial involved the blocking of an investigation of financier Robert L. Vesco and a subsequent contribution by Vesco, but Mitchell's role in antitrust actions was central to the unrelated Hughes gift and milk fund controversies.

According to committee sources, U.S. Attorney Paul J. Curran of New York had called Ervin to request a delay in public hearings at least until a jury had been chosen and sequestered.

Although the committee's mandate was scheduled to expire Feb. 28, the Senate was reportedly willing to grant an extension, but only for limited purposes. Committee chief counsel Samuel Dash insisted Jan. 28 that hearings would resume eventually and instructed the staff to continue preparations.

In a 4–3 party-line vote Jan. 23, the committee had accepted a staff recommendation to resume hearings despite the suggestion by Vice Chairman Howard H. Baker Jr. (R, Tenn.) that the "focus had shifted" to the House Judiciary Committee's inquiry into the impeachment of Nixon, and that it would be an act of "statesmanship" for the Ervin panel to "step aside." Sen. Lowell P. Weicker Jr. (R, Conn.) had also raised the question of interference with the Mitchell-Stans trial.

GAO: No legal basis for Agnew guard. A General Accounting Office report Jan. 29 said there was no legal authority for the Secret Service protection given Spiro T. Agnew after his resignation as vice president in 1973.

President Nixon had directed that the guard be provided the day Agnew resigned. The GAO found no statutory authority for the directive and concluded that the directive itself "does not constitute legal authority to provide" the guard, which cost $89,222 through Dec. 15, 1973.

Federal funds also were being used to provide Agnew with a staff of six persons for his transition out of office.

The GAO report had been requested by Rep. John E. Moss (D, Calif.).

Congressional donations listed. Common Cause, the public interest lobby, disclosed Jan. 31 that 35 contributors gave $1.4 million to Congressional candidates for use in the 1972 elections. More than half of the total amount collected, $62.3 million, was received by incumbents.

The 10-volume 2,000 page computer printout was compiled from diverse documents filed with the clerk of the House of Representatives and the secretary of the Senate as required by the 1971 law mandating public disclosure of campaign finances.

The Common Cause list documented only gifts totaling at least $500 which had been filed since April 7, 1972, the deadline for the disclosure rule.

The 35 major donors each gave more than $20,000 which was distributed almost equally between Republican and Democratic candidates.

Cordelia Scaife May, an heir to the Mellon fortune, was the largest single contributor, giving $110,000 to 64 Republican candidates. Her brother, Pittsburgh banker Richard Scaife, gave $56,-000 to 37 Republican candidates. A total of $251,000 was contributed by persons associated with Gulf Oil Corp., a cornerstone of the Mellon family fortune. The Pew family of Philadelphia, which controlled Sun Oil Co., donated $63,000 to 52 candidates.

While a congressman in Michigan, Vice President Gerald Ford built a $100,000 campaign chest, the study reported, although his challenger received only $10,-000 in donations. (Among contributors to Ford's campaign was Associated Milk Producers Inc. The dairy co-op, which gave $4,000, was under federal investigation.)

Other major contributors:

Lawrence Weinberg, California real estate executive, gave $87,087 to 38 Democrats; John M. Olin of Olin Corp., gave $83,000 to 54 Republicans; Leonard Davis, founder of Penn Colonial Insurance Corp., gave $76,000 to 26 candidates (mostly Democrats); Howard Saft, New York jeweler, gave $71,500 to 35 Democrats; W. Clement Stone, Chicago insurance magnate, gave $23,312 to eight Republicans and Sen. Jennings Randolph (D, W. Va.); Mary W. Lasker, New York philanthropist, gave $39,000 to 29 Democrats; Joan Whitney Payson, owner of the New York Mets, gave $58,500 to 22 Republicans; Carroll Rosenbloom, owner of the Los Angeles Rams, gave $25,000 to nine Democrats and one Liberal; John Mulcahy, New York industrialist, and wife, gave $50,000 to six Republicans; and Stanley Goldblum, former Equity Funding Corp. chairman, gave $49,000 to 38 Democrats.

Surveillance of Nixon's brother. Investigators for the Senate Watergate Committee said the Secret Service was ordered during President Nixon's first term to keep the President's brother, F. Donald Nixon, under physical surveillance, the New York Times reported Feb. 4. Fearful that his brother's business activities might embarrass the President and undermine 1972 re-election prospects, the White House kept a record of the younger Nixon's activities to be used in the event he became an issue in the 1972 election, the Times said.

According to one Times source, information supplied by the White House to Charles G. Rebozo, President Nixon's personal friend, led to dismissal of John Meier, an employe of the Howard Hughes organization whom Rebozo previously had asked be kept away from F. Donald Nixon.

Times sources indicated that Rebozo had prevailed on aides to Hughes to order Meier to stay away from F. Donald Nixon. Rebozo and White House officials close to the President feared Meier would try to "use" the President's brother. When Rebozo subsequently learned of a meeting between Meier and F. Donald Nixon, he phoned Hughes aide Richard Danner to express his displeasure, the Times said. Three months later—October 1969—Meier left the Hughes organization. While Meier denied he had been fired, Times sources linked his departure directly to the complaints by Rebozo.

(It had been revealed in 1960 that F. Donald Nixon had received a partially secured loan of $205,000 from Hughes which he used in an unsuccessful attempt to rescue a failing fast-food business he owned.)

Senate panel delays report. The Senate Watergate Committee voted unanimously Feb. 7 to delay issuing a report on its investigation until May 28. Further hearings on campaign fund issues had already been postponed, but the panel had reportedly been considering preparation of at least an interim report by Feb. 28.

Chairman Sam. J. Ervin Jr. (D, N.C.) said the committee had acted at the request of special prosecutor Leon Jaworski, who had told Ervin to expect "a number of indictments" during February. Ervin said he had been "led to believe" that an early report could hamper efforts to obtain guilty pleas.

The committee also voted unanimously to give the House Judiciary Committee access to its files for the House panel's impeachment inquiry.

Senate panel's tape suit dismissed. U.S. District Court Judge Gerhard A. Gesell Feb. 8 dismissed the Senate Watergate Committee's suit to enforce its subpoena of five presidential tape recordings on the ground that publicity surrounding the panel's hearings might be harmful to criminal prosecutions. [For further details, see p. 25G1]

$24.3 million campaign chest amassed. Candidates and political parties already had $24.3 million on hand for use in the 1974 elections and beyond, according to the Center for Public Financing of Elections Feb. 12. The bipartisan research and lobbying group also reported that $17.9 million was spent on campaigns during the last four months of 1973 when very few elections were held.

Thirteen candidates from the 1972 national election held surplus funds, including Nixon's Finance Committee to Reelect the President [See above] and Sen. George McGovern (D, S.D.). Nearly $470,000 remained from McGovern's race as the Democratic presidential candidate. Groups reporting large sums on hand were the Republican party committees—$2.8 million; Democratic party committees—$2.2 million; and Associated Milk Producers, Inc.—$1.3 million.

Milk funds reported 'laundered.' The Senate Watergate Committee was investigating allegations that at least $200,000 in contributions from the dairy lobby was donated to two Republican Congressional campaign committees in 1972 in a scheme to conceal and "launder" money actually intended for President Nixon's re-election campaign, the New York Times reported Feb. 15.

According to Congressional sources, Senate committee members informed their Republican colleagues in Congress that an investigation showed that of $300,-000 given to the Republican Senatorial Campaign Committee and the Republican Congressional Campaign Committee, $200,000 was diverted to the Finance Committee to Re-elect the President.

The Congressional donations had been made public earlier, but the transfer to Nixon's campaign had remained secret. Until this report, it was believed that the dairy group's total contributions to the presidential race had been $422,500.

Disclosure of the dairymen's previous contributions given immediately after Nixon reversed an Agriculture Department ruling in 1971 and allowed an increase in the federal support price for milk had resulted in widespread adverse publicity.

According to the Times, in mid-October 1972 presidential fund raiser Lee Nunn visited George Mehren, general manager of Associated Milk Producers (AMPI) which was one of the nation's largest dairy cooperatives, and asked for additional contributions from the industry. (The group reportedly had promised to donate $2 million if the President permitted the support price increase to take effect.)

Mehren reportedly told Nunn he feared further negative reaction if more contributions were offered. Nunn then proposed that AMPI funnel the money through Congressional committees, the Times reported. On Oct. 27, 1972 AMPI donated $150,000 to each Republican Senate and House committee; between Oct. 31 and Nov. 7, 1972, the Congressional campaign committees transferred $221,000 to the Republican National Finance Committee. They in turn sent $200,000 to the Nixon finance committee from Nov. 7 to Nov. 13, 1972. Former Commerce Secretary Maurice Stans was chairman of both committees. [See below] (Additional AMPI payments of $25,000 were later made to each of the two Congressional organizations.)

Because the Congressional transactions were reported March 10, 1973 as required by law, no illegality was involved. But because the money was received just prior to the pre-election deadline for revealing campaign donations, no publicity was given the contributions until after the election.

Gov. Wendell Anderson (D, Minn.) and Sen. Robert Dole (R, Kan.) announced Feb. 8 that they had returned campaign contributions from AMPI. Anderson's $5,000 donation was refunded in November 1973. Dole returned a $6,000 AMPI gift and $9,000 from two other dairy co-ops in February, a spokesman said.

Jacobsen indicted—Jake Jacobsen, a former AMPI attorney currently practicing in Austin, Tex., was indicted by one of the Watergate grand juries in Washington Feb. 21 for having made a false declaration before the grand jury in connection with his role in handling dairy industry political contributions. The indictment was the first in the special Watergate prosecution's milk fund investigation. Jacobsen was a former White House assistant to the late Lyndon B. Johnson.

The indictment stated that within two months after milk price supports were raised in 1971, Jacobsen "had solicited and received" $10,000 from the AMPI, saying the money was "to be paid to a public official for his assistance in connection with the price support decision."

Jacobsen had told the grand jury that the money had remained untouched in a safe deposit box from mid-1971 until November 1973, when the box was opened in the presence of a Federal Bureau of Investigation agent. The prosecution contended this statement was false.

The charge carried a maximum penalty of five years in prison and a $10,000 fine.

Jacobsen had been indicted by a federal grand jury in Abilene, Tex. Feb. 6 in an unrelated case involving the misapplication of funds of the First Savings and Loan Association of San Angelo, Tex. Jacobsen was also charged with conspiracy and false declaration. Also indicted was Ray Cowan, an Austin businessman currently living in Nicaragua.

NIH politization charged. Rep. Paul G. Rogers (D, Fla.), chairman of the Public Health and Environment Subcommittee of the House Committee on Interstate and Foreign Commerce, accused the Nixon Administration Feb. 15 of making political appointments to the advisory boards of the National Institutes of Health (NIH)—jobs traditionally considered non-political.

Rogers cited as evidence a letter from Richard M. Rosenbaum, chairman of the New York Republican State Committee, informing Dr. James G. Hirsch of New York City's Rockefeller University that he had received GOP clearance for an appointment to the advisory board of the National Institute of Allergy and Infectious Diseases. Hirsch, who later refused the offer, said Rosenbaum's letter was the first notice he had received concerning the post.

According to an informed source in the NIH, political screening for NIH posts had begun in 1969, the Washington Post reported Feb. 16. Recently, the source said, an informal agreement had been reached allowing the NIH to make scientific appointments, while the Department of Health, Education and Welfare concerned itself with political appointments to the advisory boards. Singer Frank Sinatra, who was named to the advisory council of the National Heart and Lung Institute and never attended a meeting, was cited as an example.

The Post reported that NIH scientists had told Congressional aides of a sharp decline in the quality of the councils since political clearances became the rule.

HEW Secretary Caspar W. Weinberger denied the proposed Hirsch appointment had been political, and he condemned such practices.

U.S. guards for Agnew removed. The Treasury Department Feb. 17 announced removal of the federal security guard for former Vice President Spiro T. Agnew. The service had been provided by the Secret Service at President Nixon's request. The department said the decision to withdraw the protection was made by the Treasury with prior knowledge by the White House and Agnew.

Rep. John E. Moss (D, Calif.) had requested the Treasury Feb. 8 to cancel the service after receiving a report from Comptroller General Elmer B. Staats that it was "beyond question" that the President had no legal authority to provide the service for Agnew after his resignation as vice president. An earlier finding by the General Accounting Office (GAO) that no statutory authority existed for the President's action had been disputed by the Treasury, which claimed Jan. 31 the action was based on the President's "inherent executive power." Staats held this "untenable" in that the President's power "must stem either from an act of Congress or from the Constitution itself," neither of which he found sustained the action. The GAO had notified the Treasury Feb. 15 that payments for the protection would be ended after Feb. 17.

Agnew was visiting singer Frank Sinatra in Palm Springs, Calif. at the time, having left from Washington Feb. 13 with his Secret Service escort. In addition to transition work remaining from his departure from government, Agnew reportedly was working on a novel. (The New York Times reported Feb. 6 that the magazine Ladies Home Journal had agreed to serialize Agnew's first novel. "We always like to encourage new writers." Lenore Hershey, editor of the Journal, said.)

Mitchell-Stans trial opens. The trial of two former Nixon Administration Cabinet members—John N. Mitchell and Maurice H. Stans—on criminal charges of conspiracy, obstruction of justice and perjury opened Feb. 19 in U.S. District Court in New York.

[For the complete chronology of events in the Mitchell-Stans case, see the fourth chapter.]

2 sentenced in Gurney fund case. Two Florida men received jail sentences for their roles in an illegal campaign fund scheme involving Sen. Edward J. Gurney (R, Fla.). Gurney's former aide and fund raiser, Larry E. Williams, was sentenced to a year in jail Feb. 21 after pleading guilty to charges of attempting to evade federal income taxes totaling $19,000 in 1971 and helping a government official collect a bribe.

Williams had been indicted Jan. 17 by a federal grand jury for channeling a $10,-000 bribe from Miami builder John J. Priestes to William F. Pelski, former director of the Federal Housing Administration (FHA) insuring office in Coral Gables and the former mayor of Pompano Beach.

Priestes received 20 FHA contracts to build subsidized housing in return for his illegal payment, according to the indictment. (He was serving a one-year jail term, the Miami Herald reported Jan. 18.)

Pelski pleaded guilty March 19 to conspiring to defraud the government by promising FHA financing to Gurney's political contributors. He was sentenced to 18 months in prison. Williams and James L. Groot, Gurney's former administrative assistant, were named as unindicted co-conspirators in the criminal information filed against Pelski. According to the government, Pelski gave Williams the names of persons seeking FHA insuring commitments for mortgages and loans. Williams used the list to solicit contributions for Gurney and turned the kickback money over to Groot, who used it to pay office expenses incurred by Gurney and his staff. Williams subsequently instructed Pelski to authorize the insuring commitments to the donors.

Nixon on Agnew. President Nixon was asked at a televised news conference Feb. 25 whether he believed Spiro Agnew had "brought dishonor upon his office, this Administration and the country." Nixon responded:

"It would be very easy for me to jump on the vice president when he's down. I could only say that in his period of service that he rendered dedicated service on all of the assignments that I gave to him. He went through, along with his family, a terribly difficult situation and he resigned as I think he thought he should, because of the embarrassment that he knew that would cause to the Administration and also because he felt that in view of the criminal offense that was charged that he should not stay in office. Now at this point I am not going to join anybody else in kicking him when he's down."

Kalmbach pleads guilty. Herbert W. Kalmbach, President Nixon's personal attorney and one of his chief fund raisers, pleaded guilty Feb. 25 to two violations of the federal law governing campaign funds. He admitted raising $3.9 million for a secret Congressional campaign committee in 1970 and also promising an ambassador a better diplomatic post in return for a $100,000 campaign contribution. The charges, the first a felony and the second a misdemeanor, were violations of the Federal Corrupt Practices Act and punishable by up to three years in prison and $11,000 in fines.

The two-count criminal information was filed in federal district court in Washington. Watergate special prosecutor Leon Jaworski indicated in a letter filed with the court that Kalmbach had been allowed to plead guilty to technical violations of the campaign finance law in exchange for his cooperation and full disclosure of "all relevant information and documents" in Jaworski's multifaceted investigation. Other Watergate-related charges against him had been dropped but Jaworski indicated that Kalmbach would be named as an unindicted co-conspirator in forthcoming indictments against former White House officials.

Kalmbach, who was released on his own recognizance by U.S. District Court Judge John J. Sirica pending preparation of a presentencing report by probation officers, refused any public comment except to say that he remained "the President's personal lawyer."

(Kalmbach announced Feb. 26 that he had resigned from his Newport Beach, Calif. law firm—Kalmbach, DeMarco, Knapp & Chillingworth—which he had founded in 1967. The resignation was effective Feb. 15.)

Deputy White House Press Secretary Gerald Warren said Feb. 25 that Kalmbach was still authorized to write checks on Nixon's personal bank account.

In the past, Kalmbach had handled sensitive matters for Nixon such as the Nixon Foundation, income tax returns and purchase of the family estate at San Clemente, Calif. Kalmbach had also admitted in previous testimony that he had collected payoff money for the Watergate burglars and paid for Donald Segretti's "dirty trick" activities.

At his press conference later Feb. 25, Nixon was questioned about Kalmbach's use of the ambassadorial quid pro quo in soliciting presidential campaign contributions:

Q. In your capacity as President, you approve of ambassadors and you send the nominations to the Senate. Were you consulted in any manner on this engagement, in this contribution by Mr. Kalmbach or anyone else in the White House, and have you done any research on this in the White House to determine who is responsible for it?

A. The answer to the first question is no; the answer to the second question is yes, and I would go further and say that ambassadorships have not been for sale to my knowledge, ambassadorships cannot be purchased and I would not approve an ambassadorship unless the man, or woman, was qualified clearly apart from any contribution.

The secret fund raising—Kalmbach admitted gathering $3.9 million in contributions for use by a surreptitious campaign finance committee whose operations were still under investigation by Jaworski's office. The project, dubbed "Operation Townhouse" or "The Public Institute," was run by the White House out of a basement in a downtown Washington house, funneling secret money to Republican House and Senate candidates in 1970 in at least 19 states, prosecutors told the court.

In previous testimony, Kalmbach had said he was enlisted for the fund raising drive by H. R. Haldeman, then White House chief of staff. According to the prosecutors, Kalmbach eventually received pledges of $2.8 million (including one of $110,000 from Associated Milk Producers Inc.) and $1.1 million in checks from a single donor, who was unidentified in court records.

Kalmbach had testified earlier in connection with the milk fund suit that he had worked with White House aide Jack A. Gleason in dispensing the money. Gleason had been on the staff of Harry Dent, a White House political adviser, before joining the secret project, according to Kalmbach.

Kalmbach's activities were judged to be in violation of the law because "three [unidentified] members of the staff of the executive office of the President" who had formed a committee in March 1970 to support Congressional candidates, had failed to name a chairman and treasurer or file reports of their operations. Another unnamed official was said to be the day-to-day director of the project and a fifth person, also unidentified, directed disbursement of the money, prosecutors said. The White House officials, most of whom had left the Administration, were expected to be named in future indictments obtained by Jaworski's office.

The promise to the ambassador—According to prosecutors, Ambassador J.

Fife Symington Jr., a retired Maryland businessman and former state Republican Party official, offered Kalmbach donations totaling $100,000 "only on condition that he be offered an ambassadorship to one of several agreed upon European countries."

Kalmbach gave the guarantee at a Los Angeles meeting with Symington Sept. 16, 1970 after telephoning an unnamed person on the White House staff and receiving "assurances" the promise would be honored. "Thereupon, the pledge was firmed and the deal was made," according to Jaworski's office.

Symington subsequently contributed $50,000 in his wife's name in 1970 and another $50,000 in 1972 to the Finance Committee to Re-elect the President "or one of its satellite committees," the prosecutors stated.

At the time of the deal, Symington was ambassador to Trinidad and Tobago, a post he retained until November 1971 when, according to the White House, he resigned for "personal reasons." (Kalmbach offered to return the money when the pledge was not fulfilled but Symington refused, prosecutors said.)

Symington was the first cousin of Sen. Stuart Symington (D, Mo.).

Nixon holds news conference. At a televised news conference at the White House March 6, President Nixon discussed the subject of campaign financing reform. [For further details, see p. 56E3]

IRS rescinds ITT tax break. International Telephone & Telegraph Corp. (ITT) announced March 6 that the Internal Revenue Service (IRS) had revoked its 1969 ruling that had enabled ITT to acquire the Hartford Fire Insurance Co. It was the largest corporate merger in history.

The merger had provoked controversy within the Administration which was divided over whether to press antitrust charges against ITT. The government's final decisions in the case, which had involved President Nixon and other high White House officials, spurred further controversy and prompted Watergate special prosecutor Leon Jaworski to investigate the ITT case.

The IRS ruling was integral to ITT's take-over plans: the 17,000 Hartford shareholders, whose approval of the merger was required, were allowed by the government to exchange their stock for ITT stock without immediately paying capital gains taxes.

With retroactive revocation of that favorable tax ruling, the former Hartford shareholders could be liable for up to $50 million in back taxes, according to the Wall Street Journal. ITT, which declared it would seek a court review of the IRS action, said March 7 that the shareholders would be reimbursed if a court refused to sustain their tax-free status. [See below]

The IRS confirmed that its 1969 order had been rescinded but refused to disclose the basis for its decision. ITT officials said March 7 that the action stemmed from the government's investigation of another aspect of the tax arrangements involving ITT's sale of a separate block of Hartford shares to Mediobanca, a Milan bank.

A class action suit brought by a former Hartford shareholder had also challenged this preliminary aspect of the merger which was a basis for the tax break given the Hartford group and ultimately for actual take-over approved by the Hartford shareholders.

The suit, brought by Hilda Herbst, alleged that ITT had obtained the IRS ruling by providing the government with false information. Under an agreement concluded by ITT with the IRS, the Hartford shareholders' tax-free arrangement depended upon ITT's pledge to sell a block of Hartford stock obtained earlier in 1969 "unconditionally to an unrelated third part"—Mediobanca. (ITT had bought the Hartford stock for cash, which violated an IRS requirement that the Hartford acquisition be completed only through an exchange of stock.) The Herbst suit charged that the Mediobanca purchase was not unconditional and that the Italian bank was not as "unrelated" as ITT had claimed.

Observers believed the IRS action could threaten the actual merger of ITT and Hartford, which was allowed to stand in July 1971 when the Justice Department accepted a consent decree by which ITT could retain Hartford if it divested itself of several other companies, including Avis, Inc., within its conglomerate structure. [See below]

Securities laws gave shareholders the right to demand that an acquisition be canceled if it could be proven there was a material misrepresentation of fact in the transaction, according to the Wall Street Journal. Herbst's class action suit sought to rescind the Hartford take-over.

The IRS acted six weeks before the statute of limitations would have precluded recovery of taxes from the original ruling. Rep. J. J. Pickle (D, Tex.), ranking Democrat on the House Commerce Committee's investigations sub-committee, had urged the IRS to act swiftly on a decision made in April 1973 by its New York regional office to rescind the 1969 decision. Pickle's subcommittee had been investigating the ITT case and the Watergate special prosecutor's office had begun a separate investigation of the matter at Pickle's request.

ITT trading halted—The New York Stock Exchange halted trading in ITT stock March 6 at the company's request. When trading resumed the next day, the stock was off more than $3 a share, closing at $24.75. ITT stock had been worth $37 a share when the Hartford deal was completed.

Reimbursement suit filed—The Wall Street Journal reported March 13 that an ITT stockholder had filed suit asking that

present and former ITT directors connected with the merger transactions be required to make any reimbursement to the former Hartford shareholders rather than the company itself. Lazard Freres & Co., a New York investment firm which had negotiated the disputed sale of stock to Mediobanca, was among the defendants.

According to the suit, ITT President Harold Geneen and Felix Rohatyn, an ITT director and Lazard partner, were aware of material facts that could invalidate the tax-free arrangements. This information was withheld from shareholders, the suit charged, and was cause to force ITT directors to assume any liabilities resulting from irregularities in the Hartford deal.

Court bars Nader ITT suit—The Connecticut Supreme Court Feb. 26 rejected an appeal by consumer advocate Ralph Nader challenging the ITT-Hartford merger. In a 4–1 ruling, the court declared that Nader lacked sufficient personal interest in the merger to justify his suit.

The suit, which originated in 1970, claimed that William R. Cotter, then insurance commissioner in Connecticut, had been under improper pressure from ITT to approve the acquisition. He had first rejected the merger but then reversed his decision in May 1970; soon after he ran for Congress as a Democrat and was elected.

Nader also sought review of the Administration's antitrust settlement allowing ITT to retain Hartford.

Diamond International admits violation. Diamond International Corp. and one of its vice presidents, Ray Dubrowin, pleaded guilty March 7 to charges they had violated a federal campaign finance law barring corporate contributions by donating $6,000 to the presidential race in 1971 and 1972.

According to a criminal information filed by the Watergate special prosecutor Leon Jaworski, Diamond, a diversified match manufacturing and paper products firm, donated $1,000 in 1971 to Sen. Edmund S. Muskie's (D, Me.) campaign for the Democratic presidential nomination and $5,000 in 1972 to a dummy committee set up for President Nixon's re-election campaign.

(Eight other companies and seven corporate officials had pleaded guilty to similar violations of the campaign finance law involving the 1972 race. Another corporation and its official were accused of making an illegal gift to the 1968 presidential campaign of Sen. Hubert H. Humphrey (D, Minn.).)

A federal district court judge in Washington imposed maximum fines; Diamond was assessed $5,000 and Dubrowin $1,000. According to a lawyer for Diamond International, the company had voluntarily admitted its wrongdoing to Jaworski's office.

After his sentencing, Dubrowin said the contributions which he authorized had been solicited by Deputy Assistant Transportation Secretary Vincent DeCain, a former Diamond International executive, and by Gov. Kenneth Curtis (D, Me.), a Muskie supporter. Curtis denied that there was any impropriety in his action, saying that he had invited Dubrowin to a fund-raising dinner and that a pledge card had been enclosed. The money was not identified as a corporate contribution when it was sent in the form of a cashier's check (drawn on Diamond International's account) and signed by Dubrowin, according to Muskie's campaign manager.

The gift was reported as Dubrowin's personal contribution in Muskie's voluntary disclosure of all contributions received before April 7, 1972, the deadline for making public reports of all subsequent contributions. The Nixon contribution, which was also received as a cashier's check before April 7, was not reported.

SEC requires disclosure—Corporations were required to inform their stockholders if the firm or its officers were charged with or convicted of making illegal campaign contributions, the Securities and Exchange Commission (SEC) ruled March 8.

A conviction on such charges "is material to an evaluation of the integrity of the management of the corporation as it relates to the operation of the corporation and the use of corporate funds," according to the SEC.

A full disclosure was required in proxy statements to shareholders voting in the election of directors and in other reports dealing with significant corporate developments.

Nixon proposes reform. President Nixon proposed a number of campaign reforms March 8, including tighter fund disclosure rules, limits on contributions and shorter presidential campaigns. Federal financing of Congressional and presidential campaigns was opposed by the President, who presented his proposals in a message to Congress and in a radio address to the nation.

Nixon called for public identification of every campaign donor and recipient; a $15,000 limit on individual contributions to presidential candidates, a $3,000 limit on contributions to House and Senate campaigns; a limit on candidates of one fund-raising committee and a single bank account; a limit on contributions in cash of $50; a restriction on "in kind" contributions—such as pay for campaign workers, printing supplies and use of corporate aircraft—to be accounted for within the $3,-000 or $15,000 ceilings; and a ban on political loans, stock donations and foreign contributions.

In proposing shorter presidential campaigns, Nixon recommended against holding any state primary before May 1 or national party convention before September. He again suggested Congress consider a single presidential term of six years and a four-year term for House members, and recommended repeal of the "equal time" provision requiring allotment of rebuttal time for all candidates, including minor party candidates. The provision was seen as a barrier to expanded broadcast coverage for major party candidates, including a TV debate.

To prevent the use of "dirty tricks" in campaigns, the President recommended federal laws barring "activities that unreasonably disrupt the opposing candidate's campaign" by forceful means, "such as the organized use of demonstrators to impede or deny entry at a campaign rally."

Nixon said he had asked the Justice Department to draft legislation to give a candidate a right to sue for libel against slanderous attacks.

Noting there was "a constitutional problem" involved, such as possible conflict with the right to free speech, Nixon objected to interpretation of court decisions as "being virtually a license to lie" in this area.

The President also objected to any ceiling on campaign expenditures by candidates. This would be "unrealistic" and "unfair," in many cases, he said, and raised "constitutional questions."

In stating his opposition to federal funding of campaigns, Nixon said, "One thing we don't need in this country is to add politicians to the federal dole." It was "a raid on the public treasury" and "taxation without representation," he said, since taxpayers would be sponsoring candidates they opposed.

Scott, Kennedy disagree—Senate Republican Leader Hugh Scott (Pa.) stated his disagreement with the President on the public financing aspect later March 8.

Other dissents came from Sen. Edward M. Kennedy (D, Mass.) and Common Cause, the citizens' lobby. "The story of his [Nixon's] 1972 presidential campaign finances," a Common Cause statement said, "constitutes the greatest case ever made for controlling campaign finance abuses through public financing of elections."

Kennedy said the President's message was "no more than a thinly veiled attempt by the President to obstruct or even kill the most effective response Congress has yet made to Watergate."

Public financing bill gains—A bill to provide public financing of federal election campaigns was approved by the Senate Rules Committee Feb. 6. Scott was one of its major sponsors, along with Kennedy and Sen. Claiborne Pell (D, R.I.). The financing, from the voluntary checkoff on income tax returns, would total about $24 million for major-party presidential candidates, $90,000 for House candidates and $175,000 for Senate candidates. Minor party candidates would be funded in proportion to their vote.

In the House, a bill under committee consideration would provide public funding only for the presidential campaigns. It also contained lower spending ceilings. Rep. Wayne L. Hays (D, Ohio), chairman of the House Administration Committee, outlined the proposals Feb. 27.

Use of the current $1 checkoff on the personal income tax form was supported March 6 by Senate party leaders Mike Mansfield (D, Mont.) and Hugh Scott (R, Pa.). A public service commercial promoting its use was sent to broadcasters accompanied by an endorsement from Mansfield and Scott. According to the Internal Revenue Service March 7, use of the checkoff was running far ahead of the 1973 rate, when $4 million was accumulated. The 1974 return by early March was $6 million, with contributions volunteered in 14.5% of the returns.

Finance Committee ends operation. The Finance Committee to Re-elect the President ended its two-year existence March 12 and transferred $3.57 million in surplus campaign funds to a trust account in a Washington bank.

Trustees of the fund, called the 1972 Campaign Liquidation Account, said they had agreed to pay the legal fees and expenses for suits arising out of the Watergate break-in filed against the committee and its officials. Legal costs related to the Watergate affair already totaled $1 million.

In a reversal of past policy, the trustees also agreed to pay legal expenses for former campaign officials acquitted of criminal charges and possibly for those found guilty of misdemeanor charges, according to the trustees. Finance Committee Chairman Maurice Stans, whose salary was not paid after Feb. 20, and former campaign director John Mitchell could make claims on the trust fund if acquitted of federal charges of conspiracy, obstruction of justice and perjury.

Trustees for the fund were Charles E. Potter, a former U.S. senator from Michigan, Guilford Dudley Jr., a Tennessee insurance executive and Stans, who participated in the Feb. 11 decision to pay legal expenses.

In a report filed with the General Accounting Office, trustees listed a $40,000 payment to Braniff Airways Inc. as a "refund of a contribution illegally made." The report also claimed that John W. Dean 3rd, the former White House counsel, owed $15,200. Dean had testified that he had partial custody of a secret cash fund in the White House and that the money had been transferred to a trustee account after his decision to leave the Administration.

In other developments related to illegal corporate contributions given to President Nixon's re-election campaign, two officials convicted of authorizing the donations were penalized for their actions. Gulf Oil Corp. announced March 21 that its vice president, Claude C. Wild Jr., who had been convicted of authorizing the illegal payment, had resigned, effective

March 1. (The Finance Committee refunded the $100,000 gift, Gulf reported.)

Carnation Co. Chairman H. Everett Olson agreed to pay the company $16,000 for fines and expenses incurred as a result of convictions arising out of an illegal $8,900 political donation, it was reported March 29.

Hoffa sues to seek union office. Former Teamsters union President James R. Hoffa sued in U.S. district court in the District of Columbia March 13 to have the court nullify the legal curb barring his union activity until 1980. The condition had been attached to the 1971 presidential commutation of his prison sentence for mail fraud and jury tampering.

The suit, naming President Nixon and Attorney General William Saxbe as defendants, charged that the condition had been arranged by former Nixon counsel Charles W. Colson and Teamsters President Frank Fitzsimmons to prevent Hoffa from challenging Fitzsimmons for the union post. The other part of the arrangement was that Colson would be named attorney for the union and Fitzsimmons would support Nixon for re-election, the suit charged.

The White House and Colson denied the allegations March 14.

Democrats also linked to AMPI gifts. A report commissioned by the board of directors of the nation's largest milk cooperative, Associated Milk Producers, Inc. (AMPI), revealed that AMPI had engaged in a broad pattern of irregularities involving campaign contributions to Democrats as well as Republicans since 1968.

The report, prepared by the Little Rock, Ark. law firm of Wright, Lindsey and Jennings, with an audit by the accounting firm of Haskins & Sells, was made public March 14 after being submitted to U.S. district court in Kansas City, Mo. in connection with an antitrust suit against AMPI. (The principal author of the report was Edward L. Wright, a former president of the American Bar Association.)

Copies also were sent to the Watergate special prosecutor's office and to the Senate Watergate committee, it was reported March 14. Both groups had been investigating alleged campaign abuses related to AMPI's secret contributions to President Nixon's re-election effort.

Items uncovered in the Wright report surfaced in the press throughout March:

■ It was reported March 14 that AMPI paid $104,521.62 to print and distribute copies of a book of President Lyndon Johnson's speeches during the 1968 presidential race in order to help the Democratic presidential candidate, Hubert H. Humphrey.

Records indicated that the book's printer was referred to the dairymen by a White House letter. If regarded as an indirect political contribution, the payment was in violation of a federal law barring donations from corporate funds.

■ According to a report March 27, AMPI donated at least $91,691 in corporate funds to Humphrey's 1968 presidential race and $34,500 to his 1970 senatorial campaign in Minnesota. (Officials of the auditing firm said the figures may not be complete because some canceled checks from 1967 and 1968 could not be located.)

The AMPI money was used to pay travel expenses and the salary of a campaign worker, to reimburse individuals for their campaign donations and for miscellaneous expenses for a Humphrey rally, parade, and dinner, according to the Wright report.

Two former AMPI officials had pleaded guilty in January to conspiring to donate $22,000 to Humphrey.

Harold S. Nelson, a former general manager of the co-op, pleaded innocent March 27 to a three-count perjury indictment in connection with that case. According to the government, Nelson lied to a federal grand jury in September 1973 when he denied authorizing the payment to the 1968 Humphrey campaign.

Other information in the Wright report indicated that after Humphrey's defeat in 1968, the dairymen made plans to donate money to President Nixon while continuing to back Humphrey and other Democrats in later elections. [See below]

■ According to reports March 26, Nelson arranged for delivery of a $100,000 cash contribution to Herbert Kalmbach, then Nixon's chief fund raiser, in August 1969.

AMPI records showed that the money, intended to "make peace" with Nixon after the co-op's prior support of Humphrey, was withdrawn from the account of AMPI's political unit, Trust for Agriculture Political Education (TAPE), and delivered to Kalmbach by Milton P. Semer. (His law partner, Jake Jacobsen, had been indicted for perjury regarding an alleged $10,000 payoff to the Nixon Administration. Jacobsen pleaded not guilty March 15.)

"Several days later," according to the Wright report, AMPI's treasurer Robert O. Isham realized that the donation was in violation of the Federal Corrupt Practices Act because it violated the $5,000 limit to any campaign organization and had not been reported to the clerk of the House of Representatives.

Subsequently, Nelson and Isham met in December 1969 with W. De Veir Pierson, a former assistant to President Johnson, and at that time one of AMPI's lawyers in Washington, to discuss an elaborate scheme to cover up the illegal contribution by using dummy payments to prominent Democrats.

The Wright report stated that these AMPI officials decided to conceal their donation to Nixon by borrowing another $100,000 from an Austin, Texas bank to replace the money withdrawn and given to Kalmbach. According to the "payback plan" detailed in the report, "this loan would then be repaid through money solicited and obtained by Mr. [Bob A.] Lilly [Nelson's assistant and a TAPE official] from lawyers and public relations consultants employed by AMPI." These persons, many of them prominent Democrats, were compensated for their donations to Lilly with increased fees (and taxes paid on the additional income) paid by AMPI. All denied knowledge of the cover-up scheme of the original $100,000 contribution to Nixon.

Among those named in the report as conduits for Lilly were Pierson; Richard Maguire, former treasurer of the Democratic National Committee and later an AMPI lawyer in Washington; Ted Van Dyk and Kirby Jones, public relations consultants who became high ranking aides in Sen. George McGovern's presidential race in 1972; James R. Jones, former White House aide to President Johnson, former AMPI lawyer in Tulsa, Okla. and editor of a dairy industry publication, and currently a Democratic congressman elected in 1972 from Oklahoma; the late Clifton C. Carter, a former executive director of the Democratic National Committee and Washington lawyer for AMPI.

Van Dyk said March 26 he was asked to give Lilly $10,000 for use as a "bonus outside of the regular AMPI channels. I had no reason to think there was anything under the table about this at all," Van Dyk declared. "These [AMPI] people were essentially country people and they operated in an extremely erratic, harum-scarum way. I had no reason to suspect anything untoward."

Lilly eventually raised $142,500 by 1971 to pay off the $100,000 loan and others, the Wright report stated.

(AMPI officials had sought return of what the company termed its "illegal" $100,000 contribution from Nixon campaign committee lawyer, Kenneth Parkinson. A letter, dated Jan. 21 and made public Feb. 27 during the antitrust trial in Kansas City, asked for return of the $100,000 and also $5,000 given in 1971 to the Nixon campaign's dummy committee, People United for Good Government. "We understand that this money ultimately wound up in the hands of the Ellsberg burglars," the letter declared.)

Another AMPI lawyer who funneled money to Lilly, it was disclosed March 26, was Stuart H. Russell. Between 1968 and 1973, Russell was paid more than $1 million by the co-op. Payments to Lilly, for which Russell subsequently was reimbursed, went to Humphrey and Rep. Wilbur D. Mills (D, Ark.). AMPI paid the salaries and Washington living expenses for two Mills campaign workers in late 1971 and early 1972 when Mills was preparing to declare his candidacy for the

Democratic presidential nomination, according to the Wright report.

■ It was reported March 24 that AMPI also spent $137,000 in 1971 on a computer mailing list for campaign use by Humphrey; Sen. James Abourezk (D, S.D.); Gov. David Hall (D, Okla.); Gov. Robert Docking (D, Kan.); and the Iowa Democratic Party. (Sen. Harold Hughes of Iowa said he refused an AMPI offer.)

The Minneapolis-based computer mail firm that compiled the list, Valentine, Sherman and Associates, admitted receiving the money and falsifying invoices to conceal the source of payments, according to the Wright report.

AMPI officials denied using the computer mailing list for company purposes, but Lilly told investigators for the Wright report that names and addresses were sought "for possible use in soliciting life insurance." Valentine, Sherman officials said they were also told this, but AMPI never entered the insurance field.

■ It was revealed March 24 that the Wright report also quoted Lilly as saying he made contributions in 1969 to Texas state legislators through another "conduit for political funds"—an official in the Texas Agriculture Commission. Several of the legislators claimed they never received the money, which, according to Lilly, was drawn on TAPE's account.

Plan to kill antitrust suit disclosed— Also included in the Wright report was a statement from Dwight L. Morris, a former AMPI executive, that the dairymen made arrangements with Herbert Kalmbach to buy their way out of the antitrust suit. The plan fell through before the money could be paid when the Nixon Administration's controversial handling of another antitrust suit against International Telephone & Telegraph Corp. was revealed, Morris claimed.

Morris also testified privately March 6 before the Senate Watergate committee and a Watergate grand jury in Washington.

Morris said he was told of the settlement plan by AMPI President John E. Butterbrodt. According to Morris' statement filed with the court March 12, he was told in April 1972 that Butterbrodt and George Mehren, Harold Nelson's successor as general manager of AMPI, had "gone to Washington in an attempt to settle the suit in February 1972." (The suit had been filed Feb. 1, 1972.)

"No one in Washington would talk to them about this—not the Justice Department, FTC [Federal Trade Commission] or the White House," Morris testified. "A suggestion was finally made to them that they should see Kalmbach." Butterbrodt told Morris that [after a meeting on the West Coast] "they had agreed with Kalmbach to pay $300,000 to Kalmbach and the antitrust suit against AMPI would die a natural death," Morris said.

"Kalmbach was to direct them where [to which committees, etc.] the money should be sent. Before this could be ac-

complished the ITT thing hit the press and Kalmbach sent word that he didn't want their money," Morris added.

Another document entered as evidence in a related milk fund suit and made public Feb. 9 was a memo dated Sept. 24, 1971 from Charles Colson, then White House special counsel, to H. R. Haldeman, then White House chief of staff. Colson, who had been identified in other court records as the "point of contact with the dairy people within the White House," warned Haldeman that "there is underway in the Justice Department at the moment an Antitrust Division investigation of the milk producer cooperatives.... If this goes too far, there will be a number of very serious adverse consequences which I would be glad to elaborate on in detail."

Colson had informed President Nixon in September 1970 that the dairymen were prepared to contribute $2 million to his 1972 campaign.

Attorney General John Mitchell's approval of a criminal investigation of the co-op's alleged monopolistic practices had been sought Sept. 9, 1971 and again Oct. 29, 1971. In early 1972 the Antitrust Division was permitted to file a civil suit against AMPI.

The Colson memo was entered as evidence in consumer advocate Ralph Nader's suit seeking to overturn a 1971 increase in the federal price support for milk. Nader contended that the dairymen had bought the favorable ruling from the White House with pledges of large campaign contributions.

According to a pretrial deposition filed Jan. 21 in the Kansas City antitrust suit, AMPI's former lawyer David Parr said the co-op's aim was "to manage or control the total supply of milk in the U.S. including imports and exports."

Democrats criticize Nixon proposals. A Democratic Party spokesman objected March 15 to President Nixon's campaign fund reform proposals and urged support for a Senate bill providing for public financing for campaigns for federal office. The spokesman, Sen. John O. Pastore (D, R.I.), replied in a radio address to Nixon's radio address March 8.

Pastore asserted that the Watergate scandals were "conclusive proof that the present system of private financing breeds corruption." Nixon's proposals, he said, would leave presidential campaigns "the private preserve of the rich and powerful interests." "How many Americans are capable of making a contribution of $15,-000?" Pastore asked, referring to Nixon's proposal for that limit on individual contributions to presidential campaigns.

"Let us not be misled by those who claim that public financing is taxation without representation and a raid on the federal Treasury," he said. "Taxation without representation is precisely what you have when you have corruption. Too many big contributors and their view-

points are all too often translated to public policy which, in turn, fattens the fat cats."

"The raid upon the Treasury," he continued, "is not to be found in the dollar checkoff [on individual income tax returns] which is freely the choice of the taxpayer—the real raid on the Treasury is the special favors being meted out to those who give big in order to receive big."

"Public funds for the public campaigns of public officials make good sense if we want to end political payola," Pastore said.

Referring to the public disclosure feature of the President's proposals, Pastore said the 1972 law barred "secret money to finance federal elections" but "full disclosure in itself is just not enough." "We had a taste of that in the 1972 campaign," he said, "when, with a full disclosure law on the books, millions upon millions of dollars were secretly contributed for public favor."

Legislative delay laid to Democrat— "There's Another Political Scandal in Town, but This One Belongs to the Democrats," was the headline on a full-page advertisement in the Washington Post March 21. Placed by Common Cause, the citizens' lobby, the ad pointed out that Rep. Wayne L. Hays (D, Ohio), chairman of the Democratic Congressional Campaign Committee and responsible for raising and dispensing funds for the Democratic Congressional campaigns, was "also the man responsible for writing legislation to reform campaign finance practices." Hays was chairman of the House Administration Committee handling such legislation which, according to the ad, had been stalled by Hays for 15 months.

The ad cautioned that "the question on voters' minds will not be, 'Which Watergate conspirator committed what misdeed?' but 'What steps did Congress take to prevent future Watergates.' "

The ad referred to a $500-a-plate dinner that evening to raise funds for the Democratic candidates in the November elections. "If you've been hankering to meet the special interests, here's your chance," it said. "They'll all be there." Hays, promoting the dinner along with Sen. Lloyd Bentsen (Tex.), chairman of the Democratic Senatorial Campaign Committee, denounced Common Cause in a speech on the House floor March 21. He said the campaign spending bill would require reporting of all contributions "to all candidates of all parties."

Business backed Democrats—A report issued by Common Cause March 21 on special interest campaign funding in 1972 showed that House Democratic candidates received $667,226 and Senate candidates $550,947. Of that, the report said, business sources supplied $196,831 for the House races and $154,981 for the Senate bids compared to $55,000 and $68,750, respectively, from labor sources.

Political hiring at HUD charged. The Civil Service Commission recommended March 19 that three key officials in the Department of Housing and Urban Development (HUD) be dismissed and six others suspended for using a "special referral unit" to circumvent civil service regulations and favor politically well-connected job applicants. Similar violations had been found in the General Services Administration in late 1973.

The commission did not identify the nine officials or disclose the number of employes hired under the illegal system. The accused officials would have the opportunity for hearings before a final commission decision.

The commission noted that it was proper for job candidates to be referred by political sources, but said HUD officials had asked about applicants' political affiliations and had used the information to discriminate.

HUD Secretary James T. Lynn said he had abolished the referral unit in November 1973 after a departmental investigation into the commission's charges, and had ordered that politically influential applicants be hired within regulations.

Presidential power assailed. A panel of experts in public administration reported to the Senate Watergate Committee March 20 that many of the abuses associated with the Watergate scandals could be traced to a "centralization of power in the presidency," under which "the prevailing view is that the whole government should be run from the White House." [For further details, see p. 77F2]

Anderson convicted of taking kickbacks. N. Dale Anderson, successor to former Vice President Spiro T. Agnew as Baltimore County (Md.) executive, was convicted by a federal jury in Baltimore March 20 on 32 counts of conspiracy, extortion and income tax evasion. The jury found Anderson, a Democrat, guilty of accepting about $40,000 in kickbacks from engineers and architects seeking government contracts and of failing to pay $59,000 in federal income tax for the years 1969–72.

Government prosecutors agreed with Anderson's claim that he had inherited a system of corruption from Agnew, but they disputed his contention that he had never accepted bribes from anybody and that, in fact, he had tried to end the corruption. The prosecutors said: "Anderson . . . didn't invent it [corruption] but he exploited it and made a lot of money out of it."

Among those testifying against Anderson was William E. Fornoff, a former key aide to Anderson and Agnew, who admitted acting as an intermediary through whom kickbacks were funneled to Anderson. Lester Matz and Jerome B. Wolff, engineers who had admitted paying bribes to Agnew, testified at the Anderson trial that they had paid bribes to Fornoff for Anderson. The witnesses testified under court-granted immunity against self-incrimination.

Indictments Presented
in Watergate Cover-up
& Fielding Break-in

Grand jury indicts 7. The historic indictment of seven former White House and campaign aides on charges of covering up the Watergate scandal was returned March 1 in a 15-minute session in the courtroom of Chief U.S. District Court Judge John J. Sirica.

The grand jury (the first of three dealing with the Watergate case) also delivered a sealed "report and recommendation" reportedly dealing with President Nixon's relation to the cover-up. The report, provisionally kept under seal by Sirica, touched off a controversy as to its disposition, with the central issue the possible access to the report by the House Judiciary Committee considering Nixon's impeachment.

The defendants, the charges and the maximum possible penalties:

John D. Ehrlichman, Nixon's former domestic affairs adviser: one count each of conspiracy, obstruction of justice and making false statements to the Federal Bureau of Investigation (FBI), and two counts of false declarations before a grand jury or court; 25 years in prison and $40,000 in fines;

H. R. Haldeman, former White House chief of staff: one count each of conspiracy and obstruction of justice and three counts of perjury (before the Senate Watergate Committee); 25 years and $16,000;

John N. Mitchell, former attorney general and director of Nixon's 1968 and 1972 campaigns: one count each of conspiracy, obstruction of justice, perjury, and false statements to the FBI, and two counts of false declarations to a grand jury or court; 30 years and $42,000;

Charles W. Colson, former presidential counsel: one count each of conspiracy and obstruction of justice; 10 years and $10,000;

Gordon C. Strachan, Haldeman's former assistant: one count each of conspiracy, obstruction of justice and false declarations; 15 years and $20,000;

Robert C. Mardian, former assistant attorney general and a 1972 Nixon campaign aide: one count of conspiracy; five years and $5,000;

Kenneth W. Parkinson, attorney for the Committee to Re-elect the President: one count each of conspiracy and obstruction of justice; 10 years and $10,000.

After accepting the indictment and the sealed report from grand jury foreman Vladimir N. Pregelj, Sirica issued a "special order" prohibiting "extrajudicial" comment on the case by the office of special prosecutor Leon Jaworski, the defendants and their attorneys and witnesses. Sirica later announced he had assigned himself to try the case. At a brief arraignment hearing March 9, the seven pleaded not guilty to all charges. The trial was scheduled to begin Sept. 9.

The charges: *conspiracy*—The overall conspiracy charge involving all seven defendants detailed the complex scenario in which the defendants—with other persons "known and unknown"—arranged "hush money" payoffs for those first charged in the Watergate burglary and wiretapping, offered executive clemency, destroyed documents and lied to various investigative bodies—all of which formed the basis for the other charges in the indictment.

A central figure in the grand jury's narrative was former presidential counsel John W. Dean 3rd, who had already pleaded guilty to one count of conspiracy and was cooperating with the prosecution.

According to the 45 "overt acts" of conspiracy cited by the grand jury, the cover-up began within hours after the break-in at Democratic Party headquarters June 17, 1972: Mitchell told Mardian to try to arrange for the intercession of Richard G. Kleindienst, then attorney general, in getting the arrested burglars out of jail.

Over the next few days, Strachan destroyed documents on Haldeman's orders, and Mitchell suggested to Jeb Stuart Magruder, deputy campaign director for the re-election committee, that other documents in Magruder's files be destroyed. Concern over G. Gordon Liddy and E. Howard Hunt Jr., the still-unarrested burglary conspirators, led Ehrlichman to direct Dean to tell them they "should leave the United States," and to tell Dean to "take possession" of the

contents of Hunt's safe.

Liddy and Hunt did not leave, and after Liddy reminded Mardian and campaign aide Frederick C. LaRue of certain financial "commitments" to those involved in the break-in, the sequence of fund-raising and clandestine payoffs began.

On June 26 and June 28, 1972, Ehrlichman approved two suggestions relating to possible sources of funds. Dean's first approach was to the Central Intelligence Agency (CIA) for "covert funds to pay for bail and salaries." Having apparently failed, Dean went to Herbert W. Kalmbach, Nixon's personal attorney. The first payoff was delivered July 7—$25,000 in cash to William O. Bittman, Hunt's attorney.

A key "overt act" of obstruction occurred in mid-July: Mitchell, in the presence of Parkinson, told Dean to obtain FBI reports on its Watergate investigation; Mardian, meeting with Dean, examined the reports July 21.

Meanwhile, according to the indictment, the payoffs continued as demands escalated. By Oct. 13, 1972, an additional $182,500 had been delivered, mostly by Anthony T. Ulasewicz, a former New York City policeman who dealt with Kalmbach and Parkinson under "code names." Kalmbach remained the major fund-raiser, under instructions from Ehrlichman at a White House meeting that the fund-raising and payments should be kept secret.

Hunt was apparently not satisfied: in a telephone conversation with Colson in mid-November 1972, Hunt pressed the need for additional payments. Colson taped the conversation, and—through Dean—the demands were relayed to Haldeman, Ehrlichman and Mitchell. In early December 1972 and early January 1973 Haldeman gave Dean his approval for the use of a $350,000 cash fund then under Haldeman's control; shortly afterwards, Strachan delivered approximately $300,000 to LaRue.

As the trial of the break-in defendants approached in early January 1973, discussions among the cover-up conspirators began to focus on the possibility of executive clemency. One such meeting of Ehrlichman, Colson and Dean centered on "assurances" for Hunt, and during the same period Mitchell instructed Dean to relay a promise of clemency to James W. McCord Jr.

Payments to Hunt continued even after the first criminal trial ended Jan. 30, 1973 with the conviction of Liddy and McCord. (Hunt had pleaded guilty Jan. 11, 1973.)

Dean was told by Ehrlichman March 19, 1973 to inform Mitchell that Hunt had demanded another $120,000, and the demand was discussed further two days later at a White House meeting "attended by" Haldeman and Dean. [See below] After telephone conversations involving Haldeman, Mitchell and LaRue, arrangements were made for a payment of $75,-000 to Hunt's lawyer.

In a March 22, 1973 meeting with Haldeman, Ehrlichman and Dean, Mitchell gave assurances that Hunt was no longer a "problem." Ehrlichman then told Egil Krogh Jr., Hunt's former superior in the special "plumbers" investigative unit, of his belief that Hunt would not "reveal certain matters."

Perjury: Haldeman, Dean and Nixon meeting—The key perjury charge against Haldeman concerned his testimony before the Senate Watergate Committee about the March 21, 1973 meeting with Dean and President Nixon.

The first hour of the meeting had involved only Nixon and Dean; Haldeman was present for the following 40 minutes, he told the Senate panel, but had listened to a tape of the entire session. (The tape was among those subpoenaed by the prosecution and eventually surrendered by the White House.)

Giving the "best of [his] recollection" of the meeting, Haldeman said Nixon, questioning Dean on Hunt's $120,000 "blackmail threat" over the "seamy things" Hunt had done for Ehrlichman, was trying to "smoke out what was really going on" and had "led Dean on." Dean said a million dollars might be needed over the years, "but the problem is that it is hard to raise." According to Haldeman, Nixon had said, "There is no problem" in raising the money, "but it would be wrong." Haldeman told the panel the tape of the meeting confirmed his recollection.

The grand jury charged that Haldeman's statements about Nixon's "it would be wrong," as Haldeman "then and there well knew, were false."

Nixon had backed up Haldeman's testimony as "accurate" in an Aug. 22, 1973 news conference, recalling that he had told Dean—concerning both clem-

ency and payoffs—"John, it's wrong, it won't work, we can't give clemency, and we've got to get this story out."

Nixon account of crucial meeting—That crucial meeting, and Haldeman's account of it, were the subject of five questions at Nixon's March 6 news conference. Nixon again denied authorizing executive clemency or payments to the original defendants, but conceded that different people might have "different interpretations" of a transcript of the meeting.

Asked if he could provide proof that he had said "it would be wrong," Nixon replied:

"... it would be improper as of course you know for me to comment on the substance of any charges or indictment that have been made against any of the defendants in this matter. However, it is proper for me to comment on what I said and what I did on the 21st of March, which is the date in question.

"On that occasion, Mr. Dean asked to see me and when he came into the office soon after his arrival he said that he wanted to tell me some things that he had not told me about the Watergate matter, and for the first time on March 21 he told me that payments had been made to the defendants for the purpose of keeping them quiet, not simply for their defense. If it had been simply for their defense, that would have been proper, I understand. But if it was for the purpose of keeping them quiet—you describe it as hush money—that of course would have been an obstruction of justice.

"I examined him at great length. We examined all of the options at great length during our discussion, and we considered them on a tentative basis, every option as to what the defendants would do as to who in the White House might be involved and other information that up to that time had been disclosed to me by Mr. Dean.

"Then we came to what I consider to be the bottom line. I pointed out that raising the money, paying the money, was something that could be done, but I pointed out that that was linked to clemency, that no individual is simply going to stay in jail because people are taking care of his family or his counsel as the case might be, and that unless a promise of clemency was made that the objective of so-called hush money would not be achieved. I am paraphrasing what was a relatively long conversation.

"I then said that to pay clemency was wrong. In fact, I think I can quote it directly. I said, 'It is wrong, that's for sure.' Mr. Haldeman was present when I said that. Mr. Dean was present. Both agreed with my conclusion.

"Now, when individuals read the entire transcript of the [March] 21st meeting or hear the entire tape where we discussed all these options, they may reach different interpretations. But I know what I meant, and I know, also, what I did.

"I meant that the whole transaction was wrong, the transaction for the purpose of keeping this whole matter covered up. That was why I directed that Mr. Haldeman, Mr. Ehrlichman, Mr. Dean and Mr. Mitchell, who was then in New York, meet in Washington that evening, if possible, but it turned out that they could not meet till the next day—so that we could find what could be the best way to get the whole story out.

"Also, I also know what I did with regard to clemency and with regard to the payment of money. I never at any time authorized clemency for any of the defendants. I never at any time authorized the payment of money to any of the defendants. ..."

Nixon added that after Dean had been unable to provide a complete report on "everything that he knew," an "independent investigation" by Ehrlichman was ordered. Nixon maintained that he had ordered his staff to "testify fully" about their own involvement "or anybody else's," if called before the grand jury. "In other words," Nixon said, "the policy was one of full disclosure and that was the decision that was made at the conclusion of that meeting."

Replying to another question on the possibility of "different interpretations" of a tape of the meeting, Nixon said: "What I say is that I know what I said, I know what I meant, I know what I did, and I think that any fair-minded person will reach the same conclusion that I have. ..."

Another reporter followed with a question whether Nixon had "figured out" why $75,000 in alleged hush money was paid the same day he disapproved the practice. Nixon replied that he had "no information as to when a payment was made, to what you have referred. All I have information on is as to my own actions and my own directions, and my actions and directions were clear and very precise. I did not authorize payments, and I did not have knowledge of payments, to which you have referred."

Nixon was also pressed on the policy of "full disclosure" said to have been decided upon at the meeting; had he considered "blowing the whistle immediately?"

Nixon's reply:

"As a matter of fact, among the options we considered was getting out a full report, a report that he would write. But one of the options we considered the next day and we started to consider it that day was to have everybody testify before the Ervin committee and waive executive privilege, which was a course of action which Attorney General Mitchell recommended. Yes, the option of a full disclosure at that time by everybody concerned was one that was considered. The difficulty that I had was that for months these matters had not been brought to my attention.

"I had not been informed of the payments to the defendants. I had not been informed with regard to the alleged cover-up. I had not been informed about the possible involvement of some White House aides. I felt it was my responsibility to conduct my own investigation with all the assistance I could get from those who could provide information before moving to what would be a proper way of getting this story out to the country.

"At all times it had been my goal to have a complete disclosure of this whole situation because, as you know, I have said there can be no cloud over the White House. I want that cloud removed; that's one of the reasons we have cooperated as we have with the special prosecutor. We will also cooperate with the Rodino committee. The facts will come out."

Nixon also said he thought the entire tape of the meeting would eventually be made public, but that for the present he would be guided by the strictures concerning publicity on the recent indictments.

Perjury: Haldeman and Mitchell; money and documents—Haldeman's Senate committee testimony on the $350,000 cash fund under his control, which according to the grand jury was used for "hush money" payments to the break-in defendants, resulted in a second perjury charge. Haldeman had said he was unaware of their use for "blackmail" until told by Dean in March 1973. This, the indictment charged, was false.

(Gordon Strachan's testimony before the grand jury on the handling of the money was the basis of the false declarations charge against him.)

Haldeman's third perjury count went back to the March 21, 1973 White House meeting, which—according to Dean's testimony before the Senate Committee—had included Dean's report on the preparation of a false story on the planning of the break-in to be used by Magruder. Haldeman later told the panel; "I don't believe there was any reference to Magruder committing perjury." This statement was false, the indictment charged.

Mitchell was charged with perjury in connection with his Watergate committee testimony on the so-called "Gemstone" file of wiretap information from Democratic Party headquarters. Asked about a meeting in his apartment June 19, 1972, Mitchell said he had not heard of the Gemstone file as of that date, nor to the "best of [his] recollection" had there been any destruction of documents. The statements were false, the grand jury charged.

False statements to probers—The indictment charged that Mitchell on two occasions testified falsely before the grand jury. On the first, Mitchell said he knew of no illegal, clandestine plans against the Democrats, "because, if there had been, I would have shut it off as being entirely nonproductive at that particular time of the campaign." Mitchell testified later that he could not recall being told by LaRue or Mardian that Liddy had confessed to a role in the break-in.

Ehrlichman was also charged with two counts of lying to the grand jury. According to the first charge, Ehrlichman testified falsely when he said he could not recall discussing Liddy's role in the break-in with Dean; nor could he recall when he first learned that Liddy was implicated. The grand jury also charged that Ehrlichman lied in testifying that he could not recall discussing with Kalmbach the purpose of Kalmbach's fund-raising or telling Kalmbach that the fund-raising should be kept secret.

Both Mitchell and Ehrlichman were accused of falsely telling the FBI that their knowledge of the break-in was limited to newspaper accounts. Mitchell's statement came less than three weeks after the break-in, but Ehrlichman was charged with saying as late as July 21, 1973 "that he had neither received nor was he in possession of any information relative to the break-in . . . other than what he had read in the way of newspaper accounts. . . ."

Nixon urges presumption of innocence—President Nixon's reaction to the cover-up indictment of his former aides was a brief statement read to reporters March 1 by Deputy Press Secretary Gerald L. Warren:

"The President has always maintained that the judicial system is the proper forum for the resolution of the questions concerning Watergate. The indictments indicate that the judicial process is finally moving toward resolution of the matter. It is the President's hope that the trials will move quickly to a just conclusion. The President is confident that all Americans will join him in recognizing that those indicted are presumed innocent unless proof of guilt is established in the courts."

Nixon was asked in his March 6 news conference about possible clemency for former assistants. He replied that clemency was an "individual" matter—"depending upon a personal tragedy or something of that sort." No one would be granted clemency simply because they "happen to be involved in Watergate."

Regarding the immunity from prosecution which had been granted some former aides, Nixon said that such a policy towards "any major White House employe would be highly improper." He added that neither Haldeman, Ehrlichman or Colson had "used the shield of the Fifth Amendment, as they could have." They had testified freely, Nixon said, and had been "convicted by the press—over and over again" and "before committees—over and over again," but "they are now before a court."

Both Colson and Parkinson issued statements proclaiming their innocence March 1, and Haldeman said in Los Angeles March 4 that he had "done nothing wrong," but he added it was "obvious some things were wrong."

Text of Indictment Returned March 1 by Watergate Grand Jury

Italicized material is underscored in the original document.

Introduction

1. On or about June 17, 1972, Bernard L. Barker, Virgilio R. Gonzalez, Eugenio R. Martinez, James W. McCord Jr. and Frank L. Sturgis were arrested in the offices of the Democratic National Committee, located in the Watergate office building, Washington, D.C., while attempting to photograph documents and repair a surreptitious electronic listening device which had previously been placed in those offices unlawfully.

2. At all times material herein, the United States attorney's office for the District of Columbia and the Federal Bureau of Investigation were parts of the Department of Justice, a department and agency of the United States, and the Central Intelligence Agency was an agency of the United States.

3. Beginning on or about June 17, 1972, and continuing up to and including the date of the filing of this indictment, the Federal Bureau of Investigation and the United States attorney's office for the District of Columbia were conducting an investigation, in conjunction with a grand jury of the United States District Court for the District of Columbia which had been duly impaneled and sworn on or about June 5, 1972, to determine whether violations of 18 U.S.C. 371, 2511 and 22 D.C. Code 1801 (b), and of other statutes of the United States and of the District of Columbia, had been committed in the District of Columbia and elsewhere, and to identify the individual or individuals who had committed, caused the commission of, and conspired to commit such violations.

4. On or about Sept. 15, 1972, in connection with the said investigation, the grand jury returned an indictment in Criminal Case No. 1827-72 in the United States District Court for the District of Columbia charging Bernard L. Barker, Virgilio R. Gonzalez, E. Howard Hunt Jr., G. Gordon Liddy, Eugenio R. Martinez, James W. McCord Jr. and Frank L. Sturgis with conspiracy, burglary and unlawful endeavor to intercept wire communications.

5. From in or about January, 1969, to on or about March 1, 1972, John N. Mitchell, the defendant, was attorney general of the United States. From on or about April 9, 1972, to on or about June 30, 1972, he was campaign director of the Committee to Re-Elect the President.

6. At all times material herein up to on or about April 30, 1973, Harry R. Haldeman, the defendant, was assistant to the President of the United States.

7. At all times material herein up to on or about April 30, 1973, John D. Ehrlichman, the defendant, was assistant for domestic affairs to the President of the United States.

8. At all times material herein up to on or about March 10, 1973, Charles W. Colson, the defendant, was special counsel to the President of the United States.

9. At all times material herein, Robert C. Mardian, the defendant, was an official of the Committee to Re-elect the President.

10. From on or about June 21, 1972, and at all times material herein, Kenneth W. Parkinson, the defendant, was an attorney representing the Committee to Re-elect the President.

11. At all times material herein up to in or about November, 1972, Gordon Strachan, the defendant, was a staff assistant to Harry R. Haldeman at the White House. Thereafter he became general counsel to the United States Information Agency.

Count One

12. From on or about June 17, 1972, up to and including the date of the filing of this indictment, in the District of Columbia and elsewhere, John N. Mitchell, Harry R. Haldeman, John D. Ehrlichman, Charles W. Colson, Robert C. Mardian, Kenneth W. Parkinson and Gordon Strachan, the defendants, and other persons to the grand jury known and unknown, unlawfully, willfully and knowingly did combine, conspire, confederate and agree together and with each other, to commit offenses against the United States, to wit, to obstruct justice in violation of Title 18, United States Code, Section 1503, to make false statements to a government agency in violation of Title 18, United States Code, Section 1001, to make false declarations in violation of Title 18, United States Code, Section 1623, and to defraud the United States and agencies and departments thereof, to wit, the Central Intelligence Agency (C.I.A.), the Federal Bureau of Investigation (F.B.I.) and the Department of Justice, of the government's right to have the officials of these departments and agencies transact their official business honestly and impartially, free from corruption, fraud, improper and undue influence, dishonesty, unlawful impairment and obstruction, all in violation of Title 18, United States Code, Section 371.

13. It was a part of the conspiracy that the conspirators would corruptly influence, obstruct and impede, and corruptly endeavor to influence, obstruct and impede, the due administration of justice in connection with the investigation referred to in Paragraph 3 above and in connection with the trial of Criminal Case No. 1827-72 in the United States District Court for the District of Columbia, for the purpose of concealing and causing to be concealed the identities of the persons who were responsible for, participated in, and had knowledge of (a) the activities which were the subject of the investigation and trial, and (b) other illegal and improper activities.

14. It was further a part of the conspiracy that the conspirators would knowingly make and cause to be made false statements to the F.B.I. and false material statements and declarations under oath in proceedings before and ancillary to the grand jury and a court of the United States, for the purposes stated in paragraph thirteen (13) above.

(Text of March 1 indictment—cont.)

15. It was further a part of the conspiracy that the conspirators would, by deceit, craft, trickery and dishonest means, defraud the United States by interfering with and obstructing the lawful governmental functions of the C.I.A., in that the conspirators would induce the C.I.A. to provide financial assistance to persons who were subjects of the investigation referred to in paragraph three (3) above, for the purposes stated in paragraph thirteen (13) above.

16. It was further a part of the conspiracy that the conspirators would, by deceit, craft, trickery and dishonest means, defraud the United States by interfering with and obstructing the lawful governmental functions of the F.B.I. and the Department of Justice, in that the conspirators would obtain and attempt to obtain from the F.B.I. and the Department of Justice information concerning the investigation referred to in paragraph three (3) above, for the purposes stated in paragraph thirteen (13) above.

17. Among the means by which the conspirators would carry out the aforesaid conspiracy were the following:

(a) The conspirators would direct G. Gordon Liddy to seek the assistance of Richard G. Kleindienst, then attorney general of the United States, in obtaining the release from the District of Columbia jail of one or more of the persons who had been arrested on June 17, 1972, in the offices of the Democratic National Committee in the Watergate office building in Washington, D.C., and G. Gordon Liddy would seek such assistance from Richard G. Kleindienst.

(b) The conspirators would at various times remove, conceal, alter and destroy, attempt to remove, conceal, alter and destroy, and cause to be removed, concealed, altered and destroyed, documents, papers, records and objects.

(c) The conspirators would plan, solicit, assist and facilitate the giving of false, deceptive, evasive and misleading statements and testimony.

(d) The conspirators would give false, misleading, evasive and deceptive statements and testimony.

(e) The conspirators would covertly raise, acquire, transmit, distribute and pay cash funds to and for the benefit of the defendants in Criminal Case No. 1827-72 in the United States District Court for the District of Columbia, both prior to and subsequent to the return of the indictment on Sept. 15, 1972.

(f) The conspirators would make and cause to be made offers of leniency, executive clemency and other benefits to E. Howard Hunt Jr., G. Gordon Liddy, James W. McCord Jr., and Jeb S. Magruder.

(g) The conspirators would attempt to obtain C.I.A. financial assistance for persons who were subjects of the investigation referred to in paragraph three (3) above.

(h) The conspirators would obtain information from the F.B.I. and the Department of Justice concerning the progress of the investigation referred to in paragraph three (3) above.

18. In furtherance of the conspiracy, and to the effect the objects thereof, the following overt acts, among others, were committed in the District of Columbia and elsewhere:

Overt Acts

1. On or about June 17, 1972, John N. Mitchell met with Robert C. Mardian in or about Beverly Hills, Calif., and requested Mardian to tell G. Gordon Liddy to seek the assistance of Richard G. Kleindienst, then attorney general of the United States, in obtaining the release of one or more of the persons arrested in connection with the Watergate break-in.

2. On or about June 18, 1972, in the District of Columbia, Gordon Strachan destroyed documents on the instructions of Harry R. Haldeman.

3. On or about June 19, 1972, John D. Ehrlichman met with John W. Dean 3rd at the White House in the District of Columbia, at which time Ehrlichman directed Dean to tell G. Gordon Liddy that E. Howard Hunt Jr. should leave the United States.

4. On or about June 19, 1972, Charles W. Colson and John D. Ehrlichman met with John W. Dean 3rd at the White House in the District of Columbia, at which time Ehrlichman directed Dean to take possession of the contents of E. Howard Hunt Jr.'s safe in the Executive Office Building.

5. On or about June 19, 1972, Robert C. Mardian and John N. Mitchell met with Jeb S. Magruder at Mitchell's apartment in the District of Columbia, at which time Mitchell suggested that Magruder destroy documents from Magruder's files.

6. On or about June 20, 1972, G. Gordon Liddy met with Fred C. LaRue and Robert C. Mardian at LaRue's apartment in the District of Columbia, at which time Liddy told LaRue and Mardian that certain "commitments" had been made to and for the benefit of Liddy and other persons involved in the Watergate break-in.

7. On or about June 24, 1972, John N. Mitchell and Robert C. Mardian met with John W. Dean 3rd at 1701 Pennsylvania Avenue in the District of Columbia, at which time Mitchell and Mardian suggested to Dean that the C.I.A. be requested to provide covert funds for the assistance of the persons involved in the Watergate break-in.

8. On or about June 26, 1972, John D. Ehrlichman met with John W. Dean 3rd at the White House in the District of Columbia, at which time Ehrlichman approved a suggestion that Dean ask Gen. Vernon A. Walters, deputy director of the C.I.A., whether the C.I.A. could use covert funds to pay for bail and salaries of the persons involved in the Watergate break-in.

9. On or about June 28, 1972, John D. Ehrlichman had a conversation with John W. Dean 3rd in the White House in the District of Columbia, during which Ehrlichman approved of the use of Herbert W. Kalmbach to raise cash funds to make covert payments to and for the benefit of persons involved in the Watergate break-in.

10. On or about July 6, 1972, Kenneth W. Parkinson had a conversation with William O. Bittman in or about the District of Columbia, during which Parkinson told Bittman that "Rivers is O.K. to talk to." ["Rivers" was a code name used by Anthony Ulasewicz.]

11. On or about July 7, 1972, Anthony Ulasewicz delivered approximately $25,000 in cash to William O. Bittman at 815 Connecticut Avenue, Northwest, in the District of Columbia.

12. In or about mid-July, 1972, John N. Mitchell and Kenneth W. Parkinson met with John W. Dean 3rd at 1701 Pennsylvania Avenue in the District of Columbia, at which time Mitchell advised Dean to obtain F.B.I. reports of the investigation into the Watergate break-in for Parkinson and others.

13. On or about July 17, 1972, Anthony Ulasewicz delivered approximately $40,000 in cash to Dorothy Hunt at Washington National Airport.

14. On or about July 17, 1972, Anthony Ulasewicz delivered approximately $8,000 in cash to G. Gordon Liddy at Washington National Airport.

15. On or about July 21, 1972, Robert C. Mardian met with John W. Dean 3rd at the White House in the District of Columbia, at which time Mardian examined F.B.I. reports of the investigation concerning the Watergate break-in.

16. On or about July 26, 1972, John D. Ehrlichman met with Herbert W. Kalmbach at the White House in the District of Columbia, at which time Ehrlichman told Kalmbach that Kalmbach had to raise funds with which to make payments to and for the benefit of the persons involved in the Watergate break-in, and that it was necessary to keep such fund-raising and payments secret.

17. In or about late July or August, 1972, Anthony Ulasewicz made a delivery of approximately $43,000 in cash at Washington National Airport.

18. In or about late July or early August, 1972, Anthony Ulasewicz made a delivery of approximately $18,000 in cash at Washington National Airport.

19. On or about Aug. 29, 1972, Charles W. Colson had a conversation with John W. Dean 3rd, during which Dean advised Colson not to send memorandums to the authorities investigating the Watergate break-in.

20. On or about Sept. 19, 1972, Anthony Ulasewicz delivered approximately $53,500 in cash to Dorothy Hunt at Washington National Airport.

21. On or about Oct. 13, 1972, in the District of Columbia, Fred C. LaRue arranged for the delivery of approximately $20,000 in cash to William O. Bittman.

22. On or about Nov. 13, 1972, in the District of Columbia, E. Howard Hunt Jr. had a telephone conversation with Charles W. Colson, during which Hunt discussed with Colson the need to make additional payments to and for the benefits of the defendants in criminal case No. 1827-72 in the United States District Court for the District of Columbia.

23. In or about mid-November, 1972, Charles W. Colson met with John W. Dean 3rd at the White House in the District of Columbia, at which time Colson gave Dean a tape recording of a telephone conversation between Colson and E. Howard Hunt Jr.

24. On or about Nov. 15, 1972, John W. Dean 3rd met with John D. Ehrlichman and Harry R. Haldeman at Camp David, Md., at which time Dean played for Ehrlichman and Haldeman a tape recording of a telephone conversation between Charles W. Colson and E. Howard Hunt Jr.

25. On or about Nov. 15, 1972, John W. Dean 3rd met with John N. Mitchell in New York City, at which time Dean played for Mitchell a tape recording of the telephone conversation between Charles W. Colson and E. Howard Hunt Jr.

26. On or about Dec. 1, 1972, Kenneth W. Parkinson met with John W. Dean 3rd at the White House in the District of Columbia, at which time Parkinson gave Dean a list of anticipated expenses of the defendants during the trial of criminal case No. 1827-72 in the United States District Court for the District of Columbia.

27. In or about early December, 1972, Harry R. Haldeman had a telephone conversation with John W. Dean 3rd, during which Haldeman approved the use of a portion of a cash fund of approximately $350,000, then being held under Haldeman's control, to make additional payments to and for the benefits of the defendants in criminal case No. 1827-72 in the United States District Court for the District of Columbia.

28. In or about early December, 1972, Gordon Strachan met with Fred C. LaRue at LaRue's apartment in the District of Columbia, at which time Strachan delivered approximately $50,000 in cash to LaRue.

29. In or about early December, 1972, in the District of Columbia, Fred C. LaRue arranged for the delivery of approximately $40,000 in cash to William O. Bittman.

30. On or about Jan. 3, 1973, Charles W. Colson met with John D. Ehrlichman and John W. Dean 3rd at the White House in the District of Columbia, at which time Colson, Ehrlichman and Dean discussed the need to make assurances to E. Howard Hunt Jr. concerning the length of time E. Howard Hunt Jr. would have to spend in jail if he were convicted in criminal case No. 1827-72 in United States District Court for the District of Columbia.

31. In or about early January, 1973, Harry R. Haldeman had a conversation with John W. Dean 3rd, during which Haldeman approved the use of the balance of the cash fund referred to in overt act No. 27 to make additional payments to and for the benefit of the defendants in criminal case No. 1827-72 in United States District Court for the District of Columbia.

32. In or about early January, 1973, Gordon Strachan met with Fred C. LaRue at LaRue's apartment in the District of Columbia, at which time Strachan delivered approximately $300,000 in cash to LaRue.

33. In or about early January, 1973, John N. Mitchell had a telephone conversation with John W. Dean 3rd, during which Mitchell asked Dean to have John C. Caulfield give an assurance of executive clemency to James W. McCord Jr.

34. In or about mid-January, 1973, the District of Columbia, Fred C. LaRue arranged for the delivery of approximately $20,000 in cash to a representative of G. Gordon Liddy.

35. On or about Feb. 11, 1973, in Rancho LaCosta, Calif., John D. Ehrlichman and Harry R. Haldeman met with John W. Dean 3rd and discussed the need to raise money with which to make additional payments to and for the benefit of the defendants in Criminal Case 1827-72 in United States District Court for the District of Columbia.

36. In or about late February, 1973, in the District of Columbia, Fred C. LaRue arranged for the delivery of approximately $25,000 in cash to William O. Bittman.

37. In or about late February, 1973, in the District of Columbia, Fred C. LaRue arranged for the delivery of approximately $35,000 in cash to William O. Bittman.

38. On or about March 16, 1973, E. Howard Hunt Jr. met with Paul O'Brien at 815 Connecticut Avenue, Northwest, in the District of Columbia, at which time Hunt told O'Brien that Hunt wanted approximately $120,000.

39. On or about March 19, 1973, John D. Ehrlichman had a conversation with John W. Dean 3rd at the White House in the District of Columbia, during which Ehrlichman told Dean to inform John N. Mitchell about the fact that E. Howard Hunt Jr. had asked for approximately $120,000.

40. On or about March 21, 1973, from approximately 11:15 a.m. to approximately noon, Harry R. Haldeman and John W. Dean 3rd attended a meeting at the White House in the District of Columbia, at which time there was a discussion about the fact that E. Howard Hunt Jr. had asked for approximately $120,000.

41. On or about March 21, 1973, at approximately 12:30 p.m., Harry R. Haldeman had a telephone conversation with John N. Mitchell.

42. On or about the early afternoon of March 21, 1973, John N. Mitchell had a conversation with Fred C. LaRue during which Mitchell authorized LaRue to

(Text of March 1 indictment—cont.).

make a payment of approximately $75,000 and for the benefit of E. Howard Hunt Jr.

43. On or about the evening of March 21, 1973, in the District of Columbia, Fred C. LaRue arranged for the delivery of approximately $75,000 in cash to William O. Bittman.

44. On or about March 22, 1973, John D. Ehrlichman, Harry R. Haldeman and John W. Dean 3rd met with John N. Mitchell at the White House in the District of Columbia, at which time Mitchell assured Ehrlichman that E. Howard Hunt Jr. was not a "problem" any longer.

45. On or about March 22, 1973, John D. Ehrlichman had a conversation with Egil Krogh at the White House in the District of Columbia, at which time Ehrlichman assured Krogh that Ehrlichman did not believe that E. Howard Hunt Jr. would reveal certain matters.

(Title 18, United States Code, Section 371.)

Count Two

The grand jury further charges:

1. From on or about June 17, 1972, up to and including the date of the filing of this indictment, in the District of Columbia and elsewhere, John N. Mitchell, Harry R. Haldeman, John D. Ehrlichman, Charles W. Colson, Kenneth W. Parkinson and Gordon Strachan, the defendants, unlawfully, willfully and knowingly did corruptly influence, obstruct and impede, and did corruptly endeavor to influence, obstruct and impede the due administration of justice in connection with an investigation being conducted by the Federal Bureau of Investigation and the United States attorney's office for the District of Columbia, in conjunction with a grand jury of the United States District Court for the District of Columbia, and in connection with the trial of criminal case No. 1827-72 in the United States District Court for the District of Columbia, by making cash payments and offers of other benefits to and for the benefit of the defendants in Criminal Case No. 1827-72 in the United States District Court for the District of Columbia, and to others, both prior to and subsequent to the return of the indictment on Sept. 15, 1972, for the purpose of concealing and causing to be concealed the identities of the persons who were responsible for, participated in, and had knowledge of the activities which were the subject of the investigation and trial, and by other means.

(Title 18, United States Code, Section 1503 and the number 2.)

Count Three

The grand jury further charges:

On or about July 5, 1972, in the District of Columbia, John N. Mitchell, the defendant, did knowingly and willfully make false, fictitious and fraudulent statements and representations to agents of the Federal Bureau of Investigation, Department of Justice, which department was then conducting an investigation into a matter within its jurisdiction, namely, whether violations of 18 U.S.C. 371, 2511, and 22D.C. Code 1801 (b), and of other statutes of the United States and the District of Columbia, had been committed in the District of Columbia and elsewhere in connection with the break-in at the Democratic National Committee headquarters at the Watergate office building on June 17, 1972, and to identify the individual or individuals who had committed, caused the commission of, and conspired to commit such violations, in that he stated that he had no knowledge of the break-in at the Democratic National Committee headquarters other than what he had read in newspaper accounts of that incident.

(Title 18, United States Code, Section 1001.)

Count Four

The grand jury further charges:

1. On or about Sept. 14, 1972, in the District of Columbia, John N. Mitchell, the defendant, having duly taken an oath that he would testify truthfully, while testifying in a proceeding before the June, 1972, grand jury, a grand jury of the United States duly impaneled and sworn in the United States District Court for the District of Columbia, did knowingly make false material declarations as hereinafter set forth.

2. At the time and place alleged, the June, 1972, grand jury of the United States District Court for the District of Columbia was conducting an investigation in conjunction with the United States Attorney's Office of the District of Columbia and the Federal Bureau of Investigation to determine whether violations of Title 18, United States Code, Sections 371, 2511 and 22D.C. Code No. 1801 (b), and of other statutes of the United States and of the District of Columbia, had been committed in the District of Columbia and elsewhere and to identify the individual or individuals who had committed, caused the commission of, and conspired to commit such violations.

3. It was material to the said investigation that the said grand jury ascertain the identity and motives of the individual or individuals who were responsible for, participated in, and had knowledge of unlawful entries into, and electronic surveillance of, the offices of the Democratic National Committee, located in the Watergate office building in Washington, D.C., and related activities.

4. At the time and place alleged, John N. Mitchell, the defendant, appearing as a witness under oath at the proceeding before the said grand jury, did knowingly declare with respect to the material matters alleged in Paragraph 3 as follows:

Q. Was there any program, to your knowledge, at the committee, or any effort made to organize a covert or clandestine operation, basically, you know, illegal in nature, to get information or to gather intelligence about the activities of any of the Democratic candidates for public office or any activities of the Democratic Party?

A. Certainly not, because, if there had been, I would have shut it off as being entirely nonproductive at that particular time of the campaign.

Q. Did you have any knowledge, direct or indirect, of Mr. Liddy's activities with respect to any intelligence-gathering effort with respect to the activities of the Democratic candidates or its party?

A. None whatsoever, because I didn't know there was anything going on of that nature, if there was. So I wouldn't anticipate having heard anything about his activities in connection with it.

5. The underscored portions of the declarations quoted in Paragraph 4, [in italics above] made by John N. Mitchell, the defendant, were material to the said investigation and, as he then and there well knew, were false.

(Title 18, United States Code, Section 1623.)

Count Five

The grand jury further charges:

1. On or about April 20, 1973, in the District of Columbia, John N. Mitchell, the defendant, having duly taken an oath that he would testify truthfully, and while testifying in a proceeding before the June, 1972, grand jury, a grand jury of the United States duly impaneled and sworn in the United States District Court for the District of Columbia, did knowingly make false material declarations as hereinafter set forth.

2. At the time and place alleged, the June, 1972, grand jury of the United States District Court for the District of Columbia was conducting an investigation in conjunction with the United States attorney's office for the District of Columbia and the Federal Bureau of Investigation to determine whether violations of Title 18, United States Code, Sections 371, 2511, and 22 D.C. Code 1801 (b), and of other statutes of the United States and of the District of Columbia had been committed in the District of Columbia and elsewhere, and to identify the individual or individuals who had committed, caused the commission of, and conspired to commit such violations.

3. It was material to the said investigation that the said grand jury ascertain the identity and motives of the individual or individuals who were responsible for, participated in, and had knowledge of efforts to conceal, and to cause to be concealed, information relating to unlawful entries into, and electronic surveillance of, the offices of the Democratic National Committee located in the Watergate office building in Washington, D.C., and related activities.

4. At the time and place alleged, John N. Mitchell, the defendant, appearing as a witness under oath at a proceeding before the said grand jury, did knowingly declare with respect to the material matters alleged in Paragraph 3 as follows:

Q. Did Mr. LaRue tell you that Mr. Liddy had confessed to him?

A. *No, I don't recall that, no.*

Q. Did Mr. Mardian tell you that he'd confessed to him? A. *No.*

Q. Do you deny that?

A. Pardon me?

Do you deny that?

A. *I have no recollection of that.*

Q. So Mr. Mardian did not report to you that Mr. Liddy had confessed to him?

A. *Not to my recollection, Mr. Glanzer.*

Q. That would be something that you would remember, if it happened, wouldn't you?

A. Yes, I would.

Q. I didn't ask you that, I asked you were you told by either Mr. Mardian or Mr. LaRue or anybody else, at the committee, prior to June 28th, 1972, that Mr. Liddy had told them that he was involved in the Watergate break-in?

A. *I have no such recollection.*

The underscored portions [set in italics above] of the declarations quoted in Paragraph 4, made by John N. Mitchell, the defendant, were material to the said investigation and, as he then and there well knew, were false.

(Title 18, United States Code, Section 1623)

Count Six

The grand jury further charges:

1. On or about July 10 and July 11, 1973, in the District of Columbia, John N. Mitchell, the defendant, having duly taken an oath before a competent tribunal, to wit, the Select Committee on Presidential Campaign Activities, a duly created and authorized committee of the United States Senate conducting official hearings and inquiring into a matter in which a law of the United States authorizes an oath to be administered, that he would testify truly, did willfully, knowingly and contrary to such oath state material matters hereinafter set forth which he did not believe to be true.

2. At the time and place alleged, the said committee was conducting an investigation and study, pursuant to the provisions of Senate Resolution 60 adopted by the United States Senate on Feb. 7, 1973, of the extent, if any, to which illegal, improper or unethical activities were engaged in by any persons, acting either individually or in combination with others, in the Presidential election of 1972, or in any related campaign or canvass conducted by or in behalf of any person seeking nomination or election as the candidate of any political party for the office of President of the United States in such election, for the purpose of determining whether in its judgment any occurrences which might be revealed by the investigation and study indicated the necessity or desirability of the enactment of new legislation to safeguard the electoral process by which the President of the United States is chosen.

3. It was material to the said investigation and study that the said committee ascertain the identity and motives of the individual or individuals who were responsible for, participated in, and had knowledge of efforts to conceal, and to cause to be concealed information relating to (A) unlawful entries into, and electronic surveillance of, the offices of the Democratic National Committee located in the Watergate office building in Washington, D.C., and (B) related activities, through such means as the destruction of documents and other evidence of said facts.

4. At the times and place alleged, John N. Mitchell, the defendant, appearing as a witness under oath before the said committee, did willfully and knowingly state with respect to the material matters alleged in Paragraph 3 as follows:

July 10, 1973:

MR. DASH. Was there a meeting in your apartment on the evening that you arrived in Washington on June 19, attended by Mr. LaRue, Mr. Mardian, Mr. Dean, Mr. Magruder—

MR. MITCHELL. Magruder and myself, that is correct.

MR. DASH. Do you recall the purpose of that meeting, the discussion that took place there?

MR. MITCHELL. I recall that we had been traveling all day and, of course, we had very little information about what the current status was of the entry of the Democratic National Committee, and we met at the apartment to discuss it. They were, of course, clamoring for a response from the committee because of Mr. McCord's involvement, etc., etc., and we had quite a general discussion of the subject matter.

MR. DASH. Do you recall any discussion of the so-called either Gemstone files or wire-tapping files that you had in your possession?

MR. MITCHELL. *No, I had not heard of the Gemstone files as of that meeting and, as of that date, I had not heard that anybody there at that particular meeting knew of the wire tapping aspects of that or had any connection with it.*

July 11, 1973:

SENATOR WEICKER. Now, on June 19, Mr. Magruder has testified and Mr. LaRue has stated that Mr. Mitchell, that you instructed Magruder to destroy the Gemstone files, to in fact, have a bonfire with them.

SENATOR WEICKER. Did you suggest that any documents be destroyed, not necessarily Gemstone?

MR. MITCHELL. To the best of my recollection.

SENATOR WEICKER. At the June 19 meeting at your apartment?

Did you suggest that any documents be destroyed, not necessarily Gemstone or not necessarily documents that relate to electronic surveillance?

(Text of March 1 indictment—cont.)

MR. MITCHELL. *To the best of my recollection, when I was there there was no such discussion of the destruction of any documents. That was not the type of a meeting we were having.*

5. The underscored portions [set in italics above] of the declarations quoted in Paragraph 4, made by John N. Mitchell, the defendant, were material to the said investigation and study and, as he then and there well knew, were false.

(Title 18, United States Code, Section 1621).

Count Seven

The grand jury further charges:

1. On or about July 30, 1973, in the District of Columbia, Harry R. Haldeman, the defendant, having duly taken an oath before a competent tribunal, to wit, the Select Committee on Presidential Campaign Activities, a duly created and authorized committee of the United States Senate conducting official hearings and inquiring into a matter in which a law of the United States authorizes an oath to be administered, that he would testify truly, did willfully, knowingly and contrary to such oath state material matters hereinafter set forth which he did not believe to be true.

2. At the time and place alleged, the said committee was conducting an investigation and study, pursuant to the provisions of Senate Resolution 60 adopted by the United States Senate on Feb. 7, 1973, of the extent, if any, to which illegal, improper or unethical activities were engaged in by any persons, acting either individually or in combination with others, in the Presidential election of 1972, or in any related campaign or canvass conducted by or in behalf of any person seeking nomination or election as the candidate of any political party for the office of President of the United States in such election, for the purpose of determining whether in its judgment any occurrences which might be revealed by the investigation and study indicated the necessity or desirability of the enactment of new legislation to safeguard the electoral process by which the President of the United States is chosen.

3. It was material to the said investigation and study that the said committee ascertain the identity and motives of the individual or individuals who were responsible for, participated in, and had knowledge of efforts to conceal, and to cause to be concealed, information relating to (A) unlawful entries into, and electronic surveillance of, the offices of the Democratic National Committee located in the Watergate office building in Washington, D.C. and (B) related activities, through such means as the payment and promise of payment of money and other things of value to participants in these activities and to their families.

4. At the time and place alleged, Harry R. Haldeman, the defendant, appearing as a witness under oath before the said committee, did willfully and knowingly state with respect to the material matters alleged in Paragraph 3 as follows:

I was told several times, starting in the summer of 1972, by John Dean and possibly also by John Mitchell that there was a need by the committee for funds to help take care of the legal fees and family support of the Watergate defendants. The committee apparently felt obliged to do this.

Since all information regarding the defense funds was given to me by John Dean, the counsel to the President, and possibly by John Mitchell, and since the arrangements for Kalmbach's collecting funds and for transferring the $350,000 cash fund were made by John Dean, and since John Dean never stated at the time that the funds would be used for any other than legal legal [sic] and proper purposes, I had no reason to question the propriety or legality of the process of delivering the $350,000 to the committee via LaRue or of having Kalmbach raise funds.

I have no personal knowledge of what was done with the funds raised by Kalmbach or with the $350,000 that was delivered by Strachan to LaRue.

It would appear that, at the White House at least, John Dean was the only one who knew that the funds were for "hush money," if, in fact, that is what they were for. The rest of us relied on Dean and all thought that what was being done was legal and proper.

No one, to my knowledge, was aware that these funds involved either blackmail or "hush money" until this suggestion was raised in March of 1973.

5. The underscored [set in italics above] portion of the statements quoted in Paragraph 4, made by Harry R. Haldeman, the defendant, was material to the said investigation and study and, as he then and there well knew, was false.

(Title 18, United States Code, Section 1621.)

Count Eight

The grand jury further charges:

1. On or about July 30 and July 31, 1973, in the District of Columbia, Harry R. Haldeman, the defendant, having duly taken an oath before a competent tribunal, to wit, the Select Committee on Presidential Campaign Activities, a duly created and authorized committee of the United States Senate conducting official hearings and inquiring into a matter in which a law of the United States authorizes an oath to be administered, that he would testify truly, did willfully, knowingly and contrary to such oath state material matters hereinafter set forth which he did not believe to be true.

2. At the times and place alleged, the said committee was conducting an investigation and study, pursuant to the provisions of Senate Resolution 60 adopted by the United States Senate on Feb. 7, 1973, of the extent, if any, to which illegal, improper or unethical activities were engaged in by any persons, acting either individually or in combination with others, in the Presidential election of 1972, or in any related campaign or canvass conducted by or in behalf of any person seeking nomination or election as the candidate of any political party for the office of President of the United States in such election, for the purpose of determining whether in its judgment any occurrences which might be revealed by the investigation and study indicated the necessity or desirability of the enactment of new legislation to safeguard the electoral process by which the President of the United States is chosen.

3. It was material to the said investigation and study that the said committee ascertain the identity and motives of the individual or individuals who were responsible for, participated in, and had knowledge of efforts to conceal, and to cause to be concealed, information relating to (A) unlawful entries into, and electronic surveillance of, the offices of the Democratic National Committee located in the Watergate office building in Washington, D.C., and (B) related activities, through such means as the payment and promise of payment of money and other things of value to participants in these activities and to their families.

4. At the times and place alleged, Harry R. Haldeman, the defendant, appearing as a witness under oath before the said committee, did willfully and knowingly state with respect to the material matters alleged in Paragraph 3 as follows:

July 30, 1973:

I was present for the final 40 minutes of the President's meeting with John Dean on the morning of March 21. While I was not present for the first hour of the meeting, I did listen to the tape of the entire meeting.

Following is the substance of that meeting to the best of my recollection.

He [Dean] also reported on a current Hunt blackmail threat. He said Hunt was demanding $120,000 or else he would tell about the seamy things he had done for Ehrlichman. The President pursued this in considerable detail, obviously trying to smoke out what was really going on. He led Dean on regarding the process and what he would recommend doing. He asked such things as—"Well, this is the thing you would recommend? We ought to do this? Is that right?" And he asked where the money would come from. How it would be delivered. And so on. He asked how much money would be involved over the years and Dean said "probably a million dollars—but the problem is that it is hard to raise." The President said, "There is no problem in raising a million dollars, we can do that, *but it would be wrong.*"

July 31, 1973:

SENATOR BAKER . . . What I want to point out to you is that one statement in your addendum seems to me to be of extraordinary importance and I want to test the accuracy of your notetaking from those tapes, and I am referring to the last, next to the last, no the third from the last sentence on page 2. "The President said there is no problem in raising a million dollars. We can do that but it would be wrong."

Now, if the period were to follow after "we can do that," it would be a most damning statement. If, in fact, the tapes clearly show he said "but it would be wrong," it is an entirely different context. Now, how sure are you, Mr. Haldeman, that those tapes, in fact, say that?

MR. HALDEMAN. *I am absolutely positive that the tapes—*

SENATOR BAKER. Did you hear it with your own voice?

MR. HALDEMAN. *With my own ears, yes.*

SENATOR BAKER. I mean with your own ears. Was there any distortion in the quality of the tape in that respect?

MR. HALDEMAN. No I do not believe so.

SENATOR ERVIN. Then the tape said that the President said that there was no problem raising a million dollars.

MR. HALDEMAN. Well, I should put that the way it really came, Mr. Chairman, which was that Dean said when the President said how much money are you talking about here and Dean said over a period of years probably a million dollars, but it would be very hard—it is very hard to raise that money. And the President said it is not hard to raise it. We can raise a million dollars. *And then got into the question of, in the one case before I came into the meeting making a statement that it would be wrong* and in other exploration of this getting into the—trying to find out what Dean was talking about in terms of a million dollars.

SENATOR ERVIN. Can you point—are you familiar with the testimony Dean gave about his conversations on the 13th and the 21st of March with the President?

MR. HALDEMAN. I am generally familiar with it, yes, sir.

SENATOR ERVIN, Well, this tape corroborates virtually everything he said except that he said that the President could be—that the President said there would be no difficulty about raising the money and you say the only difference in the tape is that the President also added that but that would be wrong.

MR. HALDEMAN. And there was considerable other discussion about what you do, what Dean would recommend, what should be done, how—what this process is and this sort of thing. It was a very—there was considerable exploration in the area.

5. The underscored [set in italics above] portions of the statements quoted in Paragraph 4, made by Harry R. Haldeman, the defendant, were material to the said investigation and study and, as he then and there well knew, were false.

(Title 18, United States Code, Section 1621.)

Count Nine

The grand jury further charges:

1. On or about August 1, 1973, in the District of Columbia, Harry R. Haldeman, the defendant, having duly taken an oath before a competent tribunal, to wit, the Select Committee on Presidential Campaign Activities, a duly created and authorized committee of the United States Senate conducting official hearings and inquiring into a matter in which a law of the United States authorizes an oath to be administered, that he would testify truly, did willfully, knowingly and contrary to such oath state material matters hereinafter set forth which he did not believe to be true.

2. At the time and place alleged, the said committee was conducting an investigation and study, pursuant to the provisions of Senate Resolution 60 adopted by the United States Senate on Feb. 7, 1973, of the extent, if any, to which illegal, improper or unethical activities were engaged in by any persons, acting either individually or in combination with others, in the Presidential election of 1972, or in any related campaign or canvass conducted by or in behalf of any person seeking nomination or election as the candidate of any political party for the office of President of the United States in such election, for the purpose of determining whether in its judgment any occurrences which might be revealed by the investigation and study indicated the necessity or desirability of the enactment of new legislation to safeguard the electoral process by which the President of the United States is chosen.

3. It was material to the said investigation and study that the said committee ascertain the identity and motives of the individual or individuals who were responsible for, participated in, and had knowledge of efforts to conceal, and to cause to be concealed, information relating to (A) unlawful entries into, and electronic surveillance of, the offices of the Democratic National Committee located in the Watergate office building in Washington, D.C., and (B) related activities, through such means as the commission of perjury and subornation of perjury.

4. At the time and place alleged, Harry R. Haldeman, the defendant, appearing as a witness under oath before the said committee, did willfully and knowingly state with respect to the material matters alleged in Paragraph 3 as follows:

SENATOR GURNEY. Let's turn to the March 21 meeting. . . . Do you recall any discussion by Dean about Magruder's false testimony before the grand jury?

MR. HALDEMAN. There was a reference to his feeling that Magruder had known about the Watergate planning and break-in ahead of it, in other words,

(Text of March 1 indictment—cont.)

that he was aware of what had gone on at Watergate. *I don't believe there was any reference to Magruder committing perjury.*

5. The underscored [set in italics above] portion of the statements quoted in Paragraph 4, made by Harry R. Haldeman, the defendant, was material to the said investigation and study and, as he then and there well knew, was false.

(Title 18, United States Code, section 1621.)

Count Ten

The grand jury further charges:

On or about July 21, 1973, in the District of Columbia, John D. Ehrlichman, the defendant, did knowingly and willfully make false, fictitious and fraudulent statements and representation to agents of the Federal Bureau of Investigation, Department of Justice, which department was then conducting an investigation into a matter within its jurisdiction, namely, whether violations of 18 U.S.C. 371, 2511, and 22 D.C. Code 801(B), and of other statutes of the United States and the District of Columbia, had been committed in the District of Columbia and elsewhere in connection with the break-in at the Democratic National Committee headquarters at the Watergate office building on June 17, 1972, and to identify the individual or individuals who had committed, caused the commission of, and conspired to commit such violations, in that he stated that he had neither received nor was he in possession of any information relative to the break-in at the Democratic National Committee headquarters on June 17, 1972, other than what he had read in the way of newspaper accounts of that incident.

(Title 18, United States Code, Section 1001.)

Count Eleven

The grand jury further charges:

1. On or about May 3, and May 9, 1973, in the District of Columbia, John D. Ehrlichman, the defendant, having duly taken an oath that he would testify truthfully, and while testifying in a proceeding before the June, 1972, grand jury, a grand jury of the United States, duly impaneled and sworn in the United States District Court for the District of Columbia, did knowingly make false material declarations as hereinafter set forth.

2. At the times and place alleged, the June, 1972, grand jury of the United States District Court for the District of Columbia was conducting an investigation in conjunction with the United States attorney's office for the District of Columbia and the Federal Bureau of Investigation to determine whether violations of Title 18, United States Code, Sections 371, 2511, and 22 D.C. Code 1801(B) and of other statutes of the United States and of the District of Columbia and elsewhere, and to identify the individual or individuals who had committed, caused the commission of, and conspired to commit such violations.

3. It was material to the said investigation that the said grand jury ascertain the identity and motives of the individual or individuals who were responsible for, participated in, and had knowledge of efforts to conceal, and to cause to be concealed, information relating to unlawful entries into, and electronic surveillance of, the offices of the Democratic National Committee located in the Watergate office building in Washington, D.C., and related activities.

4. At the times and place alleged, John D. Ehrlichman, the defendant, appearing as a witness under oath at a proceeding before the said grand jury, did knowingly declare with respect to the material matters alleged in Paragraph 3 as follows:

May 3, 1973:

Q. Mr. Ehrlichman, going back to that first week following the Watergate arrest, did you have any conversations besides those on Monday with Mr. Dean?

A. Yes, I did.

Q. Will you relate those to the ladies and gentlemen of the grand jury?

A. Well, I don't recall the content specifically of most of them. I know that I saw Mr. Dean because my log shows that he was in my office. I think it was four times that week, once in a large meeting—excuse me, more than four times.

He was in alone twice on Monday, and in the large meeting that I have described. He was in twice alone on other occasions, and then he was in a meeting that I had with Patrick Gray—well, that was the following week. It was a span of seven days, within the span of seven days.

Q. All right. Now at any of those meetings with Mr. Dean, was the subject matter brought up of a person by the name of Gordon Liddy?

A. *I can't say specifically one way or the other.*

Q. So you can neither confirm nor deny that anything with respect to Mr. Liddy was brought up at any of those meetings, is that correct, sir?

A. I don't recall whether Mr. Liddy was being mentioned in the press and would have been the subject of an inquiry by somebody from the outside. If he would have, then it is entirely probable that his name came up.

Q. All right. Let's assume for a moment that Mr. Liddy's name did not in that first week arise in the press. Can you think of any other context in which his name came up excluding any possible press problem with respect to the name of Liddy?

A. *I have no present recollection of that having happened.*

Q. So you can neither confirm nor deny whether or not the name of Gordon Liddy came up in the course of any conversation you had with Mr. Dean during that week or for that matter with anyone else?

A. *That's right, unless I had some specific event to focus on. Just to take those meetings in the abstract, I can't say that I have any recollection of them having happened in any of those.*

Q. All right. Let's take the example or did anyone advise you, directly or indirectly, that Mr. Liddy was implicated or involved in the Watergate affair?

A. Well, they did at some time, and *I don't know whether it was during that week or not.*

Q. To the best of your recollection, when was that done, sir?

A. *I'm sorry but I just don't remember.*

Q. Well, who was it that advised you of that?

A. I think it was Mr. Dean, but I don't remember when he did it.

Q. Would it have been within a month of the investigation? Within three months of the investigation?

A. *I'm sorry but I just don't know.*

Q. You can't even say then whether it was within a week, a month, or three months? Is that correct, sir?

A. Well, I think it was fairly early on, but to say it was within a week or two weeks or something, I just don't know.

Q. Now Mr. Dean advised you that Mr. Liddy was implicated. Did you advise the United States attorney or the attorney general, or any other law enforcement agency immediately or at any time after?

A. *No. I don't think it was private information at the time I heard it.*

Q. Well, did you inquire to find out whether or not it was private information?

A. *To the best of my recollection, when I first heard it it was not in the nature of exclusively known to Dean, or anything of that kind.*

Q. Well, was it in the newspapers that he was involved?

A. *I'm sorry. I just don't remember. It probably was, but I just don't recall.*

Q. You mean the first time you found out from Mr. Dean that Liddy was involved, Mr. Ehrlichman, it was in the same newspaper or the newspapers that you yourself could have read?

A. No, no. I am telling you that I cannot remember the relationship of time, but my impression is that he was not giving me special information that was not available to other people.

A lot of Mr. Dean's information came out of the Justice Department apparently, and so I think the impression I had was whatever he was giving us by way of information was known to a number of other people. That's what I meant by special information.

May 9, 1973:

Q. When did you first become aware that Mr. Liddy was involved?

A. I don't know.

Q. You don't know?

A. No, sir.

Q. Did you ever become aware of it?

A. Well, obviously I did, but I don't know when that was.

Q. Was it in June?

A. *I say I don't know.*

Q. Who told you?

A. *I don't know.*

Q. How did you learn it?

A. *I don't recall.*

The underscored portions [set in italics above] of the declarations quoted in Paragraph 4, made by John D. Ehrlichman, the defendant, were material to the said investigation and, as he then and there well knew, were false.

(Title 18, United States Code, Section 1625.)

Count Twelve

The grand jury further charges:

1. On or about May 3 and May 9, 1973, in the District of Columbia, John D. Ehrlichman, the defen-

dant, having duly taken an oath that he would testify truthfully, and while testifying in a proceeding before the June, 1972, grand jury, a grand jury of the United States, duly impaneled and sworn in the United States District Court for the District of Columbia, did knowingly make false material declarations as hereafter set forth.

2. At the time and place alleged, the June 1972, grand jury of the United States District Court for the District of Columbia was conducting an investigation in conjunction with the United States attorney's office for the District of Columbia and the Federal Bureau of Investigation to determine whether violations of Title 18, United States Code, Sections 371, 2511, and 22 D.C. Code 1801(B), and other statutes of the United States and of the District of Columbia had been committed in the District of Columbia and elsewhere, and to identify the individual or individuals who had committed, caused the commission of, and conspired to commit such violations.

3. It was material to the said investigation that the said grand jury ascertain the identity and motives of the individual or individuals who were responsible for, participated in, and had knowledge of efforts to conceal, and to cause to be concealed, information relating to unlawful entries into, and electronic surveillance of, the offices of the Democratic National Committee located in the Watergate office building in Washington, D.C., and related activities.

4. At the times and place alleged, John D. Ehrlichman, the defendant, appearing as a witness under oath at a proceeding before the said grand jury, did knowingly declare with respect to the material matters alleged in paragraph 3 as follows:

May 3, 1973:

Q. Now with respect to that, what further information did you receive that really related to this fundraising for the defendants and the defense counsel and their families?

A. I had a call from Mr. Kalmbach within four or five days to verify whether or not I had in fact talked to John Dean. I said that I had.

Q. This was a telephone call, sir?

A. I think it was. It may have been during a visit. I'm not sure. I used to see Mr. Kalmbach periodically about all kinds of things.

It may have been during a visit, but I think it was just a phone call.

He said substantially that John Dean had called me and said that I had no objection, and I said, "Herb, if you don't have any objection to doing it, I don't have any objection to your doing it, obviously."

He said, "No, I don't mind," and he went ahead.

Q. So far as you recall the only conversation that you recall is Mr. Kalmbach saying to you, "John Dean has asked me to do this," and you stated that you had no objection. He said that he was checking with you to determine whether you had any objection or not?

A. He was checking on Dean.

Q. On Dean?

A. Yes.

Q. And you said to him, "If you don't have any objection then I don't have any objection?"

A. *Right.*

Q. Was there any discussion between the two of you as to the purpose for which this money was to be raised?

A. I don't think so.

Q. Did you in any way approve the purpose for which this money was being given?

A. *No, I don't think so. I don't recall doing so.*

Q. Based on your testimony for the background of this, there would have been no basis for your approval or for you to affirm that?

A. That's right. That's why I say that I don't believe that I did.

Q. And your best recollection is that you did not?

A. That's right.

Q. Do you have any recollection of Mr. Kalmbach inquiring of you whether or not this was appropriate, sir?

A. Are you questioning me with respect to that?

Q. Yes.

A. *No, I don't.*

Q. He did not, to the best of your recollection?

A. *I don't have any recollection of his doing so.*

May 9, 1973:

Q. You have never expressed, say back six or seven months ago, to Mr. Kalmbach that the raising of the money should be kept as a secret matter, and it would be either political dynamite, or comparable words, if it ever got out, when Mr. Kalmbach came to see you?

A. *No, I don't recall ever saying that.*

5. The underscored portions of the declarations [in italics above] quoted in Paragraph 4, made by John D. Ehrlichman, the defendant, were material to the

(Text of March 1 indictment—cont.)
said investigation and, as he then and there well knew, were false.
(Title 18, United States Code, Section 1623.)

Count Thirteen

The grand jury further charges:

1. On or about April 11, 1973, in the District of Columbia, Gordon Strachan, the defendant, having duly taken an oath that he would testify truthfully, and while testifying in a proceeding before the June 1972, grand jury, a grand jury of the United States, duly impaneled and sworn in the United States District Court for the District of Columbia, did knowingly make false material declarations as hereafter set forth.

2. At the time and place alleged, the June, 1972, grand jury of the United States District Court for the District of Columbia was conducting an investigation in conjunction with the United States attorney's office for the District of Columbia and the Federal Bureau of Investigation to determine whether violations of Title 18, United States Code, Sections 371, 2511, and 22 D.C. Code 1801 (B), and of other statutes of the United States and of the District of Columbia had been committed in the District of Columbia and elsewhere, and to identify the individual or individuals who had committed, caused the commission of, and conspired to commit such violations.

3. It was material to the said investigation that the said grand jury ascertain the identity and motives of the individual or individuals who were responsible or participated in, and had knowledge of efforts to conceal, and to cause to be concealed, information relating to unlawful entries into, and electronic surveillance of, the offices of the Democratic National Committee located in the Watergate office building in Washington, D.C., and related activities.

4. At the time and place alleged, Gordon Strachan, the defendant, appearing as a witness under oath at a proceeding before the said grand jury, did knowingly declare with respect to the material matters alleged in Paragraph 3 as follows:

Q. Did you, yourself, ever receive any money from the Committee for the Re-election of the President, or from the Finance Committee to Re-elect the President?
A. Yes, sir, I did.
Q. Can you tell the ladies and gentlemen of the grand jury about that?
A. Yes, sir. On April 6, 1972, I received $350,000 in cash.
Q. From whom?
A. From Hugh Sloan.
Q. What was done with the money after you received it from Mr. Sloan on April 6th?
A. I put it in the safe.
Q. Was the money ever used?
A. Pardon?
Q. Was the money ever used?
A. No, the money was not used.
Q. To your knowledge, was it ever taken out of the safe?
A. No.
Q. To your knowledge, it is still there?
A. No, it is not.
Q. Where is it?
A. *I returned it to the committee, at Mr. Haldeman's direction, at the end of November.*
Q. November of '72?
A. Yes, '72, or early December.
Q. To whom did you return it?
A. To Fred LaRue.
Q. Where did that transfer take place?
A. I gave it to Mr. LaRue in his apartment.
Q. That was either late November or early December?
A. That's correct.
Q. Well, let me ask you this: Why would it have

been given to Mr. LaRue at his apartment as opposed to being given to the committee?
A. Well, Mr. LaRue is a member of the committee and he just asked me to bring it by on my way home from work.
Q. After Mr. Haldeman told you to return the money, what did you do? Did you contact someone to arrange for the delivery?
A. Yes, I contacted Mr. LaRue.
Q. That was at Mr. Haldeman's suggestion or direction?
A. No.
Q. Why is it that you would have called Mr. LaRue?
A. I don't think Stans was in the country at that time. He was not available.
Q. What position did Mr. LaRue occupy that would have made you call him?
A. He was the senior campaign official.
Q. That's the only reason you called him?
A. *That's correct.*
Q. No one suggested you call him?
A. *No.*
Q. Was anyone present in Mr. LaRue's apartment at the hotel when you delivered the money to him?
A. No.
Q. Did you ever tell anyone to whom you had given the money? Did you report back to either Mr. Haldeman or anyone else that you had delivered the money?
A. I don't think so. I could have mentioned that I had done it. When I received an order, I did it.
Q. Did you get a receipt for the money?
A. No, I did not.
Q. Did you ask for it?
A. No, I did not.
JUROR. Why?
THE WITNESS: I did not give a receipt when I received the money, so I didn't ask for one when I gave it back.
JUROR. Did someone count the money when it came in and when it went out, so they knew there were no deductions made from that $350,000?
THE WITNESS: Yes, I counted the money when I received it, and I counted it when I gave it back.
JUROR. You solely counted it; no one else was with you?
THE WITNESS: I counted it when I received it alone, and I counted it in front of Mr. LaRue when I gave it back.
JUROR. You had that money in the White House for seven months and did nothing with it?
THE WITNESS. That's correct.

Q. So who told you to give it to Mr. LaRue?
A. *I decided to give it to Mr. LaRue.*
Q. On your own initiative?
A. *That's correct.*
Q. Who do you report to?
A. Mr. Haldeman.
Q. Did you report back to Mr. Haldeman that you gave it to Mr. LaRue?
A. No, I did not.
Q. You just kept this all to yourself?
A. He was a senior official at the campaign. I gave it back to him. He said he would account for it, and that was it.
Q. Who told you to go to Mr. LaRue and give him the money?
A. *I decided that myself.*
Q. Do you have a memo in your file relating to this incident?
A. No, I do not.
Q. Did you discuss this incident with anybody afterwards?
A. Yes, I told Mr. Haldeman afterwards that I had given the money to Mr. LaRue.
Q. What did he say to you?
A. Fine. He was a senior campaign official
Q. What time of day was it that you gave it to Mr.

LaRue?
A. In the evening, after work.
Q. Does the finance committee or the Committee to Re-Elect the President conduct its business in Mr. LaRue's apartment?
A. No. It was a matter of courtesy. He's a senior official. He asked me to drop it by after work.
THE FOREMAN. Do you have any idea why Mr. LaRue asked you to return this money to his apartment, where actually you could just walk across 17th Street?
THE WITNESS. No, I do not.
THE FOREMAN. And you could have had the protection of the Secret Service guards with all that money, if you were afraid someone might snatch it from you.
THE WITNESS. I wouldn't ask for the Secret Service guards protection.
A JUROR. Why not?
THE WITNESS. They protect only the President and his family.
THE FOREMAN. Or the White House guards, whoever. I mean, I find it somewhat dangerous for a person to be carrying this amount of money in Washington, in the evening, and you accompanied by your brother, when it would have been much easier and handier just to walk across 17th Street.
THE WITNESS. I agree, and I was nervous doing it, but I did it.
THE FOREMAN. I'm still puzzled. You get the money from the treasurer or whatever Mr. Sloan's position was in the committee—shall we say on an official basis, between the disburser and you as the receiver, and the money sits in the safe for seven months; then Mr. Haldeman decides it has to go back to the committee. You call Mr. LaRue—you don't call Mr. Sloan and say "Hugh, seven months ago you gave me this $350,000 and we haven't used any of it; I'd like to give it back to you since I got it from you," but you call Mr. LaRue.
THE WITNESS. Mr. Sloan was no longer with the committee at the time.
THE FOREMAN. Well, whoever took Mr. Sloan's place.
THE WITNESS. Mr. Barret took Mr. Sloan's place.
THE FOREMAN. Why didn't you call him?
THE WITNESS. *I honestly don't know.*
Q. When you got to Mr. LaRue's apartment was he expecting you?
A. Yes. I said I would be by.
Q. And no one was present when you were there?
A. No, sir.
Q. Was the money counted?
A. Yes sir, I counted it.
A JUROR. It must have taken a long time to count that money.
THE WITNESS. It did. It took about 45 minutes. It takes a long time to count it.
Q. How did you carry this money?
A. In a briefcase.
Q. Did you take the briefcase back, or did you leave it?
A. No, I left the briefcase.
Q. Whose briefcase was it?
A. Gee, I think it was mine. I'm honestly not sure.
Q. Did you ever get the briefcase back?
A. I don't think so.
Q. Have you spoken to Mr. LaRue since that day?
A. No—well, I ran into him at a party two weeks ago.
Q. Did you have a discussion?
A. No, just talked to him.
5. The underscored portions [set in italics above] of the declarations quoted in Paragraph 4, made by Gordon Strachan, the defendant, were material to the said investigation and, as he then and there well knew, were false.
(Title 18, United States Code, Section 1623.)

Secret report linked to probe. After the grand jury had returned its Watergate cover-up indictment March 1, it transmitted to Judge John J. Sirica a sealed two-page report and covering letter, accompanied by a bulging briefcase of documents, reportedly containing evidence on President Nixon's relationship with the cover-up. According to prosecution sources, any grand jury action toward indicting Nixon had been squelched by spe-

cial prosecutor Leon Jaworski, who advised the jurors that no such action could be taken against a President in office.

Sirica read the covering letter, resealed it and called "interested parties" to a March 6 hearing on disposition of the report. Although the grand jury's recommendation was not formally made public, the jury had, by all indications, suggested that the evidence be sent to the House Ju-

diciary Committee.

The impact of the hearing was blunted by special presidential counsel James D. St. Clair's opening statement to the court that Nixon would surrender to the House panel all tapes and documents that had already been sent to the special Watergate prosecutor. In addition, St. Clair said, Nixon would be willing to respond in writing to the committee's questions and would, if necessary, grant an interview to some members of the panel. Nixon expanded upon—and limited—the new offer of cooperation later at his news conference and in letters to the committee. [See below]

St. Clair also complained about the "serious breach of grand jury secrecy" and "gross distortions" in news reports on the content of the two-page covering letter. St. Clair said he had, with Sirica's permission, read the letter March 4 and informed Nixon of its contents.

Attorneys for the seven indicted in the cover-up strongly opposed release of the report to the House committee on the ground of prejudicial pretrial publicity about their clients. John J. Wilson, an attorney for former presidential advisers H. R. Haldeman and John D. Ehrlichman, argued that leaks in Congress "are big enough to drive a truck through." (Wilson had also submitted a letter to Sirica contending that the grand jury had no legal right to issue the report.)

At one point, Sirica asked chief Judiciary Committee counsel John M. Doar if impeachment proceedings might be delayed until after the cover-up trial, which was scheduled to begin Sept. 9. Both Doar and committee minority counsel Albert E. Jenner Jr. replied that the House's constitutional mandate to investigate the impeachment issue was "overriding." Jenner added that the source of the report was irrelevant; the House's need for evidence was paramount. St. Clair said Nixon "would not be interested in delaying the impeachment process."

Philip A. Lacovara, counsel for the special prosecutor, argued that the grand jury had the power to submit the report and that it would be "unthinkable" for Sirica to decide that the grand jury "must remain mute when it has evidence which seems to bear on this matter."

Lacovara noted that the grand jury's report might contain "other items" in addition to what might be covered by Nixon's offer to surrender evidence already held by the prosecutor. Sirica reserved decision on the issue.

Nixon delimits cooperation—The President at his news conference March 6 was asked half a dozen questions about the impeachment probe, most of them about the extent of his cooperation with the House Judiciary Committee.

In reference to the announcement that he would give the committee all the data he supplied to the special prosecutor, [See below] he was asked "what about other materials that the committee might want to see that the prosecutor didn't see?"

He considered the announcement "a very forthcoming offer," Nixon answered. He would respond to any written questions under oath and if that was not satisfactory, "in order to bring the matter to a complete and, we hope early conclusion," he would be glad to meet with members of the committee, "perhaps the chairman and the ranking minority member," at the White House "to answer any further questions under oath that they may

have."

As for other materials, his counsel would continue discussions about them. "It is the goal for all of us, I think, the goal of the committee, I think it would be theirs, it certainly is mine, to get a prompt conclusion to this matter as soon as possible." He had already turned over to the special prosecutor 19 tapes and over 700 documents "and enough material" that Leon Jaworski, the prosecutor, "was able to say that he knew all and that the grand jury had all the information that it needed in order to bring to a conclusion its Watergate investigation."

Would it not serve the purpose of a speedy conclusion, he was asked, for him to give the committee whatever materials it considered pertinent to its investigation?

It would not, Nixon replied. "It would delay it . . . because if all that is really involved in this instance is to cart everything that is in the White House down to a committee and to have them paw through it on a fishing expedition, it will take them" months and perhaps even as long as a year.

He would furnish the information given to Jaworski, "all of which he considers to be relevant," the President said, as well as written responses "on any other relevant material," and he would also agree to meet with the ranking members of the House panel and answer "any other questions they may have." "I believe that that will serve the purpose."

Would he take questions in a public forum from the entire House Judiciary Committee?

His counsel would work out a proper procedure in this area. "What I want is one that will get the facts, get them quickly, and one that will not delay the proceedings."

Were there circumstances under which he would submit to cross-examination? Nixon's response: "I will do nothing to weaken the office of the Presidency, and to submit to cross-examination under circumstances that would in effect put the President in the box when he was not indicted, in effect, by the House of Representatives, where he would be in the box if he went to the Senate, I think would be improper."

The President was asked about the narrow view of impeachment asserted by his attorneys, that it should be limited to very serious crimes committed in an official capacity. Would he consider the crimes returned in the recent indictments against his former top aides—perjury, obstruction of justice and conspiracy—"to be impeachable crimes if they did apply to you?"

"Well, I've also quit beating my wife," Nixon began, indicating he held the question hostile. Of course, he said, perjury and obstruction of justice were serious crimes and would be impeachable offenses. "And I do not expect that the House committee will find that the President is guilty of any of these crimes

to which you have referred," he said.

Nixon objected to the questioner's reference to "a narrow view" of impeachment. Some would take an inaccurate connotation from the question, he said, while, actually, "it's the constitutional view." "The Constitution is very precise. Even Sen. [Sam J.] Ervin [Jr., chairman of the Senate Watergate committee] agrees that that view is the right one and if Sen. Ervin agrees, it must be the right one."

The President was asked about the opinion of Attorney General William B. Saxbe that at some point in the impeachment process the President might have to start paying for his own legal defense.

Of course, he replied, if the attorney general so ruled he would abide by it. He pointed out "that I am not a defendant until the House passes a bill of impeachment. I would then be a defendant. And if the attorney general . . . should rule that the president should pay for his defense, I'll find somebody to loan me the money."

Ford: House should get jury report. Vice President Gerald R. Ford said March 2 the sealed report of the Watergate grand jury should be turned over to the Judiciary Committee because the committee was the "proper place" to consider President Nixon's involvement or non-involvement in the cover-up.

Ford made the comment at a news conference in Phoenix, Ariz., a stop during his extensive travels around the country.

At a breakfast meeting with reporters March 12 in Washington, Ford said presidential defiance of the committee's request for tapes could be a "catalyst" to impeachment by the House. Refusal to respond to a reasonable request "certainly adds fuel to the fire when you consider 435 members have to make up their minds," he said, although it was his impression that the committee's request "goes far beyond any act relevant to" the constitutional bounds of impeachable crimes. Ford also said it was his opinion that "any indictable crime" could be grounds for impeachment, including tax fraud.

In Boston March 11, Ford said "I don't happen to believe on the basis of the evidence I am familiar with—and I think I'm familiar with most of it—that the President was involved in Watergate per se or involved in the cover-up, but time will tell."

Appearing before the Harvard College Republican Club, Ford said he would not join those asking Nixon to resign for the good of the country or the party. "That would be asking a person to admit guilt when he believes he is innocent."

"You don't have a president and vice president going off in two directions," he said. "Policywise, this Administration has done a good job and I have no hesitancy to approve its policies."

In Bal Harbour, Fla. March 8, Ford said he knew of no further Watergate "bombshells" and "I don't think there will be any."

His theme in his GOP appearances around the country, as expressed in New York City March 9, was the "peace and prosperity" espoused by the President and the "failings" of the Democratic-led Congress. In Omaha, Neb. Feb. 15, at the end of a three-day trip through the Midwest, Ford said he hoped "both the President and Congress can improve their image."

The Democrats' issue: Nixon—Democratic National Chairman Robert S. Strauss' advice to Democratic candidates March 9: "Run on the issues, and the issue is very clear—the Nixon leadership. I'd run on the failure of Richard Nixon in the leadership of the country."

Vermont town meetings—The subject of impeachment of the President came up in at least 13 of the annual town meetings in Vermont the first week in March. Resolutions calling for Nixon's impeachment were approved by eight; five voted against or sidetracked the issue.

Watergate cover-up linked to 'plumbers'. A New York Times report March 3, attributed to "well-placed sources" in the office of Watergate special prosecutor Leon Jaworski, said the prosecutor's office had determined that a principal motive behind the Watergate cover-up was a desire to hide the 1971 break-in at the office of Dr. Lewis J. Fielding, the psychiatrist who had treated Pentagon Papers defendant Daniel Ellsberg.

The sources indicated that the Watergate cover-up indictment returned March 1 was based in part on the Watergate grand jury's belief that President Nixon and his key advisers were aware that the Fielding break-in was not justified by national security considerations. The reference in the March 1 indictment to the covering up of "other illegal and improper activities," the sources said, was to actions by the White House investigative unit, the "plumbers," which was responsible for the Fielding burglary.

The March 1 indictment, the sources pointed out, also cited a threat by Watergate conspirator E. Howard Hunt Jr. "to tell about the seamy things" he had done as a member of the "plumbers."

Democrat wins Ohio GOP seat. Thomas A. Luken (D) won a special election in Ohio's 1st Congressional District March 5, defeating Willis D. Gradison Jr. (R) by a vote of 55,171–51,057. The Democrats had won the seat only three other times in this century (1912, 1936, 1964). It marked the Republican Party's third consecutive loss in special Congressional elections.

The Ohio seat had been held by William J. Keating (R), who won with 70% of the vote in 1972. He resigned Jan. 3 to become president of the Cincinnati Enquirer.

Both Ohio candidates were former Cincinnati mayors. Luken, 48, was a councilman, Gradison, 45, a stockbroker.

Watergate was a factor in the campaign, although not as overt an issue as the economy. Abortion and busing also were raised as issues. Luken avoided a direct attack upon President Nixon during most of the campaign but in the final week stressed the scandal-beset aspect of his opponent's party. After the federal Watergate indictments in the final week, Luken sharpened his attack and said Nixon should be impeached if his appointees were found guilty of high crimes or misdemeanors. He urged voters to "send a signal to Washington" by his election.

Gradison had received help from a team from the Republican National Committee, Luken from a team sent by the AFL-CIO. Both employed prominent outside speakers.

GOP retains California seat—The Republican Party retained its hold on the 13th Congressional district of California, which became vacant Jan. 1 when Rep. Charles M. Teague died. State Sen. Robert J. Lagomarsino (R), of Ventura, won a majority of votes (53%) against seven Democratic opponents in a special election held March 5.

Lagomarsino, a state senator, cautioned the Republican National Committee "not to interpret it as a vindication of the President. I don't think he won anything in this race."

The winner said he was confident when he undertook the race that he could win without a runoff. But, he said, "by the time the first returns came in yesterday, I was sweating bullets."

Aside from the issue of President Nixon's handling of Watergate, from which Lagomarsino dissociated himself, the focal point of the campaign was offshore drilling for oil in the Santa Barbara Channel, where a well blowout in 1969 caused an environmental crisis. Lagomarsino promised to seek a 400,000-acre, oil-well-free sanctuary among islands in the channel.

Murtha wins Pennsylvania recount—John Murtha (D) was officially declared winner of the Feb. 5 election in Pennsylvania's 12th Congressional District Feb. 28. His margin of victory was 122 votes. The loser, Harry Fox (R), had requested a recount because of the close vote.

Casey Exim Bank president. William J. Casey, undersecretary of state for economic affairs since February 1973, was confirmed March 5 as president of the U.S. Export-Import Bank, succeeding Henry Kearns.

Casey's nomination had been submitted to the Senate Dec. 7, 1973 but the Senate Banking Committee voted to delay action on the appointment until Special Watergate Prosecutor Leon Jaworski supplied it with "additional information" on Casey's

role in the controversial International Telephone & Telegraph Corp. case.

As former chairman of the Securities and Exchange Commission (SEC), Casey also was involved in another Nixon Administration controversy—the alleged attempt by former Cabinet officials John Mitchell and Maurice Stans to block an SEC investigation of Robert Vesco.

Although the nomination appeared stalled indefinitely, the White House renewed its support for Casey and the nomination was resubmitted Feb. 27 after Congress reconvened. Casey was confirmed before appearing as a witness for the prosecution in the Mitchell-Stans trial in New York.

IRS rescinds ITT tax break. International Telephone & Telegraph Corp. (ITT) announced March 6 that the Internal Revenue Service (IRS) had revoked its 1969 ruling that had enabled ITT to acquire the Hartford Fire Insurance Co. It was the largest corporate merger in history.

The merger had provoked controversy within the Administration which was divided over whether to press antitrust charges against ITT. The government's final decisions in the case, which had involved President Nixon and other high White House officials, spurred further controversy and prompted Watergate special prosecutor Leon Jaworski to investigate the ITT case. [For further details, see p. 42D1]

Nixon news conference held. President Nixon held a televised evening news conference at the White House March 6, his second in nine days.

During its course, he maintained that he had never authorized payment of "hush money" or offers of executive clemency to Watergate defendants, although he admitted the tape recording relating to the matter might be open to different interpretation by others.

The President offered to give the House impeachment inquiry all the tapes and documents the White House had supplied to the special Watergate prosecutor, and he said he would supply sworn testimony in writing or in a meeting with the committee's Democratic chairman and senior Republican.

The Watergate case and impeachment questions dominated the 35-minute conference; 15 of 19 queries dealt with them. The other questions covered inflation, the defense budget, campaign fund reform and the oil embargo. The President had opened the conference with a statement on his energy proposals before Congress.

Among the highlights:

Campaign financing reform—In answer to a question, Nixon said his legislative proposal to reform campaign funding practices would contain a prohibition against contributions from foreign sources. Another feature of the legislation, he continued, would be restrictions on cash contributions—nothing over $50 and limits of $15,000 per person per candidate in presidential campaigns and $3,000 in Congressional campaigns.

A proposal was being considered for some way to give candidates the right to defend themselves "against false charges that are made during a campaign, whether by their opponents or by the press."

Nixon opposed public financing of campaigns from the U.S. Treasury because that would mean that "a taxpaper would be taxed to support a candidate or a party to whom he was opposed" and "that is not right." He thought that it was "a healthy thing" for people to contribute to campaigns, particularly in small donations, and that "campaigns should be financed by the candidates and not by the taxpayer."

Watergate effect on elections—The President said he did not believe that the off-year elections were good indicators of the results in the general election, except possibly in a reverse way. He cited Congressional off-year losses by both parties after landslide presidential elections.

He said "that the dire predictions that are made as to what is going to happen in November because of what has been happening this spring will be proved to be wrong."

'Hush money' silence questioned. New controversy over President Nixon's possible role in the Watergate cover-up arose during the week following his March 6 news conference statement that he had learned on March 21, 1973 that payments had been made to the original Watergate burglary defendants "for the purpose of keeping them quiet, not simply for their defense."

The controversy revolved around three issues:

■ Nixon had said in an Aug. 15, 1973 statement that during the March 21 meeting with John W. Dean 3rd, then his counsel, and H. R. Haldeman, then White House chief · of staff, he was told that money for the defendants was used for "attorneys' fees and family support, not that it had been paid to procure silence from the recipients."

■ Federal law required that anyone knowing of the commission of a felony—such as obstruction of justice—report it to proper authorities. (Violation of the law is known as "misprision.") Nixon had said he ordered staff investigations, first by Dean, then by domestic affairs adviser John D. Ehrlichman.

■ The March 1 indictment of seven former White House and campaign aides had charged that a payment of $75,000 to an attorney for convicted conspirator E. Howard Hunt Jr. was arranged on the evening of March 21, 1973; the Nixon-Dean-Haldeman meeting had been around mid-day.

White House comment on discrepancies in Nixon's accounts of the meeting was sparse, at least temporarily. Promising to address the issue "some time in the future," Press Secretary Ronald L. Ziegler March 11 cited only "semantic differences" in Nixon's remarks involving "ambiguities" in the Nixon-Dean conversation.

News organizations received a letter from convicted Watergate conspirator James W. McCord Jr. March 8 charging that Nixon had "deliberately concealed and suppressed" evidence of improper government conduct in the case. If the facts made known in Nixon's "astounding admission" during the news conference had been revealed in March 1973, McCord said, the convictions and pleas of the seven original Watergate defendants might have been overturned.

McCord noted that at the time of the crucial meeting his trial was still technically in progress. (He was scheduled to be sentenced March 23, 1973.) McCord also recalled that his pivotal letter to U.S. District Court Judge John J. Sirica—which began the unraveling of the cover-up—was first read by Sirica on March 20.

McCord added that the Watergate prosecution had since gained access to tapes and other information on presidential meetings but had failed to request dismissal of the original convictions.

In a brief filed with Sirica March 14, McCord formally asked that his conviction be overturned because of Nixon's actions. McCord requested an evidentiary hearing on the issue and subpoenas for Nixon and six others allegedly involved in the payoffs, along with tapes of six White House conversations, including the March 21, 1973 meeting. McCord had also petitioned the House March 11 to impeach Nixon on the same grounds outlined in his letter.

In a New York Times interview March 11, special presidential counsel James D. St. Clair dismissed the issue of misprision as one which "doesn't make much sense as a legal question," since Nixon "is the chief law enforcement officer in the country." The President's legal obligation, St. Clair contended, was "to see" that the judicial process is carried out. St. Clair cited as evidence that Nixon had fulfilled that duty the March 1 cover-up indictment of his former aides.

(St. Clair also maintained repeatedly that in all the Watergate and impeachment issues he was representing "the office of the presidency," not Nixon "individually." St. Clair said many of his duties centered on insuring that there were no "unwarranted" incursions on the office.)

St. Clair sought to minimize the significance of the March 21 meeting and the payments around the same time. First, St. Clair pointed out, Dean's public testimony before the Senate Watergate Committee had placed the date of Nixon's comments on payoffs and clemency as March 13, 1973, not March 21. (Dean, however, had reportedly amended his testimony later before Senate investigators and Watergate prosecutors. And Haldeman had recalled the meeting taking place March 21.)

St. Clair also pointed to uncertainty about the date of the final payment to Hunt's lawyer, citing "sworn testimony" before the Senate committee. Hunt had said he received the money March 20 or March 21, 1973; Frederick C. LaRue, the campaign aide who allegedly arranged the payment, was similarly uncertain.

But, according to the New York Times March 13 and the Washington Post March 15, the prosecutors and the grand jury had managed to pinpoint the final payoff to the evening of March 21, 1973, as alleged in the cover-up indictment.

Citing informed sources, the Post said the key element in the sequence was a dinner attended by LaRue, campaign aide Manyon M. Millican and an unnamed personal friend of LaRue, who was visiting Washington for one day.

Under questioning by the prosecutors, LaRue was at first unable to remember the precise date of the transaction, only that it had been in March after the dinner with Millican and the out-of-town friend. At LaRue's request, Millican had delivered an envelope containing $75,000 to the home of William O. Bittman, Hunt's lawyer. Millican reportedly did not know the contents of the envelope or the purpose of his mission. Bittman was also unable to recall the exact date.

According to the Post, the prosecutors then subpoenaed the credit card records of LaRue's friend and set the date of the friend's trip to Washington and the dinner as March 21, 1973. His recollection refreshed, LaRue was able to give sworn testimony that the payment was sent to Bittman about 10 p.m.

Regarding Nixon's comments during the meeting earlier that day with Dean and Haldeman, the Post's sources reported that there were different interpretations of the content of the White House conversation, a possibility conceded by Nixon in his news conference.

While Nixon had said he considered both offers of executive clemency and payoffs "wrong," the Post said that "some who have· heard the tape" concluded that Nixon's statement was not necessarily in the context that such actions would be legally or morally wrong, but essentially impractical—or "wrong" to think that a payoff and clemency scheme would succeed in keeping the defendants quiet.

Ford, Saxbe comment—Vice President Gerald R. Ford said March 12 that "in retrospect" it would have been "the better procedure" for President Nixon to report the information on payments to Watergate defendants directly to the attorney general, "if it's perfectly clear that was what was told him." Ford said he was concerned, as "anybody would be," that Nixon might have left himself open to a charge of obstruction of justice. Ford added, without elaboration, that "you can also get good legal questions" supporting Nixon.

Reminded of the discrepancies between Nixon's Aug. 15, 1973 account of the conversation with Dean and the latest news conference, Ford said he wanted to "refresh my memory" on what Nixon had said "and what the other evidence might be." He said he might then reconsider his earlier decision not to examine evidence the White House had maintained would exonerate Nixon.

Attorney General William B. Saxbe said March 13 that White House officials were "no different from any other citizens," having the legal duty to report crimes to proper authorities. Asked specifically whether Nixon would be covered by the law concerning misprision, Saxbe responded: "I think he's no different from any other citizen, but whether it's applicable in this case I don't know."

Colleagues reject Sirica plan. Judges of the U.S. District Court for Washington rejected a proposal by Chief Judge John J. Sirica that he and two other judges—George L. Hart Jr. and Gerhard A. Gesell—be the justices assigned to all Watergate-related cases, it was reported March 6. After a "heated," closed meeting March 4, judges on the court decided to postpone action on Sirica's plan, court sources said.

Sirica's proposal, which asked that he be relieved of cases not relating to Watergate, said "expeditious handling of these cases will require...a considerable degree of coordination," which would not be possible if the cases were randomly distributed among all the judges.

Governors' conference. The impeachment issue was the dominant subject behind the scenes at the winter meeting of the National Governors' Conference in Washington March 6–7. The major topic discussed in public was the energy crisis, highlighted by an appearance March 7 by William Simon, director of the Federal Energy Office.

A Republican governor, Francis W. Sargent (Mass.), said March 6 the country would be better served if President Nixon turned his office over to Vice President Gerald R. Ford. Gov. William G. Milliken (R, Mich.) said it would be a "plus" for Republicans to have Ford in the White House, but he felt it was even more important that the impeachment proceedings continued to fully reveal the truth. If Nixon resigned, Milliken said, "we'll never know what the facts are."

Several Democratic governors—Patrick J. Lucey (Wis.) and Milton J. Shapp (Pa.)—called for Nixon's resignation March 6. Another, Gov. John J. Gilligan (D, Ohio), repeated a prediction he had made earlier that Nixon would be out of office by "the Ides of March."

At the close of the session March 7, Gov. Wendell Ford (Ky.), chairman of the Democratic Governors' Conference, said the Democratic governors were being subjected to "premeditated and methodical harassment" by federal investigative agencies, such as the Justice Department, the Internal Revenue Service and the General Accounting Office. Several other Democratic governors supported his charge.

Many of the governors left before the final event, a White House dinner. One who did remain, Gov. Winfield Dunn (Tenn.), chairman of the Republican Governors' Conference, reported March 8 he was so inspired by Nixon's speech at the dinner that he was "going to break my neck" to help keep him in office.

Bumpers, Meskill announce plans—Gov. Thomas J. Meskill (R, Conn.) announced March 11 that he would seek "a new and different challenge" instead of re-election to a second term.

Gov. Dale Bumpers (D, Ark.) announced March 11 that he would seek the Senate seat held by Sen. J. W. Fulbright (D). The nation was "pleading for leadership" in this "troublesome time," Bumpers said. Fulbright, chairman of the Senate Foreign Relations Committee and running for his sixth term, agreed that the nation was troubled and said it stemmed "from the President of the United States." Bumpers was serving his second two-year term in Arkansas, where there was no limit on the number of terms.

Six indicted in Ellsberg burglary. A second Watergate grand jury March 7 indicted six men in connection with the September 1971 burglary of the office of Dr. Lewis J. Fielding, the Los Angeles psychiatrist who had treated Pentagon Papers defendant Daniel Ellsberg. The burglary had been carried out under the aegis of the special White House investigative unit known as the "plumbers," which had been formed to stop news leaks of government information.

The charge was conspiring to violate Fielding's civil rights by acting together to "oppress, threaten and intimidate" Fielding by entering his office "without legal process, probable cause, search warrant or other lawful authority" and by concealing "the involvement of officials and employes of the United States Government."

Those charged with conspiracy were:

John D. Ehrlichman, President Nixon's former domestic affairs adviser, who had also been indicted March 1 in connection with the Watergate cover-up;

Charles W. Colson, former presidential counsel, also indicted in the Watergate cover-up;

G. Gordon Liddy, Bernard L. Barker and Eugenio R. Martinez, all of whom had been convicted in the Watergate break-in;

Felipe DeDiego, who had previously been named as an unindicted co-conspirator in a California state case relating to the Fielding burglary.

The latest indictment named as unindicted co-conspirators E. Howard Hunt Jr., Egil Krogh Jr., and David R. Young Jr. Krogh had been sentenced following a guilty plea on a conspiracy charge, and Young was a co-defendant with Ehrlichman and Liddy on state charges of burglary and conspiracy.

Ehrlichman was also charged with three counts of false declarations to the grand jury and one count of lying to the Federal Bureau of Investigation (FBI).

The conspiracy charge carried a maximum penalty of 10 years in prison and a $10,000 fine; the false statements charges against Ehrlichman provided total penalties of 15 years and $30,000 in fines.

In a separate indictment, Liddy was charged with two counts of contempt stemming from his refusal in July 1973 to testify or be sworn before the House Armed Services Committee's Subcommittee on Intelligence Operations, which was investigating the Central Intelligence Agency's connections with the Watergate case. Each count carried a penalty of one year in prison and a $1,000 fine.

The conspiracy—In a list of 19 "overt acts," the indictment related that the conspiracy began July 27, 1971 with a memorandum from Krogh and Young [the co-directors of the "plumbers"] to Ehrlichman dealing with a request for a psychiatric study of Ellsberg. Ehrlichman was told three days later that the request had been directed to the Central Intelligence Agency.

In the interim, Hunt sent Colson a memo entitled "Neutralization of Ellsberg" containing a proposal to "obtain Ellsberg's files" from the psychiatrist's office. Krogh and Young later informed Colson they would "look into" Hunt's suggestions.

Ehrlichman approved a "covert operation" Aug. 11, provided he was given the "assurance it is not traceable." By Aug. 30, Krogh and Young were able to give Ehrlichman the assurance he required.

Meanwhile, Colson, Young and Krogh began discussing raising covert funds to pay the actual burglars. Young and Colson also concentrated on how to get "the information out" on Ellsberg. Ehrlichman instructed Colson to prepare a "game plan" on possible use of the materials taken from Fielding's office under what Ehrlichman still called Hunt's "proposed" plan.

The money problem was solved around the first of September: Colson arranged to obtain $5,000 in cash, which was repaid by a transfer from the Trust for Agricultural Political Education. [A dairy industry group]; Krogh delivered the money to Liddy Sept. 1, and Liddy and Hunt went immediately to Los Angeles to meet with Barker, DeDiego and Martinez. The latter three broke into Fielding's office Sept. 3.

The final act of conspiracy cited by the grand jury came March 27, 1973, when Ehrlichman "caused the removal of certain memoranda" on the burglary "from files maintained at the White House in which such memoranda would be kept in the ordinary course of business."

Ehrlichman's false statements—The one count charging Ehrlichman with lying to the FBI involved the agency's probe into whether the Fielding burglary might taint the prosecution of the Ellsberg trial. [The charges against Ellsberg were ultimately dismissed because of government actions; Ehrlichman told the FBI May 1, 1973 that he had not seen material on the White House investigation of the Pentagon Papers affair in more than a year.

Ehrlichman appeared before a grand jury May 14, 1973 and maintained repeatedly that he knew of the burglary and the instructions to prepare a psychological profile of Ellsberg only "after the fact." In one set of questions, Ehrlichman contended that only Krogh had files relating to the case.

Colson maintains innocence—In a statement issued through his attorney March 7, Colson called the charges against him especially "hard to take" because, he said, he had undergone a lie detector test which "determined that I did not know in advance of the Fielding break-in." He said the test results had been given to special prosecutor Leon Jaworski.

"There is much that the public has not been told about the circumstances surrounding this matter. A great deal more may be revealed. . . ."

In Miami, Fla., Barker—speaking for himself, DeDiego and Martinez—said they would fight the charges. They did what they believed, Barker said; "we believed we acted on proper authority from the U.S."

A White House spokesman declined comment other than a rereading of Nixon's March 1 statement on the Watergate cover-up indictment.

Text of March 7 Indictment in Ellsberg Burglary Conspiracy

Count One

The grand jury charges:

1. At all times material herein up to on or about April 30, 1973, John D. Ehrlichman, the defendant, was acting in the capacity of an officer and employe of the United States government, as assistant for domestic affairs to the President of the United States.

2. At all times material herein up to on or about March 10, 1973, Charles W. Colson, the defendant, was acting in the capacity of an officer and employe of the United States government, as special counsel to the President of the United States.

3. From on or about July 20, 1971, up to on or about Dec. 19, 1971, G. Gordon Liddy, the defendant, was acting in the capacity of an officer and employe of the United States government, as staff assistant to the President of the United States.

4. From on or about July 1, 1971, up to and including the date of the filing of this indictment, in the District of Columbia and elsewhere, John D. Ehrlichman, Charles W. Colson, G. Gordon Liddy, Bernard L. Barker, Felipe de Diego, and Eugenio R. Martinez, the defendants, and Egil Krogh Jr., David R. Young, E. Howard Hunt Jr., named herein as co-conspirators but not as defendants, unlawfully, willfully and knowingly did combine, conspire, confederate and agree together and with each other to injure, oppress, threaten, and intimidate Dr. Lewis J. Fielding, a citizen of the United States, in the free exercise and enjoyment of rights and privileges secured to him by the Constitution and laws of the United States, in violation of Title 18, United States Code, Section 241 (A).

5. It was part of the conspiracy that the conspirators would, without legal process, probable cause, search warrant, or other lawful authority, covertly and unlawfully enter the offices of Dr. Lewis J. Fielding at 450 North Bedford Drive, Beverly Hills, Calif., with intent to search for confidential information concerning Daniel Ellsberg, thereby injuring, oppressing, threatening, and intimidating Dr. Lewis J. Fielding in the free exercise and enjoyment of the right and privilege secured to him by the Fourth Amendment to the Constitution of the United States to be secure in his person, house, papers and effects against unreasonable searches and seizures, and that they would thereafter conceal such activities, so as to prevent Dr. Lewis J. Fielding from securing redress for the violation of such right and privileges.

6. Among the means by which the conspirators would carry out the aforesaid conspiracy were the following: (a) On or about Sept. 1, 1971, the conspirators would travel and cause others to travel to the State of California; (b) on or about Sept. 3, 1971, the conspirators would, without legal process, probable cause, search warrant or other lawful authority, covertly and unlawfully enter and cause to be entered the offices of Dr. Lewis J. Fielding located in Beverly Hills, Calif., (c) On or about Sept. 3, 1971, the conspirators would unlawfully and unreasonably search and cause to be searched the said offices of Dr. Lewis J. Fielding; and (d) On or about Sept. 3, 1971, the conspirators would conduct such unlawful and unreasonable search in a manner designed to conceal the involvement of officials and employes of the United States government.

7. In furtherance of the conspiracy, and in order to effectuate the objects thereof, the following overt acts, among others, were committed in the District of Columbia and elsewhere:

Overt Acts

1. On or about July 27, 1971, Egil Krogh Jr. and David R. Young sent a memorandum to John D. Ehrlichman, which discussed a request for the preparation of a psychiatric study on Daniel Ellsberg.

2. On or about July 28, 1971, E. Howard Hunt Jr. sent a memorandum to Charles W. Colson entitled "Neutralization of Ellsberg" which discussed a proposal to "obtain Ellsberg's files from his psychiatric analyst."

3. On or about July 30, 1971, Egil Krogh Jr. and David R. Young sent a memorandum to John D. Ehrlichman which informed Ehrlichman that the Central Intelligence Agency had been "instructed to do a thorough psychological study on Daniel Ellsberg."

4. On or about Aug. 3, 1971, Egil Krogh Jr. and David R. Young sent a memorandum to Charles W. Colson which referred to the memorandum described in overt act No. 2 and which stated that "we will look into" the suggestions made by E. Howard Hunt Jr.

5. On or about Aug. 11, 1971, John D. Ehrlichman approved a covert operation proposed by Egil Krogh Jr. and David R. Young to examine all the medical files still held by Ellsberg's psychoanalyst if he were given an "assurance it is not traceable."

6. On or about Aug. 23, 1971, John D. Ehrlichman and David R. Young had a conversation in which Ehrlichman and Young discussed financing for "special project H1," a planned entry into the offices of Dr. Lewis J. Fielding to obtain confidential information concerning Danel Ellsberg.

7. In late Aug. 1971, Charles W. Colson had a telephone conversation with Egil Krogh Jr. in which Colson and Krogh discussed providing money for E. Howard Hunt Jr. and G. Gordon Liddy.

8. During the week of Aug. 22, 1971, Charles W. Colson and David R. Young had a conversation in which Colson and Young discussed providing money for E. Howard Hunt Jr. and G. Gordon Liddy and preparing a plan to disseminate information regarding Daniel Ellsberg.

9. On or about Aug. 26, 1971, David R. Young sent a memorandum to John D. Ehrlichman which referred to "Hunt/Liddy Project No. 12 and stated that Charles W. Colson would get "the information out" on Ellsberg.

10. On or about Aug. 27, 1971, John D. Ehrlichman sent a memorandum to Charles W. Colson entitled "Hunt/Liddy Special Project No. 1" which requested Colson to prepare a "game plan" for the use of materials to be derived from the "proposed undertaking by Hunt and Liddy."

11. On or about Aug. 30, 1971, G. Gordon Liddy had a meeting with Egil Krogh Jr., David R. Young and E. Howard Hunt Jr. in which there was a discussion of the means by which there would be a nontraceable entry into the office of Dr. Lewis J. Fielding.

12. On or about Aug. 30, 1971, John D. Ehrlichman had a telephone conversation with Egil Krogh Jr. and David R. Young in which Krogh and Young assured Ehrlichman that the planned entry into the office of Dr. Lewis J. Fielding would not be traceable.

13. On or about Aug. 31, 1971, Charles W. Colson had a telephone conversation in which he arranged to obtain $5,000 in cash.

14. On or about Sept. 1, 1971, Charles W. Colson arranged for the transfer of $5,000 from the Trust for Agricultural Political Education in order to repay the $5,000 cash described in overt act No. 13.

15. On or about Sept. 1, 1971, Charles W. Colson caused the delivery of $5,000 in cash to Egil Krogh Jr.

16. On or about Sept. 1, 1971, Egil Krogh Jr. delivered $5,000 in cash to G. Gordon Liddy.

17. On or about Sept. 1, 1971, G. Gordon Liddy and E. Howard Hunt Jr. traveled from Washington, D.C., via Chicago, Ill., to Los Angeles, Calif., for the purpose of meeting with Bernard L. Barker, Felipe de Diego and Eugenio R. Martinez.

18. On or about Sept. 3, 1971, Bernard L. Barker, Felipe de Diego and Eugenio R. Martinez searched the offices of Dr. Lewis J. Fielding located in Beverly Hills, Calif., for the purpose of obtaining confidential information concerning Daniel Ellsberg.

19. On or about March 27, 1973, John D. Ehrlichman caused the removal of certain memoranda related to the entry into the offices of Dr. Lewis J. Fielding from files maintained at the White House in which such memoranda would be kept in the ordinary course of business.

(Title 18, United States Code, Section 241.)

Count Two

The grand jury further charges:

On or about May 1, 1973, in the District of Columbia, John D. Ehrlichman, the defendant, did knowingly and willfully make false, fictitious and fraudulent statements to agents of the Federal Bureau of Investigation, Department of Justice, which department was then conducting an investigation into a matter within its jurisdiction pursuant to an order of the United States District Court for the Central District of California to investigate whether, as a result of an entry conducted by White House employes into the offices of Dr. Lewis J. Fielding located in Beverly Hills, Calif., there had been obtained information which might taint the prosecution in the criminal case of United States of America v. Russo (No. 93 73-CD-WMB), the trial of which was then pending before said court, in that he stated that it had been over a

(Text of March 7 indictment—cont.)

year since he had seen anything on the "Pentagon papers" investigation, and that he had not seen any material covering the White House investigation of the "Pentagon papers" case for more than a year.

(Title 18, United States Code, Section 1001.)

Count Three

The grand jury further charges:

1. On or about May 14, 1973, in the District of Columbia, John D. Ehrlichman, the defendant, having duly taken an oath that he would testify truthfully in a proceeding before the June, 1972, grand jury, a grand jury of the United States duly empaneled and sworn in the United States District Court for the District of Columbia, did make false material declarations as hereinafter set forth.

2. At the time and place alleged, the said grand jury was conducting an investigation in conjunction with the United States attorney's office for the District of Columbia, and the Federal Bureau of Investigation to determine whether violations of 18 U.S.C. Secs. 371, 1001, 1503, 1621, 1623, 2511, and 22 D.C. Code 1801 (b), and of other statutes of the United States and of the District of Columbia, had been committed in the District of Columbia and elsewhere, and to identify the individual or individuals who had committed, caused the commission of and conspired to commit such violations.

3. It was material to said investigation that the grand jury ascertain, among other things, the identity and motives of the individual or individuals who were responsible for, participated in, and had knowledge of an entry into the offices of Dr. Lewis J. Fielding, located in Beverly Hills, Calif., and related activities.

4. At the time and place alleged, John D. Ehrlichman, the defendant, appearing as a witness under oath before the said grand jury, did knowingly declare with respect to the aforesaid material matters alleged in Paragraph 3 as follows:

Q. Very well, sir. Now there came a time when this operation became concerned with Dr. Ellsberg himself, is that not correct? A. Yes.

Q. And then there was an attempt or a decision made to find out as much about Dr. Ellsberg as could be done, is that correct? A. Yes.

Q. And even part of that investigation was going to center on his psychological profile, his mental attitudes, his habits, and possible motivations. Is that correct?

A. *Well, I learned about that after the fact,* but that is my understanding of the decision that was made.

Q. When you say you learned about it after the fact, what do you mean by that, sir?

A. *Well, I learned after the break-in that they were looking for information for what they call a psychological profile. I was not aware of that before the fact.*

Q. So before the fact you were not aware that there was an attempt by Mr. Krogh, or persons working under his supervision or authority, to—there was no attempt made by these people to ascertain information that would be helpful in drawing out the psychological profile if I understood what you just said. Is that right?

A. I didn't know if they made an attempt or not. I was just saying that I didn't learn of it until after I learned of the break-in.

Q. Just so that the grand jury and we are clear on this, prior to receiving information about the break-in, you had no information, direct or indirect, that a

psychological profile of Dr. Ellsberg was being drawn up?

A. *I can't recall hearing of a psychological profile until after I had heard of the break-in.*

5. The (italicized) portions of the material declarations quoted in Paragraph 4, made by John D. Ehrlichman, the defendant, were material to the said investigation and, as he then and there well knew, were false.

(Title 18, United States Code, Section 1623).

Count Four

The grand jury further charges:

1. On or about May 14, 1973, in the District of Columbia, John D. Ehrlichman, the defendant, having duly taken an oath that he would testify truthfully in a proceeding before the June, 1972, grand jury, a grand jury of the United States duly empaneled and sworn in the United States District Court for the District of Columbia, did make false material declarations as hereinafter set forth.

2. At the time and place alleged, the said grand jury was conducting an investigation in conjunction with the United States attorney's office for the District of Columbia and the Federal Bureau of Investigation to determine whether violations of 18 U.S.C. Secs. 371, 1001, 1503, 1621, 1623, 2511, and 22 D.C. Code 1801 (b), and of other statutes of the United States and of the District of Columbia, had been committed in the District of Columbia and elsewhere, and to identify the individual or individuals who had committed, caused the commission of, and conspired to commit such violations.

3. It was material to said investigation that the grand jury ascertain, among other things, the identity and motives of the individual or individuals who were responsible for, participated in, and had knowledge of an entry into the offices of Dr. Lewis J. Fielding, located in Beverly Hills, Calif., and related activities.

4. At the time and place alleged, John D. Ehrlichman, the defendant, appearing as a witness under oath before the said grand jury, did knowingly declare with respect to the aforesaid material matters alleged in Paragraph 3 as follows:

Q. Now were you aware before this break-in, which took place on or about Sept. 3, 1971, that an effort was going to be directed towards obtaining information from Dr. Ellsberg or Dr. Ellsberg's psychiatrist?

A. *Ahead of the fact? No.*

5. The (italicized) portions of the material declarations quoted in Paragraph 4, made by John D. Ehrlichman, the defendant, were material to the said investigation and, as he then and there well knew, were false.

(Title 18, United States Code, Section 1623.)

Count Five

The grand jury further charges:

1. On or about May 14, 1973, in the District of Columbia, John D. Ehrlichman, the defendant, having duly taken an oath that he would testify truthfully in a proceeding before the June, 1972, grand jury, a grand jury of the United States duly empaneled and sworn in the United States District Court for the District of Columbia, did make false material declarations as hereinafter set forth.

2. At the time and place alleged, the said grand jury was conducting an investigation in conjunction with the United States attorney's office for the District of Columbia and the Federal Bureau of Investigation to determine whether violations of 18 U.S.C.

Secs. 371, 1001, 1503, 1621, 1623, 2511, and 22 D.C. Code 1801 (b), and of other statutes of the United States and the District of Columbia, had been committed in the District of Columbia and elsewhere, and to identify the individual or individuals who had committed, caused the commission of and conspired to commit such violations.

3. It was material to said investigation that the grand jury ascertain, among other things, the identity and motives of the individual or individuals who were responsible for, participated in, and had knowledge of an entry into the offices of Dr. Lewis J. Fielding, located in Beverly Hills, Calif., and related activities.

•4. At the time and place alleged, John D. Ehrlichman, the defendant, appearing as a witness under oath before the said grand jury, did knowingly declare with respect to the aforesaid material matters alleged in Paragraph 3 as follows:

Q. You indicate here that you did maintain a newspaper clipping file on the Pentagon papers case. A. Right.

Q. But you say there were other papers in addition? A. I think there were some others. There was a small file and it just went out. I didn't have occasion to look at it before it went, but it went.

Q. You mentioned a moment ago, in response to Mr. Silbert's question, that there were some files. Did you have a file relating to . . . A. No. I don't believe I kept a file.

Q. Who had a file? A. I think Mr. Krogh had a file. Q. Anybody else have a file? A. *I don't know.*

Q. So as far as you know, prior to the break-in, whenever that was, I think it was sometime in September, Sept. 3, the only person that had a file that you knew of was Mr. Krogh?

A. *I believe that's right.* I, of course, had a great many other things going on. He would, from time to time, post me on the whole Pentagon papers matter.

This was not just Ellsberg. At that time there were all kinds of things going on. There were lawsuits involving the New York Times. There was a lot of activity going on.

He would inform me from time to time of things that would happen. But I kept no paper as I recall. I would move paper out if any came in on this, and usually sign it over to Krogh.

Q. And subsequent to the break-in, did you learn that there were any files anywhere in existence? A. I think there were a number of files both before and after.

Q. In whose hands? A. Well, I assume Krogh. I think that he would be the one that I would always look to for paper work on this with the exception of— I do recall running across this very bulky clipping file that we had in our office, and why we had it I don't know.

But at sometime or another we accumulated a tremendous amount of newspaper clipping on this case. That was the whole Pentagon papers case.

Q. Any other files in the custody of anybody else involved in this operation? A. *Not that I know of. I would assume that Krogh had them all.*

Q. Did you ever learn that anybody had any files before or after Sept. 3?

A. *No, I don't believe so.*

5. The (Italicized) portions of the material declarations quoted in Paragraph 4, made by John D. Ehrlichman, the defendant, were material to the said investigation and, as he then and there well knew, were false.

(Title 18, United States Code, Section 1623.)

Watergate book film rights sold. Film rights for "All the Presidents Men," a book about the Watergate scandals written by Bob Woodward and Carl Bernstein, investigative reporters for the Washington Post, were bought March 6 for $450,000 by a movie company owned by actor Robert Redford.

House panel defers subpoena. Special presidential counsel James D. St. Clair, in a letter sent March 7 to House Judiciary Committee Chairman Peter W. Rodino Jr. (D, N.J.), said President Nixon would provide the committee with the

same materials already given to special Watergate prosecutor Leon Jaworski. At the same time, St. Clair stated that the President would not comply with requests for further materials, as the 700 documents turned over to the Watergate grand jury were "more than sufficient to afford the Judiciary Committee with the entire Watergate story."

"In the President's opinion, the Watergate matter and widespread allegations of obstruction of justice in connection therewith are at the heart of this matter. By making available to the committee without limitation all of the materials fur-

nished to the grand jury, . . . he feels that he will have provided the committee with the necessary materials to resolve any questions concerning him."

Committee counsel Doar told the committee March 7 that he interpreted the letter as follows: "This seems to say to me, 'Mr. Doar, your case against the President is simply the Watergate cover-up.'" To this, Doar responded, "No one outside this committee should set the limits of this inquiry."

Doar said if the committee were to issue subpoenas for the materials in question and the President were to defy or ignore them, his actions could lead to a contempt of Congress citation, which in itself could be an impeachable offense.

Doar told the committee that St. Clair's letter had been silent on the committee's request for six tape recordings not given to Jaworski.

Rep. Robert F. Drinan (D, Mass.), seconded by Rep. Charles B. Rangel (D, N.Y.), proposed that the committee subpoena the six tapes to see if the "White House is going to cooperate or the President is going to operate in contempt of this Congress."

However, Doar and chief Republican counsel Jenner urged the panel to give them more time to seek White House compliance. Rep. John Conyers Jr. (D, Mich.), who appeared to reflect the sentiments of a majority of the panel members, said he would accept a delay in issuing subpoenas as "going the last mile with the President and his representatives."

Conceding he lacked the votes, Drinan dropped his motion, but not before warning the committee that it was making a "profound mistake."

In a related action, the committee voted unanimously to urge U.S. District Court Judge John J. Sirica to supply the committee "forthwith" with the sealed report of the Watergate grand jury, which purportedly contained evidence concerning the President's role in the Watergate cover-up. Doar told the committee that it was "unthinkable" for the committee to continue its investigation without the sealed report.

Nixon proposes reform. President Nixon proposed a number of campaign reforms March 8, including tighter fund disclosure rules, limits on contributions and shorter presidential campaigns. Federal financing of Congressional and presidential campaigns was opposed by the President, who presented his proposals in a message to Congress and in a radio address to the nation. [For further details, see p. 43E1]

Mills believes Nixon should resign. Rep. Wilbur D. Mills (D, Ark.) said March 8 he expected the pressure for President Nixon's resignation to intensify when the Congressional Joint Committee on Internal Revenue Taxation investigating Nixon's income tax returns reported its findings. Mills was a member of the committee. [For further details, see p. 90E1]

Confrontation over tapes looms. White House Press Secretary Ronald L. Ziegler said March 12 it would be "constitutionally irresponsible" for President Nixon to give the House Judiciary Committee all the White House data it was seeking for its impeachment inquiry. He said the request for data threatened the separation of powers of the Constitution.

Unlimited "perusing of White House files cannot be tolerated" by the President, Ziegler said, and "the mere fact of an im-

peachment inquiry does not give Congress the right to back up a truck and haul off White House files."

Ziegler said the committee was requesting "more and more and more" before it had received and assimilated the data the White House was sending to it. (Delivery of the data to the committee began March 8.) The data not only included that already provided to the special Watergate prosecutor, which had been promised by the White House, but "boxes of materials," Ziegler said, of additional data. (In a report to the committee March 5, its counsel John Doar had indicated that the probe was covering cases not commonly associated with the Watergate scandals and involving charges that environmental, oil import and antitrust decisions were influenced by political contributions or friendship.)

"We feel that once they begin to assess what we are now in the process of furnishing," Ziegler said, "they will conclude that they have sufficient materials to complete their inquiry and to complete it quickly."

Ziegler said before the probe went any further the committee should define what it considered an impeachable offense and specify its charges against the President.

Ziegler chided reporters March 8 for "too much dwelling on Watergate" at the recent presidential news conference March 6. While the questions were "proper and legitimate," he said, they contained "a little too much point of view." The questioning failed to reflect what Nixon "has been doing with his time as President," he said.

Presidential counselor Bryce Harlow said later March 12 Nixon wanted the committee to adopt tighter "rules of relevance" as well as action by the committee itself, rather than its staff, on what material it needed from the White House. However, he said, the President had not foreclosed release of further data.

The White House had objected to the committee's request for data through an unidentified official March 11. (The official was later identified in press reports as Kenneth W. Clawson, director of communications.) He complained the panel wanted "carte blanche to rummage through every nook and cranny in the White House on a fishing expedition." As documentation, he released the committee letter requesting the material and cited its proposal that the committee's staff members be given access to the White House files to find the material they considered necessary to the House probe.

The official also pointed out that the committee was seeking, beyond the material submitted to the Watergate special prosecutor, 42 tape recordings covering six different subject areas. There was a general misimpression, the official said, that the committee was seeking only six additional tapes apart from the federal prosecution material. The letter revealed that the new tapes being sought covered conversations between the President and

key aides in the period before and after the March 21, 1973 conversation in which Nixon said he learned of the Watergate cover-up.

The misimpression apparently stemmed from a Judiciary Committee meeting March 7 when its counsel reported the White House refusal to furnish material beyond what had been furnished the special prosecutor. In keeping with its security rules to safeguard the White House data, committee secrecy was such that only its two senior members had been apprised of the specific requests for the White House data. Thus most of the members learned of the committee's requests through the White House, which irritated some of them.

The White House remarks about a "fishing expedition" also rankled members of the committee from both parties. At a meeting March 12, Chairman Peter W. Rodino Jr. (D, N.J.) assured that the material requested was vital. "It bears on matters that leave a lot of questions unanswered," he said, and was "not intended by this committee as part of any fishing expedition." Rep. Charles W. Sandman Jr. (R, N.J.) said, "All I hear about is how far the President is willing to go or is not willing to go. When are we going to start running this investigation?" Rep. Jack Brooks (D, Tex.) said release of the letter was "an affront to the comity" between the White House and Congress but "the hucksterism of the White House should not detract from the decency and forbearance of the committee." It was clear, he said, that "the White House is not going to cooperate."

Democratic committee members were so irritated over the White House stance that Rodino assembled them in caucus March 13 to urge a judicial, rather than intemperate, response. Rep. Robert F. Drinan (D, Mass.) later reported "an overwhelming consensus" at the meeting that "we'll have to subpoena the material at some time—it's just a matter of time."

At a joint news conference March 13, Rodino and the committee's ranking Republican, Edward Hutchinson (Mich.), stood firm about the request for data from the White House. The data was "necessary to a full and complete explanation of the events," Rodino said, and "we expect full cooperation from all persons. The Constitution permits nothing less." Hutchinson denied the committee was on a "fishing expedition." Its requests for data were "very reasonable and relevant," he said, and the White House should be "totally cooperative."

Both opposed the White House suggestion that the committee define impeachable behavior. Each congressman must make his own decision, they said. As for presenting its charges against the President, another White House suggestion, Hutchinson said: "There are no charges. We hope we will find none. We are simply making an inquiry."

Both rejected a suggestion raised by Sen. Norris Cotton (R, N.H.) that Nixon told him he was considering allowing an "independent person" or third party to examine the White House data to determine the relevant items. It was the responsibility of the House, they said, and could not be discharged by an outside party.

In rebutting the "fishing expedition" charge, counsel for the committee said they had discussed their requests in detail with the President's counsel and there was no misunderstanding. The proposal for committee representatives to search the White House files for relevant data, they said, came up because the White House had no index of its papers and documents.

The counsel informed the committee of receipt of an index from Watergate special prosecutor Leon Jaworski of the White House materials he had requested but had not been furnished. On the list were at least 27 tapes and some data on the "plumbers" and dairy industry contributions.

The committee dispatched a letter to the federal Watergate court March 12 declaring its right without precondition to the sealed grand jury report within the court's custody.

Finance Committee ends operation. The Finance Committee to Re-elect the President ended its two-year existence March 12 and transferred $3.57 million in surplus campaign funds to a trust account in a Washington bank.

Trustees of the fund, called the 1972 Campaign Liquidation Account, said they had agreed to pay the legal fees and expenses for suits arising out of the Watergate break-in filed against the committee and its officials. [For further details, see p. 43C3]

California charges dropped. State charges of burglary and conspiracy stemming from the 1971 break-in at the Los Angeles office of Dr. Lewis J. Fielding, the psychiatrist who treated Pentagon Papers trial defendant Daniel Ellsberg, were dropped in Los Angeles Superior Court by Judge Gordon Ringer March 13.

The dismissal of the charges against former White House aides John D. Ehrlichman, David R. Young Jr. and G. Gordon Liddy followed a meeting March 11 between Watergate special prosecutor Leon Jaworski and Joseph Busch, district attorney for Los Angeles County. Liddy and Ehrlichman were among the six defendants named in Watergate grand jury indictments returned March 7 through Jaworski's office in connection with the break-in. Young was granted immunity from prosecution in return for his testimony.

However, a perjury charge against Ehrlichman, which resulted from his testimony before a Los Angeles grand jury, was allowed to stand. A spokesman for Busch's office said Ehrlichman's alleged perjury "represents a separate and independent assault upon the integrity of the grand jury."

Judge Ringer also vacated a subpoena served on President Nixon by the defendants.

In Washington, Ehrlichman and Charles W. Colson, both also indicted for obstruction of justice in connection with the Watergate break-in, pleaded not guilty March 9 to charges stemming from the Fielding burglary. Defendants G. Gordon Liddy, Bernard L. Barker, Eugenio Martinez and Felipe DeDiego entered similar pleas March 14.

Democrats also linked to AMPI gifts. A report commissioned by the board of directors of the nation's largest milk cooperative, Associated Milk Producers, Inc. (AMPI), revealed that AMPI had engaged in a broad pattern of irregularities involving campaign contributions to Democrats as well as Republicans since 1968.

The report, prepared by the Little Rock, Ark. law firm of Wright, Lindsey and Jennings, with an audit by the accounting firm of Haskins & Sells, was made public March 14 after being submitted to U.S. district court in Kansas City, Mo. in connection with an antitrust suit against AMPI. (The principal author of the report was Edward L. Wright, a former president of the American Bar Association.)

Copies also were sent to the Watergate special prosecutor's office and to the Senate Watergate committee, it was reported March 14. Both groups had been investigating alleged campaign abuses related to AMPI's secret contributions to President Nixon's re-election effort.
[For further details, see p. 44D1]

Shultz quits Treasury. George P. Shultz, the last member of President Nixon's original Cabinet, would leave his post as secretary of the Treasury in May, the White House announced March 14. Shultz, whose policy role in economic affairs had been compared to Secretary of State Henry Kissinger's predominant role in foreign affairs, said he was resigning for personal reasons.

"I am well into my sixth year [in the Cabinet, having served also as labor secretary and director of the Office of Management and Budget] and it is demanding work," Shultz said. "There is a tendency to stay too long [in government]. You don't have the ability to 'get up' for a wide variety of topics as you once did," he added. The "distressing" Watergate scandal, which had caused other Administration officials to resign, was not a factor in his decision, Shultz said.

Mitchell & Stans Acquitted
in Vesco Fund Case

Senate panel postpones hearings. Sen. Sam J. Ervin Jr. (D, N.C.), chairman of the Watergate Committee, announced Jan. 26 that public hearings on contributions to President Nixon's 1972 re-election campaign would be postponed indefinitely.

Ervin said the delay had been decided upon to avoid prejudicing the trial of former Attorney General John N. Mitchell and former Commerce Secretary Maurice H. Stans on charges of perjury and obstruction of justice, scheduled to begin Feb. 19 in New York City. [For further details, see p. 38G3]

Mitchell-Stans trial opens. The trial of two former Nixon Administration Cabinet members—John N. Mitchell and Maurice H. Stans—on criminal charges of conspiracy, obstruction of justice and perjury opened Feb. 19 in U.S. District Court in New York.

Although a number of Administration officials were under criminal indictment, Mitchell and Stans were the first leading officials to stand trial. Their case also was the first involving alleged criminal wrongdoing by Cabinet members since Interior Secretary Albert B. Fall and Attorney General Harry M. Daugherty stood trial on charges arising from the Teapot Dome scandal in the administration of President Warren G. Harding.

Mitchell and Stans were indicted May 10, 1973 on charges they had hindered a Securities and Exchange Commission investigation of financier Robert Vesco who had donated $250,000 to President Nixon's re-election campaign. Mitchell had resigned as attorney general to head the campaign and quit that post shortly after the Watergate break-in. Stans remained chairman of the Finance Committee to Re-elect the President.

Vesco, who also was named in the indictment, fled the country early in 1973 and several efforts to obtain his extradition had proven unsuccessful. The trial of another co-defendant, former New Jersey State Sen. Harry Sears (R), was separated from that of Mitchell and Stans.

The Mitchell-Stans trial had been postponed three times. The court rejected another defense motion Feb. 19 requesting that charges be dropped or a change of venue be ordered because of prejudicial pretrial publicity. Jury selection began immediately. Special Watergate prosecutor Leon Jaworski was expected to announce indictments against other principal Administration figures in the Watergate case after the jury was sequestered.

Federal prosecutors revealed Feb. 8 that they had obtained two more White House tape recordings of conversations involving President Nixon and his former counsel John W. Dean 3rd. The tapes of conversations March 13 and March 20, 1973 were provided to the court for possible use by defense attorneys in testing Dean's veracity as a witness against Mitchell and Stans.

Mitchell-Stans mistrial denied. The trial of former Attorney General John N. Mitchell and former Commerce Secretary Maurice Stans on charges of conspiracy, obstruction of justice and perjury continued in New York after presiding Judge Lee P. Gagliardi March 4 rejected a defense motion for a mistrial.

Stans' lawyer had objected to opening remarks made March 1 by Assistant U.S. Attorney James W. Rayhill. After telling the jury that the government would prove that the defendants had conspired to quash the Securities & Exchange Commission's (SEC) investigation of financier Robert Vesco in return for a secret $200,000 cash contribution to President Nixon's re-election campaign, Rayhill said, "as you listen to the witnesses testifying before you, put yourselves in the place of the grand jurors who investigated this case, citizens like yourselves."

When Stans' lawyer contended that Rayhill's statement suggested that the indictment was proof of guilt rather than solely accusatory in nature, Gagliardi recessed the trial briefly. Following the jury's return, the judge said he was "gravely concerned" at the prosecutor's "apparent excesses." Gagliardi then abruptly adjourned the proceedings until March 4 to consider the mistrial motion.

The defense's motion for a mistrial was especially critical to other related Watergate cases, coming on the day that a Watergate grand jury returned a long awaited indictment against seven former officials in the White House and Nixon re-election campaign, including John Mitchell.

Action on the indictment had hinged on expediting the delayed Mitchell-Stans trial: return of the 24-charge indictment had been held up while a jury was sequestered in the Mitchell-Stans trial. A mistrial would have necessitated dismissal of that jury and selection of a new group whose impartiality could have been challenged on grounds of prejudicial pretrial publicity.

Gagliardi denied the defense motion March 4, saying that "an inference of guilt from the fact of the indictment was not planned by the prosecutor" and that he himself had explained "the nature of an indictment and the presumption of innocence" to the jury on five other occasions.

The trial was allowed to proceed and defense attorneys presented their opening remarks. Mitchell's lawyer described Vesco's $200,000 secret contribution as "less than .33% of the $60 million" raised by Stans and others on the Finance Committee to Re-elect the President.

"It is as if in an election costing $10,000, Vesco had contributed $33. It is as if in an election costing $100,000, Vesco had contributed $300. It is as if in an election costing $100, Vesco had contributed I think 33¢," Peter E. Fleming Jr. told the jury.

The question was "in essence whether John Mitchell would sell his life for 33¢," Fleming declared.

Sears testifies at Mitchell-Stans trial. Harry Sears, former Republican majority leader in the New Jersey State Senate, who had headed President Nixon's New Jersey re-election campaign, testified March 5-12 in the trial of former Attorney General John Mitchell and former Commerce Secretary Maurice Stans.

Sears' initial testimony appeared to support the prosecution's contention that the defendants had accepted a campaign gift from financier Robert Vesco in return for their efforts to block a Securities and Exchange Commission (SEC) investigation of Vesco.

But under cross examination by defense attorneys, Sears, who described himself as Mitchell's "friend," said he knew of "absolutely no attempts ever made to fix" the SEC probe and that "never at any time" did he ask Mitchell to arrange the fix.

Sears, who had been Vesco's intermediary with Mitchell and Stans, was originally a co-defendant, but his case had been separated from that of Mitchell and Stans. Sears was granted "transactional" immunity from prosecution March 5 after taking the Fifth Amendment in response to the prosecution's first question.

Sears was expected to be a crucial witness in determining whether Mitchell and Stans had perjured themselves in sworn testimony before a grand jury investigating the alleged conspiracy. Mitchell had claimed that Stans first briefed him on Vesco's legal troubles with the SEC in February 1972; that Sears had never provided him with documents on Vesco's situation; and that he could not recall Sears asking him to persuade William J. Casey, then chairman of the SEC, to attend a meeting between SEC investigators and Vesco. Stans had testified he had not sought a cash contribution from Vesco.

Sears' earlier testimony before the grand jury had obscured or omitted the roles played by Mitchell and Stans in the alleged conspiracy, resulting in charges of perjury being filed against him.

Sears described his preliminary efforts to help untangle Vesco's legal troubles stemming from the SEC investigation. Sears testified that he first introduced Vesco to Mitchell, then attorney general, at a New Jersey fund raising dinner in March 1971. (Vesco had been a contributor to Sear's unsuccessful bid for the gubernatorial nomination and later helped pay off campaign debts.)

The meeting coincided with the beginning of SEC's formal investigation of Vesco's mutual funds empire, a probe that culminated in the filing of a $224 million civil suit in November 1972 Vesco, complaining of SEC "harassment," already had enlisted Sears (an attorney) to file a suit limiting the SEC probe. Sears testified that Vesco had asked him to let the federal judge hearing the case know privately that Vesco "wasn't a bad guy." Sears said he refused.

In May 1971, Vesco asked him to use his "good offices" with Mitchell to do something about the SEC "witch hunt." Sears complied, testifying that he wrote Mitchell a personal letter about the situation and enclosed a copy of a letter from Vesco to Casey.

Further discussion of Vesco took place in May 1971 between Mitchell and Sears, who brought up Vesco's friendship with the President's brothers, Edward and F. Donald Nixon. On July 6, 1971, Sears said he talked to Mitchell at the Justice Department and discussed the Vesco matter "in some detail." Mitchell promised to "talk to Bill Casey" but Sears said he heard nothing from Mitchell about it.

On Nov. 30, 1971 Sears called Mitchell seeking help for Vesco who had been jailed without bond in Switzerland on the complaint of a stockholder in Vesco's company, International Controls Corp. (ICC) (also the subject of the SEC investigation). According to Sears, Mitchell called the U.S. embassy there and within 24 hours, Vesco was released on bond. (The charge was later dropped.)

In December 1971, Sears testified that he received a "gift" of $10,000 from Vesco but he later denied that he took the money "to get John Mitchell to help get Vesco out of jail." Shortly thereafter, Sears joined ICC as an attorney and director. In that capacity, he said he was expected "to get John Mitchell" to aid Vesco.

Vesco's arrest in Switzerland continued to trouble him because in Jan. 4, 1972, Sears said Mitchell telephoned about a memo he had received from John Ehrlichman, then President Nixon's domestic affairs adviser. (He introduced Ehrlichman to Vesco in September 1972 at a New York political dinner, Sears said.) According to the memo, Vesco "wanted a good word put in for" him at U.S. embassies, and Mitchell asked Sears for more background information on Vesco. Sears said he brought papers dealing with Vesco to a meeting with Mitchell in Washington Jan. 12, 1972.

In February 1972, Mitchell discussed an internal SEC memo regarding the Vesco probe with Sears at another Washington conference.

Sears said discussion about a large campaign contribution occurred at a March 8, 1972 meeting with Stans, then chairman of the Finance Committee to Re-elect the President. Stans twice asked that the donation be made in cash, a fact which Vesco verified by sending Edward Nixon to talk with Stans later that month, Sears testified. Sears saw Stans April 3, 1972 to discuss the contribution and Stans told him he had "had some discussion about that [Vesco's legal troubles] with John [Mitchell]."

According to Sears, Stans did not object to receiving the cash contribution on April 10, 1972, three days after the federal campaign finance law required public disclosure of all receipts and expenditures.

The money was delivered April 10, 1972 to Stans' office. Sears accompanied Laurence B. Richardson Jr., ICC president, to Washington. Stans accepted the money without counting it. Sears recalled Richardson saying, " 'Mr. Vesco wants me to deliver a message. He wants help.' " Stans replied, " 'That's not my department' or 'my bailiwick. That's John Mitchell's department,' " Sears testified.

Sears said he jumped to his feet and ended the meeting abruptly, saying, "What we brought here today is a political contribution. There's nothing else involved."

But several hours later, he met with Mitchell, mentioned delivery of the cash, and got an immediate appointment with Casey that day. G. Bradford Cook, SEC general counsel, also attended.

Despite the meeting with Casey and Cook, Vesco said in July 1972 that the SEC probe was "gaining momentum." He asked Sears to see Stans again. Sears said he objected to the tactic, saying "that would be the worst thing we could do." Vesco, frustrated, replied, " 'But by God, I gave all that money,' " Sears testified.

Sears said he met with Stans in August 1972 at the Republican National Convention. Stans declined to become involved, noting obliquely that there was no record of Vesco's cash contribution. "In effect," Sears said, Stans was saying "the SEC situation has gotten too hot to handle." Despite the warning, Sears said Vesco asked him in October 1972 to "tell that Stans to get the SEC off my back."

Sears said Vesco grew increasingly frustrated and as the election grew closer, emphasized that disclosure of his secret contribution could prove as worrisome to the Administration as the SEC investigation was to him. Sears said Vesco told him he had been talking with " 'Newport Beach [Calif., the home of F. Donald Nixon.] It's about time I got some help from the brothers. I have been discussing [it] with them and trying to get their help. I want to get a message to the top.' "

On Nov. 20, 1972 Sears said Mitchell called him to his office and showed him an envelope left for Donald Nixon at a Manhattan hotel by Vesco. Sears took the material home and eventually turned it over to the grand jury.

It was not revealed how Mitchell obtained the documents but the contents were introduced as evidence March 11. In a seven-page unsigned memo, purportedly written by Vesco, the need to stop the SEC investigation "promptly" was discussed.

"It is in the best interests of the U.S.A. to cause the SEC to drop the entire action," the memo read, because Vesco's influence "can uniquely assist U.S. objectives in Morocco, Spain, Costa Rica, the Bahamas, Dominican Republic and many South American countries. This capability is available for official use by the U.S. on a clandestine basis."

According to the memo, Spain's Generalissimo Francisco Franco threatened to make an "international incident" if the SEC "harassment" of shareholders in another Vesco company under SEC scrutiny, Investors Overseas Services (IOS), did not cease. Control of IOS had been sold in the fall of 1972 to the "financial establishment of Spain, the royal family and representatives of certain foreign governments," the memo said, adding that Vesco had personally discussed the transaction with Franco and Costa Rican President Jose Figueres. (Sears said Figueres had also written Nixon expressing concern about the SEC investigation and his hope that the situation would be "ameliorated." " 'Mr. John Mitchell, your former attorney general, is familiar with the matter,' " Figueres wrote Nixon.)

The memo reminded Donald Nixon that Vesco had been a "historic, undisclosed major contributor to Republican campaigns" and had been the "tutelary mentor" of his son, Donald Jr.

Just a month earlier in October 1972, Sears said, Mitchell agreed to "go through the White House . . . to talk to John Dean" about SEC subpoenas served on Vesco and associates because disclosure of the secret contribution could prove a major embarrassment to the Administration just prior to the election. Mitchell was "grateful" that Vesco already had taken the Fifth Amendment and refused to talk about the political gift in earlier testimony, Sears said. Vesco knew the value of his silence, telling Sears " 'I hope that will make them happy because that's just like another contribution.' "

Sears was cross-examined by a defense attorney March 12. He was asked whether there was a connection between the Vesco contribution and the subsequent meeting between Sears, Casey and Cook. "Absolutely none," Sears replied. He added that he had "never asked for more" than a review of the case by the SEC before it took "precipitous" action against Vesco.

Sears admitted he would not be testifying without the grant of immunity promised in August 1973 but he denied that he feared disbarment. "I have an absolute conviction that I have committed no crime and I don't fear any consequences," he declared.

Finance Committee ends operation. The Finance Committee to Re-elect the President ended its two-year existence March 12 and transferred $3.57 million in surplus campaign funds to a trust account in a Washington bank.

Trustees of the fund, called the 1972 Campaign Liquidation Account, said they had agreed to pay the legal fees and expenses for suits arising out of the Watergate break-in filed against the committee and its officials. Legal costs related to the Watergate affair already totaled $1 million.

In a reversal of past policy, the trustees also agreed to pay legal expenses for former campaign officials acquitted of criminal charges and possibly for those found guilty of misdemeanor charges, according to the trustees. Finance Committee Chairman Maurice Stans, whose salary was not paid after Feb. 20, and former campaign director John Mitchell could make claims on the trust fund if acquitted of federal charges of conspiracy, obstruction of justice and perjury.

Mitchell-Stans trial hears 10 witnesses. The trial of former Nixon cabinet officials John Mitchell and Maurice Stans on charges of conspiracy, obstruction of justice and perjury continued March 13–20 in

federal district court in New York.

Ten witnesses were called by the prosecution but the most significant testimony was given by William J. Casey, currently president of the Export-Import Bank. Casey, former chairman of the Securities and Exchange Commission (SEC), was a central figure in the government's case, which alleged that the defendants accepted a large, secret contribution for President Nixon's re-election campaign from financier Robert Vesco in return for attempting to hinder the SEC's investigation of Vesco's mutual fund empire.

Casey testified March 20 that John W. Dean 3rd, then counsel to the President, talked with him by telephone several times to discuss Vesco's troubles with the SEC. In a call Nov. 2, 1972, Casey testified, Dean asked him to delay the SEC's subpoenas of Vesco associates until after election day to prevent a "last minute campaign smear." (According to the prosecution, Vesco had threatened to reveal that he had secretly donated $200,000 to the race in an effort to increase the pressure on Mitchell and Stans.)

According to the prosecution, Dean telephoned at Mitchell's behest but Casey said Dean did not mention Mitchell's name. The prosecution did not contend that Casey was party to the conspiracy or that he knew of Vesco's cash donation at that time. Dean had been named an unindicted co-conspirator.

After consulting with his staff, Casey testified, he had not ordered a delay in the questioning of Vesco's aides, and he had informed Dean of this.

Casey described Dean's other phone calls: in the summer or early fall of 1971, Dean had made a preliminary query to determine the seriousness of the SEC's investigation of Vesco; in October 1972, Dean expressed concern about the involvement of the President's nephew, Donald Nixon Jr., who was employed by Vesco (Casey said he advised Dean that Donald Nixon could prove an embarrassment to the President); on Nov. 1, 1972 Casey was not in to receive a call from Dean but he returned it the next day; in February 1973, Dean called on a "complaint from Mr. Mitchell!" that an SEC official had leaked to the press contents of a deposition about the SEC's civil suit against Vesco. "He complained that the staff of the commission was reaching beyond the proper scope of the investigation," Casey said. Casey's testimony about another call made by Dean at Mitchell's behest was blocked by the defense.

Casey also testified that he had discussed the Vesco case with Mitchell April 6, 1972 (prior to the date of Vesco's donation). In a talk with Mitchell in December 1971 or January 1972, Casey said, they discussed Vesco's jailing by Swiss authorities on charges related to his stock problems with the SEC. Mitchell cautioned him not to exceed the agency's authority in the Swiss matter, Casey testified.

Under cross examination, Casey denied that the defendants had tried to quash the SEC case. Like an earlier witness, Harry Sears, Casey described himself as still a friend of Mitchell. The effect of his testimony was diminished by his evidently reluctant responses to prosecution questions. (Sears conceded March 13 that he had lied to a grand jury to protect Mitchell and also had lied to Vesco.)

In testimony, March 13–14, Laurence B. Richardson Jr., former president of Vesco's International Controls Corp. (ICC), denied that in delivering the $200,000 cash contribution to Stans' office in April 1972, he had acted as Vesco's "bagman." But Richardson testified that when he handed the money over and said Vesco expected help with the SEC problem, Stans told him " 'Mitchell and Sears are handling that.' "

Vesco and Stans first discussed a proposed contribution in connection with the SEC matter March 8, 1972, Richardson said, adding that Stans requested the contribution be in "currency." Following the meeting, Stans arranged an appointment that day for Vesco with Mitchell, Richardson said, but he added that since he was not present, he could not be certain it had occurred.

Richardson, who had been named an unindicted co-conspirator in the Mitchell-Stans case, said he objected to Vesco's initial plan to contribute $500,000 to Nixon's campaign, but was told that the donation was "a lot cheaper than legal fees."

Daniel W. Hofgren, a former Stans aide, March 15 corroborated Richardson's recollection of the March 8 meeting. He also said he asked Mitchell about the subsequent meeting with Vesco and was told to "stay away from that."

W. Mark Felt, a former Federal Bureau of Investigation (FBI) official, testified the same day that Mitchell had sought his help in aiding the jailed Vesco in Switzerland. On Jan. 19, 1972, Felt said, Mitchell asked him to send a message of support for Vesco to the U.S. ambassador in Switzerland through FBI channels "because he [Mitchell] didn't want to go through the State Department channel."

The final witness March 15, Hugh W. Sloan Jr., Stans' treasurer at the Finance Committee to Re-elect the President, testified that Stans twice had him remove Vesco's name from lists of prospective contributors. Vesco's cash donation was listed at Mitchell's request under the initials JM, Sloan testified. That record eventually was destroyed on Stans' order, Sloan added.

President Nixon's personal secretary, Rose Mary Woods, testified March 16 that Vesco's name was not on a master list, in her custody, of pre-April 7, 1972 contributors (those persons not required to disclose their contributions under federal law). Vesco's money was delivered April 10, 1972 but Stans claimed confidentiality for the donation because he said it was pledged prior to the deadline. (An official with the General Accounting Office testified March 18 that Vesco had not been listed as a donor in the post April 7, 1972 period.)

Another list of purported contributors was used to determine invitations to White House social functions and Vesco's name appeared on this, but with a question mark beside it, Woods testified. The list was given to her Nov. 29, 1972, two days after the SEC filed its civil suit against Vesco.

Vesco's secretary, Shirley Bailey, testified March 19 that she had typed a memo for Vesco and delivered it to a New York hotel. The message, for the President's brother, Donald Nixon, threatened to expose Vesco's contribution if the SEC probe were not quashed.

Leonard Hall, former Republican national chairman, also testified that another Vesco associate, Howard Cerny, had asked him several times to arrange a meeting with SEC Chairman Casey and that Cerny did meet with Casey in September 1972. Cerny had been named an unindicted co-conspirator.

Dean, Cook testify. Two of the prosecution's most important witnesses testified March 25–28 in the trial of former Attorney General John Mitchell and former Commerce Secretary Maurice Stans on charges of conspiracy, obstruction of justice and perjury.

Ousted White House Counsel John W. Dean 3rd, Mitchell's former protege, and G. Bradford Cook, who had resigned as Securities and Exchange Commission (SEC) chairman because of his involvement in the Mitchell-Stans case, gave testimony supporting government charges that Mitchell and Stans had attempted to block an SEC investigation of financier Robert Vesco in return for receiving a large, secret cash contribution from Vesco for President Nixon's re-election campaign.

The trial, in U.S. District Court in New York, had adjourned March 21 because of the illness of an elderly juror, Violet Humbert. She was replaced with an alternate juror, Andrew Choa, a banker, March 25 and the trial resumed with Dean's testimony.

Dean, who conceded he was once known as "Mitchell's man at the White House," testified he had discussed the SEC probe of Vesco with Mitchell at least 19 times. In October of 1972, before the presidential election and before the SEC filed its civil suit against Vesco for securities laws violations, Dean said Mitchell called and asked him to seek a postponement from the SEC in taking depositions from Vesco associates until after the election. Dean said Mitchell feared a disclosure of Vesco's secret $200,000 contribution and politically damaging reaction to news that the President's brother and nephew were involved in the transaction. Mitchell told him " 'this

whole thing is just something we don't need before the election,' " Dean testified.

Dean phoned William Casey, then SEC chairman, saying he was calling at Mitchell's behest. Dean said he later reported to Mitchell that Casey had said " 'It's going to be very hard to do anything about this [postponing deposition taking].' "

According to Dean, Mitchell first talked to him about Vesco July 14, 1972 when he asked Dean to call Casey and inquire about the status of the SEC's investigation of Vesco. Dean said he told Mitchell that John Ehrlichman, President Nixon's domestic affairs adviser had made the same request several months earlier and that Casey had told him Vesco was " 'a bad man and one that Don Nixon Jr. [the President's nephew] shouldn't be hanging around with.' " (Dean added that Ehrlichman was the youth's "keeper," and that he, Dean, also took on that role.) After rechecking with Casey, Dean testified he reported to Mitchell that the SEC was conducting a "major" investigation of Vesco.

Dean also contradicted a point in Casey's testimony March 20. According to Dean, he had discussed the Vesco contribution with Casey in the fall of 1972. Casey contended he had not known of the secret gift until February 1973.

According to Dean, he first learned of the circumstances of Vesco's gift from Stans in September or October 1972.

Dean said he subsequently met with Stans and Mitchell twice in November to discuss the Vesco donation. At the Nov. 15, 1972 meeting, Dean said, Stans and Mitchell agreed to return the money and Stans mentioned that he had talked with G. Bradford Cook, then SEC general counsel and soon to be named Casey's successor as chairman. Stans said Cook was a " 'good and trusted man' " who " 'might be helpful' " in limiting politically embarrassing details in the forthcoming SEC suit, Dean testified.

Mitchell also complained to him that he had been through " 'a hell of grilling' " before the grand jury which eventually indicted him, Dean testified. Mitchell asked him to inform then-Attorney General Richard Kleindienst that it was a "runaway grand jury" and that he hoped Kleindienst would intercede, Dean said. Kleindienst's reply was not made a part of the record.

Under cross examination March 26–27, Dean described three conversations with President Nixon relating to the Vesco case. The defense questioned Dean on the basis of partial transcripts of White House tape recordings made of the Feb. 28, 1973 and March 20, 1973 meetings and a summary of the March 13, 1973 meeting that was obtained from the White House by the Senate Watergate committee. It was the first time any excerpts of White House tapes had been made public at a trial.

The defense also led Dean through a

lengthy admission of his role in the Watergate coverup and his efforts to obtain immunity from prosecution. With these facts and portions of the tapes alluding to figures in the Watergate affair made a part of the record, defense attorneys succeeded in raising the Watergate issue in the trial. They contended that Dean's testimony had forced them to disclose information which could taint the case with prejudicial publicity and moved for a mistrial. The motion was denied.

The Feb. 28, 1973 conversation with Nixon took place one day after the SEC had revealed Vesco's secret contribution to his campaign. In response to Nixon's concern at his brother Edward's role in the contribution, Dean testified he told Nixon that Vesco was " 'sandbagging your brother.' " (Dean also testified that he questioned Edward Nixon about the contribution and that the President's brother had talked to Stans before discussing it with Dean.)

Regarding disclosure of the contribution, Nixon was told " 'Stans would like to get his side of the story out. It would be rough and tumble but he can take it,' " Dean recalled.

On March 13, 1973, Dean said, he assured the President that it would be "legal" to keep details of the Vesco contribution secret even though the money had been received after the deadline for making donations public.

Dean testified that on March 20, 1973, he had told Nixon that "no one in the White House had done anything for Vesco, as far as I know." Although he talked with Nixon 30 minutes after Mitchell had asked him to pass his complaints about the "runaway" grand jury to Kleindienst, Dean said he did not mention the request to Nixon. Dean said he had informed Nixon that the grand jury had questioned Mitchell about alleged Watergate conspirators and Nixon family members, as well as the Vesco case.

Cook, who had resigned as chairman of the SEC May 16, 1973 after serving less than three months, testified March 27 that while he was SEC general counsel, Stans asked him on four occasions to limit the SEC's investigation of Vesco's contribution or to conceal circumstances surrounding the giving of the cash.

Cook testified that he first discussed the case with Stans during a goose hunting trip in Texas that had been arranged by his father, a Nixon fund-raiser in Nebraska, to further his son's ambitions to succeed Casey at the SEC. Stans and two other Nixon fund-raisers, Herbert Kalmbach and Kenneth Dahlberg, were among those present during the trip Nov. 11–13, 1972.

Cook recalled his talk with Stans Nov. 13 while they rested in a rice field. After mentioning his desire to head the SEC, Cook discussed the mysterious handling of Vesco's $250,000 on April 6, 1972, the last day before the deadline requiring public disclosure of campaign donors. ($50,000 of the total was given in check form and duly reported.) Stans told him, " 'I don't think we took any money from Vesco, but if we did, it was in checks,' " Cook testified, adding that Stans promised to look into the matter.

Stans called him on Nov. 15, 1972, Cook said. He told Stans that the civil suit being readied against Vesco would describe the circuitous routing of the $200,000 in cash and the refusal of anyone involved to discuss it. Stans said, " 'That gives me a problem. Do you need all of that in your case?' " Cook testified.

He said he agreed to check with other SEC officials and then decided to revise a paragraph of the complaint, mentioning only the unspecified use of "large sums of cash" in certain Vesco transactions.*

Stans was pleased with the change when told on Nov. 17, 1972, Cook said, but asked him not to make public the testimony about the cash transfer.

Cook said Stans admitted Feb. 1, 1973 that he had accepted the cash contribution from Vesco but showed him a letter at the same time indicating the donation had been returned. Cook said he urged Stans to make the contribution and the refund public before it was revealed in the SEC's continuing investigation of Vesco.

During their talk in the White House "mess", Stans asked Cook to limit the SEC inquiry to the source of the money and ignore its eventual use. Cook said he consulted with Stanley Sporkin, chief of the SEC enforcement bureau and was told the request was an impossible one.

When Stans asked him Feb. 5, 1973 to "de-emphasize" the date of the contribution, Cook said, he immediately rejected the request.

Cook's testimony March 28 was the most damaging yet against Stans. According to Cook, he agreed at Stans' request to lie to a federal grand jury investi-

*Original and revised paragraph in SEC complaint:
Original version:
In possible furtherance of the aforesaid scheme to defraud, defendants Vesco and Clay, on April 6, 1972, caused Bahamas Commonwealth Bank to wire Barclays Bank International, New York City office, with instructions to pay $250,000, in cash in $100 bills to Ralph P. Dodd and charge our account with you. On that same day, Ralph P. Dodd, who, prior to his resignation on March 9, 1972, was vice president—office of the Chairman assistant secretary and director of International Controls, acting on instructions from defendants Vesco and Clay, received the above $250,000 ($200,000 in $100 bills and $50,000 in 50 bills) from Barclays Bank and delivered it to defendant Richardson's office at International Controls, Fairfield, New Jersey. The money was subsequently delivered to defendant Vesco's home in New Jersey. On April 7 or 8, 1972, Dodd, acting on instructions from Vesco's secretary, picked up $200,000 (of the original amount) from defendant Vesco's home and transferred it to Richardson at his office at International Controls. There has been no disclosure or accounting by International Controls, Vesco or Richardson with respect to the use or distribution of this $250,000 in cash. Further, defendants Vesco, Richardson and Clay have refused to testify concerning this matter among others.
Revised version:
In addition to the above described transactions, other large sums of cash have been transferred among and between Vesco and his group, Bahamas Commonwealth Bank, International Controls, and other parties. The source, ownership, use of, and accountability for, said monies are unknown. Defendants Vesco, Richardson, Clay and other persons have refused to testify on this matter, among others.

gating the Vesco contribution.

Their meeting took place in the White House mess March 7, 1973, just after Cook had been confirmed as SEC chairman. According to Cook, Stans said, " 'Let's have one of those conversations that doesn't take place.' " Stans then described his testimony given earlier that day before the grand jury. He said Stans told the grand jury that "he hadn't discussed the Vesco matter with me until after the [SEC] complaint was filed. And he said that in connection with our meeting at that time, that the meeting would be—it was being held to discuss a trip to Haiti which both he and myself had been invited to attend," Cook recalled.

Cook said his response was, " 'Well, if that's the way it is going to be, I guess that's the way it is going to be,' or words to that effect."

Cook said Stans sought another discussion with him about the Vesco case May 7, 1973, just before Cook was scheduled to testify for the third time before the grand jury. According to Cook, he refused Stans' request, threatened to report any further talks and informed him he was " 'going to tell it like it was.' "

Cook also testified about efforts his father made to secure his appointment as SEC chairman. In January 1973, he said, Stans promised to back Cook's candidacy if he agreed to name an accountant to the next vacant post on the commission. (Stans was an accountant.) Cook said he also met with Mitchell on Dec. 31, 1972 to talk about the chairmanship but that Mitchell was noncommittal.

The subject of Vesco came up during the meeting, Cook said, when Mitchell told him " 'there was some concern in New York about the tenacity and exuberance of certain staff attorneys' " at the SEC. Cook defended the staff, citing their determination in bringing the lengthy Vesco investigation to a conclusion.

Cook said he told Mitchell that his name had been mentioned by U.S. officials in Switzerland in connection with a phone call allegedly made to obtain Vesco's release from jail. Mitchell at first denied but then admitted calling the embassy, Cook said. Mitchell defended his action, saying, " 'Anybody would make a phone call to get an American citizen out of a foreign jail,' " Cook testified.

Prosecution rests its case. The government rested its case April 3 against former Attorney General John Mitchell and former Commerce Secretary Maurice Stans, accused of conspiracy, obstruction of justice and perjury in connection with financier Robert Vesco's alleged attempt to block a Securities and Exchange Commission (SEC) investigation of his mutual funds empire by making a large secret cash contribution to President Nixon's re-election campaign. Mitchell and Stans, who at one time were Nixon's chief campaign officials, accepted the money and exerted pressure on the

SEC to limit the case against Vesco, according to the government.

The jury heard testimony from three major witnesses—G. Bradford Cook, former SEC chairman; Stanley Sporkin, former chief of the SEC's enforcement division and currently an SEC commissioner; and F. Donald Nixon, the President's brother.

Under cross examination March 29, Cook admitted that he had lied under oath and "perjured" himself five times—twice before two Congressional committees investigating the SEC's role in the Vesco case and three times before the federal grand jury which eventually indicted Mitchell and Stans.

Cook had testified March 28 that Stans had asked him to lie about their discussions which resulted in significant changes being made in the SEC's civil complaint against Vesco. Cook told the court March 29 that he had committed perjury "as a result of my conversations with Mr. Stans and my feelings for Mr. Stans and . . . in connection with my own position at the SEC and the fact that I did not want to bring any discredit or dishonor to the commission as to the fact that I had these conversations with Mr. Stans."

He had lied, Cook said, in telling the grand jury on April 19, 1973 and May 3, 1973 that he and Stans had not discussed Vesco until after the SEC suit had been filed in November 1972. In the previous day's testimony, Cook had left the impression he had told the whole truth May 7, 1973 in his third appearance before the grand jury, but testimony elicited March 30 indicated he had not completely told "it like it was."

Cook testified he had lied to a Senate committee May 14, 1973 (and also May 1, 1973 when he was not under oath). He also perjured himself May 21, 1973 before a House committee, Cook said.

Defense attorneys attempted to destroy Cook's credibility by asking whether Cook was not "also lying now to avoid prosecution." Cook, who had not been indicted or named a co-conspirator, denied the charge, adding that he had not been promised immunity for his testimony against Stans and Mitchell.

Sporkin's testimony April 1 corroborated earlier testimony that pressure had been brought on the SEC to postpone until after the presidential election subpoenas that could have exposed Vesco's contribution to Nixon's campaign and that pressure also was exerted to alter a paragraph in the SEC's formal complaint against Vesco. The subpoenas were not delayed but the paragraph, which could have alerted investigators to Vesco's political activities, was changed.

Sporkin testified that he had no direct knowledge that Stans had talked to Cook about the Vesco case but said he did have "a general knowledge" that William J. Casey, then SEC chairman, "had been talking to Mr. Mitchell about the Vesco case."

According to Sporkin, Casey called him Nov. 1, 1972 and determined that subpoenas would be issued to two Vesco associates in connection with a $200,000 cash transaction (the SEC later confirmed Sporkin's suspicion that the money had been channeled to the Nixon campaign). In another call later that day, Casey asked him to "postpone" the subpoenas, Sporkin said. Casey "said to me he believed they [the Vesco associates] could be politically embarrassing if their testimony came out," Sporkin continued. Sporkin refused to permit a delay and said he asked Casey to "rely on my judgment in this matter." (The witnesses took the Fifth Amendment and nothing was revealed at the time about the donation.)

Sporkin said he was responsible for including mention of the $200,000 transaction in the SEC complaint, but at Cook's insistence, the paragraph was revised and no specific mention was made of the $200,000.

Cook discussed the Vesco case with him three other times, Sporkin testified—when Cook urged him not to worry about the disposition of the $200,000 but only to determine its source and to delay taking a deposition from Harry L. Sears in connection with the handling of the money; in January 1973 when Cook again asked a delay in Sears' deposition (Sporkin said he rejected the request); and in February 1973 when Cook told him "in confidence" that the Vesco money had been a contribution to Nixon and asked the SEC to delay making the fact known until the Finance Committee to Re-elect the President (headed by Stans) disclosed the information. Sporkin said he again refused the request. He asked Cook to have the finance committee stop payment on the check (refunding Vesco's donation), Sporkin said, but Cook told him later that the check had already cleared.

F. Donald Nixon, the older of the President's two brothers, appeared under subpoena April 2. Like other reluctant witnesses for the prosecution, Nixon said he was Mitchell's friend. Nixon also revealed that Mitchell acted as the President's intermediary with him. "I never talked to my brother about anything," Nixon said. "John Mitchell was the man that I was assigned to."

In his brief appearance, Nixon described two attempts made on Vesco's behalf to exploit his family connections. Howard F. Cerny (named in the indictment as a co-conspirator), a mutual friend, had introduced him to Vesco, Nixon testified; but the relationship was only casual and Nixon added that he had met or spoken to Vesco only five or six times.

Other ties were maintained by his son, Donald F. Nixon Jr. Vesco had employed the younger Nixon since shortly before the SEC began its investigation in March 1970 and Nixon said he believed his son was still with the Vesco family in exile in Costa Rica. (Vesco, who had fled the country in early 1973, had successfully fought two efforts at extradition.) The President's nephew also was implicated in Vesco's alleged efforts to use the contribution to quash the SEC probe.

Nixon testified that his son called sometime during Nov. 11–12, 1972 and asked him to call Vesco. Nixon said he complied and agreed to Vesco's request for help in getting an "envelope" to Mitchell. According to Nixon, he refused to supply Vesco with Mitchell's room number at the Essex House hotel in New York but did arrange for delivery of the package by the hotel manager. (The manager had confirmed the delivery in previous testimony.)

The material sent to Mitchell had been entered in evidence during the trial. In it, Vesco allegedly threatened to expose the secret donation unless the SEC investigation were halted. The government also introduced as evidence records showing a call was made to New York from a public phone in Nixon's home in Newport Beach, Calif. (The President had admitted wiretapping his brother's phone calls.)

Nixon said Vesco had made an earlier attempt to use his influence when Cerny asked help in sending a message to the President "just prior to the election" that the continuing SEC investigation "very likely would expose [Vesco's] cash contribution." Nixon testified he replied "there was no way I could do anything." However, "John Mitchell's name came up" and Nixon said he suggested Cerny talk with Mitchell.

In previous testimony before a grand jury, Nixon had said Cerny called Mitchell in his presence, but at the trial Nixon could not recall any phone call being made.

(Nixon was scheduled to retire as an executive of the Marriott Corp., which owned the Essex House hotel, April 15, a company spokesman announced March 22. The decision to leave had been made in January because of Nixon's "ill health" and a company austerity program necessitated by the energy crisis, according to the spokesman. Nixon had sought to quash the subpoena to appear at the Mitchell-Stans trial because of ill health but the motion had been denied.)

The prosecution rested its case April 3 after government lawyers read to the jury a transcript of testimony given by Mitchell and Stans before the grand jury. A total of 40 witnesses had testified for the prosecution.

(Richard E. Clay, an associate of Vesco, a co-defendant in the SEC civil suit and a co-conspirator in the Mitchell-Stans suit, was found in contempt of court March 9 for failing to testify before a federal grand jury. Like Vesco, Clay was believed to be in Costa Rica. His lawyers claimed he had renounced U.S. citizenship in April 1973 and sworn allegiance to Costa Rica.)

Mitchell, Stans present defense. Presiding Judge Lee P. Gagliardi April 5 dismissed one of three obstruction of justice charges against former Cabinet officials John Mitchell and Maurice Stans, who were also accused of conspiracy and perjury in connection with an influence peddling case. According to the government, financier Robert Vesco secretly gave a large campaign donation to Mitchell and Stans for use in President Nixon's 1972 re-election race in payment for their efforts to halt a Securities and Exchange Commission (SEC) investigation of Vesco's mutual funds dealings.

The charge alleging that Mitchell and Stans intervened on Vesco's behalf before March 18, 1971 when the SEC launched its formal investigation of him was dismissed, the court said, because the government produced no evidence of obstruction before this date.

Gagliardi, however, refused a defense motion to dismiss the other 15 charges and the first witness to testify for Mitchell and Stans took the stand April 5. He was Edward C. Nixon, the President's youngest brother. F. Donald Nixon, another brother, earlier had been a reluctant witness for the prosecution.

Edward Nixon refuted prior testimony that Stans had sought a cash (and thereby secret) contribution from Vesco. Stans had expressed no preference as to the form the donation should take, Nixon said, adding that he had relayed the information to Vesco and advised him that a cash contribution would insure anonymity.

According to Nixon, Howard Cerny, a Vesco associate named as a co-conspirator in the trial, called him March 29, 1972 and demanded that he fly to Vesco's New Jersey headquarters. (Nixon said he was working in Washington for the Committee to Re-elect the President at the time.)

At the meeting with Vesco, Cerny, Harry Sears and Laurence Richardson, Nixon said they discussed how to arrange delivery of a secret contribution before a new campaign fund law took effect April 7, 1972 requiring public disclosure of all transactions.

Nixon testified that they asked him to contact Stans, whom Vesco had not been able to reach. He recounted his meeting that same day with Stans in a New York club:

Stans told him, Nixon testified, " 'If they were really concerned so much about anonymity that the contribution should probably be in cash to be absolutely anonymous, but as far as the [finance] committee goes, it made no difference at all how it would be done.' "

Vesco called him in early 1973 to warn him he might be named in Sears' testimony during the conspiracy trial, Nixon testified. He then called Stans, who agreed that their recollections of the conversation "coincided," and also called

Mitchell, Nixon added.

Implying that his testimony had been rehearsed, the prosecution won an admission from Nixon that he "may have tried to call" Murray Chotiner, a political adviser to President Nixon, before he talked with Stans about the conversation. (Chotiner died in January.)

Three lawyers testified April 8 in an effort to prove that Vesco was being harassed by the SEC and that he merely sought the defendants' aid in obtaining relief from his harassment.

Defense strategy suffered a major setback April 9 when Judge Gagliardi refused to permit testimony from four of President Nixon's wealthiest campaign backers. The court ruled that testimony from W. Clement Stone (who contributed $2.1 million), Richard M. Scaife (who gave $1 million), John Mulcahy, Jr. (who gave $600,000) and Max M. Fisher (who gave $125,000), all of whom made their donations anonymously in the pre-April 7, 1972 period, was irrelevant to the case. The defense contended that they would show that Stans' handling of the Vesco donation followed "accepted practices, not fraudulent practices" and would refute the government's implication that Vesco's "$200,000 could buy the country." The contributors would testify they "never expected, never asked for and never received anything in return" for their huge donations, the defense said.

Stone was permitted to testify on another subject. He said Mitchell missed a reception and arrived late at a political dinner Stone had attended March 8, 1972. This conflicted with earlier testimony that Mitchell had talked to an aide just before dinner that evening advising him to "stay away from" the Vesco affair.

Two other witnesses—Robert H. Finch, former Nixon aide and Cabinet official, and DeVan. L. Shumway, former campaign committee official—testified that they had attended a meeting in March 1972 with Stans when it was decided to "honor" pledges made to donors that their pre-April 7, 1972 contributions would be kept secret.

Mitchell takes stand—John Mitchell took the stand in his own defense April 10, 15 and 16. He denied under oath April 10 that he had ever attempted to "fix or quash" the SEC probe of Vesco and that he involved himself in the investigation only once, when he called SEC Chairman William Casey to discuss Vesco's claims of harassment by the SEC staff.

But the impact of Mitchell's emphatic denials of the prosecution's broad charges was lessened by his lapses of memory on crucial points in testimony given by Sears, John Dean, Mark Felt and other government witnesses.

Mitchell, who claimed he "never solicited a [political] contribution in my life," described his first involvement in

President Nixon's campaign. Because of a "rather close relationship" with Nixon, Mitchell said, he "made the mistake that so many people make in getting involved in politics. I was invited to a meeting. It developed that in four or five months someone had to run the [1968] campaign. I was the unfortunate one." (During the period of the alleged conspiracy, Mitchell served as attorney general and then campaign director of the 1972 re-election effort. He resigned shortly after the Watergate break-in in June 1972 to return to private law practice.)

The trial was recessed April 11 and 12 but resumed April 15 with Mitchell's cross-examination. He admitted that he had "willingly contacted" Casey at Sears' request to arrange a meeting for the two men about the Vesco case, but Mitchell denied that the act was at all "improper."

Mitchell said he had been told there was "trench warfare" between Vesco's lawyers and the SEC staff regarding the investigation, which, he said, he believed to involve only minor matters. At the time of the phone call in February 1972, Mitchell testified that he had no knowledge Vesco intended to make a contribution to the Nixon campaign.

He first discussed Vesco with Sears in November 1971, Mitchell testified, when he agreed to get in touch with the U.S. embassy in Switzerland regarding Vesco's jailing on the complaint of a stockholder in Vesco's Swiss-based mutual fund. Rather than using his influence as attorney general to secure Vesco's release, Mitchell said, he merely wanted to "find out what it was all about."

Mitchell claimed to have no recollection of a phone call made April 10, 1972—the day Vesco's cash donation was delivered to Stans—to set up a meeting for Sears and Casey that afternoon. The government showed that the call had been logged in Mitchell's office records.

Under questioning, Mitchell said it "never occurred to me in any form, shape or manner" that Vesco sought a favor in return for the contribution.

"If Mr. Vesco was looking for a favor in return for the $200,000," Mitchell declared, "it would be more than just a meeting with the chairman of the SEC."

Mitchell also denied any knowledge about two "Dear John" letters on the Vesco matter from Sears mailed to Mitchell's home in May and June 1971. Mitchell, who claimed his secretary answered the letters, denied ever seeing them before the trial.

He had "no idea," Mitchell said, why Stans ordered bookkeepers at the finance committee to enter Vesco's secret cash contribution with the notation "JM."

The government concluded its cross examination of Mitchell April 16, focusing on Vesco's threatening memo delivered to Mitchell with the aid of F. Donald Nixon. Mitchell said he regarded Vesco's threat to reveal his secret campaign contribution "'unless the investiga-

tion by the SEC is stopped promptly'" as Vesco's "crude attempt to use muscle on this Administration." But Mitchell conceded he did not report the incident to the SEC or law enforcement officials.

The government contended that the document was evidence of Vesco's attempt to obstruct justice in the SEC probe.

After reading the Vesco memo, Mitchell said he called John Ehrlichman, Nixon's top domestic affairs adviser. Ehrlichman told him "that there had been an attempt by Donald Nixon Jr. [a Vesco aide and son of F. Donald Nixon] and somebody else, a Mr. Straub [another Vesco associate], to go to Key Biscayne [site of the President's Florida villa] and talk to people about the SEC investigation," Mitchell testified. "Ehrlichman had run them off," Mitchell said, "and told them he didn't want to hear anything about it."

The final witness appearing on Mitchell's behalf was Richard Kleindienst, who had succeeded him as attorney general and had also resigned in the aftermath of the Watergate scandal. Kleindienst, testifying April 16, was asked about John Dean's statement that Mitchell asked him to call Kleindienst and complain about his treatment by a "runaway grand jury" in New York investigating the Vesco case.

Kleindienst said he had "no recollection" of the phone call. "I don't believe it [the conversation described by Dean] happened," Kleindienst declared.

Kleindienst described Mitchell as "one of the closest and most intimate friends I've had in my life." He also knew Dean "very well," Kleindienst said, adding that he had brought Dean to the Justice Department and that they had had a "friendly" working relationship.

Under cross-examination, Kleindienst admitted telling the prosecution in September 1973 that "if John Dean said so [regarding the Mitchell conversation], I wouldn't dispute it."

Mitchell had admitted calling Dean, but said it was about "another matter," and he denied complaining about "a hell of a grilling" before the grand jury. The government introduced evidence from a White House tape of Dean's talk with President Nixon subsequent to Mitchell's phone call. According to the transcript, Dean said Mitchell had undergone a "grilling" by a "runaway grand jury."

Mitchell's defense rested after the court ruled it could not summon Sen. Edward Kennedy (D, Mass.) to testify, presumably about a phone call he had allegedly made to William Casey regarding a pending SEC case.

Prosecution: Vesco financed Watergate—In a legal memorandum filed with the court April 4, the government contended it had evidence that Vesco's secret cash contribution was used to finance the Watergate break-in.

A

"Clearly, it is more than just coincidence that Vesco's $200,000 in cash comes in on April 10, 1972 and $200,000 in cash is disbursed to three 'Watergate' figures after April 10, 1972 and neither the receipt nor the disbursements are reported to the General Accounting Office as required by law," the prosecution declared.

B

2 cited for contempt—Two more Vesco business associates were cited for failing to appear before a federal grand jury investigating possible criminal fraud charges against Vesco, the Wall Street Journal reported April 9.

Milton F. Meissner, former president of Vesco's Investors Overseas Services Ltd. (IOS), and Gilbert R. J. Straub were named in the contempt citation. Richard Clay had also been found in civil contempt for failing to testify before the grand jury. Vesco, Clay, Meissner, Straub and others were defendants in the SEC's suit charging them with "looting" $224 million from IOS and other Vesco-controlled companies.

C

Straub was reported to be in Costa Rica with Vesco, a fugitive from several U.S. warrants for his arrest. Meissner, released on bail in March after spending nearly a year in a Luxembourg jail on charges of fraud related to the IOS affair, was believed to be in the Bahamas with Clay.

D

Stans testifies—Maurice Stans testified in his own defense April 17–19, consistently denying that Vesco had received special considerations for the campaign contribution and that the contribution had been kept secret for devious purposes.

Under direct examination April 17, Stans maintained that the $200,000 cash gift was kept secret because privacy was Vesco's "constitutional right under the law." According to Stans, the contribution was committed before the April 7, 1972 cutoff date for keeping such gifts legally secret, and it was therefore legal to maintain the "privacy" Vesco had requested, although the money was not received until April 10, 1972. Vesco was not unique in requesting and receiving anonymity, Stans said: "I was doing my best to protect Robert Vesco and every other contributor up to April 7."

E

F

Refuting prosecution testimony that he had requested the donation be made in cash, Stans described the key meeting with Vesco on March 8, 1972, when the money was pledged. Vesco offered the money, Stans said, but demanded "maximum privacy." Stans said he replied that this might require making the donation before April 7, possibly in cash, but that "it's the money that counts, not the form."

G

Stans added that it was he who brought up the matter of the SEC investigation at the meeting, not Vesco. As Stans quoted Vesco's reply: "That has been going on almost a year. We have been trying to resolve it. But the problem was that the SEC was harassing us and we haven't been able to sit down and settle it." Stans told Vesco that it "should be no problem. Anybody having trouble with a government agency should be able to go to the head of that agency." Stans said he added "something to the effect that 'I hope you work out your SEC matter satisfactorily.' "

Stans said, however, that he held back on accepting the gift until he could "check [Vesco] out" with Mitchell. In a subsequent conversation, he and Mitchell agreed that "under the circumstances that existed at that time" it would be proper to accept the money. But Stans denied that he had asked Mitchell for an appointment with Vesco, had sent Vesco to Mitchell's office, or had said anything about arranging a meeting with the SEC chairman through Mitchell.

Stans recounted that when the money was delivered on April 10, 1972 by Laurence B. Richardson Jr., a Vesco associate, Richardson "mumbled" something like "Vesco hopes this will be of some help."

Stans denied, however, that Richardson had referred to the "SEC problem" or that Stans had replied "Mitchell and [Harry] Sears [a co-defendant scheduled for separate trial] are handling that," as Richardson had testified earlier.

Still under direct examination, Stans sought to blunt the damaging testimony of prosecution witness G. Bradford Cook, former general counsel and later chairman of the SEC.

Stans said that when Cook first mentioned the secret $200,000 in November 1972, Cook had said the SEC knew that Vesco had brought that amount in cash into the U.S., but that the agency did not know the purpose of the money. Stans said he declined to give Cook any further information and later sought the advice of John W. Dean 3rd, then White House counsel, as to whether Cook should be told of the campaign gift. According to Stans, Dean suggested that Stans was not obligated to volunteer the information and that "if the SEC wants information they should ask for it in a more formal way."

Stans testified that, contrary to Cook's testimony, Cook had later offered, without any urging from Stans, to delete a specific reference to the amount of the campaign gift from the complaint against Vesco.

When a grand jury later began investigating the handling of the Vesco case, Stans had—according to Cook—asked Cook to perjure himself to conceal the alleged political interference in the SEC probe. But Stans denied having opened a meeting with Cook with the comment: "Brad, let's have one of those conversations that doesn't take place," and denied urging Cook during that and subsequent meetings to lie in order to back up Stans' own grand jury testimony.

Near the conclusion of Stans' direct testimony April 18, Judge Lee P. Gagliardi overruled prosecution objections and allowed Stans to describe his anguish over his wife's serious illness, which, Stans said, could have clouded his memory of events between August and December 1972 and accounted for discrepancies in his grand jury testimony.

In cross-examination April 18–19, prosecutor John R. Wing attacked Stans' contention that Vesco had been treated the same as others who had donated before the April 7, 1972 deadline. After conceding that Vesco "was the largest contributor who gave exclusively in cash," Stans said "thank-you letters" had been sent to major contributors making secret donations. Wing asked whether such a letter was sent to Vesco. "I don't know," Stans replied. Wing also established that others who promised gifts before the deadline were not told they could deliver the funds later, and questioned the propriety of Stans' considering the money as "cash on hand" even before it was delivered.

In one heated exchange, Wing confronted Stans with statements before the grand jury and his trial testimony on the reasons for the anonymity of Vesco's contribution, suggesting that Stans had testified falsely on both occasions. When Wing accused Stans of giving the grand jury "complete fabrications," Stans replied that he had given his "best recollections," and again cited the "anxiety" over his wife's illness. The answer was stricken from the record after Wing's objection.

The prosecution also managed to imply that the Vesco money might have been involved in financing the Watergate break-in and cover-up, suggesting that a $350,000 bank deposit—which included the Vesco gift—was intended to cover the earlier withdrawal of the same amount for a cash fund controlled by presidential aide H. R. Haldeman. Stans denied knowledge of specific cash disbursements by the re-election committee and maintained that the identical amounts were "purely coincidental." The line of questioning led to an unsuccessful mistrial motion by the defense.

Testimony in the trial ended April 22 with the appearance of prosecution rebuttal witnesses. John Dean, who had testified earlier, took the stand again to refute aspects of Stans' direct testimony. Contrary to Stans' contentions, Dean said he had not advised Stans to withhold details of the Vesco contribution from Cook and the SEC. Dean also testified that at a meeting he attended with Stans and Mitchell, Stans had said he could have the SEC eliminate references to the $200,000 from the formal complaint against Vesco.

Washington Post reporter Sally Quinn testified in rebuttal of Mitchell's testimony that he had arrived at a campaign fund-raising affair too late to have told campaign aide Daniel W. Hofgren to "stay away from" the Vesco matter.

While Hofgren had said Mitchell made the remark during a cocktail reception preceding a dinner, Mitchell denied the statement and maintained that he had arrived only in time for the dinner. Quinn, however, said she had spoken to Mitchell at the reception and had seen him circulate among other guests.

Mitchell-Stans case goes to jury. A federal jury in New York City April 25 began deliberating conspiracy, obstruction of justice and perjury charges against former Attorney General John N. Mitchell and former Commerce Secretary Maurice H. Stans, who were also top officials in President Nixon's 1972 re-election campaign.

The case went to the jury after 42 days of testimony from 59 witnesses. The final days of the trial were highlighted by the often emotional testimony of Stans, who sought to explain that his alleged false statements to a grand jury were not intentional, but attributable to a faulty memory caused by distress over his wife's serious illness. And, Stans swore, he "never did anything to help Robert Vesco."

Mitchell, Stans acquitted. John N. Mitchell and Maurice H. Stans, former Cabinet officials in the Nixon Administration and directors of President Nixon's 1972 re-election campaign, were acquitted by a federal district court jury in New York City April 28 of all charges stemming from a secret cash campaign contribution from Robert L. Vesco, the financier whose mutual funds dealings were under investigation by the Securities and Exchange Commission (SEC).

The government had accused Mitchell and Stans of conspiracy, obstruction of justice and perjury for attempting to block the SEC investigation and later lying to a grand jury about their roles.

The verdict was widely seen as a significant boost to Nixon's campaign against impeachment, partly because the Vesco issue would be effectively removed from consideration by the House Judiciary Committee, but more importantly to some observers, because the credibility of former presidential counsel John W. Dean 3rd was brought into question. Dean had been a principal witness against Mitchell and Stans and was one of the President's chief accusers.

(Nixon's official reaction was relayed by a spokesman: "The President was very pleased for the two men and their families.")

Interviewed after the verdict, jurors on the panel of nine men and three women said the basic issue in their 26 hours of deliberations had been the credibility of government witnesses vs. that of the defendants.

According to forewoman Sybil Kucharski, a bank teller, the jury turned to the perjury charges after reaching an early impasse on the conspiracy and obstruction of justice counts. Verdicts of not guilty were reached on the perjury counts after lengthy debate, Miss Kucharski said; after that, "the rest was easy."

Miss Kucharski said she did not "want to say Mr. Dean was lying, but he was often unbelievable." A factor in the jury's consideration of Dean's testimony, she said, was the fact that he had already pleaded guilty to other Watergate charges and therefore had something to gain—leniency in sentencing—for cooperating with the government in other cases. On the other hand, she said, "We didn't feel [Mitchell and Stans] had the need" to lie. "They were credible men."

Other prosecution witnesses also suffered credibility problems, according to some jurors. Harry L. Sears, the politician, Vesco attorney and head of the Nixon campaign in New Jersey who had given lengthy testimony, was one of those—along with Vesco—who "seemed to want to get something going" to block the SEC probe, according to juror Clarence Brown, a letter carrier. "I don't think the defendants ever fell for it," Brown added. (Both Sears and Vesco had also been indicted, and Sears was scheduled for a separate trial.)

Another juror, who did not want to be named, said of former SEC Chairman G. Bradford Cook—who had given seemingly damaging testimony against Stans: "How could we believe [Cook] when he had lied so many times before. And he admitted his perjury on the stand."

In an interview April 29, juror Andrew Choa, a bank vice president, said Dean's

testimony had actually played a "relatively minor part" in the case. While Dean "certainly was not ignored" in the deliberations, Choa said, his only substantive role was in connection with one of the six perjury counts against Mitchell.

(Vice President Gerald R. Ford, who had created controversy with his earlier comments on Dean's veracity in relation to Nixon, said in a statement April 29 that the Mitchell-Stans verdict "says to me that John Dean's credibility has been severely eroded.")

According to some jurors and chief prosecutor John R. Wing, another major factor in the case was the absence of Vesco, who had escaped extradition and was a fugitive in Costa Rica. Wing said, "If we could have gotten Vesco back it would have been different."

Vesco was quoted by CBS News from Costa Rica April 28 as being "very pleased" with "the first fair verdict in a long time." Vesco added, however, "I have no desire to come back, favorable verdict or not."

St. Clair on acquittals. President Nixon's special counsel James D. St. Clair, referring April 30 to the recent acquittal of former Nixon Cabinet members John N. Mitchell and Maurice H. Stans in their New York trial, said they "demonstrate the wisdom of the President's actions in insisting that the orderly process of the judicial system be utilized to determine the guilt or innocence of individuals charged with crime, rather than participating in trials in the public media."

Questions raised in Silbert nomination. Sen. Sam J. Ervin (D, N.C.), chairman of the Senate Watergate committee, June 18 criticized the Justice Department for prosecuting Mitchell and Stans for conspiracy while not bringing felony charges against them for accepting the Vesco contribution. Ervin's comments came during Senate Judiciary Committee hearings on the nomination of Earl J. Silbert as U.S. attorney for the District of Columbia. [For further details, see p. 173E1]

Nixon Fights Subpoenas & Impeachment

Nixon's Chicago appearance. In a Chicago appearance March 15, President Nixon stressed his determination not to resign and to resist the demand of the House impeachment committee for more White House documents and tapes. The televised appearance, at a luncheon of the Executives' Club of Chicago, was attended by about 2,000 persons. The format was an hour-long question and answer period.

The questions were diverse and largely general, and the President's answers were well-received. More than 1,000 demonstrators, pro- and anti-Nixon, gathered outside the meeting site. He had been greeted at the airport the night before by Chicago Mayor Richard J. Daley, who attended the luncheon with the President.

Most of the questions covered domestic issues, and most of these involved Watergate and impeachment or resignation issues. The energy shortage drew three queries, inflation one. The only other topics raised were about politics as a profession—should youth enter it—and the presidency—should the U.S. adopt a procedure for a vote of confidence in the presidency between elections? Nixon opposed the latter, saying the founders of the U.S. had rejected the principle because of "a need for stability in the chief executive." "If a president is always watching the polls to see what he should or should not do," Nixon said, "he will be a weak president." He did not think "that a vote of confidence coming up, with the people or the Congress for that matter, being able to throw a president out because he happens to be unpopular, would be in the national interest, apart from the president's interest."

He thought the Republican prospects in 1976 were good if the Administration accomplished some of its goals—prosperity without war; less inflation, crime and drug addiction; welfare reform and a health care program.

Among his other remarks:

Resignation—In brief opening remarks, Nixon promised to return before the group after he had completed his term of office—"which I expect to do three years from now."

He amplified this position in response to a query whether it would not be better, because of the adverse effect of Watergate on the nation, if he were to resign and "allow yourself the public forum as a private citizen to answer all accusations on all parts."

Nixon replied that "the nation and the world needs a strong president" and, from a personal standpoint, "resignation is an easy copout; resignation, of course, might satisfy some of my good friendly partisans who would rather not have the problem of Watergate bothering them.

"On the other hand, apart from the personal standpoint, resignation of this President on charges of which he is not guilty, resignation simply because he happened to be low in the polls, would forever change our form of government. It would lead to weak and unstable presidencies in the future and I will not be a party to the destruction of the presidency of the United States of America."

If a president resigned when he was not guilty of charges, Nixon said, "then every president in the future could be forced out of office by simply leveling some charges and getting the media to carry them and getting a few congressmen and senators who were on the other side to exploit them."

He conceded that Watergate "has had a disturbing effect" on people and it was "wrong and very stupid to begin with." But he believed it had been "over-publicized and a lot of charges have been made that frankly have proved to be false." He said charges against him were "totally false."

He was sure many had heard of such charges: "That the President helped to plan the Watergate thing before and had knowledge of it; that the President was informed of the cover-up on Sept. 15 of 1972; that the President was informed that payments were being made on March 13, [1973] and that a blackmail attempt was being made on the White House on March 13, rather than on March the 21st when I said was the first time those matters were brought to my attention. That the President had authorized the issuance of clemency or a promise of clemency to some of the defendants, and that the President had

ordered the burglarizing—again, a very stupid act, apart from the fact that it's wrong and illegal—of Dr. Ellsberg's psychiatrist's office in California. Now all of those charges have been made. Many Americans—perhaps a majority—believe them. They are all totally false and the investigation will prove it, whatever the Congress does—the tapes, etc.—when they all come out, will establish that they are false."

March 21 meeting again cited—Nixon again directed remarks at that March 21, 1973 meeting, when he said he first learned "that a blackmail attempt was being made on the White House." He learned then for the first time, Nixon said, "that payments had been made to the defendants. And let me point out that payments had been made, but—correcting what may have been a misapprehension, when I spoke to the press on March the 6th in Washington—it was alleged that the payments that had been made to the defendants were made for the purpose of keeping them still. However Mr. Ehrlichman, Mr. Haldeman, Mr. Mitchell had all denied that that was the case and they certainly should be allowed the right in court to establish their innocence or guilt without our concluding that that was the case."

(A White House official said March 15, in reference to Nixon's Chicago remarks, that "the President doesn't want to prejudge the case. He was told allegations. He was only dealing with allegations." The President had been expected to deal with apparent conflicts in his previous versions of the March 21, 1973 meeting. White House spokesman Gerald L. Warren said March 18 the President "covered the point" in his Chicago appearance.)

In response to a query about who should define "an impeachable offense," Congress or the judiciary, Nixon said the Constitution defined it "as being treason, bribery or other high crimes or misdemeanors." "Now this President is not guilty of any of those crimes," he said, "and as far as the Congress is concerned, it would seem to me that particularly members of the Judiciary Committee . . . would want to follow the Constitution rather than to broaden that definition to include something that the Constitution framers did not have in mind."

Cooperation with House inquiry—Nixon said "we have cooperated" with the House impeachment inquiry, and had turned over to it the material furnished the special prosecutor plus "several caseloads of documents" from five different executive departments and two agencies. It seemed "reasonable" to him that the committee should first examine that material because the special prosecutor "said that he had what he considered to be the full story of Watergate—and we want the full story out."

Nixon again opposed giving the committee "a fishing license or a complete right to go in and go through all the Presidential files in order to find out whether or not there is a possibility that some action had been taken which might be and might result in an impeachable offense."

"It isn't the question that the President has something to hide," he said. It was necessary to protect the confidentiality of presidential conversations "and if that confidentiality principle is completely destroyed, future presidents will not have the benefit of the kind of advice that an executive needs to make the right decision. He will be surrounded by a group of eunuchs insofar as their advice is concerned . . . In order to make the right decision you have to have opinion expressed very freely, discussed very freely from a completely wide range."

"But when you come to the point of simply saying to a committee of Congress," Nixon continued, "without regard to relevancy, before they determine what they say is an impeachable offense, just come in and paw through the documents, it would lead" to delay of resolution of the matter and erode the principle of confidentiality.

The President was asked if he would consider testifying on behalf of former colleagues if it was vital to their defense. Nixon said for the President to appear in court for such a purpose "would be setting a precedent that would be most unfortunate."

Personal taxes—Nixon said Sen. Russell B. Long (D, La.), chairman of the Congressional panel investigating his tax returns, and the panel's ranking Republican, Sen. Wallace Bennett (Utah), were correct in indicating "there's been no evidence of fraud on the part of the President. There may be evidence that he may owe more taxes, due primarily, apparently, to the debatable technical point as to whether a gift of three-quarters of a million dollars worth of Presidential papers, which was delivered three months before the deadline, whether the paperwork on it was completed in time to qualify for the deduction.

"If it was completed in time, as I understand it, I get the deduction. If it was not

completed in time, I don't get the deduction. I pay the tax and the government gets to keep the papers.

"Well, under the circumstances that's hard for me to realize, but the President, when the I.R.S. is concerned, I assure you, is just another citizen and even more so. And that's perfectly proper."

Nixon visits Nashville. President and Mrs. Nixon attended the dedication ceremonies for a new building housing the Grand Ole Opry in Nashville, Tenn. March 16. Nixon told the 4,400 persons present, who responded enthusiastically, that "country music radiates a love of this nation—patriotism." The President also tried out a yo-yo given him on-stage by country music star Roy Acuff and rendered a few old favorites on the piano.

Mrs. Nixon had just returned from her visit to Latin America.

At the airport, the Nixons were greeted after their separate arrivals by Gov. Winfield Dunn (R) and a campaign-style rally of supporters gathered in a hangar. Anti-Nixon demonstrators protested outside.

(The Nixons returned to Washington that night and the President was host at church services in the White House March 17 conducted by the Rev. Dr. Norman Vincent Peale.)

Nixon's Houston news conference. President Nixon followed his Chicago appearance with a similar session in Houston March 19 before a convention of the National Association of Broadcasters (NAB).

The same topics dominated the hour-long question and answer appearance— the Watergate scandal, his resignation and cooperation with the impeachment inquiry. Nixon discussed his Middle East and European policies, and reiterated his optimistic assessment of the economy—a leveling off of inflation by midyear, especially in food prices.

A group of invited broadcast journalists, mainly from the South and Southwest, asked about his attitude toward the press and about the GIs still listed as missing in action in Southeast Asia.

The audience response, as in Chicago, was predominantly friendly, although several sharp questions also drew applause and there was a visible tension in the President's reaction to two of the sharpest questions posed by regular White House network correspondents, Dan Rather of CBS and Tom Brokaw of NBC.

Among the highlights:

Cooperation with House inquiry—Nixon reiterated his stand that he had cooperated with the House impeachment committee and would cooperate because he wanted to get the story out. "We want them to have all the facts they need to

conduct a thorough inquiry," he said. "Dragging out Watergate drags down America, and I want to bring it to a conclusion as quickly as we can."

But, he said, "the committee has enough information to conduct its investigation" and he was "following the precedent that every President, Democrat and Republican, since the time of Washington has followed, and that is defending the confidentiality of presidential conversations and communications."

Presidential advisers must have the assurance, Nixon said, "that anything they say, even though it's very unpopular at the moment," was not going to be made public later or the president would find only "a bunch of yes men around him, or ones that are going to play it so safe that he isn't going to get the variety of views he needs to make the right kind of decision."

Network correspondents Rather and Brokaw pursued the point. How could the House meet its constitutional responsibility to pursue the impeachment inquiry if "you, the person under investigation, are allowed to limit their access to potential evidence?" Rather asked.

The House, like the President, Nixon said, was bound by the Constitution and it specifically stated "that a president shall be impeached for treason, bribery or other high crimes or misdemeanors. It is the Constitution that defines what the House should have access to and the limits of its investigation. And I am suggesting that the House follow the Constitution. If they do, I will."

Brokaw suggested the President's reference to precedent—that past presidents withheld or championed withholding of material from Congress in the course of an impeachment inquiry—was "historically inaccurate or at least misleading." Nixon replied that the principle of confidentiality "still stands" because "if all that a Congress, under the control of an opposition party, has to do in order to get a president out of office was to make an unreasonable demand to go through all of the files of the presidency— a demand which a president would have to refuse—then it would mean that no president would be strong enough to stay in office, to resist that kind of demand and that kind of pressure. It would lead to instability. And it would destroy, as I've indicated before, the principle of confidentiality."

He was trying to meet the demands of Congress, Nixon said, and "trying to be as forthcoming as possible," but he also had "another responsibility. I must think not of myself, but I must think also of future presidents of this country, and I am not going to do anything, and I am not going to give up to any demand I believe would weaken the presidency."

March 21, 1973 conversation—The President was again asked about his recollection of the Watergate meeting on

March 21, 1973. His recent statement (March 6) was incorrect, Nixon said "insofar as it said that I learned that payments had been made prior to the time that the demand for blackmail by Mr. Hunt—alleged demand for blackmail, I should say, since it has not yet been tried—that payments had been made for the purpose of keeping defendants still. I should have said they were alleged to have been made, because, as a matter of fact, those who were alleged to have made payments to defendants for their defense fees and for their support—Mr. Ehrlichman, Mr. Haldeman, Mr. Mitchell—all have denied that that was the case. They have said it was only for the support of the defendants, and only for their attorneys' fees, which would be completely proper."

Further comment would be inappropriate because of pending court cases, he said.

Running his own campaign—Would the country have been better served if the Watergate break-in had gone undetected? the President was asked.

"Certainly not," Nixon replied. It was "wrong" and "stupid" and "should never have happened" and "should not have been covered up and I have done the very best that I can over the past year to see that it is uncovered."

"When something happens like this, to say, cover it up, forget it, when it is wrong, this of course is completely against our American system of values and I would very, very seriously deplore it."

After his 1960 campaign, Nixon said, he had been criticized "that I always ran my own campaigns." But in 1972 he had been "too busy" with foreign affairs and "frankly paid too little attention to the campaign." His advice to candidates was "run your own campaign, regardless of what the press says."

Attitude toward press—A questioner referred to Nixon's remark after losing the 1962 California gubernatorial election "that the press wouldn't have Nixon to kick around any more." Did Nixon still feel that the press was "kicking" him around again?

An adversary relationship between the President and the press was "healthy" and "good," Nixon replied. The press had a right to criticize the President and the President had the right of self defense, he said. He suggested a rule: "The President should treat the press just as fairly as the press treats him."

A Nixon charge in October 1973 that network broadcast reporting was "vicious" and "distorted" was also brought up. Did he still feel victimized by television reporting?

Nixon said he realized "bad news is news and good news is not news" and that "people don't win Pulitzer prizes by being for. They usually win them by being against."

"I am not upset by how the press reports me. I'm going to do my job, and I am not going to be diverted by any criticism from the press—fair or unfair—from doing what I think I was elected to do, and that's to bring peace abroad and I trust, prosperity without war and without inflation."

Space Center visit—President Nixon toured the National Aeronautics & Space Administration's Johnson Space Center in Houston March 20 and presented Distinguished Service Medals to Skylab III crewmen, Gerald P. Carr, Edward G. Gibson and William R. Pogue. Supporters and protesters were on the scene.

Nixon told a crowd of workers that the unknown should be explored. "You're only a failure when you give up," he said.

Before touring the center, the President met with Texas Republican leaders at a closed meeting, where he received a "very supportive introduction" from his former Treasury secretary, John B. Connally, Jr., according to GOP National Chairman George Bush, who also attended.

GOP leader backs panel. Rep. John B. Anderson (Ill.), chairman of the House Republican Conference, said March 17 that President Nixon should release all evidence requested by the Judiciary Committee for its impeachment study. Continued resistance by the President, Anderson warned, would cost him support among House Republicans.

In a television interview, Anderson praised Chairman Peter Rodino for restraining "the somewhat more impatient members" of the panel from a confrontation with the White House on the issue of executive privilege. The committee's procedures, Anderson said, had been "careful" and "in accordance with the mandate we have under the Constitution."

Anderson warned that it would be a mistake for Nixon to adopt a strategy in his public appearances of going to the country "over the heads" of Congress and the committee; the committee, he added, should not be "reviled" or "demeaned in any way."

Mills predicts Nixon to quit. Rep. Wilbur D. Mills (D, Ark.) predicted March 17 that President Nixon would be forced to leave the presidency by November. Mills, chairman of the House Ways and Means Committee, made the statement during questioning on CBS-TV's Face the Nation program.

Asked whether Nixon would leave office by resignation or impeachment, Mills replied, "one or the other." If the House voted on impeachment, Mills predicted, a surprising number of Republicans would vote in favor of it.

Mills offered to sponsor legislation to grant Nixon immunity from "persecution or prosecution" in the event he resigns. "If it takes this to protect him, and he's willing to resign under that condition," Mills asserted, "certainly I would make every effort to pass such legislation in the House." Mills said he doubted the House would vote such protection if Nixon was impeached.

Standing at record lows—President Nixon's standing was at its lowest level ever in both the Gallup and Harris surveys, published March 20. Gallup reported a 25% approval rating (64% disapproval), Harris 26% approval (71% disapproval). The Gallup survey was conducted Feb. 22–25 and March 1-4. The Harris sampling was taken March 3–7.

The previous Gallup rating published March 3 (sampling Feb. 8–11 and Feb. 15–18) was 27% approval, 63% disapproval. Nixon's Harris standing on March 7 (sampling Feb. 18–22) was 29%. Harris also found a 46%–41% plurality for the statement that Nixon had "reached the point where he can no longer be an effective President and should resign."

Sirica directs report to House panel. U.S. District Court Judge John J. Sirica ruled March 18 that a secret grand jury report and compilation of evidence dealing with President Nixon's role in the Watergate case should be released to the House Judiciary Committee for its impeachment investigation. The grand jury had submitted the material to Sirica March 1 with its indictment of seven former White House and campaign aides in connection with the Watergate cover-up.

The U.S. Court of Appeals upheld the decision March 21. [See below]

Noting that "the person on whom the report focuses, the President," had not objected to its release to the committee, Sirica emphasized the "compelling need" for an "unswervingly fair" impeachment inquiry "based on all the pertinent information." He added that it was the committee's "responsibility to determine the significance of the evidence," and that he was offering no opinion as to relevance.

Sirica said Nixon was referred to in the report "in his public capacity, and, on balance with the public interest, any prejudice to his legal rights caused by disclosure to the committee would be minimal." The report was not an indictment, Sirica noted, "and the President would not be left without a forum in which to adjudicate any charges against him that might employ report materials."

All of these considerations, Sirica said, "might well justify even a public disclosure of the report, but are certainly ample basis for disclosure to a body that in this setting acts simply as another grand jury."

Sirica emphasized that the report drew no "accusatory conclusions" and was "not a substitute for indictments." It contained no recommendations, advice or statements that might "infringe on the prerogatives of other branches of government"; in fact, Sirica added, the grand jury's only recommendation was to the court and therefore sustained separation of powers principles rather than "injuring" them. The report rendered "no moral or social judgments," and according to Sirica, was "a simple and straightforward compilation of information gathered by the grand jury, and no more."

In reaching his decision, Sirica dealt with two objections by attorneys for the cover-up defendants, who, he noted, were the only parties protesting release of the report. The form and content of the report were central to Sirica's rejection of their contention that the grand jury had no right to issue such a report. Citing numerous precedents—including some in which other grand jury reports had been suppressed—Sirica said the Watergate grand jury had "obviously taken care" to assure that its report contained no "objectionable features" that might taint it. Sirica added that the grand jury had "acted in the interests of fairness" and had "respected its own limitations and the rights of others"; therefore, he ruled, the court should "respect the jury's exercise of its prerogatives."

Regarding the objection that disclosure might harm the rights of the cover-up defendants, Sirica said mention of them in the report was only "incidental" and that their trials would provide "ample opportunity" for them to respond to such references, none of which went beyond allegations in the indictment. Considerations of possible adverse publicity were both "premature and speculative," Sirica ruled.

Sirica added, however, that while the House committee had taken measures to prevent improper disclosures of evidence, he should caution them again to use the report "with due regard for avoiding any unnecessary interference" with fair trials for the accused.

Sirica sidestepped the White House's only request regarding the report: that presidential counsel be allowed to review and copy the material. He said the request was, "more properly the committee's concern" and that he would defer to the chairman for a response to the White House.

Appeal denied—The U.S. Circuit Court of Appeals in Washington March 21 upheld Judge Sirica's decision to release the grand jury report on Nixon to the House Judiciary Committee. In a 5–1 decision (three judges had disqualified themselves) the court cited the significance of the fact that President Nixon—"described by all parties as the focus of the report and who presumably would have the greatest interest in its disposition"—had not objected to its release.

Judge George E. MacKinnon, who concurred in part with the majority decision, filed a dissent in which he argued that instead of the "selective evidence" compiled by the grand jury, the House panel should have access to all the grand jury's proceedings. Such a procedure, MacKinnon suggested, would insure that the committee received "potentially exculpatory material" favoring Nixon. The court, which had taken custody of the file late

the previous day, did not indicate whether it had reviewed the material.

Having failed in an attempt the previous day to persuade Sirica to reconsider his decision and grant an indefinite stay of the release order, attorneys for cover-up defendants H. R. Haldeman and Gordon C. Strachan argued before the appeals court that release of the report would create an "avalanche" of publicity prejudicial to their clients. John J. Wilson, representing Haldeman, contended that Sirica's order was an "abuse" of judicial discretion, because the material would almost certainly be made public.

Philip A. Lacovara, counsel for the special prosecutor, called Wilson's arguments "sheer speculation." Under questioning by Chief Judge David L. Bazelon, Lacovara said the prosecution was aware of the risk that the indictments might have to be dismissed because of publicity. Citing the safeguards available to insure fair trials, Lacovara said the prosecution was willing to assume this risk.

The court gave the defense lawyers until March 25 to file an appeal with the Supreme Court.

House panel focuses on evidence request—Members of the House Judiciary Committee March 18 praised Judge Sirica's decision that the panel was entitled to the grand jury's report on Nixon, but emphasized that their primary concern was still the request for tapes and documents refused by the White House.

Rep. Tom Railsback (R, Ill.) cited one section of Sirica's opinion as a "summary" of the committee's position: in Sirica's words, the "compelling need" for a fair inquiry "based on all the pertinent information."

Rep. Jerome R. Waldie (D, Calif.) said that with Sirica's decision, "the impeachment process now moves to a climax," and warned that lack of cooperation from the White House "will not prevent the committee from performing its constitutional responsibility."

A similar position was expressed by Rep. Lawrence J. Hogan (R, Md.), who added that he was "frankly disturbed" by recent presidential comments which "presume to dictate to the committee its responsibilities."

Regarding appeal of the decision by the cover-up defendants, Chairman Peter W. Rodino (D, N.J.) said the committee would not take part directly in litigation but would make known its position that it had a constitutional right to all evidence relating to the President's conduct.

Rodino said that while he did not yet want to state an official position on the White House request to examine and copy the grand jury report, his personal inclination would be to reject it. Rep. John J. Conyers Jr. (D, Mich.) said Sirica's deference to Rodino on such a decision gave the panel new leverage in its struggle for presidential tapes. He added he would not want the White House "to pull up to the . . . committee and paw through our

files and cart documents away in a truck."

Official White House reaction to Sirica's decision was Deputy Press Secretary Gerald L. Warren's reiteration that Nixon did not object to release of the report. Other officials said there would be no appeal by anyone representing the President and denied speculation that John J. Wilson, the attorney for H. R. Haldeman, was acting indirectly for Nixon in filing an appeal.

Sirica steps down as chief judge—Sirica's decision on the grand jury's secret report on the President came on the last day of his term as chief judge for the D.C. district. Sirica reached the mandatory retirement age of 70 the next day. He was to continue as a judge, however, and remain active in the Watergate case. He had already assigned himself to the trial of the cover-up defendants.

Sirica's successor as chief judge was George L. Hart Jr.

Buckley urges resignation. Sen. James L. Buckley (Conservative-Republican, N.Y.) urged President Nixon March 19 to resign because he had lost his 1972 election mandate to carry out his proclaimed goals.

In a public statement, Buckley proposed "an extraordinary act of statesmanship," the act of "Richard Nixon's own voluntary resignation." The "trauma" of Watergate had stripped Nixon of the ability to fulfill his mandate, Buckley said, and there was a "spreading cynicism" about the policical process and "a perception of corruption that has effectively destroyed the President's ability to speak from a position of moral leadership." There was also a "widespread conviction," he said, "that Watergate and all that it has brought in its wake has done unique and perhaps irrevocable damage to our entire system of government."

Referring to Nixon's defense that his resignation would weaken the office of the presidency, Buckley said "precisely the opposite is the case." The office had been "irrevocably weakened by a long slow agonizing inch-by-inch process of attrition," and was "in danger of succumbing to the death of a thousand cuts," he said. "The only way to save it is for the current President to resign, leaving the office free to defend itself with a new incumbent."

Buckley agreed with Nixon's argument that loss of office from low poll standings would destroy the presidency, but he said it did not apply in current circumstances since Nixon's popularity loss reflected "a cumulative loss of faith that has eroded his credibility and moral authority . . . beyond repair."

Buckley said a resignation would be "an act of sacrifice" for achievement of his goals since he would be succeeded by a person who upheld his policies.

"We need the balance wheel that alone can be provided by a president able to exercise the full authority of his office," Buckley said, "or we run the risk of a runaway Congress that could commit us to new and dangerous programs from which we may never be able to extricate ourselves."

"There is little point in protecting the office of the president if at the same time irreparable damage is done to the republic as we have known it."

Resignation was the only way to resolve the crisis, Buckley said, impeachment could not. A Senate trial would be "a Roman circus" and either verdict—to convict or not to convict—would leave an "embittered" segment of the electorate. One would think "that the media had hounded" Nixon out of office, the other that "Congress had placed political expediency above its duty."

In another reference to the media, Buckley said he was "reluctant to provide any degree of satisfaction to those in and out of the media who have been exploiting the Watergate affair so recklessly," those who "have made such wholesale use of slanderous gossip, violations of grand jury secrecy, leaks of confidential documents and meetings" and other devices.

Nixon reaction—Nixon said at his news conference later March 19 that Buckley's plea "does not cause me to reassess my position." While it might be an act of courage "to run away from a job that you were elected to do," he said, "it also takes courage to stand and fight for what you believe is right, and that's what I intend to do."

To resign because of false charges and a popularity decline, Nixon said, "might be good politics but it would be bad statesmanship. . . . It would mean that our system of government would be changed for all presidents . . . [and it would mean] a very unstable government."

Congressional reaction—Buckley's call for Nixon's resignation did not generate a positive response from conservatives in Congress, but the impact of his announcement was clear. (The only other Republican senator to call for Nixon's resignation was Edward W. Brooke [Mass.], liberal.)

Buckley's statement was described as "devastating" by Sen. Bill Brock (R, Tenn.) March 19. Sen. Charles H. Percy (R, Ill.) said Buckley's stand made the situation "more perilous" for the President.

Sen. Barry Goldwater (R, Ariz.) said Nixon's resignation at this time would involve questions of fair play and of precedent, "whereby any man in the White House who was philosophically unacceptable to certain politicians and segments of the media might be forced to resign." But, he said, "if any evidence of criminal act on the part of the President is proven, I shall change my position and support the Buckley proposal."

Sen. Jesse A. Helms (R, N.C.) agreed that Nixon should resign only if he was guilty.

Rep. Dan Kuykendall (R, Tenn.) objected to Buckley's call as "most dangerous." "His willingness to see a man forced out of office without proof of impeachable conduct," he said, "shows a lack of understanding as to how this republic was formed and how it operates."

Among the comment March 20: Sen. Jacob K. Javits (R, N.Y.) said that he preferred "to press forward with early action by the House of Representatives on impeachment." As for resignation, "it's not my bag," he said, "at this time."

Senate Republican whip Robert P. Griffin (Mich.) said Buckley's call "is bound to have a profound impact."

Rep. John Rousselot (R, Calif.) said "there is quite a lot of disgust with what has been going on" but "conservatives don't want to lead the charge." If the House voted impeachment, "and I don't know that they will," he said, "and the Senate started the proceeding and it became obvious that events were going against the President, he might take another view of resignation." "Maybe this is what Wilbur Mills was trying to say," he added.

Buckley said during an NBC television interview March 20 that conservatives were "deeply concerned over much of what we have learned about the activities of some of the people in and around the Presidency, activities that are inherently shocking, inherently indefensible."

(Howard Phillips of the American Conservative Union said March 20 that "What Buckley has done is pull a plug on the President's most important political reservoir." While it did not mean "that all the water will flow out," he said, "it does mean that conservatives will reassess whether the issues they care most about can be served by continued support for President Nixon." The ACU had sent the White House that week statements from 35 conservative members of Congress scoring Nixon's proposed $304 billion budget. Among them were statements from Goldwater, Helms, Brock, Buckley and Sen. Carl Curtis [R, Neb.].)

Presidential power assailed. A panel of experts in public administration reported to the Senate Watergate Committee March 20 that many of the abuses associated with the Watergate scandals could be traced to a "centralization of power in the presidency," under which "the prevailing view is that the whole government should be run from the White House."

The report, by a 12-member panel from the National Academy of Public Administration, had been commissioned by the Senate committee in preparation for the final report on its investigations.

While noting that many of the problems in the federal government had begun in earlier administrations, the report stated that Watergate was an "aberration" and culmination of "converging trends" which had seriously damaged the image of the public service.

Much of the report dealt with the White House staff system under which presidential assistants had become "assistant presidents," interposed—possibly illegally—between the President and departmental and agency heads. The panel concluded that the apparent policy of the Nixon Administration was that agency officials "must obey orders from the White House staff even in those areas where statutory powers" were vested in the agency official. Suggestions from presidential assistants were "to be construed as orders coming directly from the oval office."

The report criticized the "increasing and disturbing" politization of the White House staff and the civil service, and a tendency to appoint "political executives" to administer "duly legislated programs," sometimes with a "clear mandate from above in the hierarchy to 'gut' these programs."

A public manifestation of these trends, the report said, came in the hearings before the Senate committee, during which "almost none" of the top witnesses "mentioned any special considerations of public service for the public interest apart from the President's interest."

The report said the Nixon Administration had shown a tendency to run the government "like a corporation" with power concentrated at the top and exercised by White House staff members and "loyal followers" in executive agencies. An example noted in the report was the Office of Management and Budget, whose director—a Cabinet-level official and assistant to the President—had become, in effect, the "general manager" of the executive branch.

The panel noted that it unanimously opposed any movement toward a parliamentary system and believed in a strong executive. But reforms were needed, the report said—possibly a tightening of civil service laws and laws dealing with delegation of presidential authority.

The report said the "most alarming" of the Watergate disclosures had been the misuse of law enforcement and intelligence agencies against supposed "enemies" and the increasingly "partisan climate" in the Justice Department. The panel urged that Congress give "special attention and oversight" to the Federal Bureau of Investigation, the Central Intelligence Agency and the Internal Revenue Service. The panel also urged Congress to prohibit the White House from conducting "intelligence activities."

The Justice Department should be "divorced from politics," the report said, and the attorney general "should be precluded from advising the President in the latter's political or personal capacity."

To deal with investigation of wrongdoing, the report suggested a permanent office of special prosecutor, established by statute and subject to Senate confirmation for a term of at least six years.

The office should also be empowered to investigate election fraud.

The report also called for stronger campaign finance laws, including a combination of public and private funding, limitation of individual contributions to perhaps $10,000 for presidential campaigns and $3,000 for Congressional races, and limitations on cash and unreported contributions to $10. The report added that the limits should be observed by the candidates as well as their constituents.

Regarding impeachment, the report acknowledged that there was a misunderstanding over constitutional language on impeachable offenses. The panel said, however, that the phrase "high crimes and misdemeanors" needed to be understood in its historical context, which would include "crimes against the state or society as well as indictable crimes." The report also suggested that the impeachment process be extended—perhaps by constitutional amendment—to cover "serious misconduct in the political campaign prior to assumption of office."

House panel split on St. Clair bid. A party-line split over the role of special presidential counsel James D. St. Clair in the House Judiciary Committee during the panel's meetings March 20-21.

In letters to the committee, made public March 20, St. Clair said that in order for him to represent President Nixon adequately, it was "imperative" that he be allowed to participate in prehearing staff proceedings as well as in the formal committee hearings. St. Clair said he should be permitted to "cross-examine witnesses, suggest witnesses to be called and introduce relevant and material evidence for the committee's consideration."

In separate closed caucuses, the panel's Republican minority voted to support the request, and the Democrats voted to oppose it. But in the March 21 session some Democrats hinted at a possible compromise. Jerome R. Waldie (Calif.) suggested that St. Clair might be allowed to participate if the White House cooperated in turning over requested materials, a condition under which, as suggested by Robert F. Drinan (Mass.), the White House would be offered "every reasonable opportunity to be heard."

Chairman Peter W. Rodino (D, N.J.) objected that the request would "pervert constitutional processes" by turning the inquiry into an adversary proceeding, which, Rodino said, would come close to intrusion on the trial prerogatives of the Senate.

John M. Doar, the committee's special counsel, agreed with a suggestion that the panel's function was analogous to a grand jury proceeding, under which no cross-examination would be allowed. Doar was joined by Republican counsel Albert E. Jenner Jr. in opposing any form of adversary proceeding, but Jenner accepted

the contention of Charles E. Wiggins (R, Calif.) that cross-examination was "often an essential vehicle for determining the truth."

Other Republicans said the committee might appear guilty of its own "cover-up" if St. Clair were excluded, and ranking GOP member Edward Hutchinson (Mich.) told reporters later March 21 that if the request were refused the White House "can be expected to whip the committee to a pulp all over the country because of an apparent attitude of unfairness." Hutchinson had urged during the committee meeting that cross-examination should be allowed as the best way to "glean the truth." Hutchinson added, however, that he would not be part of a "deal" to permit St. Clair's participation in return for White House release of requested materials.

The issue was not resolved after the two days of meetings, and St. Clair's role in the impasse over committee access to presidential tapes and documents created additional controversy.

House Republican leader John J. Rhodes (Ariz.)—who was not a member of the Judiciary Committee—said March 20 that he had met twice during the previous week with St. Clair for briefings on the status of the panel's data request to the White House. St. Clair had reportedly held a similar meeting with Senate GOP leaders.

While giving assurances that he was not speaking for the White House, Rhodes proposed at a news conference that "some highly respected neutral source" be selected to review the requested material and eliminate items irrelevant to the panel's inquiry. Rhodes suggested that the committee's case had been weakened by the broadness of its request and its failure to define impeachable offenses. The panel should ask for material, Rhodes said, "only if it fits an offense."

Another approach to the evidence impasse—involving a special role for St. Clair—was proposed by presidential counselor Bryce Harlow March 21: Nixon would be willing to have St. Clair screen tape transcripts and release the edited material to the committee. Harlow said the committee could trust St. Clair to deal properly with specific requests for evidence because "his whole professional reputation" would be at stake.

The possibility of White House cooperation with the committee, Harlow said, still depended on the specificity of requests, a definition of impeachable offenses and a "bill of particulars" from the panel.

Kalmbach disputes Rebozo on Hughes gift. Herbert W. Kalmbach, who was personal attorney to President Nixon, gave sworn testimony to the Senate Watergate Committee March 21 that the President's personal friend Charles G. Rebozo had given or loaned portions of a $100,000 campaign contribution from billionaire in-

dustrialist Howard R. Hughes to Nixon's personal secretary Rose Mary Woods and his brothers F. Donald and Edward C. Nixon, it was reported April 6 and 7. Kalmbach repeated his testimony to investigators from the office of the Watergate special prosecutor. [For further details, see p. 129C1]

Prosecution subpoenas more data. Special presidential counsel James D. St.Clair disclosed March 21 that special Watergate prosecutor Leon Jaworski had subpoenaed the White House for additional documents following President Nixon's refusal to release material voluntarily.

The subpoena had been served March 15 and was to be answered within 10 days.

Neither Jaworski nor White House spokesmen would reveal the nature of the material sought, but sources in the prosecutor's office said the subpoena did not involve further investigation of the Watergate cover-up or the "plumbers" burglary conspiracy relating to the Pentagon papers case.

St.Clair said he did not think the subpoena would cover material Jaworski had already been denied. "Let's just say we recently have received a subpoena," he added.

The original special prosecutor, Archibald Cox, had been dismissed after he subpoenaed White House documents in 1973.

Deputy presidential press secretary Gerald L. Warren conceded that Nixon had been aware of the subpoena when he said March 19 that the White House had given the prosecution all the material it needed. Asked why Nixon did not mention the subpoena during the televised questioning session in Houston, Warren replied that Nixon had not been asked a direct question on the subject.

Ford to GOP: work to avoid disaster. Vice President Gerald R. Ford's advice to the Republican Party March 23 was that it must work to avoid disaster in the November elections. At a rally in Millburn, N.J., Ford said predictions by some Democrats of a gain of between 50 and 100 seats in the House were "not impossible" and would be "disastrous to our party." "I don't like Watergate, and you don't like it either," he said, "but none of your congressmen had anything to do with Watergate."

Ford also spoke in Atlantic City March 23 at another GOP fund-raiser to help pay off the gubernatorial campaign debt of Rep. Charles W. Sandman Jr.

In Charleston, S.C. March 15-16, Ford lauded and defended President Nixon before a GOP group and the next day pledged, "I shall remain my own man" before a non-political group. At a news conference March 15, he expressed concern that the staff of the House Judiciary Committee "may be wanting to dictate the impeachment proceedings."

White House stiffens stance. The White House continued to assert its refusal to release further data requested by the House Judiciary Committee for its presidential impeachment inquiry. The stand evoked a warning from Senate Republican Leader Hugh Scott (Pa.) that a continued confrontation on the issue would lead to impeachment. Strong statements on the issue also came from Democratic leaders.

The White House stand was emphasized in a series of statements by presidential press secretary Ronald L. Ziegler. The first statement came March 23 in response to two articles in that day's Los Angeles Times. One quoted unidentified Congressional sources as saying the White House was prepared to give the Judiciary Committee the additional tapes it was seeking because of Scott's warning. The other reported that a key tape of the March 21, 1973 meeting between Nixon and his former counsel John W. Dean 3rd was not ambiguous about the President's involvement in the Watergate cover-up.[See below]

Ziegler denied both stories and accused the House Judiciary Committee of being responsible for divulging confidential materials. "This lack of regard for the responsible handling of the materials provided to the committee cannot help but influence the White House attitude with respect to providing additional materials in the future," he said.

Ziegler said "the White House position has not changed" on release of the 42 tapes it said the committee sought and no decision had been made on the issue. The House panel should assimilate the mass of White House material already provided, he said, and "define the scope of the charges" against Nixon before demanding further data.

The President, he emphasized, was determined "not to irreversibly erode the office of the presidency."

As for the story of the March 21, 1973 Dean tape, Ziegler said there were "interpretations far different" from "the one-sided, partial, out-of-context" account in the Los Angeles newspaper. He expressed alarm at such "partisan" interpretations and "the malicious intentions of the people who planted this story."

(Congressional sources also were said to have rumored that the committee, in return for access to the tapes, would drop certain of its areas of inquiry and give Nixon's counsel the right to cross-examine witnesses during public hearings. The areas of inquiry to be eliminated were said to be the secret bombing of Cambodia, impoundment of Congressionally mandated funds, dismantling of the poverty program and, possibly, Nixon's tax problems, assuming there was no evidence of fraud.)

(Rep. Robert F. Drinan [D, Mass.], a member of the Judiciary Committee, said March 27 he had been assured that the committee had "not dropped any areas

from its investigation" and that "the committee would be informed of any recommendation that a specific area of inquiry appeared unnecessary.")

(Sen. Harold E. Hughes [D, Iowa] suggested March 27 that there was another area for the House committee to probe as possible impeachable grounds—the secret U.S. ground troop operations in Laos and Cambodia after Congress banned such activity in December 1969. In a Senate speech, Hughes said "no commander, including the Commander in Chief, should feel free to act beyond the limits of the Constitution or in violation of the law, even if his actions may successfully be concealed for months or years.")

'Hush money' tape called 'explosive'—Sources familiar with the tape of the March 21, 1973 meeting during which Nixon was told of "hush money" payments to the original Watergate defendants said there could be only one "explosive" interpretation of the meeting: that Nixon had not disapproved of the payments. The sources, said to be in both Congress and the executive branch, were cited in a Los Angeles Times report March 23.

Nixon had said that a tape of the meeting with John W. Dean 3rd and H. R. Haldeman—then his counsel and chief of staff—could be subject to different interpretations; the Times' sources, however, maintained that the tape was "not ambiguous." "When you hear the tape," one said, "you have a lot more respect for Dean's integrity and what he told the Senate Watergate Committee. It is that explosive."

According to the Times, the tape corroborated Dean's earlier statements and contained other "surprises" showing that Nixon had not given orders to stop the cover-up.

Deputy White House Press Secretary Gerald L. Warren called the sources' remarks an "expected" story "planted by someone with apparent political motives." There would be no further comment on the report, Warren said, "no matter how false it is."

Scott's warning—Scott's warning to the White House to cooperate was delivered to Nixon's counsel James D. St. Clair during a meeting, sought by St. Clair, in Scott's office March 19. Also present were Nixon counselor Dean Burch, Senate Republican whip Robert P. Griffin (Mich.); Sen. Wallace F. Bennett (Utah), secretary of the Senate Republican Conference; and Sen. Bill Brock (Tenn.), chairman of the Senate Republican Campaign Committee.

Reports quoting Scott did not appear until March 24. According to the New York Times account, Scott said he had warned St. Clair that Nixon "would be impeached" if the confrontation on the tapes continued. "I gave a clear message," Scott said, and he also reported cautioning St. Clair that defiance of the House committee would

"imperil" Nixon's position in the Senate, if the House voted to send it a bill of impeachment.

Ziegler criticized the House committee again March 25. He suggested that its staff "should perhaps work late into the evening" to complete assessment of the White House material on hand. "We feel that they should move within a matter of weeks" to finish that job, he said, whereupon the White House attorneys would "stand ready to hold cooperative discussions" about access to further material.

The White House position was not outright rejection, Ziegler said, which "would be a difficult matter to deal with." "We stand ready to cooperate," he said. As for the contrasting White House response to the special Watergate prosecutor, particularly its attempt to delay its response to a subpoena, Ziegler said the issues were not the same. The subpoena was "relatively routine in nature," he said.

10 of requested tapes 'non-existent'—Questioned by reporters at the daily White House news briefing March 27 about the tapes sought by the House panel, Ziegler indicated that some of the tapes might not exist. He understood that "a good deal" of the conversations being sought had been tape-recorded but "I don't know how much." Asked if all the 42 tapes the White House said the committee sought were intact, he said "it would depend on where the conversations took place." He gave assurance that "there has been no tampering with the tapes" that did exist.

Later, after Ziegler conferred with St. Clair, a White House statement was issued stating that "no decision has been made by the President with respect to this request pending the committee's assessment of the extensive material now before it and more specific and detailed references to the need for any additional material."

Deputy Press Secretary Gerald L. Warren appeared at the daily news briefing March 28. He was asked about a report in the Baltimore Sun that at least 10 of the 42 tapes did not exist. Warren said that was a matter of court record and he was under orders not to discuss the situation further.

The court record referred to covered the 1973 revelation by the White House that an April 15, 1973 tape did not exist because the tape recorder in the Executive Office Building had run out of tape. The President had held many conversations in the room that day, and 10 of the 42 conversations being sought by the House panel presumably occurred after the recorder had run out of tape.

Albert, Byrd defend committee—President Nixon's recent remarks about the Judiciary Committee's request for additional White House data were assailed March 25 by House Speaker Carl Albert

(D, Okla.). The President, he said, was "damaging the atmosphere in which he operates in the House," Albert said, and the President "would be well advised to cooperate, because there's nothing that can be done when one of the big issues is cover-up."

Albert made his remarks during an interview broadcast by the Public Broadcasting Service. He especially objected to Nixon's assertion, to the National Association of Broadcasters in Houston March 19, that he would not allow the House committee to "come in and bring your U-Haul trailer" to take the requested material away. Albert said he considered this "a wild defensive maneuver and almost beneath the dignity of the office of the President of the United States."

In a letter March 25 to Rep. John Conyers Jr. (D, Mich.), a member of the Judiciary Committee, Albert said he was perturbed "by any staged or contrived effort to create the impression that the committee is not acting responsibly or properly." Albert rejected Conyers' suggestion he seek equal broadcast time on behalf of the committee to rebut such assertions by the President. "I am convinced," Albert said, "that history will judge the House by what it does, not by what the President and his spokesman say."

Senate Democratic Leader Robert C. Byrd (W. Va.), addressing the National Capital Democratic Club March 27, assailed the President's use of his broadcast appearances to "launch subtle but sustained and unjustified attacks upon the legislative branch." Such a strategy, he said, "can only mislead the people and it is calculated to sabotage the legitimate and constitutional impeachment inquiry by the House of Representatives and avoid the disaster of a possible trial and conviction by the Senate."

Byrd's attack was denounced as partisan later March 27 by White House communications director Ken W. Clawson, who said "it sounds as if Sen. Byrd is trying to divert public attention from his lack of legislative leadership."

Byrd had accused the President March 20 of "deliberately distorting the truth when he says that he is cooperating with the courts and the special prosecutor" and with the House committee on the Watergate matter.

Byrd also attacked the President March 20 for an "unjustified vicious attack on Congress" for its handling of the energy problem, an attack joined by Albert and House Democratic Leader Thomas P. O'Neill Jr. (Mass.). Albert said "we passed one [energy] bill and he vetoed it."

Mansfield: vote to impeach 'there'—Senate Democratic Leader Mike Mansfield (Mont.) told reporters March 28 "the votes are there" for the House to impeach President Nixon. He attributed the situation in part to the White House's "dilatory tactics" on the materials requested by the House committee.

Mansfield said that if the House voted impeachment, the Senate's trial should begin within two weeks, regardless of any possible conflict with the fall elections. "The election will be secondary," he said.

He favored telecasting of any Senate impeachment trial because of its "extraordinary importance" and the "salutary exposure of democracy in action." He rejected Sen. James L. Buckley's view that a televised Senate trial would be "a Roman circus."

Mansfield stated his opposition to proposals to grant the President immunity from subsequent criminal prosecution as an inducement for his resignation. "The matter should take its regular course," he said.

Baker & other views—The view that the country wanted to hear the controversial tapes and that the President should turn all "relevant" material over to the House committee was voiced March 24 by Sen. Howard H. Baker Jr. (Tenn.), ranking Republican on the Senate Watergate committee. Appearing on the CBS-TV's "Face the Nation" program, Baker said "that magnificent confrontation" of an impeachment proceeding should not be conducted on a basis of "narrow legalism." The country and the presidency "would be better served by a forthcoming spirit and supplying voluntarily whatever is decently relevant or arguably relevant," he said, and the committee on its part should honor "whatever reasonable request the President makes, such as the presence of counsel in the principal deliberations and investigation of the committee."

A Republican member of the House Judiciary Committee, Rep. Thomas F. Railsback (Ill.), objected March 26 to Ziegler's remark that the committee should work longer hours. "Most members of the committee really resent that attempt to discredit their work," Railsback said.

The White House attempted to downgrade the controversy the same day. Presidential counselor Bryce N. Harlow said that he did not believe the House panel was engaged in a fishing expedition or in delaying tactics. There was a procedural problem in the request for data, he suggested, to bring the scope of the committee's probe more into focus. He predicted a vote against impeachment by the end of May.

Panel gets jury report on Nixon. The House Judiciary Committee March 26 took custody of a Watergate grand jury's secret report and compilation of evidence on President Nixon's possible role in the Watergate cover-up.

The briefcase of material went to the committee automatically after attorneys for H. R. Haldeman and Gordon C. Strachan, the two Watergate defendants trying to block release of the evidence,

had declined to appeal to the Supreme Court to overturn lower court decisions directing the material to be given to the House panel.

After a two-hour meeting with U.S. District Court Judge John J. Sirica to check the material, committee counsel transferred the briefcase to the panel's offices.

Under committee rules, only the two top members—Chairman Peter W. Rodino (D, N.J.) and ranking Republican Edward Hutchinson (Mich.)—and the two chief counsel—special counsel John M. Doar and minority counsel Albert E. Jenner Jr.—would have direct access to the evidence.

Saxbe enters Ervin panel tape suit. Attorney General William B. Saxbe asked the U.S. Court of Appeals in Washington March 27 to uphold a lower court's refusal to give the Senate Watergate Committee access to five White House tape recordings. The Justice Department's brief was filed in the committee's appeal of District Court Judge Gerhard A. Gesell's dismissal of its suit for the tapes because of possible harm to Watergate criminal prosecutions.

Committee Chairman Sam J. Ervin Jr. (D, N.C.) said March 28 that Saxbe's action was a violation of the "solemn agreement" the attorney general made "before his confirmation that he would leave all matters related to Watergate to special prosecutor Leon Jaworski." The Justice Department, Ervin added, was "not supposed to be the lawyers for the White House."

At the invitation of the court, Jaworski also filed a brief March 27 in which he took no firm position on what action the court should take. The court had not solicited the intervention by the attorney general.

Saxbe denied through a spokesman March 28 that he had violated his agreement, since the brief dealt with "institutional issues" rather than the merits of President Nixon's refusal to comply with the committee's subpoena. The spokesman said Saxbe had been advised by Solicitor General Robert H. Bork of the need to ensure that "the department's position regarding separation of powers" was "included in the record." Saxbe was, however, still "leaving Watergate to Mr. Jaworski."

Acting Assistant Attorney General Irving Jaffe contended that the Department was not "taking sides" with Nixon but had acted "on behalf of the United States." The department had been concerned about two principles, Jaffe said; executive privilege and "the integrity of the criminal justice system," which could be compromised by excess publicity. Jaffe said the department had not been sure these principles would be cited by other parties. "Our interest is broader than Jaworski's," Jaffe contended, noting that Jaworski had not wanted "to come down four-square on the fair trial issue."

Jaffe also said the department needed to enter the case because Gesell's decision, while dismissing the committee's suit, had done "a little bit of violence to the executive privilege principle" in its rejection of Nixon's blanket claims of confidentiality.

Nixon aide cites TV news bias examples. Bruce Herschensohn, deputy special assistant to President Nixon, suggested in a March 26 interview with the New York Times that "subtle and sophisticated" techniques employed by the television networks and other media had contributed to an unfavorable impression of the Nixon Administration in the public mind.

Techniques of distortion cited by Herschensohn were the failure to report certain news stories, use of derisive labels for the President's actions, employment of certain audiovisual tricks and "news judgments that always seem to go against us rather than for us."

As examples of omission, Herschensohn cited the failure of the networks to report a theory suggested by columnist Joseph Alsop on how erasures on some of the Watergate tapes could have been accidental, and a report by New York Times columnist William Safire suggesting that the portion of the Senate Watergate hearings transcript used a basis for the perjury indictment against former White House aide H.R. Haldeman was a paraphrase of what President Nixon said at a March 21, 1973 White House meeting and was not a verbatim recounting.

Herschensohn criticized use of the phrase "Saturday night massacre" to describe the sudden departures Oct. 20, 1973 from the Administration of former special Watergate prosecutor Archibald Cox, former Attorney General Elliot L. Richardson and former Deputy Attorney General William D. Ruckelshaus. "Why didn't they [the media] call it the 'Monday night massacre' when [John W.] Dean was fired and Haldeman and [John D.] Ehrlichman resigned?" Herschensohn asked.

He also questioned the use by the media of the term "Operation Candor," which he said had been coined by the Washington Post and was unfair because it implied that Nixon had not been candid prior to the onset of "Operation Candor."

Herschensohn noted that the Columbia Broadcasting System had titled its documentary on the 1973 Middle East war alert, "The Mysterious Alert," a title carrying the implication that something was strange about the alert, when, in fact, "numerous points in the documentary indicated there was nothing mysterious about the alert."

During the interview, Herschensohn stated these examples were "off the top of my head" and did not necessarily represent criticism that President Nixon had in mind when he castigated network reporting at his Oct. 26, 1973 news conference.

Nixon advises GOP candidates. At a $1,000-a-plate Republican dinner March 27 to raise funds for fall election campaigns, President Nixon was optimistic the situation "will be different" and the party would win as long as candidates stressed "the two great issues that move people in campaigns—peace and prosperity." "Candidates who support this Administration will have a strong case to take to the people this fall," he said.

Meeting March 25 with GOP National Chairman George Bush, Nixon pledged his full support to Republican candidates and said he would continue his campaign to win public support. Also attending the meeting were Sen. William Brock (Tenn.) and Rep. Robert H. Michel (Ill.), Republican campaign committee chairmen of their respective chambers.

In a survey of 11 Republican senators seeking re-election, the Associated Press reported March 27 that only Sen. Henry Bellmon (Okla.) had asked Nixon to campaign for him. Seven reported they did not want Nixon to campaign for them. Two said he could campaign for them but they were not going to ask him. Another said most people would regard close association with the Administration as "the kiss of death."

Segretti freed. Donald Segretti, convicted as a political "dirty tricks" man in the Watergate scandal, was released after serving four months and 20 days of a six-month sentence, it was reported March 27.

Schlesinger calls U.S. policy firm. U.S. Defense Secretary James R. Schlesinger cautioned the Soviet Union against thinking it could take advantage of President Nixon's troubles over the Watergate scandal to obtain concessions on a strategic arms limitation agreement. "Anyone who knows Mr. Nixon, knows full well he would do nothing to compromise national security . . . irrespective of any political disputes that exist within the United States," he said.

The remarks were made at a Pentagon news conference March 28 after the issuance of a joint U.S.-Soviet communique in Moscow following talks between Secretary of State Henry A. Kissinger and Soviet leaders.

Nixon yields on subpoena. President Nixon avoided a showdown with the Watergate prosecution March 29 by surrendering the materials subpoenaed two weeks earlier. The original deadline for response was March 25, but special prosecutor Leon Jaworski had granted an extension at the request of special White House counsel James D. St. Clair.

White House Press Secretary Ronald L. Ziegler said he had been told by St. Clair that "all the materials requested by subpoena" would be delivered, and a spokesman for Jaworski said St. Clair had given no indication that any material might be missing. According to both spokesmen, the subpoena did not involve tape recordings.

Neither the White House nor the prosecutor's office revealed the subject matter of the documents, but news reports March 30, citing informed sources, said the subpoena had sought information on campaign contributions, including those made by persons later named to ambassadorships.

Jaworski's office noted in a statement April 1 that requests for data in other areas of investigation were still outstanding. The information had not yet been subpoenaed, the statement said, but subpoenas would be issued if there were "noncompliance" from the White House.

Ford scores Nixon re-election panel. Vice President Gerald R. Ford drew cheers from a group of Midwest Republican Party leaders March 30 with a denunciation of President Nixon's 1972 re-election committee, the Committee for the Re-election of the President.

"The political lesson of Watergate is this," Ford told the group in Chicago, "never again must America allow an arrogant, elite guard of political adolescents like CREEP [an acronym for the committee] to bypass the regular party organization and dictate the terms of a national election."

He said the party's potential presidential candidates for 1976 should "sign in advance on the dotted line that they will not set up outside committees without the specific approval of the party itself."

"If there are any more cliques of ambitious amateurs who want to run political campaigns," Ford said, "let the Democrats have them next time."

Ford said "the fatal defect of CREEP" was that it "violated the historic concept of the two-party system in America and ran literally roughshod over the seasoned political judgment of the regular Republican Party."

Ford told reporters later his remarks should not be interpreted as criticism of President Nixon personally. "I'm not blaming the President for CREEP," he said. "He picked people he thought would do a good job. Unfortunately, they made mistakes."

Midwest conference—The 13-state GOP conference drew more than 1,000 party workers and major party figures.

Most of the speakers spoke of the party's accomplishments, rather than the Nixon Administration's, and attacked the Democratic record in Congress. Ford's attack on the re-election committee struck the most enthusiastic response. But former Gov. Nelson A. Rockefeller (R, N.Y.) was applauded when he said: "Let's face it: Watergate is a tragedy, but

A everyone is entitled to a fair trial and that applies to the President of the United States. Those who would push him out of office or force his resignation would be circumventing the constitutional process."

Gov. Ronald Reagan (R, Calif.), another participant, said, "I have always thought the President is innocent. I've taken his word for it, but this is in the legal process to be determined."

B Sen. Charles Percy (R, Ill.) flatly predicted that the House would impeach Nixon. Percy charged that the White House was responsible for the move toward impeachment because Nixon publicly pushed for quick resolution of the issue while his counsel was doing "everything conceivable" to delay the resolution. "That contradiction has not escaped the Congress," he said. "It has not escaped the American people." [See p. 237D1]

C At a reception he gave for participants March 29, Percy said it was important "that we deal with the real world, with the political facts of life, if we are to avoid political disaster." "Our immediate problem, of course, is that the leader of our party, the President of the United States, is in danger of being forced from office," he said. "The question that now confronts us, both individually and collectively, is how we can constructively respond to this agonizing situation." The first thing, Percy said, was to "reject Watergate in all its dimensions." Watergate, he said, "does not represent the traditional values and beliefs of the Republican Party and [we must] prove that our party's commitment to law and orderly process is not an empty promise."

D At a luncheon in Washington April 2, Ford told reporters he disagreed with contentions that the House was inclined to impeach Nixon, but he added that "a solidification of votes in the House" toward impeachment would be brought about by presidential defiance of the House impeachment inquiry. He was of the opinion that if the disputed tapes requested by the House panel contained "relevant" information, they "ought to be made available."

E *Mills says there are enough votes*—Rep. Wilbur D. Mills (D, Ark.) said April 1 "there is no doubt in my mind that there are enough votes for the articles of impeachment in the House." He also attributed the feeling within the House largely to "what the membership feels is lack of cooperation on the part of the White House" with the House probe.

F **Union men cheer attack on Nixon.** A strong attack on the Nixon Administration evoked cheers from a meeting in Washington April 1 of the AFL-CIO Building and Construction Trades Department, leaders of the construction unions. The speakers were AFL-CIO President George Meany, House Speaker Carl Albert (D, Okla.) and Sen. Henry M. Jackson (D, Wash.).

Meany said "the American people have completely lost confidence" in President Nixon and his Administration. Urging a drive in the Congressional elections, Meany told the group, which was meeting in a legislative conference, "We, as a group of workers millions strong, can play our part in giving America back to its people," Meany did not restrict his attack to domestic policy. "I pray every night," he said, "that [Secretary of State] Henry Kissinger won't give the Russians the Washington Monument—he's given them every . . . thing else."

Albert said the economy was "in a shambles" and "this country needs a Nixon-proof, veto-proof, impoundment-proof Congress."

Jackson said "mismanagement of our economy is so bad that President Nixon may be the first President to get his picture on a postage-due stamp." He predicted that the first quarter reports of oil corporations would disclose "obscene levels" of profit.

Haldeman: Nixon 'didn't know.' Former White House chief of staff H. R. Haldeman said April 2 that President Nixon "didn't know a damned thing about Watergate" and "didn't know about a cover-up of Watergate." Haldeman, under indictment in connection with the cover-up, appeared in a question-and-answer session with the Young Presidents' Organization, a business executives' group meeting in Acapulco, Mexico.

Haldeman predicted that Nixon would emerge from the Watergate scandals "stronger than he was before, and stronger than he would have been had this not happened."

Asked Nixon's greatest weakness, Haldeman—conceding that his audience might not find his answer "credible"—said it was Nixon's "softheartedness at the personal level" and his inability to dismiss or discipline people. Nixon was a "very tough guy in the abstract," Haldeman said, but it was "very hard for him to deal with personal problems." Nixon's usual action, Haldeman added, would be to call people in, "except for a few of us,"—for an indirect and delicate "chewing out."

Asked why Nixon had fought the release of White House tapes, Haldeman replied that "an awful lot of information" was being made public which in his—and Nixon's—opinion would be better kept secret "in the interest of the nation." He said "the American people do not have the means by which to determine the entire truth in ample or adequate perspective."

Javits vs. 'impeachment politics.' Sen. Jacob K. Javits (R, N.Y.) said April 3 it would be "tragic if the President began to play impeachment politics" with domestic or foreign policy "to please a given number of senators: 33 plus one." The

reference was to the minimum 34 votes necessary to prevent Senate conviction on impeachment, which required a two-thirds vote for conviction.

"The fact is," Javits said, "there has been a pulling away on domestic legislation." He cited apparent Administration policy shifts pleasing to conservatives on mass transit, welfare reform, land use and consumer protection. There were "some disquieting tendencies in the air," Javits said, and he felt compelled to speak out "before they develop into a serious deterioration of the capacity of government and the actual operation of the presidency."

Javits broached the alternative open to the President of temporary resignation, "one of his options" under the 25th Amendment, until the impeachment question was resolved. He stressed that he was not urging such a course, merely stating that such a course was open.

Buckley: Nixon 'burned out'—Sen. James L. Buckley (R-Conservative, N.Y.) told a college audience April 3 "the Nixon presidency is burned out.... There may be signs of energy, but there can never again be life. The spirit of the Nixon Administration has been shattered forever, irrevocably."

Speaking at the University of Delaware at Newark, Del., Buckley said the public had hoped for candor from the President in the impeachment inquiry but "the President has sought to narrow the focus to one of a technical, legal character." Buckley had called for Nixon's resignation March 19.

Reinecke indicted in ITT probe. California Lt. Gov. Ed Reinecke, a candidate for the Republican nomination for governor, was indicted by a Watergate grand jury in Washington April 3 on three counts of perjury in connection with the 1972 Senate Judiciary Committee investigation of the settlement of antitrust suits against the International Telephone & Telegraph Corp. (ITT). [For further details, see p. 129G3]

Panel sets data deadline. The House Judiciary Committee April 4 gave the White House until April 9 to decide whether to surrender tapes of presidential conversations the panel was seeking for its impeachment investigation. After that deadline, Chairman Peter W. Rodino (D, N.J.) said, "we will subpoena them if we must."

Rodino told a committee meeting that the request for tapes had been made "not out of curiosity but because it is our responsibility." "We have gone forward assuming good faith and cooperation," Rodino said, and "we have been respectfully patient. The courts were patient. The House has been patient. The people have been patient for a long, long time." Rodino asserted that the committee would not "be thwarted by inappropriate legalisms or by narrow obsta‹s to our inquiry."

The White House declined comment on the deadline other than to repeat that the tapes issue was the subject of meetings between counsel for President Nixon and the committee. The deadline reportedly stemmed from such a meeting April 2, when special presidential counsel James D. St. Clair had asked for more information justifying the committee's request.

The deadline was in a letter from committee counsel John M. Doar to St. Clair, which declared that the tapes were relevant in that they could determine Nixon's "knowledge or lack of knowledge, participation or lack of participation in the acts of obstruction of justice" charged in the March 1 indictment of seven former campaign and presidential aides.

Setting of the deadline was approved unanimously. If the White House rejected the request, Rodino said, a separate vote would be taken on issuing a subpoena.

Edward Hutchinson, the panel's ranking Republican, said he believed sufficient justification had been given for the data request. The committee was "not after any state secrets," he said, but was simply seeking evidence to "bring this matter to a conclusion."

Another issue facing the committee—St. Clair's role in the inquiry—remained unresolved after the meeting, but appeared to be moving towards a compromise.

Rodino had said April 1 that he did not want to be "inflexible" on a limited role for St. Clair, adding that the proceedings should not only be, but appear to be, "fair." Rodino indicated that he would not support the Republican-backed proposal that St. Clair be allowed to cross-examine witnesses. Other Democrats said April 4 that they were inclined towards allowing St. Clair to play limited role in the final stages of the inquiry.

Doar and minority counsel Albert E. Jenner Jr. presented a staff report April 4 which cited precedents showing a "definite trend" toward allowing counsel for the subject of an impeachment investigation to be present at committee sessions to state his client's case, more as a matter of "grace, not right." Doar said, however, that in no earlier case was such counsel permitted to participate in preliminary inquiry at the staff level.

GOP staff members submitted a separate brief urging that presidential counsel be allowed to cross-examine witnesses and join in all stages of the investigation.

Steinbrenner indicted. George M. Steinbrenner 3rd, chairman of American Ship Building Co. of Cleveland and a major partner in the New York Yankees baseball team, was indicted April 5 on 14 felony counts in connection with illegal contributions to the campaigns of President Nixon and Republican and Democratic members of Congress. The in-

dictment, returned by a federal grand jury in Cleveland, was signed by special Watergate prosecutor Leon Jaworski. [For further details, see p. 130D3]

Chapin convicted. Dwight L. Chapin, former appointments secretary to President Nixon, was convicted by a federal jury in Washington April 5 on two counts of perjury in connection with grand jury testimony on his dealings with Donald H. Segretti, the "dirty trickster" of the 1971–72 presidential campaign. The case was the first brought to trial by the special Watergate prosecutor.

After 11½ hours of deliberation, the jury found that Chapin had lied during the following exchanges with a Watergate grand jury in April 1973.

Q. To your knowledge, did Mr. Segretti ever distribute any statement of any kind or any campaign literature of any kind?
A. Not that I am familiar with.
Q. Did you ever express any interest to him or give him any instructions with respect to any single or particular candidate?
A. Not that I recall.

The jury acquitted Chapin on a charge of falsely denying that he had told Segretti to avoid talking to the Federal Bureau of Investigation about his activities.

A fourth count in the indictment was dismissed by Judge Gerhard A. Gesell, who ruled April 3 that the prosecution had produced insufficient evidence that Chapin lied in telling the grand jury he did not know the details of arrangements for paying Segretti.

Segretti, who had been released March 25 after serving 4½ months of a six-month sentence for his political sabotage, appeared April 2 as the first prosecution witness, repeating much of what he had told the Senate Watergate Committee.

Segretti testified that Chapin had recruited him in the summer of 1971 for a job which he said Chapin had referred to as "pulling pranks." During the following year, Segretti said, he met with Chapin personally at least seven times to report on his activities. On one occasion, Chapin told him he should "concentrate" on Sen. Edmund S. Muskie (D, Me.), then the frontrunner in the Democratic primary campaigns. Segretti conceded on cross-examination that Chapin might not have been so direct in the instructions on Muskie, perhaps mentioning Muskie as the focus of sowing dissension among Democrats simply "because he entered more primaries."

One of the techniques used against Muskie, Segretti said, was to distribute scurrilous—and false—material about other Democrats on Muskie stationery. Regarding one such letter—accusing Sens. Hubert H. Humphrey and Henry M. Jackson (Wash.) of drunkenness and sexual misconduct—Segretti said he had told Chapin specifically how much the dis-

tribution had cost ($20). Segretti said that on another occasion Chapin had laughed when told of a false press release saying that Rep. Shirley Chisholm (D, N.Y.) had once been confined to a mental institution.

Segretti said his usual practice was to send Chapin copies of the phony material, but conceded under cross-examination that "I don't recall any discussion with Chapin where I sat down and said I personally distributed . . . this literature."

Testifying in his own defense April 3, Chapin portrayed himself as too concerned with important White House affairs to pay much attention to Segretti's political pranks. Chapin explained that he had quickly become "bored" with the "junk" in Segretti's reports and began discarding Segretti's envelopes unopened.

Chapin testified that he had never discussed distribution of campaign material with Segretti, was not familiar with material Segretti had distributed "personally," and, regarding the instructions on Muskie, that he had only told Segretti to focus on "frontrunning candidates." Shown a note in his own handwriting directing Segretti to disrupt Muskie's campaign, Chapin said he did not recall the note and was unable to recall it when he testified before the grand jury.

Chapin was also confronted with a secret chronology he had prepared for John W. Dean 3rd, then presidential counsel, detailing Segretti's activities and mentioning specific Democratic candidates. Regarding the specific listing of candidates, Chapin said that in his grand jury testimony he had only meant to deny that there was any "master plan against any particular candidate."

Asked about blank spaces in the memo, Chapin testified they represented the names of those who had originally approved the Segretti project: former White House Chief of Staff H. R. Haldeman and former Attorney General John N. Mitchell.

Dean, whose reliability as a witness had been the focus of pretrial controversy, appeared briefly for the prosecution April 3 to corroborate the authenticity of the memo from Chapin.

Chapin's sentencing was set for May 15. He faced up to five years in prison and a fine of up to $10,000 on each of the two counts.

Nixon attends Pompidou rites. President Nixon conferred with leaders of seven nations in Paris April 6–7 after attending a memorial mass for the late French President Georges Pompidou.

White House assistants said Nixon's stay in Paris showed that despite the Watergate scandal and his threatened impeachment, the President commanded respect abroad.

Between his meetings in Paris, Nixon went into the streets to mingle with generally friendly French crowds. These forays and the meetings were criticized by French officials and newspapers as "funeral summitry" and attempts by Nixon to improve his personal popularity.

In a letter circulated among journalists and reported by the New York Times April 9, a high French official charged Nixon had "shamelessly substituted a publicity campaign for the mourning of an entire nation, introducing an atmosphere of loud feverishness, the discourtesy of which is equaled only by its clumsiness."

Le Monde, France's leading newspaper, agreed April 8 in an editorial titled "The Nixon Festival." Le Figaro, a conservative Paris daily, called Nixon's activities "Operation Charlemagne," and printed a cartoon in which a crowned woman, representing Europe, knelt and kissed the hand of Nixon, who sat with his feet resting on a death notice, presumably for Pompidou.

Political use of IRS detailed. Sen. Lowell P. Weicker Jr. (R, Conn.), a member of the Senate Watergate Committee, accused the Internal Revenue Service (IRS) April 8 of acting as a "public lending library" for White House efforts to aid political friends and harass political enemies. [For further details, see p. 131D1]

House bars study of October alert. The House April 9 by voice vote killed a resolution requiring Secretary of State Henry Kissinger to provide information to Congress on President Nixon's order that placed U.S. military forces on alert during the Middle East War of October 1973. The resolution, introduced by Reps. Michael Harrington (D, Mass.) and Fortney H. Stark (D, Calif.), would have required Kissinger to turn over the texts of all communications between Nixon and Soviet officials, as well as a chronological list of orders and actions by the U.S. during the alert. (The military alert had been viewed with skepticism by some Administration critics at the time as a possible attempt by Nixon to distract public attention from Watergate goings-on.)

Prior to the vote by the full House, the Foreign Affairs Committee had disapproved the resolution. Committee Chairman Thomas E. Morgan (D, Pa.) and three other committee members had met with Kissinger, who gave them much of the information demanded in the Harrington-Stark resolution. After hearing reports from Morgan and the others, the committee voted 26–2 that Kissinger's response had been sufficient and that it was in the interest of national security that the information not be made public. Not satisfied with Kissinger's answers, Harrington and Stark brought their resolution to the House floor where it was defeated.

Prosecution to probe taxes. Attorney General William B. Saxbe said April 9 that the Internal Revenue Service (IRS)

had forwarded to the special Watergate prosecutor the information on President Nixon's discredited 1969–72 income tax returns. The IRS had ruled that Nixon owed $465,000 in additional taxes and interest, which Nixon said would be paid, while disclaiming responsibility for the preparation of the returns. [For further details, see p. 93B1]

Nixon campaigns in Michigan race. President Nixon April 10 campaigned in the 8th Congressional District of Michigan on behalf of James Sparling, a Republican seeking the seat vacated Jan. 31 by Rep. James Harvey (R) who resigned to take a federal judgeship in Michigan. The special election to be held April 16, was billed as a test of Nixon's political strength.

Nixon, in the 8th district at the invitation of Sparling, followed an itinerary during his day-long trip that included a speech at the airport near Saginaw, where he landed, and a 53-mile motorcade through the heavily Republican farmland areas of the district. Along the motorcade route, Nixon made brief speeches before crowds numbering around 2,000 in the towns of Bad Axe, Cass City and Sandusky, none of which had populations over 3,000.

Although Sparling said at the time he extended the invitation that the President had been asked to come to speak out on Watergate and economic issues, rather than the 8th district race, Nixon avoided mention of Watergate. He focused instead on Sparling and Sparling's Democratic opponent, State Rep. J. Robert Traxler. Nixon echoed accusations by Sparling that Traxler was a tool of the labor unions and that his record of absenteeism as a state representative disqualified him for service in the House. Nixon said the voters needed "a man who will be a full-time congressman."

Traxler, embracing the strategy used by Rep. Richard F. Vander Veen (D, Mich.) in his successful effort to fill the seat left vacant by the elevation of Rep. Gerald Ford (R, Mich.) to the vice presidency, said Nixon and his record were the only issues in the campaign. Nixon's visit, he said, helped him. Traxler's strength lay in the Democratic tri-city region of Saginaw, Bay City and Midland, where he hoped a large voter turnout, coupled with apathy among Republicans in rural areas, would send him to Washington as the 8th district's first Democratic congressman since the Depression.

Nixon's campaign foray, his first since 1972, provoked controversy among Michigan Republicans. Sen. Robert Griffin (R, Mich.) warned in a fund-raising letter that the GOP might lose the 8th District. Saginaw County Republican Chairman Robert Grant Jr. had openly opposed Nixon's visit.

Porter sentenced to 30 days. Herbert L. Porter, former scheduling director for the Committee to Re-elect the President, was sentenced to 30 days in prison April 11 on a charge of making false statements to the Federal Bureau of Investigation. Porter had pleaded guilty Jan. 28.

U.S. District Court Judge William B. Bryant actually handed down a sentence of 15 months in prison but suspended all but 30 days. Porter was also placed on unsupervised probation for a year.

In arguing for leniency, Porter's attorney said President Nixon had been an "idol" to Porter and that when Jeb Stuart Magruder, Porter's superior on the campaign committee, invoked the President's name, Porter quickly went along with the plan to concoct a false story for the FBI.

Assistant special prosecutor Richard Ben-Veniste told the court that Porter had cooperated fully and that Porter's involvement in the cover-up was "less in degree than others who pleaded guilty to felony charges."

Nixon subpoenaed. The House Judiciary Committee April 11 voted 33–3 to issue a subpoena ordering President Nixon to turn over to it by April 25 all tape recordings and other materials related to 42 presidential conversations the committee deemed relevant to its impeachment inquiry. The subpoena was served on special presidential counsel James St. Clair that same day by Benjamin Marshall, chief security officer to the committee.

In effect, the committee's vote was a rejection of a compromise offered by St. Clair in an April 9 letter to John Doar, chief counsel to the Judiciary Committee. St. Clair's letter said President Nixon had ordered a review of the material in question and would furnish by April 22 "additional materials" that would "permit the committee to complete its inquiry promptly." St. Clair's letter did not indicate which tapes or material would be turned over to the committee.

White House Press Secretary Ronald L. Ziegler, speaking to the press after the subpoena had been delivered, said the President would give an answer by April 25 that would allow the House panel "to draw a prompt and just conclusion," as well as "bear out the President's statement that he will cooperate consistent with his constitutional responsibilities." Reiterating a White House position that the President's lawyers "all along indicated . . . [a] desire to proceed quickly with the proceedings," Ziegler said that it was not until April 4 that Doar specified what the committee wanted.

The three votes against serving the subpoena were cast by Rep. Edward Hutchinson (R, Mich.), ranking Republican on the committee*; Charles E. Wiggins (R, Calif.), whose vote was by proxy; and Trent Lott (R, Miss.). Reps. Charles W. Sandman Jr. (R, N.J.) and Harold V. Froehlich (R, Wis.) were absent at the time of the vote.

The 42 presidential conversations cited in the subpoena took place from Feb. 20, 1973 to April 18, 1973. The subpoena demanded records—"all tapes, dictabelts or other electronic recordings, transcripts, memoranda, notes or other writings or things"—of meetings the President had with former White House aides H. R. Haldeman, John D. Ehrlichman and John W. Dean 3rd; former Attorney General Richard G. Kleindienst; and Henry E. Petersen, assistant attorney general in charge of the criminal division of the Justice Department.

St. Clair made a last effort to head off a subpoena 45 minutes before the committee met the morning of April 11. He called Doar and offered to turn over "within a day or two" records of conversations involving the President, Haldeman, Ehrlichman and Dean between Feb. 20 and March 30, 1973. The offer did not include conversations Nixon had with Haldeman, Ehrlichman, Kleindienst and Petersen between April 15 and April 18, 1973.

Before the committee took its vote on issuing the subpoena, it engaged in partisan debate focusing on a compromise amendment and a rule limiting each member to one minute of debate. Over Republican arguments that the committee was embarking on a great constitutional confrontation and that it was "ridiculous" to make a judgment after only 30 minutes of debate, the committee voted 21-17 along party lines to uphold the rule limiting debate. The second vote concerned a motion by Rep. David Dennis (R, Ind.) to limit, as St. Clair had in effect proposed that morning, the subpoena to conversations that occurred between Feb. 20 and March 30, 1973. The motion was defeated 22-16, with M. Caldwell Butler (R, Va.) voting with the Democrats. However, the Democrats agreed to amend the subpoena to meet Dennis' ob-

*One reason Hutchinson cited for voting against subpoenaing the tapes was that a subpoena was "unenforceable." Anticipating that question, Doar had prepared a staff memorandum on the committee's power to subpoena documents from the President. It admitted that if the President refused to comply with the subpoena, "the practical difficulties of enforcing the subpoena may well be insurmountable."

Congress might seek the aid of the judicial branch in enforcing the subpoena, although the power to impeach was vested solely in the legislative branch. But "as a practical matter," the memorandum said, the courts had no means of enforcement not already available to the House. Legislation resolving legal tangles arising from use of the courts was possible, the memo said, but consideration had to be given to considerable delays that might result.

Conceding that it was not realistic to think that the President could be "compelled" to comply, the memorandum suggested two alternate approaches: the Judiciary Committee could infer that Nixon's noncompliance resulted from the fact that the evidence was "unfavorable," or the committee could declare noncompliance "a derogation of authority explicitly vested by the Constitution in the House" and, therefore, an impeachable offense.

jection that the subpoena did not sufficiently describe the April 1973 conversations. An amendment by Rep. Delbert L. Latta (R, Ohio), introduced after a lunchtime recess, carefully specifying which conversations were sought in the subpoena, was approved unanimously by the committee.

Until the adoption of the Latta amendment, committee Republicans had expressed a preference to settle for voluntary compliance by the President. Confronted at the morning committee meeting of April 11 with a subpoena already drafted by the Democrats, Rep. Robert McClory (Ill.), second ranking Republican on the committee, said: "The partisan steps now taken are a mistake. My feeling is that we ought to take what we are offered voluntarily and not subpoena." Hutchinson, who said April 10 that St. Clair's offer April 9 "was offensive to the House, I'm sorry to say," commented after the final vote that the White House "had offered to turn over voluntarily the material and I think in the end [the White House] would have turned it all over. . . . the subpoena is not returnable until after the Easter recess, [April 22] and they offered us some material sooner."

Replying to Hutchinson, Rep. John Conyers Jr. (D, Mich.) said: "That's ludicrous. It is clear that even most of the Republicans can't go along with the kind of cavalier treatment this committee has received from Mr. St. Clair and the White House."

Committee Chairman Peter W. Rodino Jr. (D, N.J.) said after the final vote: "This clearly demonstrates the Committee on the Judiciary's discharge of the responsibility it feels it owes to the people of the United States and Congress to conduct the kind of inquiry that reflects credit on the Congress of the United States."

GOP warning to Nixon—Senate Republican leaders had issued a unanimous warning to the President that unless he promptly produced all the materials sought by the House Judiciary Committee, he was "aching for impeachment," the Washington Post reported April 12. At the meeting convened by presidential assistant Dean Burch April 9, the senators were presented with a draft of the White House's response to Doar's letter of April 4. [See above] The first draft of the letter, which proposed an indefinite delay on the Judiciary Committee's request for evidence, was rejected by the senators, the Post reported. A second letter, approved by the senators, was sent by St. Clair that evening.

Told by Burch that the White House was having difficulty transcribing the tapes because of their poor quality, the senators warned him that if the White House continued to delay, "the first article in the bill of impeachment well could be contempt of Congress," the Post quoted one senator as saying. (After

the letter was sent April 9, Burch commented publicly that he was "surprised that there is apparently so much consternation [among House Judiciary Committee members]. . . . We're going to turn over all materials St. Clair deems relevant.")

Senators present at the meeting were Republican leader Hugh Scott (Pa.), Republican whip Robert Griffin (Mich.), policy chairman John Tower (Tex.), conference chairman Norris Cotton (N.H.), conference secretary Wallace Bennett (Utah), and campaign chairman William Brock (Tenn.)

Particulars of the subpoena—The Judiciary Committee subpoena called for President Nixon to produce all tape recordings and other materials covering these conversations:

■ Conversations between the President and Haldeman Feb. 20, 1973 concerning the appointment of Jeb Stuart Magruder, deputy director of the Committee to Re-elect the President, to a government position.

■ Conversations Feb. 27, 1973 between Nixon, Haldeman and Ehrlichman concerning the assignment of Dean to work directly with the President on Watergate and related matters.

■ Conversations between the President and Dean March 17 to March 20, 1973 concerning the break-in at the office of the psychiatrist who treated Pentagon Papers defendant Daniel Ellsberg, and the involvement of White House aides in the Watergate burglary and its subsequent cover-up.

■ Conversations between Nixon and Ehrlichman March 27 and 30, 1973 concerning involvement of White House aides in the Watergate burglary, and the President's request to Ehrlichman to take over from Dean the White House inquiry into Watergate.

■ All conversations between Nixon and Haldeman, and Nixon and Ehrlichman from April 14 to April 17, 1973 inclusive.

■ All conversations between the President and Kleindienst, and the President and Petersen from April 15 to April 17, 1973 inclusive.

St. Clair to observe inquiry—The Democratic majority on the Judiciary Committee had informally agreed April 9 to allow presidential counsel St. Clair to sit in on sessions in which evidence on the President's conduct in office was presented to the committee. Committee chairman Rodino said April 11 that he would recommend that after all the evidence was in that St. Clair be permitted to file comments on the evidence, to recommend additional witnesses and to question those witnesses. A formal vote by the committee was scheduled for after the panel's Easter recess.

Ford Cabinet talk. Vice President Gerald Ford's thoughts about his possible Cabinet in the event he assumed the presidency was reported by John Osborne in the New Republic magazine April 13. Osborne, specifying it was an account of Ford's thinking "as I've been led to understand it," indicated that Ford favored retaining many key Nixon Cabinet officers, including Henry Kissinger as secretary of state, but was dubious about James Schlesinger as his defense secretary since he felt he would be ineffective in dealing with Congress. The Osborne article also indicated that Ford was bothered by hours of "small talk" with President Nixon and had broken off recent conversations with the President to escape.

Ford later conceded he was the source of the article, during an interview with Osborne he thought was off the record. Ford aides stressed his repeated assertions that he expected Nixon to serve out his full term. As for the "small talk" item, Ford corrected what he considered Osborne's exaggeration. What he meant, Ford said, was he sometimes felt he was taking too much of the President's time.

White House Press Secretary Ronald L. Ziegler, who would not be retained in any Ford Administration according to the Osborne article, was reported April 14 to have criticized Ford's remarks on his future plans as "inappropriate." The report was in a UPI dispatch from Key Biscayne, Fla. attributed to Ziegler as a comment to a TV interviewer as he left church services. A later clarification had Ziegler using the word "inappropriate" to any comment on his part.

Harlow resigns. Bryce N. Harlow, who joined the White House staff as counselor to the President June 14, 1973, at the peak of the Watergate scandal, resigned April 13, to return to private life.

Democrat wins in Michigan. J. Robert Traxler (D) was elected to Congress in a special election in Michigan's 8th Congressional District April 16. He defeated James M. Sparling Jr. (R), 59,918 (51.4%)–56,575 (48.6%). Traxler had used President Nixon as the major issue in the race. Nixon had visited the district in an effort to help Sparling April 10.

It was the first time a Democrat had won the seat since 1932. Seven-term Rep. James Harvey (R), who resigned the seat Jan. 31 to take a federal judgeship, won in 1972 with 59% of the vote.

Sparling, 45, had been Harvey's administrative assistant for 13 years and served as a Congressional liaison in the White House for a time in 1973.

Traxler, 42, was a lawyer and member of the Michigan House of Representatives. He had campaigned against Nixon's policies and "moral leadership." Traxler's comment after the verdict was in: "We're going to Washington with a message—throw the rascals out."

It was the fourth Republican defeat in five recent special Congressional elec-

tions. Traxler's victory raised the Democratic majority in the House to 247. Republicans held 187 seats (one vacancy).

The President was not "dismayed or disheartened" by the outcome, according to White House Deputy Press Secretary Gerald Warren April 17. He indicated that the results were closer than expected before Nixon's visit to the area. "The President believes that Jim Sparling fought a good fight," Warren said, "and if a man is willing to run hard and campaign hard on the issues, the President will never turn away an opportunity to help him."

Vice President Gerald R. Ford conceded April 17 that the Republicans had taken "a licking" and that the Watergate issue was at least partially responsible. "Certainly, Watergate is a factor that is going to have an adverse impact" on the fall Congressional elections, he said. "It tends to prove what I've been saying for the last month or so—if our people don't get aroused, then we could have a substantial loss." He warned that the situation could lead to a "legislative dictatorship" by the Democrats.

Jaworski gets new subpoena. U.S. District Court Judge John J. Sirica April 18 ordered a subpoena issued on the White House for tapes, transcripts and other documents relating to 64 presidential conversations. Sirica acted at the request of special Watergate prosecutor Leon Jaworski, who had petitioned the court April 16 to issue the subpoena. In papers filed with the court, Jaworski said the materials would be needed for the trial of the seven cover-up defendants, scheduled Sept. 9.

Sirica set a deadline of May 2 for response to the subpoena.

(Under procedural rules, a trial subpoena would be issued through the clerk of the court, unlike the grand jury subpoenas issued automatically by Jaworski. To have the subpoena made returnable before trial, Jaworski had to petition the court for a ruling on the subpoena request.)

The 64 conversations listed by Jaworski were between President Nixon and former key aides H. R. Haldeman, John D. Ehrlichman and Charles W. Colson, all cover-up defendants, and former counsel John W. Dean 3rd. The dates ranged from June 20, 1972, three days after the Watergate break-in, to June 4, 1973, the date said by Nixon to have included his personal review of some tapes. Most of the conversations were in February, March and April, 1973. (Colson filed a motion April 17 saying that he was joining in Jaworski's request and asking that he be allowed to inspect all materials examined by the prosecution.)

Jaworski told the court the material had been requested "as early as" Jan. 9, and despite repeated requests since then, there had been "no definitive response" as to whether the material would be released.

In a letter to special presidential counsel James D. St. Clair, dated April 11 and released April 16, Jaworski warned

that if the President declined to produce the materials voluntarily, he would be compelled to seek "appropriate judicial process." Jaworski noted that he was presently seeking no more than an assurance that the material would be provided "sufficiently in advance of trial to allow thorough preparation."

Jaworski noted that St. Clair's latest reply had been that the prosecution would receive "any materials" released to the House Judiciary Committee for its impeachment inquiry. Regarding other material, St. Clair had replied that the request would not be considered until the White House had decided what to give the House panel.

Jaworski said he had "emphasized repeatedly" that his request was "in no way" tied to those of the House committee and was "distinguishable both factually and legally." Nonetheless, Jaworski said, St. Clair had refused to consider the requests separately and had failed to "assure us when we will receive a definite response."

(Of the 64 conversations listed by Jaworski, 24 had been included in the Judiciary Committee's subpoena.)

Ford says Nixon not the issue. Vice President Gerald R. Ford urged Republicans April 20 not "to become endlessly embroiled" in the Watergate issue or the party would "forfeit elections from coast to coast." Speaking to the California Republican State Convention in San Jose, Ford said: "Our task is difficult. The Democrats are seeking maximum exploitation on a national basis of what may be the greatest controversy ever generated about a President of the United States." But, he said, "the issue is not R.M.N.," it is whether "Republicans can mobilize a return to the A.B.C.'s of politics on a personal and precinct level."

He was proud "to be involved in this Administration," Ford said, "but that is not to say that we are perfect. We must correct what is wrong, strengthen what is right and move forward rather than backward."

Others in GOP disagree—In Sen. Charles H. Percy's (R, Ill.) view, stated in Chicago April 18, Nixon's resignation "would be somewhat of an advantage to the party and possibly to the country."

Sen. Clifford Case (R, N.J.) was reported by the UPI April 21 as advocating a Nixon resignation in the event the House voted impeachment and there was a delay in the Senate trial.

Gov. Mills E. Godwin Jr. (R, Va.) said April 18 in Wakefield, Va. that the Watergate episode should be resolved and impeachment "might be the only answer to the crisis of leadership."

William A. Barnstead of Massachusetts became the first Republican state chairman to call for Nixon's resignation. A long-time Nixon supporter, Barnstead said in Boston April 17, "I believe he is guilty, at least of covering up the facts on Watergate."

Democratic governors confer. A meeting of Democratic governors in Chicago April 21–22 focused primarily on the November elections and the 1976 presidential election.

Optimism about the November results, because of an expected Watergate fallout against Republican candidates, was so high that a fear of beneficial underdog status for the Republicans surfaced at the meeting, which was attended by 15 of the 32 Democratic governors. As Gov. Thomas P. Salmon (Vt.) put it, "We've almost reached the point where the President and the Republican Party could achieve certain benefits from the martyrdom people now perceive in Watergate and its preempting of other national events." The opinion was reinforced by pollster Peter D. Hart, who cautioned the governors April 22 that there was a danger of surfeit of success in talk of electing a "veto-proof" Congress. "People are looking for checks and balances at this point," he said.

Another speaker, Sen. Hubert H. Humphrey (D, Minn.), said April 22 "I think we can get a veto-proof Congress but then there can be no excuse for our failure to act." Humphrey recommended a full agenda of domestic programs, most of them designed to rescue "the average citizen from the inflation-battered economy." And by 1976, he said, "we won't be running against President Nixon. The Republican candidate will have systematically gone far from the programs and policies of Nixon. What we need is action of our own in the form of positive, people-oriented programs." If that were done, he said, "we don't need Watergate to win or any presidential abdication either."

Humphrey volunteered some advice about the type of candidate the party should have in 1976. "We don't need a case of charisma, or image, or Madison Avenue," he said. "What we need is a man who will watch the store. Not a genius. A man who will run this government."

Another main speaker April 22 was Democratic National chairman Robert S. Strauss, who advised against calls for Nixon's resignation. "Let us remember what this President was and did when he perceived himself a hero," he said. "I ask you what horrors await this nation if he is able to portray himself as a resigned martyr."

Gov. Milton Shapp (Pa.) disagreed. "I think he ought to resign," he said April 22. "At any rate, we need a new president now to get the country's business done."

Questions raised in Silbert nomination. Senate Judiciary Committee hearings on the nomination of Earl J. Silbert as U.S. attorney for the District of Columbia focused on the adequacy of the original Watergate investigation. Silbert, 37, who headed the original Watergate prosecution team while he was an assistant U.S. attorney, was nominated by President Nixon Jan. 29 to be U.S. attorney. Silbert appeared before the committee April 23

and 24. [For further details, see p. 172G3]

Watergate panel wins IRS data access. The Internal Revenue Service (IRS) agreed to provide the Senate Watergate Committee with tax returns and other politically sensitive materials from its files on President Nixon's friend Charles G. Rebozo and the President's brother F. Donald Nixon, the New York Times reported April 24.

The IRS decision, an abrupt reversal of its previously stated position, included an agreement to provide a wide variety of tax returns and other data deemed essential by the committee to its investigation of Rebozo's handling of the $100,000 cash presidential campaign contribution by billionaire industrialist Howard Hughes in 1969 and 1970, the Times reported. [For further details, see p. 132B2]

House panel to probe tax issue. The House Judiciary Committee planned to send a written questionnaire to President Nixon to explore whether there was any criminal fraud on the part of the President on the matter of his federal income tax returns for 1969 through 1972.

Pursuit of the tax issue as a priority area of search in the committee's impeachment inquiry was disclosed April 25 as the committee met to hear a report from its legal staff on the scope of the inquiry and to consider a follow-up in the course of its subpoena to the White House for information.

The committee voted 34–4 to extend the deadline for compliance with the subpoena from that day, April 25, to April 30. The extension had been requested April 22 by Nixon's counsel James D. St. Clair. The votes against extension were cast by Democrats Jerome R. Waldie (Calif.), Robert F. Drinan (Mass.), Charles B. Rangel (N.Y.) and Elizabeth Holtzman (N.Y.).

Committee Chairman Peter W. Rodino Jr. had told reporters April 23 he expected the committee to agree to extend the deadline because "we don't want to have a confrontation." He said St. Clair had said in his telephone request for delay that "he was having a difficult time getting the material together and the President has not had a chance to review it." Asked at that time if some of the material could be provided on time, St. Clair said "the President wanted to review it all at once," Rodino reported.

There had been reports that the White House response to the subpoena would be in the form of edited transcripts of the tapes requested with material deemed irrelevant or impinging on national security deleted.

The possibility of such a response was not dispelled by White House spokesman Gerald L. Warren April 23 when he spoke of the need for more time to "prepare the materials" to be submitted to the committee. Talking of the President's "response" to the subpoena, Warren steered a middle course between "com-

pliance," a word he avoided, and "outright rejection," which he ruled out.

Rodino made known his opposition to a partial response April 18. Appearing on the NBC "Today" broadcast, he said the committee would not accept any procedure in which the White House made "the final determination" of what evidence was relevant to the House inquiry. Furthermore, he said, anything less than full compliance with the subpoena could become in itself part of an impeachment bill. At his news conference April 23, Rodino said a partial transcript of the tapes would be considered by the committee an "emphatically" unsatisfactory response.

Reporters questioned Rodino April 23 about another report that the committee was seeking additional tapes and documents from the White House apart from the subpoenaed material. Rodino confirmed the report. The new material being sought involved Watergate, the 1971 antitrust settlement involving the International Telephone and Telegraph Corp. (ITT) and dairy industry campaign funds.

As for the scope of the inquiry, as outlined in the staff report, the focus was to be narrowed to seven priority areas: the Watergate cover-up attempt; clandestine domestic surveillance; the ITT issue; the dairy industry issue; the $200,000 campaign contribution of Robert L. Vesco; the $100,000 donation from Howard R. Hughes to Nixon's friend, Charles G. Rebozo; and Nixon's personal finances.

Some of the committee's original areas of inquiry were to be sidetracked as the panel intensified its probe in the priority areas. The staff report said 15 of the 56 original charges against the President were in this category and would be dormant because of either lack of "substantial" evidence against the President or "insufficient" evidence to warrant further pursuit at this time.

However, the committee did not decide to drop such areas from its probe. Several Democrats objected to dropping any subjects of the inquiry, just as several Democrats opposed extension of the deadline for compliance with the subpoena.

Mitchell, Stans acquitted. John N. Mitchell and Maurice H. Stans, former Cabinet officials in the Nixon Administration and directors of President Nixon's 1972 re-election campaign, were acquitted by a federal district court jury in New York City April 28 of all charges stemming from a secret cash campaign contribution from Robert L. Vesco, the financier whose mutual funds dealings were under investigation by the Securities and Exchange Commission (SEC).

The government had accused Mitchell and Stans of conspiracy, obstruction of justice and perjury for attempting to block the SEC investigation and later lying to a grand jury about their roles.

The verdict was widely seen as a significant boost to Nixon's campaign against impeachment, partly because the Vesco issue would be effectively removed from consideration by the House Judiciary Committee, but more importantly to some observers, because the credibility of former presidential counsel John W. Dean 3rd was brought into question. Dean had been a principal witness against Mitchell and Stans and was one of the President's chief accusers. [For further details, see p. 71F1]

Colson cites national security defense. Former Presidential counsel Charles W. Colson said April 29 that President Nixon in a June 1971 meeting told him and H. R. Haldeman, then White House chief of staff, that leaks of classified information had to be stopped, "whatever has to be done . . . whatever the cost."

Colson, under indictment in connection with the September 1971 break-in at the office of the psychiatrist who had treated Pentagon Papers defendant Daniel Ellsberg, made the statement in a pretrial sworn affidavit submitted to U.S. District Court Judge Gerhard A. Gesell. Filed in support of a defense move to use national security as a defense against conspiracy charges, the statement was the most detailed account of President Nixon's anger over leaks of classified information to be made public.

Besides citing concern by the President and his national security adviser Henry Kissinger over the leaks, Colson asked the court for access to many classified government documents to prepare his case. These included federal investigatory reports "concerning the suspicion that Dr. Ellsberg was acting on behalf of some foreign government in releasing classified information." He also sought other classified information to which Ellsberg had access as a Defense Department official.

In his account of the June 1971 White House meeting, Colson said Nixon in effect said to him and Haldeman: "I don't give a damn how it is done, do whatever has to be done to stop these leaks and prevent further unauthorized disclosures; I don't want to be told why it can't be done. This government cannot survive, it cannot function if anyone can run out and leak whatever documents he wants to . . . I want to know who is behind this and I want the most complete investigation that can be conducted. The President went on: I want to know how and why the 'counter-government' is at work. If we do not stop them, if we do not find out who is involved and why, we will endanger everything that this government is trying to do in the most sensitive foreign policy and national security areas. I don't want excuses, I want results. I want it done, whatever the cost."

At another point, Colson said "Kissinger was even more alarmed over the leaks than the President. He believed that the leaks must be stopped at all costs, that Ellsberg must be stopped from making further disclosures of classified information. . . ." Colson stated that he had the "clear impression" that Kissinger, like the President, feared that Ellsberg's activities would "undermine the most critical and sensitive foreign policy negotiations."

Colson's affidavit also mentioned an April 1973 conversation with White House domestic affairs adviser John D. Ehrlichman, who told him that the President had informed Assistant Attorney General Henry E. Petersen that he [Nixon] had approved the "Ellsberg operation" after consultation with Federal Bureau of Investigation Director J. Edgar Hoover. The affidavit did not explain what was meant by the "Ellsberg operation."

Nixon's $465,000
Tax Debt Disclosed

IRS to re-examine Nixon tax returns. The Internal Revenue Service (IRS) announced Jan. 2 that it was re-examining President Nixon's tax returns. The President had made public his 1969–1972 income tax returns Dec. 8, 1973 when he disclosed personal financial data to "remove doubts" that had arisen and "correct misinformation."

At that time, he had asked a Congressional tax committee to re-evaluate two controversial items that substantially reduced his federal income tax obligations and promised to pay any tax deemed delinquent by the panel. The items involved a gift to the government of his vice presidential papers, for which continuing large deductions were made, and the sale of some California property for which no capital gain tax was paid. The committee, the Joint Committee on Internal Revenue Taxation, decided not to limit its inquiry to the two items.

The IRS announcement was authorized by Nixon through his private tax lawyer, Kenneth W. Gemmill of Philadelphia. It was the practice of the IRS not to disclose information on individual cases unless a court dispute arose.

The IRS noted the two investigations of the Nixon returns. "Questions have been raised in the press," it said, "as to the relationship of the consideration of the President's tax returns" by the IRS and the Congressional committee, which was a party to the announcement. Their inquiries would not be a joint effort, the announcement said, but arrangements were under way for "an exchange of information" and "the representatives of the President are cooperating fully" with both groups.

On a case of nonfraudulent underpayment of federal income tax, a three-year statute of limitations existed from the due date of the return. There was no statute of limitations for civil fraud on a tax return.

State tax status promised—President Nixon's California tax lawyer, Dean S. Butler of Los Angeles, said Jan. 2 full details of Nixon's state income tax status would be made public "some place along the line." Nixon's statement in December 1973 disclosed that he had paid no state income tax while President.

IRS auditing Nixon Foundation. An Internal Revenue Service investigation of the tax returns of the Richard Nixon Foundation was disclosed Jan. 18 by the President's accountant, Arthur Blech, who was also accountant for the foundation. Blech informed the New York Times that an audit was under way in response to the newspaper's queries about the tax returns of the foundation, which was established in 1969 to finance and construct a library for Nixon's presidential papers. The foundation listed its net worth at the end of 1972 at $114,076. It was regarded as a public charity by the IRS, which entitled it to exemption from the annual tax of 4% of its income required of a private foundation.

One of the Times' queries concerned a payment of $20,000 by the foundation to Nixon's brother, Edward, a foundation trustee, as a site consultant fee. The fee was not reported to the IRS, as normally required, Blech said, on legal advice that the brother was "a nominal trustee without any powers" and only compensation to "executive trustees" with power need be reported. The payment was reported to California authorities, Blech said, because a breakdown had been requested of expenditures listed for building construction in process.

Backdating of tax claim reported. A California state official reported Jan. 25 that the deed for President Nixon's gift of vice presidential papers to the National Archives was falsely backdated to a period prior to July 25, 1969, the effective date of a law curbing tax deductions for such gifts. Nixon had claimed deductions of $482,000 over the past four years for the gift.

The matter was under investigation by the office of Secretary of State Edmund G. Brown Jr. Deputy Secretary Thomas Quinn said principals involved in the case had informed the office that the deed, dated March 27, 1969, actually was signed and notarized April 10, 1970.

The state investigation had discovered that the deed had been typed on a typewriter that was not purchased until July 1969. The typewriter belonged to the law office of Frank DeMarco Jr., Nixon's California tax lawyer. Quinn said DeMarco testified a draft of the deed was drawn in April 1969 but he had no copy of it. Quinn said neither the original nor copies of it had been found.

DeMarco defended the procedure as proper since the intention to donate the papers was known prior to the deadline and the papers delivered to the archives.

Edward L. Morgan, who handled the matter at the White House for Nixon as a presidential aide, resigned as an assistant Treasury secretary Jan. 18. Asked if the resignation was connected to the papers matter, he said: "It's not directly related, but I can't say it's totally unrelated. Of course, I feel badly about it; it's something I'm clearly involved in and I'm giving the President another problem." Asked to explain, he said, "If he is going to have to pay considerable tax, it's a problem. Obviously, I'm questioning what I did." Morgan said he now knew he did not have authority to sign the deed turning over the papers to the government, but that he did not know it at the time.

Sen. Russell B. Long (D, La.) chairman of the Congressional committee investigating Nixon's tax returns, predicted Jan. 23 that the President would be asked to pay back taxes because of his erroneous deduction for the gift of the papers. "It looks more and more that there was a tax liability on the President's part," he said.

Impeachment probe covers finances. The House Judiciary Committee's impeachment probe extended into the area of President Nixon's personal finances. Committee members reported Feb. 14 that special counsel John Doar had informed them that two staff investigators were in California for that purpose and staffers had been assigned as liaison with the joint Congressional panel investigating Nixon's tax returns. [For further details, see p. 29G3]

White House news conference. At a televised news conference Feb. 25, President Nixon indicated that "the paper-work" for legalizing the large tax deductions for his gift of vice presidential papers to the government "apparently was not concluded" until after the deadline for making such gifts. [For further details, see p. 30C2]

'Zero taxpayers' list' published. A Treasury Department report based on 1972 tax returns showed that 402 persons with incomes greater than $100,000 paid no federal income tax for the year. In 1971, 276 persons in the same category had paid no taxes.

Included were 99 individuals whose incomes were in excess of $200,000 and four millionaires. They paid no federal taxes in 1972. No persons making illegal claims for tax exemption were included on the "zero taxpayers' list," which was released March 2 by Sen. Walter F. Mondale (D, Minn.).

Mills believes Nixon should resign. Rep. Wilbur D. Mills (D, Ark.) said March 8 he expected the pressure for President Nixon's resignation to intensify when the Congressional Joint Committee on Internal Revenue Taxation investigating Nixon's income tax returns reported its findings. Mills was a member of the committee.

During an interview in Little Rock, after he announced plans to seek reelection to a 19th term, Mills said he believed "very strongly" Nixon would resign. He said he thought Nixon should resign. Asked why, he replied, "That will come out later. You will know about it in 30 or 40 days."

Asked if he believed the report would provide more pressure for resignation than the Watergate scandal, Mills replied, "Yes, I do." He said he had talked to "some key Republican members of Congress who say that if he is still in office by the month of June, they will ask him to resign."

An unidentified White House spokesman later March 8 denounced Mills' interview as "a dirty, cheap shot." Mills used "a scare tactic by referring to a report that I believe is nonexistent," the spokesman said.

Presidential counselor Bryce Harlow said March 11 that Mills should make the facts known if he had them to support his allegations. Mills "should put up or shut up," he said. The next day Harlow denounced the remarks as typical of "guilt by innuendo" attacks associated with the late Sen. Joseph R. McCarthy (R, Wis.).

Mills had reportedly told colleagues he believed the public would be outraged by the forthcoming report because of the picture of narrow legality or morality in so many areas. "What I said," Mills explained in Washington March 12, "was that the tax issue could hurt the President more than Watergate, simply because people understand taxes. If the figures that have been talked about—$250,000 to $300,000 owed—are correct, people certainly will be asking questions."

Mills was reported as indicating to colleagues that the tax owed by Nixon could go as high as $500,000. The $500,000 figure could be reached in back taxes and interest if all the big controversial items on Nixon's returns were assessed against him, even without a finding of fraud, which carried a further penalty of 50% of all delinquent taxes owed during any tax year. Mills denied March 12 he was accusing the President of tax fraud.

Sen. Russell B. Long (D, La.), chairman of the joint committee studying the Nixon returns, had expressed doubt Feb. 8 that Nixon was guilty of fraud on the back tax issue but indicated the likelihood of a finding that back taxes would be owed. Long repeated his views March 8. "I have said that evidence thus far indicates the President will owe more taxes but that we do not have proof of fraud," he said. "That statement still stands."

Tax scrutiny of predecessors denied—The White House denied March 12 that Nixon played any role in having the tax returns of his predecessors reviewed to ascertain whether he was taking all possible deductions. Press Secretary Ronald L. Ziegler said Nixon had never seen the returns of a previous president and "does not recall" ever asking an aide to review such returns.

The denial was in response to reports by syndicated columnist Jack Anderson and the New York Times, based on a June 1969 White House memorandum, that Nixon pushed for business deductions for "all allowable items" and suggested a review of the returns of previous presidents "for guidance."

According to the Times March 12, the memorandum was written by John D. Ehrlichman, then domestic affairs adviser to Nixon, and addressed to Edward L. Morgan, then Ehrlichman's deputy.

Among the "allowable items" suggested were the use of Nixon's homes in California and Florida. According to the Times, the memorandum also said:

"The President holds the view that a public man does very little of a personal nature. Virtually all of his entertainment and activity is related to his 'business.' He wants to be sure that his business deduction include all allowable items. For instance, wedding gifts to congressmen's daughters, flowers at funerals, etc. He has in mind that there is some kind of a $25 limitation on such expenses. He suggests that we might review the returns of one or more previous presidents for guidance."

According to the documents revealed by the Times, the suggested "allowable items" included payment from Nixon's personal funds for his daughter Julie Eisenhower's summer work in the White House as a tour guide. This deduction was not claimed, apparently on the advice of Internal Revenue Service aide Roger V. Barth, who had been approached for the advice. Barth also advised appointment of an accountant to handle the President's records and promised to work closely with the accountant in handling any problems that arose.

The Anderson column, published March 8, also said the Congressional committee studying Nixon's taxes was in possession of testimony that Nixon had "carefully checked each page" of his 1969 tax return with his two tax attorneys before signing it April 10, 1970, and the deed for Nixon's gift of vice presidential papers to the government was notarized at the White House that day. California officials claimed that the deed had been falsely backdated.

Nixon discusses Finances. In a televised appearance at a luncheon of the Executives' Club of Chicago March 15, President Nixon discussed the investigations of his income tax returns. [For further details, see p. 74G1]

U.S. aid to homes put at $17 million. A House subcommittee report approved March 21 put federal spending on President Nixon's private estates in California and Florida at $17 million. The figure was higher than the $10 million reported by federal agencies in 1973 because of the addition of $7.1 million in personnel costs, largely pay and maintenance costs for permanently assigned personnel at three sites, the third being the home of Nixon's friend Robert H. Abplanalp on Grand Cay in the Bahamas.

The report was sent to the House Government Operations Committee by a 6–4 party line vote. The Republicans, in the minority, objected vigorously to the report and to release of some of its findings by subcommittee chairman Jack Brooks (D, Tex.), who issued a statement disclosing the $17 million figure.

The statement said the report's findings concerned "the loose arrangements" for U.S. payment of items "not requested by the Secret Service," submission of "after-the-fact requests, procurement of items far in excess of security needs, the obligation of federal funds by nongovernmental personnel and other such practices . . ." Brooks spoke of the possible necessity for legislation setting guidelines for such spending, such as limiting it to one site, and more exact record-keeping.

The White House also denounced the report. Its communications director, Kenneth W. Clawson, said March 21 the report was based "on runaway partisanship and not facts" and was constructed "to unjustly malign the President." Brooks was "trying to deceive the American people," Clawson said.

Deputy Press Secretary Gerald L. Warren criticized Brooks March 22 for citing the $17 million figure and the press for reporting it. Federal spending on the Nixon homes was under $1 million, Warren said, according to a report by the

General Accounting Office (GAO). Asked to comment on the view that most of the expense could have been avoided if Nixon had not spent so much time at his two estates, Warren said the American people "do not want the President to be a prisoner in the White House."

Rep. John Buchanan (Ala.), the subcommittee's ranking Republican, attacked the report March 22 as a "total distortion" of the facts. He said "only" $205,000 was spent on Nixon's two homes and a little over $1 million on surrounding property.

GSA Administrator Arthur F. Sampson also complained about the report March 23. He said he detected "a partisan grandstand play" and accused Brooks of trying to "purposely mislead the public."

Brooks defended the report March 25 as documentation of "how $17 million of the taxpayers' money was spent that would not have been spent but for the President's desire" to maintain his two estates, which Brooks called "vacation spas." He also indicated reluctance of the White House to supply full data on such spending. The $17 million, he said, was "at least the fifth version of 'total expenditures' and an even closer look at the situation might find that we are still short of what actually was spent."

Congressional panel, IRS disclose findings; Nixon to pay $465,000 in taxes. A White House announcement April 3 said President Nixon would pay $432,787.13 in back taxes plus interest on the basis of a report from the Internal Revenue Service (IRS) that he owed that amount. With interest, the total amount was about $465,000.

The announcement followed by about four hours release of a staff report of the Congressional Joint Committee on Internal Revenue Taxation that found Nixon's income tax delinquency totaled $476,431 during his first term.

The IRS and the committee closed their investigations of Nixon's taxes April 4.

The IRS specified it would not seek a civil fraud penalty against the President for the years involved because it "did not believe any such assertion was warranted."

The committee, by a 9–1 vote, with Sen. Carl Curtis (R, Neb.) in dissent, approved a statement endorsing the staff report and commending Nixon for his "prompt decision" to pay the tax deficiencies and interest. Announcing the decision to conclude its inquiry, the statement said the committee members "agree with the substance of most of the recommendations made by the staff."

The White House statement—Details of the IRS report, which the President said he received April 2, were not released, al-

though the White House statement said it "rebuts any suggestions of fraud on the part of the President." The Nixon statement also said the Congressional report "offers no facts which would support" any charge of fraud. It added that "any errors which have been made in the preparation of the President's returns were made by those to whom he delegated the responsibility for preparing his returns and were made without his knowledge and without his approval."

The statement said Nixon's counsel believed the largest item involved in the claimed tax delinquency—charitable deductions of $482,018 from 1969–1972 for a gift of papers to the government—could be "sharply and properly contested in court proceedings such as are open to an ordinary taxpayer to review the decisions" of the IRS. It said the President also believed his counsel could make "a very strong case against the major conclusions" of the Congressional staff report.

Since Nixon had requested the committee to examine his tax returns and stated he would abide by its judgment, he was directing that the back taxes be paid. Noting that the Congressional staff report indicated that the proper amount to be paid must be determined by the IRS, he was using the IRS-calculated amount, the statement said.

The Congressional staff report—Release of the Congressional staff report was decided by a 9–1 committee vote, with only Sen. Curtis in dissent. Its release prior to formal assessment by the committee was decided upon to prevent news leaks about it.

The staff report itself stressed that it was "a report only" and "not a demand for payment of taxes," which was a matter between the taxpayer and the IRS. It also stressed that no attempt had been made "to draw any conclusions whether there was, or was not, fraud or negligence involved" on the part of the President or his representatives. This aspect was shunned to avoid prejudgment, it said, by committee members in light of the current impeachment investigation.

The staff report made other observations. One was that the committee inquiry was not confined to the two items mentioned by Nixon in his request to the panel for the probe—the gift of the papers and the sale of some property at San Clemente, Calif. A broader examination was necessary, it said, because of the possible interrelationship of items on a tax return and because in this case, "so many questions have been raised" and "the general public can only be satisfied by a thorough examination." It cited the necessity of public "confidence in the basic fairness of the collection system."

The report also noted that "because of the office held by the taxpayer, it has not been possible to call upon him for the usual substantiation," although counsel to Nixon—Kenneth W. Gemmill and H. Chapman Rose—had "been helpful in the

staff examination" of the returns and "supplied most of the information requested." "As is true in any examination of a tax return," the report said, it was "not possible to give assurance that all items of income have been included." The staff report, it continued, "contains recommendations on two categories of income which it believes should have been included but were not; namely, improvements made by the government to the San Clemente and Key Biscayne properties which the staff believes primarily represent personal economic benefits to the President, and economic benefits obtained by family and friends from the use of government aircraft for personal purposes."

One final comment in the report was that the staff limited its recommendations to income tax matters "although in this examination it found instances where the employment taxes were not paid and gift tax returns not filed."

The staff report figures—The committee staff found a total tax deficiency in Nixon's returns for 1969–1972 of $444,022. With interest due as of April 3 of $32,409, the deficiency would total $476,431.* The breakdown by year:

	Proposed Deficiency	Interest	Deficiency Plus Interest
1969	$171,055		$171,055
1970	93,410	$16,638	110,048
1971	89,667	10,547	100,214
1972	89,890	5,224	95,114
Total	$444,022	$32,409	$476,431

No interest payment was included for 1969 because the general statute of limitations had expired for that year's return. The report noted that any payment by the President for that year would be voluntary. If interest were to be included, it said, the amount would be $40,732.

The report also cited deductions the President would be entitled to if certain reimbursements were made to the government as a result of the report's findings. These involved $106,262 for General Services Administration improvements "which the staff believes were primarily personal in nature"; $27,015 the staff found represented the cost for personal trips of family and friends; and $4,816.84 for a Cabinet table purchased by Nixon but which the staff believed the government should have bought.

A summary of the report's 10 parts:

1. The staff disallowed the $482,018 deductions for Nixon's gift to the government of his vice presidential papers "because the gift was made after July 25, 1969," the effective date of the Tax Reform Act eliminating such deductions. The deed of the gift, dated March 27, 1969, "which purportedly was signed on April 21, 1969, was not signed (at least by

*President Nixon paid $78,651 in federal income taxes in 1969–1972 on income of $1,122,266. The payments were $72,682.09 in 1969, $792.81 in 1970, $878.03 in 1971 and $4,298.17 in 1972 on listed income in those years. They were: 1969-$328,161.52; 1970-$262,942.56; 1971-$262,384.75; and 1972-$268,777.54.

all parties) until April 10, 1970 and was not delivered until after that date." It was signed by Edward Morgan rather than the President "and the staff found no evidence that he was authorized to sign for the President."

Furthermore, the staff found the gift was "so restricted" it was "a gift of a future interest in tangible personal property, which is not deductible currently under law, even if the gift was valid in all other respects."

Nixon's 1968 gift of papers, it found, "contains the same restrictions as the second gift so that in the staff's opinion, it, too, is a non-deductible gift of a future interest. As a result, the staff believes that the amount of the 1968 gift in excess of what was deducted in 1968 is not available to be carried over into 1969."

2. In 1970, "no capital gain was reported on the sale of the President's excess San Clemente acreage. The staff believes that there was an erroneous allocation of basis between the property retained and the property sold and that a capital gain of $117,835 should have been reported."

3. A capital gain of $151,848 should have been declared, the report said, on the 1969 sale of Nixon's New York City apartment because the staff "does not view the San Clemente residence in which he reinvested the proceeds of the sale (within one year) as his principal residence." The capital gain figure was larger than the $142,912 reported on Nixon's 1969 tax return "because the President's cost basis should be reduced by the depreciation and amortization allowable on the New York apartment resulting from its use in a trade or business by Mr. Nixon." The amount of depreciation and amortization allowable was put at $8,936.

4. The report found "that depreciation on the San Clemente house and on certain furniture purchased by the President, business expense deductions taken on the San Clemente property, as well as certain expenditures from the White House 'guest fund' are not proper business expenses and are not allowable deductions. These deductions totaled $91,452."

Among the items disallowed was $5,-391.43 for a "masqued ball" given by Nixon's daughter Tricia in 1969 and $22.50 for cleaning Mrs. Nixon's bathroom rug.

5. Nixon reported 60% of a capital gain on the 1972 sale of Cape Florida development lots, his daughter, Patricia, reported 40%. The report said "the entire amount should be reported as income to the President," and that he should report $11,617, the amount allocated to his daughter, as a capital gain in 1972 and the remainder of the gain in 1973. His daughter should file an amended return for 1972 and the President could deduct as interest part of the payment he made in 1973 to his daughter on the money she loaned him and she should report the interest as income in 1973.

6. The President should declare as income, the report said, the value of flights in government planes taken by his family and friends "when there was no business purpose for the furnishing of the transportation." "The staff was given no information about family and friends on flights where the President was a passenger," it noted, but "for other flights the first-class fare costs of his family and friends are estimated to be $27,015." The reported noted that Nixon had paid for most of such travel expense himself from April 1971 through March 1972 and again after Nov. 7, 1972.

7. Nixon should declare as income $92,-298 in improvements made to his Key Biscayne and San Clemente estates, the report said, since the improvements were "undertaken primarily for the President's personal benefit."

The total amount of the federal spending at the two estates, not counting the cost of the federal offices supporting presidential use of the estates, was said to be $1.4 million.

The staff cited the expenditures it believed should have been declared as income. They included public funding for such items as landscaping and landscape maintenance, boundary surveys, sewer and paving, a cabana and repair to a gazebo.

At San Clemente, in a den of the house, four bullet-proof picture windows were installed facing the ocean, at a cost of $1,-600. They had not been requested by the Secret Service. The report concluded that their purpose was aesthetic rather than useful and that Nixon should have paid their entire cost. On an $18,494 heating system in the house, installed at Secret Service request, the staff decided that Nixon should pay $12,988 of the amount since some system, although possibly not the type insisted upon by the Secret Service, would have had to be installed anyway and Nixon intended to install it on his own.

At Key Biscayne, a security fence was installed at a cost of $71,000, but it had been remodeled since Nixon desired it to look like the fence around the White House. The report said $12,679 of the cost

should be considered taxable income because of the "additional cost resulting from the President's personal tastes." A $400 concrete shuffleboard court ruined in construction of security facilities was replaced by a $2,000 terrazzo tile court; the report held the $1,600 difference was taxable income.

8. The staff found that Nixon "should be allowed an additional $1,000 in sales tax deductions."

9. On state gasoline tax deductions, the staff found that $148 should not be allowed for 1969 through 1971 but an additional $10 was allowable for 1972. The deductions were taken for a pickup truck used at San Clemente and based on more than 10,000 miles use a year, which the staff considered excessive.

10. The staff found that several other income items should be reported but they were entirely offset by deductions and did not increase taxable income.

Addenda—The staff reported it had submitted a series of questions for consideration by the President, questions relating "to issues still not fully answered." It was hopeful that the answers would be forthcoming and could be made public.

Information also was requested, it said, "with respect to a so-called 'special projects fund,'" because "the staff was made aware that certain expenditures out of this fund possibly had been made for personal items of the President relating to his San Clemente residence." It reported an answer from Nixon's counsel indicating only one possible instance, a $6.30 expenditure for light bulbs at San Clemente.

Nixon borrowing foreseen. The back-tax assessment "almost virtually wiped out" Nixon's personal savings, a White House spokesman said April 4. "The President is going to have to borrow a substantial amount in order to meet this obligation," he said.

Deputy White House Press Secretary Gerald L. Warren gave assurance April 4 that "the President will pay his taxes" and would not contest the IRS assessment

White House Statement on Taxes April 3

We have learned of the decision by the Joint Committee on Internal Revenue taxation to release a staff analysis of the President's taxes before the committee itself has had opportunity to evaluate the staff views, and before the President's tax counsel could advise the committee of their views on the many legal matters in dispute in that report.

Yesterday the President received a statement from the Internal Revenue Service indicating its view, also, that he should pay an additional tax.

The President's tax counsel have advised him that the positions they have sought to present to the committee, as outlined in their brief, are valid and compelling. His intent to give the papers was clear. Their delivery was accomplished in March 1969, four months before the July deadline. His intent as to the amount of the gift was stated to his counsel. Because of these facts the President's tax counsel strongly affirm that those various issues could be sharply and properly contested in court proceedings such as are open to an ordinary taxpayer to review the decisions of the Internal Revenue Service.

The President believes that his tax counsel can make a very strong case against the major conclusions set forth in the committee's staff report. However, at the time the President voluntarily requested the committee to conduct its examination of his tax returns, he stated that he would abide by the committee's judgment. In view of the fact that the staff report indicates that the proper amount to be paid must be determined by the Internal Revenue Service, he has today instructed payment of the $432,-787.13 set forth by the Internal Revenue Service, plus interest.

It should be noted that the report by the Internal Revenue Service rebuts any suggestions of fraud on the part of the President. The committee's staff report offers no facts which would support any such charge.

Any errors which may have been made in the preparation of the President's returns were made by those to whom he delegated the responsibility for preparing his returns and were made without his knowledge and without his approval.

against him, which was due within 30 days. He said the payment would have "a major impact" on Nixon's financial position. Nixon's net worth as of May 31, 1973, according to his financial statement in December 1973, was $988,000, of which $432,000 was in cash and most of the rest in real estate. Part of this, the home at San Clemente, had been pledged by the President as a gift to the American people. This residential property was listed in the financial statement as worth $571,000. A final mortgage payment of $226,660 on the estate was due on July 15.

Prosecution to probe taxes. Attorney General William B. Saxbe said April 9 that the Internal Revenue Service (IRS) had forwarded to the special Watergate prosecutor the information on President Nixon's discredited 1969–72 income tax

returns. The IRS had ruled that Nixon owed $465,000 in additional taxes and interest, which Nixon said would be paid, while disclaiming responsibility for the preparation of the returns.

Saxbe pointed out, however, that the prosecutor should not deal with whether Nixon himself was involved in criminal fraud but with the role of those who had actually prepared the returns. Questions about the President, Saxbe said, should be left to the House Judiciary Committee's impeachment inquiry.

(Chief committee counsel John M. Doar said April 8 that tax fraud was clearly part of his staff's investigation and that IRS records on Nixon's taxes had been requested. Chairman Peter W. Rodino (D, N.J.) had indicated earlier that instead of the fraud issue the panel should concentrate on whether Nixon's handling of tax matters had impeded

government operation by diminishing confidence in the taxation system.)

The only person mentioned by Saxbe as a possible target of a prosecution investigation was Frank DeMarco, Nixon's tax attorney, but the New York Times reported April 11 that the IRS had given prosecutor Leon Jaworski a list of former White House aides and other presidential associates allegedly involved in Nixon's personal tax affairs.

Citing "well-placed sources," the Times said IRS Commissioner Donald C. Alexander had met privately with Jaworski the previous week, submitted the list, and urged Jaworski to begin a grand jury inquiry into possible criminal conspiracy relating to the claim of $576,-000 as a deduction for the gift of Nixon's vice presidential papers, $482,018 of which had been claimed through 1972.

Document Reporting Undeclared Nixon Income and Impermissible Deductions*

*This table prepared by Congressional investigators lists President Nixon's adjusted gross income (AGI) as reported by him on Line 1. It shows calculations made by the Congressional staff and on Line 16, the deficiencies found which totaled $444,022. Of this amount, Nixon agreed to pay $432,787, or $11,234 less, not counting the interest listed on Line 17.

Recommended Deficiency and Interest, 1969–72

SCHEDULE A	1969	1970	1971	1972
1. Income as reported on return (AGI)	$328,162	$262,943	$262,385	$268,778
2. Additions to income	142,367	85,994	13,592	18,011
a. Gain on sale of New York apartment (50% of NLTCG)[1]	$75,924			
b. Improvements to San Clemente and Key Biscayne properties	62,442	$17,800	$8,956	$3,101
c. Personal use of government airplanes by family and friends	4,001	9,276	4,636	9,102
d. Gain on sale of San Clemente property (50% of NLTCG)		58,918		
e. Gain on sale of Florida lots (50% of NLTCG)				5,808
3. Deductions from income improperly taken as itemized deductions (item 6)[2]	−6,294	−5,510	−5,517	−5,332
4. Corrected income (AGI) (1 + 2 − 3)	464,235	343,427	270,460	281,457
5. Deductions reported on return	178,535	307,182	255,677	247,570
6. Deductions improperly taken as itemized deductions but allowable in arriving at AGI (item 3)[2]	−6,294	−5,510	−5,517	−5,332
7. Deductions not allowable	$117,184	$140,976	$152,102.	$157,303
a. Charitable contribution deduction for gift of papers	95,298	123,959	128,668	134,093
b. Amounts treated on return as business deductions	21,833	16,954	23,402.	23,210.
i. San Clemente residence	4,700	7,808	10,237	9,422
ii. Key Biscayne residence	292	646	614	583
iii. Depreciation of White House furniture		1,347	1,095	889
iv. Guest fund deductions	16,841	7,153	11,456	12,316
c. Gasoline tax	53	63	32	
8. Additional deductions allowed:				
a. Sales tax	1,274			
b. Gasoline tax				10
9. Allowable itemized deductions (5 − 6 − 7 + 8)	56,331	160,696	98,058	84,945
10. Corrected taxable income (4 − 9 − personal exemptions)[3]	406,104	180,856	171,052	195,012
11. Ordinary tax determined on corrected taxable income	137,394	58,820	90,545	86,927
12. Alternative capital gain tax (if applicable)	84,185	32,512		7,261
13. Total corrected ordinary income tax liability (11 + 12)	243,737	94,203	90,545	94,188
14. Total tax (13 plus minimum tax)	[4]243,737	[5]94,203	90,545	94,188
15. Tax as shown on return	72,682	793	878	4,298
16. Deficiency (14 − 15)	171,055	93,410	89,667	89,890
17. Interest	[6]	16,638	10,547	5,224
18. **Total deficiency and interest**	**171,055**	**110,048**	**100,214**	**95,114**

[1]Net long term capital gain.
[2]This amount represents those deductions claimed because of the business use of the Key Biscayne residence. The President had claimed these expenses as itemized deductions, but the committee staff believes that they should be allowed as expenses incurred in connection with maintaining investment property (sec. 212). This means that it now is a deduction to arrive at AGI, rather than an itemized deduction and is treated accordingly.

[3]Personal exemptions for 1969 totaled $1,800 ($600 × 3); $1,875 for 1970 ($625 × 3); $1,350 for 1970 ($675 × 2); and $1,500 for 1972 ($750 × 2).
[4]Includes $22,158 of income tax surcharge at 10 percent.
[5]Includes $2,283 of income tax surcharge at 2.5 percent and minimum tax of $588.
[6]Since 1969 is a closed year and any payment by the President would be voluntary, the staff did not include an interest payment for the deficiency in this year. However, if interest were to be included, the amount would be $40,732.

The Times' sources said Jaworski had decided to begin a formal investigation after receiving Saxbe's permission, which was necessary because Nixon's personal employes—as distinct from the White House staff and other appointees—were outside the prosecution's statutory mandate.

Lawyer, accountant answer White House—Frank DeMarco, Nixon's tax attorney, and Arthur Blech, his tax accountant, said in separate interviews that Nixon and the White House staff had paid closer attention to his tax affairs than had been suggested by the official White House disclaimer of responsibility.

In a statement reported by the Los Angeles Times April 5, DeMarco said it would be ridiculous to believe that he and Blech had made important decisions on Nixon's returns without instructions from the President or his representatives. Regarding the 1969 return, DeMarco said that he and Herbert W. Kalmbach, Nixon's former personal attorney and fund raiser, had met with the President and gone over the return "page by page." DeMarco contended that Nixon's questionable deductions might still be legally defensible but did not show "political astuteness."

According to the Los Angeles newspaper, DeMarco had also been privately expressing concern that he and Blech would become "scapegoats" for Nixon's tax improprieties.

In an interview reported by the New York Times April 8, Blech said he and DeMarco had operated on instructions from key White House aides, including former domestic affairs adviser John D. Ehrlichman and former counsel John W. Dean 3rd. "Any illusion that we had options is crazy," Blech said. "The pattern was set in 1969 and the deductions for 1970, 1971 and 1972 just followed suit."

As an example of the White House instructions, Blech cited the order—relayed through DeMarco—to deduct as business expenses 100% of the cost of operating Nixon's Key Biscayne, Fla. home and 50% of costs for the San Clemente, Calif. estate. Blech said he reduced the deduction to 25% on his own initiative. Even the lower amount was disallowed by the Congressional committee report on Nixon's taxes.

Blech recalled that he had become concerned that the low amount of taxes to be paid for 1970 ($783) was "politically unwise" and asked for a meeting with Nixon. A promised meeting at San Clemente was canceled, Blech said, and he had never talked to Nixon.

The Times also reported that other sources supported Blech's account of the orders from the White House, and according to one source, Nixon knew of all the tax actions in his behalf and had not objected to any of the procedures. The source cited a 1969 memo from Ehrlichman to Nixon detailing the plans for the large deduction for the gift of the President's papers to the National Archives. The single word "good" was at the bottom of the memo in Nixon's handwriting.

California asks $5,302 in back taxes. A California tax board ruled April 12 that President and Mrs. Nixon owed the state $4,263.72 in back taxes, about $1,000 in (6%) interest on the delayed settlement and a penalty of $39.17 (for failing to file a 1970 return). Martin Huff, executive officer of the Franchise Tax Board, in announcing the ruling, said the President's attorneys had agreed to pay the back taxes promptly.

The ruling was based on Nixon being a nonresident with income generated from within the state. Part of the President's salary was prorated by the state as California income on the basis of the time he was at San Clemente on "working vacations" (94 days in 1969 and 1970). The assessment also included income of a 1970 capital gain on sale of some San Clemente land, improvements to his estate, royalty income from sale of his book, "Six Crises," and income from his mother's estate.

The board found that Nixon owed the state $4,107.04 on gross California income of $66,140 for 1969, and $156.68 on gross income of $116,317 for 1970. The low 1970 tax figure reflected a large interest payment by Nixon on his loan for the San Clemente purchase.

Although the President would have to file 1971 and 1972 returns, the board said, he would not owe any state taxes for those years because his deductions would more than offset his income as computed for state purposes.

Huff said there was no evidence of fraud or criminal negligence in the failure of the President to file California returns since he had not believed he had a requirement to file.

White House to return donations—White House Communications Director Ken W. Clawson said April 15 the President was "heartened and moved in the past 10 days by an outpouring of public support" for his tax debt but he had decided to pay "every penny" himself.

The outpouring—5,649 letters and telegrams as of noon April 13, all but 113 favorable to the President—indicated, according to Clawson, that "the citizens of this country are getting tired of the President being kicked in every conceivable manner and they ought to be." Some 5,000 of the letters contained contributions ranging from 6¢ to $5,000 and totaling $43,657.71. The contributions were to be returned to the donors or if made anonymously, to be turned over to the Red Cross for aid to victims of the recent tornados.

IRS silent on negligence—Internal Revenue Service (IRS) Commissioner Donald C. Alexander declined to reveal April 7 whether a 5% negligence penalty was included in the $432,787 back-tax assessment on President Nixon. The White House had not disclosed the details of the IRS report on Nixon's taxes.

Appearing on the Columbia Broadcasting System program "Face the Nation," Alexander said his refusal to answer was based on the principle of confidentiality between the IRS and taxpayers. Alexander noted, however, that there had been no fraud penalty.

Reminded that the White House had partially waived the privacy privilege, Alexander insisted that he would not give a "further breakdown" of the aggregate figure released by the White House. "All taxpayers, including this one," were entitled by law "and sound IRS practice" to the basic right of privacy, "and we don't propose to go behind that."

Alexander acknowledged that his agency had not done "as thorough an audit as it should have" when Nixon's returns were first examined. Alexander

Congressional Staff Table on Nixon Estates

Additional Taxable Income Because of the Expenditure of Federal Funds at the President's Properties in San Clemente and Key Biscayne

	1969	1970	1971	1972
San Clemente expenditures:				
Exhaust fan			$388.78	
Den windows in residence	$1,600.00			
Heating system	12,988.00			
Point gazebo			4,981.50	
Boundary surveys	5,472.59			
Sewer	3,800.00			
Handrails	998.50			
Paving	5,866.66			
Cabana, stair rail to beach, railroad crossing and warning signals	3,500.00			
Landscape construction	3,600.00			
Landscape maintenance	5,799.00	$15,635.00	1,593.00	$391.00
Total San Clemente expenditures	**43,624.75**	**15,635.00**	**6,963.28**	**391.00**
Key Biscayne expenditures:				
Shuffleboard court	1,600.00			
Fence and hedge system	12,679.00			
Landscape construction	3,414.00			
Landscape maintenance	1,124.00	2,165.00	1,992.00	2,710.00
Total Key Biscayne expenditures	**18,817.00**	**2,165.00**	**1,992.00**	**2,710.00**
Total Federal expenditures at San Clemente and Key Biscayne	**62,441.75**	**17,800.00**	**8,955.28**	**3,101.00**

said the apparent preferential treatment given earlier presidents' returns might explain the IRS laxity on Nixon, but that procedural reforms would assure that the IRS would meet "its obligations" in the future. Alexander declined to detail the new procedures, saying that the second audit on Nixon "speaks for itself."

On another issue, Alexander conceded that the IRS had in the past furnished the White House with information on "sensitive" tax cases of certain people, but that the practice had been stopped.

In a related development, Nixon's tax accountant Arthur Blech said April 6 that Nixon had been granted an extension in filing his 1973 return, which would have to be "reworked" to comply with IRS decisions on procedures used in Nixon's 1969–72 returns.

Archives claims Nixon papers—Among plans to help the President pay his back-tax debt were several to purchase his vice presidential papers. The biggest item in Nixon's federal back-tax debt—some $235,000—derived from disallowance of $482,018 in deductions through 1969–72 for his gift to the National Archives of the papers, which had been valued at $576,-000. The remainder of the deduction presumably was to have been claimed for 1973. The deductions were disallowed because of inadequate compliance with the tax law.

A spokesman for the General Services Administration, the parent agency of the National Archives, said April 12 that despite the disallowance of the deductions for the papers, the gift itself was legally binding and the papers were government property.

White House Deputy Press Secretary Gerald Warren said it had always been the President's contention that a valid gift had been made.

House panel to probe tax issue. The House Judiciary Committee planned to send a written questionnaire to President Nixon to explore whether there was any criminal fraud on the part of the President on the matter of his federal income tax returns for 1969 through 1972.

Pursuit of the tax issue as a priority area of search in the committee's impeachment inquiry was disclosed April 25 as the committee met to hear a report from its legal staff on the scope of the inquiry and to consider a follow-up in the course of its subpoena to the White House for information. [For further details, see p. 87B2]

Pulitzer Prizes. The 58th annual Pulitzer Prizes in journalism, letters and music were presented in New York May 7. For the second consecutive year prizes went to journalists who investigated the activities of President Nixon and irregularities in his re-election campaign.

The national reporting awards, with two coequal winners of $1,000, went to

James R. Polk of the Washington Star-News for his disclosure of alleged irregularities in the financing of the 1972 Nixon campaign, and Jack White of the Providence (R.I.) Journal-Bulletin for disclosure of the President's income tax returns. The decision to give White an award came amid dissent from the approval committee, some of whom considered the publication of the tax returns, normally confidential material, as "illegal" reporting.

Gifts to Nixon family. The White House acknowledged May 14 that Mrs. Nixon and her daughters, Tricia Cox and Julie Eisenhower, had received gifts of jewelry from the Saudi Arabian royal family, but spokesmen accused the Washington Post, which had uncovered the heretofore secret gifts, of reporting a story that was "blown completely out of proportion and sensationalized."

Columnist Maxine Cheshire had reported May 13 that Mrs. Nixon received a matched set of emeralds and diamonds from Prince Fahd, half brother to King Faisal, on Oct. 14, 1969. An appraisal, requested by the Nixons in February 1970, set the gems' value at $52,400. She also received diamond and ruby earrings from King Faisal on May 28, 1971.

Prince Sultan, another of the king's half brothers, gave her a diamond watch bracelet, in July 1972, along with a diamond and ruby pin for Julie and a diamond and sapphire pin for Tricia.

According to the Post, the jewelry was removed from Mrs. Nixon's bedroom wall safe March 28. The gems were sent to a gifts unit in the Executive Office Building, where their receipt was recorded, when the newspaper attempted to verify reports of the jewelry's existence.

The gifts unit processed the estimated 3,500 gifts received by the White House each year, according to the Post. Few of the gifts were of great monetary or historical value.

White House spokesmen rejected any charges of impropriety regarding the gifts, saying that the family had intended to "turn them over" when Nixon left office and had always considered the gems to be the government's property, although their receipt had not been publicly acknowledged.

White House Counsel J. Fred Buzhardt Jr. refused to allow reporters to inspect records in the gifts unit, contending they were the President's private papers.

Article One of the Constitution forbids any officeholder from accepting gifts, offices or titles without the consent of Congress. Legislation passed by Congress in 1966 revised another bill passed in 1881 holding such gifts to be illegal. The updated law prohibited anyone related to government officials by "blood, marriage or adoption" from accepting gifts valued at more than $50.

State gifts, exchanged between heads of state, were "deemed to have been ac-

cepted on behalf of the United States," the law stated.

Buzhardt termed the jewelry "private gifts" from the Saudi Arabian ruling family, but said they were "in the same category as state gifts and they must go to a public repository when the President's term ends."

Federal regulations implementing the two statutes charged that gifts be "deposited" with the U.S. chief of protocol and authorized him to keep records of all items received by officials in the three branches of government. Soon after Nixon took office in 1969, it was decided by presidential assistant John Ehrlichman and Emil Mosbacher, then chief of protocol, that the Nixon family was exempt from the revised rules, Buzhardt said, although he conceded that the issue was not tested in the courts.

It was also agreed, he continued, that "precise records" would be kept at the White House should the courts rule otherwise. Ehrlichman and Mosbacher decided that records kept by the protocol office, designated by law as watchdog for the gifts, would be abolished, but that the protocol chief could have access to the information, Buzhardt told the Post.

House unit OKs Nixon homes' report. The House Government Operations Committee approved 36–0 May 14 a report that $17.1 million in federal funds had been spent in connection with President Nixon's homes. The report recommended that action be taken by agencies involved to recover any "improper expenditures," although no improper items were specified.

The report recommended recovery, if possible, of security costs enhancing the value of a president's property and limitation of permanent security systems to one of a president's private homes.

LBJ home cost put at $5.9 million—The committee reported May 24 that federal costs attributed to security for the late President Lyndon B. Johnson in Texas totaled $5.9 million. Part of the funds, $770,-000, was for Johnson's office in a federal building in Austin, Tex.

Impeachment panel asks Nixon data. The confidentiality of President Nixon's tax returns was upheld by Attorney General William B. Saxbe May 25 over the authority of the House impeachment process. However, the White House announced later May 25 that the President would give the House Judiciary Committee information on his income taxes "under appropriate safeguards."

In pursuit of its impeachment inquiry, the committee had asked the IRS for its audit of the Nixon returns. Treasury Secretary William E. Simon requested a legal opinion from Saxbe, who held that the committee was not entitled to the data without further action by the House (a) designating it a "select committee" authorized to investigate tax returns or (b) transmitting the data from committees specified under the IRS code as entitled to such data.

More officials report gifts. Following reports of disclosures of gifts by the President and his family, dozens of valuable gifts from U.S. officials and their families had flowed into the State Department's Protocol Office, the Washington Post reported June 12.

In April, former Vice President Spiro Agnew turned in gifts he and his family had received from the Saudi Arabian government in 1971. Sen. and Mrs. J. W. Fulbright (D, Ark.) received jewelry from the petroleum minister of Abu Dhabi in December 1972, but did not turn them in until 14 months later. Former Secretary of State and Mrs. William P. Rogers received jewels from the Republic of Kuwait in September 1973 but did not report them until May. Sen. Hubert Humphrey (D, Minn.) returned to the State Department June 12 an eight-carat diamond, worth over $100,000, which he was given in 1968 by Congo President Joseph Mobutu. Humphrey had also received leopard pelts which were sold for charity, and therefore could not be returned.

The delays were all in violation of Article One of the Constitution and legislation passed by Congress in 1966 which prohibited an officeholder from taking official gifts valued at more than $50. State Department officials attributed the delays in turning over the gifts to the "weakness" of the 1966 law, legislation they considered "vague, ambiguous" and lacking in sufficient enforcement procedures.

The committee's June 20 session focused on Nixon's personal income tax situation. Afterwards, several members confirmed reports that the Internal Revenue Service report on Nixon's taxes, in which it assessed him $432,000 in unpaid taxes for the years 1969-72, included a negligence finding and 5% penalty against Nixon. The White House had not acknowledged the negligence finding in announcing the IRS report in April. [For further details, see p. 171D2]

Cover-up sessions concluded. The House Judiciary Committee's closed hearings to study staff evidence moved past the Watergate cover-up phase June 19.

It also became known after the session that Nixon had not as yet paid the delinquent taxes assessed against him for 1969, a year for which the statute of limitations had expired. Nixon's intention to pay the 1969 taxes, announced in April, was reaffirmed at the White House June 20. The President was reported to have paid the taxes for 1970, 1971 and 1972.

(Nixon's tax lawyer, Frank DeMarco Jr., resigned his state notary commission on the eve of hearings scheduled June 17 on an alleged false notarization by DeMarco on Nixon's donation of pre-presidential papers to the government. The

donation was the basis of a hugh tax deduction claimed by Nixon for his presidential years but disallowed by the IRS in its finding of back-taxes due. Edmund G. Brown Jr., California secretary of state, announcing he had received DeMarco's resignation letter June 14, said June 17 it was "clear" that the documents on Nixon's donation, dated April 21, 1969, had been signed a year later, on April 10, 1970, after a law barring such deductions took effect.)

Cover-up sessions concluded. The House Judiciary Committee's closed hearings to study staff evidence moved past the Watergate cover-up phase June 19.

The committee's June 20 session focused on Nixon's personal income tax situation. Afterwards, several members confirmed reports that the Internal Revenue Service report on Nixon's taxes, in which it assessed him $432,000 in unpaid taxes for the years 1969-72, included a negligence finding and 5% penalty against Nixon. The White House had not acknowledged the negligence finding in announcing the IRS report in April. [For further details, see p. 171E2]

Impeachment inquiry enters new phase. The House Judiciary Committee completed its closed evidentiary hearings June 21 and moved June 24 to accelerate its impeachment inquiry in an effort to conclude its work by the latter part of July.

Evidentiary hearings end—The committee's June 21 session was its 18th and final closed hearing over a six-week period to hear the evidence gathered by its staff. The subjects were President Nixon's personal income tax status for 1969-72 and the secret bombing of Cambodia ordered by Nixon in 1969. [For further details, see p. 173E3]

St. Clair presents rebuttal. President Nixon's defense against impeachment was presented to the House Judiciary Committee in closed sessions June 27-28 by his chief defense counsel James D. St. Clair. The material was said to have dealt with the Watergate burglary, the cover-up, Administration transactions with the International Telephone & Telegraph Corporation and milk producers, the White House "plumbers," wiretapping and Nixon's income taxes. [For further details, see p. 177D1]

Watergate committee details abuses. In its last official action, the Senate Select Committee on Presidential Campaign Activities, known as "the Watergate Committee" or "the Ervin Committee," released the final report July 13 on its investigation of the Watergate and other scandals related to the 1972 presidential campaign.

Rebozo linked to $50,000 spent on Nixon—The committee's final report pre-

sented lengthy evidence that Charles G. Rebozo, President Nixon's friend, spent more than $50,000—including presidential campaign funds—for the President's personal benefit. The section of the report dealing with Rebozo was first made public July 10, but was included in the final report issued July 13.

Mrs. Nixon's earrings—The committee's final report also concerned the March 17, 1972 purchase by Rebozo of platinum and diamond earrings, a birthday present from the President to Mrs. Nixon.

Property improvements—The committee's report likewise raised questions about $45,621 in improvements made on the President's two Key Biscayne properties.

[For complete details on the committee's findings, see p. 185]

Nixon mortgage date extended. President Nixon received a six-month extension of time to meet the final mortgage payment on his San Clemente, Calif. property. A payment of $600,000 had been due July 14. Nixon's share of the payment due was $226,660, and the remainder was due from the B & C Investment Co., owned by Nixon's friend, industrialist Robert H. Abplanalp.

A White House spokesman said July 13 Nixon could not afford to pay the entire amount at the current time but had agreed to pay interest (7½%) of $16,999.52 and an unspecified amount of the principal.

Interview with Rabbi Korff. President Nixon told Rabbi Baruch Korff, leader of a pro-Nixon group, that Watergate would be remembered as "the broadest but the thinnest scandal in American history." The interview, held on May 13, was released by the President's press office in San Clemente, Calif. July 16, when Nixon met again with Korff, president of the National Citizens Committee for Fairness to the Presidency. [For further details, see p. 195C1]

The President also spoke of his personal finances. He did not mind having his tax returns "gone over with a fine tooth comb," he said, and would pay the "extra money." "I have never cared much about money," he said, "If I did, I would have a lot of it because I was out of office for eight years" and, despite the fact he was "a fairly accomplished lawyer," "still only entered here [the presidency] with a net worth of less than $600,000." [For further details, see p. 195C1]

Doar says evidence merits impeachment. John M. Doar, special counsel to the House Judiciary Committee, urged committee members July 19 to recommend the impeachment of President Nixon on one or more charges. Doar was seconded by Albert E. Jenner Jr., special Republican counsel to the committee. [For further details, see p. 200D1]

Cox dismissal prelude disclosed. According to evidence released by the House Judiciary Committee July 20, Archibald Cox, the first Watergate special prosecutor, was warned by the White House as early as July 3, 1973 that his investigations were going too far and that he might be dismissed. Cox was fired Oct. 20, 1973 during a dispute over access to presidential tapes.

The panel's evidence included an affidavit by Elliot L. Richardson, the attorney general during Cox's tenure, who related that on July 3, 1973 he had received a complaint from White House chief of staff Alexander M. Haig Jr. about reports that Cox was investigating expenditures on Nixon's estate at San Clemente, Calif. [For further details, p. 198E2]

Evidence release continues. Internal Revenue Service (IRS) investigators reported to Commissioner Donald C. Alexander that if presidential aides connected with preparation of President Nixon's 1969 income tax return could be compelled to testify, they could "possibly connect the taxpayer with the preparation of the return," thus providing the basis for a fraud penalty against the President, according to testimony released by the House Judiciary Committee July 26. [For further details, see p. 206F2]

Panel rejects articles on Cambodia, finances. The House Judiciary Committee recessed July 30 after approving three articles of impeachment charging President Nixon with obstruction of justice in connection with the Watergate scandal, abuse of presidential powers and attempting to impede the impeachment process by defying committee subpoenas for evidence. The committee rejected two other proposed articles, one charging that

Nixon had usurped the powers of Congress by ordering the secret bombing of Cambodia in 1969, the other concerning income tax fraud and the unconstitutional use of government funds to make improvements on his properties in California and Florida. [For further details, see p. 207C3]

Rebozo subpoena compliance ordered. U.S. District Court Judge George L. Hart Jr. Aug. 22 ordered attorneys for Charles G. Rebozo, a close friend of former President Nixon, to surrender to the Watergate special prosecutor their records concerning funds possibly spent for Nixon's personal benefit.

The subpoena called for bank records, memoranda and other items in the custody of the law firm headed by Thomas H. Wakefield, records which—according to the prosecution—related to expenditures of more than $36,000 by Rebozo on his own behalf and for Nixon. [For further details, see p. 236C3]

Edited Transcripts
of Watergate Tapes Released

Nixon releases transcripts. President Nixon, in a televised address April 29, said he would turn over to the House Judiciary Committee the next day, and also make public, 1,200 pages of edited transcripts of his conversations with key aides concerning Watergate. Asserting he had "nothing to hide," Nixon said the transcripts included "all the relevant portions of all of the subpoenaed conversations that were recorded and related to Watergate or the cover-up. The transcripts also covered other conversations, he said, which were not subpoenaed by the committee "but which have a significant bearing on the question of Presidential action with regard to Watergate." [Text begins on Page 100]

The President pointed repeatedly to a double stack of binders nearby containing the transcripts, which, he said, together with material already made available, "will tell it all" as far as what he personally knew and did with regard to Watergate and the cover-up.

Nixon offered a verification procedure. He invited the committee's chairman and ranking Republican member "to come to the White House and listen to the actual full tapes of these conversations so that they can determine for themselves beyond question that the transcripts are accurate and that everything on the tapes relevant to my knowledge and my actions on Watergate is included. If there should be any disagreement over whether omitted material is relevant, I shall meet with them personally in an effort to settle the matter." Nixon said he personally had decided the questions of relevancy and he believed it appropriate that the committee's review "should also be made by its own senior elected officials and not by staff employes."

Nixon reasserted his duty to defend the principle of executive privilege, but said he believed it was vital now "to restore the principle itself by clearing the air of the central questions" involved and to provide the evidence "which will allow this matter to be brought to a prompt conclusion." He said he felt that the public was entitled to the facts because of "the current impeachment climate." "I want there to be no question remaining about the fact that

the President has nothing to hide in this matter," Nixon said.

The President cited the "wrenching ordeal" for the nation of an impeachment proceeding and "the impact of such an ordeal" throughout the world. Therefore, he was making the transcripts public and would also make public transcripts of all the parts of the tapes already turned over to the special prosecutor and the committee that related to his actions or knowledge of Watergate.

During the past year, Nixon said, "the wildest accusations have been given banner headlines and ready credence as well," leaving "a vague, general impression of massive wrongdoing, implicating everybody, gaining credibility by its endless repetition."

"The basic question at issue today," he continued, "is whether the President personally acted improperly in the Watergate matter. Month after month of rumor, insinuation and charges by just one Watergate witness, John Dean [former counsel to the President], suggested that the President did act improperly. This sparked the demand for an impeachment inquiry."

Nixon said he expected the transcripts to become "grist for many sensational stories in the press." "Parts will seem to be contradictory with one another, and parts will be in conflict" with testimony in the Senate Watergate hearings, he said. The tapes "will embarrass me and those with whom I have talked" and would "become the subject to speculation and even ridicule" and parts "will be seized upon by political and journalistic opponents."

Returning to the principle of confidentiality, he believed a reading of the raw transcripts made it "more readily apparent why that principle is essential and must be maintained in the future." "The same kind of uninhibited discussion," he said, the "same brutal candor is necessary in discussing how to bring warring factions to the peace table or how to move necessary legislation through the Congress."

The transcripts, Nixon said, would demonstrate his concern during the period covered. "The first and obvious one," he

said, "was to find out just exactly what had happened and who was involved." He also was concerned, he said, for the people involved and, "quite frankly," about the political implications. "This represented potentially a devastating blow to the Administration and to its programs."

"I wanted to do what was right," he stressed. "But I wanted to do it in a way that would cause the least unnecessary damage in a highly charged political atmosphere to the Administration."

His other concerns were not to prejudice the rights of potential defendants and "to sort out a complex tangle" not only of facts but also of legal and moral responsibility. "I wanted, above all, to be fair," Nixon said.

In speaking of the tapes themselves, the President referred to the 18½-minute gap in a June 1972 tape. "How it was caused," he said, "is still a mystery to me" but he was "absolutely certain" that "it was not caused intentionally by my secretary, Rose Mary Woods, or any of my White House assistants."

Nixon specifically cited several conversations with Dean. The transcripts "show clearly," he said, that, contrary to Dean's charge he was fully aware of the cover-up in September 1972, "I first learned of it" from Dean on March 21, 1973 some six months later. He learned in that conversation, Nixon said, that Watergate defendant Howard Hunt was "threatening blackmail" unless $120,000 was extended to legal fees and family support, and that the blackmail involved exposure not on Watergate but on "extremely sensitive, highly secret national security matters [such as, presumably the Ellsberg case break-in]."

Later, Nixon said, he learned "how much there was that he [Dean] did not tell me then; for example, that he himself had authorized promises of clemency, that he had personally handled money for the Watergate defendants, and that he had suborned perjury of a witness."

In his March 21 talk, he said, he kept returning to the blackmail threat, "which to me was not a Watergate problem but one which I regarded, rightly or wrongly, as a potential national security problem of very serious proportions." "I considered long and hard," Nixon said, "whether it might in fact be better to let the payment go forward, at least temporarily." In the course of this consideration "and of just thinking out loud," he suggested several times that meeting Hunt's demands "might be necessary."

But then, he said, he also "traced through where that would lead."

"The money could be raised," he continued. "But money demands would lead inescapably to clemency demands, and clemency could not be granted, I said, and I quote directly from the tape—It is wrong, that's for sure."

Nixon also quoted from the transcripts that "in the end we are going to be bled to death" and "it is all going to come out anyway and then you get the worst of both worlds" and in effect it would "look like a cover-up. So that we cannot do."

Recognizing that the tape could be interpreted differently by different people, Nixon said in the end it showed his decision to convene a new grand jury "and to send everyone before" it with instructions to testify.

Nixon tracked his subsequent actions—assigning Dean to write a report and, when it was not forthcoming, giving the task to his aide John D. Ehrlichman; having another aide H. R. Haldeman pursue other independent lines of inquiry; having Ehrlichman inform the attorney general of his findings; and agreeing to have Assistant Attorney General Henry Petersen put in charge of the investigation and his follow-up and cooperation with Petersen.

"I made clear there was to be no cover-up," Nixon stressed. He quoted his own remarks against extending clemency and for doing "the right thing," his advice "to prick the boil and take the heat" and for Dean to "tell the truth. That is the thing I have told everybody around here."

In essence, the transcripts would show, Nixon said, "that what I have stated from the beginning to be the truth has been the truth, that I personally had no knowledge of the break-in before it occurred, that I had no knowledge of the cover-up" until March 21, 1973 that he never offered clemency and that, after March 21, "my actions were directed toward finding the facts and seeing that justice was done."

He said he was confident that the evidence he was releasing would be found to be "persuasive and, I hope, conclusive," by those who studied it "fully, fairly and objectively."

Never before in the history of the presidency, Nixon said, "have records that are so private been made so public. In giving you these records—blemishes and all—I am placing my trust in the basic fairness of the American people."

11 conversations missing—The transcripts, which were released April 30, did not cover 11 of the 42 conversations subpoenaed by the committee. Four of them, according to White House counsel J. Fred Buzhardt, occurred on April 15, 1973 and were not recorded because the machine ran out of tape; five occurred on telephones that were not connected to a recorder; and tapes of two others were not

found, the implication being that the conversations did not occur.

The transcripts themselves were found to be liberally sprinkled with deletions marked "unintelligible," "expletive deleted" or "inaudible." Many passages actually were unintelligible because of the markings. One entire comment attributed to Nixon, whose conversation was dotted with "expletives," was: "P. [expletive removed]! [unintelligible]"

A brief attached as an introduction to the volume of transcripts said the expletives had been removed, except where necessary to maintain relevancy, in the interest of good taste. Other deletions, allowable on the relevancy test, it said, were made to eliminate characterization of third persons and material not relating to the President's conduct.

The House Judiciary Committee received a 1,308-page volume measuring 2¼ inches thick; reporters obtained an eight-by-10-inch book, the pages typewritten and double-spaced, about the size of a big-city phone directory.

Copies of the transcripts, at $12.25 each, were available from the Government Printing Office. Its Washington bookstore sold 800 copies in three hours May 1.

Former White House Communications Director Herbert G. Klein was brought back to the White House on temporary assignment as a media consultant to help coordinate the effort to distribute the material released by the President.

Transcript of President Nixon's April 29 Address to Nation

Good evening. I have asked for this time tonight in order to announce my answer to the House Judiciary Committee's subpoena for additional Watergate tapes and to tell you something about the action I shall be taking tomorrow, about what I hope they will mean to you, and about the very difficult choices that were presented to me.

These actions will at last once and for all show that what I knew and what I did with regard to the Watergate break-in and cover-up were just as I have described them to you from the very beginning. I spent many hours during the past few weeks thinking about what I would say to the American people if I were to reach the decision I shall announce tonight. And so my words have not been lightly chosen. I can assure you they are deeply felt.

It was almost two years ago in June 1972, that five men broke into the Democratic National Committee headquarters in Washington. It turned out that they were connected with my re-election committee, and the Watergate break-in became a major issue in the campaign.

The full resources of the FBI and the Justice Department were used to investigate the incident thoroughly. I instructed my staff and campaign aides to cooperate fully with the investigation. The FBI conducted nearly 1,500 interviews. For nine months, until March 1973, I was assured by those charged with conducting and monitoring the investigations that no one in the White House was involved.

Nevertheless, for more than a year there have been allegations, insinuations, that I knew about the planning of the Watergate break-in and that I was involved in an extensive plot to cover it up. The House Judiciary Committee is now investigating these charges.

On March 6, I ordered all materials that I had previously furnished to the special prosecutor turned over to the committee. These included tape recordings of 19 Presidential conversations and more than 700

documents from private White House files.

On April 11, the Judiciary Committee issued a subpoena for 42 additional tapes of conversations which it contended were necessary for its investigation. I agreed to respond to that subpoena by tomorrow.

In these folders that you see over there on my left are more than 1,200 pages of transcripts of private conversations I participated in between Sept. 15, 1972, and April 27 of 1973 with my principal aides and associates with regard to Watergate. They include all the relevant portions of all of the subpoenaed conversations that were recorded; that is, all portions that relate to the question of what I knew about Watergate or the cover-up, and what I did about it.

They also include transcripts of other conversations which were not subpoenaed, but which have a significant bearing on the question of Presidential action with regard to Watergate. These will be delivered to the committee tomorrow. In these transcripts, portions not relevant to my knowledge or actions with regard to Watergate are not included, but everything that is relevant is included—the rough as well as the smooth, the strategy sessions, the exploration of alternatives, the weighing of human and political costs. As far as what the President personally knew and did with regard to Watergate and the cover-up is concerned, these materials, together with those already made available, will tell it all.

I shall invite Chairman Rodino and the committee's ranking minority member, Congressman Hutchinson of Michigan, to come to the White House and listen to the actual full tapes of these conversations so that they can determine for themselves beyond question that those transcripts are accurate and that everything on the tapes relevant to my knowledge and my actions on Watergate is included. If there should be any disagreement over whether omitted material is relevant, I shall meet with them personally in an effort to settle the matter.

I believe this arrangement is fair and I think it's ap-

propriate. For many days now, I have spent many hours of my own time personally reviewing these materials and personally deciding questions of relevancy. I believe it is appropriate that the committee's review should also be made by its own senior elected officials and not by staff employes.

The task of Chairman Rodino and Congressman Hutchinson will be made simpler than was mine by the fact that the work of preparing the transcripts has been completed. All they will need to do is to satisfy themselves of their authenticity and their completeness.

Ever since the existence of the White House taping system was first made known last summer, I have tried vigorously to guard the privacy of the tapes. I have been well aware that my effort to protect the confidentiality of Presidential conversations has heightened the sense of mystery about Watergate and, in fact, has caused increased suspicion of the President.

Many people assumed that the tapes must incriminate the President, or that otherwise he wouldn't insist on their privacy. But the problem I confronted was this: Unless a President can protect the privacy of the advice he gets, he cannot get the advice he needs. This principle is recognized in the constitutional doctrine of executive privilege, which has been defended and maintained by every President since [George] Washington and which has been recognized by the courts whenever tested as inherent in the Presidency. I consider it to be my constitutional responsibility to defend this principle.

Three factors have now combined to persuade me that a major, unprecedented exception to that principle is now necessary:

First, in the present circumstances, the House of Representatives must be able to reach an informed judgment about the President's role in Watergate.

Second, I am making a major exception to the principle of confidentiality because I believe such action is now necessary in order to restore the principle itself by clearing the air of the central questions that have brought such pressures upon it, and also to provide the evidence which will allow this matter to be brought to a prompt conclusion.

Third, in the context of the current impeachment climate, I believe all the American people, as well as their representatives in Congress, are entitled to have not only the facts but also the evidence that demonstrates those facts.

I want there to be no question remaining about the fact that the President has nothing to hide in this matter.

The impeachment of the President is a remedy of last resort. It is the most solemn act of our entire constitutional process. And, regardless of whether or not it succeeded, the action of the House in voting a formal accusation requiring trial by the Senate would put the nation through a wrenching ordeal it has endured only once in its lifetime, a century ago, and never since America has become a world power with global responsibilities. The impact of such an ordeal would be felt throughout the world and it would have its effect on the lives of all Americans for many years to come.

Because this is an issue that profoundly affects all the American people, in addition to turning over these transcripts to the House Judiciary Committee, I have directed that they should all be made public, all of these that you see here.

To complete the record, I shall also release to the public transcripts of all those portions of the tapes already turned over to the special prosecutor and to the committee that relate to presidential actions or knowledge of the Watergate affair.

During the past year, the wildest accusations have been given banner headlines and ready credence as well. Rumor, gossip, innuendo, accounts from unnamed sources of what a prospective witness might testify have filled the morning newspapers and then are repeated on the evening newscasts.

Day after day, time and again, a familiar pattern repeated itself. A charge would be reported the first day. That's what it was—just an allegation. But it would then be referred back to the next day and thereafter as if it were true. The distinction between fact and speculation grew blurred. Eventually, all seeped into the public consciousness as a vague, general impression of massive wrongdoing, implicating everybody, gaining credibility by its endless repetition.

The basic question at issue today is whether the President personally acted improperly in the Watergate matter. Month after month of rumor, insinuation and charges by just one Watergate witness, John Dean, suggested that the President did act improperly. This sparked the demand for an impeachment inquiry. This is the question that must be asnwered, and this is the question that will be answered by these transcripts that I have ordered published tomorrow.

These transcripts cover hour upon hour of discussion that I held with Mr. [H. R.] Haldeman, John Ehrlichman, John Dean, John Mitchell, former Attorney General [Richard] Kleindienst, Assistant Attorney General [Henry] Petersen and others with regard to Watergate. They were discussions in which I was probing to find out what had happened, who was responsible, what were the various degrees of responsibility, what were the legal culpabilities, what were the political ramifications, and what actions were necessary and appropriate on the part of the President.

I realize that these transcripts will provide grist for many sensational stories in the press. Parts will seem to be contradictory with one another, and parts will be in conflict with some of the testimony given in the Senate Watergate Committee hearings.

I've been reluctant to release these tapes not just because they will embarrass me and those with whom I have talked—which they will—and not just because they will become the subject of speculation and even ridicule—which they will—and not just because certain parts of them will be seized upon by political and journalistic opponents—which they will.

I've been reluctant because in these, and in all the other conversations in this office, people have spoken their minds freely, never dreaming that specific sentences or even parts of sentences will be picked out of the subjects of national attention and controversy. I've been reluctant because the principle of confidentiality is absolutely essential to the conduct of the Presidency.

In reading the raw transcripts of these conversations, I believe it will be more readily apparent why that principle is essential and must be maintained in the future. These conversations are unusual in their subject matter, but the same kind of uninhibited discussion—and it is that—the same brutal candor is necessary in discussing how to bring warring factions to the peace table or how to move necessary legislation through the Congress.

Names are named in these transcripts. Therefore, it is important to remember that much that appears in them is no more than hearsay or speculation exchanged as I was trying to find out what really had happened while my principal aides were reporting to me on rumors and reports that they had heard while we discussed the various, often conflicting stories that different persons were telling.

As the transcripts will demonstrate, my concerns during this period covered a wide range. The first, and obvious one, was to find out just exactly what had happened and who was involved. A second concern was for the people who had been or might become involved in Watergate. Some were close advisers, valued friends, others whom I had trusted. And I was also concerned about the human impact on others, especially some of the young people and their families who had come to Washington to work in my Administration, whose lives might be suddenly ruined by something they had done in an excess of loyalty or in a mistaken belief that it would serve the interests of the President.

And then I was quite frankly concerned about the political implications. This represented potentially a devastating blow to the Administration and to its programs, one which I knew would be exploited for all it was worth by hostile elements in the Congress as well as in the media. I wanted to do what was right. But I wanted to do it in a way that would cause the least unnecessary damage in a highly charged political atmosphere to the Administration.

And fourth, as a lawyer, I felt very strongly that I had to conduct myself in a way that would not prejudice the rights of potential defendants. And fifth, I was striving to sort out a complex tangle, not only of facts, but also questions of legal and moral responsibility.

I wanted, above all, to be fair. I wanted to draw distinctions, where those were appropriate, between persons who were active and willing participants on the one hand, and on the other those who might have gotten inadvertently caught up in the web and be technically indictable but morally innocent.

Despite the confusions and contradictions, what does come through clearly is this: John Dean charged in sworn Senate testimony that I was fully aware of the cover-up at the time of our first meeting on Sept. 15, 1972. These transcripts show clearly that I first learned of it when Mr. Dean himself told me about it in this office on March 21, [1973] some six months later.

Incidentally, these transcripts, covering hours upon hours of conversation, should place in somewhat better perspective the controversy over the 18½-minute gap in the tape of a conversation I had with Mr. Haldeman back in June of 1972.

Now how it was caused is still a mystery to me, and I think to many of the experts as well. But I am absolutely certain, however, of one thing—that it was not caused intentionally by my secretary, Rose Mary Woods, or any of my White House assistants.

And certainly if the theory were true that during those 18½ minutes Mr. Haldeman and I cooked up some sort of a Watergate cover-up scheme that so many have been quick to surmise, it hardly seems likely that in all of our subsequent conversations—many of them are here, which neither of us expected would see the light of day—there is nothing remotely indicating such a scheme, indeed quite the contrary.

From the beginning, I have said that in many places on the tapes there were ambiguities—statements and comments that different people with different perspectives might interpret in drastically different ways, that although the words may be ambiguous, though the discussions may have explored many alternatives, the record of my actions is totally clear now and I still believe it was totally correct then.

A prime example is one of the most controversial discussions, that with Mr. Dean on March 21, the one on which he first told me of the cover-up, with Mr. Haldeman joining us midway through the conversation. His revelations to me on March 21 were a sharp surprise, even though the report he gave to me was far from complete, especially since he did not reveal at that time the extent of his own criminal involvement.

I was particularly concerned by his report that one of the Watergate defendants, Howard Hunt, was threatening blackmail unless he and his lawyers were immediately given $120,000 for legal fees and family support, and that he was attempting to blackmail the White House, not by threatening exposure on the Watergate matter, but by threatening to reveal activities that would expose extremely sensitive, highly secret national security matters that he had worked on before Watergate. **A**

I probed, questioned, tried to learn all Mr. Dean knew about who was involved, what was involved. I asked more than 150 questions of Mr. Dean in the course of that conversation. He said to me—and I quote from the transcripts directly—"I can just tell from our conversation that these are things that you had no knowledge of."

It was only considerably later that I learned how much there was that he did not tell me then: for example, that he himself had authorized promises of clemency, that he had personally handled money for the Watergate defendants, and that he had suborned perjury of a witness. **B**

I knew that I needed more facts. I knew that I needed the judgments of more people. I knew the facts about the Watergate cover-up would have to be made public, but I had to find out more about what they were before I could decide how they could best be made public.

I returned several times to the immediate problem posed by Mr. Hunt's blackmail threat, which to me was not a Watergate problem but one which I regarded, rightly or wrongly, as a potential national security problem of very serious proportions. I considered long and hard whether it might in fact be better to let the payment go forward, at least temporarily, in the hope that this national security matter would not be exposed in the course of uncovering the Watergate cover-up. **C**

I believed then, and I believe today, that I had a responsibility as President to consider every option, including this one, where production of sensitive national security matters was at issue—protection of such matters.

In the course of considering it, and of just thinking out loud as I put it at one point, I several times suggested that meeting Hunt's demands might be necessary. But then I also traced through where that would lead. **D**

The money could be raised. But money demands would lead inescapably to clemency demands, and clemency could not be granted. I said—and I quote directly from the tape—"It is wrong, that's for sure."

I pointed out—and I quote again from the tape—"but in the end we are going to be bled to death. And in the end it is all going to come out anyway. And then you get the worst of both worlds. We're going to lose, and people are going to"—then Mr. Haldeman interrupts me and says: "And look like dopes." And I responded, "And in effect look like a cover-up, so that we cannot do." **E**

Now I recognize that this tape of March 21 is one which different meanings could be read into by different people, but by the end of the meeting, as the tape shows, my decision was to convene a new grand jury and to send everyone before the grand jury with instructions to testify.

Whatever the potential for misinterpretation there may be as a result of the different options that were discussed at different times during the meeting, my conclusion at the end of the meeting was clear, and my actions and reactions, as demonstrated on the tapes that follow that date, show clearly that I did not intend the further payment to Hunt or anyone else be made. **F**

These are some of the actions that I took in the weeks that followed in my effort to find the truth to carry out my responsibilities to enforce the law.

As the tape of our meeting on March 22, the next day, indicates, I directed Mr. Dean to go to Camp David with instructions to put together a written report. I learned five days later, on march 26, that he was unable to complete it, and so on March 27 I assigned John Ehrlichman to try to find out what had happened, who was at fault, and in what way and to what degree. **G**

One of the transcripts I am making public is a call that Mr. Ehrlichman made to the attorney general on March 28, in which he asked the attorney general to report to me, the President, directly any information he might find indicating possible involvement of John Mitchell or by anyone in the White House. I had Mr.

Haldeman separately pursue other independent lines of inquiry. Throughout, I was trying to reach determinations on matters of both substance and procedure, on what the facts were and what was the best way to move the case forward.

I concluded that I wanted everyone to go before the grand jury and testify freely and fully. This decision, as you will recall, was publicly announced on March 30, 1973. I waived executive privilege in order to permit everybody to testify.

I specifically waived executive privilege with regard to conversations with the President and I waived the attorney-client privilege with John Dean in order to permit him to testify fully and, I hope, truthfully.

Finally on April 14, three weeks after I learned of the cover-up from Mr. Dean, Mr. Ehrlichman reported to me on the results of his investigation. As he acknowledged, much of what he had gathered was hearsay, but he had gathered enough to make it clear that the next step was to make his findings completely available to the attorney general, which I instructed him to do.

And the next day, Sunday, April 15, Attorney General Kleindienst asked to see me, and he reported new information which had come to his attention on this matter. And although he was in no way whatever involved in Watergate because of his close personal ties not only to John Mitchell but to other potential people who might be involved, he quite properly removed himself from the case.

We agreed that assistant Attorney General Henry Petersen, a Democrat and career prosecutor, should be placed in complete charge of the investigation. Later that day, I met with Mr. Petersen. I continued to meet with him, to talk with him, to consult with him, to offer him the full cooperation of the White House—as you will see from these transcripts—even to the point of retaining John Dean on the White House staff for an extra two weeks after he admitted his criminal involvement because Mr. Petersen thought that would make it easier for the prosecutor to get his cooperation in breaking the case if it should become necessary to grant Mr. Dean's demand for immunity.

On April 15, when I heard that one of the obstacles to breaking the case was Gordon Liddy's refusal to talk, I telephoned Mr. Petersen and directed that he should make clear not only to Mr. Liddy but to everyone that—and now I quote directly from the tape of that telephone call—"as far as the President is concerned, everybody in this case is to talk and to tell the truth." I told him, if necessary, I would personally meet with Mr. Liddy's lawyer to assure him that I wanted Liddy to talk and to tell the truth.

From the time Mr. Petersen took charge, the case was solidly within the criminal justice system, pursued personally by the nation's top professional prosecutor with the active personal assistance of the President of the United States. I made clear there was to be no cover-up.

Let me quote just a few lines from the transcripts; you can read them to verify them, in that you can hear for yourself the orders I was giving in this period.

Speaking to Haldeman and Ehrlichman I said, "It is ridiculous to talk about clemency. They all knew that."

Speaking to Ehrlichman, I said, "We all have to do the right thing, we just cannot have this kind of a business."

Speaking to Haldeman and Ehrlichman, I said, "The boil had to be pricked. We had to prick the boil and take the heat. Now that's what we are doing here."

Speaking to Henry Petersen, I said, "I want you to be sure to understand that you know we are going to get to the bottom of this thing."

Speaking to John Dean, I said, "Tell the truth. That is the thing I have told everybody around here."

And then speaking to Haldeman, "and you tell Mc-Gruder, 'now, Jed, this evidence is coming in. You ought to go to the grand jury. Purge yourself if you're perjured and tell this whole story.'"

I'm confident that the American people will see these transcripts for what they are—fragmentary records from a time more than a year ago that now seems very distant, the records of a President and of a man suddenly being confronted and having to cope with information which, if true, would have the most far-reaching consequences not only for his personal reputation but more important for his hopes, his plans, his goals for the people who had elected him as their leader.

If read with an open and a fair mind and read together with the record of the actions took, these transcripts will show that what I have stated from the beginning to be the truth, has been the truth, that I personally had no knowledge of the break-in before it occurred, that I had no knowledge of the cover-up until I was informed of it by John Dean on March 21.

But I never offered clemency for the defendants, and after March 21, my actions were directed toward finding the facts and seeing that justice was done fairly and according to the law.

The facts are there. The conversations are there. The record of actions is there. To anyone who reads his way through this mass of materials I have provided, it will be totally, abundantly clear that as far as the President's role with regard to Watergate is concerned, the entire story is there.

As you will see, now that you also will have this mass of evidence I have provided, I have tried to cooperate with the House Judiciary Committee. And I repeat tonight the offer that I had made previously—to answer written interrogatories under oath—and if there are then issues still unresolved, to

meet personally with the chairman of the committee and with Congressman Hutchinson to answer their questions under oath.

As the committee conducts its inquiry, I also consider it only essential and fair that my counsel, Mr. [James] St. Clair, should be present to cross-examine witnesses and introduce evidence in an effort to establish the truth.

I am confident that for the overwhelming majority of those who study the evidence that I shall release tomorrow, those who are willing to look at it fully, fairly and objectively, the evidence will be persuasive and, I hope, conclusive.

We live in a time of very great challenge and great opportunity for America. We live at a time when peace may become possible in the Middle East for the first time in a generation. We are at last in the process of fulfilling the hope of mankind for a limitation on nuclear arms, a prospect that will continue when I meet with the Soviet leaders in Moscow in a few weeks. We are well on the way toward building a peace that can last, not just for this, but for other, generations as well.

And here at home, there is vital work to be done in moving to control inflation, to develop our energy resources, to strengthen our economy so that Americans can enjoy what they have not had since 1956—full prosperity without war and without inflation.

Every day absorbed by Watergate is a day lost from the work that must be done by your President and by your Congress, work that must be done in dealing with the great problems that affect your prosperity, affect your security, that could affect your lives.

The materials I make public tomorrow will provide all the additional evidence needed to get Watergate behind us and to get it behind us now. Never before in the history of the Presidency have records that are so private been made so public. In giving you these records—blemishes and all—I am placing my trust in the basic fairness of the American people.

I know in my own heart that, through the long painful and difficult process revealed in these transcripts, I was trying in that period to discover what was right and to do what was right. I hope, and I trust, that, when you have seen the evidence in its entirety, you will see the truth of that statement.

As for myself, I intend to go forward to the best of my ability with the work that you elected me to do. I shall do so in a spirit perhaps best summed up a century ago by another President when he was being subjected to unmerciful attack. Abraham Lincoln said, "I do the very best I know how, the very best I can, and I mean to keep doing so until the end. If the end brings me out all right, what is said against me won't amount to anything. If the end brings me out wrong, ten angels swearing I was right would make no difference."

Thank you and good evening.

Brief asserts innocence. A White House legal brief accompanying the transcripts April 30 asserted President Nixon's innocence in the Watergate matter. Released several hours before the transcripts, it maintained that "the raw material of these recorded confidential conversations establishes that the President had no prior knowledge of the break-in and that he had no knowledge of any cover-up to March 21, 1973."

Written by Nixon's special counsel James D. St. Clair, the brief said: "In all of the thousands of words spoken, even though they are unclear and ambiguous, not once does it appear that the President of the United States was engaged in a criminal plot to obstruct justice."

The brief, as the President did in his speech, attacked in particular John Dean's credibility. It indicated Dean had repeatedly perjured himself in sworn testimony and accused him of trying to blackmail the President in an effort to gain immunity from prosecution.

It said Assistant Attorney General Henry E. Petersen had reported to Nixon on April 27, 1973 that Dean's lawyer was threatening to "bring the President in—not in this case [the cover-up] but in other things" if Dean did not get immunity. Nixon's reply, according to the brief, was: "All right. We have the immunity problem resolved. Do it [grant immunity] to Dean if you need to, but I am telling you—there ain't going to be any blackmail." (Dean was not extended full immunity. He pleaded guilty to one count of conspiracy to obstruct justice and was awaiting sentencing. Dean's attorney, Robert C. McCandless, denied ever making such a threat April 30.)

As another contradiction, the brief cited Dean's testimony that Nixon had never asked him to write a report on his Watergate investigation, that it was not until he went to Camp David that he received a call from a Nixon aide asking for the report. According to the March 22, 1973 transcript, Nixon told Dean "I

want a written report."

St. Clair referred to the recent acquittal of former Nixon Cabinet members John N. Mitchell and Maurice H. Stans in their New York trial. The acquittals, he contended, "demonstrate the wisdom of the President's actions in insisting that the orderly process of the judicial system be utilized to determine the guilt or innocence of individuals charged with crime, rather than participating in trials in the public media."

Dean had been a witness for the prosecution in the case and the verdict was seen as a blow against his credibility. In addition to bringing up the case, the brief pointed out Dean's plea of guilty to a felony.

The brief's interpretation of the controversial Sept. 15, 1972 conversation between Dean and the President was that the transcript did "not in any way" support Dean's testimony that the President was fully aware of the cover-up. It referred to

Nixon's compliment then to Dean that he had handled things skillfully by "putting your fingers in the leaks that have sprung here and sprung there." This was "said in the context not of a criminal plot," St. Clair contended, but "in the context of the politics of the matter, such as civil suits, counter-suits, Democratic efforts to exploit Watergate as a political issue and the like. The reference to 'putting your fingers in the leaks' was clearly related to the handling of the political and public relations aspect of the matter."

In addition to supplying the brief, St. Clair buttressed the President's position in meeting with newsmen and in a television interview with Walter Cronkite of CBS. The President's stance also had been previewed by Dean Burch, counselor to the President, in a meeting with the Republican National Committee April 26.

Burch told the group Nixon would be releasing "a massive body of evidence" that would be "compelling and persuasive." "Out of this factual record," he said, "the whole story will emerge and the whole truth become known." Burch asked the Republicans to return "loyalty for loyalty" to Nixon, who was "our President and the leader of our party," and the "two roles are indistinguishable; our hopes and our goals and our fortunes are as one."

In his news conference May 1, St. Clair contended, as Nixon had in his TV speech, that the full story of his Watergate role was now available. St. Clair indicated also that the White House felt that further disclosure on other issues was unnecessary. "The name of this problem we are facing is called Watergate," St. Clair said. In

reply to a question if the Judiciary Committee should "forget about milk and ITT," the subjects of other material requested by the committee, St. Clair said:

"Based on what I know about it, the answer is yes. The President has published a white paper, so-called, on each of these. I don't know that anyone has seriously challenged the accuracy of them, and a fair reading of those white papers would make it reasonably clear ... there is no basis for a charge against the President."

Vice President Gerald R. Ford added his voice in support of the President's action. In a statement April 29, he said the Judiciary Committee should be "satisfied," that Nixon was being "more than cooperative" and supplying it with "more than enough" data to carry out its investigation.

Digests of Transcripts of White House Tapes

These are digests of the tape transcripts concerning the Watergate case as edited and made public by the White House April 30:

Sept. 15, 1972 (5:27–6:17 p.m.)

The President, Haldeman and Dean in the Oval Office:

The meeting was held on the same day the original Watergate indictments were returned and, according to Dean's testimony before the Senate Watergate Committee, signaled Nixon's early awareness that efforts were being made to keep various investigations contained.

According to the White House transcript, the meeting focused on possible ramifications of the break-in and the investigations, means of keeping them within bounds, and a counterattack against Democrats and others who were "less than our friends."

The meeting opened on press treatment of the affair and the role of the Federal Bureau of Investigation (FBI):

H. How did it all end up? **D.** Ah, I think we can say well at this point. The press is playing it just as we expect.

H. Whitewash? **D.** No, not yet—the story right now—

P. It is a big story. **H.** Five indicted plus the WH former guy and all that. **D.** Plus two White House fellows.

H. That is good that takes the edge off whitewash really that was the thing Mitchell kept saying that to people in the country Liddy and Hunt were big men. Maybe that is good.

P. How did MacGregor handle himself? **D.** I think very well he had a good statement which said that the Grand Jury had met and that it was now time to realize that some apologies may be due.

H. Fat chance. **D.** Get the dam[inaudible]. **H.** We can't do that.

P. Just remember, all the trouble we're taking, we'll have a chance to get back one day. How are you doing on your other investigations?

H. What has happened on the bug? **P.** What bug?

D. The second bug there was a bug found in the telephone of one of the men at the DNC [Democratic National Committee].

P. You don't think it was left over from the other time?

D. Absolutely not, the Bureau has checked and re-checked the whole place after that night. The man had specifically checked and re-checked the telephone and it was not there.

P. What the hell do you think was involved? **D.** I think DNC was planted.

What Initials Mean

Identities of persons described by initials in the transcripts of the White House tapes:

P. President Nixon
D. John W. Dean 3rd, former counsel to the President.
E. John D. Ehrlichman, former assistant to the President for domestic affairs.
H. H. R. Haldeman, former White House chief of staff
K. Richard G. Kleindienst, former attorney general
H.P. Henry E. Petersen, assistant attorney general in charge of the Criminal Division
M. John N. Mitchell, former attorney general
Z. Ronald L. Ziegler, press secretary to the President
R. William P. Rogers, former secretary of state

P. You think they did it. **D.** Uh huh.

P. [Expletive deleted]—do they really want to believe that we planted that?

H. Did they get anything on the finger prints? **D.** No, nothing at all—either on the telephone or on the bug. The F.B.I. has unleashed a full investigation over at the DNC starting with O'Brien right now.

H. [Laughter] Using the same crew—

D. The same crew—the Washington Field Office.

P. What kind of questions are they asking him?

D. Anything they can think of because O'Brien is charging them with failing to find all the bugs. **H.** Good, that will make them mad.

D. So Gray is pissed and his people are pissed off. So maybe they will move in because their reputation is on the line. I think that is a good development.

P. I think that is a good development because it makes it look so [adjective deleted] funny. Am I wrong?

D. No, no sir. It looks silly. If we can find that the DNC planted that, the whole story will reverse.

P. But how could they possibly find it, though?

D. Well, they are trying to ascertain who made the bug. It is a custom made product. If they can get back to the man who manufactured it and who he sold it to and how it came down through the chain.

P. Boy, you never know when those guys get after it—they can really find it.

D. The resources that have been put against this whole investigation to date are really incredible. It is truly a larger investigation than was conducted against the after inquiry of the JFK assassination. **P.** Oh.

Regarding the FBI, Nixon added later: "We want it cleared up. If anybody is guilty over here we want to know."

A good job by Dean—Dean's report to Nixon indicated that potentially harmful

effects of the break-in might already be well in hand, and Nixon commended his efforts:

D. Three months ago I would have had trouble predicting there would be a day when this would be forgotten, but I think I can say that 54 days from now nothing is going to come crashing down to our surprise.

P. That what? **D.** Nothing is going to come crashing down to our surprise.

P. Oh well, this is a can of worms as you know a lot of this stuff that went on. And the people who worked this way are awfully embarrassed. But the way you have handled all this seems to me has been very skillful putting your fingers in the leaks that have sprung here and sprung there. The grand jury is dismissed now?

D. That is correct. They have completed and they have let them go so there will be no continued investigation prompted by the Grand Jury's inquiry. The GAO report referred over to Justice is on a shelf right now because they have hundreds of violations—they have violations of McGovern, of Humphrey, violations of Jackson, and several hundred Congressional violations. They don't want to start prosecuting one any more than they prosecute the other.

P. They definitely will not prosecute us unless they prosecute the others.

Later in the meeting, after discussion of the various investigations and the Democrats' civil suit against the Republicans, Nixon concluded that they "really can't sit and worry about it all the time ... So you just try to button it up as well as you can and hope for the best, and remember basically the damn business is unfortunately trying to cut our losses."

Dean replied that at least there had been "no effect" on Nixon, and Haldeman interjected that aside from minor "lower level" connections and references to presidential counsel Charles W. Colson, the affair had been kept "away from the White House."

A counterattack—Dean noted that there were problems among Republicans, including dissension between the re-election committees, as well as the political effects of the break-in. The discussion then moved to some strong measures that might be taken:

P. We are all in it together. This is a war. We take a few shots and it will be over... Don't worry. I wouldn't want to be on the other side right now. Would you?

D. Along that line, one of the things I've tried to do, I have begun to keep notes on a lot of people who are emerging as less than our friends because this will be over some day and we shouldn't forget the way some of them have treated us.

P. I want the most comprehensive notes on all those who tried to do us in. They didn't have to do it. If we had a very close election and they were playing the other side I would understand this. No—they were doing this quite deliberately and they are asking for it and they are going to get it. We have not used the power in this first four years as you know. We have never used it. We have not used the Bureau and we have not used the Justice Department but things are going to change now. And they are either going to do it right or go.

D. What an exciting prospect.

P. Thanks. It has to be done. We have been [adjective deleted] fools for us to come into this election campaign and not do anything with regard to the Democratic Senators who are running, et cetera. And who the hell are they after? They are after us. It is absolutely ridiculous. It is not going to be that way any more.

H. Really it is ironic that we have gone to extremes. You and your damn regulations. Everybody worries about not picking up a hotel bill.

D. I think you can be proud of the White House staff. It really has had no problems of that sort. And I love this GAO audit that is going on now. I think they have some suspicion that even a cursory investigation is going to discover something here. I don't think they can find a thing. I learned today, incidentally, and have not confirmed it, that the GAO auditor who is down here is here at the Speaker of the House's request. P. That surprises me.

H. Well, [expletive deleted] the Speaker of the House. Maybe we better put a little heat on him. P. I think so too.

H. Because he has a lot worse problems than he is going to find down here.

D. That's right.

H. That is the kind of thing that, you know, we really ought to do is call the Speaker and say, "I regret to say your calling the GAO down here because of what it is going to cause us to do to you."

Dealing with the investigations—A pending inquiry by the House Banking and Currency Committee was a point of concern at the meeting. Dean was doubtful about "whether we will be successful in turning that off," but various courses of action were explored.

Dean cited a plan to have attorneys for the break-in defendants tell the committee that hearings would prejudice the defendants' rights. Dean also suggested that John B. Connally Jr., then Treasury secretary, might "talk turkey" with Chairman Wright Patman (D, Tex.), and that Gerald R. Ford, then the House Republican leader, might play some role with the GOP panel members. (Dean noted that Ford was "not really taking an active interest in this matter," but might be briefed by campaign official Maurice Stans.)

Nixon replied,

"What about Ford? Do you think so? Connally can't because of the way he is set up. If anybody can do it, Connally could, but if Ford can get the minority members. They have some weak men and women on that committee, unfortunately. . . ."

Nixon added later that efforts should be made to "push it. No use to let Patman have a free ride."

Dean reported that favorable action might be ahead on the Democrats' civil suit and Republican countermeasures.

Dean cited Judge Charles R. Richey's action to delay depositions in Democrats' suit because of conflict with the criminal indictments and suggested that Richey had indicated sympathy for the libel countersuit filed by Stans. In any case, Dean suggested, there would be delays and harmful publicity before the election might be avoided. The GOP countersuits and the depositions taken in them would be useful, Dean said near the end of the meeting. Nixon agreed, Haldeman laughed, and Dean concluded: "We can blunder down the road anyway."

Feb. 28, 1973 (9:12–10:23 a.m.)

The President and Dean in the Oval Office:

Much of the meeting centered on, as Nixon said at the outset, "what kind of line to take" with the upcoming hearings of Sen. Sam J. Ervin's (D, N.C.) Watergate Committee: how to limit testimony by White House aides, the use of the executive privilege doctrine, how to deal with committee members.

Nixon suggested that Richard Kleindienst, then attorney general, might deal with Vice Chairman Howard H. Baker (R, Tenn.), but should try to avoid the appearance of making "a deal." Baker, whom Nixon characterized later in the meeting as "a smoothy—impressive," was going to keep "at arm's length," but could be talked to through Kleindienst. Nixon suggested a "back-up position"; "one of a [inaudible] if Kleindienst wants to back [inaudible] for [inaudible]. . . ."

Nixon discussed other suggestions offered by Haldeman and Ehrlichman: an agreement that Ervin and Baker could question under "very restricted" conditions; written interrogatories—which, as Dean suggested, would show "publicly you are not withholding any information and you are not using the shield of the presidency;" or "stalking horse" witnesses to be used as "defusing factors" in the hearings.

Nixon said, however, that: "we ought to cooperate in finding an area of cooperation. Here it is. You see, the Baker theory is that he wants to have a big slambang thing for a whole week and then he thinks interest in the whole thing will fall off. And he is right about that. But his interest in having a big slambang for a week is that we bring all the big shots up right away. The big shots you could bring up. They could bring up Stans. They have to put him on, and they've got to put Mitchell on. They would like, of course, to get Haldeman, Ehrlichman and Colson."

Nixon added later that Kleindienst should emphasize to the committee it should conduct the "model of a Congressional hearing. That will disappoint the [adjective deleted] press. No hearsay! No innuendo! No leaks!"

Near the end of the meeting, Nixon suggested the perspective on the break-in to be followed with the committee:

P. It will be somewhat serious but the main thing, of course, is also the isolation of the President. D. Absolutely! Totally true!

Some Persons Mentioned in Digests of Tape Transcripts

Robert H. Allen (Spelled Allan in transcripts)—A contributor to the Republican Party

Jack Anderson—Syndicated columnist.

Bernard Barker—Convicted Watergate conspirator

William O. Bittman—Attorney for E. Howard Hunt

John J. Caulfield—Former aide to John W. Dean 3rd

Dwight L. Chapin—Former Presidential appointments secretary

John B. Connally Jr.—Former Treasury secretary

Frank De Marco Jr.—Nixon's California tax lawyer

Walter E. Duncan—Contributor to Republican Party

Fred Fielding—Former aid to Dean

Leonard Garment—Presidential counsel

Seymour Glanzer—Assistant U.S. attorney, District of Columbia

L. Patrick Gray 3rd—Former acting director of the FBI

Lawrence M. Higby—Former aid to Haldeman

E. Howard Hunt Jr.—Convicted Watergate conspirator

Bruce A. Kehrli—White House aide

Egil Krogh Jr.—Former chief assistant to John D. Ehrlichman

Frederick C. LaRue—Chief aide to Mitchell at the Committee to Re-elect the President

C. Gordon Liddy—Convicted Watergate conspirator

Robert C. Mardian—Former deputy manager, CRP

Peter Maroulis—Attorney for Liddy

James W. McCord Jr.—Convicted participant in the Watergate break-in; former head of security for CRP

Richard W. McLaren—Former head of Justice Dept. Antitrust Division

Richard A. Moore—Special presidential counsel

Lawrence F. O'Brien—Democratic National Committee chairman at the time of the Watergate burglary

Paul O'Brien—Attorney for CRP

Kenneth W. Parkinson—Attorney for CRP

Herberg L. Porter—Scheduling director for CRP

Charles R. Richey—U.S. District Court judge, District of Columbia

H. Chapman Rose—Lawyer and presidential consultant

Henry B. Rothblatt—Attorney for four of the original Watergate defendants

Donald H. Segretti—California lawyer convicted of sabotaging Democratic campaigns

Charles Shaffer—Attorney for Dean

Earl J. Silbert—First chief prosecutor in Watergate case

Hugh Sloan—Former treasurer of CRP

Joseph Sneed—Former deputy attorney general

Gordon Strachan—Former assistant to H. R. Haldeman

Frank Strickler—Attorney for Haldeman and Ehrlichman

William C. Sullivan—Former FBI official

Harold H. Titus—Former U.S. attorney, District of Columbia

John J. Wilson—attorney for Haldeman and Ehrlichman

P. Because that, fortunately, is totally true. D. I know that, sir! P. [expletive deleted] Of course, I am not dumb and I will never forget when I heard about this [adjective deleted] forced entry and bugging. I thought, what in the hell is this? What is the matter with these people? Are they crazy? I thought they were nuts! A prank! But it wasn't! It wasn't very funny. I think that our Democratic friends know that, too. They know what the hell it was. They don't think we'd be involved in such.

D. I think they do too.

P. Maybe they don't. They don't think I would be involved in such stuff. They think I have people capable of it. And they are correct, in that Colson would do anything. Well, O.K.—Have a little fun. And now I will not talk to you again until you have something to report to me. D. Alright, sir.

P. But I think it is very important that you have these talks with our good friend Kleindienst. D. That will be done.

P. Tell him we have to get these things worked out. We have to work together on this thing. I would build him up. He is the man who can make the difference. Also point out to him what we have. [Expletive deleted] Colson's got [characterization deleted], but I really, really—this stuff here—let's forget this. But let's remember this was not done by the White House. This was done by the Committee to Re-Elect, and Mitchell was the chairman, correct? D. That's correct!

P. And Kleindienst owes Mitchell everything. Mitchell wanted him for Attorney General. Wanted him for Deputy, and here he is. Now, [expletive deleted]. Baker's got to realize this, and that if he allows this thing to get out of hand he is going to potentially ruin John Mitchell. He won't. Mitchell won't allow himself to be ruined. He will put on his big stone face. But I hope he does and he will. There is no question what they are after. What the committee is after is somebody at the White House. They would like to get Haldeman or Colson, Ehrlichman. D. Or possibly Dean.—You know, I am a small fish.

P. Anybody at the White House they would—but in your case I think they realize you are the lawyer and they know you didn't have a [adjective deleted] thing to do with the campaign.

D. That's right.

There was some concern over the possible appearance of Herbert W. Kalmbach, then Nixon's personal attorney, as a witness before the committee, but Nixon and Dean agreed that he would probably be a good witness:

D. The one I think they are going to go after with a vengeance—and I plan to spend a great deal of time with next week, as a matter of fact a couple of days getting this all in order—is Herb Kalmbach.

P. Yes. D. Herb—they have subpoenaed his records, and he has records that run all over hell's acres on things. You know Herb has been a man who has been moving things around for Maury and keeping things in tow and taking care of— P. What is holding up his records?

D. They already have gotten to the banks that had them, and what I think we will do is that there will be a logical, natural explanation for every single transaction. It is just a lot of minutia we've got to go through, but he is coming in next week and I told him we would sit down and he is preparing everything—all that is available, and we are going to sit down with Frank DeMarco and see if we can't get this whole thing—

P. They can't get his records with regard to his private transactions? D. No, none of the private transactions. Absolutely, that is privileged material. Anything to do with San Clemente and the like—that is just so far out of bounds that— P. Did they ask for them? D. No. No indication. P. Kalmbach is a decent fellow. He will make a good witness. D. I think he will. P. He is smart.

P. Oh, well, it will be hard for him. I suppose the big thing is the financing transaction that they will go after him for. How does the money get to the Bank of Mexico, etc. D. Oh, well, all that can be explained. P. It can? D. Yes, indeed! Yes, sir! They are going to be disappointed with a lot of the answers they get. When they actually get the facts—because the Times and the Post had such innuendo—when they get the facts, they are going to be disappointed.

Clemency and the seven defendants—At one point in the meeting, Nixon abruptly asked about the sentencing situation regarding the convicted burglary conspirators. After a brief colloquy on the harshness of sentences and the high level of the appeal bonds, the transcript was interrupted by "[Material unrelated to Presidential deleted.] Then, following a brief discussion on unrelated news leaks, Nixon said:

I feel for those poor guys in jail, particularly for Hunt with his wife dead. D. Well, there is every indication they are hanging in tough right now.

P. What the hell do they expect though? Do they expect clemency in a reasonable time? What would you advise on that? D. I think it is one of those things we will have to watch very closely. For example,—

P. You couldn't do it, say, in six months. D. No, you couldn't. This thing may become so political as a result of these hearings that it is a vendetta. This judge may go off the deep end in sentencing, and make it so absurd that it's clearly injustice that they have been heavily—

P. Is there any kind of appeal left? D. Right. Liddy and McCord, who sat through the trial, will both be on appeal and there is no telling how long that will last. It is one of these things we will just have to watch.

P. My view though is to say nothing about them on the ground that the matter is still in the courts and on appeal. Second, my view is to say nothing about the hearings at this point, except that I trust they will be conducted the proper way and I will not comment on the hearings while they are in process. Of course if they break through—if they get muckraking—It is best not to cultivate that thing here at the White House. If it is done at the White House again they are going to drop the [adjective deleted] thing. Now there, of course, you say, but you leave it all to them. We'll see as time goes on. Maybe we will have to change our policy. But the President should not become involved in any part of this case. Do you agree with that?

D. I agree totally, sir. Absolutely. That doesn't mean that quietly we are not going to be working around the office. You can rest assured that we are not going to be sitting quietly.

March 13, 1973 (12:42–2 p.m.)

The President and Dean in the Oval Office:

The means of handling the Senate Watergate Committee hearings, how various witnesses might conduct themselves and possible retaliatory publicity actions by the White House—all remained major concerns. But, as Dean pointed out midway through the meeting, the political crisis might pass, but "after the Ervin hearings, they are going to find so much—there will be some new revelations. I don't think that the thing will get out of hand."

Nixon and Dean dealt first with Watergate committee witnesses: former aides Chapin and Colson might be put back under the protection of executive privilege by making them White House "consultants." Nixon said it would be an "obvious fraud" that "won't work" to have both as consultants, but Colson could be accorded the status—to be "kept in the drawer" and used as needed.

Later in the discussion, Nixon asked about other possible witnesses:

P. Who is going to be the first witness up there? D. Sloan. P. Unfortunate. D. No doubt about it— P. He's scared?

D. He's scared, he's weak. He has a compulsion to cleanse his soul by confession. We are giving him a lot of stroking. Funny thing is this fellow goes down to the Courthouse here before Sirica, testifies as honestly as he can testify, and Sirica looks around and called him a liar. He just said—Sloan just can't win! So Kalmbach has been dealing with Sloan. Sloan is like a child. Kalmbach has done a lot of that. The person who will have a greater problem as a result of Sloan's testimony is Kalmbach and Stans. So they are working closely with him to make sure that he settles down . . . John Mitchell will be ready, as Maury Stans will be ready.

P. Mitchell is now studying, is he? D. He is studying. Sloan will be the worst witness. I think Magruder will be a good witness. This fellow, Bart Porter, will be a good witness. They have already been through the grand jury. They have been through trial. They did well. And then, of course, people around here.

P. None will be witnesses. D. They won't be witnesses?

P. Hell, no. They will make statements. That will be the line which I think we have to get across to Ziegler in all his briefings where he is constantly saying he will provide information. That is not the question. It is how it is to be furnished. We will not furnish it in a formal session. That would be a breakdown of the privilege. Period. Do you agree with that?

D. I agree. I agree. I have always thought that's the bottom line, and I think that is the good thing that is happening in the Gray hearings right now. If they send a letter down with specific questions, I send back written interrogatories sworn. He knows, the lawyer, that you can handle written interrogatories, where cross examination is another ball game.

P. That's right! D. You can make a person look like they're inaccurate even if they are trying to tell the truth.

P. Well now, really, you can't mean that! All the face-making and all that. Written interrogatories you can handle? D. Can be artfully, accurately answered and give the full information.

'New revelations'—When Dean predicted there would be "new revelations" after the Ervin committee hearings, Nixon agreed. They discussed the possibilities:

D. They would be quick [inaudible] They would want to find out who knew— P. Is there a higher ~~up~~? D. Is there a higher up? P. Let's face it, I think they are really after Haldeman. D. Haldeman and Mitchell.

P. Colson is not big enough name for them. He really isn't. He is, you know, he is on the government side, but Colson's name doesn't bother them so much. They are after Haldeman and after Mitchell. Don't you think so.?

D. Sure. They are going to take a look and try to drag them, but they're going to be able to drag them into the election—

P. In any event, Haldeman's problem is Chapin isn't it? D. Bob's problem is circumstantial. P. Why is that? Let's look at the circumstantial. I don't know, Bob didn't know any of those people like the Hunts and all that bunch. Colson did, but Bob didn't. OK? D. That's right.

P. Now where the hell, or how much Chapin knew I will be [expletive deleted] if I know. D. Chapin didn't know anything about the Watergate.

P. Don't you think so? D. Absolutely not. P. Strachan? D. Yes. P. He knew? D. Yes. P. About the Watergate? D. Yes.

P. Well, then, he probably told Bob. He may not have. D. He was judicious in what he relayed, but Strachan is as tough as nails. He can go in and stonewall, and say, "I don't know anything about what you are talking about." He has already done it twice you know, in interviews.

P. I guess he should, shouldn't he? I suppose we can't call that justice, can we? D. Well, it is personal loyalty to him. He doesn't want it any other way. He didn't have to be told. He didn't have to be asked. It just is something that he found was the way he wanted to handle the situation.

P. But he knew? He knew about Watergate? Strachan did? D. Yes.

D. Yes. P. I will be damned! Well that is the problem in Bob's case. Not Chapin then, but Strachan. Strachan worked for him, didn't he? D. Yes. They would have one hell of a time proving that Strachan had knowledge of it, though. P. Who knew better? Magruder? D. Magruder and Liddy. P. Oh, I see. The other weak link for Bob is Magruder. He hired him et cetera. D. That applies to Mitchell, too.

P. Mitchell—Magruder. Where do you see Colson coming into it? Do you think he knew quite a bit and yet, he could know quite a great deal about a lot of other things and not know a lot about this. I don't know. D. Well, I have never—P. He sure as hell knows Hunt—that we know—was very close to him. D. Chuck has told me that he had no knowledge, specific knowledge, of the Watergate before it occurred. There have been tidbits that I have raised with Chuck, I have not played any games with him. I said, "Chuck, I have indications—"

P. What indications? The lawyer has to know everything. D. That's right. I said, "Chuck, people have said that you were involved in this, involved in that, involved in all of this." He said, "That is not true, etc." I think that Chuck had knowledge that something was going on over there, but he didn't have any knowledge of the details of the specifics of the whole thing.

P. There must have been an indication of the fact that we had poor pickings. Because naturally anybody, either Chuck or Bob, were always reporting to me about what was going on. If they ever got any information they would certainly have told me that we got some information, but they never had a thing to report. What was the matter? Did they never get anything out of the damn thing?

D. I don't think they ever got anything, sir. P. A dry hole? D. That's right. P. (Expletive deleted) D. Well, they were just really getting started.

P. Yeah. Bob one time said something to me about something, this or that or something, but I think it was something about the convention, I think it was about the convention problems they were planning something. I assume that must have been MacGregor—not MacGregor, but Segretti. D. No, Segretti wasn't involved in the intelligence gathering piece of it at all. P. Oh, he wasn't? Who the hell was gathering intelligence? D. That was Liddy and his outfit.

P. Apart from Watergate? D. That's right. Well you see Watergate was part of intelligence gathering, and this was their first thing. What happened is—

P. That was such a stupid thing! D. It was incredible—that's right. That was Hunt.

P. To think of Mitchell and Bob would have allowed—would have allowed—this kind of operation to be in the campaign committee! D. I don't think he knew it was there.

P. I don't think that Mitchell knew about this sort of thing. D. Oh, no, no! Don't misunderstand me. I don't think that he knew the people. I think he knew that Liddy was out intelligence gathering. I don't think he knew that Liddy would use a fellow like McCord [expletive removed], who worked for the committee. I can't believe that.

P. Hunt? D. I don't think Mitchell knew about Hunt either.

P. Well Mitchell thought, well, gee, and I hired this fellow and I told him to gather intelligence. Maybe Magruder says the same thing.

D. Magruder says—as he did in the trial—well, of course, my name has been dragged in as the guy who sent Liddy over there, which is an interesting thing. Well what happened they said is that Magruder asked—he wanted to hire my deputy over there as Deputy Counsel and I said, "No way, I can't give him up."

P. Was Liddy your deputy? D. No, Liddy never worked for me. He wanted this fellow Fred Fielding who works for me, Look, he said, Magruder said to me, "Will you find me a lawyer?" I said, "I will be happy to look around." I checked around the White House, Krogh said, "Liddy might be the man to do it—he would be a hell of a writer. He has written some wonderful legal opinions over here for me, and I think he is a good lawyer." So I relayed that to Magruder.

P. How the hell does Liddy stand up so well? D. He's a strange man, Mr. President. P. Strange or strong? D. Strange and strong. His loyalty is—I think it is just beyond the pale. Nothing—P. He hates the other side too, doesn't he? D. Oh, absolutely! He is strong. He really is.

'The hang-out road'—After discussing the ramifications of the break-in, the President and his counsel returned to a point touched on earlier in the meeting when they had been exploring possible news conference questions: whether to take a "here it all is" approach, for which Nixon had concluded, "we have passed that point." Dean had agreed, adding "plus the fact they are not going to believe the truth!" They addressed the problem again:

P. Is it too late to go the hang-out road? D. Yes, I think it is. The hang-out road— P. The hang-out road [inaudible]. D. It was kicked around Bob and I and—

P. Ehrlichman always felt it should be hang-out. D. Well, I think I convinced him why he would not want to hang-out either. There is a certain domino situation here. If some things start going, a lot of other things are going to start going, and there can be a lot of problems if everything starts falling. So there are dangers, Mr. President. I would be less than candid if I didn't tell you there are. There is a reason for not everyone going up and testifying. P. I see. Oh no, no, no! I didn't mean to have everyone go up and testify.

D. Well, I mean they're just starting to hang out and say here's our story— P. I mean put the story out PR people, here is the story, the true story about Watergate.

D. They would never believe it … They would never buy it as far as one White House involvement in Watergate which I think there is just none for that incident which occurred at the Democratic National Headquarters. People here we just did not know that was going to be done. I think there are some people who saw the fruits of it, but that is another story. I am talking about the criminal conspiracy to go in there.

The Mexican checks—Responding to a Nixon question about "this Texas guy that gets his money back," Dean went into the problem of the allegedly "laundered" campaign gift linked to the Watergate break-in:

D. All hell broke loose for him that week. This was Allan— P. No, no. Allan— D. Allan, not Duncan nor (unintelligible). All hell broke loose for Allan for this reason: He—the money apparently originally came out of a subsidiary of one of Allan's corporations down in Mexico. I went to a lawyer in Mexico who put it down as a fee billed to the subsidiary, and then the lawyer sent it back into the States, and it came back up here. But the weakness of it is that the Mexican lawyer: (1) didn't have a legitimate fee; (2) It could be corporate contribution. So Allan had personally put a note up with the corporation to cover it. Allen, meanwhile, is having problems with his wife, and a divorce is pending. And tax problems—

P. (inaudible Watergate— D. I don't know why that went in the letter. It wasn't used for the Watergate. That is the interesting thing. P. It wasn't?

D. No, it was not. What happened is that these Mexican checks came in. They were given to Gordon Liddy, and said, "why don't you get these cashed?" Gordon Liddy, in turn, put them down to this fellow Barker in Florida, who said he could cash these Mexican checks, and put them with your Barker's bank account back in here. They could have been just as easily cashed at the Riggs Bank. There was nothing wrong with the checks. Why all that rigamarole? It was just like a lot of other things that happened over there. God knows what it was all done. It was totally unnecessary, and it was money that was not directly involved in the Watergate. It wasn't a wash operation to get money back to Liddy and the like.

The 'offensive'—Early in the meeting Nixon asked Dean about "my project of getting on the offensive," particularly in using former FBI official William C. Sullivan (who had access to wiretap and other records) in kicking "a few butts around."

Dean said he had gathered information on wiretaps and other domestic intelligence operations by earlier administrations. Nixon urged that a probe of McGovern funds be pushed and asked, "Do you need any IRS stuff?" Dean replied that there were no need for the IRS "at this hour," but there were "a couple of sources over there that I can go to … we can get right in and get what we need."

At various points in the meeting, Nixon and Dean returned to the question of Sullivan, whom Nixon called "a valuable man." Nixon suggested that he would be even "a little bit more pleased" if they "would get Kennedy into it." The reference reminded Dean of an earlier White House investigation of Sen. Kennedy and the problems that might arise:

D. Let me tell you something that lurks at the bottom of this whole thing. If, in going after Segretti, they go after Kalmbach's bank records, you will recall sometime back—perhaps you did not know about this—I apologize. That right after Chappaquidick somebody was put up there to start observing and within six hours he was there for every second of Chappaquidick for a year, and for almost two years

he worked for Jack Caulfield. P. Oh I have heard of Caulfield.

D. He worked for Caulfield when Caulfield worked for John, and then when I came over here I inherited Caulfield and this guy was still on this same thing. If they get to those bank records between the start of July of 1969 through June of 1971, they say what are these about? Who is this fellow up in New York that you paid? There comes Chappaquidick with a vengeance. This guy is a twenty year detective on the New York City Police Department.

P. In other words we—D. He is ready to disprove and show that—

P. [unintelligible] D. If they get to it—that is going to come out and this whole thing can turn around on that. If Kennedy knew the bear trap he was walking into—

P. How do we know—why don't we get it out anyway? D. Well, we have sort of saved it.

P. Does he have any records? Are they any good? D. He is probably the most knowledgeable man in the country. I think he ran up against walls and they closed the records down. There are things he can't get, but he can ask all of the questions and get many of the answers as a 20 year detective, but we don't want to surface him right now. But if he is ever surfaced, this is what they will get.

P. How will Kalmbach explain that he hired this guy to do the job on Chappaquidick? Out of what type of funds? D. He had money left over from the pre-convention—

P. Are they going to investigate those funds too? D. They are funds they are quite legal. There is nothing illegal about those funds. Regardless of what may happen, what may occur, they may stumble into this in going back to, say 1971, in Kalmbach's bank records. They have already asked for a lot of his bank records in connection with Segretti, as to how he paid Segretti.

P. Are they going to go back as far as Chappaquidick? D. Well this fellow worked in 1971 on this. He was up there. He has talked to everybody in that town. He is the one who has caused a lot of embarrassment for Kennedy already by saying he went up there as a newspaperman, by saying: "Why aren't you checking this? Why aren't you looking there?" Calling the press people's attention to things. Gosh, the guy did a masterful job. I have never had the full report.

Closing the meeting, Nixon affirmed that Sullivan would be a "very effective" source for getting information to the press and to friendly contacts on the Ervin panel.

Dean agreed, but added:

". . . if I have one liability in Sullivan here, it is his knowledge of the earlier [unintelligible] that occurred here. P. That we did? D. That we did.
P. Well, why don't you just tell him—he could say, "I did no political work at all. My work in the Nixon Administration was solely in the national security." And that is thoroughly true! D. That is true.

March 17, 1973 (1:25–2:10 p.m.)

The President and Dean, in the Oval Office:

The Ellsberg burglary—The transcript opens with Nixon's admonition that the affair of Donald H. Segretti's political sabotage operations must be dealt with openly: "I think you've just got to—Chapin, all of them have just got to take the heat . . . you've got to admit the facts.
"
Dean agreed, adding that the Segretti matter was not "that serious."

Then the following dialogue on the burglary of the office of the psychiatrist who had treated Pentagon papers defendant Daniel Ellsberg:

D. The other potential problem is Ehrlichman's and this is—P. In connection with Hunt? D. In connection with Hunt and Liddy both. P. They worked for him?

D. They—these fellows had to be some idiots as we've learned after the fact. They went out and went into Dr. Ellsberg's office and they had, they were geared up with all this CIA equipment—cameras and the like. Well they turned the stuff back in to the CIA some point in time and left film in the camera. CIA has not put this together, and they don't know what it all means right now. But it wouldn't take a very sharp investigator very long because you've got pictures in the CIA files that they had to turn over to (unintelligible).

P. What in the world—what in the name of God was Ehrlichman having something (unintelligible) in the Ellsberg (unintelligible)? **D.** They were trying to—this was a part of an operation that—in connection with the Pentagon papers. They were—the whole thing—they wanted to get Ellsberg's psychiatric records for some reason. I don't know. **P.** This is the first I ever heard of this. I, I (unintelligible) care about Ellsberg was not our problem. **D.** That's right. **P.** (Expletive deleted) **D.** Well, anyway (unintelligible), it was under an Ehrlichman structure, maybe John didn't ever know. I've never asked him if he knew. I didn't want to know. **P.** I can't see that getting into, into this hearing.

D. Well, look. No. Here's the way it can come up. **P.** Yeah.

D. In the CIA's files which they—which the committee is asking for—the material they turned over to the Department of Justice. **P.** Yeah.

D. There are all the materials relating to Hunt. In there are these pictures which the CIA developed and they've got Gordon Liddy standing proud as Punch outside this doctor's office with his name on it. And [unintelligible] this material, it's not going to take very long for an investigator to go back and say, well, why would this—somebody be at the doctor's office and they'd find out that there was a break-in at the doctor's office and then you'd find Liddy on the staff and then you'd start working it back. I don't think they'll ever reach that point. **P.** [Unintelligible]

D. This was the way, this was—**P.** It's irrelevant. **D.** It's irrelevant. Right.

P. That's the point. That's where—that's where—where Ervin's rules of relevancy [unintelligible].

P. Now what the hell has this got to do with it. **D.** It has nothing as a lot of these things that they should stumble along into is irrelevant.

March 20, 1973 (7:29–7:43 p.m.)

The President and Dean in a telephone conversation:

Dean offered his suggestions on an unidentified letter Nixon was preparing and other means of making some sort of public statement, and perhaps a report to the Cabinet on the Watergate issue. Dean said that too much openness could create too many problems and suggested the "stonewall, with lots of noises that we are always willing to cooperate, but no one is asking us for anything."

Dean cited the seemingly favorable FBI report ("There is not one scintilla of evidence."), but counseled against publishing it. Nixon suggested a general perspective:

P. You've got to have something where it doesn't appear that I am doing this in, you know, just in a—saying to hell with the Congress and to hell with the people, we are not going to tell you anything because of Executive Privilege. That, they don't understand. But if you say, "No, we are willing to cooperate," and you've made a complete statement, but make it very incomplete. See, that is what I mean. I don't want a, too much in chapter and verse as you did in your letter, I just want just a general—**D.** An all around statement.

P. That's right. Try just something general. Like "I have checked into this matter; I can categorically, based on my investigation, the following: Haldeman is not involved in this, that and the other thing. Mr. Colson did not do this; Mr. so and so did not do this. Mr. Blank did not do this." Right down the line, taking the most glaring things. If there are any further questions, please let me know. See? **D.** Uh, huh. I think we can do that.

P. That is one possibility, and then you could say that such things—and then use the FBI report to the Cabinet and to the leaders. It might just be very salutary. You see our own people have got to have confidence or they are not going to step up and defend us. You see our problem there, don't you?

Dean had also said there were "soft spots" and "potential problem areas" in the overall situation, and he wanted to "draw all my thoughts together" before briefing Nixon. They made the appointment for the key meeting the next day.

March 21, 1973 (10:12–11:55 a.m.)

The President and Dean in the White House Oval Office, later joined by Haldeman:

D. The reason that I thought we ought to talk this morning is because in our conversations, I have the impression that you don't know everything I know and it makes it very difficult for you to make judgments that only you can make on some of these things. . . . I think that there is no doubt about the seriousness of the problem we've got. We have a cancer within, close to the presidency, that is growing. It is growing daily. It's compounded, growing geometrically now, because it compounds itself. That will be clear if I, you know, explain some of the details of why it is. Basically, it is because (1) we are being blackmailed; (2) people are going to start perjuring themselves very quickly that have not had to perjure themselves to protect other people in the line. And there is no assurance—**P.** That that won't bust? **D.** That that won't bust. . . .

Dean told Nixon that Watergate began as an innocent request by the White House for campaign intelligence against the Democrats. However, Liddy became involved and the final result was the bugging of the Democratic National Committee at its Watergate headquarters. When the burglars were arrested, they demanded money to see them through the November elections, as well as attorney's fees.

D. All right, so arrangements were made through Mitchell, initiating it. And I was present in discussions where these guys had to be taken care of. Their attorneys fees had to be done. Kalmbach was brought in. Kalmbach raised some cash. . . .

P. They put that under the cover of a Cuban committee, I suppose? **D.** Well, they had a Cuban committee and they had—some of it was given to Hunt's lawyer, who in turn passed it out. . . .

D. That's the most troublesome post-thing because (1) Bob is involved in that; (2) John is involved in that; (3) I am involved in that; (4) Mitchell is involved in that. And that is an obstruction of justice. . . . Here is what is happening right now. What sort of brings matters to the (unintelligible). One, this is going to be a continual blackmail operation by Hunt and Liddy and the Cubans. No doubt about it. . . . Hunt now is demanding another $72,000 for his own personal expenses; another $50,000 to pay attorneys' fees; $120,000. Some (1) he wanted it as of the close of business yesterday. He said, "I am going to be sentenced on Friday, and I've got to get my financial affairs in order." . . . Hunt has now made a direct threat against Ehrlichman. As a result of this, this is his blackmail. He says, "I will bring John Ehrlichman down to his knees and put him in jail. I have done enough seamy things for he and Krogh, they'll never survive it."

P. Was he talking about Ellsberg? **D.** Ellsberg, and apparently some other things. I don't know the full extent of it. **P.** I don't know about anything else. . . .

D. So that is it. That is the extent of the knowledge. So where are the soft spots on this? Well, first of all, there is the problem of the continued blackmail which will not only go on now, but it will go on while these people are in prison, and it will compound the obstruction of justice situation. It will cost money. It is dangerous. People around here are not pros at this sort of thing. This is the sort of thing Mafia people can do: washing money, getting clean money, and things like that. We just don't know about those things, because we are not criminals and not used to dealing in that business.

P. How much money do you need? **D.** I would say these people are going to cost a million over the next two years. **P.** We could get that. On the money, if you need the money you could get that. You could get a million dollars. You could get it in cash. I know where it could be gotten. It is not easy, but it could be done. But the question is who the hell would handle it? Any ideas on that?

D. That's right. Well, I think that is something that Mitchell ought to be charged with.

P. I would think so too. **D.** And get some pros to help him.

D. When I say this is a growing cancer, I say it for reasons like this. Bud Krogh, in his testimony before the Grand Jury, was forced to perjure himself. He is haunted by it. Bud said, "I have not had a pleasant day on my job." . . .

P. He might be able to—I am just trying to think. Perjury is an awful hard rap to prove. If he could just say that I—Well, go ahead.

A

D. Well, so that is one perjury. Mitchell and Magruder are potential perjurers. There is always the possibility of any one of these individuals blowing. Hunt. Liddy. Liddy is in jail right now, serving his time and having a good time right now. I think Liddy in his own bizarre way the strongest of all of them. . . .

P. Just looking at the immediate problem, don't you think you have to handle Hunt's financial situation damn soon?

D. I think that is—I talked with Mitchell about that last night and—

P. It seems to me we have to keep the cap on the bottle that much, or we don't have any options. **D.** That's right.

B

P. Either that or it all blows right now? **D.** That's the question. . . .

D. Now we've got Kalmbach. Kalmbach received, at the close of the '68 campaign in January of 1969, he got a million $700,000 to be custodian for. That came down from New York, and was placed in safe deposit boxes here. Some other people were on the boxes. And ultimately, the money was taken out to California. Alright, there is knowledge of the fact that he did start with a million seven. Several people know this. Now since 1969, he has spent a good deal of this money and accounting for it is going to be very difficult for Herb. For example, he has spent close to $500,000 on private polling. That opens up a whole new thing. It is not illegal, but more of the same thing.

C

P. Everybody does polling. **D.** That's right. There is nothing criminal about it. It's private polling.

P. People have done private polling all through the years. There is nothing improper.

D. What really bothers me is this growing situation. As I say, it is growing because of the continued need to provide support for the Watergate people who are going to hold us up for everything we've got, and the need for some people to perjure themselves as they go down the road here. If this thing ever blows, then we are in a cover up situation. I think it would be extremely damaging to you and the—

P. Sure. The whole concept of Administration justice. Which we cannot have!

D

D. That is what really troubles me. For example, what happens if it starts breaking, and they do find a criminal case against a Haldeman, a Dean, a Mitchell, and Ehrlichman? That is—

P. If it really comes down to that, we would have to [unintelligible] some of the men.

D. That's right. I am coming down to what I really think, is that Bob and John and John Mitchell and I can sit down and spend a day, or however long, to figure out one, how this can be carved away from you, so that it does not damage you or the Presidency. It just can't. You are not involved in it and it is something you shouldn't—**P.** That is true!

E

D. I know, sir. I can just tell from our conversation that these are things that you have no knowledge of.

P. You certainly can! Buggings, etc.! . . . So what you really come to is what we do. Let's suppose that you and Haldeman and Ehrlichman and Mitchell say we can't hold this? What then are you going to say?

What are you going to put out after it. Complete disclosure, isn't that the best way to do it? **D.** Well, one way to do it is—**P.** That would be my view.

D. One way to do it is for you to tell the Attorney General that you finally know. Really, this is the first time you are getting all the pieces together.

F

P. Ask for another Grand Jury? **D.** Ask for another Grand Jury. The way it should be done though, is a way—for example, I think that we could avoid criminal liability for countless people and the ones that did get it could be minimal. . . .

D. Well, I have been a conduit for information on taking care of people out there who are guilty of crimes.

P. Oh, you mean like the blackmailers? **D.** The blackmailers. Right.

P. Well, I wonder if that part of it can't be—I wonder if that doesn't—let me put it frankly: I wonder if that doesn't have to be continued? Let me put it this way: let us suppose that you get the million bucks, and you get the proper way to handle it. You could hold that side? **D.** Uh, huh.

G

P. It would seem to me that would be worthwhile. **D.** Well, that's one problem.

P. I know you have a problem here. You have the problem with Hunt and his clemency.

D. That's right. And you are going to have a clemency problem with the others. They all are going to expect to be out and that may put you in a position that is just untenable at some point. You know, the Watergate Hearings just over, Hunt now demanding clemency or he is going to blow. And politically, it's impossible for you to do it. You know, after everybody—

P. That's right! **D.** I am not sure that you will ever
A be able to deliver on the clemency. It may be just too hot.

P. You can't do it politically until after the '74 elections, that's for sure. Your point is that even then you couldn't do it. **D.** That's right. It may further involve you in a way you should not be involved in this.

P. No—it is wrong that's for sure. **D.** Well—there have been some bad judgments made. There have been some necessary judgments made.

P. Before the election? **D.** Before the election and in the wake the necessary ones, you know, before the election. You know, with me there was no way, but the burden of this second Administration is something that is not going to go away.

P. No, it isn't. **D.** It is not going to go away, Sir! . . .

B **D.** What I am coming in today with is: I don't have a plan on how to solve it right now, but I think it is at the juncture that we should begin to think in terms of how to cut the losses; how to minimize the further growth of this thing, rather than further compound it by, you know, ultimately paying these guys forever. I think we've got to look—

P. But at the moment, don't you agree it is better to get the Hunt thing that's where that—**D.** That is worth buying time on.

P. That is buying time, I agree. . . . Suppose the worst—that Bob is indicted and Ehrlichman is indicted. And I must say, we just better then try to tough it through. You get the point. **D.** That's right.

C **P.** If they, for example, say let's cut our losses and you say we are going to go down the road to see if we can cut our losses and no more blackmail and all the rest. And then the thing blows, cutting Bob and the rest to pieces. You would never recover from that, John. **D.** That's right.

P. It is better to fight it out. Then you see that's the other thing. It's better to fight it out and not let people testify, and so forth. And now, on the other hand, we realize that we have these weaknesses,—that we have these weaknesses—in terms of blackmail.

(Haldeman enters the room.)

P. I was talking to John about this whole situation and he said if we can get away from the bits and pieces that have broken out. He is right in recommending
D that there be a meeting at the very first possible time. . . . Mitchell, Ehrlichman, yourself [Dean] and Bob, that is all. Now, Mitchell has to be there because he is seriously involved and we are trying to keep him with us. We have to see how we handle it from here on. We are in the process of having to determine which way to go, and John has thought it through as well as he can. . . . But it is the kind of thing that I think what really has to happen is for you to sit down with those three and for you to tell them exactly what you told me. . . .

P. It may take him about 35 or 40 minutes. In other words he knows, John knows, about everything and also what all the potential criminal liabilities are, . . .
E Then we have to see what the line is. Whether the line is one of continuing to run a kind of stone wall, and take the heat from that, having in mind the fact that there are vulnerable points there;—the vulnerable points being, the first vulnerable points would be obvious. That would be one of the defendants, either Hunt, because he is most vulnerable in my opinion, might blow the whistle and his price is pretty high, but at least we can buy the time on that as I pointed out to John. . . .

P. The point is this, that it is now time, though, that Mitchell has got to sit down, and know where the hell all this thing stands, too. You see, John is concerned,
F as you know, about the Ehrlichman situation. It worries him a great deal because, and this is why the Hunt problem is so serious, because it had nothing to do with the campaign. It has to do with the Ellsberg case. I don't know what the hell the—[unintelligible] . . . What is the answer on this? How you keep it out, I don't know. You can't keep it out if Hunt talks. You see the point is irrevelant. It has gotten to this point—**D.** You might put it on a national security grounds basis.

H. It absolutely was. **D.** And say that this was—

H. [unintelligible]—CIA—**D.** Ah—**H.** Seriously.

P. National Security. We had to get information for national security grounds.

G **D.** Then the question is, why didn't the CIA do it or why didn't the FBI do it? **P.** Because we had to do it on a confidential basis. **H.** Because we were checking them.

P. Neither could be trusted. **H.** It has basically never been proven. There was reason to question their position. . . .

P. You really only have two ways to go. You either decide that the whole (expletive deleted) thing is so full of problems with potential criminal liabilities, which most concern me. I don't give a damn about the publicity. We could rock that through that if we had to let the whole damn thing hang out, and it would be a lousy story for a month. But I can take it. The point is, that I don't want any criminal liabilities. . . .

P. He [Hunt] is playing hard ball with regard to Ehrlichman for example, and that sort of thing. He knows what he's got. **H.** What's he planning on, money? **D.** Money and—**H.** Really?

P. It's about $120,000. That's what, Bob. That would be easy. It is not easy to deliver, but it is easy to get. Now. **H.** If in the case is just that way, then the thing to do if the thing cranks out. . . .

P. If, for example, you say look we are not going to continue to—let's say, frankly, on the assumption that if we continue to cut our losses, we are not going to win. But in the end, we are going to be bled to death. And in the end, it is all going to come out anyway. Then you get the worst of both worlds. We are going to lose, and people are going to—

H. And look like dopes!

P. And in effect, look like a cover-up. So that we can't do. Now the other line, however, if you take that line, that we are not going to continue to cut our losses, that means then we have to look square in the eye as to what the hell those losses are, and see which people can—so we can avoid criminal liability. Right? **D.** Right.

P. And that means keeping it off you. Herb has started this Justice thing. We've got to keep it off Herb. You have to keep it, naturally, off of Bob, off Chapin, if possible, Strachan, right? **D.** Uh, huh.

P. And Mitchell. Right? **D.** Uh, huh. **H.** And Magruder, if you can. . . .

P. John Dean's point is that if Magruder goes down, he will pull everybody with him.

H. That's my view. . . .

P. Another way to do it then Bob, and John realizes this, is to continue to try to cut our losses. Now we have to take a look at that course of action. First it is going to require approximately a million dollars to take care of the jackasses who are in jail. That could be arranged. But you realize that after we are gone, and assuming we can expend this money, then they are going to crack and it would be an unseemly story. Frankly, all the people aren't going to care that much. . . . And the second thing is, we are not going to be able to deliver on any of a clemency thing. You know Colson has gone around on this clemency thing with Hunt and the rest?

D. Hunt is now talking about being out by Christmas. **H.** This Year? **D.** This year. . . . **H.** By Christmas of this year? **D.** Yeah.

H. See that, really, that is verbal evil. Colson is—That is your fatal flaw in Chuck. He is an operator in expediency, and he will pay at the time and where he is to accomplish whatever he is there to do. And that, and that's—I would believe that he has made that commitment if Hunt says he has. I would believe he is capable of saying that.

P. The only thing we could do with him would be to parole him like the [unintelligible] situation. But you couldn't buy clemency.

D. Kleindienst has now got control of the Parole Board, and he said to tell me we could pull Paroles off now where we couldn't before. So—

H. Kleindienst always tells you that, but I never believe it.

P. Paroles—let the [unintelligible] worry about that. Parole, in appearance, etc., is something I think in Hunt's case, you could do. Hunt, but you couldn't do the others. You understand. . . . The point is, your feeling is that we just can't continue to pay the blackmail of these guys? **D.** I think that is our great jeopardy.

P. Now, let me tell you. We could get the money. There is no problem in that. We can't provide the clemency. Money could be provided. Mitchell could provide the way to deliver it. That could be done. See what I mean? . . . I just have a feeling on it. Well, it sounds like a lot of money, a million dollars. Let me say that I think we could get that. I know money is hard to raise. But the point is, what we do on that—Let's look at the hard problem—

D. That has been, thus far, the most difficult problem. That is why these fellows have been on and off the reservation all the way along.

P. So the hard place is this. Your feeling at the present time is the hell with the million dollars. I would just say to these fellows I am sorry it is all off and let them talk. Alright? **D.** Well,— **P.** That's the way to do it isn't it, if you want to do it clean?

H. That's the way. We can live with it, because the problem with the blackmailing, that is the thing we kept raising with you when you said there was a money problem. When you said we need $20,000, or $100,000, or something. We said yeah, that is what you need today. But what do you need tomorrow or next year or five years from now? . . .

D. One of the things that I think we all need to discuss is, is there some way that we can get our story before a Grand Jury, so that they can really have investigated the White House on this. I must say that I have not really thought through the alternative. We have been so busy on the other containment situation.

P. John Ehrlichman, of course, has raised the point of another Grand Jury. I just don't know how you could do it. On what basis. I could call for it, but I—**D.** That would be out of the question.

P. I hate to leave with differences in view of all this stripped land. I could understand this, but I think I want another Grand Jury proceeding and we will have the White House appear before them. Is that right John? **D.** Uh huh.

P. That is the point, see. Of course! That would make the difference. I want everybody in the White House called. And that gives you a reason not to have to go before the Ervin and Baker committee. . . .

H. You are in a hell of a lot better position than you are up there. **D.** No, you can't have a lawyer before the Grand Jury.

P. Oh, no. That's right. **H.** But you do have rules of evidence. You can refuse to talk. **D.** You can take the 5th Amendment.

P. That's right. **H.** You can say you have forgotten too can't you? **D.** Sure but you are chancing a very high risk for perjury situation.

P. But you can say I don't remember. You can say I can't recall. I can't give any answer to that that I can recall. **H.** You have the same perjury thing on the Hill don't you? **D.** That's right.

P. Oh hell, yes. **H.** And the Ervin Committee is a hell of a lot worse to deal with. **D.** That's right. . . .

D. No. Well, that is one possibility. But also when these people go back before the Grand Jury here, they are going to pull all these criminal defendants back before the Grand Jury and immunize them. **P.** Who will do this? **D.** The U.S. Attorney's Office will. . . . **H.** It's Hunt opportunity.

P. That's why for your immediate things you have no choice but to come up with the $120,000, or whatever it is. Right? **D.** That's right.

P. Would you agree that that's the prime thing that you damn well better get that done?

D. Obviously he ought to be given some signal anyway. . . .

P. (Expletive deleted), get it. In a way that—who is going to talk to him? Colson? He is the one who is supposed to know him?

D. Well, Colson doesn't have any money though. That is the thing. That's been one of the real problems. They haven't been able to raise a million dollars in cash. [unintelligible] has been just a very difficult problem as we discussed before. . . .

P. Well look, what it is you need on that? When—I am not familiar with the money situation. **D.** It sounds easy to do and everyone is out there doing it and that is where our breakdown has come every time. . . . As I say, we are a bunch of amateurs in that business.

H. That is the thing that we thought Mitchell ought to be able to know how to find somebody who would know how to do all that sort of thing, because none of us know how to.

D. That's right. You have to wash the money. You can get a $100,000 out of a bank, and it all comes in serialized bills. **P.** I understand.

D. And that means you have to go to Vegas with it or a bookmaker in New York City. I have learned all these things after the fact. I will be in great shape for the next time around. **H.** [Expletive deleted]

P. Well, of course you have a surplus from the campaign. Is there any other money hanging around? **H.** Well, what about the money we moved back out of here? **D.** Apparently, there is some there. That might be what they can use. I don't know how much is left.

P. Kalmbach must have some. **D.** Kalmbach doesn't have a cent.

P. He doesn't? **H.** That $350,000 that we moved out was all that we saved. Because they were afraid to because of this. That is the trouble. We are so [adjective deleted] square that we get caught at everything.

P. Could I suggest this though: let me go back around—**H.** Be careful—**P.** The Grand Jury thing has a feel. Right? It says we are cooperating well with the Grand Jury. **D.** Once we start down any route that involves the criminal justice system, we've got to have full appreciation that there is really no control over that. . . .

P. But you see, the Grand Jury proceeding achieves this thing. If we go down that road—[unintelligible] We would be cooperating. We would be cooperating through a Grand Jury. Everybody would be behind us. That is the proper way to this. It should be under the klieg lights of the Committee. Nobody questions a Grand Jury. And then we would insist on Executive Privilege before the Committee, flat out say, "No we won't do that. It is a matter done in the Grand Jury, not up there that's that." . . .

P. Now, the other possibility is not to go to the Grand Jury. We have three things. (1) You just say the hell with it, we can't raise the money, sorry Hunt you can say what you want, and so on. He blows the whistle. Right? **D.** Right.

P. If that happens, that raises some possibilities about some criminal liabilities, because he is likely to say a hell of a lot of things and will certainly get Magruder in on it. **D.** It will get Magruder. It will start the whole FBI investigation going again. . . .

P. Seems we're going around the track. You have no choice on Hunt but to try to keep— **D.** Right now, we have no choice.

P. But my point is, do you ever have any choice on Hunt? That is the point. No matter what we do here now, John, whatever he wants if he doesn't get it—immunity, etc., he is going to blow the whistle. . . . Hunker down and fight it and what happens? Your view is that is not really a viable option. **D.** It is a high risk. It is a very high risk.

P. Your view is that what will happen on it, that it's going to come out. That something is going to break loose, and— **D.** Something is going to break and—

P. It will look like the President **D.** is covering up—

P. Has covered up a huge [unintelligible] **D.** That's correct. . . .

P. As a matter of fact, your middle ground of Grand Jury. I suppose there is a middle ground of a public statement without a transcript. . . . You see that the point is that the reason time is of the essence, we can't play around on this. If they are going to sentence on Friday, we are going to have to move on the (expletive deleted) thing pretty fast. See what I mean? **D.** That's right. **P.** So we really have a time problem. **D.** The other thing is that the Attorney General could call Sirica, and say that, 'The government has some major developments that it is considering. Would you hold sentencing for two weeks?' If we set ourselves on a course of action. **P.** Yep, yep. . . .

D. I will tell you the person that I feel we could use his counsel on this, because he understands the criminal process better than anybody over here does. **P.** Petersen?

D. Yes, Petersen. It is awkward for Petersen. He is the head of the criminal division. But to discuss some of the things with him, we may well want to remove him from the head of the Criminal Division and say; 'That related to this case, you will have no relation.' Give him some special assignment over here where he could sit down and say, 'Yes, this is an obstruction, but it couldn't be proved,' so on and so forth. We almost need him out of there to take his counsel. I don't think he would want that, but he is the most knowledgeable.

P. How could we get him out? **D.** I think an appeal directly to Henry—

P. Why couldn't the President call him in as Special Counsel to the White House for the purpose of conducting an investigation. Rather than a Dean in office, having him the Special Counsel to represent us before the Grand Jury.

D. I have thought of that. That is one possibility.

H. On the basis that Dean has now become a principal, rather than a Counsel. . . .

March 21, 1973 (5:20–6:01 p.m.)

Attended by the President, Dean, Haldeman and Ehrlichman at the Executive Office Building, the meeting concerned how the White House was to deal with the upcoming Senate Watergate Committee investigation as well as a U.S. district court grand jury that was going to look further into Watergate.

There was general agreement that it was better for the President and them if the White House took the initiative in getting out information on Watergate, rather than having the scandal uncovered by the Watergate committee or the grand jury. However, the problem was to offer some sort of report that would limit the scope of the inquiries. After the possibility of a blue ribbon investigative panel of top Justice Department officials was rejected,

Ehrlichman proposed that Dean write a report:

E. The Dean statements, where the President then makes a bold disclosure of everything which he then has. And is in a position if it does collapse at a later time to say, "I had the FBI and the Grand Jury, and I had my own Counsel. I turned over every document I could find. I placed in my confidence young people and as is obvious now [inaudible].

P. [inaudible] It doesn't concern me. I mean as far as the policy is concerned. You as White House Counsel, John. I asked for a written report, which I do not have, which is very general understand. I am thinking now in far more general terms, having in mind the facts, that where specifics are concerned, make it very general, your investigation of the case. Not that "this man is guilty, this man is not guilty," but "this man did do that." You are going to have to say that, John. Segretti [inaudible] That has to be said And so under the circumstances,

E. Could he do this? To give some belief to this, that he could attach an appendix, listing the FBI reports that you had access to: interview with Kalmbach, interview with Segretti, interview with Chapin, Magruder, and whoever and me. So that the President at some later time is in a position to say, "I relied." . . . I think the President is in a stronger position later. The President is in a stronger position later, if he can be shown to have justifiably relied on you at this point in time. . . .

H. If we worry about the timeliness, and try to hang it on a sense thing, then we have to ignore the trial, and say Dean has given you a report. We basically said it was an oral report. The thing is that Dean has kept you posted from time to time with periodic oral reports as this thing, as it becomes convenient. You have asked him now to summarize those into an overall summary.

P. Overall summary. And I will make the report available to the Ervin Committee. And then I offer the Ervin Committee report this way, I say "Dear Senator Ervin. Here is the report before your hearings. You have this report, and as I have said previously, any questions that are not answered here, you can call the White House staff member, and they will be directed to answer any questions on an informal basis." [inaudible] **H.** Yeah.

After further discussion, Ehrlichman asked what impact sending Dean's written report to Justice Department would have. When no one was sure what consequences would result and with whom criminal liability would stop, the President said that Petersen, an expert in criminal law, should be approached for an opinion, but Dean said that would be a mistake.

P. And the point is, but you see here is the way I would see that statement that we would put out: Everything we would intend to say in a general statement that I have already indicated with regard to the facts as we send them in, we say people are to cooperate, without executive privilege, et cetera. Statement, it is true, is temporary. But it will indicate that the President has looked into the matter, has had his Counsel report to him and this is the result of the matter. We tell the Committee "we will cooperate." The Committee will say no. And so we just stand right there.

Some discussion followed that the Watergate burglars would be forced to testify before a grand jury, but that was left unfinished when the President ended the meeting because of an appointment.

March 22, 1973 (1:57–3:43 p.m.)

The meeting at the Executive Office Building, attended by the President, Mitchell, Dean, Haldeman and Ehrlichman, for the most part concerned White House strategy for dealing with the Senate Watergate Committee. The participants agreed that the doctrine of executive privilege should be invoked whenever possible, so as to limit the number of White House employes appearing before the committee. However, the consensus was that executive privilege

should not be invoked to the point of giving the impression that the President was trying to cover up wrongdoing. Haldeman pointed out that Dean might not have to testify before the Senate committee because of his lawyer/client relationship with the President. The participants also agreed that testimony before the committee by White House aides should, if possible, be given in executive session rather than public session.

At one point Mitchell suggested that Dean provide a written report on Watergate:

P. It is a negative in setting forth general information involving questions. Your consideration—your analysis, et cetera. You found this, that. Rather than going into every news story and every charge, et cetera, et cetera. This, this, this—put it down—I don't know but **D.** I don't think I can do it until I sit down this evening and start drafting. **H.** I think you ought to hold up for the weekend and do that and get it done. **P.** Sure. **H.** Give it your full attention and get it done.

P. I think you need—why don't you do this? Why don't you go up to Camp David? **D.** I might do it, I might do it. **P.** Completely away from the phone. Just go up there and [inaudible] I want a written report.

E. That would be my scenario. He presents it to you at your request. You then publish—[inaudible] I know that but I don't care.

H. You are not dealing with the defendants on trial. You are only dealing with White House involvement. You are not dealing with the campaign. **D.** That's where I personally . . .

P. You could write it in a way that you say this report was not comment on et cetera, et cetera, but "I have reviewed the record, Mr. President, and without at all compromising the right of defendants and so forth, some of whom are on appeal, here are the facts with regard to members of the White House staff et cetera, et cetera, that you have asked me about. I have checked the F.B.I. records; I have read the Grand Jury transcripts—et cetera, et cetera.

March 27, 1973 (11:10 a.m.–1:30 p.m.)

The President, Haldeman, Ehrlichman and Ziegler in the Executive Office Building:

Nixon was concerned with the "lines of defenses that everybody's going to take here," but a primary subject throughout the meeting was the role of John Mitchell and Jeb Stuart Magruder, whose positions on the campaign committee and possible involvement in both the planning of the break-in and the cover-up made them particularly vulnerable.

One possibility, the subject of this and later conversations, was that Mitchell might be persuaded to take the blame for the entire Watergate affair and—as a high-level figure—take the pressure off the White House.

Part of the reasoning behind the concern, according to Haldeman, was the displeasure voiced by campaign officials Paul O'Brien and Kenneth W. Parkinson with seeing "all the people getting whacked around in order to keep the thing from focusing on John Mitchell when inevitably it is going to end up doing that anyway. . . ."

After a review of the circumstances leading to the break-in (Liddy's bizarre intelligence plans and the possibility that Mitchell might have given at least indirect approval to a watered-down version), Nixon asked about O'Brien and Parkinson:

P. They aren't involved in the damn thing are they? O'Brien and Parkinson? **H.** Yes. **P.** They ran this all from the beginning? **H.** Oh, no. **P.** Well, that is what I thought. **H.** But they are involved in the post-discovery, post-June 17th.

P. [expletive removed]! [unintelligible]

H. O'Brien says, "Everything with the Committee—what you might want to consider is the possibility is to waive our retainer, waive our privileges and instruct us to report to the President all of the facts as they are known to us as to what really went on at the Committee to Re-Elect the President."

P. For me to sit down and talk to them and go through—

H. I don't know. He doesn't mean necessarily personally talk to you, but he means talk to Dean or whoever you designate as your man to be working on this.

Haldeman also voiced concern on "other facts": "Hunt is at the grand jury today. We don't know how far he is going to go. The danger area for him is on the money, that he was given money." Haldeman noted, however, that O'Brien had reported Hunt "not to be as desperate today as he was yesterday but to still be on the brink or at least shaky." The shakiness, Haldeman added, was caused by the wide-ranging statements by James McCord (who also was "pointing a finger" at Magruder and Dean, Haldeman said later in the meeting).

But Mitchell was still what Nixon later called the "real problem." Nixon had noted that "Mitchell could be telling the truth and Liddy could be too. Liddy just assumed he had abstract approval. Mitchell could say, 'I know I never approved this damn plan.'"

Nixon asked later:

Suppose you call Mitchell and say to him, will you—what do you learn—for what. And Mitchell says, "Yes, I did it." Then what do we say?

H. Its greater knowledge than we possess right now—if he would only confess. **E.** I was just going to say, maybe if Rogers said it to him—

P. Mitchell? **H.** Bill thinks—

P. Mitchell? Mitchell despises him. **H.** Yeah, I know he does. That's all it is—I didn't call Mitchell because I need [unintelligible] but we should go ahead with Magruder, I think.

E. Right now? **P.** Oh, I agree.

H. [unintelligible] **P.** [unintelligible]

E. I say any idea of a meeting between you and Mitchell ought to wait until the Magruder, Haldeman, Mitchell meeting. **P.** Oh, really?

E. And see what transpires there. Maybe the idea that Magruder says he [unintelligible]

P. What about the other way around. How about me getting Mitchell in and say, look [unintelligible] you've got to tell us what the score is, John. You have to face up to where we are. What do we say? How do we handle [unintelligible].

H. My guess is Mitchell would turn on you. I think Mitchell would say, "Mr. President, if it will serve any useful purpose for you I would come—"

P. Isn't it just as well for me to call and ask him to meet with Magruder? Or what do you think, John? I have not really had from Mitchell but I have had from Haldeman. I have had from Ehrlichman, I have had from Colson cold, flat denials. I have asked each of you to tell me, and also Dean. Now the President, therefore, has not lied on this thing. I don't think that yet has been charged. Liability has been charged, but they haven't charged the President with any offense. They are [unintelligible] in trying to protect his people who are lying. But I don't—doesn't anybody suggest that I [unintelligible] this whole damn thing?

H. As of now it is all saying that you are being ill-served by [unintelligible]. **P.** By my people. But I don't know about Mitchell. I never asked him.

H. [unintelligible]. It can't hurt anything. [unintelligible]. **P.** I should get Mitchell down rather than ask him, don't you think? **H.** Yeah.

P. What I've got to do is think in terms of my own plans. I will spend my day today on this, but I will have to clear the deck for tomorrow [unintelligible]. . . .

P. Well, what is Mitchell's option though? You mean to say—let's see what he could do. Does Mitchell come in and say, "My memory was faulty. I lied?"

E. No. He can't say that. He says—ah, ah—

P. "That without intending to, I may have been responsible for this, and I regret it very much but I did not realize what they were up to. They were—we were—talking about apples and oranges." That's what I think he would say. Don't you agree?

H. I think so. He authorized apples and they bought oranges. Yeah.

P. Mitchell, you see, is never never going to go in and admit perjury. I mean he may say he forgot about Hunt-Liddy and all the rest, but he is never going to do that.

H. They won't give him that convenience, I wouldn't think, unless they figure they are going to get you. He is as high up as they've got.

E. He's the big Enchilada.

H. And he's the one the magazines zeroed in on this weekend. **P.** They did? What grounds?

H. Yeah. [unintelligible] has a quote that they maybe have a big fish on the hook.

P. I think Mitchell should come down. **E.** To see you, me, Magruder.

Magruder and perjury—Haldeman had said early in the meeting that Magruder believed the entire "super-intelligence operation" that led to the Watergate break-in had been "put together" by the White House—"Haldeman, Dean and others."

Nixon said later:

I don't know really know what he is saying about the White House, but I understand he is saying that you signed off on it. Is that what Magruder is saying?

H. If Magruder goes public on this, then you know— **P.** Incidentally, if Magruder does that, let's see what it does to Magruder. **E.** It depends on how he does it. If he does it under immunity, it doesn't do anything to him. **P.** All right—except ruin him. **H.** Well, yeah. It ruins him in a way he becomes a folk hero to the guys—

P. He becomes an immediate hero with the media. You know, in terms of—I know how these things work. . . .

H. And look at the alternative that he now sees. It is either that or he goes to jail on perjury. **P.** How are they going to prove it? **E.** With other witnesses, not through his own mouth. **P.** What other witnesses? **H.** Beats me. I don't know how they can prove perjury. **P.** Hunt?

H. He has to be a great big gamble because he knows—let's assume—he knows he did perjure himself and if you know that you are guilty, you have to be pretty concerned about someone's ability to prove it. **P.** That's right.

E. And Liddy and McCord, and Sloan and that little thing in McCord's letter about Sloan has to worry him. **H.** If it's about Sloan. That's another thought. It may be about Barker. **E.** Is he [unintelligible] **H.** And it is more likely because Barker worked for him. **E.** I see. Well—

H. Barker said he couldn't remember who he delivered the tap reports to. [Material unrelated to Presidential actions deleted] . . .

P. Magruder has got to know—I just don't—my own feeling is, Bob,—the reason I raise the question of Magruder is what stroke have you got with Magruder? I guess we've got none.

E. I think the stroke Bob has with him is in the confrontation to say, "Jeb, you know that just plain isn't so," and just stare him down on some of this stuff and it is a golden opportunity to do that. And I think you will only have this one opportunity to do it. **P.** [unintelligible] said it isn't so before.

E. That's all the better, and in his present frame of mind I am sure he will rationalize himself into a fable that hangs together. But if he knows that you are going to righteously and indignantly deny it, ah— **P.** Say that he is trying to lie to save his own skin. **E.** It'll bend—it'll bend him.

H. Well, but I can make a personal point of view in the other direction, and say, "Jeb, for God's sake don't get yourself screwed up by—solving one lie with a second. You've got a problem. You ain't going to make it better by making it worse. **P.** Hero for the moment, but in the minds of— **H.** Well, then you've got Magruder facing all—. . . .

H. Let's go another one. So you persuade Magruder that his present approach is (a) not true; I think you can probably persuade him of that; and (b) not desirable to take. So he then says, in despair, "Heck, what do I do? Here's McCord out here accusing me." McCord has flatly accused me of perjury—He's flatly accused Dean of complicity. Dean is going to go, and Magruder knows of the fact that Dean wasn't involved, so he knows that when Dean goes down, Dean can testify as an honest man. . . .

P. Do you think he can get immunity? **H.** Absolutely.

P. Then what would he say? **E.** He would say, "I thought I was helping. It is obvious that there is no profit in this route. I did it on my own motive. Nobody asked me to do it. I just did it because I thought it was the best thing to do. Everybody stands on it. I was wrong to do it." That's basically it.

H. Magruder's viewpoint that to be ruined that way which isn't really being ruined is infinitely preferable to going to jail. Going to jail for Jeb will be a very, very, very difficult job. **E.** [unintelligible] he says he is a very unusual person. The question now is whether the U.S. Attorney will grant immunity under the circumstances. **H.** Well he would if he thought he was going to get Mitchell. **E.** Yeah, that's right.

H. The interesting thing would be to watch Mitchell's face at the time I recommend to Magruder that he go in and ask for immunity and confess. . . .

H. In other words, if all Magruder is going to do is take the dive himself, then we are not going to hear about it. If he makes us worry that he is going to get Mitchell and you and me—

P. John, do you see any way though, any way, that Magruder can stick to his story? No. **E.** Yes, because he's an ingenious—

P. Stick to his story? **E.** He is an ingenious witness. I think, I am told, if he is really as good as they say he is as a witness, it is possible that he could get away with it. Ah, it's arguable.

P. It's his word against McCord. **E.** And he is flowing with the stream, you see. He is saying the things they want him to say.

P. No, no, no. I don't mean if he says—**E.** Oh if he sticks to his old story—I see, I see. I thought you meant the story he is laying out here.

P. Oh, no no. This story. They would take that in a minute. **E.** I tell you I am to the point now where I don't think this thing is going to hold together, and my hunch is that anybody who tries to stick with a story that is not susceptible to corroboration is going to be in serious difficulty.

P. So, what do you feel then? **E.** Well, that is why I said I thought he ought to move to a real and immune confession of perjury if he can do it. There's too many cross-currents in this thing now.

P. Yeah. This is my view. If Magruder is going to lie about it, you know, I am sure he checked it out. If Magruder is going to say then—then what the hell is in it for him. **H-E.** Immunity.

The Ellsberg burglary—Nixon and Ehrlichman also returned to the national security aspects of the burglary of Daniel Ellsberg's psychiatrist's office, which—according to an earlier transcript—had been brought to Nixon's attention March 17. Ehrlichman repeated that he had not known of the burglary until afterwards, adding that Colson also seemed "totally nonplussed, the same as the rest of us."

Ehrlichman referred later, however, to the problem of former "plumbers" co-chief Egil Krogh, who had said he would confess to authorizing the operation, resign his government job and "get out of town . . ." Then the following exchange:

P. Should he?

E. I don't think he will have to. Number one, I don't think Hunt will strike him. If he did, I would put the national security tent over this whole operation. **P.** I sure would.

E. And say there are a lot of things that went on in the national interest where they involved taps, they involved entry, they involved interrogation, they involved a lot of things and I don't propose to open that up to [unintelligible] just hard line it.

P. I think is what you have to do there.

The "super panel"—As a means of circumventing normal court procedures in dealing with Watergate, Haldeman suggested the creation of a "super panel" of judges or other prominent citizens to determine the extent of White House involvement. As Haldeman suggested, "it will take the panel a long time to get set up . . . and make its findings, and then you'll probably be past the '74 elections, which'll be desirable." Haldeman added Nixon would have the "ultimate stroke on it," since he would be able to pardon anyone convicted by the panel at the expiration of his term in January, 1977—so that the maximum penalty "in this process could be about two years."

Nixon rejected the idea in this statement:

Let's face it. They'll have special prosecutors who will want to make a name for themselves. Everybody wants to make a name for themselves in this [unintelligible]. They'll drag it on and on and on. The idea that a commission might go through the '74 election, etc.—my view is I can't have this [unintelligible] I think the damn thing is going to come out anyway, and I think you better cut the losses now and just better get it over much sooner and frankly sharper."

March 28, 1973

Ehrlichman and Kleindienst, telephone conversation:

Ehrlichman and Kleindienst first disposed of an issue involving Sen. Lowell P. Weicker (R, Conn.), a member of the Watergate Committee, who had made public statements that he had information on White House involvement in Watergate. According to Ehrlichman, Weicker's information concerned Segretti's political sabotage operations, not Watergate directly; he suggested that Kleindienst "take a swing at that" in a news conference and say that the White House was exercising "diligence" and was "determined to track down every lead."

Kleindienst replied that they should avoid "provoking" Weicker, that Weicker was "essentially with us," and that his vote might be needed later.

Ehrlichman turned to a second problem:

O.K., now, the President said for me to say this to you. That the best information he had and has is that neither Dean nor Haldeman nor Colson nor I nor anybody in the White House had any prior knowledge of this burglary. He said that he's counting on you to provide him with any information to the contrary if it ever turns up and you just contact him direct. Now as far as the Committee to Re-elect is concerned he said that serious questions are being raised with regard to Mitchell and he would likewise want you to communicate to him any evidence or inferences from evidence on that subject.

Kleindienst said he was also concerned about Mitchell and suggested that if the problem led to further legal procedures, a special prosecutor should be appointed. Kleindienst cited the conflict of interest in his own personal relationship with Mitchell and Mitchell's prior position as attorney general. Ehrlichman left the suggestion hanging after being assured that appointment of a special prosecutor would be under the jurisdiction of the President, not the courts.

March 30, 1973 (12:02–12:18 p.m.)

The President, Ehrlichman and Ziegler in the Oval Office:

The entire transcript dealt with details of "talking points" to be used by Ziegler with the press, and other informal, nonpublic dissemination of the White House position to members of Congress.

Nixon suggested that Ziegler say that the President had called for an investigation of the White House staff and that every member of the staff "who has been … mentioned as a — has submitted a sworn affidavit to me denying any knowledge of."

E. Any prior knowledge. P. Any knowledge of or participation in. Could we say this? E. No, I wouldn't. P. Why? Not true? Too defensive?
E. Well, No. 1—It's defensive—it's selfserving. No. 2—then that establishes the existence of a piece of paper that becomes the focal point of a subpoena and all that kind of thing."

Further discussion refined the language to preclude saying that members of the staff "would welcome" appearing before the grand jury, but that they would appear "at the direction of the President to give information on their "alleged knowledge."

Nixon also suggested that Ziegler deflect certain questions on grounds that they were under "informal discussion" with members of the Ervin Committee, and maintain publicly that the Administration will insist on separation of powers, but not as a cover-up: there would be "total and complete cooperation" with investigative agencies, while observing executive privileges.

(The meeting transcript is followed by an excerpt from Ziegler's March 30 press briefing—listed as a separate transcript section—in which he gives a "restatement of a policy that has been in effect": that members of the White House staff, "by direction of the President," will testify before a grand jury as to their "alleged knowledge or possible involvement in the Watergate matter."

April 8, 1973 (7:33–7:37 a.m.)

The President and Ehrlichman, telephone conversation:

Lines of defense and the positions of Mitchell and Magruder were again the subject in Ehrlichman's report on his meeting with Dean.

Ehrlichman said Dean wanted the message relayed to Magruder that Dean was to appear before the grand jury, and that Dean felt Liddy had already "pulled the plug" on Magruder. Ehrlichman added "there isn't anything he, Dean, knows or could say that would in any way harm John Mitchell." But it would harm Magruder.

Regarding Magruder, Nixon asked:

"But what about the theory of your idea that Magruder ought to come in and say, 'Look, my recollection has been refreshed' and so forth.
E. Well, yeah, but he said that he's satisfied that they are not really after Magruder on perjury. They are after him— P. On Watergate. E. They are after somebody as the instigator of the plot. P. I see. E. And that, cleaning up the— P. What does he think Magruder will do? Whether Magruder will— E. Well, nobody knows. P. Magruder could be the loose [unintelligible] of the whole plan. E. He's entirely vulnerable and nobody knows. P. Uh-huh.
E. But Dean's very strong feeling is that this is a time when you just have to let it flow. And that's his— P. I tend to agree with him, you know. Do you? E. Yes, I do. I do. P. Basically, Mitchell must say—go on in and hard-line it, John, etc. We cannot, we can't claim privilege for Dean on this kind of a matter, can we? E. I don't believe on acts prior to the investigation, no.

Ehrlichman said Dean would consult with Mitchell before giving grand jury testimony. Nixon suggested an approach: "But he's got to let it off pretty hard with Mitchell … he hasn't got any choice on it, that he will not testify to anything after the fact. And that he'll not testify except … and then he'll be damn careful he's protective about it. Is that what he's going to say? We don't want Mitchell, you know, popping off."

April 14, 1973 (8:55–11:31 a.m.)

With the President, Haldeman and Ehrlichman in attendance, this meeting at the Executive Office Building opened with a report to the President by Ehrlichman that Colson felt Mitchell should testify before the Watergate grand jury. After speculating what Hunt would say in an upcoming appearance before the grand jury, the meeting's participants turned to the problem of convincing Mitchell to talk to the U.S. attorney's office about what he knew concerning Watergate. The bulk of this conversation then dealt with arguments that might be used to convince Mitchell to talk. "I'm not convinced he's [Mitchell] guilty," Nixon said, "but I am convinced he ought to go before a grand jury."

After exploring alternatives, the three decided that Mitchell would be called to Washington and Ehrlichman would talk to him. The arguments that they finally decided to use to convince Mitchell were as follows:

E. Well, if he asks me, what do you want me to do? I am going to say, "If you will do what I ask you, what I would suggest, you would pick up the phone or you would allow me to pick it up, and call Earl Silbert and make an appointment today and go over and talk with the U.S. Attorney about this case with counsel." …
E. "Well, you're asking me in effect to go down and enter a guilty plea." And I would say, "Look, John, you're the only who knows the basic [unintelligible] to go and to decide whether there's any room with what you know and the ultimate action of the jury through which you might pass unpunished. I can't make that judgment for you and I don't have any right to make it for you. All I'm saying is that if we're looking at this thing from the standpoint of the President, today is probably the last day that you can take that action, if you're ever going to take it to do the President a bit of good."
P. "Do you realize, John, that from the White House, I mean, Colson, maybe Haldeman are going to get involved in this thing too?"
E. Well, here again, we're looking at this thing not from the standpoint of any other individual. "We are looking at it from the standpoint of the Presidency and that's the only way I think you and I can approach this."
P. And I'd go further and say, "The President has said let the chips fall where they may. He will not furnish cover for anybody." I think you ought to say that. E. That's right.
P. Don't you agree, Bob? That isn't it? …
E. And this is one that will permit him, one that might help the Presidency rather than damage it.
P. Bob, do you think there's something to be said for having John wait to talk to Magruder until after he sees Mitchell? Suppose you get stone-walled with Mitchell.
H. Well, I think John's in a stronger position if he's talked with Magruder than if he hasn't but I, maybe I. E. I tell you, it is not what Mitchell says that matters today. It is the fact that you have acted on information you have today. P. Yeah.
E. Now, let's suppose Mitchell turns us down cold, and says I'm going to preserve all my rights. I'm going to fight every inch of turf and so on and so forth. O.K. That's right. But at least you, having accumulated all this knowledge this week, have tried to get this thing out, so that sometime two months from now, three months from now, a year from now when there's a panic you can say on the 14th of April— …
E. When somebody comes to [unintelligible], what the hell was the White House doing all this time? Then you're in a position to say, "Well, we began to investigate personally the external circumstances and we came to some conclusions—we acted on those conclusions."
P. "John Ehrlichman conducted an investigation for the President." E. "And we made an effort." Now, it may be that what should happen here is that if they both stonewall, I ought to sit down with Silbert and just say, "Now, I don't have a lot of evidence."
P. I agree with that. E. But I have an accumulation of hearsay—
P. And the President wants you to go forward on this.

A E. And I'll turn over to you the report that I made for the President, for whatever it's worth. And I want to tell you that I have had contact with two of your targets to make clear to them that nobody in the White House wanted them in any way to be reticent. Beyond that, I don't have anything to say to you. . . .

At one point in the meeting, the matter of whether or not to fire Dean was raised.

P. That's the point. All right. One final thing. Dean. You don't think we have to bite it today? E. Well, I'm not so sure. I'd be inclined. When you say bite it isn't simply a matter of making a decision, in my opinion—

P. I have made a decision. He's to go.

E. Well, I'm not sure that's the right decision. By forcing the isue, I don't mean to imply that. P. Oh, I see. [Unintelligible.]

B E. Uh, [unintelligible.]

P. When you said you didn't think you agreed with the decision, I thought that was one of the recommendations you made.

E. No, my recommendation is that you recognize that there's a go, no go decision that has to be made because— P. Oh, I see.

E. Here's your situation. Look again at the big picture. You now are possessed of a body of fact. P. That's right. E. And you've got to—you can't just sit here. P. That's right.

E. You've got to act on it. You've got to make some decisions and the Dean thing is one of the decisions that you have to make. You may decide—. . .

C E. "I'll tell you, I am still heavily persuaded that we affect the grand jury and U.S. Attorney treatment of Dean favorably by keeping him on. P. O.K. E. And that that's important. Now—

P. Why is that?—because they like him? E. No, no. No, no. Because they can treat him differently as the President's Counsel than as a dismissed person. E. Exacty. P. Yeah. . . .

E. There were 8 or 10 people around here who knew about this, knew it was going on. Bob knew, I knew, all kinds of people knew.

P. Well, I knew it. I knew it. . . .

D P. I must say though, I didn't know it but I may have assumed it though but you know, fortunately—I thank you both for arranging it that way and it does show the isolation of the President, and here it's not so bad—But the first time that I knew that they had to have the money was the time when Dean told me that they needed $40,000. I had been, frankly, [unintelligible] papers on those little envelopes. I didn't know about the envelopes [unintelligible] and all that stuff.

E. The point is that if Dean's, if the wrongdoing which justifies Dean's dismissal is his knowledge that that operation was going on, they you can't stop with him. You've got to go through a whole place wholesale. P. Fire the whole staff.

E E. That's right. It's a question of motive. It's a question of role and I don't think Dean's role in the aftermath, at least from the facts that I know now, achieves a level of wrongdoing that requires that you terminate him.

P. I think he made a very powerful point to me that of course, you can be pragmatic and say, [unintelligible] cut your losses and get rid of 'em. Give 'em an hors d'oeuvre and maybe they won't come back for the main course. Well, out, John Dean. On the other hand, it is true that others did know. . . .

F H. What Dean did, he did with all conscience in terms that the higher good— P. Dean, you've got to have a talk with Dean. I feel that I should not talk to him. E. I have talked to him. P. I mean about motive. E. I have talked to him. P. What's he say about motive? He says it was hush-up? E. No. He says he knew, he had to know that people were trying to bring that result about. P. Right. . . .

P. When he came in to see Bob and you what would he say was the problem? E. He'd say, "These guys. Hunt's getting jittery, and says that he's got to have umpty-ump thousand dollars, and Mitchell's terribly worried about it," and it was never expressed, but it was certainly understood—

P. On the question of motive then, though, I guess in those conversations with you with respect to motive was never discussed. E. Never discussed with me in those terms.

G P. Right. The motive was to help defendants who were, by golly, who had worked for the campaign committee. E. It never really got that far because, we, at least my conversation with John always was, "Well, you know that's interesting, but I just don't know what to do for you."

P. Yeah. He may have gone further with you, Bob. Did he? H. No. We referred him to Kalmbach. You aimed it at Kalmbach, I aimed it at Mitchell. I said, "John, you can't come here and ask for help, we don't have it." The one thing where it did go further, if you want to argue about it, it was in the sense that the 350.

P. That we had. H. Which was not our money, we did move back over there. P. For this purpose? H. [Unintelligible]. Yeah, yeah. P. Who asked for it? H. Nobody.

P. I mean how, who asked for the move on the 350? H. Hunt did.

P. How did you know? Somebody came to you? H. Gordon Strachan came to me after the election and said you have $350,000 in cash. What do you want to do with it. P. This was not requested by LaRue? H. No. P. Of Gordon? H. No, the problem was getting them to take it back. They wouldn't take it, cause they didn't know how—

P. Well, that money— H. LaRue wanted it but Mitchell wouldn't let him take it. E. They just didn't know how to account for it. Well, then, frankly, he wouldn't have to account for it, in my opinion. H. Well but he didn't—he was P. 1970 money.

H. He will have to account for it now, because Fred LaRue is in personal receipt under grand jury knowledge of $328,000 in cash delivered to him at night at his apartment by Gordon Strachan. The witnesses to that transaction were Strachan and LaRue.

P. LaRue testified— H. But Strachan just testified that that's what happened. Well, LaRue's got a problem. What did he do with it? At that point, it's income to him. He's got an I.R.S. problem if he can't get that accounted for.

P. He'll use it. What does he say? He says, "I used it for hush money"? H. I don't know what he'll say. He'll probably say, "I packaged it up."

April 14, 1973 (1:55–2:13 p.m.)

In this short conversation in the White House Oval Office, Haldeman informed the President of Magruder's intention to tell all he knew to the U.S. attorney. Certain that the prosecutor was going to learn all the facts about Watergate, Magruder said in a phone conversation with Haldeman, he hoped he could lighten the jail sentence facing him by cooperating with the prosecutor. What was ironic, Magruder told Haldeman, was that all the material derived from the Watergate intelligence operations was "trash." Magruder had told him "The tragedy of this whole thing is that it produced nothing," Haldeman said.

April 14, 1973 (2:24–3:55 p.m.)

Ehrlichman met with the President and Haldeman in the Oval Office to report on his just-completed meeting with Mitchell. Ehrlichman recounted that he told Mitchell the President did not feel that Mitchell's only option was to agree to a guilty plea with the U.S. Attorney's office:

E. And he [Mitchell] said, well, he appreciated that, but he had not been taking the position he had for the reason that he thought he was necessarily helping or hurting the Presidency, but he said, "You know, these characters pulled this thing off without my knowledge." He said, "I never saw Liddy for months at a time." And he said, "I didn't know what they were up to and nobody was more surprised than I was. . . . I didn't press him on it and I tried to play him with kid gloves. I never asked him to tell me anything. He just told me all this stuff. He says that actually Magruder is going to have a problem with all of this because Dean talked Magruder into saying the wrong things to the grand jury, and so Magruder's got a problem. . . .

E. Well it goes on like that. His characterization of all this is that he was a very busy man, that he wasn't keeping track of what was going on at the committee—that this was engendered as a result of Hunt and Liddy coming to Colson's office and getting Colson to make a phone call to Magruder and that he, Mitchell, was just not aware that all that happened until Van Shumway brought Liddy into Mitchell's office sometime in June and that's the first he had knowledge of it. . . .

E. Well, I said I understand that one version of the fact is that Magruder brought you a memo with a number of targets on it, and that you checked off the targets that you wanted. And he said, "Why nothing could be further from the truth than that."

P. That was John Dean's version. H. That's right. P. That's what he said to Mitchell. H. Right. Then what Mitchell said to me was that he did not—he said I checked—I signed off on it.

P. Go ahead. H. I said you mean you initialed it and he said no.

E. Then I said they had testimony saying Hunt and Liddy, having a conversation, and Liddy saying to Hunt, "Yes, I know how you don't like this stuff, but we have to do it because Mr. Mitchell insists on it." He said, "I never saw Liddy for five months. From February to June, I never laid eyes on him." He said, "I think Liddy is the source of a lot of my problems here, using my name, etc."

Told by Ehrlichman that the President felt that the body of information on Watergate gathered by the White House should be turned over to the Justice Department, Mitchell agreed that was the proper course. Ehrlichman said he told Mitchell that Kleindienst felt he should step aside from any case involving Mitchell:

He [Mitchell] got a very wide smile on his face, and he said, "Well, it's great to have friends, isn't it?" He says, "Especially the way we stuck by them"—meaning the I.T.T. business, I assume, because of Kleindienst. So that was an interesting little aside. He said, "I would be very grateful if you would all kind of keep me posted," . . .

P. Oh, I get the point. Now does he know that Magruder is going to confess?

E. I said that in the course of calling to invite people to come talk with me today, and I indicated that there were more than two, that the persons who called was told that Dean intended—pardon—that Magruder intended to make a clean breast of it and that was first party information and very reliable, and that that would tend to begin to unravel the saint from the sinner in both directions. And he agreed with that. Now he said, "Which version is it that Magruder is going to testify to? Is it the one that he gave Bob and me in Bob's office, or is it some other version?" H. That's not true. . . .

E. He said, "You know in Bob's office, Magruder said that Haldeman had cooked this whole thing up over here at the White House and—" . . .

E. Mitchell's theory—

P. Whatever his theory is, let me say, one footnote, is that throwing off on the White House won't help him one damn bit.

E. Unless he can peddle the theory that Colson and others were effectively running the committee through Magruder and freezing him out of the operation, which is kind of the story line he was giving me.

H. Did he include me in the others? E. Yep. H. That I was freezing him out of the operation?

E. That you, in other words—he didn't say this baldly or flatly, but he accumulated a whole bunch of things: its Colson, Dean and Bob working with Magruder, and that was sort of the way the line went.

P. No. The White House wasn't running the campaign committee.

H. He's got an impossible problem with that. The poor guy is pretty sad if he gets up there and says that. . . .

Ehrlichman finished his summary, and they turned to the question of indictments: who was likely to talk, what would those who talked say, and who would be indicted.

Following a short discussion on dealing with the Senate Watergate Committee, they considered Ehrlichman's remark that what he knew about Watergate couldn't be made public without prejudicing the rights of Watergate defendants under indictment. Both Haldeman and Ehrlichman expressed interest in creating publicity that would prejudice the rights of defendants—Magruder and Mitchell—and ultimately bring about their acquittal. However, Nixon apparently did not favor that course, as he moved to another area of discussion. The remainder of the meeting, for the most part, concerned getting out a public statement on Watergate that would do the least damage to the President and the White House.

April 14, 1973 (5:15–6:45 P.M.)

With Haldeman and the President at the Executive Office Building, Ehrlichman had just come from a meeting with former Nixon re-election campaign official Jeb Stuart Magruder. Magruder, Ehrlichman recounted, had held an "informal" conference with the U.S. attorney to lay out his own involvement in Watergate.

The bugging of the Watergate headquarters of the Democratic National Committee, Magruder related to Ehrlichman, came after Mitchell had "chewed" out Liddy for his failure to obtain useful political intelligence against the Democrats. Moreover, the bugging operation was part of an overall plan that had been approved by Mitchell with reluctance, Magruder said:

E. In the conversation, Mitchell orally approved it. Now it involved other things besides tapes, and he was not specific. He said, "In all honesty this was a kind of a non-decision. Nobody felt comfortable in this thing but we were sort of bull-dozed into it." was the way he put it. Ah—P. By Colson? E,. That's the inference. . . .

E. The one copy [of Liddy's intelligence report] that Magruder had had pictures of the kinds of papers that you'd find around with campaign headquarters. He sent a synopsis of the pictures to Mitchell. He thought it was so bad he picked up the phone and called Liddy and chewed him out. . . . Liddy was badly embarrassed by the chewing out he got. He met in a meeting with him, and said to John Mitchell, "Mr. Mitchell I'll take care of it." That was all that was said. So the next break-in was entirely on Liddy's own notion. Magruder says neither Mitchell nor Magruder knew that another break-in was contemplated. . . . He [Magruder] said, "No one else." He said, "The U.S. Attorney is hot after Colson:—they know he was close to Hunt. The only thing they have him on right now is the phone call to Magruder," so far as Jeb knows. But his attorney then chimed in, and said, "I think the U.S. Attorney has a good deal more because the U.S. Attorney told the lawyer that Hunt had re-perjured himself with respect to Colson."—when he was called back in under immunity and testified as to the break-in, and the capture of the burglars, and the cover-up. Mitchell, LaRue, Mardian and the lawyers basically—

P. Plus Magruder.

E. Dean devised a cover story, in concert with these other people, and enlisted Bart Porter who went to the Grand Jury and perjured himself in concert with the cover story. Dean prepared Magruder and others for the testimony at the Grand Jury, cross-examining and getting them ready.

E. Likewise, he leaked out information from the Grand Jury to the people at the Committee for the Re-election. The U.S. Attorney knows that he did that. It is illegal to do so. . . . P. What about Haldeman? E. Haldeman's very much a target of the U.S. Attorney. So far they indicated that he was implicated only by association with other people—meaning Strachan presumably. . . .

P. What is, what about Strachan? Strachan says you did not know about this. H. Can I give Strachan a report on this? P. Sure. What is your view about his perjury? E. I don't know. H. He's going to the Grand Jury Monday morning. That's why it's better that he be given this information so he doesn't perjure himself.

P. Right. H. I don't think he's testified on any of this so I don't think he has any perjury problem. What he has to do is prove the defense that—P. Meets these points. H. Meets these points and—P. Good.

H. And he could—he can keep himself as an office boy, which is what he was. An office boy. If he lied about a thing—he persuaded Gordon to keep Liddy on—Jeb to keep Liddy on—I would think he would argue back that—"Jeb said to me, 'well, what should we do?' and I said, 'I think you better keep him on—he's getting good stuff' " Don't you think so? . . .

P. Let me ask you, John, about Colson. Everything that has been said, despite the fact of how accurate—it would be consistent with Colson's not knowing the Watergate defendants? E. Magruder doesn't lay a glove on him.

P. But he says they're hot after him. Of course, the only thing they would be hot after him is on the—ah—

Hunt. E. His connection with Hunt. Their premise apparently is, according to their lawyers, that everything Hunt knew, Colson knew.

Turning to his phone conversation with Kleindienst, Ehrlichman told the President of Kleindienst's desire to have a special prosecutor take care of Watergate. Nixon's reaction was completely negative and he continued to question Erhlichman about Magruder:

P. Now the question is what do you do about Dean. That may be moot. For that reason I would say—I—H. Does Magruder guess that Mr. Dean's going to be indicted? E. Magruder does not link Dean with the break-in and the bugging.

P. No, but he says he was there—E. He's in the inception. P. Yeah. E. But they have that on him. H. But he's in a wholly [unintelligible] all he had to do—reject this plan—E. Sir? And he is not a participant in the Liddy, Magruder quarter-million—take it to Florida—plan. He is no link at all to the plan that was carried out.

P. All right then—so they get him for what? They get him for the aftermath, the aftermath, and the obstruction. He has have a chance. Not much. They'll say that he believed that he has a constructive immunity on that, E. But he doesn't have it any more.

After some more discussion concerning who was implicated in Watergate, the three turned to the question of resignations among the White House staff. Haldeman was disturbed that his connection to political trickster Donald Segretti might force him to resign, but Nixon rejected that course.

H. You've got a really—a punchy decision which is whether you want me to resign or whether you don't. That's one you've got to figure out. The problem with that is if I go on the basis of the Segretti matter, you've got to let Dean go on the basis of his implication, which is far worse. P. Yeah.

H. Strachan's already out of the White House so that's no problem. If he's going to ring Ehrlichman in, you are going to have to let him go. E. He's got sort of a hypothesis in that he is developing our conversation that—that—referring him to Kalmbach—which is actual. As a matter of fact, I didn't refer him to Kalmbach. He came to me and said, "May I go to Kalmbach." [unintelligible.]

P. Go to Kalmbach for the purpose of—E. For the purpose of getting Herb to raise some money. For the purpose of paying the defendants. For the purpose of keeping them "on the reservation." P. Right. With that they could try to tie you and Bob in a conspiracy to obstruct justice. E. That's his theory. P. It's rather questionable.

April 14, 1973, Approximately 6 p.m.

Telephone conversation, Ehrlichman and Kleindienst:

Ehrlichman reported to Kleindienst on the course of his investigation of White House involvement in Watergate, remarking at one point that he had been talking to "everybody but the milkman": persons inside and outside Nixon's staff, and lawyers. There had been problems, he noted: some who "appeared to be reticent to come forward because they somehow felt that the presidency was served by their not coming forward." Nixon had told him to "straighten them out on that point."

Ehrlichman said he had been "a little late" in talking to Magruder, who had "just come back from telling everything to the U.S. Attorney"—information "dramatically inconsistent" with his earlier grand jury testimony. And, Ehrlichman added, Magruder "implicates everybody in all directions up and down in the Committee to Re-elect," including Mitchell. Ehrlichman said later that Magruder had also implicated Dean.

Kleindienst asked if there was a "substantial" case of perjury against Mitchell and Magruder. "No question," Ehrlichman replied, adding that it was "more than just a participation in a conspiracy . . . they are principals." Ehrlichman noted that Mitchell had been "steadfast in his protestations of innocence," but that the Magruder case was "persuasive to me."

Ehrlichman later brought up another matter:

E. Let me spoil your afternoon completely, will you? One of the things Magruder told me was—and his attorney who was with him corroborated—was that they are very concerned about Dean's facility for advising people at the Committee of the proceedings of the Grand Jury.

K. [unintelligible]. E. Well, he was apparently informing Magruder and others of what the Grand Jury was saying and doing.

K. [unintelligible]. E. And Silbert or someone else said to his attorney, well, we know the source of Dean's information and it was from higher up.

K. That is pretty speculative, because I don't think Henry Petersen would have told him. E. Well, anyway, there— K. I couldn't have because I didn't know.

Near the end of the conversation, Kleindienst counseled:

Yours is a very God damn delicate line as to what you do to get information to give to the President and what you can do in giving information to the Department of Justice, you know, to enforce the law. E. Well you are my favorite law enforcement officer. K. [unintelligible]

April 14, 1973 (11:02–11:16 P.M.)

Telephone conversation, the President and Haldeman:

Reflecting on Magruder's discussions with the Watergate prosecutors, Nixon surmised that some of what Magruder was saying could be "exaggerated," adding:

P. I don't know. I can't tell. He is obviously flailing around like a wild man at the present time. H. No, no, he's not really. I think he was earlier. He was frantic, but once he figured out where he was going, I think he—P. He thinks this is what he remembers now? H. Yep. Uh, huh.

P. I am not sure that his interpretations on various things—they could be interpreted either way you know, like his interpretation on Dean, his interpretation on Strachan, for example. H. Yep, yep. P..Certainly—H. That's right and there—P. I just don't know how it is going to come out. That is the whole point, and I just don't know. And I was serious when I said to John at the end there, damn it all, these guys that participated in raising money, etc. have got to stick to their line—that they did not raise this money to obstruct justice. H. Well, I sure didn't think they were. P. Huh? J. I didn't think they were and I don't think they did. P. Well—H. With maybe some exceptions.

P. Right, right. Of course, I suppose there they will say, like McCord has said, that that was the purpose. That somebody told him that. That doesn't mean anything. H. Yeah.

P. The question, of course, is Liddy and the others. But we shall see. It is the word of the felons against the word of the men that raised the money, huh? H. That's right. Well, you just—You don't know how much will come out in what way either. I mean that—

P. No, we, at least I think now, we pretty much know what the worst is. I don't know what the hell else they could have that is any worse. You know what I mean. Unless there is something that I don't know, unless somebody's got a piece of paper that somebody signed or some damn thing, but that I doubt.

Regarding other witnesses, Nixon asked about Colson; Haldeman replied there was nothing "inconsistent" between statements by Magruder and Colson.

P. Oh, that could be right. Chuck could say, yes, the Liddy project, sure but I thought the Liddy project was something else. H. That's right. That's what he does say.

P. He does, huh? **H.** Yeah. And as Ehrlichman said—under questioning, they specifically said that he didn't get into any specifics on it, and they have nothing that hits him on any specifics.

P. I think he believes that, Bob, I know—**H.** I do too. **P.** I think he believes that. **H.** I have thought that all along.

They later turned to the question of Gordon Strachan, and Strachan's conversations with Ehrlichman:

P. . . . You do one person you do tell and I—and he can still say that he just told him to tell the truth. You ought to tell Strachan, but tell him—. **H.** John is telling him. **P.** John is, but not in a way that Strachan indicates that he knows what the other fellow said. **H.** That's right. **P.** Is Strachan smart enough to do that? **H.** Yes.

P. He has to be prepared that he is going to be asked this and is going to be asked that. John should put him through a little wringer there. **H.** Yep.

P. John is the one who should do it. He is conducting an investigation for the President. **H.** Well, and he's got the information. I don't. I can reconstruct—**P.** No. **H.** Part of it. **P.** That's right. I agree. But John will know the questions too. **H.** The specific points is what he needs to cover.

April 14, 1973 (11:22–11:53 P.M.)

Telephone conversation, the President and Ehrlichman:

At various points in the conversation, Nixon and Ehrlichman dwelt on White House dealings with the Ervin Committee. Discussing the merits of televised public hearings, Nixon suggested that Ziegler tell the press Nixon felt that White House staff members who had been charged should have a chance to be heard publicly, "under certain proper ground rules." Nixon also suggested that televised hearings might be better than having the press speculate on what had happened in closed sessions.

P. You know—you see a man looking honest and earnest etc., denying it in a public forum—**E.** Yeah, yeah **P.** where he just—you know I just have a feeling—**E.** There is something to be said for splitting the time with them.

Later, concerning legal tactics Magruder's lawyers might use to delay a criminal trial, Nixon asked:

P. Won't that take a little time? **E.** Yes sir, you bet it will! My hunch is that the soonest you could get a case like that to trial would be the Fall. September or October—**P.** Really? **E.** Something of that kind. **P.** That leaves the committee hanging for a while, I suppose. I don't know whether that is good or not. **E.** Well I don't thing they would let the committee proceed in the meantime.

P. You don't really? **E.** They would use every effort to stop it, and I am just guessing, but just common sense tells me they could stop it. I don't know the law.

P. One long shot, should you talk to Ervin? **E.** Should I? **P.** Yes. **E.** Confide in him? **P.** [Characterization deleted] **E.** No, I can't—I just wouldn't dare. Kleindienst might at some time later.

P. He should make the deal. I think, frankly, let's get off the damn executive privilege. **E.** Get a little ride on it huh—while we can?

P. Well at least I do think it would cool a little of the Congressional stuff, you know. **E.** Uh, huh. **P.** I really do. As I read the Congressional stuff, they say—they can't understand this or that or the other thing. Allright now we are—basically, also, its bold. The President just says there is enough of this nonsense? We are going to fight. You see what I mean? **E.** Uh, huh, I get you. OK, it suits me.

P. Puts the President in the position of being as forthcoming as we can—and the facts out. **E.** Yep

Haldeman's position—Nixon was concerned about dealing with his closest staff, especially Haldeman:

. . . And the thing about Bod, as I say, is this: I get back to a fundamental point. Is he guilty or is he not? In my view, he is not, you know. **E.** Yep.

P. And if he isn't—even if it means that the whole country and the Congress and all the members of the Senate and House say resign, resign, the President says. No. I will not take a resignation from a man who is innocent. That is wrong. That is contrary to our system and I am going to fight for him. **E.** Uh, huh.

P. If evidence is brought out to the contrary, fine. Then we will take a look at it. . . . Well you know you get the argument of some, anybody that has been charged against, you should fire them. I mean you can't do that. Or am I wrong? **E.** No, you are right.

P. Well, maybe I am not right. I am asking. They say, clean the boards. Well, is that our system? **E.** Well that isn't a system. You know, that is a machine. That's—

P. That's right. I feel, honestly,—I mean, apart from the personal feeling we both have for Bob, don't you? But you know, I raised this myself. One way out is to say, well look, as long as all these guys have been charged, out they go and they can fight this battle and they can return when they get cleared. It is not good, is it? **E.** You know I don't think it is. I don't think that is anyway to run a railroad. I think—

P. I suppose that would probably be the deal of purists. What does Len think on that? Does he think that, or—**E.** I don't know. I think you have to show—**P.** Well, that is irrelevant—**E.** some heart on the thing.

P. Well, the point is, whatever we say about Harry Truman, etc. while it hurt him a lot of people admired the old bastard for standing by people. **E.** Sure—**P.** who were guilty as hell **E.** Yep.

P. And damn it I am that kind of person. I am not one who is going to say, look, while this guy is under attack, I drop him. Is there something to be said for that, or not?

E. I don't think, number one, I don't think you would gain anything by it. The problem doesn't go away. **P.** No they will say, oh, that Nixon's top person, closest man to him, in the office for four or five hours a day, and out he goes. Everything must be wrong! **E.** Yep-that is it. That is liking separating Siamese twins.

Dealing with Dean—Nixon turned to Ehrlichman's upcoming conference with Dean:

P. What are you going to say to him? **E.** I am going to try to get him around a bit. It is going to be delicate. **P.** Get him around in what way? **E.** Well to get off this passing the buck business. **P.** John that's—**E.** It is a little touchy and I don't know how far I can go.

P. John, that is not going to help you. Look he has to look down the road to one point that there is only one man who could restore him to the ability to practice law in case things go wrong. He's got to have that in the back of his mind. **E.** Uh, huh.

P. He's got to know that will happen. You don't tell him, but you know and I know that with him and Mitchell there isn't going to be any damn question, because they got a bad rap.

[Material not related to Presidential actions deleted]

P. You say that Dick was really shaken? **E.** Yeah, he was.

P. Damn it, I told him once, I said, Dick, the real target here is Mitchell. He said, oh, no, It can't be! He's got sort of the idea that probably it is Haldeman or Colson. **E.** Well I am sure he is going to call me the first thing in the morning.

P. Yeah, but with him I would be very tough. I would say Dick—just don't mess around—they are after Mitchell, and they are going to get him at the present time. At least, that's what our information indicates and so here is where we go.

E. He is probably doing a little checking with his U.S. Attorney tonight.

P. Would he do that? **E.** Oh sure, sure. He has to make the ultimate prosecution decision, or else he has to delegate it to somebody, so he is entitled to—

P. Your point is that he would delegate it to Dean. I think that Dean is the best one to delegate it to, rather than, John, the suggestion that he resign and then we will put in another Attorney General. That would be a hell of an admission that, that we thought—**E.** He isn't going to want to do that would be my guess. He isn't going to want to resign at this point.

Near the end of the conversation, Nixon asked:

Well, with Dean I think you can talk to him in confidence about a thing like that, don't you? He isn't going to—. **E.** I am not sure—I just don't know how much to lean on that reed at the moment. **P.** I see. **E.** But I will sound it out.

P. Well you start with the proposition, Dean, the President thinks you have carried a tremendous load, and his affection and loyalty to you is just undiminished. **E.** All right. **P.** And now, let's see where the hell we go. **E.** Uh, huh.

P. We can't get the President involved in this. His people, that is one thing. We don't want to cover up, but there are ways. And then he's got to say, for example? You start with him certainly on the business of obstruction of justice. **E.** That's right.

P. Look, John—we need a plan here. And so that LaRue, Mardian and the others—I mean, **E.** Well, I am not sure I can go that far with him. **P.** No. He can make the plan up.

April 15, 1973 (10:35–11:15 a.m.)

The President and Ehrlichman in the Oval office:

The first transcript from the day on which, according to the White House, the recorders eventually ran out of tape because of Nixon's many meetings, was highlighted by a discussion of what various witnesses might tell the prosecution about Watergate, and explorations of how the White House should deal with the Justice Department. The transcript was also marked by numerous clusters of "unintelligible" notations—more so than many of the other transcripts.

Nixon queried Ehrlichman on the status of evidence:

P. I suppose Colson is [unintelligible] Hunt, and Bittman which, of course, could tie Colson in, right? **E.** Yeah.

P. Up to his navel. There's not a damn thing you can do about that is there John? **E.** No, really not, not at this point. You have to depend on Hunt's natural secrecy and secretiveness. **P.** John, there is nothing in it for Hunt. Let me ask this, [unintelligible] go back over everything he's done prior to that time. **E.** Well . . .

P. There might be something? **E.** Well, he's up on, apparently, he has perjured himself a second time. Gee, he perjured himself at the trial, then he was granted immunity, came back into the grand jury, and perjured himself again. The U. S. Attorney is looking down his throat and could say to him look, I can forget some of these counts if you're a good boy now.

P. Yeah, but the point that I make is this—is really, of course, you know, its the limits of his testimony. **E.** mmhuh-mmhuh. **P.** If he testifies just on Watergate that's fine. He isn't going to get a damn thing more than anybody else. **E.** I don't see any incentive for him to go broader, and I haven't heard a whiff of that. **P.** [Unintelligible] give him immunity for that? I suppose, or would they? **E.** I don't know. I don't think they can give him immunity at this point.

The Colson-Hunt situation came up again later in the meeting:

P. But Magruder said they are hot after Colson. **E.** Suspicion. **P.** Or Magruder's attorneys say that. Magruder had nothing on Colson. **E.** No. The one phone call is the only incident that he has to relate. **P.** His attorney says I think they're hot in going after Colson. **E.** Yeah. **P.** The reason there of course is Hunt. **E.** Right—the association. **P.** Yeah. **E.** And that's natural. You've got a guy in the case that . . . **P.** Well Hunt [unintelligible] Colson. **E.** Yeah. Hunt has to know it.

P. What do you do about Colson, John? **E.** I don't think there's much to do at this point. He's **P.** Yeah. **E.** He's building his own defenses. I assume that he's doing whatever has to be done with Hunt—that only he could do.

P. So, but, but . . . **E.** Well you know he's, I'm sure, has had surreptitious contact with Hunt. **P.** Yeah. He says [unintelligible] take care of your kids. **E.** And I think Chuck's natural proclivities will **P.** Do everything. **E.** do anything we can possibly do.

P. See [unintelligible]. There isn't a hell of a lot more they can tell us that Magruder hasn't told [unintelligible] **E.** That's right.

Nixon asked about Strachan; Ehrlichman replied he had talked to him

"Just about ten minutes ago. And I've been doing all the talking so far. **P.** [Unintelligible] trying to talk [unintelligible] **E.** What Magruder had said about him and so forth. So. **P.** [Unintelligible] any [unintelligible] for removing him? **E.** Not yet. Not yet. **P.** He's a good man—good man. **E.** I think he, I think he'll do fine. You see . . .

P. [Unintelligible] you expect anyone [unintelligible] I was cogitating last night, and we've got the people that can—I mean on the obstruction of justice thing, which I think is our main problem at this time—well of course it is the main problem because it involves the other people. **E.** Yeah.

P. Otherwise it's just Chapin. **E.** Yes, Chapin. **P.** and Mitchell. **E.** Yeap. **P.** Magruder. **E.** Yeah. **P.** Possibly Dean, but a . . . **E.** Mardian and LaRue.

P. [Unintelligible] on the [unintelligible] of the case? **E.** LaRue. **P.** They got him on that too? **E.** Yeah. Yeah. **P.** You mean Magruder has? **E.** Yeah.

P. That's going to be hard. This fellow's lied twice to [unintelligible]? **E.** That's right. That's true. **P.** The people you've got with obstruction are Hunt and Goldblatt and Bittman, right? **E.** Oh, Rothblatt the lawyer. **P.** Rothblatt? **E.** Yeah, right. Well, I don't think Bittman is going to testify. I would be very surprised if he did. **P.** Why? **E.** Well.

P. Get him involved in obstruction of justice? **E.** Well I just don't think—I think, I'm just guessing here, my guess is that he's worked himself out a haven in all of this.

P. Wouldn't serve his interests to get involved in the obstruction of justice. He's basically almost a bag man, not a bag man, but a message carrier, isn't he? **E.** No. No.—was an instigator—. He was concerned about his fee. And a . . . **P.** Oh really John? **E.** Yeah. Yeah. So he was one of the active promoters of that as near as I can tell.

P. [Unintelligible] me what you and [unintelligible] say on the obstruction thing. What was involved? I mean, from our side, our guys.

E. Well you had defendants who were concerned about their families. That's understandable. You had lawyers who were concerned about their fees and that's less understandable.

P. Oh, yes. It's understandable. **E.** Well I mean in terms of the end result. You had a campaign organization that was concerned about the success of its campaign . . . **P.** Yes. **E.** And didn't want these fellows to say anything in public that would disrupt the campaign. . . . If you were talking about keeping [unintelligible] if you know the defendants were guilty, and if you didn't know who else was [unintelligible]. **E.** That's correct. **P.** And you just thought that they [unintelligible]. **E.** Well you know, the thing that ran through my mind . . . **P.** Yeah. **E.** Was Howard Hunt has written 40 books, and **P.** Yeah.

E Howard Hunt was worried about the support of his family. And I could see Howard Hunt writing an inside expose of how he broke into the Democratic National Headquarters at the request of the Committee to Re-elect the President. **P.** Yeah.

E. Now, if I had a choice between getting contributions for the support of Howard Hunt's family. **P.** Yeah. And that's . . . **E.** And that was pretty easy. **P.** And I suppose they would say though that . . .

E. Oh, didn't care what Howard Hunt said to the Prosecutor. He can say anything he wanted to the prosecutor in a secret—in a secret session. That didn't hurt us. **P.** It was all secret then. **E.** The Grand Jury was secret. **P.** The Grand Jury was all operating at that time. **E.** Sure. **P.** It hadn't come to trial? **E.** Sure—it didn't come to trial until after the election. **P.** Yeah. [Unintelligible]. **E.** So.

P. I think [unintelligible] it was—nobody was trying to keep him from telling the truth to the Grand Jury—to shut him up to the Grand Jury?

E. I can say in truth and candor that Dean never explained to me that there was any kind of a deal to get these guys to lie or to change their stories or to refuse to testify to the trial of the action or anything of that kind. That was just never discussed. So I don't feel too uncomfortable with this.

A statement by Ehrlichman that Magruder had given the prosecution all the information Liddy had refused to give prompted Nixon to ask, "How do you get Liddy's sentence cut down? [Unintelligible]

E. It may be too late for him. **P.** I wonder if it is. Huh? Or is it? **E.** Yeah. He was only . . . **P.** Why didn't he talk [Unintelligible]"

Dean and the grand jury—Ehrlichman also reported on Dean's (and the White House's) use of grand jury information:

E. . . . the U.S. Attorney now feels that Dean overreached them by providing information out of the grand jury to the Committee for the Re-election. I think that may be legitimate criticism if he in fact did that. On the other hand, for him to provide us with information inside, for the orderly operation of the government, is another matter. That's two quite different things. If you peddle information from a grand jury to the outside, or if you peddle it inside to people who are responsible. **P.** [Unintelligible]

E. Oh that was, let me think. **P.** [Unintelligible] Grand Jury at that point. **E.** He had information on who was going to be called as witnesses so that apparently Mardian was able to get around and coach witnesses. **P.** Did Mardian coach them?

E. In some cases Mardian, I guess, was very heavy-handed about it, and— **P.** Well, is there anything wrong with that? **E.** Yeah, well there's something wrong with— **P.** He was not their attorneys is the problem? **E.** Well, no, the problem—the problem is he asked them to say things that weren't true. **P.** Oh. **E.** When I say coach I use the word loosely, and— **P.** [Unintelligible]

Another aspect of the White House relationship with the prosecution had been brought up earlier in the meeting—the then-unresolved issue of a special Watergate prosecutor. Ehrlichman mentioned one person already in the Justice Department, Deputy Attorney General Joseph Sneed, who did not share Kleindienst's legal problem of a personal closeness with Mitchell, . . . "and Sneed is controllable within limits, and I think he is credible. I may be wrong about his credibility.

P. I agree with this, I think he's credible. The reason I think he's credible is something else—is that the grand jury I assume [unintelligible] come through with some indictments. I mean, suppose they just indict Magruder and Mitchell [unintelligible]. **E.** Yeah. **P.** Well, that's the fish. **E.** Yeah. **P.** The big fish. **E.** Yeah.

P. Damn it, what more do they want? Now what's the problem with the special prosecutor? As I see it, it just puts another [unintelligible] loose [unintelligible] around there. **E.** Well the special prosecutor . . . **P.** Reflects on **E.** Will second-guess Silbert. I assume will feel that his mandate is to . . . **P.** Tear hell out of the place? **E.** Yeah—yeah. **P.** That's right. **E.** And—that's just an additional risk which you wouldn't have with the Dean who's been a part of the process. I just—I don't think.

P. [Unintelligible] with him [unintelligible] myself [unintelligible]. If not then, let's face it, he hasn't been very helpful throughout this thing. **E.** That's right. [Unintelligible] he stood as far away from it as he could get.

ITT mentioned—During a discussion of an upcoming conference with Kleindienst, Nixon referred to the controversial antitrust case involving the International Telephone and Telegraph Corp. (ITT)

P. I can say on I.T.T., of course, we didn't—my basic responsibility [unintelligible] McLaren settled this case or something like that, and a **E.** Yeah. **P.** [unintelligible] **E.** No. that wasn't to settle a case. **P.** No, not settle **E.** That was not to file an action. You remember they were about to file a law suit and

P. How did we know about it? **E.** Flanigan found out about it. **P.** You came and told me? **E.** I came and told you about it. **P.** Why [unintelligible] may have forgotten the details.

P. Why didn't we think they should file an action? **E.** Well **P.** I am sure it was a good reason. **E.** Yeah. We had a run **P.** [unintelligible] we had a runaway antitrust division at that point.

P. Yeah, and I had been raising hell with McLaren **E.** That's right. **P.** on all this, and I said now this is a violation of my policy— **E.** not on. **P.** [unintelligible] a violation of rules that I had laid down with McLaren. **E.** And I will testify to my dying day that our approach to antitrust cases has [unintelligible] virtually without variation, on policy rather than the merits of the individual case.

April 15, 1973 (1:12–2:22 p.m.)

The President and Kleindienst in the EOB Office:

Kleindienst said the "primary reason" for talking to Nixon was the "very serious question" that had come up regarding the possible indictment of Haldeman and Ehrlichman. At several points Nixon reiterated his hesitation about removing them from his staff when they might be innocent, but Kleindienst counseled Nixon to keep in mind that the presidency should be protected.

According to Kleindienst's information from the prosecutors, Strachan would implicate Haldeman:

K. . . . they believe this fellow Strachan is just about ready to [unintelligible]—on the face of it. **P.** Some of this—got some of the take in other words. Haldeman had—if Haldeman was furnished the reports. **K.** Either the reports or papers that would indicate that Liddy was doing something like this.

P. Oh—papers? **K.** Apparently there was the sum of three hundred fifty thousand dollars. **P.** Yeah—I know about that. **K.** Transferred from the White House to LaRue. **P.** Right. **K.** That Bob indeed indicated that the transfer of that money. [unintelligible].

K. Might have just thought that [unintelligible]. That would implicate **P.** That I would think would mean that he had some of it—the reports from the bugging. **K.** Either the reports or budgetary or—

Dean, who was becoming increasingly recognized as a problem for the White House, could be harmful to Ehrlichman, Kleindienst said:

K. . . . Dean intimated two things with respect to Ehrlichman. One, Dean had in his possession some documents that were taken out of Hunt's office—that's number one. **P.** He's told the U.S. Attorney this?

K. Yes. Other item he issued a directive that—to get Hunt out of the country. Instances, standing by themselves—nothing more to say on one side or the other can constitute an obstruction of justice. . . . .

P. What Dean—Dean had told 'em, but he hasn't testified? **K.** Right—and that other point about Dean's posture with the United States Attorney—that's why I wanted to talk to you about this. That these are conditional statements. If Dean worked out an arrangement satisfactory to Dean the U.S. Attorney's office and Dean agree that they are not going to have knowledge of these statements.

P. So what would happen? **K.** Well, in the event they don't work something out then Dean presumably wouldn't testify this way with respect to Ehrlichman or he might, depending upon what [unintelligible] If they work something out, probably it would be for the purpose of—no, no sir. There's going to be no immunity offered. **P.** Well, then why would he get it? Work something out—why?

K. Well that's—that hasn't been resolved because Dean and his lawyers are being very, very careful there. **P.** I'm sure.

Later in the meeting, Nixon asked:

P. What about Hunt? **K.** Hunt doesn't know anything. He knows about the obstruction of justice—somebody gave him the money. Isn't that the one where Mrs. Hunt or somebody—I don't know what that is—I don't know. **K.** You know as much about it as I do. **P.** [unintelligible] say something [unintelligible] and I don't want to get so deeply involved. . . .

P. If Dean does not testify about deep sixing documents and getting Hunt out of the country they have nobody else that can say that. **K.** What they want initially. **P.** Yeah—will they work out. I think they'll honor their agreement between them.

P. Well, as you know, Dean put it out for press. **K.** No—no sir. **P.** They're decent men. **K.** Yes they are. **P.** Good. **K.** Yes sir. **P.** But Dean. **K.** They raised questions whether or not I should even mention that to you because of the (unintelligible). **P.** No, (expletive removed) you should tell me. **K.** Oh (expletive removed) I didn't argue with them about that.

Payments to defendants—Early in the meeting Nixon asked Kleindienst to explain the "legal point" regarding payments to the original defendants:

P. Of course I was thinking of the Berrigans and all the funds that have been raised through the years, Scottsboro, etc. Nobody ever raised any question about it. If you raise money for the defense and it's for support—and Ellsberg—[expletive removed] in Ellsberg, the defense—

K. And likewise in this case. If I had committed a crime and you know about it and you say, "Kleindienst, you go in the Court and plead guilty to the commission of that crime and here is ten thousand dollars, you know, to tide you over and so forth." **P.** That isn't a crime?

K. No. On the other hand, if you know that I committed a crime. **P.** Right. **K.** And you say, "you go in there and plead guilty, and here is twenty-five thousand dollars on the condition that thereafter you'll say nothing. You just make the plea, take the Fifth Amendment, the judge cites you for contempt, you've got to continue to testify you don't. You do not take it." Then you are now in a position of obstructing justice.

P. Excuse me. If you'd explain that again. If you tell 'em—if you tell 'em—if you raise the money for the purpose of telling them not to talk. **K.** After he's pleaded guilty. Let's take the— **P.** Well, they were all before the Grand Jury at this point, Right?

K. And the judge says, "I'm going to give you immunity—I have ordered you to testify to what you know." He refuses, takes the Fifth Amendment and he's punished for contempt. And you give him twenty-five thousand dollars. [unintelligible]

P. There was some thought that—that was all after the election that that happened, huh? K. I don't know but that happened after the conviction—after Liddy's conviction.

P. Oh, in other words, the obstruction they are talking about is what happened after the conviction? K. Yes sir. P. Rather than before the conviction? K. Yes sir. P. Well, who the hell would—you mean—but I can't see Haldeman or Ehrlichman or anybody in that [unintelligible]

K. Well. P. No—I'm just asking. Or Dean, ah, you mean that after that that they raised—they gave money for that purpose? K. For whatever they gave—let's say that money was given to Liddy in connection with—and.

P. Let me say this—there isn't any question that money that they have had on that or whatever—Mitchell's defense frankly—it would be—you know—these people had worked for the committee and they were provided with money for their legal fees and for their support. That is—this is before their conviction. Now comes the point of after their conviction. That's when the case may be, that's when you get the jeopardy. K. Or if people are up for trial, Mr. President, you say.

P. No-no-no-I'm sorry—not conviction—but after their indictment. K. Yes. After the indictment "Here's fifty thousand dollars. You plead guilty and thereafter take the Fifth Amendment. If they offer you immunity, you know, not testify about anything." If that's.—

P. And then you given 'em money? K. Yes. P. That's—I agree. K. Yes—obstruction of justice.

P. Yeah. If the purpose of it is to get them not to talk. In other words, not to carry out what the judge said. I can see that. Sure.

After further discussion of potential evidence and the advisability of appointing a special prosecutor, Nixon referred to his and his closest aides' isolation from the 1972 campaign:

P. . . . we were on our way to China and then we were on our way to Russia. K. I know.

P. We weren't in the campaign—they were. We couldn't and that's why we had no control. Well, anyway, I'm not making excuses. The thing to do now is to. K. Deal with the facts as you have them. P. Go forward. K. It would have to be by you, Mr. President.

Nixon and Kleindienst then debated various names as possibilities for special prosecutor, and Kleindienst advised that "responsibility for the entire matter" should be delegated to Henry Petersen, whom Kleindienst described as a respected career man in the Justice Department. Nixon expressed tentative agreement, and Kleindienst urged haste "before this stuff gets out of hand."

At the end of the transcript shortly afterwards came the notation "[No more sound—tape runs out.]

April 15, 1973 (3:27–3:44 p.m.)

Telephone conversation, the President and Haldeman:

Haldeman reported on his conversation with William Rogers, then secretary of state, who—according to Haldeman—had surmised that the Ervin Committee hearings might be delayed because of possible conflict with the rights of criminal defendants in pending indictments.

Haldeman said Rogers advised pursuing what Nixon called the "Executive Session commitment" with the panel.

P. Puts us in a good forthcoming position. H. That's his point, that that is a very sound offer, just as your offer to work with the Grand Jury was a sound offer that produced results. You say we will be perfectly willing to work with the Senate.

Haldeman noted that Rogers favored appointment of a special prosecutor.

Nixon replied that he had come to the same conclusion, but for a prosecutor such to "see that the indictments run to everybody they need to run to, so that it isn't just the President's men. . . ." Nixon added later, "the Special Prosecutor thing helps in another way. It gets one person between me and the whole thing."

Much of the remainder of the conversation was devoted to the credibility of such witnesses as Magruder and Strachan, and the public impact of the indictment of such a prominent figure as Mitchell.

(The Nixon-Haldeman conversation was followed in the transcript by a separate entry for a one-minute telephone call at 3:48 p.m. from Nixon to Kleindienst, in which Kleindienst asked if he might bring Henry Petersen along to a meeting. Nixon replied, "Yeah, I want to ask him to do something.")

April 15, 1973

Telephone conversation between Higby and Haldeman.

Higby said he had a message for Nixon from Dean, which Dean wished Haldeman to relay. Dean's message: that his actions were "motivated totally out of loyalty" to Nixon; that Ehrlichman had asked to meet him that night, but Dean felt such a meeting "inappropriate at this time;" that Dean was willing to meet with Nixon to discuss "these matters" at any time; and that Nixon should take counsel from Petersen "who I assure you does not want the Presidency hurt."

April 15, 1973 (8:14–8:18 p.m.)

Telephone conversation between Nixon and Petersen. Nixon asked Petersen if he had any further information to report before their meeting scheduled for the next day. Petersen said that in preliminary negotiations with Dean's counsel, the counsel indicated Dean would plead not guilty and go to trial "unless we come to some agreement with him. His counsel's position is that it would be a travesty to try Dean and not try Ehrlichman and Haldeman."

Nixon asked how the prosecutors could use information obtained from Dean if Dean did not plead guilty, and Petersen replied they could not use it "for any purpose."

Nixon then asked about the propriety of his talking immediately with Dean, and Petersen gave his approval. Nixon asked Petersen what he should ask Dean, and an exchange ensued concerning Liddy:

P. What do you want me to say to him? Ask him to tell me the whole truth? H.P. Yes, sir. And there is one other thing: that is a signal from you might bring out the truth from Liddy. P. From Liddy? H.P. Yes sir.

P. A signal from me? What do I do? H.P. He went to John Mitchell, I am told, and indicated that he would do whatever he was told to do.

P. I never met the man. I don't know what I can do with him. H.P. Uh, huh. P. How do I give him the signal? H.P. Well, I will do it for you. P. He, Liddy has talked to John Mitchell and said a signal from the President? H.P. No, he said a signal from Mitchell.

P. From Mitchell? H.P. Yes, sir, and so indicated that he was going to stand firm. P. Then, what am I trying to get at, how do I get—I then would go over Mitchell to you, Liddy and you're telling me that? H.P. No. We just go and say that we have discussed this situation with the President of the United States and he thinks it is vitally important that you tell us everything you know. P. I get it. Uh huh. OK . . .

April 15, 1973 (8:25–8:26 p.m.)

Telephone conversation between Nixon and Petersen.

Nixon told Petersen that he was trying to get in touch with Dean. In the meantime, he said, concerning Liddy: "you are to tell him the President wants everybody involved in this to tell everything they know." Petersen agreed and said he would get in touch with Liddy's lawyer first thing in the morning; Nixon urged that he do this immediately, and Petersen agreed.

Nixon continued:

P. Fine. One thing I want to be sure of Henry; you understand as far as Liddy is concerned I have no control over him—don't know the man at all and I just want, since he has raised the question, that maybe not talking because of me— H.P. No, no—I don't want to leave that impression.

P. Because of Mitchell, huh? H.P. He is taking orders from higher authority. The decision is mine but since you are the highest authority he will stand in line if we handle it discreetly.

P. I just want him to be sure to understand that as far as the President is concerned everybody in this case is to talk and to tell the truth. You are to tell everybody, and you don't even have to call me on that with anybody. You just say those are your orders. H.P. Yes, Sir.

April 15, 1973 (9:39–9:41 p.m.)

Telephone conversation between Nixon and Petersen.

Nixon told Petersen he had been talking with Dean, and Dean recommended that Nixon personally tell Liddy's lawyer that he wanted Liddy to tell all he knew. Nixon said he still preferred for Petersen to give Liddy's lawyer the message, but if the lawyer would not accept it from him, Nixon would be willing to deliver it personally. Petersen agreed.

Nixon added that if it was necessary to bring the lawyer to the President's office, "you come with him. I don't want any things where he comes in and makes any motion—you see what I mean?" Petersen agreed.

April 15, 1973 (11:45–11:53 p.m.)

Telephone conversation between Nixon and Petersen. Nixon rescheduled their meeting the next day for an hour later than they had planned, and then told Petersen of his talk with Dean:

P. . . . I got him in finally and heard his story and I said directly to him, "Now when do you want to resign?" And, he said, "Well I will resign but I would prefer to wait until I have testified." Now I want to ask your judgment on that. I can bring him in the morning and tell him, "Look, I want your resignation." But, what do you want me to do? I don't want to interfere with your process?

H.P. Mr. President, I don't think that we ought to— P. Tip our hand? H.P. Not yet. He is the first one who has really come in. P. Oh, I see. H.P. He came in a week ago Sunday.

P. Right. Let me say this. The main thing Henry we must not have any question, now, on this, you know I'm in charge of this thing. You are and I am. Above everything else and I am following it every inch of the way and I don't want any question, that's of the fact that I am a way ahead of the game. You know, I want to stay one step ahead of the curve. You know what I mean? H.P. I understand.

P. So—if you think on Dean— H.P. I think we ought to hold the line. P. Alright and you will let me know. H.P. Yes, sir. I will indeed. P. as soon as—then I will call him in and naturally he will have to resign. H.P. Yes, sir.

Nixon said he had informed Haldeman and Ehrlichman of "The charges that have been generally made," and both had agreed that if the charges stood up they would resign. Nixon said he was "perfectly prepared" to ask them to resign immediately, but Petersen advised that he wait "until we hear their testimony, which is, well we want to put them off until we can fashion all the . . . things into a pattern."

Nixon asked how long that would take, and Petersen replied at least a week and possibly two. Nixon expressed a fear that during that time "the damn thing will leak out." He asked Petersen to prepare a written assessment of Haldeman's and Ehrlichman's "vulnerabilities" for their meeting the next day, so he could "act on it," and Petersen agreed.

Petersen later said of Haldeman and Ehrlichman:

H.P. . . . we are going to have to weave all of the facts with respect to them into a pattern. It is not going to come out neat and clean— P. And clear— H.P. with respect to either one of them.

P. Because, in both cases they have a—basically in both of their cases, as I look at the thing since it is basically the obstruction of justice case for the most part, with the possibility of Haldeman of knowledge, although that is questionable to believe. But you have to hear Strachan before you decide that. H.P. Yes sir.

P. But that's a matter which is going to involve your hearing them too, what they know, I suppose, as well as hearing the others.

H.P. Oh, I think that is right and I think with respect to the obstruction of justice thing is concerned, it is easy for me to see how they fell into that, if you like.

P. Yeah. Uh huh. Rather than being directly conspirators? H.P. That's right. That's right.

P. And there is a difference in that respect, I suppose. H.P. That's right. A difference, at least, in moral culpability.

P. Sure. Motive.

H.P. In plain terms of ultimate embarrassment, I think that— P. The embarrassment is there, but in terms—basically in terms of motive which might be the legal culpability, they might be off but in terms of embarrassment they would have to be out of the government? H.P. Yes sir.

P. I get your point and, frankly, either one is enough. I understand that totally because that was what was involved in the Adams' case, as you recall. H.P. Yes.

P. He was not legally guilty of a damn thing. Well, he might have been, I suppose, making the telephone call, if they had ever brought him to trial. But because of the possibility, we had to move on him. Well in any event, I am glad to get your view on it but I want you to know that having talked to Dean and told him to wait, I wanted you to know that I had told him to wait because I had agreed with him that I would not do it until I heard from him, but let me say I am going to wait until I hear from you then, on Dean. Is that fair enough? H.P. Fine, yes sir.

Nixon then asked about Magruder, and Petersen replied:

H.P. We've had him in and we have to get his testimony in before the grand jury, and we are trying to work out with his lawyers as to whether or not—

P. Well, he will come in and plead guilty so you can. Because it seems to me, that your idea of getting him on and pleading guilty and beating the damn press and the Ervin Committee to it is a very good one. Otherwise, you know, they are going to say they forced you to do it. And that is very important, don't you agree?

H.P. There are negotiations under way with counsel now and obviously they are very much afraid of Sirica. They are afraid Sirica is going to clap him in jail immediately. P. Oh. H.P. We have to see Sirica, too.

P. Now, Sirica's got to see the point of this. My goodness, because the point is Sirica's got to realize he is getting bigger fish. H.P. That's right.

April 16, 1973 (9:50–9:59 a.m.)

Conversation between Nixon, Haldeman and Ehrlichman in the Oval Office:

Nixon began by asking advice on how to proceed with two resignation letters he had had prepared for Dean's signature. Ehrlichman recommended he have Dean sign both of them—"Then you could use

whichever one he wanted or none, depending on how circumstances unfold."

E. Unless he won't. You know, you know what to do at that point. H. You go to Petersen and ask him not to [unintelligible]

P. That is why, John, I want to nail down what Dean said about other bugs on the White House and so forth, and so on. I assume that is the Plumbers operation. E. No, no. What he is referring to is the FBI's bugs on the journalists in the first year he was nominated. P. [Unintelligible].

E. Hold on. No, no. These were almost all FBI bugs. What I said all National Security— P. But I was wondering what your advice if I should not tell him today that anything in that area is National Security [unintelligible]

E. I think you should, and I think it should cover not only that but Plumbing operation and anything else of which he has knowledge that I am [unintelligible] that with Executive Privilege right now . . .

E. Now if you remember the whole operation was because you were afraid there were leaks out at the NSC and you were trying to find them. P. I thought they were due to the F.B.I.

E. Well, all the [unintelligible] were but there was one in Georgetown at somebody's house that actually was never put on. It was [unintelligible] but it was explored and how Dean knows about that, I don't know. The F.B.I. files— P. [Unintelligible] E. I can't say. I doubt it. I think it was before his time.

Ehrlichman later said:

There is one point before you talk to Dean that I heard last night that didn't fit together. Maybe it doesn't matter. And that is that Dean said, last night, as I understood it, that Petersen had told you that Liddy has not talked. They can't get Liddy to talk. P. Yeah.

E. Dean told us that Liddy had told him everything. Told the U.S. Attorney. P. I know that, I know that, but I—

E. Petersen lying to you or [unintelligible]. P. Well, maybe a little both. E. Well, I think it is probably [unintelligible]. P. A snow job. E. Either that or Dean is [unintelligible] cover-up in case anything starts to seep out.

Ehrlichman said he had held a meeting with Ziegler earlier in the morning, and Ziegler wanted Nixon:

"to get out the fact that Dean [unintelligible] you that the Dean report was inadequate [unintelligible] that several weeks ago you reinstituted an examination of the personal investigation and that this culminated in a whole series of actions over the weekend.

P. I spent the weekend working on it. [Unintelligible] got to say. E. The report did not. This is the week that Mitchell being here [unintelligible]. P. [Unintelligible].

E. Well, now, If I am going to be splashed on this thing you are better off now having another scrap with Dean. P. Well, somebody is going to be. E. Well, we could not [unintelligible]— P. Investigation of the matters. E. I think that that is the way, the investigation of the matter.

P. But I didn't talk to Mitchell. E. Well, they say who did it, delegating him to do that. I mean that, that's— P. [Unintelligible] look one damn thing. E. Well, I think there is a full Ehrlichman report, unquote. [Unintelligible].

As the meeting ended, Ehrlichman advised Nixon to ask Dean whether he intended to plead guilty or not.

April 16, 1973 (10–10:40 a.m.)

The President and Dean in the Oval Office:

As presidential action on Dean drew nearer, Nixon asked Dean to sign two already-prepared alternative letters to be held in reserve: "straight resignation" if Dean pleaded guilty, and a request for immediate leave of absence if Dean were to "go in on some other basis." Dean agreed with the general course of action, and received Nixon's permission to draft his own letters. Dean also received assurance that similar action was being taken with regard to Haldeman and Ehrlichman, and Nixon

suggested later that Dean's version might be used by others who might have to resign.

Nixon then took Dean through a recapitulation of Dean's reports on Watergate and an assessment of the status of the evidence. Nixon asked about payments to defendants, offers of clemency and the obstruction of justice implicit in such action:

P. What was the situation, John? The only time I ever heard any discussion of support for the defense fund was [inaudible]. I guess I should have assumed somebody was helping them. I must have assumed it. But I must say people were good in a way because I was busy. . . .

P. I said, "Why, John, how much is it going to cost to do this?" That is when I sent you to Camp David and said [expletive removed] "Let's see where this thing comes out." D. That's right. P. And you said it could cost a million dollars. D. I said it conceivably could. I said, "If we don't cut this thing—"

P. How was that handled? Who handled that money? D. Well, let me tell you the rest of what Hunt said. He said, "You tell Dean that I need $72,000 for my personal expenses, $50,000 for my legal fees and if I don't get it I am going to have some things to say about the seamy things I did at the White House for John Ehrlichman." Allright, I took that to John Ehrlichman, Ehrlichman said, "Have you talked to Mitchell about it?" I said, "No, I have not." He said, "Well, will you talk to Mitchell?" I said, "Yes I will." I talked to Mitchell. I just passed it along to him. And then we were meeting down here a few days later in Bob's office with Bob and Ehrlichman, and Mitchell and myself, and Ehrlichman said at that time, "Well, is that problem with Hunt straightened out?" He said it to me and I said "Well, ask the man who may know: Mitchell." Mitchell said, "I think that problem is solved."

P. That's all? D. That's all he said. P. In other words, that was done at the Mitchell level? D. That's right. P. But you had knowledge; Haldeman had knowledge; Ehrlichman had knowledge and I suppose I did that night. That assumes culpability on that, doesn't it? D. I don't think so. P. Why not? I plan to be tough on myself so I can handle the other thing. I must say I did not even give it a thought at the time. D. No one gave it a thought at the time.

P. You didn't tell me this about Ehrlichman, for example, when you came in that day. D. I know.

P. You simply said, "Hunt needs this money." You were using it as an example of the problems ahead. . . .

P. Well, you take, for example, the clemency bit. That is solely Mitchell apparently and Colson's talk with Bittmann where he says he will do everything I can because as a friend. D. No, that was with Ehrlichman. P. Hunt? D. That was with Ehrlichman.

P. Ehrlichman with whom? D. Ehrlichman, and Colson and I sat up there. Colson presented his story to Ehrlichman regarding it and then John gave Chuck very clear instructions on going back and telling him, "Give him the inference he's got clemency but don't give him any commitment."

P. No commitment. D. Right. P. That's allright. No commitment. I have a right to say here—take a fellow like Hunt or a Cuban whose wife is sick or something and give them clemency for that purpose—isn't that right? D. That's right.

P. But John specifically said, "No commitment," did he? D. Yes. P. And then Colson went on apparently to—D. I don't know how Colson delivered it— P. To Hunt's lawyer—isn't that your understanding? D. Yes, but I don't know what he did or how—

P. Where did this business of the Christmas thing get out, John? What in the hell is that all about it? That must have been Mitchell, huh? D. No, that was Chuck again. P. That they would all be out by Christmas? D. No, I think he said something to the effect that Christmas is the time the clemency generally occurs.

P. Oh yeah. Well, I don't think that is going to hurt him. Do you? D. No.

P. Clemency is one thing. He is a friend of Hunt's. I am just trying to put the best face on it, but if it is the wrong thing to do I have to know.

D. Well, one of the things, I think you have to be very careful. And this is why the issue should be very good is, if you take a set of facts and let the prosecutors who have no PR judgment but they will give you the raw facts as they relate to the law, and it's later you have to decide what public face will be put on it. P. Oh, I understand. You can help on that, John.

Nixon's interwoven themes at various points in the conversation were the White House's public posture in its dealings with the prosecution, and how Dean should conduct himself:

A

B

C

D

E

F

G

P. Don't you agree with me that it is better that we make the first announcement and not the Justice Department. D. Yes I do. On your own staff. P. Oh hell, I am going to make the announcement on Magruder too. (expletive omitted) It was our campaign. I am not going to have the Justice Department—we triggered this whole thing. Don't you agree? You helped to trigger it. You know what I mean. D. When history is written and you put the pieces back together, you will see why it happened. Because I triggered it. I put everybody's feet to the fire because it just had to stop. P. That's right. D. And I still continue to feel that.

P. You put Magruder's feet to the fire. Where did you see Magruder? D. I didn't. In fact, I refused to see him. That was one of the problems. P. Oh, and that's why—D. I started to talk with—I met with him in one of these outer offices at a meeting.

P. What got Magruder to talk? I would like to take the credit. D. Well. P. I was hoping that you had seen him because—D. He was told, one, that there was no chance. . . . The situation there is that he and Mitchell were continuing to talk. Proceeding along the same course they had been proceeding to locking their story, but my story did not fit with their story. And I just told them I refused to change, to alter my testimony. But would repeat it just as I had given it. This had to do with a number of meetings in the Department of Justice.

P. Oh yes, I remember. You told me that. I guess everybody told me that. Dean said, "I am not going down there and lie," because your hand will shake and your emotions. Remember you told me that.

D. Yes, I said that. I am incapable of it. P. Thank God. Don't ever do it John. Tell the truth. That is the thing I have told everybody around here. (expletive omitted) tell the truth! All they do John is compound it. . . .

Dean agreed again later that Nixon was the one breaking the case:

D. Well, (expletive omitted) that is what we have done. That's right. P. I could have told you to go to Camp David and concoct a story couldn't I? and you have never heard that said, have you? D. No Sir.

P. In fact, I think I covered a little of that (inaudible). But on the other hand, it was your job to tell me, wasn't it. D. Uh, huh.

P. And you have. Basically what you have done—no, you told me the truth though. You've told me the truth. It was your job to work for the President, the White House staff and they were not involved in the pre-thing. But then you thought the post-thing. You thought about it and that is why you decided, as you said. D. I thought we should cut the cancer right off because to keep this whole thing—

P. Look, one thing I want to be sure. When you testify, I don't want you to be in a position, and I don't want the President to be in a position, that his counsel did not level with him. See my point?

D. There is no point that I have not leveled with you, as you should know.

P. Now when they say, "Now Mr. Dean, why didn't you tell the President—did you know about this? Why didn't you tell the President?"

D. That is a P.R. situation Mr. President. The U.S. Attorneys are not going to ask me questions asking what I said to the President and what I didn't.

P. Well, I frankly think—I would hope you can help on the P.R. there by saying—D. I will be happy to help on it.

P. I would like for you to say—and you are free to talk. You are to say, "I told the President about this. I told the President first there was no involvement in the White House. Afterwards, I told the President that I—" And the President said, "Look, I want to get to the bottom of this thing, period." See what I am driving at—not just the White House. You continued your investigation et cetera, and the President went out and investigated on his own. Which I have done, believe me. I put a little pressure on Magruder and a few of D. Uh, huh.

P. And as a result of the President's actions this thing has been broken. D. That's right. P. Because also I put pressure on the Justice Department—I told Kleindienst—(expletive omitted)

D. No, I think you are in front right now and you can rest assured everything I do will keep you as far as—P. No, I don't want, understand when I say don't lie. Don't lie about me either. D. No, I won't sir—you—

P. I think I have done the right thing, but I want you to—if you feel I have done the right thing, the country is entitled to know it. Because we are talking about the Presidency here.

April 16, 1973 (10:50–11:04 a.m.)

The President, Haldeman and Ehrlichman in the Oval Office:

Haldeman returned for a discussion of the "scenario" the White House would follow in dealing with the cover-up. Nixon said he was satisfied that Dean would use executive privilege protection if questioned on matters Nixon had decided involved "national security." Ehrlichman said he would follow the same course.

Nixon asked how the scenario had "worked out." Haldeman began the outline:

H. Well, it works out very good. You became aware sometime ago that this thing did not parse out the way it was supposed to and that there were some discrepancies between what you had been told by Dean in the report that there was nobody in the White House involved, which may still be true.

P. Incidentally, I don't think it will gain us anything by dumping on the Dean Report as such. E. No. P. What I mean is I would say I was not satisfied that the Dean Report was complete and also I thought it was my obligation to go beyond that to people other than the White House.

E. Ron has an interesting point. Remember you had John Dean go to Camp David to write it up. He came down and said, "I can't." P. Right. E. That is the tipoff and right then you started to move. P. That's right. He said he could not write it. H. Then you realized that there was more to this than you had been led to believe, (unintelligible)

P. How do I get credit for getting Magruder to the stand? E. Well it is very simple. You took Dean off the case right then. H. Two weeks, the end of March. P. That's right. E. The end of March. Remember that letter you signed to me? P. Uh, huh. E. 30th of March. P. I signed it. Yes.

E. Yes sir, and it says Dean is off of it. I want you to get into it. Find out what the facts are. Be prepared to—

P. Why did I take Dean off? Because he was involved? I did it, really, because he was involved with Gray.

E. Well there was a lot of stuff breaking in the papers, but at the same time— H. The scenario is that he told you he couldn't write a report so obviously you had to take him off. P. Right, right.

E. And so then we started digging into and we went to San Clemente. While I was out there I talked to a lot of people on the telephone, talked to several witnesses in person, kept feeding information to you and as soon as you saw the dimensions in this thing from the reports you were getting from the staff—who were getting into it—Moore, me, Garment and others.

H. You brought Len Garment in. E. You began to move. P. I want the dates of all those— E. I've got those. P. Go ahead. And then— E. And then it culminated last week. P. Right.

E. In your decision that Mitchell should be brought down here; Magruder should be brought in; Strachan should be brought in.

P. Shall I say that we brought them all in? E. I don't think you can. I don't think you can. H. I wouldn't name them by name. Just say I brought a group of people in. E. Personally come to the White House. P. I will not tell who because I don't want to prejudice their rights before (unintelligible)

E. But you should say, "I heard enough that I was satisfied that it was time to precipitously move. I called the Attorney General over, in turn Petersen,"

P. The Attorney General. Actually you made the call to him on Saturday. E. Yes. P. But this was after you heard about the Magruder strategy. E. No, before. P. Oh. E. We didn't hear about that until about three o'clock that afternoon. P. Why didn't you do it before? This is very good now, how does that happen? E. Well—

P. Why wasn't he called in to tell him you had made a report, John? H. That's right. John's report came out of the same place Magruder's report did— P. No. My point is—E. I called him to tell him that I had this information. P. Yeah but, why was that? That was because we had heard Magruder was going to talk? E. No. Oh, I will have to check my notes again. H. We didn't know whether Magruder was going to talk. E. That's right. H. Magruder was still agonizing on what he was going to do. . . .

April 16, 1973 (12–12:31 p.m.)

The President and Haldeman in the Oval Office:

Haldeman offered suggestions as to how the press and public might be dealt with as the more serious revelations by Magruder and others became known. One alternative was a statement by Petersen reflecting the "diligence" with which the White House had pursued and would continue to pursue the case.

Haldeman addressed his own problems:

H. . . . your action has to include cutting cleanly and that you've got to remove me and probably Ehrlichman, although he has an interesting thesis, according to Ron—I have not talked to Len—which is at least worth considering, which is that I move ahead of the game now, put out my whole story, including the factual details without pulling any punches of my, you know, that $350,000 fund. Yes, I sent it back to the committee—and I go into specifics. That I understand that Mr. Strachan delivered it to Mr. LaRue and that my motive was not to provide funds for the defendants. My motive was to move these funds back where they belonged, but I have to agree that I fully recognized that LaRue's motive in accepting money was, as I had been told at least, was a need to provide money for the defendants, to provide legal fees and to provide support for their families. And I acted at all times at the instigation of and through John Dean. In other words I didn't do any of this. John Dean came to me and said we need this and I knew I wanted to get rid of the money and said this is the way to do it, etc.

Haldeman said he would add that Dean, "through whom I was working and who was my only contact in this matter," had not advised him that he was involved in anything "illegal or improper." But Nixon was concerned that such action might push Dean into other revelations:

P. But the whole point is whether he then gets off and gets on other things. See what I mean? I don't want him—he is in possession of knowledge about things that happened before this. I told him that was all national security.

Despite other ramifications of the case, Haldeman was still concerned that:

H. They are going to get into the money and where the money went. If we haven't told them by then, they are going to drag it out of us drop by drop.

P. That right. H. I can see it is a weak appearing case in terms of what did I think I was giving the money back to them for. Where did the money go? Now there is no question about that, some of it. I don't think all of it did. But I knew where some of it was going to go.

P. But again you guys have to see what in the hell, again what LaRue testifies. What the money was for: to shut them up, or was it to provide help for their families. H. You see, that is the whole point. In my viewpoint it wasn't to shut them up but that is a hard case for anybody to believe I suppose.

P. Yeah, they will say it was to keep them quiet. H. Well, absolutely. But that—so they can't make the legal case.

After a discussion about what form public statements might take, the transcript ends with a prophetic exchange:

P. Well in the country it is not that big. It is just a little bit in the evening news and it should be handled as a news story. I am not going to go on and say, look, we are in a hell of a shape. It will be a big news story, it will be a big story for a couple or three weeks. Let's face it,— H. Yep, that's right. P. But it is not going to be at the moment. We are going to have one hell of a time.

April 16, 1973 (1:39–3:25 p.m.)

The President and Petersen met at the Executive Office Building and were joined for a short time by White House Press Secretary Ronald L. Ziegler.

Moving quickly through several preliminary matters, the President informed Petersen that he had asked Dean to draft a letter of resignation. Did Petersen have objections, Nixon wanted to know. As the prosecutor, Petersen replied, he would prefer to wait until Dean had agreed to plead guilty to criminal charges, but he understood the President's position and had no objection to Nixon's taking the resignation immediately.

However, Petersen said, he was worried about the announcement. Some discussion followed before Petersen suggested that the President say he had been conducting his own investigation into Watergate. "That I designated Henry Petersen as a my special counsel," Nixon added. In addition, the President said he would state that Dean had been assigned to write a report on Watergate but the report had not been full enough. When Nixon added to his proposed statement that Ehrlichman had taken over the Watergate investigation from Dean, Petersen stopped him, questioning the inclusion of Ehrlichman, who might have ordered the destruction of Watergate evidence. Dean said he was instructed by Ehrlichman to "deep six" documents that had been taken from E. Howard Hunt's White House safe, Petersen said.

Petersen changed the subject, turning to the question of subornation of perjury by Dean. Magruder had told the U.S. attorney of a call from Dean, in which Dean had told Magruder that Magruder had successfully perjured himself before the Watergate grand jury. Dean, Magruder said, had learned this in a phone conversation with Petersen:

H.P. Dean then calls Magruder, according to Magruder, and says Petersen says you've passed. Now that has great relevance in terms of the subornation of perjury charge. And the possibilities are ... And I didn't tell him any testimony in any event. P. I see.
P. You characterized it rather than give him the substance of it. H.P. That's right. That's right.

The involvement of Colson was another concern voiced by the President. Petersen answered that the U.S. attorney had nothing specific linking Colson to Watergate.

Nixon returned to the matter of a statement to the press. Petersen did not mind if his own name appeared, but he preferred not to have "putative defendants" named in the statement. At that point, Nixon asked Ziegler to aid them in putting out a statement. Ziegler cautioned that anything in a statement was bound to raise more questions. Discussion followed and a short statement was drafted: the President was conducting a personal investigation of Watergate; he was utilizing all the facilities available to him; the report to him by Dean had been inadequate; and he did not wish to make any more comments for fear of jeopardizing the rights of prosecution and defendants alike.

At one point, Petersen and the President had discussed the strategy used by Dean's lawyer in bargaining with the U.S. attorney. Dean wanted to plead guilty to an offense that would not result in his disbarment, Petersen said.

H.P. Oh Dean. The negotiations on Dean are still wide open. P. Dean isn't going to plead guilty? H.P. No sir. P. He's got this defense of being an agent? Right? H.P. That's right. ... Well, you know, the jury appeal unless you—in a sense jury notification of sympathy—that the jury will not convict because they think he's the fall guy. P. Oh I see—well [inaudible]—the Cubans. H.P. Depends on how sympathetic an appeal is made. P. That's my point.
H.P. But Dean's appeal's much more sympathetic. Dean's out for anyone on instructions, and he hasn't gone out and committed an overt criminal act. He hasn't broken anything the Cubans did—which is what detracted from their attempt to do this. Dean

has done—performed neutral acts which in the circumstances they were performed take on the traces of criminality, and he excuses that with, one—he wasn't fully informed; two, he was only an agent; three, he didn't have enough authority to countermand Mitchell—or he told Haldeman and Haldeman didn't countermand. Dean was impotent in the circumstance. That will be his defense. P. I see. ... Oh I see. going to go out as an agent? H.P. Yes, Sir.
P. No agent for the President, that's for sure, because— H.P. He's agent for Haldeman and— P. He hasn't testified that he's an agent for the President in any of this, has he? H.P. No sir. P. If he has, I need to know it. H.P. Yes, Sir—I know. P. [Inaudible] see Dean until a month ago. Never even saw him.

Other discussion between Nixon and Petersen related to the resignations of Haldeman and Ehrlichman. While Ehrlichman and Haldeman might not be legally culpable, their roles in Watergate were sufficient to probably necessitate their resignations for political reasons, Petersen advised Nixon.

April 16, 1973 (3:27–4:04 p.m.)

Having just seen Petersen, Nixon then conferred with Ehrlichman. They were joined by Ziegler.

In conversation with Petersen, Gray had denied receiving documents from Hunt's White House safe, Nixon said. Was this true, Nixon asked Ehrlichman. He would have to dispute Gray, Ehrlichman replied. He did not know the contents of the envelope, Ehrlichman said, but he was certain that Gray had been given it by Dean.

Ziegler entered the room. White House counsel Richard Moore and H. Chapman Rose opposed issuing a statement to the press, as envisaged by Nixon, Petersen and Ziegler in the previous meeting, he said. Rose felt that the President was too closely tied into Watergate as an investigator and too closely tied to the grand jury proceedings, Ziegler said.

P. We just won't try to get out in front. We got anything else you can say. Don't say, don't—we seem to, we've gotten into enough trouble by saying nothing so we'll say nothing today. You know, actually, thank God we haven't, thank God we haven't had a Haldeman statement. Believe me. (Unintelligible) thank God we didn't get out a Dean report. Right? Thank God. So, we've done a few things right. Don't say anything. ...
P. Well let me say, I'll—I've got Petersen on a short leash.

Petersen had also told him, Nixon continued, that Dean's lawyer was threatening to implicate the President, Haldeman and Ehrlichman in Watergate:

P. That he's informed the President and the President didn't act? He can't say that can he? I don't think, I've been asking for his damned report, you know. E. The fact that he put the chronology all together—he comes up with a hell of a lot of egg on his face.
P. I think he blames—he would blame you and Haldeman. E. Well, he's going to have a little trouble with that. P. Is he? Good. E. And I put together my log today. And I have seen him on the average of five times a month since the Watergate breakin. See, Bruce Kehrli (unintelligible) you know (unintelligible). I've seen none of his memos routinely. I don't supervise any of his work, so I think he's going to have a tough time making that stick. And some of those were on your estate plan. P. Yeah. E. Some of them were on the Library. P. Good. E. Some of them were on the leak scandal. So, he's not seen me five times a month on Watergate.

April 16, 1973 (4:07–4:35 p.m.)

Dean had been summoned to Nixon's Executive Office Building office to give a progress report on statements he had been preparing for the President.

A statement by the President would say that all members of the White House staff appearing before the grand jury would be given administrative leaves of absence until the grand jury had completed its work, Dean said, opening the meeting. In addition, his own letter would read that he (Dean) was requesting an indefinite leave of absence, having been informed that Ehrlichman and Haldeman had verbally tendered similar requests to the President.

P. You don't want to go if they stay— D. There is a problem for you of the scapegoat theory. P. You mean making use of it. D. That's right. P. Like Magruder being the scapegoat for Mitchell? D. That's right. You know, everybody is appearing before the Grand Jury. This does not impute guilt on anybody.
P. Let me put it this way I think rather [unintelligible] I could say that you, as Counsel—that you have been responsible for the investigation. We already have said that about this case haven't we? D. That's right. The only man you are dealing with and the only role I have is to help fill in any information I can to deal with the Public Relations of the problem. You know—
P. You can say it that way John. You can say the President sought your advice until it is cleared up. D. That's right.

Nixon was concerned about having to ask for Haldeman's and Ehrlichman's resignations. Dean commented:

D. That is a tougher question because one that is putting you in the position of being the judge of the entire facts before all the facts are in necessarily.
P. That is really my problem in a nutshell. So those fellows say that—this fellow says that— .D. Maybe that is the way this ought to be handled. You say, "I have heard information about allegations about [inaudible] some publicly and some have not become public yet. I am not in a position to judge because all the facts are not in yet [inaudible]

Another topic raised by Nixon was the question of Haldeman's involvement in the Watergate bugging operation:

D. Well, Bob tells me he did not know. Now I know the question is—the other thing is—I cannot, I couldn't describe twenty minutes after the meeting what Liddy was presenting was the most spectacular sales pitch you have ever seen in codes and charts and [unintelligible] operations. P. You mean Gemstone?
D. Well, that is what I am told now later after the fact they called it. I told Bob, "They are talking about bugging. They are talking about kidnapping. They are talking about mugging squads, taking people south of the border in San Diego, etc." P. What did Bob say? D. He said, "Absolutely NO." P. You will so testify? D. That is right—absolutely.

April 16, 1973 (8:58–9:14 p.m.)

Telephone conversation between the President and Petersen:

P. Well, ... Let me say first, I just want to know if there are any developments I should know about and, second, that of course, as you know, anything you tell me, as I think I told you earlier, will not be passed on. H.P. I understand, Mr. President. P. Because I know the rules of the grand jury.
H.P. Now—LaRue was in and he was rather pitiful. He came down with O'Brien and said he didn't want private counsel at all. He just wanted to do what he did. He told John Mitchell that it was "all over." ... LaRue, admits to participating in the [unintelligible] and obstruction of justice. He admits being present, as Dean says he was, at the third meeting, budget meeting, but— ... . He is reluctant to say at this point that Mitchell specifically authorized the budget for the electronic eavesdropping at that point. But I think he is going to come around. He is just so fond of John Mitchell. He admits that it could not have been activated without Mitchell's approval, however. ... Liddy confessed to Dean on June 19th—Dean then told Ehrlichman.
P. Liddy confessed that he did the deal, or what? H.P. That he was present in the Watergate. P. Uh, huh.
H.P. Ah, then you also asked about Colson. Colson and Dean were together with Ehrlichman when Ehrlichman advised about Hunt to get out of town and thereafter—P. Colson was there? H.P. Colson was there so he is going to be in the grand jury. With

respect to Haldeman, another matter. In connection with payments of money after—

P. The fact. H.P. June 17th, Mitchell requested Dean to activate Kalmbach. Dean said he didn't have that authority and he went to Haldeman.

P. Uh, huh. H.P. Haldeman gave him the authority.

P. Uh, huh. H.P. He then got in touch with Kalmbach to arrange for money, the details of which we really don't know as yet.

Had Magruder agreed to plead guilty, Nixon asked Petersen. No, Magruder wanted a deal in which he would not go to jail before others did, Petersen replied.

H.P. Now the other concern we have on that issue is how to charge.

P. How to charge? H.P. In terms of how we charge Magruder. In terms of the things we are concerned with, we don't feel like we ought to put Haldeman and Ehrlichman in there as unindicted coconspirators at this point, but we are afraid not to. If we don't and it gets out, you know, it is going to look like a big cover-up again.

P. Hmph. H.P. So we are trying to wrestle our way through that.

P. Whether you indict Haldeman and Ehrlichman along with the others, huh? H.P. Well we would name them at this point only as unindicted coconspirators, but anybody who is named as an unindicted co-conspirator in that indictment is in all probability going to be indicted later on.... Sirica's habit in court, and he certainly is going to do it in this case, is to interrogate the defendant himself. P. Right. H.P. And— P. The defendant who pleads guilty?

H.P. That's right. If he interrogates Magruder, that brings out the Ehrlichman/Haldeman facts and if we haven't mentioned them or included them in the conspiracy charge, then we are all going to have a black eye....

P. My second point is that—let me see about the 19th—Dean says that—H.P. On the 19th. P. Yeah. H.P. Liddy confessed to Dean. P. Dean says that? H.P. Dean says that. P. Liddy confessed to him and that he told Ehrlichman? H.P. Right. He told Ehrlichman.

P. Humph—that's a new fact isn't it? H.P. It's at least—yes, sir, and that's a terribly important fact I think because there was no disclosure made by either one of them. P. Either Dean or Ehrlichman? H.P. Yes, sir. P. Humph....

P. You see the point is, Dean didn't tell me that. That is the thing that discourages me. H.P. Well, Mr. President, you have to remember that we are de-briefing him on what has transpired over the last 18 months. P. I see. H.P. It is very difficult, you know, to get it all in. P. I know. I am not talking about you, but I am talking about what he didn't tell me, you see. That's a key fact that he should have told me, isn't it? H.P. Yes....

H.P. Let me go back over my notes. The principal thing that I wanted to point out to you on Haldeman is that Dean went to Haldeman to get authority to go to Kalmbach. P. Oh yes, yes, yes. That was it. When Mitchell told him to go to Haldeman. H.P. Mitchell told Dean simply to activate Kalmbach to handle the money. P. I see. H.P. Dean then went to Haldeman to get authority to contact Kalmbach. Thereafter, Kalmbach took care of the money. Now—details on the $350,000 which you indicated you knew about—P. I knew about the fund. I don know how it all went—

H.P. This is how it developed. It developed, as related to us, as money over which Haldeman exercised control. That money was delivered to LaRue to be used for payments, at least a portion of it. P. Some of it. Right. I think Haldeman would say that's true. I think he would. I don't know, but we'll see. You should ask, I guess, Kalmbach.

April 17, 1973 (9:47–9:59 a.m.)

Conversation between Nixon and Haldeman, Oval Office:

Nixon began by saying he thought "we ought to use John Connally more to hammer out what our strategy is here on Watergate." Haldeman agreed.

Haldeman then urged that they meet "earlier" that day to be ready to "move" by 3 p.m. or 3:30 in response to breaks in the Watergate story, particularly information received by the Los Angeles Times ("About [unintelligible]," Nixon said.) Nixon agreed, setting a meeting for 1

p.m., and asked Haldeman to meet with Ehrlichman before that.

The following exchange ensued:

P. Dean met with Liddy on June 19th, must have been when he did it. He was in California in January but that is irrelevant. But they keep banging around and banging around. The prosecution gets out the damn stuff. Did John talk with you about it?

H. Yeh, he mentioned it. Dean did tell us that story in Ehrlichman's office last week or two weeks ago. P. But not to go all through this. H. I don't think so. P. Yeh.

H. I think I mentioned it to you. Remember I described the story to you in some detail (unintelligible) walked down 17th Street—P. This was all after we had started our own investigation. H. Oh, yeah. P. I mean it wasn't back then. It wouldn't indicate that we knew about all this, etc. Another thing, if you could get John and yourself to sit down and do some hard thinking about what kind of strategy you are going to have with the money. You know what I mean. H. Yeh.

(Material unrelated to President's actions deleted.)

P. Look, you've got to call Kalmbach so I want to be sure. I want to try to find out what the hell he is going to say he told Kalmbach? What did Kalmbach say he told him? Did he say they wanted this money for support or—H. I don't know. John has been talking to Kalmbach.

P. Well, be sure that Kalmbach is at least aware of this, that LaRue has talked very freely. He is a broken man. The other thing is that this destruction of the [unintelligible] things is troublesome, of course. John tells me, too, and basically the culprit is Pat Gray. Does Colson know about that? Is that why they are calling Colson because Colson was in the room when it was handed to Gray? H. No, he wasn't. Well, apparently he wasn't.

P. He says he wasn't H. Colson thought, well there was a meeting before that, where they talked about the deep-sixing and all that supposedly. P. He was in that meeting? H. Which Colson was supposed to have been in.

P. Right, right, right. H. Colson doesn't remember being in it, but Colson flatly says that there was never anything where he was where there was a discussion of Hunt getting out of the country. Kehrli says the same thing. He was supposed to be at the same meeting. In fact, Ehrlichman has checked everyone who was at that meeting and nobody recalls that being said except Dean. And we now have the point that Dean is the one who called Liddy and told him to telephone Hunt to get out of the country and then called him later and said not to.

P. I would like a policy. I think, Bob, we have to think, I must say, we've got to think about a positive move. I think it ought to be money. H. I agree.

Nixon noted that "the prosecutor has been pretty clever. They got Magruder. Well Magruder just caved, but it had to come."

P. The other point, is the other element. The question now that is coming as far as Dean is concerned. He basically is the one who surprises me and disappoints you to an extent because he is trying to save his neck and doing so easily. He is not, to hear him tell it, when I have talked to him, he is not telling things that will, you know—

H. That is not really true though. He is. P. I know, I know, I know. He tells me one thing and the other guy something else. That is when I get mad. Dean is trying to tell enough to get immunity and that is frankly what it is Bob.

H. That is the real problem we've got. It had to break and it should break but what you've got is people within it, as you said right at the beginning, who said things and said them, too, exactly as Dean told them. The more you give them the better it will work out.

April 17, 1973 (12:35–2:20 p.m.)

The President, Haldeman and Ehrlichman in Oval Office, later joined by Ziegler:

The meeting focused on formulation of a public statement by the President on Watergate and on what to do about Dean, who was talking on his own to the Watergate prosecution. Concern kept cropping up about what the President had said to Dean in a meeting in March about payment of money to a Watergate defendant, Haldeman's link to a fund channeled to such payments and potential vul-

nerability from his aide Strachan's handling of material tied to the Watergate break-in plans, and Ehrlichman's possible jeopardy from reports of his advice to "deep-six" some material discovered in Watergate defendant Hunt's safe and of whether Ehrlichman was "an affirmative actor" in the scene or just had "knowledge of the general transactions."

Should Dean be fired, as Colson was recommending? "Colson would like to discredit him," Ehrlichman observed. "Well, I know," Nixon said. "But the question is what he could do to discredit us?" "That's a problem," Nixon said.

Colson also argued, according to Ehrlichman, that Dean should not get immunity from prosecution, that it was known Dean had little or no access to Nixon but that "knowledge imputed to us is knowledge imputed to you" and if Dean testified "that he imputed great quantities of knowledge to us . . . it will be very easy to argue—that all you have to do is read Dean's testimony—look at the previous relationships—and there she goes!"

Colson wanted to see Nixon, Ehrlichman continued. "He says you have total and complete control over whether Dean gets immunity through Petersen. Now that's what he says. He said he would be glad to come in and tell you how to do it, why, and all that stuff."

P. I don't want Colson to come in here. I fell uneasy about that, his ties and everything. I realize that Dean is the (unintelligible), Dean, of course, let's look at what he has, his (unintelligible) and so forth about (unintelligible) go popping off about everything else that is done in the government you know, the bugging of the—

E. Well, the question is, I suppose is which way he is liable to do it most.

P. First of all, if he gets immunity he'll want to pay just as little price as he can. E. Well, the price that—the quid-pro-quo for the immunity is to reach one through us to all of us. Colson argues that if he is not given immunity, then he has even more incentive to go light on his own malefaction and he will have to climb up and he will have to defend himself.

Nixon said he had brought up with Dean the "the tactic of all three re-signing"—Dean, Haldeman and Ehrlichman—and Dean refused to leave his post unless Haldeman and Ehrlichman left theirs.

Ehrlichman objected:

E. Well, he's not in any position to bargain with you on that. Now when the time comes that I'm charged with anything wrong—P. Well, John, you have been by a U.S. Attorney and by Petersen to me. Petersen is not charging you legal—E. That's what I mean. See I understand the difference. You see Dean has broken the law on the face of his (unintelligible) to you—

P. Petersen has said to me, he says that there is—because of the evidence that has come in here—that Haldeman and Ehrlichman should (unintelligible) now I'm faced with that damned hardship.

Nixon told Haldeman and Ehrlichman "candidly" that if he did not suspend them Petersen would probably give Dean immunity. "Dean is the guy that he's got to use for the purpose of making the case," he told them.

H. Yes, but, even Ehrlichman, which he already admits he doesn't have a case on (unintelligible) significance.

P. Well, he says legally, yes, he does. In the case of Haldeman, it'll discuss—the Strachan things have—determine a lot to do with what Strachan says and what Kalmbach says—the 350 thing and that sort of thing. H. Kalmbach has no relation to me on that. E. That ah—

P. Have you thought when you say before it gets to (unintelligible) thing out of the way. Have you given any thought to what the line ought to be—I don't mean a lie—but a line, on raising the money for these defendants? Because both of you were aware of what was going on you see—the raising of the money—you were aware of it, right? E. Yes, sir.

P. And you were aware—You see, you can't go in and say I didn't know what in hell he wanted the $250 for. H. No-I've given a great deal of thought (unintelligible) P. Well I wonder. I'm not—look—I'm concerned about the legal thing, Bob, and so forth. You say that our purpose was to keep them from talking to the press.

E. Well, that was my purpose—and before I get too far out on that, ah, I want to talk to an attorney to find out what the law is—which I have not yet done. P. Right! H. That's just what I want to do too. This is only a draft.

P. Right. Good. The only point is I, I think it is not only that but you see that involves all our people. That's what I feel—it involves Kalmbach—E. Well. P. And what to hell Kalmbach was told. E. Well, Mr. President, when the truth and fact of this is known, that building next door is full people who knew that money was being raised for these people.

P. E.O.B.? E. Yes, sir, just full of them. P. Many who know, but there were not so many actors. In other words, there's a difference between actors and noticees.

At that point, Ehrlichman stressed "the difference here between knowledge of the general transactions going on . . . and being an affirmative actor . . . because that's the difference between Dean and me."

The question came up of how much information the press really had. Haldeman did not think much more information was out on the White House, "unless," he mused, "I don't know what it could be unless they got Colson stuff—that would be the only area. P. (unintelligible). H. Yeah. That's the only area where you have any jeopardy in the White House."

Nixon asked Ehrlichman how he felt about getting his story out. "Well, subject to attorney's advice," Ehrlichman replied. "That's what I was going to say," Haldeman said. "I will not make this statement until I have worked it out." He went on that he would argue "that the better off I come out of this the better off you [Nixon] come out of it—vis-a-vis me. In other words, anything I do in my interest is to your interest."

This was not true for Ehrlichman when the talk turned to whom Dean actually reported to in the White House. Ehrlichman said that if "we are put in a position of defending ourselves, the things that I am going to have to say about Dean are: that basically Dean was the sole proprietor of this project, that he reported to the President, he reported to me only incidentally."

P. Reported to the President? E. Yes sir, in other words—P. When? E. Well, I don't know when, but the point is—

P. You see the problem you've got there is that Dean does have a point there which you've got to realize. He didn't see me when he came out to California. He didn't see me until the day you said, "I think you ought to talk to John Dean." I think that was in March. E. All right. But, but the point is that basically he was in charge of this project. P. He'll say he reports to the President through other people.

E. Well, O.K. Then you see what you've got there is an imputation. He says—as that kind of a foundation—"I told Ehrlichman that Liddy did it." What he is saying is that, "I told the President through Ehrlichman that Liddy did it." H. Which means that it was perfectly acknowledged as far as Ehrlichman was concerned and there was nothing that you were required to do about it anyway. E. That's right. But you see I get into a very funny defensive position then vis-a-vis you and vis-a-vis him, and it's very damned awkward. And I haven't thought it clear through. I don't know where we come out.

P. Yeah. You see Dean's little game here [unintelli-

gible]. One of the reasons this staff is so damned good. Of course he didn't report to me. . . .

The question then, Nixon asked, was "who the hell did he report to?" In many cases, Ehrlichman replied, "to no one. He just went ahead and did things."

Nixon brought up that Dean's "highly sensitive information was on only one count . . . believe me guys we all know—Well—the [unintelligible] stuff regarding Bob. Strachan has got to be worked out. I don't know how that's going to work out. Bob, did Strachan have a—the plan? What he says was about whether he did have a plan—whether he did show it to you—remains to be seen." Haldeman said he apparently said he did not.

A little later, Nixon said "the main thing is this, John, and when you meet with the lawyers—and you Bob, and I hope Strachan has been told—believe me—don't try to hedge anything before the damned grand jury. I'm not talking about morality, but I'm talking about the vulnerabilities."

"You guys—dammit—I know you haven't done a damned thing," Nixon told them.

The President had told them earlier in the conversation "I know that as far as you're concerned, you'll go out and throw yourselves on a damned sword. I'm aware of that. I'm trying to think the thing through with that in mind, because, damn it, you're the two most valuable members of the staff. I know that. The problem is, you're the two most loyal and the two most honest. We don't have to go into that. You know how I feel about that. It's not bull—it's the truth."

Nixon told them that "we've got to remember whatever he [Dean] is doing . . . He's going to do anything to save his ass. That's what is involved." and "you got to remember [unintelligible] he put this a lot higher," he said. "He could say, 'Well, I told the President about $127,000 that we needed $127,000 and the President said, 'well I don't know where we could get it, I don't know'."

Nixon pursued this point, a reference to the payment sought by Hunt. Earlier, he had referred to it as the "$120,000 for clemencies."

Haldeman reminded Nixon he was president when the $127,000 talk came up.

P. Good, What did we say? Remember he said, "How much is it going to cost to keep these, these guys (unintelligible). I just shook my head. Then we got into the question— H. If there's blackmail here, then we're into a thing that's just ridiculous. P. He raised the point—

H. (unintelligible) but you can't say it's a million dollars. It may be $10 million dollars. And that we ought not to be in this—P. That's right. That's right.

H. We left it—that—we can't do anything about it anyway. We don't have any money, and it isn't a question to be directed here. This is something relates to Mitchell's problem. Ehrlichman has no problem with this thing with Hunt. And Ehrlichman said, (expletive removed) if you're going to get into blackmail, to hell with it." P. Good [unintelligible]. Thank God, you were in there when it happened. But you remember the conversation? H. Yes sir.

P. I didn't tell him to go get the money, did I? H. No. P. You didn't either did you? H. Absolutely not! I said you got to talk to Mitchell. This is something you've got to work out with Mitchell—not here—there's nothing we can do about it here. P. We've got a pretty good record on that one, John at least.

Later, Nixon said, "Well [inaudible]. I suppose then we should have cut—shut it

off, 'cause later on you met in your office and Mitchell said, 'That was taken care of ' " H. The next day.

Haldeman added later "and there was no further squeak out of it so I now do assume that Mitchell took care of it."

As for the application to Haldeman for the funds, Haldeman said "all the input to me about the 350 came from Dean, and all the output came from Dean."

P. Then Dean was the one that said, "Look Bob, we need 350 for or need the rest of this money." H. No, they didn't even come that way. Dean said, "They need money for the defense, for their fees." And it was always put that way. That's the way it was always discussed. P. Right—that's why I want that line. I think that's most important. You can work on—Get a lawyer.

Returning to the problems for the others, Nixon said, suppose charges were filed, "charges might be that Haldeman had knowledge, and that he participated—cover-up—I'm trying, Bob, to put my worse—"

H. Sure. P. Do you agree Bob, they might make that a charge—the heat would really go on. H. Sure. P. In John's case they make the deep six charge [unintelligible]. I'd [unintelligible] with you on that. E. It's up to you.

On the press plan needed for that day, Ehrlichman suggested "it would involve the suspension [of Dean] because it would involve a recounting of how you happened to get into the personal investigation of this by reason of Dean's being unable to reduce his full report to writing for you. And that that rang a bell, and you personally turned to and have spent a great deal of your time in the last several weeks on this—and have seen dramatic progress in the grand jury in the last several days. That would be Step 1. Now in addition to that you would say the Ervin committee has come up with a good set of ground rules. . . ."

The ground rules, Ehrlichman said, provided for executive session and in open sessions executive privilege would be reserved.

P. Executive privilege is reserved, fine. H. At this point, the way we're in the soup now, we can lose nothing by going. P. That's right. H. I think we may gain. P. That's right, I couldn't agree more. So if you can prepare me with at least that much, I'll agree. That I can say that today. H. Well, that's a hell of a bomb shelter right there.

Nixon brought up "Garment's scenario:" that the President had asked any government people who were directly or indirectly subjects of the investigation to be relieved of duties pending grand jury action and anyone refusing would be dismissed.

Ehrlichman said he thought "it should be a very tight statement—very conservative—well at least you should think it through so that you can stay away from the soft places." "People are waiting to see your face on the evening news talking about the Watergate case," he said. "And making more assurances."

You know where the Watergate story was in the Washington Post today? Haldeman asked. "Page 19."

Nixon: "I know. I know. And it'll be page 19 five months from now if we handle it right."

Ehrlichman told Nixon newspaper editorials would be appearing about the cancer at the heart of the presidency and the need for drastic surgery. "And that in a case like this you lean over backwards and fire and so forth," that "Dean has raised serious charges and so on so forth." "Maybe the thing to do," he said, "is for Ziegler—if he gets a question about suspension or firing—to say, 'This is the President's general policy'—without regard to individuals—'any individual whose bound by the grand jury' . . ."

P. Why don't I say that today? E. That's fine. P. Fine. Alright. I think I got the message. If you will write up a brief, brief, brief statement. . . .

Nixon also planned to have Petersen in and tell him the President could not let people go simply because charges were made "and second, 'I've thought over the immunity thing and I want nobody on the WH staff given immunity. I don't want anybody shown any consideration whatever.' "

Nixon said he would also tell Petersen he was directing everybody to cooperate but "I will not have a member of the White House staff testifying in the Senate against others."

E. Yes, sir, and I think that the fourth point that you should cover with him is that if I'm before that grand jury and I am asked about Dean's information within the grand jury, I will have to say that Dean told me that it came from Petersen. P. Yeah. E. And, there's no point in your getting way out by saying out here to the press that I'm relying on Henry Petersen as my good right hand and then have him compromised at a later time. P. That's right.

April 17, 1973 (2:39–2:40 p.m.)

Telephone conversation between Nixon and Ehrlichman:

Nixon called "to check the points you want with Petersen," with whom Nixon would meet in 10 minutes. The first was "no immunity. However, I would say that for any of the top three." Ehrlichman agreed.

P. In other words, so that I can, if it sort of appears that if you want to give it to Strachan, that is ok. See? Don't you think that is a good line? E. I think that is good. Any of the people in—The four points as I wrote them down were to inform him that you were making a statement; Your policy with regard to suspension and firing.

P. Which is charges or indictment? E. Indictment for suspension and firing for conviction, which will be in the statement that I am drafting.

P. Wait a minute. E. He'll tell the press that. P. Right. E. Then privately to him, your policy with regard to immunity for top people. P. Yeah, and leaks from the Grand Jury. E. I wouldn't limit it to three. I would say any top person, like Dean or up. P. Yeah. E. It will sell.

P. Then I will say, as far as a fellow like Strachan, that is fine. You can do what you want. E. Yeah.

P. That strengthens the position. E. Colson, Dean, anybody of that kind, no dice.

P. He has mentioned these four to me. I will just say that. E. And then, of course, the leaks out of the Grand Jury. And put it to him whether he doesn't think that later exposure would prejudice the whole investigation and whether he shouldn't withdraw at an appropriate time so that a replacement can be obtained.

P. Charges and—I am going to follow a policy of accepting resignation on charges or indictment. Is that it? E. No. Suspension on indictment and a resignation on conviction.

P. Of course. That is right. Everybody would know that. Suspension on indictment and resignation on refusing to cooperate. Right? E. Or conviction.

P. Right. And what about charges? I mean remember we had that gray area. E. Well, there again you will have to reserve the right, depending on the seriousness of the charge—

P. Yeah. I will say if there is a serious corroborated charge,—E. Then you want him to bring it to you and you will reserve judgment on the individual case.

April 17, 1973 (2:46–3:49 p.m.)

Conversation between Nixon and Petersen in the Oval Office:

Nixon asked if Petersen had anything Nixon needed to know, and Petersen answered negatively. They then briefly discussed what was legal for Nixon to know.

P. As a matter of fact, I don't want you really to tell me anything out of the Grand Jury unless you think I need to know it. If it corroborates something or anybody here I need to know it—otherwise I don't want to know about it. H.P. No, Sir.

P. That's good, because I find—Incidentally, if I might—I don't think I like—for example, I haven't been in touch with John Mitchell but he might call me sometime and I don't want to be a position of ever saying anything, see? H.P. Well, I understand how you feel—it's a—

P. I guess it would be legal for me to know? H.P. Well yes, I think it is legal for you to know. P. Is it? Well, but don't do it, right.

Nixon reiterated his concern over leaks from the grand jury, and mentioned that Dean had talked freely with Mitchell. Petersen said he knew this.

P. The point is I think you will have to assume that Dean in this period, who was basically sort of in charge of it for the White House (and the rest of us were out campaigning-traveling, so forth, so on) will probably have told people that he has information from the Grand Jury. Now you just have to evaluate that yourself. I just don't want the Department of Justice, and you particularly, after your, ah—the way you have broken your— H.P. Mr. President— I am sure that is so. P. I don't want to get embarrassed, see? H.P. I have no concern about that.

Petersen said Dean was "probably getting information from the grand jury." Nixon said he was particularly concerned about grand jury leaks during the summer months.

Petersen later described his talks with Dean:

H.P. Well with respect to John Dean it is almost awkward to say it—my conversation with Dean touched upon three things: (1) leaks—which frankly I tell you I don't take very seriously—see what I mean—that's part and parcel of the Washington business; P. Yeah.

H.P. (the second) was Dean's personal involvement—this is to say P. What did he do.

H.P. Well we didn't suspect him but what did he do with respect to the securing of equipment and records in Hunt's office in connection with the motion to suppress where he was a potential witness for the defense on the motion to suppress. And the third was status reports—now from those status reports: I spoke to him in terms of ultimates. Magruder was a good witness in his own behalf. Magruder—the Grand Jury didn't believe what he said about the money—but not the testimony itself—the result of the testimony. So I don't have any problems. . . . P. That has no problem of (inaudible)?

H.P. No sir, and I can disclose to an attorney for the government in the course of my work. Dean was in addition to Counsel for the President, obviously an attorney for the government—and there is not anything improper in that. P. Right—well good, I am relieved to hear that.

H.P. Now, politically if someone wants to say—as they said to Pat Gray—you shouldn't have been talking to John Dean. Well, there is no way out of that. P. You see that is why I am raising the point. H.P. There is no way out of that.

P. That was perfectly proper for Pat Gray to talk to Dean you know—as a matter of fact, it would be improper for him not to. . . . H.P. Indeed.

P. Dean was running the investigation of the damn thing and I certainly expected him to get all of the FBI information he could H.P. Yes. P. What the hell is the FBI for? H.P. That's right. You know—I don't—

P. Gray got a bad rap on that. H.P. I don't think that—that's demoguery I think—I don't take that seriously. P. That's right—quite right.

Nixon then said he was working on a statement, like the one they had worked on the day before, but which also covered the Ervin Committee. He said they had

"worked out a deal with [the committee] now where everything on . . . executive privilege we have in executive session." Petersen agreed.

P. The right of executive privilege will be reserved and all witnesses will appear in public session—that's the way the deal was signed. So they will take all of our people in executive sessions discuss matters—you know like they bring—the judge brings the lawyers around the bench. H.P. I understand—yes sir.

P. Does that sound like a good procedure to you? H.P. Yes sir—I've only got one reservation and we alluded to this earlier in connection with the Magruder plea, and that is—whether or not Senator Ervin will be willing to hold off public sessions that might interfere with the right of fair trial for the others.

Nixon said he did not want "the damn Ervin Committee to go forward . . . they should drop the committee investigation the day the grand jury took it up seriously."

The conversation then shifted to the cases against Haldeman, Ehrlichman and Dean, and what Nixon should do about his top aides.

P. Haldeman and Ehrlichman at this point had [inaudible] with Rogers—I not only let him read what you had given me but then I elaborated everything I knew about this thing. His judgment is this that on Ehrlichman it is a very thin [inaudible]. H.P. Very thin indeed.

P. Did we do any good on the Liddy call? H.P. I don't know—Maroulis, P. (inaudible) H.P. his lawyer, flew down P. (inaudible) H.P. and we had Liddy brought over to a cell block of DC Court and made him available—and that was yesterday and of course I am sure Liddy is thinking it over—but we'll see. That man is a mental case . . . (inaudible)

The statement Nixon had been working on was brought into the office, and Petersen helped the President revise it.

They later returned to Haldeman and Ehrlichman:

P. Never going to [inaudible]—he said particularly he said if they have any witnesses for the fact that he handed a packet to the Director of the FBI and Hunt didn't leave the country [inaudible] discussions. I don't know—I am not trying to judge it—but. H.P. No, I understand—I agree that it is very thin. P. They better have a damn lot more than that or they are not going to get Ehrlichman. H.P. That's right.

P. On that—they may get him on something else. And the other point was, that you made, was Dean said that he had talked—that Liddy had told him everything on June 19th. You remember? H.P. Yes, sir.

P. Do you know when he told Ehrlichman? H.P. No, sir. P. In California after Ehrlichman had been there in March—February?—in March.

H.P. Dean told Ehrlichman then? P. That's right. So, it is a curious thing as to—Gray's concern to me. I said Dean hasn't told you he didn't tell him ahead of Ehrlichman but I mean that he didn't run right over and tell him. H.P. No. No.

P. The point is that Dean conducted his investigation and did not come to Ehrlichman and say "look we have to go on Mitchell" because that's what that was really about. H.P. Yeah. P. Liddy had involved himself and subsequently said Mitchell and Magruder. That's what I understood to be the truth of the case.

H.P. Well what Liddy in effect said was—what he admitted was that he was present at the Watergate—Dean already knew from prior dealings that Liddy was involved; you see? P. Oh, I see—present at Watergate H.P. That's right.

P. Oh, I thought he also—I thought you said—he told everything—that you had copies of everything . . . H.P. Well I think that is correct. He probably filled in the details but you recall at least from the meeting in February in Mitchell's office, Dean knew what Liddy was up to. P. Yeah.

Nixon noted that he could face the problem "in terms that of the fact that anybody who this touches should go out . . ."

P. Therefore, you advice—on Sunday or least it was now—sack Haldeman, Ehrlichman and Dean now—all three—because in the one case Dean should know he has admitted complicity—in the other case there is a possibility of charges which may not be true and which may not be indictable but which from the standpoint of the public will so involve them that it will cut off their legs. And let me say—I understand the point as well—the only thing is the question of how and when you do it—and as that I [inaudible]. And so I have decided to handle each on an individual basis—and by that I mean that our policy generally will be that anyone who refused to cooperate will, of course, be sacked immediately. Anyone who is indicted at this time will be put on leave—indefinite leave—'until he is tried. You don't—That is our system. Now, if you indict somebody, I will then put them on leave indefinitely which means he is out of a job—he'll have to go. What would happen in that instance I think, of course, is that most of the people that are involved here would resign immediately so that—I am just saying

H.P. I understand.

Nixon expressed concern as to whether Haldeman and Ehrlichman would be cited in the prosecution's statement when Magruder went to court. Petersen said the prosecution intended to file a "one count conspiracy indictment that would name Magruder and unindicted co-conspirators."

Nixon asked Petersen to explain what an unindicted co-conspirator was, and Petersen obliged. "... In other words," Nixon subsequently said, "I would then say—anybody that was an unindicted co-conspirator would then be immediately put on leave." Petersen agreed, and Nixon proceeded to discuss immunity.

P. I have thought about it a lot—I don't care what you do on immunity to Strachan or any other second people but you can't give immunity to any top people —not Dean—needless to say you don't want to to Haldeman or Ehrlichman. Dean is the counsel to the President—after the flap with Gray—I went over this with Rogers—he says—after your flap on the Gray thing and the rest—it would like that you're ...

H.P. Right—you know why I asked.

P. I just want you to know that you if give immunity but I will have to talk (inaudible). **H.P.** OK, well, let me put it this way, I will not do that without my knowledge. If it is necessary for me to do that I will come to you first and then we can reach an agreement that yes you will have to disavow it and that was the decision of the prosecutor. I don't want to make that decision, Mr. President. I don't want to immunize John Dean; I think he is too high in the echelon but— it's a—

P. The prosecutor's got the right to make the decision? **H.P.** Yes, sir. **P.** You better, I think ... **H.P.** I think it would—look—because your close relationship with Dean—which has been very close—it would look like a straight deal—now that's just the way you've got to figure it. **H.P.** That's right.

"The thing that scares the hell out of me is this," Petersen continued:

suppose Dean is the only key to Haldeman and Ehrlichman and the refusal to immunize Dean means that Haldeman and Ehrlichman go free. That is the decision that we are going to ultimately come down to.

P. Well you will have to come into me with what you've got (inaudible) then there ... **H.P.** I will. **P.** And let me handle Haldeman and Ehrlichman. **H.P.** I will sir.

P. If it comes down to that—I may have to move on Haldeman and Ehrlichman—then for example you come to me and say look here's what—Look I am not going to do anything to Haldeman and Ehrlichman just because of what Dean says—I can't do that. It's got to be corroborated. **H.P.** I agree with that.

P. Do you agree with that? **H.P.** Yes sir—I am not going to do anything with those two unless it is corroborated either.

P. Dean is—I find, has told two or three different stories. I didn't realize it until lately. I guess when a guy is scared he doesn't— **H.P.** He is a man under great pressure.

Nixon then posed the example of Ehrlichman as a possible co-conspirator:

P. Right, let's take Ehrlichman—let's say that the only testimony we have is something about (inaudible) —and so far and so on—something about that Dean is supposed to have told him about the Liddy operation or something—March. All right—so is he a co-conspirator? Let's suppose you cannot get anybody to corroborate that—All right, then the question is, however, then that is one thing. If on the other hand—

you wouldn't sack Ehrlichman for that? **H.P.** Mr. President, I wouldn't prosecute Ehrlichman for that. **P.** But you might sack him? **H.P.** Yes sir.

P. Now the second point is, let us suppose ... **H.P.** I mean if he were a junior partner in the Petersen-Nixon law firm out in Oshkosh, I would not. But as senior advisor to the President of the United States I would. That is the difference.

"I have made it clear," Petersen later said, "that I think they [Nixon's top aides] have made you very, very vulnerable ... to rather severe criticism because of their action. At least in public forums they eroded confidence in the office of the Presidency ..."

Petersen then asked if Nixon had decided to accept Dean's resignation, and Nixon answered: "No, I have decided to treat them all the same." Petersen agreed this was wise. "I am not going to condemn Dean until he has a chance to present himself," the President asserted. He said the same rule applied to Strachan.

Petersen said the prosecution probably lacked enough evidence to implicate Strachan as a principal, and therefore would not prosecute him, but ask him to testify as "a witness rather than a defendant," without a formal granting of immunity.

"That is much better basically than immunity..." Nixon commented. "If you go the immunity route [with Dean] I think we are going to catch holy hell for it." Petersen agreed. "It is the toughest decision I have facing me," he said.

"The ideal position," Petersen continued, "would be for Dean to agree to plead guilty to a one-count felony indictment, with a possible maximum jail sentence of five years, as Magruder had. However, Petersen noted that Dean's lawyers "say we will try this whole damn administration."

The two men then expressed dismay at the entire Watergate case and the fate of Mitchell. Nixon offered the following account of what actually had happened:

P. But what happened we know is this: These jackasses got off ... see this Liddy is crazy and Hunt and that whole bunch conducted this (inaudible) Mitchell wasn't minding the store and Magruder is a weak fellow—and the damn thing—and then afterwards they compounded it by what happened afterwards. **H.P.** That's right.

P. They were caught in it and they said—Oh we can't—and basically they were trying to protect Mitchell—let's face it. You know that.

Returning to Haldeman and Ehrlichman:

P. Yeah, well what you are in effect saying to me, as I say, I want to be very clear on the Haldeman/Ehrlichman thing. That if they were left out of the non-indictable list it gives me a little running room. I want to be very clear, that understood? **H.P.** That's right, that's right. **P.** It doesn't mean that they aren't eventually be indicted if you get the facts. **H.P.** That's right.

P. But it does mean that they have an oppor ... they aren't canned as a result of the fact—that is what we are really getting down to isn't it—you would have to put Dean on that list, wouldn't you? **H.P.** Yes Sir.

P. I guess you would have to with everything with him because basically Magruder is going to name him. **H.P.** That's right. **P.** Hmp. **H.P.** And, if we get down to ...

P. Magruder is not naming Haldeman and Ehrlichman though. That is the problem is it? **H.P.** Yes but he does—but not in firsthand sense—**P.** Only by hearsay. **H.P.** But you see, if he makes that statement in open court—

P. Yeah, I get it. **H.P.** It seems to me it makes your practical difficulties just as severe as if we had named him in the first place. **P.** Well I am glad to get this kind of stuff so I get a clear view of everything—what the

options are. **H.P.** And if we frankly—if we think that Sirica is going to elicit that kind of statement we will include him in the charge to the extent that we can.

Nixon continued:

P. You would anticipate then that if you didn't include Haldeman and Ehrlichman in your general thing that Sirica will question the defendant—Magruder—and he then will bring in—**H.P.** If he brings that out—if we think that is a real possibility then we will have to decide whether or not as a matter of conscience and professional ethics we can put them in. If we can answer that yes—then we will put them in. If on the other hand, we think there is no basis for it—even if Sirica does bring out the hearsay—we will just have to take the knuckle for it. ...

H.P. Here's one thing—in the earlier stages of the proceedings when they had Segretti in the Grand Jury—**P.** Yeah.

H.P. I told Silbert—now—damn it Silbert keep your eye on the mark—we are investigating Watergate—we are not investigating the whole damn realm of politics and I don't want you questioning him about the President's lawyer. **P.** Right.

H.P. Well, he didn't. Well now Kalmbach comes up and you heard on the news I am sure today—he apparently is going to be called by the Senate Committee—but he also comes up in this investigation with respect to actually Kalmbach raising money—or passing money at Mitchell's direction for the co-conspirators. So we are going—**P.** Sure. **H.P.** To have Kalmbach back into the Grand Jury. **P.** Well in that instance, I suppose there you've got to prove what he thought he was raising it for.

H.P. Well, even if he didn't know or he was misled—the fact that he **P.** (inaudible) **H.P.** did at the time we may very well end up with him being a witness. **P.** Damn right—oh I know that. I would seriously—I mean. And again on that particular count—I guess you were the one, I think who said the question is motive—what they raised the money for. **H.P.** That's right.

P. If you are trying to help them out with their defense—that is one thing—but if you are helping them out to keep them quiet that is a hell of (inaudible)—that is an obstruction job. **H.P.** That's right—you know if you are acting out of Christian charity— **P.** Right **H.P.** that is fine. **P.** That would be Mitchell's defense on that. **H.P.** Of course all the inferences run the other way and that is a hell of a defense to have to put to the Jury.

Petersen then assured Nixon he would give him 12 hours' notice before indicting any of his aides, and would not indict anyone at least until the next day, and possibly not until the day after.

Finally, there was this exchange on Mitchell:

P. Mitchell will never plead guilty, never. Fight it all the way down the line. (inaudible) What would you do if you were Mitchell? **H.P.** I think I would probably go to Saudi Arabia to tell you the truth.

P. Poison **H.P.** When I think the former Attorney General of the United States being subject to criminal trial is just—**P.** For obstruction of justice—not the bugging—the obstruction of justice. **H.P.** It is just terrible.

April 17, 1973 (3:50–4:35 p.m.)

Conversation between Nixon, Haldeman, Ehrlichman and Ziegler in the Oval Office:

Nixon briefed Haldeman and Ehrlichman on his meeting with Petersen, particularly regarding their possible resignation. Both complained about being put "in the same bag" with Dean, and Nixon repeated that, according to Dean's lawyers, "Dean is going to make a case against this administration."

Haldeman and Ehrlichman acknowledged that if they took leaves of absence, they could not later return to their White House posts.

Haldeman then complained about the "most bloodthirsty way" the Watergate prosecution was being conducted, particularly the way Strachan was allegedly being bullied by Silbert and other U.S. attorneys.

They then began to work on the statement Nixon would deliver later in the afternoon. They agreed the statement would sound stronger if they picked a date on which Nixon "began new inquiries" into the Watergate case, and settled on March 21. They also decided that Nixon's announced policy should be to suspend any aide indicted by the grand jury and dismiss anyone convicted, and to oppose the granting of immunity to anyone "holding a position of major importance" in the White House.

They agreed to meet with Secretary of State Rogers later in the afternoon, after Haldeman and Ehrlichman conferred with their lawyer. Nixon said he felt Rogers' advice on his aides' resignations was "wrong... Look, the point is (unintelligible) throwing you to the wolves with Dean. What does that accomplish?"

Haldeman offered, as a possible alternative, that he and Ehrlichman request leaves of absence "on the basis of the information you have, which we have, because we've been involved in the investigation too." Haldeman noted that if their names appeared on the list of Magruder's co-conspirators, they would have to ask for leaves anyway.

Nixon later said, "Well, maybe it's too soon for Rogers," apparently agreeing his aides should not yet resign. "Well, I guess we just let Dean go ahead and try the administration," he said. Ehrlichman asserted Dean was going to "do his work with or without immunity... Ervin is going to get him up there... and will take him over the jumps."

Ehrlichman said Nixon's statement would "lay a ground rule for Ervin on immunity which is going to be very tough for him to live with if there are Ervin hearings." All agreed there would be hearings because, as Ehrlichman asserted, "The more battles the President wins, like the economical stabilization performance, the more urgent the Ervin hearings become. It's the only thing they have left, now. You're winning all the big ones."

April 17, 1973 (5:20–7:14 p.m.)

The President, Rogers, Haldeman and Ehrlichman met in Nixon's office in the Executive Office Building:

The bulk of the Nixon-Rogers discussion, which was joined midway by Haldeman and Ehrlichman, dealt with how to proceed in light of a statement Nixon made to the press less than an hour before the conversation recounted in the edited transcript took place.

In the press statement, Nixon announced that members of the White House staff would appear voluntarily before the Senate Watergate Committee and that any person indicted would be suspended immediately. Nixon also said that he did not support any effort to grant immunity to persons holding positions of "major importance" either past or at present in the Administration.

The matter of immunity was of vital importance to Haldeman and Ehrlichman because, as Nixon said, "Dean is the only one who can sink Haldeman and Ehrlichman."

Petersen had urged him to suspend Haldeman and Ehrlichman if they were named as unindicted co-conspirators in forthcoming legal proceedings, Nixon told Rogers. According to the edited transcript, Nixon was unwilling to take this action without testimony corroborating Dean's charges.

Nixon said the prosecutors had "made a deal with Dean. And that's why I put in that statement, I hope—that's the point." Nixon said he invoked Rogers' name in his earlier talk with Petersen. "I said, 'We think we have a grave problem in giving immunity to the President's counsel.' He [Petersen] said, 'But suppose that it's Dean's testimony that we need to get Haldeman and Ehrlichman. Then should we give him immunity—shouldn't we give him immunity?' I said, 'No—not unless you have corroboration.'"

Nixon said he asked Petersen to continue to report to him. "I said, 'If you get any corroborating testimony [regarding Haldeman's and Ehrlichman's alleged culpability], I'd like to know.' And if I get some corroborative testimony, I said, 'I'd like to be warned and I can call in my people and say, Look I found this out and I've got information and you—therefore, you ought to consider whether you shouldn't resign.'"

(Later in the conversation, Nixon said Petersen had promised him 12 hours notice before making public any evidence in Magruder's statement to the U.S. attorney's office if it implicated Haldeman and Ehrlichman.)

In offering his own assessment of their chances, Nixon said he thought Ehrlichman "was going to beat it" but that Haldeman was "probably in trouble."

"I'm not sure he'll be indicted," Nixon said, but he conceded that Haldeman faced legal problems in "staying too close to the money. He never can explain that. In terms of legal involvement though but he could never explain to people and you (unintelligible) some of that damn money back there for 'em. Testified by Mitchell, by Dean. Was it a (unintelligible) of the defense?"

"You know I am concerned about my people," Nixon continued.

I know that Haldeman and Ehrlichman are not guilty of a damn thing. You know what I mean. It's only tangential on that, Bill—tangential. Sure they knew we were raising money for these damn defendants, but they were (unintelligible) in the campaign. I mean, I mean (unintelligible) Dean at the meeting, wasn't he? **R.** Yeah.
P. Ehrlichman was handling the whole domestic thing and Haldeman was working with me at the time. They didn't work in the campaign. It was all over with Mitchell. Mitchell was—in this whole thing, and frankly, Dean was handling it for the White House. (unintelligible). Our people were aware that he was. We were aware about that.

Rogers said he thought Haldeman and Ehrlichman "ought to resign." Nixon sought clarification, asking, "But you would wait until their names were mentioned [in corroborative testimony]? That's the whole point." "Yeah," Rogers replied.

Nixon and Rogers also discussed the involvement of other high Administration officials in the widening Watergate affair.

"My feeling," Nixon said,

was that Mitchell—basically always thought Magruder knew the damn thing. Mitchell just wasn't tending the shop. That's what I understand.
R. I'm surprised about Dean. I thought—I thought. Well from the beginning, I thought Magruder lied and I thought Mitchell probably—he may well have given the go ahead and said, "Oh yeah, to hell with this," and the damn thing was then approved. **P.** Yeah. "Don't tell me about it." **R.** "Go ahead. Don't tell me. Go ahead and do it." Well I'm surprised about Dean because I didn't think—
P. Now Dean claims that he didn't have anything to do with having them go ahead. Understand that. After that, Dean came in terms of the obstruction of justice. There's where he's vulnerable. That's all. He's not vulnerable on the first part in my opinion. I think he—Dean handled the whole thing. He was depending upon—regarding the fact—when I started my investigation of the 21st of March. I saw Dean at least (unintelligible) times. At Camp David, he was to write the (expletive deleted) up so we could put out a statement. He said, "I really can't write a statement that you can put out." So I must say, I've done everything I can to get to the bottom, Bill, as you can see. I said, "John, you got to let it all hang out—now find out—you got to tell me what the hell the score is so we'll know how to deal with this. We're not going to be nibbled to death by a thousand hurts." That's exactly what we've done. So we've got just (unintelligible) The time when McCord, which I—I don't know what he's talking about. There are—at least, he's made a lot of allegations that he can't prove. But there's enough there that would put anybody on notice that without a doubt there's something wrong. **R.** Yeah.

When Rogers inquired as to Dean's intentions in cooperating with the U.S. attorney's office, Nixon said Dean was "going to try this whole Administration I would expect. And my view on that is let him try the whole Administration. Ron Ziegler has an interesting point. He said, 'Dean had in February, had said, "I, for nine months conducted this investigation," Now he comes in and charges inaction.' Dammit, why didn't he come in earlier, and tell me these things, Bill? Why didn't he do it? If he knew, I would think that—"

Tangential references to other figures in the Watergate affair were few and the conversation quickly returned to Nixon's principal concern: the legal problems facing his two top aides. Nixon was fearful that they faced imminent indictment and asked Rogers to "put your mind to the problem... because I really think we've got to start helping 'em. Help advise them. They're in the eye of the hurricane."

Haldeman and Ehrlichman joined the meeting immediately after conferring with their lawyer, John J. Wilson, whose name had been suggested to them by Rogers.

The four men discussed the dilemma facing the President in whether to seek the resignation of his chief aides.

R. Being compelled to leave the government. Hell, as far as the public is concerned, you are already indicted. **E.** Really, the job—they have this capacity by using that process. They could ruin you and never give you a day in court. **R.** Of course. **E.** They could list you as a co-conspirator, don't call you to the grand jury, don't take an indictment against you—**H.** Force the President to suspend you and—
E. You are cooked forever. You are a conspirator in the Watergate case. **R.** As far as the public is concerned, you are indicted even if they don't call it that. **E.** That's right. **R.** That's what it is nowadays. The President has been forced to have you leave. **E.** It's nonactionable. It's privileged. You can't sue for slander. **H.** We do have a public record in that regard in that we have a public position that commands substantial attention. **R.** See, Bob, the protection of the grand jury gives a citizen that first the charge is heard in public. **H.** That's right. To turn this around.
R. Then the charge—then everybody shuts up. The evidence is not disclosed. Nobody says a word and

the judge cautions everybody to take the oath not to repeat the evidence and then you go to trial. And everything is then controlled by the rules of evidence. Then the jury makes a decision based on that evidence. That's the system. Now if you do it the other way, you don't get the trial. You both would be indicted and convicted by the public beforehand.

During the discussion, Ehrlichman inextricably linked his and Haldeman's defense strategy to that of Nixon's. "Our relationship to Dean—was probably client to attorney," Ehrlichman declared, adding that their conversations could involve a "question of privilege."

E. The question is, if requested by the prosecutor, to waive the privilege. It is that Dean conversation where he says he came and told me that Liddy had confessed.

P. But he did it in California, didn't he? E. Well, the only reason to tell me was not for me as me but because I was one of two conduits that he had to the Boss. He didn't have, I mean, the organizational setup was that way. H. The President's log is very interesting. I don't know if you've gotten through all of this, but from the time of the Watergate break-in until the end of August when he signed your votes in the office, you never saw John Dean. P. That's of course— H. During July and August the President had no communication with Dean at all.

E. Now, he gave a lot of legal advice about this case. A lot of traffic and all that, but there's also developed a poor relationship with Dean and sooner or later the President is going to have to decide whether he wants to consider privilege—if Dean becomes—P. My privilege? Lawyer-client privilege?

E. Yes. In Dean's communications to me and my communications to him. And the same with Bob. I think. That's a tough problem. You probably won't want to reserve it. P. I'll take a look.

R. How did he contact the President? H. Dean? He dealt with one of us. E. In our capacity to make decisions. He was really an advisor in that situation. Not a (unintelligible) and sometimes he followed and sometimes he didn't. P. That's common. Everyone wants to carve his place. H. Yeah.

R. Problem is, what do other people say about him? E. He's a jerk. Sure, that's right. P. And I deferred to him in this damned investigation. Remember you said, "I think you ought to talk to John Dean." Remember. And I called him in there. And,—I listened ad infinitum and carted him off to Camp David. H. (unintelligible) I deferred to him on most occasions.

The gravity of Dean's possible testimony incriminating Haldeman and Ehrlichman was apparent to all of the participants, especially Nixon, who said, "I think what we ought to do [is] make our deal or not with Dean within a week.... The way this guy talks, I think all of you, all of you, everybody may get it."

Nixon concluded with a strong statement of support for his two chief aides. "I want you to go forward," Nixon declared, "and if this thing comes out, which I can't believe, I want you to go forward at all costs to beat the damned rap. They'll have a hell of a time proving it."

When Ehrlichman voiced some fear that Dean "may be provoked to make a public statement which is slanderous and hostile," Nixon urged them (and Haldeman "particularly") to get "the most vicious libel lawyer there is. I'd sue every (expletive deleted) (unintelligible). There have been stories over this period of time. That will make—that also helps with public opinion. Sue right down the line. It doesn't make any difference now about the taking depositions and the rest, does it? The important thing is the story's big and I think you ought to go out and sue people for libel."

Sen. Lowell P. Weicker (R, Conn.), a member of the Senate Watergate Committee, was mentioned as a specific target of a libel suit. When told that Weicker's comments made to the press

were not protected by Congressional immunity privileges, Nixon said, "Good, sue him. I think you should.... You may as well get at the libel thing and have yourself a little fun." "Might make expenses," Ehrlichman added.

The meeting concluded on a grim note as Nixon cautioned them to "expect the worst." Ehrlichman said he feared an end not only to his government career but also to his ability to practice law. Nixon tried to reassure them, reminding them that "the [Nixon] foundation is going to be a hell of big thing. It's bound to be."

Haldeman was equally grim. "If we have to get out of here, I think the foundation funding is one thing—but there is a lot of intrigue too—I hope to get funding for the ability to clear my name and spend the rest of my life destroying what some people like Dean and Magruder have done to the President."

April 18, 1973 (2:50–2:56 p.m.)

Telephone conversation between Nixon and Petersen:

Nixon asked if there was "anything I need to know today." Petersen said there were "no significant developments," but added that he would be seeing Strachan and his lawyer. Petersen then mentioned the problem of news leaks from the grand jury:

The only copy of the grand jury transcript has been locked up in the prosecutor's office. We have the F.B.I. checking out the reporter on the ground that they have leaked it. The judge called us in about it this morning. P. Uh, huh. Sirica did. H.P. Yeah. P. About what? About part of it leaking?

H.P. He was concerned about leaking and, of course, Anderson has been printing some of it. We have changed reporters. We haven't even been bringing it over here for security reasons. P. Yeah. I would hope to keep the grand jury from leaking. But—

H.P. Well, you know that it's just wrong. Now we are handling it over here, I trust, aren't we? I just told Ziegler he won't comment on anything because it might affect the rights of either the prosecution or the rights of innocent people or the rights of defendants. H.P. We are not taking any calls from them over here. P. So that is all we are saying. H.P. You can't talk to them at all. P. Fine.

Nixon then asked Petersen whether he had "finished the thing with Magruder yet," and Petersen replied negatively. As for Dean, Petersen said: "we have just backed off of him for a while. His lawyers want time to think."

P. I have deliberately, Henry—I left Dean in a position where I said look he was going to be treated like everybody else because it wasn't fair, I mean for him to be at all, you know—what I mean, like when we talked about resignation, etc., since he was making some charges. Well, it isn't that. Since he has at least had some private discussions, but they haven't yet been in the grand jury forum, so I have to respect those.

H.P. I think that is right. P. So that was your suggestion, at least, that we should not do anything on Dean at this point. H.P. I think that is right. I think you ought to just let him sit.

P. All I have is just information—H.P. That's right. P. Basically from you and from him, but it is information the gravity of which I just can't judge until I see whether it is corroborated. H.P. You have to treat that as private, in any event. P. Private, don't I? Yeah. And for that reason if I were to move to do it—so I think we are in the right position and, then, fine. OK—Then I won't expect any more from you today. I won't bother you.

H.P. No. I am a little concerned about Senator Ervin's Committee. They have just, under the agreement Kleindienst worked out with Senator Ervin, have

called the Bureau and asked to see the interview statements of Magruder, Porter, Sloan and LaRue. P. Oh, my (expletive removed).

H.P. Ah, and I feel like I am sitting on a powder keg there, but I don't feel like I can dare go to Senator Ervin until I get a definite commitment from Magruder. P. Yeah, yeah. On Magruder, what's waiting besides the Committee with him? Oh, the deal with the DC jail and—

H.P. Well that is right and whether or not the Judge is going to clap him in right away, and whether or not the Committee is going to put pressure on him.

P. In other words, you think— you haven't yet tried to talk to Ervin? H.P. No, Sir, and I don't want to until I can tie him down. P. Til you've got him tied? I get it. H.P. Well, I've got to be able to say that I am coming out with something public in terms of a charge.

P. I see. Right, right. H.P. You know, have a valid basis for asking him to slow it up.

Finally, Nixon said he was glad Petersen thought his statement the previous day had gone well, as Petersen told him earlier in the conversation:

P. I worked on it to be sure that it didn't compromise anybody one way or the other and as you noticed too I put the immunity thing. It leaves the ball in your court, but—H.P. I noticed.

P. On the other hand, I had to express the view because basically people are going to ask me, what about Mitchell, what about, you know, a lot of people and you know I just can't be in this position. H.P. I agree wholeheartedly. P. Lower people are different. But you know, upper people, you know, they might think I am protecting (unintelligible) H.P. I agree.

April 19, 1973 (8:25–9:32 p.m.)

The President met with John J. Wilson and Frank Strickler, attorneys retained by Haldeman and Ehrlichman:

Having had several meetings with Haldeman and Ehrlichman, it was their assessment, Wilson told Nixon, that neither man could be successfully prosecuted for his role in Watergate. In addition, they had seen Assistant U.S. Prosecutor Seymour Glanzer, who had assured them that no action by the prosecutor against Haldeman or Ehrlichman would be taken without its first being communicated to them (Wilson and Strickler).

Nixon said he had learned from Petersen that Haldeman and Ehrlichman might be named as unindicted co-conspirators in one of the Watergate prosecutions. Wilson said he understood that. Wilson only hoped that Nixon would not seek the resignations of Haldeman and Ehrlichman, as resignation would be viewed in the public mind as an admission of guilt. Nixon agreed. If they were indicted, they would be let go, having been given every chance, Nixon said.

April 27, 1973 (5:37–5:43 p.m.)

The President and Petersen in the Oval Office:

Nixon said he had heard reports that Dean had made statements to the prosecution implicating the President. "We've got to head them off at the pass," Nixon said, "Because it's so damned—so damn dangerous to the Presidency, in a sense."

Nixon suggested the rumors might become widespread. Then came the following dialogue:

P. Now, Henry, this I've got to know. Now, understand—I have told you everything I know about this thing. H.P. I don't have any problem with that, Mr. President, and I'll get in touch with them immediately, but—P. Who? H.P. With Titus, Silbert and Glanzer and Campbell? Who are— P. Do you mind calling them right now? H.P. No, sir. P. OK. Say, "Now, look. All of your conversations with Dean and Bittman, do they implicate the President?" Because we can't—I've got—if the U.S. Attorney's office and, ah

H.P. Mr. President, (unintelligible) I had them over
A there—we had a kind of crisis of confidence night before last. I left to come over here and I left my two principal assistants to discourse with Silbert and the other three. And in effect it concerned me—whether or not they were at ease with my reporting to you, and I pointed out to them that I had very specific instructions, discussed that with them before on that subject, and—well P. Yes.

H.P. As a consequence—I kind of laid in to Titus yesterday and it cleared the air a little bit, but there is a very suspicious atmosphere. They are concerned and scared. Ah—and I will check on this but I have absolutely no information at this point that—P. Never heard anything like that—H.P. No, sir.
B Absolutely not.P. My gosh—As I said—

H.P. Mr. President, I tell you, I do not consider it, you know, I've said to Titus, "We have to draw the line. We have no mandate to investigate the President. We investigate Watergate." and I don't know where that line draws, but we have to draw that all the time.

P. Good. Because if Dean is implicating the Presidency—we are going to damned well find out about it. That's—that's—because let me tell you the only conversations we ever had with him, was the famous March 21st conversation I told you about, where he told me about Bittman coming to him. No, the Bittman request for $120,000 for Hunt. And I then finally began to get at them. I explored with him
C thoroughly. "Now what the hell is this for?" He said "It's because he's blackmailing Ehrlichman." Remember I said that's what it's about. And Hunt is going to recall the seamy side of it. And I asked him, "Well how would you get it? How would you get it to them?" so forth. But my purpose was to find out what the hell had been going on before. And believe me, nothing was approved. I mean as far as I'm concerned—as far as I'm concerned turned it off totally.

H.P. Yea. My understanding of law is—my understanding of our responsibilities, is that if it came to that I would have to come to you and say, "We can't do that." The only people who have jurisdiction to do that is the House of Representatives, as far as I'm concerned. P. That's right. But I want you to know,
D you tell me, because as far as I'm concerned—H.P. I'll call them. Do you want me to call from here or outside?

P. Use the Cabinet Room and you will be able to talk freely. And who will you call, who will you talk to there? H.P. I'll call Silbert. If he's not there, I'll get Titus.

P. You'll say that "This is the story some New York Times reporter has and Woodward of the Post, but Hersh is reporting that Dean had made a statement to the prosecutors." Now understand that this is not a grand jury thing. Now damnit, I want to know what it is. H.P. I'll call right away. P. And I need to know. H.P. Yes, sir.

E

April 27, 1973 (6:04–6:48 p.m.)

The President, Petersen and Ziegler in the Oval Office.

Ziegler had not yet entered when Petersen returned to report on the phone call to the prosecutors Nixon had urged in the previous conversation. Petersen said that during the "negotiations" with Charles Shaffer, an attorney for Dean, Shaffer had repeated an earlier statement
F that they would "bring the President in," not in this case but in "other areas."

When Ziegler joined the meeting, Nixon alluded to the reports that the New York Times and Washington Post would soon publish stories that Nixon had been implicated. "It is a totally false story. Needs to be totally knocked down." Petersen repeated Shaffer's emphasis on "other areas." Nixon added:

G P. That's not Watergate, but in other areas. H.P. Whatever that means. P. Well, that's fine. Just let them tie us in. H.P. Now, to put that in context, they had previously said that if we insisted on trying Dean and not Ehrlichman and Haldeman, that they would be "trying this Administration," the President and what have you.

P. So basically that's the game they are playing. Z. I can understand how—you indicated that their attorney, the other day, said they would resist in tying in—did you say? In not the Watergate, but—

H.P. They would be tying in the President. I mean, it was an emotional statement. P. Emotion at tying in the President, not in Watergate, but in other things. Right. H.P. Not in the Watergate, but in other things. Whatever they would be—

P. When was this? H.P. Monday. Monday of this week. P. Monday of this week. H.P. Monday of this week. P. Well, I thing this— —I think this thing we just hit back on.

H.P. Well, that's the only thing. And I don't know that. And they had no idea. P. But Dean gave them. H.P. What? P. But Dean give them. H.P. Oh, yes, but, but— P. That basically ties in the White House. H.P. That was one of the reasons that was so important to disclose that because they could have hung that over our heads, you see and—

P. You remember my call from Camp David. I said, "Don't go into the national security stuff." I didn't mean—H.P. Oh, I understand. P. 'Cause I remember I think we discussed that silly damned thing. I had heard about it, just heard about. You told me that. That's it, you told me. What (expletive removed) did they break into a psychiatrist's office for? I couldn't believe it.

Nixon later told Ziegler to "take a hard line" with the newspapers. Regarding the Post, he added:

P. Anything on that they better watch their damned cotton picking faces. Because boy, if there's one thing in this case as Henry will tell you, since March 21st when I had that conversation with Dean, I have broken my ass to try to get the facts of this case. Right?

Nixon continued that he had brought in acting FBI Director William Ruckelshaus, told him to cooperate with Petersen and the prosecutors, and to "leave no stone unturned and I don't give a damn who it hurts. Now believe me, that's what he's been told . . ."

P. So there you are. You've got to knock that—Crack down. If there's one thing you have got to do, you have got to maintain the Presidency out of this. I have got things to do for this country and I'm not going to have—now this is personal. I sometimes feel like I'd like to resign. Let Agnew be President for a while. He'd love it. H.P. I don't even know why you want the job?

Nixon returned to his and the prosecution's dealings with Dean:

P. Let me say this, let me ask you about (unintelligible). First, on Dean—I would not want to get into a position—You have told me now, "You can do what you want with Dean." You have given up. You mean, in other words, fire him, hire him, leave him, treat him like the others, wait until the grand jury acts, or something. You see, I have three courses: I can wait until the grand jury acts, I can take leaves of absence, or I can take resignations, I have three different courses on all three men. I can do different things with each one of them. Right? H.P. Yes, sir.

P. These are the options, but what I will do remains to be seen. Now in Dean's case, I do not want the impression left that—I have gone over with you before, that by saying "Don't grant immunity to a major person," that in so doing I am trying to block Dean giving evidence against Haldeman or Ehrlichman. H.P. I understand that. P. I have applied that to others, and I don't want to—no. Do I make myself clear? H.P. Yes, let me make myself clear. P. Yes.

H.P. I regard immunity authority under the statutes of the United States to be my responsibility, of which I cannot divest myself. P. Right. H.P. And—ah—we take opinions, but I would have to treat this as advisory only. P. Right. Well understand, I only expressed an opinion. H.P. I understand. P. And understand you have got to determine who is the major culprit too. H.P. Yes, sir.

P. If you think Dean is an agent—let me say—if Dean, I—I think Haldeman and Ehrlichman in the case of themselves with Dean. But my point is, you have got to—ah—I don't know what you prosecutors think, but if your prosecutors believe that they have got to give Dean immunity, in whole or in part, in order to get the damned case, do it. I'm not— I'm not telling you what to do, but—you understand? Your decision. . . .

P. All right. We have got the immunity problem resolved. Do it. Dean if you need to, but boy I am tell you—there ain't going to be any blackmail. H.P. Mr. President, I—

P. Don't let Dick Kleindienst say it. Dean ain't—"Hunt is going to blackmail you." Hunt's not going to blackmail any of us. "It is his word, basically, against yours." It's his word against mine. Now for—who is going to believe John Dean? We relied on the damned so—Dean, Dean was the one who told us throughout the summer that nobody in the White House was involved when he, himself apparently, was involved, particularly on the critical angle of subornation of perjury. That's the one that—I will never, never understand John.

They later explored details of others involved in the "hush money" scheme:

P. What about Bittman? H.P. What he's concerned about is the allegation that he, in behalf of Hunt, was attempting to blackmail the White House for substantial sums of money in return for Hunt's silence. That's the allegation. And that's what McCord said—ah

P. McCord said that Bittman— H.P. McCord said that Dorothy Hunt told him all this sort of thing.

P. And so how do you get to them? Do you have to call Bittman? What do you do? H.P. Well, we may get into the fee. Fees are not privileged. P. I see. H.P. Now— P. You say, "Where did you get your fee?" H.P. That's right.

P. And how would you go about that one? H.P. We'll have to subpoena the fee records out of the law firm. P. And then if he got the fees, you say, "Did blackmail the White House for this?" H.P. Well, ah.

P. How did he pay the fee? H.P. No, no. I think that—one, we try and find out whether or not the amount of fees reflected on the books of the law firm were consistent with the amount of money that was—oh—to have gone to the law firm. In other words, what we think happened is that a considerable amount within the law firm was paid out in fees and the balance went on to Dorothy Hunt for distribution to the Cubans and what have you.

P. For support. H.P. The strange thing about this one, Mr. President, is that they could have done it openly.

P. Why, of course! . . . H.P. And we're going to help these—They were doing this—Once you do it in a clandestine fashion, it takes on elements—P. Elements of a cover-up. H.P. That's right, and obstruction of justice. P. That's what it is, a question of the way it was done. H.P. Sir

After Petersen gave further details on how "the case was being built," Nixon said:

P. Well, there's only this one charge I give to you, among many others, and that is: If any of this— I mean, I can't allow it. Believe me that even prosecutors shouldn't even have informed you of this one. Or me—I—

The Ellsberg trial—At the end of the transcript, Nixon and Petersen returned to the Ellsberg case:

P. But what are you going to do? What will happen now? The FBI will now interview Dean on that report in California? H.P. Yes, sir. They will interview Ehrlichman and they will, ah, attempt to identify the psychiatrist. They will interview the psychiatrist named as Ellsberg's psychiatrist to determine whether or not they were burglarized or know they were burglarized. They will attempt to determine if there's any police report of a burglary. We will check with the Defense Department since they have been involved in this thing. We will recheck the FBI. We've already checked them once.

P. What did they find? H.P. Well, nothing. We've checked our own people— P. Now, the FBI did not do anything. H.P. I understand. But . . . we're talking about the evidence of information that may have been stemmed from that source. P. Yeah. Well they got into the trial. H.P. Whether any of that has gotten into the file in any way. And when we do that and we do that, we have to file a report to the Court and we will and ah we'll see what develops.

April 30, 1973

The final transcript appendix was the text of Nixon's televised address in which he accepted basic responsibility for the Watergate affair but denied that he was personally involved in the break-in or the cover-up. The speech also included announcement of the resignations of Haldeman, Ehrlichman, Dean and Kleindienst.

Soviets report impeachment moves. Developments in the Watergate affair and U.S. Congressional moves to impeach President Nixon were reported in the Soviet press April 12 and 30, marking an apparent shift in Moscow's earlier policy of silence regarding the President's domestic troubles. The shift reflected, according to the New York Times April 13 and May 1, the Kremlin's growing concern over Nixon's ability to favorably influence Soviet-U.S. relations.

An April 12 article in the foreign affairs weekly Novoye Vremya disclosed that the President was facing the possibility of impeachment and raised the connection between "the income-tax scandal" and the impeachment bid. The government newspaper Izvestia reported April 30 that Nixon was turning over to the House Judiciary Committee "shorthand records made from his tape-recorded conversatons with his chief assistants concerning [the Watergate] affair."

Although the tone of the articles was sympathetic to the President, the April 30 report noted that "various assertions and rumors were under way for more than a year that the President had allegedly been involved in a cover-up attempt."

Sirica bars disqualification bid. U.S. District Court Judge John J. Sirica April 30 rejected motions by five of the seven Watergate cover-up defendants that he disqualify himself as presiding judge in their trial, scheduled to begin in September.

The motions had been filed April 10 by former Attorney General John N. Mitchell and former presidential aides Charles W. Colson, John D. Ehrlichman and Gordon C. Strachan. They were later joined by Kenneth W. Parkinson, an attorney for President Nixon's re-election committee.

The defendants, who asked that Sirica step aside voluntarily or that a three-judge panel choose a new presiding judge, argued that Sirica had shown a "prosecutorial interest" in his conduct of the trials of the original Watergate burglary conspirators in early 1973 by questioning witnesses and defendants about the involvement of others and by using sentencing procedures "designed to pressure ... defendants into making further disclosures."

The cover-up defendants also argued that Sirica should be disqualified because he had listened privately to White House tapes subpoenaed by the prosecution, some of which were related to the cover-up indictment, and that he had examined and transmitted to the House Judiciary Committee the grand jury report on Nixon's role in the cover-up. In the history of the Watergate scandal, the defendants argued, Sirica had become "inextricably intertwined" in the public mind with the prosecution and would therefore be prejudicial to the pending case.

In a brief filed April 26, special prosecutor Leon Jaworski defended Sirica's fitness to preside at the trial while acknowledging that a three-judge panel might best render a decision on the disqualification issue that would bear the heaviest weight in case of appeal. In any event, Jaworski argued, justice would be helped rather than hindered by Sirica's familiarity with the Watergate case.

In his response to the motions April 30, Sirica rejected all points raised by the defendants, ruling that "every action, decision and comment" had arisen "in the course of official judicial activities," and reflected, "if anything, a judicial state of mind rather than a personal bias."

Nixon approved Ellsberg break-in. John D. Ehrlichman, former domestic affairs adviser to President Nixon, said in a sworn affidavit that the President twice "indicated his after-the-fact approval" of the Labor Day 1971 break-in at the office of Dr. Lewis J. Fielding, the psychiatrist who had treated Pentagon Papers defendant Daniel Ellsberg. The affidavit also stated that Nixon had ordered Assistant Attorney General Henry E. Petersen to keep his Watergate investigators away from the break-in because matters of national security were involved.

Ehrlichman, indicted March 7 in connection with the Fielding break-in, submitted the affidavit to the U.S. district court in Washington April 30. The break-in, Ehrlichman's affidavit contended, was legally justified by requirements of national security.

Denying any advance knowledge of the break-in, which was perpetrated by the special White House investigations unit called "the plumbers," Ehrlichman said the President discussed the burglary twice when he had been present. The first discussion occurred during an April 18, 1973 phone conversation between Nixon and Petersen, in which the President said to Petersen in substance: "You and your department stay out of that. This is strictly a national security matter. I know you have to enforce the laws, but, as President, I have to protect the national security and that comes first. As President I am instructing you to take no action whatsoever on that matter." After hanging up, Ehrlichman said, the President said the conversation had dealt with the Fielding burglary. The President "said in substance that the break-in was in furtherance of national security and fully justified by the circumstances."

The second conversation related in the Ehrlichman affidavit took place in early May 1973 in the White House Oval Office, where the President told Ehrlichman in effect: "While I did not know of the break-in attempt in advance, I surely recognize the valid national security reasons why it was done."

At another point in his affidavit, Ehrlichman said Henry A. Kissinger, then the President's national security adviser, had been present at the 1971 meeting at the Presidential retreat in San Clemente, Calif., during which Nixon had named Kissinger's aide David R. Young Jr. a co-director of the "plumbers" unit. Kissinger had testified at Senate hearings on his appointment as secretary of state that he "did not know of the existence of the plumbers group."

Ehrlichman changes counsel—Ehrlichman disclosed March 30 that he had retained William S. Frates of Miami to represent him in upcoming Watergate trials. Frates was also associated with Charles G. Rebozo, the President's friend. John J. Wilson, who had represented Ehrlichman and former White House chief of staff H. R. Haldeman at the Senate Watergate hearings, would remain as counsel to Haldeman, Ehrlichman said. "I have concluded that it is important for me to have separate counsel," Ehrlichman said.

ITT & Milk Fund
Developments

Kalmbach disputes Rebozo on Hughes gift. Herbert W. Kalmbach, who was personal attorney to President Nixon, gave sworn testimony to the Senate Watergate Committee March 21 that the President's personal friend Charles G. Rebozo had given or loaned portions of a $100,000 campaign contribution from billionaire industrialist Howard R. Hughes to Nixon's personal secretary Rose Mary Woods and his brothers F. Donald Nixon and Edward C. Nixon, it was reported April 6 and 7. Kalmbach repeated his testimony to investigators from the office of the Watergate special prosecutor.

According to the Washington Post April 6, Kalmbach told the Watergate panel that Rebozo had summoned him to a meeting at the White House April 30, 1973—the same day Nixon fired his counsel John W. Dean 3rd and accepted the resignations of aides H. R. Haldeman and John D. Ehrlichman. Informing Kalmbach that the meeting had been called at the President's request, Rebozo said he was seeking legal advice concerning an inquiry by the Internal Revenue Service (IRS) into the Hughes contribution. The Post reported April 7 that Kalmbach testified he had concluded from Rebozo's statements at the meeting that the President was aware that part of the Hughes contribution had gone to Miss Woods and F. Donald Nixon. The sources added, however, that Kalmbach testified Rebozo did not specifically tell him that.

When Rebozo related that the money had been given to Miss Woods and the President's brothers, Kalmbach advised him "to make a clean breast of it" to the IRS, the New York Times reported April 7. According to Times sources, Kalmbach also testified that he received a phone call from Rebozo in January 1974, during which Rebozo said the earlier conversation had been a mistake. The money, in $100 bills, was still in its original wrappers in a safety deposit box, Rebozo reportedly said.

William S. Frates, counsel for Rebozo, said his client denied Kalmbach's allegations. Rebozo did have a conversation with Kalmbach at the President's suggestion, Frates said, but it was only one of several with people in the White House on

how to return the money to Hughes. Charles F. Rhyne, attorney for Miss Woods, called Kalmbach's testimony "preposterous." F. Donald Nixon also denied the allegations.

According to Post sources, Rebozo turned next for advice to Kenneth Gemmill, a Philadelphia lawyer who had handled tax matters for the President. Gemmill, who Post sources said had no knowledge that any money might have been funneled to Miss Woods or the President's brothers, recommended that the gift be returned to Hughes to avoid any embarrassment with the IRS.

Deciding to follow Gemmill's advice, Rebozo sought to return the money, only to encounter difficulty in finding someone to take the $100,000. Rebozo, in an interview with the Miami Herald in 1973, had admitted he had trouble finding a Hughes agent willing to accept the money. "I wanted to make absolutely sure that there was no question about it being the identical bills. I had the money inventoried, and I had the serial numbers taken down . . . just before I returned it." Rebozo also said President Nixon had not learned of the Hughes gift until after the 1972 election, although he (Rebozo) had informed Miss Woods of it 1970, shortly after receiving the second of two $50,000 cash installments from Richard G. Danner, a Hughes aide.

In a related development, the Times reported April 8 that Watergate committee investigators had established that Rebozo flew to the New York fishing retreat of Robert H. Abplanalp, the President's millionaire friend, about a week before the Hughes contribution was returned. Rebozo, who in sworn testimony to the Watergate committee denied the allegations by Kalmbach, confirmed meeting with Abplanalp. However, Rebozo said "he just flew up for lunch."

Sources close to the committee, the Times reported, said the panel's investigative team, led by committee attorney Terry F. Lenzner, felt that Rebozo had originally sought out Kalmbach in the hope that Kalmbach, one of the President's chief campaign fund raisers, could be induced to help raise the $100,000 needed to replace the contribution. When

Kalmbach merely urged Rebozo to tell the IRS about the distribution of the money, Times sources said, Rebozo sought other avenues, such as Abplanalp.

Gross convicted. Nelson G. Gross, former state chairman of the New Jersey Republican Party, was found guilty by a Newark, N.J. federal jury March 29 of five counts of tax fraud and perjury. Gross was sentenced to two years in prison and fined $10,000 June 16.

Chairman of the 1969 gubernatorial campaign of former Gov. William T. Cahill, Gross had been charged with advising trading stamp executive William H. Preis to disguise a $5,000 campaign contribution as a tax-deductible business expense and with subsequently urging Preis to lie to a grand jury investigating the contribution.

In a related development, John A. Kervick, a former N.J. state treasurer who pleaded guilty to bribery and extortion charges in 1973, was fined $10,000 and placed on three years probation by a federal judge in Trenton June 17. Kervick, 68, was said to be suffering from cancer.

Ford scores Nixon re-election panel. Vice President Gerald R. Ford drew cheers from a group of Midwest Republican Party leaders March 30 with a denunciation of President Nixon's 1972 re-election committee, the Committee for the Re-election of the President. [For further details, see p. 81C3]

Reinecke indicted in ITT probe. California Lt. Gov. Ed Reinecke, a candidate for the Republican nomination for governor, was indicted by a Watergate grand jury in Washington April 3 on three counts of perjury in connection with the 1972 Senate Judiciary Committee investigation of the settlement of antitrust suits against the International Telephone & Telegraph Corp. (ITT).

The indictment was the first resulting from the Watergate prosecution's investigation of the ITT case.

Reinecke's testimony before the Senate panel had concerned efforts in 1971 to bring the 1972 Republican national con-

C

D

E

F

G

vention to San Diego with financial aid from ITT, which was then facing the Justice Department's antitrust suits.

Two counts of the indictment centered on Reinecke's 1971 conversation with John N. Mitchell, then attorney general, on convention details and the ITT commitment of funds. When the committee summoned Reinecke because of statements to newsmen that such a conversation had occurred in May 1971 (the antitrust settlement was announced July 31, 1971), he testified that the conversation—his only one with Mitchell on the subject—had not occurred until September. This, the indictment charged, was false.

The grand jury also charged that Reinecke lied in telling the committee that he had "no way of knowing" whether Mitchell had heard of ITT's commitments before September 1971.

The third count accused Reinecke of lying when he testified that the idea of bringing the convention to San Diego was "really hatched" April 27, 1971 during discussions with San Diego businessmen at a "social" gathering in Washington.

Reinecke told a news conference in Sacramento that the indictment was "shocking, incredible and unbelievable in terms of fairness of the special prosecutor." Reinecke said he was innocent, would not plead guilty or engage in plea bargaining and was "in the gubernatorial race to stay." He said he would seek a change of venue to California, charging that no one "gets a fair trial in Washington, D.C. these days."

The indictment was returned to U.S. District Court Judge George L. Hart Jr., who broke the usual routine of an indictment announcement with an angry statement that there had been a premature leak of the charges, a clear violation, he said, of rules governing grand jury secrecy. Hart said an aide to Rep. Jerome R. Waldie (D, Calif.)—also a candidate for governor—had asked his office for a copy of the indictment 27 minutes before it was to be returned in court.

Summoned to explain the leak, special prosecutor Leon Jaworski surmised that it was probably a case of newsmen "putting two and two together" and telling Waldie's office. The prosecution noted that Reinecke's attorneys had been notified in advance of the pending announcement, and that Reinecke had then scheduled his news conference.

Reinecke had sought during February to have the prosecution clarify his status in the ITT investigation. After a letter to Jaworski and a meeting between his attorneys and the prosecutor, Reinecke reported Feb. 15 that Jaworski had refused to give him an "immediate and official clearance" of the "cloud hanging over" his campaign for governor.

Reinecke had told a news conference Feb. 20 that he had not deliberately lied to the Senate panel but conceded that he had not told all he could. He attributed this to advice from Clark MacGregor, then President Nixon's adviser on Congres-

sional relations and Reinecke's "good friend" from their service in the House.

Reinecke said MacGregor had advised him to answer only direct questions and not to volunteer information. Senators had asked only whether he had "met" with Mitchell before September 1971, Reinecke contended, not if he had conferred by telephone. But Reinecke conceded to the newsmen that he had discussed the ITT money offer with Mitchell in three phone conversations during May and June 1971.

According to reports April 4, Reinecke's effort to clear himself with the Watergate prosecution continued into March. With Jaworski's permission, he underwent two days of lie detector tests administered by the Federal Bureau of Investigation. The test results were not made public.

Maheu says Humphrey got '68 Hughes gift. Robert A. Maheu, a former aide to billionaire recluse Howard R. Hughes, said under oath April 4 that he personally delivered $50,000 in cash to Hubert H. Humphrey in July 1968, when Humphrey, then vice president, was campaigning for the presidency. The charge was made by Maheu during testimony he gave in his $17.3 million libel suit against Hughes.

According to Maheu, he met Humphrey by prearrangement outside a Los Angeles hotel after a fund-raising dinner for Humphrey. (A Humphrey aid had denied Maheu's request to meet privately with Humphrey, and Maheu agreed to see Humphrey during a ride to the airport.) Maheu said he sat on a jump seat in the rear compartment of the limousine carrying Humphrey. After he made a reference to Humphrey to "the matter we discussed," Maheu testified, the car was stopped and he got out, leaving behind a briefcase containing $50,000 in cash. "I had the impression that the vice president was aware that I had left the briefcase," Maheu said.

In a sworn affidavit Feb. 19 in connection with Maheu's suit, Humphrey denied that he had personally received a gift from the Hughes organization in 1968. However, Humphrey said March 19 that the cash contribution might have been made to someone on his campaign staff, but he reiterated that he had not been personally involved.

In testimony April 5, Maheu said Humphrey called him the morning after the 1968 election to thank him for the $100,000 in contributions given him by Hughes. Half the money, Maheu said, had been channeled to the Humphrey campaign by way of Nevada Democrats who were issued checks by the Hughes organization. The remaining amount, an issue because Maheu's suit focused on Hughes' remark to the press that Maheu "stole me blind," was given to Humphrey in the ride to the airport, Maheu testified. A countersuit against Maheu filed by Hughes charged that Maheu had misappropriated money entrusted to him—possibly the $50,000 allegedly given Humphrey.

Testimony from three witnesses April

3 corroborated elements of Maheu's contention. Joseph R. Cerrell, a campaign aide for Humphrey in 1968, said he seen Maheu enter the limousine, but could not remember if Maheu carried an attache case. Lloyd Hand, a campaign aide who was with Humphrey when Maheu entered the limousine, said he had the impression that Maheu had left a briefcase, but Hand did not know its contents. Los Angeles attorney Gordon S. Judd, who was employed by the Hughes organization in 1968, remembered bringing an attache case to Maheu just before the alleged transaction was made. Judd said he was not told what was in the briefcase.

Hughes buys Bahamas hotel—Hughes purchased the luxury Xanadu Princess Hotel from billionaire shipping magnate D. K. Ludwig for an estimated price of $15 million, it was reported Feb. 20. Hughes, who was living in the hotel located in the Bahamas city of Freeport, owned five hotel-casinos in Las Vegas, Nev., as well as casinos in Las Vegas and Reno, Nev.

Chapin convicted. Dwight L. Chapin, former appointments secretary to President Nixon, was convicted by a federal jury in Washington April 5 on two counts of perjury in connection with grand jury testimony on his dealings with Donald H. Segretti, the "dirty trickster" of the 1971–'72 presidential campaign. [For further details, see p. 83B2]

Steinbrenner indicted. George M. Steinbrenner 3rd, chairman of American Ship Building Co. of Cleveland and a major partner in the New York Yankees baseball team, was indicted April 5 on 14 felony counts in connection with illegal contributions to the campaigns of President Nixon and Republican and Democratic members of Congress. The indictment, returned by a federal grand jury in Cleveland, was signed by special Watergate prosecutor Leon Jaworski.

Steinbrenner was charged with one count of conspiracy, five counts of willful violation of campaign finance laws, two counts of urging others to give false statements to the Federal Bureau of Investigation, four counts of obstruction of justice and two counts of obstructing a criminal investigation.

American Ship Building was charged with one count of conspiracy and one count of making an illegal campaign contribution. Robert E. Bartlome, company secretary, and Stanley J. Lepkowski, treasurer and controller, were named as unindicted co-conspirators.

Steinbrenner pleaded not guilty April 19. The company also pleaded not guilty.

The indictment charged that "trusted employes" were selected to receive "bonuses," the proceeds of which were then sent to candidates of Steinbrenner's choosing. To conceal the bogus bonus system and other employe political contributions ordered by Steinbrenner, the indictment charged that Steinbrenner directed the submission of fictitious vouchers to create a cash contributions fund, and caused "the destruction and alteration" of other company records.

The indictment listed 19 contributions made between 1970 and 1973, including $31,200 to the Committee to Re-elect the President and $23,500 to other candidates.

In a subsequent development, John H. Melcher Jr., executive vice president and general counsel of American Ship Building, pleaded guilty in Washington April 18 to a misdemeanor count of helping Steinbrenner conceal the circumstances surrounding transmittal of the $25,000 in employe checks to the Nixon re-election committee.

After a separate investigation, the Securities and Exchange Commission (SEC) April 15 accused Steinbrenner of making illegal political contributions with corporate funds and attempting to disguise the gifts as ordinary business expenses. The SEC requested the U.S. district court in Washington to appoint a "special master" to examine American Ship Building's records and require Steinbrenner to reimburse the company for the total amount of illegal contributions, which the SEC complaint estimated to be "in excess of" $120,000.

Political use of IRS detailed. Sen. Lowell P. Weicker Jr. (R, Conn.), a member of the Senate Watergate Committee, accused the Internal Revenue Service (IRS) April 8 of acting as a "public lending library" for White House efforts to aid political friends and harass political enemies.

Appearing at a joint hearing of Senate Judiciary Subcommittees on Constitutional Rights and Administrative Practice and Procedure, and the Foreign Relations Subcommittee on Surveillance, Weicker disclosed a collection of documents, gathered by the Watergate Committee, showing politically motivated tax audits, undercover White House investigations and military spying on civilians.

One 1969 IRS memo describing the creation of a special activists "study unit" advised that the unit's function of examining tax returns of "ideological, militant, subversive, radical or other" organizations must not become publicly known, since disclosure "might embarrass the Administration." The unit was abolished in August 1973 after, according to Weicker, assembling tax data on about 10,000 persons.

According to the documents, former presidential counsel John W. Dean 3rd and former White House and Treasury Department official John J. Caulfield—both involved in the Watergate cover-up—were central characters in political use of the IRS.

A 1971 set of Dean-Caulfield memos suggested that the Administration was interested in helping evangelist Billy Graham and actor John Wayne, both supporters of President Nixon, with their tax problems. One memo referred to a "back-

door" copy of an audit on Graham and promised similar material on Wayne. Dean was later supplied with audit histories of several entertainment figures "whose economic condition is similar to that of John Wayne."

Another 1971 series of memos from Caulfield to Dean outlined possible measures to conduct "discreet" audits on Emile DeAntonio, producer of "Millhouse: A White Comedy," a film satirizing Nixon, and on the film's distributors. Caulfield also referred to the release of derogatory Federal Bureau of Investigation data on DeAntonio.

Weicker also gave the committees a list of 54 undercover White House investigations by Anthony T. Ulasewicz, some of which had been disclosed earlier. Subjects of Ulasewicz' efforts ranged from possible "improper conduct" by Donald F. Nixon Jr., the President's nephew, "scandals" in the backgrounds of Democratic Sens. Edmund S. Muskie (Me.) and Hubert H. Humphrey (Minn.), to a check "on a comedian named Dixon who was doing imitations of the President."

Other material submitted by Weicker documented earlier charges that Army intelligence units had infiltrated a group of American civilians in West Germany supporting 1972 Democratic presidential nominee George S. McGovern, and suggestions that former White House counsel Charles W. Colson had intervened in the parole case of Calvin Kovens, a 1972 campaign contributor who had been convicted of mail fraud with labor leader James Hoffa.

Reinecke pleads innocent. California Lt. Gov. Ed Reinecke pleaded not guilty to perjury charges in federal district court in Washington April 10. Reinecke, a candidate for the Republican nomination for governor, had been indicted on three counts of lying to a Senate committee investigating the political implications of antitrust settlements involving the International Telephone & Telegraph Corp.

Heeding Reinecke's plea for a trial before the June 4 state primary election, Judge Barrington D. Parker said April 11 that trial could begin immediately after a mid-May hearing on a defense motion to move the trial to California. Parker had originally scheduled the trial for June 19.

McGovern unit charged. The Citizens for McGovern Committee of St. Louis was cited by the General Accounting Office (GAO) April 10 for apparent violations of federal campaign fund laws during the 1972 presidential campaign. The GAO report was referred to the Justice Department for action.

The alleged violations involved failure to maintain complete and accurate financial records and inability to provide information required by law. The GAO

said the committee's records of contributions and expenses which failed to indicate actual dates of receipts, types of receipts, or sufficient identification of contributors.

Senate OKs campaign reform bill. A comprehensive campaign reform bill was passed by the Senate April 11 by a 53–32 vote (38 D & 15 R vs. 23 R & 9 D). The Senate took a total of 51 roll-call votes on the bill, which had been debated since March 26. One of the votes was to impose cloture, which carried April 9 by a 64–30 vote (44 D & 20 R vs. 20 R & 10 D), one more than the required two-thirds majority. A 60–36 cloture vote had fallen four short of the required margin April 4. The filibuster against the bill was led by Sen. James B. Allen (D, Ala.).

Comment on the bill was split. Sen. William Brock (R, Tenn.) considered it "an insult to the American people," Sen. George D. Aiken (R, Vt.) "worse than no bill at all." Sen. Edward M. Kennedy (D, Mass.) described passage as "one of the finest hours of the Senate in this or any other Congress."

The major feature of the bill was public funding for presidential and Congressional campaigns. The funds would come from the $1 income tax checkoff established in 1971, with Congress authorized to appropriate any additional funding necessary. Beginning in 1976, major party candidates for federal office would be entitled to the federal financing of their campaigns. Other candidates would be entitled to funding in proportion to their share of the popular vote in the prior election, if they received at least 5% of the vote, or in the current election if it was their first. Candidates also would have a choice of using private contributions or a combination of public and private funding.

A matching grant system would be used for primaries. A presidential candidate would have to raise $250,000 in contributions of $250 or less to be eligible for the same amount from the government. Additional contributions would be matched dollar for dollar up to the prescribed limit of a candidate's spending. Limits were set for private contributions and a candidate's spending.

In Senate and Congressional primary contests, a Senate candidate would have to raise $25,000 to $125,000, depending on the population of his state, in contributions of $100 or less to become eligible for matching funds; candidates for the House would have to raise $10,000 in contributions of $100 or less.

In general elections, the candidates would be eligible for federal payments equal to their overall spending limits. These were: 12¢ per eligible voter, or about $17 million, for president; 12¢ per voter or $175,000, whichever was greater, for the Senate; 12¢ per voter or $90,000, whichever was greater, for the House.

The same formula on an 8¢-per-voter basis, would be used to limit primary campaign spending. This would make the key figures about $11.5 million for a presidential candidate, $125,000 for the Senate and $90,000 for the House.

The rules for contributions would be no more than $3,000 from an individual, or $6,000 from an organization, to a candidate for each election year; no more than $25,000 in one year from an individual to all candidates for federal office, political parties or political committees. Contributions by foreigners and cash contributions of more than $100 would be prohibited.

Personal campaign spending by a candidate or his immediate family would be limited to $50,000 in presidential races, $35,000 in Senate races and $25,000 in House races.

A candidate would be required to keep his major funding records in one central committee and his actual funding through clearly designated channels. Presidential campaign expenditures in excess of $1,000 would have to be approved by the chairman of the candidate's national party or his delegate.

Among the provisions added to the bill during the debate were ones to require top federal officials, including the president, to disclose the federal and state income taxes they paid each year and to subject them to annual income tax audits by the General Accounting Office.

Other provisions of the bill called for repeal of the equal-time provision for campaign broadcasts by candidates; creation of an independent federal elections commission with subpoena power to enforce the new law; designation of election day as a legal holiday; setting elections for federal offices on the first Wednesday after the first Monday in November; requiring a uniform closing hour for polls across the country; and prohibiting disclosure of presidential election returns until midnight, Eastern Standard Time, on election day.

Sen. Herman Talmadge (D, Ga.) planned to introduce an amendment to prohibit publication of defamatory statements about candidates but withdrew it April 8 in view of the possibility it could have been used to inhibit good faith reporting. It would have made it a criminal offense for a person to "cause to be published a false and defamatory statement of fact about the character or professional ability of a candidate for federal office with respect to the qualifications of that candidate for that office if such person knows that such statement is false."

Questions raised in Silbert nomination. Senate Judiciary Committee hearings on the nomination of Earl J. Silbert as U.S. attorney for the District of Columbia focused on the adequacy of the original Watergate investigation. Silbert, 37, who headed the original Watergate prosecution team while he was an assistant U.S. attorney, was nominated by President Nixon Jan. 29 to be U.S. attorney.

Silbert appeared before the committee April 23 and 24 and defended himself

against criticism of the original Watergate probe from Sens. Philip A. Hart (D, Mich.) and Birch Bayh (D, Ind.). He had only two assistants to prepare for a trial with 90 witnesses, Silbert said.

[For further details, see p. 172G3]

House panel seeking ITT, milk Fund data. House Judiciary Committee Chairman Peter W. Rodino Jr. (D, N.J.) told reporters April 23 that the committee was seeking tapes and documents, aside from those already subpoenaed concerning the ITT anti-trust settlement and dairy industry contributions. [For further details, see p. 87B3]

Watergate panel wins IRS data access. The Internal Revenue Service (IRS) agreed to provide the Senate Watergate Committee with tax returns and other politically sensitive materials from its files on President Nixon's friend Charles G. Rebozo and the President's brother F. Donald Nixon, the New York Times reported April 24.

The IRS decision, an abrupt reversal of its previously stated position, included an agreement to provide a wide variety of tax returns and other data deemed essential by the committee to its investigation of Rebozo's handling of the $100,000 cash presidential campaign contribution by billionaire industrialist Howard Hughes in 1969 and 1970, the Times reported.

The Times had reported April 21 that Terry Lenzner, assistant chief counsel to the Watergate panel, had circulated a memorandum to committee members that in effect charged the IRS with obstructing his investigation into the handling of the Hughes gift. Contrary to an agreement for full exchange of data made with IRS agents in January, Lenzner's memo said, the IRS had not been forthcoming and stated April 12 that the committee would receive no additional data, pending resolution of a disagreement over language in the agreement.

The IRS responded to the charges in Lenzner's memorandum April 21: "The IRS flatly denies that it has engaged in any cover-up . . . and asserts that it has been cooperating . . . to the fullest extent consistent with the disclosure limitations in the tax laws."

The latest exchange agreement between the IRS and the committee, Times sources said, contained a proviso limiting access to the data to Carmine Bellino, chief investigator for the full committee, and Richard Schultz, an assistant minority counsel. Neither Lenzner nor his direct aides was to receive direct access to the materials, although relevant findings were to be made available, the sources said.

Lenzner's investigation had been enlarged March 21 when Herbert W. Kalmbach, personal attorney to President Nixon, told the committee of an April 30, 1973 meeting he had with Rebozo, in which Rebozo had admitted distributing parts of the Hughes campaign gift to the President's brothers, F. Donald Nixon

and Edward C. Nixon, the President's personal secretary Rose Mary Woods and "others." Rebozo sought his legal advice, Kalmbach reportedly testified, because the IRS was then investigating Rebozo's handling of the money. (Kalmbach's testimony was partly confirmed by Stanley Ebner, general counsel to White House Office of Management and Budget, who said Kalmbach had outlined, without mentioning names, Rebozo's problem to him and had asked for his advice, the Washington Star-News reported April 16.)

In his memorandum, Lenzner had also charged that the IRS had used the White House as a go-between in its investigation of the Hughes gift. Before the IRS got in touch with him, Rebozo had already been informed by White House aide John D. Ehrlichman of the IRS's interest in the Hughes cash. The Times also reported April 22 that committee investigators were felt to believe that J. Fred Buzhardt Jr., President Nixon's counsel, had taken over the role of intermediary between the IRS and Rebozo when Ehrlichman resigned his post April 30, 1973.

In another development, the Times reported April 11 that special Watergate prosecutor Leon Jaworski had subpoenaed the federal income tax returns of Rebozo and Robert H. Abplanalp, the President's millionaire friend. It had been revealed earlier that Rebozo, Abplanalp and Richard G. Danner, an aide to Hughes, had met at a New York State fishing retreat owned by Abplanalp about a week before William E. Griffin, general counsel to Abplanalp's Precision Valve Corp., returned the $100,000 to a representative from the Hughes organization.

Gurney indicted in Florida. Sen. Edward J. Gurney (R, Fla.) was indicted by a Leon County grand jury in Tallahassee, Fla. April 26. It charged him with violation of a state law requiring reporting of campaign contributions.

The indictment was disclosed by Gurney's office in Washington April 29. Gurney immediately declared his innocence and denounced the action as a "political Pearl Harbor attack" by Democrats seeking his Senate seat. Gurney, who had announced his intention to seek re-election, expressed faith in "the process of justice and courts."

The charge, a misdemeanor carrying a maximum penalty of one year in prison and a $1,000 fine, stemmed from a televised news conference in December 1973 when Gurney admitted that $100,000 had been raised in his name without his knowledge. The money was reportedly part of $400,000 taken by a Gurney aide from builders seeking influence for federal housing permits. Gurney denied knowledge of the activity. When he learned about it in mid-1972, he had ordered it halted, Gurney said, but could not report it then because he was not a candidate. He said he could not report it since becoming a candidate because he did not know who contributed the funds.

Nixon releases edited tapes transcripts. President Nixon April 29 announced he would release edited transcripts of his key conversations with White House aides concerning Watergate. [For portions of the transcripts containing references to the use of campaign funds, see pp. 99–126]

Among the transcripts was one which concerned the ITT settlement. [For further details, see p. 115D2]

St. Clair comments. In a news conference May 1, President Nixon's special counsel James D. St. Clair contended that the full story of Nixon's Watergate role was now available. St. Clair indicated also that the White House felt that further disclosure on other issues was unnecessary. "The name of this problem we are facing is called Watergate," St. Clair said. In reply to a question if the Judiciary Committee should "forget about milk and ITT," the subjects of other material requested by the committee, St. Clair said: "Based on what I know about it, the answer is yes. The President has published a white paper, so-called, on each of these. I don't know that anyone has seriously challenged the accuracy of them, and a fair reading of those white papers would make it reasonably clear ... there is no basis for a charge against the President."

Northrop admits violation. Northrop Corporation, a Los Angeles-based aerospace company and major Defense Department contractor, and two of its top executives pleaded guilty May 1 to charges of making illegal contributions totaling $150,000 to President Nixon's 1972 re-election campaign.

A federal district court in Los Angeles imposed maximum fines; Northrop and Thomas V. Jones, chairman and chief executive, were each fined $5,000. Jones could have received up to five years in prison. The Watergate special prosecutor's office, which brought the case, said it was the first such action under a 1940 statute prohibiting political contributions by government contractors. Previous illegal campaign financing charges had been filed under provisions prohibiting corporate campaign contributions in general.

At the same hearing, Northrop Vice President James Allen pleaded guilty to the corporation-contribution statute and received the maximum $1,000 fine. Both executives were charged with "nonwillful" misdemeanor violations.

The special prosecutor's charges said that on Jan. 25, 1973, Jones substituted $100,000 in personal money for corporate funds and then had documents backdated to show falsely that all contributions were made from personal, rather than corporate money. The charges stated that Allen partially reimbursed other Northrop officers for contributions they had made to the 1972 election campaign.

Herbert Kalmbach, President Nixon's attorney, had told the Senate Watergate committee in 1973 he had received $75,000 from Jones.

Anderson sentenced. N. Dale Anderson, successor to former Vice President Spiro T. Agnew as Baltimore County (Md.) executive, was sentenced to five years in prison May 1. Anderson, who had been convicted on 32 counts of conspiracy, extortion and income tax evasion, had resigned his office April 23.

William E. Fornoff, formerly Anderson's administrative officer and later a chief witness against him, was given a two-year suspended sentence and fined $5,000, it was reported May 1.

Agnew disbarred. Former Vice President Spiro T. Agnew was barred from the practice of law May 2 by the Maryland Court of Appeals, the state's highest court. The court held unanimously that "automatic disbarment" resulted from conviction on a charge involving moral turpitude in the absence of "compelling reason to the contrary." Agnew had pleaded no contest to a tax evasion charge in October 1973. His counsel, in arguments before the court, had contended that Agnew should be suspended rather than disbarred. Maryland was the only state where Agnew was a member of the bar.

The court held that the crime to which Agnew pleaded no contest was "infested with fraud, deceit and dishonesty." "It is difficult to feel compassion," the court said, "for an attorney who is so morally obtuse that he consciously cheats for his own pecuniary gain that government he has sworn to serve, completely disregards the words of the oath he uttered when first admitted to the bar and absolutely fails to perceive his professional duty to act honestly in all matters."

Milk fund developments. According to court papers filed in the government's antitrust case against Associated Milk Producers Inc. (AMPI), a Texas-based cooperative, the firm's lobbyist, Robert Lilly, claimed that AMPI had made a "commitment" of campaign funds to President Nixon's re-election race "in conjunction with the 1971 price support" increase authorized by Nixon.

Lilly's statement, reported in the press May 2, was made to Edward L. Wright, a lawyer who had been hired by AMPI's directors to investigate the alleged payoff. Wright's report was made public March 14. His notes of the interview with Lilly had been subpoenaed for the antitrust trial.

Lilly said he was told of the arrangement April 4, 1972 during a meeting with AMPI's general manager, George L. Mehren, and Mehren's predecessor, Harold S. Nelson. "The commitment [of a campaign contribution] was made in March of 1971 by Nelson, [David] Parr, Marion Harrison, and [Jake] Jacobsen," Lilly told Wright.

"There was a big argument over how much money had been committed," Lilly said. "The figures ranged from $500,000 to $1 million. Jacobsen contacted Connally in March of 1971 about the contribution. Connally said there had to be new money or additional money." (Administration documents already made public cited a campaign pledge of $2 million made by the dairy industry.)

Mehren disputed President Nixon's defense of his controversial price support decision made in an Administration white paper on the milk fund controversy, the Washington Post reported May 5. Nixon claimed that he had been pressured to authorize the price increase because of overwhelming Congressional backing for the legislative proposal. Mehren contested that assertion in statements made to Congressional investigators. "We had lined up quite a bit of support [in Congress]," Mehren said, "but not in my opinion sufficient to override a presidential veto."

When he and other industry officials met with Nixon March 23, 1971, Mehren said, they were not hopeful about their chances to win White House support for the increase. However, the Nixon campaign received a check for $25,000 from the political arm of Dairymen Inc. the next day, and on March 25, 1971, the Agriculture Department announced that it had reversed a previous ruling and would allow an increase in the support price of milk.

Herbert Kalmbach, the President's personal attorney and chief fund-raiser, also gave an account of the circumstances surrounding the dairy industry's pledge of campaign funds, it was reported May 6.

Kalmbach told the Senate Watergate Committee staff that a secret midnight meeting was held March 24, 1971 in his Washington hotel room for the purpose of asking dairymen to reconfirm their offer (made in 1970) to contribute $2 million to Nixon's campaign. Murray Chotiner, a Nixon confidant who had left the Administration three weeks earlier and set up private law practice, conveyed the message to Harold Nelson. (Chotiner had also just been retained by AMPI as its Washington counsel.) Nelson reaffirmed the pledge, Kalmbach testified.

The information was passed on to the House Judiciary Committee, according to the Washington Post, and formed the basis of the committee's request for White House tapes and other documents relating to the milk fund controversy. Sources close to the Senate Watergate Committee said testimony from Kalmbach and others caused the committee to conclude that the efforts to seek reconfirmation of the $2 million pledge were launched with Nixon's approval by John Ehrlichman, his top domestic affairs aide. Ehrlichman telephoned White House Special Counsel Charles Colson, who then met with Chotiner, investigators said. The arrangements were concluded March 23, 1971, immediately after Nixon had met with Ehrlichman and other aides and decided to authorize the milk price increase.

(Nixon had met earlier that day with the dairy representatives.) Later that night, the dairymen agreed to make an immediate donation of $25,000—Dairymen Inc. met the deadline with its contribution March 24, 1971, according to Congressional investigators. Public announcement of the price increase was not made until March 25, 1971 when the White House was certain it would receive additional campaign funds, investigators charged.

Democrats linked to milk fund—Court documents filed in the antitrust case also yielded evidence supporting charges that dairy industry payoffs also involved prominent Democrats, including the late President Lyndon B. Johnson and Rep. Wilbur D. Mills (D, Ark.), it was reported May 7 and 9.

According to subpoenaed interview notes, AMPI comptroller Robert O. Isham told Edward Wright that "phony bonuses" paid to AMPI employes were subsequently used to make contributions to Johnson's "$1,000 Club," a group comprised of major campaign donors. The payments were later restored to the co-op when the corporation set up a legitimate political spending arm, TAPE (Trust for Agricultural Political Education).

AMPI continued to maintain a close relationship with Johnson after Nixon's election, according to subpoenaed statements.

Another court document quoted George Mehren as saying that AMPI leased a plane from a holding company for the Johnson financial interests for $94,000 a year. The lease, which Mehren termed "lush" and Johnson family spokesmen labeled "a bargain," was signed by Mehren's predecessor, Harold Nelson, despite opposition from AMPI's board of directors, the document stated. When he became general manager, Mehren said, he tried to cancel the agreement but was unable to win Johnson's approval. He agreed to cosign the lease, Mehren stated, when "it became plain to me that AMPI was in no position to charge the immediate past president of the U.S. with being party to a fraudulent transaction."

He also told Wright that Johnson welcomed the payments on the plane as a "supplement" to his "retirement income." Mehren also claimed that Johnson had told him in 1972 that "the dairy people in his last campaign had agreed to give $250,000 but had not done so and he had forgotten it."

It was reported May 5 that David Parr, an Arkansas attorney for AMPI and at one time the dairy co-op's second ranking official, hoped to raise $2 million in cash for Rep. Mills' race for the Democratic presidential nomination. (Mills, who was chairman of the House Ways and Means Committee, had been one of the chief backers of legislation mandating an increase in the federal support price of milk.)

Parr assigned five-seven salaried employes of AMPI to work for the Mills campaign, according to statements from Lilly and Isham. The assistance was ended in early 1972 when Mehren was named general manager in a corporate shakeup.

Nader criticizes Mills' funding—The Tax Reform Research Group, which was affiliated with consumer advocate Ralph Nader, April 1 accused Mills of obtaining campaign aid from groups that had "some special interest in receiving favorable legislation from the House Ways and Means Committee."

"Mills was heavily supported by big business interests" representing "milk, oil, beer and medicine," the report stated.

The research group investigated the sources of $231,027 in contributions. (The total cost of Mills' campaign was $274,836.) The two largest contributions received by Mills were from the dairy industry ($60,100) and energy interests ($33,400).

Jacobsen indictment dismissed. A false declaration indictment against Jake Jacobsen, a Texas lawyer accused of lying in connection with money allegedly given to the Administration in return for an increase in federal milk price supports by major dairy cooperatives, was dismissed on a technicality May 3 by Federal Judge George L. Hart Jr.

Hart ruled that Jacobsen's answers to a question posed by the Watergate prosecutors were "literally true." Jacobsen had been asked about his role in an alleged $10,000 payoff made by Associated Milk Producers Inc., a Texas-based co-op, to John B. Connally Jr., then Treasury secretary.

Jacobsen had replied, "That is correct," to the prosecution's question, "And it is your testimony that the $10,000 was the $10,000 which you put into that [safe deposit] box within a number of weeks after it was given to you by Mr. [Robert] Lilly [an AMPI executive] and it was untouched by you between then and the time you looked at it with the FBI agent [on Nov. 27, 1973]?"

Hart ruled that in the poorly worded question the government had not asked Jacobsen whether the statement was true or false.

Lehigh Valley co-op pleads guilty. Lehigh Valley Cooperative Farmers, an Allentown, Pa. dairy co-op, pleaded guilty May 6 to charges that it had illegally contributed $50,000 in corporate funds to President Nixon's re-election race.

Federal court in Washington imposed the maximum fine for the criminal offense—$5,000. No corporate official was named in the charge. According to the Watergate prosecutors' office, two separate $25,000 donations (in $100 bills) were given to the Nixon campaign between April 19-27, 1972, and became part of the money used by campaign official Frederick C. LaRue to buy the silence of the Watergate break-in defendants.

Pulitzer Prizes. The 58th annual Pulitzer Prizes in journalism, letters and music were presented in New York May 7. For the second consecutive year prizes went to journalists who investigated the activities of President Nixon and irregularities in his re-election campaign. [For further details, see p. 95G1]

Kleindienst pleads guilty. Former Attorney General Richard G. Kleindienst pleaded guilty May 16 to a misdemeanor charge that he had refused to testify "accurately and fully" before a Congressional committee investigating the Administration's handling of the controversial International Telephone & Telegraph Corp. (ITT) antitrust settlement. The guilty plea was entered in federal district court in Washington.

The minor criminal offense related to Kleindienst's testimony in March and April 1972 before the Senate Judiciary Committee, which was considering his nomination to succeed John Mitchell as attorney general.

Kleindienst was the first person who had served as the nation's top law enforcement officer to be convicted of criminal misconduct. (Another former attorney general, Harry Daugherty, was indicted but not convicted for his role in the Harding Administration's Teapot Dome Scandal.) At the time of the Senate hearings, Kleindienst was serving as acting attorney general. While supervising the Justice Department's ITT cases, he was deputy attorney general, the department's second ranking post. Kleindienst resigned as attorney general in April 1973 as a consequence of the widening Watergate affair.

Kleindienst pleaded guilty to concealing from the committee his communication about ITT with President Nixon and John Mitchell and circumstances surrounding the Justice Department's decision to appeal one of the antitrust cases against ITT to the Supreme Court. In sworn committee testimony, Kleindienst had said, "I was not interfered with by anybody at the White House. I was not importuned. I was not pressured. I was not directed."

Later statements issued by Kleindienst and White House documents released recently contradicted this testimony.

In a talk with reporters after court, Watergate Special Prosecutor Leon Jaworski defended his decision not to bring perjury charges, which involved the commission of felonies, against Kleindienst. Reports had been circulating for several months that Kleindienst was engaging in plea bargaining with Jaworski's office in order to prevent the filing of felony charges that would have resulted in his automatic disbarment as a lawyer.

Jaworski confirmed the plea bargaining reports in a letter to Kleindienst's attorney Herbert J. Miller, setting out the terms of an arrangement allowing Kleindienst to plead guilty to the lesser offense in return for cooperating with the prosecution's ITT investigation. (The letter, dated May 10, was released May 16.)

According to the plea bargaining arrangement, if Kleindienst agreed to plead guilty, "this will dispose of all charges of which this office is presently aware arising out of his testimony at his confirmation hearings, arising out of his handling of documents during his hearings, and arising out of his appearance before the August 1973 grand jury on Dec. 21, 1973, unless substantial new evidence develops demonstrating that Mr. Kleindienst has failed to disclose material matters relating to the ITT matter .... If evidence is developed that Mr. Kleindienst was involved in any criminal obstruction of the ITT antitrust cases or any other matter within the Justice Department, this [guilty plea] disposition will not bar his prosecution for that offense."

In his letter, Jaworski declared that the "investigation has failed to disclose any criminal conduct by Mr. Kleindienst in the manner in which he handled the ITT antitrust cases." Jaworski also praised Kleindienst for defying a direct "presidential order to abandon an appeal and leave the government without any relief [in an ITT case]." (Kleindienst said previously he had threatened to resign if the order were not rescinded.)

(After court, Jaworski told reporters that in bringing charges against Kleindienst, there was "no implication intended" that President Nixon had acted illegally by issuing instructions about the ITT case.)

Under an arrangement with the judge, Kleindienst was allowed to leave the court without talking with reporters. In a statement issued later that day, Kleindienst admitted he was "wrong in not having been more candid with the [Senate] committee." He said he pleaded guilty to the misdemeanor charge "out of respect for the criminal justice system of the U.S. and the indisputable fact that the system must have equal application to all. This same respect for the criminal justice system required that I voluntarily and fully cooperate with the Watergate special prosecution force," and Kleindienst added, "I am morally certain that I have done so."

Sentencing was postponed pending a probation officer's report. Kleindienst told the court he had been promised no specific sentence in return for his cooperation. The law provided for a fine ranging from $100–$1,000 and up to one year in jail, but the court could suspend sentence.

The only other person indicted in connection with the ITT investigation was California Lt. Gov. Ed Reinecke.

Gurney indictment dismissed. Leon County (Fla.) Judge Charles McClure May 17 dismissed a misdemeanor indictment that had charged Sen. Edward J. Gurney (R, Fla.) with violating a state law on campaign contributions. Characterizing the indictment as "fatally defective," McClure said the law under which Gurney had been indicted was unconstitutional. He also said that the grand jury that had indicted Gurney had heard "highly improper" and "prejudicial" legal advice, an apparent reference to State Sen. Marshall Harris (D, Miami), who had taken the case to the grand jury.

Dairy officials plead guilty. Two officials of the Lehigh Valley Cooperative Farmers entered guilty pleas in federal district court in Washington in connection with illegal contributions made by the dairy co-op to President Nixon's re-election campaign. The co-op had pleaded guilty to a misdemeanor charge May 6.

Richard L. Allison, who was recently dismissed as president of the co-op because of his role in authorizing the $50,000 contribution, pleaded guilty May 17 and was given a suspended fine of $1,000 for his misdemeanor offense.

Francis X. Carroll, Lehigh's Washington-based attorney and lobbyist who had also been fired by the co-op, pleaded guilty May 28 to a misdemeanor charge of aiding Allison in the transaction. Carroll's fine was also suspended.

Allison disputed the Nixon finance committee's version of the contribution. He said a $35,000 cash honorarium was paid April 20, 1972 when Agriculture Secretary Earl Butz addressed a co-op meeting. Subsequently, Carroll "came back and said it would cost more money," Allison testified. Another $25,000 was then turned over.

Lawyers for Allison and Carroll said they did not know what happened to the remaining $10,000.

Court rejects Reinecke plea. A federal district court judge May 20 refused to dismiss a perjury indictment against California Lt. Gov. Ed Reinecke, who had been charged in connection with the Administration's handling of antitrust suits against the International Telephone & Telegraph Corp. (ITT). Reinecke had contended that he had been misled with promises of leniency and trapped by the Watergate special prosecutor's staff into cooperating with their ITT investigation.

The court also refused Reinecke's request that the trial, scheduled to begin in Washington in July, be moved to California.

Nixon rejects requests. President Nixon informed the House Judiciary Committee May 22 that he would not comply with two subpoenas for Watergate-related tapes and documents the panel had issued a week before for its impeachment inquiry. Nixon also said that any future subpoenas "allegedly dealing with Watergate" would be rejected.

Earlier in the day, presidential counsel James D. St. Clair informed the committee that its requests for additional material on the International Telephone and Telegraph Corp. (ITT) antitrust controversy and campaign contributions by the dairy industry would not be met, with the possible exception of an edited transcript of one conversation on the ITT case. [For further details, see p. 147D1]

Watergate panel loses tape appeal. The U.S. Court of Appeals for the District of Columbia ruled 7–0 May 23 that the Senate Watergate Committee had not shown a compelling enough need for tapes of five presidential conversations to require enforcement of its subpoena for the tapes. The decision upheld and expanded upon a lower court ruling which, while dismissing the panel's suit to enforce the subpoena, had rejected President Nixon's blanket claim of confidentiality over presidential communications. [For further details, see p. 148B1]

Jaworski seeks 'enemies' conversation. Special prosecutor Leon Jaworski petitioned U.S. District Court Judge John J. Sirica May 28 to release a previously-withheld portion of a presidential conversation which, according to Jaworski, could contain evidence of Administration attempts to "abuse and politicize" the Internal Revenue Service (IRS). Part of the tape of the Sept. 15, 1972 conversation, involving President Nixon, former aide H. R. Haldeman and former counsel John W. Dean 3rd, had been turned over to a grand jury, but Sirica had upheld a White House claim of executive privilege regarding a 17-minute section. [For further details, see p. 149C2]

No ITT antitrust crime seen. Special Watergate prosecutor Leon Jaworski said May 30 that his staff had uncovered no evidence that International Telephone & Telegraph Corp. (ITT) officials had committed any criminal offenses in connection with a 1971 settlement of the government's antitrust suits against the firm.

Jaworski's comments were contained in a letter to Rep. J. J. Pickle (Tex.), the ranking Democrat on the Special Investigations Subcommittee of the House Commerce Committee, one of several Congressional panels examining various aspects of ITT's links to the Administration. However, Jaworski said the case against ITT "was not closed." Allegations that ITT officials had improperly influenced the Internal Revenue Service (IRS) and the Securities and Exchange Commission (SEC) would be "vigorously pursued," he said.

Jaworski also assured Pickle that the staff would continue to investigate charges that ITT officials had committed perjury during Congressional hearings.

Pickle had written Jaworski in November 1973 to complain of inaction on the ITT investigation begun by Jaworski's predecessor, Archibald Cox. The probe had centered on charges that the antitrust settlement resulted from ITT's pledge to underwrite the 1972 Republican Convention, then scheduled for San Diego.

Jaworski said his investigation focusing on the IRS and SEC would continue "under new leadership and a reorganized staff," a reference to the recent resignations of three staff lawyers, Joseph J. Connolly, Paul R. Hoeber and Lawrence A. Hammond. They had reportedly quit out of dissatisfaction with the decision to allow former Attorney General Richard Kleindienst to plead guilty to a misdemeanor charge related to the ITT case.

Nixon bars release of Stans' papers. President Nixon filed a formal claim of executive privilege May 30 in an effort to block the release of his correspondence with Maurice Stans regarding persons under consideration for federal appointments. Stans, who had served as commerce secretary from 1969–72, had been Nixon's chief fund raiser during the 1968 and 1972 elections and had headed the Finance Committee to Re-elect the President.

Chief U.S. District Court Judge George L. Hart Jr. May 24 had ordered Stans to comply with a subpoena and turn over his files on Nixon campaign contributions to a Watergate grand jury investigating charges of bribery and campaign finance law violations. Stans had challenged the grand jury's request in a three-month legal battle.

In ordering compliance with the subpoena, Hart rejected Stans' claim that the records were his personal papers and were protected by constitutional guarantees against unlawful search and seizure.

The material sought by the Watergate prosecutor's staff dated from 1968 until February 1974 (when Stans was still chairman of the finance committee) and included the period when Stans served as commerce secretary.

Hart had ordered Stans May 17 to produce the documents for in camera (private) inspection by the court. In his ruling May 24, Hart said that records in 17 files "show conclusively that Mr. Stans had frequent contacts with [political] contributors during his tenure" as commerce secretary. Six other folders, Hart said, were personal in nature and were not subject to the subpoena.

It was revealed during the May 17 hearing that Stans had transferred his papers to the finance committee's office when he became chairman in 1972. The documents remained there, but keys to the files had been turned over to Stans Feb. 25, when the grand jury's subpoena was served. Stans had refused to release the documents since then.

The Watergate prosecutor's office argued that the papers were the property of the finance committee and that records throughout the 1968–74 period dealt with campaign donations. According to the grand jury subpoena, the political papers sought included lists of major donors and others entitled to federal jobs as rewards for their contributions, lists of noncontributors and names of those Stans felt had not given enough. This latter group was known as the "S" list, according to the special prosecutor's office.

In his May 30 letter to Hart, Nixon said he was asserting "the constitutional privilege to refuse to disclose confidential information when disclosure would be contrary to the public interest."

"As a result of certain unusual circumstances," however, Nixon said he was waiving that claim in connection with an investigation of four persons who had been major donors to his campaign and who had been offered or nominated for ambassadorial posts—Ruth Farkas, Vincent de Roulet, Cornelius V. Whitney and J. Fife Symington Jr.

According to Senate sources, Whitney had told the Senate Watergate Committee that he had secretly contributed $250,000 to the Nixon campaign in expectation he would be named ambassador to Spain, the Washington Post reported May 31. Whitney's money was later returned and he was not named to the post. The prosecutor's office was investigating charges of job-buying in connection with the other persons named.

House panel warns Nixon. The House Judiciary Committee formally notified President Nixon May 30 that his refusal to comply with its subpoenas "might constitute a ground for impeachment" that the committee could take before the House. The committee also approved May 30 issuance of another subpoena for White House tapes and documents and voted to continue its impeachment hearings on evidence in closed sessions. [For further details, see p. 150F3]

Nixon's Support Erodes
as Impeachment Hearings Begin

Committee votes noncompliance. The House Judiciary Committee voted 20–18 May 1 to inform President Nixon by letter that he had "failed to comply with the committee's subpoena" requesting White House tapes and documents.

The vote was almost along party lines. Two of the panel's 21 Democrats—Reps. John Conyers Jr. (Mich.) and Jerome R. Waldie (Calif.)—voted against the motion because they considered it too weak; they favored holding the President in contempt of the House. One of the committee's 17 Republicans, Rep. William S. Cohen (Me.). voted for the Democratic motion to send the letter and became the deciding vote.

Earlier, Cohen had proposed adding to a letter of noncompliance the committee's hope that a compromise could be worked out. This was rejected by a 27–11 vote; the Democrats generally felt it was too weak and the Republicans did not care to join in the noncompliance view.

Conyers' motion to recommend contempt action against the President was rejected 32–5.

The committee decision came during a long evening session. In addition to the absence of 11 of the 42 subpoenaed conversations, because they had not been recorded or could not be found [See above], the President's response to the subpoena did not cover notes or memorandums or Dictabelts requested under the subpoena.

The committee's special counsel John M. Doar also informed the panel the White House transcripts were "not accurate." After comparison with some overlapping material obtained previously, some of it from the special prosecutor, the staff's own tape experts, Doar said, had been able to "pick up parts of conversations" that were marked "unintelligible" in some of the White House transcripts.

Doar also said there were sections of the White House transcripts where words had been omitted without any notation that the deletion had been made. Doar stressed that he was not suggesting there had been any "intentional distortion" in the White House version, only that the committee staff could detect, if the actual tapes were available, many of the parts marked "unintelligible" by the White House.

Doar advised the committee it would not be "prudent" for the two senior committee members, as the President offered, to attempt to verify the accuracy of the transcripts without professional help. Chairman Peter W. Rodino Jr. (D, N.J.), who would be one of the verifiers along with Rep. Edward Hutchinson (R, Mich.), agreed. Rodino said "it would be absolutely impossible for me to adequately and fully and responsibly authenticate" the transcripts.

(Nixon's special counsel James D. St. Clair said April 30 if the proposed verification procedure was not satisfactory to the committee as a whole there was "no insuperable bar" to seek the President's consent for other members of the committee to hear the tapes. It was "a matter of practicality," he said, not a constitutional issue.)

The partisan split in the committee on the transcript issue was apparent from the outset. Even before the President's offer of the transcripts April 29, Rodino said the actual tapes were "necessary and relevant" to the House inquiry and transcripts would not suffice. However, Hutchinson said if the transcripts displayed by Nixon on TV represented "the complete record of Watergate, which the President says it does, then I think it would be adequate."

The same day, Rep. Robert McClory (R, Ill.) said the transcripts would be "both an adequate compliance with the committee's subpoena and sufficient for the committee's investigation." But Waldie described Nixon's response to the committee as "condescending and contemptuous" and said "his duty is to respond to the subpoena."

The committee's Republicans met April 30 with the House Republican leadership. House GOP Leader John J. Rhodes (Ariz.) reported afterwards "the overwhelming majority" believed Nixon was in "substantial compliance" with the subpoena.

The split exended to interpretation of the transcripts. McClory said May 1 he found the March 21, 1973 transcript "ambiguous" and unlikely either to "help or hurt" Nixon. Rep. George E. Danielson (D, Calif.) said the same transcript was "pretty damning of the President" and would provide grounds for impeachment unless rebutted.

Hearings set, rules adopted—Rodino announced May 1 the committee planned to begin hearings the following week on the evidence in hand. The staff would present the material to the members at the initial sessions, which would be closed.

In rules of procedure for the hearings adopted unanimously May 2, the committee approved television and radio coverage of open sessions and of participation within limits, for presidential counsel James D. St. Clair. St. Clair would be permitted to attend all the sessions, open or closed; to call witnesses for the President, although he would be required to tell the committee in advance "precisely" what the testimony was expected to be; to make objections relating to examination of witnesses or admissibility of testimony, subject to the chair's rulings; to question any witness, subject to the chair's decisions on length and scope of the questioning.

A Republican motion to give St. Clair the full right to cross-examine witnesses was rejected by the committee 23–15. Democratic attempts to limit St. Clair's participation also were rejected by similar margins. Rodino, who urged extension of the privilege of objection to St. Clair, assured the committee "I will not tolerate any obstruction."

The committee adopted by a 19–17 vote a rule reducing the quorum number for the hearings to 10, half the customary

*Text of the letter:

Dear Mr. President: The Committee on the Judiciary has directed me to advise you that it finds as of 10 a.m. April 30 you have failed to comply with the Committee's subpoena of April 11, 1974.

Signed
Peter W. Rodino

number. The rule was supported by Rodino and Hutchinson, who considered it necessary to avoid forced adjournment during long sessions.

White House rejects view—Deputy White House Press Secretary Gerald L. Warren May 2 rejected the committee's finding that the President was not in compliance with the subpoena. "We feel it is complete," he said of submission of the transcripts, "and we feel it gives the House Judiciary Committee the facts with which to make a fair judgment."

Quashing of Jaworski subpoena asked. President Nixon's lawyers sought to quash another subpoena from the special Watergate prosecution May 1, and U.S. Judge John J. Sirica May 2 postponed a decision on the issue until at least May 8, when he scheduled a hearing. A response to the subpoena, which covered 64 White House conversations, had been due May 2.

The taped conversations were being sought by the prosecution as further necessary data in preparation for the trial of seven men in the Watergate cover-up conspiracy case and as potential exculpatory information for the defendants.

The bid to quash the subpoena was based on the claim of executive privilege, or the President's prerogative to assert confidentiality of presidential communication, and the contention that the prosecutor had not shown that the materials being sought were either relevant or admissible as evidence at the trial. The claim of executive privilege was extended only to the portions of the subpoenaed materials that had not yet been made public. According to the White House brief, this would exclude 20 of the 64 subpoenaed conversations, "portions" of which were contained in the transcripts released April 30 to the House Judiciary Committee.

The President's counsel asserted it was the President's decision, "rather than for a court, to determine when it was constitutionally permissible for a president to refuse to produce information."

As for the exculpatory evidence, the White House counsel said the rule requiring disclosure of material for defendants did not apply to material protected by executive privilege and, in any case, the President "would be willing to consider" specific requests by defendants on the issue.

In court May 2, Philip A. Lacovara, counsel for the special prosecutor, bid for immediate release of the conversations bereft of confidentiality through issuance of the transcripts. White House lawyer John McCahill contended that privilege had been waived on the transcripts but not on the tapes from which the transcripts were drawn.

The move to fight the subpoena was disclosed to reporters April 30 by Nixon's Watergate counsel, James D. St. Clair.

Albert, Sullivan deny Dean statements. House Speaker Carl Albert (D, Okla.) May 1 dismissed as "complete fabrication" the statement by John Dean in the White House tape transcripts that Albert had requested the General Accounting Office (GAO) to investigate Republican campaign practices.

Regarding the Sept. 15, 1972 conversation involving Nixon, Dean and H. R. Haldeman, Albert said he had "never talked to the GAO in my life or the controller general about doing anything to the White House." Albert also said he was unaware of any White House pressure being applied to him, as Nixon and Haldeman had suggested during the meeting.

William C. Sullivan, former assistant director of the Federal Bureau of Investigation (FBI), called Dean a "liar" and "double-crosser" who had betrayed him by giving information on political use of the FBI by previous administrations to sources other than the White House, the Boston Globe reported May 7.

Sullivan denied Dean's suggestion to Nixon during the March 13, 1973 meeting that Sullivan would be willing to disclose FBI secrets in return for a job as director of a proposed domestic security agency.

Nixon speaks in Phoenix. President Nixon was cheered by a partisan crowd of about 15,000 persons in Phoenix, Ariz. May 3. In his first appearance outside Washington since public release of transcripts of Watergate conversations, the President said "the time has come to put Watergate behind us and get on with the business of America" and "I intend to stay on this job." Most of his speech was devoted to the themes of world peace and domestic prosperity.

Anti-Nixon demonstrators were present, about 1,500 outside the hall and 150 inside.

Also present were Arizona's Republican senators, Barry M. Goldwater and Paul J. Fannin, and Gov. John R. Williams. The state's two Republican members of Congress also were present, House minority leader John J. Rhodes and Sam Steiger.

The state's only other member of the House, Democrat Morris K. Udall, delivered the official Democratic rebuttal to the Nixon speech, at another site (both speeches were carried over a statewide radio broadcast). "The fate of Richard Nixon lies not in political oratory, the maneuvers of clever White House lawyers or advance men who gather crowds to hear him speak in selected states before selected audiences," Udall said. "Mr. Nixon's fate rests in the truth and in the judgment of his fellow citizens will make when they get that truth."

Jacobsen indictment dismissed. A false declaration indictment against Jake Jacobsen, a Texas lawyer accused of lying in connection with money allegedly given to the Administration in return for an increase in federal milk price supports by major dairy cooperatives, was dismissed on a technicality May 3 by Federal Judge George L. Hart Jr. [For further details, see p. 134D2]

Lehigh Valley co-op pleads guilty. Lehigh Valley Cooperative Farmers, an Allentown, Pa. dairy co-op, pleaded guilty May 6 to charges that it had illegally contributed $50,000 in corporate funds to President Nixon's re-election race.

Federal court in Washington imposed the maximum fine for the criminal offense—$5,000. No corporate official was named in the charge. According to the Watergate prosecutors' office, two separate $25,000 donations (in $100 bills) were given to the Nixon campaign between April 19–27, 1972, and became part of the money used by campaign official Frederick C. LaRue to buy the silence of the Watergate break-in defendants.

Kalmbach testifies. Herbert Kalmbach, the President's personal attorney and chief fund-raiser, told the Senate Watergate Committee staff that a secret midnight meeting was held March 24, 1971 in his Washington hotel room for the purpose of asking dairymen to reconfirm their offer (made in 1970) to contribute $2 million to Nixon's campaign, it was reported May 6.

The information was passed on to the House Judiciary Committee, according to the Washington Post, and formed the basis of the committee's request for White House tapes and other documents relating to the milk fund controversy. [For further details, see p. 133D3]

Glenn defeats Metzenbaum. Sen. Howard M. Metzenbaum lost the Democratic senatorial primary in Ohio May 7 to John H. Glenn Jr., the first U.S. astronaut to orbit the earth. The contest was bitterly fought on a personal level, with frequent Glenn references to Metzenbaum's tax problems.

Glenn, against the Watergate background and President Nixon's tax problems, stressed the need for integrity in government.

GOP criticism mounts. Senate Republican Leader Hugh Scott (Pa.) severely criticized and renounced support May 7 for the "immoral" activities delineated in the transcripts of White House conversations on Watergate issued by President Nixon April 30. Scott said the transcripts revealed "deplorable, disgusting, shabby, immoral performances" by all participants in the conversations.

In a Senate speech, Scott said: "I am not going to take any position supporting any action which involved any form of immorality or criminality as the transcripts indicate. At the same time, I call for a suspension of judgment. I hope that all of us will assume the presumption of innocence and that we will withhold our judgment as to specific individuals, pending the operation of our great constitutional system. It works; it always has; it will this time."

This major blow to the President's Watergate defense was followed by others. House Republican Leader John J. Rhodes (Ariz.) said May 7 he "wouldn't quarrel" with Scott's description of the transcript performances. Rhodes said May 9 "the content of the transcripts was devastating" and resignation a "possible option." He did not see "much choice" between resignation and impeachment, since both were "traumatic." Rhodes said as a lawyer he preferred the impeachment process as the best way to reach the truth, but he was unsure if it were worth the agony or could "settle the dust."

Rhodes thought Nixon could continue to operate effectively as President at the moment, but he said "we might have to reconsider it" if "the erosion" of the President's position continued. He said Nixon's departure and the accession of Vice President Gerald Ford would be "beneficial" to the Republican Party.

Rep. John B. Anderson (Ill.), chairman of the House Republican Conference, predicted May 9 Nixon would be impeached if he did not resign. Nixon had "damaged himself irreparably" in disclosing the conversations, Anderson said. "The transcripts make it quite clear he was deeply involved in Watergate on the 13th of March [1973]." The President had repeatedly stated he was unaware of the cover-up until March 21, 1973.

Interior Secretary Rogers C. B. Morton said in a speech at Springfield, Mo. May 9 "we have seen a breakdown in our national leadership." "We have seen a breakdown in our ethics of government," he said, "which I deplore and which I am having a very difficult time in living with."

Sen. Marlow W. Cook (R, Ky.) suggested May 9 that Nixon seriously consider resigning because of the "moral turpitude" revealed in the transcripts.

Vice President Gerald R. Ford mixed his reaction to the transcript material, which he deplored, with renewed support for the President. He was "a little disappointed" by the transcripts, he said in Myrtle Beach, S.C. May 3. In reply to a reporter's question, "Is this the President you have known for 25 years?" he said "the answer is no." In Ann Arbor, Mich. May 4, in a commencement address at his alma mater, the University of Michigan, Ford said the transcripts "do not exactly confer sainthood on anyone concerned." In a New York speech May 6, he added: "But when you add it all up, I haven't lost my faith in the capability of the President to do a great job."

At Eastern Illinois University in Charleston May 9, Ford spoke of "a continuous series of revelations and reports of corruption, malfeasance and wrongdoing in the federal government, not the least of which is the sorry mess which carries the label of Watergate." These were "hammer blows to the confidence the American people have placed in their government," he said, and "a grave situation" did exist. At a news conference later in Chicago, he expressed hope the President would "survive, because I think he's innocent."

Among other GOP comment:

May 6—Rep. John Ashbrook (R, Ohio): "I listened to him [President Nixon] last Monday night [April 29] and for the first time in a year I believed him. Then I read the March 21st [1973] transcript and it was . . . unbelievable."

Rep. Robert McClory (Ill.), second-ranking Republican on the House Judiciary Committee: The "level of conversation" in the transcripts was "injurious to the President and to the presidency."

Rep. William Steiger (R, Wis.): The "biggest disappointment" in the transcripts "is that there is no explicit statement by the President or his staff that any of the activities were morally or governmentally wrong." He did not think the transcripts "conclusively establish either guilt or innocence."

May 7—Sen. John G. Tower (R, Tex.): The transcripts "show there is a lot of cynicism in the White House, that the President did delegate away a lot of authority—inordinately—and that he was not aware of all that was going on."

Sen. Jacob K. Javits (R, N.Y.): The transcripts were "very clearly marked by no basic concern with the public's business."

Rep. Robert H. Michel (Ill.), chairman of the House Republican Campaign Committee: Recalling his campaign work for Nixon in 1972 and the portrait of Nixon drawn in the transcripts, "This is not the kind of man I was recommending."

Key editorial support lost—William Randolph Hearst Jr., editor of the Hearst newspapers and a firm Nixon supporter, said in his Sunday column May 5 (published May 3) the transcript conversations "add up to as damning a document as it is possible to imagine short of an actual indictment." The conversations, he said, revealed Nixon as a man "with a moral blind spot" and made his impeachment inevitable. "The gang talking on the tapes, even the censored version, comes through in just that way—a gang of racketeers talking over strategy in a jam-up situation," Hearst said. "Perhaps the kindest way of putting it is that they amount to an unwitting confession, in which he stands convicted by his own words as a man who deliberately and repeatedly tried to keep the truth from the American people."

The Chicago Tribune, an influential Republican newspaper, in an editorial in its May 9 edition (published May 8), called for Nixon to leave office for the sake of "the presidency, the country and the free world." Speaking of the transcripts, it said "We have seen the private man and we are appalled." "The key word is immoral," it said of Nixon. "Two roads are open. One is resignation. The other is impeachment. Both are legitimate and would satisfy the need to observe due process."

The Omaha World-Herald called May 7 for Nixon's resignation. Although it had endorsed Nixon's presidential candidacy three times, the paper said his accomplishments were "overshadowed now by the appallingly low level of political morality in the White House."

Editorials urging impeachment of the President were published May 10 by the Los Angeles Times and the Cleveland Plain Dealer.

Initial poll results unfavorable—The Gallup Poll reported May 4 that 42% of those who watched or read President Nixon's recent Watergate speech came away with a less favorable opinion of the President. The poll, on the basis of 654 telephone interviews May 2, found only 17% had a more favorable opinion of Nixon, 35% had unchanged opinions (no determination of original opinion).

Other results from the survey: pluralities felt there was enough evidence against Nixon for the House to vote impeachment (44%–41%) but did not want him removed from office (49%–38%); 62% backed the House Judiciary Committee dissatisfaction with the transcripts and insistence on the original tapes; in a credibility test between Nixon and John W. Dean 3rd, Nixon had a slight edge, 38% to 36%.

White House rebuttal—The mounting adverse reaction from Republicans to the revelations of the transcripts led to repeated assertions from the White House that no impeachable offense had been disclosed and President Nixon had no intention of resigning.

While the President was in Spokane May 4, White House Press Secretary Ronald L. Ziegler stressed the necessity not to draw conclusions unless the transcripts were read "in their entirety." He continued the assault begun by the President and his counsel on the credibility of his former counsel John W. Dean 3rd. There were "a very great number of contradictions" between Dean's Senate testimony and the transcripts, Ziegler said. The White House made public that day a paper claiming "misstatements" by Dean "in 16 separate areas, on dozens of occasions."

Reports that the transcripts corroborated much of Dean's testimony before the Senate Watergate committee appeared in the press May 4 from the committee's chairman, Sen. Sam J. Ervin Jr. (D, N.C.), and Republican members Howard H. Baker Jr. (Tenn.) and Lowell P. Weicker Jr. (Conn.).

Support for Nixon also came May 5 from White House chief of staff Alexander M. Haig Jr., who appeared on the ABC "Issues and Answers" program, and Nixon's chief lawyer, James D. St. Clair, who appeared on NBC's "Meet the Press."

"At what point in the review of wrongdoing," Haig asked, "does the review itself involve injustice, excesses and distortions which, in effect, result in the cure being worse than the illness itself?" While he was not condoning "what alleged wrongdoing may have occurred" in Watergate, he said, the time had come "to bring this matter to a conclusion."

St. Clair also stressed that the White House had made a complete accounting of Watergate. He said an important consideration in not releasing the material previously was its possible effect on third persons. "But when it gets down to the fact that by not publishing these," he said, "people begin to believe that he is hiding criminal conduct on his own part, to the extent that it might even threaten the presidency, then something has to give."

On the CBS "Face the Nation" broadcast May 5, Rep. Thomas F. Railsback (R, Ill.) considered the transcripts "a very constructive first step" but only "partial compliance" with the House Judiciary Committee's subpoena for the presidential tapes. Rep. Paul S. Sarbanes (D, Md.) said on the same program the impeachment probe was "a very serious matter indeed" and further material from the White House was necessary. Both were members of the Judiciary Committee.

White House Counselor Dean Burch told reporters May 7, speaking of the transcripts, he tended "to temper my analysis a bit by trying to imagine the human problems that were involved" because some of Nixon's "best and closest assistants and, indeed, friends, were in a hell of a lot of trouble." The March 21, 1973 conversation in the transcript he found "troublesome," he said, because of "the discussion of a payment" to Watergate defendant.

But, Burch stressed, "I don't think the President is impeachable" and he expected Nixon to remain in office. The President, he said, would not resign if impeachment was voted by the House.

Deputy Press Secretary Gerald L. Warren made the same points May 8. "We don't believe the President will be impeached," he said, and the President had made "very clear" there was no consideration of resigning.

"The President will not quit even if hell freezes over," White House Communication's Director Ken W. Clawson said May 9. Presidential counselor Anne L. Armstrong said the same day "I don't see an impeachment offense" and Nixon was "very much against resignation. I think he has the guts to see it through in the proper way."

Dr. John McLaughlin, a Jesuit priest who was a special assistant to Nixon, held a news conference May 8 to assert that "the President acquitted himself throughout these [transcript] discussions with honor." Any conclusion that they were amoral or immoral, he said, "is erroneous, unjust and contains elements of hypocrisy." The transcript material, he said, represented only a fraction of the President's confidential conversations while in office and "we ought to look at the extent to which he has produced a climate of charity in the international community and at home.

Pulitzer Prizes. The 58th annual Pulitzer Prizes in journalism, letters and music were presented in New York May 7. For the second consecutive year prizes went to journalists who investigated the activities of President Nixon and irregularities in his re-election campaign. [For further details, see p. 95G1]

Nixon bars release of more tapes. Special presidential counsel James D. St. Clair announced May 7 that President Nixon would "respectfully" decline "to produce any more Watergate tapes" for use in the House Judiciary Committee's impeachment inquiry, and that Nixon had instructed him to "press forward" with the effort to quash special prosecutor Leon Jaworski's subpoena for tapes of 64 White House conversations.

The surprise announcement came only a few hours after presidential counselor Dean Burch had said St. Clair was attempting to negotiate a settlement with Jaworski, and one day after U.S. District Court Judge John J. Sirica had delayed to May 13 a hearing on the White House motion to quash the prosecution subpoena. Sirica had said he was granting the delay to facilitate "discussions leading to possible compliance with the subpoena."

In his news conference, St. Clair said discussions with Jaworski had broken off, and that Nixon had definitely decided that there would be no "accommodation" with Jaworski or any "further adjustments" in the White House stance against compliance.

Regarding the impeachment panel's request for additional evidence, St. Clair said Nixon would release material on "non-Watergate" matters such as the International Telephone & Telegraph Corp. antitrust controversy and the dairy industry campaign fund issue. But on the Watergate issue, St. Clair said, if the committee issued a subpoena "we are going to have a confrontation, because the President is firm in his resolve that he has done more than is necessary."

Reaction on the Judiciary Committee indicated that there might be further subpoenas on the White House. Chairman Peter Rodino (D, N.J.) and ranking GOP member Edward Hutchinson (Mich.) said May 8 that the panel would begin reviewing the evidence it had, and whenever gaps were found the White House would be requested to provide the necessary additional material. Rodino reportedly presented a plan to committee Democrats under which separate subpoenas would be voted on for each phase of the hearings to fill the gaps.

While reiterating his opposition to subpoenas, which he said were unenforceable, Hutchinson told a news briefing that "a request" should be made if "unavailable" material appeared to be necessary.

Chief committee counsel John M. Doar said May 8 that Nixon had "definitely not" provided the full story on Watergate, adding that he would recommend that the panel subpoena the tapes St. Clair said would be withheld.

Dean's house sold. Sen. Lowell P. Weicker Jr. (R, Conn.) one of the members of the Senate Watergate Committee, bought a house in Alexandria, Va. for $135,000 from John Dean 3rd. Dean, a witness for the Watergate committee, bought the house two years before for $72,500, it was reported May 8.

Judiciary committee begins hearings. The House Judiciary Committee May 9 opened its long-awaited hearings to determine whether to recommend the impeachment of President Nixon.

The committee's leaders pledged in an 18-minute public ceremony to conduct a fair and nonpartisan inquiry. Then, after a brief procedural debate, the committee went into a closed three-hour session to hear a presentation of the events leading up to the June 1972 Watergate burglary.

Well-placed sources said that during the closed meeting the committee briefly discussed the possibility that evidence existed showing that Nixon knew in April 1972 of the political intelligence-gathering scheme that led to the Watergate break-in, the New York Times reported May 10. [See below]

Committee Chairman Peter W. Rodino Jr. (D, N.J.) opened the hearings by stressing "the importance of our undertaking and the wisdom, decency and principle we must bring to it. We understand our high constitutional responsibility. We will faithfully live up to it."

"For some time," Rodino continued, "we have known that the real security of this nation lies in the integrity of its institutions and the trust and informed confidence of its people. We conduct our deliberations in that spirit."

Rodino declared the committee would "thoroughly" examine six areas of inquiry, beginning with "the question of presidential responsibility for the Watergate break-in and its investigation by law enforcement agencies."

"First," he said, "we will consider detailed information assembled by the [committee] staff. This consists of information already on the public record, information developed in executive session by other Congressional committees, information furnished by the federal grand jury of the District of Columbia and other information." After the May 9 session, the committee would meet regularly three days a week for all-day sessions, beginning May 14, Rodino said.

Rodino noted that special presidential counsel James D. St. Clair was present at the ceremony and would attend the committee's sessions. "After the initial proceedings are completed," Rodino said, "Mr. St. Clair will be afforded the opportunity to respond to the presentation orally or in writing, as determined by the committee."

St. Clair and his assistants "understand the committee's rules of procedure and the committee's rules of confidentiality, and they are bound by those rules,"

Rodino asserted.

(St. Clair had told newsmen earlier that he was confident Nixon "will not be impeached. The House of Representatives will not impeach.")

Rep. Edward Hutchinson (Mich.), the ranking Republican on the committee, followed Rodino and noted that impeachment of a president was "the most awesome power constitutionally vested in the House of Representatives . . . one of those great checks and balances written in our Constitution to ameliorate the stark doctrine of the separation of powers."

"I trust that the members of this committee embark upon their awesome task, each in his own resolve to lay aside ordinary political considerations and to weigh the evidence according to the law," Hutchinson said.

Rep. Harold D. Donohue (D, Mass.) rose after Hutchinson concluded his remarks and moved that during the initial presentation of evidence the committee go into executive session, in accordance with a House rule governing "evidence of testimony at an investigative hearing [that] may tend to defame, degrade or incriminate any person."

After a few procedural questions were answered, the committee passed the motion by a vote of 31-6. Those who voted negatively were all Democrats. One committee member, Walter Flowers (D, Ala.) did not vote because he was in his home state attending a ground-breaking ceremony.

Two opponents of the motion later issued statements protesting the private examination of evidence. Rep. John Conyers (D, Mich.) asserted: "It is absurd for us to slam the door on the American people. It was exaggerated governmental secrecy which led to Watergate, and now, as we begin to hear the information which ties the horrors of the past years together, we impose the same secrecy on ourselves."

Rep. Joshua Eilberg (D, Pa.) protested that the White House would leak secret information from the committee to further "a public relations campaign on [Nixon's] behalf." He warned that closed sessions "can only lead to rumor and speculation at a time when the public must know what was truly said and done."

Under the committee's rules of confidentiality, St. Clair was allowed to report evidence only to the President. He told reporters after the closed session that he would consult with Nixon "regularly."

Staff presents evidence—In the closed session May 9 the committee's special counsel, John M. Doar, reportedly read a memorandum outlining the relationship between high White House officials and officials of Nixon's 1972 re-election campaign, and the committee's staff presented documents and testimony related to planning by agents of the re-election campaign for the political intelligence-gathering operation that led to the Watergate break-in.

Authoritative sources quoted by the New York Times May 10 said the most substantial issue raised in the session was whether Nixon was given a general briefing on the intelligence operation on April 4, 1972, when he met with John N. Mitchell, then Nixon campaign manager, and H. R. Haldeman, then White House chief of staff. The sources said a tape recording of that meeting (which was among 75 Watergate-related tapes that St. Clair had said would not be turned over to the committee) might be a "key" piece of evidence.

The April 4 meeting occurred five days after Mitchell allegedly approved a broad-scale intelligence-gathering operation. Gordon Strachan, a former aide to Haldeman, had testified under oath that he had sent a memorandum to Haldeman in early April advising him on the intelligence operation, and that it was referred to in a "talking paper" that Haldeman took with him to the April 4 meeting.

Committee members said after the session that they had learned nothing new from the evidence presented by the staff, but Rep. Don Edwards (D, Calif.) noted that the presentation was "very responsibly done, a very scholarly, fair job."

President to 'fight' to keep office. The White House acted May 10 to squelch rumors flooding Washington that President Nixon would resign.

In the evening, Press Secretary Ronald L. Ziegler telephoned the New York Times with this message: "The city of Washington is full of rumors. All that have been presented to me today are false, and the one that heads the list is the one that says President Nixon intends to resign. His attitude is one of determination that he will not be driven out of office by rumor, speculation, excessive charges or hypocrisy. He is up to the battle, he intends to fight it and he feels he has a personal and constitutional responsibility to do so."

Earlier May 10, White House chief of staff Alexander M. Haig Jr., in an interview with the Associated Press, said: "I think the only thing that would tempt resignation on the part of the President would be if he thought that served the best interests of the American people. At this juncture, I don't see anything on the horizon which would meet that criterion. Admittedly, that's a subjective view on my part, and I think it is one the President shares very strenuously."

(Haig later emphasized that this was not a softening of Nixon's position against resignation but rather an assertion that the public interest was paramount over Nixon's personal interest.)

The rumors of resignation had intensified May 10 with Vice President Gerald Ford's hasty return to Washington from a speaking tour to meet privately with the President. [See below]

Congressional comment critical of the President, continued in the wake of his release of transcripts of his Watergate conversations.

Sen. Richard S. Schweiker (Pa.) May 10 joined those calling for the President's resignation. He was the third Republican senator to urge that course. "I cannot remain silent in the face of the now obvious moral corrosion destroying and debasing the presidency," Schweiker declared.

Sen. Milton R. Young (R, N.D.) said May 10 "it would be a whole lot easier for members of Congress and myself" if Nixon "used the 25th Amendment and stepped aside until this thing is cleared up." The amendment permitted the vice president to assume executive authority if he and the Cabinet persuaded Congress the President was unable to discharge the powers and duties of office. Nixon was "getting in deeper trouble all the time," Young said, and "it's a question of whether he can continue as President." "I doubt if there is anyone in the Senate who'd urge him to stay," Young said. "There wouldn't be over five who you'd call hard-core supporters."

White House response came May 11 from Nixon's daughter, Mrs. David (Julie Nixon) Eisenhower, who reported on a family gathering the night before aboard the presidential yacht on the Potomac. At a press conference with her husband at the White House, Julie, speaking of her father said: "He said he would take this constitutionally down to the wire. He said he would go to the Senate and he said if there were one senator that believes in him, that that is the way it would be."

"I feel that as a daughter it is my obligation to come out here and say, no he is not going to resign," she said, even though "I know that he doesn't want me out here. He doesn't want anyone to construe that I'm trying to answer questions for him."

As for the transcripts, they portrayed "a human being reacting in a difficult situation," she said.

(The President's wife's response was given May 10 by her spokesman, Helen Smith. "Mrs. Nixon is a loyal person herself and she thinks it's time to rally," Mrs. Smith reported. Mrs. Nixon "can stand these things because she feels she knows the truth," she said.)

Later May 11, the President flew to Stillwater, Okla. to address the Oklahoma State University graduating class. On his arrival at the airport, he told a crowd of several thousand persons, "I have that old Okie spirit. I've got it down deep in my heart, and we never give up." At the university, before a crowd of more than 25,000, Nixon said he knew many persons were "concerned about political problems in Washington." "I can say," he continued, "that having presented all the evidence to the House of Representatives,

I hope it will act promptly so the President and Congress can get on with the people's business, as we should."

His speech largely followed the pattern of his recent speeches citing world peace efforts, a strong economy and defense. Several hundred anti-Nixon demonstrators were in the audience, but most of them left as the President began speaking.

Nixon, Ford hold private meeting—The widespread rumors of May 10 that Nixon might soon resign or take some other major step were largely fueled by news that Vice President Ford had been summoned to a private meeting with Nixon.

Questioned about the meeting later in the day, Ford said the subject of resignation had not come up, "but I could infer that he had no intention of resigning."

Ford said Nixon had not expressed displeasure with Ford's bluntly-worded speech in Illinois the previous day, in which Ford had referred to the "grave" situation in government. "As a matter of fact," Ford said, "the President was mostly concerned about the fact that I was working too hard at the job" and had "cautioned me to be a little less on the road and not work so hard on behalf of candidates of the party and speaking to the public generally."

Ford said he was not at liberty to discuss the details of the meeting, but said it covered "a great many subjects": foreign policy, "some of the problems before Congress," and the White House role in the impeachment inquiry.

In a commencement address at Texas A. & M. University May 11, Ford said he had told Nixon that he was not among those "trying to jump off" Nixon's "ship of state." Ford added that his message to all graduates in his series of commencement appearances was that "the government in Washington wasn't about to sink." Ford told a Republican fundraising dinner in Dallas that evening that he "very strongly" disagreed with GOP leaders calling for Nixon's resignation.

In three appearances in the South May 13, Ford stressed positive themes: "America's contributions" to "everything that is right in the world" to state legislators in Baton Rouge, La., and military preparedness in New Orleans and in Pensacola, Fla.

In Pensacola, Ford said he had "diligently read" the White House Watergate transcripts and had "read the news media reports and listened to them." The "overwhelming weight of the evidence," Ford said, "proves the President innocent of any of the charges.

Erosion continues—The erosion of Nixon's leadership continued May 11. "There's an awful lot of pulling and hauling going on," House Republican Leader John Rhodes (Ariz.) said of the continuing signs of Republican disillusionment with the President. House GOP Conference Chairman John Anderson (Ill.) said that "the most propitious time

to convince him to resign would be now," that "once the impeachment resolution is voted on, the lines may have hardened again and the President may have been persuaded that he can last a little longer." Anderson said "he should spare the nation one last agony. . . . If he is capable of a last act of nobility, he should resign."

There was more reaction from the White House. The President would not be "pressured out of office," Haig said May 11, and "we just can't succumb to the firestorms of public opinion." "If anything, there is a greater conviction here," he said, "that the system must work its way. To do anything else would do serious damage."

Republican talk of a resignation focused, as it had in the past, on Sen. Barry Goldwater (R, Ariz.) as a possible bearer of the party's feelings to the President. But Goldwater dissociated himself from such a move. "If anybody tried that right now," he told the Washington Post May 11, "I think he'd [Nixon] tell them to go to hell." "When the time comes to resign, he'll know it" without outside advice, Goldwater said.

Goldwater said at the Naval Academy at Annapolis, Md. May 7 that he did not think Nixon should resign but that, if the House voted impeachment, Nixon would then resign "rather than let the country be dragged through two or three months of terror" in a Senate trial.

Patrick J. Buchanan, a special consultant to the President, told reporters May 14 if a Republican delegation should confront Nixon with a demand for resignation "he would receive them respectfully, he would say he should not resign and he would not resign."

Democratic leaders vs. resignation—Senate Democratic leaders and prominent Senate conservatives voiced opposition to resignation May 13.

Senate Democratic Leader Mike Mansfield (Mont.) said "resignation is not the answer." He said it was "time to keep cool, the evidence must be forthcoming."

Senate Democratic whip Robert Byrd (W. Va.) said if the President resigned under current conditions a significant number of citizens would feel he had been driven from office by his political enemies. "The question of guilt or innocence would never be fully resolved," he said, "the country would remain polarized" and "confidence in government would remain unrestored."

Sen. William E. Brock 3rd (R, Tenn.), who said the transcripts had caused "deep concern and depression" among conservatives, said "the President has a right to decide what he wants to do and to have a trial if he wants it, which he seems to."

Other statements May 13 against resignation were made by Sen. Carl T. Curtis (R, Neb.), who warned against "mob rule," and Sen. Strom Thurmond (R, S.C.), who said Nixon was "the only President we have," and Sen. Henry L.

Bellmon (R, Okla.), who said a resignation "would create a disastrous precedent for future presidents."

The stand by the Democratic leaders was endorsed May 14 by the party's national chairman, Robert S. Strauss, who met in Washington with the House and Senate Democratic leaders along with Gov. Wendell Ford (Ky.), chairman of the Democratic Governors Conference. House Speaker Carl Albert (D, Okla.), a participant, said he did not believe Nixon should or would resign.

Senate Republican Leader Hugh Scott (Pa.) also agreed with the Democrats May 14 "to allow the system to function." "I think our nation is strong enough to withstand the functioning of its own Constitution," Scott said.

Nixon: 'Don't worry,' not resigning—Health, Education and Welfare Secretary Caspar W. Weinberger emerged from a meeting with Nixon May 13 with direct assurance on the matter. He had urged the President not to resign, Weinberger reported, and said Nixon had told him: "Don't worry. There isn't any chance of that whatever."

Transportation Secretary Claude S. Brinegar told the National Press Club May 14 he opposed a resignation. He said he was "shocked, offended and discouraged" by the Watergate "mess" but he made it clear he was "a non-political type" and "such events are beyond my comprehension."

Commerce Secretary Frederick B. Dent told a Greensboro, N.C. audience May 14 Nixon was innocent of criminality, attacked the media for "vindictiveness" and contended the impeachment drive was being led by political enemies who opposed Nixon's policies and his support of free enterprise.

Among other developments: May 11—Former Treasury Secretary John B. Connally Jr. told a GOP group in Milwaukee "the portions of the transcript I've read tell a sad, even sordid story" but no impeachable offense was revealed. He said he believed the impeachment inquiry should "proceed at deliberate speed."

Rep. Mark Andrews (R, N.D.) said "things have reached a point where his leaving office one way or another is the best course for the presidency and the country."

The Americans for Democratic Action approved unanimously in convention resolutions reaffirming its call for Nixon's impeachment, opposing immunity for Nixon from prosecution in return for a possible resignation and advocating that Nixon turn over his duties to the vice president if he were impeached until the Senate trial ended.

The Miami Herald, a 1972 Nixon supporter, called for his impeachment.

May 12—The Chattanooga News-Free Press, another 1972 Nixon supporter, urged Nixon to "stand fast" and said presidents should not be "shouted out of office by clamor."

Indianapolis Mayor Richard Lugar (R) said Nixon had "recorded and transcribed a moral and spiritual tragedy" and "weakened the trust which I cherished in his words and deeds and I am heartsick for him and for our country."

May 13—White House Director of Communications Ken W. Clawson said Nixon was being accused over the transcripts of immorality and "that is not much of a charge for an impeachment trial."

Alf M. Landon, the 1936 GOP presidential nominee, told the Associated Press that resignation was "the easy way." While not advocating impeachment, Landon said the procedure was "the best way to settle all the questions involved in President Nixon's official conduct of this critical, sordid Watergate matter."

May 14—The Greensburg (Pa.) Tribune-Review said in an editorial Nixon "makes us feel, somehow, unclean." It urged impeachment and said Nixon should step aside pending the Senate trial. The publisher was Richard Mellon Scaife, the second-largest contributor ($1 million) to Nixon's 1972 campaign.

Nixon again vows he will not resign— President Nixon said May 16 he was determined to stay in office, even if impeached by the House and tried by the Senate. The statement was made to syndicated columnist James J. Kilpatrick during an interview requested by Nixon.

"I would have to rule out resignation. And I would have to rule out the rather fatuous suggestion that I take the 25th Amendment and just step out and have Vice President Ford step in for a while," Nixon told Kilpatrick. Nixon asserted that the office of the Presidency would be fatally weakened if he resigned.

If impeached, Nixon said, he would defend himself before the Senate, while continuing to perform his presidential duties.

Kilpatrick described the 80-minute session as "more of a monologue than an interview." The President, he said, "looked well and strong," but seemed to have "lost some of the edge of sharp incisiveness that he exhibited a few years ago." Nixon's "conversation tends to run off on tangents" and was "littered with broken sentences," Kilpatrick wrote.

Hunt denies blackmail. Convicted Watergate conspirator E. Howard Hunt Jr. said May 10 that his requests for money from the Nixon administration—a central subject of the edited transcripts released by the White House—were not intended as blackmail, but were "routine" actions to provide security for his family and to pay overdue legal fees.

Hunt commented at a taping of "Firing Line," the television interview program conducted by columnist William F. Buckley Jr., a long-time friend of Hunt.

Hunt said the "blackmail" characterization by former presidential counsel John W. Dean 3rd in a March 21, 1973

meeting with President Nixon was a "total misperception" on Dean's part caused by Dean's "youth, inexperience," and "total unfamiliarity with clandestine activities." Hunt contended that there was a traditional and unwritten agreement that an intelligence agent's employer would provide family support if the agent was captured.

Hunt recounted that he had submitted his request for $120,000 to Paul O'Brien, an attorney for the Committee to Re-elect the President, but did not "threaten" to disclose any "seamy" activities. Hunt quoted himself: "Look, you people are in arrears. . ., I'm going to jail in a few days, and if you didn't know it, I also took part in some seamy activities for the White House on the West Coast." Hunt said O'Brien apparently relayed the request to Dean, who "construed it according to his likes, and like Chicken Little he went running to the President." Hunt replied "no" when Buckley asked if he had considered revealing the acts if the money had not been paid.

The portrayal of him as a blackmailer, Hunt said, was a White House strategy to make him a scapegoat for the Watergate affair.

Liddy in contempt of Congress. G. Gordon Liddy, one of the original Watergate defendants, was found guilty of contempt of Congress May 10 for refusing to answer questions before the House Armed Services Subcommittee on Intelligence Operations. Liddy, who had refused to even be sworn in before the committee, did not contest the facts or ask for a jury trial. U.S. District Court Judge John H. Pratt gave Liddy a six-month suspended sentence and placed him on probation for one year. Liddy's sentence was light, Pratt noted, because of other prison sentences already given him.

Pratt rejected defense arguments that the subcommittee had committed procedural errors in summoning Liddy to testify.

Buzhardt criticizes slur reports. J. Fred Buzhardt Jr., counsel to the President, May 12 criticized reports that ethnic slurs allegedly made by the President had been deleted from the White House transcripts released April 30. Appearing on the CBS television program "Face the Nation," Buzhardt said the reports were part of "a concerted campaign . . . to poison the public mind against the President by any means, foul or fair."

He had listened to some 40 White House tapes, Buzhardt said, and was unable to find anything he would construe as an ethnic slur.

The New York Times had reported May 12 that Nixon had referred to two staff members of the Securities and Exchange Commission (SEC) as "Jew boys" and to U.S. District Court Judge John J. Sirica as a "wop."

An unidentified White House spokesman confirmed that the Feb. 28, 1973 transcript did contain reported references to Jews, but denied they were anti-Semitic.

Transcript error noted. The White House conceded May 13 that the edited transcript of one of Nixon's Watergate conversations contained two different versions of a short section of that conversation.

In the transcript of an April 16, 1973 meeting between Nixon and Assistant Attorney General Henry E. Petersen—as published by the Government Printing Office—the first version covering about one page was followed by the second on the facing page. The following example fell about mid-way in the section: First version:

Nixon speaking: "Can't have the President—after all—after all these months and what we've gone through and now once I have learned something of it I say 'bah.' "

Second version: "You can't have the press—after all these months and what we have gone through and all. Once, I find something out—I say—ACT!"

Another statement by Nixon shortly afterwards contained 13 notations of "inaudible"; the second contained four.

The error became known when brought to the attention of the Washington Post by John B. Northrop, a vice president of a New York City brokerage firm. Deputy White House Press Secretary Gerald L. Warren confirmed the mistake, saying "We did the best we could." Warren repeated Nixon's offer to let the two ranking members of the House Judiciary Committee listen to the actual tapes if the panel was dissatisfied with the transcripts.

Questioned further on the issue the next day, Warren said that in transcribing the tapes, White House secretaries had gone "over and over the various portions" to "pull out all the words possible." Warren explained that apparently "one of the revisions was just added onto one of the earlier versions." He asserted, however, that "the substance of the tapes is there."

Chapin sentenced. Dwight L. Chapin, former appointments secretary to President Nixon, was sentenced May 15 to a prison term of 10-30 months May 15 for lying to a grand jury about his involvement in political sabotage operations during the 1972 presidential campaign. Chapin had been convicted on two perjury counts April 5.

In passing sentence, U.S. District Court Judge Gerhard A. Gesell told Chapin he "apparently chose loyalty to your superiors above obligations as a citizen and a public servant." Chapin's "resort to the convenience of swearing falsely" could not be condoned, Gesell said.

Chapin was released pending the result of his appeal.

House panel hearings continue. The House Judiciary Committee issued two new subpoenas May 15 for White House tape recordings and other data to further the committee's impeachment inquiry.

The subpoenas, directed at Watergate-related activity, required compliance by May 22. One sought 11 conversations occurring on three dates—(1) April 4, 1972, five days after alleged approval of a political intelligence-gathering plan prior to the Watergate break-in; (2) June 20, 1972, the first day Nixon was at the White House after the break-in three days earlier; (3) June 23, 1972 when moves allegedly were made to involve the Central Intelligence Agency (CIA) in curbing the Watergate probe by the Federal Bureau of Investigation (FBI).

Committee counsel John M. Doar said the tapes were being sought to determine "whether or not" Nixon knew of the intelligence-gathering plan, what his "action or inaction" may have been in the early days of the cover-up attempt and "what approach" Nixon wanted the CIA and FBI to take in the investigation.

The committee vote approving this subpoena was 37-1, with Rep. Edward Hutchinson (Mich.), the senior Republican member, dissenting on the ground it was unenforceable and posed a constitutional confrontation between the President and Congress.

The second subpoena issued sought diaries of Nixon's White House meetings over four periods Doar considered "crucial" to the Watergate affair. The committee took separate votes on each of the periods after several Republicans objected to the subpoena. Rep. David W. Dennis (Ind.) considered many of the listings of the President's activities irrelevant to the inquiry. Rep. Wiley Mayne (Iowa) said the subpoena would be "an invitation to go out and ransack presidential files on every conceivable subject." In each instance the committee voted to include the period in the subpoena's coverage. The votes:

36-2, Hutchinson and Mayne against, for the diaries from April through July 1972, the period just before and after the break-in;

32-6 for diaries from February through April 1973, a period related by Doar to the President's attitude toward the Watergate investigation. In dissent were Hutchinson, Mayne, Dennis and three other Republicans, M. Caldwell Butler (Va.), Delbert L. Latta (Ohio) and Trent Lott (Miss.);

29-9 for diaries from July 12 through July 31, 1973, a period related to the disclosure of the White House recording system. The six dissenters above were joined by two more Republicans, Henry P. Smith 3rd (N.Y.) and Carlos J. Moorhead (Calif.) and one Democrat, Ray Thornton (Ark.).

32-6 for diaries for October 1973, the month the first special Watergate prosecutor Archibald Cox was dismissed. Dissenters were Hutchinson, Smith, Dennis, Butler, Lott and Latta.

The committee also was pursuing its request for other material from the White House not as yet covered by any of its subpoenas, and committee chairman Peter W. Rodino Jr. (D, N.J.) said May 15 that the issue of another subpoena from the committee would be taken up the following week if the White House continued to defer its decision on releasing the material.

The President's chief defense attorney, James D. St. Clair, attended the committee's meeting, which was an open business session. Rodino ruled that St. Clair's role at such a session was "as a spectator, as any other member of the public," but he permitted St. Clair to submit informally two memorandums opposing the new subpoenas on the ground that the panel already had enough evidence to complete its Watergate probe.

Closed evidence hearings continue— Following the committee's three-hour public meeting on the subpoenas, the committee returned to its closed hearings, its third, on evidence assembled by its staff. Its second evidentiary session May 14 reportedly dealt with the period immediately after the Watergate break-in. Committee member William L. Hungate (D, Mo.) commented later that the tenor of the session was "just like piano lessons—we're learning the keyboard."

At the third session May 15, the members listened to two tapes in its possession—a June 30, 1972 tape and a Sept. 15, 1972 tape. Afterwards, some Democrats contended that deletions had been made in the Nixon transcripts covering the same period, because of content, and not because it was inaudible, while some Republicans said nothing was deleted from the transcripts except expletives. Rodino said he had not yet concluded "if the failure to include some of the material was deliberate or otherwise."

Press reports emanating from the third session, attributed to a "committee source," said the Sept. 15 tape contained a threat, not included in the Nixon transcript, by the President to take action against the Washington Post and its attorney, Edward Bennett Williams. According to the source, the committee's tape contained a specific reference by Nixon to the Post's ownership of a television station and his remarks that, "The main thing is the Washington Post is going to have a damnable, damnable thing out of this one" and "I think we're going to fix" Williams.

Two groups aligned politically with Nixon later challenged the Post's TV licenses in Jacksonville and Miami Fla.

White House Press Secretary Ronald L. Ziegler criticized the committee later May 15 for the leak. "This is serious business," he said, and the leak of such material was contrary to the committee's stated intent "of a fair and disciplined proceeding."

St. Clair took the protest against the leak a step further May 16, requesting in a letter to Rodino that all the panel's proceedings be public because the "selective" leaking of information from closed sessions was "prejudicing the basic right of the President to an impartial inquiry on the evidence."

St. Clair said he was acting at Nixon's direction in asking that the record of previous executive sessions be made public and that all future sessions be open "so that the American people can be fully in-

formed with regard to all the evidence presented."

At a news briefing before one of the three separate closed sessions May 16, Rodino rejected the request to open all committee proceedings, contending that the best way for the public to be fully informed would be for Nixon to release all the material the panel had requested. Rodino said, however, that the record of the closed sessions would eventually be made public.

Most committee members reportedly favored opening all the proceedings, but cited the pledge of confidentiality regarding evidence transmitted by the Watergate grand jury and certain other sources.

Rodino said after the May 16 meetings that the panel had heard evidence on possible perjury during the original Watergate investigation and on White House conduct in response to the creation of the Senate Watergate Committee in early 1973.

Other committee sources said the focus of the day's evidence was the gathering and distribution of money paid to the original Watergate defendants. The sources said most of the evidence duplicated public testimony before the Senate Watergate Committee.

The committee also listened to the tape of the Feb. 28, 1973 meeting between Nixon and John W. Dean 3rd, then presidential counsel. According to the sources, the edited White House transcript was a reasonably accurate version of the tape.

White House defends Sept. 15 deletion— Deputy White House Press Secretary Gerald L. Warren and special counsel James D. St. Clair contended May 16 that Nixon's threat against the Washington Post and its television stations was irrelevant to the Watergate issue and thus justifiably deleted from the transcript of the Sept. 15, 1972 meeting involving Nixon, Dean and H. R. Haldeman.

Warren denied that Nixon's statements meant the Administration intended to use the Federal Communications Commission's (FCC) licensing procedures against the Post. Warren said he did not know whether it was simply a "coincidence" that the Post's TV licenses were challenged a few months after the meeting.

The transcripts told "the complete story of the actions relating to the Watergate matter," Warren said, reiterating that the transcripts had been released "in full awareness" that the Judiciary Committee already had access to eight of the tapes transcribed.

Regarding the TV license challenges, which were pending before the FCC, former FCC Chairman Dean Burch—currently a counselor to the President—said Nixon was "entitled to be displeased" with the Post, but emphasized that the FCC "was not leaned on by anyone at the White House."

Larry H. Israel, president of the Washington Post Co., said in a statement May 16 that "it should be deeply disturbing to every citizen" that the White House would try to use the processes of a regulatory agency "for economic retaliation against a newspaper exercising its proper journalistic responsibilities and to attempt to intimidate it from doing so."

Rep. Jerome R. Waldie (D, Calif.), a member of the Judiciary Committee, said the staff had already begun an investigation of the licensing issue. According to an FCC spokesman, Committee Chairman Rodino had written to FCC Chairman Richard Wiley in late February inquiring about the incident.

St. Clair was asked by newsmen May 16 if Nixon's remarks might have implied an improper use of a federal agency. St. Clair replied: "You can't incriminate a man for what he says. It has to be something he does."

Deletion disputed—Former presidential counsel John W. Dean 3rd was quoted by friends May 2 as saying that there were "major deletions" in the edited transcripts of Nixon's Watergate conversations. Dean, who was under court order to refrain from public comment on Watergate, reportedly said the transcript of his Sept. 15, 1972 meeting with Nixon and H. R. Haldeman omitted a long discussion on using the Internal Revenue Service (IRS) against political enemies and Dean's report on an IRS investigation of former Democratic National Chairman Lawrence O'Brien.

Deputy White House Press Secretary Gerald L. Warren said in response to the report that the section of the tape omitted from the transcript had been ruled irrelevant to Watergate by U.S. District Court Judge John J. Sirica when he screened the tape before releasing it to a grand jury. In the latest transcript release, the White House had reportedly decided to give the public and House Judiciary Committee what the grand jury had received.

Berger scores St. Clair defense. An academic attack on President Nixon's legal defense appeared in the Yale Law Journal published May 15. Written by Raoul Berger of the Harvard Law School, the article described the defense against impeachment put forward by Nixon's attorney James St. Clair as "instant history," "far-fetched theories" and "sheer effrontery." He said St. Clair's legal memorandum on impeachment consisted of "a pastiche of selected snippets and half-truths, exhibiting a resolute disregard of adverse facts." When St. Clair "wraps himself in the cloak of pseudo-history," Berger wrote, "he lays himself open to the suspicion that he is not so much engaged in honest reconstruction of history as in propaganda whose sole purpose is to influence public opinion in favor of a client who is under grave suspicion."

Kleindienst pleads guilty. Former Attorney General Richard G. Kleindienst

pleaded guilty May 16 to a misdemeanor charge that he had refused to testify "accurately and fully" before a Congressional committee investigating the Administration's handling of the controversial International Telephone & Telegraph Corp. (ITT) antitrust settlement. The guilty plea was entered in federal district court in Washington.

The minor criminal offense related to Kleindienst's testimony in March and April 1972 before the Senate Judiciary Committee, which was considering his nomination to succeed John Mitchell as attorney general. [For further details, see p. 134B3]

In a talk with reporters after court, Watergate Special Prosecutor Leon Jaworski defended his decision not to bring perjury charges, which involved the commission of felonies, against Kleindienst. Reports had been circulating for several months that Kleindienst was engaging in plea bargaining with Jaworski's office in order to prevent the filing of felony charges that would have resulted in his automatic disbarment as a lawyer. [For further details, see p. 134G3]

GOP election concern. Vice President Gerald Ford urged Republicans meeting in Honolulu May 17 to work to prevent the Democrats from turning November's general elections "into a national referendum on Watergate." The "horrors" of Watergate, he said, were not their responsibility.

National Chairman George Bush May 19 conceded that the Republicans were concerned about damage to the party by the Watergate affair. The scandal, he said, on the ABC "Issues and Answers" broadcast, had already "hurt" the party at the polls. However, Bush said, the low public rating of Congress could reflect against the Democrats. Congressional failure was "Democratic failure," he said, and the "people are going to understand that."

The Republican Party's fate, Bush said, was "not inextricably interwoven" with President Nixon's fate. Asked if the President's troubles were caused by a political "vendetta" against him, Bush replied, "Absolutely not." There were "enough things" in Watergate "that we all deplore," he said, and, in fact, "it is the Republicans" rather than their opponents "that care the most about ₊ Watergate. . . . We always thought the Democrats did more of that kind of thing."

In an interview with the New York Times May 19, Bush admitted he was "more concerned than ever" about the political fallout from Watergate. It "can't possibly help us," he said.

He did not think President Nixon would resign. "The constitutional process has to be allowed to work," he said, "no matter what the result, and it's not my job to tell congressmen how to vote or what to think."

Bush said he was "deeply troubled" about the Nixon transcripts because of

the "amorality of tone" in the conversations. "The transcripts turn me off," he commented. He described his own job as "extremely tough" because he and other party officials were being criticized as Nixon apologists if they defended the President and as turncoats if they did not.

Sen. William E. Brock (Tenn.), chairman of the GOP Senatorial Campaign Committee responsible for raising funds for the Senate candidates, admitted the difficulty of his job May 19. "I am having a great deal of trouble," he said. "Watergate has done us a considerable amount of harm. There is no question about that, and you can't hide from it. It is there."

Nixon-Jaworski conflict deepens. The dispute between President Nixon and the special Watergate prosecution over access to presidential tapes and documents took on the appearance of history repeating itself May 20, as U.S. District Court Judge John J. Sirica ordered Nixon to comply with a subpoena for evidence, and special prosecutor Leon Jaworski charged that the White House had attempted to "undercut" his role as an independent prosecutor. In a situation similar to that which led to the 1973 dismissal of Archibald Cox, the first special prosecutor, the White House said Sirica's order would be appealed.

Sirica's ruling was a point-by-point rejection of arguments advanced by special presidential counsel James D. St. Clair in an effort to have the subpoena quashed. Shortly after the ruling was released, Jaworski sent a letter to Senate Judiciary Committee Chairman James O. Eastland (D, Miss.), to whom he had promised to report on any conflicts with the White House.

Sirica backs prosecution—The prosecution subpoena in question had been issued for tapes and other records covering 64 conversations relating to the Watergate cover-up. Jaworski had said the evidence was necessary for the trial of the seven cover-up defendants, and could be used by the prosecution and by the defense as possible exculpatory evidence.

Sirica's May 20 ruling supporting access to the evidence by both the court and the prosecutor came a week after a closed hearing, during which—according to the decision—St. Clair had argued that the subpoena did not conform with evidentiary rules of relevance and necessity, and that the dispute between Nixon and Jaworski was an "intra-branch" affair in which the courts should have no role.

Sirica rejected the White House contention that Jaworski's role could be limited by presidential order, noting that the prosecutor was "vested with the powers and authority conferred upon his predecessor pursuant to regulations which have the force of law." Sirica said Jaworski had full authority to determine whether to contest a presidential assertion of executive privilege, and added that the

A

B

C

D

E

F

G

prosecutor's independence had been "affirmed and reaffirmed by the President and his representatives."

Nixon's attempt to "abridge" this independence with an argument that Jaworski "cannot seek evidence from the President by court process is a nullity and does not defeat the court's jurisdiction," Sirica concluded.

Regarding the relevance of the subpoenaed evidence, Sirica noted that 20 of the 64 conversations were included in the edited transcripts made public by the White House on April 30. The content of the transcripts, Sirica ruled, showed that they were relevant to the cover-up trial, and the act of releasing them had, to a certain extent, destroyed claims of confidentiality. Sirica also said that a memorandum submitted by Jaworski (which was kept under seal) had demonstrated the potential relevance of the evidence and a "sufficiently compelling" need for the tapes to be surrendered.

Sirica ordered that the material be submitted to the court for his private examination, along with "particularized" claims of privilege, a procedure which had been followed in dealing with tapes in late 1973.

Sirica ordered the material turned over by May 31, but stayed execution of the order pending completion of appeals.

Jaworski criticizes White House role—Jaworski's letter to Sen. Eastland and the Judiciary Committee May 20 followed the release of Judge Sirica's decision and cited the fact that Sirica had "pointedly" rejected the White House contention that it could unilaterally limit the prosecutor's role.

Jaworski said presidential counsel St. Clair's argument that the prosecutor had no standing in court vis-a-vis the President had first been advanced after he and St. Clair agreed to secret proceedings before Sirica. The argument which prompted the letter, Jaworski said, was the White House contention that the President had ultimate authority "to determine when to prosecute, whom to prosecute, and with what evidence to prosecute."

The challenge to the prosecution's right to "take the President to court," Jaworski said, was a direct contravention of the conditions under which he had agreed to accept the position of special prosecutor.

Jaworski conceded that Nixon had the right to "raise ... defenses, such as confidential communications, executive privilege, or the like," which should be subject to court ruling as to their soundness. Jaworski added, however, that any claim by the White House which "challenges my right to invoke judicial process against the President ... would make a farce of the special prosecutor's character" and violate the understanding accepted by the committee members when he was appointed.

Meeting in closed session May 21, the committee adopted, 14–1, a resolution stating that Jaworski was "acting within the scope of the authority conferred upon him," and commending him for the "fidelity for the duties imposed upon him."

The dissenting vote was cast by Sen. Edward M. Kennedy (D, Mass.), who said later that the resolution was "an inadequate response" to a "serious and substantial problem."

The committee also agreed to send a letter to Attorney General William B. Saxbe urging him to "use all reasonable and appropriate means to guarantee" Jaworski's independence. Eastland said the letter represented the unanimous view of the panel. A spokesman for Saxbe said the next day that Saxbe "still subscribes" to the promise he had made during his confirmation hearings to "fight for" Jaworski's "right to proceed as he sees fit."

A proposal to hold open hearings on the issue was defeated by a vote of 9–5 because, according to one member, the panel did not want to create a "diversion."

Richardson sees parallels—Former Attorney General Elliot L. Richardson, who had resigned in October 1973 when ordered to discharge Archibald Cox, said May 20 that the current confrontation between Nixon and Jaworski and the arguments used by St. Clair virtually duplicated the circumstances in which Cox had been fired.

Richardson added that in view of the guidelines set when Jaworski replaced Cox, there should be "no conceivable question" of the prosecutor's right "to challenge an assertion of executive privilege" in the courts.

White House spokesmen May 21 dismissed the suggestion that Jaworski might be fired. Deputy Press Secretary Gerald L. Warren said Nixon was not considering such a move, and St. Clair said that "in the first place, there wouldn't be any basis for dismissal."

In related developments May 22, Sen. Adlai E. Stevenson 3rd (D, Ill.) introduced legislation providing for emergency appointment of an interim special prosecutor by a panel of federal judges if the office should become vacant, and Vice President Gerald R. Ford said Nixon should compromise and surrender tapes "which are relevant to a criminal proceeding."

Watergate costs up to $6.5 million. Federal spending on the Watergate affair was nearing the $6.5 million mark, according to an estimate of the General Accounting Office (GAO) released May 20. The estimate, released by Rep. Edward R. Roybal (D, Calif.), who requested the study, showed that $382,474 of the total was spent by the White House on attorney fees, salaries and travel.

The total, which covered costs to March 24, also included $2.8 million for the budget of the Watergate special prosecutor, $1.5 million each for the probes by the House Judiciary Committee

($500,000 of it pending appropriation by Congress) and the Senate Watergate committee, $225,000 for grand jury costs, and $100,000 for GAO probes of spending on presidential homes.

The GAO noted that its survey of White House costs included interviews since "the White House office does not maintain accounting or other records which would permit us to obtain precise information on the costs incurred on Watergate." It also noted that five lawyers had been assigned to the White House from departments or agencies, including the Federal Communications Commission, without shifting their payrolls. Two others brought into the White House were put on payrolls of departments in which they had never worked, the GAO said.

Deputy White House Press Secretary Gerald L. Warren said May 21 the practice of shifting employes from executive departments and independent agencies from time to time to the White House was authorized under the U.S. Code.

Court rejects Reinecke plea. A federal district court judge May 20 refused to dismiss a perjury indictment against California Lt. Gov. Ed Reinecke, who had been charged in connection with the Administration's handling of antitrust suits against the International Telephone & Telegraph Corp. (ITT). Reinecke had contended that he had been misled with promises of leniency and trapped by the Watergate special prosecutor's staff into cooperating with their ITT investigation.

The court also refused Reinecke's request that the trial, scheduled to begin in Washington in July, be moved to California.

Warren upholds federal structure. Former Chief Justice Earl Warren cautioned May 21 against hasty revision of the governmental structure in response to the Watergate scandal. Speaking at Morehouse College in Atlanta, Warren said "the scandal has shaken the faith of people, not only in the individuals involved, but also the procedures which brought them to their high places."

Some "dangerous" changes in the federal structure were being proposed, Warren said, because of the doubt and cynicism of the period. "The sponsors fail to recognize," he said, "that the conditions they recoil against do not flow from public officials following constitutional procedures, but, on the contrary, from circumventing them. As a result, they ignore the old truism that we do not tear down good buildings merely because they have been occupied by bad tenants."

Magruder sentenced. Jeb Stuart Magruder, former deputy director of the Committee to Re-elect the President, was sentenced to a prison term of 10 months to four years May 21 for his role in plotting the Watergate break-in and cover-up. Magruder had pleaded guilty Aug. 16, 1973 to a one-count indictment covering a variety of charges, including perjury, conspiracy and obstruction of justice.

Magruder, who had been cooperating with the prosecution for more than a year, was a principal character in the edited White House tape transcripts released by President Nixon April 30, in which Nixon and his aides expressed increasing concern over the impact of Magruder's statements to the prosecutors and the grand jury.

In a statement to the court before sentencing, Magruder said he was "confident that this country will survive its Watergates and its Jeb Magruders." For his own part, Magruder said: "my ambition obscured my judgment."

U. S. District Court Judge John J. Sirica, who delivered the sentence without further comment, ordered Magruder to begin serving his term in a minimum security institution by June 4.

Subpoenas rejected. President Nixon informed the House Judiciary Committee May 22 that he would not comply with two subpoenas for Watergate-related tapes and documents the panel had issued a week before for its impeachment inquiry. Nixon also said that any future subpoenas "allegedly dealing with Watergate" would be rejected.

Earlier in the day, presidential counsel James D. St. Clair informed the committee that its requests for additional material on the International Telephone and Telegraph Corp. (ITT) antitrust controversy and campaign contributions by the dairy industry would not be met, with the possible exception of an edited transcript of one conversation on the ITT case.

In a letter to Judiciary Committee Chairman Peter W. Rodino Jr. (D, N.J.), Nixon reiterated the basic White House argument that production of additional material "would merely prolong the inquiry without yielding significant additional evidence." "More fundamentally," Nixon continued, compliance "with an endless series of demands would fatally weaken this office" in his own Administration and for future presidents.

Nixon contended that the subpoenaed White House diaries were obviously "intended to be used to identify even more presidential conversations, as a basis for even more subpoenas."

Nixon said the House panel had "the full story of Watergate, in so far as it relates to presidential knowledge and presidential actions." Nixon added, however, that he was prepared to answer, under oath, "pertinent written interrogatories, and to be interviewed, under oath," by Rodino and ranking Republican Edward Hutchinson (Mich.).

St. Clair's two letters to committee counsel John M. Doar on the ITT and milk fund issues stated that in both in-

stances the panel had already been given "voluminous documents" from the White House and Justice and Agriculture Departments, as well as pertinent tapes.

Regarding the ITT case, St. Clair said the dates covered in the committee's latest request (Feb. 29, 1972–April 5, 1972) indicated a focus on the period when Richard G. Kleindienst was undergoing confirmation hearings on his nomination as attorney general. St. Clair said the White House was "not aware of any allegation that the President had anything to do with these hearings or the preparation of testimony. . . ."

With the exception of a conversation involving Nixon, former aide H. R. Haldeman and former Attorney General John N. Mitchell on April 4, 1972, St. Clair continued, there was "no evidence that this subject matter was ever discussed during any of the conversations" covered by the request. St. Clair said the tape would be reviewed and a transcript "of the pertinent portion thereof, if any," would be furnished in a few days.

On the milk fund issue, St. Clair said the panel already had tapes on the "operative discussions" relating to the decision to increase price supports, and that Nixon "does not believe that any further production of materials would serve any useful purpose."

St. Clair concluded both letters with a reminder that Nixon had published "a definitive paper" on each subject. "In case you do not have a copy," St. Clair said, "one is enclosed for your information."

Committee critical—In a statement issued on behalf of the Judiciary Committee May 22, Chairman Rodino said Nixon's response to the subpoenas was "a very grave matter" to which the panel would give "careful consideration" as it determined whether there were grounds for impeachment.

Reaction among other members was uniformly critical, but there were differences of opinion on how the committee should proceed. Some Republicans reportedly favored seeking a Supreme Court ruling ordering Nixon to comply, while Democrats favored further subpoenas and construction of a record of presidential noncompliance with its requests.

Rodino said formal action on Nixon's response would be deferred until the following week and that a decision on possible subpoenas in the non-Watergate phases would follow hearings on those issues.

Closed evidence presentation continues—The committee continued its closed hearings May 21–22, where impeachment evidence was presented by the committee's staff.

After the May 21 session, Chairman Rodino issued a statement in which he suggested that President Nixon had learned of the Watergate cover-up earlier than he had previously admitted and that

Nixon had edited this fact out of one of the Water transcripts made public by the White House April 30.

Noting Nixon's claim that he had no knowledge of the cover-up until March 21, 1973, when White House counsel John W. Dean 3rd so informed him, Rodino cited a June 4, 1973 recording of a presidential conversation with White House Press Secretary Ronald L. Ziegler. The June 4 recording indicated that Nixon had spent "a number of hours" listening to the Watergate tapes and that Nixon had described some of the conversations in the tapes to Ziegler, Rodino said. Included was a discussion of the President's March 17, 1973 meeting with Dean, which involved, Rodino said "a discussion of the Watergate matter and the possible involvement of White House personnel and others."

The committee had subpoenaed the actual recording of the March 17 meeting, but the White House provided only an edited transcript concerning primarily the break-in at the office of Pentagon Papers defendant Daniel Ellsberg's psychiatrist by the special White House investigative unit known as the "plumbers."

During the committee session May 21, panel members had also listened to the recording of the March 21, 1973 meeting between Nixon and Dean, later joined by H. R. Haldeman, White House chief of staff. Committee member Jerome Waldie (D, Calif.) said he had detected a significant difference between the recording and the edited White House transcript. Waldie cited a section of the edited transcript in which Nixon discussed meeting hush-money demands made by Watergate conspirator E. Howard Hunt Jr. According to the transcript version, Nixon said to Haldeman, "Hunt . . . might blow the whistle and his price is pretty high, but at least we can buy the time on that, as I pointed out to John [Dean]." However, Waldie said that the tape actually had Nixon saying, "But at least we should buy time on that. . . ."

Another controversial point about the March 21 meeting concerned Nixon's and Dean's discussion of raising $120,000 to pay Hunt. The White House transcript version read:

President: "That's why for your immediate things, you have no choice but to come up with the $120,000, or whatever it is. Right?"

Dean: "That's right."
President: "Would you agree that that's the prime thing that you damn well better get that done?"

Dean: "Obviously he ought to be given some signal, anyway."

President: "(expletive deleted), get it . . ."

According to committee members, the missing expletive was "for Christ sakes" or "Jesus Christ." Another committee member said the deleted expletive was "goddam it."

A The committee May 22 heard a 15-minute Dictabelt recording made by Nixon the night of March 21, 1973. Nixon described the day, during which Dean said he had informed him of the Watergate cover-up, as "uneventful." Ziegler said May 23 that the remark had been taken out of context and that the full quotation actually read: "As far as the day was concerned, it was uneventful except for the talk with Dean."

B **Watergate panel loses tape appeal.** The U.S. Court of Appeals for the District of Columbia ruled 7–0 May 23 that the Senate Watergate Committee had not shown a compelling enough need for tapes of five presidential conversations to require enforcement of its subpoena for the tapes. The decision upheld and expanded upon a lower court ruling which, while dismissing the panel's suit to enforce the subpoena, had rejected President Nixon's blanket claim of confidentiality over presidential communications.

C Speaking for the court, Chief Judge David L. Bazelon said such a claim of executive privilege was valid and necessary to the conduct of the presidency so long as another "institution of government" did not make a sufficiently strong showing of need. Under these conditions, Bazelon said, the ruling against the Senate committee was consistent with the same court's October 1973 decision that a Watergate grand jury should have access to presidential tapes.

D Bazelon said there were "peculiar circumstances" in the current case which militated against the Senate panel's position. Among these were the President's release of edited transcripts of some of his conversations, including the five sought by the committee, and the fact that the House Judiciary Committee had obtained copies of the same five tapes for its impeachment inquiry.

E Since the "investigative objectives" of the committees "substantially overlap," Bazelon said, the Senate panel's demand was, from a Congressional standpoint, "merely cumulative" and unsupported by its legislative function.

F Regarding the White House transcripts, Bazelon said the committee should be able to get the information needed for legislative recommendations from the transcripts despite their "ambiguities."

G Committee chief counsel Samuel Dash and other committee sources declined comment on whether the case might be appealed to the Supreme Court.

Senate OKs panel extension—By voice vote May 21, the Senate approved a resolution giving the Watergate Committee until June 30 to file its final report and extending the life of the committee, with subpoena powers, until that date. The panel's mandate had been scheduled to expire May 28 under an earlier extension.

The resolution also provided that the committee should continue in existence past June 30 if a final court decision on its suit to obtain presidential tapes had not been issued by then. The committee had voted unanimously May 15 to request the extension.

Impeachment panel asks Nixon data. The confidentiality of President Nixon's tax returns was upheld by Attorney General William B. Saxbe May 25 over the authority of the House impeachment process. However, the White House announced later May 25 that the President would give the House Judiciary Committee information on his income taxes "under appropriate safeguards."

In pursuit of its impeachment inquiry, the committee had asked the IRS for its audit of the Nixon returns. Treasury Secretary William E. Simon requested a legal opinion from Saxbe, who held that the committee was not entitled to the data without further action by the House (a) designating it a "select committee" authorized to investigate tax returns or (b) transmitting the data from committees specified under the IRS code as entitled to such data.

Ford differs with Nixon on tapes. Vice President Gerald Ford acknowledged May 26 he disagreed with President Nixon on the issue of providing relevant information to a House impeachment inquiry. Ford said the difference "was laid out quite candidly" during a meeting with Nixon May 23. The meeting came after Ford had called several times for White House cooperation with the House probe.

At a news conference in New York May 22, Ford said he planned to "talk to the White House about the content" of further taped Watergate conversations being sought by the House Judiciary Committee. "I hope," he said, "that when the committee gets through the present vast amount of evidence, if it needs any additional evidence relating to impeachment, the White House would cooperate."

Later May 22 Ford told a Republican rally in Wilmington, Del., "I don't think when all the evidence is in, they've got a case" but "let's get it all out there, the quicker the better."

A few hours after his meeting with Nixon May 23, about which little immediate detail was available, Ford told ABC correspondent Bill Zimmerman, in an interview broadcast May 24, "a stonewall attitude" in refusing to provide the committee with relevant information "isn't necessarily the wisest policy." It "could be" the issue that could bring about House impeachment, he thought, and he wanted the House "to make its judgment on the facts, not on some emotional, institutional issue."

Ford visited Lansing, Mich. May 24, for appearances at Michigan State University and before the Michigan Legislature, but mentioned Watergate only briefly as "a traumatic" experience for the nation. His reception by the Legislature was enthusiastic, but 300–400 demonstrators attended his campus visit, chanting "Nixon must go" and "Gerald Ford's nothing new, tricky Dicky No. 2."

At a news conference in Danbury, Conn. May 26, Ford related some details of his May 23 meeting with Nixon. He was asked about reports of differences between him and Nixon on the issue of White House release of information to the House Judiciary Committee. "This difference existed before the meeting," he replied. "It was laid out quite candidly during the meeting, and I haven't backed off from it since." Ford said he "wants the facts out in the open so that the House committee can act on the facts," that he felt there "should be as much disclosure as possible." "Obviously, he [Nixon] has a somewhat different opinion and I respect it," he said. He said he told the President a refusal to provide relevant information "could lead to an emotional institutional confrontation."

White House Press Secretary Ronald L. Ziegler said May 27 "the vice president has no difficulties with the President at all." Ford, in Charlotte, N.C. May 28, affirmed that "the President and I have had, do have and expect to have very good personal relations."

Easing his stand on the issue, Ford told reporters in Birmingham, Ala. May 29 he thought Nixon's position was "proper" at the current time. "I will keep pressing the committee to open up their hearings, I will keep pressing them to call these witnesses," he said. "Until they have done that, I think the President's attitude is proper."

48% favor ouster. A Gallup Poll issued May 26 showed that a plurality of those interviewed, by a 48%–37% margin, believed that President Nixon's actions were serious enough to warrant his removal from the presidency. In mid-April, the finding was 46%–42% in favor of removal from office. The latest survey was taken May 10–13.

Louis Harris pollsters found a 49%–41% call for Nixon's impeachment and removal from office. Results of the survey were published May 11. The previous finding on the question in April was 42%–42%.

The Harris interviewers also asked if there was any belief that Nixon "will be found to have violated the law." The replies: 51% yes, 30% no (previous month's survey, 40% yes, 34% no).

Gallup reported very little change in a year in the public belief about Nixon's involvement in the Watergate scandal. In the May 10–13 survey, interviewers found that 73% believed Nixon was involved to some extent, similar to the 71% finding in February and 67% finding in June 1973.

Both major polling groups found that release of the White House transcripts had little or no effect on the President's popularity rating. Gallup put the rating at 25%, a drop of one point from April; Harris at 32%, a one point increase over March and April. Results of both surveys were issued May 22. The Gallup polling period was May 10–13, Harris's May 7–8. Harris found that 66% of those interviewed had a positive reaction to Nixon's foreign policy performance, a 3% increase from February's reaction. Gallup reported finding for the first time that Nixon received less than majority approval from all major population groups, including Republicans.

Dairy officials plead guilty. Two officials of the Lehigh Valley Cooperative Farmers entered guilty pleas in federal district court in Washington in connection with illegal contributions made by the dairy co-op to President Nixon's re-election campaign. The co-op had pleaded guilty to a misdemeanor charge May 6.

Richard L. Allison, who was recently dismissed as president of the co-op because of his role in authorizing the $50,000 contribution, pleaded guilty May 17 and was given a suspended fine of $1,000 for his misdemeanor offense.

Francis X. Carroll, Lehigh's Washington-based attorney and lobbyist who had also been fired by the co-op, pleaded guilty May 28 to a misdemeanor charge of aiding Allison in the transaction. Carroll's fine was also suspended.

[For further details, see p. 135B2]

Fulbright defeated in Arkansas. Sen. J. W. Fulbright (D, Ark.), 69, was defeated by Gov. Dale Bumpers, 48, in a primary bid May 28 for a sixth term. Fulbright had been a member of the Senate for 30 years and chairman of its Foreign Relations Committee since 1959. The vote was 380, 348–203, 135.

Bumpers campaigned for "fresh leadership," with frequent references to the "mess" in Washington. With his victory over Fulbright, he had defeated three top Arkansas politicians in the past four years. Bumpers had defeated former Gov. Orval Faubus (D) in the 1970 gubernatorial primary and Gov. Winthrop Rockefeller (R) that fall.

Jaworski seeks 'enemies' conversation. Special prosecutor Leon Jaworski petitioned U.S. District Court Judge John J. Sirica May 28 to release a previously-withheld portion of a presidential conversation which, according to Jaworski, could contain evidence of Administration attempts to "abuse and politicize" the Internal Revenue Service (IRS). Part of the tape of the Sept. 15, 1972 conversation, involving President Nixon, former aide H. R. Haldeman and former counsel John W. Dean 3rd, had been turned over to a grand jury, but Sirica had upheld a White House claim of executive privilege regarding a 17-minute section.

Jaworski also requested Sirica to reconsider the withholding of Haldeman's notes of that portion of the meeting, which had been included in the claim of privilege.

Jaworski said that while the White House had contended the privileged section concerned Nixon's "conduct of his official duties . . . unrelated to Watergate," other evidence refuted such an assertion, although the material might be "only indirectly related to Watergate." Jaworski noted that the court had long known the prosecution was investigating misuse of the IRS for "political and personal objectives."

The evidence, Jaworski contended, supported allegations that in September 1972 the White House had presented lists of "enemies" to the IRS with instructions "that they be audited or otherwise harassed." Jaworski also said the White House "unlawfully" tried to have the IRS investigate former Democratic National Chairman Lawrence F. O'Brien during August and September 1972.

Among the evidence cited by Jaworski were testimony by Dean and Haldeman before the Senate Watergate committee; material gathered by the grand juries; a summary of the meeting prepared by presidential counsel J. Fred Buzhardt Jr. for the Senate committee staff, which noted that "Dean reported on the IRS investigation of Larry O'Brien;" and a transcript of part of the meeting by the House Judiciary Committee staff for the impeachment inquiry indicating that Haldeman was aware Dean was investigating "the McGovern people" through the IRS.

Jaworski also noted that the withheld section might be relevant to the Watergate cover-up trial of seven former Nixon aides, including Haldeman.

(The edited White House transcript of the meeting, released April 30, contained a section on an Administration "counterattack" using federal agencies. But neither O'Brien nor the IRS was mentioned in that context.)

Nixon adamant on 'plumbers' evidence. James D. St. Clair, special White House counsel, said May 30 that President Nixon intended to retain control of evidence purported to be relevant to the defense of two former aides in the so-called Ellsberg break-in trial, even if it resulted in dismissal of the case. The statement was made in a letter to the U.S. District Court Judge Gerhard A. Gesell, who had warned St. Clair May 24 that by withholding documents sought by former aides John D. Ehrlichman and Charles W. Colson, Nixon "must know he is acting deliberately . . . [in] aborting this trial."

St. Clair had appeared in court May 24 to block two subpoenas sought by Ehrlichman and Colson for portions of their own White House files. These documents, the defendants contended, would prove they had legitimate national security reasons for meeting with members of the White House investigation unit called the "plumbers," which allegedly conceived and executed the 1971 burglary of the office of the psychiatrist who had treated Pentagon Papers defendant Daniel Ellsberg. Specifically, Ehrlichman and Colson sought their private notes of conversations with the President, and Colson wanted use of the secret 10-page "damage assessment" by the White House in connection with the release of the Pentagon Papers.

In his attempt to quash the proposed subpoenas May 24, St. Clair asserted that the scope of the subpoenas was too broad. St. Clair also brought a personal note from Nixon to Gesell, in which the President claimed executive privilege on the documents.

Gesell responded with a stern lecture to St. Clair, stating that Nixon had lost any privilege to withhold when the federal government, which Nixon headed, brought an indictment causing the defendants to require the documents. "You are quite out of focus," he told St. Clair. "If these documents are not produced, the case must be dismissed.... It is not up to the President to decide what documents to produce. I want those documents produced."

In his May 30 letter, St. Clair said the President was "not desirous of having ... any indictments of former government officials dismissed without a full and fair trial, but he must implement the constitutional responsibilities of his office by not jeopardizing the national security, even if it means...that these cases must ultimately be dismissed."

As a compromise, Colson, Ehrlichman and their counsel would be allowed to inspect the defendants' personal notes and then inform the President as to which documents they considered relevant to their defense. The President would then decide "whether the documents should be produced," St. Clair said. Such documents would also be made available to the prosecution.

However, the "damage assessment" requested by Colson could not "be made public without substantial risk to the security of the United States," St. Clair stated. Instead, the assessment would be given to Judge Gesell for his personal inspection and to the defendants under a specific order not to disclose its contents. Should the court find "all or any part of the document relevant and material, the decision of whether the document or the relevant portion of it shall be declassified shall remain one for the Chief Executive and will not be assumed by the court," St. Clair stated. (Gesell had told St. Clair May 24, "This is a public trial. We don't have in camera [private] hearings here.")

Gesell bars national security defense— Gesell ruled May 24 that the defendants in the trial were not entitled to cite "national security" as a legal justification for the break-in at the office of Ellsberg's psychiatrist. Moreover, he held that the President was without constitutional right to authorize any break-in or search without a warrant, even when national security was involved. "The 4th Amendment," Gesell said, "protects the privacy of citizens against unreasonable and unrestrained intrusion by government officials and their agents. It is not theoretical. It lies at the heart of our free society."

Conceding that "warrantless invasion" of a home or office had been approved by the Supreme Court "under carefully delineated emergency circumstances," Gesell asserted that no exceptional circumstances obtained in this case. "On the contrary," he said, "it [the burglary] had

been meticulously planned over a period of more than a month. The search of Dr. [Lewis J.] Fielding's office was therefore clearly illegal under the unambiguous mandate of the 4th Amendment."

The defendants' contention—that the President, by reason of his special responsibility over foreign relations and national security, had the right to suspend requirements of the 4th Amendment—was rejected by Gesell. Recent Supreme Court decisions allowing limited warrantless wiretapping for gathering intelligence did not apply to this case, Gesell said.

Not only did the President not have the right to authorize the break-in, Gesell went on, "he did not in fact give any specific directive permitting national security break-ins, let alone this intrusion." Gesell quoted from a letter Nixon had submitted to the court April 29. The President's letter referred to a 1971 meeting he had held with Ehrlichman and Egil Krogh Jr., a co-director of the "plumbers." At that meeting "it was my intent," the President's letter said, "...that the fullest authority of the President under the Constitution and the law should be used if necessary to bring a halt to these disclosures.... I did not have prior knowledge of the break-in..., nor was I informed of it until March 17, 1973."

Gesell continued:

"Of course, since the President had no such authority in the first place, he could not have delegated it to others. Beyond this, however, the court rejects the contention that the President could delegate his alleged power to suspend constitutional rights to non-law enforcement officers in the vague, informal, inexact terms noted above.... Whatever accomodation is required between the guarantees of the 4th Amendment and the conduct of foreign affairs, it cannot justify a casual, ill-defined assignment to White House aides and part-time employes granting them an uncontrolled discretion to select, enter and search the homes and offices of innocent American citizens without a warrant."

Charges against DeDiego dismissed— Gesell May 21 dismissed all charges against Filipe DeDiego in connection with the break-in at the office of Ellsberg's psychiatrist. DeDiego was charged with one count of conspiring to violate the civil rights of Dr. Lewis J. Fielding by breaking into his office.

The charges were being dropped because DeDiego had been given immunity by state prosecutors in return for his testimony about the break-in. It was "not practical," Gesell said, to hold the necessary hearings to determine if the evidence used by federal prosecutors had been tainted by their access to the immunized state testimony.

Ruckelshaus admitted to bar. William D. Ruckelshaus, former deputy attorney general was admitted to the Washington bar, it was reported May 30; former Attorney

General Richard G. Kleindienst was his sponsor.

No ITT antitrust crime seen. Special Watergate prosecutor Leon Jaworski said May 30 that his staff had uncovered no evidence that International Telephone & Telegraph Corp. (ITT) officials had committed any criminal offenses in connection with a 1971 settlement of the government's antitrust suits against the firm. [For further details, see p. 135E3]

Access to federal data. A bill to amend the Freedom of Information Act to ease public access to government documents and information was approved by the Senate May 30 by a 64–17 vote. The bill was sent to conference with the House.

The Senate version contained two controversial amendments specifying ground rules on which information could be withheld and eliminating ground rules for federal judges reviewing government claims of national security to bar release of data.

Book rights sold. Carl Bernstein and Bob Woodward, investigative reporters for the Washington Post, sold paperback rights for their book on Watergate, "All the President's Men" for $1 million, it was reported May 30.

Nixon bars release of Stans' papers. President Nixon filed a formal claim of executive privilege May 30 in an effort to block the release of his correspondence with Maurice Stans regarding persons under consideration for federal appointments. Stans, who had served as commerce secretary from 1969–72, had been Nixon's chief fund raiser during the 1968 and 1972 elections and had headed the Finance Committee to Re-elect the President. [For further details, see p. 136C1]

House panel warns Nixon. The House Judiciary Committee formally notified President Nixon May 30 that his refusal to comply with its subpoenas "might constitute a ground for impeachment" that the committee could take before the House. The committee also approved May 30 issuance of another subpoena for White House tapes and documents and voted to continue its impeachment hearings on evidence in closed sessions.

The committee's actions had strong bipartisan backing. Rep. Robert McClory (Ill.), the panel's second-ranking Republican, said: "We are reviewing allegations that the President obstructed the [Watergate] inquiry of the Department of Justice, the Senate [Watergate] committee and the special prosecutor. His current conduct does not make it easier for this member to conclude that such allegations are without merit."

The warning to Nixon—The warning to the President, a letter* from the chairman, Rep. Peter W. Rodino Jr. (D, N.J.), also cautioned Nixon that the committee members would "be free to consider whether your refusals warrant the drawing of adverse inferences concerning the substance of the materials," or inferences, that is, that the materials withheld were incriminating.

Such inferences could not properly be drawn, according to James D. St. Clair, Nixon's chief defense lawyer later May 30, because the President's stand was based on his constitutional duty to protect the presidency.

The letter was sent following a 28-10 vote by the panel favoring the action. All but one of the committee's 21 Democrats—Rep. John Conyers Jr. (Mich.)—voted to send the letter. They were joined by eight of the 17 Republicans. The eight: Reps. William S. Cohen (Me.), Henry P. Smith 3rd (N.Y.), Hamilton Fish Jr. (N.Y.), Charles W. Sandman (N.J.), Lawrence J. Hogan (Md.), M. Caldwell Butler (Va.), Robert McClory (Ill.) and Tom Railsback (Ill.).

Conyers wanted stronger action by the committee on the issue. He proposed seeking an immediate House vote to impeach the President for "contempt for and obstruction of the constitutional process" of impeachment, but the committee rejected this by a 29-9 vote. The committee also rejected, by a 27-11 vote, a proposal by Rep. Jerome R. Waldie (D, Calif.) to seek a House decision to cite the President for contempt of Congress.

The committee also rejected two alternative proposals, by votes of 32-6, suggested by Republicans. One of these, from Railsback, called for seeking legislation to give the federal courts jurisdiction to decide whether the President had a constitutional right to refuse impeachment evidence. The other, from Rep. David W. Dennis (Ind.), would have the committee enter, as an amicus curiae (friend of the court) the Supreme Court suit brought by the special Watergate prosecutor in his pursuit of White House tapes for criminal trials. [See below]

Both court procedures were opposed by chief Republican counsel Albert E. Jenner Jr. because of the "serious legal and constitutional problems" raised by submission to the judiciary of the impeachment issue on which Congress had sole constitutional authority.

Subpoena approved 37-1—The committee's fourth subpoena to the White House was approved by a 37-1 vote, Rep. Edward Hutchinson (Mich.), the panel's ranking Republican, in dissent (by proxy, since he was recuperating from surgery). The subpoena demanded 45 Watergate-related conversations occurring between Nov. 15, 1972 and June 4, 1973 plus any related documents from the files of key presidential aides.

Closed sessions voted 23-15—The committee's vote to continue closed hearings until completion of presentation of evidence by its staff was by a 23-15 margin. The vote rejected a motion by Rep. Wayne Owens (D, Utah) to open the hearings scheduled to hear evidence relating to Administration involvement with the International Telephone and Telegraph Corp. and the dairy industry during the 1972 Nixon re-election campaign. Committee officials had tentatively planned to open those phases of the hearings. Defeat of the open hearings was brought about by Republicans, despite the strong public pressure by the President for open hearings. All but two Republicans voted to reject the Democratic motion. Rep. Charles E. Wiggins (R, Calif.), who led the drive for rejection, said St. Clair was "wrong" in his argument for open hearings. Evidence presented in public could jeopardize the rights of defendants at impending Watergate trials, he said, and "far more important is that we not prejudice a trial of the President of the United States in the Senate."

Prior developments—The committee's counsel recommended to the members May 23 and took a public stand that the President's Watergate transcripts could not be accepted as a substitute for the subpoenaed tape recordings. Special counsel John M. Doar said the transcripts were "inadequate and unsatisfactory" for a fair and thorough carrying out of the committee's constitutional impeachment obligation. Jenner agreed. The American people "cannot accept" unverified transcripts to resolve the issue, he said, and the House "would not be acting responsibly if it does."

Both rejected the verification procedure offered by the President for Rodino and the ranking Republican to listen to the withheld tapes. Doar said every member of the committee and the House was required under the Constitution to make a personal judgment on the issue and the responsibility could not be delegated.

Chairman Rodino buttressed their argument with a statement that the transcripts were marred by, among other things, paraphrases in place of verbatim quotes. "There are misstatements," he said. "There are omissions of words and paragraphs. There are misattributions of statements made by individuals. There are additions [paraphrases longer than the verbatim talk]. There are 'inaudibles.'" These were in addition to the deleted material, he added, and "what that material is we do not know."

The argument was rejected by the White House May 24 as "diversionary tactics." Press Secretary Ronald Ziegler said "our view, and St. Clair's view, is that it is not a reasonable position that is being taken by the counsel and the chairman" to reject the transcripts.

Ziegler criticized the committee May 25 on another matter, involving a report that day in the New York Times that the committee possessed what its investigators believed was "conclusive evidence"—from Cincinnati lawyer Sherman E. Unger, who was not involved in the affair—that a hush money payment to a Watergate defendant was initiated on March 21, 1973, a few hours after Nixon discussed the payment with his counsel. Ziegler accused the committee of leaking the information "to create a negative inference against the President." "The fact is," he said, "the President did not authorize or know about such a payment."

Watergate phase completed—The committee's closed hearings on the Watergate phase of its inquiry were completed May 29. Comments from members afterwards indicated the panel was split on whether the evidence presented implicated or exonerated the President in impeachable activity.

Rep. William L. Hungate (D, Mo.) interpreted the evidence as "a prima facie case" against the President.

Rep. Charles E. Wiggins (R, Calif.) said, "If the staff has presented the best evidence, it most assuredly is not overwhelming."

Rep. Robert McClory (R, Ill.) said there was "no clear-cut evidence one way or the other" to implicate or exonerate the President.

Nixon's counsel St. Clair described the evidence as "not very substantial." St. Clair said the committee should complete its Watergate phase entirely, by calling witnesses, among other things, before continuing with a "disjointed" inquiry into the non-Watergate phases.

Sirica bars tape plea—U.S. District Court Judge John J. Sirica May 30 rejected the House Judiciary Committee's request for access to the complete tapes of four White House conversations currently in his custody. The tapes had been delivered to Sirica for his examination in late 1973; he had subsequently released portions to a grand jury and withheld others as unrelated to Watergate, pursuant to claims of executive

*Text of Letter to the President: Dear Mr. President:
The Committee on the Judiciary has authorized me to reply to your letter of May 22 in which you decline to produce the tapes of Presidential conversations and Presidential diaries called for in the committee's subpoenas served on you on May 15, 1974. You also decline to produce any other material dealing with Watergate that may be called for in any further subpoenas that may be issued by the committee.
The Committee on the Judiciary regards your refusal to comply with its lawful subpoenas as a grave matter. Under the Constitution it is not within the power of the President to conduct an inquiry into his own impeachment, to determine which evidence, and what version or portion of that evidence, is relevant and necessary to such an inquiry. These are matters which, under the Constitution, the House has the sole power to determine.
In meeting their constitutional responsibility, committee members will be free to consider whether your refusals warrant the drawing of adverse inferences concerning the substance of the materials, and whether your refusals in and of themselves might constitute a ground for impeachment.
The committee's decisions on these matters will be contained in the recommendation the committee will make to the House of Representatives.
Respectfully,
Peter W. Rodino Jr.
Chairman.

privilege by Nixon. The Judiciary Committee had received the same portions released to the grand jury.

In his latest ruling, Sirica said that in upholding his function of screening the tapes for the grand jury, the U.S. Court of Appeals had not intended that he act as a "conduit" for "other parties demonstrating an interest," adding that committee requests "should be directed to the President."

Sirica noted that the courts should not become a part of the impeachment controversy, "particularly when both parties have consciously avoided attempts to invoke the court's jurisdiction."

The tapes involved two meetings on June 20, 1972 with former aides John D. Ehrlichman and H. R. Haldeman (including the tape with the 18½-minute "gap," which was under investigation as a separate issue by a grand jury; a June 30, 1972 meeting with Haldeman and former Attorney General John N. Mitchell; and the meeting on Sept. 15, 1972 with Haldeman and former counsel John W. Dean 3rd. (The withheld portion of the September tape was also being sought by special prosecutor Leon Jaworski. [See below])

Supreme Court to hear tape case. The Supreme Court May 31 granted special Watergate prosecutor Leon Jaworski's plea for prompt consideration of President Nixon's claim of executive privilege over tapes of 64 White House conversations, which Jaworski had said were essential to the trial of seven former Nixon aides accused in the Watergate cover-up.

Jaworski had petitioned the court directly May 24, within hours after special presidential counsel James D. St. Clair had filed notice with the U.S. Circuit Court of Appeals, appealing District Court Judge John J. Sirica's May 20 decision that Nixon must comply with Jaworski's subpoena for the tapes.

In its terse, four-sentence order May 31, the high court said only that the petition for early review had been granted, initial briefs should be filed by June 21, replies should be filed by July 1, and that oral arguments would be heard July 8; no vote was announced. Associate Justice William H. Rehnquist took no part in the decision, and no reason was announced. (Before his appointment to the court, Rehnquist was an assistant attorney general under John N. Mitchell, a defendant in the cover-up case.)

Jaworski's petition requested that the Supreme Court take immediate charge of the dispute under rules permitting such a step upon a showing that a case "is of such imperative public importance as to justify the deviation from normal appellate processes."

Jaworski argued that if the Supreme Court did not enter the case until after all other remedies had been exhausted, the cover-up trial scheduled for Sept. 9

might have to be postponed until the spring of 1975. (The Supreme Court was scheduled to recess in June and would not resume a regular term until October.)

Immediate consideration of the case, Jaworski added, would not "sacrifice any benefits" of intermediate review, since the Circuit Court of Appeals had previously "considered and ruled at length" on the principal constitutional issues involved in the current case.

Among the issues listed as "worthy of review," Jaworski cited the one which had recently become paramount in the proceedings before Sirica: whether the evidence dispute was internal within the executive branch, and whether the special prosecution had been "validly authorized to resort to the judicial process to secure physical evidence from the President himself."

Other overriding questions, Jaworski said, were: whether the courts have the ultimate authority to judge the applicability of executive privilege to evidence "demonstrably material" to judicial proceedings, whether privilege could be invoked "in the face of a prima facie showing that the conversations at issue involved a criminal enterprise," and whether Nixon had not already "irretrievably waived" such privilege by releasing edited transcripts of Watergate-related conversations.

A White House brief in opposition to immediate Supreme Court review was filed May 30, arguing that while the case posed "exceedingly important" constitutional issues, "hasty decision" would be inappropriate. It was because of the weight of the issues, the brief stated, "that the President opposes any attempt to shortcut the usual judicial process."

The brief argued that the issues cited in Jaworski's petition had never been definitively decided by the court, providing all the more reason for the case to run a normal course through intermediate review and, ultimately, careful consideration by the highest court.

Noting that Jaworski had cited as precedent the 1952 Supreme Court decision to bypass the appeals court on the question of President Truman's seizure of the steel industry, the White House argued that in the present case the urgency of a "trial of persons charged with crimes" could not be equated with the "magnitude and irreparable effect to the nation" involved in the steel case.

In conclusion, the White House brief argued that a "rush to judgment" would be questionable "in the midst of an impeachment inquiry involving intrinsically related matters," noting also that the ability of the White House to properly participate in an early Supreme Court proceeding would be hampered by the impeachment inquiry, which required "full time effort by the President's special counsel and staff."

(The brief marked the reappearance of White House legal consultant Charles

Alan Wright, who was a central figure in earlier proceedings involving presidential tapes. Wright's name appeared on the brief above St. Clair's.)

At a news conference later May 30, St. Clair declined to predict whether Nixon would comply with a Supreme Court decision, calling it a "hypothetical situation."

In a related development concerning Jaworski's complaint that the White House had been trying to impair his independence, Attorney General William B. Saxbe told the Senate Judiciary Committee by letter May 23 that he would "use appropriate means" to support the special prosecutor. Saxbe also told newsmen "no one can fire him except me, and I have no intention to do so."

Staff report on milk fund. In its findings from an investigation of links between an Administration price decision and dairy industry campaign contributions, the staff of the Senate Watergate committee concluded that campaign pledges made by major dairy cooperatives (totaling $2 million) "apparently [were] directly linked to a favorable milk price support decision by the President worth hundreds of millions of dollars to the industry—and costing the same amount to the government and consumers."

The staff's draft report, published May 31, also challenged claims by Nixon in a White Paper issued Jan. 8 to justify the 1971 decision increasing federal milk price supports. [For further details, see p. 213C1]

Criticism of Nixon continues. Criticism of President Nixon continued, with the White House denying that delaying tactics were being employed in the Watergate and impeachment inquiries on several fronts.

Chesterfield Smith, president of the American Bar Association, said May 26, "I've been shocked and annoyed that the White House doesn't clearly state 'Yes, I am subject to the rule of law. I'm not a king. I'm only a man elected by the people and when the Supreme Court decides that I have to do something, certainly I'm going to do it.'" "All men in this nation are subject to the rule of law," Smith said.

Smith's comments followed a refusal May 25 by White House Press Secretary Ronald L. Ziegler to "get into" the question of whether Nixon intended to abide by a ruling of the Supreme Court on the release of subpoenaed tapes to the special Watergate prosecutor. In 1973 Nixon had said he would obey a "definitive" ruling of the Supreme Court. Deputy Press Secretary Gerald L. Warren said June 3, "The matter is before the Supreme Court." Warren added, "I am not going to practice law from this podium."

Smith said "the President has not been interested in expediting this [the Watergate investigations] in any way." "It is clear to me," he said, "that he has impeded it for reasons of his own, that I don't believe he has been thinking of himself as the chief enforcement officer of the nation. I think he is thinking of himself as somebody being investigated."

Senate Democratic Whip Robert C. Byrd (W.Va.) said May 26 the situation had somewhat "hardened" in the Senate against Nixon, partly because of "the stonewalling that the President and his lawyer have been exhibiting all the way down the line." Byrd said he could not repeat his March 3 estimate doubting that two-thirds of the Senate was ready to vote to convict Nixon on impeachment.

Byrd told reporters May 29 the Nixon strategy of "delay, delay, delay" raised the possibility that a Senate vote on the issue would not come before the November elections and might well be delayed until 1975.

(Delay into 1975 beyond expiration of the current Congress would raise serious constitutional and legal questions about carrying over the impeachment proceeding, according to Senate Republican leaders May 30. The Senate Democratic leaders believed an impeachment trial could be carried over into the next Congress because the Senate was a "continuing body" carrying over two-thirds of its membership.)

Archibald Cox, who was ousted as special Watergate prosecutor during the 1973 tapes dispute with Nixon, said May 30 "if the President pursues his refusal to give the committee all evidence it deems relevant, that would be grounds for impeachment on which I would say he ought to be convicted." Cox had said May 27 failure by the President to submit evidence ordered by the courts, either to the committee or the special Watergate prosecutor, constituted "the most serious of impeachable offenses."

Elliot L. Richardson, who resigned as attorney general in 1973 rather than obey Nixon's order to fire Cox, said May 25 that the President "has an obligation" to make information subpoenaed by the special prosecutor "available to any inquiry."

Henry Ford 2nd, chairman of the Ford Motor Co. and a contributor to Nixon's re-election campaign ($50,000), said in an interview May 26 that he felt "let down" by the Washington situation and the President should give the impeachment inquiry everything it requested. "I think the country is in real trouble because of Watergate," he said, because of Nixon's preoccupation with the issue.

Evangelist Billy Graham, in a statement May 28, reaffirmed that President Nixon remained "my friend and I have no intention of forsaking him now," but he said reading the Nixon transcripts had been "a profoundly disturbing and disappointing experience." "What comes through in these tapes is not the man I have known for many years," Graham said, and indicated that as a nation "we

have lost our moral compass." He added, however, that "it would be nothing less than hypocrisy to call for a moral housecleaning at the White House unless we are willing to do the same at your house and my house."

Vice President Gerald Ford May 29 disagreed with Graham's view that America had lost its moral compass. Ford said he had "great faith in the basic morality of the American people." "We're going through a very difficult period in Washington," he said, but "we're very fortunate that the institutions we have, both in the courts and in the Congress, are strong enough to take care of any of the problems that have arisen."

Ford joined Graham later May 29 in a foursome at the Kemper Open Invitation Golf Tournament in Birmingham, Ala.

Ford appeared at a GOP fund-raising event in Manchester, N.H. May 31, the same day the Manchester Union Leader, the state's largest circulation newspaper, published a front-page editorial by its publisher, William Loeb, denouncing Ford for "treacherous" disloyalty to Nixon. "Jerry is a jerk," it said, "and we can't stand any more jerks in the White House if we are to survive as a free nation."

Ford denied in an interview June 1 that he was "zigging and zagging" in his comments about Watergate and impeachment and said those who accused him of wavering about Nixon were trying to undercut the President.

According to a survey of more than 100 leading newspapers in 45 states, conducted by Editorials on File, (results released May 31), 47 had called for President Nixon's resignation (32) or impeachment (15), and nine continued to support the President without significant reservations. Some 50 other newspapers surveyed were generally critical of Nixon's refusal to turn over all evidence to the House Judiciary Committee but did not specifically conclude whether or not he should give up his office.

Editorials on File was a New York City-based publication that surveyed U.S. and Canadian editorial opinion.

White House rebuttal—White House spokesmen denied that delaying tactics were being employed against the Watergate and impeachment inquiries. The President, Press Secretary Ziegler asserted May 25, "weighs every factor as he reviews the various proceedings." "He has a unique responsibility," Ziegler said. "He has to act not on what he considers the popular political appeal but on how he views his constitutional responsibilities and the duties of his office. He is determined that his defense against successive encroachments on the confidentiality of his office is right."

The office of the White House counsel was considering "each issue on its merits," Deputy Press Secretary Warren said May 29, and such consideration was not a delaying tactic. "We feel the impeach-

ment proceedings should be conducted at an appropriately fast pace," he said.

Alexander M. Haig Jr., White House chief of staff, admitted Watergate "has diverted a great deal of time and energy of the President and other key public officials." But, he continued, "notwithstanding the difficulties we've made further progress in bringing the government back to the people, in suppressing drug traffic, in bringing back normalcy—the return to sanity, if you will—within our society. This includes the racial area, on the campuses and in our streets." Despite the impact of Watergate, he said, "we've been able to move ahead at home and abroad" and the President had been very active "in doing the business of the American people." Haig's comments were in an interview in U.S. News & World Report magazine June 3.

Nixon to visit Mideast, Moscow. President Nixon's plans to make separate trips to the Soviet Union and the Middle East were announced May 31 and June 4.

The week-long visit to the Soviet Union for conferences with Soviet Communist Party General Secretary Leonid Brezhnev was to begin June 27.

Nixon was to leave June 10 on the trip to the Middle East. The itinerary included Syria, where relations with the U.S. were broken in 1967. Secretary of State Henry A. Kissinger was to accompany the President on the trip, which was expected to last nine or 10 days.

Soviet stress U.S. bipartisan support—In commenting on the President's visit to the Soviet Union, the Communist Party newspaper Pravda stressed June 2 that the summit meeting enjoyed the support of Democrats as well as Republicans in Congress. It avoided earlier partisan attacks, such as issued by the Soviet press agency Tass May 16, contending that the Watergate troubles were "being fanned by the President's political adversaries."

Recent reports in the Soviet press informing readers of Nixon's tax and Watergate problems and the growing threat of impeachment had shown Moscow to be growing increasingly wary of the President's political strength and future. Only eight days before the May 31 announcement, a strong assertion by Nixon that he still planned to make the trip went unreported by the Soviet press.

Brooke, Meany vs. Moscow trip—Domestic opposition to Nixon's planned trip to the Soviet Union was expressed within the context of the impeachment probe.

Sen. Edward W. Brooke (R, Mass.) May 22 "seriously" questioned "the wisdom of a summit meeting in June" when the "question of impeachment could be coming to a head in the House of Representatives." He cautioned that if substantive issues were at stake "the Kremlin might be tempted to seek undue advantage of a weakened President who desperately needs a dramatic gesture to counterbalance his political liabilities." The President, he said, "might compromise to a greater degree than he should or normally would were his position at home more secure" or he "might overreact to an attempted Soviet squeeze" and revert to a stance of Cold War confrontation.

"The possibility of this type of reaction," Brooke said, "cannot be totally dismissed in view of the fact that a hard-line approach by the President could find favor with some members of Congress at a time when the impeachment question would be before them."

Brooke said there was "increasing evidence that the Russian leaders may doubt that the President can effectively make commitments that will be supported by the U.S. Congress and the American people. Hence, they may be unwilling to deal with him on substantive issues during his Moscow visit."

Brooke specifically referred to the strategic arms limitation talks (SALT) between the two countries. He urged the President to forego the Moscow trip until a SALT accord was set, publicized and supported by Congressional leaders.

AFL-CIO President George Meany urged the President June 4 to call off the Soviet trip. Addressing the convention of the AFL-CIO International Ladies Garment Workers Union in Miami Beach, Meany said, "I don't ever want an American president to meet with Mr. Brezhnev except from a position of strength. Mr. Nixon does not occupy a position of strength, and I doubt that he ever will again. Not because he has been crippled by partisan enemies, but because he has crippled himself by his own conduct."

Nixon in command, Haig asserts—Nixon chief of staff Alexander M. Haig Jr. assured Administration officials May 23 that President Nixon was in command of American foreign policy. Haig "made it rather clear" at a meeting with about 250 sub-Cabinet level officials, special presidential assistant Charles M. Lichenstein reported, "that in his view the President was wholly in command and was performing effectively and in detail in all the major trouble areas."

House Republican Leader John J. Rhodes (Ariz.) said May 22 Nixon was "the toughest individual I've ever known" and if anybody thought that he was "going to Moscow and sell anybody out, then they just don't know the man very well."

Poll: public critical of Nixon's handling of economy. The public was critical of President Nixon's handling of economic issues, according to a Louis Harris poll published June 3. In a sample of 1,555 households taken May 4–7, 82% of those surveyed said they did not approve of the "way [Nixon] has handled the economy," and 60% said they felt the Administration's economic policies were doing "more harm than good." (Those favoring Nixon in each poll totaled 15% and 20% respectively.)

Those interviewed were critical of the Administration's ties to business—72% said the Administration and the Republican Party were "too close to big business," 38% said the Administration "has given too many advantages, made too many special deals with business," and 69% said the Administration had been "too easy" on big business.

Charles Colson pleads guilty. Charles W. Colson, former special counsel to President Nixon, pleaded guilty in Washington federal court June 3 to a felony charge that he "unlawfully ... did ... endeavor to influence, obstruct and impede" the trial of Pentagon Papers defendant Daniel Ellsberg. In return for the plea, the Watergate special prosecutor's office agreed to drop all other charges pending against Colson.

As part of his understanding with the prosecutor's office, Colson consented to give it sworn testimony and provide relevant documents in his possession, and in other Watergate-related cases, which observers took to mean the impeachment inquiry against the President. He was still subject to charges of perjury if any future testimony he gave were false, the prosecutor's office said.

Colson pleaded guilty to a one-count criminal information accusing him of "devising and implementing a scheme to defame and destroy the public image and credibility of Daniel Ellsberg and those engaged in the legal defense of Daniel Ellsberg, with the intent to influence, obstruct and impede the conduct and outcome" of the 1973 Ellsberg trial.

Colson faced a maximum prison sentence of five years and a fine of $5,000 or both. Colson was also subject to disbarment from the practice of law as a result of the felony plea.

In a statement issued after his plea had been entered, Colson maintained that he had been innocent of charges contained in the two indictments previously returned against him—the Watergate cover-up and the Ellsberg break-in. But he admitted he was guilty of the charges in the information.

"I have watched," his statement said, "with a heavy heart the country I love being torn apart by one of the most divisive and bitter controversies in our history. The prompt and just resolution of other proceedings, far more important than my trial, is vital to our democratic process. I want to be free to contribute to that resolution no matter who it may help or hurt—me or others. ... That is the dictate of my conscience."

Colson's statement said he was affected by a statement by U.S. District Court Judge Gerhard A. Gesell during pretrial arguments that "for this to be a government of laws and not men, then those men entrusted with enforcing the law must be held to account for the natural consequences of their own actions. ... We cannot accept the principle that men in high government can act in disregard of the rights of even one individual citizen."

Colson also stated that in negotiating a plea with the special prosecutor's office, he had not bargained on the basis of any future testimony he might give.

A White House spokesman said June 4, "We welcome his decision to step forward and tell the truth." Another spokesman said he was certain any testimony Colson might give "would be highly supportive of the President."

Plea linked to conversion—Sen. Harold E. Hughes (D, Iowa) told the Washington Post June 3 that Colson's guilty plea was the result of his "conversion to Christ." According to Hughes, at an informal prayer group attended by Colson, Hughes and three others, Colson said he was not guilty of what he had been charged. "He went in search of what he had done that was criminal," Hughes said. "When he accepted Christ, full truthfulness was the inevitable result."

Ehrlichman subpoena issue resolved—The Colson plea came at the beginning of a hearing called by Gesell to discuss subpoenas sought by Colson and John D. Ehrlichman, a co-defendant in the Ellsberg break-in trial. Colson's subpoenas no longer at issue, Gesell accepted a White House plan that would give Ehrlichman and his attorneys full access to Ehrlichman's personal White House notes. After examining the documents, Ehrlichman would submit a list of needed documents to the court. Reversing a previous position, Gesell also consented to having some "national security" material submitted to him in camera (private) for a determination of relevancy.

However, Gesell repeated his warning that sanctions might be necessary if the White House refused to release the notes deemed relevant to the trial by Ehrlichman and the court. For the first time, Gesell added that failure to produce the evidence could result in a contempt of court citation.

Santarelli quits LEAA post. Donald E. Santarelli's resignation as administrator of the Law Enforcement Assistance Administration (LEAA) was accepted by President Nixon June 4, following publication of a statement by Santarelli that Nixon should resign. In an interview published in the Philadelphia Inquirer June 2, Santarelli was quoted as saying, "There is no White House. There is no White House anymore. It pains me, but I think he [Nixon] should resign. After all, you've got the cleanest vice president in history over there. His whole life's been gone over by every agency imaginable." In an earlier interview with the Associated Press, Santarelli had said he would "very assiduously avoid" using the President's name in public. He was not worried about criticism from the Administration, Santarelli said, because "there is nobody to can me ... no White House to deal with."

In his letter of resignation, Santarelli said he was quitting because of "misleading reports" that had compromised his "ability to continue to serve as a credible and effective administrator" of LEAA.

Experts report on tape gap. U.S. District Court Judge John J. Sirica June 4 released the final report by a court-appointed panel of technical experts on an $18\frac{1}{2}$-minute gap in one of the Watergate tapes surrendered by President Nixon. It confirmed the panel's earlier finding that the gap and buzzing sounds had been put on the tape during a process of manual erasing and rerecording.

The panel said it drew "no inferences about such questions as whether the erasure and buzz were made accidentally or intentionally, or when, or by what person or persons."

(The gap was still under investigation by a grand jury.)

The report, which included a lengthy appendix of back-up data, concluded that the Uher 5000 recorder used by Rose Mary Woods, Nixon's personal secretary, in transcribing tapes had "probably produced the entire buzz section" on the June 20, 1972 recording of the conversation between Nixon and H. R. Haldeman, then White House chief of staff. Magnetic markings on the tape, the panel said, could not have been caused by operation of a foot pedal, contrary to a possible explanation offered earlier by Miss Woods.

The panel said it had examined the hypothesis that the gap and buzz might have been caused by a defective part or other machine malfunction, and conceded that, "when viewed apart from the total body of data, certain individual marks on the evidence tape might be accounted for in ways other than we have described." The report concluded, however, that only its explanation "accounts for the data in their entirety and the patterns they form."

In a statement June 4, special presidential counsel James D. St. Clair criticized the report for creating "the false impression that all portions of the erasure were done manually and deliberately."

St. Clair also issued a report (which had been submitted to the court) prepared by Michael Hecker of the Stanford Research Institute (SRI), which had been retained as White House consultant.

Hecker said the SRI group was in "general agreement" with the court-appointed panel, but was "uncomfortable with the degree of certainty" with which the panel had rejected machine malfunction as a possible explanation for the gap.

According to Hecker, the machine used by Miss Woods was probably defective when the erasure was produced; such a faulty machine, he contended, could produce marks "similar to those observed on the evidence tape."

Hecker's explanation centered on the rectifier in the recorder's power supply, which if defective could cause significant amplitude variations; these variations, in turn, could produce markings closely resembling the so-called "K-1 pulses"—signatures of an internal switch activated from the recorder's keyboard.

(During the court panel's testing, Hecker pointed out, the recorder had failed to operate, and the trouble had been traced to a defective rectifier. The court panel's report had noted, however, that it had tested the machine for about 50 hours before the failure.)

In conclusion, Hecker agreed with the court panel that the presence of a "genuine K-1 pulse" would be "strong evidence of manual operation of the keyboard controls."

Charles S. Rhyne, an attorney for Miss Woods, also took issue with the court panel's report, citing other studies pointing to defects in the recorder as an explanation for the disputed gap. Rhyne had filed a motion with Sirica urging that the panel's report not be received as evidence. The panel was "unqualified," Rhyne argued, and had produced a report "replete with error" and "incompetent opinion based on wrong assumptions."

Governors conference. The National Governors Conference was held in Seattle June 2–5. Former Attorney General Elliot L. Richardson, who spoke June 5, commented on the appropriateness of the time and site when power was shifting from federal to state hands, "from the city of Washington to the state of Washington." The theme was a major undercurrent during the convention as the governors exhibited confidence in the strength of the state as an institution in contrast to a Watergate-weakened Washington. Part of the confidence flowed from a renewed vigor of state financial structure attributed to revenue sharing.

The governors focused June 4 on "ethics in state government" at which the press and reform organizations, specifically Common Cause, were subjected to some criticism. However, Common Cause Chairman John Gardner, who addressed the session, praised the states for being responsive to "the citizens' concern for a housecleaning in politics" and "many governors" for playing "distinguished roles in advancing the causes of responsive, accountable government."

The governors also held separate party caucuses June 4 with their party chairmen Robert S. Strauss (D) and George Bush (R). Kenneth R. Cole Jr., Nixon aide for domestic affairs and the second Administration representative at the conference, warned that a "veto-proof" Congress resulting from the November elections "would continue the federal big-daddy approach for another 40 years."

On opening day, six of the governors appeared on NBC's "Meet the Press" program broadcast from Seattle June 2. All six, including two Republicans, asserted that President Nixon should comply in full with the House Judiciary Committee's request for evidence for its impeachment inquiry.

Some went even further. Gov. Jimmy Carter (D, Ga.) said "I personally think that the President is guilty and I think that the release of evidence will prove it." Gov. Tom McCall (R, Ore.) said impeachment was a "completely ludicrous procedure" and Nixon should resign immediately.

The others on the panel were Govs. Daniel J. Evans (R, Wash.), outgoing conference chairman, Wendell Ford (D, Ky.), Daniel Walker (D, Ill.) and Wendell R. Anderson (D, Minn.).

Impeachment inquiry continues. The House Judiciary Committee continued its closed hearings June 4–6 to consider evidence gathered by its staff in the impeachment inquiry.

The first two sessions focused on Nixon Administration dealings with the International Telephone and Telegraph Corp. and the dairy industry; the June 6 session considered the Administration's secret domestic surveillance activities, including 17 wiretaps effected in 1969 against government officials and reporters.

Conflicting reports emerged from the sessions on whether the material presented helped or hurt President Nixon in his stand against impeachment.

Much of the wiretap material consisted of summaries of FBI transcripts of recorded conversations, with the names of those subjected to the taps excised. The committee also was said to be in possession of court papers from the civil lawsuit filed by Morton H. Halperin, a former presidential aide, because of the government's wiretap against him.

The wiretap session led to renewed speculation concerning the extent of the role played by Secretary of State Henry A. Kissinger, whether he initiated any of the surveillance or saw or utilized information gleaned from it. At a press conference June 6, Kissinger declared he "did not make a direct recommendation" for such surveillance and he reiterated his Senate testimony that his role had been limited to supplying names of some aides who had access to sensitive material that had been leaked and thus became targets of the surveillance.

When he was pressed by reporters for details, Kissinger bristled. "This is a press conference and not a cross-examination," he said, "I do not conduct my office as a conspiracy."

[For the complete chronology of events in the Kissinger wiretap controversy, see the chapter on domestic spying]

Staff reports 'responsiveness' plan. The staff of the Senate Watergate Committee, in a draft report circulated among committee members June 7, said White House officials had conducted a "concerted and concealed endeavor" to "politicize" the executive branch "to insure that the Administration remained in power" in the 1972 election. The so-called "responsiveness program," according to the report, was "among the most dangerous activities discovered" by the committee, and "may rise to the level of a conspiracy to interfere with the lawful functioning of government.

Alluding to possible "conspiracy to defraud the U.S.," the staff contended that the White House efforts were not "politics as usual," but had involved "the diverting of millions of taxpayers' dollars . . . to the political goal of re-electing the President."

The staff said the program was designed (in 1971) and later largely supervised by Frederic V. Malek, then a special assistant to Nixon and currently deputy director of the Office of Management and Budget. But according to documents and testimony compiled by the staff, the program was known, in varying degress of detail, to former Nixon aides H. R. Haldeman, John D. Ehrlichman and Charles Colson, former Attorney General and campaign director John N. Mitchell and former Treasury Secretary George P. Shultz. According to one memorandum by Malek, the program had "the President's full backing."

In analyzing the program, the staff noted several levels of operation in the executive branch which were used to promote Nixon's re-election: "selective funding" with federal contracts and grants to key states and voting blocs; the shaping of "legal and regulatory action to enhance campaign goals"; political ratings of applicants for federal jobs subject to Civil Service regulations; withdrawal of federal aid to punish groups deemed to be too close to the Democrats; and solicitation by government officials of campaign contributions from aid recipients.

Especially strong efforts were directed at black and Spanish-speaking voters, the report said. Quoting a memo on black programs, the report cited instructions that projects should be identified and promised funding through the White House in return for "a strong vote commitment for the President from the recipient."

Regarding Spanish-speaking groups, the staff cited "substantial—if not overwhelming—evidence" that "political

elements" in the Administration and re-election committee had sought direct control over the awarding of grants and contracts. The report also cited an attempt by the White House and campaign committee to prevent the release of Census Bureau statistics on minority economic achievements that might reflect adversely on the Administration.

Other efforts were directed toward the aged, including official agency brochures promising aid and designed to help the re-election campaign, and grants to an organization which, according to the report, was of questionable efficacy as a social service institution but was known to be "friendly to the Administration."

The report conceded that it was "hardly unprecedented" for an administration to aid disadvantaged groups in hopes that political benefits might result; but, the report charged, "the present Administration ventured far beyond the normal course."

According to the report, the "responsiveness" program was apparently abandoned after the Watergate break-in June 17, 1972.

Military Spies
& 'Security' Wiretaps*

White House military spy ring disclosed. Until its exposure in late 1971, a military spy ring, operating within the National Security Council (NSC), passed highly secret information concerning U.S. diplomatic initiatives to officials in the Pentagon, it was reported Jan. 11.

David R. Young Jr., a member of the Special White House investigative unit known as the "plumbers," concluded in a book-length report he submitted to President Nixon in early 1972 that confidential information from the office of Henry A. Kissinger, head of the NSC, had been supplied by the ring to Adm. Thomas H. Moorer, chairman of the Joint Chiefs of Staff (JCS), the New York Times reported Jan. 14. Moorer labeled the report "ludicrous."

The Times had reported Jan. 11 that data from Kissinger's NSC office had been obtained by "ransacking of classified files and the unauthorized photocopying of documents." According to the Times, Young stumbled across the spy ring while investigating the publication by syndicated newspaper columnist Jack Anderson of secret minutes of NSC meetings concerning the India-Pakistan war of 1971.

Implicated in the ring were Rear Adm. Robert O. Welander, in 1971 liaison officer between the NSC and the JCS, and his chief aide, Yeoman 1.C. Charles E. Radford, who had also been on Moorer's Pentagon office staff. Welander, whose post was later abolished, and Radford were subsequently transferred to new assignments.

Anderson said Jan. 17 neither Welander nor Radford had been his source for the notes of the NSC meetings on the India-Pakistan war. However, Anderson agreed that military aides attached to Kissinger had "filched" secret data from Kissinger's files. Frustrated over President Nixon's "obsessive secrecy" with regard to diplomatic moves that affected the armed forces, Anderson reported, Moorer had

set up his own "pipeline" to the White House. Anderson named Navy Capt. Arthur K. Knoizen, Moorer's executive assistant, as the recipient of information obtained by Welander. Anderson said Knoizen also received detailed minutes from Navy Capt. Howard N. Kay who represented the Pentagon at meetings of Kissinger's secret Washington Special Action Group. Kay's minutes were considerably more detailed than the ones sent to the Pentagon through official channels, Anderson said.

The Washington Post reported Jan. 13 that the spy ring had been the product of Pentagon efforts to acquire data on Kissinger's secret diplomatic initiatives to China, North Vietnam and the Soviet Union. In order to bring changes in basic U.S. foreign policy, the Post said, Kissinger felt the need to shut out those committed to a traditional Cold War doctrine. Post sources in and out of the Pentagon challenged suggestions that the spy ring had been a military effort to usurp civilian authority. "The military was trying to maintain what had been legally accessible in the past and which was being choked off," one Post source said.

An unnamed Justice Department official, cited by the Times Jan. 15, refused to say no illegalities had occurred, but he pointed out that Moorer, the nation's highest military officer, was almost certainly "cleared for everything."

Other Times sources familiar with the workings of the NSC said a separate distribution system was used to deny officials—regardless of classification—access to materials about which they had no need to know. A former NSC staff member, the Times reported, indicated that Pentagon officials would be privy to formal NSC position papers but not to private presidential papers or documents dealing with Kissinger's private demarches.

White House reaction—Apprised of the story Jan. 10, the White House said the accounts of the spy ring "convey an incorrect impression of the knowledge and actions" of Moorer; that the source of the leaks had been "a low-level employe whose clerical tasks gave him access to highly classified information"; and that the accounts were "fragmentary."

Privately, the Times reported Jan. 17, White House officials Jan. 10 had depicted the matter as extremely serious and said the President had chosen not to disclose the situation in order to protect the "whole military command structure." However, the Times said the White House changed its tack Jan. 15, describing the spy ring incidents as the work of an "eager-beaver" Navy enlisted man (Radford).

The Post Jan. 13 suggested that President Nixon had been talking about the military spy ring when he said at a November 1973 press conference that the plumbers had uncovered "leaks which were seriously damaging to the national security, including one that I have pointed out that was so serious that Sen. Ervin and Sen. Baker agreed it should not be disclosed." (Sens. Sam J. Ervin Jr. (D, N.C.) and Howard Baker (R, Tenn.) were respectively chairman and vice chairman of the Senate Watergate Committee.)

The Post also cited informed sources who said White House attorney J. Fred Buzhardt Jr. had attempted to discourage criminal investigation of members of the plumbers squad. Buzhardt had warned that indictments might threaten national security because members of the plumbers might be forced to disclose national security matters as part of their defense. Buzhardt was reported to have mentioned three specific national security items: the military spy ring; the existence of a double agent in the Soviet embassy who was working for U.S. intelligence, and a Central Intelligence Agency (CIA) informer in the Indian government. Post sources said the informer in the Indian government had been compromised by a story that appeared in the New York Times in 1971, and that the value of Soviet agent had long been questioned by many in the U.S. intelligence community.

Blackmailer tried to use spy ring—The Times reported Jan. 13 that a government official—whose identity could not be learned—who participated in the plumber's investigation of the military spy ring, attempted to "blackmail" his way into an important job by threatening to make the secret information public. According to Times sources, President Nixon rejected the demand but did not order the official discharged or arrested,

*For a complete listing of references to developments relating to the undercover activities of the White House 'plumbers' and the trial of former presidential adviser John D. Ehrlichman for his role in that group's break-in at the office of Dr. Daniel Ellsberg's psychiatrist's office, consult the Index under the following headings: EHRLICHMAN, John D.; PENTAGON Papers.

C

D

E

F

G

as he feared such a move would generate unwanted publicity.

Wiretap story disputed—The White House branded as "inaccurate" a report appearing in the Chicago Sun-Times Jan. 12 that in 1971 Kissinger ordered a wiretap placed on the Pentagon office phone of Melvin Laird, then secretary of defense, who Kissinger felt might be a recipient of leaked NSC data. The New York Times had also reported Jan. 12 that Young during the course of his investigations was ordered to report directly Gen. Alexander M. Haig Jr., then Kissinger's chief deputy in the NSC. Kissinger had denied knowledge of the plumbers' activities.

Probes announced—Secretary of Defense James R. Schlesinger announced Jan. 15 that he had launched an informal investigation into charges that a spy ring had passed secret documents to the Pentagon without authorization. A Pentagon spokesman noted that Laird had ordered an investigation into news leaks concerning the India-Pakistan war, but, the spokesman said, he did not know whether a formal report had been filed.

Sen. John C. Stennis (D, Miss.), chairman of the Senate Armed Services Committee, said Jan. 14 that he planned to begin an informal probe of the alleged spy ring. (Stennis, 72, had announced his decision to seek re-election Jan. 10.)

Wiretap disclosure ordered. U.S. District Court Judge Aubrey E. Robinson Jr. ruled in Washington Jan. 11 that the Justice Department must reveal the nature and extent of wiretaps and other surveillance of antiwar activists in 1968-69.

The ruling came in a civil suit filed in 1969 under the Omnibus Crime Act of 1968 providing compensation for victims of illegal wiretapping. The suit had been delayed during criminal trials of some of the plaintiffs, including the "Chicago Seven." Other plantiffs were the War Resisters League, the Catholic Priests Fellowship, the Southern Conference Education Fund and the Black Panther Party.

Judge Robinson rejected Justice Department contentions that the wire taps should be kept secret for national security reasons and refused as "highly irregular" a government request that he examine the information privately.

Kissinger denies role in leak probe. Secretary of State Henry A. Kissinger said Jan. 22 that his role in the White House investigation of a military spy ring passing secret documents from the National Security Council (NSC) to the Pentagon was limited to listening to a tape-recorded interrogation of Rear Adm. Robert O. Welander, liaison officer between the NSC and the Joint Chiefs of Staff (JCS).

Kissinger admitted that he knew his former aide, David R. Young Jr., had been the interrogator of Welander but he denied that this new disclosure in any way contradicted his testimony before the Senate Foreign Relations Committee during hearings on his confirmation as secretary of state. Kissinger had testified to the committee Sept. 7, 1973: "I have no knowledge of any such activities that David Young may have engaged in. I did not know of the existence of the plumbers group. . . . Nor did I know that . . . Young was concerned with internal security matters."

At a State Department news briefing Jan. 22, during which he also discussed the Middle East situation, Kissinger recounted that an investigation of leaked NSC documents concerning the India-Pakistan war of 1971 had been placed in the hands of John D. Ehrlichman, then domestic affairs adviser to President Nixon, who was in overall charge of the White House investigative unit known as the "plumbers." Subsequently, Kissinger said, Ehrlichman asked him to listen to a tape-recorded interrogation of Welander. Although he conceded that he learned from Ehrlichman that Young was the interrogator, Kissinger insisted he did not know Young had been in charge of the probe. (During the interrogation Welander had revealed the existence of the NSC military spy ring.)

Moorer plays down data importance—Appearing on the National Broadcasting Co. (NBC) program "Today" Jan. 18, Adm. Thomas H. Moorer, chairman of the JCS, conceded that he received "file" documents taken from the NSC in 1971, but he said he had paid little attention to them because they were "essentially useless and duplicated material obtained through normal channels."

Yeoman Charles E. Radford, a Navy stenographer assigned to Welander, had assembled a file of copies of documents he had typed for Kissinger's office, Moorer said. Welander delivered the copies to him (Moorer) with the explanation that his "yeoman had retained these in his clerical duties," Moorer said. Since it was "readily apparent," Moorer said, "I was familiar" with the subjects, "I simply did not follow through as to the precise origin of these papers."

Claiming that his problem was not finding information but dealing with the excessive amount he had, Moorer said when he eventually learned of the full import of the matter, he instructed Welander to return any such papers to the NSC. He stressed that Radford had been "overzealous" in providing the extra data.

Moorer also disclosed that Welander had been the one who discovered that Radford had "leaked" the NSC minutes concerning the India-Pakistan war to syndicated columnist Jack Anderson. Asked why Radford had not been punished, Moorer cited a lack of firm evidence.

Blackmailer identified—The New York Times reported Jan. 25 that W. Donald Stewart, inspector general of the Defense Investigative Service, had been identified by "informed sources" as the man who tried to blackmail his way into a high level government job by threatening to reveal what he knew about the military spy ring passing documents from the NSC to the Pentagon.

Stewart, who was in charge of the Pentagon's investigation of Yeoman Radford, sent a communication to President Nixon in May or June 1973, in which he requested the post of director of the Federal Bureau of Investigation (FBI), the Times said. The communication was given to Alexander M. Haig Jr., Nixon's chief of staff, who subsequently told Stewart, Times sources said, "to go to hell." Haig, who confirmed the incident to the Times, without identifying the blackmailer, said the extortionist had not been fired from his Pentagon job for fear he would make his information public.

According to the Times, Stewart had also given his information about the passing of documents to Senate Watergate Committee minority counsel Fred D. Thompson, who relayed it to Sen. Howard Baker (R, Tenn.), vice chairman of the Senate committee.

During public committee interrogation of Ehrlichman, Baker attempted to raise the matter of the spy ring, the Times said. However, Ehrlichman balked at responding and asked for a private meeting concerning the matter. At the private meeting attended by White House aides and Watergate Committee leaders, the blackmail scheme was revealed by the Nixon aides, the Times reported.

Schlesinger backs Moorer—Stating he was no "great admirer" of the "plumbers," Secretary of Defense James R. Schlesinger said Jan. 24 that he was "inclined to doubt" the conclusion drawn by David Young that a military spy ring had passed secret NSC documents to Moorer. He agreed there had been "improprieties" in the way data had been passed between the NSC and the JCS, but asserted there was "no evidence of illegalities" nor indication that a "spy ring" had existed.

Acknowledging that Moorer might have been more observant of documents passing through his office, Schlesinger added that Moorer had not been familiar with the "exuberant" methods used to obtain the material.

Schlesinger also disclosed that White House counsel J. Fred Buzhardt Jr. had refused him access to the tape-recorded interrogation of NSC liaison Welander by Young. The denial, Schlesinger speculated, might have been because the tape had been impounded as evidence in the forthcoming trials of members of the "plumbers" unit.

Nixon on privacy. In his State of the Union Message delivered before a joint session of Congress Jan. 30, President Nixon spoke on the right of personal privacy. These were his remarks:

One measure of a truly free society is the vigor with which it protects the liberties of its individual citizens. As technology has advanced in America, it has increasingly encroached on one of those liberties what I term the right of personal privacy. Modern information systems, data banks, credit records, mailing list abuses, electronic snooping, the collection of personal data for one purpose that may be used for another—all these have left millions of Americans deeply concerned by the privacy they cherish.

And the time has come, therefore, for a major initiative to define the nature and extent of the basic rights of privacy and to erect new safeguards to insure that those rights are respected.

I shall launch such an effort this year at the highest levels of the Administration, and I look forward again to working with this Congress and establishing a new set of standards that respect the legitimate needs of society but that also recognize personal privacy as a cardinal principle of American liberty.

Nixon's brother ordered spied upon. The New York Times reported Feb. 4 that the Secret Service was ordered to spy on the President's brother, F. Donald Nixon. [For further details, see p. 39G2]

Moorer sought Radford court-martial. Adm. Thomas H. Moorer, chairman of the Joint Chiefs of Staff (JCS), said he twice recommended institution of court-martial proceedings against Navy Yeoman 1.C. Charles E. Radford for leaking secret National Security Council (NSC) documents to the press in 1971, but in both instances civilian authorities overruled him. Uncertain as to who made the decision not to court-martial Radford, Moorer, who spoke to newsmen after giving secret testimony to the Senate Armed Services Committee Feb. 6, was not clear why the proceedings had not been begun, except that he "guessed it was concluded the evidence was circumstantial."

The committee also heard secret testimony from Secretary of State Henry Kissinger, who reiterated an earlier stated position that he had nothing to do with the investigation of the NSC spy ring.

In a letter sent Jan. 30 to Sen. John C. Stennis (D, Miss.), chairman of the Armed Services Committee, Moorer said that on two occasions only had he received secret NSC documents purloined by Radford, a Navy stenographer often assigned to NSC Director Kissinger. Moorer claimed that Radford had retained "miscellaneous staff papers, roughs and questionnaires" from Kissinger's July 1971 trip to Pakistan and China.

Subsequently, Moorer said, he received from Rear Adm. Robert O. Welander, liaison officer between the NSC and the JCS, "working papers" kept by Radford. A second group of documents came to him from Welander, Moorer said, after Radford returned from a trip to Southeast Asia he made in September 1971 with Brig. Gen. Alexander M. Haig Jr., then Kissinger's chief aide in the NSC.

On neither occasion did he inquire about the exact source of the documents, Moorer said, since they contained information he already possessed. When he learned that Radford had collected the papers in an unauthorized manner, Moorer said he ordered the documents returned to the NSC. Moreover, Moorer denied he had any part in the pilfering of NSC documents. He emphasized he had "easy access" to Kissinger.

In contrast to Moorer's explanation, the New York Times reported Feb. 3 that

military spying of the NSC had begun in the fall of 1970 and continued for 15 months until December 1971 when Radford confessed to Pentagon investigators.

Among the documents taken by Radford and shown to Moorer, the Times reported, were copies of "eyes only" messages from the U.S. ambassadors in South Vietnam and Cambodia that were intended solely for President Nixon and Kissinger. The Washington Post reported Jan. 25 that Radford had access to Kissinger's secret handwritten notes and papers from Kissinger's first top secret visit to China.

The Times also reported Feb. 3 that the passing of NSC documents to the Pentagon had begun under Welander's predecessor, Rear Adm. Rembrandt C. Robinson, who was killed in a helicopter crash in Southeast Asia in 1972. Under Robinson, the Times said, very little of importance was taken.

Radford disputes Moorer on spy ring. Yeoman 1.C. Charles E. Radford told Seymour M. Hersh, a reporter for the New York Times, Feb. 8 that he had pilfered hundreds of top-secret National Security Council (NSC) documents while he served as a stenographer-clerk for the military liaison office in the NSC. He said he had been instructed by two admirals to obtain the documents, which were subsequently forwarded to the Pentagon office of Adm. Thomas H. Moorer, chairman of the Joint Chiefs of Staff (JCS). The two rear admirals named by Radford were Rembrandt C. Robinson and Robert O. Welander, both former heads of the NSC military liaison office and both direct superiors of Radford.

In contradicting statements made by Moorer, Radford said he had always believed that Moorer was aware of his activities. Radford claimed that Robinson on several occasions conveyed this fact to him. Radford indicated that at least four different officers assigned to Moorer received documents from late 1970 to the end of 1971. Those documents, he said, were "sanitized"—all identifying marks were clipped off and the material was pasted on plain white paper. Material solely intended for Moorer, Radford added, was delivered with all the original markings intact.

Radford met privately with Sen. John C. Stennis, chairman of the Senate Armed Services Committee Feb. 10. Radford and Stennis declined comment.

IRS returns Times phone records. The Internal Revenue Service (IRS) Feb. 13 returned to the Chesapeake and Potomac Telephone Co. (C&P) telephone records of the Washington bureau of the New York Times that it had secretly subpoenaed Jan. 8. Not among the returned records, however, were logs of toll calls made from the Maryland home of Washington-based Times reporter David E. Rosenbaum, whose name had appeared on the Jan. 8 IRS subpoena for the Times records. (Rosenbaum said Feb. 12 that

the IRS might have been interested in the calls he made when he was investigating charges of tax evasion against a major contributor to President Nixon's 1972 campaign.)

The IRS said it had subpoenaed the records as part of an investigation into a leak of information by an IRS employe. The records were procured by an "administrative summons," a legal instrument normally reserved for tax evasion cases and one not giving notice to the person or organization under scrutiny.

Reporters' panel to seek injunction—The Reporters Committee for Freedom of the Press said Feb. 11 it would seek a court order enjoining the American Telephone & Telegraph Co. (AT&T) from secretly providing law enforcement agencies with telephone records of newsmen.

The suit, aimed at insuring newsmen of notice of service so they would be able to fight the subpoenas in court, followed disclosure by the St. Louis Post-Dispatch Feb. 1 that the Justice Department had issued secret subpoenas in 1971 for the telephone records of the Post-Dispatch, Knight Newspapers Inc. and Leslie H. Whitten, an associate of syndicated columnist Jack Anderson.

AT&T promises notice of subpoenas—AT&T announced Feb. 15 that it would notify its customers when records of their long distance phone calls were subpoenaed by government investigators. The phone company also agreed to supply the records only in response to subpoenas, not simply to written requests as had been the policy in the past. However, AT&T qualified its announcement, saying subscribers would be notified in all cases except when "the agency requesting the records directs the company not to disclose, certifying that such a notification could impede its investigation and interfere with enforcement of the law."

A spokesman for the Reporters Committee for Freedom of the Press said the exception potentially nullified AT&T's entire commitment to advance notification.

Yeoman and admiral disagree on roles. Appearing before the Senate Armed Services Committee Feb. 20 and Feb. 21 respectively, Yeoman 1.C. Charles E. Radford and Rear. Adm. Robert O. Welander gave contradictory testimony concerning their roles in a military spy ring alleged to have passed top secret documents from the National Security Council (NSC) to the office of Adm. Thomas H. Moorer, chairman of the Joint Chiefs of Staff (JCS).

Under oath, Welander denied he had ever "ordered or directed" Radford to "obtain or save" documents in an unauthorized fashion. Instead, Welander suggested, Radford had implicated him in the passing of the documents in order to shift the focus of a White House investigation linking the yeoman to the leaking of NSC minutes to syndicated columnist Jack Anderson.

According to a prepared statement released by Welander after his closed door testimony before the committee, he was called to the White House by former presidential adviser John D. Ehrlichman, who was the nominal supervisor of the Administration's investigative unit known as the "plumbers," which was assigned to probe the Anderson leak. "After a few preliminary questions ... [Ehrlichman] presented me a prepared statement on White House stationery for my signature. This statement would have had me admit to the wildest possible, totally false charges of political spying," Welander testified. Welander said he refused to sign and Ehrlichman backed down.

Welander said Ehrlichman's questions about the passing of documents from the NSC to the JCS had been based on information given the "plumbers" by Radford, who at that time was the "prime suspect in an offense," the Anderson leak, which, Welander said, "in another time would have been branded treason."

Welander conceded that he had received "a collection of tissue copies and rough drafts of staff reports, memoranda of conversations and outgoing cables" from Radford, after Radford had returned from two secret negotiating trips to Asia. Acknowledging that this information did "supplement" and "highlight" data he received through normal channels, Welander denied that he had any reason to doubt Radford's statements "that he acquired the documents in the regular course of his clerical duties."

Radford had given secret sworn testimony to the Senate panel the previous day and afterward released a prepared statement. He recounted that soon after he was assigned to the liaison unit between the NSC and the JCS, his superior, the late Rear Adm. Rembrandt C. Robinson, told "me that I was in an important position ... of great trust. He told me I would be seeing things that in some cases, he would not see and that, as I became more familiar with his files, I would know what he was interested in; that I should make sure of what he saw, or knew about what I saw, by bringing him a copy."

In July 1971, Radford testified, while at the President's home in San Clemente, Calif., having just returned from a trip to Asia, during which he was a stenographic aide to NSC Director Henry A. Kissinger, Radford received a telephone call from Welander, who asked him to obtain an agenda to a later Presidential meeting that was to be attended by Moorer. The yeoman said he followed instructions and was later told by Welander that he (Radford) "had no idea how helpful it was for the chairman of the joint chiefs to walk into a meeting and know what was going to be said."

In addition, Radford said, he had obtained a copy of a report from Kissinger to Nixon meant for the President's "eyes only." The report dealt with Kissinger's personal notes about secret conversations he had in July 1971 with Chou En-lai, the Chinese premier, the yeoman said. After-

ward, Moorer's personal aide "walked through the office and said, 'Radford, keep up the good work.' I knew what he meant. Nothing else was said," Radford testified.

Radford named 10 Pentagon officers who received documents he had purloined from the NSC files, including Moorer, Adm. Elmo R. Zumwalt, chief of naval operations, and Air Force Gen. John W. Vogt Jr., the current Pacific commander who was then assigned to the JCS. Also cited by Radford were two Navy captains, who served as Moorer's executive assistants in 1970 and 1971: Harry D. Train 2nd and Arthur K. Knoizen.

Radford did not submit direct evidence that Moorer had been involved in the spying scheme but said he "assumed" and "believed" Moorer had received the purloined materials.

After hearing testimony from Radford and Welander, committee member Sen. Harold E. Hughes (D, Iowa) said Feb. 21: "At this point there seems to be a direct conflict. One or the other would have to be committing perjury."

In a related development Feb. 21, the Senate committee released secret testimony given it by Kissinger. Kissinger testified that none of his personal communications to the President had been made available to the Pentagon, and only some information about secret negotiations with North Vietnam had been forwarded.

Nixon barred charges in NSC spying case. Sources close to the inquiry by the special White House investigative unit, the "plumbers," said Feb. 23 that President Nixon had personally ordered his former domestic affairs adviser John D. Ehrlichman, also nominal head of the "plumbers," not to seek prosecution of any of the military personnel suspected of passing top secret documents from the National Security Council (NSC) to the office of Adm. Thomas H. Moorer, chairman of the Joint Chiefs of Staff (JCS).

According to the Times, a closely involved source quoted Ehrlichman as saying: "The President called me off it. He said, 'John, if you prosecute this, you'll blow the whole thing open.'"

Picturing Nixon as irate over the pilfering of NSC documents not intended for Pentagon eyes, the sources said the President decided against bringing charges, for fear White House secrets would be compromised during the legal proceedings.

This explanation was challenged by Sen. Harold E. Hughes (D. Iowa), a member of the Senate Armed Services Committee: "As far as I know, there are no classified secrets involved that could have gotten out. Any court-martial proceedings would have been held behind closed doors, and none of it would have been available to the public."

Ex-JCS aide admits receipt of papers— Marine Corps Col. James A. MacDonald (ret.), a JCS staff officer in 1971, told the

New York Times Feb. 22 that he received four illicitly obtained NSC documents that provided the Pentagon with advance information on later high-level White House meetings attended by the President and Henry A. Kissinger, then director of the NSC.

Claiming that Rear Adm. Robert O. Welander, liaison officer between the NSC and the JCS, routinely provided Pentagon officials with purloined NSC documents in the last half of 1971, MacDonald said he returned the documents which had been previously stripped of all identifying marks to prevent tracing, to Adm. Moorer's office.

"I had no feeling of being devious," MacDonald said, adding that the information provided in the documents given him by Welander was officially made available to Moorer at a later time. "Maybe the admiral [Moorer] didn't know all this at 11 a.m., but he'd get it anyway at 3 p.m."

Nixon handling of spying probed—The Times reported Feb. 26 that the office of special Watergate prosecutor Leon Jaworski had begun an investigation of President Nixon's handling of military spying in the NSC in 1971. Investigators for Jaworski's office were allowed to see the classified report on the snooping prepared by David R. Young Jr, a member of the plumbers, the Times reported

Privacy panel announced. President Nixon announced in a radio address Feb. 23 that he was creating a "top-priority" Cabinet-level committee to recommend measures to protect individual privacy against computerized data banks and other developments of "advanced technology" used by both government and private institutions.

Hart scores 'political spying'—The Democrats' "equal time" reply to Nixon's address was delivered March 2 by Sen. Philip A. Hart (Mich.), who called on the President to "immediately" ban any wiretapping or electronic surveillance not authorized by court order and to "state without equivocation that the label of 'national security' will not be used again to hide or excuse illegal acts." Instead of "the naming of a new committee," Hart said, Nixon should have ordered "everyone in his Administration to refrain from political spying of any kind."

"Perhaps understandably in the light of Watergate," Hart said, "the President chose to paint the primary threat as one of technology. We have learned to our regret that, with or without sophisticated technology, unprincipled men can find ways to invade our privacy."

Hart noted that in addition to the acts of the Watergate burglars and the White House "plumbers" unit, the government had used Army personnel "to spy on peaceful political meetings" and had used the confidential files of the Internal Revenue Service "to harass persons on a White House enemies list."

Buzhardt testifies on military spying. J. Fred Buzhardt Jr., former chief counsel to the Defense Department, disputed suggestions that the Nixon Administration had decided not to prosecute a military liaison officer and an aide for passing secret documents from the National Security Council (NSC) to the Pentagon for fear that such a disclosure would compromise the government's case against Daniel Ellsberg, who was accused of leaking the Pentagon Papers.

Buzhardt, currently counsel to the President, testified in secret March 7 before the Senate Armed Services Committee, which was investigating the spy ring. After his testimony, Buzhardt spoke to reporters.

Buzhardt acknowledged that the Administration accepted and then overruled a Defense Department recommendation not to indict and prosecute Ellsberg. At the time, Buzhardt said, he believed the case was "too complex" to be presented effectively and that the risk of Ellsberg's acquittal was too high. He denied a story in the New York Times March 7 that Pentagon objections were based on national security reasons and added that he did not know who made the final decision to prosecute Ellsberg.

A suggestion by the Times that the President's decision to prosecute Ellsberg for reasons of national security was politically motivated was rejected by Buzhardt, who asserted that national security "didn't matter one way or the other" in the Ellsberg case.

Buzhardt said the cases against Adm. Robert O. Welander and Yeoman 1.C. Charles E. Radford for passing documents from the NSC to the Pentagon were circumstantial and not prosecutable. He added that the investigation of the alleged spying by the White House unit, the "plumbers," did not depict a "military spy ring."

White House used secret Pentagon link—At the time military officers were allegedly passing secret documents from the NSC to the Pentagon, the White House was using its own private channel to the Pentagon and receiving information from the military without the knowledge of the secretary of defense, the Washington Post reported March 3.

The exchange of information was between Adm. Thomas H. Moorer, chairman of the Joint Chiefs of Staff (JCS), and Henry A. Kissinger, director of the NSC. Although the secretary of defense was the superior of the chairman of the JSC, a technical provision under law allowed direct communication between the JCS and the White House, the Post said.

According to the Post, former Secretary of Defense Melvin R. Laird and his deputy David Packard were upset when they became aware of the private channel.

The material passed in the private channel primarily involved Pentagon policy on withdrawal from Vietnam, with civilian Pentagon officials backing one approach, and the military, allied with the White House, supporting another.

White House files personnel data—Computerized data was kept by the White House personnel office on all full-time noncareer employes in the federal government. A Washington Star-News report May 15 said some 6,000 persons were informed by letter of the data file and invited to review the information for accuracy. Half of the persons involved were top-level federal employes, the others were those who had applied for the posts. In addition to usual personnel statistics, the data included ethnic and political background "when available."

Impeachment inquiry continues. The House Judiciary Committee continued its closed hearings June 4–6 to consider evidence gathered by its staff in the impeachment inquiry.

The first two sessions focused on Nixon Administration dealings with the International Telephone and Telegraph Corp. and the dairy industry; the June 6 session considered the Administration's secret domestic surveillance activities, including 17 wiretaps effected in 1969 against government officials and reporters.

Conflicting reports emerged from the sessions on whether the material presented helped or hurt President Nixon in his stand against impeachment.

Much of the wiretap material consisted of summaries of FBI transcripts of recorded conversations, with the names of those subjected to the taps excised. The committee also was said to be in possession of court papers from the civil lawsuit filed by Morton H. Halperin, a former presidential aide, because of the government's wiretap against him.

The wiretap session led to renewed speculation concerning the extent of the role played by Secretary of State Henry A. Kissinger, whether he initiated any of the surveillance or saw or utilized information gleaned from it. At a press conference June 6, Kissinger declared he "did not make a direct recommendation" for such surveillance and he reiterated his Senate testimony that his role had been limited to supplying names of some aides who had access to sensitive material that had been leaked and thus became targets of the surveillance.

When he was pressed by reporters for details, Kissinger bristled. "This is a press conference and not a cross-examination," he said, "I do not conduct my office as a conspiracy."

Kissinger threatens to resign over taps. Secretary of State Henry A. Kissinger threatened to resign June 11 unless charges that he had participated in "illegal or shady" wiretapping activity were cleared up. The secretary made the remark during an emotional news conference in Salzburg, Austria, during President Nixon's stopover preparatory to his Mideast tour.

Appearing to be hurt and angry, Kissinger, in a shaking voice, complained of "innuendoes" and said he did not believe it was possible to conduct the foreign policy of the nation "under these circumstances when the character and credibility of the secretary of state is at issue." "And if it is not cleared up, I will resign," he declared.

Kissinger's surprise threat to quit his post was prompted by reports from unidentified Congressional sources that Kissinger had a more extensive role in federal wiretapping efforts than he had led senators to believe at his confirmation hearing in 1973.

The reports suggested: he had initiated the wiretapping—which was undertaken by the government against 13 federal officials and four newsmen from 1969–71; he had prior knowledge of formation of the White House investigation unit known as the "plumbers" in 1971; the order to end the "national security" wiretaps came from his office; and then-National Security Council (NSC) aide Alexander M. Haig Jr., presumably acting for Kissinger, vetoed at least two, and possibly three, FBI proposals in mid-1969 to terminate one tap, at the home of Morton I. Halperin, because it was unproductive.

Before leaving with the presidential party on the Mideast trip, Kissinger appeared before the Senate Foreign Relations Committee June 7 to defend his credibility on the issue. According to unpublished White House transcripts, circulating to members of the House Judiciary Committee, President Nixon had remarked on Feb. 28, 1973 in a White House talk that Kissinger had asked that the 1969 taps be instituted. Sen. Edmund S. Muskie (D, Me.) asked Kissinger at the hearing June 7 if he had originated the recommendation for the wiretapping program. "I did not," Kissinger replied. He said he "had the impression" that the President's comments were "based on a misapprehension."

Kissinger said his role "was in supplying names as part of a program instituted by the President, the attorney general and the director of the Federal Bureau of Investigation (FBI) to protect the national security."

The day before, during a news conference at which he expected to deal primarily with his Mideast diplomacy, Kissinger's role in the wiretapping was again raised. One question was whether he had retained counsel "in preparation for a defense against a possible perjury indictment." Kissinger, stung, retorted he did not conduct his office as a conspiracy.

After Kissinger's Salzburg news conference, Senate Democratic Leader Mike Mansfield (Mont.) disclosed that he had met Kissinger June 8 and "he was in some distress" because of the wiretapping thing "hanging over him." Kissinger had, indicated, Mansfield said, "he might have to consider resigning." Mansfield added: "I told him not to even think of it."

At Salzburg, Kissinger reaffirmed his testimony before the Senate that he only provided names of individuals with access to sensitive information in the wiretapping effort from 1969 to 1971. He denied instigating the wiretapping or having prior knowledge of creation of the "plumbers."

"I find wiretapping distasteful," Kissinger said. "I find leaks distasteful, and therefore a choice had to be made. So, in retrospect, this seems to me what my role has been." Because of his concern about "egregious violations" of national security items, or leaks of classified material, he said, he had spoken to the President in 1969 and Nixon had ordered, on the advice of John N. Mitchell, then attorney general, and FBI Director J. Edgar Hoover, "the institution of a system of national security wiretaps." Kissinger said his office supplied the names of persons with access to the security data.

"The fact of the matter is that the wiretaps in question were legal," Kissinger declared. "They followed established procedures."

Kissinger said he had sent a letter to the Senate Foreign Relations Committee requesting a new review of the wiretapping charges. He read parts of the letter: "The innuendoes which now imply that new evidence contradicting my testimony has come to light are without foundation." "All the available evidence is to the best of my knowledge contained in the public and closed hearings which preceded my confirmation."

Nixon reluctant to accept—White House Press Secretary Ronald L. Ziegler issued a statement June 11 in response to Kissinger's news conference that the President would be very reluctant to accept Kissinger's resignation. The President recognized Kissinger's "desire to defend his honor against false charges," the statement said, "and the secretary's strong feeling that he be able to carry out his responsibilities unencumbered by the diversions of the kind of anonymous attack that has so poisoned our national dialogue. As far as the President is concerned, he is sure that those in the United States and in the world who seek peace and are familiar with Secretary Kissinger's contributions to international trust and understanding share his view that the secretary's honor needs no defense."

Senate panel accepts review—Kissinger's request for a review of his testimony was accepted unanimously June 11 by the Senate Foreign Relations Committee. Chairman J. W. Fulbright (D, Ark.) said the panel would renew its request to the Justice Department to provide it with documents on the original authorization of the wiretaps. The department had declined to provide the data.

There were indications of support for Kissinger and opposition to his re-

signation from both Democrats and Republicans on the committee.

52 senators express support—A resolution backing Kissinger was introduced in the Senate late June 12 with early sponsorship of 39 Republicans and Democrats. By June 13, 52 senators had signed the resolution, including Majority Leader Mansfield and Minority Leader Hugh Scott (R, Pa.). The resolution, submitted by Sen. James B. Allen (D, Ala.), said the Senate "holds in high regard Dr. Kissinger and regards him as an outstanding member of this Administration, as a patriotic American in whom it has complete confidence, and whose integrity and veracity are above reproach."

In a Senate speech, Sen. Barry Goldwater (R, Ariz.) urged an end to the "incessant nit-picking" over the wiretapping incident and called for "a determined inquiry" to stop leaks of secret information. It was time to decide "once and for all," he said, "whether it is more important to protect secret information relative to our government or more important to provide more circulation for newspapers, more viewers and listeners to the electronic media, and more money and adulation for people willing to turn against their government."

Strong expressions of support for Kissinger came June 12 from Vice President Gerald Ford and Dean Burch, counselor to the President. Both accused the House Judiciary Committee of having leaked derogatory information about Kissinger and urged the panel's hearings to be opened to the public.

"I think generally the people who are leaking this information are pro-impeachment," Ford said. Burch accused chairman Peter W. Rodino Jr. (D, N.J.) of having lost control of his Judiciary Committee, a charge denied by Rodino and Rep. Robert McClory (Ill.), second-ranking Republican on the committee.

After his Senate speech June 12, Goldwater accused the Washington Post of committing an "act of treason" by publishing secret FBI documents that indicated Kissinger had initiated some of the wiretaps in question. "It's very obvious to me that any information that the government has can be obtained by the Washington Post or any other newspaper that wants to pay the price," he said. "This is plain, outright treason, and I won't stand for it."

Benjamin C. Bradlee, executive editor of the Post, in a statement later June 12, said: "That's really an outrageous charge. We neither stole the documents nor bought them." "We have a right to look at any information given to us by responsible government officials, whether it's a senator or a president or a bureaucrat," he said. "And we have a responsibility to print all information that is relevant and newsworthy."

Reports on the FBI documents had been published June 12 by the Post, the New York Times and the Boston Globe, along with reports of Kissinger's Salzburg

news conference.

According to one document, entitled "Sensitive Coverage Placed at Request of White House" and dated May 12, 1973, specific requests for the wiretaps had come from either Kissinger, then national security adviser, or his aide, Gen. Alexander M. Haig Jr., currently White House chief of staff. The document was addressed to Leonard M. Walters, then assistant director of the FBI, now retired.

The narrative at the beginning of the document read: "The original requests were from either Dr. Henry Kissinger or General Alexander Haig (then Colonel Haig) for wiretap coverage on knowledgeable NSC personnel and certain newsmen who had particular news interest in the SALT talks. The specific requests for this coverage were made to either former Director J. Edgar Hoover or former Assistant to the Director William C. Sullivan (and on one occasion by General Haig to SA Robert Haynes, FBI, White House liaison). Written authorization from the Attorney General of the United States was secured on each wiretap."

Another document, dated May 13, 1973, said "it appears that the project of placing electronic surveillance at the request of the White House had its beginning in a telephone call to Mr. J. Edgar Hoover on May 9, 1969, from Dr. Henry A. Kissinger."

Kissinger was said in the documents to have received 37 FBI summaries of the wiretapped information and to have received the summaries as late as Dec. 28, 1970. An FBI document dated May 31, 1973 was reported to have contained Kissinger's assertion that "what he was learning as a result of the [wiretap] coverage was extremely helpful to him while at the same time very disturbing." The document also said a preliminary estimate of the wiretap operation was that there had been no evidence of federal illegality gleaned from the wiretaps nor any instance that data had been leaked to unauthorized persons.

Ex-NSC aide files new wiretap suit—William Anthony K. Lake, a former staff member of the National Security Council (NSC), filed suit against Kissinger and Nixon June 12, charging that wiretaps were unconstitutionally placed on his home telephone. Lake, who served on Kissinger's NSC staff from June 1969 to June 1970, argued that the wiretap violated his civil liberties, since it was not based on evidence that he had disclosed or was likely to disclose classified information.

Lake's suit, which named other Nixon Administration officials as well as the Chesapeake & Potomac Telephone Co. as defendants, contended that the tap had been placed after he had left the NSC. The tap was ordered, Lake asserted, because he was believed to oppose some Administration policies.

A second wiretap suit by former NSC staff member Richard M. Moose, a

Kissinger aide from January to September 1969, was withdrawn June 12, only hours after it had been filed. Moose's attorney, Nathan Levin, said the action came at the request of Sen. Fulbright, who thought it inappropriate for Moose, a consultant to the Senate Foreign Relations Committee, to be involved in such litigation, since the committee had agreed to review Kissinger's role in initiating the wiretaps.

Morton H. Halperin, also a former NSC staff member, had filed a similar wiretap suit against Kissinger in 1973.

Ruckelshaus backs Kissinger. William D. Ruckelshaus, former acting director of the Federal Bureau of Investigation, supported Secretary of State Henry A. Kissinger June 16 in his account of his wiretapping role in 1969–71. Renewed charges concerning Kissinger's involvement in the government effort to plug security leaks by tapping officials and newsmen during that period had evoked a Kissinger threat to resign unless he was cleared on the issue.

Ruckelshaus, who first investigated the wiretapping effort and reported on it a year earlier, said Kissinger's role was "pretty much as he's described it." Appearing on the CBS "Face the Nation" program, Ruckelshaus suggested an explanation for one of the questions involved: whether Kissinger did or did not initiate the wiretaps. "In the sense that he supplied the names, he initiated it," he said. "But his definition of initiation is that it wasn't his idea to tap; he simply complained about the leaks." Ruckelshaus said "in the process of supplying those names it may well have been described in FBI memoranda that this was a request coming from the National Security Council or Mr. Kissinger."

Ruckelshaus agreed there were "some questions" about one aspect of the wiretapping effort, that some persons with "only a peripheral, if any, relationship to national security" were among those tapped.

On Watergate, Ruckelshaus said he expected "more surprises" in the investigation. "There is information that I'm aware of that has not as yet become public," he said.

Government documents relating to the authorization of the wiretaps were being sent to the Senate Foreign Relations Committee, a Justice Department spokesman said June 14. The committee, which had accepted Kissinger's request for a review of the issue, had let it be known the data had been requested but withheld up to this point. The record of the wiretaps was under court control arising from a civil lawsuit brought by one of the tap targets, Morton Halperin. The Justice Department, in announcing it was supplying the committee with material "directly or indirectly" relating to Kissinger's role, said permission for transfer of documents had been authorized by U.S. Judge John L. Smith, presiding judge in the Halperin case. Procedures to safeguard the secrecy of the material were worked out between the committee and the department.

Smith June 19 refused a request from Halperin's counsel to make the wiretap files public, since much of it had already been publicized. Smith said Halperin would not benefit by release of the data and "it would prejudice the defendants in this case and other parties not in this case."

Adverse leaks continue—Reports of Kissinger's wiretapping role continued to appear. The New York Times reported June 20, according to a memorandum prepared by a House Judiciary Committee staff member, that Kissinger testified at a closed session of the Senate Foreign Relations Committee in the fall of 1973 that the instigation for the wiretaps came either from him or H. R. Haldeman, President Nixon's former chief of staff. Kissinger was asked at the hearing, according to the memo, whether his aide at the time, Gen. Alexander M. Haig Jr., currently White House chief of staff, "might have initiated these taps on his own." Kissinger's reply was said to be, "It would be inconceivable to me that Haig would go off on his own, so it would have to be they are on instructions from me or Mr. Haldeman."

The Times reported that the memo was prepared by William P. Dixon, a Democratic staff member, at the request of Democratic members of the Judiciary Committee and that the memo was made available to the newspaper by a Republican member of the committee who had generally supported Nixon in the impeachment inquiry.

Moorer cleared of spy ring charges. The Senate Armed Services Committee cleared Adm. Thomas H. Moorer, chairman of the Joint Chiefs of Staff, of charges he engaged in military spying on the White House, it was reported June 26. Recommending that Moorer be retired with the full rank, pension and honors of an admiral, the committee concluded that Moorer was "not culpable" in the unauthorized transfer of secret documents from the National Security Council to the Pentagon by two White House military liaison officers in 1971.

Moorer acknowledged receipt of the documents but claimed that he thought they had been sent to him through authorized channels.

St. Clair presents rebuttal. President Nixon's defense against impeachment was presented to the House Judiciary Committee in closed sessions June 27–28 by his chief defense counsel James D. St. Clair. The material was said to have dealt with the Watergate burglary, the cover-up, Administration transactions with the International Telephone & Telegraph Corporation and milk producers, the White House "plumbers," wiretapping and Nixon's income taxes. [For further details, see p. 177C1]

Evidence Release Continues: *Clandestine activities*—The Judiciary Committee July 18 released a four-volume 2,090-page record of the evidence accumulated by its staff including clandestine activities sponsored by the White House. A 225-page rebuttal by the President's special counsel, James D. St. Clair, accompanied the publication of the evidence. [For further details, see p. 196G2]

Senate panel clears Kissinger. The Senate Foreign Relations Committee Aug. 6 reaffirmed its support for Secretary of State Henry A. Kissinger after probing his role in the wiretapping of 17 officials and newsmen from 1969 to 1971. Kissinger had requested the investigation and threatened to resign unless cleared of allegations concerning his role.

In a report unanimously approved, the committee concluded that there were "no contradictions" between Kissinger's testimony at his confirmation hearings in 1973 "and the totality of the new information available." In reaffirming its 1973 finding that Kissinger's role in the wiretapping did not constitute grounds to bar confirmation, the panel stated "if the committee knew then what it knows now it would have nonetheless reported the nomination favorably to the Senate."

The report noted that there were some "unexplained contradictions" between testimony of and individuals and documents in the case, but it said the committee "did establish to its satisfaction" that Kissinger's role "was essentially as he described it in testimony last year."

The report cited a letter from President Nixon of July 12 asserting his full responsibility for the wiretap program.

In its closed hearings, the committee took testimony from Attorney General William B. Saxbe July 10, FBI Director Clarence M. Kelley July 15, Kissinger July 23 and Nixon chief of staff Alexander M. Haig Jr. July 30.

A State Department spokesman said Aug. 6 that Kissinger was "gratified" by the report and "no longer sees any reason for resignation."

Impeachment Investigation
& Trial Developments

Jury named Nixon co-conspirator. The White House acknowledged June 6 that a Watergate grand jury had voted in February to name President Nixon as an unindicted co-conspirator with his former aides, who were indicted for the cover-up of the Watergate break-in.

The grand jury's vote, reported to be unanimous, had been kept secret under an order by U.S. District Court Judge John J. Sirica. But after a report of the jury's action appeared in the June 6 editions of the Los Angeles Times, special presidential counsel James D. St. Clair said he had been informed of the vote three or four weeks earlier by special Watergate prosecutor Leon Jaworski.

St. Clair related that when he had told Nixon, the President responded: " 'They just don't have the evidence and they are wrong.' " St. Clair said Nixon "regretted" the jury's action and considered it "inappropriate."

For his own part, St. Clair contended that Nixon was "not a co-conspirator only because a grand jury says he is." "It won't be the first time a grand jury was wrong. Grand jury allegations are far from proof and have no legal effect."

(An unindicted co-conspirator could not be prosecuted under the indictment in which he was named, but would not be immune from future indictments involving the same alleged offenses.)

Later in the day, St. Clair requested that Sirica unseal the records citing Nixon and release the list of other co-conspirators. St. Clair said that because of the disclosures there was no longer any "compelling" need for secrecy. (The indictment had cited only "other persons to the grand jury known and unknown" as being involved in the cover-up conspiracy.)

According to news reports, the grand jury had at first been inclined to indict Nixon, but had been dissuaded by Jaworski's contention that such action could not be taken against a President in office. Deputy White House Press Secretary Gerald L. Warren contended June 6 that all the evidence taken together "proves the President's innocence." A reporter noted that included among the edited White House tape transcripts was Nixon's statement to Assistant Attorney General Henry E. Petersen on April 17, 1973 that "an unindicted co-conspirator

would then be immediately put on leave." Warren replied that he was "not going to accept questions such as that relating to the President of the United States."

Members of the House Judiciary Committee, questioned about the impact of the jury's action on the impeachment inquiry, generally responded that while the disclosure would not be ignored, the committee had much of the same evidence—as well as the grand jury's secret report—and could reach its own independent conclusions.

One major effect, according to an attorney for one of the cover-up defendants, would be to strengthen Jaworski's position in his efforts to obtain additional White House tapes related to the cover-up. The attorney noted that with Nixon officially cited by the grand jury, many of his conversations could be deemed relevant and admissible in the pending cover-up trial.

(One of the indicted aides, Charles W. Colson, pleaded guilty to a charge in another case June 3. In return, the Watergate prosecutor agreed to seek dismissal of criminal conspiracy indictments against Colson in the Watergate cover-up.)

Grand jury term extended—The term of the original Watergate grand jury, which had named Nixon as an unindicted co-conspirator in the cover-up case, was extended six months May 31.

U.S. District Court Judge George L. Hart Jr. granted the extension at the request of special prosecutor Jaworski. The jury was one of three considering Watergate-related evidence.

Suspended sentence for Kleindienst. Former Attorney General Richard Kleindienst, who had pleaded guilty to a misdemeanor charge of failing to testify "accurately" before a Senate hearing, received a suspended sentence for his criminal offense June 7.

Chief U.S. District Court Judge George L. Hart Jr. imposed the minimum sentence under law—a $100 fine and one month jail term—and suspended both penalties. Kleindienst, who wept openly in

court, was placed on one month unsupervised probation.

Hart praised Kleindienst as a man who had exhibited the "highest integrity throughout his personal and official life." The crime to which he had pleaded guilty was a "technical violation" of the law, Hart said in announcing the sentence. It "is not the type of violation that reflects a mind bent on deception.... Rather, it reflects a heart that is too loyal and considerate of the feelings of others."

Had Kleindienst testified "accurately and fully," Hart said, "it would have reflected great credit on this defendant—but would have reflected discredit upon another individual," an apparent allusion to President Nixon.

Kleindienst was the first former Cabinet official to be convicted of a crime arising out of official acts since 1929 when former Interior Secretary Albert B. Fall was convicted for his role in the Teapot Dome scandal. Kleindienst's sentence also was the lightest yet imposed on those convicted of Watergate-related crimes. Minimum sentences had ranged from a 30-day prison term for Herbert Porter to a six-year jail term for G. Gordon Liddy.

Staff reports 'responsiveness' plan. The staff of the Senate Watergate Committee, in a draft report circulated among committee members June 7, said White House officials had conducted a "concerted and concealed endeavor" to "politicize" the executive branch "to insure that the Administration remained in power" in the 1972 election. The so-called "responsiveness program," according to the report, was "among the most dangerous activities discovered" by the committee, and "may rise to the level of a conspiracy to interfere with the lawful functioning of government.

Alluding to possible "conspiracy to defraud the U.S.," the staff contended that the White House efforts were not "politics as usual," but had involved "the diverting of millions of taxpayers' dollars.... to the political goal of re-electing the President."

[For further details, see p. 155G3]

C

D

E

F

G

A Sirica reverses privilege ruling. U.S. District Court Judge John J. Sirica ruled June 7 that special Watergate prosecutor Leon Jaworski should have access to the tape of a portion of a presidential conversation that had been withheld under a privilege claim by President Nixon. According to Jaworski's petition, the tape of a Sept. 15, 1972 conversation could contain evidence bearing on alleged White House misuse of the Internal Revenue Service.

B In reversing his earlier affirmation of Nixon's claim that the portion was not relevant to Watergate, Sirica said his first evaluation of the tape had been based on the narrowest definition of Watergate—the break-in and cover-up. After re-hearing the tape, Sirica said he considered the tape "unquestionably relevant" to Jaworski's mandate to investigate Watergate in its "broadest sense."

The White House announced June 10 that Nixon would stand on the claim of C privilege and appeal the decision.

Ford continuing travels. Vice President Gerald R. Ford June 8 defended his cross-country travels since assuming office Dec. 6, 1973. Speaking at Utah State University in Logan, Ford said "I categorically reject the demand that I listen only to the strident voices on the banks of the Potomac." He was "not going to barricade myself in Washington," he said. "I D am going right on meeting my fellow citizens around the country."

"It is not so much what I am telling the American people that matters," he continued, "but what they are telling me," and that was "a lot different from what I hear in Washington, D.C. And I like it a lot better."

Since becoming vice president, Ford had made more than 350 appearances in 35 states.

E In addition to the advice he said he was getting from friends and others to remain in Washington and do his job, Ford said he was being asked, "Why do I uphold the President one day and the next day side with the Congress, which is deliberating his impeachment?" His answer: he felt it was his duty "to try to head off deadlock and seek a reasonable and prompt resolution of the nagging Watergate issue that is sapping the valuable time of our elected leaders and political strength of our nation."

F In an appearance in Chicago June 14, Ford deplored the "doom-sayers and woe-criers." "We have people who say all those in government are bad, corrupt or dishonest," he said. "You and I know that it is utterly ridiculous to tar the entire government and everyone in it because of the mistakes or misdeeds of a handful or a few individuals."

G In San Diego June 20, Ford called for a domestic "disengagement" following the Watergate affair and a new initiative "on a domestic impasse which has this nation spinning its wheels."

Ford told reporters in Monterey, Calif.

June 22 the House impeachment inquiry had come down to the one issue of whether Nixon was involved in the Watergate cover-up and "it's becoming even more clear the preponderance of the evidence favors the President."

In an interview with columnist William F. Buckley Jr. broadcast by the Public Broadcasting Service June 30, Ford said he expected the House Judiciary Committee to report a bill of impeachment by a close margin and the House to reject it.

Nixon attends rally by supporters. President Nixon, at a rally in his support June 9, pledged to serve out his term and leave office with his head "held high." "I shall do nothing that will weaken this office while I am President," he said. The occasion was a rally at the Shoreham Hotel in Washington sponsored by the National Citizens Committee for Fairness to the President. The committee was launched in 1973 by Rabbi Baruch Korff of Providence, R.I.

The President's brief speech was devoted largely to foreign policy and the need for a strong presidency. "A strong American presidency is essential if we are to have peace in the world," he told the group.

The group, about 1,400 persons, shouted approval of a resolution read by Rabbi Korff declaring "our faith in God and country, in constitutional government, in the presidency and in our beloved President who is one of the strongest links in the chain of the presidency."

The resolution deplored "the climate of hysteria being engendered" by the press against Nixon and "the impeachment syndrome within the House Judiciary Committee," which was conducting an impeachment inquiry.

The press came under repeated attack from speakers. Nixon told the group "what we say here will be little noted by the media but what you have done here and throughout the United States will be long remembered."

Sen. Carl Curtis (R, Neb.), one of the speakers, assailed "the get-Nixon crowd, including those who continue to conduct a trial by press," the Watergate grand jury—"the make-up of which can hardly be described as representative of our country," and character "assassination of public officials." "Lynching hasn't stopped in the United States," he said. "It's just that different people are doing it."

The rally was attended by Mrs. Nixon and the President's daughters, Tricia Nixon Cox and Julie Nixon Eisenhower. Members of the Administration attending included Treasury Secretary William E. Simon, Agriculture Secretary Earl L. Butz, Roy Ash, director of the Office of Management and Budget, economic adviser Herbert Stein and Ambassador to Italy John Volpe.

"Support the President" demonstrators picketed the office of Judiciary Com-

mittee Chairman Peter W. Rodino (D, N.J.) and the Washington Post building June 10.

Nixon defies House subpoena. President Nixon informed the House Judiciary Committee by letter June 10 that he would refuse to comply with further subpoenas for Watergate evidence. He would draw "a line," he said, since the committee would not.

Invoking executive privilege and the doctrine of separation of powers, Nixon cited the necessity to protect the presidency from unlimited search and seizure by the legislative branch.

Nixon also cited his "extensive and unprecedented cooperation" with the committee and said it already possessed a "voluminous body of materials" that gave "the full story of Watergate" as it related to presidential knowledge and activity.

He rejected the committee's view that "it should be the sole judge of presidential confidentiality." Executive privilege, he contended, was part of the basic doctrine of separation of powers and each branch historically had been "steadfast" in upholding its own independence.

The President asserted that this doctrine took precedence even over an impeachment inquiry. "If the institution of an impeachment inquiry against a president were permitted to override all restraints of separation of powers," he argued, "this would spell the end of the doctrine of separation of powers; it would be an open invitation to future Congresses to use an impeachment inquiry, however frivolous, as a device to assert their supremacy over the executive, and to reduce executive confidentiality to a nullity."

Nixon also rejected the committee's warning to him that members would be free to draw "adverse inferences" from his refusal to supply evidence. Such inferences would be legally wrong, he said, inasmuch as it was established law that no inference may be drawn from "a valid constitutional claim." The President also cited a "common sense argument" that a valid claim of privilege must be accepted without adverse inference "or else the privilege itself is undermined and the separation of powers nullified."

Nixon expressed his determination "to do nothing which by the precedents it set would render the executive branch henceforth and forevermore subservient to the legislative branch and would thereby destroy the constitutional balance. This is the key issue in my insistence that the executive must remain the final arbiter of demands on its confidentiality."

The President suggested that instead of pursuing "the chimera of additional tapes" the committee call witnesses to testify.

Albert: House acts responsibly—In response to the President's letter, House Speaker Carl Albert (D, Okla.) issued a statement later June 10 saying the House was acting responsibly but "the President has not responded responsibly." "The presidency is not at stake in this matter," he said, "and those who say it is are simply going beyond the realm of reason. We want a strong President, we want a strong Congress, we want a strong judicial system, but all of us must live within the bounds of mutual responsibility under the Constitution."

Nixon challenges jury citation. Attorneys for President Nixon disclosed June 11 that they had petitioned the Supreme Court to decide whether a grand jury had the right "to charge an incumbent President as an unindicted co-conspirator in a criminal proceeding." And in papers filed June 11 with U.S. District Court Judge John J. Sirica, the White House asked for access to the secret grand jury evidence relating to the citation of Nixon in connection with the Watergate cover-up, and requested that the evidence be sent to the Supreme Court for a "factual analysis of the grand jury's action."

In the Supreme Court petition, special presidential counsel James D. St. Clair argued that the grand jury citation "seriously impinges" on the constitutional powers of impeachment vested in the House of Representatives. "The prejudicial nature and irreparable effect of such a grand jury finding cannot be seriously questioned," the petition stated.

In the affidavit filed with Sirica, St. Clair contended that the jury had acted "outside its authority . . ., but even if it were acting properly, the evidence presented was and is totally insufficient to support the action taken and, in fact, contradicts that action."

St. Clair asked that the evidence be sent to the Supreme Court as part of the record for the upcoming hearing on special prosecutor Leon Jaworski's subpoena for tapes and documents relating to the cover-up. St. Clair argued that the grand jury's action must be analyzed before the subpoena issue could be decided.

Because of the tape subpoena issue, the Supreme Court had already been given material on the cover-up, including the papers naming Nixon as a co-conspirator. In response to a White House request, Sirica had ruled June 7 that the material on the Nixon citation need no longer be kept secret. However, Sirica said public release of the documents would be at the option of the Supreme Court.

The Supreme Court developments came amid a series of pretrial hearings in the cover-up case, during which, among

other rulings, Sirica said June 11 that the prosecution must provide the six defendants with a complete list of unindicted co-conspirators by July 1. Sirica also denied motions by each defendant for a separate trial, overruling defense arguments that because of antagonism and conflicting goals among the defendants, some might suffer in the "crossfire."

At a second session June 12, Sirica turned to the problem of access to White House files by defendants H.R. Haldeman and John D. Ehrlichman, which in Ehrlichman's case had jeopardized the conduct of the "plumbers" trial, in which he was also a defendant. [See below]

Offering what he called a nonbinding "suggestion," Sirica said that instead of the broad subpoena Ehrlichman had used in the plumbers case, the two should approach Nixon for "a nice heart-to-heart talk" about possible voluntary access. Sirica noted that Nixon had on several occasions praised his two former aides, and suggested that this "easy way" could avoid time-consuming and abrasive court proceedings.

Sirica and defense attorneys said the other defendants were not in a position to try a similar approach.

Sirica's trial role upheld—In a 5–1 decision June 7, the U.S. Court of Appeals for the District of Columbia rejected motions by four of the cover-up defendants that Judge Sirica be disqualified from presiding at their trial. The defendants had argued that Sirica had shown a "prosecutorial interest" in earlier Watergate proceedings and might be prejudiced in the cover-up case.

The ruling, based solely on written arguments, was issued without an opinion, but the court left open the possibility of a lengthier decision later. Dissenting Judge George E. MacKinnon said in a statement that oral arguments should have been heard. Based on the existing record, MacKinnon added, he would have granted the disqualification motions.

Impeachment inquiry. The House Judiciary Committee continued closed hearings June 11–13 on its staff's evidence of the Nixon Administration's involvement in the 1971 burglary at the office of Dr. Daniel Ellsberg's former psychiatrist; the White House approach to the Ellsberg trial judge, W. Matthew Byrne Jr., for his possible appointment as director of the

Federal Bureau of Investigation; and the alleged White House attempt to use the Internal Revenue Service (IRS) for political benefit.

In reference to the IRS subject, Chairman Peter W. Rodino Jr. (D, N.J.) said after the hearing June 13 the issues raised went "to the heart of whether there have been serious abuses of power by the President or members of his official family." "This is a subject that the committee will not dismiss lightly," he said. Rep. Robert McClory (Ill.), second-ranking Republican committee member, commented, however, that he did not "feel the presentation was too serious insofar as the President is concerned."

At the June 11 hearing on the Ellsberg break-in, the panel's second session on activities of the White House "plumbers" unit originally set up to plug leaks of government secrets, Rodino rejected an attempt by Nixon's chief defense counsel James D. St. Clair to give the committee a 10,000-word defense statement on Nixon's conduct in the Watergate affair. Rodino ruled the presentation was "premature" before completion of the staff's presentation of evidence. He said the St. Clair paper would "give a distorted picture to the public" of the impeachment inquiry, which was not restricted to the Watergate area.

Impoundment report issued—The committee released a staff report June 12 on one of the non-Watergate areas, presidential impoundment of Congressionally mandated funds. It ruled out the issue as grounds for impeachment in this case. While the President might have overreached his authority, it concluded, he did abide by final court orders in the matter and "there appear to be alternative remedies" for Congress to consider to regain the power allotted it by the Constitution to allocate federal funds.

The report said the impoundment issue went "to the heart" of the constitutional principle of separation of powers, that "an unjustified, sustained and deliberate refusal by or failure of the executive branch to carry out spending statutes enacted by Congress may be said to represent grounds for impeachment." But, in a practical sense, it said, each of the three separate branches of government would occasionally try "to exercise its constitutional power to its fullest extent, and in doing so may temporarily abrade the powers of prerogatives of another branch." From the historical viewpoint, it found, not every abrasion "need lead to the impeachment of a president."

(The Administration June 13 released $500 million of transportation funds it had impounded. Of the total, $370 million was allocated for highways and $130 million for mass transit. Another $8 billion in transportation funds remained under impoundment.)

Memo pinpoints 'stonewall' advice—A memorandum prepared by committee staff lawyer William P. Dixon reported that President Nixon had advised John N. Mitchell, then attorney general, in a March 22, 1973 discussion, to "stonewall it" and "plead the Fifth Amendment." The memo, first disclosed by the Los Angeles Times June 12, reported quotes not contained in the White House transcripts released previously to the committee.

Nixon told Mitchell, according to the memo: "And, uh, for that reason, I [unintelligible] I don't give a s . . . what happens. I want you to [unintelligible] stonewall it, plead the Fifth Amendment [unintelligible] else, if it'll [unintelligible]. That's the big point. . . ." Another Nixon quote to Mitchell was: "But that's the way [unintelligible]. Even up to this point, the whole theory has been containment, as you know, John."

Mitchell's attorney denied June 12 that Nixon ever told Mitchell to plead the Fifth Amendment.

Dixon's memo also said the material "may be interpreted to support the assumption that the President never asked [his counsel at the time, John W.] Dean to write a report for the purpose of giving him additional facts, but merely so it could be relied on as an excuse in the event things came 'unstuck' and the President needed justification for his inaction." The memo quoted Nixon discussing with Dean and others on March 22, 1973, the contents of a report, that it would be "a negative setting," that he had found that "this individual, that individual," etc. were not "involved in any [unintelligible]."

The memo suggested that the discussion also turned to use of the Dean report to prevent or restrict testimony by Administration aides before the Senate Watergate Committee. If Dean were called, Nixon suggested, according to the memo, ". . . You'd simply say, 'Now that's out . . . Dean has—he makes the report. Here's everything Dean knows. That's where, that's why the Dean report is critical.' "

In the same context, according to the memo, Nixon said: ". . . We can't have a complete cave and have the people go up there and testify. You would agree on that?" Mitchell replied, "I agree." Nixon said, "Particularly if, particularly if we have the Dean statement that may have been given out. . . ." Mitchell said, "Give it to the committee for the purpose . . . [unintelligible] to limit the number of witnesses which are called up there, instead of a buckshot operation."

The memo also was reported by the New York Times June 13 with another Dixon memo also citing conversations that differed or were absent from the Nixon transcripts. Among the conversations cited were Nixon's advice to Dean on March 17, 1973 to try to prevent implication of Nixon aide H.R. Haldeman in the Watergate cover-up, to "cut that off," "We can't have that go to Haldeman"—and Nixon's insistence March 21, 1973, despite Dean's remark it was not true, that the White House claim a committee

of Cuban-Americans in Miami was the source of large cash payments to the Watergate burglars.

Senate Watergate Committee leaks. Staff reports to the Senate Watergate Committee also were being leaked to the press. One reported by United Press International June 14 asserted that President Nixon "must be held responsible and accountable" for the campaign of "dirty tricks" against 1972 Democratic presidential candidates. "Not only was he the candidate on behalf of whom these activities were undertaken," it said, "he also set the moral and ethical standards by which his re-election campaign operated." [For further details, see p. 215D1]

Ehrlichman trial severance reversed. U.S. District Court Judge Gerhard A. Gesell reversed himself June 14 and ordered former Presidential aide John D. Ehrlichman to stand trial June 26 with three other defendants for the 1971 break-in at the Los Angeles office of the psychiatrist who had treated Pentagon Papers trial defendant Daniel Ellsberg. Gesell had ordered Ehrlichman's trial delayed indefinitely June 11, because of what he called President Nixon's "resistance to lawful trial subpoenas" by Ehrlichman, who sought access to his personal White House papers.

In his order June 14, Gesell said Nixon had agreed to give Ehrlichman sufficient access to his White House files. Moreover, Gesell indicated that he agreed with the White House position that most of the documents sought by Ehrlichman were irrelevant to his defense.

A last-minute motion by attorneys for the Watergate special prosecutor's office June 12 had asked Gesell to reconsider his order and warned that delaying Ehrlichman's trial might result in "perhaps no trial at all." To buttress their motion, the prosecuting attorneys also provided Gesell with a sworn affidavit by J. Fred Buzhardt Jr., the White House counsel. Buzhardt said in the sworn statement that, since the court session the previous day during which Gesell had severed Ehrlichman's trial, Buzhardt had reviewed Ehrlichman's personal notes in the White House files and had found nothing "which bears on the issue of guilt or innocence of defendant Ehrlichman." (Buzhardt, 50, suffered an apparent heart attack June 13 and was reported to be in serious condition. Hospital spokesmen said his condition had stabilized.)

In the process of preparing an order directing the White House to comply with Ehrlichman's subpoenas when he received the prosecution's motions and the Buzhardt affidavit, Gesell immediately called a public hearing to announce that a compromise had been achieved. "We have progressed substantially. The claim of executive privilege has been removed," Gesell said at the hearing. However, Gesell delayed until June 14 issuance of a final ruling, pending a challenge by Ehrlichman's lawyers.

Buzhardt, under questioning from the judge, waived executive privilege on a

series of White House documents supplied to the court in secret during the previous week. However, when Buzhardt was subsequently asked by newsmen if the President had any less privilege than the day before when Gesell had ordered the severance, Buzhardt replied, "No, I don't know of any instance where we've changed our position."

The latest in the series of confrontations between Gesell and the White House over use of documents under Presidential control began June 4 when the White House refused to give Ehrlichman and his attorneys full and direct access to Ehrlichman's personal notes of meetings with the President. Instead, Buzhardt and Presidential counsel James D. St. Clair took the position that the notes would have to be screened and extraneous matters removed before they were turned over. (St. Clair had told Gesell June 3 that he saw "no problem" with Ehrlichman's lawyers' request for direct access to Ehrlichman's personal notes.)

In court June 7, St. Clair defended the switch in the White House's position before an angry Judge Gesell. It was the White House's view, St. Clair stated, that Ehrlichman should go through his files alone, select possibly relevant material, and, if the court agreed on its relevance, "we'll [the White House] review it with the President and determine whether it could be released."

Incensed at White House alteration of its position, Gesell told St. Clair, "I hope you will lend your best efforts . . . to reverse this obvious affront to the process of justice. I've been astounded by the position taken today—totally astounded. The point that the President of the United States will not let this man be represented by counsel is offensive. I think it borders on obstruction."

Gesell's remarks were made at a hearing he had called after William C. Frates, one of Ehrlichman's lawyers, formally moved to place in contempt of court "those in control" of Ehrlichman's personal notes. Establishing that President Nixon was in control of the notes, Gesell consented to an oral motion by Frates for an immediate hearing on the issuance of a show cause order. Ehrlichman then took the witness stand to explain the relevance of the notes to his defense, and Buzhardt followed him to describe how the White House had screened documents to which Ehrlichman had been given access. A White House lawyer not familiar with the case had examined Ehrlichman's raw notes for relevancy, and Buzhardt had re-screened the first White House lawyer's work, Buzhardt testified. Gesell then took the testimony under advisement and said he would issue a subsequent ruling.

Break-in convictions appealed. Counsel for the seven men convicted in the Watergate break-in argued before the U.S. Court of Appeals in the District of Columbia June 14 for new trials or dismissal of charges. The arguments were that there had been errors by the judge and prosecution in the case, that subsequent developments altered the situation, that their clients were on, or believed they were on, official government business.

One of the attorneys, William G. Olhausen, argued in behalf of James W. McCord Jr. that "there is such a stench attached to this case that it has to be thrown out." In corroboration, counsel referred to perjured testimony and withheld or destroyed evidence and claimed selective prosecution. Sidney M. Glazer of the special Watergate prosecutor's staff replied that McCord had been captured during the illegal break-in and he could have come forward with his legal complaints during the trial but had not.

Supreme Court widens tape case. The Supreme Court June 15 widened its consideration of the Presidential tapes case to include the issue of whether the Watergate grand jury had the right to name President Nixon as an unindicted co-conspirator in the Watergate cover-up. Consideration of the grand jury's citation against the President had been sought by special presidential counsel James D. St. Clair.

The court refused a request from both sides—St. Clair and special Watergate prosecutor Leon Jaworski—to make public the record of the tapes case, which involved access by the special prosecution to 64 presidential tape recordings Nixon refused to surrender. The court refused to unseal the record except for the one sentence citation by the grand jury of Nixon. It read:

"On Feb. 25, 1974, in the course of its consideration of the indictment in the instant case, the June 5, 1972, grand jury, by a vote of 19–0, determined that there is probable cause to believe that Richard M. Nixon (among others) was a member of the conspiracy to defraud the United States and to obstruct justice charged in Count I of the instant indictment, and the grand jury authorized the special prosecutor to identify Richard M. Nixon (among others) as an unindicted co-conspirator in connection with subsequent legal proceeding in this case."

The court decided to keep briefs to be filed under seal and cautioned counsel, in their arguments, to "refrain from disclosing" any of the record under seal.

Counsel on both sides were requested by the court to prepare arguments on the question of whether District Court Judge John J. Sirica's May 20 order for the White House to submit the tapes to him for private court inspection was "an appealable order." Lower court orders normally were not appealable unless they were considered "final" action. Such action in this case would have taken defiance of the subpoena to a contempt citation against the President, an action both sides resisted as too drastic in this case simply to obtain higher court review.

In a memo filed with Sirica June 14, Jaworski disclosed that the President's counsel had asked that court to "expunge" the grand jury's naming of the President as an unindicted co-conspirator from the record on the ground that the jury could not so act against an incumbent president because of the impeachment

clause. This clause also was cited by Jaworski in contending that St. Clair could not argue in court, but only in the Congressional impeachment proceeding, the merit or lack of merit of the special prosecutor's case on which the grand jury's finding was based.

The memo was filed to oppose St. Clair's request to the court for release of the grand jury evidence relating to Nixon to the Supreme Court and to the President. Jaworski's arguments: St. Clair had not challenged the factual underpinning of the grand jury's finding during Sirica's proceeding, thus the issue could not be raised before the Supreme Court; the President's counsel had presented no supportive showing for his assertion that the finding against Nixon was unjustified, and, in fact, St. Clair had heard only "part of the evidence submitted to the grand jury," that "additional" evidence had been given the House Judiciary Committee by the jury and the jury had considered some evidence not forwarded to the committee; the question of whether a grand jury had probable cause to make a finding was an area that was "traditionally eschewed" by the courts; and the naming of the President was "merely incidental" to the indictment of others, Nixon "was not the focus or target" of the jury's action.

Sirica June 18 rejected the request for release of the material. Counsel had failed to show "any need or basis for lifting the traditional secrecy of grand jury proceedings," he said. Sirica agreed with Jaworski's argument that the issue before the Supreme Court was the legality of the grand jury's action and not the merits of the evidence, which "probably could not be attacked in any event," he said.

Books published. The following two Watergate-related books were published in June:

All the President's Men. By Carl Bernstein and Bob Woodward. Illustrated. Simon & Schuster, 349 pp., $8.95.

Executive Privilege. A Constitutional Myth. By Raoul Berger. Harvard University Press, 384 pp., $14.95.**

Nixon gains in polls. President Nixon's popularity rating increased slightly from a low of 25% in early May to 28% approval in early June, the Gallup Poll found in a survey conducted May 31–June 3 (results published June 16).

The percentage of those disapproving of the way Nixon was handling his job remained the same at 61%, the 3% rise in approval coming from the "no opinion" respondents (11% in the June survey, 14% in May).

Gallup also found the percentage of respondents who thought Nixon should be compelled to leave office had declined to 44% from the 48% level in May. The interviewers found almost no change in the number of those thinking there was enough evidence of possible wrongdoing to bring Nixon to trial be-

fore the Senate. In the latest sampling, it was 50%, the month before 51% in April it was 52%.

A Louis Harris survey published June 17 found majorities opposed Nixon's trip to the Soviet Union (52%) and Middle East (51%) while the House was considering his impeachment and a plurality (46%–39%) agreeing that Nixon was "using the trips abroad as a grandstand play to prevent Congress from impeaching and removing him from office." The survey period was June 1–4.

Ruckelshaus backs Kissinger. William D. Ruckelshaus, former acting director of the Federal Bureau of Investigation, supported Secretary of State Henry A. Kissinger June 16 in his account of his wiretapping role in 1969–71. Renewed charges concerning Kissinger's involvement in the government effort to plug security leaks by tapping officials and newsmen during that period had evoked a Kissinger threat to resign unless he was cleared on the issue. [For further details, see p. 163B1]

On Watergate, Ruckelshaus said he expected "more surprises" in the investigation. "There is information that I'm aware of that has not as yet become public," he said.

French wary of Nixon. The French government was reported to have adopted an aloof stance toward an invitation issued by NATO Secretary General Joseph Luns June 14 to the heads of state of the 15 NATO members to attend an Atlantic summit meeting in Brussels June 26. The French newspaper Le Monde reported June 16–17 that France might be represented by Premier Jacques Chirac instead of President Valery Giscard d'Estaing, thus reasserting a Gaullist distance from what was being interpreted as an attempt by Nixon to "gather his allies around him for a 'family photograph'." The newspaper charged that Nixon was calling for the meeting in an attempt "to glean the maximum success from external affairs before returning to his Watergate difficulties."

In announcing the Brussels meeting, Luns said he had acted "on a suggestion from President Nixon." The Washington Post reported June 15 that Luns had been asked to call the meeting only after a favorable response had been received from other NATO members to feelers put out by Secretary of State Henry Kissinger.

Kerner appeal rejected. Supreme Court without comment or recorded dissent, refused to hear June 17 an appeal by Otto Kerner, the first sitting federal appellate judge to be convicted of a felony. Kerner had argued that he could not be convicted of any crime until he had been removed from the bench by Congress, a process involving impeachment by the House and conviction by two-thirds of the Senate.

Kalmbach sentenced. President Nixon's personal attorney, Herbert Kalmbach, who had pleaded guilty Feb. 25 to two criminal offenses related to the Watergate investigation, was sentenced June 17 by Judge John Sirica of the U.S. district court in Washington.

Kalmbach was sentenced to a jail term of 6–18 months and ordered to pay a $10,-000 fine for violating a federal disclosure law governing campaign funds. The maximum penalty for the offense, which was a felony, was two years in prison and a $10,000 fine.

Kalmbach was ordered to serve a concurrent six-month prison term for promising an ambassadorial appointment in return for a $100,000 contribution to the Nixon campaign, a misdemeanor offense. (He could have received up to one year in jail and been fined $1,000.)

Sirica recommended that Kalmbach be placed in a minimum security federal prison. He was allowed two weeks to clear up his personal affairs before beginning his sentence.

Before sentence was imposed, Kalmbach told the court "how deeply embarrassed I am and how much I regret that I am standing before you this afternoon." In pleading for a light sentence, his attorney said Kalmbach was a "man who accepts without hesitation the truth of statements by those he accepted as his friends." While serving as an "intermediary" for the "White House management team," Kalmbach's "blind spot for his friends" was used in a "deplorable, shameful way," his attorney declared.

Saxbe criticizes Nixon's conduct. Attorney General William B. Saxbe, in a public television interview June 17, said President Nixon had acted wrongly when he relayed secret Watergate grand jury testimony to his former aides, who were interested parties in the grand jury proceedings. Speaking of the edited White House tape transcripts made public April 30, Saxbe focused on conversations (April 16 and 17, 1973) between Nixon and Henry E. Petersen, assistant attorney general. In the conversations, Nixon assured Petersen that secret grand jury information given him by Petersen would not be passed on.

Interviewer: "So your reading of the transcripts is that they call into question not the behavior of Mr. Petersen but the behavior of Mr. Nixon." Saxbe: "That's right, Mr. Petersen is a pro ... He presumed that the President was working on the case with him. He was his only superior."
Interviewer: "So the President lied to him?" Saxbe: "I don't know whether he lied to him or not."
Interviewer: "Does this ... reflect a kind of casual attitude towards seeing that the laws are enforced on the part of the President?" Saxbe: "Either that or a lack of knowledge about grand jury proceedings."

President ends Mid-East tour. Nixon concluded a five-nation tour of the Middle East with visits to Saudi Arabia, Syria, Israel and Jordan June 14–18. The remainder of the President's one-week visit to the region was highlighted by a joint announcement in Damascus June 16 by Nixon and President Hafez al-Assad of resumption of U.S.-Syrian diplomatic relations, and by Nixon's pledge in Jerusalem June 17 of long-term military and economic aid to Israel and the promise to that country of nuclear technology for peaceful purposes. Nixon had visited Egypt June 12–14 and created a storm of controversy in domestic circles by pledging atomic aid to the Egyptians.

Rush refuses Senate testimony. Kenneth Rush, recently named counselor to the President for economic affairs, refused to testify before a Congressional committee on economic policy, Sen. William Proxmire (D, Wis.) said June 14. Proxmire was co-chairman of the Joint Economic Committee, which had planned hearings June 17 on President Nixon's mid-year economic report.

Proxmire said the hearings were canceled after Rush informed the panel he would meet with them informally but declined formal testimony, invoking executive privilege to protect his responsibility to give the President "candid and uninhibited advice."

Proxmire said Rush's stance was "unacceptable and ridiculous" and "based on the same arrogance of power and immaturity of thought that led to Watergate." "What we are interested in," he said, "are not Mr. Rush's conversations with the President but his views as the new economic czar on the immensely important and topical issues over which he will exercise great power and authority such as inflation, unemployment and economic growth."

Rush also declined a Senate panel's invitation to testify on the East-West trade situation. Chairman Frank Church of the Subcommittee on Multinational Corporations, called Rush's refusal "totally unwarranted" June 19.

Jaworski defends plea bargaining. Watergate Special Prosecutor Leon Jaworski June 18 defended his office's use of plea bargaining as a fair, legal and necessary way to prosecute Watergate criminals. Jaworski's comments were in response to public criticism that his office had engaged in too much plea bargaining and that resulting prison sentences were too light. (In plea bargaining, the prosecutor and the defendant agreed on a charge or charges less serious than potential charges against the defendant. Often, in return for having all other charges against him dropped, the defendant would agree to testify for the prosecution.)

Attorney General William B. Saxbe told the annual convention of the National Association of Attorneys General in Coeur D'Alene, Idaho June 24, "It is

hardly reassuring when one man goes to prison for years for theft while another man involved in a conspiracy to steal our freedoms is in and out of jail in the wink of an eye."

Richard A. Sprague, special U.S. prosecutor in the murder case of United Mine Workers union insurgent Joseph A. Yablonski, was critical of the plea bargain struck with former Attorney General Richard Kleindienst. Writing in the New York Times June 21, Sprague said Jaworski "perverted the law to find the most minimal charge, one that was in fact a fiction." (It was previously reported that three assistant Watergate special prosecutors had resigned in protest over Jaworski's decision to accept a guilty plea by Kleindienst to a misdemeanor and not perjury, a felony.)

Kleindienst was guilty of lying to a Senate committee, not refusing to testify, Sprague said. "What right does Mr. Jaworski have to take the law into his own hands or to make up his own statute?... It is as much a perversion of the legal process for Mr. Jaworski to distort the law for his purposes as it was for Mr. Kleindienst to have deceived the Senate committee," Sprague said.

In his defense, Jaworski cited American Bar Association (ABA) guidelines, which stated that prosecutors should consider negotiated pleas. Among the justifications for plea bargaining cited in the ABA rules were: if evidence against a defendant were not strong, and willingness of a defendant to provide information on other cases.

Regarding the record of his own office, Jaworski noted that all defendants who plea bargained—except Kleindienst and defendants in cases involving illegal corporate campaign contributions—had pleaded guilty to felonies punishable by up to five years in prison. Those who pleaded guilty had also agreed to testify for the prosecution. He pointed out that it was not he but federal judges who imposed prison sentences. "Is it in the public interest, if a plea can be taken today, to wait for trial next year?" he asked.

Judiciary panel leaks attacked. The continuing news leaks from the House Judiciary Committee were attacked by White House spokesmen June 18–19.

Kenneth W. Clawson, communications director, denounced them June 18 as "a purposeful effort to bring down the President with smoke-filled room operations by a clique of Nixon-hating partisans." The latest leak, another Dixon memo reported that day by the Washington Post, Clawson said, showed that the committee and its chairman "intend to do nothing about this trial by innuendo." The memo and others prepared by Dixon, he said, "were written for the purpose of slandering President Nixon."

The memo reported by the Post June 18 quoted President Nixon as having told an aide on April 16, 1973 that he was "planning to assume some culpability" in the payment of hush money to a Watergate defendant because of the President's knowledge of the proposed transaction. The quote was not in the Nixon transcripts released to the committee.

Presidential speechwriter Patrick J. Buchanan denounced the committee's leaks June 19 as "nameless, faceless character assassination" of the President, Kissinger and other officials. Buchanan attributed an article in that day's Washington Post to a leak from the committee. The article cited a Buchanan memo of July, 1971 arguing against a White House campaign to defame Dr. Daniel Ellsberg, who released the Pentagon papers. Buchanan's argument, appaarently not heeded, was that attacks on Ellsberg "while good for the country, would not, it seems to me, be particularly helpful to the President politically." An account of the Buchanan memo also had been published by the St. Louis Post-Dispatch June 11.

Judiciary Committee Chairman Peter W. Rodino Jr. (D, N.J.) defended the committee later June 19. "We have a job," he said, "and we're going to go forward to do the best we can, despite some unfortunate leaks." The panel's second-ranking Republican member, Rep. Robert McClory (Ill.), also commented: "We don't appreciate attacks when they blanket the committee and its staff. We deplore the leaks, but this is not the pattern of the committee. Leaks are the exception."

Dixon reportedly had been instructed to stop the practice of writing memos for various Democratic members of the panel, and Rodino reportedly had agreed to a request from Republican members to make his memos, 14 in all, available to the minority.

Another attack against the committee, and another statement of support, came from other quarters June 19. Senate Democratic Leader Mike Mansfield (Mont.), referring to the Rodino panel, said he was "disturbed and in a sense depressed by the delay and postponement on the one hand and the leaks on the other." "It's not facing up to the issue squarely or fairly," he said, "it's creating impressions and innuendoes and speculations and rumors which ought to be considered only by the committee concerned and the courts." Mansfield attributed the delay, according to the UPI, to the White House and the leaks to the committee.

A view that Rodino was not being unfair came from James D. St. Clair, President Nixon's chief defense lawyer. "From my vantage point, which is not Mr. Buchanan's," he said, "Chairman Rodino is doing his level best to stop the leaks. It may just not be possible."

Among other Dixon memos that had surfaced in the press:

■ The Los Angeles Times reported June 13 from a Dixon memo quoting Nixon as having said on March 21, 1973 to an aide that "we should buy time" by making the hush money payment to a Watergate defendant. The quote differed from the Nixon transcript version which had Nixon saying "we can buy time."

■ A copy of a Dixon memo obtained by the Los Angeles Times June 14 suggested that Nixon began to meet regularly with John W. Dean 3rd, then his counsel, in February 1973 to give Dean an excuse to claim executive privilege and refuse testimony before Watergate investigating bodies and that Jeb Stuart Magruder, then an aide at the Nixon campaign committee, was kept on the government payroll despite perjury before a grand jury for much the same reason, to insure his silence about the cover-up.

The memo had a cover letter by Dixon, which also was reported, saying, "This memo is interpretative on my part and the facts presented herein may be interpreted differently by others."

Appeals court accepts tape case. The U.S. Court of Appeals for the District of Columbia agreed June 19 to review Judge John J. Sirica's ruling to give the special Watergate prosecutor part of a White House tape originally withheld under a claim of executive privilege. The conversation in question, held Sept. 15, 1972, pertained to possible White House intervention with the Internal Revenue Service for political purposes.

Cover-up sessions concluded. The House Judiciary Committee's closed hearings to study staff evidence moved past the Watergate cover-up phase June 19.

The committee had begun its sixth week of closed evidentiary sessions June 18 with a review of material relating to President Nixon's earliest awareness of the cover-up. The next day the panel looked at the evidence pertaining to the firing of the first special Watergate prosecutor, Archibald Cox, Oct. 20, 1973. It also heard a technical discussion of the controversial 18-1/2-minute gap in the tape of a presidential conversation sought by the committee.

In a statement issued after the June 19 meeting, Chairman Peter W. Rodino Jr. (D, N.J.) said the evidence inspected pertained to "certain events" between Oct. 19, 1973, the day before Cox's ouster, and June 10, 1974. Talking with reporters during a recess, Rodino said it was "a very pertinent question" whether the cover-up might still be continuing.

The committee's June 20 session focused on Nixon's personal income tax situation. Afterwards, several members confirmed reports that the Internal Revenue Service report on Nixon's taxes, in which it assessed him $432,000 in unpaid taxes for the years 1969-72, included a negligence finding and 5% penalty against Nixon. The White House had not acknowledged the negligence finding in announcing the IRS report in April.

It also became known after the session that Nixon had not as yet paid the delinquent taxes assessed against him for 1969, a year for which the statute of limitations had expired. Nixon's intention to pay the 1969 taxes, announced in April, was reaffirmed at the White House June 20.

The President was reported to have paid the taxes for 1970, 1971 and 1972.

(Nixon's tax lawyer, Frank DeMarco Jr., resigned his state notary commission on the eve of hearings scheduled June 17 on an alleged false notarization by DeMarco on Nixon's donation of pre-presidential papers to the government. The donation was the basis of a hugh tax deduction claimed by Nixon for his presidential years but disallowed by the IRS in its finding of back-taxes due. Edmund G. Brown Jr., California secretary of state, announcing he had received DeMarco's resignation letter June 14, said June 17 it was "clear" that the documents on Nixon's donation, dated April 21, 1969, had been signed a year later, on April 10, 1970, after a law barring such deductions took effect.)

World leadership cited. House Republican whip Leslie C. Arends (Ill.) told reporters after meeting with President Nixon June 20 that the President's recently-concluded trip to the Middle East "should put to rest any questions about whether he is leading this nation now." "He is a world leader," Arends said. Nixon met with a group of Democrat and Republican Congressional leaders to brief them on his trip.

At the regular White House news briefing June 20, Deputy Press Secretary Gerald L. Warren was asked whether Nixon's tour had improved his chances to fend off impeachment. Warren said the trip demonstrated that "the President's foreign policy is respected in that part of the world." The U.S. approach to the Mideast "is a highly credible approach and is recognized as such in that area," he said, "but I would not link it directly to impeachment."

Moscow summit negotiations lag tied to Watergate. Both Moscow and Washington appeared anxious to draft new trade and nuclear agreements that could be signed during President Nixon's June 27–July 3 Moscow talks. Despite Brezhnev's test and arms pacts proposals, however, concern was being expressed that preparations for the visit were lagging: the White House advance team had flown to Moscow June 20, only a week before the President's arrival and negotiations on the desired agreements were dragging. Soviet sources noted that this contrasted sharply with the pace of preparations for the two previous Nixon-Brezhnev summits, the New York Times reported June 21. Many observers viewed the Administration's preoccupation with its Watergate problems as a possible reason for the lack of preparations for the summit.

In a Pentagon press conference June 17, Secretary of Defense James Schlesinger conceded that "we have had less chance to review these problems [of arms control] than we might prefer." However, he sought to give reassurances that "the President would do nothing intentionally that would damage the national security."

U.S. negotiator quits SALT—Paul H. Nitze resigned from the U.S. negotiating team at the Strategic Arms Limitation Talks (SALT) June 14, citing "the depressing reality of the traumatic events now unfolding in our nation's capital and of the implications of those events in the international arena." In quitting SALT, he also relinquished his post as special adviser to the secretary of defense on strategic nuclear matters.

A former Defense Department deputy secretary, Nitze had been appointed to the U.S. SALT delegation in 1969 when preliminary talks opened and was retained as the top Pentagon representative through the second phase of discussions, SALT II, which had convened in November 1972.

In addition to a terse notice of his resignation to the President, Nitze also released a statement to the press in which he said: "Until the office of the presidency has been restored to its principal function of upholding the Constitution . . . I see no real prospect for reversing certain unfortunate trends in the evolving situation," a thinly veiled assessment that the Watergate scandals had weakened the ability of the Nixon administration to effectively negotiate new arms agreements.

A lifelong Democrat who had served under the past three Administrations, Nitze was known to be the only member of the U.S. SALT negotiating team who had openly disagreed with Secretary of State Henry Kissinger. According to the New York Times June 15, Nitze believed Kissinger was too anxious to reach an agreement with Moscow and thus was not a sufficiently tough negotiator.

The Department of Defense June 14 named Dr. James Wade, a member of the defense research and engineering group at the Pentagon, to replace Nitze.

Krogh released. Egil Krogh, who pleaded guilty to "conspiracy to violate the civil rights" of Dr. Lewis Fielding, Daniel Ellsberg's psychiatrist, was released June 22 after serving four months of a six-month sentence.

Colson sentenced to prison term. Charles W. Colson, former special counsel to President Nixon, was sentenced to one-three years in prison and fined $5,000 by U.S. District Court Judge Gerhard A. Gesell June 21. Colson had pleaded guilty June 3 to a charge that he obstructed justice by disseminating derogatory information in 1971 about Pentagon Papers trial defendant Daniel Ellsberg and one of Ellsberg's lawyers, Leonard Boudin.

Before Gesell passed sentence, Colson read to the court a statement reiterating his innocence of the offenses for which he had been indicted but accepting responsibility for the charge for which he was about to be sentenced. "As to the specific offense charged, the President on numerous occasions urged me to disseminate damaging information about Daniel Ellsberg . . . I endeavored to do so—and willingly. I don't mean to shift my responsibility to the President. I believed what I was doing was right."

"The President," Colson said, "I am convinced, believed he was acting in the national interest. I know I did." Colson added that Ellsberg, who made public the Pentagon Papers, was viewed by the White House as a threat to national security since he had access to secret information, which he might disclose. The White House felt that Ellsberg's actions bordered on "treasonous" and feared that Ellsberg might rally the public against the policies the President believed right for the country, Colson said.

"In all fairness to the President, it should be remembered that this government was engaged at the time in the most sensitive and closely guarded foreign policy negotiations, which could affect . . . perhaps the future stability of the world for a long period to come," he said. "I had one rule—to get done that which the President wanted done. And while I thought I was serving him well and faithfully, I now recognize that I was not—at least in the sense that I never really questioned whether what he wanted done was right or proper." At another point, Colson said, "During the time I served in the White House, I rarely questioned a presidential order. Infrequently did I question the President's judgment."

After sentencing, Colson, a convert to evangelical Christianity, told newsmen, "I have committed my life to Jesus Christ. I can work for the Lord in prison or out of prison, and that's how I want to spend my life. What happened today is the Lord's will and the court's will, and, of course, I accept that fully."

As a result of his guilty plea, Colson, an attorney, was disbarred June 25 by the U.S. District Court for the District of Columbia.

White House reaction to the sentence was sharp: Ken W. Clawson, director of communications, issued a statement June 21 charging that Colson was being sentenced for a felony that had been "standard practice of members and staff of the Senate Watergate Committee for more than a year and the same felony being committed daily by some partisan members of the House Judiciary Committee. I just wish the Watergate special prosecutor would pursue these felons with the same ardor with which he investigated Mr. Colson."

Nixon leg ailment disclosed. The disclosure that President Nixon had a leg ailment diagnosed as phlebitis was confirmed at the White House June 24. The disclosure was broadcast earlier that day by CBS News. The initial reports from the White House described the condition as a "mild" one that had "all cleared up." It was said to have originated before his Middle East trip. The President's physician, Dr. Walter K. Tkach, was quoted as saying "the President is in good health." The spokesmen declined further immediate comment.

The next day, as Nixon was flying the Atlantic for his trip to Western Europe and the Soviet Union. Tkach told reporters the President first noticed his leg was swollen the weekend before he departed for the Middle East on June 10 but did not reveal it until at least 24 hours later when he reached Salzburg, Austria. Upon being told he had phlebitis, Tkach reported, Nixon refused recommendations for medical treatment, and ordered that the condition be kept secret so that it would not interfere with his trip. Tkach said hot packs were administered and Nixon's leg kept elevated as much as possible. He reported that there was no danger of a blood clot moving to another part of the body, one of the possible problems of the condition.

"He's in no pain, and the swelling has gone down," Tkach said, and added that Nixon was taking no medication.

White House Press Secretary Ronald L. Ziegler reported in Brussels June 26 that there was "still some swelling" in the President's leg but that Nixon told him the night before he was not experiencing the pain he had during the Middle East trip. Ziegler said the President had not wanted the condition publicized to avoid concern about it from others meeting him on his tour, during which he wore an elastic stocking.

Tkach expressed confidence June 26 "that the matter has resolved itself."

Watergate believed stalling summit pacts. The Administration was predicting that no major agreements would emerge from the Moscow summit meeting, officials acknowledged June 25. Asked why a summit meeting was being held, a top official said: "If we did not go to the summit, we would be saying we are not a functioning government." The statement was viewed by most observers as a commentary on the current state of affairs in Washington as a result of the Watergate affair.

Mitchell linked to Hughes' hotel bid. A Senate Watergate Committee staff report charged that former Attorney General John N. Mitchell bypassed his antitrust division and approved an effort in 1970 by billionaire Howard Hughes to buy the Dunes Hotel in Las Vegas, Nev., it was reported June 25. [For further details, see p. 215G2]

Questions raised in Silbert nomination. Senate Judiciary Committee hearings on the nomination of Earl J. Silbert as U.S. attorney for the District of Columbia focused on the adequacy of the original Watergate investigation. Silbert, 37, who headed the original Watergate prosecution team while he was an assistant U.S. attorney, was nominated by President Nixon Jan. 29 to be U.S. attorney.

Silbert appeared before the committee April 23 and 24 and defended himself against criticism of the original Watergate probe from Sens. Philip A. Hart (D, Mich.) and Birch Bayh (D, Ind.). He had only two assistants to prepare for a trial with 90 witnesses, Silbert said.

Another member of the committee, Sen. Sam J. Ervin Jr. (D, N.C.), chairman of the Senate Watergate committee, April 30 urged an "in depth" investigation of Silbert's handling of the original probe. Sen. John V. Tunney (D, Calif.) joined in the call.

Two witnesses attacked Silbert's handling of the case. Robert S. Vance, president of the Association of State Democratic Chairmen, said April 30 that whatever the reasons, Silbert's "course of conduct had the unquestioned effect of keeping the lid on until after the November elections." James W. McCord Jr., one of the seven convicted in the original Watergate break-in case, testified May 1 that Silbert had given the White House the minutes of the grand jury investigation of his case.

The senators' criticism was directed at the failure of the original investigators to pursue indications of further involvement by Nixon's re-election committee and the White House. Hart wanted to know why the grand jury was not continued after the initial indictments, and why more immunity was not granted to gain more information.

Ervin directed his questions at former Attorney General Richard G. Kleindienst June 18 and Assistant Attorney General Henry E. Petersen June 19 and 20, officials in the department at the time of the original Watergate probe.

Ervin questioned the repeated public assurances by the department of no White House involvement in the case and of an exhaustive investigation. He criticized the department for undertaking a difficult conspiracy case against former Attorney General John N. Mitchell and former Commerce Secretary Maurice H. Stans while not bringing felony charges against them for accepting the secret $200,000 cash contribution from Robert L. Vesco. Ervin asked why the department had indicted the Finance Committee to Re-elect the President but none of its officers, and he deplored the decision to spare Stans a personal appearance before the Watergate grand jury by allowing him to present a written statement. A grand jury "can't cross-examine a piece of paper," Ervin said.

Kleindienst June 18 defended Silbert's and Petersen's roles and lauded the professionalism of the department. While he had been in "constant contact" with Petersen, he said, he thought it best, as a political appointee, to largely remove himself from the probe because of the "very grave, sensitive, political nature" of the case. While he took full responsibility as attorney general "for everything that was done," Kleindienst said, he had "tried to assume the posture at the very outset to leave it to Mr. Petersen and Mr. Silbert."

Kleindienst said he had not put pressure on subordinates in the case. He had told Petersen he would like to have indictments by Sept. 1 of that year but that was not pressure. "I was expressing a desire and hope," he said, "to avoid criticism

in an election year in a situation involving a political crime."

Petersen angrily protested Ervin's questioning June 19. "This is a terrible, terrible thing," he shouted. "Do us justice, will you?" He accused Ervin of being unfair. They clashed over whether the department's probe had been blunted out of deference to the high-level politicians involved. Petersen claimed much of their involvement was not known at the time.

At one point, Ervin commented in reference to the theory of equality before the law, "Well, then, justice as administered by the Department of Justice is not blind."

"I hope justice is not blind, senator," Petersen replied. "I do not apply it blindly." "I deal with restraint," Petersen explained. "I don't agree with the blunderbuss approach on political cases. I thought it ought to be done with surgical precision, with restraint."

At another point, Petersen admitted, "If you mean did we accept the lies of all these people who lied to us, I guess we did. You know something, we were snookered."

Petersen returned before the committee June 20, 24 and 26. He contended June 20 the prosecution headed by Silbert had stated in a still-secret memorandum that there would be further investigations after the first case was completed. He said the prosecution believed "when the jail doors started clanging shut, someone would crack."

Petersen agreed with Tunney's speculation June 24 that approval of the Silbert nomination could be construed as approval of the original Watergate investigation. "Are we saying [if we approve the nomination] that the President as chief law enforcement officer fulfilled his duty?" Tunney asked. "I think that inference might be drawn," Petersen said.

Under questioning from Tunney June 26, Petersen conceded he had failed to check out a lead from the Central Intelligence Agency (CIA) potentially connecting two Watergate conspirators, G. Gordon Liddy and E. Howard Hunt Jr., to the office break-in of Dr. Daniel Ellsberg's psychiatrist. The CIA had sent him on Dec. 5, 1972 copies of photographs, one showing Liddy outside the office, and copies of false identification documents issued by the CIA to Liddy and Hunt, the aliases similar to those used in renting rooms near the Watergate building in that burglary. Petersen said he and Silbert studied the data but did not know what to make of it.

"But it seems so easy to ask for an FBI check," Tunney said. "In 20-20 hindsight," Petersen said, "I've asked myself a hundred times" why that was not done. He said it was a "faux pas" but "I'm not prepared to criticize Mr. Silbert for what I didn't have sense enough to tell him to do."

Another member of the panel, Sen. Roman L. Hruska (R, Neb.), called attention June 26 to the "very splendid letters of recommendation" for Silbert from special Watergate prosecutor Leon Jaworski and his predecessor, Archibald Cox.

French snub NATO meeting. Government leaders of the 15 member states of the North Atlantic Treaty Organization

(NATO) met in Brussels June 26 and signed a declaration on Atlantic relations that had been approved by their foreign ministers in Ottawa June 18. The notable absence from the Brussels meeting of French President Valery Giscard d'Estaing was interpreted by many as a snub to Nixon. France was represented by Premier Jacques Chirac, who, it was reported, was not received by President Nixon, who attended the conference. The French government had earlier reported to be viewing the meeting as a public relations stunt by Nixon to focus domestic attention away from the Watergate scandal.

In remarks upon his arrival in Brussels June 25, President Nixon stressed the role of NATO in Soviet-U.S. relations: "Without the alliance, it is doubtful that detente would have begun. Without a continuing strong alliance, it is doubtful detente would continue." Nixon attended the NATO meeting en route to his June 27–July 3 summit meeting in the Soviet Union.

Impeachment inquiry enters new phase. The House Judiciary Committee completed its closed evidentiary hearings June 21 and moved June 24 to accelerate its impeachment inquiry in an effort to conclude its work by the latter part of July.

The committee also voted June 24 to issue four new subpoenas for White House tape recordings of Presidential conversations.

In other action, marked by partisan dispute, the panel decided June 25 to make public the evidence it had gathered and June 26 to take testimony from at least five witnesses.

Evidentiary hearings end—The committee's June 21 session was its 18th and final closed hearing over a six-week period to hear the evidence gathered by its staff. The subjects were President Nixon's personal income tax status for 1969–72 and the secret bombing of Cambodia ordered by Nixon in 1969.

Comments from committee members afterwards reflected a wide divergence of interpretation on the tax evidence. Chairman Peter W. Rodino Jr. (D, N.J.) said a serious question was raised "whether the President was treated like any other taxpayer." Rep. Charles E. Wiggins (R, Calif.), an articulate Nixon defender throughout the committee proceedings, said the tax matter was "a nonissue" and "there isn't any fraud here."

The committee heard evidence, according to the New York Times, that the Internal Revenue Service (IRS) investigation of Nixon's tax status was incomplete, as far as a potential fraud finding was concerned, and the matter was recommended by the IRS to a grand jury for further consideration. A letter, obtained by the Times from a Democratic member of the committee, reportedly was presented at the closed session in which IRS Commissioner Donald C. Alexander told special Watergate prosecutor Leon Jaworski that "we have been unable to complete the processing of this matter in view of the lack of cooperation of some of the witnesses and because of many inconsistencies in the testimony of individuals. . . ."

Interest in Colson statement—Several committee members expressed interest June 21 in former Nixon aide Charles W. Colson's courtroom statement that day that he had engaged in an attempt to obstruct the trial of Daniel Ellsberg on orders of the President. Asked to comment on the allegation of a Presidential directive to commit a felony, Wiggins noted that Colson was in "a plea bargaining situation" and said it was "a novel theory" to call dissemination of derogatory material an "obstruction of justice."

White House counsel Leonard Garment, on the CBS "Face the Nation" broadcast June 23, saw no illegality in such a Nixon directive to Colson and suggested that "what was done" to carry out the directive was "a matter that remains to be determined on the basis of evidence that's presented to the Judiciary Committee or to other forums."

New subpoenas issued—The four new subpoenas authorized by the committee June 24 covered 49 tapes, bringing to 147 the number sought by the panel from the White House.

Two of the subpoenas were approved by voice vote without dissent. The first requested 10 tapes involving discussions of the White House special investigations unit, five bearing on talks between Nixon and Colson. The second subpoena demanded two tapes of Sept. 15, 1972 talks concerning alleged White House efforts to intervene with the IRS for political gain.

The two other subpoenas were authorized by votes of 34–4, the dissent coming from Republican Reps. Edward Hutchinson (Mich.), Wiggins, Trent Lott (Miss.) and Delbert L. Latta (Ohio). They covered 19 tapes potentially related to knowledge of false testimony by Presidential subordinates at the 1972 Senate hearings on the nomination of Richard G. Kleindienst to be attorney general and 18 White House meetings concerning the 1971 decision to raise federal milk price supports and pledges by dairy producer organizations for Nixon re-election funds.

The panel rejected on a 23–15 party line vote a Republican proposal to subpoena the Sept. 15, 1972 tapes from Judge John J. Sirica of the U.S. district court, which had temporary custody of the tapes. The majority opposed putting the panel in confrontation with the courts.

St. Clair rebuttal scheduled—The committee approved unanimously June 24 a resolution permitting oral and written rebuttal of its evidence by Nixon's chief defense attorney, James D. St. Clair. The resolution specified that the rebuttal must be factual and not interpretative or argumentative.

Evidence to be made public—The vote June 25 for disclosure of the committee's evidentiary record was 22–16. The White House later praised the action to move the hearings "to a conclusion," but the split within the committee crossed party lines. The majority included six Republicans, while five Democrats voted not to release the material.

Various groupings argued against publication of the record. Several Nixon critics opposed publication because of the possibility of violating the civil rights of third parties. Some Republicans wanted publication, eventually, only of the material on which proposed impeachment charges were based. Some Southern Democrats opposed publication of evidence without interpretation.

The resolution to release evidence excluded classified material on the Cambodia bombing and empowered Chairman Rodino and ranking Republican Hutchinson to exclude other material. Rep. Robert McClory (R, Ill.), the author of the latter provision, explained that "any irrelevant material, any sensitive material, any material impinging on human rights" should be excluded.

Discord over witnesses—The committee's closed session June 26 to consider summoning witnesses was marked by sharp partisan discord. The decisions were to call five witnesses, to interview five others as potential witnesses and to conclude the testimonial phase by July 12. Debate over proposed articles of impeachment would follow that. (Rodino had announced June 24 that the committee planned to take testimony from witnesses the following week and that the hearings might extend through the Congressional recess for Independence Day in an attempt to finish the impeachment inquiry "some time in the latter part of July.")

The witnesses selected were Alexander P. Butterfield, head of the Federal Aviation Administration who formerly was an aide to H.R. Haldeman, former chief of staff for Nixon; Herbert W. Kalmbach, Nixon's personal attorney; Assistant Attorney General Henry E. Petersen; former White House counsel John W. Dean 3rd; and Frederick C. LaRue, former official of the Nixon re-election campaign.

The five potential witnesses selected were Charles W. Colson, former special counsel to the President; former Attorney General John N. Mitchell; Haldeman; William O. Bittman, former lawyer for Watergate conspirator E. Howard Hunt Jr.; and Paul L. O'Brien, a lawyer for the Nixon re-election committee.

The divisive argument within the committee reached a climax on a motion to call all 10 persons as witnesses. It failed by a 19–19 vote. On one side were 19 Democrats. Two Democrats—Reps. Wayne Owens (Utah) and Walter Flowers (Ala.) —joined the 17 Republicans.

Nixon's lawyer St. Clair proposed, by letter, a witness list of Dean, Mitchell, Haldeman, LaRue, Bittman and O'Brien. It drew strong support from the Republicans, who also objected to the July 12 deadline for testimony. The Democrats argued against indefinite prolongation of the proceedings.

The Democrats showed some disarray. A preliminary motion in favor of St. Clair's list carried by a 21–17 vote when four of them joined the Republican side. Rodino, who favored calling witnesses only to fill in gaps in the record, called a caucus of the Democrats, who emerged from it to reverse the earlier vote 22–16. The vote to hear five witnesses and decide later on the other five carried 33–5.

California break-in probed. John D. Ehrlichman, former domestic affairs adviser to President Nixon, and three others went on trial in Washington federal court June 28 on charges stemming from the 1971 break-in at the Los Angeles office of Dr. Lewis J. Fielding, the psychiatrist who had treated Pentagon Papers trial defendant Daniel Ellsberg. Ehrlichman, G. Gordon Liddy, Eugenio Martinez and Bernard L. Barker were indicted on the charge that they conspired to deprive Fielding of his civil rights. Ehrlichman also faced three counts of making false declarations to a grand jury and a single count of lying to the Federal Bureau of Investigation (FBI).

Selection of a jury had been relatively smooth, requiring less than two days. The racial make-up of the jury—nine blacks and three whites—conformed to the racial make-up of Washington, which was more than 70% black. Two of Ehrlichman's four attorneys were black.

The first major witness to take the stand was David R. Young Jr., a co-director of the White House investigative unit known as the "plumbers." Young had supplied the original Watergate prosecutor's office with a series of memorandums dealing with the break-in and agreed to testify for the prosecution in return for a grant of immunity from prosecution.

Direct examination of Young by associate Watergate prosecutor William H. Merrill July 1 had a dual focus. Merrill tried to show that Ehrlichman had been involved in the planning of the break-in and that in two 1973 meetings with Young, Ehrlichman reacknowledged his role in the operation. Young's testimony was generally supported by the memorandums he had given the prosecution, but he rarely went beyond the memos when asked to relate specific conversations with the alleged conspirators.

Young testified that he and Egil Krogh Jr. had been given "co-responsibility" for tracking down leaks of classified information to the newspapers. As co-directors of the "plumbers," he said, they were to report to Ehrlichman. (Krogh had pleaded guilty to violating Fielding's civil rights Nov. 30, 1973.)

The idea of obtaining a psychiatric profile of Ellsberg originated with convicted Watergate conspirator E. Howard Hunt Jr., who then was a member of the "plumbers" unit, Young testified. Hunt also first raised the possibility of a "covert operation" to get information from Ellsberg's psychiatrist, Young added. Young and Krogh then met with Ehrlichman Aug. 5, 1971 and recommended a covert operation to examine Ellsberg's psychiatric files, Young said. Young testified Ehrlichman's response was "Let's think about it."

Merrill then introduced an Aug. 11, 1971 memorandum from Young and Krogh to Ehrlichman, on which Ehrlichman had initialed his approval of a "covert operation" as long as "it was not traceable." An Aug. 30, 1971 meeting at the Executive Office Building attended by Young, Krogh, Liddy and Hunt was convened to discuss final plans for the break-in, Young testified. There was no decision at the time, he said, on whether the covert operation would proceed. Instead, Young and Krogh phoned Ehrlichman, who was vacationing on Cape Cod.

Krogh told Ehrlichman that "our investigators" were back from California and "feel the operation can be undertaken," Young said. (Krogh's statement referred to a trip to Los Angeles by Hunt and Liddy to determine the feasibility of entering Fielding's office.) When he and Krogh told Ehrlichman that the operation should be undertaken, Young said, Ehrlichman responded, "All right, let me know if anything substantive was recovered."

Young said that when Liddy later told him that the operation had not been successful and that Fielding's office had to be ransacked to hide the real intent of the break-in, he told Liddy, "That's not what I understood a covert operation to be."

This was his last contact with the Ellsberg operation until shortly after the President's re-election, Young testified. On his "own initiative," Young said, he decided to review the files relating to break-in. Besides limiting to one copy any memo relating to the operation, Young stated, he altered the Aug. 11, 1971 memorandum so that it contained no references to the break-in.

In March 1973, Young testified, he was contacted by Ehrlichman, who asked to see any Ellsberg-related files Young possessed. Subsequently they met March 27, 1973.

According to Young's notes of the meeting, written May 4, 1973, ". . . Mr. Ehrlichman interjected that then I did not know about it (the break-in) either. I said no, I had known about it beforehand and my clear recollection was that he also had known about it. I explained that, in fact, his approval of the matter was reflected in a couple of the memos in the briefcase and I pointed to the briefcase. Mr. Ehrlichman replied that there was no question about what had actually happened, but that he had taken those memos out and thought he should keep them because they were a little too sensitive and showed too much forethought. I said . . . that someone else might have copies. Mr. Ehrlichman replied that he would have to take that chance."

Young testified that he did not tell Ehrlichman he had made his own copies of the memorandums.

Young also told of a later meeting with Ehrlichman April 30, 1973, the day Ehrlichman resigned as adviser to the President. At that meeting, Young testified, Ehrlichman told of just having met with two FBI agents. Ehrlichman said he told the agents, Young testified, that he knew that Liddy and Hunt had gone to California on a "covert operation" involving Ellsberg, but that he did not know they would be involved in a break-in.

Young said he expressed his disappointment that Ehrlichman did not tell the FBI that he (Ehrlichman) "had approved the Hunt and Liddy mission beforehand." "They didn't ask me," Young quoted Ehrlichman as saying.

Young cross-examined—During cross-examination July 2 by William Frates, Ehrlichman's chief attorney, Young's mo-

tives for testifying were attacked. (The defense asserted in its opening statement in the trial that Young's supplying of the memorandums to the prosecution and his agreeing to testify were part of an effort "to save his own neck.") At one point in his questioning, Frates asked if Young had altered the Aug. 11, 1971 memorandum because it was personally incriminating. Young answered, "I deleted it not only because it involved me, but also Mr. Ehrlichman, Mr. Krogh and the White House."

Frates also dealt with the meaning of "covert." Asked by Frates if he considered the word to mean "illegality," Young responded, "I did not."

Frates asked Young if he had authorized the break-in at Fielding's office. "I recommended a covert operation. I had no authority to authorize it," Young replied. Did he ever discuss a break-in with Ehrlichman? Frates asked Young. "As I understand the question, using the word 'break-in,' we never discussed it."

During further questioning by Merrill, Young was asked if he considered "persons being in Dr. Fielding's office to examine his files without his knowledge or consent to be something . . . prohibited by law."

Young replied, "I did not at that time focus on whether or not it was legal or illegal. I focused on the object—which was to examine the files without his [Ellsberg's] consent. I recognize it as a serious invasion of privacy. I don't know whether I perceived it as violation of law."

Peter Maroulis, attorney for Liddy, asked Young July 2 to give the purpose of the operation. Young answered: "The purpose was to determine, in part, to what extent Mr. Ellsberg was involved with a wider effort to make unauthorized disclosure or find out if he had furnished classified material . . . to his psychiatrist, and . . . the motive side, . . . whether he was acting on his own or taking blame for a whole group of people."

Ehrlichman denied notes—Ruling them irrelevant, U.S. District Court Judge Gerhard A. Gesell said June 27 that he had decided not to permit Ehrlichman and his lawyers to have access to a collection of Ehrlichman's personal White House notes that had been subpoenaed. Gesell said he had seen the notes and they "contained irrelevancies."

Gesell also announced that he would not act on a suggestion by the prosecution that it would not seek to prove that Ehrlichman had sought to conceal the illegal activities of the "plumbers." The motion by the prosecution had been an effort to head off a subpoena by Ehrlichman, which asked for access to his personal White House notes that allegedly showed he had concealed the activities of the "plumbers" for reasons of national security.

Nixon bombing remarks reported. The Los Angeles Times reported June 29 that the House Judiciary Committee had been given another tape transcript in which President Nixon referred to Vietnam bombing and a public relations effort to explain the reason for shifting the site of

the 1972 Republican National Convention from San Diego to Miami Beach. The transcript of an April 4, 1972 conversation was said to have been given the committee by Nixon's defense lawyer James D. St. Clair.

According to the report, Nixon said in the transcript, "The bastards [North Vietnam] have never been bombed like they're going to be bombed this time, but you've got to have weather." He also was reported to have made disparaging remarks about the command of the Air Force and Navy bombing.

The reported talk about San Diego involved the Sheraton Hotel, which was to be a convention hub, and the disclosure that ITT-Sheraton Corp. had pledged up to $400,000 to help finance the convention. Nixon remarked about "the admission of guilt in ITT" involved in the change of site, that "maybe that's better than just having the damned story rehashed again." Former Attorney General John N. Mitchell also expressed concern that "the television cameras [would be] on the Sheraton Hotel all through the convention."

The President then talked of a "PR" campaign to base the shift on a conflict, to be created, with the ownership of the convention arena. (The site change, announced May 5, 1972, was related to labor problems.)

Weicker charges abuse of Constitution. In a separate personal report, first released June 29, Sen. Weicker charged that "every major substantive part of the Constitution was violated, abused and undermined during the Watergate period."

Emphasizing that his statement was based on the "known" facts of Watergate and related scandals gathered by the Ervin Committee and other investigative bodies—not on "new facts of scandal"—Weicker listed examples which he said illustrated how the White House had overstepped its constitutional and statutory authority: domestic intelligence plans "containing proposals that were specifically identified as illegal," the "enemies" list and misuse of the IRS, use of campaign funds for payoffs to the Watergate burglars, warrantless wiretaps of government officials and reporters and obstruction of House and Senate investigations.

Weicker said First Amendment guarantees had been subverted by intimidation of the press and issuance of false information by Administration spokesmen. "The President himself," Weicker said, "misled the press in news conferences and official statements, as to the investigation, its results, and the substance of evidence involving himself and the Watergate matter."

Weicker noted that his report implied no conclusions on individuals' criminal guilt, "except as the courts have already passed judgment," nor did it imply a position on Nixon's possible impeachment.

The report concluded with 17 legislative recommendations, including:

■ Prohibition of "all forms of domestic electronic surveillance."

■ Transforming the post of attorney general into an elective office.

■ Requiring that all nominations for federal office be by direct primary, with unaffiliated voters free to participate in the party primary of their choice.

■ Granting the Supreme Court original jurisdiction over disputes involving "any privilege asserted by the President with respect to Congress or federal law enforcement agencies, thereby making the Supreme Court the first and final arbiter of the issue."

■ Requiring that senior White House staff personnel be confirmed by the Senate.

■ Requiring that after a presidential nominee was selected, the campaign be run by the candidate's party.

Bittman resigns. William O. Bittman, the first defense attorney for Watergate conspirator E. Howard Hunt Jr., resigned from his seven-year partnership with the law firm of Hogan & Hartson effective June 30.

Charges of partisanship. As the House Judiciary Committee entered the phase of taking testimony from witnesses in its impeachment inquiry, there were attacks on Chairman Peter W. Rodino Jr. (D, N.J.) and charges that the inquiry was "a partisan lynch mob." The discord between the committee's Democrats and Republicans had erupted June 26 over the list of witnesses.

The committee's decision to schedule testimony from five witnesses, including only two of six requested by President Nixon's attorney, James D. St. Clair, was assailed by White House spokesmen June 27. Committee Chairman Rodino was denounced, and defended himself in a floor speech June 28, after a report was published attributing to him a statement that all 21 Democrats on the committee were prepared to vote to recommend impeachment of the President. Rodino announced his readiness July 1 to allow all six witnesses sought by Nixon's lawyer to testify, but the partisan breach was not healed. The committee split along party lines July 1 in voting to continued closed hearings and the House July 1 rejected a proposal urged by Rodino to expedite the hearings by restricting the right of committee members to interrogate the witnesses.

Meanwhile, the committee's inquiry continued with St. Clair's rebuttal on Nixon's behalf June 27–28 and testimony from the first witness July 2.

Panel called a 'lynch mob'—The committee's failure to schedule all six witnesses requested by St. Clair came under strong attack from the White House June 27. Dean Burch, special counselor to the President, characterized the committee's

impeachment inquiry as a "partisan lynch mob." "The Constitution indicates," he said, "that the defendant, in any kind of proceeding that has a smack of fairness, is entitled to have witnesses." To curb that right, he said, was "patently unfair" and the President was being deprived of basic 6th Amendment rights* he would have if he had "stolen a loaf of bread." Burch said he believed the committee was rushing to bring the issue to a vote, "at the expense of the rudiments of due process," in response to "pressure within the Democratic hierarchy." He attributed the "remarkable step-up in the tempo" of the committee's inquiry to "blatant partisanship."

At the Overseas Press Club, the Rev. John McLaughlin, a deputy special assistant to the President, attacked Rodino June 27 on the witness issue for trying to "railroad" the President's impeachment and "denying Mr. Nixon his day in court."

Rodino ouster urged—The attack on Rodino intensified after a report in the Los Angeles Times June 28 by Jack Nelson quoted Rodino as saying that all 21 Democrats on the panel were prepared to vote to recommend Nixon's impeachment. Nelson had met with Rodino June 27. Another reporter at the meeting, ABC correspondent Sam Donaldson, corroborated Nelson's account but said Rodino was giving only his personal assessment of the mood of the way committee members were reacting to the evidence, "that he believed all 21 Democrats would most likely reach that conclusion."

Ken W. Clawson, White House director of communications, said later June 28, "Chairman Rodino's partisanship and the bias of other Democrats on the House Judiciary Committee was confirmed today out of Mr. Rodino's own mouth." He called for Rodino to be "discharged as chairman and replaced by a fair-minded Democrat."

At the urging of House Speaker Carl Albert (D, Okla.), Rodino went to the floor of the House June 28 to deny the newspaper report and affirm his intention to conduct the inquiry fairly. "I want to state unequivocally and categorically that this statement is not true," he said of the newspaper report. He had never asked any of the committee members "how he or she will vote" on the issue, Rodino said, and had insisted throughout the inquiry that "only when there is a complete presentation of evidence should members

*The 6th Amendment: In all criminal prosecutions, the accused shall enjoy the right to a speedy and public trial, by an impartial jury of the State and district wherein the crime shall have been committed, which district shall have been previously ascertained by law, and to be informed of the nature and cause of the accusation; to be confronted with the witnesses against him; to have compulsory process for obtaining witnesses in his favor, and to have the Assistance of Counsel for his defence.

draw a conclusion." If it became apparent he had prejudged the evidence and could not conduct the inquiry fairly, he said, "I assure you that I would not be sitting as chairman and I would withdraw myself from that capacity."

House Republican whip Leslie C. Arends (Ill.) said June 28 the newspaper article about Rodino was "one of the most disturbing things I've seen since this thing started." Rep. Lawrence J. Hogan, a Rodino committee member who announced June 27 his candidacy for the Republican nomination for governor of Maryland, told the House June 28 he thought the impeachment inquiry "has been biased and it has been unfair."

But other Republicans on the committee supported Rodino June 28. Ranking GOP member Edward Hutchinson (Mich.) said he was "satisfied" that Rodino had not acted improperly. Rep. Robert McClory (Ill.), speaking after Rodino, told the House "I know the chairman has tenaciously avoided statements that would prejudge the case." Rep. Wiley Mayne (Iowa) said "most members of the committee discounted the story as soon as they saw it. I know I did."

Nixon's attorney St. Clair said June 28 he was "satisfied the committee members are going to wait until all the evidence is in." He said he did not believe Rodino should resign his post.

Talk of censure, not impeachment—There were reports June 29–30 of an effort by conservative Republicans to turn the case against Nixon into a vote of censure, rather than impeachment. But House Republican Leader John J. Rhodes (Ariz.) opposed it strongly June 29 as "exactly the wrong thing to do." "What we are trying to do," he said, "is to strengthen the presidency one way or another, not weaken it. To censure the President and leave him in office would be doing the country a grave disservice. It would completely cripple the man and would be giving him the worst of two worlds."

House Democratic leaders were exhibiting concern about maintaining a schedule for the impeachment proceedings. A tentative schedule circulated June 27 set July 12 for completion of examination of witnesses by the committee, July 15 for the start of debate on proposed articles of impeachment and a vote during the week of July 22. The House vote on impeachment was tentatively set for Aug. 23.

Rodino agrees to hear witnesses—Rodino announced July 1 it was his intention to recommend that all of the witnesses requested by St. Clair be summoned for testimony before the committee following staff interviews.

The chairman made the announcement as the House was about to consider a proposal to expedite the committee's hearings by suspending a House rule giving each of the committee's 38 members the right to question witnesses. Instead, the members could submit written questions to the committee's two senior lawyers to be asked if deemed relevant and not repetitive.

The proposal was backed by Rodino and senior GOP committee member Hutchinson, Speaker Albert and House GOP Leader Rhodes, but it was vigorously attacked by Republicans led by committee member David W. Dennis (Ind.). "Why should an investigation of this magnitude be conducted entirely by the hired help?" Dennis asked. Another committee member, Trent Lott (R, Miss.), complained of "gag rule."

The proposal, requiring a two-thirds majority for waiver of the rule, was defeated, 207 (including 31 Republicans) to 140 (including 120 Republicans), just short of the necessary two-thirds.

Later July 1, the committee voted, after heated partisan debate, to hear all witnesses in closed sessions. The vote, was 23–15, with Hutchinson and Lott joining the 21 Democrats to keep the hearings private.

St. Clair presents rebuttal—President Nixon's defense against impeachment was presented to the committee in closed sessions June 27–28 by his chief defense lawyer St. Clair. The material was said to have dealt with the Watergate burglary, the cover-up, Administration transactions with the International Telephone and Telegraph Corp. and milk producers, the White House "plumbers," wiretapping and Nixon's income taxes.

St. Clair reportedly focused June 27 on Nixon's argument that he never condoned the payment of hush money to a Watergate defendant. St. Clair reportedly quoted former Nixon counsel John W. Dean 3rd's testimony before the Senate Watergate committee in which Dean said he had discussed the payment with Nixon but "there was no further discussion of the matter and it was left hanging" when the meeting ended.

On the milk producers' issue, St. Clair reportedly produced evidence June 28 that a $2 million campaign pledge, allegedly in return for an increase in federal milk price supports, had been "tossed around" only in jest.

The first session reportedly was again marked by partisan dispute. The Democrats repeatedly challenged St. Clair for offering what they considered unsubstantiated conclusions. The Republicans asserted that some data supporting the President produced by St. Clair had been disregarded by the committee's staff in its presentation of evidence.

First witness heard—Alexander P. Butterfield testified in closed session July 2 as the first witness in the committee's impeachment inquiry. Currently administrator of the Federal Aviation Administration, Butterfield had been staff secretary at the White House during Nixon's first term.

Rebozo plea vs Watergate unit held moot. U.S. District Court Judge John Lewis Smith Jr. July 2 dismissed as moot a plea by Charles G. Rebozo, President Nixon's friend, for an order barring the Senate Watergate Committee from inquiring further into his affairs or citing him for contempt. Smith held that there was no longer any issue since the committee's authority had lapsed June 28. [For further details, see p. 216F3]

Minority report on CIA involvement. A report by the Watergate Committee's minority staff on the Central Intelligence Agency's involvement in the Watergate scandal was made public July 2. The 43-page document had been prepared under the direction of Sen. Howard H. Baker Jr. (R, Tenn.), the committee's vice chairman.

While the preparers of the report expressly refrained from drawing conclusions, they did reveal, among other things, that the CIA had used a Washington public relations firm as a "cover" for agents outside the U.S., that the agency had destroyed its own records despite a request by Senate majority leader Mike Mansfield (D, Mont.) to keep them intact, that a CIA agent might have functioned as a domestic operative in violation of the agency's charter, that there were unanswered questions about the agency's foreknowledge of the 1971 break-in at Daniel Ellsberg's psychiatrist's office, and that a CIA employe fought within the agency against withholding data from the Watergate committee. In addition, the report detailed instances in which the CIA attempted to frustrate committee investigators by refusing to make its employes available as witnesses and by ignoring, resisting or refusing requests for documents and other materials.

■ The report said that the public relations firm of Robert R. Mullen & Co. had employed convicted Watergate conspirator E. Howard Hunt Jr., a retired CIA operative, at the time of the burglary of the Watergate headquarters of the Democratic National Committee. Mullen, the report said, was serving as a cover for two CIA agents stationed abroad, and employed retired CIA agents.

Robert F. Bennett, head of Mullen, in the weeks following the Watergate break-in, "was supplying information to the CIA about many aspects of the Watergate incident and was at that time serving as liaison between Hunt and [Watergate conspirator G. Gordon] Liddy, [and] there is no indication that these facts were disclosed to the FBI [Federal Bureau of Investigation]," the report said.

■ The report also dealt with the CIA's knowledge of the Sept. 3, 1971 break-in at the Los Angeles offices of Daniel Ellsberg's psychiatrist, Dr. Lewis J. Fielding. At the request of John Ehrlichman, the CIA had supplied a camera to Hunt, who used it to take photographs near Fielding's office. According to the report, the CIA developed the negatives, realized they were "casing" photographs, and terminated its assistance to Hunt. In testimony, however, agency officials said that aid to Hunt had been discontinued because of his escalating demands for agency assistance.

The report contradicted the CIA's claims that it had no contact with Hunt after Aug. 31, 1971. "Recent testimony and secret documents indicate that Hunt had extensive contact with the CIA after" Aug. 31, 1971, that he had a "large role" in the preparation of a CIA psychological profile of Ellsberg completed in November 1971, and that Hunt had other contacts with the CIA.

In discussions with a CIA psychiatrist who aided them in preparation of the profile, the report said, Hunt and Liddy stated that they wanted to "try Ellsberg in public, render him the 'object of pity as a broken man' and be able to refer to Ellsberg's 'Oedipal complex.'" The psychiatrist, "extremely concerned about Hunt's presence and remarks," ignored Hunt's requests that he not reveal Hunt's activities to anyone else in the CIA and voiced his apprehension to his superiors.

The report said the committee asked to see the memorandums of the psychiatrist, but the CIA refused.

■ The report expressed concern at the activities of CIA operative Lee R. Pennington, who assisted the wife of Watergate burglar James W. McCord Jr.—a former CIA employe—in destroying papers at her home shortly after the Watergate break-in. There was an effort by agency officials, the report noted, to keep from the FBI, the Watergate committee and other Congressional committees information about Pennington's visit.

Subsequently, when FBI agents asked about "Mr. Pennington," the CIA furnished information about a former employe with a similar name—the wrong Mr. Pennington. In January 1974, the agency's former director of security attempted to exclude material on the Pennington visit from a CIA Watergate file made available to the Watergate and other Congressional committees. Only when a lower echelon security officer protested did the agency reverse itself, the report said. The Pennington material was provided, and the chief of security was reportedly forced to retire.

"The Pennington matter," the report said, apparently "was extremely sensitive . . . because Pennington may have been a domestic agent" in violation of the agency's charter, which forbade intelligence activities in the U.S. However, the report did not make clear what domestic activities might have been involved, although it did contain a passing reference to a CIA file on syndicated columnist Jack Anderson.

Kalmbach debarred. Herber W. Kalmbach, former personal attorney to President Nixon who began serving a prison term July 1 for illegal campaign fund raising practices, was suspended from law practice by the California Supreme Court July 3.

Kissinger acknowledges Watergate impact on Moscow summit. U.S. Secretary of State Henry A. Kissinger acknowledged June 28 that the impact of Watergate and impeachment efforts would hamper attempts by President Nixon to exert leadership at the Moscow summit negotiations. In a Moscow press conference July 3, Kissinger laid blame for failure to achieve more substantial agreements on factionalism within both governments: "Both [Washington and Moscow] have to convince their military establishments of the benefits of restraint, and that does not come easily to either side." Kissinger and U.S. Secretary of Defense James Schlesinger had expressed contrasting views on the issue of limiting nuclear arms. President Nixon and Soviet Communist Party General Secretary Leonid I. Brezhnev had signed a number of limited documents on nuclear relations July 3, concluding a one week's visit by Nixon to the Soviet Union. None of the agreements constituted a hoped-for breakthrough toward permanent agreements on limiting offensive nuclear weapons. In first revealing the agreements July 2, Brezhnev had observed that the arms accords "could have been broader."

Soviets seen drifting from Nixon—In his Moscow dinner addresses June 27 and July 2, President Nixon underscored the "personal" basis on which Soviet-U.S. negotiations were conducted and the vital role of "personal relationships" in the evolution of detente. In his June 27 speech, Nixon said previous Soviet-U.S. agreements had been possible "because of a personal relationship that was established between the general secretary [Brezhnev] and the President of the United States." He stated July 2 that "our differences ... could never be solved unless we met as friends."

Brezhnev, for his part, was less inclined to balance detente on the shoulders of individuals. While he too, in his addresses at the Moscow welcome and farewell dinners, noted the good personal relations between himself and the President, Brezhnev did not repeat the theme as forcefully as Nixon. Observers viewed this as an acknowledgement of the collective structure of the Soviet leadership, which would discourage founding detente on individual

personal relations. Moscow and Washington sources also saw it as an indication that Moscow was not anxious to link detente to a President whose viability was undermined by the threat of impeachment. The Soviet Union had recently begun to stress the role of Democrats in improving U.S.-Soviet relations.

A brief controversy arose June 28 over the official Soviet translation of Nixon's June 27 speech. As published in the Soviet newspapers, the Tass translation omitted the word "personal" from a phrase in which it had been used by the President: "Because of our personal relationship," Nixon had said, "there is no question about our will to keep these agreements [that had been made in the past] and to make more where they are in our mutual interest."

Leonid Zamyatin, director general of Tass, the Soviet news agency, denied June 28 that there was any significance to the alteration of the text.

Nixon ailment dangerous during trip. President Nixon's personal physician, Dr. Walter Tkach, disclosed July 4 that the President had undertaken his recent Middle East trip despite some danger to his life from his leg ailment, described after the trip as phlebitis, inflammation of a vein. The condition actually was thrombophlebitis, Tkach said, involving clotting as well as inflammation. While the danger was "pretty much gone" as of July 4 there had been "an outside chance" that the clot could have broken loose during the Middle East trip and caused death by reaching the heart or lungs, Tkach said.

The disclosure of the gravity of the ailment was made by the New York Daily News in an interview with Tkach, who said he apprised Nixon of the possible complications when the President first revealed his trouble to him in Salzburg, Austria en route to the Middle East. Tkach said he advised Nixon not to make the trip, and hospitalization had been considered, but Nixon "took a calculated risk" to go through with it because he said he had "an obligation to make the trip."

At a news conference after the initial report July 4, Tkach said the gravity of the condition had abated somewhat by the President's later trip to the Soviet Union. At the current time, Tkach reported, there still was some swelling in Nixon's left leg. The clot, he said, "will always be there," having become "fixed" or attached to the wall of the vein and hence, the "danger is pretty much gone." The prescription for the ailment was physical exercise and rest.

The President, at his home in Key Biscayne since his return from the U.S.S.R., was reported by the press office there July 4 to be "feeling fine." Deputy White House Press Secretary Gerald L. Warren said July 5 that the gravity of the ailment had not been publicized during the President's trips so as

not to interfere with his negotiations with foreign leaders.

The President, accompanied by his friend, Charles G. Rebozo, took a helicopter trip to Palm Beach July 7 to inspect the Mar-A-Lago Estate willed to the government by the late Mrs. Marjorie Merriweather Post as a possible presidential retreat.

Court voids 1971 Nixon import surcharge. The U.S. Customs Court in New York City ruled July 8 that President Nixon had exceeded his constitutional authority in 1971 when he imposed a 10% import surcharge tax. In its unanimous decision, the three-judge panel ordered the Treasury Department to refund the $481 million it had collected during the last four months of 1971 when the tax was in effect.

Designed to reverse the U.S.'s deteriorating international balance of payments position, the surcharge was imposed Aug. 15, 1971, the same date that Nixon announced a 90-day wage-price freeze.

In a strongly worded opinion, Chief Judge Nils A. Boe concluded that Nixon's action "exceeded authority delegated to the President." The court could not "fail to recognize the efforts of the President to achieve stability in the international trade position and monetary reserves of this country." But, Boe wrote, "neither need nor national emergency will justify the exercise of a power by the executive that isn't inherent in his office nor delegated by Congress." Only Congress had the power to levy and collect taxes, duties, imposts and excises and to regulate foreign commerce, Boe said.

After imposing the surcharge, the government allowed importers to pass on the tax to consumers through higher prices. The Customs Court ruling did not require the importers to make refunds to consumers.

Court hears tapes case. The Supreme Court July 8 heard oral arguments in the historic cases captioned "The United States vs. Richard M. Nixon" and "Richard M. Nixon vs. the United States." The primary issue had long been central to the Watergate case: the disputed doctrine of executive privilege and access to presidential tapes and documents by the special prosecutor. A second question had arisen more recently: whether a grand jury had the authority to name President Nixon as an unindicted co-conspirator in the Watergate cover-up.

In three hours of oral presentation, punctuated with questions from the eight justices considering the case, (Justice William H. Rehnquist had withdrawn the two sides re-emphasized positions they had taken in lower court proceedings, special prosecutor Leon Jaworski insisting that there was no constitutional basis for a sweeping claim of privilege—especially when a criminal conspiracy was involved, and special presidential counsel James D. St. Clair maintaining that compliance with

Jaworski's subpoena for tapes of 64 White House conversations would irrevocably weaken the presidency. St. Clair also emphasized that the issues were unavoidably intertwined with the House impeachment inquiry, and that the court should not even hear the case in that "political" context.)

Speaking first, Jaworski attacked Nixon's contention that the President alone could determine the limits of executive privilege and decide which records would be surrendered for a criminal inquiry. In urging the court to sustain District Court Judge John J. Sirica's decision that the tapes be turned over, Jaworski said constitutional government would be in "serious jeopardy if the President—any President—is to say that the Constitution means what he says it does, and that there is no one, not even the Supreme Court, to tell him otherwise."

Jaworski stressed that the current circumstances presented special requirements for judicial intervention: ". . . there is at stake the matter of the supplying of evidence that relates to two former close aides and devotees." Jaworski added that Nixon had publicly stated his belief that H. R. Haldeman and John D. Ehrlichman "would come out all right in the end." And, Jaworski noted, "the President has a sensitivity of his own involvement."

Responding to questions, Jaworski said that while "executive privilege" was not specifically mentioned in the Constitution, the issue had broad constitutional overtones. But in the current case, he continued, the question was "a very narrow one . . . whether the President, in a pending prosecution, can withhold material evidence from the court, merely on his assertion that the evidence involves confidential communications." Relating the issue to the general question of separation of powers, Jaworski added: "if the courts are the ultimate interpreters of the Constitution and can restrain Congress to operate within constitutional bounds, they certainly shouldn't be empowered any less to measure presidential claims of constitutional powers."

In response to questions by Justices William O. Douglas and Potter Stewart, Jaworski said the grand jury's action naming Nixon as a co-conspirator was not an effort to influence or intervene in the impeachment inquiry but an important link in establishing the relevance and necessity of the subpoenaed evidence, and acknowledged that the action "admits some evidence that would otherwise not be admissible" in the pending cover-up trial.

Jaworski also acknowledged to Justice Lewis F. Powell Jr. that the co-conspirator citation tended to foreclose Nixon's claims of privilege, but disagreed with Powell's assertion that it reduced the President "to the status of any other person accused of a crime." Jaworski added later that, "painful as it is," the grand jury's action "must be considered as being valid and sufficient to show . . . that the President was involved in the proceedings in the course and in the continuation of the particular conspiracy that was charged."

Regarding the court's position on the grand jury's action, Justice Stewart observed that while the sufficiency of the grand jury's evidence behind naming Nixon was at most a collateral issue, the action itself was important in that Jaworski had tied it to the validity of the subpoenas, and the White House had contended that the jury had overstepped its authority. Justice Thurgood Marshall noted, however, that "whether or not they had the authority, they did it. . . and so I don't see how we have anything to do with whether they had the authority or not."

St. Clair argued that because of the impeachment inquiry and its "realistic fusion" with the special prosecutor's criminal proceedings, the subpoena issue had already influenced and would continue to have an effect on the restricted legislative function of impeachment. For that reason, St. Clair said, the essentially political question should remain outside the purview of the courts.

St. Clair contended that the influence on the impeachment probe was pervasive, since the White House tapes, if surrendered, would also eventually go to the House Judiciary Committee. In the same context, St. Clair argued that the prosecutor had acted improperly in keeping the co-conspirator citation secret while Judge Sirica was deciding whether to send the grand jury's compilation of evidence to the impeachment panel.

Justice Stewart inquired whether the courts should "stop dead in their tracks" in a matter involving the President "even tangentially" if an impeachment inquiry was under way. St. Clair rejected the strength of the suggestion, but said that since the same subject matter was involved in the two proceedings, the court "should not go forward at this time."

Justice Marshall asked about the contents of the tapes and their relevance to the impeachment investigation. St. Clair replied that he did not know, but that the fact of the President's participation in the conversations should be sufficient, regardless of the actual content.

In a later hypothetical but noteworthy argument, St. Clair suggested that confidentiality of presidential conversations should be absolute in order to insure proper functioning of the office.

St. Clair was asked:

"Don't you think it would be important in a hypothetical case if an about-to-be-appointed judge was making a deal with the President for money? St. Clair: Absolutely.

"Question: But under [your argument] it couldn't be. In public interest you couldn't release that. St. Clair: I would think that that could not be released, if it were a confidential communication. If the President did appoint such an individual, the remedy is clear, the remedy is he should be impeached.

"Question: How are you going to impeach him if you don't know about it?

"St. Clair: Well, if you know about it, then you can state the case. If you don't know about it, you don't have it.

"Question: If you know the President is

doing something wrong, you can impeach him; but the only way you can find out is this way; you can't impeach him, so you don't impeach him. You lose me some place along there. St. Clair: Human experience has not demonstrated that's a fact. Very few things forever are hidden."

In another exchange involving the actual cover-up conspiracy, St. Clair was asked what public interest there would be in "preserving secrecy with respect to a criminal conspiracy." St. Clair replied that "a criminal conspiracy is criminal only after it's proven to be criminal."

Regarding the President's position in relation to the court and St. Clair's argument that jurisdiction was questionable, Marshall suggested that the White House was willingly submitting Watergate issues to the court in the present case. St. Clair agreed, to the extent that the questions were submitted for the court's "guidance and judgment with respect to the law." On the other hand, St. Clair added, the President "has his obligations under the Constitution."

Addressing the grand jury citation, St. Clair said the President "was not above the law by any means. But law as to the President has to be applied in a constitutional way which is different from anyone else." Given this, St. Clair added, the citation was an "intrusion" on a function "that is solely legislative and not judicial."

At one point, St. Clair said the White House would be willing to release to the prosecution the tapes of 20 conversations of which edited transcripts had been made public and sent to the impeachment panel. [See below] In response to a question, St. Clair said such a decision was not inconsistent with claims of absolute privilege, since the release of selected material was a legitimate political decision within the framework of executive privilege. But the release of any additional evidence to the House would be another political decision reserved to the President, St. Clair asserted; "the court ought not to be drawn into that decision," as it would be in granting Jaworski's petition.

Regarding the White House contention that the tapes dispute was an internal affair within the executive branch, St. Clair argued that a special prosecutor was a "constitutional anomaly" and that his appointment did not create an additional branch of government; "executive power is vested in a President." Jaworski had been delegated certain authority to prosecute, St. Clair said, but "was not delegated the right to tell the President what of his conversations are going to be made available as evidence." By the same token, it was not the function of the courts "to direct or rule what evidence will be presented to it by the executive in the executive's duty of prosecuting."

In a rebuttal argument, assistant special prosecutor Philip A. Lacovara maintained that both the subpoena for evidence and the grand jury's citation were valid because a showing had been made that the conversations occurred in "furtherance of a criminal conspiracy," not in the course of "legitimate governmental processes." Lacovara added that the remote possibility that another grand jury might abuse the authority to name a President as co-conspirator was not sufficient to invalidate the current citation.

Regarding St. Clair's contention that the impeachment inquiry should require removal of the tapes issue from the court's consideration, Lacovara argued that the cover-up prosecution had been "brought to a head without regard to the impeachment inquiry," and was an independent, separate constitutional process. A central issue, Lacovara said, was simply the "ordinary, prosaic remedy" being used for that trial—a subpoena for evidence.

Written briefs filed—In preliminary actions laying the groundwork for oral arguments, both sides had filed briefs with the court June 21 and July 1. Addressing the privilege and impeachment issues in the first set, the White House argued that the intermingling of the Watergate prosecution and the impeachment inquiry was "manifestly unfair" to Nixon, and that the courts should not be used as a "back-door" circumvention of the impeachment process.

Jaworski maintained that while evidence in the two proceedings might overlap, the President could not be the proper judge of whether the public interest required the subpoenaed materials be released. "Shall the evidence from the White House," Jaworski asked, "be confined to what a single person, highly interested in the outcome, is willing to make available?"

In his July 1 brief, St. Clair said the grand jury's citation of Nixon as a "criminal co-conspirator, even an unindicted one," had crippled the presidency and was, in effect, an act of impeachment. Jaworski maintained, however, that such an action was not constitutionally proscribed, but was, in fact, a necessary evidentiary prelude to the cover-up trial.

Tape offer rejected—Assistant special prosecutor James Neal told Judge Sirica July 11 that a White House offer of tapes of 20 presidential conversations was "illusory" and meaningless because, according to Neal, access would be granted only to portions identical with the edited transcripts already released to the public and the impeachment inquiry. The offer had been made during the July 8 Supreme Court hearing on the prosecutor's subpoena for tapes of 64 conversations. [See above]

Neal said that under the offer, Sirica would not be allowed to screen the complete tapes, and the tapes themselves could not be used as courtroom evidence in the cover-up trial.

Sirica and attorneys for the cover-up defendants agreed that such tapes would be of little use for the trial. Overruling White House objections, Sirica ordered that the transcript of the hearing be sent to the Supreme Court.

In another development during the July 1 hearing, assistant special prosecutor Richard Ben-Veniste disclosed that a blank space lasting about 19 minutes had been discovered on the tape of a March 20, 1973 conversation between Nixon and former adviser John D. Ehrlichman.

The tape had not been subpoenaed but, according to Ben-Veniste, was part of another compromise offer by the White House.

Ben-Veniste revealed the "gap" in requesting that Sirica order the White House to determine whether any of the withheld tapes at issue in the Supreme Court case were missing or incomplete. Also urging that precautions be ordered to insure integrity of the tapes, Ben-Veniste noted that at least one original tape had been torn and "to some extent mangled" during preparation of the White House transcripts.

Sirica declined to issue the order.

Cover-up defense pleas denied. U.S. District Court Judge John J. Sirica July 9 denied a series of motions by the six Watergate cover-up defendants for separate trials, dismissal, delaying the start of the trial, and moving the trial out of Washington.

Sirica rejected as premature the defense contentions that inflammatory publicity had made a fair trial impossible. He added, however, that his decision not to move the trial would be reconsidered if a jury could not be selected in Washington.

Sirica scheduled a secret hearing for July 29 on the contention by defendant Gordon C. Strachan that he had given information to the original Watergate prosecutors with an informal understanding that it would not be used against him. Strachan's attorneys also maintained that the government's case against him was further tainted because his testimony before the Senate Watergate Committee was given under a grant of limited immunity.

In a related development July 9, defendants John N. Mitchell and Kenneth W. Parkinson petitioned the Supreme Court to disqualify Sirica from presiding in the cover-up trial. The petition sought review of an appeals court decision upholding Sirica's refusal to withdraw.

Discrepancies noted in taped transcripts. The House Judiciary Committee July 9 released its own transcripts of some Watergate conversations by President Nixon that varied in many instances from the White House transcripts of the same talks released April 30.

The committee's transcripts of eight White House conversations occurring between Sept. 15, 1972 and April 16, 1973, contained indications that the President was more involved in the cover-up than portrayed in the White House version. One section of the committee's transcripts, not contained in the White House version, showed awareness by the President and esteem for the activities of John W. Dean 3rd, then his counsel, in the aftermath of the Watergate break-in. Dean later became a key Nixon accuser and was denounced by the White House.

In nearly all cases where substantial discrepancies between the White House and committee transcripts existed, the White House version put the President in a better light.

The committee's transcripts were prepared by its staff from tape recordings and transcripts received from the White House and the Watergate grand jury. Along with them, the committee released a side-by-side comparison of certain passages from the committee and White House versions. Many of the discrepancies had been previously leaked to the press.

Among the discrepancies (the dates of the conversations, and participants, indicated; Judiciary Committee version first):

Feb. 28, 1973 (Nixon, Dean, discussing the situation that Nixon's personal attorney Herbert W. Kalmbach had been questioned by authorities and had not yet disclosed damaging information)—Nixon: "It'll be hard for him,—'cause it'll, it'll get out about Hunt." E. Howard Hunt Jr. was one of the Watergate defendants who received money raised by Kalmbach. Nixon's statement was not in the White House transcripts.

March 13, 1973 (Nixon and Dean)—P. Uh, is it too late to, to, frankly, go the hang-out road? Yes it is.

D. I think it is. I think—here's the—the hang-out road—

P. The hang-out road's going to have to be rejected. I, some, I understand it was rejected.

"Hang-out" was used to mean reveal the truth. The White House version did not have Nixon saying "Yes it is" nor his remarks about having that road rejected.

In the same conversation, there was a discussion about how Nixon campaign director John N. Mitchell would have allowed an operation like the June 1972 bugging of the Democratic headquarters in the Watergate office building in Washington.

Dean. I don't think he knew it was there.

P. You kidding?

D. I don't.

P. You don't think Mitchell knew about this thing?

D. Oh, no, no, no.

The White House transcripts: D. I don't think he knew it was there.

P. I don't think that Mitchell knew about this sort of thing.

D. Oh, no, no!

March 21, 1973 (Nixon and Dean discussing the question of hush money to Hunt)—Committee version: P. Would you agree that that's a buy-time thing, you better damn well get that done, but fast?

White House transcripts: P. Would you agree that that's the prime thing that you damn well better get that done?

Committee version: P. Well, your, your major, your major guy to keep under control is Hunt. D. That's right. P. I think. Because he knows. D. He knows so much. P. About a lot of other things. D. He knows so much. Right . . .

White House transcripts: P. Your major guy to keep under control is Hunt? D. That is right. P. I think. Does he know a lot? D. He knows so much. . . .

Punctuation, such as a question mark, also varied elsewhere in the two versions of the March 21 conversation.

Still talking of the Hunt demand for money, Dean noted that Mitchell and another campaign official were "aware" of the situation. Nixon's comment, according to the committee version, was: "True, [unintelligible] do something." The White House transcript was: "True. Are they going to do something?"

Also on March 21, Nixon talked of the payments to the Watergate defendants, several of whom were Cuban Americans, in this fashion on the committee version: "As far as what happened up to this time, our cover there is just going to be the Cuban committee did this for them up through the election." In the White House transcript, he said: "These fellows though, as far as what has happened up to this time, are covered on their situation, because the Cuban committee did this for them during the election?"

The same day, joined by Nixon chief of staff H. R. Haldeman, Nixon talked of grand jury testimony in this way in the committee version: "Just be damned sure you say I don't (Haldeman interjected "yeah") remember: I can't recall, I can't give any honest, an answer to that that I can recall." In the White House transcripts, Nixon said: "But you can say I don't remember. You can say I can't recall. I can't give any answer to that that I can recall."

March 22, 1973 (discussing the use of executive privilege before the Senate Watergate committee)—Committee version: P. "But now—what—all that John Mitchell is arguing, then, is that now we, we use flexibility in order to get on with the cover-up plan."

White House transcript: P. "Well, all John Mitchell is arguing then, is that now we use flexibility in order to get off the cover-up line."

The committee's March 22 transcript contained a 16-page dialogue between Nixon and Mitchell that was not in the White House version. In it, Nixon was critical of President Eisenhower for ousting his aide Sherman Adams over a gift scandal. Referring to Eisenhower, Nixon said: "He only cared about—Christ, 'Be sure he was clean.' Both in the fund thing and the Adams thing. But I don't look at it that way. And I just—that's the thing I am really concerned with. We're going to protect our people, if we can."

In the same context, Nixon remarked: "And, uh, for that reason, I am perfectly willing to—I don't give a shit what happens. I want you all to stonewall it, let them plead the Fifth Amendment, cover-up or anything else, if it'll save it—save the plan. That's the whole point."

The President continued, suggesting that Mitchell, however, "do it the other way," an apparent reference to a limited disclosure in a report by Dean to the Senate hearings.

"On the other hand, uh, uh, I would prefer, as I said to you, that you do it the other way," Nixon told Mitchell. "And I would particularly prefer to do it that other way if it's going to come out that way anyway. And that my view, that, uh, with the number of jackass people that they've got that they can call, they're going to—the story they get out through leaks, charges, and so forth, and innuendoes, will be a hell of a lot worse than the story they're going to get out by just letting it out there."

Mitchell said, "Well" and Nixon continued. "I don't know. But that's, uh, you know, up to this point the whole theory has been containment, as you know, John."

The dialogue deleted from the March 21 transcript, according to the committee, also contained praise for Dean. With Dean and Mitchell present, Nixon remarked, "John Dean is, uh [unintelligible] got—put the fires out, almost got the damn thing nailed down till past the election and so forth." After Dean left the room, Nixon continued. "I was going to say that Dean has really been, uh, something on this."

M. That he has, Mr. President, no question about it. He's a very . . .

P. Son-of-a-bitching tough thing.

M. You've got a very solid guy that's handled some tough things. And, I also want to say these lawyers that you have think very highly of him.

In a "few" instances, committee chairman Peter W. Rodino Jr. (D, N.J.) noted in a foreward to the transcripts, material had been deleted by the committee—by Rodino and the committee's senior Republican Edward Hutchinson (Mich.)—on their judgment it was "irrelevant material which was considered to be defamatory, degrading or embarrassing." One such deletion was at the end of the March 22 conversation.

White House reaction. White House Press Secretary Ronald L. Ziegler defended President Nixon's position on the transcripts July 9 and deplored the Judiciary Committee's "dribbling out" of evidence in a "hypoed public relations campaign."

Nixon's defense lawyer, James D. St. Clair, joined in the defense rebuttal by declaring there were no "significant differences" between the White House and committee versions.

Both continued the rebuttal at separate news conferences July 10. "Squabbling over words is not a fruitful exercise," St.

Clair told reporters. "It is the overall gist of it that counts." Ziegler said "the overall weight of the evidence shows that the President did want this material [the cover-up] out. The thrust of the transcripts in no way contradicts what the President has said."

Ziegler said that in the areas of the transcripts where Nixon seemed to be suggesting violation of the law, the President simply was acting as a "devil's advocate."

Ziegler defended the 2,500-word deletion of part of the March 22, 1973 conversation involving potential appearances by White House aides before the Senate Watergate committee. [See above] "The President was examining the various theories on how to deal with a political situation before the Senate Watergate committee," Ziegler said, "and not in reference to grand jury proceedings or other proceedings."

Nixon personally made the decision to delete the material, Ziegler said, on the ground it was of "dubious relevancy."

Rodino panel hears witnesses. Five witnesses were called before the House Judiciary Committee July 3–11 to testify in closed sessions of its impeachment inquiry. All five were on the list of witnesses requested by President Nixon's defense lawyer, James D. St. Clair. A sixth on his list, H. R. Haldeman, former White House chief of staff, informed the committee July 2 he would not testify voluntarily and would invoke his constitutional privilege against self-incrimination if subpoenaed and the committee did not make a decison to summon him under those circumstances.

The others were Paul L. O'Brien, a former lawyer for President Nixon's re-election campaign committee, who testified July 3; Frederick C. LaRue, a former official of that committee, who testified July 3 and 8; William O. Bittman, former attorney for E. Howard Hunt Jr., one of the convicted Watergate conspirators, who testified July 9; former Nixon campaign director John N. Mitchell, who appeared before the committee July 9 and 10; and former White House counsel John W. Dean 3rd, who came before the panel July 11.

St. Clair had requested the witnesses because of their "first-hand knowledge critical" to Nixon's defense, which St. Clair was focusing on the alleged payment of hush money to a Watergate defendant, Hunt. St. Clair's argument was that the payment, $75,000, was arranged and effected for legitimate reasons, support for Hunt and his family and for legal fees, without direct instruction from the President.

Mitchell, whose involvement was on the authorization end, reportedly gave consent to the payment as legitimate expenses for legal fees and family support. He reportedly told the committee frequently he had no specific recollection of the data under question.

Dean's appearance July 11 gave St. Clair the opportunity to confront a key accuser of the President, and, according to the reports, he subjected the testimony to fierce attack.

'Plumbers' trial defense rests. The defense in the "plumbers" trial rested its case July 10 after presiding U.S. District Court Judge Gerhard A. Gesell read aloud to the jury sworn testimony from President Nixon, who had provided written replies to six questions submitted by the defense. Prior to the reading of Nixon's testimony, Secretary of State Henry A. Kissinger had appeared as a defense witness.

Except for Nixon's and Kissinger's testimony, the defendants had concluded their defense July 9. John D. Ehrlichman, former domestic affairs adviser to Nixon, denied he authorized the 1971 break-in at the Los Angeles office of Dr. Lewis J. Fielding, the psychiatrist who had treated Pentagon Papers trial defendant Daniel Ellsberg. Testifying on his own behalf July 8 and 9, Ehrlichman attempted to refute earlier testimony by David R. Young Jr. and Egil Krogh Jr., co-directors of the White House "plumbers" unit, that Ehrlichman had authorized a break-in at Fielding's office for the purpose of obtaining information for a proposed psychiatric profile of Ellsberg.

Defendants Eugenio Martinez and Bernard L. Barker, who along with Ehrlichman and G. Gordon Liddy were charged with conspiring to violate Fielding's right against illegal search and seizure, made short appearances on the witness stand July 9. Barker said he had never heard of Ellsberg until a few minutes before the entry into Fielding's office. Barker added that he was told that the break-in involved "matters of national security—a traitor to this country who was passing material to the Soviet embassy." Martinez offered similar testimony.

The questions to Nixon had been delivered to the White House July 9. In a letter accompanying the replies, the President said he had decided to respond "as a matter of discretion and in the interest of justice." (Judge Gesell said the submission of written interrogatories was "not an order, merely a request" to which the President had acceded.)

The six questions and Nixon's replies were:

Q. What duties and responsibilities, if any, did you authorize the special investigations unit located in Room 16 of the Executive Office Building to perform?

A. I authorized the special investigations unit to prevent and halt leaks of vital security information and to prepare an accurate history of certain critical national security matters which occurred under prior Administrations.

Q. What instructions, if any, did you personally give John D. Ehrlichman concerning his role in the activities of the unit? (If so, please give details, including where and when such instructions were given.)

A. I instructed John D. Ehrlichman to exercise general supervisory control over the special investigations unit.

Q. Did you ever instruct John D. Ehrlichman not to discuss the activities of the unit with either (A) the

FBI [Federal Bureau of Investigation] and-or (B) members of the White House staff not directly involved in the work of the unit? Please detail each such instruction and indicate the date on which it was given, the reasons for giving it and the period during which it remained in effect.

(Nixon gave a single reply to the third and fourth questions.)

Q. Did you ever instruct John D. Ehrlichman not to discuss the activities of the unit at any time after Sept. 3, 1971, as they related to Dr. Fielding's files with either (A) the FBI and-or (B) members of the White House staff not directly involved in the work of the unit? Please detail each such instruction and indicate the date on which it was given, the reasons for giving it and the period during which it remained in effect.

A. I do not have a precise recollection of instructions given to Mr. Ehrlichman with respect to any specific agencies. In substance, however, I do recall repeatedly emphasizing to Mr. Ehrlichman that this was a highly classified matter which could be discussed with others only on an absolutely "need to know" basis. I conveyed these instructions because I believed that the unit could not function effectively if its existence or the nature and details of its work were compromised by disclosure. These instructions were given at various times after the special investigations unit was formed, which was shortly after June 13, 1971. [the date of newspaper publication of the Pentagon papers]

Q. On what date were you first informed of the Fielding break-in?

A. March 17, 1973.

Q. Did you ever authorize anyone on the White House staff to search the files of Dr. Fielding for information about Dr. Ellsberg, without a warrant or the permission of Dr. Fielding, or hire others to do so? (If yes, please give details and state whether or not you authorized the CIA to cooperate with the unit by assisting it in any way in any such search of Dr. Fielding's files for information concerning Dr. Ellsberg.)

A. No.

Kissinger spent only 108 seconds on the witness stand. Asked if he had authorized, directly or indirectly, Young before Aug. 12, 1971 to request from the Central Intelligence Agency (CIA) a psychological profile of Ellsberg, Kissinger responded that he had not. Did he know that the CIA or Young was working on a profile? Kissinger was asked. "I had no such knowledge," he replied. Finally, "Did you have any knowledge whether there was a plan to obtain psychological information regarding Daniel Ellsberg or his psychological files from his psychiatrist?" Again Kissinger said, "I had no such knowledge."

Ehrlichman's testimony—Under direct examination by defense attorney Henry H. Jones July 8, Ehrlichman denied having authorized or having seen plans for the break-in.

Associate special Watergate prosecutor William Merrill then directed a series of questions at Ehrlichman designed to show that the defendant had known about the plan for a psychological profile of Ellsberg and that Ehrlichman, in authorizing a "covert operation" to examine Fielding's files on Ellsberg, had been aware he was authorizing an unlawful entry into Fielding's office.

Much of what Merrill asked Ehrlichman centered on an Aug. 11, 1971 memorandum, on which Ehrlichman initialed his approval of a "covert operation" as long as it was "not traceable" to the White House. Asked by Merrill what he considered a "covert operation" to be, Ehrlichman responded that it was "a private investigation, where the people

don't identify themselves as from the FBI—a conventional investigation like the FBI would conduct."

Questioned about the methods that would be used to obtain the information, Ehrlichman responded that it "didn't enter my thought processes." Ehrlichman said he thought perhaps the files could be examined "by request" or "by a third party." He added that he had not known where the files were and supposed that Fielding was an employe of the Rand Corp., where Ellsberg had worked at the time of the disclosure of the Pentagon Papers. "It occurred to me they might be going to the Rand management," Ehrlichman testified.

Under other questioning by Merrill and Judge Gesell, Ehrlichman said he had sought assurances that the operation would not be traceable to the White House because he feared it would become a "cause celebre in the press," as well as have a "big brother is watching appearance."

"What did you think you were approving when you signed the memorandum?" Gesell asked. "I thought I was approving a legal, conventional investigation," Ehrlichman responded.

Ehrlichman also testified that he was unable to remember a telephone call from Krogh and Young in late August 1971. During that call, Krogh and Young testified, Ehrlichman gave final approval for the project. Actually, Ehrlichman testified, he had not learned of the break-in until after it had occurred.

In other testimony, Ehrlichman said he had met Young March 21, 1973—not March 27 as Young had stated—and Young "volunteered to send papers over to me." Contrary to Young's testimony that Ehrlichman had admitted removing memos from the "plumbers" file because they were "too sensitive" and showed "too much forethought," Ehrlichman asserted that he had been too busy to look at the file Young had supplied and had subsequently returned it to Young.

Ehrlichman also maintained that he couldn't remember many details testified to by Krogh and Young, although many of them were documented by memorandums. Ehrlichman said his faulty memory was a function of training himself "not to pack around in my memory" the great mass of information with which he dealt. "A great deal of this was just grist I was glancing at and setting aside because it wasn't of any great moment," he explained.

At another point, Ehrlichman said he did not remember talking to former White House counsel Charles W. Colson about the financing of the project. Colson July 3 had testified he received a phone call from Ehrlichman in late August 1971. "Mr. Ehrlichman said that Mr. Krogh needed $5,000 and could I obtain it," Colson said. (Colson, who secured the money from Joseph D. Baroody, a Washington public affairs consultant, denied that either he or Baroody knew the purpose of the money.

Krogh's testimony—Krogh, in testimony July 2, said he and Young had met with Ehrlichman Aug. 5, 1971 to tell him that the FBI had been unsuccessful in interviewing Fielding and that if the "plumbers" were to succeed in gathering information for the Ellsberg profile, "we would have to conduct an operation on our own." After he had received the Aug. 11 memo on which Ehrlichman initialed his approval, Krogh said, "It was clear to me that an entry operation would have to be undertaken to examine those files."

Regarding their Aug. 30, 1971 call to Ehrlichman, Krogh said he and Young had conveyed to Ehrlichman that the investigation could be conducted. While unable to recall Ehrlichman's specific words, Krogh insisted, "We felt it had been approved, authorized." However, like Young, Krogh conceded that Ehrlichman had never used the term "break-in."

Closing arguments—In his closing arguments to the jury July 11, Merrill altered his tactics, announcing that he was no longer accusing Ehrlichman of authorizing a "break-in." Instead, Merrill contended, Ehrlichman should be found guilty of plotting a "covert operation." Pointing out that the operation had been covert so it would be "nontraceable," Merrill asserted it had been illegal because the "plumbers" lacked a search warrant. "No one says covert means illegal," Merrill said, but he added that this operation had been without a warrant and was, therefore, illegal.

Merrill's arguments caused William Frates, Ehrlichman's chief attorney, to charge that the prosecutor was trying to bewilder the jury by backing off from his original complaint. The prosecutors "are trying to make you believe the word 'covert' is an illegal operation," Frates told the jury.

Merrill and Frates also clashed over the difference between "lying" and "failing to recollect." At issue was Ehrlichman's testimony that he "failed to recollect" certain memos and telephone calls.

Frates argued that Ehrlichman testified before the grand jury after he had left the White House and did not have access to either his files or his telephone logs. Moreover, given the amount of paperwork that confronted him, Ehrlichman could easily have forgotten many things, Frates said. To this, Merrill retorted, "What he says he's forgotten are the incriminating things."

Frates' final arguments also focused on the veracity of Young's and Krogh's testimony. Young "couldn't answer a question straight if he wanted to," Frates said. Turning to Krogh, Frates read aloud to the jury Krogh's letter of resignation as assistant secretary of transportation, in which Krogh said the break-in had not been authorized by his superiors.

Daniel Schultz, who jointly represented

Barker and Martinez, characterized his clients as "little men" who had been duped into believing they were participating in a legal CIA operation. In contrast, Merrill contended that Barker and Martinez knew the law. "Can we allow these things to happen because someone in the government doesn't like someone?" he asked. "That's not patriotism—it's anarchy, the beginnings of a police state."

Committee issues Watergate evidence. The House Judiciary Committee released July 11 an eight-volume, 4,133-page record of the evidence assembled by its staff dealing with the Watergate break-in and its aftermath. Seven volumes consisted of the material presented by the staff to the committee members in closed sessions in May and June. The eighth volume was President Nixon's rebuttal presented to the committee by his lawyer, James St. Clair.

The staff material consisted of statements of information and supporting material; there was no attempt to present findings. "A deliberate and scrupulous abstention from conclusions, even by implication was observed," committee Chairman Peter W. Rodino Jr. (D, N.J.) said in a foreword to the record.

The St. Clair material—242 pages—did contain conclusions and was much narrower in scope than the staff record. It focused primarily on the controversial payment of $75,000 to Watergate conspirator E. Howard Hunt Jr. St. Clair restated the President's position that he first learned of the Watergate cover-up on March 21, 1973, then launched an inquiry and took action to bring the facts to the proper authorities. "The President had no knowledge of an attempt by the White House to cover up involvement in the Watergate affair," it declared.

The bulk of the evidence released was already on the public record, but there were some new disclosures. Among them, contained in secret grand jury testimony released as supportive material, was Hunt's admission that his demand for the money was accompanied by a threat. He was asked, according to the evidence released by the committee, if there was "any other interpretation other than the clear meaning of the words that you would review your options for alternatives other than that you would tell about these so-called seamy things unless they met your demands?" Hunt's reply was "No" and he also explained to the grand jury what the "seamy things" were—the burglary of the office of Daniel Ellsberg's psychiatrist, the forging of State Department cables and the political dirty tricks of Donald Segretti.

Also among the material released was grand jury testimony by former Nixon aide John D. Ehrlichman that when he learned of Hunt's demand, from then Nixon counsel John W. Dean 3rd, "I said it looked to me like blackmail."

Among other disclosures in the committee's record:

■ Nixon expressed hope on June 30, 1972, 13 days after the Watergate break-in, that there would be no further disclosures and commented on the risk of disclosure. Part of the evidence was a taped conversation with his aide H. R. Haldeman and John N. Mitchell about Mitchell's possible resignation as campaign director.

HALDEMAN: Well, there maybe is another facet. The longer you wait the more risk each hour brings. You run the risk of more stuff, valid or invalid, surfacing on the Watergate caper—type of thing—
MITCHELL: You couldn't possibly do it if you got into a—
HALDEMAN: —the potential problem and then you are stuck—
PRESIDENT: Yes, that's the other thing, if something does come out, but we won't—we hope nothing will. It may not. But there is always the risk.
HALDEMAN: As of now there is no problem there. As, as of any moment in the future there is at least a potential problem.
PRESIDENT: Well, I'd cut the loss fast. I'd cut it fast. If we're going to do it I'd cut it fast. That's my view, generally speaking. And I wouldn't—and I don't think, though, as a matter of fact, I don't think the story, if we, if you put it in human terms—I think the story is, you're positive rather than negative, because as I said as I was preparing to answer for this press conference, I just wrote it out—as I usually do, one way—terribly sensitive [unintelligible]. A hell of a lot of people will like that answer. They would. And it'd make anybody else who asked any other question on it look like a selfish son-of-a-bitch, which I thoroughly intended them to look like.
MITCHELL: [Unintelligible] Westchester Country Club with all the sympathy in the world.
PRESIDENT: That's great. That's great.
MITCHELL: [Unintelligible] don't let—
HALDEMAN: You taking this route—people won't expect you to—be a surprise.
PRESIDENT: No—if it's a surprise. Otherwise, you're right. It will be tied right to Watergate. [Unintelligible] tighten if you wait too long, till it simmers down.
HALDEMAN: You can't if other stuff develops on Watergate. The problem is, it's always potentially the same thing.
PRESIDENT: Well if it does, don't just hard-line.
HALDEMAN: [Unintelligible] That's right. In other words, it'd be hard to hard-line Mitchell's departure under—
PRESIDENT: That's right. You can't do it. I just want it to be handled in a way Martha's not hurt.
MITCHELL: Yeah, okay.

■ Nixon described Jeb Stuart Magruder, a re-election committee official who had begun to cooperate with Watergate prosecutors, as a "rather weak man who had all the appearance of character but who really lacks it when the, uh, chips are down." He described Gordon C. Strachan, Haldeman's aide who allegedly destroyed files and committed perjury, as "a real, uh, courageous fellow through all this." Both descriptions were on part of a dictated recollection of that day's events, March 21, 1973.

■ Nixon told an aide on June 4, 1973 that a tape of his March 17, 1973 meeting with Dean included a discussion of the substance of Watergate. (Nixon had refused the committee's subpoenaed request for the March 17 tape.)

■ White House telephone directories were recalled shortly after the Watergate break-in and reissued with Hunt's name missing.

■ A Feb. 1, 1972 memo from Strachan to Haldeman suggested that "230 green [$230,000] be held under [Herbert W.] Kalmbach's personal control; and that any polling be paid for by regular Nixon finance committees." On the memo, under his initialed approval, Haldeman wrote, "make it 350 green and hold for us." Strachan informed Haldeman in a later memo that Kalmbach, Nixon's personal lawyer at the time, would provide "350 in green under your unquestioned personal control. A separate box of green is being developed for the campaign." Haldeman's testimony about the $350,000 cash fund, which provided payments to the Watergate defendants, was that it had been held for special private political polls.

Watergate hampers Nixon's role. Top executives of the nation's largest companies concluded overwhelmingly that Watergate had seriously impaired Nixon's ability to manage the nation's economy, according to a survey conducted by the New York Times.

The poll was published July 11. Questionnaires had been mailed late in June to officials of the nation's 500 largest industrial firms. Responses were received from 167 persons, or 34%, a number considered statistically significant. Of those responding, 80% agreed that Nixon's economic performance had suffered because of Watergate.

Nixon's political support among the businessmen polled also had suffered. (Comments indicated that the erosion followed the White House release of edited tape transcripts.) Although 58% of those responding opposed his impeachment, 42% favored it and 56% said they believed the House would vote to impeach him. (38% of the group believed Nixon's removal from office or resignation was warranted.) A Times survey of business executives in November 1972 had shown 91.4% of those responding (430) planned to vote for Nixon's re-election.

Of those surveyed, 28% favored Nixon's conviction in the Senate, but only 6% said they believed the Senate would take such action; 28% of those responding felt Nixon should resign but only 1% said they felt he would.

Nixon aide convicted in 'plumbers' case. John D. Ehrlichman, former domestic affairs adviser to President Nixon, was found guilty July 12 by a federal jury in Washington of conspiring to violate the civil rights of Dr. Lewis J. Fielding, the psychiatrist of Pentagon Papers defendant

Daniel Ellsberg. Three other defendants in the trial—G. Gordon Liddy, Bernard L. Barker and Eugenio Martinez—were convicted of the same charge. Ehrlichman was also found guilty of three of four counts of making false statements.

Each defendant faced a maximum sentence of 10 years in prison and a $10,000 fine on the conspiracy charge. Ehrlichman faced five years in prison and a fine of up to $5,000 on each of the other counts. Sentencing was set for July 31.

Instructing the jury on the conspiracy charge July 12, U.S. District Court Judge Gerhard A. Gesell said that it need not find Ehrlichman had known in advance of plans for a "covert entry" into Fielding's office files to obtain Ellsberg's psychiatric records. Moreover, Gesell told the jurors, an illegal search need not entail "physical break-in," which only tended to emphasize "lack of permission." The law had been broken if the government attempted to acquire private information without a search warrant, he said. "When a government agency invades an area in which there is a legitimate expectation of privacy to look through such papers without permission, that is a search," the judge stated.

Gesell's instructions struck at the heart of Ehrlichman's defense that he had not authorized an illegal break-in but merely a legal "covert operation." Ehrlichman's attorneys objected that the judge had failed to charge the jury with Ehrlichman's theory of the case. Gesell replied, out of the hearing of the jury, that Ehrlichman's "defense has been one of guarding and dodging around various issues of the case...."

In his other instructions, Gesell said, "An individual cannot escape criminal liability simply because he sincerely but incorrectly believes that his acts are justified in the name of patriotism, of national security or the need to create an unfavorable press image or that his superiors had the authority to suspend without a warrant the protections of the Fourth Amendment." (The 4th Amendment guaranteed against unreasonable searches.)

Ehrlichman was acquitted on a charge of false testimony to a grand jury May 14, 1973. At that time, Ehrlichman stated that he did not know who, other than Egil Krogh Jr., co-director of the White House "plumbers" unit, had files on the unit's investigation of Ellsberg. However, the

jury concluded that Ehrlichman had twice made false statements to the grand jury when he said he had not been aware before the break-in of the plan to obtain Ellsberg's psychiatric files. In addition, the jury convicted Ehrlichman of the charge of falsely stating to the Federal Bureau of Investigation May 1, 1973 that he had not seen any material relating to the White House investigation of the Pentagon Papers affair for more than a year.

Ford: Evidence clears Nixon. Vice President Gerald R. Ford expressed confidence after meeting with President Nixon July 13 that the House would not vote to impeach the President. There was a "possibility" that the House Judiciary Committee would vote a bill of impeachment, he said, but he felt "strongly" that the House would reject it because the "preponderance of the evidence favors the President."

The meeting, at San Clemente, Calif., was Ford's sixth with Nixon that week. Ford attributed the meetings to Nixon's desire to have the Vice President play an active role in the Administration's fight against inflation. The July 13, session was devoted "99.9%" to economic problems, Ford told reporters afterwards.

At a news conference in Albuquerque, N.M. July 12, Ford said that the "new evidence as well as the old evidence" exonerated Nixon of any impeachable offense.

Dallas motorcade 'sniping' discounted— The shattering of a window in a police car escorting Ford on a visit to Dallas, Tex. July 6 evoked fear of a sniper attack on his motorcade, but that interpretation was discounted by officials later.

Inflation: No. 1 national concern. Inflation worries had replaced the energy problem as the nation's overriding concern, according to a Gallup Poll published July 14.

Forty-eight percent of those surveyed named the rising cost of living as the nation's paramount problem, followed by 15% who cited "lack of trust in government" and 11% who named "corruption in government" and "Watergate" as the principal areas of concern.

(In a survey conducted in January, 46% of those polled had named the energy crisis as the nation's "most important problem," followed by 25% who cited inflation.)

Ervin Panel Reports on Campaign Financing

Watergate panel issues report. In its last official action, the Senate Select Committee on Presidential Campaign Activities, known as "the Watergate Committee" or "the Ervin Committee," released the final report July 13 on its investigation of the Watergate and other scandals related to the 1972 presidential campaign.

The committee, whose televised hearings in 1973 had focused public attention on the scandals, said in an introduction to the 2,250-page report that its investigation had not been conducted, nor its report prepared, "to determine the legal guilt or innocence of any person or whether the President should be impeached."

The panel said, however, that "to be true to its mandate from the Senate and its constitutional responsibilities," it "must present its view of the facts" of the Watergate affair and related matters in addition to recommending remedial legislation to "safeguard the electoral process."

Announcing the report's release at a news conference in the committee's hearing room July 12, Chairman Sam J. Ervin Jr. (D, N.C.) contended that the report was not weaker because it did not make specific accusations. Ervin said, "There are two ways to indicate a horse. One is to draw a picture that is a great likeness. And the other is to draw a picture that is a great likeness and write under it, 'This is a horse.' We just drew the picture."

The report said the picture presented by its compilation of evidence demonstrated that "campaign practices must be effectively supervised and enforcement of the criminal laws vigorously pursued against all offenders—even those of high estate—if our free institutions are to survive." Accordingly, the report presented 35 recommendations for election campaign reform, including some endorsing legislation already passed by the Senate.

Among the major proposals: [See excerpts of committee text, pp. 192–194]

■ An independent and permanent office of "public attorney" with powers similar to those of the existing special prosecutor.

■ A federal elections commission with supervisory and enforcement powers.

■ Restrictions on domestic intelligence activities by the White House staff.

■ Extension of the Hatch Act (forbidding campaign activities by civil service employes) to cover the entire Justice Department.

■ Limits on cash campaign contributions by individuals, reforms in reporting procedures and restrictions on solicitation of campaign funds by presidential staff.

■ Tightening of laws involving use of federal agencies to aid the election of political candidates.

Although the report was adopted unanimously, two Democrats—Daniel K. Inouye (Hawaii) and Joseph M. Montoya (N.M.)—filed a joint statement advocating public campaign financing, a measure opposed by the full report.

In separate statements, two Republicans, Committee Vice Chairman Howard H. Baker Jr. (Tenn.) and Sen. Edward J. Gurney (Fla.) expressed opposition, in different terms, to the report's proposal for a permanent public attorney. While agreeing in principle, Baker questioned the constitutionality of such an appointment through the judiciary. Gurney, however, said he totally opposed the "creation of a czar" outside the executive branch "who could hound and intimidate governmental officials in the proper exercise of their responsibilities." (Gurney was indicted July 10 for bribery, conspiracy and lying to a grand jury.)

Baker also urged repeal of the two-term limitation on a President "to make a second-term incumbent more politically responsive," and recommended stronger Congressional monitoring of all intelligence activities than was proposed in the committee report. (Baker had also released a separate report on his investigation of Central Intelligence Agency connections with the Watergate affair.

Lowell P. Weicker Jr. (R, Conn.) had already released a separate report condemning abuses of executive power. Herman E. Talmadge (D, Ga.) was the only committee member who did not file a separate statement.

Sen. Ervin appended to the report a "statement of individual views" studded with historical references and verbal equivalents of the arched eyebrows that had marked his appearance during the televised hearings. Ervin condemned the "illegal and unethical activities" by campaign officials and White House aides, which he said corrupted both the electoral process and the workings of government.

Answering his own question, "Why was Watergate?" Ervin said presidential aides' "lust for political power blinded them to ethical considerations and legal requirements. . . . They had forgotten, if they ever knew, that the Constitution is designed to be a law for rulers and people alike at all times and under all circumstances; and that no doctrine involving more pernicious consequences to the commonwealth has ever been invented by the wit of man than the notion that any of its provisions can be suspended by the President for any reason whatsoever."

The committee's report dealt only briefly with an aspect of presidential power which had arisen from its hearings and had subsequently become a central issue in criminal prosecutions and the House inquiry into President Nixon's possible impeachment: the existence of tape recordings of many of Nixon's conversations and the question of access to the recordings by the committee, the special prosecutor and the House Judiciary Committee.

Taking note of the committee's difficulties in pursuing a suit for access to the tapes, the report recommended that Congressional bodies be given statutory standing in the courts to subpoena and sue the executive branch, including the President.

The committee's evidence—Although much of the Ervin committee's evidence and findings had been made public earlier through open testimony, news leaks or officially-released draft reports, the final draft report issued July 13 presented a more detailed and collated account of the intricacies of political intelligence operations, campaign fund raising, and the use of government agencies for campaign purposes.

The account was based on testimony taken in public and executive sessions, documents submitted voluntarily and under subpoena, and in some cases on the edited White House transcripts of some of the President's conversations released by Nixon April 30.

The committee's report covered the following major areas:

A ■ Political intelligence plans—some stillborn, others implemented—leading to the Watergate break-in, and the subsequent attempts to conceal the involvement of the White House and high campaign officials. A central element was the testimony of former presidential counsel John W. Dean 3rd.

■ Misuse and attempted misuse of government agencies, particularly the Internal Revenue Service (IRS) against the Administration's political "enemies."

B ■ The political sabotage "dirty tricks" operations directed against Democratic candidates during the 1972 campaign.

■ The so-called "responsiveness program," under which federal agencies were, with varying degrees of success, urged to use their powers to set regulations and award government funds to best meet Nixon's re-election needs. According to the report, the program was designed to gain favor with minority groups, "neu-

C tralize" potential opponents and inspire willingness to make campaign contributions.

■ Illegal contributions by corporations, most of which had led to indictments and convictions or guilty pleas.

■ Political contributions as a means of gaining favorable consideration for ambassadorships.

■ Contributions by labor unions.

D ■ The relationship between contributions by the dairy industry and the Administration's decision to raise milk price support payments.

■ Contributions to the early campaign efforts of Sen. Hubert H. Humphrey (D, Minn.) and Rep. Wilbur D. Mills (D, Ark.), and post-campaign use of funds by Sen. George McGovern (D, S.D.).

E ■ Payments by industrialist Howard R. Hughes to Charles G. Rebozo, a close personal friend of the President. Presenting 350 pages of sometimes conflicting evidence, the report examined the circumstances surrounding the delivery of the funds, the dispute over Rebozo's storage of the money in a safe deposit box, White House efforts to intervene in an IRS investigation of Rebozo, and Rebozo's alleged disbursal of Hughes funds for Nixon's personal use.

In its introduction to the report, the committee cautioned that it had not ob-

F tained all the information it sought, and certain findings thus were "tentative, subject to re-evaluation when the full facts emerge." But the panel said it could make "appropriate" general observations based on its evidence: that the Watergate affair reflected "an alarming indifference displayed by some in high public office or position to concepts of morality and public responsibility and trust. Indeed, the conduct of many Watergate participants

G seems grounded on the belief that the ends justified the means, that the laws could be flaunted to maintain the present Administration in office."

The committee said that its own efforts, and the public awareness of them, had

"provided the atmosphere necessary to support other essential governmental responses to Watergate such as the work of the special prosecutor and the activities of the House Judiciary Committee on impeachment."

Political intelligence and cover-up. The Senate Watergate Committee's report declared that the June 17, 1972 Watergate break-in had to be viewed in the context of earlier political intelligence plans and operations: a 1970 domestic spy plan proposed by presidential aide Tom Charles Huston but reportedly discarded; the White House "plumbers" unit; and, moving closer to the 1972 campaign, "Project Sandwedge," which was rejected by presidential adviser John D. Ehrlichman. According to the report, the latter plan, for a political "detective agency," was presented to then-Attorney General John N. Mitchell in 1971, with the proposal that it operate directly under the Committee to Re-elect the President, (CRP), but Mitchell rejected it.

Intelligence plans were resurrected after the hiring of G. Gordon Liddy as counsel to CRP. The report described the series of meetings on the question involving Mitchell, Liddy, campaign aide Jeb Stuart Magruder and presidential counsel John W. Dean 3rd. Various plans, including the Watergate operation, were discussed, rejected, changed and ultimately approved.

The report noted that one meeting (Jan. 27, 1972) at which Liddy's plans were rejected as too expensive took place in Mitchell's office while he was still attorney general. Despite the rejection of the proposal, Liddy retained his position as CRP counsel and "continued to have the responsibility of developing an intelligence-gathering plan."

Although a plan was eventually approved, the committee said it had been unable to establish the exact circumstances. The report, however, cited testimony by several witnesses that Mitchell, by then the director of the Nixon campaign, had reluctantly approved it, possibly with the knowledge of White House officials.

Within hours after the arrest of the Watergate burglars, a "massive cover-up" had begun and "eventually encompassed destruction and secretion of documents, obstruction of official investigations, suborrnation of perjury and offers of money and executive clemency to the Watergate defendants to secure silence."

The report noted that existence of a cover-up could not be "seriously disputed" in view of the guilty pleas by some of the participants. (The steps taken by the alleged cover-up conspirators were covered in detail by the indictment of seven former Nixon aides.)

While refraining from direct accusations, the report addressed the question of the motivations for payments made to the original Watergate break-in defendants: "None of those who authorized or participated in the making of those pay-

ments used their own money. To the contrary, they used campaign funds contributed by others who had no knowledge that their money was being employed to pay the legal fees of the Watergate defendants and to support their families. Also relevant is the clandestine nature of the payoffs, which were made with $100 bills and placed in 'drops' by an unseen intermediary using a code name."

Citing the White House tape transcripts, the report noted that "even the President recognized that the payoffs smacked of a cover-up."

The 'responsiveness program.' The Watergate committee's final report included documentation of an effort, which began in 1971, to use the funding and regulatory powers of the executive branch to insure that Nixon would be re-elected the following year. Most of this section of the report had been made public earlier.

In addition to the previously-cited funding efforts toward minority groups, misuse of government employment procedures and withdrawal of funds to "neutralize" politically-suspect recipients, the final report cited an effort to use labor safety regulations to please the industrial community.

In this regard, the report cited what it called "interesting statements" in a June 14, 1972 memorandum from George C. Guenther, then head of the Labor Department's Occupational Safety & Health Administration (OSHA) to Laurence H. Silberman, then undersecretary of labor. Guenther's memo stated in part: "While promulgation and modification activity must continue, no highly controversial standards ... will be proposed...." Guenther continued that OSHA would concentrate on "priorities and long-range planning," and that occupational safety activities would remain "low-keyed" during the campaign period. The committee noted that Silberman testified he did not order Guenther to "discontinue the plan."

Guenther's memo stated further that he had discussed with others the "great potential of OSHA as a sales point for fund raising and general support from employers," and asked for Silberman's suggestions "as to how to promote the advantages of four more years of properly managed OSHA for use in the campaign...." The report said no action was taken on the request.

Although the panel's earlier draft report said the entire "responsiveness program" had apparently ended shortly after the Watergate break-in on June 20, 1972, the final report cited "numerous documents" indicating that similar activities continued until the end of the campaign. The report cited only one document, a Nov. 2, 1972 memorandum suggesting that a potentially hostile Mexican-American group might remain neutral if programs affecting its interests "could be sprung loose within the next few days."

Campaign financing abuses. The Senate committee's report stated that "at least

13 corporations made [political] contributions totaling over $780,000 in corporate funds," donations that were in violation of a federal statute prohibiting campaign contributions from corporations and unions.

Of this total, an estimated $749,000 was given to President Nixon's re-election campaign. (The donations Nixon received from the dairy industry were not included in this figure).

"While there is no evidence that any fund raiser for President Nixon directly solicited a corporate contribution," the report said, "there is evidence that a number of them were indifferent to the source of the money or, at the very least, made no effort whatsoever to see to it that the source of the funds was private rather than corporate. In any event, there is no evidence that any fund raiser who was involved in these contributions sought or obtained assurances that the contribution was legal at the time it was made."

The committee concluded that there was "no clear pattern to the solicitations." Sources of the corporate money also varied but "the most utilized source" of the illegal contributions was foreign subsidiaries. "In the great majority of cases, the contributions were in the form of cash," the report stated, and "the bulk" of the donations were made prior to April 7, 1972—the date on which a new federal reporting law took effect—in order to cloak the contributions.

There was no disclosure of any of the donations until July 6, 1973—15 months after most of the money was received. "The main impetus" for these disclosures was a suit brought by Common Cause to compel the Finance Committee to Re-elect the President to name its secret donors and the amounts of their gifts.

When the finance committee, realizing it might be forced by the courts to reveal the sources of its contributions, sent letters to corporations seeking the names of individuals who had actually made the donations, responses from the corporations varied, the committee report declared.

Some corporate officials prepared false lists of individual employe donors, some made voluntary disclosures, "and in at least one case, an elaborate scheme to conceal the corporate nature of a contribution was indulged in, and involved lying to the FBI," according to the committee. [See below]

Corporations cited for illegal contributions:

American Airlines, Inc.—$55,000 was given in March 1972 to the Nixon campaign. The gift, given in cash, was laundered through the Swiss bank account of the firm's Lebanese agent.

American Ship Building Co.—$100,000 in cash was given April 6, 1972, of which $25,000 originated from corporate funds. The remaining amount was credited to the firm's chairman, George M. Steinbrenner, but the source of that money has not been determined, according to the committee.

Evidence obtained by the committee indicated that Steinbrenner attempted to conceal the source of the donation in August 1973, when he instructed company officials to "arrange a 'legitimate bonus payment plan' to camouflage" the transaction. The committee said that eight persons who participated in the deception, including Steinbrenner, signed false FBI statements about it. Steinbrenner and the company were indicted on charges related to the donation and both pleaded not guilty.

Ashland Oil Co., Inc.—$100,000 in cash was given April 3, 1972 after the money was laundered through a Gabon subsidiary.

Braniff Airways, Inc.—$40,000 in cash was given between March 28, 1972 and April 7, 1972. Officials conceded that the gift was made from corporate funds but contended they had intended to reimburse the company. No steps were taken, however, until July 1973, when informed by the finance committee that public disclosure of their contribution might be required.

Carnation Co.—A total of $7,900 in two contributions was made to the Nixon campaign.

Diamond International Corp.—$5,000 was given to the Nixon campaign and $1,000 to Sen. Edmund S. Muskie's (D, Me.) campaign for the Democratic presidential nomination.

Goodyear Tire & Rubber Co.—$40,000 in cash was given to the Nixon campaign.

Gulf Oil Corp.—$100,000 in cash was given to the Nixon campaign, $10,000 to Sen. Henry M. Jackson's (D, Wash.) campaign for the Democratic presidential nomination and $15,000 to Rep. Wilbur D. Mills (D, Ark.) in the same race.

Hertz Corp.—An estimated $8,000–$9,000 in car rentals were provided the Muskie campaign in 1971 and 1972. More than half was written off and the remainder that was billed, $4,103.29, was actually paid by Hertz. Officials were authorized "to provide funds to outside lawyers to enable them to make contributions to the Muskie campaign in the total amount of the outstanding bills," according to committee evidence. (The lawyers were also paid an extra 25%-30% more than the donation "for the purpose of reimbursing them for their income tax obligation," the report stated.)

Lehigh Valley Cooperative Farmers, Inc.—$50,000 in cash was given to the Nixon campaign and was used to pay hush money to the original Watergate defendants.

Minnesota Mining & Manufacturing Co.—A total of $36,000 in two contributions was given to the Nixon campaign, and two Democratic contenders for the nomination, Rep. Mills and Sen. Hubert Humphrey, each received $1,000 in cash. According to the committee, 3M had maintained a secret slush fund since the 1950s. The money had been obtained by overstating prepaid insurance and was then transferred to a Swiss bank account. In 1967 this procedure was changed—a

Swiss attorney was paid for fictitious services and he returned the money in cash to a 3M official.

Northrop Corp.—$150,000, laundered through Luxembourg, was given to the Nixon finance committee in several transactions. Two deliveries of $50,000 each were made in March 1972 and on April 5, 1972. Another $50,000 in cash, was given secretly to Herbert Kalmbach in July 1972. Northrop officials later pleaded guilty to violations of the federal campaign law, but, the committee declared, "the information contained in the indictments, to which the defendants pleaded guilty, is in direct contradiction with the information supplied . . . to the committee during the fall of 1973." Northrop Chairman Thomas V. Jones, "among others, also represented to the General Accounting Office, the FBI, and the [Watergate] grand jury that the $100,000 contribution was part of a personal commitment unrelated to the corporation," the report stated. "Jones represented that a post-April 7 contribution of $50,000 came from a personal cash fund which he kept," the report added.

Phillips Petroleum Co.—$100,000 in cash was given to the Nixon campaign.

The report also traced the course of five checks, totaling $114,000, that originated from the corporate funds of Gulf Resources and Chemical Corp. of Texas. The money had been laundered in Mexico and Miami and the cash was found in the possession of Watergate burglar Bernard Barker during the break-in.

The committee report described fund raising attempts by the National Hispanic Finance Committee, involving Miami contractor John Priestes, and his efforts to obtain a quid pro quo from the Administration in return for making a secret cash contribution.

Two fund raising programs, organized by the Nixon campaign and aimed at business groups, were described—the Corporate Conduit Program, and the Industry-by-Industry Campaign.

Part of the committee's report was based on information obtained from questionnaires sent to 700 individual contributors, corporate officers and union executives in the fall of 1973.

Responses were received from officials of every corporation and union and from about 80% of the unaffiliated individuals. The questionnaire "may have been responsible for uncovering two [illegal] corporate contributions [Diamond International and Carnation] and evidence of a third [Hertz]," according to the committee.

Abuses by Democrats—The report was critical of Sen. George McGovern's (D, S.D.) resolution of his presidential campaign debt. Evidence was developed, the report stated, that as McGovern's campaign finance committees were "settling bills with creditors, including corporations, at 50% of their face value, these presidential committees were making substantial transfers of funds to McGovern

Senatorial committees in anticipation of a 1974 contest for his re-election to this Senate seat."

A total of $340,416.96 was transferred for use in the Senate campaign under these transactions, the report claimed. Debts incurred during the presidential race were reduced by $35,322.32 in negotiations with business creditors.

The report also cited evidence that cash contributions totaling $10,000 were given to the campaign of New York City Mayor John V. Lindsay (D) by officers of two companies doing business with the city. The money was donated in the pre-April 7, 1972 period and no campaign finance report was filed by Lindsay.

Union contributions—No comprehensive attempt was made by the committee to survey union political activity, but two unusual campaign activities involving unions were cited in the report. In one instance, campaign contributions totaling $4,134.15, were given to the United Farm Workers' political education fund. The money, given by the McGovern Central Control Fund, originated with El Pueblo con McGovern, a fund raising committee composed of union leaders and supporters.

In another instance, the Seafarers International Union's political committee applied for a $100,000 loan from a New York bank on Oct. 31, 1972. One day later, the loan was approved and on the following day a check for $100,000 was sent by the union to the Nixon finance committee. The report questioned whether the political donation was made from "voluntary contributions by rank and file members of the union," as required by law.

Committee questionnaires on campaign contributions made by union political committees revealed "no evidence of illegal union contribution activity," the report declared.

Data on the donations showed that McGovern received $678,782 from 19 unions; Humphrey received $176,556 from 15 unions; Sen. Vance Hartke (D, Ind.) received $14,250 from six unions; Muskie received $5,736 from two unions. President Nixon received $44,500 from six unions (Seafarers' union gift excluded).

(McGovern also was loaned large amounts by two unions but little of that money was repaid. The Communications Workers union was repaid $10,000 of its $100,000 loan, with the remainder forgiven and the United Auto Workers union was repaid $82,000 of its $150,000 loan, with the remainder forgiven.)

The selling of ambassadorships—Although President Nixon denied that ambassadorships were "for sale" to persons making large campaign contributions, the report noted that his principal fund-raiser, Herbert Kalmbach admitted promising an ambassadorial post to one contributor, J. Fife Symington, and informed the special prosecutor's office that a similar pledge was made to another contributor, Vincent de Roulet.

Information obtained by the committee showed that since Nov. 7, 1972, Nixon had appointed 13 non-career ambassadors whose campaign contributions totaled $706,000. Eight of that group had each donated at least $25,000. "In fact, over $1.8 million in presidential campaign contributions can be attributed in whole, or in part, to persons holding ambassadorial appointments from the President," the report declared. "Six large contributors, who gave an aggregate of over $3 million, appear to have been actively seeking appointments at the time of their contributions," the report added.

Nixon fund raisers told committee investigators that "they went to great pains to tell prospective contributors who might be interested in ambassadorial posts that there was no quid pro quo in exchange for any contributions they might give," the report stated, but evidence showed that that policy was violated on at least two instances when Kalmbach made promises to Symington and de Roulet.

"In a third case involving Cornelius Vanderbilt Whitney," the report stated, a $250,000 contribution was returned to Whitney in the expectation that he would have to testify before the Senate Foreign Relations Committee and that the return would eliminate any suggestion that the anticipated appointment was related to a campaign gift." According to Whitney, Administration officials told him that this action made it possible for him to truthfully say that he did not buy the appointment.

When eventually denied the appointment in December 1971 because of his age (74), Whitney did not offer to recontribute the $250,000, although he later donated $50,000 to the re-election campaign, the report stated.

(Another case involving Ruth Farkas, currently ambassador to Luxembourg, was not investigated at the request of the special prosecutor's office, the committee said.)

The report cited testimony given by Nixon fund raisers about major contributors who sought diplomatic posts. John Safer, a Washington developer, gave $250,000 and asked to "be considered . . . for an ambassadorship," the report said. Roy Carver, chairman of the Board of Bandag, Inc., contributed Bandag stock worth about $257,000, but never received an appointment, according to testimony.

Vincent de Roulet, who had been a contributor to Nixon's 1968 campaign and who had been named ambassador to Jamaica in September 1969, said of his 1968 contribution: "I was seeking some position in government for which I considered myself qualified and I knew that there were only three or four ways to get it, one of which was money."

De Roulet subsequently contributed $50,000 for White House use in the 1970 Senate races and the same amount to Nixon's 1972 campaign—a practice also followed by Symington, according to the committee report.

(The money given in 1970 was used for the secret "Town House project.")

Despite the gift, de Roulet was unable to obtain the more prestigious diplomatic posting that he sought and he resigned in August 1973.

The committee examined Herbert Kalmbach's role as the President's chief fund raiser during the first 1½ years of the re-election campaign. "In all," the report declared, "Kalmbach solicited pledges of over $13.4 million," of which $10.66 million was received. Most of this amount, $8.8 million, was given in the pre-April 7, 1972 period.

"Kalmbach's efforts thus amounted to a committment for one-third of the total campaign budget, virtually all of which was committed prior to April 7, 1972," the report stated.

Kalmbach resigned his position at the finance committee when the new disclosure law took effect, although he later raised hush money for the Watergate defendants.

Ambassadors in eight Western European countries were major contributors to the Nixon re-election campaign: Walter Annenberg (Great Britain)—$250,000; Shelby Davis (Switzerland)—$100,000; Ruth Farkas (Luxembourg)—$300,000; Leonard Firestone (Belgium)—$112,600; Kingdon Gould (Netherlands)—$100,900; John Humes (Austria)—$100,000; John Irwin (France)—$50,500 and Arthur Watson, Irwin's predecessor and father-in-law, $300,000; John Moore (Ireland)—$10,442. Total figure—$1,324,442.

Major contributors in Caribbean posts: Sumner Gerard (Jamaica, replacing de Roulet)—$38,867; Lloyd Miller (Trinidad and Tobago, replacing Symington)—$25,000.

The milk fund. The thrust of the committee's report on its investigation of the circumstances surrounding the dairy industry's large campaign fund pledges and contributions to the Nixon re-election campaign differed considerably from the draft report prepared by the committee staff and published in May.

The staff report's accusatory tone was tempered in the report issued by the committee, which concluded that the "dual role played by many Nixon officials of both policy maker and fund raiser gave at the very least, the appearance of impropriety and provided circumstances that were ripe for abuse. Whether or not these two roles were directly tied, they *appeared* [committee emphasis] to be linked, and this had a significant impact on the approach taken by the dairymen. [Harold] Nelson [general manager of Associated Milk Producers, Inc.] said they gave the first $100,000 in 1969 because 'it appeared we were not going to get any place if we did not.' And when called upon in March 1971 to re-affirm the $2 million pledge [made the previous September], Nelson explained that he felt he had no choice. . . ."

According to the committee, the dairy lobby eventually contributed a total of $632,500 to the Nixon re-election campaign, "including $245,000 furnished to the campaign just prior to the election."

Nixon's decision, announced in March 1971, to raise federal price supports for milk, "was worth at least tens of millions of dollars to the milk producers and they spared no effort in seeking that favorable action," the report stated.

However, the report continued, "price supports were just one item on the dairymen agenda. In fact, the milk producers, representing one of the wealthiest political funds in America and one of the largest groups of contributors to the 1972 campaign, had actively sought favorable action from the Nixon Administration throughout its first term on a number of matters of great financial importance to dairy farmers at the same time that they were pledging hundreds of thousands, and even millions to President Nixon's re-election campaign—with the knowledge of the President himself and with the encouragement of top presidential aides and fund raisers."

(Some of these matters of importance to dairy farmers "included dairy import quotas, government cheese purchases and school milk programs, and the approach taken by the Antitrust Division of the Justice Department toward certain practices of the dairy co-ops," the report said.)

The committee focused on charges that Nixon's decision to raise milk price supports was directly related to the dairy co-ops' promised campaign contributions. The committee noted that the President, his key advisers and dairy representatives denied that any quid pro quo was involved. The report also declared that "much of what the President says [in defense of his decision to authorize the increase] is supported by the surrounding events," especially, the report added, Nixon's assertion that "his action was influenced primarily by Democratic Congressional pressure (generated by the dairymen) coupled with his fear of losing dairymen support in his 1972 re-election bid if he opposed them."

But, the report also stated that the committee had uncovered other "key facts" that "shed light on the type of potential 'support' the dairymen represented" to Nixon. "The crux of the committee's investigation was, thus, not whether it was the correct decision but whether the President made that decision for the 'wrong' reason," the report stated.

Over a hundred persons were interviewed in the course of the committee investigation, the report noted, but it added that its inquiries were limited by the White House's withholding of key documents and tapes. Nixon also refused to permit the committee to take testimony from his former agriculture secretary, citing executive privilege.

Despite these limitations, the report said, the committee discovered that "a presidential aide was instructed [March 23, 1971] to 'alert' the dairymen of the decision" reached that day in a meeting of the President and his top aides. Earlier that

day, Nixon had met with the dairy representatives at the White House.

The message received by the dairymen before a public announcement was made "carried an additional twist," the report stated. "The co-op leaders were informed that an increase was a good possibility but not certain. . . . A key dairy leader (Harold Nelson) was expected to re-affirm the $2 million pledge at a late night meeting prior to the public announcement. . . . At the pre-arranged meeting [arranged by John Ehrlichman], [Herbert] Kalmbach [Nixon's chief fund raiser and Nixon associate Murray Chotiner were] . . . informed of the re-affirmation 'in view of' the price support increase which had been set for the next day."

According to the report, the dairymen began meeting their promised campaign obligations within one week after the price decision was announced. By early September 1971, the report stated, nearly all of the entire $250,000 [promised] was in fact contributed—and at the same time, AMPI "accomplished one of its long sought after objectives. The President attended and addressed an AMPI annual convention."

According to the report, an additional contribution was made during the convention "at the special request of Charles Colson. Colson testified before a state grand jury that [$5,000 in] milk money was used to pay for the break-in of the office of Daniel Ellsberg's psychiatrist."

"Even before these contributions were made, the milk producers made at least one, and perhaps two, payments to [AMPI lawyer] Jake Jacobsen for [Treasury] Secretary [John] Connally's use," the report charged. Separate payments of $10,000 and $5,000 were cited.

"Both Connally and Jacobsen deny tha Connally ever took or used $10,000," the report stated. "Jacobsen has testified that the $10,000 remained in his safe deposit box untouched for over 2½ years," the report continued. "However, the committee has obtained documentation from the Bureau of Engraving and the Federal Reserve System indicating that some of the bills of the $10,000 were not even placed into circulation until almost two years after Jacobsen says he placed them in his box. Jacobsen denies even requesting, much less receiving, the $5,000 payment, and Connally denies any knowledge of the $5,000 matter."

The dairymen also sought Connally's assistance in terminating an antitrust suit brought by the Justice Department against AMPI. The dairy industry also sought the aid of other high level White House officials, such as H. R. Haldeman and John Mitchell, in halting the antitrust suit, but most of their efforts were directed at Herbert Kalmbach, who was offered a "substantial and secret pre-April 7, 1972 contribution" in exchange for help on the antitrust matter, according to the report.

Humphrey campaign abuses. "It should be noted," the report declared, "that improprieties in campaign financing were not limited to any particular candidate or party." Sen. Hubert Humphrey was cited for several apparent violations of campaign financing laws, but the committee's investigation was hampered by his refusal to be interviewed by the committee staff, and by his campaign manager's refusal to testify under oath. Humphrey also did not fully comply with the committee's request for campaign records, the report stated.

The committee's investigation centered on four general areas:

■ Humphrey's relationship to the dairy lobby: According to the report, Humphrey received services worth $25,000 from a Minneapolis firm specializing in computerized political services, Valentine, Sherman and Associates (VSA). The bill was paid by AMPI, the report stated, adding, "there is evidence that . . . [Jack Chestnut, Humphrey's campaign manager] was aware of and promoted this payment." The report also charged that under terms of a "covert arrangement" set up in 1970, Chestnut was paid a monthly retainer by AMPI and it was concealed as payment to another lawyer.

The report alleged that AMPI funded a number of other political services performed by VSA for Humphrey and other Democratic candidates and party groups in Iowa, South Dakota, Kansas and Oklahoma in 1971. The total amount AMPI paid VSA in 1971 for the benefit of Humphrey and other Democratic officials was $137,000, according to the report.

In addition to the $25,000 payment from AMPI, the report stated, Humphrey also received $17,225 for his presidential campaign from dairy producers' trusts (which, like political committees established by the unions, could legally dispense funds to candidates and parties if the money was contributed voluntarily by members of the dairy cooperatives. Contributions originating from the personal funds of corporate officials and employes also were allowed under law.)

The committee noted that Humphrey, a supporter of dairy industry legislation since 1949, had introduced legislation in March 1971 that would have raised the federal price support for milk. Humphrey had stated that there was "no relationship between his receipt of dairy contributions and his support of the price increase legislation," the report said.

■ Large individual contributions: Under the law in effect until April 7, 1972, the report noted, it was illegal for any individual to donate more than $5,000 in any calendar year to a presidential candidate or to any national campaign committee operating in his behalf, yet "more than $500.000 was contributed to the Humphrey presidential campaign in 1971 and 1972 (up to April 7) in the form of donations in excess of $5,000."

Unlike other presidential candidates, Humphrey made no effort to circumvent this rule by establishing dummy committees to receive subdivided, hence legal, contributions.

Evidence gathered by the committee showed that Humphrey received four contributions of stock, each worth at least $86,000 channeled through a limited partnership, Jackson & Co., which sold the stock and distributed the proceeds to a Humphrey committee.

A "purported personal loan" of $100,000 also was made by Paul Thatcher, an official in the Humphrey campaign, to Humphrey through a trust account maintained by Chestnut, the report said.

One of Humphrey's principal backers, Dwayne O. Andreas, was said to have served as trustee for a "blind trust" maintained for Humphrey's benefit. (Andreas, and three others had donated more the than 10,000 shares of stock in Archer-Daniels-Midland Co., the nation's largest soybean processing firm, to Jackson & Co. Andreas was chairman of the firm.)

Two separate payments of $23,000 and $86,000 (of Humphrey's own money) were transferred from the blind trust in January and February 1972 for use in the presidential campaign. As of April 7, 1972, the report noted, candidates were prohibited from using more than $50,000 in personal funds in their own campaigns. (Gift tax was paid on the money originating from the blind trust, the report stated.)

■ Corporate funds received from 3M: A Humphrey aide, the report declared, solicited a contribution from an official of Minnesota Mining and Manufacturing Co. in February 1972. The campaign received a total of $1,000 in April 1972 from 10 of the firm's executives, who were later reimbursed for the contributions from 3M's secret cash reserves used for political activities. [See above]

■ The Loeb contribution: Humphrey personally solicited a contribution from John L. Loeb Sr., a partner in a prominent Wall Street investment banking house, according to the report. A violation of campaign financing laws was committed when Loeb tried to conceal that he was the source of the $50,000 donation. It was also a violation of federal statutes for a campaign committee to accept a contribution by one person in the name of another, but it was not clear from the committee's report whether Humphrey's fund raisers were aware of the deception practiced by Loeb.

Mills campaign abuses. Alleged campaign abuses also occurred in Rep. Wilbur D. Mills' brief race for the Democratic presidential nomination.

The committee said it was unable to make a complete study of Mills' campaign practices, however, because Mills ignored repeated requests from the committee for an interview and his campaign manager, like Humphrey's, refused to testify, citing his 5th Amendment rights against self-incrimination.

The investigation also was limited by Mills' refusal to make a voluntary disclosure of his pre-April 7, 1972 receipts

and disbursements. The disclosures were not required by law, but other Democratic contenders for the nomination had made their finance records public.

(Unofficial figures cited by the report put Mills' pre-April 7, 1972 receipts at about $200,000. According to the General Accounting Office, Mills received $293,000 in the period after April 7.)

The committee's probe centered on Mills' relationship to the dairy industry, principally Associated Milk Producers, Inc. (AMPI) Evidence obtained by the committee showed that Mills received $185,000, or 38% of his total campaign revenues, from dairy industry sources. Of that total, TAPE and the group which replaced it in 1972, CTAPE, contributed $26,500, SPACE donated $12,500, ADEPT contributed $16,000 and members, employes and officers of AMPI gave $40,000.* In addition to these sums, Mills also received $15,000 from the corporate funds of Mid-America Dairymen Inc. and "up to $75,000 in money, goods and services from AMPI corporate assets."

"This limited investigation has not uncovered any direct evidence that . . . Mills' support of the March 1971 dairy legislation constituted a specific quid pro quo for the money, goods and services given to him," the committee declared, but it added that Mills' "failure" to make himself available for committee interview "prevented a full development of the facts."

The committee also noted that David Parr, an AMPI official in Arkansas, ordered the dairy cooperatives' records relating to political activities or contributions destroyed in March/April 1971.

Joseph Johnson, Mills' campaign manager, had been on AMPI's payroll while working on the Mills campaign in 1971, the report said, and he refused to testify under oath before the committee.

The committee also cited evidence that Mills' fund raisers solicited corporate contributions from Gulf Oil Corp. and from 3M. [See above] The $15,000 Gulf donation, laundered through a subsidiary in the Bahamas, was delivered in cash prior to April 7, 1972. A 3M executive contributed $1,000 in July 1972, the report stated, and was reimbursed from 3M's slush fund.

Rebozo linked to $50,000 spent on Nixon. The committee's final report presented lengthy evidence that Charles G. Rebozo, President Nixon's friend, spent more than $50,000—including presidential campaign funds—for the President's personal benefit. The section of the report dealing with Rebozo was first

made public July 10, but was included in the final report issued July 13.

Focusing on $150,100 in cash collected by Rebozo during the President's first term of office, the report detailed how Rebozo, a Key Biscayne, Fla. banker, funneled money through various trust accounts to pay for $46,000 in previously unreported improvements on Nixon's Key Biscayne property. Similarly, the report traced through other trust accounts $4,562 left over from the 1968 campaign that was used by Rebozo to buy diamond and platinum earrings for the First Lady.

The report did not suggest, however, that Nixon knew the source of Rebozo's expenditures and did note that Nixon reimbursed him for $13,642 of the home improvement expenses. In a letter to the committee June 20, James D. St. Clair, the President's special counsel, said he wished to convey the "President's assurance that he never instructed C. G. Rebozo to raise and maintain funds to be expended on the President's personal behalf, nor, so far as he knows, was this ever done."

Rebozo fund raising—A Feb. 16, 1969 confidential memorandum from H. R. Haldeman, the White House chief of staff, to John Ehrlichman, then counsel to the President, described Rebozo's effort to obtain money from oil billionaire J. Paul Getty. The memo, reprinted in part in the committee's report, said, "Bebe Rebozo has been asked by the President to contact J. Paul Getty in London regarding major contributions. . . . The funds should go to some operating entity other than the [Republican] National Committee so that we can retain full control of their use. Bebe would appreciate your calling him with this advice as soon as possible since the President has asked him to move quickly."

Instead of Rebozo, Herbert W. Kalmbach, the President's personal attorney, was dispatched to solicit a contribution from Getty, but, the report said, Rebozo did collect $100,000 in two cash installments from a representative of billionaire recluse Howard Hughes in 1969 and 1970, and $50,000 in currency from supermarket chain executive A. D. Davis shortly before a new campaign finance disclosure law became effective April 7, 1972.

The report said that Watergate committee investigators had been unable to resolve a number of questions concerning the disposition of these contributions. Rebozo testified to the committee that right after he received the Davis money he called the Finance Committee to Re-elect the President, which sent Frederick LaRue, a committee official, to Miami to pick up the contribution. Rebozo's testimony was contradicted by LaRue, who asserted that he received no money from Rebozo until October 1972. Told by

*The dairy cooperatives' political trusts: AMPI's political arm was TAPE (Trust for Agricultural Political Education). It was replaced in 1972 by CTAPE (Committee for Thorough Agricultural Political Education). The political arm of Dairymen, Inc. was SPACE (Trust for Special Political Agricultural Community Education). Mid-America Dairymen, Inc.'s political group was ADEPT (Agricultural and Dairy Educational Political Trust).

former Attorney General John N. Mitchell that Rebozo had money on hand to help finance the Kentucky senatorial campaign of Louis Nunn, LaRue said he contacted Rebozo and arranged a pick-up. How much LaRue received from Rebozo Oct. 12, 1972 was unclear, the report said, because LaRue first told committee interviewers that the amount was $25,000-$30,000, only to recollect later that it could have been $50,000 or more. In any case, LaRue was certain that the money was comingled with funds used to pay the Watergate break-in defendants. LaRue further testified to giving to a Nunn campaign courier a sum of cash of "about the amount" received from Rebozo. The Nunn campaign, however, said it received no such cash.

The report said committee investigators were confronted with a number of unanswered questions involving the much-publicized Hughes contribution. Moreover, the report stated, investigators were not able to establish beyond a doubt when Rebozo received each of the two $50,000 cash payments. On the basis of all relevant evidence, the report concluded that the deliveries most likely took place in September 1969 and July 1970, but these dates were open to doubt and at least four other dates were possible. Richard G. Danner, carrier of the Hughes gift and a personal friend of Rebozo since the late 1940s, originally testified to one set of dates of delivery and later, after conferring with Rebozo, testified to two other times.

The dates of delivery were important to committee investigators seeking to determine if the money Rebozo returned to the Hughes organization June 27, 1973 was the same money he had been given, as Rebozo asserted. The committee report said that serial numbers of 1,001 $100 bills returned to a Hughes representative were recorded and attempts were made to trace the money through records of the Federal Reserve Bank of San Francisco, the distributor of newly printed bills to Las Vegas, Nev., where the Hughes-owned Silver Slipper Casino—the source of the $100,000—was located. The search, hampered by the incompleteness of federal reserve records, was inconclusive.

Wholly unresolved, the report said, was the issue of Kalmbach's testimony to committee about an April 30, 1973 White House meeting with Rebozo, at which Rebozo said he had disbursed portions of the Hughes $100,000 to the President's secretary, Rose Mary Woods, the President's brothers—F. Donald and Edward C. Nixon—and "unnamed others." While the committee's report simply recounted the Kalmbach testimony it disclosed for the first time a sworn affidavit from Kalmbach's personal attorney, James O'Connor. Following his meeting with Rebozo, Kalmbach immediately told O'Connor all the details, including the fact that Rebozo said he had

disbursed some of the Hughes money to Woods and the Nixon brothers.

Mrs. Nixon's earrings—The committee's final report also concerned the March 17, 1972 purchase by Rebozo of platinum and diamond earrings, a birthday present from the President to Mrs. Nixon. According to the committee, the complicated transaction was arranged as follows: At the time of Nixon's election in 1968, Rebozo maintained in his Key Biscayne bank an account in the name of The Florida Nixon for President Committee, account No. 1-0455. On April 15, 1969 Rebozo issued a $6,000 check payable to Thomas H. Wakefield—Special Account, drawn on the Florida Nixon for President account. He used the check to open a new account, the Thomas H. Wakefield—Special Account No. 2-1691. The signatories were Wakefield, who was Rebozo's attorney, and Rebozo himself. Rebozo said he created the special account in his attorney's name to receive funds owed to him "for one thing or another" and so as not to attract attention. He signed all checks until the account was closed.

On June 28, 1972, Rebozo transferred $4,562 in the Wakefield Special Account, the remaining balance, to the account of Wakefield's law firm, Wakefield, Hewitt & Webster Trust Account No. 1-673 in the Key Biscayne bank. That same day, a $5,000 check was drawn against No. 1-673 and the proceeds were deposited in the Wakefield, Hewitt & Webster Trust Account No. 11-611-1 in the First National Bank of Miami. Also on the same day, a check was issued from account 11-611-1 for the purchase of a $5,000 cashiers check payable to Harry Winston, the New York City jeweler from whom the platinum and diamond earrings were purchased March 17, 1972.

A check of Winston's records revealed that the jeweler had also received a $560 check from the President and a $90 check from Rose Mary Woods. The earrings were delivered on March 17, 1972 to Lt. Cmdr. Alex Larzelere, a White House military attache.

In summary, the committee report said, ". . . $4,562.33 of funds originally derived from campaign contributions were used to purchase . . . earrings. This complex four stage process of payment . . . concealed the fact that the funds originated from contributions to the 1968 campaign and were ultimately used by Rebozo on behalf of President Nixon."

Property improvements—The committee's report likewise raised questions about $45,621 in improvements made on the President's two Key Biscayne properties. These included $18,435 for a swimming pool, $6,508 to extend a roof, $11,900 to convert a garage into living quarters, $3,586 for a fireplace, $1,138 for a billiard table, $395 for an architectural model, $243 for a putting green and $3,-

335 for architects' fees and tile repairs. The report pointed out that records reflecting the expenditure of $45,621 were "withheld" from Coopers & Lybrand when the accounting firm prepared the President's financial statement in 1973.

Rebozo paid for these improvements, the report said, by checks drawn on his own personal account at the Key Biscayne bank ($13,361), with cash ($9,046), and with checks drawn on trust accounts in the name of Wakefield ($23,213). Shortly after the 1972 presidential election, Rebozo deposited $20,000 in $100 bills into two of the Wakefield trust accounts, the report said. (These were the same currency denominations received from Hughes and Davis.)

The committee claimed that Rebozo would not honor committee subpoenas for the trust account records and other financial data. As a result, the committee was unable to determine to what degree Nixon reimbursed Rebozo for the improvements. The committee staff located one 1973 reimbursement check for $13,642, an amount not listed as a liability on the President's financial statement.

Contrasting IRS investigations—The committee's report pointed out the disparity in treatment accorded Rebozo and Lawrence O'Brien, the former Democratic national chairman, both of whom were the subjects of investigations by the Internal Revenue Service (IRS). During the course of the IRS investigation of the Hughes organization that turned up the $100,000 campaign gift to Rebozo, it was revealed that O'Brien's public relations firm had been paid a "substantial" sum by Hughes Tool Co. in 1970.

The report said that the committee took testimony from IRS officials, who said that O'Brien's tax returns were audited and, except for a small deficiency, they were found in order. In late 1971 or early 1972 top IRS officials decided that with the election approaching, it would be wise to postpone until after the election investigations that were "politically sensitive." Because of this policy, the report said, the IRS did not interview Rebozo or F. Donald Nixon until six months after the election. In contrast, "the IRS . . . did succumb to pressures from the Administration and interviewed O'Brien before the 1972 election," the report stated.

In addition, the committee recounted testimony by Ehrlichman that "I wanted them [IRS] to turn up something and send [O'Brien] to jail before the election and unfortunately it didn't materialize." Ehrlichman similarly testified to what he told then-IRS Commissioner Johnnie Walters about what he (Ehrlichman) thought about the audit, ". . . it was my first crack at [Walters] . . . this was the first chance I had to tell the commissioner what a crappy job he had done. . . ."

A

Excerpts from Senate Watergate Committee Recommendations

Watergate Break-In and Cover-Up

I

The Committee recommends that Congress enact legislation to establish a permanent office of public attorney which would have jurisdiction to prosecute criminal cases in which there is a real or apparent conflict of interest within the executive branch. The public attorney would also have jurisdiction to inquire into (with power to gain access to executive records) the status and progress of complaints and criminal
B charges concerning matters pending in or involving the conduct of federal departments and regulatory agencies. The public attorney would be appointed for a fixed term (e.g., five years), be subject to Senate confirmation and be chosen by members of the judicial branch to ensure his independence from executive control or influence.

In each of the nation's two major scandals during the past half century, Teapot Dome and Watergate, the appointment of a special prosecutor was essential to preserve the integrity of the criminal justice system and public confidence in the rule of law. In both situations, the office was created after serious abuses had occurred . . .

C It is thus essential that an independent public attorney's office be created to investigate and prosecute where conflicts of interest in the executive branch exist. This office should be given power to inquire fully into corruption in the executive branch and have access to all records relating to such corruption. The operations of the current special prosecution force demonstrate the effective role such an entity can play.

The preventative role this office could fulfill must be emphasized. Permanent status for this office could help ensure responsible action by executive branch officials who have primary responsibility to administer and enforce the law. Indeed, it is reasonable to speculate that the existence of a public attorney's
D office might have served as a deterrent against some of the wrongful acts that comprise the Watergate scandal. Because of this preventive role, it is unwise to wait until another national crisis to re-institute the office of special prosecutor. It is far better to create a permanent institution now than to consider its wisdom at some future time when emotions may be high and unknown political factors at play.

The public attorney we recommended would not be only a "special prosecutor" but an ombudsman having power to inquire into the administration of justice in the executive branch. With the power of access to executive records, he could appropriately respond to complaints from the public, the Congress,
E the Courts and other public and private institutions. If he became aware of misconduct in the executive branch, he could assume the role of special prosecutor. The public attorney should also be required to make periodic reports to Congress on the affairs of his office and the need for new legislation within his jurisdiction, a function that should be of great assistance to the relevant Congressional oversight committees.

The Attorney General should find such an office advantageous in cases involving charges against Administration officials or persons otherwise close to high executive officers, particularly where a proper exercise of discretion not to prosecute would give rise
F to public suspicion of cover-up. Such cases could be referred by the Attorney General to the public attorney. The public attorney would also have jurisdiction to prosecute all criminal cases referred to it by the Federal Elections Commission, which is elsewhere recommended in this report.

It is not anticipated that there would be substantial jurisdictional disputes between the Justice Department and the public attorney. The statute establishing the public attorney should grant him discretionary jurisdiction in any situation where there is a reasonable basis to conclude that a conflict of interest exists. He should have exclusive jurisdiction over criminal cases referred to him by the Federal Elections Commission. As to cases where a ju-
G risdictional dispute cannot be resolved, provision should be made for special judicial determination on an expedited basis. Deciding such jurisdictional disputes is well within the competence of the courts for the question would primarily be one of statutory interpretation. . . .

The present immunity statute would have to be amended to allow the independent prosecutor to grant use immunity without the consent of the Attorney General. The procedure by which the public attorney obtains immunity should be made similar to that applicable to Congressional requests for immunity. The Attorney General would be informed of an immunity request, but he could only delay the immunity, not prevent it. Similarly, the Attorney General would inform the public attorney of his immunity decisions; the public attorney would have the power to delay, not prevent, immunity.

To guarantee true independence from the executive branch, the public attorney should be appointed for a fixed term. . . . He should be removable only by the appointing authority. . . . for gross improprieties. Because it is highly important that the special prosecutor act solely in the interest of justice and not for personal benefit, he should be ineligible for appointment or election to federal office for a period of two years after his term expires or he resigns or is removed.

Crucial to the independence of the public attorney is the appointing authority. If the appointing authority is vested in the President or the Attorney General (who is responsible to the President), the appearance of political influence would remain even if the public attorney has such tenure. The argument in favor of Presidential appointment is that criminal prosecution is an executive function and there is a presumption of regularity respecting the exercise of Presidential power that should not be discarded because of the unique abuses of Watergate. But Watergate at least teaches that the abuse of power must be anticipated. . . .

. . . the Congress should vest the appointment power as follows: the Chief Justice should be given the power and duty to select three retired circuit court judges who, in turn, would appoint the public attorney. After the Chief Justice makes the initial appointment of the three circuit court judges, the Chief Justice's responsibilities would be ended; the three retired circuit court judges—who would not sit on any cases either at trial or in an appellate capacity in which the public attorney's office was involved—would make the actual appointment, which would be subject to confirmation by the Senate. . . . At the end of the five-year period, the Chief Justice would appoint (or reappoint) three retired circuit judges and they, in turn, would choose a new public attorney, or reappoint the outgoing public attorney for one additional term only. . . .

II

The Committee recommends that, in connection with its revision of the federal criminal code, Congress should treat as a separate federal offense, with separate penalties, any felony defined in the code (except those felonies that specifically relate to federal elections) that is committed with the purpose of interfering with or affecting the outcome of a federal election or nominating process.

The purpose of this proposal is primarily to establish as a separate federal crime the commission of certain traditional common law offenses such as burglary and larceny where these crimes are committed with the intent of interfering with or affecting a federal election or nominating process. . . .

Adoption of the above proposal would not add redundancy to the criminal law. Rather, it would allow the prosecution of crimes in which there is a federal interest in the federal courts. . . .

III

The Committee recommends that Congress enact legislation making it unlawful for any employe in the Executive Office of the President, or assigned to the White House, directly or indirectly to authorize or engage in any investigative or intelligence gathering activity concerning national or domestic security not authorized by Congress.

The evidence received concerning the establishment, by direction of the President, of a special investigative unit in the White House (the Plumbers) and the operations of the Plumbers illustrates the danger to individual rights presented by such a secret investigative activity. . . .

IV

The Committee recommends that the appropriate Congressional oversight committees should more closely supervise the operations and internal regulations of the intelligence and law enforcement "community." In particular, these committees should continually examine the relations between federal law enforcement and intelligence agencies and the White House, and promptly determine if any revision of law is necessary relating to the jurisdiction or activities of these agencies.

From its beginning, the Central Intelligence Agency has been prohibited from performing police and internal security functions within the United States. . . .

Notwithstanding this clear and long-standing prohibition, the select committee found that the White House sought and achieved CIA aid for the Plumbers and unsuccessfully sought to involve the CIA in the Watergate cover-up. . . .

As for law enforcement agencies, testimony of the former acting director of the Federal Bureau of Investigation, Patrick Gray, as well as evidence received by the Committee of efforts by the White House to interfere with the IRS, indicate that similar oversight functions should be strengthened with regard to the FBI, and IRS and similar agencies.

V

The Committee recommends that Congress amend:

(1) The false declaration prohibition of 18 U.S.C. 1623 to make it equally applicable to Congressional proceedings under oath.

(2) Section 1621 of Title 18 to provide that, once the oath has been properly administered by a Congressman in a public or private Congressional hearing, it is not a defense to a perjury charge that subsequently a quorum was absent or no Congressman was present when the alleged perjurious statement was made. . . .

VI

The Committee recommends that the Congress refrain from adopting proposed revisions of Title 18 which would unjustifiably broaden the present defenses to criminal charges of official mistake of law and execution of public duty. The Committee supports the predominant rule of law adopted in the American Law Institute's model penal code, that any reliance on a mistake of law or superior orders must be objectively reasonable to constitute a valid defense. . . .

VII

The Committee recommends that the appropriate committees of Congress study and reconsider Title III of the Omnibus Crime and Safe Streets Act of 1968 for the purpose of determining whether the electronic surveillance provisions contained in that act require revision or amendment.

The Committee's investigation has revealed incidents of unlawful violations of privacy through electronic surveillance, some . . . directly or indirectly under federal branch auspices in whose trust Congress placed the protection of privacy under the provisions of Title III of the Safe Streets Act of 1968. The restrictions contained in that act have proved to be inadequate to protect individuals against unjustified invasions of privacy.

Campaign Practices

I

The Committee recommends that Congress enact criminal legislation to prohibit anyone from obtaining employment, voluntary or paid, in a campaign of an individual seeking nomination or election to any federal office by false pretenses, misrepresentations or other fraudulent means for the purpose of interfering with, spying on, or obstructing any campaign activities of such candidate. Furthermore, such legislation should make it unlawful for anyone to direct, instruct, or pay anyone to join any such campaign by such means or for such purposes as are outlined above.

New legislation is needed to prevent the infiltration of Presidential and federal campaigns. The activities of Donald Segretti, Robert Benz, Michael McMinoway, Elmer Wyatt, Tom Gregory and others are abundant documentation of the numerous infiltration efforts in the 1972 campaign.

The dangers of this infiltration range from the confusion and suspicion resulting from leaked information to the opponents or newspapers to more systematic disruption and sabotage of the opposition campaign. . . .

II

The Committee recommends that Congress enact legislation to make it unlawful to request or knowingly to disburse or make available campaign funds for the purpose of promoting or financing violations of federal election laws.

This recommendation is an effort to deter individuals with control over campaign funds from blindly and automatically providing money for campaign activities whenever they are so instructed. For example, Herb Kalmbach, the custodian of left-over 1968 campaign funds, funded Tony Ulasewicz's activities for nearly three years as well as the travels and illegal activities of Donald Segretti.

III

The Committee recommends that Congress enact new legislation which prohibits the theft, unauthorized copying, or the taking by false pretenses of campaign materials, documents, or papers not available for public dissemination belonging to or in the custody of a candidate for federal office or his aides.

IV

The Committee recommends that Congress should make it unlawful for any individual to fraudulently misrepresent by telephone or in person that he is representing a candidate for federal office for the purpose of interfering with the election.

Responsiveness Program

I

Prosecution for violations of the existing criminal statutes [relating to impairment of government agency functions], insofar as they relate to federal elections, and the criminal statutory enactments recommended below should be entrusted to the public attorney. . . .

II

The Federal Elections Commission . . . should be given authority to investigate and restrain violations of federal civil and criminal statutes insofar as those violations relate to federal elections. The commission should also be empowered to refer evidence of such violations to the public attorney. . . .

III

The Committee recommends that Congress enact legislation making it a felony to obstruct, impair or pervert a government function, or attempt to obstruct, impair or pervert a government function, by defrauding the government in any manner. . . .

. . . there is currently in the federal code a statute (18 U.S.C. 371) making it unlawful to conspire to defraud the United States. The Supreme Court has ruled that a conspiracy to interfere with the lawful functioning of government is prosecutable under this provision. The Committee's recommendation . . . would make illegal *individual* conduct that fraudulently interferes with lawful government function. . . .

IV

The Committee recommends that Congress preserve as part of the United States Code 18 U.S.C. 595, which makes it illegal for a government official connected with the awarding of federal grants and loans to use his official authority to affect a federal election, but recommends that his offense be upgraded to a felony. The committee recommends that 18 U.S.C. 600, which makes illegal the promise of government benefit for political support, be upgraded to a felony.

The Committee also recommends that the scope of Section 595 be expanded to include misuse of official authority in connection with the dispensing of other federal funds such as government contracts payments and federal subsidies. . . .

V

The Committee recommends that Congress preserve in the United States Code 18 U.S.C. 611, which proscribes political contributions by or solicitations to government contractors, and 18 U.S.C. 602, which makes illegal political solicitations by persons receiving federal compensation for services rendered to other such persons—but appropriately amend these provisions to make illegal contributions by or knowing solicitations to (a) any person receiving, during the calendar year a contribution or solicitation is made, other federal monies (e.g. grants, loans, subsidies) in excess of $5,000, and (b) the principals or dominant shareholders of corporations receiving, during the calendar year a contribution or solicitation is made, . . . federal funding designed to benefit disadvantaged and minority groups. . . .

The evidence before the Committee indicates that, respecting minority groups, plans were laid to solicit recipients of grants or loans. Also, there appear to have been particular pressures to contribute on minority businessmen whose corporations were quite dependent on government business. . . .

The current major bills to revise the criminal code before Congress . . . generally weaken the proscriptions in Sections 602 and 611 and lessen the penalties for their violation. In view of the abuses discovered, a weakening of the law in this area seems unwise.

VI

The Committee recommends that Congress amend the Hatch Act to place all Justice Department officials—including the Attorney General—under its purview.

The evidence the Select Committee has gathered indicated that various federal officials took an active part in the President's 1972 re-election campaign. Some of the officials apparently involved were covered by the Hatch Act, which prohibits certain federal employees from engaging in political campaigns and political management, but some were not. Some of the federal officials involved in political activities were employed at the Department of Justice. . . .

VII

The Committee recommends that the appropriate committees of both houses of Congress, in accordance with their constitutional responsibilities, maintain a vigilant oversight of the operations of the executive branch in order to prevent abuses of governmental processes to promote success in a federal election. . . .

Campaign Financing

In making its legislative recommendations the Select Committee has made a number of proposals that it believes will reduce the likelihood of future abuses. In so doing, it wishes to emphasize two points. First, full disclosure of contributions and expenditures as well as of governmental action affecting contributors is the critical minimum of campaign financing reform. But for even this minimum to be an effective tool, the data must be accessible and reviewed by those with an interest in the government process, including candidates and the press. Second, the temptation to over-regulate must be viewed in terms that such action would have on the willingness of citizens to participate voluntarily in the electoral process. . . .

I

The Committee recommends that the Congress enact legislation to establish an independent, nonpartisan Federal Elections Commission which would replace the present tripartite administration of the clerk of the House, secretary of the Senate, and GAO Office of Federal Elections and would have certain enforcement powers. With . . . exceptions . . . the Committee adopts sections 308 and 309 of S. 3044 which would create a Federal Elections Commission and vest in it certain enumerated powers.

Under the Senate bill, the commission would be composed of seven members appointed by the President with the advice and consent of the Senate who would serve seven-year terms. Not more than four of the commissioners would be members of the same political party. . . .

II

The Committee recommends enactment of a statute prohibiting cash contributions and expenditures in excess of $100 in connection with an election for nomination and election for federal office.

III

The Committee recommends enactment of a statute requiring each candidate for the office of President or Vice President to designate one political committee as his central campaign committee with one or more banks as his campaign depositories. . . .

Laundering of funds is often accomplished by contributing and transferring funds from committee to committee so as to obscure the original source and make it impossible to trace the money to the intended beneficiary or use. The Select Committee believes that the requirements of a central campaign committee and a designated depository increase the traceability of campaign funds by putting the responsibility for collecting and reporting campaign financial information in a centralized place.

IV

The Committee recommends enactment of a statutory limitation on over-all campaign expenditures of Presidential candidates. The committee proposes a limit of expenditures of 12 cents times the voting age population during a general election. . . .

The Select Committee further recommends a limitation on expenditures of Presidential candidates in primary elections . . . provided for in Section 504(a)(2)(a) of S. 2044. This section provides for an expenditure limit of "two times the amount which a candidate for nomination for election to the office of Senator from that State may expend in that State in connection with his primary election campaign.". . . .

V

The Committee recommends enactment of a statutory limitation of $3,000 on political contributions by any individuals to the campaign of each Presidential candidate during the prenomination period and a separate $3,000 limitation during the post-nomination period. A contribution to a Vice-Presidential candidate of a party would be considered, for purposes of the limitation, a contribution to that party's Presidential candidate.

A necessary corollary to a limit on contributions to Presidential candidates is a limitation on independent expenditures on behalf of a candidate without his authorization. Such expenditures, if unrestricted, could be used to avoid and thereby undermine any limitation on contributions . . . On the other hand, there are serious constitutional arguments against an outright prohibition on independent campaign expenditures in view of the right of expression guaranteed by the First Amendment. A reasonable solution seems to be the adoption of a rule to the effect that if an individual acted on his own, and not at the suggestion or request of the candidate, he could expend a separate $1,000 on behalf of one or more candidates during the prenomination and general election periods and would have the responsibility for reporting expenditures aggregating over $100 on behalf of any candidate. Such independent expenditures on behalf of a candidate would not count toward the over-all expenditure limit of the candidate.

VI

The Committee recommends that the Internal Revenue Code be amended to provide a credit in a substantial amount of individual and joint federal income tax returns for any contribution made in a calendar year to a political party or any candidate seeking election to any public office, federal, state, or local.

The incentive which the committee suggests is a 100 per cent tax credit for contributions up to a certain level, for example, $25 for an individual return and $50 for a joint return.

VII

The Committee recommends against the adoption of any form of public financing in which tax monies are collected and allocated to political candidates by the federal government. . . . While recognizing the basis of support for the concept of public financing and the potential difficulty in adequately funding campaigns in the midst of strict limitations on the form and amount of contributions, the committee takes issue with the contention that public financing affords either an effective or appropriate solution. Thomas Jefferson believed "to compel a man to furnish contributions of money for the propagation of opinions which he disbelieves and abhors, is sinful and tyrannical."

The Committee's opposition is based like Jefferson's upon the fundamental need to protect the voluntary right of individual citizens to express themselves politically as guaranteed by the First Amendment. Furthermore, we find inherent dangers in authorizing the federal bureaucracy to fund and excessively regulate political campaigns. . . .

VIII

The Committee recommends enactment of a statute prohibiting the solicitation or receipt of campaign contributions from foreign nationals.

Under present law . . . it is a felony to solicit, accept or receive a political contribution from a foreign principal or an agent of a foreign principal . . . Since the term "principal" connotes the existence of an agency relationship, it is the [Justice] Department's view that a foreign national is a foreign principal . . . only if the principal has an agent within the United States. . . .

Thus the present statute permits political contributions from individuals who neither reside in the United States nor have the right to vote in elections within the United States. . . .

In addition to direct contributions by foreign nationals during 1972, hundreds of thousands of dollars were laundered through foreign banks and foreign companies. . . .

The proposed statute would prohibit political contributions by foreign nationals whether or not they have agents within the United States. . . .

IX

The Committee recommends that no government official whose appointment required confirmation by the Senate or who was on the payroll of the Executive Office of the President be permitted to participate in the solicitation or receipt of campaign contributions during his or her period of service and for a period of one year thereafter.

During the 1972 campaign there was a widespread transfer of key Administration officials from the White House and from departments and agencies to high positions in the campaign effort. In certain cases, these officials or their assistants went to the very persons over whom they previously wielded regulatory or other power to solicit campaign contributions. Particularly in view of the likelihood that many of

A

B

C

D

E

F

G

these officials would return to the government, solicitation by them may well have had undesirable coercive aspects. While the entire practice of carving the campaign force out of the Administration on a temporary basis seems highly questionable, the committee recommends as a minimum step that high Administration officials who leave to enter the campaign be barred from engaging in fund-raising activities for a period of one year.

X

The Committee recommends that stringent limitations be imposed on the right of organizations to contribute to Presidential campaigns.

One of the major abuses investigated by the Select Committee was the apparent attempt on the part of several large dairy cooperatives to utilize their contribution potential of millions of dollars to influence Administration decisions. The power of associations and organizations . . . individuals, corporations or unions—to band together and pool their contributions has given rise to enormous contributions. . . . In the context of a Presidential race it appears that a limit of $6,000—the figure contained in S. 3044—would tend to avoid the problem of undue influence by organizations while providing them an opportunity to participate in the political process. . . .

XI

The Committee recommends that violations of the major provisions of the campaign financing law, such as participating in a corporate or union contribution in excess of the limit, and making a foreign contribution shall constitute a felony.

Rebozo-Hughes Investigation and Related Matters

I

Communications between the White House and the Internal Revenue Service should be more strictly regulated, specifically:

1. Any requests, direct or indirect, for information or action made to the IRS by anyone in the Executive Office of the President, up to and including the President, should be recorded by the person making the request and by the IRS. Requests and responses by the IRS (i.e. whether information was provided), should be disclosed at least once a year to appropriate Congressional oversight committees.

2. On "sensitive case reports," which cover special cases, the IRS should be permitted to disclose to persons in the Executive Office of the President, up to and including the President, only the name of the person or group in the report and the general nature of the investigation.

3. All persons in the Executive Office of the President, up to and including the President, should be prohibited from receiving indirectly or directly any income tax return.

4. All requests for information or action and all IRS responses should be disclosed periodically to the appropriate Congressional oversight committees.

There were numerous efforts by the White House to use the IRS for political purposes between 1969 and 1972. Particularly striking examples, such as attempts to use the IRS to harass persons perceived as "enemies," have already been exposed and discussed at great length by the Select Committee and other groups. In addition, there was misuse of the IRS by the White House regarding the IRS investigations of Rebozo, the President's brothers, and people connected with the Hughes operation. Because of the close relationship of several of the parties to the President, questions of improper White House influence in this case are particularly acute. . . .

II

Congress should enact legislation requiring full financial disclosure by the President and Vice President of the United States to the Government Accounting Office each year of all income, gifts and things of value that they or their spouses have received during the year or expenditures made for their personal benefit or the benefit of their spouses by other individuals.

Presently, legislation requires that Congressmen and Senators file statements of financial disclosure each year. Certainly, the head of the executive branch of the government should be held to no less a standard than the members of the legislature, and perhaps even held to a higher standard of disclosure because of the significance of his position. . . .

Examples of items which should be disclosed include the following:

(a) Copies of tax returns, declarations, statements, or other documents which were made individually or jointly for the preceding year in compliance with the provisions of the Internal Revenue Code;

(b) The identity of each interest in real or personal property having a value of $10,000 or more which the President or Vice President or spouses owned at any time during the preceding year;

(c) The identity of each trust or other fiduciary relation in which the President or Vice President or spouses held a beneficial interest having a value of $10,000 or more, and the identity, if known, of each interest of the trust or other fiduciary relation in real or personal property in which he or she held a beneficial interest having a value of $10,000 or more at any time during the preceding year;

(d) The identity of each liability of $5,000 or more owned by the President or Vice President or by them jointly with their spouses, at any time during the preceding year; and

(e) The source and value of all gifts received by the President, Vice President, or spouses in the aggregate amount or value of $50 or more from any single source received during the preceding year.

III

Suggestion: State and local bar associations should conduct a study of the attorney-client privilege in light of the abuses of the privilege uncovered during the Select Committee's investigations. . . .

In at least four instances . . . the lawyer-client privilege has been pleaded as part of an attempt to cover up illegal or questionable activities that had nothing to do with the rendering of legal advice:

(1) Mardian and Liddy in the Watergate cover-up;

(2) Dean and Segretti in the Watergate dirty-tricks cover-up;

(3) Kalmbach and Rebozo in the Hughes-Rebozo cover-up;

(4) Wakefield-Rebozo, also in the Hughes-Rebozo area. . . .

The Courts

I

The Committee recommends that Congress enact legislation giving the United States District Court for the District of Columbia jurisdiction over suits to enforce Congressional subpoenas issued to members of the executive branch, including the President. This statute, which would apply to all subpoenas issued by Congressional bodies, would replace the special statute passed for and limited to the Select Committee that is now codified as 28 U.S.C. 1364. The statute should provide that a Congressional body has standing to sue in its own name and in the name of the United States and may employ counsel of its own choice in such a suit. The statute should provide that suits brought to enforce Congressional subpoenas must be handled on an expedited basis by the courts.

II

The Select Committee recommends that Congress give careful consideration to the bill now before the Senate (S. 2567) that would establish a Congressional Legal Service and thus give Congress a litigation arm that would allow it to protect its interest in court by its own counsel.

III

The Select Committee recommends that Congress amend 2 U.S.C. 190a-1(b) to allow a senatorial committee or its staff to take testimony and evidence in private session upon an express determination by the committee that the requirements of efficient and productive investigation so require and that the investigation would be materially harmed if a regimen of confidentiality were not imposed. The amended statute, however, should provide that testimony or evidence taken in confidence for these reasons should be released to the public as soon as the requirements of efficient investigation no longer demand confidentiality.

Supreme Court Upholds Jaworski; House Panel Votes Impeachment

Interview with Rabbi Korff. President Nixon told Rabbi Baruch Korff, leader of a pro-Nixon group, that Watergate would be remembered as "the broadest but the thinnest scandal in American history." The interview, held on May 13, was released by the President's press office in San Clemente, Calif. July 16, when Nixon met again with Korff, president of the National Citizens Committee for Fairness to the Presidency.

After their July 16 meeting, Korff told reporters that Nixon had agreed with him that the recent conviction of former Nixon aide John Ehrlichman for conspiracy and lying was "a blot on justice." [See below]

In the May 13 interview, Nixon said the Watergate figures had been "tried and convicted in the press and on television" and it would be "extremely difficult" for them to get "a fair trial" in Washington.

Belittling the Watergate affair, Nixon said it had not been been brought about by greed for money. "Now, of course," he said, "I do not mean that crime can only be measured in terms of whether or not you were paid something. But when they said this is like Teapot Dome, that is comparing apples with oranges, and, shall we say, rather poor oranges, too."

Watergate "caught the imagination of the press," Nixon said, because "I am not the press' favorite pin-up boy. If it hadn't been Watergate, there would probably have been something else. So now they have this. But I will survive it and I just hope they will survive it with . . . as much serenity as I have."

The President said "if one good thing could come out of Watergate, and some good comes out of every adversity, it would be a greater sense of responsibility on the part of the press, on the part of investigators and the rest, for the rights of individuals." He deplored the "harassment" tactics and "abusive process" employed by some staff members of the special Watergate prosecution.

As for impeachment, Nixon said "when a Congressman and Senator gets right down to the tough call, he is going to think a long time before he wants to impeach a President, unless he finds wrongdoing." He thought his own impeachment would have "devastating consequences" on foreign policy, would "jeopardize"

world peace and would have a "very detrimental effect on our political system for years to come."

The President also referred to critics of the "tone" of his Watergate conversations, as disclosed in transcripts. If such critics "were to tape the conversations of Presidents that I have known," he said, "they wouldn't like their tone, either."

The President also spoke of his personal finances. He did not mind having his tax returns "gone over with a fine tooth comb," he said, and would pay the "extra money." "I have never cared much about money," he said, "If I did, I would have a lot of it because I was out of office for eight years" and, despite the fact he was "a fairly accomplished lawyer," "still only entered here [the presidency] with a net worth of less than $600,000."

The May 13 interview was incorporated in a book written by Korff, "The Personal Nixon: Staying on the Summit."

Evidence on IRS misuse released. The House Judiciary Committee July 16 released evidence collected in its impeachment inquiry concerning possible White House attempts to misuse the Internal Revenue Service for political gain. The committee previously released eight other volumes of evidence on the Watergate affair.

The ninth volume detailed repeated attempts by the White House, some successful, to gain confidential tax information on individuals from the IRS and to use its tax-return audits to hurt political enemies and protect friends of the President.

Among the evidence was testimony from both of the Nixon Administration's first two commissioners of Internal Revenue that they had offered their resignations in protest against what they considered improper White House pressures and actions. One of them, Randolph W. Thrower, did resign in January 1971 after he tried without success to see Nixon to warn him, as Thrower put it in an affidavit, "that any suggestion of introduction of political influence into the IRS would be very damaging to him and his administration, as well as to the revenue system and the general public interest."

Thrower's successor, Johnnie Walters, testified that former White House counsel John W. Dean 3rd gave him a list in September 1972 of 490 supporters of the Democratic presidential nominee, Sen. George McGovern (D, S.D.), and asked the service to inspect their taxes. Walters said he advised Dean "that compliance with the request would be disastrous for the IRS and for the administration."

Walters said he also had intense pressure from Nixon aide John D. Ehrlichman in the summer of 1972 to create a tax problem for Lawrence F. O'Brien, then Democratic national chairman. O'Brien had been audited and his return closed, Walters said, but Ehrlichman continued to press for action, with some of the requests relayed through then-Treasury Secretary George P. Shultz. Walters said he told Ehrlichman over the telephone, with Shultz on an extension, that the IRS file on O'Brien's return was closed. Ehrlichman was said to have replied angrily, "I'm goddamn tired of your foot-dragging tactics." Walters said he then had told Shultz "that he could have my job any time he wanted it."

The committee included in its data Ehrlichman's statement at a closed hearing of the Senate Watergate committee, that IRS personnel "down in the woodwork" had "75 well-selected reasons why they shouldn't audit him [O'Brien], and they weren't having any of the same reasons with regard to Republicans at that time, and I thought there was a little unevenhandedness." "I wanted them to turn up something and send him to jail before the election," Ehrlichman told the Senate committee, "and unfortunately it didn't materialize."

The IRS did pass along to the White House a report requested in March 1970 by Clark Mollenhoff, then White House special counsel, on the taxes of Gerald Wallace, brother of Gov. George C. Wallace (D, Ala.). Mollenhoff's affidavit said he sought the report only after Nixon aide H. R. Haldeman assured him "the report was to be obtained at the request of the President." Mollenhoff delivered the report to Haldeman, he said, but later was accused by Haldeman, among others, of being the source of a "leak" of derogatory material from the report to columnist Jack Anderson.

Anderson's column, apparently based on the leaked report, appeared three weeks before the Alabama gubernatorial primary in 1970. Mollenhoff asserted in the affidavit that the leak came from "the highest White House level." (Anderson said he had been shown the report by the late Murray Chotiner, a long-time political adviser to Nixon.)

Confidential information from the IRS was obtained on several occasions by Dean, according to the evidence. In September 1971 Dean received data on an IRS audit of evangelist Billy Graham, a friend of Nixon's, which he relayed to Haldeman with a note, "Can we do anything to help?" Haldeman's answer was, "No, it's already covered." In October 1971 Dean obtained a copy of a tax audit of actor John Wayne, a supporter of Nixon. The evidence included Dean's testimony at a closed hearing of the Senate Watergate committee that Nixon requested that tax audits "be turned off on friends of his."

Other evidence indicated Nixon's desire to have the IRS harass left-wing organizations. "Nearly 18 months ago, the President indicated a desire for IRS to move against leftist organizations taking advantage of tax shelters," White House aide Tom Huston wrote Haldeman in September 1970. Huston added he had pressed the IRS on the issue "to no avail."

Nixon's interest in pressing for probes of his political opponents was indicated in a transcript of a Sept. 15, 1972 White House tape. According to the text, Haldeman told the President that Dean was "moving ruthlessly on the investigation of McGovern people, Kennedy stuff, and all that too . . . and Dean's working the thing through IRS. . . ."

The latter part of the tape was missing from the evidence because of presidential defiance of a committee subpoena. The section had been turned over to U.S. Judge John Sirica but was in litigation on the issue of executive privilege.

Dean had told the Senate Watergate committee that the conversation turned eventually to "use of the Internal Revenue Service to attack our enemies." Dean said he cited the White House lack of "clout" at the IRS because of Democratic holdovers in the agency and "the President seemed somewhat annoyed and said that the Democratic administrations had used this tool well, and after the election we would get people in these agencies who would be responsive to White House requirements."

Dean told Nixon on March 13, 1973, according to another transcript, that "we have a couple of sources" at the IRS and "we can get right in and get what we need."

One of the sources was revealed in the committee's evidence to be Vernon D. Acree, assistant commissioner of Internal Revenue, who was promoted in April 1972 to be commissioner of customs.

Activity on ambassadorships noted—The evidence released by the committee July 16 included data indicating that John Mitchell had a hand in ambassadorial appointments while he was attorney general. A memorandum to Nixon chief of staff Haldeman from his aide Gordon C. Strachan Dec. 2, 1971 said, "Concerning ambassadorships, Kalmbach will get a case-by-case determination from the attorney general as he did in the case of John Safer." Safer, a Washington, D.C. real estate developer, was said to have been solicited for a contribution and to have donated $250,000 to the Nixon campaign with the comment "that he wanted to be considered for an ambassadorship." According to the Strachan memo, "apparently, Safer was also referred to Herbert Kalmbach, who reiterated that his interest in an ambassadorship would be forwarded to the proper persons but that no quid pro quo could follow from the contribution."

Kalmbach currently was in prison for violation of election laws and promising an ambassadorship as reward for a campaign donation. The incident did not involve Safer, who had not been nominated for such a post. The Senate Watergate committee report issued July 13 cited a conflict on the issue between Kalmbach and White House aide Peter M. Flanigan, who reportedly was responsible for filling ambassadorships. Flanigan wrote the Senate committee that Kalmbach had been "misinformed" about his authorization to make the commitment. But Kalmbach testified that the commitment "came right out of Bob's [Haldeman] office."

Final witnesses heard. The Judiciary Committee concluded hearing witnesses July 17 with testimony from Herbert W. Kalmbach, President Nixon's former personal attorney.

Kalmbach, the ninth witness called, began his testimony July 16 after the panel completed two consecutive days of taking testimony from Charles W. Colson, a former special counsel to Nixon.

Both men currently were serving prison terms—Colson for obstruction of justice, Kalmbach for election law violations and promising an ambassadorship as reward for campaign contribution.

On July 12, the witness was Assistant Attorney General Henry E. Petersen, who had been in charge of the original Watergate investigation.

All of these sessions were closed.

Evidence release continues: *clandestine activities*—The House Judiciary Committee July 18 released a four-volume 2,090-page record of the evidence accumulated by its staff concerning clandestine activities sponsored by the White House. A 225-page rebuttal by the President's special counsel, James D. St. Clair, accompanied the publication of the evidence.

The evidence, much of which was already a part of the public record, specifically dealt with the operations of the "plumbers" investigative unit, wiretaps on 13 government officials and four newsmen, the White House-financed activities of political trickster Donald H. Segretti, activities by John J. Caulfield and Anthony T. Ulasewicz, who made secret inquiries for the White House, and the stillborn domestic surveillance plan of 1970, which called for the lifting of restraints against certain illegal activities.

The mass of evidence suggested that clandestine White House activities originated because of national security concerns but later became overtly political operations. The documents also showed that Nixon and his top aides were aware in March and April 1973 that some of the activities of the White House "plumbers" investigative unit were illegal.

The evidence cited White House concern about leaks of national security information and the highly secret wiretap program that was instituted in 1969 to combat the leaks. In 1970, the evidence indicated, the President was ready to approve implementation of the domestic surveillance plan proposed by White House aide Tom Charles Huston. Nixon rescinded his approval at the last minute because of objections from FBI Director J. Edgar Hoover, who refused to countenance the illegalties of the plan.

In 1971, White House efforts against news leaks took the form of 17 wiretaps against government officials and newsmen, as well as the creation of the "plumbers." Part of the evidence released was Nixon's assessment of the wiretaps, which he made known to John W. Dean 3rd, his counsel, Feb. 28, 1973. "They never helped. Just gobs and gobs of material: gossip and bullshitting," Nixon said. The evidence pointed out that two of the taps remained in effect even after the two officials in question—unnamed in the report, but widely known to be former National Security Council advisers Morton Halperin and Anthony Lake—had left the Administration and become foreign policy advisers to one of the 1972 Democratic presidential hopefuls.

As for the "plumbers," one previously unreleased document showed that Nixon was warned March 21, 1973 of the possible illegality of the "plumbers" 1971 break-in at the office of Daniel Ellsberg's psychiatrist. "That's an illegal search and seizure that may be sufficient for at least a mistrial," Nixon was told by aide John D. Ehrlichman, who was apparently referring to the then-ongoing trial of Ellsberg.

One previously unpublished memorandum, dated Sept. 20, 1971, discussed extensive plans by the "plumbers" to leak classified material about the 1963 assassination of South Vietnamese President Ngo Dinh Diem and the unsuccessful Bay of Pigs invasion of Cuba in 1961. In both instances, the emphasis was on placing the Democratic Party and President Kennedy in an adverse light.

St. Clair's defense of the President consisted of White House memorandums, including a hitherto unpublished 1973 affidavit by Kissinger, demonstrating Administration anxiety over leaks of classified information from 1969 through 1971. In addition, the defense volume reprinted many of the newspaper articles that supposedly prompted the President to authorize both the 17 wiretaps and the "plumbers." The defense did not deal with the main thrust of the Judiciary committee's presentation—that the two major White House intelligence gathering programs became highly politicized.

The ITT controversy—Two volumes of evidence on the Administration's handling of antitrust suits against International Telephone & Telegraph Corp. (ITT) were released by the committee July 19. St. Clair presented a 208-page collection of information defending Nixon's role in the ITT case to the House panel that same day.

No evidence in the material published by the House committee appeared to substantiate allegations that Nixon had ordered the Justice Department to drop its appeal of an antitrust case involving ITT because of ITT's promise to underwrite the 1972 Republican National Convention, then scheduled for San Diego. No government document supported the original contention of ITT's Washington lobbyist, Dita Beard, that the two were linked.

But the documents revealed numerous meetings in the 1969-1971 period between high Administration officials and ITT executives who waged an intense lobbying campaign in an effort to have the antitrust charges dropped.

The only new evidence included in the committee's information, most of it published previously, was a transcript of tape recorded conversation between Nixon and John Ehrlichman during a White House meeting April 19, 1971. George Shultz, then director of the Office of Management and Budget, was also present at the meeting, which was interrupted when Nixon telephoned then-Deputy Attorney General Richard Kleindienst, ordering him to drop a Justice Department appeal of one of the antitrust suits against ITT. Prior to the phone call, Nixon told Ehrlichman, "I don't want to know anything about the case. . . . I don't want to know about Geneen. I've met him and I don't know—I don't know whether ITT is bad, good or indifferent. But there is not going to be any more antitrust actions as long as I am in this chair."

In his phone conversation with Kleindienst a few minutes later, Nixon was explicit in his instructions regarding the ITT matter. "I want something clearly understood," Nixon said, "If it is not understood, [Richard] McLaren's ass is to be out within one hour. The IT&T thing—stay the hell out of it. Is that clear? That's an order." [McLaren was chief of the Justice Department's antitrust division.]

Nixon continued:

The order is to leave the God damned thing alone. Now, I've said this, Dick, a number of times, and you

fellows apparently don't get the me—, the message over there. I do not want McLaren to run around prosecuting people, raising hell about conglomerates, stirring things up at this point. Now, you keep him the hell out of that. Is that clear?

Or either he resigns. I'd rather have him out anyway. I don't like the son-of-a-bitch.

The question is, I know, that the jurisdiction—I know all the legal things, Dick, you don't have to spell out the legal—

That's right.

That's right. Don't file the brief.

Your—my order is to drop the God damn thing. Is that clear?

Nixon also vented his anger about McLaren's handling of antitrust matters during a conversation with Ehrlichman and Shultz that followed his call to Kleindienst.

Shultz's remark that he felt "conglomerates have taken a bum rap" on antitrust matters prompted Nixon to focus on McLaren. He was "a nice little fellow," Nixon said, "who's a good little antitrust lawyer out in Chicago. Now he comes in and all these bright little bastards that worked for the Antitrust Department for years and years and years and who hate business with a passion—any business—have taken over. . . ."

Nixon continued, "They've gone off on a kick, that'll make them big God damn trust busters. That was all right fifty years ago. Fifty years ago maybe it was a good thing for the country. It's not a good thing for the country today. . . ."

Nixon was so furious that he ordered McLaren fired "in one hour," adding that it would not be a face-saving departure with McLaren rewarded for his services by being named a federal judge.

In the aftermath of Nixon's phone call to Kleindienst, the Justice Department delayed bringing an appeal on the ITT case to the Supreme Court. On April 21, Nixon was persuaded by then Attorney General John Mitchell that it would be "political dynamite" to abandon the ITT appeal. (A transcript of this taped conversation also was published by the committee). Shortly thereafter, the ITT case was settled out of court while the delayed appeal was still pending and McLaren left the government after having been named a federal judge in Illinois.

Although Nixon yielded on the matter, the transcript showed that he complained to Mitchell that the business community "believes . . . we're a hell of a lot rougher on them in the antitrust than our predecessors were."

Although the committee established no direct link between ITT's promised campaign contributions and the Administration's settlement of the antitrust suits, Mitchell and Kleindienst were charged with having given "false testimony" about their roles in the case before the Senate Judiciary Committee. The House committee also questioned whether Nixon knew that his Administration's chief law enforcement officials had testified falsely in the committee's hearings on Kleindienst's nomination to succeed Mitchell as attorney general.

No determination was possible on the question of whether Nixon had willfully

concealed knowledge that his aides had testified untruthfully, the committee said, because Nixon had failed to comply with subpoenas for copies of the daily news summaries provided him during the Senate hearings, or with tapes of talks with his aides about the testimony given by Mitchell and Kleindienst.

In his defense of Nixon, St. Clair declared, "There exists no testimonial or documentary evidence to indicate that the President had any part, directly or indirectly, in the settlement of the ITT antitrust cases." St. Clair relied heavily on McLaren's sworn statement that neither the White House nor Mitchell nor Kleindienst had influenced his decision regarding settlement of the suit. However, St. Clair made no mention of the April 19, 1971 transcript.

The milk fund—The House committee released two volumes of evidence July 19 relating to charges that President Nixon had raised the federal support price of milk in March 1971 in return for pledges of large campaign contributions from major dairy cooperatives.

The panel drew no conclusions about the alleged link between the donations and the price increase, but it noted that the "President's refusal to comply with the committee's subpoena has left the evidence incomplete as to whether the milk producer contributions were made with the intent to influence the President's official acts or whether the President acquiesced in their acceptance with this knowledge." "If these elements were present," the committee concluded, "then the President's acceptance constituted bribery, whether or not the contributions actually influenced the price support decision."

In rebuttal, St. Clair declared, "There isn't a scintilla of evidence to demonstrate that any action was taken by the President because of any campaign contributions or pledges of contributions made by the dairymen to the President's re-election campaign. . . ." "Economic and traditional political considerations were the only basis of the decision to increase the price support level," St. Clair said, repeating arguments previously advanced by the White House.

Most of the material gathered by the committee, much of which had been obtained from the Senate Watergate committee, had already been published.

One of the few new pieces of evidence was the transcript of Nixon's meeting March 23, 1971 with seven top aides, including John Ehrlichman, John Connally, George Shultz and Clifford Hardin, at that time secretary of agriculture. Nixon asked Connally, who had briefed him earlier in the day, to review the price increase issue for those present at the White House meeting.

At the President's request, Connally focused on the political reasons warranting White House support of a milk price increase, although he also asserted that the action could be justified on economic grounds as well. Connally emphasized that the dairy co-ops were "organized, adamant and militant." They utilized a check-off system to levy funds from their large memberships, and Connally added, "they're amassing an enormous amount of money that they're going to put into political activities."

These political considerations, Connally said, necessitated swift action on the dairymen's request for a price increase. Rejecting arguments for postponement until the following year, Connally said, "They're going to make their association and their alliances this year and they're going to spend a lot of money this year in various Congressional and Senatorial races all over this United States. . . . If, if you do something for them this year, they think you've done it because they got a good case and because you're their friend. . . . If you wait, . . . it's still going to cost you an enormous amount of money next year, and you get no political advantage out of it."

Nixon then referred to a danger that the Administration could be outflanked because legislation pending in the House and Senate authorizing the increase seemed certain of passage. The dairy lobby had warned that a veto of the bill could "cost you Missouri, Wisconsin, South Dakota for sure [and a] veto will probably cost you Ohio, Kentucky, and Iowa," Connally told Nixon.

Nixon then summed up the discussion and indicated the action he would take: "My political judgment is that the Congress is going to pass it. I could not veto it. Not because they're milkers, but because they're farmers. And it would be just turning down the whole damn middle America. Uh, where, uh, we, uh, where we, uh, need support. And under the circumstances, I think the best thing to do is to just, uh, relax and enjoy it."

With the decision made to approve the increase, Connally then urged Nixon to make the best bargain possible. "Trade for this year and next" with the dairy industry, Connally said, suggesting that the Administration extract a pledge that no requests for another price increase would be made in 1972. "All right, make the best deal you can," Nixon said. "Let's let them know what we're doing," he added. Ehrlichman agreed: "Let's get credit." Subsequent references to the "two year deal" were cryptic:

Connally: Well, let's don't, let's don't trade the, uh, uh, through Agriculture, uh, on the merits.
President: Yeah.
Connally: Until, uh, some other conversations are had.
President: Yeah.
Hardin: [Unintelligible] we've got a little work to do. We've got to let [former Rep.] Page [Belcher, R, Okla.] that, uh—
Unidentified: What?
Hardin: I mean—[Sen.] Bob Dole [R, Kan.].
Connally: All I'm saying is you—
Ehrlichman: No. Later, because they're—
Connally: You're in this thing for everything you, you can get out of it. [Unintelligible]
Unidentified: Yeah.
Ehrlichman: You either hold your position now till you get the green light, couldn't you?
Connally: Oh, sure.

President: What?
Ehrlichman: Yeah, as I say, that Agriculture doesn't need to do anything right away.
Unidentified: He—
President: You, you're now thinking of the political offer?
Ehrlichman: In a day or so.

Nixon also suggested that before any public announcement of the price increase, the Administration should reap some political gain by telling two powerful Congressional leaders, House Ways and Means Committee Chairman Wilbur Mills (D, Ark.) and Speaker Carl Albert (D, Okla.), both strong backers of the pro-dairy industry legislation, that their support of the bills had caused the Administration to reverse itself in favor of their dairy constituents.

Just before the meeting concluded, Ehrlichman reminded Nixon that Special Counsel Charles Colson should be brought in with Dole to coordinate these complex maneuvers. Nixon responded: "Well, because Colson dealing with the, uh—Well, in any event, I think you got a good game plan."

(Colson had been the White House contact with the dairy industry and had told Nixon in a September 1970 memo of their pledge to contribute $2 million to his re-election campaign. Dole, who also served as Republican national chairman, had been another source of information about the proposed donations.)

Ehrlichman concluded the milk price discussion with a quip: "Better go get a glass of milk. Drink it while it's cheap."

The committee cited evidence, also published in the Senate Watergate report, that immediately following Nixon's meeting with his advisers, efforts were made by Ehrlichman and Herbert Kalmbach, Nixon's chief fund raiser, to seek reaffirmation of the dairymen's pledge of $2 million. It was also alleged that Nixon's decision authorizing the price increase was kept from public and the dairy leaders until their offer was confirmed.

Cox dismissal prelude detailed—According to evidence released by the committee July 20, Archibald Cox, the first Watergate special prosecutor, was warned by the White House as early as July 3, 1973 that his investigations were going too far and that he might be dismissed. Cox was fired Oct. 20, 1973 during a dispute over access to presidential tapes.

The panel's evidence included an affidavit by Elliot L. Richardson, the attorney general during Cox's tenure, who related that on July 3, 1973 he had received a complaint from White House chief of staff Alexander M. Haig Jr. about reports that Cox was investigating expenditures on Nixon's estate at San Clemente, Calif.

Richardson's affidavit, dated July 17, said that Haig had warned Nixon might "move on this to discharge Mr. Cox, and that it could not be a matter of Cox's charter to investigate the President." At Richardson's request, Cox issued a statement disclaiming the San Clemente investigation, but in a subsequent tele-

phone conversation, Haig told Richardson that the statement was inadequate. Richardson recalled that at this point Nixon interrupted the conversation to demand that Cox issue a stronger statement of denial within an hour.

Richardson said Haig called again on July 23 with a warning that "the 'boss' was very 'uptight' about Cox and . . . various of his activities, including letters to the IRS and the Secret Service . . . seeking information on guidelines for electronic surveillance." Haig said Nixon wanted "a tight line drawn with no further mistakes" and that "if Cox does not agree, we will get rid of Cox."

Richardson also recalled that at the end of a conversation with Nixon about Vice President Spiro Agnew in late September or early October 1973, (Agnew resigned Oct. 10, 1973) "the President said in substance, 'Now that we have disposed of that matter, we can go ahead and get rid of Cox.' There was nothing more said."

In addition to the Richardson affidavit, the committee's evidence included an account of Cox's requests to the White House, beginning May 30, 1973, that files possibly relating to Watergate be kept intact and that certain security measures be taken. Cox requested an inventory of files left by several of Nixon's former aides and—after former counsel John W. Dean's testimony before the Senate Watergate committee—a "detailed narrative," to be furnished by Nixon, covering the "conversations and incidents" mentioned by Dean.

According to the evidence, Cox complained on several later occasions that few of his demands were being met.

Recalling a brief conversation with Nixon on May 25, 1973, Richardson indicated in his affidavit that Cox's mandate was to have been restricted from the beginning. Referring to his statement three days earlier that executive privilege would not be invoked as to "testimony" or "discussions" concerning possible criminal conduct, Nixon told Richardson that such a waiver of privilege would not apply to "documents." Richardson said he had been unaware of the condition until then.

Nixon reviews Dean tapes—Evidence released by the Judiciary Committee July 20 included its transcript of a June 4, 1973 White House meeting during which Nixon reviewed still-secret tapes of potentially damaging conversations with former counsel John W. Dean 3rd. Reports of what Dean had been telling the Senate Watergate Committee staff had already begun to appear.

During the reviewing session with chief of staff Alexander M. Haig, press secretary Ronald Ziegler and White House assistant Stephen B. Bull, Nixon expressed concern over the disputed March 21 conversation and its implications of cover-up and hush money:

"Nixon: Well, as I told you, we do know we have one problem: It's the damn conversation of March 21 due to the fact that, uh, for the reasons (unintelligible). But I think we can handle that.

Haig: I think we ca—, can. That's the—

Nixon: Bob [Haldeman] can handle it. He'll get up there and say that—Bob will say, 'I was there; the President said—"

At several points in the meeting, Nixon repeated that the cover-up had first been fully disclosed to him on March 21, but conceded that he should have "reacted" before then: "Dean shouldn't have had to come in . . . which to his credit he did."

Apparently referring to all of his conversations with Dean, Nixon assessed his position: "Really the goddamn record is not bad, is it?" But it would not be "comfortable for me," he added, "because I was sitting there like a dumb turkey."

Returning to the March 21 problem, Nixon summarized the situation near the end of the June meeting:

"What I was saying about this crap is that it's reassuring up to a point, but in fact, uh, at least, in this whole business we, we sat there and we conspired about a coverup [unintelligible] or not. We did talk about it on the twenty-first. That's a tough conversation. Unless Haldeman explains it—which he will. [Sighs] But I think we can survive that, too."

In an exchange with Bull, Nixon referred to a Dean meeting (April 15, 1973) of which, according to White House statements, a tape was never made:

"Nixon: March twenty-first. I don't need April, I don't need April fifteen. I need the sixteenth. (Unintelligible) correct. There were two on April sixteenth. I just want the second (unintelligible). You can skip the—April fifteenth.

Bull: And March twenty-first.

Nixon: March twenty-first, that's right. I have those."

Nixon's, Haldeman's strong roles described—President Nixon was always "very, very much in charge" of Administration activities, and H. R. Haldeman—Nixon's "alter ego" and chief of staff—was the "implementer," according to testimony released by the committee July 24.

Former presidential assistant Alexander P. Butterfield (currently head of the Federal Aviation Administration) had told the committee that Nixon had been in firm control of the 1972 re-election campaign.

"He made the big decisions . . . Anything having to do with strategy would emanate from the President and be carried to the [re-election] committee via Haldeman and Gordon Strachan," Butterfield said.

Describing White House operations, Butterfield called Haldeman "almost the other President," adding "I can't emphasize that enough." Butterfield said he knew of no occasion when Haldeman withheld information from Nixon.

Cautioning that he was not speaking in a "derogatory manner," Butterfield described Nixon as being intensely interested in the more mundane details of the Administration, engaging in a year's ex-

change of memorandums on the location of the White House tennis court, sending a memo on the "fine restrooms" in Yugoslavia compared with the "shabby" facilities along the Washington Mall, expressing concern as to whether salad should be served at state dinners.

The President "was 100 per cent in charge," Butterfield said.

St. Clair defends the President. St. Clair's defense of Nixon took the form of oral arguments before a closed session of the Judiciary committee July 18 and a 151-page written brief made public July 20. His written brief contended that there was no "conclusive evidence" of Presidential actions that would warrant impeachment.

According to committee members, St. Clair's oral arguments were consistent with his strategy of focusing on the payment of "hush money" to Watergate conspirator E. Howard Hunt Jr., which, the President's special counsel argued, was the only charge that could potentially constitute an impeachable offense.

In his final arguments, St. Clair surprised the committee by introducing the edited transcript of part of a taped conversation that the President had refused to turn over to the committee despite a subpoena. The transcript was of part of a March 22, 1973 conversation between Nixon and Haldeman and it concerned aid to the Watergate defendants. St. Clair later told newsmen that the gist of Nixon's remarks to Haldeman was that he was unaware of and disapproved of blackmail payments to Hunt.

The transcript excerpt, as given the committee, was reprinted in the Baltimore Sun July 19:

H.—Well—What's the (inaudible)—still the Cubans seem to be the least matter of concern—they're they're fanatics—and they don't seem to be really too concerned about their (inaudible) and their needs are fairly minimal. And Dean confirms again that Liddy—Liddy is enjoying—Liddy's in jail—he didn't stay out—he just said I want to start serving my term—and he's at Danbury and thoroughly enjoying it. It's a little strange.

P.—That uh judge gave him 35 years.

H.—(inaudible) As long as he thinks we are going to be of some help to him someday then he thinks (inaudible) has five kids. And all he is concerned about is that is there is enough income to take care of his kids and that's being taken care of right now by his father (inaudible).

P.—Damn it—when people are in jail there is every right for people to raise money for them. (inaudible) And that's all there is to it. I don't think we ought to (inaudible)—there's got to be funds—I'm not being—I don't mean to be blackmailed by Hunt—that goes too far, but for taking care of these people that are in jail—My God they did this for—we are sorry for them—we do it out of compassion, yet I don't (inaudible) about that—people have contributed (inaudible) report on that damn thing—there's no report required (inaudible) what happens. Do you agree? What else (inaudible).

H.—That's why I—it seems to me that there is no real problem on obstruction of justice as far as Dean is concerned, and, I think, it doesn't seem to me we are obstructing justice.

P.—Yeah.

H.—People have pled guilty.

P.—Yeah.

H.—When a guy goes and pleads guilty are you · obstructing justice? (inaudible). His argument is that when you read the law that uh

P.—Yeah—but Dean didn't do it. Dean I don't

think—I don't think Dean had anything to do with the obstruction. He didn't deliver the money—that's the point. I think what really set him off was when Hunt's lawyer saw him at this party, and said Hunt made $120,000—well that was—kind of very (inaudible)—that was a shot across the bow. You understand that that would look like a straight damn blackmail if Dean had gotten the money (inaudible). You see what I mean? Let's come to the other. When you talk about the wagons around the White House, Bob, what really happens here is, uh, that you really have to take a hard look at the situation (inaudible). I realize the weak (inaudible). I don't think that we (inaudible) had anybody candidly suggested that Magruder is not aware that there is a (inaudible).

H.—I don't think I really don't know—but I had—my opinion. I had no knowledge—my opinion is that he knew and—uh from the way he talks that's the point. (inaudible) is convinced of that. Dean thinks so.

P.—Although (inaudible) it's Magruder's word against the others (inaudible).

(The reference in the transcript to the 35-year prison sentence given by U.S. District Court Judge John J. Sirica caused some observers to question the accuracy of the date of the March 22 transcript. Sirica sentenced Hunt and Liddy March 23, 1973.)

St. Clair's maneuver provoked sharp criticism from committee chairman Peter W. Rodino Jr. (D, N.J.), who said it showed "an effort to keep from the committee evidence that it should rightly have had." There was little support among other committee members for St. Clair's tactic. Rep. George Danielson (D, Calif.) said it was improper for a lawyer in a closing argument to offer evidence that was not already on the record. Rep. Robert McClory (R, Ill.) called it a "bad tactic." But Rep. David W. Dennis (R, Ind.) said, "I want all the evidence we can get."

St. Clair justified his action, contending that the reason for the late introduction was that Dean appeared to have changed his testimony regarding the March 21, 1973 meeting with Nixon. After telling the Senate Watergate Committee that the question of money had been "left hanging," St. Clair said, Dean had testified to the Judiciary panel that "maybe something had been resolved." Accordingly, the President decided to turn over the March 22 transcript to show that he was against blackmail payments to Hunt, St. Clair said.

In his written brief, St. Clair asserted that "in light of the complete absence of any conclusive evidence demonstrating Presidential wrongdoings sufficient to justify the grave action of impeachment, the committee must conclude that a recommendation of impeachment is not justified."

Citing the March 22, 1973 conversation between Haldeman and Nixon, St. Clair declared that Nixon should not have been named an unindicted co-conspirator by the Watergate grand jury. "Like a composite photograph," the brief said, "the individual parts of this portion of the indictment may be literally correct; but the artful language and distorted juxtaposition of the parts resulted in a total impression that is grossly distorted insofar as the imputed involvement of the President in the Watergate cover-up is concerned." Moreover, the President's role in the critical March 21, 1973 meeting with Dean was that of a devil's advocate, as the President sought to learn about all facets of the problem, the brief said.

On the other allegations of wrongdoing, St. Clair said:

■ Nixon would have been derelict in his duties if he had not authorized both the 1969 wiretapping program and the 1971 "plumbers" unit to stop national security leaks. In neither case did Nixon know of or order any illegal activities.

■ The decision to settle the antitrust suit against ITT did not result from a promised campaign contribution. Nor was the President under a legal obligation to reveal alleged false testimony by Mitchell and then-Deputy Attorney General Richard Kleindienst in the ITT case, since neither had been charged with perjury.

■ The President's decision to raise milk price supports in 1971 was unrelated to a campaign pledge by milk producers.

■ There was no indication that the IRS harassed White House political enemies, although there were suggestions that the agency be used to do so.

Doar says evidence merits impeachment. John M. Doar, special counsel to the House Judiciary Committee, urged committee members July 19 to recommend the impeachment of President Nixon on one or more charges. Doar was seconded by Albert E. Jenner Jr., special Republican counsel to the committee.

Abandoning the neutrality that had characterized his staff's 10-week presentation of evidence, Doar presented to the panel five sets of proposed articles of impeachment and a 306-page summary of evidence, which he said buttressed his arguments. Asked by newsmen after the committee's closed session that day if he had doubts about his pro-impeachment stance, Doar replied, "No, I don't regard it as a close call."

The proposed articles of impeachment, 29 in all, were composed by both the members and staff of the committee. Essentially, the articles centered on four allegations against the President:

He obstructed justice by participating in the cover-up that followed the Watergate break-in.

He abused the powers of the presidency by invading the civil rights and privacy of U.S. citizens and by misusing or attempting to misuse agencies of the U.S. government.

His refusal to honor subpoenas by the Judiciary Committee was contemptuous of Congress.

He committed fraud in connection with his income taxes and expenditure of public funds on his personal property.

The summary of evidence presented by Doar was intended to draw together the mountain of impeachment data into a cohesive argument that, in the view of the committee staff, "demonstrates various abuses of Presidential power." The

document provided a detailed narrative of the Watergate case and information on the other alleged abuses of power.

"Circumstances strongly suggest," the summary said, "that President Nixon decided, shortly after learning of the Watergate break-in, on a plan to cover up the identities of high officials of the White House and the Committee for the Re-election of the President directly involved in the illegal operation." Until after the 1972 election, the summary added, "President Nixon's policy of containment—of 'cutting the loss'—worked . . . because two of the President's assistants, John Dean, counsel to the President, and Herbert Kalmbach, personal attorney to the President, assigned to carry out the President's policy, did their jobs well—with the full support of the power and authority of the office of President of the United States."

Contrary to Nixon's statement that on Sept. 15, 1972 he knew nothing of the case, the summary contended he had already done the following things: met with H.R. Haldeman, his chief of staff, and John N. Mitchell, his campaign manager, both of whom were "fully apprised of" White House connections to Watergate; arranged a misleading explanation for Mitchell's resignation; received from L. Patrick Gray 3rd, then acting director of the Federal Bureau of Investigation (FBI), a warning about White House interference in the FBI's Watergate inquiry; "prevented" a personal appearance before the Watergate grand jury by Maurice H. Stans, his chief campaign fund raiser and former commerce secretary; and "made an untrue public statement about Dean's 'complete investigation' of the Watergate matter," when in fact Dean "acted to narrow and frustrate the FBI investigation" and "conducted no independent investigation of his own."

The summary also reviewed Nixon's March 21, 1973 meeting with Dean, during which Dean detailed the payment of "hush money" to the convicted Watergate conspirators: "The President did not condemn the payments or the involvement of his closest aides. He did not direct that the activity be stopped. The President did not express any surprise or shock. He did not report it to the proper investigatory authorities." Subsequently, the summary added, the President repeatedly modified his accounts of the meeting.

"The 'report' that the President . . . requested Dean to make in March 1973 was one that was designed to mislead investigators and insulate the President from charges of concealment," the summary asserted.

When his associates lied or "stonewalled" to sustain the cover-up, the summary said, "the President condoned this conduct, approved it, directed it, rewarded it and, in some cases, advised witnesses on how to impede the investigators." Moreover, when the cover-up began to unravel in late March 1973,

"there is clear and convincing evidence that the President took over in late March the active management of the cover-up," the Doar summary stated.

Other areas touched by the summary: wiretapping and other "illegal and improper" intelligence gathering activities; the burglary of Daniel Ellsberg's psychiatrist's office and the concealment of those activities; use of the Internal Revenue Service (IRS) in improper ways; the International Telephone & Telegraph (ITT) case; the milk-fund case; and expenditures on Nixon's personal properties in Florida and California.

GOP counsel cautions vs impeachment. Samuel A. Garrison, the newly designated special Republican counsel, cautioned the Judiciary committee July 22 against impeaching the President unless it appeared probable he would be convicted and removed from office by the Senate. (Garrison, who was deputy minority counsel, was given the title of chief minority counsel July 21, replacing Jenner, who the panel's Republican leadership thought had been too pro-impeachment. Jenner remained as an associate counsel.)

Even if Nixon were shown to have committed an impeachable offense, it might not be in "the best interests of the country" to impeach and remove him from office, Garrison said. The primary purpose of impeachment was not to punish the President, Garrison stated, but "to protect the country's system of government, and thereby protect the people."

Other arguments advanced by Garrison were that Nixon should not be impeached for "abuse of power" unless he had done things other presidents hadn't. While not passing on Nixon's guilt or innocence of tax fraud, Garrison questioned if the framers of the Constitution had intended such an offense to be impeachable. The President should not be impeached for refusing to comply with committee subpoenas, he said, unless Nixon's refusal was not "justifiable or excusable." Garrison also suggested to the committee that Nixon's reliance on executive privilege to withhold evidence was analogous to invocation of the 5th Amendment against self-incrimination. In that context, he said, committee members should not draw adverse inferences from Nixon's refusal to honor the subpoenas.

Hogan will vote to impeach. Rep. Lawrence J. Hogan (R, Md.) July 23 became the first Republican member of the House Judiciary Committee to announce that he would vote for President Nixon's impeachment. In a surprise announcement, Hogan said, "Nixon has, beyond a reasonable doubt, committed impeachable offenses, which, in my judgment, are of sufficient magnitude that he should be removed from office."

Hogan, a moderate conservative who had been a staunch defender of the President in the past, charged that Nixon had "lied repeatedly, deceiving public officials and the American people. He has withheld information necessary for our system of justice to work. Instead of cooperating with prosecutors and investigators, as he said publicly, he concealed and covered up evidence, and coached witnesses so that their testimony would show things that really were not true. He tried to use the CIA to impede and thwart the investigation of Watergate by the FBI. He approved the payment of what he knew to be blackmail to buy the silence of an important Watergate witness."

Nixon "praised and rewarded those whom he knew had committed perjury," Hogan continued. "He personally helped to orchestrate a scenario of events, facts and testimony to cover up wrongdoing in the Watergate scandal and to throw investigators and prosecutors off the track. He actively participated in an extended and extensive conspiracy to obstruct justice. To my mind," Hogan concluded, "he is guilty beyond a reasonable doubt of having committed these impeachable offenses."

Dean Burch, President Nixon's political adviser, immediately denounced Hogan's defection, charging that his decision was motivated by political considerations. Hogan was seeking the Republican nomination for governor.

Hogan conceded that his decision could cost him the party nomination, but most observers believed the vote for impeachment would aid him in the general election where Democrats outnumbered Republicans 3 to 1.

Nixon aides condemn panel, staff—White House press secretary Ronald L. Ziegler July 19 accused Judiciary Committee chief counsel John M. Doar of conducting a "kangaroo court," charged the committee with making a "total shambles of what should have been a fair proceeding," and said Chairman Peter Rodino had presented a false "picture of fairness."

Referring to Doar's presentation of proposed impeachment articles and strong condemnations of Nixon's conduct, Ziegler said Doar was acting in a "partisan" and "radical" manner "to run the President out of office."

Ziegler maintained that the evidence absolved Nixon of authorizing hush money payments, adding that the committee "can either look at the facts and make their judgment on facts or they can do it in a partisan, duplicitous, false way, like Mr. Doar and the partisans on that committee are doing."

Ziegler said Nixon would have no direct comment on the proceedings, but stated, "I am speaking as the President's spokesman."

Presidential counselor Dean Burch continued the attack July 20, calling Doar and minority counsel Albert E. Jenner Jr. "hired guns" using a "blunderbuss" approach to attack Nixon. Burch called the committee's proceedings "a black spot on jurisprudence."

Ford discloses hearing tapes—Vice President Gerald R. Ford told a news conference July 18 that because he was concerned about discrepancies between White House and House Judiciary Committee transcripts of presidential tapes he had requested and received permission to listen to portions of two tapes.

Although he had said earlier that it would be improper for him to hear the White House recordings, Ford said he had concluded that it was now in his "interest" to "find out the quality."

Ford said he now understood how there "could be a different interpretation of the words that were spoken." Asked which version was more accurate, he replied, "I think you could read it either way."

Ford did not identify the tapes he had heard, but said he had listened to one at the White House and the other at an unidentified location.

Replying to an unrelated question, Ford said he would be "highly selective" in his campaigning for Congressional candidates in the fall elections. Ford indicated that in areas where there were "first-class" Democrats running, he might not aid the Republicans.

Broad presidential privilege denied. The Supreme Court ruled 8–0 July 24 that President Nixon must provide "forthwith" the tapes and documents relating to 64 White House conversations subpoenaed by special Watergate prosecutor Leon Jaworski for the pending Watergate cover-up trial of six former presidential aides.

The decision did not mention presidential impeachment or the current impeachment inquiry in the House, and it defined the limits on presidential privilege on the relatively narrow grounds of the evidentiary needs imposed by Watergate criminal cases. But the decision was expected to have broad impact on Congressional and public opinion and further erode Nixon's position in relation to the Watergate scandals.

In an opinion written by Chief Justice Warren E. Burger, a Nixon appointee, the court said that a generalized claim of executive privilege, while not explicitly provided by the Constitution, was "constitutionally based." But in the current case, Burger continued, such an assertion of privilege "must yield to the demonstrated, specific need for evidence in a pending criminal trial." [See text, pp. 202–206]

In a statement issued late the same day from San Clemente, Calif., Nixon said he had instructed special counsel James D. St. Clair, who had argued for the President before the court, to "take whatever measures are necessary" to comply with the decision "in all respects."

Addressing a secondary issue in a footnote to the opinion, the court left standing a grand jury citation of Nixon as an unindicted co-conspirator in the cover-up case. Calling this issue "unnecessary" to resolution of the privilege question, Burger said the court had "improvi-

dently" granted a White House petition for review of District Court Judge John J. Sirica's refusal to expunge the citation. The court also denied a White House request that the court examine the grand jury's evidence to determine if the citation was justified.

Before dealing with the primary issue of confidentiality of presidential conversations, Burger rejected White House contentions that the tape dispute was an internal issue within the executive branch and should not be considered by the court. A "mere assertion of a claim of 'intra-branch' dispute," Burger wrote, was insufficient. The court noted that regulations establishing the independence of Jaworski's office had the force of law and had not been revoked by the attorney general. Under such conditions, the court said, Jaworski had the standing to pursue specific requests for applicable evidence through the courts, if necessary.

Burger also ruled that Jaworski had made sufficient preliminary showing that the potential evidence in the tapes and documents was both relevant and necessary to a criminal proceeding. And, because of the co-conspirator citations of Nixon and others, their statements could be preliminarily deemed admissible at trial.

Turning to the White House argument that the separation of powers doctrine should preclude judicial review of a claim of presidential privilege, Burger wrote that while one branch's interpretation of its powers "is due great respect from the others," the court must currently reaffirm a principle enunciated by an earlier court (in Marbury vs. Madison, 1803): "it is emphatically the province and duty of the Judicial department to say what the law is."

Burger said the powers constitutionally vested in the courts "can no more be shared with the executive branch than the chief executive, for example, can share with the judiciary the veto power, or the Congress share with the judiciary the power to override a presidential veto. Any other conclusion would be contrary to the basic concept of separation of powers and the checks and balances that flow from the scheme of a tripartite government."

Burger conceded that a President's need for candor and objectivity from advisers deserved "great deference from the courts." But a claim of privilege based solely on the "broad, undifferentiated claim of public interest in the confidentiality of such conversations," Burger continued, causes a confrontation with "other values."

Without a claim of need to protect "military, diplomatic or sensitive national security secrets," the court said, the confidentiality of presidential communications would not be "diminished" by submission of the material to Judge Sirica for private inspection under strict security precautions.

On the other hand, the court said, the impediment imposed upon the administration of justice by such a claim of ab-

(Continued on Page 206)

Text of Supreme Court Decision in Presidential Tapes Case

A

Supreme Court of the United States

United States Petitioner, 73-1766 V. Richard M. Nixon, President of the United States, Et)

Richard M. Nixon, President of the United States, Petitioner, 73-1834 V. United States.

On Writs of Certiorari to the United States Court of Appeals for the District of Columbia Circuit Before Judgment.

B

(July 24, 1974)

Mr. Chief Justice Burger delivered the opinion of the Court.

These cases present for review the denial of a motion, filed on behalf of the President of the United States, in the case of United States v. Mitchell et al. (D.C. Crim. No. 74-110), to quash a third party subpoena duces tecum issued by the United States District Court for the District of Columbia, pursuant to Fed. Rule Crim. Proc. 17 (c). The subpoena directed the President to produce certain tape recordings and documents relating to his conversations with aides and advisers. The Court rejected the President's
C claims of absolute executive privilege, of lack of jurisdiction, and of failure to satisfy the requirements of Rule 17 (c). The President appealed to the Court of Appeals. We granted the United States' petition for certiorari before judgment, [1] and also the President's responsive cross-petition for certiorari before judgment, [2] because of the public importance of the issues presented and the need for their prompt resolution. — U.S. —. — (1974).

On March 1, 1974, a grand jury of the United States District Court for the District of Columbia returned an indictment charging seven named individuals [3] with various offenses, including conspiracy to defraud the United States and to obstruct justice.
D Although he was not designated as such in the indictment, the grand jury named the President, among others, as an unindicted co-conspirator. [4] On April 18, 1974, upon motion of the special prosecutor, see N. 8, infra, a subpoena duces tecum was issued pursuant to Rule 17 (c) to the President by the United States District Court and made returnable on May 2, 1974. This subpoena required the production, in advance of the September 9 trial date, of certain tapes, memoranda, papers, transcripts, or other writings relating to certain precisely identified meetings between the President and others. [5] The special prosecutor was able to fix the time, place and persons present at these discussions because the White House daily logs and appointment records had been delivered to him.

E On April 30, the President publicly released edited transcripts of 43 conversations; portions of 20 conversations subject to subpoena in the present case were included. On May 1, 1974, the President's counsel filed a "special appearance" and a motion to quash the subpoena, under Rule 17 (c). This motion was accompanied by a formal claim of privilege. At a subsequent hearing, [6] further motions to expunge the grand jury's action naming the President as an unindicted co-conspirator and for protective orders against the disclosure of that information were filed or raised orally by counsel for the President.

On May 20, 1974, the District Court denied the motion to quash and the motions to expunge and for pro-
F tective orders. —F. Supp.— (1974). It further ordered "the President or any subordinate officer, official or employee with custody or control of the documents or objects subpoenaed," id. at—, to deliver to the District Court, on or before May 31, 1974, the originals of all subpoenaed items, as well as an index and analysis of those items, together with tape copies of those portions of the subpoenaed recordings for which transcripts had been released to the public by the President on April 30. The District Court rejected jurisdictional challenges based on a contention that the dispute was nonjusticiable because it was between the special prosecutor and the chief executive and hence "intraexecutive" in character; it also rejected the
G contention that the judiciary was without authority to review an assertion of executive privilege by the President. The court's rejection of the first challenge was based on the authority and powers vested in the special prosecutor by the regulation promulgated by the Attorney General; the court concluded that a justiciable controversy was represented. The second challenge was held to be foreclosed by the decision in Nixon v. Sirica, —U.S. App. D.C.—, 487 F 2d 700 (1973).

The District Court held that the judiciary, not the President, was the final arbiter of a claim of executive privilege. The court concluded that, under the circumstances of this case, the presumptive privilege was overcome by the special prosecutor's prima facie "demonstration of need sufficiently compelling to warrant judicial examination in chambers. . . ." —F. Supp., At—. The court held, finally, that the special prosecutor had satisfied the requirements of Rule 17 (c). The District Court stayed its order pending appellate review on condition that review was sought before 4 P.M., May 24. The court further provided that matters filed under seal remain under seal when transmitted as part of the record.

On May 24, 1974, the President filed a timely notice of appeal from the District Court order, and the certified record from the District Court was docketed in the United States Court of Apeals for the District of Columbia Circuit. On the same day, the President also filed a petition for writ of mandamus in the Court of Appeals seeking review of the District Court order.

Later on May 24, the special prosecutor also filed, in this Court, a petition for a writ of certiorari before judgment. On May 31, the petition was granted with an expedited briefing schedule. —U.S.—(1974). On June 6, the President filed, under seal, a cross-petition for writ of certiorari before judgment. This cross-petition was granted June 15, 1974, —U.S.—(1974), and the case was set for argument on July 8, 1974.

I—JURISDICTION

The threshold question presented is whether the May 20, 1974, order of the District Court was an appealable order and whether this case was properly "in," 28 U.S.C. Section 1254, the United States Court of Appeals when the petition for certiorari was filed in this court. Court of Appeals jurisdiction under 28 U.S.C. Section 1291 encompasses only "final decisions of the District Courts." Since the appeal was timely filed and all other procedural requirements were met, the petition is properly before this court for consideration if the District Court order was final. 28 U.S.C. Section 1254(1); 28 U.S.C. section 2101 (E).

The finality requirement of 28 U.S.C. Section 1291 embodies a strong Congressional policy against piecemeal reviews, and against obstructing or impeding an ongoing judicial proceeding by interlocutory appeals. See, e.g. Cobbledick v. United States, 309 U.S. 232, 324-326 (1940). This requirement ordinarily promotes judicial efficiency and hastens the ultimate termination of litigation. In applying this principle to an order denying a motion to quash and requiring the production of evidence pursuant to a subpoena duces tecum, it has been repeatedly held that the order is not final and hence not appealable. United States v. Ryan, 402 U.S. 5330, 532 (1971); Cobbledick v. United States, 309 U.S. 322 (1940); Alexander v. United States, 201 U.S. 117 (1906). This court has

"Consistently held that the necessity for expedition in the administration of the criminal law justifies putting one who seeks to resist the production of desired information to a choice between compliance with a trial court's order to produce prior to any review of that order, and resistance to that order with the concomitant possibility of an adjudication of contempt if his claims are rejected on appeal." United States v. Ryan, 402 U.S. 530, 533 (1971).

The requirement of submitting to contempt, however, is not without exception and in some instances the purposes underlying the finality rule require a different result. For example, in Perlman v. United States, 247 U.S. 7 (1918), a subpoena had been directed to a third party requesting certain exhibits; the appellant, who owned the exhibits, sought to raise a claim of privilege. The Court held an order compelling production was appealable because it was unlikely that the third party would risk a contempt situation in order to allow immediate review of the appellant's claim of privilege. id., at 12–13. That case fell within the "limited class of cases where denial of immediate review would render impossible any review whatsoever of an individual's claims." United States v. Ryan, Supra, at 533.

Here too the traditional contempt avenue to immediate appeal is peculiarly inappropriate due to the unique setting in which the question arises. To require a President of the United States to place himself in the posture of disobeying an order of a court merely to trigger the procedural mechanism for review of the ruling would be unseemly, and present an unnecessary occasion for constitutional confrontation between two branches of the Government. Similarly, a Federal judge should not be placed in the posture of issuing a citation to a President simply in order to invoke review. The issue whether a President can be cited for contempt would itself engender protracted litigation and would further delay both review on the merits of his claim of privilege and the ultimate termination of the underlying criminal action for which his evidence is sought. These considerations lead us to conclude that the order of the District Court was an appealable order. The appeal from that order was therefore properly "in" the Court of Appeals, and the case is now properly before the Court on the writ of certiorari before judgment. 28 U.S.C. section 1254; 28 U.S.C. section 2101 (E). Gay v. Ruff, 292 U.S. 25, 30 (1934). [7]

II—JUSTICIABILITY

In the District Court, the President's counsel argued that the court lacked jurisdiction to issue the subpoena because the matter was an intra-branch dispute between a subordinate and superior office of the executive branch and hence not subject to judicial resolution. That argument has been renewed in this Court with emphasis on the contention that the dispute does not present a "case" or "controversy" which can be adjudicated in the Federal courts. The President's counsel argues that the Federal courts should not intrude into areas committed to the other branches of Government. He views the present dispute as essentially a "jurisdictional" dispute within the executive branch which he analogizes to a dispute between two Congressional committees. Since the executive branch has exclusive authority and absolute discretion to decide whether to prosecute a case, Confiscation Cases, 7 Wall. 454 (1869), United States v. Cox, 342 F. 2D 167, 171 (CA5), cert. denied, 381 U.S. 935 (1965), it is contended that a President's decision is final in determining what evidence is to be used in a given criminal case.

Although his counsel concedes the President has delegated certain specific powers to the special prosecutor, he has not "waived nor delegated to the special prosecutor the President's duty to claim privilege as to all materials . . . which fall within the President's inherent authority to refuse to disclose to any executive officer." Brief for the President 47. The special prosecutor's demand for the items therefore presents, in the view of the President's counsel, a political question under Baker v. Carr, 369 U.S. (1969), since it involves a "textually demonstrable" grant of power under Art. II.

The mere assertion of a claim of an "intra-branch dispute," without more, has never operated to defeat Federal jurisdiction; justiciability does not depend on such a surface inquiry. In United States v. ICC, 337 U.S. 426 (1949), the Court observed, "Courts must look behind names that symbolize the parties to determine whether a justiciable case or controversy is presented," id., at 430, see also: Powell v. McCormack, 395 U.S. 486 (1969); ICC v. Jersey City, 322 U.S. 503 (1944): United States ex rel Chapman v. FPC, 345 U.S. 153 (1953); Secretary of Agriculture v. United States, 347 U.S. 645 (1954); FMB v. Isbrandsten Co. 356 U.S. 481, 482 N. 2 (1958); United States v. Marine Bank Corp., —U.S.—(1974), and United States v. Connecticut National Bank, —U.S. — (1974).

Our starting point is the nature of the proceeding for which the evidence is sought—here a pending criminal prosecution. It is a judicial proceeding in a Federal court alleging violation of Federal laws and is brought in the name of the United States as sovereign. Berger v. United States, 295 U.S. 78, 88 (1935). Under the authority of Art. II, Sec. 2, Congress has vested in the Attorney General the power to conduct the criminal litigation of the United States Government. 28 U.S. C. Sec. 316. It has also vested in him the power to appoint subordinate officers to assist him in the discharge of his duties. 28 U.S.C. Secs. 509, 510, 515, 533. Acting pursuant to those statutes, the Attorney General has delegated the authority to represent the United States in these particular matters to a special prosecutor with unique authority and tenure. [8] The regulation gives the special prosecutor explicit power to contest the innovation of executive privilege in the process of seeking evidence deemed relevant to the performance of these specially delegated duties. [9] 38 Fed. 4EG. 30739.

So long as this regulation is extant it has the force of law. In Accardi v. Shaughnessy, 347 U.S. 260 (1953), regulations of the Attorney General delegated certain of his discretionary power to the Board of Immigration Appeals and required that board to exercise its own discretion on appeals in deportation cases. The Court held that so long as the Attorney General's regulations remained operative, he denied himself the authority to exercise the discretion delegated to the board even though the original authority was his and he could reassert it by amending the regulations. Service v. Dulles, 354 U.S. 363, 388 (1957), and Vitarelli v. Seaton, 359 U.S. 535 (1959), reaffirmed the basic holding of Accardi.

Here, as in Accardi, it is theoretically possible for the Attorney General to amend or revoke the regulation defining the special prosecutor's authority. But he has not done so. [10] So long as this regulation remains in force the executive branch is bound by it, and indeed the United States as the sovereign composed of the three branches is bound to respect and to enforce it. Moreover, the delegation of authority to the special prosecutor in this case is not an ordinary delegation by the Attorney General to a subordinate officer: With the authorization of the President, the acting Attorney General provided in the regulation that the special prosecutor was not to be removed without the "consensus" of eight designated leaders of congress. Note 8, Supra.

The demands of and the resistance to the subpoena present an obvious controversy in the ordinary sense, but that alone is not sufficient to meet Constitutional standards. In the Constitutional sense, controversy means more than disagreement and conflict; rather it means the kind of controversy courts traditionally resolve. Here at issue is the production or nonproduction of specified evidence deemed by the special prosecutor to be relevant and admissible in a pending criminal case. It is sought by one official of the Government within the scope of his express authority; it is resisted by the chief executive on the ground of his duty to preserve the confidentiality of the communications of the President. Whatever the correct answer on the merits, these issues are "of a type which are traditionally justiciable." United States v. ICC, 337 U.S., at 430.

The independent special prosecutor with his asserted need for the subpoenaed material in the underlying criminal prosecution is opposed by the President with his steadfast assertion of privilege against disclosure of the material. This setting assures there is "that concrete adverseness which sharpens the presentation of issues upon which the Court so largely depends for illumination of difficult constitutional questions," Baker v. Carr, 369 U.S., at 204. Moreover, since the matter is one arising in the regular course of a Federal criminal prosecution, it is within the traditional scope of Art. III Power. id., at 198.

In light of the uniqueness of the setting in which the conflict arises, the fact that both parties are officers of the executive branch cannot be viewed as a barrier to justiciability. It would be inconsistent with the appliable law and regulation, and unique facts of this case to conclude other than that the special prosecutor has standing to bring this action and that justiciable controversy is presented for decision.

III—RULE 17 (C)

The subpoena duces tecum is challenged on the ground that the special prosecutor failed to satisfy the requirements of Fed. Rule Crim. Proc. 17 (c), which governs the issuance of subpoenas duces tecum in Federal criminal proceedings. If we sustained this challenge, there would be no occasion to reach the claim of privilege asserted with respect to the subpoenaed material. Thus we turn to the question whether the requirements of Rule 17 (C) have been satisfied. See Arkansas-Louisiana Gas Co. v. Dept of Public Utilities, 304 U.S. 61, 64 (1938); Ashwander v. Tennessee Valley Authority, 297 U.S. 288, 346–347 (1936). (Brandeis, J. concurring.)

Rule 17 (C) provides:

"A subpoena may also command the person to whom it is directed to produce the books, papers, documents or other objects designated therein. The Court on motion made promptly may quash or modify the subpoena if compliance would be unreasonable or oppressive. The Court may direct that books, papers, documents or objects designated in the subpoena be produced before the Court at a time prior to the trial or prior to the time when they are to be offered in evidence and may upon their production permit the books, papers, documents or objects or portions thereof to be inspected by the parties and their attorneys."

A subpoena for documents may be quashed if their production would be "unreasonable or oppressive," but not otherwise. The leading case in this Court interpreting this standard is Bowman Dairy Co. v. United States, 341 U.S. 214 (1950). This case recognized certain fundamental characteristics of the subpoena duces tecum in criminal cases: (1) It was not intended to provide a means of discovery for criminal cases. 10., at 220; (2) Its chief innovation was to expedite the trial by providing a time and place before trial for the inspection of subpoenaed materials. [11] id. As both parties agree, cases decided in the wake of Bowman have generally followed Judge Weinfeld's formulation in United States v. Iozia, 13 I.R.D., 335, 338 (SDNY 1952), as to the required showing. Under this test, in order to require production prior to trial, the moving party must show: (1) that the documents are evidentiary [12] and relevant; (2) that they are not otherwise procurable reasonably in advance of trial by exercise of due diligence; (3) that the party cannot properly prepare for trial without such production and inspection in advance of trial and that the failure to obtain such inspection may tend unreasonably to delay the trial; (4) that the application is made in good faith and is not intended as a general "fishing expedition."

Against this background, the special prosecutor, in order to carry his burden, must clear three hurdles: (1) relevancy; (2) admissibility; (3) specificity. Our own review of the record necessarily affords a less comprehensive view of the total situation than was available to the trial judge and we are unwilling to conclude that the District Court erred in the evaluation of the special prosecutor's showing under Rule 17 (c). Our conclusion is based on the record before us, much of which is under seal. Of course, the contents of the subpoenaed tapes could not at that stage be described fully by the special prosecutor, but there was a sufficient likelihood that each of the tapes contains conversations relevant to the offenses charged in the indictment. United States v. Gross, 24 F.R.O. 138 (SDNY 1959). With respect to many of the tapes, the special prosecutor offered the sworn testimony or statements of one or more of the participants in the conversations as to what was said at the time. As for the remainder of the tapes, the identity of the participants and the time and place of the conversations, taken in their total context, permit a rational inference that at least part of the conversations relate to the offenses charged in the indictment.

We also conclude there was a sufficient preliminary showing that each of the subpoenaed tapes contains evidence admissible with respect to the offenses charged in the indictment. The most cogent objection to the admissibility of the taped conversations here at issue is that they are a collection of out-of-court statements by declarants who will not be subject to cross-examination and that the statements are therefore inadmissible hearsay. Here, however, most of the tapes apparently contain conversations to which one or more of the defendants named in the indictment were party. The hearsay rule does not automatically bar all out-of-court statements by a defendant in a criminal case. [13] Declarations by one defendant may also be admissible against other defendants upon a sufficient showing, by independent evidence [14] of a conspiracy among one or more other defendants and the declarant and if the declarations at issue were in furtherance of that conspiracy. The same is true of declarations of coconspirators who are not defendants in the case on trial. Dutton v. Evans 400 U.S. 74, 81 (1970). Recorded conversations may also be admissible for the limited purpose of impeaching the credibility of any defendant who testifies or any other coconspirator who testifies. Generally, the need for evidence to impeach witnesses is insufficient to require its production in advance of trial.

See, e.g., United States v. Carter, 15 F.R.D. 367, 371 (D.D.C. 1954). Here, however, there are other valid potential evidentiary uses for the same material and the analysis and possible transcription of the tapes may take a significant period of time. Accordingly, we cannot say that the District Court erred in authorizing the issuance of the subpoena duces tecum.

Enforcement of a pretrial subpoena duces tecum must necessarily be committed to the sound discretion of the trial court since the necessity for the subpoena most often turns upon a determination of factual issues. Without a determination of arbitrariness or that the trial court finding was without record support, an appellate court will not ordinarily disturb a finding that the applicant for a subpoena complied with Rule 17 (c). See, e.g., Sue v. Chicago Transit Authority, 279 F. 2D, 416, 419 (CA7 1969); Shotkin v. Nelson, 146 F.20 402 (CA10 1944).

In a case such as this, however, where a subpoena is directed to a President of the United States, appellate review, in deference to a coordinate branch of Government, should be particularly meticulous to ensure that the standards of Rule 17 (c) have been correctly applied. United States v. Burr, 25 Fed. Cas. 30, 34 (No. 14.6920) (1807). From our examination of the materials submitted by the special prosecutor to the District Court in support of his motion for the subpoena, we are persuaded that the District Court's denial of the President's motion to quash the subpoena was consistent with Rule 17 (c). We also conclude that the special prosecutor has made a sufficient showing to justify a subpoena for production before trial. The subpoenaed materials are not available from any other source, and their examination and processing should not await trial in the circumstances shown. Bowman Dairy Co., Supra; United States v. Iozia, Supra.

IV—THE CLAIM OF PRIVILEGE

A

Having determined that the requirements of Rule 17 (c) were satisfied, we turn to the claim that the subpoena should be quashed because it demands "confidential conversations between a President and his close advisers that it would be inconsistent with the public interest to produce," App. 48A. The first contention is a broad claim that the separation of powers doctrine precludes judicial review of a President's claim of privilege. The second contention is that if he does not prevail on the claim of absolute privilege, the Court should hold as a matter of constitutional law that the privilege prevails over the subpoena duces tecum.

In the performance of assigned constitutional duties each branch of the Government must initially interpret the Constitution, and the interpretation of its powers by any branch is due great respect from the others.

The President's counsel, as we have noted, reads the Constitution as providing an absolute privilege of confidentiality for all Presidential communications. Many decisions of this Court, however, have unequivocally reaffirmed the holding of Marbury v. Madison, 1 Cranch 137 (1803), that "it is emphatically the province and duty of the Judicial department to say what the law is." ID., at 177.

No holding of the Court has defined the scope of judicial power specifically relating to the enforcement of a subpoena for confidential Presidential communications for use in a criminal prosecution, but other exercises of powers by the executive branch and the legislative branch have been found invalid as in conflict with the Constitution. Powell v. McCormack, Supra; Youngstown, Supra.

In a series of cases, the Court interpreted the explicit immunity conferred by express provisions of the Constitution on members of the House and Senate by the speech or debate clause. U.S. Const. Art. 1, Sec. 6. Doe v. McMillan, 412 U.S. 306 (1973); Gravel v. United States, 403 U.S. 606 (1973); United States v. Brewster, 408 U.S. 501 (1974); United States v. Johnson, 383 U.S. 169 (1966). Since this Court has consistently exercised the power to construe and delineate claims arising under express powers, it must follow that the court has authority to interpret claims with respect to powers alleged to derive from enumerated powers.

Our system of Government "requires that Federal courts on occasion interpret the Constitution in a manner at variance with the construction given the document by another branch." Powell v. McCormack, supra, 549. And in Baker v. Carr, 369 U.S., at 211, the Court stated:

"Deciding whether a matter has in any measure been committed by the Constitution to another branch of Government, or whether the action of that branch exceeds whatever authority has been committed, is itself a delicate exercise in constitutional interpretation, and is a responsibility of this Court as ultimate interpreter of the Constitution."

Notwithstanding the deference each branch must accord the others, the "judicial power of the United States" vested in the Federal courts by Art. III, Section 1 of the Constitution can no more be shared with the executive branch than the chief executive, for example, can share with the judiciary the veto power, or the Congress share with the judiciary the power to override a Presidential veto. Any other conclusion would be contrary to the basic concept of separation of powers and the checks and balances that flow from the scheme of a tripartite Government. The Federalist, No. 47, P. 313 (C. F. Mittel ed. 1938). We therefore reaffirm that it is "emphatically the province and the duty" of this court "to say what the law is" with respect to the claim of privilege presented in this case. Marbury v. Madison, supra,at 177.

B

In support of his claim of absolute privilege, the President's counsel urges two grounds one of which is common to all governments and one of which is peculiar to our system of separation of powers. The first ground is the valid need for protection of communications between high government officials and those who advise and assist them in the performance of their manifold duties; the importance of this confidentiality is too plain to require further discussion. Human experience teaches that those who expect public dissemination of their remarks may well temper candor with a concern for appearances and for their own interests to the detriment of the decision making process. [15] whatever the nature of the privilege of confidentiality of Presidential communications in the exercise of Art. II powers the privilege can be said to derive from the supremacy of each branch within its own assigned area of constitutional duties. Certain

A
B
C
D
E
F
G

powers and privileges flow from the nature of enumerated powers; [16] the protection of the confidentiality of Presidential communications has similar constitutional underpinnings.

The second ground asserted by the President's counsel in support of the claim of absolute privilege rests on the doctrine of separation of powers. Here it is argued that the independence of the executive branch within its own sphere, Humphrey's Executor v. United States, 295 U.S. 602, 629–630; Kilbourn v. Thompson, 103 U.S. 168, 190–191 (1880), insulates a President from a judicial subpoena in an ongoing criminal prosecution, and thereby protects confidential Presidential communications.

However, neither the doctrine of separation of powers, nor the need for confidentiality of high level communications, without more, can sustain an absolute unqualified Presidential privilege of immunity from judicial process under all circumstances. The President's need for complete candor and objectivity from advisers calls for great deference from the courts. However, when the privilege depends solely on the broad, undifferentiated claim of public interest in the confidentiality of such conversations, a confrontation with other values arises. Absent a claim of need to protect military, diplomatic or sensitive national security secrets, we find it difficult to accept the argument that even the very important interest in confidentiality of Presidential communications is significantly diminished by production of such material for in camera inspection with all the protection that a District Court will be obliged to provide.

The impediment that an absolute, unqualified privilege would place in the way of the primary constitutional duty of the judicial branch to do justice in criminal prosecutions would plainly conflict with the function of the courts under Art. III. In designing the structure of our Government and dividing and allocating the sovereign power among three coequal branches, the framers of the Constitution sought to provide a comprehensive system, but the separate powers were not intended to operate with absolute independence.

"While the Constitution diffuses power the better to secure liberty, it also contemplates that practice will integrate the dispersed powers into a workable Government. It enjoins upon its branches separateness but interdependence, autonomy but reciprocity. Youngstown Sheet & Tube Co. v. Sawyer, 343 U.S. 579, 635 (1952) (Jackson, J., concurring).

To read the Art. II powers of the President as providing an absolute privilege as against a subpoena essential to enforcement of criminal statutes on no more than a generalized claim of the public interest in confidentiality of nonmilitary and nondiplomatic discussions would upset the constitutional balance of "a workable government" and gravely impair the role of the courts under Art. III.

C

Since we conclude that the legitimate needs of the judicial process may outweigh Presidential privilege, it is necessary to resolve those competing interests in a manner that preserves the essential functions of each branch. The right and indeed the duty to resolve that question does not free the judiciary from according high respect to the representations made on behalf of the President. United States v. Burr, 25 Fed. Cas. 187, 190, 191–192 (No. 14,694) (1807).

The expectation of a President to the confidentiality of his conversations and correspondence, like the claim of confidentiality of judicial deliberations, for example, has all the values to which we accord deference for the privacy of all citizens and added to those values the necessity for protection of the public interest in candid, objective, and even blunt or harsh opinions in Presidential decision-making. A President and those who assist him must be free to explore alternatives in the process of shaping policies and making decisions and to do so in a way many would be unwilling to express except privately. These are the considerations justifying a presumptive privilege for Presidential communications. The privilege is fundamental to the operation of government and inextricably rooted in the separation of powers under the Constitution. [17] In Nixon v. Sirica,—U.S. App. D.C.—, 487 F, 2D 700 (1973), the Court of Appeals held that such Presidential communications are "presumptively privileged," id., at 717, and this position is accepted by both parties in the present litigation.

We agree with Mr. Chief Justice Marshall's observation, therefore, that "in no case of this kind would a Court be required to proceed against the President as against an ordinary individual." United States v. Burr, 25 Fed.: as. 187, 191 (No. 14, 694) (CCD Va. 1807).

But this presumptive privilege must be considered in light of our historic commitment to the rule of law. This is nowhere more profoundly manifest than in our view that "the twofold aim [of criminal justice] is that guilt shall not escape or innocence suffer." Berger v. United States, 295 U.S. 18, 88 (1935). We have elected to employ an adversary system of criminal justice in which the parties contest all issues before a court of law. The need to develop all relevant facts in the adversary system is both fundamental and comprehensive. The ends of criminal justice would be defeated if judgments were to be founded on a partial or speculative presentation of the facts. The very integrity of the judicial system and public confidence in the system depend on full disclosure of all the facts, within the framework of the rules of evidence.

To ensure that justice is done, it is imperative to the function of courts that compulsory process be available for the production of evidence needed either by the prosecution or by the defense.

Only recently the Court restated the ancient proposition of law, albeit in the context of a grand jury inquiry rather than a trial.

"'That the public . . . has a right to every man's evidence' except for those persons protected by a constitutional, common law, or statutory privilege, United States v. Bryan, 339 U.S., at 331 (1949); Blackmer v. United States, 284 U.S. 421, 438, Branzburg v. United States, 408 U.S. 665, 688 (1973)."

The privileges referred to by the Court are designed to protect weighty and legitimate competing interests. Thus, the Fifth Amendment to the Constitution provides that no man "shall be compelled in any criminal case to be a witness against himself."

And, generally, an attorney or a priest may not be required to disclose what has been revealed in professional confidence. These and other interests are recognized in law by privileges against forced disclosure, established in the Constitution, by statute, or at common law. Whatever their origins, these exceptions to the demand for every man's evidence are not lightly created nor expansively construed, for they are in derogation of the search for truth. [18]

In this case the President challenges a subpoena served on him as a third party requiring the production of materials for use in a criminal prosecution on the claim that he has a privilege against disclosure of confidential communications. He does not place his claim of privilege on the ground they are military or diplomatic secrets. As to these areas of Art. II duties the courts have traditionally shown the utmost deference to Presidential responsibilities. In C. & S. Air Lines v. Waterman Steamship Corp., 333 U.S. 103, 111 (1948), dealing with Presidential authority involving foreign policy considerations, the Court said:

"The President, both as commander-in-chief and as the nation's organ for foreign affairs, has available intelligence services whose reports are not and ought not to be published to the world. It would be intolerable that courts, without the relevant information, should review and perhaps nullify actions of the executive taken on information properly held secret." id., at 111.

In United States v. Reynolds, 345 U.S. 1 (1952), dealing with a claimant's demand for evidence in a damage case against the Government the Court said:

"It may be possible to satisfy the Court, from all the circumstances of the case, that there is a reasonable danger that compulsion of the evidence will expose military matters which, in the interest of national security, should not be divulged. When this is the case, the occasion for the privilege is appropriate, and the Court should not jeopardize the security which the privilege is meant to protect by insisting upon an examination of the evidence, even by the judge alone, in chambers."

No case of the Court, however, has extended this high degree of deference to a President's generalized interest in confidentiality. Nowhere in the Constitution, as we have noted earlier, is there any explicit reference to a privilege of confidentiality, yet to the extent this interest relates to the effective discharge of a President's powers, it is constitutionally based.

The right to the production of all evidence at a criminal trial similarly has constitutional dimensions. The Sixth Amendment explicitly confers upon every defendant in a criminal trial the right "to be confronted with the witnesses against him" and "to have compulsory process for obtaining witnesses in his favor." Moreover, the Fifth Amendment also guarantees that no person shall be deprived of liberty without due process of law. It is the manifest duty of the courts to vindicate those guarantees and to accomplish that it is essential that all relevant and admissible evidence be produced.

In this case we must weigh the importance of the general privilege of confidentiality of Presidential communications in performance of his responsibilities against the inroads of such a privilege of the fair administration of criminal justice. [19] The interest in preserving confidentiality is weighty indeed and entitled to great respect. However we cannot conclude that advisers will be moved to temper the candor of their remarks by the infrequent occasions of disclosure because of the possibility that such conversations will be called for in the context of a criminal prosecution. [20]

On the other hand, the allowance of the privilege to withhold evidence that is demonstrably relevant in a criminal trial would cut deeply into the guarantee of due process of law and gravely impair the basic function of the courts. A President's acknowledged need for confidentiality in the communications of his office is general in nature, whereas the constitutional need for production of relevant evidence in a criminal proceeding is specific and central to the fair adjudication of a particular criminal case in the administration of justice.

Without access to specific facts a criminal prosecution may be totally frustrated. The President's broad interest in confidentially of communications will not be vitiated by disclosure of a limited number of conversations preliminarily shown to have some bearing on the pending criminal cases.

We conclude that when the ground for asserting privilege as to subpoenaed materials sought for use in a criminal trial is based only on the generalized interest in confidentiality, it cannot prevail over the fundamental demands of due process of law in the fair administration of criminal justice. The generalized assertion of privilege must yield to the demonstrated, specific need for evidence in a pending criminal trial.

D

We have earlier determined that the District Court did not err in authorizing the issuance of the subpoena. If a President concludes that compliance with a subpoena would be injurious to the public interest he may properly, as was done here, invoke a claim of privilege on the return of the subpoena. Upon receiving a claim of privilege from the chief executive, it became the further duty of the District Court to treat the subpoenaed material as presumptively privileged and to require the special prosecutor to demonstrate that the Presidential material was "essential to the justice of the [pending criminal] case." United States v. Burr, Supra, at 192. Here the District Court treated the material as presumptively privileged, proceeded to find that the special prosecutor had made a sufficient showing to rebut the presumption and ordered an in camera examination of the subpoenaed material.

On the basis of our examination of the record we are unable to conclude that the District Court erred in ordering the inspection. Accordingly we affirm the order of the District Court that subpoenaed materials be transmitted to that court. We now turn to the important question of the District Court's responsibilities in conducting the in camera examination of Presidential materials or communications delivered under the compulsion of the subpoena duces tecum.

E

Enforcement of the subpoena duces tecum was stayed pending this Court's resolution of the issues raised by the petitions for certiorari. Those issues now having been disposed of, the matter of implementation will rest with the district court. "(T)he guard, furnished to (President) to protect him from being harassed by vexatious and unnecessary subpoenas, is to be looked for in the conduct of the (District) Court after the subpoenas have issued; nor in any circumstances which is to precede their being issued."

United States v. Burr, supra, at 34. Statements that meet the test of admissibility and relevance must be isolated; all other material must be excised. At this stage, the District Court is not limited to representations of the special prosecutor as to the evidence sought by the subpoena; the material will be available to the District Court. It is elementary that in camera inspection of evidence is always a procedure calling for scrupulous protection against any release or publication of material not found by the Court, at that stage, probably admissible in evidence and relevant to the issues of the trial for which it is sought. That being true of an ordinary situation, it is obvious that the District Court has a very heavy responsibility to see to it that Presidential conversations, which are either not relevant or not admissible, are accorded that high degree of respect due the President of the United States. Mr. Chief Justice Marshall sitting as a trial judge in the Burr case, supra, was extraordinarily careful to point out that:

"I[n] no case of this kind would a court be required to proceed against the President as against an ordinary individual." United States v. Burr, 25 Fed. Cases 187, 191 (No. 14,694).

Marshall's statement cannot be read to mean in any sense that a President is above the law, but relates to the singularly unique role under Art. II of a President's communications and activities related to the performance of duties under that article. Moreover, a President's communications and activities encompass a vastly wider range of sensitive material than would be true of any "ordinary individual." It is therefore necessary [21] in the public interest to afford Presidential confidentiality the greatest protection consistent with the fair administration of justice. The need for confidentiality even as to idle conversations with associates in which casual reference might be made concerning political leaders within the country or foreign statesmen is too obvious to call for further treatment. We have no doubt that the District Judge will at all times accord to Presidential records that high degree of deference suggested in United States v. Burr, supra, and will discharge his responsibility to see to it that until released to the special prosecutor no in camera material is revealed to anyone. This burden applies with even greater force to excised material; once the decision is made to excise, the material is restored to its privileged status and should be returned under seal to its lawful custodian.

Since the matter came before the Court during the pendency of a criminal prosecution, and on representations that time is of the essence the mandate shall issue forthwith.

Affirmed.

Mr. Justice Rehnquist took no part in the consideration or decision of these cases.

FOOTNOTES

[1]—See 28 U.S.C. sections 1254 (1) and 2101 (E) and our Rule 20. See, e.g., Youngstown Sheet & Tube Co. v. Sawyer, 343 U.S. 937, 579, 584 (1952); United States v. United Mine Workers, 329 U.S. 708, 709, 710 (1946); 330 U.S. 258, 269 (1947); Carter v. Carter Coal Co., 298 U.S. 238 (1936); Rickert Rice Mills v. Fontenot, 297 U.S. 110 (1936); Railroad Retirement Board v. Alton R. Co., 295 U.S. 330, 344 (1935); United States v. Bankers Trust Co., 294 U.S. 240, 243 (1935).

[2]—The cross-petition in No. 73-1834 raised the issue whether the grand jury acted within its authority in naming the President as a coconspirator. Since we find resolution of this issue unnecessary to resolution of the question whether the claim of privilege is to prevail, the cross-petition for certiorari is dismissed as improvidently granted and the remainder of the opinion is concerned with the issues raised in No. 73-1766. On June 19, 1974, the President's counsel moved for disclosure and transmittal to this Court of all evidence presented to the grand jury relating to its action in naming the President as an unindicted coconspirator. Action on this motion was deferred pending oral argument of the case and is now denied.

[3]—The seven defendants were John N. Mitchell, H. R. Haldeman, John D. Ehrlichman, Charles W. Colson, Robert C. Mardian, Kenneth W. Parkinson, and Gordon Strachan. Each had occupied either a position of responsibility on the White House staff or the committee for the re-election of the President. Colson entered a guilty plea on another charge and is no longer a defendant.

[4]—The President entered a special appearance in the District Court on June 6 and requested that court to lift its protective order regarding the naming of certain individuals as coconspirators and to any additional extent deemed appropriate by the court. This motion of the President was based on the ground that the disclosures to the news media made the reasons for continuance of the protective order no longer meaningful.

On June 7, the District Court removed its protective order and on June 10, counsel for both parties jointly moved this Court to unseal those parts of the record which related to the action of the grand jury regarding the President. After receiving a statement in opposition from the defendants, this court denied that motion on June 15, 1974, except for the grand jury's immediate finding relating to the status of the President as an unindicted coconspirator.—U.S.—(1974).

[5]—The specific meetings and conversations are enumerated in a schedule attached to the subpoena, 42A-46A of the APP.

[6]—At the joint suggestion of the special prosecutor and counsel for the President, and with the approval of counsel for the defendants, further proceedings in the District Court were held in camera.

[7]—The parties have suggested this Court has jurisdiction on other grounds. In view of our conclusion that there is jurisdiction under 28 U.S.C. Sec. 1254(1) because the District Court's order was appealable, we need not decide whether other jurisdictional vehicles are available.

[8]—The regulation issued by the Attorney General pursuant to his statutory authority, vests in the special prosecutor plenary authority to control the course of investigations and litigation related to "all offenses arising out of the 1972 Presidential election for which the special prosecutor deems it necessary and appropriate to assume responsibility, allegations involving the President, members of the White House staff, or Presidential appointees, and any other matters which he consents to have assigned to him by the Attorney General." 38 Fed. Reg. 30739, as amended by 38 Fed. Reg. 32805. In particular, the special prosecutor was given full authority, inter alia, "to contest the assertion of 'executive privilege' . . . and handle [e] all aspects of any cases within his jurisdiction." Ibid. The regulations then go on to provide:

"In exercising this authority, the special prosecutor will have the greatest degree of independence that is consistent with the Attorney-General's statutory accountability for all matters falling within the jurisdiction of the Department of Justice. The Attorney General will not countermand or interfere with the special prosecutor's decisions or actions. The special prosecutor will determine whether and to what extent he will inform or consult with the Attorney General about the conduct of his duties and responsibilities. In accordance with assurances given by the President to the Attorney General that the President will not exercise his constitutional powers to effect the discharge of the special prosecutor or to limit the independence he is hereby given, the special prosecutor will not be removed from his duties except for extraordinary improprieties on his part and without the President's first consulting the majority and minority leaders and chairman and ranking minority members of the Judiciary Committees of the Senate and House of Representatives and ascertaining that their consensus is in accord with his proposed action."

[9]—That this was the understanding of acting Attorney General Robert Bork, the author of the regulations establishing the independence of the special prosecutor, is shown by his testimony before the Senate Judiciary Committee:

"Although it is anticipated that Mr. Jaworski will receive cooperation from the White House in getting any evidence he feels he needs to conduct investigations and prosecutions, it is clear and understood on all sides that he has the power to use judicial processes to pursue evidence if disagreement should develop." Hearings before the Senate Judiciary Committee on the special prosecutor, 93d Cong. 1st Sess., Pt. 2, at 470 1 (1974).

Acting Attorney General Bork gave similar assurances to the House Subcommittee on Criminal Justice. Hearings before the House Judiciary Subcommittee on Criminal Justice on H. J. Res. 784 and H. R. 10937, 93d Cong., 1st Sess. 266 (1973). At his confirmation hearings, Attorney General William Saxbe testified that he shared acting Attorney General Bork's views concerning the special prosecutor's authority to test any claim of executive privilege in the courts. Hearings before the Senate Judiciary Committee on the nomination of William B. Saxbe to be Attorney General, 930 Cong. 1st Sess. 9 (1973).

[10]—At his confirmation hearings Attorney General William Saxbe testified that he agreed with the regulations adopted by acting Attorney General Bork and would not remove the special prosecutor except for "gross impropriety." Hearings, Senate Judiciary Committee on the nomination of William B. Saxbe to be Attorney General, 93d Cong., 1st Sess., 5-6, Section-10 (1973). There is no contention here that the special prosecutor is guilty of any such impropriety.

[11]—The Court quoted a statement of a member of the advisory committee that the purpose of the rule was to bring documents into court "in advance of the time that they are offered in evidence, so that they may then be inspected in advance, for the purpose . . . of enabling the party to see whether he can use [them] or whether he wants to use [them]." 341 U.S., at 220 N. 5. The manual for complex and multi-district litigation published by the administrative office of the United States courts recommends that Rule 17(c) be encouraged in complex criminal cases in order that each party may be compelled to produce its documentary evidence well in advance of trial and in advance of the time it is to be offered. P. 142, CCH, Ed.

[12]—The District Court found here that it was faced with "the more unusual situation . . . where the subpoena, rather than being directed to the Government by the defendants, issues to what, as a practical matter, is a third party." United States v. Mitchell,—F. Supp.—(D.C. 1974). The special prosecutor suggests that the evidentiary requirement of Bowman Dairy Co. and Iozia does not apply in its full vigor when the subpoena duces decum is issued to third parties rather than to Government prosecutors. Brief for the United States 128-129. We need not decide whether a lower standard exists because we are satisfied that the relevance and evidentiary nature of the subpoenaed tapes were sufficiently shown as a preliminary matter to warrant the district court's refusal to quash the subpoena.

[13]—Such statements are declarations by a party defendant that "would surmount all objections based on the hearsay rule . . ." and at least as to the declarant himself" would be admissible for whatever inferences" might be reasonably drawn. United States v. Matlock,—U.S.—(1974). On Lee v. United States, 343 U.S. 747, 757 (1953). See also McCormick on evidence, Sec. 270, at 651-652 (1972 Ed.).

[14]—As a preliminary matter, there must be substantial, independent evidence of the conspiracy, at least enough to take the question to the jury. United States v. Vaught, 385 F. 2d 320, 323 (CA4 1973), United States v. Hoffa, 349 F. 2d 20, 41-42 (CA6 1965), Aff'd on other grounds, 385 U.S. 293 (1966); United States v. Santos, 385 F. 2d 43, 45 (CA7 1967), cert. denied, 390 U.S. 954 (1968) United States v. Morton, 483 F. 2d 573, 575 (CA 1973); United States v. Spanos, 462 F. 2d 1012, 1014 (CA9, 1972); Carbo v. United States, 314 F. 2d 718, 737 (CA9 1963); cert. denied, 377 U.S. 953 (1964). Whether the standard has been satisfied is a question of admissibility of evidence to be decided by the trial judge.

[15]—There is nothing novel about governmental confidentiality. The meetings of the Constitutional Convention in 1787 were conducted in complete privacy. I Farrand, the records of the Federal Convention of 1787, XI-XXV (1911). Moreover, all records of those meetings were sealed for more than 30 years after the convention. See 3 U.S. Stat. at large, 15th Cong. 1st Sess. Res. 8 (1818). Most of the framers acknowledged that without secrecy no Constitution of the kind that was developed could have been written. Warren, "The Making of the Constitution," 134-139 (1937).

[16]—The special prosecutor argues that there is no provision in the Constitution for a Presidential privilege as to his communications corresponding to the privilege of members of Congress under the speech or debate clause, but the silence of the Constitution on this score is not dispositive. "The rule of constitutional interpretation announced in McCulloch v. Maryland, 4 Wheat, 316, that that which was reasonably appropriate and relevant to the exercise of a granted power was considered as accompanying the grant, has been so universally applied that it suffices merely to state it." Marshall v. Gordon, 243 U.S. 521, 537 (1917).

[17]—"Freedom of communication vital to fulfillment of wholesome relationships is obtained only by removing the specter of compelled disclosure . . . (g)overnment . . . needs open but protected channels for the kind of plain talk that is essential to the quality of its functioning." Carl Zeiss Stiftung v. V.E.B. Carl Zeiss, Jena. 40 R.F.D. 318, 325 (D.C. 1966). See Nixon v. Sirica.—U.S. App. D.C.—, —487 F. 20 700, 713 (1973); Kaiser Aluminum & Chem. Corp. v. United States. 157 F. Supp. 939 (Ct. Q. 1958) (per Reed, J.); The Federalist No. 64 (S.F. Mittel ed. 1938).

[18]—Because of the key role of the testimony of witnesses in the judicial process, courts have historically been cautious about privileges. Justice Frankfurter, dissenting in Elkins v. United States, 364 U.S. 206, 234 (1960), said of this: "Limitations are properly placed upon the operation of this general principle only to the very limited extent that permitting a refusal to testify or excluding relevant evidence has a public good transcending the normally predominant principle of utilizing all rational means for ascertaining truth."

[19]—We are not here concerned with the balance between the President's generalized interest in confidentiality and the need for relevant evidence in civil litigation, nor with that between the confidentiality interest and Congressional demands for information, nor with the President's interest in preserving state secrets. We address only the conflict between the President's assertion of a generalized privilege of confidentiality against the constitutional need for relevant evidence to criminal trials.

[20]—Mr. Justice Cardozo made this point in an analogous context. Speaking for a unanimous Court in Clark v. United States, 289 U.S. 1 (1933), he emphasized the importance of maintaining the secrecy of the deliberations of a petit jury in a criminal case. "Freedom of debate might be stifled and independence of thought checked if jurors were made to feel that their arguments and ballots were to be freely published in the world." id., at 13. Nonetheless, the

Court also recognized that isolated inroads on confidentiality designed to serve the paramount need of the criminal law would not vitiate the interests served by secrecy.

"A juror of integrity and reasonable firmness will not fear to speak his mind if the confidences of debate are barred to the ears of mere impertinence or malice. He will not expect to be shielded against the disclosure of his conduct in the event that there is evidence reflecting upon his honor. The chance that now and then there may be found some timid soul who will take counsel of his fears and give way to their repressive power is too remote and shadowly to shape the course of justice." id. at 16.

[21]—When the subpoenaed material is delivered to the district judge in camera questions may arise as to the excising of parts and it lies within the discretion of that court to seek the aid of the special prosecutor and the President's counsel for in camera consideration of the validity of particular excisions, whether the basis of excision is relevancy or admissibility or under such cases as Reynolds, supra, or Waterman Steamship supra.

(Continued From Page 201)

solute privilege would "upset the constitutional balance" of government and "gravely impair the role of the courts."

Burger also discounted the possibility that presidential advisers would be "moved to temper the candor of their remarks" because such conversations might "be called for in the context of a criminal prosecution."

Affirming Sirica's order that the material be submitted to him for inspection and determination of relevance and admissibility, the court emphasized Sirica's "very heavy responsibility" to accord irrelevant and sensitive portions the confidentiality and "high degree of respect due the President." Under the procedures set by Sirica, particular claims of privilege by the White House would be considered before the material was sent to Jaworski.

Justice William H. Rehnquist, once an assistant attorney general under cover-up defendant John N. Mitchell, did not take part in the decision.

Nixon pledges compliance—President Nixon's reaction to the Supreme Court order that he surrender subpoenaed tapes and documents was read to reporters later July 24 by special counsel James D. St. Clair near the "western white house" in San Clemente, Calif.:

"My challenge in the courts to the subpoena of the special prosecutor was based on the belief that it was unconstitutionally issued, and on my strong desire to protect the principle of presidential confidentiality in a system of separation of powers.

While I am, of course, disappointed in the result, I respect and accept the court's decision, and I have instructed Mr. St. Clair to take whatever measures are necessary to comply with that decision in all respects. For the future it will be essential that the special circumstances of this case not be permitted to cloud the right of Presidents to maintain the basic confidentiality without which this office cannot function. I was gratified, therefore, to note that the court reaffirmed both the validity and the importance of the principle of executive privilege, the principle I had sought to maintain. By complying fully with the court's ruling in this case, I hope and trust that I will contribute to strengthening rather than weakening this principle for the future, so that this will prove to be not the precedent that destroyed the principle but the action that preserved it."

St. Clair added that the President "has always been a firm believer in the rule of law, and he intends his decision to comply fully with the court's ruling as an action in furtherance of that belief." In accordance with Nixon's instructions, St. Clair said, the "time-consuming process of reviewing the tapes subject to the subpoena" would begin immediately.

Nixon's statement, issued about eight hours after the court's decision, ended growing speculation that he might defy the court's order. During the period following the court's agreement to hear the case, St. Clair and other White House spokesmen consistently had refused to predict Nixon's reaction. On the last such occasion, a news conference July 22, St. Clair deflected questions with the assertion that comment on a case still before the court would be improper.

Sirica disqualification bid denied. The Supreme Court July 25 declined to review an appeals court decision that U.S. District Court Judge John J. Sirica was properly qualified to preside at the Watergate cover-up trial. Defendants John N. Mitchell and Kenneth W. Parkinson had petitioned to have Sirica removed because of prosecutorial bias.

Stans letters ordered released. U.S. District Court Chief Judge George L. Hart Jr. July 25 rejected President Nixon's claim that the confidentiality of his correspondence with former Commerce Secretary Maurice Stans was protected by executive privilege. Hart ordered the material turned over to the Watergate special prosecutor.

Stans, who later had served as chairman of Nixon's 1972 fund raising committee, was under investigation for possible violations of campaign finance laws involving the promise of federal jobs, including diplomatic posts, to donors.

Hart based his opinion on the Supreme Court's unanimous ruling ordering Nixon to release tapes and documents for use in the Watergate cover-up trial.

Hart adopted the language of the higher court decision when he ruled, "the court concludes that any privilege attaching to the papers in question and sought for use before the grand jury cannot prevail over the fundamental demands in the fair administration of criminal justice."

Evidence release continues. Internal Revenue Service (IRS) investigators reported to Commissioner Donald C. Alexander that if presidential aides connected with preparation of President Nixon's 1969 income tax return could be compelled to testify, they could "possibly connect the taxpayer with the preparation of the return," thus providing the basis for a fraud penalty against the President, according to testimony released by the House Judiciary Committee July 26.

The committee staff's volume of evidence on Nixon's 1969-72 tax payments concentrated on 1969, when he began taking charitable deductions (eventually totaling $482,018) for the gift of his presidential papers to the National Archives.

According to the evidence, IRS investigators advised Alexander in late March (1974) that a grand jury should investigate the roles of former White House aides John D. Ehrlichman and Edward L. Morgan, Nixon lawyers Herbert Kalmbach and Frank DeMarco, and appraiser Ralph Newman, in the gift of the papers and the preparation of the 1969 return, especially in relation to the backdated deed which placed conveyance of the gift before a law barring such deductions went into effect.

The evidence cited testimony by Alexander that he had referred the matter to special Watergate prosecutor Leon Jaworski April 2, and on the same day notified Nixon that he would be assessed a 5% negligence penalty instead of a 50% fraud penalty.

According to other data released by the committee, the IRS disallowed Nixon's claim that $10,384.50 in 1971 royalties from his book "Six Crises" had been assigned to the Nixon Foundation. The IRS ruled that no assignment of title to the manuscript had been made and that Nixon should pay personal taxes on the royalties.

Alexander also testified that he had decided on a re-audit of Nixon's 1970-72 returns on Nov. 28, 1973 and formally informed Nixon Dec. 7. (The next day, Nixon disclosed data on his personal finances and requested that a joint Congressional committee review his tax returns.

Another item of unreported income included in the committee's IRS data was a total of $67,388 in government expenditures on Nixon's homes in San Clemente, Calif. and Key Biscayne, Fla. The IRS had found the expenditures to be unrelated to official needs and thus taxable personal income. (The Joint Committee on Internal Revenue Taxation had set the amount at $92,298.

The impeachment panel also disclosed that Nixon had not yet paid the deficiency assessment of $148,080.97 for 1969. Absent a finding of fraud, Nixon was not legally bound to pay the additional tax because the general statute of limitations had expired. A White House spokesman said July 26 that Nixon intended to pay as soon as possible.

Colson relates early warnings—Former presidential counsel Charles W. Colson told the Judiciary Committee that he had warned President Nixon in January and February, 1973 that former Attorney General John N. Mitchell and White House aides might have been more deeply involved in Watergate than had been previously supposed, according to testimony released July 26. Nixon had maintained that he first learned of his aides' involvement in Watergate and the cover-up in March 1973.

Colson testified that he had told Nixon that Mitchell "had to know" about the intelligence plans which included the Watergate break-in. Colson said he also warned Nixon that the scandal could "spread into the White House staff." Nixon asked if this meant top aides H. R. Haldeman and John D. Ehrlichman, and Colson told the committee: "Since I didn't know, I just shrugged my shoulders."

Colson said he had met with Nixon after an unsatisfactory conversation with Haldeman on Watergate problems. According to Colson, Haldeman said he had been aware of a meeting in Mitchell's office before the break-in at which wiretapping was discussed, and that, in Haldeman's opinion, the discussions were no cause for concern. Colson related that he then raised the subject of payments to the Watergate defendants, which "could get smelly" and be "interpreted as hush money." Haldeman replied, according to Colson, that "there is no reason why friends can't go out and raise money to help people pay for their legal defenses. It happens all the time."

Dean suggests earlier money talk—According to testimony released by the Judiciary Committee July 25, former presidential counsel John W. Dean 3rd maintained that he and Nixon had discussed the problem of raising up to $1 million for the original Watergate defendants before the March 21, 1973 meeting usually associated with the subject.

Dean alluded to an earlier meeting as he was attempting to explain to the committee and presidential counsel James D. St. Clair why he had told the Senate Watergate Committee in 1973 that the discussion had occurred on March 13, but had later changed his testimony for the special Watergate prosecutor.

Dean testified to the impeachment panel he still had the "strong impression" and "recollection" that he discussed the money with Nixon sometime "preceding the 21st," but that he was unable to recall the exact date.

Dean also told the committee that he always considered Nixon to be fully "in charge" during meetings concerning the Watergate cover-up. Regarding the March 21 session, Dean said his first intention had been to dissuade Nixon from approving payments to the defendants, but that he was "shortly turned around." Dean maintained that Nixon felt the payments were "desirable." "The President was taking the lead at this time," Dean said, "I was just sort of following along. . . ."

Reinecke guilty of perjury. California Lt. Gov. Ed Reinecke (R) was convicted July 27 of one count of lying to the Senate Judiciary Committee during testimony about the alleged link between International Telephone & Telegraph Corp.'s (ITT) pledge of a contribution to fund the 1972 Republican Convention, then scheduled for San Diego, and the Administration's settlement of antitrust suit against ITT. [For further details, see p. 218F1]

Connally charged with bribery, perjury. Former Treasury Secretary John B. Connally Jr. was indicted July 29 by a Watergate grand jury on five counts of accepting a bribe, conspiring to obstruct justice and perjury. He was accused of accepting $10,000 in two cash payments from Jack Jacobsen, a lawyer for Associated Milk

Producers, Inc. (AMPI), on May 14, 1971 and Sept. 24, 1971.

According to the indictment, the payments, which occurred while Connally was serving as Treasury secretary, were made "for and because of official acts performed by him, to wit, his recommendations in his official capacity concerning an increase in the federal milk price support level to be fixed by the secretary of agriculture, announced on March 25, 1971."

Jacobsen was also indicted on one count of giving the bribe. Another milk fund-related charge against him had been dismissed in May on a technicality.
[For further details, see p. 218B3.]

Milk fund case widens—Charges were also filed against four other persons as a result of the nearly 12-month investigation conducted by the Watergate special prosecutor's office.

AMPI's former general manager, Harold S. Nelson, pleaded guilty July 31 to a charge that he conspired to bribe Connally in connection with AMPI's effort to secure the milk price support increase.
[For further details, see p. 219E1.]

Nixon economic address. President Nixon reiterated his intention to fight inflation with stringent fiscal and monetary policies—conservative measures that his aides termed "the old time religion"—in an address before four California business groups. The speech, which was delivered July 25 in Los Angeles, was nationally broadcast.

Nixon announced no new policy measures designed to curb rising prices.

Rush assesses Nixon's economic policies—Nixon economic adviser Kenneth Rush July 29 defended Administration economic policies in Congressional testimony.

Kenneth Rush had declined previous invitations to testify before Congress on grounds that as economic adviser to the President, his relationship with Nixon was "confidential" and that their need for a "candid and uninhibited" exchange of views could be hampered by Congressional examinations. Rush relented when Sen. William Proxmire (D, Wis.), chairman of the Joint Economic Committee, threatened to hold up action on appropriations for Rush's salary.

Rush revealed little July 29 during the Joint Economic Committee's annual hearings on the mid-year state of the economy. He endorsed the Administration's policies of "moderate" budget and monetary restraint and rejected Proxmire's charge that the White House had "no policy" on economic matters because the President "cannot cope" with inflation problems while he was preoccupied with Watergate

and impeachment problems. "I see no problem of leadership," Rush responded. No new economic policies were being utilized to combat rising prices, he said, because "what people need now is certainty, a period of feeling that we're on the right track and plan to stay on the right track."

(Rush altered his views July 31 when, following the House Judiciary Committee's vote, he observed that the threat of impeachment was exerting a "disturbing influence" on the economy by generating uncertainty within the business community.)

House Judiciary panel approves 3 impeachment articles. The House Judiciary Committee recessed July 30 after approving three articles of impeachment charging President Nixon with obstruction of justice in connection with the Watergate scandal, abuse of presidential powers and attempting to impede the impeachment process by defying committee subpoenas for evidence. The committee rejected two other proposed articles, one charging that Nixon had usurped the powers of Congress by ordering the secret bombing of Cambodia in 1969, the other concerning income tax fraud and the unconstitutional use of government funds to make improvements on his properties in California and Florida.

The committee's final deliberations, which were nationally televised, began July 24 with a motion by Rep. Harold D. Donohue (Mass.), second ranking Democrat on the panel. "I move that the committee report to the House a resolution, together with articles, impeaching the President of the United States, Richard M. Nixon."

In so moving, Donohue asked the committee to adopt two broad articles of impeachment. The first accused the President of obstructing justice by engaging in a cover-up of the Watergate affair. The second charged Nixon with abuses of presidential power, including defiance of committee subpoenas.

Opening statements by committee chairman Peter W. Rodino Jr. (D, N.J.) and ranking Republican Edward Hutchinson (Mich.) preceded Donohue's motion. In his remarks, Hutchinson noted the Supreme Court's ruling earlier that day that Nixon must surrender tape recordings of 64 Watergate-related conversations to U.S. District Court Judge John J. Sirica for determination of relevancy to the upcoming Watergate cover-up trial. The committee should entertain postponement of consideration of the articles until the contents of the tapes could be made available to the committee, Hutchinson said. However, Rodino declined to act on the suggestion. The committee sustained Rodino July 26, rejecting 27–11 a motion to delay.

(Continued on Page 209)

Judiciary Committee's Articles of Impeachment

Article I *(Approved 27-11)*

In his conduct of the office of President of the United States, Richard M. Nixon, in violation of his constitutional oath faithfully to execute the office of President of the United States and, to the best of his ability, preserve, protect, and defend the Constitution of the United States, and in violation of his constitutional duty to take care that the laws be faithfully executed, has prevented, obstructed, and impeded the administration of justice, in that:

On June 17, 1972, and prior thereto, agents of the Committee for the Re-election of the President:

Committed unlawful entry of the headquarters of the Democratic National Committee in Washington, District of Columbia, for the purpose of securing political intelligence. Subsequent thereto, Richard M. Nixon, using the powers of his high office, engaged personally and through his subordinates and agents in a course of conduct or plan designed to delay, impede, and obstruct the investigation of such unlawful entry; to cover up, conceal and protect those responsible; and to conceal the existence and scope of other unlawful covert activities.

The means used to implement this course of conduct or plan have included one or more of the following:

1. Making or causing to be made false or misleading statements to lawfully authorized investigative officers and employes of the United States.

2. Withholding relevant and material evidence or information from lawfully authorized investigative officers and employes of the United States.

3. Approving, condoning, acquiescing in, and counseling witnesses with respect to the giving of false or misleading statements to lawfully authorized investigative officers and employes of the United States and false or misleading testimony in duly instituted judicial and Congressional proceedings.

4. Interfering or endeavoring to interfere with the conduct of investigations by the Department of Justice of the United States, the Federal Bureau of Investigation, the office of Watergate Special Prosecution Force, and Congressional committees.

5. Approving, condoning and acquiescing in the surreptitious payment of substantial sums of money for the purpose of obtaining the silence or influencing the testimony of witnesses, potential witnesses or individuals who participated in such illegal entry and other illegal activities.

6. Endeavoring to misuse the Central Intelligence Agency, an agency of the United States.

7. Disseminating information received from officers of the Department of Justice of the United States to subjects of investigations conducted by lawfully authorized investigative officers and employes of the United States, for the purpose of aiding and assisting such subjects in their attempts to avoid criminal liability.

8. Making false or misleading public statements for the purpose of deceiving the people of the United States into believing that a thorough and complete investigation had been conducted with respect to allegations of misconduct on the part of personnel of the executive branch of the United States and personnel of the Committee for the Re-election of the President, and that there was no involvement of such personnel in such misconduct: or

9. Endeavoring to cause prospective defendants, and individuals duly tried and convicted, to expect favored treatment and consideration in return for their silence or false testimony, or rewarding individuals for their silence or false testimony.

In all of this, Richard M. Nixon has acted in a manner contrary to his trust as President and subversive of constitutional government, to the great prejudice of the cause of law and justice and to the manifest injury of the people of the United States.

Wherefore Richard M. Nixon, by such conduct, warrants impeachment and trial, and removal from office.

Article II *(Approved 28–10)*

Using the powers of the office of President of the United States, Richard M. Nixon, in violation of his constitutional oath faithfully to execute the office of President of the United States, and to the best of his ability preserve, protect and defend the Constitution of the United States, and in disregard of his constitutional duty to take care that the laws be faithfully executed, has repeatedly engaged in conduct violating the constitutional rights of citizens, impairing the due and proper administration of justice in the conduct of lawful inquiries, of contravening the law of governing agencies of the executive branch and the purposes of these agencies.

This conduct has included one or more of the following:

1. He has, acting personally and through his subordinates and agents, endeavored to obtain from the Internal Revenue Service in violation of the constitutional rights of citizens, confidential information contained in income tax returns for purposes not authorized by law; and to cause, in violation of the constitutional rights of citizens, income tax audits or other income tax investigations to be initiated or conducted in a discriminatory manner.

2. He misused the Federal Bureau of Investigation, the Secret Service and other executive personnel in violation or disregard of the constitutional rights of citizens by directing or authorizing such agencies or personnel to conduct or continue electronic surveillance or other investigations for purposes unrelated to national security, the enforcement of laws or any other lawful function of his office.

He did direct, authorize or permit the use of information obtained thereby for purposes unrelated to national security, the enforcement of laws or any other lawful function of his office. And he did direct the concealment of certain records made by the Federal Bureau of Investigation of electronic surveillance.

3. He has, acting personally and through his subordinates and agents, in violation or disregard of the constitutional rights of citizens, authorized and permitted to be maintained a secret investigative unit within the office of the President, financed in part with money derived from campaign contributions which unlawfully utilized the resources of the Central Intelligence Agency, engaged in covert and unlawful activities, and attempted to prejudice the constitutional right of an accused to a fair trial.

4. He has failed to take care that the laws were faithfully executed by failing to act when he knew or had reason to know that his close subordinates endeavored to impede and frustrate lawful inquiries by duly constituted executive, judicial and legislative entities concerning the unlawful entry into the headquarters of the Democratic National Committee and the cover-up thereof and concerning other unlawful activities including those relating to the confirmation of Richard Kleindienst as Attorney General of the United States, the electronic surveillance of private citizens, the break-in into the offices of Dr. Lewis Fielding and the campaign financing practices of the Committee to Re-Elect the President.

5. In disregard of the rule of law he knowingly misused the executive power by interfering with agencies of the executive branch including the Federal Bureau of Investigation, the Criminal Division and the office of Watergate special prosecution force of the Department of Justice, and the Central Intelligence Agency, in violation of his duty to take care that the laws be faithfully executed.

In all of this Richard M. Nixon has acted in a manner contrary to his trust as President and subversive of constitutional government to the great prejudice of the cause of law and justice and to the manifest injury of the people of the United States.

Wherefore, Richard M. Nixon by such conduct warrants impeachment and trial and removal from office.

Article III *(Approved 21–17)*

In his conduct of the office of President of the United States, Richard M. Nixon, contrary to his oath faithfully to execute the office of President of the United States and, to the best of his ability, preserve, protect, and defend the Constitution of the United States, and in violation of his constitutional duty to take care that the laws be faithfully executed, has failed without lawful cause or excuse to produce papers and things as directed by duly authorized subpoenas issued by the Committee on the Judiciary of the House of Representatives on April 11, 1974, May 15, 1974, May 30, 1974, and June 24, 1974, and willfully disobeyed such subpoenas. The subpoenas, papers and things were deemed necessary by the Committee *in order to resolve by direct evidence fundamental, factual questions relating to Presidential direction, knowledge or approval of actions demonstrated by other evidence to be substantial grounds for impeachment of the President.* In refusing to produce these papers and things *Richard M. Nixon, substituting his judgment as to what materials were necessary for the inquiry, interposed the powers of the presidency against the lawful subpoenas of the House of Representatives, thereby assuming to himself functions and judgments necessary to the exercise of the sole power of impeachment vested by the Constitution in the House of Representatives.*

In all of this, Richard M. Nixon has acted in a manner contrary to his trust as President and subversive of constitutional government, to the great prejudice of the cause of law and justice, and to the manifest injury of the people of the United States.

Wherefore, Richard M. Nixon by such conduct, warrants impeachment and trial, and removal from office.

Article IV *(Rejected 26–12)*

In his conduct of the office of President of the United States, Richard M. Nixon, in violation of his constitutional oath faithfully to execute the office of President of the United States and to the best of his ability to preserve, protect and defend the Constitution of the United States and in disregard of his constitutional duties to take care that the laws be faithfully executed, on and subsequent to March 17, 1969, authorized, ordered and ratified the concealment from the Congress of the facts and the submission to the Congress of false and misleading statements concerning the existence, scope and nature of American bombing operations in Cambodia in derogation of the power of the Congress to declare war, to make appropriations and to raise and support armies and by such conduct warrants impeachment and trial and removal from office.

Article V *(Rejected 26–12)*

In his conduct of the office of President of the United States, Richard M. Nixon, in violation of his constitutional oath faithfully to execute the office of the President of the United States, and to the best of his ability preserve, protect and defend the Constitution of the United States, and in violation of his constitutional duty to take care that the laws be faithfully executed, did receive emolument from the United States in excess of the compensation provided by law pursuant to Article II, Section 1 of the Constitution; and did willfully attempt to evade the payment of a portion of Federal income taxes due and owing by him for the years 1969, 1970, 1971, and 1972 in that (1) he during the period for which he had been elected President unlawfully received compensation in the form of Government expenditures at and on his privately owned property located in or near San Clemente, Calif., and Key Biscayne, Fla.; (2) he knowingly and fraudulently failed to report certain income and claimed deductions in the years 1969, 1970, 1971 and 1972 on his Federal income tax returns which were not authorized by law, including deductions for a gift of papers to the United States valued at approximately $576,000.

Roll Call Votes on Articles

	I	II	III	IV	V
Democrats					
Rodino (NJ)	Yes	Yes	Yes	No	Yes
Donohue (Mass)	Yes	Yes	Yes	No	No
Brooks (Tex)	Yes	Yes	Yes	Yes	Yes
Kastenmeier (Wis)	Yes	Yes	Yes	Yes	Yes
Edwards (Cal)	Yes	Yes	Yes	Yes	Yes
Hungate (Mo)	Yes	Yes	Yes	Yes	No
Conyers (Mich)	Yes	Yes	Yes	Yes	Yes
Eilberg (Pa)	Yes	Yes	Yes	No	Yes
Waldie (Cal)	Yes	Yes	Yes	Yes	No
Flowers (Ala)	Yes	Yes	No	No	No
Mann (SC)	Yes	Yes	No	No	No
Sarbanes (Md)	Yes	Yes	Yes	No	No
Seiberling (Ohio)	Yes	Yes	Yes	No	Yes
Danielson (Cal)	Yes	Yes	Yes	No	Yes
Drinan (Mass)	Yes	Yes	Yes	Yes	No
Rangel (NY)	Yes	Yes	Yes	Yes	Yes
Jordan (Tex)	Yes	Yes	Yes	Yes	Yes
Thornton (Ark)	Yes	Yes	Yes	No	No
Holtzman (NY)	Yes	Yes	Yes	Yes	Yes
Owens (Utah)	Yes	Yes	Yes	Yes	No
Mezvinsky (Iowa)	Yes	Yes	Yes	Yes	Yes
Republicans					
Hutchinson (Mich)	No	No	No	No	No
McClory (Ill)	No	Yes	Yes	No	No
Smith (NY)	No	No	No	No	No
Sandman (NJ)	No	No	No	No	No
Railsback (Ill)	Yes	Yes	No	No	No
Wiggins (Cal)	No	No	No	No	No
Dennis (Ind)	No	No	No	No	No
Fish (NY)	Yes	Yes	No	No	No
Mayne (Iowa)	No	No	No	No	No
Hogan (Md)	Yes	Yes	Yes	No	No
Butler (Va)	Yes	Yes	No	No	No
Cohen (Me)	Yes	Yes	No	No	No
Lott (Miss)	No	No	No	No	No
Froelich (Wis)	Yes	Yes	No	No	No
Moorhead (Cal)	No	No	No	No	No
Maraziti (NJ)	No	No	No	No	No
Latta (Ohio)	No	No	No	No	No

(Continued from Page 207)

Following Donohue's motion, Rodino opened 10 hours of general debate, after which the committee concerned itself with amending and voting on each proposed article. Generally each member used his allotted 15 minutes to announce his stand. By the end of the general debate July 25, it was clear that the committee would recommend impeachment by a large bipartisan margin.

Whether the impeachment articles would have bipartisan support had not been certain before the general debate. Pro-impeachment forces feared that White House charges of partisanship would be substantiated if no more than one or two Republicans supported impeachment. Proponents also felt that failure by the committee's Southern Democrats to back impeachment would have an adverse affect on other Southern Democrats when the full House considered the committee's recommendations.

Thus, the opening debate allowed some members of the committee to explain the "agony" they felt over impeaching a President. It provided an opportunity for others to explain to a constituency that had voted overwhelmingly for the President in 1972 why in their opinions it was necessary to impeach the President.

Rep. Tom F. Railsback (R, Ill.)—"I am one that has agonized over this particular inquiry. . . . In my opinion Richard Nixon has done many wonderful things for this country. . . . I have two serious areas of concern in respect to allegations of misconduct . . . against the President. . . . If the young people in this country think that we are not going to handle this thing fairly, if we are not going to really try to get to the truth, you're going to see the most frustrated people, the most turned-off people, the most disillusioned people, and it's going to make the period of LBJ [Lyndon B. Johnson] in 1968–67—it's going to make it look tame."

Rep. Walter Flowers (D, Ala.)—"The alternatives are clear: to vote to impeach . . . or to vote against impeachment. . . . We do not have a choice that, to me, represents anything desirable. I wake up nights . . . wondering if this could not be some sordid dream. . . . The people I represent . . . really want to support the President. Surely we want to support the Constitution and the best interests of the country. . . . What if we fail to impeach? Do we ingrain forever in . . . our Constitution a standard of conduct in our highest office that in the least is deplorable and at worst is impeachable? This is indeed a terrible choice we have to make."

Rep. M. Caldwell Butler (R, Va.)—"It . . . has [been] argued that we should not impeach because of comparable conduct in previous administrations. There are frightening implications for the future of our country. . . . If we fail to impeach, we have condoned and left unpunished a course of conduct totally inconsistent with the reasonable expectations of the

American people. . . . In short, a power appears to have corrupted. It is a sad chapter in American history, but I cannot condone what I have heard, I cannot excuse it and I cannot and will not stand for it."

Article I: obstruction of justice—The first article, a substitute for the Donohue proposal by Paul Sarbanes (D, Md.), was adopted July 27 by a 27-11 vote. Six Republicans joined the panel's 21 Democrats in voting for impeachment. The Sarbanes substitute specifically charged Nixon with failure "to take care that the laws be faithfully executed" by engaging "personally and through his subordinates and agents in a course of conduct or plan designed to delay, impede and obstruct" the investigation into the June 17, 1972 break-in at the headquarters of the Democratic National Committee at the Watergate complex in Washington. The article also accused Nixon of covering up for, concealing and protecting those responsible, as well as concealing "the existence and scope of other unlawful covert activities."

The Sarbanes substitute listed nine methods by which Nixon was alleged to have carried out the obstruction. The methods included allegations that Nixon had made "false and misleading statements" to investigators, had withheld evidence of criminal wrongdoing, had counseled associates to commit perjury, had interfered in lawful investigations of Watergate, had condoned payment of hush money, had "endeavored to misuse the Central Intelligency Agency," had passed on to prospective defendants secret grand jury information, had made "false and misleading" statements that a complete investigation had cleared White House and campaign personnel of involvement in Watergate, and had caused prospective defendants to expect "favored treatment" in return for their "silence or false testimony."

The final vote on the Sarbanes substitute came after two days of debate, during which the anti-impeachment bloc of Republicans attacked the article for its lack of specificity. The President, they asserted, was entitled, like any other defendant, to know the exact details of any offense he had allegedly committed. They said the general nature of the Sarbanes substitute showed that its proponents lacked specific evidence directly tying Nixon to any wrongdoing and were relying on "inferences upon inferences."

Pro-impeachment committee members responded that general charges were preferable because they allowed later introduction of evidence currently not on hand and were easier to prove. As for lack of evidence tying Nixon to the cover-up, the proponents insisted that the evidence, while circumstantial in nature, was overwhelming. The article's backers also contended that the President's attorney, James D. St. Clair, had been present at the time of presentation of evidence to the committee and fully knew the allegations against which he would have to defend the

President.

The first formal vote on the Sarbanes amendment was taken July 26 on a motion by Rep. Charles W. Sandman Jr. (R, N.J.), who sought to delete the first of the nine elements listed in the obstruction charge. The amendment was defeated 27–11.

The second day of debate on the Sarbanes substitute went quickly. Conceding he lacked votes for his motions to be successful, Sandman withdrew his amendments to strike the other elements of the Sarbanes article. Attempting to answer GOP charges that pro-impeachment forces lacked specific evidence against Nixon, Flowers reintroduced for purposes of debate several of Sandman's motions so that impeachment proponents could present such data. The Flowers motions were each defeated, with their sponsor voting "present." The committee then approved five technical changes in the Sarbanes article.

In answer to Republican charges that the Sarbanes substitute was not specific enough, John M. Doar, special counsel to committee, also drew up and presented to the committee July 27 a list of 50 incidents to defend the charge that President Nixon made a decision to participate in the Watergate cover-up. "This decision by the President," the preamble to the list said, "is the only one that could explain a pattern of undisputed incidents that otherwise cannot be explained." (Doar's list, written hurriedly overnight, was not meant to be an official committee document but a check-off list for purposes of debate.)

Article II: abuse of power—The second article, a substitute set of charges offered by Rep. William L. Hungate (D, Mo.), was approved July 29 by a 28-10 vote. Rep. Robert McClory (Ill.), second ranking Republican on the committee who opposed Article I, joined six Republican colleagues and 21 Democrats in recommending Nixon's impeachment for abuse of power.

This omnibus charge against Nixon, which McClory called the "crux" of the matter, specifically focused on the following allegations:

Personally and through his subordinates and agents, Nixon attempted to use the Internal Revenue Service to initiate tax audits or obtain confidential tax data for political purposes He initiated a series of secret wiretaps under the guise of "national security" and misused the results of the taps. He authorized and permitted to be maintained in the White House a secret, privately financed investigative unit which engaged in "covert and unlawful activities," including the 1971 burglary of the office of the psychiatrist of Pentagon Papers trial defendant Daniel Ellsberg. He failed to act on the knowledge that "close subordinates" endeavored to impede the Watergate investigation and related matters. He "knowingly misused the executive power by interfering" with the lawful activities of the Federal Bureau of Investigation, the

Central Intelligence Agency, the Justice Department, and the Watergate special prosecutor's office.

Rep. Charles E. Wiggins (R), whose district in California approximated the one from which Nixon was first elected to Congress in 1946, charged that the Hungate article represented a "step toward a parliamentary system of government" by trying to make Nixon accountable, after the fact, for subjective "notions of morality and propriety."

Another charge by Wiggins that the article was out of order was answered by Rep. George E. Danielson (D, Calif.), who said, "The offenses charged against the President . . . are uniquely presidential offenses. No one else can commit them. . . . You or I . . . can violate any of the statutes in our criminal code, but only the President can violate the oath of office of the President. Only the President can abuse the powers of the office of the President."

Defenders of the President challenged elements of the Hungate substitute dealing with the wiretaps and the use of a special investigations unit against Ellsberg. They said the President would have been derelict in his duty had he not acted against leaks of classified information.

However, proponents of the articles countered that while Nixon's intentions might have been well meant at the outset, his wiretaps were in contravention of existing wiretap laws and degenerated into political surveillance in the 1972 presidential campaign. Regarding the special investigation unit, the "plumbers," Rep. Joshua Eilberg (D, Pa.) remarked, "The Nixon White House made secret police a reality in America."

Article III: defiance of subpoenas—The third article in the bill of impeachment, approved July 30, charged that the President had sought to impede the impeachment process by refusing to comply with eight committee subpoenas for 147 recorded White House conversations and other evidence. Although the article was introduced by McClory, it failed to gain broad bipartisan backing and passed by the narrow margin of 21-17. Rep. Lawrence J. Hogan (R, Md.) joined McClory and 19 Democrats to insure passage. Democrats Walter Flowers (Ala.) and James R. Mann (S.C.) voted to oppose the article.

Opponents of Article III warned their colleagues that it was "political overkill" and predicted a bitter debate on the House floor. Other opponents, noting the Supreme Court's ruling against Nixon with regard to the tapes demanded by the Watergate special prosecutor, contended that the committee should have gone to the court for a definitive ruling, or, failing that, declared Nixon in contempt of Congress.

In contrast, backers of Article III insisted that failure to hold Nixon responsible for his defiance would, as Rep. Don Edwards (D, Calif.) put it, "destroy the only safety valve in the Constitution to

protect ourselves against a President who so misbehaves that he poses a threat to the country." In defense of his own article, McClory added that the committee could not conduct a "thorough and complete and fair investigation" if the President were the "sole arbiter" on questions of relevant evidence.

Rep. Ray Thornton (D, Ark.) offered an amendment, adopted 24-14, designed to make clear that Presidential defiance of a Congressional subpoena was an impeachable offense only in an impeachment inquiry and not in response to a committee drafting legislation.

Article IV: Cambodia issue rejected— The fourth article, proposed by Rep. John J. Conyers Jr. (D, Mich.), charged that Nixon had usurped Congress' power to declare war by approving and then concealing from Congress the secret bombing of Cambodia in 1969. After limited debate July 30, the committee rejected the article 26–12. Nine Democrats joined the committee's 17 Republicans in opposing it.

Opponents of this article asserted that Congress should bear much of the blame. While Nixon's decision to bomb constituted a usurpation of Congress' power, Rep. William S. Cohen (R, Me.) said, this seizure of prerogative came about "not through the bold power of the President but rather through the sloth and default on the part of Congress." Rep. Flowers said that if Nixon were impeached for Cambodia, then President Johnson should be impeached posthumously for Laos and Vietnam, President Kennedy for "Santo Domingo and the Bay of Pigs," President Eisenhower for the U-2 incident, and President Truman for the Korean conflict. Rep. Elizabeth Holtzman (D, N.Y.) countered that there had never been a vote in Congress ratifying the bombing and, hence, Nixon had acted illegally.

Article V: personal finances issue rejected—The last article to be considered by the impeachment panel concerned the President's personal finances. This article, sponsored by Rep. Edward Mezvinsky (D, Iowa), failed by a vote of 26-12 July 30. Nine Democrats and 17 Republicans voted to oppose.

According to Mezvinsky's charge, the President abused his office by "knowingly" underpaying his federal income taxes and by accepting government-paid-for improvements to his personal property in San Clemente, Calif. and Key Biscayne, Fla.

By and large, committee debate on this motion did not center on the substance of the charges but on their appropriateness as an article of impeachment. Reps. Jerome Waldie (D, Calif.), Wayne Owens (D, Utah) and Cohen agreed that Nixon's activities in these areas bordered on criminality, but each felt that an impeachable offense should be of greater magnitude. "Impeachment . . . is . . . designed to redefine Presidential powers in cases . . . [of] enormous abuse . . . and to limit the power as a concluding result of the impeachment process. . . . I do not find a

Presidential power [in this instance] that has been so grossly abused that it deserves redefinition and limiting."

Proponents of the fraud charge insisted that the President, like every other U.S. taxpayer, had to be held accountable under the tax laws. Moreover, Rep. Jack Brooks (D, Tex.) said, with reference to the matter of direct evidence of Nixon's guilt of criminal violations, the committee possessed "specific proof of the execution of fraudulent deeds, the filing of false returns, the failure to report income, [and] the enrichment of one's personal estate at public expense." No President was any less accountable for his personal misdeeds than he was for his public misdeeds, Brooks said.

(Brooks, chairman of the Government Activities Subcommittee of the Government Operations Committee, oversaw the investigation of federal expenditures on the Presidential properties in San Clemente and Key Biscayne. While Mezvinsky was the official sponsor of this article, Brooks was its chief proponent and defender during the debate.)

Committee members call inquiry fair— A bipartisan group of members of the Judiciary Committee said on the ABC television program, "Issues and Answers," July 21 that the impeachment inquiry against the President had been conducted fairly.

Rep. Charles E. Wiggins (R, Calif.), who emerged in subsequent committee debate as one of the President's chief defenders, said that "by and large it has been fair." "I have no great quarrel" with the investigation, he remarked, adding that it had been essentially nonpartisan "up until the last few days."

Others, who appeared on the program and basically agreed with Wiggins' characterization, were Reps. Don Edwards (D, Calif.), Walter Flowers (D, Ala.) and Robert McClory (R, Ill.).

White House stance wavers. White House reaction to developments in the impeachment proceedings ranged from expressions of total confidence July 27 to subsequent concessions that President Nixon faced serious problems as the issue moved to consideration by the full House.

Shortly after the first article of impeachment (obstruction of justice) was adopted by the Judiciary Committee July 27, Press Secretary Ronald L. Ziegler said Nixon remained "confident that the full House will recognize that there simply is not the evidence to support this or any other article of impeachment and will not vote to impeach." Ziegler added that Nixon was "confident because he knows he has committed no impeachable offense."

Alexander M. Haig Jr., White House chief of staff, said July 28 that Nixon's chances of escaping impeachment were uncertain because of the "very severe losses" suffered over the previous several days, but both Haig and Ziegler maintained Nixon would be vindicated.

Deputy Press Secretary Gerald L. Warren said the next day that Nixon would not resign if impeached in the House and reiterated Nixon's confidence that the House would not approve articles of impeachment. Warren said the White House was doing no "traditional" lobbying on the issue among House members and that no formal head count was being taken, adding, however, that "there may be some people who are mentally counting."

A possible shift in strategy was hinted but was subsequently discredited by presidential aide Patrick J. Buchanan July 31. Buchanan said Nixon had "not ruled out" a plan under which he would ask the House to vote unanimous impeachment without lengthy debate, assuring a speedy trial in the Senate.

Buchanan explained that there had been "serious slippage" in the President's strength in the House, and that if it seemed there was "no chance" there, the White House should seek to "maximize" its Senate position. Buchanan added that the tactic would also take the pressure off many House Republicans worried about their re-election prospects.

Later in the day, however, Buchanan said chances of following such a plan were slim. Reaction in the White House, he said, ranged from "skepticism to outright opposition."

Rep. Charles E. Wiggins (R, Calif.), one of Nixon's principal defenders, said the House would be shirking its constitutional duty by such action. Minority leader John J. Rhodes (Ariz.) termed the idea "cosmetically attractive," but said opposition was widespread among members.

Warren told reporters Aug. 1 that he would no longer answer questions on the President's impeachment strategy. He repeated that the White House remained confident about the House outcome, but conceded that the situation was "dynamic" and "unpredictable."

Warren also denied that Ziegler had been silenced by his superiors, who reportedly considered Ziegler's strong condemnations of the Judiciary Committee to have been a serious tactical error.

Ford backs Nixon—Vice President Gerald R. Ford criticized Democrats on the House Judiciary Committee July 27 for failing to give specific details in the first article of impeachment. Ford said if the full House considered impeachment "on the facts," Nixon would be found innocent. Ford said he was convinced that Nixon was innocent of any impeachable offense.

Referring to the committee's vote on the obstruction of justice article, Ford said the fact that all 21 Democrats approved the article "tends to make it a partisan issue." Asked about the six Republicans who voted for the article, Ford said he was "disappointed."

Campaigning for Rep. David W. Dennis (R, Ind.), one of Nixon's strongest supporters on the Judiciary Committee, Ford

had said in Muncie July 25 that Nixon was the victim of "Democratic partisan politics." If Nixon were impeached, Ford said, "the impact on the country would be very, very bad."

Ford said in a speech at a fund-raising dinner: "I can say from the bottom of my heart, the President of the United States is innocent and he is right."

Conservative impeachment group formed—Howard J. Phillips, once President Nixon's director of the Office of Economic Opportunity, announced July 29 the formation of Conservatives for the Removal of the President (dubbed by Phillips "CREEP 2," a reference to Nixon's 1972 Committee to Re-elect the President.)

Phillips said he preferred that Nixon resign, but if he did not he should be impeached and removed from office. Phillips said Nixon would "fall when conservative constituencies make it possible for conservative legislators to vote for his impeachment."

A letter distributed by the organization accused Nixon of following a "survival strategy" to the detriment of principled decision-making.

Deputy White House Press Secretary Gerald L. Warren said July 30 expressed doubt that Phillips represented "the view of conservative congressmen or other conservatives around the country."

Polls on public support for Nixon—A nationwide Gallup Poll, conducted before the Supreme Court ruled that President Nixon must surrender subpoenaed tape recordings and other evidence, indicated, it was reported July 26, that 24% of those surveyed approved of his performance in office, while 63% disapproved. A Harris Survey, conducted July 17–21 and reported Aug. 1, showed that 29% of those asked rated Nixon's performance as excellent or good but that 68% rated it as fair to poor.

Another Harris Survey taken July 17–21 and made public July 28 found that Americans felt by a 53%–34% margin that the House should impeach Nixon "so he can be tried by the U.S. Senate." Asked what the Senate should do, 47% of the same sample group said the Senate should convict Nixon, and 34% said it should not.

1st tapes surrendered; one gap revealed. The White House turned over to U.S. District Court Judge John J. Sirica July 30 the tapes of 20 Watergate-related conversations, beginning the process of compliance with the previous week's Supreme Court decision that tapes and documents relating to 64 conversations must be surrendered for the pending Watergate cover-up trial.

Special presidential counsel James D. St. Clair said in submitting the tapes that he knew of no gaps or "abnormalities," but in a statement outlining claims of privilege submitted the next day, St. Clair

noted that five minues and 12 seconds of an April 17, 1973 meeting had not been recorded. St. Clair attributed the missing segment to a delay in replacing a reel of spent tape with a fresh one.

(The conversation, one of those included in the edited transcripts released by the White House April 30, involved Nixon, key aides John D. Ehrlichman and H. R. Haldeman, and Press Secretary Ronald L. Ziegler. At the point in the transcript where St. Clair said the lapse occurred—page 1125 in the transcripts as published by the Government Printing Office—there was no notation of a missing segment.

In the July 31 statement outlining claims of privilege, the White House contended that 23 segments totaling about 48 minutes were unrelated to Watergate and should not be transmitted to special prosecutor Leon Jaworski.

(Deputy White House Press Secretary Gerald L. Warren said July 30 that Nixon had been working "alone" in the Lincoln Room of the White House listening to the tapes, reviewing related documents and noting sections he wanted withheld.)

The surrender of 20 tapes was part of an agreement reached July 26 by Jaworski and St. Clair at Judge Sirica's behest. Jaworski had petitioned Sirica July 25 to order that all 64 conversations be turned over, in installments, within 10 days, arguing that further delay could be harmful to the cover-up trial scheduled to begin Sept. 9. After Sirica said he might impose his own timetable if an agreement were not reached voluntarily, the parties announced that the first installment would include the 20 subpoenaed conversations that were among the edited transcripts made public by the White House. Aug. 2 was set as a "target date" for surrender for as many additional tapes as possible, with St. Clair agreeing to abide by a priority list submitted by Jaworski.

One sidelight of the July 26 hearing was Jaworski's account of an abortive attempt at compromise over the subpoenaed tapes in early May. Jaworski recounted that he had offered to pare his demands to 38 of the 64 conversations—the 20 for which edited transcripts had been released and 18 others deemed especially crucial. He also told the White House that if he received these tapes he might not have to reveal in court that Nixon had been named a co-conspirator by the grand jury.

According to Jaworski, the White House rejected the offer after Nixon had listened to some of the 18 additional conversations.

Ehrlichman sentenced in 'plumbers' case. John D. Ehrlichman, former domestic affairs adviser to President Nixon who was found guilty July 12 of conspiring to violate the civil rights of Daniel Ellsberg's psychiatrist, was sentenced to 20 months to five years in prison July 31. He received the same sentence for each of two other perjury charges on which he was convicted. The sentences, a minimum of 20 months, were to run concurrently.

Ehrlichman had been found guilty of lying to the Federal Bureau of Investigation, but U.S. District Court Judge Gerhard A. Gesell dismissed that charge July 22, ruling that it had been too vague.

G. Gordon Liddy, a co-defendant found guilty on the conspiracy charge, received a sentence of one to three years in prison, to be served concurrently with his present sentence of six years, eight months to 20 years.

The two other defendants convicted of conspiracy, Bernard L. Barker and Eugenio Martinez, were placed on probation for three years by Gesell. Gesell said they had been "duped" by high government officials and had been punished enough.

Democrats' funds probed. Records from the Senate Watergate Committee's investigation of campaign finances continued to be made public. It was revealed Aug. 1 that Rep. Wilbur D. Mills (Ark.), a candidate for the Democratic presidential nomination in 1972, received a $100,000 contribution that was secretly funneled into dummy campaign committees by two top executives of Electronic Data Systems, a computer firm owned by Texas millionaire H. Ross Perot. [For further details, see p. 220C1]

Dean sentenced. John W. Dean 3rd, the former White House counsel who became President Nixon's principal accuser in the Watergate scandals, was sentenced to one-four years in prison Aug. 2 for his role in the Watergate cover-up. Dean had pleaded guilty to one count of conspiracy to obstruct justice Oct. 19, 1973, and had faced a maximum penalty of five years in prison and a $5,000 fine.

Before pronouncing sentence, U.S. District Court Judge John J. Sirica rejected a plea by Dean's attorney that sentencing be delayed pending Sirica's examination of presidential tapes surrendered under Supreme Court order for the pending cover-up trial.

Charles N. Shaffer argued that some of the tapes might show that Dean was an agent and subordinate in the cover-up rather than a principal. Shaffer cited the conversation of Feb. 27, 1973, during which, he said, Dean had "explained the negative aspects of the cover-up to the President."

Pleading for leniency, Shaffer said Dean should be given credit for breaking the Watergate case, and that a "retributive" sentence might discourage others from volunteering evidence in similar cases. The prosecution agreed that Dean had cooperated "fully and unhesitatingly."

Dean was ordered to begin serving the sentence Sept. 3 in a minimum security institution.

Nixon resignation is again asked. President Nixon asked Congress Aug. 2 to establish a "cost of living task force" that could monitor wage, price, supply and productivity developments. According to the Administration's proposed legislation, however, the new group would not have enforcement powers to delay or reduce wage and price increases—powers that had been held by the defunct Cost of Living Council.

The proposal had wide bipartisan support in Congress.

Two opponents of President Nixon's economic policies called on him to relinquish his office to Vice President Gerald Ford in an effort to restore leadership during a time of economic crisis. Sen. William Proxmire (D, Wis.), chairman of the Joint Economic Committee, said Aug. 4 that Nixon should step aside under provisions of the 25th Amendment of the Constitution because impeachment developments would make it "extremely hard" for Nixon to "pull the country together" to "appeal to labor . . . [and] management" in a sustained fight against inflation.

AFL-CIO President George Meany criticized the Administration's policies Aug. 5 and suggested that Ford could cope with the current economic problems better than Nixon. While noting that he was not impressed by Ford's previous Congressional voting record or by his performance as vice president, Meany said Ford was a "conservative with integrity [and that] is far better than what we have today in the White House."

"All I want is for the President to go away," Meany declared. The Administration's tight money policies had pushed the economy to "the brink of disaster," Meany added.

"A depressed home-building industry, declining national production and increased unemployment had added to runaway inflation," Meany said. "The threat of business failures, drawn-out recession and continuing inflation hang over the nation as the result of the present money crunch."

Jacobsen pleads guilty. Jake Jacobsen, a former counsel for the nation's largest dairy cooperative, Associated Milk Producers Inc. (AMPI), pleaded guilty Aug. 7 to a federal charge that he had bribed former Treasury Secretary John B. Connally Jr. in an effort to secure Administration support for an increase in federal milk price supports.

Co-op fined for campaign violations— Associated Milk Producers Inc. (AMPI) was fined $35,000 Aug. 1 after pleading guilty to a six-count criminal information charging conspiracy and illegal campaign giving.

[For further details on both these developments, see p. 220G2]

Abuses & Reforms
in Campaign Financing

Staff report on milk fund. In its findings from an investigation of links between an Administration price decision and dairy industry campaign contributions, the staff of the Senate Watergate committee concluded that campaign pledges made by major dairy cooperatives (totaling $2 million) "apparently [were] directly linked to a favorable milk price support decision by the President worth hundreds of millions of dollars to the industry—and costing the same amount to the government and consumers."

The staff's draft report, published May 31, also challenged claims by Nixon in a White Paper issued Jan. 8 to justify the 1971 decision increasing federal milk price supports.

The staff report was submitted for consideration to members of the Senate panel chaired by Sen. Sam Ervin (D, N.C.). White House Press Secretary Ronald Ziegler immediately denounced the paper as "one of the crudest and most obvious political reports I've yet seen come from the Ervin committee."

In analyzing the President's decision to overturn an Agriculture Department ruling and authorize the price support, the report said Nixon "ignored the opinion of every agriculture expert in his Administration and the criteria of the government statute" in allowing the price increase to take effect.

Staff disputes about Nixon's defense of his action centered on three points:

■ Nixon had said he acted largely because legislation that would also have raised milk price supports was pending in Congress in early 1971 and had such backing that a presidential veto would likely have been overridden. This claim was "overstated," according to the staff.

"At the very least," the report declared, "the President's decision was an act of political one-upmanship calculated to outdo the Democratic members of Congress who supported milk price support legislation." Nixon had claimed in his White Paper that during the period he considered the decision, 30 separate bills authorizing the increase were introduced in the House and that legislation in the Senate had the backing of 29 senators. According to the report, eight of the 30

House bills were not introduced until after Nixon acted and 27 of the 29 co-sponsors of a Senate bill were not added until April 5, 1971. (The Administration had announced its approval of the increase March 25, 1971.)

Only one Republican senator, and 29 GOP House members co-sponsored milk price legislation in early 1971, the report stated, observing that Republican support needed to override any presidential veto would not have been forthcoming.

■ In another disputed point, the report claimed that Nixon understated the cost of his decision to consumers. The higher price support level backed by Nixon was $4.93 per hundredweight, "a level 1¢ higher than that called for in virtually every bill introduced [in Congress] in 1971," the report asserted. Total costs of Nixon's action were said to be at least $300 million, or "$10 million more than 34 of the 36 bills introduced in Congress," according to the staff paper.

By making the decision in the spring when milk production and supply were high, the report added, Nixon's "decision raised the support level just in time to have the maximum impact on milk prices."

■ The committee staff also accused Nixon of misrepresenting the significance of the co-ops' campaign pledges in his re-election race. Nixon had admitted he was aware that major dairy co-ops had pledged $2 million but said this information had not influenced his decision. The White Paper had also emphasized that the dairymen eventually contributed an estimated $427,500, or "less than 1% of the total" received by the Nixon campaign.

In rebuttal, the staff report charged that Nixon and his fund raisers had no reason "not to expect the full amount of the pledge," which, "even by the standards of the 1972 presidential campaign" was "enormous." It "represented one of the three largest pledges of his campaign and a full 1/20th of this entire projected campaign budget of $40 million," the report stated.

The dairy donations were important for other reasons, according to the staff paper: the money, which was pledged in 1970, "represented the 'early money' which is critical to every campaign;" the commit-

ments also represented a "potential loss of $2 million" to the Democratic campaign which had benefitted from dairy industry donations in the past. Hence, the pledge could have been worth $4 million to Nixon, the report concluded.

In March 1971, the polls showed Sen. Edmund S. Muskie (D, Me.), a leading contender for the Democratic nomination, to be running a close race with Nixon, the report continued. "The pledge thereby took on even greater significance," the staff paper declared.

AMPI antitrust suit developments—The trial of Associated Milk Producers Inc. (AMPI), the nation's largest dairy co-op, on federal antitrust charges continued in Kansas City, Mo.

Court documents, published in news reports May 4, alleged that AMPI's general manager George Mehren offered $150,000 to President Nixon's re-election campaign in an effort to secure Administration efforts that would "slow down the antitrust action" and then "reduce it to just a wrist slap."

The charges were made by former AMPI lobbyist Robert Lilly in a statement to Edward Wright, who had been hired by AMPI directors to investigate charges of a political payoff by co-op officials.

Another AMPI official had testified earlier that co-op officials offered money to the Nixon campaign in return for allowing the antitrust case to "die a natural death."

Lilly claimed that 30 checks for $5,000 each, with the payee unspecified, were drawn up and signed by Mehren April 4–5, 1972, but were later voided. Mehren was reported to have told Senate investigators that he "had no recollection" of the checks, according to the Washington Post May 4.

Lilly said the decision to make the contribution grew out of a Washington meeting held March 16, 1972 between Treasury Secretary John B. Connally Jr. and AMPI officials. According to Mehren, "Connally called Attorney General [John] Mitchell and said rather harshly, 'Get off your [expletive deleted]. You're losing votes in the Midwest.'" Connally then suggested that AMPI delay making any more contributions "until

C

D

E

F

G

near the end of the election,' " Mehren told Senate investigators.

The deal to quash the antitrust suit was never carried out, according to Mehren, because Herbert Kalmbach, one of President Nixon's chief fund raisers, called off the request for more AMPI contributions at another Washington meeting April 24, 1972. No reason was given, Mehren said.

The former executive director of another major dairy co-op, Dairymen Inc., told Senate investigators that he was asked at a predawn meeting March 24, 1971 with officials of two other dairy co-ops to raise $300,000 immediately for use in Nixon's campaign, the Post reported May 11.

D. Paul Alagia said he was unable to raise $300,000, $200,000 or $100,000 as requested by executives from AMPI and Mid-America Dairymen, Inc. Instead, $25,000 was quickly put up and sent by messenger to Washington.

Kalmbach had testified that Nixon's aides sought to confirm dairy industry campaign pledges in a meeting March 24, 1971 with co-op leaders one day after President Nixon decided to increase federal price supports. After securing the commitment and receiving a token contribution, the Administration announced the price decision March 25, 1971, according to Senate investigators.

Nader's milk suit delayed—U.S. District Court Judge William B. Jones May 14 granted a government request and ordered an indefinite postponement of a civil suit brought by consumer advocate Ralph Nader seeking to overturn the controversial 1971 milk price support increase. The government had contended that the case would "impinge" on the impeachment proceedings.

Other developments. Blagdon H. Wharton pleaded no contest May 17 to a misdemeanor charge that he had accepted free food and drink for a 1972 fund raising event honoring Spiro T. Agnew, then vice president. Two other perjury charges were dropped. Wharton was treasurer of the committee which had organized the dinner.

The Justice Department announced April 23 that its investigation of alleged campaign fund irregularities by Rep. Shirley Chisholm (D, N.Y.), a contender for the 1972 Democratic presidential nomination, had been "substantially closed." The General Accounting Office had referred the case, citing four apparent violations of the federal disclosure law, in November 1973.

William J. Riley, chairman of the First National Bank of East Chicago (Ind.), pleaded no contest May 8 to 10 counts of violating a 1948 law prohibiting campaign contributions from a national bank or any corporation organized by authority of Congress. Riley was fined $10,000 and the bank was fined an additional $15,000 on the same counts.

The donations totaling $14,200 were made from 1970-72 to Gov. Otis R. Bowen (R), a former governor, Sen. Vance Hartke (D) and Rep. Ray Madden (D), all of Indiana.

There were added ramifications to the convictions of other corporations and executives on charges of illegal campaign donations.

George A. Spater, who admitted authorizing an illegal contribution from American Airlines, resigned as the airline's chairman and chief executive in September 1973. The New York City Bar Association issued a rare public reprimand April 24 charging Spater with professional misconduct, but the group did not institute disbarment proceedings against him.

William W. Keeler resigned as chief executive of Phillips Petroleum Co. in January (after pleading guilty the previous month) and relinquished his post as chairman in April, according to the Wall Street Journal May 10.

Spater and Keeler had reached retirement age, but both also decided not to stand for re-election as directors of their firms.

The Journal also reported that James Allen had resigned as a Northrop Corp. director after pleading guilty to campaign donation violations.

Stockholders in American Airlines and Gulf Oil Corp. filed damage suits against the corporations and executives, alleging "loss of goodwill" had resulted from their violation of campaign fund laws. The suits, filed in Washington and New York March 27, sought reimbursement of the $5,000 fines levied against each of the corporations, interest on the fines and repayment to the corporation of legal expenses resulting from the guilty pleas. A similar suit to collect all costs incurred because of the illegal contribution was filed against Minnesota Mining & Manufacturing, the Journal reported May 13.

A shareholder in Bethlehem Steel Corp. won the right to sue Bethlehem and its officers to recover more than $500,000 allegedly spent to influence the outcome of the 1972 presidential election. A federal appellate court ruled April 17 that Richard Ash was entitled to a court hearing on his charges that Bethlehem had improperly prepared and disseminated advertisements in support of President Nixon.

Agnew to pay for improvements. The government agreed to accept payment of $1,100 by former Vice President Spiro Agnew for nearly $180,000 in security improvements made to his Washington home at government expense, it was reported June 3. The house was being sold.

California approves election reform. California voters, by a more than 2-1 margin, approved a proposal June 4 that provided for strict campaign finance disclosure, limited campaign spending and strict regulation of lobbying activity.

The proposition, called the "Political Reform Initiative," passed despite opposition from businessmen, organized labor, politicians and lobbyists.

It required that Californians contributing $50 or more to any political campaign disclose for the public record their names, occupations, and employers. Incumbents seeking statewide office would be limited to spending 90% of the amount spent by their opponents, and lobbyists would be prohibited from spending more than $10 a month to influence any state official. Besides creating a Fair Political Practices Commission with broad enforcement powers, the measure barred state and local officials from voting on matters involving personal financial conflicts of interest.

Impeachment inquiry continues. The House Judiciary Committee continued its closed hearings June 4-6 to consider evidence gathered by its staff in the impeachment inquiry.

The first two sessions focused on Nixon Administration dealings with the International Telephone and Telegraph Corp. and the dairy industry.

Sirica reverses privilege ruling. U.S. District Court Judge John J. Sirica ruled June 7 that special Watergate prosecutor Leon Jaworski should have access to the tape of a portion of a presidential conversation that had been withheld under a privilege claim by President Nixon. According to Jaworski's petition, the tape of a Sept. 15, 1972 conversation could contain evidence bearing on alleged White House misuse of the Internal Revenue Service. [For further details, see p. 166A1]

Staff reports 'responsiveness' plan. The staff of the Senate Watergate Committee, in a draft report circulated among committee members June 7, said White House officials had conducted a "concerted and concealed endeavor" to "politicize" the executive branch "to insure that the Administration remained in power" in the 1972 election. The so-called "responsiveness program," according to the report, was "among the most dangerous activities discovered" by the committee, and "may rise to the level of a conspiracy to interfere with the lawful functioning of government. [For further details, see p. 155G3]

Court overturns IRS ruling. A 1972 ruling by the Internal Revenue Service (IRS) allowing donors of large campaign contributions to divide a single donation into $3,000 portions to avoid paying gift taxes was overturned June 7 by federal district court in Washington.

The ruling was expected to have broad significance: it would render useless the numerous dummy fund raising committees established in Washington to conceal the source and amount of campaign donations; and it could allow public interest groups to challenge the way the IRS enforced tax laws for other groups (previously, legal "standing" had been restricted to citizens who were permitted to contest only their own tax liabilities).

Judge June Green's ruling in favor of the Washington-based tax reform group, Tax Analysts and Advocates, was not retroactive. The IRS had permitted donors to split their gifts and avoid tax liability in the past, but no formal ruling had been made until 1972, when the White House requested it in the name of the Committee to Re-elect the President. A further clarification had been issued in December 1973, following an investigation of alleged abuses by one of President Nixon's principal backers, W. Clement Stone, much of whose 1972 donations, estimated at more than $2 million, had been divided into $3,000 portions. Clarifying its earlier ruling, the IRS warned that multiple fund raising committees for the same candidate must exist "in fact rather than in form" in order to claim exemption for contributors from the gift tax provision.

Suspended sentence for Kleindienst. Former Attorney General Richard Kleindienst, who had pleaded guilty to a misdemeanor charge of failing to testify "accurately" before a Senate hearing, received a suspended sentence for his criminal offense June 7. [For further details, see p. 165G2]

Impeachment inquiry. The House Judiciary Committee continued closed hearings June 11–13 on its staff's evidence of the Nixon Administration's involvement in the 1971 burglary at the office of Dr. Daniel Ellsberg's former psychiatrist; the White House approach to the Ellsberg trial judge, W. Matthew Byrne Jr., for his possible appointment as director of the Federal Bureau of Investigation; and the alleged White House attempt to use the Internal Revenue Service for political benefit.

In reference to the IRS subject, Chairman Peter W. Rodino Jr. (D, N.J.) said after the hearing June 13 the issues raised went "to the heart of whether there have been serious abuses of power by the President or members of his official family." "This is a subject that the committee will not dismiss lightly," he said. Rep. Robert McClory (Ill.), second-ranking Republican committee member, commented, however, that he did not "feel the presentation was too serious insofar as the President is concerned."

Senate Watergate Committee leaks. Staff reports to the Senate Watergate Committee also were being leaked to the press. One reported by United Press International June 14 asserted that President Nixon "must be held responsible and accountable" for the campaign of "dirty tricks" against 1972 Democratic presidential candidates. "Not only was he the candidate on behalf of whom these activities were undertaken," it said, "he also set the moral and ethical standards by which his re-election campaign operated."

According to the New York Times June 17, a staff report to the committee cited a "civil and criminal conspiracy" to use for Nixon's political benefit funds appropriated by Congress for social and economic programs for special groups. The report specified such use of funds to gain support from the elderly. One plan, according to the report, was to cut the funding of two established organizations for the elderly, considered "enemies" of the President, and fund instead groups created by the White House.

The committee was preparing its final report on its investigation. Chairman Sam

J. Ervin Jr. (D, N.C.) and Vice Chairman Howard H. Baker Jr. (R, Tenn.) told reporters after a closed session June 19 that there was no intention at present to cite anyone for contempt stemming from its probe. Ervin remarked that findings of guilt or innocence were "not our function" and reaffirmed that the panel's goal was to recommend remedial legislation.

Kalmbach sentenced. President Nixon's personal attorney, Herbert Kalmbach, who had pleaded guilty Feb. 25 to two criminal offenses related to the Watergate investigation, was sentenced June 17 by Judge John Sirica of the U.S. district court in Washington.

Kalmbach was sentenced to a jail term of 6–18 months and ordered to pay a $10,000 fine for violating a federal disclosure law governing campaign funds. The maximum penalty for the offense, which was a felony, was two years in prison and a $10,000 fine. [For further details, see p. 170A1]

Appeals court accepts tape case. The U.S. Court of Appeals for the District of Columbia agreed June 19 to review Judge John J. Sirica's ruling to give the special Watergate prosecutor part of a White House tape originally withheld under a claim of executive privilege. The conversation in question, held Sept. 15, 1972, pertained to possible White House intervention with the Internal Revenue Service for political purposes.

Impeachment inquiry enters new phase. The House Judiciary Committee completed its closed evidentiary hearings June 21 and moved June 24 to accelerate its impeachment inquiry in an effort to conclude its work by the latter part of July.

The committee also voted June 24 to issue four new subpoenas for White House tape recordings of Presidential conversations.

New subpoenas issued—The four new subpoenas authorized by the committee June 24 covered 49 tapes, bringing to 147 the number sought by the panel from the White House.

Two of the subpoenas were approved by voice vote without dissent. The first requested 10 tapes involving discussions of the White House special investigations unit, five bearing on talks between Nixon and Colson. The second subpoena demanded two tapes of Sept. 15, 1972 talks concerning alleged White House efforts to intervene with the IRS for political gain.

The two other subpoenas were authorized by votes of 34-4, the dissent coming from Republican Reps. Edward Hutchinson (Mich.), Wiggins, Trent Lott (Miss.) and Delbert L. Latta (Ohio). They covered 19 tapes potentially related to knowledge of false testimony by Presidential subordinates at the 1972 Senate hearings on the nomination of Richard G. Kleindienst to be attorney general and 18 White House meetings concerning the 1971 decision to raise federal milk price supports and pledges by dairy producer

organizations for Nixon re-election funds.

The panel rejected on a 23–15 party line vote a Republican proposal to subpoena the Sept. 15, 1972 tapes from Judge John J. Sirica of the U.S. district court, which had temporary custody of the tapes. The majority opposed putting the panel in confrontation with the courts.

Mitchell linked to Hughes' hotel bid. A Senate Watergate Committee staff report charged that former Attorney General John N. Mitchell bypassed his antitrust division and approved an effort in 1970 by billionaire Howard Hughes to buy the Dunes Hotel in Las Vegas, Nev., it was reported June 25.

Made without analysis by the Justice Department's antitrust lawyers, Mitchell's "secret, ad hoc" decision was "clothed with the appearance of impropriety" and was a "classic case of government decision-making for friends" of the Nixon Administration, the report asserted.

The report also said the $100,000 cash campaign contribution by Hughes to Charles G. Rebozo, President Nixon's personal friend, might have been connected with Mitchell's decision.

According to the report, the Hughes organization had been warned by the antitrust division in 1968 that further additions to its Las Vegas holdings—four casino-hotels—would violate merger guidelines set forth in the Clayton Antitrust Act. However, Hughes was later allowed to purchase a fifth casino-hotel under the so-called "failing company doctrine," which provided for antitrust exemption in cases where the only alternative was financial failure.

When the Dunes became available in late 1969, the staff report said, Richard G. Danner, the Hughes aide who also delivered the $100,000 to Rebozo, was dispatched to Washington to deal directly with Mitchell, whom Danner knew from the 1968 presidential campaign.

Three meetings between Mitchell and Danner in January, February and March 1970 followed, the report stated. Mitchell testified to committee investigators that he recollected only one such meeting, but Danner, buttressed by Justice Department appointment logs, asserted there had been three, the report said.

The argument put to Mitchell by Danner entailed changing the definition of the relevant market. Instead of considering the impact of the purchase of the Dunes on Las Vegas alone, Danner suggested, the Justice Department should view the acquisition in terms of the whole state market.

At their February meeting, Danner supplied Mitchell with statistics on concentrations of hotel rooms in Las Vegas. A third meeting, requested by Mitchell, followed March 19. According to Danner, Mitchell said, "From our review of these figures, we see no problem. Why don't you go ahead with the negotiations" [for the Dunes.] (Negotiations for purchase of the Dunes by Hughes later fell through for unrelated financial reasons.)

Richard McLaren, head of the antitrust division at the time, told Watergate committee investigators that he first learned of the proposed acquisition March 12, 1970, two months after Danner broached the idea with Mitchell. He informed Mitchell that the purchase would violate merger guidelines, McLaren testified, but Mitchell ended their discussion without indicating his final position. One week later, the report said, Mitchell approved the purchase.

St. Clair presents rebuttal. President Nixon's defense against impeachment was presented to the House Judiciary Committee in closed sessions June 27–28 by his chief defense counsel James D. St. Clair. The material was said to have dealt with the Watergate burglary, the cover-up, Administration transactions with the International Telephone & Telegraph Corporation and milk producers, the White House "plumbers," wiretapping and Nixon's income taxes. [For further details, see p. 177D1]

GAO cites McGovern unit. The General Accounting Office, which had been designated by Congress as the watchdog for the Federal Election Campaign Act, June 27 cited a Connecticut committee that raised funds for Sen. George McGovern's (D, S.D.) 1972 presidential race for "apparent violations" of the campaign spending law. The committee could not account for $21,000 of its total $193,500 in expenditures, the GAO said.

Common Cause suit dismissed, 'hit list' disclosed. Judge Joseph C. Waddy of U.S. district court in Washington dismissed a suit June 28 brought by Common Cause, the public interest lobby, to compel disclosure of President Nixon's secret campaign contributors.

Waddy ruled that with the election past, Common Cause no longer had legal standing to sue to force disclosure of the money received and spent by the Finance Committee to Re-elect the President in the period prior to April 7, 1972. (On that date, a new federal law requiring public reporting of all financial transactions took effect.)

Aided by a court order, Common Cause in September 1973 had obtained what the finance committee had said were complete records dealing with pre-April 7, 1972, but Common Cause lawyers later told the court they had uncovered nearly $2 million in secret donations that were not recorded in the campaign documents. The attorneys sought permission from the court to search for more material.

Judge Waddy denied this move, accusing the group of "harassment" of Nixon contributors, but he agreed to unseal new campaign records uncovered by Common Cause.

Among the documents was a so-called "hit list" or "prospects for solicitation" naming the finance committee's potential donors, target contributions, assigned so-

licitors and comments. Among those cited were:

■ "East family, Sarita [Texas], target amount 100/200 [thousands of dollars], ask big. Won't get much. Needs to be scared." (The East family owned a 200,-000 acre ranch in Texas.)

■ "Howard Boyd, Houston, target amount 100—El Paso Natural Gas Co.—antitrust—Algeria (FPC)." Boyd was chairman of El Paso, which was involved in the longest pending antitrust case ever before the courts and also was seeking a Federal Power Commission ruling on the right to import liquified natural gas from Algeria.

■ "Walter R. Davis [former Occidental Petroleum Co. executive], assigned to MHS [Maurice H. Stans, finance committee chairman], target amount 50—dangerous."

■ Elmer Holmes Bobst [long a Nixon friend and retired chairman of Warner-Lambert Pharmaceutical Co.], assigned to HWK [Herbert W. Kalmbach, Nixon's personal attorney and a chief fund raiser], target amount 100/200, amount received 100,000."

Other papers showed that the finance committee's records filed in September 1973 excluded donations estimated by Common Cause lawyers at $1,825,000 and also omitted pre-April 7, 1972 expenditures of $1,175,000. (Some of the transactions had been concealed by strips of white paper glued over information that was submitted under court order.) Another document showed that convicted Watergate conspirator G. Gordon Liddy had set up two previously unknown fund raising committees in Delaware and Illinois while serving as the finance committee's general counsel.

Laundering of gifts to end—Common Cause won agreement from two Congressional officials to end the practice of concealing contributions earmarked for specific candidates by laundering the money through committees, the New York Times reported May 20.

W. Patrick Jennings, clerk of the House, and Francis Valeo, secretary of the Senate, agreed to end the system, which Common Cause lawyers termed "using a third party as a false front."

With the out-of-court settlement, Common Cause's suit testing the 1971 Federal Election Campaign Act was dismissed.

Weicker charges abuse of Constitution. In a personal report issued separately from the Watergate committee panel's report on campaign abuses, Connecticut Sen. Lowell P. Weicker (R.) charged June 29 that "every major substantive part of the Constitution was violated, abused and undermined during the Watergate period." [For further details, see p. 175D3]

Democratic telethon raises $7 million. The third annual fund-raising telethon held by the Democratic Party June 29–30 produced more than $7 million in pledges.

Nixon bombing remarks reported. The

Los Angeles Times reported June 29 that the House Judiciary Committee had been given another tape transcript in which President Nixon referred to Vietnam bombing and a public relations effort to explain the reason for shifting the site of the 1972 Republican National Convention from San Diego to Miami Beach. The transcript of an April 4, 1972 conversation was said to have been given the committee by Nixon's defense lawyer James D. St. Clair. [For further details, see p. 175G2]

Maheu wins libel suit against Hughes. A Los Angeles federal jury July 1 ruled in favor of Robert A. Maheu in his libel suit against billionaire industrialist Howard Hughes. U.S. District Court Judge Harry Pregerson ordered the six-person jury to return Oct. 8 to determine damages to be awarded to Maheu, who was seeking $17.5 million.

Maheu's suit stemmed from a statement by Hughes during a 1972 telephone news conference that he had dismissed Maheu as a staff aide because Maheu "stole me blind." Hughes, who employed Maheu from 1953 until his firing in 1970, had convened the unusual press conference to disclaim any connection with a purported biography by Clifford Irving.

Summa Corp., wholly owned by Hughes, accepted responsibility for the remarks, which it contended were true. In turn, Summa Corp. filed a $4.5 million counterclaim against Maheu, an action ultimately rejected by the jury. Hughes did not appear at the trial.

To resolve the dispute, attorneys for both sides undertook an extensive review of Maheu's financial relationships with Hughes. Among the revelations was the $100,000 cash campaign contribution by Hughes to Charles G. Rebozo, President Nixon's personal friend. In all, it was disclosed during the trial, Hughes contributed $1 million to U.S. political candidates, $600,000 of which came from the Silver Slipper, a Las Vegas, Nev. gambling casino personally owned by Hughes. This made the political contributions legal personal gifts, as opposed to corporate contributions which were illegal.

Rebozo plea vs Watergate unit held moot. U.S. District Court Judge John Lewis Smith Jr. July 2 dismissed as moot a plea by Charles G. Rebozo, President Nixon's friend, for an order barring the Senate Watergate Committee from inquiring further into his affairs or citing him for contempt. Smith held that there was no longer any issue since the committee's authority had lapsed June 28.

Rebozo had accused the panel May 20 of trying to humiliate him by subpoenaing records of every financial institution and every business he had dealt with since 1968.

Rebozo's legal actions against the committee stemmed from his complaint that the committee had obtained from Herbert W. Kalmbach, who was personal attorney to Nixon, "false" information and had relayed it "maliciously" to the press.

Priestes released. John J. Priestes, who was sent to prison in a Federal Housing Administration scandal that led to an investigation of a political fund for Sen. Edward J. Gurney (R, Fla.), was released July 2 after serving six months of a one-year prison sentence.

Gurney indicted on bribery charges. Sen. Edward J. Gurney (R, Fla.) was charged by a federal grand jury July 10 with bribery, conspiracy, and lying to the grand jury in connection with an influence-peddling and extortion scheme to raise campaign funds.

Gurney and six others also indicted were accused of having conspired since December 1970 to demand money from Florida contractors and developers "who had matters pending before" the Department of Housing and Urban Development (HUD). "In return for the contributions and payments, pressure and influence would be exerted on HUD to give favored treatment to the contributors in awarding contracts for HUD housing projects and mortgage insurance," the indictment charged.

Gurney was alleged to have extorted $223,160 over a 3½-year period for use as "personal, political and travel expenses" and for use in the operation of his Washington and Florida offices. Gurney also was accused of having "corruptly solicited and accepted a bribe on Aug. 15, 1971 from the owner of a Vero Beach, Fla. condominium apartment in return for Gurney's assistance." The bribe, according to the government, was a "fifth floor, ocean-front apartment," valued at $67,000.

Indicted with Gurney were James L. Groot, Gurney's former administrative assistant; Joseph Bastien, Gurney's executive assistant in his Winter Park, Fla. office; Earl M. Crittenden, an Orlando, Fla. citrus grower and former state Republican chairman; George Anderson, an Orlando banker and former state GOP treasurer; Wayne Swiger, director of HUD's Tampa, Fla. insurance office; and Ralph Koontz, special assistant to the Florida area director for HUD. Forty-two persons, including 39 real estate developers, were named as unindicted co-conspirators. Another unindicted co-conspirator, Larry E. Williams, had been hired to "demand" and collect the payments, according to the government.

The indictment cited 115 overt acts in the conspiracy, including some that occurred while Gurney was serving as a member of the Senate Watergate Committee. He was charged with one count of bribery, one count of conspiracy, one count of receiving unlawful compensation and four counts of making false statements to a grand jury in May 1973. If convicted, Gurney faced up to 42 years in prison and fines totaling $40,000.

Gurney issued an immediate denial: "I maintain my absolute innocence of any wrongdoing," he said. "I have an abiding faith in the American system of justice and I firmly believe that I will be proved innocent of any wrongdoing in this affair. As in the case of the Tallahassee [Fla.] indictment, I intend to fight this move just as hard as I can and I will be vindicated." (State charges against him alleging election law violations had been dismissed in May.)

Gurney was the first senator in 50 years indicted on federal charges while holding office. (Sen. Burton K. Wheeler [D, Mont.] had been acquitted of malfeasance in 1924.)

Committee issues Watergate evidence. The House Judiciary Committee released July 11 an eight-volume, 4,133-page record of the evidence assembled by its staff dealing with the Watergate break-in and its aftermath. Seven volumes consisted of the material presented by the staff to the committee members in closed sessions in May and June. The eighth volume was President Nixon's rebuttal presented to the committee by his lawyer, James St. Clair.

A Feb. 1, 1972 memo from Strachan to Haldeman suggested that "230 green [$230,000] be held under [Herbert W.] Kalmbach's personal control; and that any polling be paid for by regular Nixon finance committees." On the memo, under his initialed approval, Haldeman wrote, "make it 350 green and hold for us." Strachan informed Haldeman in a later memo that Kalmbach, Nixon's personal lawyer at the time, would provide "350 in green under your unquestioned personal control. A separate box of green is being developed for the campaign." Haldeman's testimony about the $350,000 cash fund, which provided payments to the Watergate defendants, was that it had been held for special private political polls.

GAO cites Agnew committee. A Los Angeles-based committee that had supported former Vice President Spiro Agnew's renomination in 1972 operated in apparent violation of federal campaign laws during 1972 and 1973, the General Accounting Office (GAO) said July 9.

The case against Americans for Agnew Committee, which solicited support for Agnew without his consent, was referred to the Justice Department for possible prosecution.

Lobbies amass $17.4 million. Special interest groups had already spent or had on hand $17.4 million for use in 1974 House and Senate elections, Common Cause announced July 10. Of the total—which was more than twice the amount spent on Congressional races in 1972—$14.7 million was being held in the lobbies' committees and $2.7 million had been donated to candidates.

Among the findings: health lobbies, led by the American Medical Association, had raised $2.9 million, or 223% above the 1972 amount. Funds raised by agriculture groups and the milk lobby were up 106% from 1972, despite adverse publicity stemming from Watergate-related disclosures. The three major dairy political committees, CTAPE, ADEPT and SPACE, had amassed more than $2 million. Labor fund raising committees had collected $5.4 million, a gain of 59% over 1972. Republican Congressional campaign committees had raised $3.5 million compared with the $900,000 raised by Democratic groups. Business and professional groups had about $8 million available for campaign use. Business lobbies had doubled their 1972 totals, and the National Education Association had on hand more than 10 times the amount spent in 1972.

Andreas not guilty on 1968 funds. A Minneapolis federal judge July 12 found Dwayne O. Andreas not guilty of violating campaign financing laws by donating $100,000 to the 1968 presidential campaign of Sen. Hubert H. Humphrey (D, Minn.).

Andreas had been accused of making four illegal corporate contributions of $25,000 each, when he withdrew the funds from First Interoceanic Corp. and sent the money to the Humphrey campaign as a loan.

The defense contended that Andreas, chairman of the corporation, had borrowed the funds from the firm and had deposited them in his own checking account. When Humphrey repaid Andreas, he in turn repaid the firm, the defense declared.

The case was heard without a jury and there were no witnesses.

Watergate panel issues report. In its last official action, the Senate Select Committee on Presidential Campaign Activities, known as "the Watergate Committee" or "the Ervin Committee," released the final report July 13 on its investigation of the Watergate and other scandals related to the 1972 presidential campaign.

[For a complete report on the committee's findings, see p. 185]

Evidence on IRS misuse released. The House Judiciary Committee July 16 released evidence collected in its impeachment inquiry concerning possible White House attempts to misuse the Internal Revenue Service for political gain. The committee previously released eight other volumes of evidence on the Watergate affair. [For further details, see p. 195E2]

Activity on ambassadorships noted—The evidence released by the committee July 16 included data indicating that John Mitchell had a hand in ambassadorial appointments while he was attorney general. [See p. 196G1]

St. Clair defends the President. St. Clair's defense of Nixon took the form of oral arguments before a closed session of the Judiciary committee July 18 and a

151-page written brief made public July 20. His written brief contended that there was no "conclusive evidence" of Presidential actions that would warrant impeachment. [For further details, see p. 199B2]

Doar says evidence merits impeachment. John M. Doar, special counsel to the House Judiciary Committee, urged committee members July 19 to recommend the impeachment of President Nixon on one or more charges. Doar was seconded by Albert E. Jenner Jr., special Republican counsel to the committee. [For further details, see p. 200D1]

ITT, milk fund evidence released. Two volumes of evidence on the Administration's handling of antitrust suits against International Telephone & Telegraph Corp. (ITT) were released by the House Judiciary Committee July 19. St. Clair presented a 208-page collection of information defending Nixon's role in the ITT case to the House panel that same day.

The House committee released two volumes of evidence July 19 relating to charges that President Nixon had raised the federal support price of milk in March 1971 in return for pledges of large campaign contributions from major dairy cooperatives.

[For further details, see p. 197B1]

Gurney quits Senate race. Sen. Edward J. Gurney (R, Fla.), who was indicted on charges of bribery, conspiracy and perjury, announced July 23 that he would not seek re-election to a second term. Gurney said he would devote his efforts to preparing a defense against the charges, to which he had pleaded innocent. Republican Party leaders in Florida had publicly urged him to withdraw from the state primary, scheduled for September.

Stans letters ordered released. U.S. District Court Chief Judge George L. Hart Jr. July 25 rejected President Nixon's claim that the confidentiality of his correspondence with former Commerce Secretary Maurice Stans was protected by executive privilege. Hart ordered the material turned over to the Watergate special prosecutor. [For further details, see p. 206C2]

Reinecke guilty of perjury. California Lt. Gov. Ed Reinecke (R) was convicted July 27 of one count of lying to the Senate Judiciary Committee during testimony about the alleged link between International Telephone & Telegraph Corp.'s (ITT) pledge of a contribution to fund the 1972 Republican Convention, then scheduled for San Diego, and the Administration's settlement of antitrust suits against ITT. The testimony was given April 19, 1972 during hearings to consider the nomination of then Deputy Attorney General Richard Kleindienst as attorney general, succeeding John Mitchell, who had been named campaign manager by Nixon.

Reinecke was found guilty of lying when, in response to a question by Sen. Hiram Fong (R, Hawaii), he claimed he had first informed Mitchell of ITT's $400,000 campaign pledge at a Sept. 17, 1971 meeting. The government contended that Reinecke had actually informed Mitchell of the offer during a telephone conversation May 21, 1971, while negotiations for the government's out of court settlement with ITT were under way. The settlement, which proved highly favorable to the conglomerate, was announced July 31, 1971.

Reinecke admitted under cross-examination that he had discussed the campaign donation with Mitchell on May 21, 1971, but the defense argued that Reinecke's answer had been technically truthful because he was not asked about phone conversations.

The jury reached no agreement about Reinecke's responses to three other questions by Fong, but found him guilty of lying in response to a fourth question:

Fong: So far as your testimony is concerned, Lt. Gov. Reinecke, [it] is that prior to the settlement of the ITT case no conversation was had by either one of you [Edgar Gillenwaters, a Reinecke aide, was included in the question] to anyone in the Justice Department that the ITT people had promised to do certain things in San Diego?

Reinecke: That is quite true.

Reinecke was indicted in April on three perjury counts but one was dismissed July 9 at the government's request. The charge that was dropped involved a conflict over Reinecke's claim that he first learned of ITT's campaign pledge in April 1971 and the government's contention that he had received that information several months earlier from Nixon's chief of staff, H. R. Haldeman. The prosecution said it was unwilling to call Haldeman, a defendant in the Watergate cover-up trial, as a witness against Reinecke.

Another perjury count was dismissed July 22 by Judge Barrington D. Parker on grounds that the question asked at the Senate hearing was "somewhat ambiguous."

Witnesses appearing at the trial included Senate Judiciary Committee member John Tunney (D, Calif.) and an aide to former White House Counsel John Dean.

Tunney testified July 16 that Reinecke had told him March 3, 1972 that he had discussed the ITT pledge with Mitchell in May 1971. At a press conference two days before the Tunney-Reinecke conversation, Mitchell had said he didn't "know the faintest thing about the convention financing," and when the ITT settlement was reached, hadn't known "what arrangements the Republican Party had with San Diego."

Dean's former aide, Darlene Housley, testified July 17 that Reinecke had met with Dean and another White House official, Clark MacGregor, before appearing at the Senate hearings and that she had briefed him on prior and conflicting testimony about ITT given at the Congressional hearings just before he testified.

Reinecke said July 29 that he would not resign his state office or take a leave of absence unless legally required to do so. (He remained free pending sentencing and appeal. Reinecke's term of office expired in 1975. He had been defeated in the Republican gubernatorial primary in June while under indictment.)

Connally charged with bribery, perjury. Former Treasury Secretary John B. Connally Jr. was indicted July 29 by a Watergate grand jury on five counts of accepting a bribe, conspiring to obstruct justice and perjury. He was accused of accepting $10,000 in two cash payments from Jack Jacobsen, a lawyer for Associated Milk Producers, Inc. (AMPI), on May 14, 1971 and Sept. 24, 1971.

According to the indictment, the payments, which occurred while Connally was serving as Treasury secretary, were made "for and because of official acts performed by him, to wit, his recommendations in his official capacity concerning an increase in the federal milk price support level to be fixed by the secretary of agriculture, announced on March 25, 1971."

Jacobsen was also indicted on one count of giving the bribe. Another milk fund-related charge against him had been dismissed in May on a technicality.

The indictment alleged that Jacobsen and Connally agreed on a "cover story" to conceal the $10,000 cash payment from the dairy industry. According to the special prosecutor's office, the cover-up conspiracy was carried out when Jacobsen testified that he twice offered money to Connally "for the purpose of enabling him to give it to candidates for public office and second as a contribution to Democrats for Nixon [a fund raising committee headed by Connally] and that . . . Connally declined the offer on each occasion."

The reason given for his rejection of the money, the indictment stated, was that Connally "was then a Democrat in a Republican Administration and did not want to appear to favor the candidacy of persons" from either party and that it also would be "prudent" to decline the offer in light of the publicity given AMPI's "problems."

Jacobsen testified falsely that he kept the unused cash in a safe deposit box, but, in fact, the indictment stated, Connally arranged to obtain $10,000 in cash "to give to Jacobsen so that he could make it available for inspection [by federal investigators] if called upon."

The indictment cited 12 overt acts in furtherance of the conspiracy, including two cash payments of $10,000 each made by Connally to Jacobsen in October and November 1973 for use as replacement money to corroborate their cover story. Jacobsen was named an unindicted co-conspirator in this effort to "influence, obstruct and impede" investigations by the Senate Watergate Committee and a

Watergate grand jury. Connally was charged with one count of conspiring to obstruct justice and commit perjury. Two other counts filed against him alleged that he made "false material declarations" before the second Watergate grand jury (which began deliberations Aug. 13, 1973) in appearances on Nov. 14, 1973 and April 11, 1974. The perjury charges related to Connally's testimony about conversations he had with Jacobsen regarding the milk fund matter.

Connally issued a statement July 29, denying he was guilty of "any wrongdoing." "For months," Connally said, "there have been leaks, rumors, and speculations concerning my role in the milk support price increase in March 1971. The matter is now in the open where it can be dealt with honestly and fairly," he said.

Connally was the fourth Cabinet official serving President Nixon to face indictment on Watergate-related charges or to plead guilty to federal charges: Maurice Stans had been acquitted on influence peddling charges with John Mitchell, who was also under indictment for his role in the Watergate cover-up scheme; Richard Kleindienst had pleaded guilty to misdemeanor charges involving the ITT case.

(Watergate Special Prosecutor Leon Jaworski, a former partner in a Houston law firm, announced July 29 that he would not take part in the case because he had once represented a private plaintiff in an antitrust suit against AMPI and because of a "long-standing acquaintanceship with Jake Jacobsen.")

Milk fund case widens—Charges were also filed against four other persons as a result of the nearly 12-month investigation conducted by the Watergate special prosecutor's office.

AMPI's former general manager, Harold S. Nelson, pleaded guilty July 31 to a charge that he conspired to bribe Connally in connection with AMPI's effort to secure the milk price support increase.

Nelson also admitted that he had conspired to make illegal campaign contributions to a number of Democratic and Republican candidates from 1968–1972.

Nelson admitted that AMPI funds were used to reimburse the co-op's political affiliate, TAPE, for the Kalmbach payment "to obviate the need for TAPE to report said payment."

Nelson's guilty plea came in a wide ranging, one-count conspiracy charge incorporating the bribery and illegal corporate contributions aspects. Among the other "overt acts" cited in the criminal information filed by the special prosecutor's office were authorizations made by Nelson for a $63,500 payment to the Democratic National Committee for tickets to a fund raising dinner in 1968 to benefit then Vice President Hubert H. Humphrey's presidential campaign; a

$23,950 donation to Humphrey's 1970 senatorial race in Minnesota; a $5,000 gift to the unsuccessful senatorial campaign conducted by then Vermont Gov. Philip Hoff (D); a $10,000 donation to Rep. Page Belcher's (R, Okla.) campaign for re-election; an $8,400 payment to committees organized for Sen. Edmund S. Muskie's (D, Me.) re-election campaign in 1970; and payments totaling $82,000 made to a computer mail service firm that performed work for "various Democratic Party candidates for federal elective office in Iowa" ($50,000), Humphrey's 1972 presidential primary race ($25,000) and Sen. James Abourezk's (D, S.D.) 1972 campaign ($7,000).

Many of the payments authorized by Nelson were carried out by TAPE official Robert Lilly, who was also said to have been on the AMPI payroll while working on the 1968 Humphrey campaign. Lilly, who had been cooperating with the special prosecutor's office under a grant of immunity, had told investigators that Jacobsen sought the Connally payment and that Nelson authorized the bribe.

According to the special prosecutor's office, Nelson's agreement to plead guilty to the felony violation came after plea bargaining negotiations in which he promised to make a "full and truthful disclosure" of all he knew about AMPI's other political dealings; however, Nelson was not granted immunity on possible violations relating to the President's March 25, 1971 decision to raise milk support prices, the special prosecutor's office added.

Nelson's former deputy at AMPI and the co-op's special counsel, David L. Parr, was the first official charged as a result of the special prosecutor's milk fund investigation. Parr pleaded guilty July 23 to a charge that he had authorized payment of more than $200,000 in illegal campaign contributions to Humphrey and other candidates of both parties.

Others named as unindicted co-conspirators were Nelson, Lilly, Robert O. Isham, also a TAPE official, and Stuart O. Russell, an Oklahoma lawyer cited for his role as a conduit of the illegal payments.

According to the special prosecutor's charge, a total of $150,450 was donated to Humphrey's 1968 presidential race, his 1970 senatorial campaign and his unsuccessful bid for the Democratic presidential nomination in 1972.

Other illegal payments which Parr admitted authorizing were a $50,000 payment to Democrat Richard Clark's 1972 election to the Senate from Iowa; a $10,000 payment to Rep. Belcher in 1972; $7,000 contribution to Abourezk in 1972; and $5,000 to Rep. Wilbur D. Mill's (D, Ark.) unsuccessful campaign for the Democratic presidential nomination in 1972.

It was also alleged that Lilly was paid by AMPI while he worked for the campaign of Patrick J. Hillings, a Republican

who lost a California race for Congress in 1972.

The criminal conspiracy to which Parr pleaded guilty did not involve President Nixon's re-election campaign or his controversial 1971 decision to raise federal milk price supports, but like Nelson, Parr's plea bargaining agreement did not extend to protection from possible bribery and conspiracy charges involving the President's price increase action. In a letter attached to the charges, the special prosecutor's office told the court, "It is expressly understood that Mr. Parr isn't receiving immunity from prosecution for possible violations in connection with the March 25, 1971 milk price support decision."

Nelson and Parr entered guilty pleas at federal district court in Washington. Both were released pending pre-sentencing investigations.

Humphrey's former press secretary, Norman Sherman, and his partner in the Minneapolis computer service firm, John Valentine, were indicted July 30 on charges of accepting $82,000 in illegal contributions from AMPI for computer mailing services performed for Humphrey, Abourezk and Democratic candidates in Iowa. [See above]

The misdemeanor charges brought by the Watergate special prosecutor's office were filed in federal district court in St. Paul, Minn.

No limit set on AMPI contributions—Former AMPI general manager Harold Nelson testified before the Senate Watergate Committee that the co-op had set no ceiling on its proposed contributions to the Nixon re-election campaign, but that the President's fund raisers "bungled" plans for collecting the money and thereby limited the dairy lobby's potential for donations.

The testimony was reported by the Washington Post July 17. According to Nelson, AMPI's total donations would have far surpassed the actual amount given (more than $500,000) if Nixon aides had not been so slow in setting up dummy committees to receive (and conceal) the subdivided contributions. "Even when they gave us the committees, they bungled it," he said. "For instance, one of the committee's address was a ballroom. . . . Another one, the chairman was a Washington lawyer whose name I cannot tell you. He had not even been consulted. . ., and it made him so mad that he blew his stack and called the clerk of the House."

Although he urged the White House to set up the conduits for donation early in 1971, Nelson said, the Administration was slow to act until many weeks after the decision was made to increase federal milk price supports. This tardiness worried him, Nelson added. "It was a constant thing in the back of my mind that if we didn't get the names of these committees, we might be read off just because of some inept—for want of a better term, I will say 'bureaucrat'—within the party hierarchy not coming forth and giving us the names of the committees."

"We told them [Nixon fund raisers] from the word go that we would make large contributions," he said. "At various times, $1 million, $2 million or even more money was discussed. And had they given us the names of the committees, they could have gotten much more money from us," he testified.

House committee charges abuse of power. The House Judiciary Committee recessed July 30 after approving three articles of impeachment charging President Nixon with obstruction of justice in connection with the Watergate scandal, abuse of presidential powers and attempting to impede the impeachment process by defying committee subpoenas for evidence. [For further details, see p. 207C3]

Democrats' funds probed. Records from the Senate Watergate Committee's investigation of campaign finances continued to be made public. It was revealed Aug. 1 that Rep. Wilbur D. Mills (Ark.), a candidate for the Democratic presidential nomination in 1972, received a $100,000 contribution that was secretly funneled into dummy campaign committees by two top executives of Electronic Data Systems, a computer firm owned by Texas millionaire H. Ross Perot.

The money was given by company president Milledge A. Hart 3rd, and a regional vice president, Mervin L. Stauffer, both of Dallas.

Stauffer denied that the money came from corporate funds. The donation was divided into installments and funneled through 17 committees March 30, 1972, just prior to the period when a new campaign financing law took effect and made such secret donations illegal. Mills did not make a voluntary disclosure of his receipts and expenditures during this period.

Stauffer said he gave the money "because I believe in Mills." The Dallas computer firm was a major processor of health insurance claims. Mills had been a chief sponsor of a national health insurance bill.

The committee Aug. 2 released a sworn statement from advertising executive Barry Nova who claimed that Jack L. Chestnut, Sen. Hubert Humphrey's campaign manager, arranged for an illegal $12,000 corporate payment from Associated Milk Producers Inc. (AMPI) in 1970.

Nova, who had worked in Humphrey's 1970 senatorial campaign as a political advertising specialist in the now bankrupt New York firm of Lennen & Newell, stated that Chestnut asked him to forward his bills for consulting fees to AMPI, "c/o Bob Lilly." Lilly, a former official with AMPI, had testified before the committee that $12,000 in dairy co-op money was paid to Chestnut to be forwarded to the advertising firm. The committee records also showed a letter from Chestnut to Lilly requesting payment of the bills.

Chestnut had refused to testify before the committee, citing his 5th Amendment rights against self-incrimination.

Rep. James R. Jones (D, Okla.) Aug. 1 acknowledged that he had written a memo to AMPI in 1972 claiming credit for President Lyndon Johnson's decision in December 1968 to maintain milk price supports at the prevailing level, but Jones dismissed the memo as "tall story" written while he ill and "dizzy on some super drug." The memo was released by the committee Aug. 1.

Jones had served as Johnson's appointment secretary and was hired by AMPI in January 1969. In his 1972 memo, written to protest AMPI's plan to terminate his employment, Jones claimed that he was responsible for Johnson's lame duck decision to authorize a continuation of price supports. (The decision was announced by the Agriculture Department Dec. 26, 1968.)

In his note, Jones also claimed that AMPI's top officials, Harold S. Nelson and David Parr, offered to hire him "early in December 1968," prior to announcement of the price decision. That statement also was in error, Jones told reporters, because he was not approached about joining AMPI until January 1969.

Committee records published Aug. 7 showed that oil millionaire Leon Hess made a secret $225,000 contribution to Sen. Henry Jackson's (D, Wash.) campaign for the Democratic presidential nomination in 1972. The contribution was disguised under the names of other persons, records showed.

Hess, who was chairman of the Amerada Hess Corp., used the same methods to conceal a $250,000 contribution to the Nixon re-election campaign in 1972 at the time of an Interior Department investigation of a Virgin Island oil refinery owned by Amerada. Jackson was chairman of the Senate Interior Committee.

Jackson also received $166,000 in secret cash contributions, of which more than half came from oil interests. A Texas oil millionaire, Walter R. Davis, donated $50,000; E. Edmund Miller, president of Time Oil, gave $5,000; Claude Wild Jr. of Gulf Oil Corp. contributed $10,000. (Gulf Oil had pleaded guilty to making an illegal corporate contribution to Jackson's campaign.)

According to the committee's records, Jackson raised $1.1 million during the campaign, nearly half of which was given by donors, including those mentioned above, who also made large contributions to Nixon's campaign. Dwayne O. Andreas, who had backed Nixon and Humphrey, had made a $25,000 cash contribution to Jackson's campaign, records showed.

Jacobsen pleads guilty. Jake Jacobsen, a former counsel for the nation's largest dairy cooperative, Associated Milk Producers Inc. (AMPI), pleaded guilty Aug. 7 to a federal charge that he had bribed former Treasury Secretary John B. Connally Jr. in an effort to secure Administration support for an increase in federal milk price supports. Connally, who had been indicted on five counts of accepting a bribe, conspiring to obstruct justice and commit perjury, and making false declarations, pleaded not guilty to the charges Aug. 9.

Jacobsen's plea was entered in Washington before U.S. District Court Chief judge George L. Hart Jr. who released Jacobsen pending a pre-sentencing investigation.

At the arraignment, Jacobsen told the court he had paid Connally, a long-time political associate in Texas, a total of $10,000 in dairy co-op funds in return for recommending the price increase in March 1971. Jacobsen had been plea bargaining with the Watergate special prosecutor's office in an effort to reduce the charges against him.

A letter to Jacobsen's lawyers detailing the special prosecutor's negotiating conditions, dated May 21, was released Aug. 7. In it, the special prosecutor's office agreed to dispose of federal charges pending against Jacobsen in Texas in connection with the alleged misapplication of funds from a savings and loan institution. "This understanding," the letter continued, "is expressly conditioned on full and truthful disclosure by Mr. Jacobsen and won't bar prosecution for any false testimony given hereafter or for any serious offenses committed by Mr. Jacobsen of which this office is presently unaware."

The single count bribery indictment to which Jacobsen pleaded guilty carried a maximum prison sentence of two years and a fine of $10,000.

Co-op fined for campaign violations— Associated Milk Producers Inc. (AMPI) was fined $35,000 Aug. 1 after pleading guilty to a six-count criminal information charging conspiracy and illegal campaign giving.

Rejecting pleas for leniency, U.S. District Court Chief Judge George L. Hart Jr. imposed the maximum fine. "The law against corporations giving political contributions has been on the books for a long, long time." Hart said. "It's been completely disregarded by Republicans, Democrats, independents and whatnot for a long, long time. This type of cavalier violation of the law has got to be put to a stop."

AMPI's lawyer had asked Hart to assess a penalty of $15,000 for the felony charges, contending that the co-op "represents a membership of 40,000 hard-working, sincere, honest dairy farmers" whose board of directors was not "sophisticated in this matter" and thereby had delegated operating authority to the co-op's general manager. (Harold S. Nelson, who was ousted from that post in January 1972, had pleaded guilty to conspiring to authorize illegal campaign payments.)

The co-op's membership had "learned a bitter lesson about giving too much power to a few," the group's lawyer told the court, adding that because of publicity linking the co-op to the "overhanging shadow" of Watergate, AMPI now was finding it awkward to deal with government officials.

Hart replied, "I can't believe the directors of the corporations, even though they are farmers, didn't know what was going on." Hart was also critical of the recipients of these illegal contributions, saying "I find it difficult to believe that these [campaign] organizations are so loose that they know so little about what is going on."

According to the criminal information filed by the Watergate special prosecutor's office, AMPI had made political contributions totaling $280,900 in corporate cash that went to Democratic and Republican candidates from 1968 through 1972. Recipients of the illegal payments had been disclosed in previous court actions. They included President Nixon, who was cited for the $100,000 donation in 1969, not the promised $2 million; Sen. Hubert H. Humphrey (D, Minn.), Sen. Edmund S. Muskie (D, Me.) and Rep. Wilbur D. Mills (D, Ark.), all of whom had been Democratic presidential hopefuls; Sen. James Abourezk (D, S.D.) and unidentified Democrats in Iowa; and two Republicans—former Rep. Page Belcher of Oklahoma and Patrick J. Hillings, an unsuccessful candidate for a California Congressional seat.

Politicians who had received the illegal money had denied any knowledge of its corporate source. AMPI President John E. Butterbrodt issued a statement Aug. 1 saying that the co-op was "aware of no evidence whatever" indicating that candidates who had accepted the dairy co-op's funds "had any knowledge whatsoever of the actions taken in their apparent behalf."

House OKs financing reform. A few hours before President Nixon announced his intention to resign Aug. 8 [see p. 223C1], the House passed a long delayed campaign financing bill intended to minimize the impact of large campaign contributions and prohibit future fundraising abuses, such as those that had characterized the Watergate scandal.

The vote Aug. 8 was 355–48. Rep. John Brademas (D, Ind.), one of the principal backers of the bill, urged legislators to take advantage of the public outcry against fund-raising excesses and the widespread violation of federal campaign financing laws. Alluding to the events that had led to Nixon's imminent ouster, Brademas said support of the bill would prevent recurrence of the "most spectacular lawlessness and corruption in the last 200 years of the country."

The House bill, which limited campaign contributions and restricted candidate spending, included provisions for the public financing of presidential elections, but a measure designed to provide public funds for Senate and House races was defeated 228–187. A Senate bill, passed April 11, provided for public financing of both presidential and congressional elections. Differences in the two bills would be reconciled in conference committee. President Nixon had strongly opposed the public financing of federal elections and had threatened to veto any bill incorporating that provision. Vice President Ford had also indicated his opposition to the public financing feature, Congressional Quarterly said Aug. 10.

Provisions of the House bill:
■ A $1 tax checkoff on individual federal income tax returns would provide total public funding for presidential elections. Expenditures in the general election by major party candidates were limited to $20 million. Presidential primary contenders could receive a maximum of $5 million—half a candidate's primary spending limit—but primary funds would be granted only on a matching basis, with every $250 or less in private donations matched by public money.
■ A limit of $100 was put on cash contributions.
■ Individual donors were limited to $1,000 contributions to candidates for federal office in the primary and general elections, and an aggregate contribution of $25,000 to all federal candidates annually.
■ Candidates could not give more than $25,000 in their own funds to the overall campaign. Existing political committees maintained by business and labor groups could give up to $5,000 to candidates in both the primary and general elections. Democratic and Republican Congressional committees could give up to $10,000 to candidates in a general election.
■ Candidates would be required to establish one principal campaign committee to report all related expenditures.
■ Democratic and Republican National Committees would be provided with $2 million in federal funds to finance their conventions. The parties were prohibited from spending more than that amount.
■ A six-member bipartisan panel would be established to enforce the campaign spending limits. The group would have subpoena power to investigate alleged violations but either the House or the Senate could overturn regulations promulgated by the elections committee. (This provision was stronger than that included in the Committee version.)
■ Although public financing was rejected for Congressional races, spending limits were set for House and Senate elections. House candidates could spend $60,000 in both the primary and the general elections. Senate candidates could spend either $75,000 or 5¢ for each citizen of that state. An additional 25% above these ceilings could be spent to raise campaign money.

Final passage of the bill came after two days of debate. There was a sharp partisan fight Aug. 7 over the "modified closed rule" imposed on the debate by the House Rules Committee. Republicans charged that the rule, which permitted only "germane" amendments to the legislation, was a "gag" rule preventing them from offering amendments barring campaign dirty tricks, and preventing groups, especially labor unions, from pooling membership contributions to concentrate these funds on specific candidates and selected races.

An effort to reject the rule was defeated on a party line vote, 219–190. The bill's final version closely resembled the measure reported out July 30 by the House Administration Committee. The committee had begun work on the bill in October 1973 and the delay had prompted sharp criticism from the Washington public interest lobby, Common Cause.

Ex-Humphrey aide pleads guilty. Sen. Hubert H. Humphrey's (D, Minn.) former press secretary, Norman Sherman, and his partner in a Minneapolis voter canvassing firm, John Valentine, pleaded guilty Aug. 12 to charges of "aiding and abetting" the illegal donation of $82,000 in corporate campaign donations.

They had been accused of accepting the money from Associated Milk Producers Inc. (AMPI) in payment of services performed for Humphrey, Sen. James Abourezk (D, S.D.) and unidentified Democratic candidates in Iowa.

In a statement to the court made also in behalf of his business partner, Sherman said they were "not only guilty of the charge against us, but ashamed and embarrassed that we needlessly brought humiliation to ourselves, our families, our business associates, and unfortunately, to several political men whose friendship we cherish," an apparent reference to Humphrey and Abourezk, who had denied any knowledge that the money paid on their behalf had been illegally donated.

Sherman and Valentine were released by a federal district court judge in St. Paul pending a presentencing investigation. In an appeal for leniency, Sherman said that although they had had "doubts about the transactions when the first AMPI check was received," they had received legal advice that the payments were proper. (It had been previously reported that Sherman consulted Jack L. Chestnut, Humphrey's campaign manager, about the money and had been assured the payment was legal.)

In a letter read to the court, the Watergate special prosecutor's office noted the "extent and value" of their cooperation and said the defendants had agreed to a "full and truthful disclosure" of any relevant information in future court action.

Government moves to settle AMPI suit. Associated Milk Producers Inc. (AMPI) Aug. 13 accepted the terms of a consent decree filed that day by the Justice Department in federal district court in Kansas City, Mo. The proposed consent agreement would become final in 60 days if approved by the court, ending a civil suit brought by the government in 1972.

The case had generated widespread public interest because of AMPI's involvement in Watergate-related campaign financing abuses, including testimony that co-op officials had tried to halt the antitrust suit with offers of a bribe to President Nixon's campaign fund raisers.

The 37,000 member co-op had been accused of illegally trying to monopolize the production and sale of milk in 14 midwest, southern and southwestern states and using coercion to force farmers to join the organization. As was standard in the settlement of other civil antitrust suits, AMPI agreed not to engage in the future in these allegedly illegal practices, but the co-op made no admission of wrongdoing. The dairy group also was prohibited from buying any new milk plants for 10 years without the Justice Department's prior consent, an unusual restriction that government lawyers acknowledged was rarely used outside of bank merger cases.

AMPI also agreed to refrain from selling cheap milk in selected areas to punish nonmembers by driving down their prices; to give members at least one year to withdraw from the co-op; and to file reports with the Justice Department for the next 10 years and allow government agents to inspect its records on request.

Civil suit settlement final. The Democratic National Committee and the financial trust representing former President Nixon's re-election committees formally agreed in court Aug. 9 to a settlement of the lawsuits resulting from the Watergate burglary and wiretapping. Tentative agreement had been announced in February.

The trust was to pay $775,000 to the Democratic Party, former Democratic National Chairman Lawrence F. O'Brien and the Association of State Chairmen. O'Brien said as part of the agreement he would turn over his share—$400,000—to the Democratic Party with the request "that it be applied to a program designed to re-enlist the confidence of the American people in the two-party system."

The accord also provided that the DNC would not file Watergate-related suits in the future. The Republicans agreed to drop libel countersuits.

Still pending were suits against the re-election committees by convicted Watergate conspirator James W. McCord Jr. and by R. Spencer Oliver, former director of the state chairmen's association, whose phone had been wiretapped.

Final acceptance of the tentative agreement had been held up partly by Rep. Shirley Chisholm (D, N.Y.), who had said June 19 that she would not sign a waiver against future lawsuits against the Republicans. As part of the tentative settlement, the 11 Democratic presidential and vice presidential candidates had been requested to sign such waivers. (Chisholm had been a target of the campaign "dirty tricks" of Donald H. Segretti.)

A DNC spokesman said Aug. 15 that the GOP trust accepted assurances in the final settlement that "good faith" efforts had been made to prevent future suits, but suits by individual Democrats would not be legally precluded.

House accepts impeachment report. The House Judiciary Committee's report on its impeachment inquiry of President Nixon was accepted by the House Aug. 20 by a vote of 412–3. The report was submitted to the House by Committee Chairman Peter W. Rodino Jr. (D, N.J.). House Democratic Leader Thomas P. O'Neill Jr. (Mass.) offered a resolution stating that the House "accepts the report," commending the committee for its "conscientious and capable" effort and calling the inquiry "full and complete."

On Article II, concerning abuse of presidential power and violation of the oath of office to execute the nation's laws, the report reaffirmed the committee's 28–10 vote for adoption on July 29.

[For further details, see p. 235C3]

Nixon's Resignation & Pardon

Nixon resigns presidency. Richard Milhous Nixon, 61, resigned as president of the United States Aug. 9 after a week of dramatic developments. Vice President Gerald Rudolph Ford, 61, was sworn in as his successor. It was the first time in the history of the nation that its president had resigned.

The resignation, a dramatic conclusion to the effects of the Watergate scandal on the Nixon presidency, was announced Aug. 8, three days after Nixon released a statement and transcript of tape recordings admitting "a serious act of omission" in his previous accounts of the Watergate cover-up.

According to Nixon's statement, six days after the break-in at the Democratic Party's national headquarters in the Watergate building in Washington, D.C. June 17, 1972, he had ordered the Federal Bureau of Investigation's probe of the break-in halted. Furthermore, Nixon stated, he had kept this part of the record secret from investigating bodies, his own counsel and the public.

The admission destroyed what remained of Nixon's support in Congress against a tide of impeachment that was already swelling. The President's support had been eroding dangerously since the House Judiciary Committee had debated and drawn, with substantial bipartisan backing, three articles of impeachment to be considered on the House floor. Within 48 hours of his statement of complicity, which he stated did not in his opinion justify "the extreme step of impeachment," the 10 committee members who had voted against impeachment reversed themselves, on the basis of the new evidence, and announced they would vote for impeachment. This, in effect, made the committee vote for impeachment unanimous.

The development was accompanied by serious defections in the Republican Congressional leadership and acknowledgment from all sides that the vote for impeachment in the House was a foregone conclusion and conviction by the Senate certain.

This assessment was delivered to the President by the senior Republican leaders of the Congress. Shortly afterwards, Nixon made his final decision to resign. He announced his decision the evening of Aug. 8, to a television audience estimated at 110–130 million persons. In his 16-minute address, Nixon conceded he had made "some" wrong judgments. He said he was resigning because he no longer had "a strong enough political base in Congress" to carry out his duties of office. He also reviewed what he hoped would be his legacy of accomplishment in office.

Nixon bade farewell to his staff Aug. 9 and departed the White House, with Vice President Ford waving farewell. At 11:35 a.m., the resignation—a single sentence, "Dear Mr. Secretary: I hereby resign the office of President of the United States. Sincerely, Richard Nixon"—was handed to Secretary of State Henry A. Kissinger, and the duties of that office devolved upon Vice President Ford.

Ford was administered the oath of office by Chief Justice Warren E. Burger, who had hastily returned to Washington from a vacation in Europe, at 12:03 p.m. in the East Room of the White House. In brief remarks, Ford stressed his awareness that he had not been elected to the office and pledged "openness and candor" in his administration. He told the nation "our long national nightmare" of Watergate was over and the nation remained "a government of laws and not of men." He urged prayer for himself, "to confirm" him in his new role, and, his voice breaking, for his predecessor so that the man "who brought peace to millions" would "find it for himself."

At the time, Ford's predecessor was aloft near Jefferson City, Mo. aboard the presidential aircraft, Spirit of '76, en route to his home at San Clemente, Calif.

The changeover took place in the second term of the Nixon presidency, after 5½ years (2,026 days) in office for the 37th president. Ford assumed the post as the 38th president to serve the remaining 2½ years of the second Nixon term. He would be eligible for only one full term in office.

Ford moved immediately to assure stability of government. He retained Kissinger as secretary of state, affirmed the Nixon Administration's foreign policy, met with foreign envoys, Congressional leaders, the Cabinet, economic advisers and the National Security Council. He solicited recommendations for a vice presidential choice. Ford appointed a four-man team to ease the transition, and he named a press secretary, pledging an "open" and "candid" Administration.

A resolution expressing support for Ford as a "good and faithful friend" was adopted unanimously by both houses of Congress Aug. 9. It stated Congress's "sincere best wishes, its assurances of firm cooperation and its fervent hopes for success in office."

Nixon's resignation speech—President Nixon's 16-minute speech of resignation was delivered from the White House Oval Office at 9 p.m. EDT and was seen by a national television audience estimated at 110–130 million people. [See text of speech]

"Throughout the long and difficult period of Watergate, I have felt it was my duty to persevere; to make every possible effort to complete the term of office to which you elected me," Nixon said.

But, the President continued, it had become "evident" in the last few days that he no longer had a "strong enough political base in the Congress to justify continuing that effort." As long as that base existed, he felt it necessary, Nixon said, to see the "constitutional process" through to its conclusion, for to do otherwise would be "unfaithful to the spirit of that difficult process, and a dangerous destabilizing precedent for the future."

"But with the disappearance of that base, I now believe that the constitutional purpose has been served, and there is no longer a need for the process to be prolonged," he said. Nixon conceded he lacked the support of Congress required for him to carry out the duties of his office.

The President said he had never been a "quitter." Nonetheless, he was resigning to spare the country a fight for his personal vindication that would absorb the attention of Congress and the President in the months ahead, when both branches needed to place their "entire focus" on the problems of world peace and domestic inflation.

Nixon said he was leaving his office in the "good hands" of Vice President Ford, who could begin the "essential" task of healing the "wounds of the nation."

Nixon said he "deeply regretted" any injuries that came in the course of the events that led to his decision to resign. "I would only say that if some of my judgments were wrong—and some were wrong—they were made in what I believed at the time to be the best interests of the nation." He thanked those who had supported him and said he held "no bitterness" toward those who had not.

Nixon then cited his efforts to achieve peace throughout the world. This, he said, "more than anything, is what I hope will be my legacy to you, to our country, as I leave the presidency."

Nixon's farewell—Before departing from the White House Aug. 9, President Nixon bade a sorrowful farewell to his Cabinet and aides gathered in the East Room. He expressed pride in the people he had appointed but conceded that "we have done some things wrong in this Administration, and the top man always takes the responsibility—and I have never ducked it." "We can be proud of it—five and a half years—no man or no woman came into this Administration and left it with more of this world's goods than when he came in."

The President reminisced about his father and, as he continued about his mother, tears welled in his eyes. She was,

he said, a saint about whom no books would ever be written.

But, he said, "we leave with high hopes, in good spirit and with deep humility, and with very much gratefulness in our hearts."

"Always remember," he told the group, "others may hate you, but those who hate you don't win unless you hate them—and then you destroy yourself."

On his arrival in California Aug. 9 as a former President, Nixon was greeted by a crowd of 5,000 persons. "Having completed one task does not mean that we will just sit and enjoy this marvelous California climate and do nothing," he told the crowd. "With all the time that I have which could

---

Text of President Nixon's Aug. 8 Address to Nation

Good evening.

This is the 37th time I have spoken to you from this office in which so many decisions have been made that shape the history of this nation.

Each time I have done so to discuss with you some matters that I believe affected the national interest. And all the decisions I have made in my public life I have always tried to do what was best for the nation.

Throughout the long and difficult period of Watergate, I have felt it was my duty to persevere; to make every possible effort to complete the term of office to which you elected me.

In the past few days, however, it has become evident to me that I no longer have a strong enough political base in the Congress to justify continuing that effort.

As long as there was such a base, I felt strongly that it was necessary to see the constitutional process through to its conclusion; that to do otherwise would be unfaithful to the spirit of that deliberately difficult process, and a dangerously destabilizing precedent for the future. But with the disappearance of that base, I now believe that the constitutional purpose has been served. And there is no longer a need for the process to be prolonged.

I would have preferred to carry through to the finish whatever the personal agony it would have involved, and my family unanimously urged me to do so.

But the interests of the nation must always come before any personal considerations. From the discussions I have had with Congressional and other leaders I have concluded that because of the Watergate matter I might not have the support of the Congress that I would consider necessary to back the very difficult decisions and carry out the duties of this office in the way the interests of the nation will require.

I have never been a quitter. To leave office before my term is completed is opposed to every instinct in my body. But as president I must put the interests of America first.

America needs a full-time president and a full-time Congress, particularly at this time with problems we face at home and abroad.

To continue to fight through the months ahead for my personal vindication would almost totally absorb the time and attention of both the president and the Congress in a period when our entire focus should be on the great issues of peace abroad and prosperity without inflation at home.

Therefore, I shall resign the presidency effective at noon tomorrow. Vice President Ford will be sworn in as president at that hour in this office.

As I recall the high hopes for America with which we began this second term, I feel a great sadness that I will not be here in this office working on your behalf to achieve those hopes in the next two and a half years.

But in turning over direction of the government to Vice President Ford I know, as I told the nation when I nominated him for that office 10 months ago, that the leadership of America will be in good hands.

In passing this office to the vice president I also do so with the profound sense of the weight of responsibility that will fall on his shoulders tomorrow, and therefore of the understanding, the patience, the

cooperation he will need from all Americans. As he assumes that responsibility he will deserve the help and the support of all of us. As we look to the future, the first essential is to begin healing the wounds of this nation. To put the bitterness and divisions of the recent past behind us and to rediscover those shared ideals that lie at the heart of our strength and unity as a great and as a free people.

By taking this action, I hope that I will have hastened the start of that process of healing which is so desperately needed in America.

I regret deeply any injuries that may have been done in the course of the events that led to this decision. I would say only that if some of my judgments were wrong—and some were wrong—they were made in what I believed at the time to be the best interests of the nation.

To those who have stood with me during these past difficult months, to my family, my friends, the many others who've joined in supporting my cause because they believed it was right, I will be eternally grateful for your support.

And to those who have not felt able to give me your support, let me say I leave with no bitterness toward those who have opposed me, because all of us in the final analysis have been concerned with the good of the country however our judgments might differ.

So let us all now join together in affirming that common commitment and in helping our new president succeed for the benefit of all Americans.

I shall leave this office with regret at not completing my term but with gratitude for the privilege of serving as your president for the past five and a half years. These years have been a momentous time in the history of our nation and the world. They have been a time of achievement in which we can all be proud—achievements that represent the shared efforts of the Administration, the Congress and the people. But the challenges ahead are equally great.

And they, too, will require the support and the efforts of a Congress and the people, working in cooperation with the new Administration.

We have ended America's longest war. But in the work of securing a lasting peace in the world, the goals ahead are even more far-reaching and more difficult. We must complete a structure of peace, so that it will be said of this generation—our generation of Americans—by the people of all nations, not only that we ended one war but that we prevented future wars.

We have unlocked the doors that for a quarter of a century stood between the United States and the People's Republic of China. We must now insure that the one-quarter of the world's people who live in the People's Republic of China will be and remain, not our enemies, but our friends.

In the Middle East, 100 million people in the Arab countries, many of whom have considered us their enemies for nearly 20 years, now look on us as their friends. We must continue to build on that friendship so that peace can settle at last over the Middle East and so that the cradle of civilization will not become its grave.

Together with the Soviet Union we have made the crucial breakthroughs that have begun the process of limiting nuclear arms. But, we must set as our goal, not just limiting, but reducing and finally destroying these terrible weapons so that they cannot destroy

civilization. And so that the threat of nuclear war will no longer hang over the world and the people, we have opened a new relation with the Soviet Union. We must continue to develop and expand that new relationship so that the two strongest nations of the world will live together in cooperation rather than confrontation.

Around the world—in Asia, in Africa, in Latin America, in the Middle East—there are millions of people who live in terrible poverty, even starvation. We must keep as our goal turning away from production for war and expanding production for peace so that people everywhere on this earth can at last look forward, in their children's time if not in our time, to having the necessities for a decent life.

Here in America we are fortunate that most of our people have not only the blessings of liberty but also the means to live full and good, and by the world's standards even abundant, lives. We must press on, however, toward a goal not only of more and better jobs but of full opportunity for every man, and of what we are striving so hard right now to achieve—prosperity without inflation.

For more than a quarter of a century in public life, I have shared in the turbulent history of this evening. I have fought for what I believe in. I have tried, to the best of my ability, to discharge those duties and meet those responsibilities that were entrusted to me.

Sometimes I have succeeded. And sometimes I have failed. But always I have taken heart from what Theodore Roosevelt said about the man in the arena whose face is marred by dust and sweat and blood, who strives valiantly, who errs and comes short again and again because there is no effort without error and shortcoming, but who does actually strive to do the deed, who knows the great enthusiasm, the great devotion, who spends himself in a worthy cause, who at the best knows in the end of triumphs of high achievements and with the worst if he fails, at least fails while daring greatly.

I pledge to you tonight that as long as I have a breath of life in my body I shall continue in that spirit. I shall continue to work for the great causes to which I have been dedicated throughout my years as a congressman, a senator, vice president and president, the cause of peace—not just for America but among all nations—prosperity, justice and opportunity for all of our people.

There is one cause above all to which I have been devoted and to which I shall always be devoted for as long as I live. When I first took the oath of office as president five and a half years ago, I made this sacred commitment: to consecrate my office, my energies and all the wisdom I can summon to the cause of peace among nations. I've done my very best in all the days since to be true to that pledge.

As a result of these efforts, I am confident that the world is a safer place today, not only for the people of America but for the people of all nations, and that all of our children have a better chance than before of living in peace rather than dying in war.

This, more than anything, is what I hoped to achieve when I sought the presidency. This, more than anything, is what I hope will be my legacy to you, to our country, as I leave the presidency.

To have served in this office is to have felt a very personal sense of kinship with each and every American. In leaving it, I do so with this prayer: May God's grace be with you in all the days ahead.

be useful, I am going to continue to work for peace among all the world" and "for opportunity and understanding among the people here in America."

Nixon then traveled by helicopter the final 14 miles from El Toro Marine Air Base to his home at San Clemente.

Ford: 'Confirm me with your prayers'—After his swearing-in, Ford made a brief address to those gathered in the East Room of the White House and to a national television audience. "I am acutely aware," the new President said, "that you have not elected me as your president by your ballots. So I ask you to confirm me as your president with your prayers. And I hope that such prayers will also be the first of many."

He added: "If you have not chosen me by secret ballot, neither have I gained office by any secret promises. I have not campaigned either for the presidency or the vice presidency. I have not subscribed to any partisan platform, I am indebted to no man and only to one woman—my dear wife—as I begin the most difficult job in the world."

Ford promised not to shirk the responsibilities he had not sought and pledged to be President of all the people. "We must go forward, now, together," he said.

Noting that "truth is the glue" holding together "not only our government, but civilization itself," Ford vowed "openness and candor" in all his public and private acts as President.

The "long national nightmare" of Watergate was over, Ford said, and he asked that its "wounds" be bound up. "Before closing," Ford said, "I again ask your prayers for Richard Nixon and his family. May our former President, who brought peace to millions, find it for himself."

Ford picks up reins. Before the Nixon resignation, but after the announcement of it, Ford assured reporters at his home near Alexandria, Va. Aug. 8 that he would retain Henry Kissinger as secretary of state and continue the foreign policy of the Nixon Administration. On Aug. 9, Ford and Kissinger met at the White House with nearly 60 ambassadors or chiefs of mission, in groups and individually, to assure continued friendly relations. A personal message from Ford was sent to Soviet Communist Party leader Leonid I. Brezhnev. The diplomatic sessions were continued at the State Department Aug. 10.

After his swearing-in Aug. 9, Ford met with a bipartisan group of Congressional leaders and the Nixon Administration's top economic advisers. The latter were told that control of inflation was a "high and first priority of the Ford Administration."

Ford also met Aug. 9 with the senior members of the Nixon White House staff, still intact except for Press Secretary Ronald L. Ziegler, who resigned and accompanied Nixon to California. Ford asked the staff to remain through the transition and appealed for their "help and cooperation." Gen. Alexander M.

Haig Jr., chief of staff, pledged the same loyalty to Ford "in our hour of common cause."

Ford Aug. 9 named a four-member committee of his own to oversee the transition: former Gov. William W. Scranton (R, Pa.); Donald M. Rumsfeld, ambassador to the North Atlantic Treaty Organization; Interior Secretary Rogers C. B. Morton; and former Rep. John O. Marsh (D, Va.), a member of Ford's vice presidential staff.

The chief of that staff, Robert T. Hartmann, was named a counselor to the President Aug. 9. Hartmann, 57, chief of the Washington bureau of the Los Angeles Times (1954–64) joined Ford's staff in 1966. (Marsh was named a counselor Aug. 10.)

Ford also appeared in the White House press room Aug. 9 to introduce his new press secretary, J. F. terHorst, 52, former Washington bureau manager of the Detroit News. "We will have, I trust," Ford told the reporters, "the kind of rapport and friendship we've had in the past. And I don't ask you to treat me any better. We will have an open, we will have a candid Administration. I can't change my nature after 61 years."

In his first full day as President Aug. 10, Ford met with the Nixon Cabinet and asked its members, as well as all federal agency chiefs, to remain in their posts in the name of "continuity and stability." He

also met with the National Security Council and announced he was seeking suggestions from Republicans and Democrats for the choice of a vice president.

Some details of the Cabinet meeting were relayed by terHorst. The new President told the department heads he expected them to come in for business "but not for chitchatting" and he wanted each of them to be "affirmative" in his relations with the press. The Cabinet received praise from the President for the way the members "had been carrying on during trying circumstances for several months." Secretary of State Kissinger responded "to express our unflagging support and total loyalty to you."

In his talk with reporters after the Nixon resignation announcement Aug. 8, Ford said, "This is one of the most difficult and very saddest periods, and one of the very saddest incidents I've ever witnessed." In addition to affirming continuity of foreign policy, he said he expected to "start out working with Democrats and with Republicans in the House as well as in the Senate to work on the problems—serious ones—which we have at home." He said he had "a good many adversaries in the political arena in the Congress, but I don't think I have a single enemy in the Congress."

He praised Nixon for having made "one of the greatest personal sacrifices for the

Text of President Ford's Aug. 9 Address

Mr. chief justice, my dear friends, my fellow Americans. The oath that I have taken is the same oath that was taken by George Washington and by every president under the Constitution.

But I assume the presidency under extraordinary circumstances never before experienced by Americans. This is an hour of history that troubles our minds and hurts our hearts.

Therefore, I feel it is my first duty to make an unprecedented compact with my countrymen. Not an inaugural address, not a fireside chat, not a campaign speech, just a little straight talk among friends. And I intend it to be the first of many.

I am acutely aware that you have not elected me as your president by your ballots. So I ask you to confirm me as your president with your prayers. And I hope that such prayers will also be the first of many.

If you have not chosen me by secret ballot, neither have I gained office by any secret promises. I have not campaigned either for the presidency or the vice presidency. I have not subscribed to any partisan platform. I am indebted to no man and only to one woman, my dear wife.

As I begin this very difficult job, I have not sought this enormous responsibility, but I will not shirk it. Those who nominated and confirmed me as vice president were my friends and are my friends. They were of both parties, elected by all the people and acting under the Constitution in their name. It is only fitting then that I should pledge to them and to you that I will be the president of all the people.

Thomas Jefferson said the people are the only sure reliance for the preservation of our liberty. And down the years, Abraham Lincoln renewed this American article of faith asking is there any better way for equal hopes in the world.

I intend on Monday next to request of the speaker of the House of Representatives and the president pro tempore of the Senate the privilege of appearing before the Congress to share with my former colleagues and with you, the American people, my views on the priority business of the nation and to solicit your views and their views. And may I say to the speaker and the others, if I could meet with you right after this—these remarks I would appreciate it.

Even though this is late in an election year, there is no way we can go forward except together and no way anybody can win except by serving the people's urgent

needs. We cannot stand still or slip backward. We must go forward now together.

To the peoples and the governments of all friendly nations and I hope that could encompass the whole world, I pledge an uninterrupted and sincere search for peace. America will remain strong and united.

But its strength will remain dedicated to the safety and sanity of the entire family of man as well as to our own precious freedom.

I believe that truth is the glue that holds governments together, not only our government but civilization itself. That bond, though strained, is unbroken at home and abroad.

In all my public and private acts as your president, I expect to follow my instincts of openness and candor with full confidence that honesty is always the best policy in the end.

My fellow Americans, our long national nightmare is over. Our Constitution works. Our great republic is a government of laws and not of men. Here, the people rule.

But there is a higher power, by whatever name we honor him, who ordains not only righteousness but love, not only justice but mercy. As we bind up the internal wounds of Watergate, more painful and more poisonous than those of foreign wars, let us restore the Golden Rule to our political process. And let brotherly love purge our hearts of suspicion and of hate.

In the beginning, I asked you to pray for me. Before closing, I ask again your prayers for Richard Nixon and for his family. May our former president, who brought peace to millions find it for himself. May God bless and comfort his wonderful wife and daughters whose love and loyalty will forever be a shining legacy to all who bear the lonely burdens of the White House.

I can only guess at those burdens although I witnessed at close hand the tragedies that befell three presidents and the lesser trials of others.

With all the strength and all the good sense I have gained from life, with all the confidence of my family, my friends and dedicated staff impart to me and with the goodwill of countless Americans I have encountered in recent visits to 40 states, I now solemnly reaffirm my promise I made to you last Dec. 6 to uphold the Constitution, to do what is right as God gives me to see the right and to do the very best I can for America. God helping me, I will not let you down. Thank you.

country and one of the finest personal decisions on behalf of all of us as Americans by his decision to resign."

The nation's reaction. The nation reacted soberly to the startling events in Washington that culminated in Nixon's resignation and the swift, smooth transfer of the powers of the presidency to Vice President Ford. Most persons expressed great relief that the "long national nightmare" of Watergate had ended and hope that the new Administration now could focus on the nation's other major problem—inflation.

In the spirit of reconciliation that marked President Ford's acceptance speech, the public rallied immediately to back the new leader. Liberals and conservatives, Republicans and Democrats, labor and business leaders, religious and civil rights spokesmen joined in the public outpouring of support for Ford Aug. 9.

Elliot L. Richardson, whom President Nixon had dismissed during the course of the Watergate developments, said of Ford: "He is genuinely a good man—decent, sensible, respectable. He works well with other people." Former New York Gov. Nelson Rockefeller, who was being mentioned as a vice presidential choice, praised Ford as a "man of integrity, dedication and abiding faith in America."

Representatives of the nation's governors, mayors and county officials sent a joint telegram Aug. 9 pledging their "fullest cooperation and assistance" to Ford in "reuniting the nation and restoring its sense of common purpose and direction."

The nation's top labor leaders, AFL-CIO President George Meany, Teamsters President Frank Fitzsimmons, Steelworkers President I.W. Abel and United Auto Workers President Leonard Woodcock urged their members to rally behind Ford, particularly in the government's effort to fight inflation. Business leaders such as Henry Ford II and E. Douglas Kenna, president of the National Association of Manufacturers, called for national reconciliation.

Religious leaders joined in praising Ford, but a few spokesmen, such as the conservative preacher, the Rev. Carl McIntire, also expressed criticism of Nixon because his resignation speech contained no sense of "guilt [and] humiliation." Evangelist Billy Graham, a long-time friend of President Nixon, said Aug. 8 that he deserved the prayers "even of those who feel betrayed and let down" because Nixon's "personal suffering must be almost unbearable."

The Rev. John Huffman, the former pastor of the Key Biscayne Presbyterian Church, which Nixon had attended frequently during his visits to Florida, said Aug. 8 that the resignation was "the very best thing for the nation." Huffman, who had made critical allusions to Watergate in a sermon preached before President Nixon in 1973, said Aug. 9, "Here is a case in which a law and order President has for over two years consistently lied to

---

Presidents Who Failed To Complete Terms

William Henry Harrison, 9th president (1841–1841), died April 4, 1841.

Zachary Taylor, 12th president (1849–1850), died July 9, 1850.

Abraham Lincoln, 16th president (1861–1865), died April 15, 1865. Assassinated.

James A. Garfield, 20th president (1881–1881), died Sept. 19, 1881. Assassinated.

William McKinley, 25th president (1897–1901), died Sept. 14, 1901. Assassinated.

Warren G. Harding, 29th president (1921–1923), died Aug. 2, 1923.

Franklin D. Roosevelt, 32nd president (1933–1945), died April 12, 1945.

John F. Kennedy, 35th president (1961–1963), died Nov. 22, 1963. Assassinated.

Richard M. Nixon, 37th president (1969–1974), resigned Aug. 9, 1974.

---

the American people. He lied to me personally. When I went to him with my concerns on Watergate personally over a year and a half ago, he told me he was doing everything in his power to get to the very heart of the matter."

Black leaders voiced support for Ford and called on the nation to unite behind him. Vernon Jordan, executive director of the National Urban League, said Aug. 9 that blacks should "not judge Jerry Ford as a congressman from Michigan, but take him at face value, then watch him, help him and then make a judgment."

Members of Congress predicted Aug. 8 that there would be an extended "honeymoon" between Congress and the White House, wiping out the antagonism and suspicion that had characterized relations between legislators and the Nixon Administration. Members of both parties claimed Ford, who had served 25 years as a representative from Michigan, as "one of ours." His efforts to maintain a close and open relationship with Congress would inaugurate a new "era of good feelings" and partnership between the executive and legislative branches, many members said.

"Jerry Ford is a personal friend," House Speaker Carl Albert (D, Okla.), said Aug. 8. "I am sure our relationship will be good." Senate Majority Leader Mike Mansfield (D, Mont.) echoed those views, adding, "He's a decent man. He's conservative but you know where he stands. He'd give consideration to Congressional views. He would get exceptional cooperation." Senate Minority Leader Hugh Scott (R, Penn.), said Aug. 8, "What we need is a strong Congress and a strong President and that's what we're getting."

Republicans in Congress expressed a special sense of relief about Nixon's departure and Ford's ascension to the office. Many lawmakers had regarded Watergate and the crippled Nixon presidency as a political albatross that threatened the entire future of the party when general elections were held in November. The divisive debate over Nixon's role in the Watergate coverup had served to bind

---

together the diverse elements in the Democratic Party. Nixon's removal from office not only ended the widespread public debate over Watergate; the healing over of those political wounds, represented by the nation's unity behind the new President, greatly improved the Republican Party's electoral prospects. It also thrust Ford into the favorite's role as incumbent for the 1976 presidential election.

Those who had been vehement Nixon defenders in the past were especially critical of his failure to confess his guilt within the context of his resignation speech. Rudy Bofchwitz, a Republican national committeeman from Minnesota said Aug. 8, "I'm really tempted to say that now Dick Nixon doesn't have us to kick around again. I'd like to say something kind about Nixon at this time but after two years of national agony and turmoil and the damage that has been done to my Republican Party—the completely innocent victim of this reckless mischief—I will have to wait to make a less emotional assessment of the Nixon Administration."

Dwight Dobbs of Illinois, who had rented billboards to voice support for the President in earlier phases of the Watergate investigation, said Aug. 8, "I have the same feeling as if someone in my own family committed a crime and lied to me."

Ronald F. Docksai, national chairman of Young Americans for Freedom, a conservative group that had been a staunch supporter of the President, said Aug. 8 that Nixon's resignation came "too late to impress conservatives with his integrity or moral firmness, but we feel his action in resigning is as necessary as it is tragic for him and our country."

Others, particularly those who had been Nixon's neighbors in Florida and California, or who had known him in his hometown of Whittier, Calif., were bitter about his resignation, contending that Nixon had been driven from office by a partisan Congress and a hostile press. Rabbi Baruch Korff, who had served as Nixon's most vocal defender in the last days of the Administration, said Aug. 8 that Nixon "for 30 years sacrificed everything for America's good [and] now has made the supreme sacrifice." Nixon was the "greatest peacemaker of this century" and will "be esteemed by future generations," Korff said.

Resignation rumors spark market rally—Prices on the New York Stock Exchange made sharp advances Aug. 5–7 as rumors circulated that President Nixon was planning to resign. During the three-day period, the Dow Jones industrial average gained 45 points to reach a high of 797.56 at the close of trading Aug. 7.

The rally ended abruptly Aug. 8 as caution replaced optimism and profit taking caused the Dow to close at 784.89. With a further drop of 7.59 points Aug. 9, the Dow closed the week at 777.3. The long awaited "Nixon rally," which it had been hoped would spark a general market recovery, produced a net gain of only 24.72 points for the week. (Just prior to Nixon's resignation, investors were so gloomy about the nation's economic and political outlook that the Dow reached its lowest level in four years, closing at 751.1 Aug. 1.)

International reaction. World leaders greeted Nixon's resignation with a mixture of regret, relief and concern over the policies to be followed by President Ford, who was largely unknown in foreign capitals.

Countries friendly to the U.S. seemed reassured by Ford's assertion Aug. 8 that U.S. foreign policy would remain unchanged under the continued leadership of Secretary of State Henry Kissinger. However, there was unease among Arab nations and among U.S. allies in Indochina over a possible change of policy, and among European nations over Ford's lack of experience in international economic affairs.

Nations hostile to the U.S., notably Cuba and North Vietnam, expressed pleasure over Nixon's departure. A Havana radio broadcast Aug. 9 called the ex-president "an enemy of Cuba . . . who has drowned in the dirty waters of Watergate." Hanoi Radio denounced Nixon the same day for committing "countless . . . horrible crimes" in Indochina and asserted Ford was "a representative of the capitalist class" who must prove he was different from Nixon.

Among the reactions:

Soviet Union—Soviet commentators emphasized that the change in U.S. presidents would not affect relations between Moscow and Washington, and pictured Nixon as a victim of partisan politics, the U.S. economic situation and malicious propaganda in the U.S. "mass media."

An article in the government newspaper Izvestia Aug. 9 by its political commentator, Vikenti Matveyev, declared: "In the development and improvement of relations between the United States and the Soviet Union and the question of detente in general, there is a basis of national support in the U.S.A., that does not depend on membership in the Democratic or Republican Party, or some other vacillation in the country's political atmosphere."

"The forces which originated [the improvement] will continue to act further, independently of inter-party struggle or other events . . ." the article stated. The optimism of the commentary was supported by publication alongside it of a new poem by Yevgeny Yevtushenko praising detente.

Nixon was portrayed as a victim of an inter-party struggle and of attacks by the media in an hour-long program on Moscow television Aug. 10. Commentators Valentin Zorin of the television network and Leonid Zamyatin of the official press agency Tass did not mention the Watergate burglary, its cover-up, Nixon's

income tax problems or any other aspect of his administration's scandals.

The commentators asserted the Democrats had fabricated "the so-called Watergate affair" after their defeat in the 1972 presidential elections, and had been aided by "brainwashing" against Nixon conducted by U.S. "radio and television." Zorin claimed a public opinion poll had shown that for 80% of the U.S. public, "inter-party squabbling" was less important than the U.S.' severe economic problems.

Western Europe—Western European leaders expressed confidence that relations between their countries and the U.S. would not change significantly, but officials questioned Ford's ability to conduct complex economic and financial affairs.

British Prime Minister Harold Wilson sent a message to Ford Aug. 9 saying he trusted the U.S. and Great Britain "will demonstrate the purpose and determination necessary" to resolve "problems of peace and economic well-being." The influential Financial Times praised Ford as a decent and honest man but wondered "whether [he] possesses the vision and intellectual ability to see domestic or international relations in a wide perspective."

French President Valery Giscard d'Estaing sent a message to Ford Aug. 9 recalling "the ancient and close ties of friendship" between the U.S. and France. French Finance Minister Jean-Pierre Fourcade had said Aug. 8 that he saw no reason why U.S.-French relations should change under Ford, but warned that "international operators" might try to profit from the uncertainty surrounding Nixon's resignation by speculating on "certain currencies."

Jens Otto Krag, who represented the European Economic Community (EEC) in the U.S., expressed confidence Aug. 9 that relations between Washington and the EEC would "continue to evolve under normal conditions."

The governments of Denmark and the Netherlands praised the U.S. political system for allowing the peaceful change of presidents. Danish Premier Poul Hartling declared Aug. 9 that "only in a society with a free press and a strong sense of justice is it possible to experience a political development as the one the world has now witnessed." A Dutch official asserted Nixon's resignation culminated a "process of democratic purification."

Middle East—Israel expressed confidence in continued U.S. friendship, but Arab leaders were concerned that Ford might lean too heavily in the Israelis' favor.

Israeli Defense Minister Shimon Peres said Aug. 9 that the change in U.S. presidents was a victory for the U.S. democratic process, but he expressed gratitude for Nixon's repeated support for Israel. Former Premier Golda Meir asserted Israelis would not forget that Nixon "has

been a faithful friend and has done great things to strengthen" Israel.

An unnamed Israeli official quoted by the Washington Post Aug. 10 said Nixon's resignation would have little impact on Israel. However, a resignation by Kissinger would have the impact of an "earthquake," the official asserted.

Lebanese Premier Takieddin Solh Aug. 9 urged Arabs to confront Ford with a united policy or risk a U.S. stand in the Middle East that was not even-handed. His nation's leading newspaper An Nahar agreed, asserting that "neither crying over Nixon nor being afraid of Ford" would help the Arab cause.

Indochina—South Vietnamese officials praised Nixon and expressed hope that Ford would follow his policies in Indochina. However, a spokesman for the Saigon government, Nguyen Quoc Cong, said Aug. 9 that the regime feared the Viet Cong would use the current period to "resume war in the South."

An official in the Laotian Foreign Ministry said he did not expect any fundamental change in U.S. policy because "Henry Kissinger is still in there," the Associated Press reported Aug. 9. However, officials in the Cambodian government worried that the U.S. might cut aid to Cambodia under Ford's presidency.

Other areas—The official Chinese news agency Hsinhua reported Nixon's resignation without commentary Aug. 9, but cited the reference in Nixon's resignation speech the night before to the U.S.' improved relations with Peking. A representative of the Nationalist government on Taiwan, Chen Yu-khing, expressed sympathy for Nixon and confidence that his policies would be followed by Ford.

Japanese Premier Kakuei Tanaka Aug. 9 said of Nixon's resignation, "what had to happen has happened." Other Japanese officials expressed the hope that U.S.-Japanese relations, strained during the Nixon Administration, would improve under Ford.

Indian Foreign Minister Swaran Singh said Aug. 9 that Nixon had resigned "in the best tradition of democracy," bowing to "the preponderant public opinion in his country."

Brazilian officials expressed hope Aug. 9 that with the Watergate crisis resolved, the U.S. would be able to give full attention to strengthening the dollar and to trade and energy questions. Finance Minister Mario Henrique Simonsen said an improvement in the U.S. economy would have a beneficial impact on Brazil.

Peruvian President Juan Velasco Alvarado, whose relations with the U.S. had improved recently after years of strain, said Aug. 9 that Nixon's resignation was "a shame, because Nixon gave himself for his country."

Blocking of investigation admitted. The presidential statement and tape transcripts that triggered the intense pressure leading to Nixon's resignation August 9 had been released August 5. They effectively constituted a confession to obstruction of justice—the charge contained in the first article of impeachment voted by the House Judiciary Committee.

The transcripts [See below] covered three meetings with H. R. Haldeman, then White House chief of staff, on June 23, 1972, six days after the Watergate break-in. Informed that the Federal Bureau of Investigation's (FBI) probe of the break-in was pointing to officials in his re-election campaign, Nixon instructed Haldeman to tell the FBI, "Don't go any further into this case period!"

While Nixon's earlier statements on the Watergate case attributed his concern over the FBI's investigations to national security problems and possible conflicts with the Central Intelligence Agency (CIA), the latest transcripts—and Nixon's own statement about them—finally indicated that political considerations had played a major role.

According to the transcripts, Nixon told Haldeman to base the curtailment of FBI activities on possible reopening of questions about the CIA's role in the abortive 1961 "Bay of Pigs" invasion of Cuba (some of the Watergate burglary conspirators had been involved in the CIA operation). Haldeman assured Nixon that the CIA ploy would give L. Patrick Gray, then acting FBI director, sufficient justification to drop the investigation of the "laundering" (through a Mexican lawyer and bank) of the campaign funds used to finance the Watergate operation.

Nixon then told Haldeman that Gray should be instructed—through CIA Director Richard Helms and Deputy Director Vernon A. Walters—to curtail the investigation.

In the written statement announcing release of the transcripts, Nixon referred to other transcripts released earlier (April 29–30), which he said then would "tell it all" concerning his role in Watergate and the cover-up.

But in early May, he continued, he had begun a "preliminary review" of some of the 64 conversations subpoenaed by Watergate special prosecutor Leon Jaworski, including two from June 23, 1972. Nixon said he recognized that the tapes "presented potential problems," but he "did not inform my staff or my counsel of it, or those arguing my case, nor did I amend my submission to the Judiciary Committee. . . ." As a result, those arguing and judging his case were proceeding with "information that was incomplete and in some respects erroneous. This was a serious act of omission for which I take full responsibility and which I deeply regret."

Nixon stated that since the July 24 Supreme Court order that the tapes be surrendered for the Watergate prosecution, he and his counsel had reviewed and analyzed many of the tapes, a process which "made it clear that portions of the tapes of these June 23 conversations are at variance with certain of my previous statements."

These included, Nixon said, the statement of May 22, 1973, in which he recalled that he had been concerned that the FBI's investigation of Watergate might expose "unrelated covert activities" of the CIA or "sensitive national security matters" involving the special White House investigative unit known as the "plumbers." He thus ordered that the FBI "coordinate" its investigation with the CIA. The May 22 statement, he said, was based on his "recollection at the time"—some 11 months after the break in—"plus documentary materials and relevant public testimony of those involved."

In his latest statement, however, Nixon acknowledged that the June 23 tapes showed he had discussed the "political aspects of the situation" at the time he gave the instructions, and that he was "aware of the advantages this course of action would have with respect to limiting possible public exposure of involvement by persons connected with the re-election committee."

Nixon said his review of additional tapes had not revealed other "major inconsistencies with what I have previously submitted," and that he had no reason to believe that there would be others.

Acknowledging that a House vote of impeachment was "virtually a foregone conclusion," Nixon addressed two points of caution to the potential Senate trial: first, as to "what actually happened" as a result of his instructions concerning the FBI, Nixon said Walters had informed Gray that the CIA would not be "compromised" by the FBI's probe. When Gray had expressed concern about "improper attempts to limit his investigation, as the record shows, I told him to press ahead vigorously with his investigation—which he did."

Nixon also urged that "the evidence be looked at in its entirety, and the events be looked at in perspective." Whatever his mistakes in handling Watergate, Nixon continued, "the basic truth remains that when all the facts were brought to my attention I insisted on a full investigation and prosecution of those guilty." Nixon concluded that the full record "does not

Text of President Nixon's Aug. 5 Statement

I have today instructed my attorneys to make available to the House Judiciary Committee, and I am making public, the transcripts of three conversations with H. R. Haldeman on June 23, 1972. I have also turned over the tapes of these conversations to Judge Sirica, as part of the process of my compliance with the Supreme Court ruling.

On April 29, in announcing my decision to make public the original set of White House transcripts, I stated, "as far as what the President personally knew and did with regard to Watergate and the cover-up is concerned, these materials—together with those already made available—will tell it all."

Shortly after that, in May, I made a preliminary review of some of the 64 taped conversations subpoenaed by the special prosecutor.

Among the conversations I listened to at that time were two of those of June 23. Although I recognized that these presented potential problems, I did not inform my staff or my counsel of it, or those arguing my case, nor did I amend my submission to the Judiciary Committee in order to include and reflect it. At the time, I did not realize the extent of the implications which these conversations might now appear to have. As a result, those arguing my case, as well as those passing judgment on the case, did so with information that was incomplete and in some respects erroneous. This was a serious act of omission for which I take full responsibility and which I deeply regret.

Since the Supreme Court's decision 12 days ago, I have ordered my counsel to analyze the 64 tapes, and I have listened to a number of them myself. This process has made it clear that portions of the tapes of these June 23 conversations are at variance with certain of my previous statements. Therefore, I have ordered the transcripts made available immediately to the Judiciary Committee so that they can be reflected in the committee's report, and included in the record to be considered by the House and Senate.

In a formal written statement on May 22 of last year, I said that shortly after the Watergate break-in I became concerned about the possibility that the FBI investigation might lead to the exposure either of unrelated covert activities of the CIA or of sensitive national security matters that the so-called "plumbers" unit at the White House had been working on because of the CIA and plumbers connections of some of those involved. I said that I therefore gave instructions that the FBI should be alerted to coordinate with the CIA and to ensure that the investigation not expose these sensitive national security matters.

That statement was based on my recollection at the time—some 11 months later—plus documentary materials and relevant public testimony of those involved.

The June 23 tapes clearly show, however, that at the time I gave those instructions I also discussed the political aspects of the situation, and that I was aware of the advantages this course of action would have with respect to limiting possible public exposure of involvement by persons connected with the re-election committee.

My review of the additional tapes has, so far, shown no other major inconsistencies with what I have previously submitted. While I have no way at this stage of being certain that there will not be others, I have no reason to believe that there will be. In any case, the tapes in their entirety are now in the process of being furnished to Judge Sirica. He has begun what may be a rather lengthy process of reviewing the tapes, passing on specific claims of executive privilege on portions of them, and forwarding to the special prosecutor those tapes or those portions that are relevant to the Watergate investigation.

It is highly unlikely that this review will be completed in time for the House debate. It appears at this stage, however, that a House vote of impeachment is, as a practical matter, virtually a foregone conclusion, and that the issue will therefore go to trial in the Senate. In order to ensure that no other significant relevant materials are withheld, I shall voluntarily furnish to the Senate everything from these tapes that Judge Sirica rules should go to the special prosecutor.

I recognize that this additional material I am now furnishing may further damage my case, especially because attention will be drawn separately to it rather than to the evidence in its entirety. In considering its implications, therefore, I urge that two points be borne in mind.

The first of these points is to remember what actually happened as a result of the instructions I gave on June 23. Acting Director Gray of the FBI did coordinate with Director Helms and Deputy Director Walters of the CIA. The CIA did undertake an extensive check to see whether any of its covert activities could be compromised by a full FBI investigation of Watergate. Deputy Director Walters then reported back to Mr. Gray, that they would not be compromised. On July 6, when I called Mr. Gray and when he expressed concern about improper attempts to limit his investigation, as the record shows, I told him to press ahead vigorously with his investigation—which he did.

The second point I would urge is that the evidence be looked at in its entirety, and the events be looked at in perspective. Whatever mistakes I made in the handling of Watergate, the basic truth remains that when all the facts were brought to my attention I insisted on a full investigation and prosecution of those guilty. I am firmly convinced that the record, in its entirety, does not justify the extreme step of impeachment and removal of a President. I trust that as the constitutional process goes forward, this perspective will prevail.

justify the extreme step of impeachment and removal of a President."

The courts, the tapes and St. Clair— Nixon's Aug. 5 statement said the three key transcripts had been made public partly as a result of the process of compliance with the July 24 Supreme Court decision. This reflected the central role played by that order in the events leading to his resignation.

In setting procedures for compliance with the order, U.S. District Court Judge John J. Sirica, who was to screen the tapes before transmitting them to the Watergate prosecution, had suggested that special presidential counsel James D. St. Clair personally review the tapes, along with Nixon. (St. Clair had told the Supreme Court that he had not listened to any of the tapes.)

According to news reports Aug. 5-6, St. Clair had first become aware of the incriminating material involving Nixon and the cover-up during this review and—threatening resignation—had insisted that the transcripts be made public and that Nixon let it be known that he had withheld evidence from his counsel.

White House Deputy Press Secretary Gerald L. Warren denied Aug. 6 that Nixon's decision to release the transcripts had been based on "any sort of ultimatum or anything like that" from St. Clair.

According to news reports Aug. 7-10, key roles in the prelude to resignation were played by White House chief of staff Alexander M. Haig Jr. and Rep. Charles E. Wiggins (R, Calif.), a spokesman for the Nixon defense in the House.

After learning the content of the tapes, Haig—along with St. Clair—reportedly sensed the inevitability of Nixon's fall. To get a reading on Congressional reaction to the evidence, Haig and St. Clair summoned Wiggins to the White House Aug. 2. Wiggins said later that he was stunned by the transcripts and the direct evidence that Nixon had ordered the cover-up. Wiggins told the Nixon aides that impeachment and conviction would no longer be in question and that Nixon should consider resigning. Haig and St. Clair reportedly agreed, setting the stage for convincing Nixon that further struggle against leaving office would be futile.

(St. Clair said Aug. 9 that he no longer represented Nixon because Nixon was no longer president. St. Clair said he would remain on the White House payroll for a few weeks to deal with the final details of the almost-completed process of compliance with the Supreme Court's July 24 order that Watergate-related presidential conversations be surrendered for the cover-up prosecution.)

The transcripts: June 23, 1972

First Meeting: the President and Haldeman in the Oval Office, joined briefly by Press Secretary Ziegler, 10:04–11:39 a.m.

Haldeman turned quickly to the ominous implications of the FBI's investigation of the Watergate break-in:

H. Now, on the investigation, you know the Democratic break-in thing, we're back in the problem area because the FBI is not under control, because Gray doesn't exactly know how to control it and they have—their investigation is now leading into some productive areas—because they've been able to trace the money—not through the money itself—but through the bank sources—the banker. And, and it goes in some directions we don't want it to go. Ah, also there have been some things—like an informant came in off the street to the FBI in Miami who was a photographer or has a friend who is a photographer who developed some films through this guy Barker and the films had pictures of Democratic National Committee letterhead documents and things. So it's things like that that are filtering in. Mitchell came up with yesterday, and John Dean analyzed very carefully last night and concludes, concurs now with Mitchell's recommendation that the only way to solve this, and we're set up beautifully to do it, ah, in that and that—the only network that paid any attention to it last night was NBC—they did a massive story on the Cuban thing.

P. That's right.

H. That the way to handle this now is for us to have Walters call Pat Gray and just say, "stay to hell out of this—this is ah, business here we don't want you to go any further on it." That's not an unusual development, and ah, that would take care of it.

P. What about Pat Gray—you mean Pat Gray doesn't want to?

H. Pat does want to. He doesn't know how to, and he doesn't have, he doesn't have any basis for doing it. Given this, he will then have the basis. He'll call Mark Felt in, and the two of them—and Mark Felt wants to cooperate because he's ambitious—

P. Yeah.

H. He'll call him in and say, "we've got the signal from across the river to put the hold on this." And that will fit rather well because the FBI agents who are working the case, at this point, feel that's what it is.

P. This is CIA? They've traced the money? Who'd they trace it to?

H. Well they've traced it to a name, but they haven't gotten to the guy yet.

P. Would it be somebody here?

H. Ken Dahlberg.

P. Who the hell is Ken Dahlberg?

H. He gave $25,000 in Minnesota and, ah, the check went directly to this guy Barker.

P. It isn't from the committee though, from Stans?

H. Yeah. It is. It's directly traceable and there's some more through some Texas people that went to the Mexican bank which can also be traced to the Mexican bank—They'll get their names today.—and (pause)

P. Well, I mean, there's no way—I'm just thinking if they don't cooperate, what do they say? That they were approached by the Cubans. That's what Dahlberg has to say, the Texans too, that they—

H. Well, if they will. But then we're relying on more and more people all the time. That's the problem and they'll stop if we could take this other route.

P. All right.

H. And you seem to think the thing to do is get them to stop?

P. Right, fine.

H. They say the only way to do that is from White House instructions. And it's got to be to Helms and to—ah, what's his name—? Walters.

P. Walters.

H. And the proposal would be that Ehrlichman and I call them in, and say, ah—

P. All right, fine. How do you call him in—I mean you just—well, we protected Helms from one hell of a lot of things.

H. That's what Ehrlichman says.

P. Of course, this Hunt, that will uncover a lot of things. You open that scab there's a hell of a lot of things and we just feel that it would be very detrimental to have this thing go any further. This involves these Cubans, Hunt and a lot of hanky-panky that we have nothing to do with ourselves. Well what the hell, did Mitchell know about this?

H. I think so. I don't think he knew the details, but I think he knew.

P. He didn't know how it was going to be handled though—with Dahlberg and the Texans and so forth? Well who was the asshole that did? Is it Liddy? Is that the fellow? He must be a little nuts.

H. He is.

P. I mean he just isn't well screwed on is he? Is that the problem?

H. No, but he was under pressure, apparently, to get more information, and as he got more pressure, he pushed the people harder to move harder—

P. Pressure from Mitchell?

H. Apparently.

P. Oh, Mitchell. Mitchell was at the point (unintelligible).

H. Yea.

P. All right, fine, I understand it all. We won't second-guess Mitchell and the rest. Thank God it wasn't Colson.

H. The FBI interviewed Colson yesterday. They determined that would be a good thing to do. To have him take an interrogation, which he did, and that—the FBI guys working the case concluded that there were one or two possibilities—one, that this is a White House—they don't think that there is anything at the election committee—they think it was either a White House operation and they had some obscure reasons for it—nonpolitical, or it was a Cuban and the CIA. And after their interrogation of Colson yesterday, they concluded it was not the White House, but are now convinced it is a CIA thing, so the CIA turnoff would—

P. Well, not sure of their analysis, I'm not going to get that involved. I'm (unintelligible).

H. No, sir, we don't want you to.

P. You call them in.

H. Good deal.

P. Play it tough. That's the way they play it and that's the way we are going to play it.

H. O.K.

P. When I saw that news summary, I questioned whether it's a bunch of crap, I thought, er, well it's good to have them off us awhile, because when they start bugging us, which they have, our little boys will not know how to handle it. I hope they will though.

H. You never know.

P. Good. . . .

After discussion of unrelated subjects, Nixon returned to the FBI-CIA problem, instructing Haldeman:

"When you get in (unintelligible) people, say, 'Look, the problem is that this will open the whole, the whole Bay of Pigs thing, and the President just feels that ah, without going into the details—don't, don't lie to them to the extent to say no involvement, but just say this is a comedy of errors, without getting into it, the President believes that it is going to open the whole Bay of Pigs thing up again. And, ah, because these people are plugging for (unintelligible) and that they should call the FBI in and (unintelligible) don't go any further into this case period!'"

Second meeting: The President and Haldeman in the Oval Office, 1:04–1:13 p.m.

The transcript in its entirety:

P. O.K., just postpone (scratching noises) (unintelligible) just say (unintelligible) very bad to have this fellow Hunt, ah, he knows too damned much, if he was involved—you happen to know that? If it gets out that this is all involved, the Cuba thing it would be a fiasco. It would make the CIA look bad, it's going to make Hunt look bad, and it is likely to blow the whole Bay of Pigs thing which we think would be very unfortunate—both for the CIA, and for the country, at this time, and for American foreign policy. Just tell him to lay off. Don't you?

H. Yep. That's the basis to do it on. Just leave it at that.

P. I don't know if he'll get any ideas for doing it because our concern political (unintelligible). Helms is not one to (unintelligible)—I would just say, lookit, because of the Hunt involvement, whole cover basically this

H. Yep. Good move.

P. Well, they've got some pretty good ideas on this Meany thing. Shultz did a good paper. I read it all (voices fade).

Third meeting: the President and Haldeman in the Executive Office Building office, joined by Ziegler, 2:20–2:45 p.m.

Haldeman reported on FBI and CIA reactions to White House directives about the Watergate investigations:

H. Well, it was kind of interest. Walters made the point and I didn't mention Hunt, I just said that the thing was leading into directions that were going to create potential problems because they were exploring leads that led back into areas that would be harmful to the CIA and harmful to the government (unintelligible)....

H. (Unintelligible) I think Helms did to (unintelligible) said, I've had no—

P. God (unintelligible)

H. Gray called and said, yesterday, and said that he thought—

P. Who did? Gray?

H. Gray called Helms and said I think we've run right into the middle of a CIA covert operation.

P. Gray said that?

H. Yeah. And (unintelligible) said nothing we've done at this point and ah (unintelligible) says well it sure looks to me like it is (unintelligible) and ah, that was the end of that conversation (unintelligible) the problem is it tracks back to the Bay of Pigs and it tracks back to some other the leads run out to people who had no involvement in this, except by contacts and connection, but it gets to areas that are liable to be raised? The whole problem (unintelligible) Hunt. So at that point he kind of got the picture. He said, he said we'll be very happy to be helpful (unintelligible) handle anything you want. I would like to know the reason for being helpful, and I made it clear to him he hasn't going to get explicit (unintelligible) generality, and he said fine. And Walters (unintelligible). Walters is going to make a call to Gray. That's the way we put it and that's the way it was left.

P. How does that work though, how, how, they've got to (unintelligible) somebody from the Miami bank.

H. (Unintelligible). The point John makes—the bureau is going on this because they don't know what they are uncovering (unintelligible) continue to pursue it. They don't need to because they already have their case as far as the charges against these men (unintelligible) and ah, as they pursue it (unintelligible) exactly, but we didn't in any way say we (unintelligible). One thing Helms did raise. He said, Gray—he asked Gray why they thought they had run into a CIA thing and Gray said because of the characters involved and the amount of money involved, a lot of dough. (unintelligible) and ah, (unintelligible).

P. (unintelligible)

H. Well, I think they will.

P. If it runs (unintelligible) what the hell who knows (unintelligible) contributed CIA.

H. Ya, it's money CIA gets money (unintelligible) I mean their money moves in a lot of different ways, too....

Presidential vignettes—In addition to the devastating comments about impeding the Watergate investigations, the latest presidential transcripts furnished relatively innocuous but revealing insights into Nixon's views on campaigning, monetary affairs and his own literary efforts.

After discussing some of the problems with hostile audiences and reporters during campaign appearances, Nixon offered some suggestions:

P. For example—now the worse thing (unintelligible) is to go to anything that you have to do with the Arts.

H. Ya, see that—it was (unintelligible) Julie giving that time in the Museum in Jackonville.

P. The Arts you know—they're Jews, they're left wing—in other words, stay away. Make a point.

H. Sure.

P. Middle America—put that word out—Middle America-type of people (unintelligible), auxiliary, (unintelligible). Why the hell doesn't Parker get that kind of thing going? Most of his things are elite groups except, I mean, do the cancer thing—maybe nice for Tricia to go up—ride a bus for 2 hours—do some of that park in Oklahoma—but my view is, Bob, relate it to Middle America and not the elitist (unintelligible). Do you agree?

H. Yep, sure do.

P. I'm not complaining. I think they are doing a hell of a job. The kids are willing—

H. They really are, but she can improve.

P. There again, Tricia had a very good thought on this, but let's do Middle-America.

H. Yep.

At one point during the first meeting, Haldeman tried to interest Nixon in foreign monetary developments, apparently with little success:

H. ...Did you get the report that the British floated the pound?

P. No, I don't think so.

H. They did.

P. That's devaluation?

H. Yeah. Flanigan's got a report on it here.

P. I don't care about it. Nothing we can do about it.

H. You want a run-down?

P. No, I don't.

H. He argues it shows the wisdom of our refusal to consider convertability until we get a new monetary system.

P. Good, I think he's right. It's too complicated for me to get into. (unintelligible) I understand.

H. Burns expects a 5-day [5–8] percent devaluation against the dollar.

P. Yeah. O.K. Fine.

H. Burns is concerned about speculation about the lira.

P. Well, I don't give a (expletive deleted) about the lira. (Unintelligible).

H. That's the substance of that.

Nixon also held his own book, "Six Crises," in high regard—both as a guide to campaigning and a work of literature:

H. I was thumbing through the, ah, last chapters of (unintelligible) last night, and I also read the (unintelligible) chapters (unintelligible). Warm up to it, and it makes, ah, fascinating reading. Also reminds you of a hell of a lot of things that happened in the campaign press you know, election coverage, the (unintelligible) etc., etc.

H. Yeah.

P. So on and so on. I want you to reread it, and I want Colson to read it, and anybody else.

H. O.K.

P. And anybody else in the campaign. Get copies of the book and give it to each of them. Say I want them to read it and have it in mind. Give it to whoever you can. O.K.?

H. Sure will.

P. Actually, the book reads awfully well—have to look at history. I want to talk to you more about that later in terms of what it tells us about how our campaign should be run, O.K.?....

Nixon returned to the subject later during the first meeting: "I suppose most of our staff (unintelligible) but that Six Crises is a damned good book, and the (unintelligible) story reads like a novel—the Hiss case—Caracas was fascinating. The campaign of course for anybody in politics should be a must because it had a lot in there of how politicians are like."

Impact in Congress devastating. President Nixon's statement and release of new tapes Aug. 5 had a devastating effect upon his support in Congress. That support had been perceptibly slipping away since the House Judiciary Committee's televised hearings and decision to bring impeachment articles to the House. The trend in the House toward a vote for impeachment was conceded even by Vice President Ford Aug. 3.

In the Senate, where a two-thirds vote was necessary for conviction, the prediction was less certain although there was a definite trend against the President. Even prior to release of Nixon's statement Aug. 5, Sen. Robert P. Griffin (Mich.), assistant Senate Republican leader, appeared before television cameras to call for Nixon's resignation. "I think we've arrived at a point where both the national interest and his own interest will best be served by resigning," he said. "It's not just his enemies who feel that way. Many of his friends, and I count myself one of them, believe now that this would be the most appropriate course. Needless to say, this would be an awesome and very difficult decision for him to reach but I believe he will see it that way too." Later in the day, Griffin expressed disappointment that Nixon seemed determined to remain in office.

Following release of the President's statement, with its concession of knowledge of the Watergate cover-up, coupled with acknowledgement that impeachment by the house was "virtually a foregone conclusion," Republican defections became epidemic.

Rep. Charles E. Wiggins (R, Calif.), Nixon's strongest defender during the Judiciary Committee hearings, asserted, while struggling to retain composure, that he had reached the "painful conclusion" that it was in the "national interest" for Nixon to resign. "The facts then known to me have now changed," he said in reference to his committee stance that there was no direct link to the President of a criminal offense. Wiggins said it was established now "beyond a reasonable doubt" that the President had agreed to a "plan of action" to obstruct the Watergate investigation. "These facts standing alone," Wiggins said, "are legally sufficient in my opinion to sustain at least one count against the President of conspiracy to obstruct justice." If Nixon did not resign, Wiggins said, "I am prepared to conclude that the magnificent career of public service of Richard Nixon must be terminated involuntarily and shall support those portions of Article I of the bill of impeachment adopted by the Judiciary Committee which are sustained by the evidence."

Wiggins was one of 10 committee Republicans who had voted against all five impeachment articles presented in the committee. Three others in that group, Reps. Wiley Mayne (Iowa), Joseph J. Maraziti (N.J.) and David W. Dennis (Ind.)—also announced Aug. 5 they would vote for impeachment on Article I. The President, Dennis said, had "destroyed his credibility" with the committee. Others of the group indicated they were reassessing their positions. One of them, Rep. Delbert L. Latta (Ohio), said, "We certainly weren't given the truth."

The President's loss of support spread Aug. 5 to the House Republican leadership. House GOP Policy Committee Chairman Barber B. Conable Jr. (N.Y.), who supported Nixon on more House votes in 1973 than any Republican, said he was prepared to vote for impeachment and predicted it would have "overwhelming support in the House." "I guess we have found the smoking gun, haven't we?" Conable observed in reference to the Republican argument that impeachment should not be voted without solid evidence of direct presidential involvement in a criminal offense.

House Republican Conference Chairman John B. Anderson (Ill.) said Aug. 5 the Nixon statement "goes to the very heart of the first article of impeachment. The President's own words seem to convict him of that article."

House Republican Leader John J. Rhodes (Ariz.) issued a statement that "the apparent attempt to use the CIA to cover up the depth of the Watergate conspiracy is shocking. The fact that the President's veracity is put in question by this disclosure is a tragedy."

A cry that "I'm still a Nixon man" was raised by Rep. Earl Landgrebe (R, Ind.), who added that the situation looked like "a mutiny on a ship—a kind of madness has broken out."

On the Democratic side, House Majority Leader Thomas P. O'Neill (Mass.) likened it to a "tidal wave" going against the President. He estimated that Nixon's support in the House had dropped to no more than 75 votes against impeachment. House Democratic Whip John J. McFall (Calif.) observed that the situation had changed for the President's supporters in the House, that they were now "off the hook." "Anyone can now vote for impeachment without any fear of criticism," he said, "because the President virtually concedes and invites it."

On the Senate side, the President's statement drew doleful comments Aug. 5 from some of his staunchest supporters. Sen. John G. Tower (R, Tex.) quoted from Greek tragedy: "And now a wave of melancholy tranquility settles over Thebes."

Sen. Peter H. Dominick (R, Colo.) called it "sorrowful news." Sen. Robert Dole (R, Kan.) said "I just think he loses. I just think everything is downhill."

Sen. Pete V. Domenici (R, N.M.) said "it's another set of inconsistencies. The whole thing weakens the position of the President substantially."

Senate Republican Leader Hugh Scott (Pa.) released a short statement that "the President took the proper action in releasing essential information prior to the House vote." "That's it," he told reporters, "there will be no further statement by the leadership."

Defection almost total—By Aug. 6, the collapse of Nixon support appeared almost total. Only two of the 435 House members took public stands against impeachment—Rep. Otto E. Passman (D, La.) joined Landgrebe.

GOP Leader Rhodes announced for impeachment. "Cover-up of criminal activity and misuse of federal agencies can neither be condoned nor tolerated," he said. Was there anything the President could do to save himself? "I suppose there might be," Rhodes replied, "but I can't think what it is."

The remaining 10 members of the Judiciary Committee who opposed the impeachment articles in that panel's hearings, reversed their stands Aug. 6. "I feel that I have been deceived," one of them, ranking GOP member Rep. Edward Hutchinson (Mich.), commented.

A conservative Southern Republican, Rep. Joel Broyhill (Va.), a longtime Nixon supporter, said simply, "He's gone."

With little prospect of debate left, the plan to allot 55 hours of general debate on the impeachment articles was pragmatically cut back by the House leadership Aug. 6 to 25 hours. It was to begin Aug. 19, and a vote was expected by Aug. 22.

Public defenders of the President in the Senate Aug. 6 had dropped to one—Carl Curtis (R, Neb.), who accused the U.S. of emulating a "banana republic." He pointed out the anomaly that if Vice President Ford succeeded Nixon and appointed his vice president, neither incumbent would have been elected to the office.

The consensus of the Senate Republican Policy Committee, which met at noon Aug. 6, was that the gravity of his situation, had worsened, that there had been "great erosion of support," should be relayed to the President. Sen. Tower, reporting the consensus, said a majority at the meeting felt that resignation would be "in the national interest."

Sen. Robert Dole (Kan.), former GOP national chairman, estimated Aug. 6 that if Nixon could count on 40 votes against conviction in the Senate a week ago, he had no more than 20 that day.

It dropped to 15 by Aug. 7. Sen. Barry Goldwater (R, Ariz.) said he and Scott had given Nixon that estimate when they, with Rhodes, met with the President at the White House that day. The estimate for the House was even worse, perhaps only 10 votes against impeachment.

Imminent resignation was in the air Aug. 7 and rumors swept the country. The Providence Journal cited "an undaunted supporter" of the President as the source of a report that Nixon had made "an irrevocable decision" to resign. Providence was the home of Rabbi Baruch Korff, leader of a recent movement to support the President, who had been meeting at the White House with Nixon.

Another rumor came from Phoenix in the home state of both Goldwater and Rhodes. A newspaper report from "a reliable Washington source" said the President would resign on Aug. 7. But Goldwater profanely denied any link to such rumors and later Aug. 7 went to the Senate floor to denounce the press.

Impeachment preparations continued—Even as President Nixon's resignation appeared more certain each day, Congressional leaders continued preparing for House consideration of the proposed impeachment articles and the Senate trial that might follow House action.

The House leadership indicated agreement on the rules for consideration of the proposed articles. Rep. John B. Anderson (R, Ill.), Republican Party Conference chairman and Rules Committee member, said Aug. 1 that the House would probably debate under a closed rule that would prohibit most amendments to the articles reported by the Judiciary Committee. Under such a rule, only amendments to strike part or all of a proposed article would be allowed.

Meanwhile, House members Aug. 5 began five days of hearing the tapes of presidential conversations already heard by Judiciary Committee members. Four specially equipped rooms in two House office buildings contained headsets for 204 representatives to listen at one time.

House majority whip John J. McFall (D, Calif.) announced Aug. 5 that special security measures had been planned for the period of the impeachment debate.

The full House voted 385–25 Aug. 7 to allow gavel to gavel television coverage of the impeachment proceedings. The previous day, the Senate Rules Committee had agreed to permit some type of television coverage of a Senate trial.

While House preparations were under way, the Senate Rules Committee began the first of a series of closed meetings July 31 on revision of rules for the trial. According to published reports, the committee focused on the role of the chief justice, who would preside in the trial, the standard of proof necessary for conviction and the limits on admissibility of evidence.

'Uphill struggle' conceded. White House Deputy Press Secretary Gerald L. Warren conceded Aug. 2 that the President faced "an uphill struggle" against the impeachment move. "We recognize the situation as it exists in the House," Warren said, and "if you had to make odds, you'd have to put the President in the role of underdog." But, he said, it was "a political struggle" and as such "you have a chance to win."

There was a Republican move that day to have the House consider censure, instead of impeachment, of the President, but it made little headway and was abandoned in favor of impeachment even by its author, Rep. Paul Findley (R, Ill.), after Nixon's Aug. 5 statement of Watergate cover-up complicity.

The word from both chambers of Congress was increasingly ominous. House Republican Leader John Rhodes (Ariz.) was expressing belief July 26 that there were not enough votes for impeachment but he also cautioned that the situation was volatile. Democratic Leader Thomas P. O'Neill (Mass.) was predicting at the same time that the House would vote impeachment by a margin of at least 60 votes and the movement was swelling. By July 30 Rhodes was expressing deep concern "about the evidence against the President" and House GOP Conference chairman John Anderson (Ill.) was noting the indecision among his Republican colleagues. "People are milling around, floundering, trying to decide upon a course of action," he said. By Aug. 3, Vice

President Ford, in Hattiesburg, Miss. in the midst of a tour on behalf of Republican House candidates, was conceding that "the situation in the House has eroded considerably," that "the odds have significantly changed."

The trend in the Senate by Aug. 3, according to a survey by the Washington Post, was that the split was near 60–40 for conviction, only seven short of the necessary two-thirds majority to carry. The Aug. 12 Newsweek, available Aug. 4, reported that the White House had a list of 36 senators it was counting on to support Nixon on the issue but that some on the list could be termed "shaky." One of those on the list, Sen. Robert P. Griffin (Mich.), assistant Senate Republican leader, notified Nixon Aug. 3 that if he defied a Senate subpoena for the tape recordings denied the House Judiciary Committee, Griffin would vote for conviction in the Senate trial.

On Aug. 3, the President retired to the presidential retreat Camp David in the Catoctin Mountains with Mrs. Nixon, his daughters and sons-in-law, David and Julie Eisenhower and Edward and Tricia Cox, and his friend, Charles G. Rebozo.

The next day, he summoned his chief lawyer, James D. St. Clair, his two top aides, Gen. Alexander M. Haig Jr. and Ronald L. Ziegler, and his speech writers, Patrick J. Buchanan and Raymond K. Price Jr. They remained at Camp David for about five hours. The decision was made to issue the statement of early complicity in the Watergate cover-up, and the supporting tapes, which was done Aug. 5. Warren told reporters Aug. 6 that the President considered, after making the decision, either resigning or stepping aside under the 25th Amendment but had rejected these alternatives and determined to fight it out.

His resolve to remain in office pending the outcome of the constitutional process of impeachment was reportedly made clear at a 90-minute meeting in Washington Aug. 6 with his Cabinet, Vice President Ford, top aides and Republican National Chairman George Bush. But reporters noted a softening of denials of resignation during the day. Warren, besieged by queries, was not flatly declaring Nixon would not resign but saying only that "he does not intend to resign."

Participants at the meeting were circumspect upon emerging. Secretary of State Henry A. Kissinger emphasized that the country's foreign policy continued on a bipartisan basis "in the national interest and the interest of world peace" and "no foreign government should have any doubts about the way in which our foreign policy will be conducted." Treasury Secretary William E. Simon stressed Nixon's dedication to the task of running the country and especially to control of inflation which was, in Nixon's estimation to aides that day, Simon said, the No. 1 issue before the nation.

Bush issued a more expressive formal statement later in the day. "I have

steadily maintained that the system can cope with whatever shocks it must absorb," it said. "Resignation is something that the President alone must decide. If it is to be an impeachable trial, I urge all in an official role to carry this process out in the most judicious and expeditious manner possible to spare the nation more trauma. I'm confident the President will do what is right—what is best for the country."

On Aug. 7, the President met in the Oval Office with Senate Republican Leader Hugh Scott (Pa.), Sen. Barry Goldwater (R, Ariz.) and House Republican Leader John J. Rhodes (Ariz.). Afterwards, the three Republican leaders met with reporters. "He invited us down this afternoon to disclose to him the actual situation in the House and Senate regarding his position," Goldwater told them. Scott said all three told the President the situation was "gloomy." "He asked me," Scott said. "I said, 'Gloomy,' He said, 'Damn gloomy?' I said, 'Yes, sir.'"

Goldwater said "we were extremely impressed with the uppermost thought on his mind, which is that whatever decision is made will be in the national interest. No decision has been made. We made no suggestions."

Scott said the question of resignation "did not even come up." Rhodes said the subject of immunity against prosecution if he resigned "was not touched on." Scott offered his opinion that "the situation will be resolved in a few days."

Soon after the meeting, Nixon met with Kissinger, who returned that evening and remained until shortly after midnight.

There were other signs pointing to resignation: Rabbi Baruch Korff, head of a movement to support the President, met with Nixon Aug. 7 and later issued a statement that "unless there is an immediate outpouring of support addressed to the White House . . . it is my opinion and only my opinion he may resign in the national interest."

Nixon's chief of staff Haig was reported to be among the group of White House staffers urging the President to take the option of resigning. The staff itself was shaken. "Everybody is rattled," Kenneth R. Cole, director of the President's Domestic Council, told newsmen.

Before noon on Aug. 8, Nixon met in the Oval Office with Ford and informed him, as he reportedly had Kissinger the evening before, that he was resigning. Press Secretary Ronald L. Ziegler appeared in the press room to announce, in stricken tones, that the President would address the nation that evening. The news of resignation was accepted and disseminated that afternoon.

Shortly before 7:30 p.m., Nixon met briefly with his family, which had stayed throughout the day in the East Wing of the White House, then he walked alone to the Executive Office Building, where Scott, Rhodes, James O. Eastland (D,

Miss.), president pro tem of the Senate, Senate Democratic Leader Mike Mansfield (Mont.) and House Speaker Carl Albert (D, Okla.), were waiting. He gave them formal notice of his resignation.

Half an hour later, Nixon returned to the White House and went to the Cabinet Room, where about 40 of his staunchest supporters in the Congress had assembled. The parting was tearful on both sides. The announcement to the nation was next; the President went to the Oval Office for his resignation speech.

The date was the anniversary of Nixon's presidential nomination six years ago on the first ballot at the Republican National Convention.

Final action—Among his last actions as President Aug. 8, Nixon vetoed a $13.5 billion bill providing appropriations for the Agriculture Department, the Environmental Protection Agency, the Consumer Product Safety Commission, the Federal Trade Commission and the National Water Quality Commission. The measure would also have provided relief to the drought-stricken farmers of the Midwest. The bill posed a "distinct threat to our fight against inflation," Nixon said, because the amount authorized exceeded his fiscal 1975 budget by "some $540 million."

Ford stands in wings—Vice President Ford removed himself from the impeachment debate Aug. 5 after release of the presidential statement admitting Nixon's knowledge of the Watergate cover-up. Returning to Washington from a weekend swing through Mississippi and Louisiana, Ford issued a statement that he had "come to the conclusion that the public interest is no longer served by repetition of my previously expressed belief that, on the basis of all the evidence known to me and to the American people, the President is not guilty of an impeachable offense under the constitutional definition of 'treason, bribery or other high crimes and misdemeanors.' Inasmuch as additional evidence is about to be forthcoming from the President, which he says may be damaging, I intend to respectfully decline to discuss impeachment matters in public or in response to questions until the facts are more fully available."

A vice president, Ford said, "is a party of interest as the constitutional successor if a president is removed from office" and "there are many urgent matters on America's agenda in which I hope to continue to serve this great country as a communicator and conciliator. The business of government must go on and the genuine needs of the people must be served. I believe I can make a better contribution to this end by not involving myself daily in the impeachment debate, in which I have no constitutional role."

The next day Ford attended a luncheon meeting of Republican senators, briefing them on the Cabinet meeting he attended with Nixon that day. He left the luncheon, according to reports, when the conversation turned to impeachment and calls for Nixon's resignation.

Early on the morning of Aug. 7, Ford met for an hour in his office with Nixon's chief of staff, Gen. Alexander M. Haig Jr. The meeting was at Haig's request.

In an interview with the New York Times that day, Ford did not respond to questions on sensitive issues. He did answer questions about whether he felt prepared to assume the presidency. "No question about that," he said. He had "worked real hard" and visited every executive department for top-level conferences and had confidential military briefings during his recent travels around the country. He had regular meetings with Secretary of State Henry Kissinger. "I think I know as much, if not more," Ford said, "about the government than any vice president" and "I think I'm well prepared for any contingency."

Jaworski: no agreement made. There was widespread speculation both before and after Nixon's resignation as to what legal action, if any, might be taken against him as a private citizen. A key element in the issue was the fact that Nixon had been named as an undicted co-conspirator in the cover-up case, even without the latest damaging transcripts. The grand jury had reportedly wanted to indict Nixon but had been dissuaded by Watergate special prosecutor Leon Jaworski.

In a statement released after the resignation announcement Aug. 8, Jaworski said that bargaining regarding possible immunity from prosecution had not played a part in Nixon's decision to leave office. "There has been no agreement or understanding of any sort between the President and his representatives and the special prosecutor relating in any way to the President's resignation," the statement said.

Jaworski said his office "was not asked for any such agreement or understanding and offered none." He added that he had been informed of Nixon's decision to resign during the afternoon.

Although there was general agreement that Congress did not have the power to grant immunity from prosecution, Sen. Edward W. Brooke (R, Mass.) and Rep. John H. Buchanan Jr. (R, Ala.) introduced companion resolutions Aug. 8 expressing the "sense of Congress" that Nixon should not be prosecuted after he left office. Such a measure would not be binding on the prosecution or the courts. Brooke said the next day, however, that he would not press for passage of the resolution because of the lack of contrition or confession in Nixon's televised announcement.

Congressional opinion on possible prosecution was divided: the New York Times reported Aug. 9 that many members felt Nixon should be subject to the same liability to prosecution as any ordinary citizen, but some members followed the general line of argument that

the disgrace of resignation was sufficient punishment. Senate Republican Leader Hugh Scott (Pa.) said Aug. 9 that the nation already had its "pound of flesh" and that it did not need the "blood that goes with it." Senate Democratic Leader Mike Mansfield (Mont.) said he would have "appreciated" some reference in Nixon's address "to the reasons which brought about this tragedy."

A telephone survey conducted by the Gallup organization Aug. 8–9 and reported Aug. 11 found that 55% of those polled opposed further criminal investigation of Nixon, while 37% believed such investigation should be pursued. The same poll found 79% believing Nixon "did the best thing by resigning, while 13% felt he "should have stayed."

A telephone poll conducted by NBC News before Nixon's Aug. 5 statement on the incriminating tapes and updated to reflect reaction to the statement found 56% opposed to a Congressional grant of immunity and 36% in favor. Asked whether they would favor seeing Nixon stand trial for obstruction of justice, 53% said yes, while 39% were opposed. The poll was concluded before the resignation announcement and reported Aug. 8.

Another legal possibility concerning Nixon's future—pardon by President Ford either before or after an indictment—was indirectly dismissed by Ford's press secretary Aug. 9. Asked about such prospects at a news briefing, J. F. terHorst said he had not spoken to Ford about the issue directly, but cited Ford's statements during his 1973 vice presidential confirmation hearings. (Ford had been asked: if a President resigned would his successor have the power to prevent further investigation or prosecution? Ford replied: "I do not think the public would stand for it.... The attorney general, in my opinion, with the help and support of the American people, would be the controlling factor.") News reports Aug. 9–10 cited doubts expressed by members of Congress and other analysts that Ford would grant such a pardon.

It remained technically possible that the process of impeachment by Congress could continue even though Nixon had resigned, but the prospect seemed unlikely. Anticipating Nixon's resignation, Mansfield had suggested Aug. 7 that the proceedings should go on "in order to lay it all out and get away from the idea that the President was being forced out" unjustly. But House Majority Leader Thomas P. O'Neill (D, Mass.) said later the same day that he and Judiciary Committee Chairman Peter W. Rodino (D, N.J.) had decided that to do so would be "overkill."

Rodino said Aug. 9 that the inquiry was over, and reportedly felt that his panel's final report on the articles of impeachment would be sufficient documentation of Nixon's role in Watergate and related scandals.

Another question left unsettled in the

wake of Nixon's resignation was the custody of presidential tapes and documents still in the White House, some of which could be relevant to criminal prosecution. Although such materials were traditionally the property of the departing officeholder, the circumstances of Watergate were seen as possibly imposing special conditions on Nixon's records.

Ford's press secretary terHorst said Aug. 9 that the material was temporarily in the custody of outgoing White House counsel James D. St. Clair (who was to continue serving the White House—but not Nixon—for a limited period.) A spokesman for St. Clair said ownership of the tapes and documents was "something that has yet to be determined."

Court gets tapes; 9 conversations missing. The White House disclosed to U.S. District Court Judge John J. Sirica Aug. 9 that 17 minutes of a subpoenaed 31-minute telephone conversation between President Nixon and former counsel Charles W. Colson on March 21, 1973 was not recorded because the White House recording equipment "ran out" of tape. The disclosure came as Nixon's attorneys neared completion of the process of complying with a Supreme Court order that 64 conversations subpoenaed by special prosecutor Leon Jaworski be surrendered to Sirica for prosecution of the cover-up case.

John A. Chester, an assistant to special White House counsel James D. St. Clair, also said Aug. 9 that another conversation between Nixon and Colson—reported Aug. 7 to have been missing—had been located. The "found" conversation occurred in January 1973.

The latest submission brought to 55 the number of conversations turned over to Sirica. Of the missing nine, St. Clair had said Aug. 7 that five were phone calls placed in the residence portion of the White House where the phones were not connected to the taping system. These included conversations with aides John D. Ehrlichman and H. R. Haldeman in April 1973, when the Watergate cover-up was falling apart.

Two of the conversations had taken place in lodges at the presidential retreat at Camp David, Md. In one lodge, according to St. Clair, the recorder had been removed a month before the conversation; the other lodge had never been connected to the system. Another conversation which could not be found occurred on Feb. 20, 1973 between Nixon and Haldeman; they reportedly discussed the questioning of former campaign aide Jeb Stuart Magruder by prosecutors.

St. Clair had told Sirica Aug. 6 that a half-hour phone conversation between Nixon and Colson on June 21, 1972 (four days after the Watergate break-in) was not recorded because Nixon had apparently placed the call from a phone not connected to the system.

St. Clair also turned over Aug. 7 Nixon's daily logs for the days on which subpoenaed conversations had occurred and White House records showing who had access to the tapes since Dec. 4, 1973.

St. Clair said he had been unable to gather notes on the conversations made by Nixon and his former aides. He also told Sirica that "working papers" made up during preparation of the transcripts made public April 30 had been destroyed. (The April release had included 20 of the 64 conversations.)

Ford addresses nation. In a nationally televised address Aug. 12, President Ford urged Congress to cooperate with him in confronting the problems of the nation, citing inflation as the major issue.

"My first priority is to work with you to bring inflation under control," Ford said. "Inflation is our domestic public enemy No. 1. To restore economic confidence, the government in Washington must provide leadership. It does no good to blame the public for spending too much when the government is spending too much."

In a well-received appearance (his speech was interrupted 32 times with applause) before an evening joint session, the new President announced several opening moves on the economic front, pledged an open Administration in domestic and foreign policy and declared his belief in "the absolute necessity of a free press."

He also pledged protection of individual privacy and declared his dedication to be President of "all the people." "There will be no illegal tappings, eavesdropping, buggings, or break-ins by my Administration," he asserted. "There will be hot pursuit of tough laws to prevent illegal invasions of privacy in both government and private activities." He promised to serve all the people, Ford said, and he meant "exactly that." To the limits of my strength and ability, he said, he would be President "of the black, brown, red and white Americans, of old and young, of women's liberationists and male chauvinists and all the rest of us in between, of the poor and the rich, of native sons and new refugees, of those who work at lathes or at desks or in mines or in the fields, and of Christians, Jews, Moslems, Buddhists and atheists, if there really are any atheists after what we have all been through."

Civil suit settlement final. The Democratic National Committee and the financial trust representing former President Nixon's re-election committees formally agreed in court Aug. 9 to a settlement of the lawsuits resulting from the Watergate burglary and wiretapping. [For further details, see p. 222B1]

Ex-Humphrey aide pleads guilty. Sen. Hubert H. Humphrey's (D, Minn.) former press secretary, Norman Sherman, and his partner in a Minneapolis voter canvassing firm, John Valentine, pleaded guilty Aug. 12 to charges of "aiding and abetting" the illegal donation of $82,000 in corporate campaign donations. [For further details, see p. 221G2]

Government moves to settle AMPI suit. Associated Milk Producers Inc. (AMPI) Aug. 13 accepted the terms of a consent decree filed that day by the Justice Department in federal district court in Kansas City, Mo. The proposed consent agreement would become final in 60 days if approved by the court, ending a civil suit brought by the government in 1972. [For further details, see p. 221E3]

Dollar posts gains on Nixon resignation. Events in Washington continued to exert a strong influence on the position of the U.S. dollar in foreign markets. The dollar gained on nearly all markets Aug. 7 in the wake of President Nixon's release of key tape transcripts and reports that he was being pressured to resign by members of his party as conviction on impeachment charges seemed more likely. In Tokyo, the dollar closed at 302.10 yen, its highest level since February 1973, and posted strong gains against most European currencies.

Demand for the dollar strengthened Aug. 8 as resignation rumors mounted and investors signaled their belief that a new Administration would restore confidence in the U.S. economy and exercise its customary leadership in world affairs. In Frankfurt, the dollar reached its highest level since March, closing at 2.5998 marks.

There followed a brief drop in the dollar's value reflecting what some observers believed was uncertainty over the direction of President Ford's policies. The dollar rebounded, however, Aug. 12 and 13 as investors were reassured by Ford's stated determination to curb runaway inflation and his firm moves to reassure world leaders that basic U.S. foreign policy would remain unchanged and that Secretary of State Henry Kissinger would remain at his post. The dollar hit a five-month high of 2.6175 marks in Frankfurt and also registered strong gains in Paris and London.

Staff developments. White House Press Secretary J. F. terHorst announced Aug. 14 that President Ford had asked Gen. Alexander M. Haig Jr., chief of staff at the White House under former President Nixon, "to stay on for the duration" and Haig had "agreed to do precisely that."

Ehrlichman subpoenas Nixon. The first legal action against former President Nixon as a private citizen was taken Aug. 15 in the form of a subpoena to appear as a witness for former aide John D. Ehrlichman in the pending Watergate cover-up trial.

The subpoena was issued through Ehrlichman's attorneys in Washington and addressed to Nixon at the "Presidential Compound, San Clemente, Calif.," accompanied by travel expenses of $302 and a witness fee.

In other developments concerning Nixon's legal status:

■ A spokesman for special prosecutor Leon Jaworski said Aug. 13 that no decision had been made regarding prosecution of Nixon in connection with the cover-up. The spokesman added that "no decision is imminent" and Jaworski "is not going to make a hasty decision on a prosecutorial decision like this one." Attorney General William B. Saxbe said the same day that he had told President Ford that any action against Nixon should be at Jaworski's option. Saxbe said he "got the feeling" that Ford intended to leave the matter in Jaworski's hands.

■ Trustees managing the funds remaining from Nixon's 1972 campaign decided that he could not use the money for legal fees, it was reported Aug. 14. The trustees said the decision was based on the fact that Nixon technically had not been an official of the campaign committees. (Funds were already being used for expenses incurred by former campaign officials Maurice H. Stans and John N. Mitchell.)

■ The Baltimore Sun reported Aug. 14 that before his resignation, Nixon had instructed his aides not to seek agreements barring future prosecution, with either Congress or the special prosecutor.

In a related pretrial development in the cover-up case, prosecution lawyers suggested to Judge John J. Sirica Aug. 15 that a "reasonable" delay in the beginning of the trial—scheduled for Sept. 9—might be in order so that defendants would have sufficient opportunity to review tapes surrendered by Nixon.

Tapes situation unclear—White House Press Secretary J. F. terHorst said Aug. 14 that former President Nixon's tape recordings and documents not under subpoena and not considered relevant to the Watergate case had been declared his personal property and would be returned to him.

TerHorst said the decision was the "formal" but unwritten opinion by White House attorneys James D. St. Clair and J. Fred Buzhardt Jr. (both of whom had been central figures in Nixon's Watergate defense), and was based on tradition rather than law.

Spokesmen for special prosecutor Jaworski said Aug. 14 that his office had been "informed" of the decision but declined to elaborate. But in a statement issued Aug. 15, Jaworski's office said prosecution and White House representatives had met earlier in the day and agreed that none of the Nixon files would be moved "pending further discussions." The statement added that the prosecution was "satisfied with these arrangements."

The tapes decision was among the last actions for the White House by St. Clair, who resigned Aug. 14. TerHorst announced the next day that Buzhardt would leave soon and that Philip W. Buchen, 58, President Ford's former law partner, had been appointed presidential counsel.

TerHorst said Buchen would take over the White House legal office "immediately."

Equal treatment resolution voted. The House of Delegates of the American Bar Association (ABA) overwhelmingly approved a compromise resolution Aug. 15 affirming the ABA's "dedication" to the principle of "fair, just and impartial application and enforcement of the law, regardless of the position or status of any individual alleged to have violated the law." The resolution was the association's response to expectations that it would take a position on the question of immunity or amnesty for former President Nixon.

The vote highlighted the ABA's 97th annual convention, held Aug. 12–16 in Honolulu.

The voice vote on the resolution came after a resolutions committee had rejected a draft resolution that would have mentioned Nixon by name and referred directly to the Watergate case. Some members reportedly felt that such a statement might prejudice any criminal action that might be brought against Nixon.

The House of Delegates also approved by voice vote a resolution stating that disciplinary rules should apply to lawyers whether or not they were practicing law. The resolution stated that this position should be called to the attention of lawyers "engaged in political activity or policy-making positions in government."

The legal profession's position in light of Watergate and related scandals had dominated earlier meetings during the convention. Sen. Daniel K. Inouye (D, Hawaii), a member of the defunct Senate Watergate Committee, reiterated recommendations made in that panel's final report: establishment of a permanent "public attorney" and independence for the Justice Department from political control.

Solicitor General Robert H. Bork and former Attorney General Elliot L. Richardson expressed opposition to such measures, Bork warning that Watergate "threatens us with a backlash of harmful reforms."

Former Watergate special prosecutor Archibald Cox voiced concern over the activities of lawyers involved in Watergate scandals and urged a "more sustained and wider study of where the balance should be struck between the duties of 'hired gun' and 'servant of the law'" for lawyers working in government.

Sen. Sam J. Ervin Jr. (D, N.C.), chairman of the Watergate committee, said most of the lawyers involved in Watergate were "non-practicing possessors of law licenses" who had the "pernicious notion" that Nixon "had the right to suspend the provisions of the Constitution."

President Ford, who had canceled a scheduled appearance at the convention after Nixon's resignation, sent a message which was read at the closing session. Ford urged the association to continue its "efforts to prevent the scales of justice from tilting." Ford commended the legal

system, both judicial and legislative, for helping carry the nation "through some of its darkest hours." "It has been demonstrated that our system works," Ford said, "and that our Constitution is a living document."

Tapes kept at White House. The White House announced Aug. 16 that President Ford and his counsel, Philip W. Buchen, had ordered that former President Nixon's tapes and documents would remain in White House custody pending resolution of Watergate legal issues raised by special prosecutor Leon Jaworski and "others."

Press Secretary J.F. terHorst added, however, that the action did not constitute a reversal of the informal decision that the materials were Nixon's personal property. TerHorst said he knew of no request by Nixon that the material be transferred to his custody.

Nixon deferred access to papers. The New York Times reported Aug. 18 that Richard M. Nixon, on the same day (Aug. 8) that he announced his intention to resign as President, changed the terms of his gift of pre-presidential papers to the National Archives, stipulating that no one should have access to the documents until Jan. 1, 1985 without his personal permission.

The papers had originally been donated under the condition that access would be restricted only as long as he was President.

The new stipulation, in a letter to the head of the General Services Administration, affected both groups of papers Nixon had donated. The first was in 1968, after Nixon was first elected President but before he took office. The second and larger gift was involved in the income tax deduction disallowed by the Internal Revenue Service.

Ford nominates Rockefeller as V.P. President Ford announced Aug. 20 that Nelson A. Rockefeller, 66, former governor of New York for 15 years, was his choice to be the 41st vice president of the U.S. The nomination was sent to Congress that day for confirmation which required a simple majority vote of each house.

Attempted smear of Rockefeller—While the President was winnowing the list, there was a brief flurry of reports that Rockefeller funds might have helped fund a project to disrupt the 1972 Democratic National Convention with hired thugs.

The White House said Aug. 17 the allegation was unfounded, but it had gained some currency from the White House itself, by a report from that source that the Watergate special prosecutor's office was investigating to see if the Rockefeller link existed. White House spokesman terHorst said Aug. 17 he had promulgated the report after syndicated columnist Jack Anderson had raised the issue,

noting it was only hearsay. Anderson mentioned the conjecture that the secret files of Watergate conspirator E. Howard Hunt Jr., which were thought to have been destroyed, could contain evidence of the link between Rockefeller and the "dirty tricks." The White House had been tipped off about the link and an investigation by the special prosecutor was ordered. Several lockboxes in undisclosed cities reportedly were opened but found to be empty; the special prosecutor concluded that the allegation against Rockefeller was baseless.

TerHorst said Aug. 17 the investigation was closed and attributed the original tip to "extremists who wished for reasons of their own to discredit" Rockefeller. He gave assurance that Rockefeller remained under consideration for the vice presidential nomination.

House accepts impeachment report. The House Judiciary Committee's report on its impeachment inquiry of President Nixon was accepted by the House Aug. 20 by a vote of 412–3. The report was submitted to the House by Committee Chairman Peter W. Rodino Jr. (D, N.J.). House Democratic Leader Thomas P. O'Neill Jr. (Mass.) offered a resolution stating that the House "accepts the report," commending the committee for its "conscientious and capable" effort and calling the inquiry "full and complete."

House Republican Leader John J. Rhodes (Ariz.) took the necessary parliamentary step of demanding a second and the resolution was voted without debate. The three votes against it were cast by Reps. Earl F. Landgrebe (R, Ind.), G. V. Montgomery (D, Miss.) and Otto E. Passman (D, La.).

The report thus became part of the official House record. It was published Aug. 22 as House Report 93-1305 and as Part II of the Congressional Record.

The committee's 528-page report contained the evidence, which it considered "clear and convincing," on which the committee recommended impeachment of Nixon under three articles on the grounds that he had obstructed justice in the Watergate case, abused his presidential powers for his personal and political benefit and defied Congressional demands for information for its impeachment probe. The report also contained personal statements by all the committee members except chairman Rodino.

The majority and minority opinions were expressed on each article after the listing of evidence.

On Article I, a finding that Nixon participated in a criminal conspiracy to cover up the Watergate burglary, there was a unanimous recommendation of impeachment. The committee had approved the article July 27 during its inquiry by a vote of 27-11. However, on Aug. 5, four days before he resigned, Nixon had released new evidence and the 11 Republicans who voted against the article reversed their stands.

This new evidence was cited by the 11 in their "minority views" of the committee's report. "We know," they said, "that it has been said, and perhaps some will continue to say, that Richard Nixon was 'hounded from office' by his political opponents and media critics. We feel constrained to point out, however, that it was Richard Nixon who impeded the FBI's investigation of the Watergate affair by wrongfully attempting to implicate the Central Intelligence Agency; it was Richard Nixon who created and preserved the evidence of that transgression and who, knowing that it had been subpoenaed by this committee and the special prosecutor, concealed its terrible import, even from his own counsel, until he could do so no longer. And it was a unanimous Supreme Court of the United States, which in an opinion authorized by the Chief Justice whom he appointed, ordered Richard Nixon to surrender that evidence to the special prosecutor, to further the ends of justice. The tragedy that finally engulfed Richard Nixon had many facets. One was the very self-inflicted nature of the harm. It is striking that such an able, experienced and perceptive man, whose ability to grasp the global implications of events little noticed by others may well have been unsurpassed by any of his predecessors, should fail to comprehend the damage that accrued daily to himself, his Administration and to the nation, as day after day, month after month, he imprisoned the truth about his role in the Watergate coverup so long and so tightly within the solitude of his Oval Office that it could not be unleashed without destroying his Presidency."

The majority's report on Article I cited 36 specific items against the President that it said formed "a pattern of undisputed acts" that "cannot otherwise be rationally explained" except as part of a conspiracy to obstruct justice.

"President Nixon's action," the majority said, "resulted in manifest injury to the confidence of the nation and great prejudice to the cause of law and justice, and was subversive of constitutional government. His actions were contrary to his trust as President and unmindful of the solemn duties of his high office. It was this serious violation of Richard M. Nixon's constitutional obligations as President, and not the fact that violations of federal criminal statutes occurred, that lies at the heart of Article I."

All in all, President Nixon's conduct, the majority concluded, "posed a threat to our democratic republic."

On Article II, concerning abuse of presidential power and violation of the oath of office to execute the nation's laws, the report reaffirmed the committee's 28–10 vote for adoption on July 29. The minority of 10 Republicans said they did "deplore in strongest terms the aspects of presidential wrongdoing to which the article is addressed." But they found the article vague and a "catch-all repository for mis-cellaneous and unrelated Presidential offenses." "It is a far-reaching and dangerous proposition," they said, "that conduct which is in violation of no known law but which is considered by a temporary majority of Congress to be 'improper' because undertaken for 'political' purposes can constitute grounds for impeachment."

The majority view on Article II cited allegations against Nixon of attempted misuse of the Internal Revenue Service, the Federal Bureau of Investigation and other agencies. It concluded that Nixon had "repeatedly used his authority as President to violate the Constitution and the law of the land. In so doing, he violated the obligation that every citizen has to live under the law. But he did more, for it is the duty of the President not merely to live by the law but to see that law faithfully applied. Richard M. Nixon repeatedly and willfully failed to perform that duty. He failed to perform it by authorizing and directing actions that violated the rights of citizens and that interfered with the functioning of executive agencies. And he failed to perform it by condoning and ratifying, rather than acting to stop, actions by his subordinates interfering with the enforcement of the laws."

In an individual statement, Rep. Wiley Mayne (R, Iowa), who had voted in committee against Article II, reversed himself because of Nixon's Aug. 5 admission of complicity in the Watergate cover-up. Mayne said on the basis of that he would have voted for impeachment on Article II on the ground of misuse of agencies.

The minority held to its view of Article III, which had been adopted by the committee July 30 by a 21–17 vote and dealt with Nixon's refusal to comply with the committee's subpoenas for tape recordings and other data. The minority held that such refusal in itself was not sufficient ground for impeachment and there was an "element of unfairness" in removing a president from office "for failure to cooperate in his own impeachment."

The majority held that "unless the defiance of the committee's subpoenas is considered grounds for impeachment, it is difficult to conceive of any president acknowledging that he is obligated to supply the relevant evidence necessary for Congress to exercise its constitutional responsibility in an impeachment proceeding. If this were to occur, the impeachment power would be drained of its vitality."

Among the statements by members in the committee report was one signed by 11 Democrats that "the evidence is overwhelming that Richard Nixon has used the office of the President to gain political advantage, to retaliate against those who disagreed with him and to acquire personal wealth."

Another signed by 10 Democrats considered the secret bombing of Cambodia "one of the most serious" offenses committed by Nixon and expressed their view that the subject should have been part of the impeachment recommendation. Nine committee members, from both parties, who had voted during the inquiry against inclusion of the Cambodia bombing issue as an impeachable offense, made it clear that they "certainly did not intend our vote to indicate approval of such conduct."

Ford: 1976 candidacy 'probable.' White House Press Secretary J. F. terHorst said Aug. 21 that President Ford had authorized him to say "He is now of the opinion he probably will run in 1976."

Reminded by reporters of Ford's previous statements that he had no intention of running for president in 1976, terHorst said that when Ford was vice president it did "not seem appropriate" for him to consider running. "His position has changed; therefore, his opinion has changed."

Rebozo subpoena compliance ordered. U.S. District Court Judge George L. Hart Jr. Aug. 22 ordered attorneys for Charles G. Rebozo, a close friend of former President Nixon, to surrender to the Watergate special prosecutor their records concerning funds possibly spent for Nixon's personal benefit.

The subpoena called for bank records, memoranda and other items in the custody of the law firm headed by Thomas H. Wakefield, records which—according to the prosecution—related to expenditures of more than $36,000 by Rebozo on his own behalf and for Nixon.

Counsel for the firm argued that since Wakefield was Rebozo's attorney and personal adviser when the expenditures were made, the records should be privileged because of the attorney-client relationship.

Assistant special prosecutor Paul R. Michel said Wakefield had handled the transactions on Rebozo's instructions, and contended that such transactions were purely business matters to which the attorney-client privilege did not apply.

Hart agreed that the privilege could not be invoked in such circumstances and, after a private hearing, announced that the records must be produced. Regarding 66 other items under subpoena, Hart said he had upheld a privilege claim for one, had denied claims for "a few" others, and had left the remainder to further discussion between the opposing sides.

In papers filed with the court Aug. 19, the prosecution had suggested that the money might have been illegally diverted from contributions to Nixon's 1972 campaign by industrialist Howard R. Hughes and Florida supermarket executive A. D. Davis. The prosecution said Rebozo had given the Wakefield firm more than $36,000 in $100 bills between May 1972 and April 1973, and that Rebozo "apparently did not have sufficient cash available" to transfer such amounts "from any known source other than the political campaign contributions."

The prosecution also alluded to bank records concerning $4,562 in funds "originally derived apparently from campaign contributions" and used as part of the purchase price for platinum and diamond earrings for Mrs. Nixon.

The prosecution's affidavit contended in summary that Rebozo had used the law firm's bank accounts in an apparent effort "to 'launder' political campaign funds in order to conceal their character."

Cover-up trial delayed. Acting at the suggestion of the U.S. Court of Appeals, District Court Judge John J. Sirica Aug. 22 postponed the beginning of the Watergate cover-up trial to Sept. 30. The trial had been scheduled for Sept. 9.

Sirica's action reversed his own decision of Aug.19, in which he had denied requests for delay filed by four of the six defendants and special prosecutor Leon Jaworski. The decision was appealed by defendants H. R. Haldeman and John D. Ehrlichman, once key aides to former President Nixon. Jaworski also repeated his request for delay.

In its 6–0 decision, the appeals court did not order Sirica to postpone the trial, but suggested that a delay might be advisable for "further trial preparation."

Later Aug. 22, attorneys for Ehrlichman petitioned the Supreme Court to stay Sirica's postponement order until further appeal proceedings could be held on Ehrlichman's request for an even longer delay.

In papers filed with the appeals court Aug. 21, Ehrlichman said Philip W. Buchen, counsel to President Ford, had, at least temporarily, denied him access to his files still in the White House. A White House spokesman said later in the day that Nixon had apparently stopped allowing defendants' access to their files shortly before his resignation, and that Buchen was reviewing current policy. The White House announced Aug. 23 that access would be reinstated, but defendants would not be allowed to make copies or take notes. Buchen's office said the decision had been cleared with Nixon.

Ford comments on Nixon pardon. President Ford held a televised afternoon news conference Aug. 28, his first since assuming office Aug. 9. The first question to the new President was whether he agreed with the American Bar Association "that the law applies equally to all men" or with Rockefeller that Nixon "should have immunity from prosecution?" "And specifically," the reporter continued, "would you use your pardon authority if necessary?" (Rockefeller had said Aug. 23, seconding a metaphor used by Senate Republican Leader Hugh Scott (Pa.), that Nixon had been "hung and it doesn't seem to me that in addition he should be drawn and quartered.")

Ford responded that "the expression made by Gov. Rockefeller, I think, coincides with the general view and the point of view of the American people. I subscribe to that point of view."

He added that "in the last 10 days or two weeks, I've asked for prayers for guidance on this very important point" and "in this situation I am the final authority. There have been no charges made. There have been no—there has been no action by the court; there's been no action by any jury, and until any legal process has been undertaken I think it's unwise and untimely for me to make any commitment."

Reporters later pursued the point. Was a pardon for Nixon "still an option that you will consider depending on what the courts will do?" Ford was asked.

"Of course I make the final decision," Ford replied, "and until it gets to me I make no commitment one way or another, but I do have the right as President of the United States to make that decision."

Q. Then you're not ruling it out.

A. I am not ruling it out. It is an option and a proper option for any President.

Q. Mr. President, do you feel the [Watergate] special prosecutor can in good conscience pursue cases against former top Nixon aides as long as there is the possibility that the former President may not also be pursued in the court?

A. I think the special prosecutor, Mr. [Leon] Jaworski, has an obligation to take whatever action he sees fit in conformity with his oath of office, and that should include any and all individuals, yes.

Ford was asked if there had been any communication between Jaworski's office and his own regarding Nixon. "Not to my knowledge," he replied.

Nixon retains new lawyer. Former President Nixon retained Herbert J. Miller Jr., a senior partner in a Washington law firm, to handle his Watergate-related legal matters, it was reported Aug. 28.

Miller had been active in representing other Watergate figures, including former Attorney General Richard G. Kleindienst, White House aide Richard A. Moore and William O. Bittman, an attorney involved in the payoffs to the original Watergate defendants.

Miller, a Republican, had been an assistant attorney general in the Kennedy and Johnson Administrations (1961–1965).

In an earlier development, Nixon had expressed concern about his Watergate problems, according to Rep. Dan Kuykendall (R, Tenn.). Relating a phone call he had received from Nixon Aug. 26, Kuykendall quoted Nixon as asking: "Do you think the people want to pick the carcass?" According to Kuykendall, Nixon said, "We've got problems with that fellow . . . uh . . . uh . . . ."

"Jaworski?" Kuykendall offered. "Yes," Nixon replied.

Further trial delay denied. Chief Justice Warren E. Burger Aug. 28 denied a request by Watergate cover-up defendant

John D. Ehrlichman that the trial be postponed until 1975.

Burger said his position as supervisory circuit justice for the District of Columbia should not involve interference in such matters as setting trial dates, which were the province of the district court, with the court of appeals as the "primary source of relief." Burger noted that he was taking no position on the issues of pre-trial publicity or the amount of time needed to prepare the case. These issues, Burger said, could be appealed after a verdict.

Burger also refused to refer the petition to the full Supreme Court.

$850,000 asked for Nixon expenses. President Ford asked Congress Aug. 29 for an appropriation of $850,000 to cover transition expenses and allowances for former President Nixon through the fiscal year ending in June 1975. Part of the money—$450,000—was sought under authority of the 1963 Presidential Transition Act, which allowed $900,000 for transfer of power between administrations, half to the outgoing and half to the incoming during a six-month transition period. The funding would be administered by the General Services Administration.

The remainder of the request—$400,-000—was to be made available Feb. 9, 1975, six months after Nixon's resignation, under the 1958 Former Presidents Act. The funds included $96,000 for staff expenses, $55,000 as the 11-month portion of Nixon's $60,000 annual pension, and $244,000 for special expenses. Among the latter were $40,000 for travel, $65,000 for furnishings, $21,000 for communications and $100,000 in a "miscellaneous" category.

Subpoenas served on Nixon—Former President Nixon was served with two unrelated subpoenas Aug. 28, according to a Justice Department announcement the next day. The subpoenas were served at Nixon's estate in San Clemente, Calif.

One subpoena, issued on behalf of Watergate cover-up defendant John D. Ehrlichman, called for Nixon's testimony at the trial scheduled to begin Sept. 30.

The second required Nixon to give a deposition in a civil suit filed by 21 persons who claimed they had illegally been denied entry to a 1971 Charlotte, N.C. rally for the Rev. Billy Graham. Nixon was a speaker at the rally.

Poll shows most favor prosecution—A Gallup Poll published Sept. 2 showed that 56% of those interviewed felt Nixon should be tried for possible criminal charges arising from the Watergate case. Of the remainder, 37% opposed such a trial and 7% had no opinion.

Democrats interviewed favored prosecution by a margin of 70%–25%; among Republicans, 33% favored a trial, while 59% were opposed. The poll was conducted Aug. 16–19.

President Ford grants Nixon full pardon. President Ford granted former President Nixon a full pardon Sept. 8 for all federal crimes he "committed or may have committed or taken part in" during his term in office.

Nixon issued a statement accepting the pardon and expressing regret that he had been "wrong in not acting more decisively and more forthrightly in dealing with Watergate." [See texts of pardon, Nixon statement]

The White House also announced Sept. 8 that the Ford Administration had concluded an agreement with Nixon giving him title to his presidential papers and tape recordings but guaranteeing they would be kept intact and available for court use for at least three years.

The pardon for Nixon was unexpected. Ford made his announcement from the Oval Office on Sunday morning after attending church. After reading a brief statement on his decision before a small pool of reporters and photographers—the event was filmed for broadcast later—Ford signed a proclamation granting Nixon the pardon.

Nixon had not been formally charged with any federal crime and the granting of a pardon in advance was a reversal of Ford's position on the issue, expressed as recently as his Aug. 28 news conference.

The announcement drew wide protest and some support. Generally, it was split along partisan lines and the Democratic protest was more heated than the Republican support for the Nixon pardon. One protester was White House Press Secretary J. F. terHorst, the first appointee of the Ford Administration, who resigned Sept. 8 as a matter of "conscience."

The controversy broadened Sept. 10 when a White House spokesman, in response to a question, said Ford was considering pardons for all Watergate defendants. Following further adverse criticism, the White House shifted its stance Sept. 11 and announced that individual requests for pardons would be considered.

In his statement, Ford said Nixon and "his loved ones have suffered enough, and will continue to suffer no matter what I do." "Theirs is an American tragedy in which we all have played a part," he said. "It can go on and on, or someone must write 'The End' to it. I have concluded that only I can do that. And if I can, I must."

There were no historic or legal precedents on the matter, Ford said, "but it is common knowledge that serious allegations and accusations hang like a sword over our former president's head and threaten his health as he tries to reshape his life."

He cited the "years of bitter controversy and divisive national debate" and the prospect of "many months and perhaps more years" before Nixon "could hope to obtain a fair trial by jury in any jurisdiction" of the country. He "deeply believe[d] in equal justice for all Americans, whatever their station or former station," Ford said, but "the facts as I see them are" that a former president, "instead of enjoying equal treatment with any other citizen accused of violating the law, would be cruelly and excessively penalized either in preserving the presumption of his innocence or in obtaining a speedy determination of his guilt in order to repay a legal debt to society."

Ford continued: "During this long period of delay and potential litigation, ugly passions would again be aroused, our people would again be polarized in their opinions, and the credibility of our free institutions of government would again be challenged at home and abroad. In the end, the courts might well hold that Richard Nixon had been denied due process and the verdict of history would be even more inconclusive with respect to those charges arising out of the period of his presidency of which I am presently aware."

His conscience told him, Ford said, "that I cannot prolong the bad dreams that continue to reopen a chapter that is closed" and that "only I, as President, have the constitutional power to firmly shut and seal this book." "My conscience says," he continued, "it is my duty, not merely to proclaim domestic tranquility, but to use every means I have to ensure it. . . . I cannot rely upon public opinion polls to tell me what is right. I do believe that right makes might. . . ."

The proclamation granting Nixon "a full, free, and absolute pardon" referred to the articles of impeachment recommended by the House Judiciary Committee in its televised "deliberations." "As a result of certain acts or omissions" occurring during his presidency, it stated, Nixon had become liable to possible indictment and trial for offenses against the U.S. "It is believed," the proclamation continued, that a trial, if it became necessary, could not "fairly" begin for a year or more and "in the meantime, the tranquility to which this nation has been restored by the events of recent weeks could be irreparably lost by the prospects of bringing to trial a former president of the United States. The prospects of such trial will cause prolonged and divisive debate over the propriety of exposing to further punishment and degradation a man who has already paid the unprecedented penalty of relinquishing the highest elective office in the United States."

Nixon's statement—In accepting the pardon Sept. 8, Nixon said he hoped that this "compassionate act will contribute to lifting the burden of Watergate from our country." His "perspective on Watergate" had changed, he said, and "one thing I can see clearly now is that I was wrong in not acting more decisively and more forthrightly in dealing with Watergate, particularly when it reached the stage of judicial proceedings and grew from a political scandal into a national tragedy."

He spoke of "the depths of my regret and pain at the anguish my mistakes over Watergate have caused the nation and the presidency." He knew, he said, "that many fair-minded people believe that my motivation and actions in the Watergate affair were intentionally self-serving and illegal. I now understand how my own mistakes and misjudgments have contributed to that belief and seemed to support it. This burden is the heaviest one of all to bear. That the way I tried to deal with Watergate was the wrong way is a burden I shall bear for every day of the life that is left to me."

The Nixon papers and tapes—The agreement on disposition of Nixon's presidential papers and tape recordings was signed Sept. 6 by Nixon and, for the government, by Arthur F. Sampson, administrator of the General Services Administration (GSA). In briefing reporters on the agreement Sept. 8, presidential counsel Philip W. Buchen denied that it was a condition for granting of the pardon. He conceded that the details had been negotiated for the Administration by Washington lawyer Benton L. Becker, who had also acted as Ford's agent on the pardon issue in San Clemente, Calif., where Nixon was residing.

Buchen said Ford had directed him about 10 days ago to resolve the Nixon files matter so the new Administration would not find itself "enmeshed for a long time" in jurisdictional disputes.

Nixon's right to the material was asserted in the agreement and in an accompanying legal opinion by Attorney General William B. Saxbe. The files were to be kept at a federal facility near San Clemente. Access to them was to be gained under a two-key system, one key held by Nixon and the other by the GSA. Nixon retained title to the data, including literary rights. He agreed not to withdraw any original materials for three years unless subpoenaed, at which point he could assert any defense or privilege he deemed appropriate. The tapes were to be left intact until Sept. 1, 1979. After that, the GSA was committed to destroy any tapes if so instructed by Nixon. All the tapes were to be destroyed on Sept. 1, 1984 or at Nixon's death, if it occurred prior to that date.

Nixon stated in the agreement his intention to donate "a substantial portion" of his papers to the nation and the reason he wanted the tapes destroyed—to prevent their use "to injure, embarrass or harass any persons and properly to safeguard" U.S. interests.

TerHorst quits in protest—Ford accepted White House Press Secretary terHorst's resignation with deep regret, saying he understood his position and the fact "that good people will differ with me on this very difficult decision." TerHorst's position was that "mercy, like justice, must also be evenhanded."

Press reports indicated that the resignation involved more than a policy disagreement, that terHorst had been misinformed, or not fully informed, on the pardon developments and had unwittingly passed on misinformation, bringing into question the integrity of his role as spokesman.

TerHorst told a New York Times reporter Sept. 9 that he felt it would have been "a little awkward" for him as press secretary to defend an absolute pardon for Nixon "but only a conditional pardon for young men who had fled to Canada to escape Vietnam as an act of conscience."

According to reports, terHorst's written resignation reached Ford shortly before the President announced the pardon for Nixon. Deputy Press Secretary John W. Hushen became acting press secretary.

Buchen: no conditions imposed—White House counsel Philip W. Buchen said Sept. 8 that the pardon for Nixon had been granted without any demands being made upon Nixon, that no effort had been made to obtain acknowledgment of wrongdoing. He also said the advice of the Watergate special prosecutor, Leon Jaworski, had not been sought.

Buchen described the pardon as an "act of mercy" and Nixon's statement as a "statement of contrition." The decision was predicated, he said, on the belief that "it was very likely" Nixon would have been indicted and ordered to stand trial.

Ford had asked him to make a study of the issue about a week before, Buchen said, and he had first consulted Jaworski on the probable timing of a Nixon trial in the event of an indictment. Jaworski responded that a trial could not be held for at least nine months to a year or more, that it would take that time to settle the legal problem of possible prejudicial pretrial publicity.

Buchen said he was assured by Jaworski that there were no new "time bombs" in the Nixon investigation.

Buchen said he had asked a friend, Washington lawyer Benton L. Becker, who also was a friend of Ford, to broach the issue with Nixon and his counsel, and said Becker had gone to San Clemente the previous week and advised Nixon that a pardon was probable. Nixon was said to have responded with his intention in that event to issue a statement.

Jaworski confirmed Sept. 8 that he had not been consulted about the pardon—

Text of Sept. 8 Ford Statement on Pardon

Ladies and gentlemen, I have come to a decision which I felt I should tell you, and all my fellow citizens, as soon as I was certain in my own mind and conscience that it is the right thing to do.

I have learned already in this office that only the difficult decisions come to this desk. I must admit that many of them do not look at all the same as the hypothetical questions that I have answered freely and perhaps too fast on previous occasions, My customary policy is to try and get all the facts and to consider the opinions of my countrymen and to take counsel with my most valued friends. But these seldom agree, and in the end the decision is mine.

To procrastinate, to agonize, to wait for a more favorable turn of events that may never come, or more compelling external pressures that may as well be wrong as right, is itself a decision of sorts and a weak and potentially dangerous course for a president to follow. I have promised to uphold the Constitution, to do what is right as God gives me to see the right, and to do the very best I can for America. I have asked your help and your prayers, not only when I became president, but many times since.

The Constitution is the supreme law of our land and it governs our actions as citizens. Only the laws of God, which govern our consciences, are superior to it. As we are a nation under God, so I am sworn to uphold our laws with the help of God. And I have sought such guidance and searched my own conscience with special diligence to determine the right thing for me to do with respect to my predecessor in this place, Richard Nixon, and his loyal wife and family.

Theirs is an American tragedy in which we all have played a part. It can go on and on, or someone must write "The End" to it. I have concluded that only I can do that. And if I can, I must.

There are no historic or legal precedents to which I can turn in this matter, none that precisely fit the circumstances of a private citizen who has resigned the presidency of the United States. But it is common knowledge that serious allegations and accusations hang like a sword over our former president's head and threaten his health as he tries to reshape his life, a great part of which was spent in the service of this country and by the mandate of its people.

After years of bitter controversy and divisive national debate, I have been advised and am compelled to conclude that many months and perhaps more years will have to pass before Richard Nixon could hope to obtain a fair trial by jury in any jurisdiction of the United States under governing decisions of the Supreme Court.

I deeply believe in equal justice, for all Americans, whatever their station or former station. The law, whether human or divine, is no respecter of persons but the law is a respecter of reality. The facts as I see them are that a former president of the United States, instead of enjoying equal treatment with any other citizen accused of violating the law, would be cruelly and excessively penalized either in preserving the presumption of his innocence or in obtaining a speedy determination of his guilt in order to repay a legal debt to society.

During the long period of delay and potential litigation, ugly passions would again be aroused, our people would again be polarized in their opinions, and the credibility of our free institutions of government would again be challenged at home and abroad. In the end, the courts might well hold that Richard Nixon had been denied due process and the verdict of history would be even more inconclusive with respect to those charges arising out of the period of his presidency of which I am presently aware.

But it is not the ultimate fate of Richard Nixon that most concerns me—though surely it deeply troubles every decent and compassionate person—but the immediate future of this great country. In this I dare not depend upon my personal sympathy as a long-time friend of the former president nor my professional judgment as a lawyer. And I do not.

As president, my primary concern must always be the greatest good of all the people of the United States, whose servant I am.

As a man, my first consideration will always be to be true to my own convictions and my own conscience. My conscience tells me clearly and certainly that I cannot prolong the bad dreams that continue to reopen a chapter that is closed. My conscience tells me that only I, as president, have the constitutional power to firmly shut and seal this book. My conscience says it is my duty, not mearly to proclaim domestic tranquility, but to use every means I have to ensure it.

I do believe that the buck stops here and that I cannot rely upon public opinion polls to tell me what is right. I do believe that right makes might, and that if I am wrong 10 angels swearing I was right would make no difference. I do believe with all my heart and mind and spirit that I, not as president, but as a humble servant of God, will receive justice without mercy if I fail to show mercy.

Finally, I feel that Richard Nixon and his loved ones have suffered enough, and will continue to suffer no matter what I do, no matter what we as a great and good nation can do together to make his goal of peace come true.

Now, therefore, I, Gerald R. Ford, president of the United States, pursuant to the pardon power conferred upon me by Article II, Section 2, of the Constitution, have granted and by these presents do grant a full, free, and absolute pardon unto Richard Nixon for all offenses against the United States which he, Richard Nixon, has committed or may have committed or taken part in during the period from July [January] 20, 1969, through August 9, 1974.

In witness whereof, I have hereunto set my hand this 8th day of September in the year of our Lord nineteen hundred seventy-four, and of the independence of the United States of America the 199th.

Text of Nixon Statement

I have been informed that President Ford has granted me a full and absolute pardon for any charges which might be brought against me for actions taken during the time I was President of the United States.

In accepting this pardon, I hope that his compassionate act will contribute to lifting the burden of Watergate from our country.

Here in California, my perspective on Watergate is quite different than it was while I was embattled in the midst of the controversy, and while I was still subject to the unrelenting daily demands of the presidency itself.

Looking back on what is still in my mind a complex and confusing maze of events, decisions, pressures and personalities, one thing I can see clearly now is that I was wrong in not acting more decisively and more forthrightly in dealing with Watergate, particularly when it reached the stage of judicial proceedings and grew from a political scandal into a national tragedy.

No words can describe the depths of my regret and pain at the anguish my mistakes over Watergate have caused the nation and the presidency—a nation I so deeply love and an institution I so greatly respect.

I know many fair-minded people believe that my motivations and action in the Watergate affair were intentionally self-serving and illegal. I now understand how my own mistakes and misjudgments have contributed to that belief and seemed to support it. This burden is the heaviest one of all to bear.

That the way I tried to deal with Watergate was the wrong way is a burden I shall bear for every day of the life that is left to me.

Ford Pardon Proclamation

Richard Nixon became the thirty-seventh president of the United States on January 20, 1969, and was re-elected in 1972 for a second term by the electors of forty-nine of the fifty states. His term in office continued until his resignation on August 9, 1974.

Pursuant to resolutions of the House of Representatives, its Committee on the Judiciary conducted an inquiry and investigation on the impeachment of the President extending over more than eight months. The hearings of the committee and its deliberations, which received wide national publicity over television, radio, and in printed media, resulted in votes adverse to Richard Nixon on recommended Articles of Impeachment.

As a result of certain acts or ommissions occurring before his resignation from the office of president, Richard Nixon has become liable to possible indictment and trial for offenses against the United States. Whether or not he shall be so prosecuted depends on findings of the appropriate grand jury and on the discretion of the authorized prosecutor. Should an indictment ensue, the accused shall then be entitled to a fair trial by an impartial jury, as guaranteed to every individual by the Constitution.

It is believed that a trial of Richard Nixon, if it became necessary, could not fairly begin until a year or more has elapsed. In the meantime, the tranquility to which this nation has been restored by the events of recent weeks could be irreparably lost by the prospects of bringing to trial a former president of the United States. The prospects of such trial will cause prolonged and divisive debate over the propriety of exposing to further punishment and degradation a man who has already paid the unprecedented penalty of relinquishing the highest office in the United States.

NOW, THEREFORE, I, Gerald R. Ford, president of the United States, pursuant to the pardon power conferred upon me by Article II, Section 2, of the Constitution, have granted and by these presents do grant a full, free, and absolute pardon unto Richard Nixon for all offenses against the United States which he, Richard Nixon, has committed or may have committed or taken part in during the period from January 20, 1969, through August 9, 1974.

IN WITNESS WHEREOF, I have hereunto set my hand this 8th day of September in the year of our Lord nineteen hundred seventy-four, and of the independence of the United States of America the 199th.

which he considered the President's prerogative under the Constitution—but had been asked only for his estimate of when a Nixon trial would be held if he were indicted.

There were press reports that Nixon had angrily rebuffed an attempt by the Ford emissaries to obtain a public confession of criminal guilt from him, but White House Acting Press Secretary John W. Hushen denied the reports Sept. 9. "There was no quid pro quo regarding the pardon," he said. "There were no requests or demands that he issue a statement."

Buchen said Sept. 10 that Ford "did not make a deal" with Nixon on the pardon before Nixon left office. He made the point, in another press briefing, that the granting of a pardon "can imply guilt—there is no other reason for granting a pardon." The fact that someone accepted a pardon, he said, "means that it was necessary for him to have the pardon."

Two memorandums were released by the White House Sept. 10—one from special prosecutor Jaworski's office listing 10 areas still under investigation at the time of the pardon—of possible criminal activity that might involve Nixon; a second memo to Jaworski's office from Nixon's counsel arguing the case against indictment and prosecution on the ground that Nixon could not get a fair trial by an impartial jury.

The first memo noted that the Watergate cover-up was an area by itself and not covered by this particular memo. It stressed that none of the other 10 matters "at the moment rises to the level of our ability to prove even a probable criminal violation" by Nixon.

The 10 areas listed were:

1. Tax deductions relating to the gift of pre-Presidential papers.
2. The [Charles W.] Colson obstruction of justice plea in the Ellsberg matter.
3. The transfer of the national security wiretap records from the FBI to the White House.
4. The initiating of wiretapping of John Sears.
5. Misuse of IRS information.
6. Misuse of IRS through attempted initiation of audits as to "enemies."
7. The dairy industry pledge and its relationship to the price support change.
8. Filing of a challenge to the Washington Post ownership of two Florida television stations.
9. False and evasive testimony at the [Richard] Kleindienst confirmation hearings as to White House participation in Department of Justice decisions about ITT [International Telephone & Telegraph Corp.].
10. The handling of campaign contributions by Mr. [C.G.] Rebozo for the personal benefit of Mr. Nixon.

Buchen told reporters Sept. 10 he had no information on the subject of Ford's reference to Nixon's state of health in his announcement of the pardon. There had been conflicting reports from visitors to San Clemente about Nixon's health—some said it was good, that Nixon was bearing up as well as could be expected, others maintained he was not bearing up well and his behavior was cause for concern.

Wide protest against pardon—There was immediate protest from Congress against the pardon to Nixon. The White House was flooded with telephone calls and telegrams from the public. A spokesman said Ford was told the evening of Sept. 8, upon inquiry, that the volume of incoming telephone calls was "very heavy and kind of unfavorable." Western Union messages into Washington had reached a volume of 110,000 by Sept. 11.

According to a Sept. 10 New York Times poll, public support for Ford had dropped sharply; 32% believed he was doing a good job, 33% a fair job, 25% a poor job and 10% had no opinion.

The Democratic Congressional leadership was outspoken in criticism Sept. 8. Senate Majority Leader Mike Mansfield (Mont.), responding that "all men are equal under the law," said "that includes presidents and plumbers." "What about the 40 or 50 already indicted and some of whom have been sent to prison?" he asked. Senate Democratic whip Robert C. Byrd (W.Va.) spoke of "a double standard."

However Senate Republican Leader Hugh Scott (Pa.) said Ford acted "with great humanity to bring an end to an American tragedy." House GOP Leader John J. Rhodes (Ariz.) said he believed Nixon had paid "a substantial price" and "anything further would be more overkill than justice."

Other comment Sept. 8: Sen. Edward Brooke (R, Mass.)—The pardon without Nixon's "full confession of his involvement in Watergate is, in my judgment, a serious mistake."

Sen. Lowell Weicker (R, Conn.)—The pardon was "neither equal justice nor leadership in a government of laws."

Sen. Edward S. Muskie (D, Me.)—"I think this is unwise. We don't know what if any crime Mr. Nixon committed."

Sen. Henry M. Jackson (D, Wash.)—"President Ford may have established a precedent which will hurt our whole system of the administration of justice for a long time to come."

Sen. Walter F. Mondale (D, Minn.)—"We don't even know what acts by Mr. Nixon the President is pardoning, because all the facts and all the evidence are not yet available."

Sen. Philip Hart (D, Mich.)—"A decision which precludes even full presentation of charges can only serve to breed cynicism and corrode a sense of justice."

Sen. Barry M. Goldwater (R, Ariz.)—The pardon was "the only decent and prudent course."

Sen. John C. Stennis (D, Miss.)—Nixon has "sustained severe and what will prove to be continued punishment." The pardon, he added, would enable full attention to be paid to the nation's problems.

Rep. Edward Mezvinsky (D, Iowa)—"I don't think anyone disagrees that justice should be tempered with mercy. But hiding from the truth is not justice and providing pardon before charges are resolved prohibits us from knowing how much mercy has been shown."

Rep. David Dennis (R, Ind.)—"Probably the President's acting now and getting the thing decided without letting it become a protracted subject of debate is a good move."

Rep. Wiley Mayne (R, Iowa)—The pardon "is premature and might well have been deferred until special prosecutor [Leon] Jaworski had indicated what if any further action would be undertaken by his office."

Rep. Jerome R. Waldie (D, Calif.)—"I thought it was a disastrous error." He said the House Judiciary Committee "ought to continue its [Nixon impeachment] inquiry." Waldie was a member of the Judiciary Committee, as were Mezvinsky, Dennis and Mayne.

Two other members—Reps. George Danielson (D, Calif.) and Don Edwards (D, Calif.)—also spoke of possible renewal of the impeachment proceedings.

Judiciary Committee Chairman Peter W. Rodino Jr. (D, N.J.) was "very upset" about the pardon, according to a spokesman Sept. 9, but opposed renewal of the proceedings. Rodino explained to House Speaker Carl Albert (D, Okla.) Sept. 10 that the impeachment inquiry was "to develop facts toward impeachment, not to determine whether a man is guilty of criminal acts. That's something that belongs to another branch of government."

Nelson A. Rockefeller, vice presidential designate, said Sept. 8 the pardon was "an act of conscience, compassion and courage."

Archibald Cox, former Watergate special prosecutor, said Sept. 8 "an advance pardon defeats three principles important to a free society"—determination of guilt or innocence by established processes, preservation of the legal process and affirmation "that the law does in truth apply to all men equally."

Comment continued Sept. 9. Senate Republican Whip Robert P. Griffin (Mich.) said in a floor speech he had no doubt Nixon's health was "a factor" in the pardon decision.

Critical statements came from Sens. William Proxmire (D, Wis.), Gaylord Nelson (D, Wis.), Frank Church (D, Idaho), George McGovern (D, S.D.), Robert Packwood (R, Ore.), Clifford P. Case (R, N.J.) and Sam J. Ervin Jr. (D, N.C.), chairman of the Senate Watergate committee. Ervin commented that "a good case can be made for the proposition that the pardon power vested in the President by the Constitution exceeds that of the Almighty, who apparently cannot pardon a sinner unless the sinner first repents of his sins." Rep. Walter Flowers (D, Ala.) a member of the House Judiciary Committee, said he considered the pardon "premature."

Supporters of the pardon were joined by Sens. James O. Eastland (D, Miss.) and Carl T. Curtis (R, Neb.).

Visit to Pittsburgh draws pickets—President Ford encountered some hostility during a quick trip to Pittsburgh Sept. 9 to address an urban transportation conference. A large crowd gathered at the conference site and Ford emerged to considerable booing and hostile picket signs, such as "Equal Justice for All? Who's all?" and "Justice Died 9/8/74."

His speech at the conference was interrupted only once with applause, when he pledged support for "limited" federal operating subsidies for transit systems. He reminded the meeting the automobile was "our chief transportation vehicle" and "what we must do is to learn how best to live with them on the urban scene."

The hostile public reception was the first for Ford since assuming office a month ago. He had been accorded repeated and enthusiastic applause Sept. 6 in Philadelphia during a visit honoring the reconvening of the First Continental Congress. His speech there focused on inflation, which he said was "the cruelest kind of taxation without representation." "We're going after—one and all, Democrats and Republicans," he said, "the public enemy of inflation in 1974 and we will lick him before July 4, 1976."

Nixon to resign from state bar—Nixon's intention to resign from the California Bar Association was disclosed by a spokesman Sept. 9. The spokesman said Nixon would be busy with "matters other than law."

The board of governors of the association recommended Sept. 12 that Nixon's letter of resignation, dated Sept. 11, be rejected.

The association had announced July 26 it was beginning an investigation of evidence that could lead to disbarment of Nixon.

Other Watergate pardons studied. Deputy Acting White House Press Secretary John W. Hushen told reporters Sept. 10 the President had authorized him to state that the "entire matter" of pardons for all persons connected with Watergate was "now under study." Hushen made the statement in response to a routine question whether Ford was considering a pardon for John W. Dean 3rd, Nixon's former White House counsel, and others connected with Watergate. Dean's wife had reportedly written the President asking for a pardon. "I am authorized to say that the entire matter is now under study," Hushen replied. Reporters asked Hushen, who was conducting his first White House press briefing, if pardons for the other Watergate figures were seriously under study and whether he realized the probable public impact of his statement. Hushen refused to amplify the statement, aside from emphasizing that the study of the matter itself did not mean that such pardons would necessarily be granted. He reiterated the authorization from Ford and gave assurance that all of the factors involved "have been taken into account."

After a day's barrage of criticism and a visit from 13 Republican Congressional leaders, Ford substantially shifted his position: pardons for Watergate figures, if sought, would be considered on a case-by-case basis; no consideration was being given to blanket amnesty or pardons; and no study was in progress.

The affirmation that "there is no study going on" was made by Senate Republican Leader Hugh Scott as he emerged from the two-hour meeting with the President Sept. 11. Scott then read a statement by Ford:

"The announcement yesterday by Mr. Hushen concerning study of the entire matter of Presidential clemency and pardons was prompted by inquiries to the White House press office concerning Mrs. John Dean's reported statement in reference to pardoning her husband and similar public statements on behalf of others. Such a study is, of course, made for any request concerning pardon of an individual. However, no inference should be drawn as to the outcome of such study in any case. Nor is my pardon of the former President, under the unique circumstances stated by me in granting it, related to any other case which is or may be under study."

Scott said "applications for pardon have not reached the President. When they do that is when a study will be necessary" and the President then would "consider it most carefully."

House Republican Leader John Rhodes, appearing with Scott, said the significance of Hushen's statement was that requests for pardons from Watergate figures would be given serious attention and "not be thrown into the wastebasket."

Hushen told newsmen Sept. 11 "there never was any consideration of blanket amnesty or pardons."

Rhodes had joined the sharp protest Sept. 10 against extending pardons to all Watergate defendants, which the White House said that day Ford had under consideration. Reiterating his support for the Nixon pardon, Rhodes said the Nixon assistants charged with Watergate offenses had not suffered "the special consequences that a fallen President must bear" and their "fates are not directly connected with the well-being of the Republic."

Scott the same day had opposed blanket clemency and advocated consideraton of other pardons on a case-by-case basis.

House Speaker Carl Albert said a pardoning of many Nixon aides "would be viewed as an abuse of presidential power."

Senate Democratic whip Robert Byrd said "making a second mistake won't help matters" but "would complete the cover-up of the cover-up."

Pretrial pardons renounced—The Senate Sept. 12 adopted a resolution urging Ford to refrain from using his pardoning power until the judicial process in each case was completed. The resolution, passed by a 55–24 vote with bipartisan support, had no

force of law but merely expressed the sense of the Senate.

The resolution opposed any pardon "to any individual accused of any criminal offense arising out of the Presidential campaign and election of 1972 prior to the indictment and completion of trial and any appeals of such individual." Such a pardon "would effectively conceal the whole truth of what happened" in the Watergate case, the resolution stated.

Senate Republican Leader Scott reported near unanimity in Congress that the judicial process should proceed on the Watergate case without interference. "The public needs to know everything it can about Watergate," Scott said.

A resolution was introduced in the House Sept. 12, calling on the President to answer some questions concerning the Nixon pardon. Among them was whether Nixon's resignation was related in any way to a promise of pardon.

The question of whether Ford had made an agreement with Nixon before the former president left office also came up at a White House press briefing Sept. 12. "That is absolutely not true," Press Secretary Hushen responded. "There was no communication regarding a pardon for Mr. Nixon." He said Ford did not intend to pardon any of the Watergate defendants before trial.

Hushen said he was uninformed on several other questions put to him, based on current press reports. According to sources reported by the Washington Post Sept. 12, former Nixon aides H.R. Haldeman and John D. Ehrlichman had unsuccessfully conveyed to Nixon urgent requests that they be granted presidential pardons. The requests, made during the last days of Nixon's presidency, were deeply resented by Nixon because of the tone and character of the pleas, according to the sources. They were described as "threatening" and being tantamount to blackmail.

According to another report, Ford, prior to granting Nixon the pardon, had talked with Nixon's son-in-law, Edward F. Cox, who told him Nixon was in poor health and suffering from phlebitis, with his leg swollen to twice its normal size.

The report about Nixon's phlebitis was confirmed by Nixon's son-in-law David Eisenhower, during a television appearance Sept. 12. He said Nixon's spirits were "not great" and he was "depressed at times."

Eisenhower told a UPI reporter Sept. 12 that Ford's emissaries had sought "some kind of confession" before the pardon decision was made. Nixon "wasn't willing to concede anything," Eisenhower said, and "views himself as an innocent man."

Jaworski aide resigns. The effect of President Ford's pardon of former President Nixon on the office of the special Watergate prosecutor was one early resignation and rumors of others. Philip A. Lacovara, one of prosecutor Leon Jaworski's key aides, announced his resignation Sept. 9, effective at the end of the month.

Lacovara's statement cited "recent events" as the reason for his resignation, and he said later that the events "certainly include" the pardon.

Rumors began circulating about Jaworski's resignation, but he said Sept. 10 there was "no substance" to them. "I have no plans for resigning at the present time," Jaworski said.

Despite conflicting reports on the status of Jaworski's office, some lawyers saw beneficial effects in the pardon. One staff lawyer said Sept. 9 that since the pardon constituted a grant of immunity, he felt willing to sacrifice the prosecution of Nixon in return for Nixon's inability to invoke Fifth Amendment privileges, either in relation to his potential appearance as a witness or to the release of tapes and documents.

In a related development Sept. 11, eight members of the Senate Judiciary Committee sent a letter to Jaworski asking that a "full and complete record" of Nixon's involvement in Watergate and related scandals be included in his final report to Congress. According to the Los Angeles Times Sept. 11, Jaworski had said he intended to make such a public report eventually, possibly in the form of a special report on Nixon.

Seven senators signing the letter were Democrats: Birch Bayh (Ind.), Quentin N. Burdick (N.D.), Robert F. Byrd (W.Va.), Sam J. Ervin Jr. (N.C.), Philip A. Hart (Mich.), Edward M. Kennedy (Mass.) and John V. Tunney (Calif.). Charles McC. Mathias (Md.) was the only Republican.

Cover-up defense motions rejected. U.S. District Court Judge John J. Sirica Sept. 12 denied petitions for delay or dismissal in the Watergate cover-up trial despite protests by defendants that President Ford's pardon of former President Nixon had created the public impression that they were guilty.

Three of the defendants—John N. Mitchell, John D. Ehrlichman and H.R. Haldeman—contended that because of publicity surrounding the pardon the trial should be postponed indefinitely or that the indictments should be dismissed. The defendants also argued that it would be "offensive" to the concept of equal justice if Nixon, an unindicted co-conspirator in the case, went unprosecuted while they—his subordinates—had to stand trial.

According to Mitchell's lawyers, Nixon's acceptance of the pardon implied that Nixon acknowledged "certain illegal acts" related to the cover-up charges and that a public assumption of guilt would be unavoidable.

Sirica agreed, however, to a one-day delay in the beginning of the trial (to Oct. 1) so that a new panel of prospective jurors could be chosen. The ruling was in response to Haldeman's contention that a questionnaire sent to 400 potential jurors was so worded that a recipient might know in advance the trial for which he was being summoned.

Sirica had issued another series of rulings Sept. 11. One denied a request for delay in which Haldeman had said higher courts should have time to consider his contention that his indictment was faulty because a 1973 law extending the life of the grand jury had been improper.

In another action Sept. 11, Sirica denied Gordon C. Strachan's petition for dismissal of his indictment. Strachan had contended the indictment was tainted because he had given information with the understanding that he had been granted immunity.

Editorial Reaction to the Watergate Affair

Cooperating Newpapers

Akron (Ohio) Beacon Journal (174,000)
Albany (N.Y.) Knickerbocker News (71,000)
Albuquerque (N.M.) Journal (66,000)
Anchorage (Alaska) Daily Times (13,000)
Ann Arbor (Mich.) News (37,000)
Atlanta Constitution (209,000)
Baltimore News American (201,000)
Baltimore Sun (165,000)
Billings (Mont.) Gazette (44,000)
Biloxi (Miss.) Daily Herald (37,000)
Birmingham (Ala.) News (76,000)
Boston Globe (261,000)
Boston Herald American (211,000)
Buffalo Evening News (284,000)
Burlington (Vt.) Free Press (45,000)
Charleston (S.C.) News & Courier (66,000)
Charleston (W.Va.) Gazette (60,000)
Charlotte (N.C.) Observer (170,000)
Chattanooga (Tenn.) Times (64,000)
Chicago Daily Defender (21,000)
Chicago Daily News (435,000)
Chicago Today (429,000)
Chicago Tribune (768,000)
Christian Science Monitor (Mass.) (216,000)
Cincinnati Enquirer (195,000)
Cleveland Plain Dealer (403,000)
Cleveland Press (374,000)
Columbia (S.C.) State (107,000)
Columbus (Ohio) Dispatch (222,000)
Dallas Morning News (243,000)
Dallas Times Herald (232,000)
Dayton (Ohio) Daily News (113,000)
Denver Post (255,000)
Des Moines (Iowa) Register (246,000)
Des Moines (Iowa) Tribune (109,000)
Detroit Free Press (593,000)
Detroit News (640,000)
Emporia (Kans.) Gazette (10,000)
Fall River (Mass.) Herald-News (42,000)

Fort Worth (Tex.) Star-Telegram (98,000)
Greenville (S.C.) News (91,000)
Hartford (Conn.) Courant (160,000)
Honolulu (Hawaii) Star-Bulletin (124,000)
Houston Chronicle (303,000)
Houston Post (295,000)
Indianapolis News ((183,000)
Indianapolis Star (225,000)
Kansas City (Mo.) Star (310,000)
Kansas City (Mo.) Times (324,000)
Lincoln (Neb.) Star (27,000)
Little Rock Arkansas Democrat (74,000)
Little Rock Arkansas Gazette (108,000)
Long Island (N.Y.) Press (418,000)
Los Angeles Times (966,000)
Louisville Courier-Journal (233,000)
Madison Wisconsin State Journal (71,000)
Manchester (N.H.) Union Leader (62,000)
Memphis Commercial Appeal (214,000)
Miami Herald (383,000)
Miami News (86,000)
Milwaukee Journal (347,000)
Minneapolis (Minn.) Tribune (238,000)
Nashville Tennessean (139,000)
Newark (N.J.) Star-Ledger (246,000)
New Bedford (Mass.) Standard-Times (73,000)
New Orleans States-Item (128,000)
New Orleans Times-Picayune (199,000)
Newsday (L.I., N.Y.) (459,000)
New York Daily News (2,130,000)
New York Post (623,000)
New York Times (846,000)
Norfolk (Va.) Ledger-Star (105,000)
Norfolk (Va.) Virginian-Pilot (129,000)
Oklahoma City Daily Oklahoman (181,000)
Oklahoma City (Okla.) Times (103,000)
Omaha (Neb.) World-Herald (129,000)
Orlando (Fla.) Star-Sentinel (129,000)
Ottawa (Ont.) Citizen (86,000)

Philadelphia Evening Bulletin (634,000)
Philadelphia Inquirer (464,000)
Phoenix Arizona Republic (170,000)
Pittsburgh Post-Gazette (236,000)
Pittsburgh Press (344,000)
Portland (Me.) Evening Express (30,000)
Portland (Me.) Press Herald (56,000)
Portland Oregonian (244,000)
Rapid City (S.D.) Journal (31,000)
Richmond (Va.) Times-Dispatch (144,000)
Roanoke (Va.) Times (63,000)
Rochester (N.Y.) Democrat & Chronicle (143,000)
Sacramento (Calif.) Bee (167,000)
Saginaw (Mich.) News (61,000)
St. Louis Globe-Democrat (293,000)
St. Louis Post-Dispatch (326,000)
St. Petersburg (Fla.) Times (163,000)
Salt Lake City (Utah) Deseret News (84,000)
Salt Lake City (Utah) Tribune (108,000)
San Diego Union (152,000)
San Jose (Calif.) Mercury (128,000)
Seattle (Wash.) Times (245,000)
Sioux Falls (S.D.) Argus-Leader (50,000)
Springfield (Mass.) Union (79,000)
Syracuse (N.Y.) Herald-Journal (126,000)
Topeka (Kans.) Daily Capital (63,000)
Toronto (Ont.) Globe & Mail (264,000)
Tulsa (Okla.) Daily World (110,000)
Vancouver (B.C.) Sun (225,000)
Wall Street Journal (497,000)
Washington Post (500,000)
Washington Star-News (302,000)
Winston-Salem (N.C.) Journal (78,000)
Winston-Salem (N.C.) Twin City Sentinel (46,000)
Worcester (Mass.) Evening Gazette (95,000)
Worcester (Mass.) Telegram (63,000)

••

ITT, MILK FUND WHITE PAPERS ISSUED; NIXON REJECTS ERVIN PANEL SUBPOENAS

President Nixon Jan. 8 released two white papers detailing his involvement in two controversial decisions made by the Administration in 1971 related to an increase in the federal price support for milk and an antitrust suit against the International Telephone & Telegraph Corp. (ITT). Nixon branded as "utterly false" charges that presidential actions were offered in the matters as a quid pro quo "either in return for political contributions or the promise of such contributions."

In the 17-page statement on the milk fund, Nixon defended as "totally proper" his decision to reverse an Agriculture Department ruling and allow an increase in the federal price support of milk, although he admitted for the first time that before he ordered the increase he was aware that the dairy industry had pledged at least $2 million to his re-election campaign. Nixon said his decision to raise the price support was based on three factors: (1) "Intensive Congressional pressure"; (2) "The economic merits of the case itself, as presented by the industry leaders in the meeting with the President, and as weighed by the President's advisers [in a meeting later that day] "; (3) "Traditional political considerations relating to needs of the farm states."

In his ITT statement, Nixon claimed that his order to Deputy Attorney General Richard Kleindienst to drop a pending appeal with the Supreme Court on one of the government's antitrust suits against ITT was based entirely on Nixon's personal philosophy that corporations should not be challenged on grounds of "bigness per se." Further, Nixon said in his eight-page statement, he was unaware of ITT's campaign pledge to fund the Republican National Convention when he personally intervened in the case in April 1971.

Among other developments involving the Watergate affair and related scandals during early January:

■ President Nixon informed the Senate Watergate Committee Jan. 4 that he would not comply with its wide-ranging subpoenas for tapes and documents, but later comments by White House aides and committee sources indicated that a compromise might be in the making. In a letter to Committee Chairman Sam J. Ervin Jr. (D, N.C.), Nixon called the three subpoenas "an overt attempt to intrude into the executive to a degree that constitutes an unconstitutional usurpation of power."

■ Chairman Peter W. Rodino Jr. (D, N.J.) of the House Judiciary Committee, which was considering the question of impeachment proceedings against President Nixon, said Jan. 7 the panel's staff "is now dealing with a consideration of the areas in which the inquiry should go, and has yet to reach any conclusions on the questions of what is an impeachable offense and what sort of evidence should be gathered." Rodino said a full report would "hopefully be ready" to be presented to the House by late April.

■ Special Watergate prosecutor Leon Jaworski said Jan. 12 he would resist, unless the courts ruled otherwise, sharing with the House impeachment inquiry any presidential tapes, documents or other information furnished him by the White House. Jaworski said his requests to the White House for information in connection with his federal probe were related to the grand jury procedures and "we have no right to access to that information otherwise. Because of that, we are bound by the rules of secrecy attached to that information."

Long Island Press

New York, N.Y., January 10, 1974

A few months ago, President Nixon launched what he called "Operation Candor" to convince the nation that "I am not a crook." Unfortunately, it has been neither very candid nor very convincing.

First Mr. Nixon released a financial statement which showed that he had taken advantage of every possible tax gimmick, including some that may be in violation of the tax laws. A congressional committee and the Internal Revenue Service are checking to see if the President owes what may amount to hundreds of thousands of dollars in taxes and interest.

On Tuesday, Mr. Nixon issued two "white papers" designed to show that he did nothing wrong in the ITT anti-trust or milk price support cases. The White House said "traditional political considerations" — but not a promise of campaign contributions — influenced the milk decision. In the ITT case, Mr. Nixon contends his only action occurred before the giant conglomerate pledged $400,000 to help underwrite the 1972 Republican convention in San Diego.

With those statements, "Operation Candor" came to a close. Administration officials said that in the "whole area of maligning the President," Mr. Nixon would not tolerate further allegations. The President, they said, has too many more important matters to tend to.

We believe Mr. Nixon has nothing more important to do than try to reestablish his own credibility.

* * *

The public wasn't satisfied last April when Mr. Nixon tried to put Watergate and related scandals behind him with the statement, "I must now turn my full attention — and I shall do so — to the larger duties of this office." We doubt that the public is any more satisfied with "Operation Candor."

Too much remains secret. Even while issuing the white paper on the ITT and milk cases, the White House refuses to give any of the material it has given to Special Prosecutor Leon Jaworski to congressional committees probing Watergate. In addition, only last week, Mr. Nixon refused to honor the Senate Watergate Committee's demand for 500 tapes and documents.

Perhaps the committee's demand was excessive. The President's staff is busy. But Mr. Nixon cannot hide forever behind claims of executive privilege and a too-heavy work load in regard to some of the tapes — not if he expects to regain public confidence.

Sen. Sam Ervin says the committee might drop its pursuit of other documents if the White House surrenders five tapes of conversations with former presidential counsel John W. Dean III.

"According to the testimony of John Dean, these five tapes, if they haven't been doctored, will reveal whether or not John Dean testified truly before the committee when he testified that these conversations indicated that President Nixon had knowledge of the Watergate coverup," Sen. Ervin said. That's a question all Americans want answered.

* * *

Vice President Ford voiced the hope the other day that a compromise could be reached in the latest tapes deadlock. Sen. Ervin's offer seems to be a fair middle ground.

If Mr. Nixon's "Operation Candor" is to have any meaning — and any positive effect on his future — the President must bend on the tapes. Otherwise, the public cannot be blamed for suspecting that the tapes and documents Mr. Nixon is so jealously guarding contain incriminating evidence.

DESERET NEWS
Salt Lake City, Utah, January 10, 1974

In accordance with the American legal tradition of pressured innocence, we're willing to accept the President's version of what happened in the ITT and milk cases unless or until it is refuted by more concrete facts than have been forthcoming so far.

The Deseret News is among those who raised serious questions when the Department of Justice settled the ITT case out of court and the firm offered to contribute $400,000 to help finance the 1972 Republican national convention.

Unhappily, the Justice Department has a long history of being deeply involved in partisan politics. President Nixon continued that tradition when he named his campaign manager, John Mitchell, as attorney general. Until the department is removed from politics, its handling of cases involving major campaign contributors will always be suspect. Moreover, how wise is it to settle anti-trust cases out of court when the practice precludes the possibility of securing authoritative judicial resolution of novel legal theories — in this case concerning the legality of conglomerates?

Even so, the Justice Department is part of the executive branch which the President oversees, and he has a right to make sure that the department's policies are in line with his policies.

His policy on anti-trust cases is that corporate mergers should not be opposed merely because they make big firms bigger — and that makes sense.

Out-of-court settlements are reached in 98 percent of all anti-trust cases to save time and expense and avoid the uncertainties of prolonged litigation. Plenty of legal experts think the government got a bargain by getting ITT to divest itself of several firms without going to court.

To this extent, it's one of those cases where there's ample room for reasonable men to disagree. As for the President's statement he was unaware of any financial offer to the GOP from ITT, if that assertion is to be successfully contradicted it will take more facts than have been produced to date.

In the milk case, the President says he approved of increasing price supports not in return for a campaign contribution from the dairy industry but because Congress would otherwise have ordered even higher supports.

That's in line with the same wishy-washy philosophy by which the White House imposed federal controls on the economy — which the administration now regrets — because Congress would otherwise impose even tighter restrictions.

The President's plea that he could not veto the price increase because it would alienate dairy farmers, makes one wonder why he wasn't more concerned about alienating milk consumers who foot the bill. But this isn't the first time the potential power of the farm bloc influenced a decision on price supports for all sorts of agricultural commodities, and it won't be the last.

At least the President can point to figures indicating the higher supports stimulated increased milk production and helped stem a long-term upward trend in prices. If the critics of his decision can point to facts as concrete and specific, it's certainly a well-kept secret.

In both the milk and ITT cases, the government took what seems to have been the path of least resistance. Brave and bold the administration's decisions weren't. But then government is often described as the art of reasonable compromise.

One final point: An incumbent American President rarely has trouble getting re-elected. That doesn't make him totally immune to partisan considerations, as even the white papers make clear. But neither does he have to stoop to making petty deals.

The burden of proof rests upon President Nixon's accusers. Let them make their case not with suspicion and innuendo but with substantiated evidence — if they can.

THE LINCOLN STAR
Lincoln, Neb., January 10, 1974

President Nixon served up the last helping of "Operation Candor" Tuesday by issuing two "white papers" which briefly explained his roles in raising milk price supports in 1971 and in the settlement of an International Telephone and Telegraph Corp. antitrust case.

Nixon candidly stated that he ordered the hike in milk price supports because of congressional pressure, the economic benefits of the plan and the "traditional political considerations" relating to the needs of the farm states, while being aware of the dairy industry's pledge of up to $2 million for his re-election campaign.

And he said he originally moved to suppress further action in an antitrust case against ITT because of his personal belief that government should not bring lawsuits against corporations simply on the basis of their size. When he first ordered the case dropped, the President said, he was not aware that ITT had guaranteed to underwrite the Republican National Convention in 1972. This latter explanation is harder to believe, in light of testimony that the White House was well aware of the ITT pledge and testimony concerning the various meetings between high administration officials and ITT corporate officers. These specific meetings were not covered in the white paper.

The White House pretty well described the last installment of Operation Candor when it said the papers "support the President's previous statements that his actions were totally proper."

That's what it was, in effect — a statement that what he said before was right.

Presidential papers, tape recordings or other documents which would have supported the statements were not released because they are "on file" with the special prosecutor and the White House said it didn't want to interfere with the judicial process. The White House also said it trusted that the evidence would remain in confidence.

Of course, it would take such palpable evidence in support of the President to make believable his claim that campaign pledges did not motivate his actions.

Without the evidence, the white papers represent nothing more than a holding action.

With the exception of the candor he briefly displayed in talking about the milk deal, the statements Tuesday were a fitting end to a flop of an operation.

Chicago Tribune
Chicago, Ill., January 10, 1974

President Nixon's white papers explaining his role in the 1971 decision to increase federal milk price supports and in the International Telephone and Telegraph antitrust case have shed no new light on the circumstances surrounding these controversial issues.

Issuance of these white papers carries out a promise to the Associated Press Managing Editors that the President would speak further about the milk price decision and the I. T. T. affair. But if these statements mark the end of Operation Candor, the finale of Mr. Nixon's explanation of his actions to the public, it is a lamentably insubstantial conclusion.

The details in the new white papers have been disclosed previously, if never in comprehensive form. Mr. Nixon does acknowledge that he took "traditional political consideration" into account when he raised the milk price support level to 85 per cent of parity, altho his secretary of agriculture wanted to hold the level to 80 per cent.

The core of Mr. Nixon's statements is that neither political contributions nor the promise of such contributions influenced his decision in either the milk or I. T. T. case. He says that if he had not acted as he did in the milk case, Congress would have raised the price supports to 90 per cent of parity and the American consumer would have paid even higher prices for milk. He points out that the milk producers, an influential lobby since the 1960s, focus the bulk of their political campaign contributions on congressional rather than Presidential campaigns.

The fact remains that President Nixon's campaign solicitors welcomed any and all contributions. They may well have gone to greater lengths in beating the bushes for money than the President realized or would have approved. But records of the 1972 campaign provide no evidence that President Nixon auctioned off favors to the highest bidders. On the contrary, there is ample proof that the hopes of many donors of large sums to President Nixon's re-election campaign were disappointed by the President's subsequent decisions.

The oil industry, for example, contributed heavily to Mr. Nixon's 1968 campaign, but Mr. Nixon put up only a token fight when Congress voted to cut the oil depletion allowance. Nor did big contributors fare well in the awarding of the controversial trans-Pacific air routes. Close to home, such big individual contributors as W. Clement Stone and Anthony Angelos did not receive the ambassadorships they apparently sought.

Like many other politicians, including Mayor Daley, President Nixon has accepted political contributions big and small without feeling any compulsion to provide political favors in return. In the future, efforts to trade big gifts for political favors will be further discouraged by the 1973 Federal Elections Campaign Practices Act, requiring contributors of $100 or more to be identified publicly.

If the issuance of the not very informative statements on I. T. T. and the milk case marks the end of Operation Candor, we can only assume that Mr. Nixon believes he is a President under threat of hostile legal action who will not voluntarily assist those who want to prosecute him. So far as his interests are concerned, this is understandable and even prudent. The public interest would be better served, however, by a more open and communicative attitude in the White House.

The Oregonian

Portland, Ore., January 11, 1974

Taken at face value, the so-called white paper issued by President Richard M. Nixon to refute charges of impropriety in the milkmen's campaign contributions and the International Telephone and Telegraph antitrust case is a reasonable and persuasive response.

News stories and comment have not done justice to the two segments of the "white paper" and perhaps have only added to the confusion of some Americans about what is fact and what fiction in the long campaign by critics to unmake a president. As a public service, the entire text, 9,500 words, will be printed in The Oregonian, beginning in Sunday's Forum section. Let those who read decide if the President is being honest and sincere.

The "white paper" from San Clemente evidently winds up "Operation Candor." Although the White House may reach a compromise with Sen. Sam Ervin's committee to release a few of the White House recordings bearing on Watergate, while rejecting committee subpoenas for nearly 500 tapes and documents on the grounds of irrelevancy and confidentiality, essentially the President seeks to end his public responses and devote his major attention henceforth to other matters.

The specific evidence on which the latest explanations are based is in the hands of Leon Jaworski, the Justice Department's special prosecutor, for examination by federal grand juries. Federal court rules assure the confidentiality of grand jury evidence, and it has not been given to John Doar, chief counsel for the House Judiciary Committee which is charged with deciding whether or not it should recommend impeachment of the President. But if the three grand juries considering Watergate-related matters, including the milk fund and ITT cases, bring out indictments, the evidence will be used in open court trials. That is where it belongs if it is material to criminal prosecutions.

As the President pointed out, inasmuch as the documents supporting his statements are on file with the special prosecutor, "It should be clear that the accounts published today are consistent with the basic facts contained in those documents and tapes."

One of the allegations denied by the President, as it was denied repeatedly in the past with less detail, is that he ordered an increase in federal support for milk in return for political contributions. The President said there were traditional political considerations involved, an admission which made headlines. But he said these considerations were not promised campaign contributions, but a desire to retain the support of farmers and knowledge that the Democratic Congress was ready to adopt legislation raising the milk support from 80 per cent of parity to a mandatory 85 or 90 per cent. This has been confirmed by members of Congress and by the milk lobby. Hardly anyone has asked whether an increase of milk support was necessary or beneficial to consumers as well as to milkmen, who by 1971 had joined the political campaigns arena along with long-established organized labor and other business and agricultural interests.

The organized milk lobby contributed more to congressional campaigns than it did to the Nixon re-election fund. Among Democratic supporters of a higher support price were Senators Hubert H. Humphrey and George McGovern and, in the House, Speaker Carl Albert and Ways and Means Chairman Wilbur Mills. But was there an economic justification, as well as political considerations?

President Nixon listed some results of the milk support increase as follows: The price of milk did not skyrocket, but rose "at the lowest rate of recent years. . . at a rate significantly below the general rate of inflation." The cost to the government of the milk support program went down, not up. Government inventories of surplus dairy products went down, instead of expanding. The level of dairy production was ample but not excessive.

In the ITT case, the President was accused of intervening in a Justice Department antitrust case in April, 1971, to order the department not to appeal a lower court ruling favoring ITT because the multinational conglomerate had pledged sums (variously mentioned as from $200,000 to $450,000) for the Republican National Convention in San Diego, where ITT's Sheraton division had a new hotel. ($100,000 was contributed to the GOP convention committee and sent back when the convention was shifted to Miami.) The President denied knowledge of any such pledge when he told the Justice Department not to appeal because he thought an appeal violated his policy of not prosecuting business just because it was big. He rescinded the order two days later when then Atty. Gen. John Mitchell advised him that Solicitor Gen. Erwin Griswold had fully prepared the case and probably would resign if ordered to drop it and that the appeal did not violate administration policy, as aide John Ehrlichman had told the President.

The ITT appeal subsequently was dropped when the firm consented to a divestiture of companies said to be the largest in antitrust history. The result was praised not only by Griswold but by former Solicitor Gen. Archibald Cox, the special Watergate prosecutor Nixon fired.

President Nixon, seeking re-election in 1972, was a veteran politican operating in the political arena. Of course he was politically sensitive to voters' lobbies, as is every member of Congress including his most vocal critics. That is the system in which democracy has survived in this nation for nearly 200 years. If there is any evidence that he sold government favors for campaign funds it has yet to be produced. His "white paper" was a political statement seeking a restoration of public confidence, a statement certainly responsible considering the prolonged attack on him and the presidency itself. It should stand unless specifically refuted by evidence, not accusation, rumor and doubt.

THE SPRINGFIELD UNION

Springfield, Mass., January 10, 1974

In taking the "white paper" course of explaining his actions on federal milk price supports and the ITT anti-trust case, President Nixon has merely added to the ammunition of his critics and the misgivings of many of his supporters.

The White House observed that no documents or tape recordings were being released because the President is determined to keep them confidential. That only confirms the obvious. What concerns the public goes deeper than that.

On one hand, charges that the President considered campaign contributions in his decisions in the milk price supports and ITT cases are not proven by his withholding of the tapes and documents. On the other hand, they are not disproven.

Many who believe, for one reason or another, that the charges are false would welcome a presidential decision to turn the controversial material over to the Senate Watergate committee. The fact that it is on file with the Nixon-appointed special prosecutor is not enough.

The nagging thought in many minds is that there is nothing in the "white papers" that would not have been said if the charges were true. This has been so in White House statements relating to the Watergate affair, as well as the ITT and milk price cases.

Perhaps the blanket of confidentiality or executive privilege or national security will leave a permanent question in the public mind. That would be a pathetic scar on an administration which has served the nation well in many ways.

ALBUQUERQUE JOURNAL

Albuquerque, N.M., January 11, 1974

Like many of President Nixon's recent public addresses, the white papers detailing his involvement in the ITT anti-trust case settlement and the hike in milk support prices are adequate for those who need not be convinced, but they serve no useful purpose for those who do.

The two white papers were virtually devoid of documentation although the only documentation available is at the exclusive disposal of the White House staff.

Thus the public is asked to accept the words and explanations of the White House staff at their face value.

This would have been feasible only a year earlier, when most of the American people not only believed their President but sincerely wanted him to be found in the right.

Today the President and his staff find themselves in a position similar to that of the lonely shepherd boy who falsely shouted "Wolf, wolf!" once too often. Repeated denials and explanations, of themselves plausible, have proved to be false or fragmentary by subsequent disclosures.

This is unfortunate not only for the administration but for an American public hopelessly groping for leadership. Indeed the two white papers were superbly prepared and, except for a year of Watergate disclosures as their context, are self-consistent in presentation. In another context the White House explanations and "traditional political considerations" would have been plausible and admirably compatible with earlier administration decisions and policy statements.

If, indeed, as commentators concluded, the two white papers mark "finis" to the White House's so-called "Operation Candor," then that operation must be denounced as a dismal flop. The American people have pleaded hopefully for bread, and they have been handed a stone.

The Washington Post

Times Herald

Washington, D.C., January 11, 1974

"In the thousands of pages of testimony and analysis regarding the ITT case since 1971, the only major charge that has been publicly made against President Nixon is that in return for a promise of a political contribution from a subsidiary of ITT, the President directed the Justice Department to settle antitrust suits against the corporation."—From the President's White Paper on ITT.

NOW THAT may well be so. And if that indeed were all there was to the ITT affair as a matter of concern to Mr. Nixon, then his ITT White Paper could even reasonably be said to lay the matter fairly persuasively to rest as far as the President is concerned. But to argue in that fashion would be to suggest that Richard M. Nixon, over the years of the ITT affair (1969 to 1972) was not in fact President of the United States—and that he was no more than a private citizen, and that Tuesday's ITT White Paper was in the nature of a defendant's brief in an ordinary criminal case. And that, in fact, is the way it reads. On the central question of a possible connection between the ITT settlement and the ITT political contribution it treats the conduct of his subordinates and advisers, including two former attorneys general, John Mitchell and Richard Kleindienst, as if they were in no real way connected with the President, no part of his administration and no part of his responsibility.

That is the first great inadequacy of the President's White Paper on ITT. For we are not dealing, of course, with Richard M. Nixon, private citizen: we are dealing with a head of government entirely responsible for the men he placed in high office and in close association with him, and also responsible, by extension, for their acts. And we are dealing with a President whose performance in office is the subject not only of an investigation by a Special Prosecutor but also of a preliminary inquiry by the House Judiciary Committee studying possible grounds for impeachment. As is argued elsewhere on this page by J. H. Plumb, a professor at Cambridge University, not the least of the tests of a President's conduct of office—and of his liability to impeachment—is his "judgment in choosing ministers" and his responsibility to hold himself "answerable at all times and on all matters, not only for keeping the law but also in choosing men of integrity and honor." It is thus no defense for the President to suggest, by way of arguing his own case, that two of his most trusted associates may have committed perjury or to claim innocence on grounds of ignorance of what was being done in his name and on his behalf by his most trusted and intimate associates.

This is not to argue that the case has been made that the out-of-court settlement of the ITT antitrust suit was arranged "in return for a promise of a political contribution" from ITT—the offer of $400,000 to help finance the Republican convention in 1972. It is only to say that the President's White Paper cannot by the nature of things disassociate him from what happened in the ITT affair. As to what actually did happen, the second great inadequacy of the President's explanation, as with the milk deal, is that the story, even as he tells it, by no means precludes the possibility of gross impropriety at the very least, and at the worst, illegality. As we observed yesterday with respect to the milk case, the distinction between a legal contribution and a criminal bribe may seem a difficult distinction to establish, and the best way to approach a judgment is through its chronology:

• When Richard W. McLaren took over as head of the Justice Department's Antitrust Division at the beginning of the Nixon administration, he immediately embarked on a much-publicized campaign against conglomerate mergers, with the plainly proclaimed intention of obtaining a Supreme Court ruling expanding the reach and powers of the Clayton Antitrust Act. Congress was already talking about moving in this direction with legislation and the leaders of this move were expressly urged by Mr. McLaren to hold off, pending a Supreme Court determination on his lawsuits, one of which was directed at halting three pending ITT acquisitions involving Hartford Fire Insurance Co., Canteen Corp., and Grinnell Corp. There was not the slightest sign at the time that either Mr. McLaren or the Justice Department was acting in any way inconsistent with Mr. Nixon's campaign promises to "make a real effort . . . to clarify this entire conglomerate situation," although the President, in his White Paper, would now have us believe that his policy is to be found in a report of a task force set up during the campaign which strongly urged him, at the time of his inauguration, not to pursue antitrust action against "conglomerate enterprises." If this was in fact administration policy, it is unclear why Mr. McLaren was even appointed, let alone unleashed to conduct his assault through the courts not only against ITT but another conglomerate, Ling-Temco-Vought, Inc., and still less clear how Mr. Nixon could have hailed the ultimate out-of-court settlement much later as "the greatest divestiture in the history of the antitrust law," and at the same time denounce, by contrast, the inaction of the two previous Democratic administrations.

• In October, 1970, the lower courts ruled against the government in the first ITT case, involving Grinnell, but not until the Spring of 1971 were Mr. McLaren and the Justice Department ready with their appeal. At this point, as the President tells it, he suddenly discovered that "the ITT litigation was inconsistent with his own views on antitrust policy," on grounds that it challenged bigness for its own sake, rather than for its effect on competition in the market place. On April 19, the President, according to the White Paper, ordered that the appeal be dropped; two days later, threatened with the resignation of the Solicitor General in protest, he reversed himself. But later in the month, again as he tells it, a "central clearing house" was set up to promulgate government-wide the President's real thinking on antitrust policy and somehow in the process Mr. McLaren was persuaded to abandon his quest for a definitive Supreme Court ruling and to seek a negotiated settlement. Mr. Nixon does not explain this change of heart, other than to cite the Solicitor General's view, as he has done in the past, that the government would probably have lost the case on appeal.

• Entirely missing from the President's recounting is the following history: According to sworn testimony, ITT President Harold Geneen had determined to block an appeal of the Grinnell case, if necessary by appealing directly to the President. ITT Special Counsel Lawrence Walsh talked Mr. Geneen out of starting at the top, however, and into an intense and comprehensive campaign directed at assorted Cabinet officers and members of the White House staff.

On April 16 Mr. Walsh wrote a letter to Deputy Attorney General Kleindienst in which he urged a high-level, interdepartmental review of the government's antitrust policies and baldly warned, in contrast to the estimate of the Solicitor General, of the "high probability" that the government would win its case, to the extreme detriment of the interests of ITT. Mr. Walsh specifically asked for a delay of the government's appeal. At about the same time, at a cocktail party, a meeting was arranged between an ITT director, Felix Rohatyn and Mr. Kleindienst, to give ITT a chance to state its case. The meeting took place on April 20; two days later, Mr. Walsh has testified, the idea of an intergovernmental review was abandoned—"the meeting between Rohatyn and Kleindienst had done so well that we never did anything more; for all practical purposes, the matter of the policy review came to a halt."

• The following month, on May 12, Mr. Geneen first broached the idea of ITT financial support for the Republican convention, by which time ITT had presented a much more detailed case for the damage that would be done by a settlement along the lines of the one Mr. McLaren had been seeking, and it was possible to

continued on the following page

continued from preceding page

perceive the rough outlines of an agreement far more favorable to ITT than the judgment Mr. Walsh feared would be handed down by the Supreme Court.

There is more, much more, to this story—the incriminating Dita Beard memo; the reports of the role of the "plumbers" in spiriting Mrs. Beard out of town and out of sight (for which E. Howard Hunt is said to have worn his fabled red wig); the persistent denials by Mr. Kleindienst and Mr. Mitchell of any role of their own in this affair and of any intervention by the White House. and the clear evidence to the contrary in sworn testimony and in the famous Colson memorandum which came to light at last summer's Ervin Committee hearings on Watergate—not to mention the President's White Paper. But the essence of it all is that at about the same time. two things occurred: there was an abrupt and fundamental reversal of what had seemed to be a firm. fixed government course of action, in a manner which precisely suited the interests of ITT; and there was an offer from ITT of financial support to the Republican Party for the convention which was to nominate Mr. Nixon for a second term as President. Nowhere in his White Paper, does Mr. Nixon so much as imply that he could see even any impropriety—let alone illegality—in this simple fact of an offer of a significant political contribution to the party in power by a powerful business concern with a vital piece of business before the government. This is the third, and in many respects the most appalling, inadequacy in the President's White Paper on the ITT affair.

The Miami Herald
Miami, Fla., January 10, 1974

ON June 7, 1971, William A. Powell, president of Mid-America Dairymen Inc., a large co-op, sat down and wrote or dictated a letter to a farmer in Cameron, Mo., as follows:

"We dairymen as a body can be a dominant group. On March 23, 1971, along with nine other dairy farmers, I sat in the Cabinet Room of the White House, across the table from the President of the United States, and heard him compliment the dairymen on our involvement in politics. He said, 'You people are my friends and I appreciate it.' Two days later an order came . . . increasing the support price for milk."

This letter appeared subsequently in The Wall Street Journal, from which we quote. It is not a part of President Nixon's lengthy denial that he granted favors to milk producers and the International Telephone and Telegraph Corp. in return for campaign contributions.

Such charges, said Mr. Nixon, are "utterly false."

Perhaps so. The Powell letter could be coincidental. There are White House tapes and there are written documents concerning the milk price support increases, which brought hundreds of millions of dollars to the producers and higher prices to the consumer. They are not offered in evidence to support Mr. Nixon's disavowal.

Other facts are known, though of course they may also be coincidental.

As early as Dec. 16, 1970, Associated Milk's Washington attorney, Patrick J. Hillings, wrote a letter to Mr. Nixon mentioning the setting up of "appropriate channels" for contributing "$2 million for your reelection." A subsequent known contribution of $422,500 fell somewhat short of this mark, supposing that there were not unknown contributions, and has been dismissed by Mr. Nixon percentagewise as peanuts.

According to the same newspaper source, drawn from the available records, Archibald Cox, former Watergate special prosecutor, "was seeking tapes of presidential conversations about milk prices when Mr. Nixon fired him. Mr. Cox intended to discover whether the President or his lieutenants knew about the promised campaign donations when they discussed milk matters at a White House meeting on the afternoon of March 23, 1971; the price boost was announced March 25."

Well, sort of. This week's White House statement discloses for the first time that the dairy's industry request for support price increases did come to him and that he acted upon it, and that he knew of the proposed $2 million campaign contribution.

In return, coincidentally, for less than $500,000 the dairy farmers got perhaps as much as $500 million when Mr. Nixon, as he said, took "traditional political consideration" into account in having the support level set by the Commodity Credit Corp. hurriedly overrun.

It makes hardly any difference that the milk lobby contributed to other politicians, as we are reminded it did. The basic decision had to be made in the White House, and there alone.

We leave the rest, including the coincidentals of the I.T.&T. case, to the American people. And Mr. Nixon to his anxiety to get on with other things, which is an habitual peroration to the exordium of innocence.

For our own part, we are reminded of Alice's Cheshire Cat. It grins and grins, and then it fades away.

Washington Star-News
Washington, D.C., January 10, 1974

The central issue in the Watergate matters that have become known as the "milk fund" and the "ITT case" is whether President Nixon sold out to private interests for campaign cash. The latest "white papers" from the White House — which, incidentally, probably constitute the last gasp of "Operation Candor" — contain no conclusive proof of innocence or guilt.

The facts are undisputed that milk producing interests pledged up to $2 million for Mr. Nixon's 1972 campaign and actually delivered some $400,000; and that a subsidiary of International Telephone and Telegraph offered a substantial sum (no one seems certain exactly how much) to underwrite the 1972 Republican convention that had been scheduled for San Diego.

The "white papers," which reiterate Mr. Nixon's claim that he was not influenced by campaign money, are narratives apparently distilled from White House tape recordings and documents. At one time, the White House gave the impression that it would release publicly the raw material on which the "white papers" were based. That it did not may be inconsequential since the background files and tapes have been turned over to special Watergate prosecutor Leon Jaworski. It is unlikely that the White House would make claims that could clearly be contradicted from material in Jaworski's hands.

It may be that there is no way of proving conclusively that Mr. Nixon did or did not sell out, and that it will boil down to each individual making his own decision as to whether to believe the President's protestations of innocence. Unfortunately for Mr. Nixon, his word is not held in high regard by the public these days.

If these latest "white papers" prove anything, it is that looking out for the President's political skin is one of the biggest factors in the administration's decision making. Running through one of the papers is unmistakable evidence that the White House was overwhelmingly concerned about political considerations in making a decision in 1971 to raise milk price supports. Whether the increase was in the national interest was incidental.

Another paper dealing with an antitrust action against ITT indicates that Mr. Nixon made one major decision in that case in direct contravention of his own policy because his solicitor general threatened to quit and the White House wanted to avoid the political repercussions.

One of the White House statements referred to "traditional political considerations" being involved in decision making. We would like to believe that most presidential decisions down through history have been based not on "traditional political considerations" but on the national interest.

Newsday
Long Island, N.Y., January 13, 1974

In a week, congressmen will head back to Washington after the year-end recess. There they will confront the gravest constitutional question of our century, the question of impeaching a President. All the signs at this point indicate that the lawmakers are undecided—and that the public is too. Richard Nixon has irretrievably damaged his capacity to lead effectively, both seem to be saying, but impeachment is just too threatening a process to set in motion.

A nationwide poll published by the Roper organization last week may hold the key to the country's mood. The poll was conducted in November, *before* the revelation of an 18-minute gap in one of the crucial White House tapes. Even so it found 79 per cent of those interviewed believing at least one of the serious accusations made against the President. But only 44 per cent favored impeachment, compared to 45 per cent opposed. How, in a nation dedicated to respect for the law and due process, can that be?

One more finding of the Roper poll gives a strong clue: Less than 50 per cent of the citizens polled understand what the word impeachment really means, the polltakers concluded on the basis of their in-depth interviews.

The majority, they found, believe impeachment is tantamount to removing the President from office. It isn't, of course; it's the process of bringing formal charges and nothing more. The charges must then be tried in the full dignity of the law—the Senate sitting as jury, the chief justice presiding—and removal takes place only if the charges are found to be true by two-thirds of the senators. In short, impeachment is not the disordered, injudicious amputation so many Americans seem to fear. It is the highest form of due process in the Constitution.

We're convinced that if all Americans understood this, the polls would show far different results and the nation's dithering would be decisively ended. We hope the legislators who are now busily pulse-taking among their constituents during the congressional recess have been explaining the impeachment process. Certainly there's no doubt about the constituents' interest, as Representative Angelo Roncallo (R-Massapequa) discovered during a 21-mile hike across his district last week.

* * *

The important thing now, we think, is to let the Constitution work as the founding fathers intended instead of conjuring up fears and doubts about the possible side-effects of impeachment.

In an effort to get at the facts on these side-effects, we solicited the opinion of some distinguished experts on the op-ed page recently. None made impeachment sound like an inviting or easy prospect. But their articles helped put the matter into focus.

Would the trial of a President halt the working of government? Emanuel Celler, for 22 years chairman of the House Judiciary Committee, noted that during the Andrew Johnson impeachment, the Senate worked on legislation in the morning and sat as a jury in the afternoon—for seven months. "But it functioned only feebly as a legislature, because Johnson's trial took up so much time and energy," Celler wrote. That prospect would be discouraging—except that Congress is already dead-centered by the twin White House policies of arrogance on legislation and intransigence on Watergate.

Would impeachment cause new damage to a faltering economy? Economist Robert Lekachman predicted that it would, depending in large part on how long it takes to resolve Nixon's guilt or innocence. But he added: "In fear and trembling, I state my judgment, partly as economist and mostly as citizen, that in the long run impeachment will be perceived as a demonstration that the American attachment to traditional democratic values is sturdy enough to survive the economic dislocations. . . ."

And what of foreign policy? Hans J. Morgenthau, a distinguished authority on international law, gave this answer in the op-ed series: "The importance of the President for American standing in the world is easily exaggerated. That standing is the result of American power and policies, and the qualities and reputation of the President are but two of many factors affecting the position. . . . The trumps Mr. Kissinger was able to play [in the Mideast] were his own ability, supported by American power, and Mr. Nixon's sagging prestige did not visibly detract from the value of these trumps."

It seems to us, putting the experts' worst predictions about impeachment up against the current news, that they've already been fulfilled. That is, the President is *already* incapacitated and the administration adrift; the nation is *already* paying a heavy economic price; confidence in the presidency and even in politics could hardly be driven lower. We seem to be paying all the costs of impeachment without gaining any of the clarification the process would surely bring. And if that's so, it seems appropriate to ask our congressmen before they return to Washington: What are we waiting for?

PORTLAND EVENING EXPRESS
Portland, Me., January 7, 1974

Many Americans are now debating, within their own minds or with their neighbors and associates, whether President Richard Nixon should be impeached or whether the country should try to endure him until the end of his term, unless he resigns.

There is a division of opinion within the country, just as there is within Congress. But the House has already made its decision, it has voted a million dollars to help the Judiciary Committee of the House launch impeachment proceedings, which means that the committee will intensively probe every aspect of the President's administration for evidence that would render him vulnerable to impeachment proceedings.

The latest Gallup poll shows that sentiment for impeachment and removal from office — which means an indictment by the House by a majority vote and then a Senate trial, and Mr. Nixon's removal by a two-thirds vote — has slightly dropped from the last reading of public sentiment. Now 35 per cent elect this course, though it would be fully as instructive if voters were asked simply if the House should impeach (indict) the President.

The basic question facing Americans is whether they wish to see the Constitution mandate pursued, or if they wish to ignore it, and take a chance that Mr. Nixon will resign, or somehow muddle through the rest of his term.

Rep. Peter Kyros said the other day, and we agree with him, that there is no way to duck the issue. The House must proceed with impeachment, regardless of the outcome in the Senate. There are too many offenses against the law linked to Mr. Nixon's administration and its officers to permit sweeping the scandal under the rug. We have heard a lot about the credibility of Mr. Nixon; now Congress must re-establish the credibility of our judicial system and pursue the role played by the President to the end.

TULSA DAILY WORLD
Tulsa, Okla., January 7, 1974

IN ANNOUNCING his plans to retire next year, Senate Watergate Committee Chairman SAM ERVIN said he hoped to do some fishing. Apparently, he decided to get an early start.

The Chairman's latest attempt to subpoena hundreds of private PRESIDENTIAL papers and tapes can only be described as a fishing expedition. Committee Staff Member RUFUS EDMISTEN admitted as much after PRESIDENT NIXON quite correctly ignored the summons.

EDMISTEN, deputy counsel to the ERVIN panel, said after the PRESIDENT'S refusal to knuckle under that the latest subpoena will be narrowed "to the essentials" and that Court action will follow.

EDMISTEN did not explain why the list of subpoenaed material was not "narrowed to the essentials" in the first place, which is an admission of at least sloppy legal procedure. But it isn't really the important issue here.

The vital question is whether the PRESIDENT of the United States is subservient to a Congressional committee in the matter of private papers and records. The issue is a complex one, but it will remain important long after the Watergate investigation has been forgotten.

Mind you, we are not saying that the PRESIDENT is above the law or that he could ignore a legal subpoena or order issued by a Court in the pursuit of justice. Nor do we defend NIXON for his frequently awkward and inconclusive role in trying to clear up the Watergate mess.

But we do not wish to see NIXON or any PRESIDENT reduced to the role of a Congressional lackey whose office and papers are open to any legislative chairman who wants to have a look.

In refusing to obey ERVIN's command, NIXON wrote the Chairman:

"Neither the judiciary nor the Congress could survive a similar power asserted by the Executive Branch to rummage through their files and confidential processes."

The PRESIDENT was absolutely right. To give one Branch of the Federal establishment the kind of unlimited fishing license that ERVIN seeks would amount to a rather drastic change in our form of Government.

THE ARIZONA REPUBLIC

Phoenix, Ariz., January 11, 1974

Operation Candor has come to an end. It was something less than a success. That's because someone had decided "to dream the impossible dream, to fight the unbeatable foe."

President Nixon's candor just has not impressed the liberal-Democratic establishment. Nothing less than tablets carved in stone, preferably given to a new Moses on Mt. Sinai, could change Nixon's foes' determination to remove him from office.

Consider his unprecedented action in turning his tapes of Oval Room conversations over to the Watergate grand jury. It has since been revealed that the presidential aides, both in writing and verbally, urged the prosecutor to treat the tapes "with the utmost confidentiality."

So one tape ended up at a Washington cocktail party and portions of others have appeared in the press with attribution to unspecified sources.

The credibility of the tapes was damaged, if not destroyed, by the revelation that two were missing and parts of another had been erased. It was not necessary to trace these discrepancies to the President. They had happened, and that was enough to damn the man in the Oval Office. His candor was of no help.

Realizing that his personal financial affairs were the subject of great criticism, President Nixon published a balance sheet of his income and outgo such as no president, and perhaps no man in public life, had ever published.

The critics, most of whom would not reveal their own income tax returns under any conditions, moved in for the kill, and it is now generally believed that the Internal Revenue Service is about to tangle with Nixon's accountants on the legitimacy of some claimed tax deductions. Obviously, candor got the President nowhere in this case.

The latest, and presumably the last, exercise in Operation Candor was President Nixon's issuance of white papers dealing with the so-called milk scandal and the ITT affair.

In the milk affair, the President quite candidly said he had authorized increases in milk support prices in 1972 and added he knew that three large dairy cooperatives had contributed funds to the Committee for the Re-election of the President.

But he denied any connection between the two facts, and pointed out that the boost in milk support levels had been supported by Speaker Carl Albert and Rep. Wilbur Mills, two of the most powerful Democrats in Congress.

The white paper brought out an interesting statement. The President, again with candor seldom appearing in a political pronouncement, said the dairy interests were "an essential part of his political constituency."

If it was wrong for Mr. Nixon to do what a large number of his political followers wanted him to do, then there has never been a president of the United States who was not guilty of wrongdoing.

Ralph Nader insists the President's action cost the milk-user money, as indeed it did. The cost would have been higher if the President had waited for Congress to act. Now Nader is pushing a class action lawsuit against the President, who may yet have to defend an executive action in a court of law.

In the second white paper, dealing with International Telephone & Telegraph Co., President Nixon denied that a promised contribution from the giant multinational corporation had anything to do with his actions on an antitrust case against the company.

It matters little that his intervention came before the money was pledged to help defray the costs of the Republican national convention in 1972. Or that the President was acting on the advice of his attorney general. Candor again failed to help the President.

What it all amounts to, unless we are mistaken, is that the liberal-Democratic bloc, with the full support of the Eastern seaboard mass media, has determined the President must resign.

They won't urge his impeachment, because they aren't sure they have the votes to win such a vote. They won't urge the Ervin committee to finish its hearings on Watergate, because those hearings will hurt Republican candidates for Congress if they are still being held this summer. But they will attack every act of Nixon in his own defense. They will insist that he prove his innocence, and ignore him when he tries.

In the words of one astute observer, Nixon is to be allowed to sit in the White House until the posse comes to take him out and hang him. It wouldn't be a literal hanging, of course.

A resignation would do. Or the complicated procedure in the 25th Amendment would make it possible to allow his vice president to take over the office of the presidency on a finding of incapacity on Nixon's part.

What really interests us about this scenario is what will happen afterward. Will the people who once wanted rapprochement with China and detente with Russia urge Gerry Ford to destroy everything Nixon has done in this direction?

Will those who hailed Harry Truman and Franklin D. Roosevelt and Jack Kennedy for supporting Israel demand that the post-Nixon United States kowtow toward the Arab sheikdoms?

Will those upon whom the President wasted his candor want to know about the tax deductions and the income tax returns and the accumulations of wealth by the Lyndon Johnsons, the Hubert Humphreys and the rest?

No one knows. For the present there is only one goal

That goal is to get rid of Richard Nixon, but only at the time most likely to have the greatest impact on the November elections.

The Boston Globe

Boston, Mass., January 10, 1974

The White House, in releasing many pages of statements on Tuesday, has announced that this ends what has been called "Operation Candor," and this is just as well. For the statements make even more clear than the events that followed the start of the operation last November that it was misnamed. It was George Orwell's "double-speak." There has been no candor from start to finish. The operation has ended, not with a bang, but with a whimper.

No sooner was the operation launched than President Nixon was assuring Republican governors there would be no more Watergate "bombshells." The very next day the White House had to disclose before Judge Sirica, and fail to explain adequately, the 18-minute "gap" in a subpoenaed Watergate tape. And soon Mr. Nixon was to startle a group of editors in Florida with the assertion, "I am not a crook."

In early December he released his tax figures, but they boomeranged. They showed that with an income of more than $200,000 he paid less Federal taxes in two years than an average worker earning $16,000, and that he paid no state tax at all in California, where he votes. And now the Internal Revenue Service is reportedly about to rule that he underpaid his Federal taxes by perhaps $30,000, and should have paid capital gains taxes on the sale of part of his San Clemente estate.

Now at the operation's end come the promised complete statements on the milk price and International Telephone & Telegraph cases — and the kindest thing to be said of them is that they raise more questions than they answer. To make it worse, the White House says no other documents or any tape-recordings concerning them will be released.

In the ITT case, the White House denies President Nixon ordered the Justice Department to settle an antitrust suit in return for a promised political contribution. But there seems now no question at all that there was such an order, and that two threatened resignations (shades of Archibald Cox!) caused Mr. Nixon to change his tactics.

The White House now claims the "only action" by Mr. Nixon was a phone call April 19, 1971 to then Deputy Atty Gen. Richard Kleindienst ordering him not to appeal a lower court ruling favoring ITT. Mr. Nixon "expressed irritation," says the report. Kleindienst has said the President called him a "vulgar name" and asked him, "Don't you understand the English language?" Only his threat to resign forced the President to let the court proceedings continue, Kleindienst said last November.

The White House does say that on April 21, two days later and after a delay was granted, then Attorney General John Mitchell advised Mr. Nixon not to interfere because if he did, Erwin N. Griswold, then Solicitor General and a former Harvard Law School dean, would resign and there would be "legislative repercussions." So at this point Mr. Nixon changed his mind.

But the White House glossed over the secret meetings between high ITT and Administration officials that began in 1970, and the propriety of giving corporate officials such private access during a cials such privtee access during a court case. It ignored the famous memo of June 25, 1971, by ITT lobbyist Dita Beard, 36 days before the out-of-court settlement was agreed to, saying ITT's $400,000 convention offer had "gone a long way" toward such a settlement. And it ignored a memo from then White House aide Charles W. Colson referring to talks between Mr. Nixon and Mitchell as to the "agreed upon ends" in the ITT settlement.

So much for ITT. Now what about the milk case? Here the White House said Mr. Nixon—who last October, in connection with a gift from Howard Hughes, had said he made it a point never to know anything about campaign contributions — did know, when he decided in 1971 to increase milk price supports and thus hand dairymen $300,000,000, of a dairy industry promise to contribute $2 million to his re-election campaign. (Again, this had already been disclosed in a Colson-to-Nixon memo.) His excuse this time was a sort of "nolo contendere," a plea that the price boost was necessary because of "congressional pressure . . . economic merits . . . (and) traditional political considerations."

All we need to know to understand this better is what happened in 13 days of March, 1971. On the 12th, Secretary of Agriculture Hardin rejected pressure for higher milk prices. On the 22d, the dairymen gave the Republicans $100,000. The next day, Mr. Nixon spent an hour with Hardin and dairy leaders. (Scheduled weeks earlier, the White House now says.) The next day, the milk producers plunked in another $25,000. And the next day, Hardin reversed himself and announced support prices were going up.

For the average tax-paying, milk-drinking and now freezing consumer, it is all simply too much. Mr. Nixon is asking his country to believe the unbelievable. And so, once again, we say he should resign.

EXPERTS REPORT ON TAPE; FORD ATTACKS CRITICS

A panel of technical experts examining the Watergate tape recordings surrendered by President Nixon reported Jan. 15 that an 18½-minute gap in the tape of a June 20, 1972 conversation between Nixon and H. R. Haldeman had been caused by at least five separate erasing and rerecording operations. The experts' report appeared to eliminate the possibility that President Nixon's personal secretary Rose Mary Woods' admitted single five-minute accidental erasure could have been responsible for the 18-minute gap, as the White House had contended.

In their written report to U.S. District Court Judge John J. Sirica, the experts said "magnetic signatures" measured directly on the tape showed that "buzzing sounds were put on the tape in the process of erasing and rerecording at least five, and perhaps as many as nine, separate and contiguous segments." Panel member Richard H. Bolt agreed with assistant special prosecutor Richard Ben-Veniste's contention that if it had been an accident, "it would have to be an accident that was repeated at least five times."

Judge Sirica recommended Jan. 18 that a grand jury investigate "the possibility of unlawful destruction of evidence and any related offenses" regarding the 18½-minute gap in the tape and the nonexistence of two other tapes subpoenaed by the special prosecutor, Leon Jaworski. Jaworski said in a statement released later in the day that his office, along with the Federal Bureau of Investigation, would "conduct an exhaustive investigation into all phases of the matter and any relevant information will be referred to the grand jury."

Among other Watergate developments during the second half of January:

■ Vice President Gerald R. Ford warned Jan. 15 that President Nixon's critics were waging "an all-out attack" in an attempt to "crush" him and his policies. Addressing members of the American Farm Bureau Federation in Atlantic City, N.J., Ford identified the President's antagonists as "a few extreme partisans" and as a "relatively small group of political activists."

■ Amidst continuing speculation in Congress and elsewhere over the possibility of President Nixon's impending resignation, Senate Republican Leader Hugh Scott (Pa.) and Vice President Ford asserted that the White House possessed information that could clear President Nixon of wrongdoing in the Watergate affair. Scott, interviewed by CBS Jan. 20, said he had "some information which is not yet public—which is enormously frustrating to me, because it seems to me to exculpate the President—but I cannot break through the shell down there of all of his advisers, who feel differently about it, who feel that the President

no longer needs to make some of these replies." Ford told reporters Jan. 22 that the information "will exonerate the President" and "will totally undercut" testimony of former presidential counsel John W. Dean 3rd that Nixon had knowledge of the cover-up prior to March 21, 1973, when Nixon said he learned of it.

■ Egil Krogh Jr., the former White House aide who once headed the special investigative unit known as the "plumbers," was sentenced to six months in prison Jan. 24 in connection with the 1971 break-in at the office of the psychiatrist who had treated Pentagon Papers defendant Daniel Ellsberg. Krogh had pleaded guilty Nov. 30, 1973 to a charge of conspiring to violate the civil rights of Dr. Lewis J. Fielding. Although there had been widespread speculation that Krogh would implicate President Nixon in illegal activities by the plumbers, Krogh said in a statement released after the sentencing that he had "received no specific instruction or authority whatsoever regarding the break-in from the President, directly or indirectly."

■ Sen. Sam J. Ervin Jr. (D, N.C.), chairman of the Watergate Committee, announced Jan. 26 that public hearings on contributions to President Nixon's 1972 reelection campaign would be postponed indefinitely. The two items remaining on the committee's schedule were the $100,000 payment from industrialist Howard R. Hughes to Nixon's friend Charles G. Rebozo, and contributions by the dairy industry. Ervin said the delay had been decided upon to avoid prejudicing the trial of former Attorney General John N. Mitchell and former Commerce Secretary Maurice H. Stans on charges of perjury and obstruction of justice, scheduled to begin Feb. 19 in New York City.

■ A California state judge said in Los Angeles Jan. 29 that he would summon President Nixon as a witness for the defense in the trial of former White House aides John D. Ehrlichman, G. Gordon Liddy and David R. Young Jr., charged in the burglary of the office of Dr. Fielding. Judge Gordon Ringer said he was "persuaded" that Nixon was a "material witness" and that he would issue a "properly prepared certificate commanding . . . Nixon to testify before this court" on Feb. 25 for a pretrial hearing and on April 15 for the trial. Deputy White House Press Secretary Gerald L. Warren said in Washington Jan. 30 that Nixon's lawyers would recommend that he "respectfully decline to appear" on constitutional grounds. Asked whether Nixon might respond to questions in writing, Warren said that "other requests" would be dealt with "as they arise."

New York Post

New York, N.Y., January 17, 1974

A sorely bruised and shamefully mistreated American people has suffered one more indignity at the hands of the President of the United States.

It has now been learned, from an exhaustive, dispassionate technical analysis of a key Watergate recording, that crucial sections of the tape, bearing directly upon the President's personal credibility, have been erased.

In other words, the White House—that is, the President or his highest ranking associates—is nakedly open to the charge of having destroyed evidence subpenaed by the special federal prosecutor appointed to investigate the worst political scandal in the nation's constitutional history.

This fresh crime adds one more count to a legal and moral indictment that is without precedent in the conduct of the Presidency. It represents another betrayal of the public's long-abused trust in President Nixon's integrity. It was committed in secret; it was, nevertheless, an open gesture of contempt for honor, decency and the countless Americans who cherish their Presidency and the generous Constitutional traditions that give it life and meaning.

The decision at the White House to resort to destruction of evidence was not some aberration, some act of sudden panic. On the contrary, it was wholly consistent with and, indeed, the inevitable climax of the repeated denials, evasions, contrived "explanations" and fraudulent appeals to alleged Constitutional privilege that have denoted the President's attempts to withhold such evidence from the moment that its existence was revealed.

The American people, and legal officials representing them, have been told, variously, that the tapes and documents could not be furnished because of "executive privilege," that tapes were suddenly found not to exist, that one tape was possibly inadvertently altered by the President's secretary and that these materials didn't really matter because the whole truth has already been officially revealed by the President.

But each of these increasingly tortuous attempts to frustrate investigation has been a failure and the vestiges of them all have now been engulfed in the technical experts' report to Federal Judge Sirica that the critical June 20, 1972 tape, the one with the 18-minute "hum," has been erased. Not "doctored," as many Americans supposed. Just erased.

Who did it? In a sense, that hardly matters any more. A proven finding that the President himself actually manipulated the buttons is not necessary.

The evidence was destroyed while it was in the custody of the White House and therefore required, pursuant to the most elementary considerations of law and judicial order, the closest and most scrupulous care. The President's responsibility for the abuse of the evidence is clear and compelling.

He cannot restore the faith and trust he has so heedlessly and selfishly squandered by resorting, once again, to the desperate, discredited tactics of the past. They have all been frantically tried, not once but often. They have all served, in the end, to demonstrate the moral flabbiness of the White House case.

*　　*　　*

There is, in fact, only one dignified way in which the President may at last clear away some part of the suffocating atmosphere into which his leadership —or, more precisely, his failures of moral leadership—have plunged his Administration and the nation.

That is for him to resign at once—to help restore this country's badly shaken morale and its old, hopeful faith in the institution of the Presidency, to demonstrate the sense of patriotism that he has often professed and to save some degree of the personal honor that every human being is entitled to claim.

The Charleston Gazette

Charleston, W.Va., January 17, 1974

It now becomes unmistakeably clear that a White House tape that goes to the very heart of the Watergate criminal conspiracy and the subsequent coverup was deliberately erased.

A panel of six technical experts, chosen jointly by the White House and the special Watergate prosecutor, submitted a report setting forth that the 18-minute gap in the crucial tape could have been made only by someone pushing the record and erase buttons at least five and perhaps as many as nine separate times.

Because of repeated objections raised by White House lawyers in a continuation of coverup tactics, the experts were not permitted to say whether the acts were deliberate. But this is of no consequence for no one in his right mind could be made to believe that a person could push the record and erase buttons five to nine times by hand accidentally. It had to be deliberate.

This amounts to destruction of evidence — and most important evidence it is, for the obliterated portion of the tape had to do with a conversation between President Nixon and White House chief of staff H. R. Haldeman three days after the break-in at Democratic party headquarters.

And if anybody believed President Nixon's secretary, Rose Mary Woods, when she testified that she may have accidentally caused part of the erasure by stepping on a foot pedal, all doubt has now been removed.

The mystery of the White House tape now involves deliberate destruction of evidence and also perjury — and this calls for a full-scale grand jury investigation to get to the bottom of what amounts to conspiracy upon conspiracy

The Detroit News

Detroit, Mich., January 17, 1974

Just when it seems that rock bottom has been reached in the Watergate mess, another revelation sends President Richard Nixon's credibility plunging to a new low.

It happened again this week when a panel of court-appointed technical experts revealed that an 18½-minute gap in a key Watergate tape was caused by repeated erasures and re-recordings.

Although the experts declined to say whether they think the erasures occurred by accident or design, they agreed under questioning that if it were an accident, the accident would have been repeated at least five times and as many as nine times to produce the results which they discovered.

Under such circumstances a skeptical public can be forgiven if it entertains the thought that someone in the White House may have tampered deliberately with the tape, thus concealing important evidence and obstructing justice.

Add to that the possibility of perjury. The White House previously had suggested that the 18½-minute gap had been been produced by a single, continuous operation: Rose Mary Woods might accidentally have pressed the wrong button and held her foot on a pedal while answering a telephone call.

From the very first, that gap in a controversial tape had the appearance of being an incredibly convenient accident. Now expert testimony effectively destroys the White House's theory of how the accident occurred.

How much is the public supposed to swallow without getting completely sick to its stomach?

The new evidence pulls the rug from under the President's loyal apologists and will certainly increase support in Congress for the movement to impeach Mr. Nixon. "This is the most serious single bit of evidence to date," observes Rep. John Anderson, leader of the House Republican Conference. "The theory that there has been a conscious effort to conceal evidence is no longer a theory."

While the latest horror story was being told in Judge Sirica's court, Vice-President Gerald Ford, doing his best to restore confidence in the administration, was out delivering a speech in which he blamed "a few extreme partisans" for stretching out the ordeal of Watergate for their own political purposes.

Extreme partisans are not above doing exactly that. However, the White House has made their work easy for them, since the White House has been at least as devious as the partisans have been partisan.

However, the Nixon crisis has long since transcended mere partisan conflict. As the President stumbles and reels from one disaster to another, public confidence in this administration sinks further and further, taking with it the ability of the nation to solve the many problems, besides Watergate, which beset it.

At this rate, if Mr. Nixon continues to refuse to leave the presidency, he will one day find that the presidency, by popular request and congressional action, has taken leave of him.

THE ARIZONA REPUBLIC

Phoenix, Ariz., January 17, 1974

Who erased and recorded "at least five and perhaps as many as nine separate and continuous segments" of a tape recording a conversation between President Nixon and White House Chief of Staff H. R. Haldeman?

That's today's prime question in the continuing drama of Watergate. It's also the question that Judge John Sirica apparently is pondering as he decides whether to submit the tape to a grand jury which, incredible as it may seem, could file a criminal charge against the President of the United States.

It has been known for several weeks that there was an 18-minute erasure in the crucial tape. But it was not publicly known how the erasure was done or who did it. Tuesday a panel of experts reported to the judge that "the recording controls must have been operated by hand" in erasing the five to nine segments that produced a buzz instead of voices when it was last played in public.

It would be easy to raise technical questions about the experts' expertise. For instance, one of them said a malfunction in the bridge rectifier made it impossible any longer to duplicate the buzzing sound in the recorder. Now, who is altering the tape?

The panel's report was a summary, not the complete report. It may be vulnerable to attack by other experts. But the damage to President Nixon's image is immense. He now is in the position of having to prove a negative, to show that neither he nor his secretary, Rose Mary Woods, erased the vital part of the tape. No ordinary man is expected, under Anglo-Saxon law, to prove his innocence, but it looks more and more as though Mr. Nixon will have to do exactly that.

It could well be that additional study will show the recording machinery was inadequate. President Nixon told the managing editors at Disneyland last November that the recording device was "a little Sony" with little lapel mikes. He said it cost only $2,500. However, the panel of experts did not blame the 18-minute erasure on the price of the instrument.

When he spoke to the Republican governors, also in November, Gov. Tom McCall of Oregon asked the President if the Republicans would be "blindsided by any more bombs." The President, according to McCall, said "if there are any he is not aware of them." Obviously he thought then that the June 20, 1972, tape was in order.

Judge Sirica deserves credit for not allowing the electronics expert to testify as to whether the erasures could have been made unknowingly or unintentionally. One of the prosecutors, asked whether he would pursue the suggestion that the erasure was intentionally made, said, "I think the point has been made."

The point he thought made, obviously, was that the President is guilty. That could well be the majority public opinion as a result of this latest bomb in the Watergate case.

But it will be a strange inversion of the legal niceties if the safeguards that apply to every other citizen do not apply to the President. Sen. Sam Ervin kept asking where the Constitution excepted the President from the legal processes applied to everyone else. The public's reaction to the tapes may well be his answer.

President Nixon, in our estimation, should never have turned the tapes over to Judge Sirica in the first place. He has since gone back

to the legal position that the tapes were protected by executive confidentiality, but the damage has been done.

The damage done to the presidency is more important than the damage done to the President. What future president will ever dare discuss personally sensitive matters with his chief of staff if he knows a federal judge can reveal that conversation to the world?

THE ATLANTA CONSTITUTION

Atlanta, Ga., January 17, 1974

A panel of technicians, including some recommended by the White House, has unanimously concluded that the now-famous 18 minute hum on a Watergate tape was caused by erasing and re-recording.

Now Judge John Sirica's court and the court of public opinion are wondering who wanted to erase what — and why.

The 18-minute segment was supposed to be a conversation between President Nixon and his top aide, H.R. Haldeman, a few days after the Watergate burglary. Haldeman's notes on the conversation indicate it was about the need to counter the Watergate burglary of Democratic headquarters with a public relations offensive.

The gap *could* have been caused accidentally—if anyone is willing to believe that the erase and re-record buttons were accidentally pushed at least five and maybe nine times in a short stretch of tape.

And, of course, there is Gen. Alexander Haig's "sinister force" to consider.

But people unwilling to accept either of those explanations are left with one alternative: the tapes were tampered with deliberately.

But who would do that? The President? Haldeman? Georgia's Sen. Herman Talmadge reminds us that Haldeman had taken some tapes home for a weekend. Did he merely listen? — or did he push buttons?

Who else had access to the tape and the UHER recording machine? Rose Mary Woods, the President's secretary did. So did Stephen Bull, an aide charged with custody of the tapes. And secret service men charged with their safe-keeping. Would any of these employes actually tamper with the President's tapes? Bull vehemently says no. Rose Mary Woods, in a remarkably gymnastic courtroom performance, admitted she may have erased five minutes, but not 18.

How can we get at the truth? Should we try to get at the truth?

There are reports of widespread public apathy over Watergate, the tapes and assorted scandals — but we believe the American people want and are entitled to the truth.

And one way to get at the truth of this particular matter is to question under oath in court all the parties involved. Including the President.

Why not? He has assured us on numerous occasions that he wants to get the truth out. Somehow his various speeches, press conferences and briefings have failed to end suspicion and mistrust.

There is nothing we can see in the Constitution that bars a President from cooperating with a court in the search for truth. Surely, after a year of personal pain for the President and travail for the nation, that is worth a try.

THE RICHMOND NEWS LEADER

Richmond, Va., January 21, 1974

Well, maybe the devil *did* do it.

After the dismaying events of the past week, it is difficult to know what to believe in the matter of The Great Gap. It may be, as the Republican Minority Leader, Senator Hugh Scott, contended yesterday, that the President possesses proof which will lead him — and the nation — out of this dark night of doubt. But as time passes without such proof being issued by the White House, the public tendency is to believe the worst about — for instance — The Gap.

So last week two prosecutors — one mini-skirted, the other fashionably mutton-chopped — made mincemeat of the White House proposition that Rose Mary Woods, super-contortionist, accidentally erased 18.5 minutes of a critical Oval Office tape. Experts who have been examining the tape for about a month testified that part of the tape had been erased at least five times, probably deliberately. White House lawyers cautioned the nation not to draw hasty conclusions from the experts' testimony, and strongly implied that come this past Friday, they would cross-examine the ex-

perts and reduce their testimony to so much hash.

What happened? Friday arrived on schedule, the White House lawyers did practically nothing to dilute the experts' testimony, and Judge John Sirica recommended that the matter of The Great Gap be referred to a grand jury. Whereupon, the White House lawyers hastened to explain helpfully to the citizenry that the judge's recommendation is neither a conviction nor even an indictment. What is more, a day earlier brief gaps were disclosed in the President's Dictabelted memoranda about the main points of two important un-taped conversations.

And so it goes. Late last month the President declined to make public transcripts or summaries of Watergate-related tapes on the grounds that such transcripts or summaries might convince many of his complicity in the cover-up. That is perhaps understandable, but his decision not to release transcripts or summaries was yet another contradiction of prior promise. Several weeks ago, with the release of White House white papers on allegations of presidential mis-

deeds in connection with the milk industry and ITT, Press Secretary Ron Ziegler announced that "operation candor" had concluded. In view of the latest developments about The Gap and the Dictabelt gaps, was the Ziegler announcement a declaration that the White House will tell the truth no more?

The ring seems to be closing; the President seems increasingly to be treed. Washington sentiment is widespread that 1974 will see the end of the Nixon presidency — with all the awful things that that would mean. Yet one of the most abject aspects of this entire matter is that problems of inflation, energy, and unemployment are worsening. All are being, or will be, blamed on Richard Nixon: The Hoover syndrome may indeed be setting in. The bewildering gaps and the apparently ludicrous explanations for them offered by the White House do not help the Nixon cause. Perhaps, as Alexander Haig said two months ago, the debbil is responsible for the gaps. But while rational men exist, devil theories never will be satisfactory substitutes for the truth.

The Greenville News

Greenville, S.C., January 17, 1974

News that an 18-minute gap on a key White House tape resulted from repeated erasing has added fresh fuel to the smoldering Watergate controversy. And, as with most other elements of the entire affair, the information raises more questions than it answers.

The facts known to date about the erasure are relatively few. A panel of qualified technical experts has testified that the gap was created by manually erasing and re-recording from five to nine times. At least five persons, including President Nixon, had access to the tapes before they were turned over to U.S. District Judge John J. Sirica.

This is just about the sum of public knowledge on the matter. The experts were not allowed to speculate on whether the erasure was caused deliberately or accidentally. The implication of their testimony, of course, was that inadvertently erasing the tape would have been difficult.

The electronic marks on the tape seem to negate earlier testimony of President Nixon's secretary, Rose Mary Woods, that she accidently pushed the record button while transcribing the tape, but for no longer than five minutes. However, it is entirely possible that without her knowledge hands other than her's toyed with the tape.

The important question, assuming the segment was deliberately erased, is why. This is much more vital than who actually performed the erasing chore. Finding an answer is not likely to be easy.

The recording, one of nine subpoenaed by the special Watergate prosecutor, was of a conversation between Mr. Nixon and H.R. Halderman on June 20, 1972 —three days after the break-in at Democratic party headquarters. Mr. Haldeman's notes indicate that the gap obliterated a conversation about Watergate.

The obvious conclusion then is that the segment was erased to eliminate a discussion on the caper possibly incriminating the President. But there are other conclusions, just as probable, that must be considered before Mr. Nixon is given a blanket indictment.

What was actually on the missing tape segment? The President has not commented and Mr. Haldeman's notes are by no means an accurate transcript of the conversation.

There is a real possibility that vital matters of national security were discussed. The recent disclosure that the joint chiefs of staff were spying on Henry Kissinger has not only added legitimacy to the White House plumbers, but also has added a degree of validity to the President's claims that release of the tapes could endanger the nation's security.

Even though public pressure forced Mr. Nixon to turn over the tapes, his legitimate fear of their damage to national security could have led him to have certain segments erased. To ignore such a possibility is to ignore the complexities of this country's position as a major world power.

All speculation on motives behind the erasure is, of course, rather academic. The courts—and the American people—will ultimately have to pass judgment on Mr. Nixon's personal and political integrity.

And, innocent or guilty, the President has been his own worst enemy. He and his associates have fumbled every chance to regain some measure of public faith. The administration has yet to successfully gain the offensive.

It would be in keeping with the manner in which the White House has handled Watergate and related matters for the President to have had a perfectly good reason for erasing the tape and yet to wait until the courts uncovered the act to speak out. The tape gap is minute compared to Mr. Nixon's credibility gap, which he and his advisors have been instrumental in creating.

The country generally is tired of the whole mess. Even the President's strongest and most faithful supporters cannot stand another year of multiple controversies without more positive aid from the White House.

ARKANSAS DEMOCRAT

Little Rock, Ark., January 20, 1974

Just as it appeared that a glimmer of light might be showing at the end of President Nixon's personal long, dark tunnel of Watergate, a panel of electronic experts has snuffed it out. It was revealed this week that one of the key tapes had been intentionally tampered with and the shadow of suspicion has again fallen close to the President and his nearest aides.

The new evidence shows that the missing 18½ minute segment of the tape was deliberately erased and then re-recorded at least five times and possibly nine. What adds to the seriousness of the findings is that other than Mr. Nixon himself, only four other persons had access to the tape. It thus appears that one of the five destroyed important evidence subpoenaed by a federal court. It is a serious crime, and all other Watergate charges and counter-charges aside, it is the most grievous blow yet to the President's sagging prestige and honesty.

Prior to this latest bombshell many believed that Mr. Nixon might have turned the corner and was on his way back toward restoring his shattered public credibility and trust. The White Papers he issued on the milk case and the ITT matter were largely accepted by the public as plausible, if not perfect, answers. His Operation Candor did him some good even while opening him up to a new ocean of criticism on the way he handled his tax matters. The people were tiring of Watergate and wanted the scandal laid to rest in the quickest, most orderly manner possible. The machinery for impeachment had been set in motion and talk of the President resigning was dimming. Many felt that even though impeachment might prolong the nation's agony, it was still the best route because it was Constitutional while the dangers in establishing a precedent of government by resignation were too horrible to risk. Then too, many believed that Mr. Nixon could weather an impeachment proceeding because no solid proof had been found that directly tied him to an impeachable crime.

This crutch may now have been kicked out from under him. If it is determined that the President had a part in the tape tampering, or knew about it, he is open to immediate indictment. It would be an act that would well fall under the Constitutional provision of "high crimes and misdemeanors" and one that could hardly be ignored by even his most partisan supporters.

Arkansas Congressman Ray Thornton is a member of the House committee that will study the evidence and recommend either for or against impeachment. Thus far Thornton has set an excellent example for his colleagues by refusing to publicly comment on the President's fate until all of the evidence is in. It is the proper posture to take and is quite in line with the dignity and decorum such grave proceedings command.

With the impeachment trauma now apparently inevitable, we would hope that the Senate Watergate committee would quietly fold its tent so that the circus overtones that have often marked its proceedings will not infect the House so that it can move with dispatch to properly settle this unpleasant business.

The moral outrage of a long suffering public demands nothing less.

Pittsburgh Post-Gazette

Pittsburgh, Pa., January 31, 1974

SHOULD the President of the United States appear in person in court under subpoena to testify in a criminal case?

The question, simmering in American legal history since 1807, is to the fore again with the issuance by a California state judge of a subpoena to President Nixon. The order came at the request of John D. Ehrlichman, a former chief aide to the President, seeking Mr. Nixon's courtroom presence as a material witness in Mr. Ehrlichman's forthcoming trial on burglary and conspiracy charges.

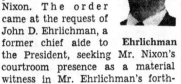

Ehrlichman

The White House has indicated Mr. Nixon will decline. Presumably that could result in appeals stretching all the way to the U. S. Supreme Court.

* * *

Here we have a clash between the trial rights of a defendant and the doctrine of separation of powers. It may be that Mr. Ehrlichman's only hope of escaping prison, loss of livelihood by disbarment, and disgrace is testimony of exoneration given in person by President Nixon, backed up by subsequent courtroom cross-examination.

On the other hand since 1807 a truce has existed between the courts and the presidency along the common sense lines that if a President were to be at the beck and call of subpoenas hither and yon across the country, he might not get anything else done.

In 1807 Chief Justice John Marshall, sitting as circuit judge in the treason trial of Aaron Burr, subpoenaed President Jefferson. "That the President of the United States may be subpoenaed, and examined as a witness, and required to produce any paper in his possession, is not controverted," Mr. Marshall declared.

But the chief justice stopped short of a head-on clash. He said in his subpoena that transmission of specified documents to the court would suffice. Mr. Jefferson subsequently produced them and offered testimony by deposition.

The outcome is described by historian Arthur Schlesinger Jr. "The matter thus ended with Marshall asserting a constitutional right to subpoena Presidents and Jefferson standing on a practical right not to show up in court. Marshall, in other words, said that the President was subject to the same law as every other American citizen, and Jefferson said: Well, yes, but the President also had more solemn responsibilities than any other American citizen, and this must be taken into account. Both Marshall and Jefferson were surely correct."

We hope something can be worked out. Certainly Mr. Nixon should be responsive to the demand for testimony, if only out of loyalty to a former close associate.

A way should be found, short of placing a President on the witness stand, of obtaining the needed information through depositions.

Beyond that, in a time when the four-decades long growth of Presidential power has aroused apprehensions that we run the risk of treating Presidents like monarchs, Mr. Nixon has an extra obligation to bear in mind the Marshall thesis that a President is subject to the same law as every other American citizen. If the courts ultimately should rule that this included a personal appearance in the Ehrlichman court case, he should comply. We hope it doesn't come to that.

The Oregonian

Portland, Ore., January 31, 1974

President Nixon's intention of refusing to honor a subpoena, if it ever reaches him, to appear personally in a California state court to testify at the trial of John Ehrlichman, David Young and G. Gordon Liddy, was anticipated. And it is a proper decision. The President, however, should be persuaded to provide written answers to questions seeking the facts in the case in which his former aides are accused.

Never before has a state court attempted to command the presence of a president in a trial. Superior Court Judge Gordon Ringer of Los Angeles, however, has ruled that Mr. Nixon is a material witness for the defense. Judge Ringer has not yet signed the subpoena. If it is issued it would have to be accepted by a District of Columbia court and served on the President, who then would reject it on constitutional grounds, or on a plea of inability to appear. Rejection of a subpoena for a personal appearance ought to be accompanied by offer or agreement to provide needed testimony in the form of written interrogatories—a response anticipated by Judge Ringer.

Citizens are frequently heard to assert that the President ought to be treated like any other American, that he is "not above the law." But the President of the United States is not just another citizen. He is the head of the executive branch of the U. S. government, which has co-equal status with the legislative and judicial branches. The person of the President is protected for a good reason. The presidency could be destroyed as an effective branch of government were the President subject to harassment, political or legal, by either of the other branches. The President is not above the law. But the ultimate law for him is impeachment, as provided in the Constitution.

It ought to be clear that if President Nixon, beset as he is by Watergate-related accusations and investigations, agreed to appear in Judge Ringer's court as a witness, the floodgates would be opened. The demands for him to testify in other cases, or to defend himself against politically-motivated or other charges, would be endless. No president could discharge his national obligations effectively under such conditions.

The President already has explained his order to a White House group, now known as "the plumbers," to investigate and stop the leaking of national security information to others not classified to receive it. He may not wish to go beyond that statement. It is more likely, however, that he will provide answers to necessary questions sought by defense counsel in the Ehrlichman-Young-Liddy trials. This, too, could open the gates to other such demands—as his release of seven tape recordings to the special prosecutor of Watergate allegations inspired the Senate Watergate committee to demand almost 500 tapes and documents by subpoena. That is a risk, however, that the President can control, while contributing to the processes of justice.

The Virginian-Pilot

Norfolk, Va., January 30, 1974

The Senate Watergate Committee isn't exactly folding its tents and stealing silently away, but it has been upstaged in recent weeks.

And maybe its members were not unhappy to be given good reason to postpone the hearings on campaign contributions from Howard Hughes and from the milk producers, scheduled to start this week. On January 23 the Committee had voted — 4 to 3, along party lines — to hold the hearings, but postponed them at the request of the Federal prosecutors who will be bringing former Attorney General John Mitchell and former Secretary of Commerce Maurice Stans to trial on charges of conspiracy and perjury, starting February 18.

The fear that the hearings might prejudice the Mitchell-Stans trial is not unrealistic and the delay is warranted. But that is not to say that the investigation ought to be called off. Why did Howard Hughes, the legendary recluse, secretly contribute $100,000 to Mr. Nixon's re-election? Why did the dairymen give $427,500 and what were they promised in return? The full story should be told.

Meanwhile, the House Judiciary Committee, which is charged with considering the impeachment of the President, is hard at work. And so is Special Prosecutor Leon Jaworski, who is expected to bring further indictments soon in the tangle of Watergate.

In the three-ring circus of Watergate, the Ervin Committee has been reduced to a sideshow.

The Ervin Committee essentially has done its job: the House Judiciary Committee and Mr. Jaworski have theirs to do yet. For the function of the Senate Watergate hearings was to alert the American public to what was done in the interests of Mr. Nixon's re-election in '72 and how our political system was subverted systematically. (Ironically, the President would have won — and won big — without all the dirty tricks and trappings that are collectively labeled "Watergate.") By now Watergate is a household word in just about every household in the United States, thanks to the hearings on television.

The question before the country is no longer who did what to whom in Watergate. The polls suggest that the American people think they know who is telling the truth — and who is lying to them. The question now is one of crime and punishment, which is a matter for the courts and the prosecutors and the judges and the juries to settle. And, of course, the biggest question is whether President Nixon should be impeached. — or impelled perhaps to resign in the course of the impeachment proceedings — as the result of Watergate. That is the constitutional responsibility of the House Judiciary Committee at the present stage of things. (If the Committee recommends impeachment, then the full House of Representatives votes whether or not to bring the President to trial before the U. S. Senate, with the Chief Justice presiding and a two-thirds vote necessary to convict and oust the President.)

Now, the Ervin Committee's prime responsibility is to frame its final report to the Senate, and to the nation, on Watergate. And that could have a major part in the drama that is unfolding, unpredictably, in Washington.

The New York Times

New York, N.Y., January 24, 1974

The White House continues to devise game plans which are an affront to the intelligence of the American people. The latest examples are the White House-inspired statements by Vice President Ford and Senator Hugh Scott to the effect that they have seen the President and have come away confident that, if only the public knew what they know, Mr. Nixon would be in the clear.

The revelations by Messrs. Ford and Scott had in common the fact that they revealed nothing. The Vice President said that Mr. Nixon had volunteered to show him the exculpatory evidence but that he had "not had the time to see it." Senator Scott said he had come into possession of hitherto unpublished information which, though he was not at liberty to disclose it, seemed "to exculpate the President." The Senator explained that this silence was imposed on him by Mr. Nixon's advisers whom he depicted as so confident about the President's case that they felt he "no longer needs to make some of these replies."

The issues at stake ought by now to be recognized as too serious to the nation to condone such verbal games. The picture of Presidential advisers too bashful to step forward with solid evidence in support of Mr. Nixon is in the same category of fantasy as Alexander Haig's courtroom musings about a "sinister force" that might have caused the eighteen-minute gap in the White House tape.

Does anyone still believe that the President would, at this stage of the investigation, voluntarily withhold from the public any favorable information? The only plausible explanation for the cryptic story put out by Senator Scott therefore is that he has joined the long list of those who have allowed themselves to be used by the White House to confuse the public and prolong the governmental crisis. His statement and that of the Vice President seem carefully orchestrated to tie in with the President's freshly proclaimed determination "to fight like hell" against impeachment.

The continued readiness of some Nixon loyalists to sacrifice their own credibility to these games of obfuscation is puzzling when viewed against the number of reputations and careers that litter the political landscape. The list of victims begins with the easily misled Cuban emigrés who were recruited for the Watergate break-in. It extends all the way to Miss Rose Mary Woods, the loyal secretary who originally was brought into Judge John J. Sirica's court under circumstances so ambiguous that she was not clear whether the lawyers who accompanied her represented her or Mr. Nixon.

The list of victims includes some of the President's lawyers whose professional reputations may well have been tarnished by the part they played, perhaps unwittingly, in bringing to the court subpoenaed evidence that had been tampered with while it was under their client's self-confessed "sole custody."

The list of victims also includes those delegations of Congressmen who, at an earlier stage of the game plan, attended confidential sessions in the White House only to come away with unsubstantiated hints of the villainy of such men as Archibald Cox and Elliot Richardson.

The list of victims includes the politically naive who, like L. Patrick Gray 3d, were sacrificed while "twisting slowly, slowly in the wind." Vice President Ford seems determined to join the list as well. He has compounded his recent blunder of playing the ventriloquist's puppet to the White House by reiterating the silly charge that the efforts to impeach the President are the work of a small group of anti-Nixon partisans.

The evidence of Mr. Nixon's responsibility in the unprecedented accumulation of political abuses and scandals has become too massive to be answered with White House-inspired statements by gullible loyalists. The hour is too late to present to the American people anything but facts.

THE KNICKERBOCKER NEWS
··· UNION-STAR ···

Albany, N.Y., January 25, 1974

"Operation Candor", which never really got off the ground, has been succeeded by "Operation Counter-attack." The opening gun was sounded when President Nixon told a group of Republican congressmen visiting the White House that he would "fight like hell" against moves to impeach him.

Almost simultaneously, Senate Republican Leader Hugh Scott said he had seen evidence disproving major Watergate charges against the President. He didn't say what the evidence was. In similar fashion, Vice President Ford said he had been assured by the President that he had evidence to disprove sworn testimony before the Senate Watergate committee of former presidential aide John W. Dean 3d. The Vice President said, however, he had not read the material President Nixon had available.

It does seem strange, does it not, that this material, in whatever form it might take, was not used by the President months ago to set the nation at ease concerning his direct Watergate role.

But let us say the President does have evidence to prove he did not participate in the Watergate coverup, as had been charged by Mr. Dean. Then, let us say, he will make it public. Would this restore to the President the respectability he has so largely lost?

It is extremely doubtful. The greater charge against the President is not that he was knowingly involved in the Watergate coverup. Nor is the strange conglomeration involving campaign funds. Nor is his avoidance—legal or not—of taxes. Nor is the matter of vast public expenditures on his homes in California and Florida.

Rather, the greatest charges against the President is that he permitted and at least tacitly condoned the creation in the White House of a climate in which the end justified the means. The end was the greater glorification of the President. The means were often illegal, often immoral, slick, slippery and casually cruel.

And to that charge the President has presented as his only defence:

"I didn't know it was loaded."

The Boston Globe

Boston, Mass., January 22, 1974

It may be a firecracker instead of a bombshell this time, but Senator Hugh Scott's statement that the White House is withholding evidence favorable to itself inescapably bolsters the suspicion that there are things so damaging in the Administration archives that even favorable material cannot be released, for fear that the rest will get out.

It now appears that at least part of the exculpatory evidence referred to by the Republican minority leader on "Face the Nation" is transcripts that would counter John Dean's sworn testimony before the Ervin Committee last June that President Nixon talked to Dean about the Watergate coverup some six months before the President claims to have had any knowledge of it.

If such evidence exists, it must have been available last summer. Why, then, wasn't it used to quash the Dean testimony at the time? The fact that it was not used and that it is now being suppressed again, after a brief exposure to selected newsmen and lawmakers in November, surely suggests either that the evidence does not hold up or that related evidence is so incriminating that its disclosure cannot be risked.

And the fact that two tapes subpoenaed by the Federal Court turned out not to exist and that 18½ minutes of a third tape related to Watergate have been erased five to nine separate times, simply adds to the impression that evidence is being kept from the court and from the public. In this connection, the Dean testimony hardly seems important any more.

What is important is the desperation that led Sen. Scott to say anything about the evidence at all. A moderate Republican who has served for 30 years on Capitol Hill, who supported the President on the bombing of Cambodia up to last year but has opposed him in such areas as busing and legal services, Mr. Scott is, one must conclude, deeply concerned about the survival of the Republican party.

Next year 16 of the party's 42 senators will be up for re-election. Five of those Republicans will not be running again. Two others, Edward Gurney of Florida and Jacob Javits of New York, are expected to face very stiff competition for their seats. And that's just for starters.

It is no wonder that Sen. Scott, on the same TV show, said he hoped that the Special Prosecutor would "indict everybody who is involved in the Watergate" and "do it as fast as possible." It is no wonder that he expressed concern that Democrats might prolong impeachment proceedings for political reasons. The Minority leader's real message, and a clearly valid one, was that full disclosure and swift legal action is the only way the Republican party can be saved. And, other considerations aside, the health of the Republican party reflects the health of this nation.

HOUSE PANEL GIVEN SUBPOENA POWER; DEMOCRAT WINS PA. HOUSE SEAT

By a vote of 410–4 Feb. 6, the House approved a resolution ratifying the Judiciary Committee's impeachment investigation and granting the panel broad subpoena power to compel testimony or production of documents from any source, including the President. (The Judiciary Committee had voted Jan. 31 to seek House approval for broad subpoena power in its impeachment inquiry.) The next day, Committee Chairman Peter W. Rodino (D, N.J.) announced that, on President Nixon's initiative, White House counsel James D. St. Clair and committee counsel would meet "promptly" to discuss the extent of Nixon's cooperation with the inquiry. (In his Jan. 30 State of the Union message, Nixon had said he would cooperate with the inquiry consistent with the responsibilities of his office. As a footnote to his address, the President said that all probes into the Watergate affair should be concluded without delay. "One year of Watergate is enough," Nixon said.

There were these other developments in the Watergate affair during early February:

■ U.S. District Court Judge Gerhard A. Gesell Feb. 8 dismissed the Senate Watergate Committee's suit to enforce its subpoena of five presidential tape recordings on the ground that publicity surrounding the panel's hearings might be harmful to criminal prosecutions. Weighing the competing assertions of the "public interest," Gesell said the committee had not demonstrated a "pressing need" for the tapes or that hearings on their content would "at this time" serve the public interest. But, Gesell said, he also rejected President Nixon's contention "that the public interest is best served by a blanket, unreviewable claim of confidentiality over all presidential communications." Gesell added that his rejection of Nixon's claim was also based on the President's unwillingness to submit the tapes for the court's private inspection "or in any other fashion to particularize his claim of executive privilege."

■ State Rep. John P. Murtha (D), 41, won a 229-vote victory over Harry Fox (R), 49, in a special election in Pennsylvania's 12th Congressional District Feb. 5. More than 120,000 votes were cast. The seat had been held for the last 24 years by a Republican, John P. Saylor, who died in October 1973, although Democrats held a slight lead in voter registrations. The election had been watched for possible political fallout from the Watergate scandal, but the close decision negated clear-cut interpretation. Both candidates avoided the issue during the campaign.

Los Angeles Times
Los Angeles, Calif., February 3, 1974

We have been hearing from both detractors and defenders of President Nixon a demand that the House Judiciary Committee hasten its vote on articles of impeachment.

His most vehement critics argue that the evidence to support Mr. Nixon's removal from office is already overwhelming and that to delay the impeachment process is to prolong the tenure of a President who has lost much of his authority to govern.

Those loyal to Mr. Nixon agree that the Judiciary Committee should move swiftly, but on the ground that a false presumption of presidential guilt held by most Americans is precisely what prevents him from governing effectively.

We believe that the demands for haste—one presuming the President's guilt, the other his innocence—serve neither the interests of justice nor of the nation. And we agree with the decision of the Judiciary Committee Thursday to reject a proposal by a number of its Republican members that the committee set an April 30 cutoff date for its investigation.

In our opinion, the cases for or against Mr. Nixon's involvement in offenses that would justify his removal from office are not conclusively proved by the evidence now at hand.

Special prosecutor Leon Jaworski, federal grand juries and the Judiciary Committee itself still have a mass of evidence to evaluate and new disclosures of possible wrongdoing in the Administration that warrant investigation. And the Senate Watergate committee, now in recess, may hold further hearings that could produce evidence bearing on the President's guilt or innocence. It is also possible that criminal prosecutions—soon to come to trial—against close associates of Mr. Nixon could develop information that the Judiciary Committee should consider.

Simply put, the impeachment case is not yet ready for trial. And it won't be until the investigations now under way are far more complete.

It is also apparent that there is no majority sentiment for impeachment in either the House or the Senate on the basis of present evidence, and a precipitous vote would almost certainly favor Mr. Nixon.

But such a verdict would satisfy only the President's most ardent defenders. His acquittal would not—and should not—dictate an end to the investigations by Jaworski, the grand juries or the Senate Watergate committee. Their inquiries involve government officials other than Mr. Nixon, and possible offenses that his own exoneration on other charges would not exempt from prosecution.

As difficult as the President's position may be now, it could only worsen if he were to survive an impeachment vote and then have new and substantive accusations emerge from the on-going investigations that should have been in the articles of impeachment on which he was tried.

No. A vote by the Judiciary Committee on articles of impeachment should not be taken until we know more than we do now. This is not to propose that we draw out the President's ordeal—and the nation's—to indefinite lengths. But we should, at the very least, wait for the evidence that we know will be forthcoming within a reasonable time.

If the President should be brought to trial—and in a proceeding from which there is no appeal—the verdict must evolve from an orderly and deliberate process. No other form of verdict would be acceptable to a majority of Americans—or to history.

THE CINCINNATI ENQUIRER
Cincinnati, Ohio, February 5, 1974

THE WORK OF the House Judiciary Committee in connection with the possible impeachment of President Nixon has scarcely begun. But there are already some clear clues to how ugly and partisan that procedure—if it eventuates—is likely to be.

The most recent development is an agreement among the 16 Republican members of the committee that neither Mr. Nixon nor any other President could be impeached because of the criminal acts of his subordinates in the absence of clear evidence that the President himself directed or was aware of them.

That position is evidence that the Republican members of the committee view impeachment as a procedure to punish presidential wrongdoing. It is at odds with the view—widely enunciated by congressional Democrats—that impeachment is essentially a political, rather than a criminal, procedure. The same view would tend to suggest that a vote to impeach a President is closely akin to a vote of no confidence under a parliamentary system.

If that proves to be the unanimous view of the 21 Democrats on the Judiciary Committee, there can be little doubt that the committee will wind up recommending Mr. Nixon's impeachment to the full House of Representatives. Such a recommendation would be likely regardless of what Mr. Nixon says or does between now and the moment the committee voted. For, according to this view of the impeachment process, Mr. Nixon, by falling from public favor to the extent the public-opinion polls suggest, has already done enough to warrant impeachment.

That sort of interpretation by Judiciary Committee Democrats may establish a plausible background for an impeachment recommendation, but it would also contribute to the creation of a precedent that Democrats, along with all other Americans, could come to rue.

For certainly there have been other Presidents who have fallen from public favor, other Presidents who have been beleaguered by problems of credibility, other Presidents whose subordinates have run afoul of the law, other Presidents whose conduct has been assailed as unconstitutional.

To inquire into the origins of the constitutional provisions concerning impeachment is to find that George Mason, for one, was gravely concerned that American Presidents might serve at the pleasure of Congress. His fears were in large part responsible for the constitutional requirement that a President be impeached only for "treason, 'bribery or other high crimes and misdemeanors" — offenses that, in Mr. Mason's time, had more than figurative significance.

As a practical matter, however, no one pretends that there will be any superior authority watching over the collective shoulder of the House Judiciary Committee as it proceeds to consider the case for or against impeachment. The full House will have the last word. And what the framers of the Constitution intended—whether impeachment was to be a political device or a criminal device—will matter not at all.

If there is any restraint at all at work on the House it will be the verdict of history—a history that will either applaud or condemn those who are determined to drive Mr. Nixon from office, regardless of the formulation required to accomplish that task.

THE ANN ARBOR NEWS
Ann Arbor, Mich., February 3, 1974

POPULAR thinking has it that if it came down to a matter of having impeachment articles voted against him with conviction by the Senate a clear possibility, President Nixon would resign first.

This kind of wishful thinking makes a certain kind of sense. Why put a president and the nation through that kind of an emotional wringer? Why not give the President an "out" that lets everybody save face?

This reasoning may be behind Rep. Wilbur Mills' suggestion that Mr. Nixon resign if the House Judiciary Committee should recommend impeachment.

Mr. Mills' experience and expertise notwithstanding, what would be the advantage of such a resignation? It would, of course, get Congress off the hook — the House from voting to impeach the President and the Senate from sitting as a trial court.

But aside from letting Congress wriggle free of its responsibilities, what is the advantage to the nation of a resignation? A resignation is first of all inconclusive. It doesn't really get at the heart of the matter, which is whether the President is guilty or innocent of the charges laid against him.

A resignation of the kind envisioned by Mills would also be premature. It could mean that any time a president sank low in the polls or sustained heavy criticism that the way out of the situation would be for him to resign. The start of government by resignation, one distinguished columnist called it.

Mills and others are also willing to grant Mr. Nixon immunity from further prosecution if that is what it takes to get him to resign. Does Congress really have that kind of power? Didn't we learn anything from the "Agnew precedent," which is that plea bargaining at the highest levels of government by any other name is still justice being compromised and the peoples' law thwarted?

IT IS of course Mr. Nixon's right to resign if he so chose. Conceivably he might resign under pressure, although he said again last week he would do no such thing. But the main thing is that people stop seeing the resignation of the President as a desirable step to take. True, it rids the nation of Richard Nixon, which surely will please the headhunters among us, but it harms the system. It would "settle" a paramount national problem in less than conclusive fashion, and perhaps create even more doubts.

Let's not compromise the constitutional process by letting loose ends abound and by permitting the President to name his own poison, so to speak, by the plea bargaining tactic.

The Oregonian
Portland, Ore., February 3, 1974

Too much probably is being made of President Nixon's statement that he intends to cooperate with the House Judiciary Committee's search for evidence on which to impeach him, but only to the degree that it does not weaken the presidency.

A vote for impeachment by a majority of the committee and thereafter by a majority of the House of Representatives would depend as much on the political mood of the House as on the evidence. This mood reflects, to some degree, the mood of the nation. Obviously, the Judiciary Committee could easily persuade itself to vote impeachment, with or without evidence that meets the constitutional test of "high crimes and misdemeanors," if it wishes to show its political muscle.

It is therefore only reasonable to anticipate that President Nixon will respond to reasonable requests for information, issued by subpoena or otherwise. We believe the limitation he placed on cooperating with the Judiciary Committee was meant as a warning that he would resist, if legally possible, such a raid on executive documents as the Ervin committee of the Senate attempted in trying to subpoena about 500 items. Unless the House committee seeks to replace the Senate committee as a public forum for dissection of the executive branch—and that is not its constitutional duty in impeachment proceedings—it will request only that information necessary to the inquiry.

The House Judiciary Committee probably is right in its contention that its authority to recommend impeachment, and therefore its right to subpoena White House material, constitutionally outweighs the doctrine of separation of powers, or executive privilege. Otherwise, there might be no way to impeach a president on the basis of evidence. But surely the committee and the President will avoid a Supreme Court test, if possible, by the method of reasonable requests reasonably granted. This is no children's game they are playing.

The Pittsburgh Press

Pittsburgh, Pa., February 7, 1974

Reflected in Washington news dispatches has been the belief that the continuing Watergate scandals will work against Republican candidates in the 1974 off-year elections for Congress.

And the results of a series of special elections have been awaited for some clues as to what the electorate might be thinking.

Well, the first of the special elections has just been held in Pennsylvania's 12th congressional district (Cambria, Armstrong, Indiana, Somerset, Jefferson and Clarion counties).

And it didn't prove anything. Those who are trying to guess which way the electorate is leaning can continue to guess. And whichever way they guess, they may be right.

★ ★ ★

The 12th district has a big Democratic majority in voter registration. But for the past 25 years it was represented by a Republican congressman, the late Rep. John P. Saylor of Johnstown.

The last time out, he won by 65,000 votes. And in 1972, President Nixon carried the district by 48,000 votes.

Tuesday, in a special election to fill Mr. Saylor's unexpired term, Democrat John P. Murtha apparently won by 230 votes. He was running against Harry Fox, Mr. Saylor's administrative assistant, who says he'll ask a recount.

So, the Democrats can claim a victory, having gained their first seat in the 1974 elections.

★ ★ ★

But how significant was it? The thin majority Mr. Murtha got bears little relationship to the huge Democratic registration majority. It would seem many Democrats who voted for Republican Saylor still voted Republican for Mr. Fox.

And what about the 1,000 votes that went for the Constitutional candidate? Those could be described as mainly conservative votes. If they had been added to the Republican total, what would have happened to Mr. Murtha's small margin?

Further, of the six counties represented in the district, four went Republican.

There appears to be no sure way to gauge what issues affected the voting.

The 12th is a district which includes a great deal of industry. With a strong contingent of organized labor, the district would be sensitive to the issue of unemployment and, like any other district, voters probably reacted also to inflation and the energy shortage. A general disillusionment with government could have been a factor, too.

In sum, no one factor appears to have affected the outcome. So the result offers no clear-cut conclusions.

★ ★ ★

One other aspect of this election may be noted. It was to fill the remainder of Rep. Saylor's two-year term—from the time the new congressman takes the oath of office until the end of the term on Dec. 31. That's a matter of less than 11 months.

In just three more months, there will be a primary election to nominate candidates for the next two-year term in Congress.

The cost of conducting an election campaign for Congress, a $42,500-a-year job, is not small. And what the candidates spent for last Tuesday's election probably will be duplicated in the regular congressional election.

So we have another example of money playing a major role in the democratic process of electing a member of Congress. And about all we can do about it now is demand full disclosure of all campaign contributions and expenditures.

The Charlotte Observer

Charlotte, N.C., February 6, 1974

The House set the stage Wednesday for the Judiciary Committee to subpoena President Nixon himself and any evidence it deems necessary in its impeachment inquiry. The 410-4 vote to give the committee full subpoena powers was far more significant than the lopsided count may indicate.

No president has ever been forced by subpoena to personally appear before a congressional committee or the House or Senate as a whole. In impeachment proceedings against President Andrew Johnson in 1867-68, neither the House nor the Senate subpoenaed Mr. Johnson himself. Nor has a president ever been required by subpoena to appear before a congressional committee on any other matter.

Only the courts have previously subpoenaed presidents, and there have been only two instances of that. One was when a federal court subpoenaed President Thomas Jefferson to testify and produce a letter in the Aaron Burr treason case; Mr. Jefferson avoided forcing a constitutional test of whether the courts could do that by yielding the letter the court wanted. The second such case was when President Nixon was subpoenaed last July 23 by the Senate Watergate Committee and by the special prosecutor to produce tapes and documents. He eventually yielded to the special prosecutor's subpoena but is still fighting the Watergate Committee's requests.

The Constitution's Intent

So a never-settled constitutional issue will arise if President Nixon is subpoenaed by the Judiciary Committee and refuses to comply. We think the answer is implicit in the Constitution.

There may be a difference between subpoenaing a president for general investigative purposes and subpoenaing him in impeachment proceedings. When the Watergate Committee issued subpoenas for President Nixon, we expressed regret. We thought that action would force a constitutional issue that might better remain unsettled and could establish a precedent for future congressional subpoenas of presidents in non-impeachment investigations: a precedent that might not always be used responsibly.

We said at the time that it would be better for the Watergate Committee to complete its inquiry and make its report without such subpoenas, leaving it to the House to initiate impeachment proceedings to obtain presidential information and testimony if necessary to determine Mr. Nixon's role in the scandals.

To Get The Truth

The House has initiated those proceedings, and it is fully proper, we think, for it to subpoena the President. In advocating impeachment on Dec. 14, we said such proceedings were the only means of establishing the President's guilt or innocence, given his refusal to cooperate. Raoul Berger, a leading authority on impeachment, has pointed out that the Founding Fathers gave Congress impeachment power in "a deliberate breach in the doctrine of separation of powers, so that no arguments drawn from that doctrine (such as executive privilege) may apply to the preliminary inquiry by the House or the subsequent trial by the Senate.

The House vote Wednesday gave the Judiciary Committee power to call the President. The ranking Republican member of the committee, Rep. Edward Hutchison, R-Mich., has said he will not go along with the committee's Democratic majority if it votes to subpoena the President. But after debate on the subpoena issue Wednesday, 410 members of the House — including almost all the Republicans — overrode those objections by giving the committee majority power to issue such a subpoena.

That, we think, is in keeping with good constitutional principle. The very nature of the impeachment process is that it gives Congress unqualified power to seek the facts where they are to be found. If Mr. Nixon is subpoenaed, he must comply or add heavily to the reasons why the House should impeach him and, further, give the Senate reason to remove him from office.

The Des Moines Register

Des Moines, Iowa, February 13, 1974

A federal judge in Washington, D.C. has blocked the Ervin Committee from obtaining five White House tapes by citing "the need to safeguard pending criminal prosecutions from the possibly prejudicial effect of pre-trial publicity." The committee had declared that if it obtained the tapes it would make them public.

Much of the testimony before the Ervin Committee has related to possible criminal conduct. The subject matter of the taped conversations has been described by John Dean and others in their appearances before the committee. It is hard to see how the contents of the tapes could be any more prejudicial than the testimony about the conversations.

If anything, the taped material would be less prejudicial. The tapes contain the actual conversations, in contrast to the recollections of them told to the committee. The U.S. Supreme Court has upheld the use in evidence of taped conversations because of their greater reliability compared to memory.

The subject matter of the tapes has been discussed widely outside the committee. President Nixon several times has quoted portions of the tapes in his own defense. The White House has been showing transcripts of the tapes to selected persons. Senator Hugh Scott (Rep., Pa.) was given access to the transcripts and he quoted from them. Scott based his condemnation of John Dean and his statement that the President would be exculpated on the transcripts he was shown.

Under these circumstances, denying the public access to the tapes serves no useful purpose. The public is being given self-serving versions of what the tapes contain, but the public is denied the opportunity to hear the tapes and decide for itself.

The Senate resolution establishing the Ervin Committee directed the committee to make "a complete investigation" and to "reveal the full facts" about Watergate. The federal court ruling denying the committee access to the tapes prevents the committee from carrying out its mandate. The court declared in effect that legal proceedings must take precedence over giving Congress and the public the facts.

The tapes may yet be made public either as a result of trials brought by the special prosecutor or in impeachment proceedings. But disclosure is not assured. Ways must be found to guarantee that the public will be informed fully about the contents of the tapes and everything else relevant to Watergate.

Chicago Tribune

Chicago, Ill., February 3, 1974

John Doar, special counsel for the House Judiciary Committee, is at work on a framework of definitions to determine whether President Nixon can be charged with "high crimes and misdemeanors" and thus impeached under the terms of the Constitution. This is a necessary task required by his job, but it is going to require a good deal of plastic surgery on a document which the Founding F a t h e r s—intentionally and wisely, we believe—drew up in very vague terms.

At the opposite extreme from Mr. Doar we find opinions such as that once expressed by former Atty. Gen. Kleindienst: "You don't need facts. You don't need evidence. All you need is votes." And Vice President Ford, back when he was seeking the impeachment of Justice William O. Douglas, said that "an impeachable offense is whatever a majority of the House of Representatives considers it to be at a given moment in history."

In a practical sense, of course, Mr. Ford and Mr. Kleindienst are right. The danger of ignoring facts and evidence, tho, is obvious: impeachment can become the tool of a vindictive Congress, as it did when President Andrew Johnson was impeached, or of a public opinion stampeded by passion. Time Magazine's essay last week echoed the concern of the 19th century French t r a v e l e r, de Tocqueville, who complained that "nothing can be more alarming than the vagueness with which political offenses are described in America."

And yet, the more we reflect on it, the wiser it seems to have some flexibility—some vagueness, if you will—in the rules covering impeachment. Facts and evidence are essential, as Mr. Doar realizes [tho it sometimes looks as if some others do not]. Without them it would be hard for the Senate to conduct a trial. But impeachment of a President is not like the indictment of a man for armed robbery. By the nature of things, it must involve some imponderables.

A man can be a bad President without being a criminal. Time quotes Philip B. Kurland, the University of Chicago's constitutional authority, as saying: "If a President spent a term fishing, it wouldn't be criminal; but it would be an abuse of office and he would be subject to removal." On the other hand there have been plenty of Presidents who have engaged in extra-constitutional activities and never been challenged, usually because what they did happened to be popular at the time.

In short, the factual evidence in the impeachment process must inevitably be seasoned with public opinion, partly because the effectiveness of a President depends on public opinion and partly because public opinion will largely determine the votes for or against impeachment in the House. There must be enough flexibility in the rules to make them realistic and durable.

The balance between the rights of the Presidency and of Congress, like the balance between the rights of a free press and a lawful government is of too awesome importance to be defined in precise and indelible terms. Each must be confident of its proper rights, yet restrained by the knowledge that it is risky to go beyond an undefined point which will vary with public opinion and the temper of the times. Even when the facts are known, we must not expect them to fit into a neat formula which will enable us to say, "This is impeachable," or "This is not."

The questions then become broader. Has the President lost confidence to the extent that he is unable to govern? Will the country be better off with impeachment? These are questions that depend on public opinion, fickle as it may be, and to this extent we don't expect ever to see a specific definition of high crimes and misdemeanors, nor in fact should we want to.

The Dallas Morning News

Dallas, Tex., February 10, 1974

THEY USED to have a saying in the Old West: Give the so-and-so (or epithets to that effect) a fair trial before we hang him.

A kangaroo court to try Richard Nixon already is assembling, and reliable sources report that construction work on the scaffold is very far advanced.

The AFL-CIO has mounted a nationwide campaign to impeach the President and remove him from office. Liberal groups like Americans for Democratic Action, the American Civil Liberties Union and Ralph Nader's Congress Watch are more restrained. They do not, mind you, necessarily want the President removed from office. But how they yearn for impeachment!

The ostensible idea is to get the charges against the President in front of Congress; to formalize them by way of an impeachment resolution. The Senate can then either convict Nixon or clear him. One way or the other, the matter is put behind us.

Not an unattractive theory, even from the President's viewpoint. It falls oddly, however, from the lips of, say, Leon Shull, head of the anti-Nixonian ADA.

If the AFL-CIO, ADA and the rest are so disinterested, why so belligerent an outcry for impeachment; why the lobbying campaign which already is supposed to have reached 15 million Americans and will be taken directly to House members?

The House Judiciary Committee has launched a formal inquiry into the necessity of impeachment. Surely, then, from Shull, a simple statement of faith in the committee's judgment would suffice. Not so, though: The committee must be lobbied as though passage of a pork-barrel bill for Secaucus, N. J., were the issue.

True enough, the House inquiry is not strictly a judicial proceeding. But there is enough of the judicial about it—offenses disallowed by the Constitution are at question—to make it very like a grand jury proceeding.

Would the ADA lobby a grand jury, urging the indictment of John Doe for wife-beating so that Doe might be tried and convicted or acquitted? If it did, the Civil Liberties Union would surely protest. Yet here is the ACLU joining the ADA in urging that the Judiciary Committee impeach (i.e., indict) Richard Nixon for "high crimes and misdemeanors."

At the very least, it must seem remarkable to many Americans that the only groups lobbying for impeachment are those which have consistently opposed the President's policies. Liberal groups, that is to say.

This makes the impeachment campaign savor all the more of a vendetta. With the President's sworn enemies calling for his impeachment, what is one to think, except that, as Vice-President Ford recently said, they want to "crush the President and his philosophy," the better to "dominate the Congress and through it the nation"?

It is all very interesting to hear them talk of how they merely wish Nixon to have his day in court. Already they want him impeached, no matter what the evidence. Would the evidence, or lack of it, matter any more when the impeached chief executive confronted his senatorial jurors—amid the sound of nails being pounded into his scaffold?

The Virginian-Pilot

Norfolk, Va., February 8, 1974

The House of Representatives has given the go-ahead to the Judiciary Committee's impeachment investigation by a whopping 410 to 4 vote.

And it armed the Committee with the full subpoena power it sought. The Committee is empowered to compel any person to testify and to order the production of any documents that it deems necessary. If it so votes, it can order the President to testify.

The last possibility is just a possibility, not a probability yet. And it isn't known whether Mr. Nixon would honor such a subpoena.

But the nature and size of Wednesday's vote is an ominous signal to the White House.

Certainly the 410 to 4 tally isn't indicative of the House's thinking on the impeachment question. (The four naysayers were Representatives Ben B. Blackburn of Georgia, Earl F. Landgrebe of Indiana, Carlos J. Moorhead of California, and David C. Treen of Louisiana. All are Republicans.) It is likely that there is less than a majority willing to vote to impeach Mr. Nixon at this time.

But the majority of House members, particularly the Republicans, are clearly scared stiff. They are afraid that they will be damned if they do impeach, and damned if they don't. They would like for the whole business to go away quietly, which it won't. (The notion that Mr. Nixon ought to resign appeals to Republicans who must face the voters, but not to the President.)

And if the feet of the 435 House members are going to be held to the fire of an impeachment vote, most of them will want to appear not as the defender or prosecutor of the President (though there will be some of those), but as a conscientious juror doing his duty in a matter of the gravest moment.

Which means that Mr. Nixon is going to be hard-pressed to defy or ignore the Judiciary Committee's wishes, as he chooses to defy Special Prosecutor Leon Jaworski's pursuit of White House tapes and as he chooses to ignore the 11 questions that the Senate Select Committee put to him this week.

For the Constitution plainly and simply states that the House of Representatives "shall have the sole power of impeachment," and now that power is vested in the House Judiciary Committee by 410 to 4 vote.

If the Committee seeks documents or tapes, or perhaps the President's testimony, and if Mr. Nixon refuses, then the President is going to seem above the law, whatever the arguments his lawyers may make. (And for obvious reasons there is a lack of legal precedent.) Is the President above the law? is not a complicated question. The public would be quick to reach its verdict, and it would not be favorable to Mr. Nixon.

Hence the refusal to cooperate with the Judiciary Committee might be a fatal step to take. Legally speaking, there is a body of opinion that in and of itself the refusal would be grounds for impeachment. Politically speaking, it would be easier to vote to impeach a defiant President than one who appeared to be cooperating to get to the truth.

But because of the conduct of the White House, there is plainly reason to think that Mr. Nixon has something to hide. Hence he may be damned if he does and damned if he doesn't, like other reluctant Republicans.

HOUSE STUDY: CRIME NOT NEEDED TO IMPEACH

In a study on the nature of presidential impeachment, counsel for the House Judiciary Committee concluded that violation of criminal law need not be a requisite for impeachment. (According to Article II, Section 4 of the Constitution: "The President, Vice President and all civil Officers of the United States, shall be removed from Office on Impeachment for, and Conviction of Treason, Bribery, or other High Crimes and Misdemeanors.") The study, released by the committee Feb. 21, was prepared by the panel's special counsel John M. Doar and its Republican counsel Albert E. Jenner Jr. and their staff.

The staff report stressed that impeachable offenses "cannot be defined in detail in advance of full investigation of the facts." It said "no fixed standards for determining whether grounds for impeachment exist" were being offered in the report, and, in fact, the framers "did not write a fixed standard" into the Constitution but had adopted from English history "a standard sufficiently general and flexible to meet future circumstances." The study found that this standard for presidential impeachment could include commission of "constitutional wrongs that subvert the structure of government, or undermine the integrity of office and even the Constitution itself." It found that a president's "entire course of conduct in office" could be considered in as much as, "in particular situations, it may be a course of conduct more than individual acts that has a tendency to subvert constitutional government." It found that, flowing from the Constitutional requirement that a president faithfully execute the laws, he was responsible "for the overall conduct of the executive branch." The study concluded that impeachment was "a constitutional remedy addressed to serious offenses against the system of government," that in the American experience of 13 impeachments criminality may or may not have been charged, and that "the emphasis has been on the significant effects of the conduct—undermining the integrity of office, disregard of constitutional duties and oath of office, abrogation of power, abuse of the governmental process, adverse impact on the system of government."

Asked at a televised news conference Feb. 25 about his views on impeachment, President Nixon said the Constitution was "very precise" in defining an impeachable offense and it was "the opinion of White House counsel and a number of other constitutional lawyers ... that a criminal offense on the part of the President is the requirement for impeachment." He said his counsel was preparing a brief on the matter for presentation to the House Judiciary Committee.

There were these other developments in the Watergate case during the latter half of February:

■ Special prosecutor Leon Jaworski said Feb. 14 that he and the White House had reached an impasse on release of presidential tapes and documents and that it was "clear that evidence I deem material to our investigations will not be forthcoming." In a letter to Senate Judiciary Committee Chairman James O. Eastland (D, Miss.)—to whom Jaworski had promised to report on the progress of his dealings with the White House—the prosecutor said he had been informed by special presidential counsel James D. St. Clair that release of the material would be "inconsistent with the public interest and the constitutional integrity of the Presidency."

■ President Nixon addressed an "Honor America Day" rally of more than 20,000 persons in Huntsville, Ala. Feb. 18 after being introduced to the crowd by Gov. George Wallace (D). At the conclusion of his "what's right with America" speech, the President added a "personal note" disparaging news reporting in Washington. There was a tendency there, he said, "for partisanship to take over from statesmanship, ... a tendency in the reporting of news—I do not say this critically, it's simply a fact of life—that bad news is news and good news is not news."

■ Richard F. VanderVeen (D) was elected to Congress Feb. 18 from Michigan's 5th District, a seat held by Republicans since 1910 and for the past 25 years by Gerald R. Ford, who vacated it in 1973 to become vice president. VanderVeen, 51, a corporation lawyer, based his campaign on the Watergate issue, calling for President Nixon's resignation. He defeated Robert VanderLaan (R), 43, State Senate majority leader, 53,008–46,159. VanderVeen had billed his campaign as a "referendum on Richard Nixon." "Our President must stand beyond the shadow of a doubt," his ads said. "Our President must be Gerald Ford."

■ The possibility that the 18½ minute gap on the tape of a meeting between H. R. Haldeman and President Nixon was accidental in nature was offered again Feb. 18 by an independent investigator. Allan D. Bell Jr., president of Dektor Counterintelligence and Security Inc. of Springfield, Va., said his firm had found that a defective part in the recorder (which had been found by the court-appointed panel), or any variations in the recorder's electric power could have caused the machine's erase and record heads to make the reported marks on the tape.

■ The Senate Watergate Committee voted Feb. 19 to hold no further public hearings but decided to continue its investigation—behind closed doors —of possible campaign fund irregularities involving industrialist Howard Hughes, President Nixon's friend Charles G. Rebozo, and the dairy industry, and links between the Central Intelligence Agency and the Watergate break-in.

THE COMMERCIAL APPEAL
Memphis, Tenn., February 22, 1974

THE HOUSE Judiciary Committee now has received from its staff a report outlining the ground rules to be followed in determining whether President Nixon has been guilty of impeachable offenses.

Since no vote on it is scheduled in the committee, the report is expected to become the basis on which the investigation now will proceed.

The report takes what is being referred to as the "broad" approach to impeachment. That is, it does not hold with the White House contention that impeachment may be only for indictable crimes.

It acknowledges that impeachment is "a grave step for the nation." But it says impeachment is to be predicated "only upon conditions seriously incompatible with either the constitutional form and principles of our government or the proper performance of the constitutional duties of the presidential office."

In defining what it considers impeachable conduct, the report includes "undermining the integrity of the office, disregard of constitutional duties and oath of office, arrogation of power, abuse of the government process, adverse impact on the system of government," all of which, it says, "can be brought about in ways not anticipated by criminal law."

THAT LATTER point is where the House committee now will break with the White House. The staff will be working on the basis that the President can do wrong without violating the law, that the presidency involves responsibilities beyond the narrowness of the law — political and moral responsibilities — and that the occupant of that office must be held accountable on that level.

This is a reasonable approach, for if the occupant of the presidency does not have such responsibility he can allow the entire system of government to be corrupted so badly that it will be beyond repair. And if that should happen, it might even become impossible to hold the occupant responsible for subsequent real violations of law.

That may seem farfetched at this time, but then, the creation of such things as the notorious "plumbers" unit in the White House would have seemed farfetched, too, if they had been publicly suggested four years ago.

THE BROAD approach to impeachment has sound historical basis. Its foundations lie in the Constitutional Convention where impeachment procedures were seriously discussed.

An early form of the impeachment statement said the president might be removed upon "conviction by the Senate, for treason or bribery." James Madison and Elbridge Gerry objected to such narrow grounds. The upshot was the extension of the definition to include "other high crimes and misdemeanors." That was the proposal of George Mason who made clear he had borrowed the term from English law. The purpose was to strike at grave offenses against the state but beyond the ordinary laws.

Alexander Hamilton said in The Federalist that the impeachment provision was designed to reach "the misconduct of public men" and "abuse or violation of some public trust." Madison extended his comments, saying the impeachment provision would make the executive responsible for the conduct of those who served under him. He said it would subject the president to impeachment if he "suffers them (his underlings) to perpetuate with impunity high crimes or misdemeanors against the United States, or neglects to superintend their conduct, so as to check their excesses."

WHETHER THE HOUSE committee now can determine that the President has been guilty of any such conduct and whether, if it does, it can convince the full House and then the Senate that its findings are sufficient remain to be seen. That is a long road ahead.

But the basis for that investigation appears sound and reasonable. It should make it possible to carry on the work in the same scholarly, nonpartisan manner that the committee has so carefully followed thus far.

DAILY NEWS
New York, N.Y., February 24, 1974

The "opinion" given by the legal staff of the House Judiciary Committee on what constitutes grounds for presidential impeachment is most likely just the opening gun in a protracted duel.

John Doar

Not unexpectedly, Committee Chief Counsel John Doar and his aides supported the view that "political" offenses—abuse of power and the like—are sufficient cause for impeaching a President.

A number of reputable constitutional scholars hotly dispute this broad interpretation of "high crimes and misdemeanors," and they no doubt will be heard from in good time.

It is not altogether certain whether the committee itself will adopt the staff's guidelines or confine its probe to actions of President Richard M. Nixon which purportedly violate specific criminal statutes.

As practical politicians, they cannot help but perceive the risks of venturing into the broad, inviting fields opened by the staff report.

Doar & Co. can well afford to deal in abstract legal philosophizing. But the political instincts of the lawmakers should warn them that the farther they stray from the narrow path of impeachment based on indictable acts the slipperier the footing becomes and the greater the danger that they, not Mr. Nixon, may wind up on trial in the public eye. The—

SNARES AND PITFALLS

—facing Congress if it yields to temptation are apparent in the aides' own report.

They submitted a series of historical examples, precedents and opinions on non-criminal causes for ouster of public officials, each keyed to a charge laid against Mr. Nixon.

Two of them—regarding impoundment of funds and the sacking of Special Watergate Prosecutor Archibald Cox—deserve study.

For example, the lawyers delved into the dusty archives of 14th-century England to find a case where Parliament jumped on one of the king's men for failing to spend money it had appropriated.

Our own history, however, is filled with instances of presidents holding back authorized outlays. Congress has fumed and raged over the practice, but never before was it seriously advanced as a reason for booting a President out of office.

To qualify the Cox ouster for impeachable status, the committee helpers really reached—citing a remark by Founding Father James Madison to the effect that "wanton removal of meritorious officers" might subject a chief executive to removal.

The staffers eagerly latched onto that vague theory, ignoring the solid—and exactly contrary—precedent established in the attempt to impeach President Andrew Johnson more than 100 years ago.

Johnson not only won acquittal in the Senate, but the "law" he was accused of violating when he fired a cabinet member against the expressed will of Congress was later declared null and void by the courts.

Committee members would be well advised to tread warily in such obviously treacherous terrain. An attempt to impeach Mr. Nixon on flimsy evidence, or for alleged presidential malpractices that were condoned previously, would label the proceedings as a partisan scalp hunt and bring discredit upon Congress. Gentlemen, beware.

Richmond Times-Dispatch

Richmond, Va., February 27, 1974

To say that merely because something has been done once is no reason that it should be done twice is to state what most laymen probably would accept as a truism. Most laymen, but not necessarily most lawyers. Lawyers have profound respect for precedent, which means that they often argue that a rule established in one case should apply to all similar future cases. Of course, this could be an excellent way to perpetuate injustice, for the precedential rule might have been wrong.

Quite naturally, lawyers involved in the inquiry to determine whether President Nixon should be impeached are scouring law and history books for precedents to support their respective points of view. The legal staff of the House Judiciary Committee has cited precedents, many of dubious validity, to support the argument that Mr. Nixon could be impeached for acts that are not indictable crimes, including such vague offenses as "undermining the integrity of office" and having an "adverse impact on the system of government." Justice Department lawyers, on the other hand, have cited precedents to support a narrower definition of impeachable offenses; and the President himself expressed the belief Monday night that he could be impeached only for committing a "criminal offense."

The Constitution would seem to be clear on the matter. It defines impeachable offenses as "treason, bribery, or other high crimes and misdemeanors." Some legal experts, however, consider this provision to be impossibly vague. It may be easy to define treason and bribery, they say, but it is not at all easy to define high crimes and misdemeanors. Some legal scholars insist that as the authors of the Constitution interpreted the word "misdemeanor" it applied not merely to criminal offenses but also to other kinds of misbehavior, including something called "maladministration."

Academically, all this concern about precedent may be of interest, but it is irrelevant to the case of President Nixon. No matter how many Keepers of the Royal Hounds may have been impeached and removed from office for non-criminal reasons in England's history, the truth is that if Congress attempts to oust Mr. Nixon on anything other than criminal grounds it will invite—and deserve—the wrath of the nation. For

while most Americans have a very low regard for the President, as they have a very low regard for Congress, polls indicate that they do not favor his forced removal from office. A politically motivated impeachment proceeding they surely would resent, and resent bitterly.

President Nixon's popularity has plummeted not because of his Vietnam war policies, his "secret" bombing of Cambodia or his impoundment of funds—to cite three reasons that some Nixon critics have given for favoring his impeachment—but because of his possible involvement in certain *criminal* aspects of the Watergate affair. Did he, the American people are asking, obstruct justice, encourage perjury, destroy evidence or commit any other *crime* in the usual meaning of the word? If Congress can find no evidence to support Mr. Nixon's conviction on these grounds, it could not justify his ouster to the American people.

DESERET NEWS

Salt Lake City, Utah, February 27, 1974

The President of the United States isn't supposed to serve merely at the pleasure of Congress.

But that's what could happen unless the ground rules on impeachment are drawn as tightly and precisely as possible so there's no room for personal vendettas.

It's not just the fate of one Richard M. Nixon that's at stake. Rather, it's ultimately the fate of the American presidency that's involved as the House of Representatives decides whether or not to impeach — which means simply indict — President Nixon for trial by the Senate.

So those who suggest that it would be proper to impeach the President "on general principles," as James Kilpatrick discusses in his column on this page, are clearly out of order.

Nor is President Nixon merely pleading his own case when he insists that the grounds for impeachment should be narrowly defined, as he did during his press conference this week. If any axes were being ground, it was also those of the men who will follow him in occupying the Oval Office in years to come and whose hands can be weakened or strengthened by what the House does now.

A few days ago the staff of the House Judiciary Committee in effect put the rule of men ahead of the rule of law when it insisted that a President can be impeached for conduct not explicitly illegal.

The 150-page staff report started sensibly enough, stressing that impeachment was "a grave step for the nation."

But then the report ventured into deep water by listing as impeachable such conduct as "undermining the integrity of the office, disregard of constitutional duties and oath of office, arrogation of power, abuse of the government process, adverse impact on the system of the government."

By standards that fuzzy and flexible, just about any President in recent history could have been subject to impeachment.

Abuse of the government process? Any President who ever impounded funds appropriated by Congress would leave himself open to impeachment on that charge. Yet the practice of impoundment as a means of keeping the government from spending more than it earns goes

back long before the days of Richard M. Nixon.

Arrogation of power? If that standard had been applied early on in the history of the republic, either Thomas Jefferson might have been impeached for the Louisiana purchase — or France could still own a major piece of this continent.

Undermining the integrity of the office? A charge that imprecise and all-encompassing would leave the White House at the mercy of every lunatic fringe that ever took issue with any presidential action. Indeed, what about applying the same rule to Congress? With the lawmakers now being rated even lower in the polls than the President, couldn't it be argued that by doing their jobs with such conspicuous ineptitude the members of Congress are "undermining the integrity" of the legislative office? Certainly they are undermining confidence.

Happily, the report of its staff is not binding upon members of the House Judiciary Committee. Indeed, with constitutional experts divided among themselves as to the precise meaning of the constitutional provisions involved, each man seems to be his own judge on what constitutes grounds for impeachment.

In making that judgment, it should be clear that impeachment is warranted only for the most serious of offenses. After specifying treason and bribery, the Constitution mentions "other high crimes and misdemeanors" as grounds for impeachment. Did the founding fathers really intend to rank conduct not explicitly illegal in the same category with treason or bribery?

Moreover, as a matter of simple justice, in deciding whether or not he should be impeached, Congress should apply to Richard Nixon the same set of standards it would be willing to apply not only to other Presidents but also to Congress itself. The Constitution specifies, after all, that it's not just the President and Vice President that can be impeached, but also "all civil officers of the United States."

Impeachment is supposed to be a method for salvaging the political system. Loosely applied, impeachment can become a method of seriously weakening the political system.

With the stakes that high, it's time for politicians to act like statesmen.

AKRON BEACON JOURNAL

Akron, Ohio, February 26, 1974

"I AM NOT a crook," President Nixon once told us on coast-to-coast, prime-time television.

Under the broad legal guidelines drawn up by the bi-partisan staff of the House Judiciary Committee, proof of that statement would not suffice to prevent Mr. Nixon's impeachment.

The lawyers poked around in legal history and past impeachment proceedings and concluded the predictable: That Richard Nixon could be impeached and removed from the presidency for actions that aren't necessarily legal crimes. We agree.

But we must also agree with their accompanying conclusion that if impeachment is based on other than indictable crimes, the offenses would have to be very serious breaches of the public interest.

For three months the Judiciary Committee has been working on ground rules and to establish what focus impeachment proceedings should take. Now it must decide whether to accept the broad opinion by its legal staff or trim it down. It seems to us the committee would be wise to accept this rather orthodox interpretation of impeachment and get down to its serious business.

This version is a moderate one, as it should be It is far more reasonable than the view from either extreme—the White House insistence that impeachment can be based only on an offense for which persons can be jailed, or the equally partisan anti-administration view that it can be based on "anything Congress wants it to be."

The White House defense is nonsense, since the only penalty for a guilty verdict in a Senate trial is removal from office anyway. And at the other extreme, a political lynching is as much a betrayal of public trust as a political cover-up.

The staff report reflects the scope the founding fathers intended in the phrase "high crimes and misdemeanors" in the impeachment section of the Constitution. The lawyers documented this: George Mason, who proposed the term, is quoted that it was his intent to encompass "attempts to subvert the Constitution" rather than strictly criminal acts. And the staff quotes the English jurist Blackstone that the first and principal high misdemeanor at the time was "maladministration of such high offices as are in public trust and employment..."

What does this mean in 1974?

It means that if the report is adopted, Congress has the option of inquiring into such diverse issues as the illegal bombing of Cambodia, refusing to spend funds appropriated by Congress, obstruction of justice in the Watergate case, and misuse of massive executive power. This is the way it should be, because the real questions revolve not only around crimes, but abuse of power and trampling on public trust.

From all indications, the White House plans to dig in and try to blunt the efforts of the legal staff and the Judiciary Committee. So far, for example, there is no indication that the administration will turn over some 700 pages of documents and 17 tape recordings the committee has requested.

But the Judiciary Committee, after three months of preliminaries, now has its staff recommendations on where to go from here. It's time for the members to decide, and to get moving.

These are still the early steps of the impeachment process. After the Judiciary Committee makes up its mind on what to consider as impeachable grounds, it will take the full House to decide whether to impeach. And it is vital to remember that all impeachment means is that the Senate holds a trial — a trial requiring a two-thirds majority to convict.

It is important to retain a proper perspective. The staff's report is merely a tool for the Judiciary Committee to accept, modify or reject. Congress, not a few staff lawyers, will decide whether impeachment is in order. First, the committee must act.

THE WALL STREET JOURNAL

New York, N.Y., February 25, 1974

The staff of the House Judiciary Committee has reported that an impeachment need not be based on a violation of criminal law. We agree with this conclusion as a point of abstract law, but it is a point without much relevance to the current proceedings.

To judge by both history and constitutional logic, the purpose of the impeachment clause is far broader than enforcing the criminal law against a President. Historically it was a means for the British Parliament to remove ministers appointed by the king. While some of the Founding Fathers argued this was not necessary for a President subject to periodic election, they borrowed the practice because of the danger of affronts that could not wait four years for correction. The most feared scenario seemed to be a President taking bribes from the English king.

Logically, impeachment is a constitutional safety-valve, a method of salvaging the political system itself. A President might have arguable legal grounds for, say, suspending elections in some emergency, but surely such an abuse would be grounds for impeachment if Congress disagreed. On the other hand, no Congress is going to impeach a President for a clear but technical violation of the criminal code. In other words, impeachment turns not necessarily on criminality, but on high political grounds.

As it happens, though, the grounds on which President Nixon conceivably could be impeached are also criminal violations. If he is guilty of a cover-up, he is also guilty of an obstruction of justice. If he is guilty of selling public policy in the milk or ITT cases, he is guilty of bribery. And if he is innocent of the criminal violations, he could scarcely be impeached on these grounds.

The committee staff report wisely observes that nothing much can be decided in the abstract. A good deal of vagueness was inevitable in the report's constitutional discussion. But the unfortunate result is to offer a definition of the impeachment power that provides no limits at all. The report defines "high crimes and misdemeanors" as "undermining the integrity of office," and so on. Another whole report could be written to define "undermining the integrity of office."

Thus the report will be cited as support by those in Congress who wish to impeach the President for, say, the bombing of North Vietnamese troops in Cambodia. Yet surely the President's powers as Commander in Chief allow him to attack belligerents who are fighting American troops in the field. And those troops were kept in the field not only by the decision of the Executive but by decision after decision of the Congress on appropriation after appropriation. Other non-criminal grounds offered by the President's critics are similarly deficient. They express little more than disagreement with the policies of the man the American people have elected.

Now, at some point an impeachment bill based on such vague grounds may provide a political out for Democrats on the Judiciary Committee. Legally unable to prove the cover-up, and politically unable to say they have no grounds for impeachment, they may decide to put forward a bill of particulars they know will lose in the full House. But since the decisive votes are held by moderates who will want more solid grounds, such a bill would signify a committee that is not serious about impeachment.

It is also possible that in the end an impeachment vote will turn on a presidential decision to refuse the committee's subpoenas. This above all should not be decided in the abstract; it will depend on what the subpoenas are for. In such a face-off, the committee will be strong if it is trying to subpoena evidence of a criminal violation and weak if it is trying to mount a fishing expedition to refight the Vietnam issue, the impoundment of funds and every other complaint rejected by the people in the 1972 election.

So despite the correct constitutional theory of the staff report, the Judiciary Committee would be wise to concentrate on the alleged criminal offenses. Yes, impeachment is based not on criminal offenses but on high political grounds. But in this case, if there were no criminal offenses there are no high political grounds.

Arkansas Gazette.

Little Rock, Ark., February 21, 1974

It has made sense from Richard Nixon's viewpoint but it has been something less than complimentary to us in the South to find Mr. Nixon, in his speaking appearances, turning up nowhere else in the country as he pursues his fight to avoid impeachment. Nixon does not appear to feel comfortable and secure anywhere else than in the South, but where he feels *most* comfortable is in a place like Huntsville, Ala., in the Deep Deep South where he joined a great patriotic celebration Monday and went over with the crowd very big indeed, especially with George Wallace there lending his blessing to the occasion.

Nixon is counting on the South—that is, on Deep South Democrats in the House of Representatives—to save him from impeachment if the House Judiciary Committee votes out an impeachment bill. So it is that a Nixon visit to Huntsville, or to Macon, Ga., is part of the clever Neo-Southern Strategy. This first Southern Strategy was designed to get him into the White House and this one is destined to keep him from going *out* of the White House, as it were, on a rail.

Certainly Mr. Nixon was at ease in Huntsville as he was earlier in Macon, Ga., where the politics is symbolized by the mayor, Ronnie Thompson, who is somewhere to the right of the John Birch Society. The next place, in perfect logic, for Mr. Nixon to show up will be Shreveport-Bossier City, L o u i s i a n a, where the citizens recently got up a great gaggle of thank-you-Mr. President petitions. In fact, we *predict* it — that Nixon's next great patriotic celebration will be at Shreveport and that he will go over bigger there than he did at Huntsville.

But no matter: Why is it an affront to the South for Nixon to keep turning up in the South? Simply because it shows that Mr. Nixon believes the Deep South to be the only section of the country where a majority of the people do not have sense enough to know hopeless corruption when they see it, or worse, where a majority of the people do not even care.

We would not want to patronize Shreveport-Bossier City, or Macon, or Huntsville, but if Nixon ever shows up in Little Rock it will be time for all of us to start worrying.

It is likely in any case, that the Nixon political strategists themselves are realizing that Nixon's continuous returning to the Deep South has become conspicuous.

The outing at Huntsville, indeed, was rendered a little more conspicuous even than it was by a coincidence, which was election day in the Republican citadel which is Jerry Ford's own congressional district. There in a stronghold of Republicanism, in a congressional district that hadn't gone Democratic in 63 years and which had been the constituency of the Vice President himself, what happened? Why the Democrat won! And his whole campaign was centered upon removing Richard Nixon from office, by resignation or impeachment.

The way things are evolving, some rethinking in the strategy against impeachment may be in prospect.

THE KNICKERBOCKER NEWS
··· UNION-STAR ···

Albany, N.Y., February 20, 1974

Appearing in one of the few places in the country where he wouldn't run the risk of being heckled right off the platform, President Nixon has told an "Honor America Day" audience in Huntsville, Ala., which is heavily dependent on federal defense contracts, that partisanship and distorted reporting in Washington make it appear that "the nation is sick."

It was, to use one of the President's own expressions, a cheap shot.

As usual, Mr Nixon has played loose with the facts. It is not America that is sick. What is sick is the Nixon administration, a regime so riddled with corruption and lack of leadership that every reputable poll indicates the President has lost the people's confidence.

If Washington is excessively partisan, it is because of the crimes committed by thugs like the "plumbers", organized and directed from the White House.

As for the "distorted reporting" bit, the National News Council, an impartial organization of distinguished citizens, has been trying, without success, to get the White House to provide specifics on the President's charges, in a news conference last Oct 26, of "outrageous, vicious and distorted reporting" on the television networks The council made more than a dozen separate requests for documentation by the White House, which at first promised to deliver the proof, then just stopped responding.

As has been the case so many times, when its bluff is called, the Nixon White House retreats into sulky silence It's evidently easier for this President to wave the flag than to adhere to the principles for which that noble banner stands.

ST. LOUIS POST-DISPATCH
St. Louis, Mo., February 17, 1974

It may well be that President Nixon's refusal to make available certain tapes and documents to Special Watergate Prosecutor Jaworski is the sort of action he had in mind when he vowed recently to "fight like hell" to stay in office. If so, however, it shows how thin Mr. Nixon's defenses have become, for what he is doing now is more in the line of shouting at the enemy and throwing stones than shooting effective bullets.

A certain similarity, to be sure, exists between Mr. Nixon's rejection of Mr. Jaworski's request and the President's refusal to cooperate with Archibald Cox that led to the sacking of the first special prosecutor last October. But a closer look reveals that Mr. Jaworski, unlike his predecessor, is all but immune to Mr. Nixon's counteroffensive. This means that in actuality there is little the President can do now but attempt to confuse the situation in the hope that it may delay the inevitable.

Partly this is due to a change in circumstances. Federal District Judge Sirica already has upheld the special prosecutor's authority to subpena evidence from the President, a ruling Mr. Nixon acceded to rather than appeal to a higher court. Thus should Mr. Jaworski choose to litigate the matter, his chances of obtaining the material would seem excellent. Another federal judge has ruled that the firing of Mr. Cox was illegal, so any arbitary dismissal of Mr. Jaworski might be considered an impeachable offense.

In an attempt to undo the damage caused by the Cox firing, the White House, too, was forced to erect a number of highly visible safeguards to protect Mr. Jaworski. On Oct. 26, for example, Mr. Nixon promised that the new special prosecutor "will have total co-operation from the Executive Branch." A month later, the acting Attorney General, Robert H. Bork, issued regulations prohibiting a change in the prosecutor's jurisdiction without the approval of eight congressional leaders. So here again, Mr. Jaworski is well fortified should he press his claims.

Partly, too, Mr. Jaworski's strong position is due to the careful manner in which he has carried out his mission. With a minimum of publicity, his assistants have gone about building a case against the Watergate principals; indeed, it is possible that indictments may be secured without the refused tapes and documents. When confronted with presidential obstinacy that amounted to a breach of promise, Mr. Jaworski, keeping *his* word, reported the difficulty to the Senate Judiciary Committee.

He thus has in reserve three powerful weapons: taking the President to court over the material, striking an immediate arrangement to share information with the House Judiciary Committee (which is considering the impeachment question) and taking the entire case before the public.

This being the situation, one might ask why Mr. Nixon has embarked on a course which probably will lead to defeat, should Mr. Jaworski contest him, and can only hurt him even more in the realm of public opinion—why, in short, at this late moment he has again asserted that in the criminal investigation of Watergate, he, a suspect, should be the one to determine what is evidence. The courts are scarcely likely to accept this monarchial claim and, more importantly, neither are Congress and the people.

The answer, it appears, lies in the hopelessness of the defense Mr. Nixon has so disastrously stuck to: Evasion, recalcitrance and misrepresentation instead of a forthright effort to get the truth out. He has lost his credibility with the people and at every significant step he has lost in the courts. So all that seems to remain is obstructionism, and with Mr. Jaworski poised to obtain damning indictments even that is unlikely to succeed.

The Des Moines Register

Des Moines, Iowa, February 16, 1974

President Nixon declared in his State of the Union address he believed he had provided "all the material that [the special prosecutor] needs to conclude his investigations and to proceed to prosecute the guilty and to clear the innocent." Special prosecutor Leon Jaworski this week notified the Senate Judiciary Committee it is "now clear that evidence I deem material to our investigation will not be forthcoming" from the White House.

President Nixon is a suspect in the Watergate cover-up and other crimes being investigated by Jaworski's office. The President's status makes it impossible for him to sit in objective judgment on the information Jaworski needs.

The President's claim that he believes he has given Jaworski enough evidence is reminiscent of the President's earlier insistence that he ought to be the sole judge of what evidence should be released to law enforcement authorities. The courts rejected that claim and forced the President to give White House tapes to the grand jury.

The special prosecutor is in the best position to know the evidence he needs to carry out his mandate. The responsibility of the special prosecutor is broad. As Jaworski declared recently in an interview, "The question really is not one of indictments. The issue is that I am charged with making a full investigation with care and thoroughness. Those are two important words — care and thoroughness. They require that all available evidence be obtained and studied."

Jaworski said in the interview that "many documents" and several tapes were being withheld by the President.

The President's refusal to furnish evidence to law enforcement officials conflicts with the oath he took to uphold and faithfully execute the laws. The refusal conflicts also with his oft-repeated promises to cooperate fully with the Watergate investigation.

The special prosecutor can — and should — go to court to obtain access to the evidence he needs. Court action would prolong the Watergate ordeal, which the President has said has gone on "long enough." Responsibility for delay would rest with the President, not with Jaworski.

The special prosecutor was handpicked by the President after Jaworski's predecessor, Archibald Cox, was fired, also in a dispute over evidence in the President's possession. The White House claimed that Cox, a Democrat, was uncooperative and intent on harassing a Republican president.

Jaworski is not subject to the same accusation. The difficulty Jaworski is having obtaining needed evidence makes it evident that the real White House objection is to revealing information the President wants to hide.

The House Judiciary Committee is considering the possibility of initiating impeachment proceedings. The President's refusal to give law enforcement officials evidence material to an investigation of criminal wrongdoing provides another strong argument for advocates of impeachment.

The Dallas Morning News

Dallas, Tex., February 16, 1974

A United Press International dispatch transmitted over the wires at 2:43 p.m., Dallas time, on Nov. 1, 1973, declared that the distinguished Houston attorney, Leon Jaworski, had been named special Watergate prosecutor by Acting Atty. Gen. Robert Bork.

Bork at that time promised that Jaworski would have the full cooperation of the executive branch, that there would be "no restrictions on his freedom" to investigate the Nixon administration's involvement in the scandal.

On Friday of this week, 107 days later, Mr. Jaworski—whose professional competence and integrity have never been questioned—revealed that evidence "material to our investigations" had been denied him by the White House.

Neither Mr. Nixon nor anyone else in his administration has any business going back on this promise.

Mr. Jaworski is fair, objective and probably knows more law than all the White House legal eagles combined.

To instruct him to go to the bottom of this mess, then deny him evidence he says is vital, is to make him a prosecutor who can't prosecute.

The News has defended certain conditions of presidential confidentiality and executive privilege.

But it regrets the breaking of an executive promise to Mr. Jaworski in a matter which the public wants resolved—and resolved promptly so that presidential emphasis can be shifted to other national issues which will be with us longer than the odors of Watergate.

Mr. Jaworski can be trusted not to reveal anything that would endanger the welfare of his country. He is that kind of man.

THE DAILY OKLAHOMAN

Oklahoma City, Okla., February 16, 1974

NOW that the question of what White House records will be made available to Special Prosecutor Leon Jaworski has again aroused the ire of the Washington press corps and a number of congressional staff members, it would be well if all of them could sit down and consider briefly what the man was appointed by President Nixon to do.

He was not named by the President to secure the impeachment of the President. He is, in effect, the President's own housecleaner, the lawyer who is to ferret out and prosecute to the full extent of the law wrongdoers within the administration or the President's 1972 campaign staff. He is also obliged by the wording of the statute enacted by Congress, in creating his office, to seek out any wrongdoers in the McGovern campaign of that same period. So far, there has been little if anything said about any such violations, but it appears that some of the same contributors who have been pilloried for their contributions to the Nixon campaign covered all bases and made at least as large donations to McGovern. In particular, the dairy industry gave more to the Democratic campaign than to the Nixon committees.

Jaworski came to Washington with no illusions, if we are to believe all his instant biographies. He inherited a legal staff of young and eager lawyers at least a number of whom joined the Archibald Cox staff in order to become participants in a historical first—the removal of a President of the United States from his office. But that is not the place for

them to do that job, if it is to be done.

The U.S. Constitution provides for the impeachment of a President by the House of Representatives and trial of any such impeachment by the Senate. It says clearly that removal from office by such a process does not exempt a convicted President from later trial in the courts for his crimes. The sense of the section is for crimes committed while serving as President.

Clearly the place to go about all investigation and possible processing of a removal from office is in the House of Representatives, which already delegated responsibility to its Judiciary Committee. There is no legal basis for the probing of the Ervin Committee of the Senate into possible grounds for any impeachment, since the Senate would sit as a trial court if one were preferred by the House.

In an impeachment, the prosecutor of the case when it comes before the Senate is known as the Manager for the House of Representatives. He is not a Special Prosecutor, and he is obviously not appointed by the President or the Attorney General.

It would violate some basic legal concepts for the executive to name his own man to make the legal case for his own removal from office. Yet Washington newsmen and others who ought to know better berate Jaworski if he does not seem intent on that job. The prosecution of law violators within the President's official family is Jaworski's job. Impeachment is another and totally distinct matter.

THE ARIZONA REPUBLIC

Phoenix, Ariz., February 18, 1974

The Watergate scandals move back into the federal courts this week, with trials scheduled to open against two Nixon aides.

Former cabinet members John Mitchell and Maurice Stans are being accused of perjury and conspiracy in connection with Robert L. Vesco's contribution of $200,000 to the Committee to Re-elect the President. Both have long since been convicted in the public mind, but belated efforts are now being made to restrict pre-trial publicity.

Last week, for instance, Judge Gerhard Gesell (who made the key ruling against the Ervin Committee's efforts to subpoena 500 White House tapes and documents) criticized Watergate prosecutor Leon Jaworski for injecting prejudicial publicity into a television talk show.

Appearing on ABC's Issues and Answers Feb. 3, Jaworski said, "We have found no basis for a charge of perjury" against John Dean, President Nixon's former counsel. Since the charges against Dwight L. Chapin, President Nixon's former appointments secretary, depend on testimony by Dean, it was obvious that Jaworski's statement was prejudicial in the extreme.

Judge Gesell rebuked Jaworski mildly, saying "It seems to me your good sense would keep you off talk shows," but he didn't stop the court action in Chapin's case. The judge also rebuked present Nixon aides for making comments about the credibility of witnesses, which was a justifiable effort to insist on the impartiality of the courts.

There have been other efforts to cut down on damaging publicity as the new Watergate cases get closer to trial. Last week the prosecutor's office announced it would hold up the filing of any new indictments until a jury had been picked in the Vesco case.

And President Nixon has refused to give the prosecutor any more evidence. There were two good reasons for this action. First, the White House doesn't want any of these documents leaked to the press at a time when they could influence the trials.

Second, according to the President's attorney, James D. St. Clair, the White House already has given prosecutor Jaworski 17 recordings of actual presidential conversations, and more than 700 documents dealing with Watergate affairs.

What more does Mr. Jaworski want? To close down the White House and send all the papers and documents in the executive branch's files to the attorney general's office?

Perhaps he doesn't want to go that far, but he has asked for 40 additional tapes that have not been reviewed by anyone and hence are clearly the object of a fishing expedition.

It would be a pleasant change, with the court cases under way and the rule of court being enforced, if the prosecutor, the press, the Congress and everyone else muted their voices and allowed a modicum of judicial calm to replace the circus atmosphere that has marred so much of the effort to really fix the guilt for Watergate.

Chicago Tribune

Chicago, Ill., February 20, 1974

Vice President Ford's 5th Congressional District seat in Michigan has been won by a Democrat for the first time in 64 years. Richard Vander Veen, who had failed in previous attempts to win public office, handily defeated Robert Vander Laan, Republican leader of the state Senate and a man who had never lost an election.

Because Mr. Vander Veen made Watergate the major issue in the campaign, and because the district is so predominantly Republican, commentators have been quick to seize upon the election as a harbinger of doom for the G. O. P. in November. If it happens in Grand Rapids, it will happen everywhere, etc., etc.

We don't think so. The mood of the voters was more anti-Nixon than anti-Republican. Many Dutch reform church Republicans in the area are highly indignant over Watergate. Mr. Vander Veen artfully made the contest into a referendum on Watergate, and even took out newspaper ads in which he promised to do his utmost to dislodge Mr. Nixon and turn the Presidency over to Mr. Ford, a political folk hero in the district. To this extent a Democrat won by clinging to the coattails of a Republican Vice President—hardly proof of impending doom for Republicans. Mr. Vander Laan, who took a softer line on Mr. Nixon, found it too soft for his own good.

Another fact overlooked in the postmortems is that the Republicans could have won the race if they had just been able to get their own regular voters to the polls. Leaders of both parties agreed that the Democrats could take the seat if 30 per cent of the Republican voters stayed home.

That is just what happened. Only about 40 per cent of the registered voters in the district went to the polls, and the turnout was heaviest in the Democratic areas of urban Grand Rapids. In overwhelmingly Republican Ionia County, only 7,000 of the 17,000 voters voted—and the Democrat, Mr. Vander Veen, won by 100 votes. Thruout the district, his total was almost unchanged from the Democratic vote in 1970, when Mr. Ford won handily. But Mr. Vander Laan, the Republican, polled barely half as many votes this year as Mr. Ford did in 1970.

In short, there still seems to be no significant migration of Republicans into the Democratic fold. The Republican Party should be able to hold its own, despite Watergate, the energy crisis, and the country's economic jitters, if it comes up with the good candidates and the positive attitudes and programs that will overcome the apathy and disappointment of Republicans and bring them out to vote.

THE SAGINAW NEWS

Saginaw, Mich., February 20, 1974

It's a bit early to predict election catastrophe for Republicans in November's congressional elections, yet the outcome of the special election in Michigan's 5th District centering around Grand Rapids clearly foreshadows trouble for the party.

The picking and sorting will go on for awhile because the contest for Vice President Ford's old seat in the House had drawn national attention. But the victory of Democrat Richard F. VanderVeen over highly favored Robert VanderLaan in a rock-ribbed Republican stronghold guarantees the kind of national attention a troubled GOP hardly needs.

If Pennsylvania's 12th District special election two weeks ago was too close to provide an accurate gauge, Grand Rapids is not. And the indication there is that the GOP is in the throes of down-clout with independent voters.

Certainly it lends credence to the harpings of Sen. Barry Goldwater who has been saying all along that the Republican party was going to pay a heavy price at the polls this year because of Watergate and the President's failure to clear himself of its ugly shadows. That factor played a big role in turning bookish attorney VanderVeen, a perennial loser in politics, into a smashing upset winner in territory held for 64 years by Republicans.

Suffice to say the jolt that has come out of Grand Rapids will produce tremors for GOP tacticians here in the 8th District where another special election is scheduled in April to fill former Congressman Jim Harvey's seat in the House. They can afford to be worried by the 5th District shocker and Democrats will take heart that this is the year they can crack a 44-year run of Republican incumbents. This one, too, will be watched closely for its national implications.

The postmortems, however, can be short and sweet.

This was a vote of disenchantment with Mr. Nixon to be sure. It was also a vote of disenchantment over the administration's failures in the economic sector. The message from Grand Rapids and surrounding area is that Watergate, soaring inflation and the energy crisis are a bad mix.

There is as much as anything abroad a yearning for new faces in Washington — an infusion, hopefully, of new ideas for dealing with the nation's domestic problems. It is a message sent special delivery to the White House and one that it ought to read most carefully. It has lost vast numbers of independent voters who have soured on credibility in the nation's capital.

THE MIAMI NEWS

Miami, Fla., February 20, 1974

The election of a Democrat in Gerald Ford's Michigan Republican district should convince political analysts that Watergate will be the principal issue of this year's Congressional elections, whether party officials agree or not.

A week ago, in the first of six such elections over a two-month period, a Pennsylvania contest went to the Democrats by less than 200 votes. Analysts thought Watergate was a relatively unimportant issue in that election, even though the Republicans had held the seat for 24 years. Certainly, said a pundit, the narrow victory didn't prove President Nixon's scandals are an intolerable burden.

But Watergate was the only topic for the Democrat who had never won an election in Michigan — until Monday, that is — Richard VanderVeen. The chairman of the Republican committee in the Wolverine State said, "There is a message; people don't like what is going on in Washington."

This is the pitfall for the Democrats who hope to sweep the fall Congressional election: A strong anti-Washington feeling prevails in much of the nation. As one Democrat put it, "All Watergate does is confirm the worst suspicions people have against government and politics."

Indeed, the Democrats must look beyond Watergate. The human needs, the faltering economy, the lack of leadership on "people" issues, are major factors which require attention. Candidates will have to come to grips with these issues if the anti-government attitudes are to be changed.

THE TENNESSEAN

Nashville, Tenn., February 20, 1974

THE LOSS of Vice President Gerald Ford's old House seat in Michigan to a Democrat Tuesday may increase the pressure on the Republican side of Congress for President Nixon's removal from office.

★ ★ ★

Many Republicans have long been convinced of the damaging effects which Watergate has had on their party. Many strong GOP members of Congress have decided to retire this year rather than face the voters with the Nixon disgrace hanging over their heads. These include such party stalwarts as Sen. Norris Cotton of New Hampshire who said Wednesday, after the Michigan election, that his decision not to run this years was "irrevocable."

Many other Republicans have clung to the fantasy that the party has not been hurt by Watergate. This is Mr. Nixon's personal problem, they say, and has no bearing on the fortunes of the party. Those in this group have generally played down the prospect of impeachment or Mr. Nixon's resignation.

Some of them may change their minds after the GOP debacle in Michigan's Fifth District Tuesday, when the Democratic candidate for Mr. Ford's old district—Mr. Richard VauderVeen — defeated the Republican candidate — Mr. Robert VanderLaan—by a substantial majority.

The congressional seat, in the conservative Grand Rapids area, had been in Republican hands for the last 61 years. A Democrat had not won the seat since 1910, and usually the elections have been no contest in favor of the GOP candidate. Voter registration in the district is about 3-2 Republican.

The losing Republican candidate was a popular and previously successful politician who was heavily favored to win. He was on the right side of the issues which are important to the district's conservative Dutch-American constituency. The only thing he had going against him, it seems, was Watergate and President Nixon.

The winning Democrat was a won an election and was unable even to win the mayor's race in his East Grand Rapids hometown in 1971. But in the congressional race he found a winning issue—what he termed the "moral bankruptcy" of the Nixon administration—and he didn't let the electorate forget it.

There is no other way to interpret the results except as an angry repudiation of President Nixon and a rebuke to the GOP for the quality of its leadership.

When a congressional seat that has been considered "safe" for the Republicans for more than 60 years is suddenly turned over to a weak Democrat, it cannot help bringing qualms of fear to Republicans in other parts of the nation—such as Tennessee—where congressional seats and governorships can never be considered safe for either party.

President Nixon may go on brushing off the unanswered questions about Watergate, unexplained gaps in pertinent White House tapes, the irregularities in his personal income tax returns, the public expenditure on his private estates, the milk fund, the ITT deal and numerous other controversies involving questions of the President's moral character. And some Republican office holders may continue to stick their heads in the sand and pretend that none of this affects their chances of re-election.

★ ★ ★

But the myth that the Republican Party has not been severely damaged by five years of Nixonism has been smashed, and the GOP could be facing one of the most disastrous off-year election defeats in its history if Mr. Nixon is still in the White House in November.

GRAND JURY INDICTS 7; PRESENTS REPORT ON NIXON

Seven former White House aides were indicted by a Watergate grand jury March 1 in the courtroom of Chief U.S. District Court Judge John J. Sirica. Those indicted were John D. Ehrlichman, H. R. Haldeman, John N. Mitchell, Charles W. Colson, Gordon C. Strachan, Robert C. Mardian and Kenneth W. Parkinson. Charges against the seven included conspiracy, obstruction of justice, false declarations and perjury. The overall conspiracy charge involving all seven defendants detailed the complex scenario in which the defendants—with other persons "known and unknown"—arranged "hush money" payoffs for those first charged in the Watergate burglary and wiretapping, offered executive clemency, destroyed documents and lied to various investigative bodies—all of which formed the basis for the other charges in the indictment. The grand jury also delivered a sealed "report and recommendation" to Sirica reportedly dealing with President Nixon's relation to the Watergate coverup. Although the grand jury's recommendation was not formally made public, the jury had, by all indications, suggested that the evidence be sent to the House Judiciary Committee. According to prosecution sources, any grand jury action toward indicting Nixon had been squelched by special prosecutor Leon Jaworski, who had advised the jurors that no such action could be taken against a President in office.

Speculation on President Nixon's possible complicity in the Watergate coverup was increased as a result of a key perjury charge in the indictment against Haldeman concerning his testimony before the Senate Watergate Committee about a March 21, 1973 meeting with John W. Dean 3rd and the President. Haldeman had testified that Dean had told Nixon that a million dollars might be needed to keep Watergate conspirator E. Howard Hunt Jr. quiet. According to Haldeman, Nixon responded, "There is no problem" in raising the money, "but it would be wrong." The grand jury charged that Haldeman's statements about Nixon's "it would be wrong" comment, as Haldeman "then and there knew well, were false." Nixon, however, had backed up Haldeman's testimony as "accurate" in an Aug. 22, 1973 news conference.

In a news conference March 6, Nixon was asked if he could provide proof that he had said "it would be wrong" to provide hush payments. The President affirmed his denial of authorizing clemency or hush payments, but said "...when individuals read the entire transcript of the [March ᴊ 21st meeting or hear the entire tape where we discussed ... these options, they may reach different interpretations. But I know what I meant, and I know, also, what I did." In his news conference, the President seemed to contradict another statement he had made earlier. Nixon said that "for the first time on March 21 he [Dean] told me that payments had been made to the defendants for

the purpose of keeping them quiet, not simply for their defense." In an Aug. 15, 1973 statement, Nixon had said, "I was told then [at the March 21 meeting] that funds had been raised for payments for the defendants.... But I was only told that the money had been used for attorneys' fees and family support, not that it had been paid to procure silence from the recipients...."

Commentators also noted that federal law required that anyone knowing of the commission of a felony—such as obstruction of justice—report it to proper authorities. The President's special counsel, James D. St. Clair, said, however, that the issue of misprision did not "make much sense as a legal question," since Nixon is the chief law enforcement officer...."

Among other Watergate-related developments during early March:

■ St. Clair announced in Judge Sirica's court March 1 that the President would surrender to the House Judiciary Committee all tapes and documents that had already been sent to the special Watergate prosecutor. In addition, St. Clair said, Nixon would be willing to respond to the panel's questions and would, if necessary, grant an interview to some members of the panel. In a letter to Committee Chairman Peter W. Rodino (D, N.J.) March 7 St. Clair said the President would not comply with requests for further materials, as the 700 documents turned over to the Watergate grand jury were "more than sufficient to afford the Judiciary Committee with the entire Watergate story."

■ Thomas A. Luken (D) won a special election in Ohio's 1st Congressional District March 5, defeating Willis D. Gradison Jr. (R) by a vote of 55,171–51,057. The Democrats had won the seat only three other times in this century (1912, 1936, 1964). It marked the Republican Party's third consecutive loss in special Congressional elections. In another special election March 5, the Republican Party retained its hold on the 13th Congressional district of California where State Sen. Robert J. Lagomarsino won a majority of votes (53%) against seven Democratic opponents.

■ A second Watergate grand jury March 7 indicted six men in connection with the September 1971 burglary of the office of Dr. Lewis J. Fielding, the Los Angeles psychiatrist who had treated Pentagon Papers defendant Daniel Ellsberg. Those charged with conspiracy were: Ehrlichman, Colson, G. Gordon Liddy, Bernard L. Barker, Eugenio R. Martinez and Felipe DeDiego. On March 13, Los Angeles Superior Court Judge Gordon Ringer dropped state charges of burglary and conspiracy in the Fielding break-in against Ehrlichman, Liddy and David R. Young Jr. Dismissal of the charges followed a meeting between Jaworski and the Los Angeles County District Attorney. Young was granted immunity from prosecution in return for his testimony.

The Charlotte Observer

Charlotte, N.C., March 10, 1974

President Nixon changes his own version of Watergate almost every time he makes a statement on the matter. His latest major contradiction is perhaps the most damaging of all. The White House said over the weekend that it will explain the latest account; but whatever the explanation, the President has now publicly admitted an important violation of law.

His admission has to do with the March 21, 1973, White House meeting at which there was discussion of paying large sums to those arrested in the Watergate break-in. Did the President approve payoffs to silence the witnesses, thereby engaging in a criminal conspiracy of the greatest magnitude? A large amount of money was sent on its way to Watergate burglars immediately after the meeting. Was that not with Mr. Nixon's approval?

On Aug. 15, 1973, Mr. Nixon said this: "I was told then (at the March 21 meeting) that funds had been raised for payments to the defendants ... But I was only told that the money had been used for attorneys' fees and family support, not that it had been paid to procure silence from the recipients."

But a week ago, on March 6, Mr. Nixon said this: " . . . . And for the first time on March 21 he (John Dean) told me that payments had been made to the defendants for the purpose of keeping them quiet, not simply for their defense."

Whether or not the President engaged in a conspiracy to silence witnesses, then, he acknowledges that he knew of one. That clearly seems to be an admission, too, that he then violated the law by not reporting such a conspiracy.

The White House promises an explanation, but what explanation can there be?

The Watergate grand jury has indicated that it believes Mr. Nixon lied about that meeting. Mr. Nixon had maintained that he discussed raising hush money but had said at the March 21 meeting that "it would be wrong." In indicting H.R. Haldeman, the grand jury charged that Mr. Haldeman lied when he testified that Mr. Nixon said of raising the money: "But it would be wrong." In short, the grand jury had concluded that Mr. Haldeman and Mr. Nixon were lying about this.

The grand jury also indicated, by not indicting John Dean, that it believed his testimony directly contradicting the Nixon-Haldeman version.

This episode thus emerges as the heaviest part of the burden that Mr. Nixon c a r r i e s in facing impeachment charges. Even the most partisan Nixon supporters are likely to balk at saying it was acceptable for the President to engage in a conspiracy to obstruct justice.

Many blunt words have been used in the Watergate affair. But none of them have been sharper than the words used by the ordinary citizens who, as members of the grand jury, studied the matter for almost two years. They concluded there was sufficient evidence to charge those they indicted with a conspiracy which, they said, has existed at the highest levels of the Nixon Administration "up to and including" the present. The grand jurors accused the alleged conspirators in these stark words, which hang over the President as well as those indicted:

"(They) unlawfully, w i l f u l l y and knowingly did combine, conspire, confederate and agree together and with each other, to commit offenses against the U n i t e d States . . . (They) would corruptly influence, obstruct and impede . . . the due administration of justice . . . and by deceit, craft, trickery and dishonest means defraud the United States."

The News American

Baltimore, Md., March 8, 1974

PRESIDENT NIXON'S decision to turn over to the House Judiciary Committee the tapes and documents already provided to the special Watergate prosecutor should go far toward restoring the presidential stature which has been increasingly diminished in the public mind by his handling of the Watergate scandal.

The decision itself amounts to little more than a consent to meeting the impeachment group half way. But the announcement — and the staging of that announcement at his televised press conference this week — demonstrated the manipulative skill and adroitness which the President has always possessed in large measure.

Millions of Americans who viewed the conference on their home sets certainly must have been convinced that their President is now doing his best — considering the dignity of his office — to co-operate with the very organization which is studying a proposal to evict him from the White House.

The timing of the President's announcement could not have been better programmed. The essence of his decision was released by his counsel and then, at the unexpectedly scheduled conference, the President calmly expanded on that decision in such a manner as to leave the public impression that he was amenable to almost any procedure the committee devised.

As could be anticipated, the House committee already is insisting that the Nixon offer does not go far enough. However, it would appear that the President at least has created an area of understanding, a platform so to speak, where he and the committee can work out their procedural difficulties. Meanwhile, by calling his second televised news conference in nine days, the President clearly has regained much ground he lost during the long periods of his post-Watergate silence.

THE ROANOKE TIMES

Roanoke, Va., March 8, 1974

President Nixon is moving toward a posture of greater openness and accessibility — not only to the press and the people through more frequent news conferences and public appearances, but also to the House committee that will investigate the possibility of impeaching him.

His first steps toward cooperation with that committee are welcome; they indicate he will avoid for now the kind of hard-line attitude that would immediately lead to a series of ditch-by-hedgerow procedural battles and to interminable delay. He will ultimately have to do more than he has promised, however. For on examination, what he is willing to give the committee is not nearly so much as it may seem.

Obviously, Mr. Nixon could not deny to the committee what the White House already has yielded (reluctantly, and with many delays) to the Watergate prosecution. And it matters little whether his lawyers resisted transmission of the grand jury report that allegedly alluded to the President; with access to the same evidence, the House committee can draw its own conclusions.

Mr. Nixon would like everyone to believe that this much evidence is all any reasonable person could want; at his news conference Wednesday night he made it seem that Prosecutor Leon Jaworski found the 19 tapes and "over 700 documents" sufficient for his purposes. In fact, the prosecutor deemed it enough only to bring indictments; for the more stringent task of seeking convictions, Mr. Jaworski has said he needs more evidence from the White House, something that has been resisted.

The President has agreed to answer written interrogatories from the House committee and even to sit down privately with its leaders — not the entire group — and answer questions under oath. That sounds like a large concession. But the Watergate grand jury rejected a similar compromise offer from the White House; its members wanted Mr. Nixon in person before the whole body, apparently feeling that only in this way could the contradictions and inconsistencies in the various Watergate accounts be pursued. And in his news conference, the President hedged when asked if he would submit to cross-examination on his answers.

The plain fact is that Mr. Nixon continues to resist disclosure of the kind that would, as he has put it, "get this story out." He insists that means of disclosure was a key aim of his meetings last March with White House associates, but the results were just the opposite.

And while he has said that during last March he ordered "intensive new inquiries" and findings to be reported directly to him, no one — not John Dean III, former FBI head L. Patrick Gray, former Atty. Gen. Richard Kleindienst, Asst. Atty. Gen. Henry Petersen, or even John Ehrlichman — supported Mr. Nixon's version in his own testimony. When the President declares, "I know what I meant," it is strange that none of his servitors seemed to get the message — as evidenced also by the payment of "hush" money to Howard Hunt even while these White House conferences were going on.

What it boils down to is that some very shady things went on around the White House, apparently carried out by people who were Mr. Nixon's long-time associates and who, one assumes, knew what his wishes were without asking him in every instance. At the very least, the President needs to undergo some very searching questioning about why the men he supervised did not behave with the openness and honesty that their leader so fervently espouses.

St. Petersburg Times
St. Petersburg, Fla., March 8, 1974

Did the President of the United States condone the payment of hush money to the original Watergate defendants?

That's the central question of Mr. Nixon's involvement in the illegal coverup to which the President addressed himself in detail at his press conference this week. He said he should be judged not only by the tapes, which he says are inconclusive, but also by his ACTIONS following that crucial meeting on March 21, 1973, when John Dean told Mr. Nixon of the payoffs.

THAT'S A fair test. Apparently that was the test used by the Watergate grand jury, which after listening to the tapes indicted former White House chief of staff H. R. Haldeman for lying when he said Mr. Nixon said the payoffs were wrong. The President contends his statement applied both to clemency and the payoff. But the facts — and the actions — seem to support the grand jury.

Here are some of the events that occurred AFTER Mr. Nixon was told on March 21 of the payoffs and of burglary leader Howard Hunt's request for $120,000 more:

✔ After the 11:15 a.m. meeting on March 21 between Mr. Nixon, Dean and Haldeman, the grand jury said Haldeman at 12:30 p.m. telephoned former Atty. Gen. John Mitchell. Later that afternoon Mitchell authorized his aide Fred C. LaRue to deliver $75,000 to Hunt's lawyer, William O. Bittman.

✔ After hearing Dean's report on March 21, Mr. Nixon said he "personally" ordered "all those

conducting the investigations to get all the facts and to report them directly to me." But neither FBI director Patrick Gray, Atty. Gen. Richard Kleindienst nor assistant Atty. Gen. Henry Petersen received any such orders. Who did investigate? Nixon aide John Ehrlichman, himself deeply implicated.

✔ On March 22, one day after Mr. Nixon first said he learned of the "serious charges," White House aide John Caulfield told Watergate burglar James McCord that the Administration would provide $100,000 in cash for his bail.

✔ As a result of the "serious charges" he learned March 21, Mr. Nixon said Wednesday night that he called a meeting the next day of Haldeman, Dean, Ehrlichman and Mitchell "so we could find out the best way to get the story out." Yet when Mitchell was asked under oath if there was any discussion of the coverup at this meeting, he answered: "None w h a t s o e v e r." Haldeman testified: "The four of us met in the morning in my office and had some discussion of Dean's report to the President, although not in any detail. Most of the discussion was regarding approaches to dealing with the situation rather than a review of the facts of the situation." If the President wants to be judged by his actions, why didn't he seek to corroborate or refute the "serious charges" at this meeting?

✔ On April 30 when Haldeman and Ehrlichman resigned and by which time Mr. Nixon certainly knew the full story, the President described the aides as "two of the

finest public servants it has been my privilege to know . . ."

THESE events AFTER Mr. Nixon learned of the payoffs certainly tend to confirm the grand jury's view. There are other contradictions in the public record.

In his August 15 statement on Watergate, Mr. Nixon said that on March 21 "I was told that the funds had been raised for payments to the defendants, with the knowledge and approval of persons both on the White House staff and at the Re-election Committee. But I was only told that the money had been used for attorneys' fees and family support, not that it had been paid to procure silence from the recipients."

Yet in his August 22 press conference at San Clemente, Mr. Nixon said: "Basically, what Mr. Dean was concerned about on March 21 was not so much the raising of money for the defendants but the raising of money for the defendants for the purpose of keeping them still. In other words, so-called hush money."

This crime of obstructing justice had not been mentioned in either the President's May 2 broadcast on Watergate or his May 23 statement on Watergate. It came only after John Dean's testimony to the Senate committee on June 25.

Since he learned of the crime on March 21, Mr. Nixon said this week, his policy has been one of full disclosure. Yet he still refused to release the tapes of that crucial March 21 meeting so that the American people can judge for themselves.

THE DAILY OKLAHOMAN
Oklahoma City, Okla., March 7, 1974

WITHIN the short interval of two weeks, two incredibly clumsy errors have been revealed in the official handling of the evidence on which the case against President Nixon has been constructed in Washington. The effect is to disclose a carefully-knotted noose that is unraveling as fast as it can be tightened.

Columnist William Safire, formerly known as one of the "house liberals" at the White House but now "the house conservative" at The New York Times, uncovered the latest blunder. This one was a lawyers' error which led to the federal grand jury basing an indictment on a supposed presidential direct quote — in the Haldeman testimony read to the Senate committee—that in truth was a stenographer's error.

The young lawyers on the staff of Special Prosecutor Leon Jaworski are a bright and eager group. They know that whatever comes out of their efforts, they are part of a historic action, which could clean up

corruption in high places in our federal government or could end with the removal from office of the President himself. They are also endowed with considerable self-esteem — not a rare thing in young professionals, nor necessarily a bad thing. But the combination of these factors with the inevitable intoxication that publicity causes has produced sloppiness in the work they were called to Washington to do.

It has already been noted that the special prosecutor is not supposed to become involved in impeachment matters. His task is to clean up any corruption and venality he may find in the administration, on behalf of the President, and that is why he is a presidential appointee. Impeachment, under the constitution, can only be undertaken by the House of Representatives. That is what the Rodino Committee is doing—investigating the charges and countercharges, to learn if there are grounds for the House bringing an impeachment.

The Jaworski lawyers were thus charged with giving evidence to the grand jury investigating those in the administration, other than the President, who may have committed crimes. And the key item on which H. R. Halderman was indicted was apparently a transcript of his testimony to the Ervin Committee, in which he is charged with lying when he said, under oath, "the President said 'there is no problem in raising a million dollars, we can do that, but it would be wrong.'"

The grand jury underlined the last five words, on the assumption that this was a direct quotation from the President. In fact, the transcript was from a recording of Halderman reading a written statement. Reference to the written statement shows that he did not put the statement in quotes, but was merely stating the sense of what he understood the President to have said.

The error was made by the law-

yers, who had months and money and staff to prepare their case. It led to an indictment for perjury. But it is not the first bit of legal clumsiness to surface in this matter. Earlier, a skeptic at the Dektor Co. questioned the "experts" appointed by Judge John Sirica about their examination of the White House tape recorder that had erased 18½ minutes of a presidential conversation.

Those court-appointed savants had been told to see if a malfunction of the machine could have produced the erasure. They found the machine was defective, repaired it, and then tested it and another machine of another make. Then they solemnly reported that the machine would not malfunction and that the erasure had to be deliberate. Later tests proved that the defect did, in fact, produce such erasures.

This kind of "legal" work would be fatal to a case in a local court. It is fast discrediting the case against the President. And it reflects no credit on those responsible for such errors.

EVEN THE President's normal sympathizers on the House Judiciary Committee seem ready now to subpoena what the committee needs if Mr. Nixon and his defense team persist in their shopworn and transparent effort to urge a quick decision while withholding vital evidence.

This readiness is encouraging A subpoena would signal House intent to examine all the relevant facts carefully, even though this means delaying the impeachment process, rather than being goaded by the White House into precipitate action that could backfire.

The White House technique, which has been a feature of the "Watergate" case from the start, is marked by pious presidential announcements of intent to cooperate in getting at "all the facts," coupled with a silent war of obstruction, confusion and delay.

At the moment, for example, it appears that Mr. Nixon's chief defense lawyer, James D. St. Clair, hopes the House panel will make such an issue of the withholding of evidence that an impeachment decision will hinge on that issue alone. But this is narrow: a removal-from-office trial in the Senate, where a two-thirds vote is required, would run considerable risk of defeat. And this could foreclose returning to other, broader charges when and if they came to light.

The committee's options

As conservative columnist Garry Wills has written, the House committee now has three choices: It could (1) drop efforts to get evidence from the White House files, and go ahead with facts already uncovered in the Ervin, Cox or Jaworski inquiries. It could (2) dramatize the uncooperativeness of lawyer St. Clair and his client, Mr. Nixon, by pursuing impeachment on the charge that locked files constitute an obstruction of justice. Or (3) it could appeal to the President, first, and then to the courts, for the tapes, papers, names and dates it needs to complete its survey of all the relevant violations of law alleged against the President. It is a sad fact that this last procedure would substantially delay giving Mr. Nixon the fair hearing to which he is entitled under the Constitution. Moreover, the hard-core defenders of the President could wield the sharp stick throughout, challenging the House to "get off the President's back" and "put Watergate behind us."

However, the House would gain two advantages through a decision to follow the subpoena-courts route. One would be the probability of success in obtaining what it requests. Judge Sirica's favorable ruling in regard to the subpoenas issued by special prosecutor Cox, before he was fired, and a recent ruling by Federal Judge Gesell in the case of the Ervin Committee subpoenas suggest this.

Secondly, recourse to the courts would expose more forcefully than ever before the ambiguity of White House promises of cooperation. These began to come to the surface on March 15, 1973, when the Ervin panel was told: "Mr. Dean will furnish information when any of it is requested, provided it is pertinent to the investigation." A month later, Mr. Nixon said, "Members of the White House staff . . . will testify under oath and they will answer fully all proper questions." In July, in a letter to Senator Ervin: "My staff is under instructions to co-operate fully with yours in furnishing information pertinent to your inquiry."

The theme of full, candid disclosure has been part of the White House armory of confusion since June 22, 1972, when the President asserted that Ron Ziegler and John Mitchell "have responded to questions on this in great detail." That was followed by the August 1972 press conference, in which the President said of Watergate: "What really hurts is if you try to cover it up." On March 24, 1973, he told

The Courier-Journal

Louisville, Ky., March 14, 1974

Senator Scott, "I have nothing to hide." Last fall, it was, "I am not a crook." And through it all has come the recurrent demand that Congress or the courts explore all the facts, make a quick decision, and let the nation go on from there.

"All the facts" were promised Prosecutor Cox before his disillusionment. According to H. R. Haldeman, "all the facts" was the President's mandate when he named John Dean to lead the White House investigation of Watergate. And, last fall, such facts were part of the President's personal promise "to see that any doubts as to the integrity of the man who occupies the highest office of the land—to remove those doubts where they exist." Yet they still exist.

As everybody knows by now, Mr. Nixon could bring this about in an instant by dropping all the legal improvisations and giving the investigators what they need to make a decision based on all the relevant facts — with the relevance to be determined not by the man who is being investigated, but by the people constitutionally instructed to explore the evidence and then decide on it. Since Mr. Nixon won't bring this about voluntarily, the House Judiciary Committee should take care of the matter itself.

THE WALL STREET JOURNAL.

New York, N.Y., March 14, 1974

At the moment the Watergate affair seems headed for an impeachment vote based not on the guilt or innocence of Richard Nixon but on the prerogatives of Congress versus the President. This means further national strife without settling anything, and while we can understand why the White House might want to force the battle into this mold we have trouble understanding why the House Judiciary Committee seems even more eager to do so.

We suspect that the White House may want to force an early impeachment vote, centering on the constitutional doctrine of Executive privilege rather than on a third-rate burglary. Its history of non-disclosure certainly gives reason to suspect that its offers of cooperation with the impeachment committee may be a facade. But even when that has been said, the White House has been doing a skillful job of structuring the issue so that it can contend it has been reasonable and the committee unreasonable.

The White House has provided the committee with some of the requested evidence on matters pertaining to the President's complicity in the Watergate cover-up. It has met demands for some information on seemingly extraneous matters, including, it says, decisions of the Environmental Protection Agency and Cost of Living Council. But it has now demurred on a further request. It has not completely closed the door on further material, but has said that a line has to be drawn somewhere, that it would like to know what charges are being investigated, and that it would like requests to come from the committee rather than its staff.

This is on its face an entirely reasonable request. If one believes that such a thing as Executive privilege exists, as we do, then one has to believe that even in an impeachment inquiry there are some limits on what Congress can demand. If it can get anything about any dispute by using an impeachment label, then no shred of privilege can continue. So at a minimum, it seems to us, the demands should be linked to some specific charge. This is what the White House says it wants, and the way to test its motives is meet reasonable demands and see what further obstructions may emerge.

Chairman Rodino seems to have some sense of this, and has delayed the actual use of subpoenas. But many members of the committee have reacted by huffing about prerogatives. We are particularly upset that the committee thinks its prerogatives would be invaded if it asked for court enforcement of eventual subpoenas. There must be some balance between the legitimate demands of the committee and the legitimate defense of Executive privilege, and only the courts are in position to strike it.

Instead of going to the courts, the committee seems prepared to enforce its subpoena by impeaching the President for refusing it. This would not be a trivial ground for impeachment if the committee could make the case that the President was withholding evidence it needed to decide his complicity in an important offense, like the Watergate cover-up. But it certainly would be trivial if the committee had showed no restraint, pressing demand after demand until at last one was refused. Indeed, if the evidence the committee has suggests the President is in fact guilty of the cover-up, why in the world does it need evidence about the environment and Cost of Living Council? A fishing expedition, it seems to us, would be the action of a committee that discovered it really didn't have any grounds for impeachment.

If the committee is really serious about impeachment, it should take the time to explore the evidence it now has and pick out the few most serious and promising charges to follow. It should seek to build a public case, for example by release of tape-recordings it wants to follow up, and go back to the White House with specific and narrowly framed demands. In short, it should try to smoke the White House out of its posture of reasonableness.

We would hope that the White House would not be smoked out, but would comply with such a request. In fact, we think the White House would be well advised to itself make public some of the evidence, in particular the March 21 tape already so widely discussed. For the soft spot in its current posture concerns not narrow questions of legality and equity, on which it would probably win, but the broader question of repeated withholding of evidence persuading the public that it has much to hide.

At this late date, a civilized way of handling the Watergate dispute probably is too much to hope for. But the last thing we need is another round in the historic but ultimately petty battle about the prerogatives of the branches of government. What we do need is an airing of the evidence on whether the President was implicated in the cover-up.

The Times-Picayune
New Orleans., La., March 14, 1974

The tired rhetoric of confrontation is being trotted out yet again to describe President Nixon's opposition to giving the House Judiciary (or Impeachment) Committee any more information than he has already given special prosecutor Leon Jaworski. But legislative-executive confrontation is hardly new to this issue, and it is time someone called a halt to the preparatory phase and a go to the action phase.

Although Mr. Jaworski has complained he was not given everything he needed for his purposes — has any case-maker ever been satisfied that

he had all or even enough evidence? — he has been able to give a federal grand jury enough to get indictments of a handful of breathtakingly high-level presidential aides, plus a sealed envelope that clearly holds the grand jury's judgment on presidential involvement.

Such grand jury indictments are the equivalent, in a different judicial procedure, of impeachment by the House of Representatives. Mr. Jaworski has yet to get his indictees convicted, of course, but the outcome of a jury trial is not always directly related to the evidence or arguments

of only one side.

The House should therefore have enough with what is already available to decide on its own true or no true bill — especially since, regardless of the outcome of the argument over what specifically constitutes an impeachable offense, a Senate decision to convict or not convict will clearly be made on far more than the physical evidence

The committee, in our view, should stop wrangling over more documents and tapes and get on with its deliberations and decision.

The Salt Lake Tribune
Salt Lake City, Utah, March 8, 1974

President Nixon belatedly moved a step closer to reasonable cooperation with the House Judiciary Committee impeachment inquiry. The change of heart is welcome news. But the President still did not go all the way and until he does so the lingering suspicion of his complicity in Watergate crimes will continue to undercut such conciliatory acts.

Mr. Nixon said he would turn over to the Judiciary Committee all documents and tapes furnished the Watergate grand jury. He said he would answer written questions from the committee and if the answers were not satisfactory would submit to limited questioning at the White House by ranking members of the committee.

So far, so good. But the President drew the line there. He reiterated that he would not provide masses of additional White House material for the committee to "paw through in a fishing expedition."

While the elements of partisan politics and curiosity cannot be eliminated from any such inquiry, there is as yet no evidence that the Judiciary Committee intends to "paw through" irrelevant executive department documents or indulge in a "fishing expedition."

The documents and tapes the committee wants are essentially the same documents that Mr. Nixon refuses to give Special Watergate Prosecutor Leon Jaworski. Mr. Jaworski spelled out what he wants and why he wants it. But in a letter to the Senate Judiciary Committee the other day he said the White House was refusing to honor the request.

If the Judiciary Committee was seeking carte blanche access to White House communications we would say the President was perfectly correct in resisting the attempt. But all it wants are certain additional tapes and documents which the special prosecutor also says are necessary to complete his investigation.

Ever since Watergate first broke, Mr. Nixon has persisted in a "if you want me come and get me" strategy while at the same time proclaiming complete innocence of any wrongdoing. That kind of tactic might be expected and accepted in an ordinary judicial proceeding involving ordinary citizens. But in a case where the vital integrity of the government in general and the presidency in particular is the crucial issue, the adversary strategy has backfired many times.

Each of Mr. Nixon's previous attempts to vindicate himself stopped short of candor. They raised as many doubts as they quieted. They left the impression that he was not being completely frank. A growing number of people concluded that the President was not telling all because to do so would mean implicating himself in one or more of the Watergate crimes.

The latest offer is in that mold. It extends presidential cooperation but it holds back just enough to nurture the widely held doubts. And by forcing the Judiciary Committee and the special prosecutor to fight for the additional documents and tapes the President once again renders hollow his often proclaimed desire for a speedy resolution of the whole Watergate affair.

Los Angeles Times
Los Angeles, Calif., March 14, 1974

President Nixon is not giving much encouragement to those who are still trying to suspend judgment on whether legitimate grounds may exist for his impeachment. He insists that he is innocent of all wrongdoing. But from the very beginning of the Watergate scandal he has fought to limit the scope of every inquiry into his own possible involvement.

Mr. Nixon did not honor his pledge of full cooperation with Archibald Cox, the first special prosecutor. To the contrary, he got rid of Cox for going to the courts to secure evidence that the White House did not want him to have.

Mr. Nixon did not honor his pledge of full cooperation with Leon Jaworski, the second special prosecutor. To the contrary, he did not fulfill requests, dating back to last August, for 40 White House tapes that Jaworski said were essential to "a complete and thorough investigation."

Mr. Nixon did not cooperate fully with the Senate Watergate Committee. To the contrary, its members had to fight every step of the way for evidence material to their public hearings, and are still pressing, unsuccessfully, for more Administration tapes and documents in order to complete their final report to Congress.

And now, it appears, the President may pursue the same contentious tactics in his relations with the House Judiciary Committee. Mr. Nixon's pledge last week to answer under oath written interrogatories from the committee and to give sworn testimony to the two ranking members of the committee at the White House was a hopeful sign that he would be far more forthcoming than he has been in the past.

But the statements of three White House officials on Tuesday indicate a stiffening of the President's position toward the committee, and threaten a major confrontation between Mr. Nixon and Congress.

Press Secretary Ronald Ziegler said it would be constitutionally irresponsible" for the President to release additional materials to the Judiciary Committee until it first defines an impeachable offense. "The fact of an impeachment inquiry doesn't give Congress the right to back up a truck and haul off executive files," he said.

Of course it doesn't. And the White House would be correct in refusing every committee request for information that has no conceivable relevance to its investigation.

But the Judiciary Committee, at the present time, is asking for many of the same tapes that the special prosecutor's office has been trying to secure from the White House since last August. And their relevance is not in doubt. The tapes contain pres-

idential conversations with five aides over a number of days before and after March 21, 1973—the date on which Mr. Nixon insists that he was first told by John W. Dean III that there was an ongoing White House conspiracy to cover up the Watergate burglary and to buy the silence of the defendants.

Not only was Ziegler's statement abrasive—a number of committee members took it as a deliberate provocation—but its logic was questionable. How can the committee specifically define the charges it may bring against the President if he refuses to turn over evidence on which it must base that determination? Clearly, the committee is the best judge of what evidence is or is not relevant and what charges that evidence may or may not sustain.

Ziegler's comment drew an immediate and predictable response from both Republicans and Democrats on the committee, who saw it as an overt challenge to their authority. And the battle-lines were drawn even more sharply later Tuesday when presidential counselor Bryce Harlow and White House counsel J. Fred Buzhardt also were critical of the committee's procedures.

Harlow was right, however, in pointing out that the committee's legal staff has not always told the members what evidence was being sought from the President. All such requests obviously should have committee approval if the investigators are to avoid straying into areas where they have no right to be.

Mr. Nixon already has paid a terrible cost in public confidence for his past reluctance to cooperate more fully with Watergate investigators. But now, as in the past, there is opportunity for compromise.

Vice President Ford believes that compromise is still possible if the committee is reasonable in its requests and if both parties are willing to deal in "practicalities rather than fine legal points."

We hope Ford is right. And we also hope the President will take the Vice President's advice that he should be as "cooperative as possible."

No one knows the House better than Ford. And he has told Mr. Nixon straight out that defiance of the committee, which could lead to a subpoena for presidential documents, would "add fuel to the fire" of the impeachment threat.

There is no doubt that it would, just as there is no doubt that continued wrangling with those who have authority to investigate Watergate adds no credence at all to Mr. Nixon's claim that he has nothing to conceal.

AKRON BEACON JOURNAL
Akron, Ohio, March 7, 1974

THE KNIGHT Newspapers survey of Tuesday's special congressional election in Cincinnati shows more trouble ahead for Republicans in November. And that means more trouble for President Nixon.

The Knight survey, conducted by Philip Meyer of our Washington bureau, showed that "voter disapproval of President Nixon was the strongest single factor in the election of Democrat Thomas A. Luken" in the traditionally Republican district.

Disapproval of Mr. Nixon was not the only factor, of course, but it was enough to swing the election and cost the Republicans a seat in Congress.

The result in Cincinnati will not make Republican congressmen suddenly turn on the President. They didn't do that after the GOP lost a seat in Pennsylvania, and they didn't do it after losing Vice President Ford's old seat in Michigan.

But the three elections, and particularly the Michigan and Ohio elections, will have a cumulative effect on the loyalty of Republican congressmen toward a President of their own party.

They may not turn tail and run from the White House, but they will back off and be awfully careful about supporting Mr. Nixon.

The Michigan district had not been represented by a Democrat in 64 years. Cincinnati's First District had gone for Democrats only in years of Republican disasters — the party split of 1912, the Roosevelt landslide of 1936 and the Johnson landslide of 1964.

If history means anything, and it usually does, 1974 will be a disastrous year for Republicans.

And just as some Republicans salvaged themselves in 1964 by opposing Barry Goldwater, others will be inclined to save their own skins this year by opposing Richard Nixon.

With impeachment proceedings under way, Mr. Nixon needs all the support in Congress he can muster. But he's losing it fast. He may want to lean on congressional Republicans and discover none willing to stand within leaning distance from him.

And who can blame them? William Keating took the Cincinnati district with more than 70 percent of the vote in the 1972 election; Bill Gradison, a reasonably attractive Republican candidate, received only about 48 percent Tuesday. Most congressmen, Republican and Democratic, won by considerably less than Keating did in 1972.

That doesn't mean all incumbent Republicans are going to lose in November, but those who aren't a little bit scared don't understand the situation.

As Mr. Nixon's liability to the Republican Party becomes clearer, the likelihood increases that he will be treated by Republicans as an enemy of the party. Between now and November, the President may find himself standing — or falling — alone.

The Detroit News
Detroit, Mich, March 7, 1974

The election of a Democrat to Congress from an Ohio district which has long been a Republican stronghold illustrates again the shattering impact of Watergate on the Republican Party.

Democrats, all making an issue of the Watergate scandals, have now won three out of four recent special elections in congressional districts where Republican candidates normally get elected with ease.

Taken by itself, the recent Pennsylvania election seemed but a very thin straw in the wind. However, the election of a Democrat to the Michigan congressional seat vacated by Vice-President Gerald Ford came as stunning evidence of disenchantment with the GOP. The election of Democrat Thomas A. Luken over Republican Willis D. Gradison Jr. in Ohio's 1st District confirms the evidence and establishes an obvious downward trend of Republican fortunes in 1974.

No doubt other issues such as economic dislocation and the fuel shortage exerted some influence on the Ohio contest. However, the Democratic candidate, who asked the voters to send "a signal to Washington" about political scandal, turned the election largely into a test of public reaction to Watergate.

Ironically, Republican Gradison also criticized President Nixon's mishandling of Watergate. Voters refused, however, to distinguish between the Nixon administration and the Republican candidate. They expressed their displeasure with the President by rejecting a candidate of the President's party. This attitude is perhaps unfair but it is nevertheless a hard political fact with which Republican candidates must grapple in the congressional elections of 1974.

The Republican Party finds a spark of encouragement, of course, in the victory of a Republican, Robert J. Lagomarsino, in Tuesday's special election in California's 13th District. Still, that district is another Republican stronghold and a Republican would be expected to win there, so the victory cannot be regarded as a gain, as can the victories by the Democrats elsewhere.

Incidentally, Democratic forces may have outsmarted themselves in the California election by entering seven Democratic candidates, perhaps intending to fragment the vote so that nobody could get the majority needed to avoid a runoff. They succeeded in fragmenting a part of the vote but leaving enough of it intact for the Republican to win outright.

Superficially, the results of Tuesday's contests in Ohio and California might be called a standoff or a split decision in the test of voter reaction to Watergate. In truth, those results constituted a net loss to the Republicans, who must expect more of the same unless the Nixon administration miraculously manages to regain the confidence of a skeptical and angry public.

The Dispatch
Columbus, Ohio, March 7, 1974

TWO SPECIAL congressional elections this week proved at least one absolute—special elections are very deceptive barometers.

In districts in both Ohio and California, voters were dinned with contentions their election could be considered a referendum on the Watergate issue.

SO WHAT happens? In Ohio, a Democrat was elected to succeed a Republican as congressional representative. And in California, a Republican was tapped for the Congress seat.

In the final analysis, the two elections reflected a reality—a congressional district is a local, not a national, political subdivision and its electorate expects its representative to represent the district rather than a national mood or movement.

THE OHIO contest was in Cincinnati and technically the district involved was considered a Republican stronghold for only three other Democrats have won this century. But was it really all that Republican? Or would it be more proper to label it as a "Taft district" since three generations of that family have had their roots in that general area?

Too, it must be considered that the two candidates, Democrat Thomas Luken and Republican Willis Gradison Jr., were no newcomers to the political arena, both having been elected to the Queen City's governing council.

OF COURSE, the Democrat pointed to the Watergate issue. That is to be expected for Watergate is pure politics. Yet the Republican candidate also criticized White House handling of the scandal.

Mr. Luken's margin of victory was decisive but not overwhelming, an indication Cincinnati voters were making their selections more between men than between issues.

AS FOR THE California poll, it fails to tell any special story. A lone Republican, Robert Lagomarsino, a veteran state senator, was pitted against seven Democrat opponents and emerged as the winner.

Here, too, the Republican candidate virtually ignored the Watergate issue. Apparently the electorate had other matters on its mind.

Public opinion polls continue to show two things. First, the electorate wants problems solved, especially in the fields of inflation and energy shortages.

SECOND, the electorate is disappointed with the representation and leadership it is getting in Washington.

What congressional officeholders and officeseekers alike should be seeing in these special elections is that the electorate is concerned about its federal government and can be expected to seek out the representation it deems best.

NATIONAL issue concerns aside, congressional elections remain primarily parochial decisions. Reading national emotional issues into them is hazardous.

PUBLIC FINANCING OF ELECTIONS REJECTED BY PRESIDENT NIXON

In a message to Congress and a radio address to the nation March 8, President Nixon proposed a number of campaign reforms. They included: public identification of every campaign donor and recipient; a $15,000 limit on individual contributions to presidential candidates; a $3,000 limit on contributions to House and Senate campaigns; a limit on candidates of one fund-raising committee and a single bank account; a limit on contributions in cash of $50; a restriction on "in kind" contributions—such as pay for campaign workers, printing supplies and use of corporate aircraft—to be accounted for within the $3,000 or $15,000 ceilings; and a ban on political loans, stock donations and foreign contributions.

Nixon also proposed shorter presidential campaigns, recommending against holding any state primary before May 1 or national party convention before September. He again suggested Congress consider a single presidential term of six years and a four-year term for House members, and recommended repeal of the "equal time" provision requiring allotment of rebuttal time for all candidates, including minor party candidates.

Nixon said he had asked the Justice Department to draft legislation to give a candidate a right to sue for libel against slanderous attacks. Noting there was "a constitutional problem" involved, such as possible conflict with the right to free speech, Nixon objected to interpretation of court decisions as "being virtually a license to lie" in this area.

The President also objected to any ceiling on campaign expenditures by candidates. This would be "unrealistic" and "unfair," in many cases, he said, and raised "constitutional questions." In stating his opposition to federal funding of campaigns, Nixon said, "One thing we don't need in this country is to add politicians to the federal dole." It was "a raid on the public treasury" and "taxation without representation," he said, since taxpayers would be sponsoring candidates they opposed.

A bill to provide public financing of federal election campaigns was approved by the Senate Rules Committee Feb. 6. The financing, from the voluntary checkoff on income tax returns, would total about $24 million for major-party presidential candidates, $90,000 for House candidates and $175,000 for Senate candidates. Minor party candidates would be funded in proportion to their vote.

Des Moines Tribune
Des Moines, Iowa, March 8, 1974

President Nixon has once again voiced objections to public financing of election campaigns. His veto threats stymied legislative moves for campaign spending reforms in the past. Now he has prepared a measure to curtail the amounts of individual contributions as a substitute for public financing.

In his press conference Wednesday night, Nixon likened public financing plans to "taxation without representation." He said that paying for election campaigns from the treasury forces a taxpayer "to support a candidate or a party to whom he was opposed."

His comment distorts the mechanics as well as the purpose of public financing. Most plans permit taxpayers to contribute to designated political parties through income tax checkoffs, as both U. S. and Iowa tax forms do, in addition to limited individual contributions. Most plans also provide means for Congress to allocate general revenue funds to carry on political campaigns to acquaint the voters with the candidates and the issues.

Public financing plans are an attempt to neutralize the influence of wealth on elections. Money merely becomes a tool for campaigning, not a measure of support for a party or its candidates. Theoretically, in the democratic system, the voters show their support for candidates with ballots, not dollars.

Nixon said, "It is a healthy thing for people to contribute to campaigns and particularly in the smaller contribution areas." He mentioned that 800,000 persons contributed amounts of $100 or less to his 1972 campaign while about 700,000 did likewise for Democrat George McGovern.

Combined, that is 1.5 million. Hardly a remarkable showing, considering that 76.2 million voted for either Nixon or McGovern in 1972. Nixon's remarks duck the main problem which is the huge gifts made by special interests.

Public financing offers a way to broaden voter participation in the electoral process, making it more representative of the American people. In view of the scandals in his own election financing in 1972, you would think President Nixon would be the first to argue for public financing. He is in a weak position to defend the traditional system of private financing.

New York Post
New York, N.Y., March 9, 1974

In the course of another incongruous exercise in political piety, President Nixon yesterday called for an array of new political campaign laws. He apparently assumed that most Americans have totally forgotten about innumerable gross violations of the old ones.

The President's midday radio speech, in which the word "Watergate" was nowhere pronounced, included pretentious recommendations for "reform" and flagrant misrepresentation of several plans designed to prevent abuse and assure wider citizen participation in politics.

Significantly, no one could conclude from listening to the Presidential admonitions on "broader public disclosure" of campaign financing that there is a law in force to promote such reporting and that it was systematically flouted by the Nixon Administration.

The law was signed by the President early in February, 1972. Designated the Federal Election Campaign Act of 1971, it provided—in the President's approving words—for "full reporting of both the sources and use of campaign funds." There then ensued the Republican Presidential reelection campaign marked by wholesale violations of the new law.

"Full reporting?" The operative policy was no reporting—of illegal corporate contributions, laundering of funds, government by cash on delivery. The General Accounting Office cited repeated abuses and transgressions. Yet when faced with demands for names of contributors, the Republican response was that this was invasion of privacy.

It might be charitably argued that a chastened President now contritely seeks true reform. No doubt the White House hoped to create that impression. But on basic issues his program is sadly deficient.

Does the President endorse public financing of campaigns, as prescribed in reform legislation pending in Congress? In fact he harshly decries it, depicting it falsely as a "raid on the Treasury" and an exercise in compulsion. Those distortions will gravely damage the campaign to encourage Americans to voluntarily authorize the use of some tax revenues by checking a box on their tax returns. The President also rejects overall limits on campaign spending. He denigrates mail registration of new voters.

Nixon's call for Congressional overthrow of the Supreme Court's liberalized libel ruling would have been more impressive if accompanied by some hint of personal repentance about his own uses of demagogy. But it has clearer overtones of private vindictiveness against what he has so often depicted as the hostile media. In part the law as it now stands provides remedies against reckless, knowing disregard for truth—a standard the White House might strengthen by some faithful observance.

We do not suggest there are no valid items in the President's package. But its negative and self-serving aspects predominate. Viewed as a whole, the document has major elements of political fraud.

San Jose Mercury

San Jose, Calif., March 11, 1974

President Nixon's proposals for election campaign reform, submitted to Congress last week, are a mixed bag at best, reflecting the incredible complexity of the problem.

Not much will come of the Nixon plan, probably, because the Democratically controlled Congress is in no mood to listen respectfully to the Republican President. Nonetheless, the President's view of the problem is worth examining because it does provide a fairly comprehensive overview of the issue.

In general, it can be said that President Nixon:

1. Favors full disclosure of campaign contributions rather than a ceiling on such donations.

2. Favors shorter campaigns as a means to reduce the cost of campaigning and to ease the physical pressure on candidates.

3. Opposes public financing of campaigns because of the "compulsory" nature of tax-money contributions.

4. Wants legislation which will make it easier for public figures to sue for slander and libel.

5. Wants an end to the "equal time" provision of the Federal Communications Act, thus making more free radio and television time available to candidates.

Everything considered, it is impossible to take more than a medium-dim view of the President's concept of election "reform."

Full disclosure, as a considerable body of experience in California has shown, is no panacea. Disclosure frequently comes too late and in indigestibly massive l u m p s; the voter has no way of evaluating the information he gets, and the influence of special interest groups remains unchecked.

The President's objection to public financing of election campaigns is actually wide of the mark, in that it is possible to write legislation which will permit the taxpayer to designate the party he wishes to benefit from his contribution. Further, public financing is the only viable alternative to abuses attaching inherently to the private contribution system—full disclosure or no.

The President is on sound ground, however, when he calls for shorter campaign periods. There is no good reason, as he observed, for turning a campaign into an endurance contest.

Two months should, indeed, be sufficient for the voters to become thoroughly conversant with the views and personalities of presidential candidates.

Finally, it appears the President has let his own difficulties with the press cloud his good judgment in the matter of libel and slander laws. Making it easier for candidates to sue would not, as the President hopes, "open up" the e l e c t o r a l process by encouraging more good but essentially timid individuals to run for office.

The controlling Supreme Court ruling holds that malice must be shown if a public figure is to collect a libel judgment; mere error committed in the heat of a campaign or under the time pressure of a deadline is not sufficient to justify legal redress.

This is a sound position, one that protects the candidate as much as the press and one that serves the larger public interest, in that it guarantees the most open kind of free-swinging campaigns.

The American people would be the big loser if this "malice-only" rule were to be abandoned by the Supreme Court or, as President Nixon has suggested, if it were to be legislated away by Congress.

The Boston Globe

Boston, Mass., March 9, 1974

We try hard not to be cynical, not to lose a measure of compassion for a President who has undergone nearly a year of uninterrupted attacks on his integrity and that of his closest associates. Few public officials have been asked to withstand as much.

But he makes it difficult.

Yesterday he unveiled his program for campaign reform. It was an opportunity to acknowledge what the country was thinking: if it were not for the foolish, unethical, unnecessary, and sometimes illegal misdeeds by him and his friends, campaign reform would not be a current subject of national debate. But instead of candor and a long view toward making the political process more responsive, he provided an insensitive, largely warmed-over litany of old ideas.

Granted, having the President lecture about campaign corruption is like listening to Noah on floods. But it is difficult to fathom how he could treat this issue as business as usual, attacking the Democrats and the media as if they and not he himself had been the subject of the disclosures of the past year.

So, the man who refused to campaign in 1972 says that there can be no spending limits on campaigns in the future because people want to see the candidate in their hometown and that takes a lot of money.

The man who financed his campaign in substantial part by large donations from special interests and illegally defied the will of the people's representatives in Congress by impounding appropriated funds calls public campaign financing a "raid on the Treasury" and "taxation without representation."

The man who provided government airplanes to bring key senators back to Washington to filibuster against campaign reform last fall now accuses Congress of inaction on the issue.

The man whose campaigns have been characterized by the use of disruptive techniques and questionable charges now suggests in a passing comment that organized and intentional disruption of opponents' campaigns should be stopped.

And in a final and shocking new chapter in his vendetta against the media, the President has proposed rolling back the most recent US Supreme Court decision establishing standards for libel of a public official.

Under the Sullivan v. New York Times doctrine, a public official must prove not only that the words were untrue, but that they were printed knowingly and with malicious intent. This is a difficult standard to meet. But since that case, we know of no man or woman who declined to seek public office because the recourse against a newspaper was thus limited. And Watergate itself is evidence of the value to this country of a press which is given wide latitude in holding politicians accountable for their deeds. The President will not restore his credibility by blaming the country's malaise on those who brought the misdeeds to light rather than those who committed them.

The President's opposition to public financing is of long standing. He worked to thwart the income tax check-off and to defeat modest public financing legislation in the past.

The saddest part of all is that what has been revealed in the past few months has not changed his view. While the storm continues to swirl around his head, the best he can do is offer a few tidbits of reform which will provide little assurance that the era of political Watergate is behind us.

St. Louis Globe-Democrat

St. Louis, Mo., March 9, 1974

"Clean" is as nice and wholesome a word as you'll find in the English language, except when applied to politics. Then it takes on a nasty tone of cynicism. In most minds the words "clean" and "elections" unquestionably are considered as antonyms.

Must it be so?

President Nixon did not cast himself as Sir Galahad in proposing election reforms to the Congress. With his White House inner circle under indictment for various abuses in the 1972 election campaign, the President certainly is an expert on things going wrong.

Yet Mr. Nixon need not apologize to anyone for having beaten George S. McGovern. The President did not steal an election that saw him carry 49 states with a popular margin of 17,409,550 votes.

In assessing the President's recommendations Friday, White House counselor Bryce Harlow readily admitted that their "relevance to Watergate problems is self-evident."

Harlow's appraisal is as undeniable as it is candid, but dirty politics did not begin with Watergate. In truth, Americans are more offended by the stupidity of Watergate than by any possible criminality.

☆ ☆ ☆

Whatever may come of Watergate, the President is positively right in opposing federal financing of election campaigns through tax dollars.

He is correct in calling such a system "taxation without representation." That's an abuse this nation revolted against in its foundation nearly 200 years ago.

Addressing the people, Mr. Nixon said, "You work too hard for your money to have it work for candidates or campaigns you don't know about or don't care about, or even oppose. One thing we don't need in this country is to add politicians to the federal dole."

Amen to that.

Predictably, Sen. Edward M. Kennedy reacted vehemently. He said the President's message is "no more than a thinly veiled attempt by the President to obstruct or even kill the most effective response Congress has yet made to Watergate."

Kennedy would like to see the federal coffers opened to him, and those like him, while denying private citizens the right to support candidates as they choose.

It is clear that the Nixon proposals will be worked over severely in Congress.

☆ ☆ ☆

While the President is correct in calling for careful accounting of contributions, his suggestion of a $15,000 limitation on gifts from individuals for presidential candidates is unrealistically low. People of wealth should have the option of making substantial contributions. Requiring all money for a candidate to pass through one committee and one bank also is not practical.

The President's recommendation that labor and business political action committees be prohibited from giving directly to candidates, but rather through political parties, with amounts earmarked for individuals, would appear to make accounting more questionable than it is now. A candidate could plead he never received the funds intended for him.

To insure clean elections, the American people must involve themselves in the two-party system to a greater degree.

Individuals must take the time, trouble and expense to back candidates who are worthy of support. The government cannot guarantee clean elections. It can only attempt to penalize those who break the laws.

Clean elections will be assured when candidates and campaign workers agree that it is no disgrace to lose, but it is dishonorable to win by foul means.

HOUSTON CHRONICLE

Houston, Tex., March 10, 1974

President Nixon is setting an exactly correct course in his proposals on campaign financing.

He takes a strong stand against public financing of campaigns and declares:

"I conclude that the single most important action to reform campaign financing should be broader public disclosure."

The President's proposals would, if enacted, open the books on election campaigns and put heavy penalties on disruptive, coercive and fraudulent campaign activities.

The Chronicle has long called for campaign reforms similar to those outlined by the President. We believe public financing of political campaigns to be unwise in principle, unworkable in practice and inherently dangerous to the electoral process. We believe solutions can be found that will preserve the present two-party system and keep our elections out from under the control that federal financing would inevitably exert.

Briefly, under the President's plan, no individual could contribute more than $3000 to any Senate or House candidate or more than $15,000 to any presidential candidate. Those limits would apply separately in primaries, runoffs and general elections. No cash contributions over $50, no donations from foreigners and no donations of assets such as stocks would be allowed. Federal laws would be enacted to prohibit disruptive and willfully misleading activities, coercive activities or fraudulent election day practices.

In addition, the President proposes that presidential campaigns be shortened by holding no state presidential primary or state nominating convention before May 1 of an election year. This we support.

We have some reservations about delaying the presidential national nominating conventions as late as September. There should be adequate time for the candidates to bring out the issues and for the public to get a good reading on the character and capabilities of those seeking the presidency. Perhaps the first week of September would leave enough time, but later would be cutting the presidential campaign too short. It would be best to trim the time from the primary campaigns, a move which would also reduce spending.

Any legislation concerning electoral reform must be carefully examined. There is a natural tendency on the part of those in office to tilt factors in favor of the incumbent. There is a danger that in seeking reform we may distort our present form of government and lessen its responsiveness to the citizenry.

We believe the President has set forth a proper approach to curing our campaign ills.

DAILY NEWS

New York, N.Y., March 10, 1974

Both Congress and President Richard M. Nixon see eye to eye on the need for election reform, and agree that the crux of the problem is a drastic overhaul of campaign financing practices.

From that point, their approaches diverge sharply.

On Capitol Hill, sentiment leans heavily toward almost complete elimination of private contributions to office-seekers in favor of funding from the public till.

Mr. Nixon opposes that approach because it forces taxpayers to underwrite the expenses of some candidates whose views and policies they oppose. He favors keeping the system of voluntary donations, with strict limits on individual gifts and full disclosure of givers' identities.

John Williams

We think the President is right on both counts. His objection to taking money from citizens indiscriminately for candidates is well taken. Another, and perhaps even greater drawback, to the scheme was raised in a recent Reader's Digest article by former Delaware Sen. John Williams (R). Williams wrote:

"Federal financing would make political parties unresponsive to the people. Guaranteed millions of dollars from the public treasury, a party could pursue extremist or outworn aims year after year simply because it would not have to go to the people for financial support."

Williams speaks from a vantage point above the political fray. Moreover, the reputation he made as Mr. Integrity during his years in Congress is sufficient assurance that his views are not colored by self-serving, ax-grinding motives.

The danger he foresees—of political parties becoming the captives of small cliques of ideologues—should prompt all Americans to think hard, and think twice, about the touted virtues of public campaign financing. Another—

THOUGHT-PROVOKING VIEW

—of the lessons to be learned from the 1972 campaign scandals has been offered by the American Enterprise Institute, one of several private groups asked by the Senate Watergate Committee to analyze data uncovered by the panel.

The AEI report, written by Yale Law Professor Ralph Winter Jr., rejects out of hand the popular notion that the availability of huge political war chests leads to political corruption. Winter argues that excessive government power, not money, is the real problem. He puts it this way:

"The furor over private campaign financing is likely to obscure one of the few clear lessons of Watergate—the lesson that unchecked discretion to bestow or give away economic favors permits governmental officials to wield arbitrary power. Only the imposition of controls on the exercise of that power can solve the underlying evil."

The point the professor is driving at is most aptly illustrated by the celebrated case of the dairymen's donations to Mr. Nixon's campaign.

Whether the President hiked milk price supports to get that contribution is hotly debated. We don't believe there can be any doubt, however, that if the government weren't up to its neck in the business of rigging markets there would have been no multimillion-dollar milk producers' slush fund.

There are scores and even hundreds of other federal programs that touch upon the lives and fortunes of vast segments of society. Persons and groups affected inevitably will vie for preference, using money and whatever other weapons are available to apply political pressure.

Mr. Nixon, the Congress and the American people would do well to ponder the wisdom of Prof. Winter's conclusions. Regardless of how the campaign funding ground rules are changed, the jostling among competing interests for favored treatment will continue as long as the government insists on keeping a meddlesome finger in affairs that concern so many people so deeply.

SEN. BUCKLEY CALLS FOR NIXON'S RESIGNATION

New York's Conservative Sen. James L. Buckley urged President Nixon to resign March 19. In a public statement, Buckley proposed "an extraordinary act of statesmanship," the act of "Richard Nixon's own voluntary resignation." The "trauma" of Watergate had stripped Nixon of the ability to fulfill his mandate, Buckley said, and there was a "spreading cynicism" about the political process and "a perception of corruption that has effectively destroyed the President's ability to speak from a position of moral leadership."

Referring to Nixon's defense that his resignation would weaken the office of the presidency, Buckley said "precisely the opposite is the case." The office had been "irrevocably weakened by a long slow agonizing inch-by-inch process of attrition," and was "in danger of succumbing to the death of a thousand cuts," he said. "The only way to save it is for the current President to resign, leaving the office free to defend itself with a new incumbent." Resignation was the only way to resolve the crisis, Buckley said, impeachment could not. A Senate trial would be "a Roman circus" and either verdict—to convict or not to convict— would leave an "embittered" segment of the electorate.

There were these other developments in the Watergate affair during the second half of March:

■ President Nixon took his case to the public with televised appearances at the Executives Club in Chicago March 15, the Grand Ole Opry in Nashville March 16 and the National Association of Broadcasters in Houston March 19. He stressed his determination not to resign and to resist demands of the House impeachment inquiry for further White House tapes and documents.

■ U.S. District Court Judge John J. Sirica ruled March 18 that a secret grand jury report and compilation of evidence dealing with President Nixon's role in the Watergate case should be released to the House Judiciary Committee for its impeachment investigation. The grand jury had submitted the material to Sirica March 1 with its indictment of seven former White House and campaign aides in connection with the Watergate cover-up. The U.S. Court of Appeals upheld the decision March 21. Sirica emphasized that the report drew no "accusatory conclusions" and was "not a substitute for indictments." The briefcase of material went to the committee automatically March 26 after attorneys for H. R. Haldeman and Gordon C. Strachan, the two Watergate defendants trying to block release of the evidence, had declined to appeal to the Supreme Court to overturn lower court decisions directing the material to be given to the House panel.

■ A party-line split over the role of special presidential counsel James D. St. Clair developed in the House Judiciary Committee during the panel's meetings March 20–21. In letters to the committee, made public March 20, St. Clair said that in order for him to represent President Nixon adequately, it was "imperative" that he be allowed to participate in pre-hearing staff proceedings, be permitted to "cross-examine witnesses, suggest witnesses to be called and introduce relevant and material evidence for the committee's consideration."

In separate closed caucuses, the panel's Republican minority voted to support the request, and the Democrats voted to oppose it. But in the March 21 session some Democrats hinted at a possible compromise. Jerome R. Waldie (Calif.) suggested that St. Clair might be allowed to participate if the White House cooperated in turning over requested materials.

Chairman Peter W. Rodino (D, N.J.) objected that the request would "pervert constitutional processes" by turning the inquiry into an adversary proceeding, which, Rodino said, would come close to intrusion on the trial prerogatives of the Senate. John M. Doar, the committee's special counsel, agreed with a suggestion that the panel's function was analogous to a grand jury proceeding, under which no cross-examination would be allowed. Doar was joined by Republican counsel Albert E. Jenner Jr. in opposing any form of adversary proceeding.

■ St. Clair disclosed March 21 that special Watergate prosecutor Leon Jaworski had subpoenaed the White House March 15 for additional documents following President Nixon's refusal to release the material voluntarily. After having been granted a delay from the original March 25 response deadline, the White House agreed March 29 to surrender the materials.

■ The White House continued to assert its refusal to release further data requested by the House Judiciary Committee for its presidential impeachment inquiry in a series of statements by presidential press secretary Ronald L. Ziegler.

Ziegler said March 23 "the White House position has not changed" on release of the 42 tapes it said the committee sought and no decision had been made on the issue. The House panel should assimilate the mass of White House material already provided, he said, and "define the scope of the charges" against Nixon before demanding further data.

Ziegler criticized the House committee again March 25. He suggested that its staff "should perhaps work late into the evening" to complete assessment of the White House material on hand. "We feel that they should move within a matter of weeks" to finish that job, he said, whereupon the White House attorneys would "stand ready to hold cooperative discussions" about access to further material.

The New York Times

New York, N.Y., March 20, 1974

In calling on President Nixon to resign as an "extraordinary act of statesmanship and courage," Senator James L. Buckley has aligned himself with a broad spectrum of opinion that places the nation's interest above partisan loyalties. The crux of the Senator's message is that only by stepping down "now" can Mr. Nixon serve "the interests of the Presidency." This appeal is diametrically opposed to the view propounded by Mr. Nixon that he must cling to his office in order to save the Presidency—a view he reiterated last night in rejecting the Buckley plea.

Senator Buckley's announcement, breaking a long silence on the matter, suggests that Mr. Nixon is not succeeding in his frantic efforts to hold the support of his party's conservative wing. There can be little comfort for Nixon loyalists in the New York Republican's assurance that he does not consider the President "legally guilty of any of the hundreds of charges brought against him" by sections of the media. A man of Senator Buckley's strong views would hardly have added his voice to the bipartisan call for the President's resignation if he were not convinced that Mr. Nixon has seriously abused his mandate and his office.

The point at issue is eloquently expressed in Senator Buckley's judgment that "the character of a regime always reflects and expresses the character of its leader" and that the leader's aides and agents "do what they sense and believe he wants them to do."

Rejecting the morally bankrupt refrain of Nixon apologists who justify Watergate by portraying political corruption as the normal state of governmental affairs, Senator Buckley called the Watergate situation "different not only in degree but in kind from any other in American history."

By any valid yardstick of executive responsibility, Mr. Nixon has demeaned the Presidency. Senator Buckley's call for resignation now is clearly an appeal to the conscience of his own party to exercise its special responsibility to press for restoration of the integrity of American government.

New York Post

New York, N.Y., March 20, 1974

According to the conventional political form charts, Sen. James Buckley might have been expected to remain a last-ditch supporter of Richard Nixon while Sen. Jack Javits led the drive for the President's resignation. Instead it was Buckley who startled the country on Tuesday by urging Nixon to step down, and 24 hours later Javits was dissociating himself from the stand of his Senate colleague.

After examining the statements of both men, we are tempted to conclude that Buckley reached the right conclusion for the wrong reasons while Javits offered strong rhetoric for a bad case.

Thus Buckley appeared to be saying that Nixon should quit not because there is already massive evidence of improper conduct unfolded against him but because it is too late for him to regain any posture of leadership.

Javits in turn contended that Nixon's departure without full-scale impeachment proceedings and conviction by the Senate would enable him to leave as "a martyred President, driven out of office by the media and a few loud members of Congress."

It would indeed be a misfortune if Nixon were able to leave in that atmosphere. But Javits has hardly helped to clear the air by, in effect, echoing Buckley's attack on the media rather than spelling out the indictment against Nixon that is a matter of public record and explains the widespread irretrievable loss of public confidence in his leadership.

A majority of Americans no longer believes what Richard Nixon says because he has repeatedly dissembled and engaged in obstruction of justice. He has changed his version of many events and hidden behind "privilege" on others. He has blocked access to vital information —at least until he could no longer find legal loopholes. His meager tax payments and numerous tax dodges, regardless of technical issues subject to litigation, have degraded his office. Is that the portrait of a "martyr" victimized "by the media and a few loud members of Congress"?

Impeachment and conviction might minimize subsequent confusion. But those procedures will require months of national distraction and turmoil. Unlike Buckley, we believe the case against Nixon is overwhelming. That is why, unlike Javits, we believe there is compelling reason for resignation now.

Chicago today American

Chicago, Ill., March 21, 1974

THERE will undoubtedly be many more appeals for President Nixon's resignation, but none is likely to be more eloquent that Sen. James L. Buckley's. We do not happen to share Buckley's view that resignation is the only way out of the "Watergate trauma," or even the best way; Mr. Nixon himself promptly dismissed it. Yet the senator's statement Tuesday, calling on Nixon to resign as "an extraordinary act of statesmanship and courage," was powerful in itself, and circumstances gave it extra force.

Buckley is a Conservative with a capital C, the Senate's only Conservative Party member. He has been an unswerving champion of the President's political views, and was one of the senators on whom Nixon relied heavily for support in impeachment proceedings. And yet Buckley — sorrowfully, but very thoroly — demolished much of the case that Nixon has been building for himself.

Mr. Nixon, for instance, has constantly compared the triviality of the Watergate incident itself — the nitwit attempt by a bunch of amateur burglars to bug Democratic headquarters — with the immense affairs of state that he was engaged in at the time. The point is clear: How can anyone think Watergate is as important as successful negotiations toward peace?

As Buckley observed, this comparison is false. "Watergate" is no longer one specific incident. It has expanded into a "crisis of the regime . . . a disorder, a trauma involving every tissue of the nation," which has destroyed "the President's ability to speak from a position of moral leadership."

Buckley also shot some holes in the Nixon contention that, by refusing to quit, he is defending future Presidents from being hounded out of office just because their popularity ratings are low. The present case, said the senator, shows "a qualitative difference that hinges not on the fact of a low rating, but on the reason for that rating . . . a cumulative loss of faith." There is little point in protecting the office of the President "if at the same time irreparable damage is done to the republic as we have known it."

What bothers us about Buckley's plea is its unconscious snobbery. The senator cannot bear the thought of impeachment proceedings because everyone would be watching them. The Senate chamber would become "a 20th Century Roman Coliseum . . . The most sordid dregs dug up by the Watergate miners would inflame the passions of the domestic audience."

This is a picture of the American public that we do not share: The idea that it would promptly turn a Constitutional procedure into an indecent circus, and that history-making decisions should be reached discreetly among gentlemen rather than letting the masses in on them. Impeachment is certainly an unpleasant prospect, but it seems to us the only way to establish all the facts for all the people.

Moreover — regardless of our feelings or Sen. Buckley's — it seems to be the only way that Mr. Nixon has left open.

St. Louis Globe-Democrat

St. Louis, Mo.
March 21, 1974

Sen. James Buckley's snipe at President Nixon is more damaging to himself than it is to the besieged chief executive. Certainly the New York senator's performance will never be mistaken for a profile in courage.

So far as political impact is concerned, it is no more than a pitty-pat. Buckley, a Conservative-Republican, is a mere curiosity to the people he attracted to his wobbly press conference.

If Buckley had called a conference to expound on conservative principles, he would have received zero attention from the same scribes who flocked to hear him give up on Mr. Nixon.

Buckley conceded he had no evidence of Mr. Nixon's guilt. Then he mused:

"As it now stands, the office of the President is in danger of succumbing to the death of a thousand cuts. The only way to save it is for the current president to resign, leaving the office free to defend itself with a new incumbent."

Bully for Buckley! The world can consider itself fortunate that he is a mini-spokesman for minority opinion.

One wonders how much thought the senator put into his anguished observation. There are shaving commercials that seem more to the point and much more profound.

Buckley cannot be taken seriously.

If Bebe Rebozo calls on the President to resign, that will be worth noting.

OKLAHOMA CITY TIMES
Oklahoma City, Okla., March 21, 1974

THE CALL by Sen. James L. Buckley, a conservative, for President Nixon's resignation should not be shocking. Nixon has gotten flak from both ends of the political spectrum, conservative and liberal.

The President's firm response to Buckley before the broadcasters at Houston—reaffirming his determination to stay in office—should be heartening to his supporters in the broad expanse at the middle of the spectrum. It should be reassuring also to responsible leaders around the world.

THE PERPLEXING thing about Buckley's statement was its reference to a Watergate-induced "governmental crisis" threatening irreparable damage to the nation.

What governmental crisis? While Buckley was speaking, the Arab oil embargo was being lifted. The Bonn government was agreeing to offset fully the costs of stationing 200,000 American troops on West German soil. Under an expiring pact, it bore only 80 per cent of the cost.

Through the good offices of the United States the Israeli and Egyptian military forces had been disengaged along the Suez Canal. And at least some progress had been made toward unraveling the complex Israeli-Syrian knot on the Golan Heights.

THESE accomplishments toward peace came while President Nixon supposedly was "swamped in Watergate." Detractors will say they were really the work of Secretary of State Henry Kissinger. But it takes nothing from Kissinger's skilled diplomacy to note he is under the President's direction and carrying out his policies.

Who could have done better? Gerald Ford? George McGovern? Scoop Jackson? Edward Kennedy?

What Nixon has achieved since Watergate came on top of the historic detente worked out with America's arch Communist foes, Russia and mainland China. The one area in which Watergate has hampered Nixon is slowing down domestic programs to reverse the swing to big, centralized government. But that has to be balanced against the other gains.

IT IS SAD to see Buckley, a respected conservative, apparently perceiving an anti-Nixon majority sentiment in his New York constituency, demonstrating more concern for his own political survival than for the welfare of the country. Like others in the Boston-New York-Washington axis, he may be misled by the so-called opinion polls, the validity of which are somewhat suspect anyway.

Nixon's visits to places like Florida, Chicago, Nashville and Houston indicate he still enjoys a broad base of support. And, surely, the people in the hitherlands of America have as much right to see him complete the term for which he was lawfully elected as those on the East Coast have to see him turned out of office.

WINSTON-SALEM JOURNAL
Winston-Salem, N.C., March 21, 1974

On election day, 1970, Conservative Party senatorial candidate Jim Buckley was riding in his limousine through the streets of New York City. The car phone rang, Buckley answered it, and a voice on the other end asked if this was Mr. Buckley. The would-be Senator said yes, and the voice told him to hold on for J. Edgar Hoover. Then Hoover came on the line with a message: Mr. Nixon, said Hoover, just wanted Buckley to know that the President would be pulling for him. Buckley thanked Hoover, put down the phone, and continued his ride toward victory.

All that was a long time ago, at least in terms of how much Watergate has flowed under the bridge. On Tuesday, now-Senator Jim Buckley called reporters together for a press conference in the Senate Caucus Room. "I propose," Buckley said solemnly, "an extraordinary act of statesmanship and courage — an act at once noble and heartbreaking, at once serving the greater interests of the nation, the institution of the presidency, and the stated goals for which (Richard Nixon) so successfully campaigned. That act is Richard Nixon's own voluntary resignation as president of the United States."

Asked about the Buckley bombshell at a press conference in Houston later the same day, President Nixon offered what has become an increasingly ritualized response: No, he would not resign. Yes, he respected the Senator's concern, but a presidential bail-out would be the antithesis of courage and statesmanship. He planned to fight on, even in the face of defections by longtime friends.

And fight on he should — provided, of course, that he is, as he says, innocent of any criminal wrongdoing. For if he is innocent — and that is a presumption seldom made any more — if he is innocent, then all the lost friends and disastrous popularity polls should not sidetrack him from his own vindication. But if, like his

first Vice President, he is merely holding out in the hope that his crookedness will go undiscovered, then the President could do no better than to give up now by invoking some variation of the Agnew Solution.

Yet interestingly enough, Jim Buckley, even as he threw in the towel, would make no comment on the possible guilt or innocence of Mr. Nixon. Buckley is worried about the President's short-term ability to govern, as well as the long-term effects of the Nixon presidency on conservative-to-moderate Republicanism. Both are legitimate concerns, but both also could be as effectively resolved by presidential vindication as by presidential resignation.

As effectively resolved — but not as easily resolved. And that fact is perhaps Senator Buckley's overriding worry: He grimly envisions a televised Senate trial in which "the ruler of the mightiest nation on earth would be starred as the prisoner in the dock." And of course he is right: A Senate trial necessarily would be televised, and necessarily would take on qualities that would make Joe McCarthy's hearings look like amateur night at the zoo.

But if the nation is still to be guided by the Constitution, then even a Christians-to-the-lions spectacle must be accepted as the price of government by law. Mr. Nixon apparently is prepared to endure such a trial, and Senator Buckley, no matter how legitimate his squeamishness, should not attempt to dictate what the President should or should not permit himself to suffer. After all, the President may well be completely innocent, and the Buckley bombshell — indeed all the bombshells from all quarters — may yet blow up in the judges' faces on the last day the President stands in the dock.

Meanwhile, one can only reflect on that election day in 1970, and ponder, with great sadness, the subsequent sea changes that led Jim Buckley to convene a press conference, rather than to return the President's call.

The Salt Lake Tribune
Salt Lake City, Utah, March 21, 1974

President Nixon has said it repeatedly — he will not resign. Latest repetition of this theme came Tuesday night in Houston before the National Association of Broadcasters. His renewed adamancy was in response to conservative Republican Sen. James L. Buckley's proposal of "an extraordinary act of statesmanship" — Mr. Nixon's resignation

The President finds resignation anything but an act of statesmanship. Or as he told the broadcasters and the nation:

"From the standpoint of statesmanship, for a president of the United States, any president, to resign because of charges made against him which he knew were false and because he had fallen in the polls, I think would not be statesmanship; it might be good politics, but it would be bad statesmanship, and it would mean that our system of government would be changed for all presidents and all generations in the future."

With nearly the same frequency that he has stated his refusal to resign, Mr. Nixon has reminded the nation that the only way to

remove a president from office is the constitutionally provided process of impeachment.

That being the case, and in full awareness of the possibility of the "Roman Circus" Sen. Buckley warns of, there is only way to proceed, the way already embarked on by the House Judiciary Committee — impeachment.

Despite Sen. Buckley's fear of the "sordid dregs dug up by the Watergate miners" that "would inflame the passions of the domestic audience and provide the guffaws, prurient curiosity, or amazement of the outside world," impeachment is the sole process by which the President's conduct can be properly and consitutionally assessed. Any public inquiry into the conduct of any public official involves risks to the system, but in the case of Mr. Nixon's possible involvement in the Watergate affair it is a necessary risk.

Watergate and its attendant incidents have drastically denigrated Mr. Nixon's effectiveness. Or as Sen. Buckley argues, the "perception of corruption . . . has effectively

destroyed the President's ability to speak from a position of moral leadership."

The impeachment process is the only consitutionally provided way in which the President can be afforded the "fair trial" so many of his defenders claim he has been denied. And in what amounts to at least partial agreement with Mr. Nixon's defenders, he is entitled to a proper and legally instituted examination of his official conduct — impeachment by the House and if subsequent events so order, trial and conviction by the U.S. Senate.

But most importantly, and particularly so in consideration of Mr. Nixon's unyielding refusal to resign, the only way the matter of the President's guilt or innocence will ever be resolved is by full employment of the impeachment process. Failure to impeach and try Mr. Nixon will always leave unsettled the plethora of doubts surrounding Watergate and its related scandals.

The Virginian-Pilot

Norfolk, Va., March 21, 1974

Senator James L. Buckley's statement urging Mr. Nixon to resign for the good of the Nation is a body blow that increases the likelihood that the President will be knocked out of the White House.

The odds on that are uncertain. Mr. Nixon was quick to respond to the Buckley statement, saying for the umpteenth time that he does not intend to quit. Before the broadcasters in Houston the President said that it "takes courage to stand and fight for what you believe is right, and that's what I intend to do."

But Mr. Nixon's political position — and impeachment is a political question ultimately — is significantly weakened by Mr. Buckley's defection.

For it breaches the conservative solidarity that anchors the President's last line of resistance. Even if the House of Representatives votes a bill of impeachment, the White House has been confident that two-thirds of the Senate will not vote to convict the President. But if the conservatives don't stick together, where will the White House find the necessary 34 votes?

Mr. Buckley's conservative credentials are impeccable. As he said in his statement, "I am a lifelong Republican who has worked actively for Richard Nixon." He is also a Buckley, intimately linked to the conservative Establishment through his brother, the columnist, and the network of National Review thinkers and writers. All of which means that Mr. Buckley cannot be counterattacked personally, as the White House has responded to critics like Representative Wilbur Mills, the Arkansas Democrat.

And with Mr. Buckley leading the way, it will be easier for other conservatives to desert the President. That may happen.

For while other conservative spokesmen, such as Arizona's Barry Goldwater and North Carolina's Jesse Helms, have rallied to the President's standard, saying they do not think he ought to resign, they are also careful to hedge their support.

What the conservatives on Capitol Hill are now saying is that Mr. Nixon shouldn't resign since he hasn't been found guilty of any criminal offense. But they are quick to add that he must resign if he is found guilty. The logic of such statements suggests that there will be little support in Congress for the White House refusal to give the House Judiciary Committee the evidence it is seeking. That is where Mr. Nixon may be most vulnerable.

Mr. Buckley's lengthy statement meanwhile is curious in what it seems to be saying, and what it is really saying.

By proposing the President resign, Mr. Buckley said, he is making no judgment of the guilt or innocence on Mr. Nixon's part. The act would not be an acknowledgement of either guilt or weakness, Mr. Buckley said. Instead, it would "be an extraordinary act of statesmanship and courage — an act at once noble and heartbreaking," and so on.

That is eyewash to flatter Mr. Nixon into resigning. Obviously he ought not to quit if he isn't guilty and doesn't deserve to be impeached. Mr. Nixon's own perception of the act of quitting is realistic. And what Mr. Buckley is really telling the President is to quit before he is fired, to quit to spare us the act of firing him.

He comes close to hysteria in describing the agony of an impeachment proceeding televised to the whole world. The Senate, Mr. Buckley said, "would become a 20th Century Roman Colosseum as the performers are thrown to the electronic lions." Even if the impeachment of Mr. Nixon weren't as lurid as that, it surely would be a traumatic undertaking. ("The audience," Mr. Buckley noted pointedly, "would hear those magical tapes in full — that could not be avoided.") And the only way out is the President's resignation.

"As it now stands, the office of the President is in danger of succumbing to the death of a thousand cuts," Mr. Buckley said. Hence, it is necessary to ditch the man to defend the office.

That is also a body blow to Mr. Nixon, since it turns the arguments of the White House topsy-turvy. All of the desperate and devious stratagems of the White House are rationalized as defending the institution of the Presidency, and not as defending Mr. Nixon. The latter ("I am not a crook") is no longer persuasive, the polls suggest.

But if Mr. Nixon is to be denied the defense of delay and obfuscation (refusing to release the tapes) and he is to be denied the defense of the institution ("In order to preserve the Presidency," Mr. Buckley said, "Richard Nixon must resign as President"), then there can be no alternative to his impeachment. ("Impeachment" doesn't mean finding guilty, but bringing to trial.) "The stage has now been reached," Mr. Buckley warned, when "Americans must come to terms with Watergate if Watergate is not to come to end up drowning us all."

And in political terms, it is the Republicans who will drown first in an election year. If Mr. Nixon resists to the bitter end in impeachment proceedings, the Republican Party will be laid waste by the voters, or so it seems to a good many of its members. And while the President is willing for Republicans to sacrifice themselves to defend the Presidency and, incidentally, the man who happens to be President, it is not a sacrifice that the average politician would be happy to make for Mr. Nixon's sake.

The sum of such thinking is that the President must resign for the good of the Nation, the good of the office, and the good of the party. If and when that perception is shared widely, the fate of Mr. Nixon will be sealed. If it is accepted by those who, like Mr. Buckley, are conservatives and lifelong Republicans, the pressure on the President to resign will become irresistible, perhaps sweetened by legislation to bar his prosecution when he leaves the White House. It is too soon to say that Mr. Nixon's days are numbered. But they are becoming more and more unpleasant.

HERALD-JOURNAL

Syracuse, N.Y., March 20, 1974

This newspaper, alone among all others in New York State, supported Sen. James L. Buckley in 1968 when he first ran for the U.S. Senate, then as a Conservative, against Sen. Jacob K. Javits, Republican.

That year, we also backed Sen. Hubert H. Humphrey in his race for the presidency against Richard M. Nixon.

We endorsed Buckley again in 1970 when he ran for the Senate against Charles E. Goodell, an appointee of Gov. Rockefeller, and Richard L. Ottinger, Democrat. In that year, practically every other newspaper in the state joined forces with us. So did Nixon who made no bones about his preference for Buckley.

We recite this brief history before saying Buckley is wrong, absolutely wrong, in his assessment of Watergate and the presidency,

leading to his call for Nixon to resign.

Today, Nixon's standing has dropped in the polls of public opinion. Buckley views this along with the impeachment inquiry in the House and the continuing media emphasis on Watergate as a crisis and believes that "the one way . . . by which the crisis can be resolved and the country pulled out of the Watergate swamp" is for Nixon to resign.

▽   ▽

Would Buckley have advised Harry S. Truman to resign when his Korean War standing dropped below Nixon's current level instead of mounting his 1948 "give-'em-hell" campaign that ended in victory despite the deep-freeze scandals?

Would Buckley have counseled President Lyndon B. Johnson to

give up 20 years later when plagued by the marching critics of Vietnam, forcing him to decide in May of 1968 not to seek another four-year term? Johnson has also attracted our support, first for reelection and next in those weeks before he was hounded out of office.

For we believe that the mandate of the people holds and not the pronouncement, in this case, of a Sen. Buckley. In 1972, Buckley should recall, Nixon returned to office with the biggest mandate ever given to a president.

Nixon's resignation would set a dangerous precedent. We would know, for certain, that presidents could be forced out of office after one misstep or upon assuming an unpopular stance.

Buckley, speaking into a cluster of microphones, seven tv cameras and 75 or more reporters, insisted he did not believe Nixon is "legal-

ly guilty" of the charges leveled against him. Nor, he said, should Nixon's resignation be taken "as in any way acknowledging either guilt or weakness."

▽   ▽

If Buckley thinks that resignation won't be taken as a sign of guilt, he has stepped out of the world of reality.

And that's a dangerous step for a senator to take when he may have to vote on Nixon's innocence or guilt if the House moves to impeach.

For Buckley has abandoned the concept of fair play, the historic belief that a man is innocent until proven otherwise (despite his protestations), countering the preachings of all conservatives.

Brought into question is Buckley's own value as a senator from the State of New York.

The Evening Bulletin

Philadelphia, Pa., March 24, 1974

The bipartisan unity of the House Judiciary Committee has been severely shaken by the request of President Nixon's lawyer, James D. St. Clair, to be allowed to take part in the committee's impeachment inquiry.

Maintaining that unity is essential.

Every step of the inquiry must be perceived as fair by the public. Bipartisanship has been the committee's great strength. Its mandate from the House of Representatives is a bipartisan one. Republican and Democratic members stood together in a remarkable fashion in supporting demands for evidence resisted by the White House.

The committee's unity is the best possible answer to Mr. Nixon's public relations campaign to persuade the electorate that the committee is being unreasonable—that it rather than he himself is dragging out Watergate to the country's detriment.

So the party-line breach that has now been opened up on Mr. St. Clair's participation in the inquiry should be healed, and it can be healed.

Although there are procedural grounds for resisting the St. Clair move, there are also procedural grounds for acceding to it. The snags are lawyers' snags. They should not be permitted to obscure the fundamental purpose of setting in motion this rarely used part of the constitutional machinery, which involves a noncriminal, a political process. The committee must consider all the facts on alleged presidential misconduct in a manner that the public will accept as in every way fair.

• • •

The committee's inquiry is not a trial. If the committee recommends and the House approves impeachment charges, Mr. Nixon would have his trial by the Senate with all his rights duly safeguarded. There is already counsel representing the Republican minority on the House Judiciary Committee. Mr. St. Clair's participation could prove harrassing or even impede the committee's work.

However, there have been past impeachment inquiries involving lesser officials than the President in which the accused has been permitted to present witnesses, cross-examine, and be represented by counsel in House committee hearings.

In this present case, it seems all-important that no privilege ever given to others now be denied to Mr. Nixon; that the committee consider every aspect of the matter, pro and con, before making its recommendation to the House; that there be no element of surprising Mr. Nixon, and that every committee action be seen as straightforward, candid, open and thoughtful.

It would be the greatest disservice to the country if the committee, for whatever reason, helped to fortify the claim that the Watergate scandal as it may involve the President is something dreamed up by liberals, press, or partisan Democrats just to "get" Mr. Nixon.

That's why the Democrats, being in the majority, should lean over backward in this instance of the St. Clair participation to accommodate themselves to the views of their Republican colleagues in the minority.

• • •

There is only one constitutional way to remove a President if removal is justified—through House impeachment and Senate trial. The Bulletin has stated several times that forced resignation is not an acceptable alternative to following constitutional processes.

The impeachment inquiry by the House must be unswervingly fair, a phrase used by Federal Judge John J. Sirica last week when he ordered a sealed report by the Watergate grand jury turned over to the Judiciary Committee.

"It would be difficult to conceive of a more compelling need," Judge Sirica declared, "than that of this country for an unswervingly fair inquiry based on all the pertinent information."

Since Mr. Nixon has resisted the effort of the committee to get all the pertinent facts (though not its demand for the grand jury report) it may be asked why the House committee should not follow other precedents and deny Mr. St. Clair a role in its hearings.

The answer is that how Mr. Nixon chooses to fight against impeachment is his affair. But Congress, in considering whether he has gravely abused his trust and the office of the Presidency, must have the country behind it.

The country must be convinced that, if anything, the committee has erred on the side of forbearance, patience, and the most scrupulous regard for Mr. Nixon's position.

That cannot be achieved by a House committee divided on party lines.

AKRON BEACON JOURNAL

Akron, Ohio, March 25, 1974

THE INSISTENCE on the part of the White House that the House Judiciary Committee "first define the charges (against the President) and be specific on what materials are wanted and why" is clearly a play on public misunderstanding of the impeachment procedure.

The fact is that there are no official charges against the President, and it is not within the power of the Judiciary Committee to bring charges.

There will be no charges against Mr. Nixon unless he is impeached by the full House of Representatives. Impeachment is simply the act of bringing charges against a high public official, and does not presume guilt. An official accused by the House is entitled to the same presumption of innocence as any citizen charged by a grand jury.

In a strictly legal sense, it would be quite unfair to Mr. Nixon for the committee to "define charges" against him before seeking evidence to support or rebut those charges.

The committee's duty is to conduct an investigation, or "inquiry," into the conduct of the President and to recommend to the full House whether impeachment is justified. The House is in no way obligated to follow the committee's recommendation.

Obviously, the committee cannot conduct a scattergun investigation, and it is not doing so. Serious allegations of misconduct have been made against the President, and the committee has to determine to the best of its ability the truth or falsehood of those allegations. Some facts are known — such as the bombing of Cambodia and the withholding of funds mandated by Congress to be spent — which the committee must judge to be either impeachable or non-impeachable.

The committee has been specific within that framework, but allegations are hardly the same thing as charges. And if it had not been specific on "what materials are wanted and why," how could the White House say it will not turn over 42 requested tapes? It would seem that 42 is a very specific number.

Impeachment, and particularly impeachment of a President, is a legal process conducted in a necessarily political atmosphere. The subject under investigation is a politician; the grand jurors, congressmen, are politicians and the petit jurors, senators, are politicians.

Mr. Nixon's planned defense against expected charges seems to be to try to take advantage of both politics and the law, even when the two are incompatible.

The play on the public confusion about the process of investigation, impeachment and Senate trial is designed to put public pressure on the committee to act in a manner inconsistent with judicial fairness.

The committee, from all appearances, is methodically sticking to the law.

THE ROANOKE TIMES

Roanoke, Va., March 18, 1974

President Nixon's lawyers are conducting a shrewd campaign to slow down and confuse the consideration of impeachment— the procedure which makes a charge but does not imply a verdict. A master stroke is Counselor St. Clair's letter that it would be irresponsible for the President to give the House Judiciary Committee more of the requested evidence until the committee reached a definition of an impeachable offense.

That is an attempt to force upon the committee, and ultimately upon the Congress, Mr. Nixon's intriguing definition of such an offense. It would be, his lawyers have written, not only limited to a criminal offense "but one of a serious nature committed in one's governmental capacity." That could lead to a long debate as to whether a President acting in his capacity as a campaigner for re-election could do things he could not do "in one's governmental capacity."

Not long ago Sen. Hugh Scott, R-Pa., minority leader, emerged from the White House proclaiming there were documents definitely proving Mr. Nixon's innocence of the Watergate cover-up. Maybe so;

we hope so. But those documents have yet to appear.

Now emerges Sen. Norris Cotton, R.-N.H., with the word that President Nixon would accept a review of the requested evidence "by an independent person." That ploy was used once, with Senator Stennis of Mississippi selected as the independent person. It collapsed in the confusion of the weekend which brought the firing of Special Prosecutor Cox and the resignation of Atty. Gen. Richardson.

So it goes. Trying to reach a sound conclusion on this question, in the face of a presidential reluctance to be forthright, is like working on a rock pile. Except for one possibility, this hedgerow strategy promises to be successful. The country doesn't really want to impeach President Nixon. If it can be kept thoroughly confused as to what impeachment is, its reluctance will be reinforced. The alternative possibility arises from the utter unpredictability of everything related to Watergate. Shrewd defenses have failed before and they may collapse again. Simple frankness long ago should have ended the problem, when it was very, very small.

The Des Moines Register

Des Moines, Iowa, March 16, 1974

The White House is complaining that the House Judiciary Committee wants to rummage through the President's files.

The White House cited as proof a request from the committee for information about how the President's papers, conversations and memoranda are indexed. The committee expressed particular interest in the indexing of the files of H.R. Haldeman, John Ehrlichman, Charles Colson and John Dean.

The committee said the inquiry would be expedited if "we could work out a way whereby members of the inquiry staff may examine these files for the purpose of selecting materials which, in our opinion, are necessary for the investigation."

The White House gave Special Prosecutor Leon Jaworski authority to "rummage" through White House files when it permitted a member of the special prosecutor's staff to examine the files of the special investigations ("plumbers") unit. The White House provided the prosecutor the documents he found and concluded he needed.

But Jaworski complained last month that in another instance the White House delivered documents from the files of a former staff member "but refused to let us review the files to make our own determination of relevance. The White House also has refused to let us review the files of another former staff member, requested as early as August, 1973."

Flipping through any and all White House files in hope of turning up some-

thing relevant obviously would be improper. But the special prosecutor and the House Judiciary Committee are not on fishing expeditions. Their inquiries relate to specific topics and categories of information.

In some cases they are aware of certain documents and conversations and can specify them by date and time. In other cases they are aware only that certain White House officials were involved in matters under investigation. The only way to learn the full story about these matters is to examine the records of the involvement by the officials and to obtain the pertinent documents.

The White House staff cannot be trusted to comb the files and turn over everything needed. The President and his staff are targets of the inquiry. No one can have confidence that the suspect in an inquiry will disclose everything that incriminates him. In a criminal investigation the suspect obviously cannot be permitted to do the investigating and decide what the prosecutor should see.

Charges of a "fishing expedition" are a smokescreen to obscure the fact that the White House is hiding evidence from the special prosecutor and the House Judiciary Committee. Both agencies are conducting properly authorized inquiries. Both are entitled to the evidence they seek unless the President invokes the Fifth Amendment guarantee against self-incrimination he is entitled to invoke under the Constitution.

The Boston Globe

Boston, Mass., March 25, 1974

As the House Judiciary Committee plods ahead with its inquiry into the possible impeachment of President Nixon, the President's chief attorney, James D. St. Clair of Boston, has seen fit to make an "imperative" request that he be allowed to take an active role in its deliberations.

Aside from the fact that there are no legal grounds for such participation, this is plainly another maneuver by the White House team to go the people over the heads of the Judiciary Committee.

The tactic is not unlike Mr. St. Clair's earlier arguments that the President need not report the hushing-up of a crime since he is the nation's chief legal officer; his argument that, because John Dean misquoted the date of the March 21 conversation with Mr. Nixon before the Ervin committee (at a time when Mr. Dean was denied access to his files), Mr. Dean should not be considered a credible witness; and his contention that the Judiciary Committee must define the grounds

for impeachment before seeking additional evidence from the White House.

To that contention, Republican committeeman Edward Hutchinson very properly replied, "There are no charges. We hope we will find none. We are simply making an inquiry." The implication is clear, that if the President has nothing to hide he should welcome the opportunity to provide evidence that could clear his name.

The White House request that Mr. St. Clair be allowed to cross-examine witnesses, suggest witnesses to be called, and introduce evidence for the committee's consideration has already succeeded, at least temporarily, in dividing the committee's Republicans from the Democrats, with Ohio Republican Delbert L. Latta stating that, if the request is denied, "the American people will certainly wonder why. . . ."

The reason the request should be denied is that the committee investi-

gation is not an adversary proceeding, but a preliminary effort to gather facts on the basis of which the full House must determine whether or not there are grounds for a trial in the Senate. To allow the President's counsel to call and cross-examine witnesses at this stage would be comparable to conducting a trial in a local police station.

The basis for an impeachment proceeding lies in English parliamentary law which differs from common law in being aimed at the dismissal of kings and ministers. Its rules and precedents are broad and unique and, if there are precedents in this country for allowing participation by counsel at the committee stage (as was done in the case of Justice William O. Douglas, whose case never went beyond the committee), it is a matter of courtesy, not of rights.

Harvard Law Professor Raoul Berger emphasizes the point that the current impeachment proceeding is a "national crisis" without parallel

since Andrew Johnson, the only American President to undergo a full trial in the Senate, never raised the question of executive privilege and, in fact, furnished all the evidence requested by Congress.

Even though there is only one potential defendant who could be named in the present impeachment process, the body of law makes it clear that his lawyers have no standing during the investigatory stage. They come onto the scene in the trial stage, after charges have been brought by the House and the case sent to the Senate for trial.

Mr. St. Clair's action at this stage can only be regarded as meddlesome and of questionable purpose. Its effect, however, is another matter. For it has served, more as the political act it was than as the legal maneuver it pretended to be, to open a party-line breach in the committee membership.

The request is without merit and should be summarily rejected.

Washington Star-News

Washington, D.C., March 21, 1974

Fairness would seem to dictate that the House Judiciary Committee allow President Nixon's attorney to participate in the examination of witnesses during its impeachment inquiry. But the Democrats on the committee, apparently laboring under the mistaken notion that the proceedings should follow the rules of a grand jury, have refused.

While the impeachment process is in some ways analogous to a grand jury proceeding, the fact is that it is heavily overlaid with politics. The House is not a grand jury. It is a political forum in which the members are influenced by self-preservation, special interests and the vagaries of public opinion. The Judiciary Committee is part of its parent body, not part of a grand jury, and it seems reasonable that its rules should be as flexible as possible.

The important thing is to get at the truth. What can be the harm in allowing the President's attorney, James St. Clair, to cross-examine witnesses? It could, in fact, be helpful to give him a chance to "shake" testimony damaging to the President. If the committee decides to recommend impeachment, it should have the strongest case possible. If there is no case, it is the committee's duty to recommend against impeachment.

A strong argument can be made that the President is entitled to know the general outline of the evidence against him before the debate begins on the House floor. This is not just a common criminal proceeding. It involves the highest official of the land and questions of the gravest national import. The President ought to have some representation during the proceedings. Ordinarily, it could be assumed that the committee's minority counsel, Albert Jenner, would keep a sharp eye out for the President's interest. But that does not seem to be the case; rather Jenner appears to be adopting a non-partisan posture.

Committee Chairman Rodino, a Democrat, has acknowledged that there are historical precedents for allowing the subject of an impeachment to be represented by counsel, but he claims this privilege rested on a "matter of grace, not of right." Rodino and his colleagues should reconsider and allow St. Clair to participate, at least to some extent. It not only would be fair but would help allay the notion held by some that the President is being railroaded.

ST. LOUIS POST-DISPATCH

St. Louis, Mo., March 21, 1974

While one prong of President Nixon's Watergate counter-offensive is clearly directed at rebuilding public support for himself, another one is proceeding at a less visible but no less important level. Here we refer to his persistent attempts to hamstring the House Judiciary Committee as it proceeds with the impeachment inquiry. Insofar as they have been discussed, Mr. Nixon has characterized these efforts as part of his responsibility to protect the presidency. In fact, however, they are a naked encroachment on the authority of the House as set forth explicitly in the Constitution.

Hitherto this tactic has had two well-defined goals: limiting the amount and the nature of the evidence the committee is entitled to and formulating a narrow definition of an impeachable offense. To these ends, the White House has asserted that information furnished by Mr. Nixon to the Special Watergate Prosecutor should be sufficient for the committee and that the impeachment inquiry should go no farther than the Watergate cover-up. Now White House Counsel St. Clair has demanded that he be allowed to cross-examine the committee's witnesses and also to subpena witnesses of his own, thus revealing a third objective. That is for the White House itself to become an active participant in the committee's proceedings.

Such an arrangement would be tantamount to allowing suspects in criminal cases to participate in grand jury deliberations, for in impeachment the House acts as the grand jury for the nation. Beyond this, the Constitution plainly says the House "shall have the sole power of impeachment." There is not a word in that document stating that the President or his lawyer has the right to interfere with it. In Houston Tuesday, Mr. Nixon suggested that both he and the House follow the Constitution on impeachment. By carrying on the inquiry, the House is doing so. By seeking to intrude on the proceedings, Mr. Nixon is not.

THE CINCINNATI ENQUIRER

Cincinnati, Ohio, March 24, 1974

IT WOULD BE IRONIC indeed if the future of Richard M. Nixon's presidency should hang upon his willingness to open even more of the White House's files and records to congressional investigators rather than on any of the substantive allegations that have been leveled against him.

Yet that remains the distinct possibility if some members of the House Judiciary Committee persist in their view that the President be cited for contempt of Congress for failure to supply every tape and record the committee believes it needs and that the citation itself serve as the basis for the President's impeachment.

Mr. Nixon contends, with much correctness, that he has been remarkably forthcoming in complying with the requests of the several investigatory bodies that have been at work for many months. Special Watergate prosecutor Leon Jaworski found the evidence accumulated in part through the administration's co-operation sufficient to indict several former aides of the White House and the Committee to Re-elect the President. The White House, moreover, acquiesced in the delivery to the House Judiciary Committee of a mass of additional evidence accumulated by the Watergate grand jury.

Yet without even making a gesture at digesting the evidence within its purview, the committee is insisting on yet more tapes, more records, more files.

The implication of the committee's representations is that despite more than half a year of work by the Senate Select Committee on Presidential Campaign Activities, despite the many months of inquiry by the Watergate grand jury, despite several months of inquiry by the Judiciary Committee's special impeachment staff, the committee still hasn't been able to assemble a credible case for the President's impeachment. That disability is all the more remarkable in view of the committee's definition of the grounds for impeachment—a definition that would prescribe impeachment for any presidential offenses "seriously incompatible with either the constitutional form and principles of our government or the proper performance of constitutional duties."

Presidential impeachment remains the more awesome weapon in the arsenal available to Congress in its struggle with the executive branch. That it has been employed on only one previous occasion underscores a long-held recognition that it involves a genuinely traumatic national experience. Surely, it should be apparent to the leadership of the Judiciary Committee that the nation is in no mood to see Mr. Nixon tricked into an impeachment action.

NIXON TO PAY $465,000 TAX DEBT AFTER IRS REPORTS ON DELINQUENCY

President Nixon April 3 agreed to pay a total of $465,000 in back taxes and interest on the basis of a report he received from the Internal Revenue Service (IRS) the previous day assessing his tax debt for the period from 1969–1972 at that amount. The IRS specified it would not seek a civil fraud penalty against the President for the years involved because it "did not believe any such assertion was warranted." Announcement of Nixon's decision to comply with the IRS findings followed by about four hours release of a staff report of the Congressional Joint Committee on Internal Revenue Taxation which independently assessed Nixon's tax delinquency at $476,431 for the same period. The Nixon statement said the Congressional report likewise "offers no fact which would support" any charge of fraud. It added that "any errors which have been made in the preparation of the President's returns were made by those to whom he delegated the responsibility for preparing his returns and were made without his knowledge and without his approval."

While details of the IRS report were not released, both it and the committee report found Nixon's largest and most widely publicized tax deduction—a claimed $482,018 from 1969–1972 for the gift of his vice presidential papers to the government—to have been invalid. The Congressional staff report disallowed the deductions "because the gift was made after July 25, 1969," the effective date of the Tax Reform Act eliminating such deductions. The deed of the gift, dated March 27, 1969, "which purportedly was signed on April 21, 1969, was not signed (at least by all parties) until April 10, 1970 and was not delivered until after that date," the report said.

Frank DeMarco, Nixon's tax attorney, and Arthur Blech, his tax accountant, said in separate interviews that Nixon and the White House staff had paid closer attention to his tax affairs than had been suggested by the official White House disclaimer of responsibility. In a statement reported by the *Los Angeles Times* April 5, DeMarco said it would be ridiculous to believe that he and Blech had made important decisions on Nixon's returns without instructions from the President or his representatives. Regarding the 1969 return, DeMarco said that he and Herbert W. Kalmbach, Nixon's former personal attorney and fund raiser, had met with the President and gone over the return "page by page." According to the Los Angeles newspaper, DeMarco had also been privately expressing concern that he and Blech would become "scapegoats" for Nixon's tax improprieties. In an interview reported by *The New York Times* April 8, Blech said he and DeMarco had operated on instructions from key White House aides, including John Ehrlichman and John Dean.

Attorney General William B. Saxbe said April 9 that the IRS had forwarded to the special Watergate prosecutor the information on President Nixon's discredited 1969–72 income tax returns. Saxbe pointed out, however, that the prosecutor should not deal with whether Nixon himself was involved in criminal fraud but with the role of those who had actually prepared the returns. Questions about the President, Saxbe said, should be left to the House Judiciary Committee's impeachment inquiry. (Chief committee counsel John M. Doar said April 8 that tax fraud was clearly part of his staff's investigation and that IRS records on Nixon's taxes had been requested.)

The New York Times

New York, N.Y., April 5, 1974

Although President Nixon has wisely decided to pay the back taxes and interest assessed by the Internal Revenue Service, his decision leaves some troubling questions unresolved.

The most serious and factually the most obscure concerns the large deduction that he claimed for the donation of his Vice-Presidential papers. On the face of it, this deduction could not stand because there is no deed of gift signed by the President prior to the deadline of July 25, 1969. Neither the I.R.S. nor the staff of the Congressional Joint Committee on Internal Revenue Taxation apparently believes the explanation that an earlier deed had been signed and lost.

At best, President Nixon showed an extraordinary failure of judgment in taking this huge deduction in a taxable year when Congress was in process of forbidding such a deduction. At worst the President was a party to a tax fraud. The issue properly should go to the House Judiciary Committee, where it can be studied anew as part of the impeachment inquiry and where witnesses can testify and evidence be introduced with regard to the suspicious timing of the President's donation of his papers.

The other deductions which the committee staff and, presumably, the I.R.S. decided had been improperly claimed by the President are not esoteric or difficult to understand. One would not have to be a lawyer —as Mr. Nixon is—to understand them. A layman reading the statement of financial net worth released in Mr. Nixon's behalf several months ago by a private accounting firm could readily perceive that the President owed a capital gains tax on the sale of his New York City apartment unless he claimed his new estate in San Clemente, Calif., as his principal residence. But that was manifestly impossible inasmuch as he lived in the White House and paid no California state income tax.

Similarly it was self-evident that he owed a sizable capital gains tax on the sale of the undeveloped portion of his San Clemente estate to two friends in 1970 at a good price while he kept the house and the more valuable ocean-front acreage. What is hard to understand is how Mr. Nixon could have had the audacity to fail to report these capital gains or how the officials of the Internal Revenue Service who ostensibly audited his returns could have acquiesced in those omissions.

The same statement of net worth showed that Mr. Nixon must either have paid virtually no income tax much of the time he was in office or had a large flow of cash from an undisclosed source. Otherwise, he could not have sustained his visible standard of living and still have acquired and maintained expensive estates in Florida and California. It was in order to quell unpleasant rumors that he had a cash flow from some occult source that Mr. Nixon referred his income tax returns to the Joint Committee and made his famous statement, "I am not a crook."

Against that background, the closing sentence of President Nixon's statement is disturbing and offensive: "Any errors which may have been made in the preparation of the President's returns were made by those to whom he delegated the responsibility for preparing his returns and were made without his knowledge and without his approval."

Such a statement would be a plausible excuse if the I.R.S. had found mistakes in arithmetic or trivial omissions. But the failure to report capital gains on his New York apartment and his San Clemente land are not small matters. Moreover, the decision to take a huge deduction for his Vice-Presidential papers was a judgment involving hundreds of thousands of dollars that only Mr. Nixon himself could have made, particularly as the deduction was claimed despite the change in the tax law that Mr. Nixon as Chief Executive was surely aware of.

Mr. Nixon is disclaiming knowledge that common sense indicates he must have had and disclaiming responsibility that cannot be disclaimed. This eagerness to disavow his own acts is as disturbing as the acts themselves.

THE SAGINAW NEWS

Saginaw, Mich., April 5, 1974

The enormity of his tax liability to the federal government casts the final dark and tragic shadow over a faltering administration and the dwindling presidency of Richard M. Nixon.

This is not a political death wish for the President. This newspaper has twice endorsed Mr. Nixon for the highest office in the land. Thus far, by comparison to other journals, this one has pursued the route of restraint in its comments toward a president in obviously deep trouble. Our position has been to question, to criticize — but also to accord every benefit of doubt.

We have refrained from calling for extreme measures preferring instead to see the impeachment process take its course. So we are not without compassion for Mr. Nixon.

Now, however, we must seriously ask if Mr. Nixon can any longer govern this nation with strength and credibility. It is time, we submit, for Mr. Nixon to ask himself this question — to make a searching reassessment of his position in light of the very office he holds.

We do so because our compassion for the stability of this country is paramount to our feelings toward a single individual who has failed to put that ahead of personal considerations.

Mr. Nixon can reverse that with a simple act of statesmanship by resigning and sparing this nation further emotional damage and the prolonged agony of impeachment.

We no longer see any profit in pursuing that course, whatever its outcome, because the credibility damage is already irreversible and it won't be erased by a political trial.

The Presidency is an office that can only be conducted effectively with the trust and the respect of the people and with the trust and respect of the Congress. We said trust and respect, freedom from doubt over questions of moral turpitude, not all-out affection or total agreement.

No president will ever attain the latter. But any president must have the former — particularly one engaged in delicate international detente with potential adversaries who claim to hew to even more stringent social-moral codes than we do in this country. .

Without that, the rock that he must appear to be standing on is cut out from under him. Reverse the positions. Let us suppose it was the regime of Brezhnev or Mao that was under a cloud of mistrust and political antagonism. Would the U.S. be prone to enter into serious agreements with either of them? We doubt it. More than likely we would be warily watching homefront developments in their countries.

This is just one of the many reasons why the President owes the government and the people something more than a payment of back taxes of astounding proportions. We are no longer persuaded that this thunderclap at credibility can be muted simply by squaring up.

We know that Mr. Nixon will pay those taxes due. He has said he would as long ago as last December when his income tax returns raised most serious and elemental questions. And we know that it will be an extremely painful financial reckoning. But these are no casual figures. And they are not a one-time slip up.

Independent professional re-audits of Mr. Nixon's tax returns done by the IRS and for the Joint Committee on Internal Revenue Taxation are a four-year trace of gross underpayments and claims to exemptions which fail to stand any test of validity.

What is particularly devastating in the official confirmation of presidential tax liability is that both reports differ little as to amount owing, not at all to specific exemptions taken which shouldn't have been — or in failure to declare capital gains on sale of properties that almost any taxpayer knows must be declared.

The reports themselves, of course, are no surprise The public has been prepared for this for a long time. It was additionally conditioned to expect the worst when Rep. Wilbur D. Mills inappropriately leaked the committee's findings almost two weeks ago.

We are deeply dismayed and saddened by the confirmation, nonetheless. Mr. Nixon owes close to $450,000 in back taxes on income of close to a million dollars over the past four years. It might have been more except for the fact that the White House refused to turn over complete information on the number of government-paid flights taken by the President and members and friends of the First Family which were not all related to official White House business. ,

In the overview, we can charitably consider this single item to be inconsequential.

For the rest of it, however, the President, the same as any other taxpayer, must bear the burden of responsibility. We do not know where he got his own tax advisers, but they, too, cast additional dismal reflection on matters of principle and judgment. Where were the value judgments, indeed, when Mr. Nixon was signing those IRS returns with tax payments of $600 and $700?

To say the least, it is an inopportune time for Mr Nixon to pay a call on the 8th Congressional District where there are unemployed taxpayers. For him to interject himself into a campaign which is already over-heated, is bad taste. He does indeed become an issue. Inescapably so.

The rising wave of doubt over what Mr. Nixon himself has done to the office of the presidency has reached the stage of tarnish which cannot be removed so casually. We regret that it has gone this far. But Mr. Nixon has taken us there. Resignation is now the highest and most selfless act he can perform to his fellow countrymen.

The Boston Globe

Boston, Mass., April 3, 1974

Under the best of circumstances, it seems inevitable that the tax return filed by a President of the United States would be a complicated document. In President Nixon's case the elemental complexity has been supplemented by changes in his place of residence, his donation of personal papers to the government, and possibly by some of his real estate transactions.

The working out of these questions presents a problem. Mr. Nixon has taken a broad view of the sanctuary afforded him by the office he holds — that, short of impeachment, he really is accountable only to himself now that he has been elected.

But in conceding that some of the deductions he has claimed might be subject to different interpretation, he agreed to let the Congressional Joint Committee on Internal Revenue Taxation come to a conclusion on the matter of his liability for taxes to California and on his deduction for donation of his vice presidential papers.

At his Feb. 25 news conference, he said that "I voluntarily asked . . . the House and Senate to look into the matter and to advise me as to whether or not the deduction was a proper one. If it was not a proper one, I, of course, will be glad to pay the tax."

Apart from his devotion to the pursuit of truth and fairness, and an understandable desire on his part to improve relations with an increasingly hostile Congress, Mr. Nixon may have been drawn to this course by the nature of the joint committee. Its most prominent members include Sen. Russell B. Long (D-La.), Rep. Wilbur Mills (D-Ark.), Sen. Herman Talmadge (D-Ga.), Sen. Wallace Bennett (R-Utah) and Sen. Carl Curtis (R-Neb.). Of its other five members, probably the most threatening from a partisan point of view might be Sen. Vance Hartke (D-Ind.). But the dominant character of the membership is conservative. And its staff enjoys the reputation of being perhaps the most professional in Congress. Mr. Nixon, in short, had no reason to fear being railroaded by a bunch of wild-eyed radicals or narrowly partisan foes.

The committee has not yet released its report on the matter although it would seem to have had ample time to have reached a conclusion on the issues. It has even been involved in public argument about when to act. And now there are vague reports, including one printed in the Wall Street Journal, that the President may decide not to adhere to the ultimate recommendations of the committee. While the suggestion includes the possibility that some members of the committee will recommend that its finding be appealable to the Tax Court, this introduces a new complication in the light of Mr. Nixon's position about his unassailability short of impeachment.

The President has every right to achieve the most favorable legitimate tax treatment available, just like all citizens. His decision to seek advice from the joint committee had the virtue of being simple and crisp—a sensible and judicious way out of a complicated tangle. If he now decides to seek appeal or to take that route if it is offered him by the committee, he may have a legal leg to stand on but he will once again have fallen back on complexity—at just the moment when most Americans are thinking rather ruefully about the meaning of Federal taxation.

ARKANSAS DEMOCRAT

Little Rock, Ark., April 9, 1974

As the Ides of April approach, the weary American taxpayer is hardly cheered by the news his President tried to avoid nearly a half million dollars in taxes. Nor is there joy in finding out just how close Mr. Nixon figured his tax bill. His use of every loophole, every shelter, every deduction says much about his attitude toward the republic and how it should be supported. Such things as taking a 25 per cent deduction on a bill of $4.64 may be an indictment more damaging than anything yet revealed by Watergate.

But the public has registered only mild dismay. In contrast to the prediction of Rep. Wilbur Mills that Mr. Nixon would be forced from office by the tax report, ad-hoc committees have sprung up to help him pay his tax bill. Instead of resigning, the President has announced he will pay what is due and has turned down the offers of help.

He has also tried to shift the full blame for his tax troubles to his subordinates. "Any errors which may have been made in the preparation of the President's returns were made by those to whom he delegated the responsibility . . ." a White House aide said. This self-serving statement has been refuted by the President's accountant and tax lawyer who say Mr. Nixon went over his tax returns page by page before they were filed.

Of greater concern to the nation than the actual dollars involved, should be the sordid portrait of Mr. Nixon as a Scrooge-like miser, pinching every penny before passing it on to the public treasury. Of equal concern and fright is the picture of the Internal Revenue Service that also emerges. The IRS, at an earlier time, said the President's returns were good in order. Someone in the IRS now has egg on his face. Maybe it's the same fellow who made the decision for the IRS to pass on to the White House the tax records of various individuals and corporations who were on the "enemies list." This is a clear violation of public law and brings Big Brotherism far too close.

A large part of Mr. Nixon's tax troubles stem from his questionable gift to the national archives of his vice presidential papers. The gift itself is surrounded with doubts, but now it has been revealed that even after the papers were delivered, some 17 boxes of the most valuable items were reclaimed. This attempt at having your cake and eating it too raises even more questions about Mr. Nixon's personal character.

It has been suggested that one of the reasons the public has taken this tax bombshell with such calm is that they are numbed by scandal and have grown shockproof. We don't think so. Sure there has been no great outcry, but at the same time people are submitting their own income tax returns as punctually and honestly — according to the IRS — as they have in past years. Mr. Nixon has not outraged them or started the demise of America's unusual voluntary income-tax system. We'd rather think that it means that in a big country like this, people are neither surprised nor influenced by sharpies in high places.

The Standard-Times

New Bedford, Mass., April 1, 1974

President Richard M. Nixon has made history—of a most undesirable and dismaying nature.

Consider the facts:

—The Internal Revenue Service has ruled that Nixon owes $432,787, plus interest—nearly a half-million dollars—in back taxes.

—Congressional investigators looking into the President's underpayments said they had found five different categories of taxable income that he should have reported and failed to report and six different categories of deductions that they said he took without being entitled to do so.

—Members of the staff of the Joint Committee on Internal Revenue Taxation found improprieties connected with nearly every one of the controversial items in Mr. Nixon's tax returns that have been widely discussed in recent months. These include the large deduction that he took for giving his pre-presidential papers to the National Archives and his not reporting capital gains on two real estate sales.

Let us assume, since the President—as with all of us—is innocent until proved guilty, that there is no question of fraud on the part of Mr. Nixon. In this connection, however, it must be pointed out that congressional investigators said they had not attempted to reach a conclusion on the matter of fraud because it is an issue that may come before the House Judiciary Committee, which is considering whether to recommend Mr. Nixon's impeachment.

But the question of fraud aside, here is the President of the United States, a lawyer, with the best professional talent in the country at his beck and call—with consultants, accountants, attorneys, secretaries, clerks, advisers and a voluminous filing system—and he has underpaid his taxes by more than $400,000 for his first four years in the White House.

And as with most of the other cloudy matters that have surrounded the White House since Watergate, this tax matter has its cloudy aspects, too. The biggest single deduction item ($428,018) for the gift of his papers was ruled out by the joint committee because the gift was made after July 25, 1969, the date when provisions of the Tax Reform Act of 1969 disallowing such deductions became effective.

The deed of conveyance (dated March 27, 1969), which purportedly was signed on April 21, 1969 was not signed, at least by all parties, until April 10, 1970 and was not delivered until after that date. Documents which Nixon's attorney has said would prove that transfer of the papers was accomplished in April, 1969 have not been produced.

Now the official White House answer to all this is that the President will pay what it has been decided he owes and that any errors in his tax returns were made "by those to whom he delegated responsibility for preparing his returns and were made without his knowledge and without his approval." We find it difficult to believe that the IRS would accept this as sufficient excuse from an ordinary taxpayer—and frankly, do not think the IRS should. The taxpayer, especially if the taxpayer is a lawyer and the President of the United States, has some kind of obligation to know what his tax return says before he signs it. And signing it surely implies approval of its content.

Moreover, it is incredible that the President, a lawyer, should not have been aware that he had to report as taxable income certain expenditures made out of public funds that solely benefited him or his family and not the public—for example $27,015 worth of purely personal airplane travel by the Nixon family and friends and $5,391 for a "masqued ball" for his daughter, Tricia.

Even if no violation of law is involved in this matter, the overriding fact is that Richard Nixon's treatment of his tax liabilities during his first term in the White House has diminished public respect for the presidency by failing to set a standard for the nation's citizens to follow.

We have made a determined effort to be fair to Mr. Nixon through the months of revelations, belated and unsatisfactory explanations, the lack of White House candor, and the whole gloomy aura of administration arrogance, ineptitude, skulduggery, and "tough-it-out" reaction that have followed Watergate. But this is the final straw and we believe that a majority of Americans—striving, and often sacrificing to meet their tax obligations to the federal government—will agree that it is.

Richard M. Nixon no longer has the public confidence necessary to provide leadership to this nation. His own actions, and those of persons whom he selected to serve with him have destroyed the overwhelming popular support that put him into the White House for a second term.

If Mr. Nixon cares about the United States—and he maintains that he does—he should resign from the presidency without delay, for the good of this nation and its troubled millions who yearn for White House leadership in which they can once more have faith.

FORT WORTH STAR-TELEGRAM
Fort Worth, Tex., April 10, 1974

President Nixon's agreement to pay some $465,000 in back taxes has fanned the flames on the long-burning fire for meaningful tax reform.

U. S. Sen. Walter Mondale, (D-Minn.), noted that 402 Americans with 1972 incomes of over $100,000 paid no federal income tax for that year. Of these, 99 had incomes of over $200,000, and four of over $1 million.

"If this can be substantiated," said Cong. Jim Wright, "It is an outrage. The average American is just bound to feel the same way I do about it."

A minimum tax was enacted in the Tax Reform Act of 1969 to get at the problem of the wealthy taxpayer who pays no taxes.

But the minimum tax is so riddled with exemptions it has been only marginally effective. In fact, Mr. Nixon used the $30,000 exemption in the minimum tax to legally escape taxation on $58,448 in tax-sheltered income in 1970, 1971 and 1972.

Among worrisome tax treatments are those dealing with capital gains, the ever-growing volume of state and local government bonds whose interest is tax exempt, depletion allowances and deductions for interest paid on debts.

And, the most worrisome aspect of all, the growing complexity of what should be the simple task of a person paying his fair tax.

We agree with Congressman Wright who, in a recent newsletter, said: "I think everybody owes something."

Mr. Wright, noting he paid an income tax of $9,293.84 last year, said most deductions and allowances written into the tax code stem from laudable public purpose.

Tax-free yields on municipal bonds help local governments raise money for improvements; depletion allowances encourage exploration; and deductions for interest paid help families buy homes.

"But it never was the intent of Congress that any one of these or any combination of them should permit any upper-bracket taxpayer escape his responsibility entirely," Mr. Wright said.

He proposed any tax reform should contain some provision to the effect that any taxpayer making, say, $50,000 or more must pay taxes on at least half his actual income, regardless of deductions he can claim.

Mr. Wright's basic figure may be the subject of debate, but there is nothing wrong with his basic idea. It certainly would provide a tax-sharing opportunity to those previously denied the privilege because of too-appealing tax loopholes.

Newsday
Long Island, N.Y., April 15, 1974

"In law school I majored in tax law," President Nixon reminded reporters at a June, 1972, press conference. "As a lawyer I used to do quite a bit of tax work. But when [Manolo Sanchez, the President's valet] came in recently and asked me to help him figure out the forms, I had to send him to a lawyer."

The President complained then that the tax laws were "hopelessly complex." Those Long Islanders who have spent the weekend struggling with tax forms and their consciences on the eve of Monday's filing deadline probably would agree. So did the late Judge Learned Hand who years ago wrote that the words of the tax statutes "merely dance before my eyes in a meaningless progress . . . They leave in my mind only a confused sense of some vitally important but concealed purpose . . ."

And that was before accelerated depreciation, investment tax credits, income averaging, oil depletion allowances, the Mexican vegetable rollover tax shelter and all the rest.

The plain truth is that the federal income tax code has degenerated into a mishmash that practically nobody can decipher. Not even the President of the United States. And certainly not the Internal Revenue Service, which originally congratulated Nixon for the "care shown in the preparation" of his returns—the very returns that have just been found wanting by nearly a half-million dollars.

It wasn't always thus. The 1913 law resulting from a constitutional amendment that called on Congress to "collect taxes on income, from whatever source derived," was put down in 26 pages. Instructions for filling out Form 1040 (it was called that even then) required only one page. Now a person would be hardpressed in an entire lifetime to read, much less absorb, the volumes of tax laws and regulations and addenda that apply to it.

That's why taxpayers who file all but the simplest of returns are—like the President—turning in growing numbers to the accountants and lawyers who earn their fees by mining the ambiguities inherent in today's tax law. These tax professionals routinely push the IRS as far as they dare to go. They know that less than three per cent of all returns are audited. And while Nixon has agreed to pay the full $467,000 in taxes and interest assessed by the IRS, in a more typical case the taxpayer's lawyer and an IRS agent would now be haggling like Persian rug dealers over what the taxpayer's actual liability should be.

The hundreds of "tax preferences" in the law cost the U.S. Treasury more than $70 billion a year in lost revenue. The average taxpayer benefits from some of them—deductions for property taxes and home mortgage interest, for instance. But the really big beneficiaries are major corporations and rich individuals. It's no accident that the tax breaks seem designed to benefit those who need them least.

This distorts the basic premise of the American tax system, which is that the heaviest burden should be shouldered by those who can best carry it. Actually, most big corporations and high-income individuals pay less than half of what the tax tables say they should be paying. Many corporations wind up paying taxes at the same rate as a $15,000 wage earner.

The President's tax troubles have created still another movement in Congress to close tax loopholes. But history teaches that Congress is likely to create at least as many loopholes as it closes. Two years ago Representative Wilbur Mills, chairman of the tax-writing House Ways and Means Committee, proposed that Congress pass legislation that would force the lawmakers to reconsider the desirability of continuing 53 major tax preferences. The idea was that those whose merit could not be proved conclusively would be phased out in easy stages.

We wish Mills would renew that proposal. It's a sad commentary on the state of the current tax law that Mills, who has been personally responsible for most of the tax legislation of the last 20 years, routinely claims only the standard deduction. He won't itemize for fear that the complex tax laws he helped to father might be subject to misinterpretation.

President Nixon's tax troubles highlight the fact that mere tax "reform" is no longer enough. The nation desperately needs laws that the average taxpayer can understand—and which make it certain that everybody pays his fair share.

RAPID CITY JOURNAL—

Rapid City, S.D., April 5, 1974

In the months this nation has wallowed in Watergate, this newspaper has recommended the impeachment process — indictment by the House of Representatives and trial in the U.S. Senate — as the proper way to determine whether President Nixon is guilty or innocent of impeachable offenses.

That position was based on our commitment to the principle of a fair trial for any accused person.

We have perhaps also been in the position of the youngster who, during the Black Sox baseball scandal of 1919, tearfully implored Shoeless Joe Jackson: "Say it ain't so, Joe!"

Our feelings were not for Richard Nixon, the man, but for Richard Nixon, president of the United States.

Whether Richard Nixon, president of the United States, is guilty of impeachable offenses still has not been determined.

But Richard Nixon, the man who is president of the United States,

owes nearly a half million dollars in back taxes. By not contesting an Internal Revenue Service ruling to that effect, Richard Nixon, for all practical purposes, admits it "is so."

The IRS report rebuts any suggestion of fraud and the Joint Committee on Internal Revenue Taxation which studied the Nixon tax issue offers no facts that would support a charge of criminality.

But the tax issue relates directly to the image of Nixon as a person, rather than a political leader. It is an issue in which Nixon's special place in our society as president cannot be used as a defense. Arguments for protecting the office of the presidency do not apply to the occupant as a taxpayer.

The findings of the congressional staff report and the IRS ruling strike home to American taxpayers. The tax issue is one every American can easily understand and translate into his own terms. More important, it further shreds the President's

credibility and virtually destroys his effectiveness and capability to lead.

It is a more debilitating wound than the President's alleged involvement in Watergate and its coverup.

We have been willing to accept the consequences of the shattering effect the impeachment process would have on this nation and its relations with the other nations of the world. Regardless of the verdict, the shadow of doubt would be removed.

However, there is no shadow of doubt surrounding the income tax issue. Nixon, himself, has removed it. In so doing, his image as president has been irreparably damaged. Even acquittal through the impeachment process cannot fully restore that image.

For that reason, and with a hollow feeling in the pit of the stomach, we say Richard Nixon, the man, would best serve this nation by resigning from the office of the presidency.

Sentinel Star

Orlando, Fla., April 7, 1974

FOR THE SAKE of argument let's say an Orange County taxpayer named Richard signs his homestead exemption form but inadvertently keeps it in his coat pocket.

The April 1 cutoff date passes before he gets it to the tax assessor's office and Richard fails to get his $5,000 exemption.

His tax bill is $100 higher than it would have been had the application reached the courthouse on time.

✿ ✿ ✿

NOW SURELY nobody would accuse Richard of cheating on his taxes.

Nobody would call him "Tricky Dick."

On the contrary, most people would feel sorry for a citizen hurt financially because of a paperwork technicality.

The Richard of Orange County is mythical.

Another Richard, the President of the United States, is real and his situation is similar except on a grander scale.

✿ ✿ ✿

THE PARALLEL isn't exact, but it's pretty close.

President Nixon is going to have to pay $467,431 in back taxes and interest, much of it because his underlings goofed by not sending a properly signed and dated deed of conveyance for the gift of his vice presidential papers to the National Archives.

Let's take a look at the technicality that wipes out Mr. Nixon's cash and cuts his net worth in half.

Late in 1968, after his election, Mr. Nixon decided to get his vice

presidential papers in order and give them to the people.

He planned to claim their appraised value as an income tax deduction — a procedure that was legal and customary at the time.

✿ ✿ ✿

THE PAPERS, later appraised at $576,000 were delivered to the Archives March 27, 1969, months ahead of a July 25, 1969, law that disallowed tax credits for such gifts.

The law, paragraph 170 (a) (1) of the Internal Revenue Code, required these elements for a gift to be valid as a tax exemption:

(1). The donor must intend to make the gift. (Obviously Mr. Nixon had this intention.)

(2). There must be a physical transfer. (There was.)

(3). There must be a deed of conveyance executed by the donor. (And this was where Mr. Nixon was done in by aides who neglected this detail and later sent the archivist a backdated deed.)

✿ ✿ ✿

THE REST of the tax claim involved capital gains on two property sales and these too were complicated and could be debated both ways.

The President is going to have to pay up without a squawk because he said he'd abide by the findings of the Joint Committee on Internal Revenue whose staff came up with the claim figure.

An ordinary citizen facing a catastrophic tax bill would head for the nearest IRS office and start bargaining. Many a tax bill has been settled by the taxpayer's ability to pay, and we've even

heard of the IRS bending its technicalities in favor of simple justice.

But being President and the most conspicuous citizen of the republic, Mr. Nixon won't be able to strike a bargain with Uncle Sam. He'll probably have to borrow from his wealthy friends, Charles "Bebe" Rebozo and Robert Abplanalp.

As for the tax claim being right or wrong, the question reminds us of the yardman who was paid his exact wage without the accustomed tip. "Is that not correct?" asked the housewife. "Yes ma'am," he said. "It's correct but it ain't right."

✿ ✿ ✿

MEANWHILE, what about the Nixon papers, still in the original crates at the Archives?

If he didn't give them, presumably he still owns them.

And the appraisal of $576,000 by Ralph G. Newman, a supposedly competent authority, is based on what the papers would have been worth on the open market as collectors' items.

President Nixon has been talking disparagingly about the House Judiciary Committee backing a U-Haul into the White House driveway to cart away the large quantity of presidential tapes it wants.

If we were in Mr. Nixon's shoes, we'd beat Congress to the punch, rent that U-Haul, pick up the papers and sell them to raise that big tax bill.

Better still, let the National Archives buy the papers at a mutually fair price.

How does $467,431 sound?

HOUSE JUDICIARY COMMITTEE ISSUES SUBPOENA FOR TAPES

The House Judiciary Committee April 11 voted 33–3 to issue a subpoena ordering President Nixon to turn over to it by April 25 all tape recordings and other materials related to 42 presidential conversations the committee deemed relevant to its impeachment inquiry. The subpoena was served on special presidential counsel James St. Clair that same day. In effect, the committee's vote was a rejection of a compromise offered by St. Clair in an April 9 letter to John Doar, chief counsel to the Judiciary Committee. St. Clair's letter said President Nixon had ordered a review of the material in question and would furnish by April 22 "additional materials" that would "permit the committee to complete its inquiry promptly." St. Clair's letter did not indicate which tapes or material would be turned over to the committee.

White House Press Secretary Ronald L. Ziegler, speaking to the press after the subpoena had been delivered, said the President would give an answer by April 25 that would allow the House panel "to draw a prompt and just conclusion," as well as "bear out the President's statement that he will cooperate consistent with his constitutional responsibilities."

In other Watergate developments:

■ President Nixon avoided a showdown with the Watergate prosecution March 29 by surrendering materials subpoenaed two weeks earlier. The original deadline for response was March 25, but special prosecutor Leon Jaworski had granted an extension at the request of St. Clair.

■ Sen. Lowell P. Weicker Jr. (R, Conn.), a member of the Senate Watergate Committee, accused the Internal Revenue Service (IRS) April 8 of acting as a "public lending library" for White House efforts to aid political friends and harass political enemies. Appearing at a joint hearing of two Senate sub-committees, Weicker disclosed a collection of documents, gathered by the Watergate Committee, showing politically motivated tax audits, undercover White House investigations and military spying on civilians. One 1969 IRS memo describing the creation of a special activists "study unit" advised that the unit's function of examining tax returns of "ideological, militant, subversive, radical or other" organizations must not become publicly known, since disclosure "might embarrass the Administration." The unit was abolished in August 1973 after, according to Weicker, assembling tax data on about 10,000 persons.

■ The Democratic majority on the Judiciary Committee informally agreed April 9 to allow presidential counsel St. Clair to sit in on sessions in which evidence on the President's conduct in office was presented to the committee.

■ President Nixon April 10 campaigned in the 8th Congressional District of Michigan on behalf of James Sparling, a Republican seeking the seat vacated Jan. 31 by Rep. James Harvey (R) who resigned to take a federal judgeship in Michigan. The special election to be held April 16, was billed as a test of Nixon's political strength.

■ As the possibility grew that impeachment hearings against the President might be held, a debate intensified over whether or not such hearings should be televised.

St. Louis Globe-Democrat
St. Louis, Mo., April 13, 1974

The Easter recess of Congress gives all parties to the Presidential impeachment inquiry a chance to cool their tempers. It is just as well that the House Judiciary Committee got a subpoena out of its system before members headed home on their spring break.

Certain Congressmen are given to popping off like corks in a cellar. Those who trumpeted about the "historic confrontation we are now in" just may not know what they are talking about.

Suppose President Nixon were to tell the committee he will not honor the subpoena. No way. Who, then, would attempt to take physical possession of the tapes? Would it be Fishbait Miller, doorkeeper of the House? An appropriate person, perhaps, because the Congressmen do appear to be on a deep-sea fishing expedition.

☆ ☆ ☆

Without as yet having defined an impeachable offense, the Judiciary Committee has demanded 42 additional tapes belonging to the President, including every conversation he had on certain days with H. R. Haldeman, John Ehrlichman, former Attorney General Richard G. Kleindienst and Assistant Attorney General Henry E. Petersen.

The Congressmen already have the files of the Senate Watergate Committee, all the material that was turned over to Special Prosecutor Leon Jaworski, and whatever was in the little black bag that Judge John J. Sirica got from the Watergate grand jury.

Doesn't this suggest that up to this point the committee has found Mr. Nixon to be clean, and that members are now carried away on a search-and-destroy mission? Spurred on by the "Get Nixon" lynch mob, there appears to be a desperate effort to strangle the President with his tapes.

Imagine how the civil libertines would scream if someone tried to convict a kidnap killer on the basis of wiretaps!

Without wanting to dismiss the House committee's action frivolously, there still exists this unresolved question: What powers over the President do the Congressmen really have? They can vote to impeach him, but can they make him do their will meanwhile? If so, where is this spelled out in the Constitution?

Those who say the President dare not "defy" the committee, or he will certainly be impeached, are admitting that the Congressmen's weapons are political and not legal.

☆ ☆ ☆

The President's defense appears to be in exceptionally capable hands, with James St. Clair as his chief counsel. St. Clair would betray his obligations were he not to use every legal safeguard to protect the President to the maximum degree.

The House Committee has the right to investigate the President's actions with possible impeachment in mind, but it has no extraterritorial rights to pry into everything Mr. Nixon has said or done in the time since the Watergate break-in occurred and a coverup was attempted.

No less a Constitutional authority than Sen. Sam Ervin says no evidence was produced in his Senate Watergate hearings to support the impeachment of President Nixon.

"I think this is one section of the Constitution on which Dick Nixon and I agree," Senator Sam said.

Now that he's calling 'em that way, you won't see Senator Sam as the cover boy of Time magazine, or in the centerfold of Newsweek.

Chicago Tribune
Chicago, Ill., April 11, 1974

The House Judiciary Committee's deadline for receiving additional tapes and documents sought in connection with its impeachment investigation has come and gone, and nothing has been delivered. Instead, President Nixon's special counsel, James St. Clair, said he had been "directed" by the President to say that a review of the material is under way, that it will be completed "by the end of the Easter recess" [April 22], and that "the material furnished at that time will permit the committee to complete its inquiry promptly."

This elusive response aroused members of the committee to predictable anger. Several Republicans who have hitherto been cool to subpenas and impeachment are wavering. It is hard to believe that in more than a year of screaming controversy over Watergate and related matters the White House has not gotten around to reviewing just about everything in its possession which might be relevant.

Once again, there is a vague promise to produce something — we're not told just what—at some time in the future; and once again there is the familiar suggestion that this something is all that is needed to satisfy the committee and enable it to finish up its work "promptly" and presumably forget about impeachment.

Every effort thus made by the White House in the past to brush aside the scandal has instead raised new questions and intensified the zeal of the President's critics. Mr. St. Clair's latest message seems almost calculated to taunt the committee.

Surely all of this must be perfectly clear to Mr. St. Clair, a skilled and experienced lawyer. And altho Mr. Nixon has been isolated from reality and fed bum advice by his staff in the past, he, too, must realize now that the course of events is being determined not just by the Judiciary Committee, but by an increasingly exasperated public opinion.

What, then, can be their motive in deliberately provoking the committee's wrath? Is there still a hope that the captain's bridge can ride out the storm while the rest of the ship founders beneath it? If so, something will have to happen pretty soon to satisfy the country or divert its attention.

Is the purpose to provoke the committee itself into behavior so rash as to discredit it in the eyes of the public? If so, at least one Democratic committee member, California's Jerome Waldie, seems to be stumbling into the trap with his belligerent talk of impeachment and his demand that the committee "no longer tolerate" the President's "contemptuous attitude." Mr. Waldie's halo was already badly dented the other day when one of his assistants showed up in Federal Court asking for copies of an indictment which, it turned out, had not yet been returned. Evidently Mr. Waldie or his assistants had been illegally siphoning information out of the special prosecutor's office.

Fortunately most of the committee members and staff have behaved well. To their credit, the Democrats on the committee agreed—before receiving Mr. St. Clair's message—to let him sit in on the impeachment inquiry. This is a right that a prospective defendant does not enjoy in ordinary indictment proceedings but which, in the present instance, seems quite justified in order to protect Mr. Nixon's interests and prevent the slightest hint of a lynching party.

The longer the committee maintains its dignity and composure, the more certainly the White House will have to recognize that the tactics of delay and evasion will not work and that more sincere evidence of the promised cooperation is necessary.

THE KNICKERBOCKER NEWS
••• UNION-STAR •••
Albany, N.Y., April 12, 1974

It is now clear beyond any question that President Nixon is trying to stall the House Judiciary Committee's impeachment inquiry and, if possible, stir up divisive bickering among committee members.

The maneuver, implicit in the White House's latest reply to the committee's month-and-a-half-old request for 42 presidential tapes, is just another example of how Mr. Nixon came by his "Tricky Dick" label. The House Judiciary committee's 33-3 bipartisan vote to issue a subpoena for the tapes indicates that the President's ploy has failed.

It was back on Feb. 25 that the House committee formally asked the President to turn over the tapes of those 42 conversations that are considered vital to the impeachment inquiry. Ever since, Mr. Nixon, while piously proclaiming his cooperation with the committee, has been using every evasive and obstructionist tactic in a lawyer's book to avoid compliance.

Now, on the day of the latest deadline given him by the committee, the President, through his Watergate counsel, James D. St. Clair, contends he needs more time to decide how to respond to the committee's request, but promises he will furnish materials, by April 22, "that will enable the committee to complete its inquiry promptly."

Note that the White House does not say whether it will turn over all, or any, of those tapes by April 22. The response also makes inevitable further delays in the inquiry, for the House can't proceed with requests for or examination of other material until it learns what tapes, if any, it will receive by April 22.

House Judiciary Committee chairman Peter Rodino, who has taken great pains to proceed prudently through the Nixon minefield, understandably is running out of patience. So should the American people. There has been enough of this White House doubletalk and devious game playing.

The mission of the House Judiciary Committee's impeachment inquiry is to get at the truth. The key to the truth is in the evidence. Much of that evidence is under Mr. Nixon's control. Either that evidence clears Mr. Nixon or it doesn't and there's only one way to find out: for the President to turn it over to the committee promptly. It seems more than curious that Mr. Nixon is so reluctant to part with the very evidence that he insists so feverishly will clear him.

Withholding or destruction of evidence that is vital to the investigation of a possible crime constitutes obstruction of justice, which is a serious crime and is grounds, in itself, for impeachment. If any other individual had done what the President has done so far to impede such an important investigation, he would have been hauled before a judge long ago, cited for contempt and slapped in jail. The President indicates, by his actions, that he considers himself above the law. It is time for him to learn that he isn't.

The American system of justice presumes a suspect or target of an investigation to be innocent until proven guilty in a trial. But it does not presume that Americans are damned fools. If more and more Americans come to the conclusion that their President is acting more and more like a guilty man while he protests his innocence, that won't be their fault; it will be his.

The Oregonian
Portland, Ore., April 13, 1974

The House Judiciary Committee sailed angrily into uncharted waters when it voted, 33 to 3, to subpoena White House tape recordings some of which the President's lawyer had offered to deliver and some of which have yet to be specified as pertinent to the committee's investigation of impeachment.

President Nixon is a stubborn man—too stubborn for his own good in his overemphasis of the sanctity of the presidency from interference by the legislative and judicial branches. Should he react to reject the House subpoena the committee may find itself no better off than before.

The committee could appeal to the courts to enforce the subpoena, with the unwelcome delays that would bring. But the President might not deliver all the tapes if ordered to do so by a court. Or the committee could ask the House of Representatives to declare the President in contempt of the Congress. That might be used as a charge in voting impeachment, but it would not produce the tapes. The committee's staff of lawyers could not point a sure way out of the maze.

Inasmuch as the procedures and powers of the impeachment process are not spelled out in either the Constitution or judicial decisions, the Judiciary Committee is making history in this first attempt by Congress to subpoena a president. Perhaps the confrontation may still be averted or modified.

The President's chief counsel, James St. Clair, has offered to provide those tapes of presidential conversations specified in earlier requests by the committee. He has insisted that the White House be given more time to audit and analyze some tapes the contents of which the committee is only guessing at or in which it is fishing for information. The subpoena deadline is 10 a.m., April 25, four days after Congress returns from its Easter holiday.

The better course for both sides would be agreement in the interim on the relevancy of the few disputed tapes or portions of them. The White House has already said that some of the conversations were not recorded. The congressional power of impeachment and trial is clearly stated in the Constitution. The methods of its accomplishment are not. Reasonable men in Congress and the White House have a national obligation to resolve the methods.

The Charlotte Observer

Charlotte, N.C., April 14, 1974

The two months of delay that President Nixon forced into the Senate's Watergate inquiry have cost him the goodwill of some supporters in Congress. But if the reason for his strategy is simply that his guilt would be established by the tapes and documents sought by the Senate Judiciary Committee, it may not have been a strategy caused by bad judgment and stubbornness.

That point seems to be overlooked by congressional supporters of the President, many of whom are expressing exasperation over the fact that he forced the Judiciary Committee to subpoena him. They still hope that he is innocent of impeachable offenses — or not probably guilty. And if he is not probably guilty, they seem to be saying, why is he damaging himself this way?

Why, indeed. Mr. Nixon cannot now claim to be making some great constitutional point about separation of powers; he already had become the first president ever subpoenaed (by a grand jury), and now he has become the first to be subpoenaed by Congress. After the Watergate grand jury issued two subpoenas for evidence, Mr. Nixon complied with one without a fight and obeyed the other after an appeal failed. So he himself has established that the President can be subpoenaed.

It will be difficult for even the White House's constitutionally imaginative lawyers to claim now that the subpoena must be ignored because to obey it would damage the presidency. But they may have a try at it.

If so, the suspicion will grow that they would like for the Judiciary Committee to recommend impeachment not on charges of obstructing justice or authorizing illegalities but on grounds that the President had refused a subpoena.

Mr. Nixon might find it much nicer to defend himself against that charge. It is easier to argue high constitutional principles than to rebut evidence of payoffs to obstruct justice. One then may quote Burke rather than precedents from United States v. Hoffa.

The Judiciary Committee requested the tapes and documents on Feb. 25. Now, six weeks later, it has been forced to subpoena Mr. Nixon for them; he has until April 25 to comply. So, even as Ron Ziegler was urging the Judiciary Committee staff to step up the pace of the inquiry and "perhaps work late into the evenings," the White House has succeeded in delaying matters two full months. That cannot be without reason. The reason was not that this delay would give Mr. Nixon time to gain congressional support: he has been steadily losing it, and already was two months ago. Perhaps the reason is just the one that comes first to mind: that the tapes and documents establish Mr. Nixon's guilt.

If so, the key tapes, notes and transcripts may never appear. The White House already has hinted that some of them may be missing. (It never seems to know what is in hand until it is forced to disclose that something has disappeared.)

Friends of Mr. Nixon in Congress then may deplore that, too, as a terribly counter-productive bit of stubbornness and wonder why he did not say earlier that this particular bit of evidence was missing. But even his greatest defenders are wearying.

We remember, almost two years ago, when the question was why Mr. Nixon did not just come forth with the facts to clear this whole thing up. Just stubbornness and bad judgment? No one has as large a supply of that as Mr. Nixon's congressional supporters have had to attribute to him. Why, indeed.

THE CINCINNATI ENQUIRER

Cincinnati, Ohio, April 15, 1974

PRESIDENT NIXON'S energetic foray into Michigan's Eighth Congressional District amounts to a political gamble of immense proportions. Whether it pays off is likely to tell us something about the condition of Mr. Nixon's long-touted political instinct.

At stake is a congressional seat vacated by Republican Rep. James Harvey, who was recently appointed to the federal bench. The seat has been widely regarded as traditionally Republican. Yet the Democratic candidate, as of last week, was close to 10% ahead in the polls.

To venture into the Eighth, accordingly, was a monumental risk in the best of circumstances. To venture into the Eighth without an enthusiastic invitation from the Republican congressional nominee and in the face of heavy layoffs in the automotive industry—a key factor in the Eighth District's economy—was a manifestation of Mr. Nixon's eagerness, even his desperate eagerness, to test himself on the hustings.

Mr. Nixon aimed his visit at the Eighth District's Republican strongholds. He evidently assumed that organized labor would work around the clock to get its minions out in force in Saginaw and its environs. He hoped, by his barnstorming, to do as much among his own followers in the small towns and rural areas of the district.

His appeal, just as obviously, was aimed at growingly popular convictions that Congress has become so obsessed with the Watergate affair and the President's possible impeachment that it has ignored the nation's more urgent needs. The President spoke in particular of the congressional bottleneck that has stymied attention to a whole series of legislative recommendations.

If Mr. Nixon loses his gamble tomorrow, he apparently figures that he will be no worse off than if he hadn't campaigned at all.

But if, by some stroke of alchemy, he should pull it off, he will have taken a significant step toward convincing actual and potential Republican candidates around the country that the Nixon administration is not the albatross it was widely assumed to be.

Whichever way the returns run tomorrow night, political history will be written.

The Salt Lake Tribune

Salt Lake City, Utah
April 10, 1974

Evidence mounts that advisers and staffmen surrounding President Nixon's first White House term participated in an alarming amount of political freewheeling. The latest such disclosure concerns tax information acquired from the Internal Revenue Service.

Ostensibly, detailed data from individual federal tax returns is confidential. No one, presumably not even the President, is afforded access to anyone else's IRS files. Now, however, material uncovered by Sen. Lowell P. Weicker, R-Conn., indicates this protective shield has been breached.

In testimony before a joint session of three Senate subcommittees investigating covert government intelligence-gathering, Sen. Weiker produced memos to the White House containing specific deficiency totals from particular IRS records. Personalities mentioned ranged from California Gov. Ronald Reagan to film actors John Wayne, Jerry Lewis, Peter Lawford and entertainer Sammy Davis Jr. Their exact income tax deficiencies for years during the early and mid-1960s were revealed to White House staffers, including John W. Dean III. The purpose is fuzzy, although Sen. Weicker maintains it was with the idea of either helping or harrassing persons or groups involved.

The senator alleges the practice fits a pattern of using federal agencies to reward friends but mostly punish foes of the administration. As substantiation he provided other documents showing Dean, then a special White House counsel, discussed, in mid-1971, an IRS investigation and a half-million dollar cut-off in federal contracts as a way of disciplining the Brookings Institution, a research organization that had produced reports uncomplimentary of administration programs. Also, Dean and other White House personnel were shown seriously considering ways of encouraging antitrust actions against the Los Angeles Times. It's a dreary picture.

First, it's distressing to learn that IRS officials actually cooperated in these obviously improper activities. And the present IRS commissioner, Donald C. Alexander, acknowledged last weekend that "certain sensitive case reports. . .were apparently forwarded to the White House." He felt strongly enough about it to add that he refused subsequent requests after he became commissioner and that the indiscretion isn't likely to recur. It shouldn't if the IRS expects to retain public confidence essential for efficient tax collection work.

Secondly, but more distasteful, is the continuing discovery that people at the presidential level were receptive to manipulating federal agencies as a help for friends or a weapon against enemies. That's old ward-heeler politics that has no place in White House responsibilities.

Evidently, few schemes of retribution—those against Brookings and the Los Angeles Times— were ever carried out. Fortunately, almost all the original "whiz kids" are gone from the White House. If anything is gained from their excesses, it's relearning that the nation's institutions are vulnerably fragile and utmost care must be taken when entrusting them to ambitious but inexperienced hands.

The Detroit News

Detroit, Mich., April 14, 1974

Both President Nixon and the House Judiciary Committee have played a reckless kind of political gamesmanship to produce the newest crisis involving White House tapes and documents.

For his part, Mr. Nixon has obviously baited the committee, promising to satisfy its demands but never quite delivering on his promise —in short, practically inviting the committee to issue its unprecedented subpena.

His most obvious purpose would be to stall for time; after all, each day he manages to hold back the tide brings him nearer the end of his term unscathed.

Another purpose, some believe, is to make the issue of the subpena itself the central question of the committee's impending vote on whether to recommend impeachment. Under this theory, he considers himself on strong ground when he defends the principle of separation of powers and he believes that if the chips were down, the House would back down on that issue; and if not the House, the Senate.

Whatever his motives, the President could not have chosen a strategy better calculated to infuriate the entire committee. He started out with defenders among the committee's Republicans but has now managed to create almost unanimous bipartisan opposition for himself. The committee is now almost certain to recommend impeachment—not only on the question of the subpena, assuming Mr. Nixon fails to respond, but on a variety of other charges.

On the other side of the coin, the committee, dominated by the Democratic majority, seems to have played a game of its own. Although the President had promised some sort of response to the committee's requests by April 22, the committee refused to wait until that date to see what material he would offer. Instead, it issued a subpena with a deadline of April 25, three days after the President's own deadline.

In taking that action, it has given him an excuse—violation of the separation of powers—for not doing what he might otherwise have done if permitted to act without compulsion.

The committee, like the President, is playing the game of delay, too— or is being unnecessarily stubborn. It's not as if the committee lacks information on which to act and absolutely needs that extra truckload of tapes and documents from the White House.

Mr. Nixon has already given the committee most of the mountain of tapes and documents previously given to the special Watergate prosecutor. The Senate Watergate committee has forwarded all the data accumulated in its exhaustive, far-ranging hearings.

Federal Judge John Sirica has given the House Judiciary Committee that suitcase full of documents from the Watergate grand jury.

In brief, there is no monumental, earnest effort on either side to get this thing over with, as both sides say they would like to do. The President, on the one hand, fails to keep his promises to cooperate; the Judiciary Committee, on the other, has long since obtained sufficient information on which to act but keeps demanding more.

While the game goes on, the people wait for action that one way or another will settle Watergate and end the permanent state of national crisis it has created.

The Washington Post

Washington, D.C., April 13, 1974

"We will have an answer to the committee regarding today's communication and previous ones by the Easter vacation. And that answer will be comprehensive and conclusive in terms of the President's actions.

"We are confident the answer will allow the committee to draw a prompt and just conclusion, that it will receive the support of the House and bear out the President's statement that he will cooperate consistent with his constitutional responsibilities."—Ronald L. Ziegler, the President's press secretary, answering reporters' questions, April 12, 1974.

HAVING SAID all that, Mr. Ziegler has said nothing —unless President Nixon intends either to comply entirely with the subpoena of the House Judiciary Committee, or to demonstrate convincingly that what he is withholding has no bearing on the case. For to the extent that the President's compliance is in any sense *selective*, there is no way for him to be either "comprehensive" or "conclusive," and no way for his performance to justify the trust or the support of the House. To see why, it is necessary not only to understand the weakness of the President's constitutional argument but to understand the process that leads responsible investigators (and it seems safe to assume the combined majority and minority staffs of the Rodino committee belong in that category) to seek tapes, documents and other material from the White House in the first place. No more than the Special Watergate Prosecutor, Leon Jaworski, are they on anything as simple as a "fishing expedition." They are presumably working from, among other records and documents, the volumes of testimony before the Watergate committee. Beyond that, however, they are taking their own testimony from potential witnesses, seeking to fill in blanks, follow up leads, and round out a coherent reconstruction of what actually happened, in detail. There is no other way to go about building a solid case —whether we are talking about establishing innocence or guilt.

Thus, in the absence of any persuasive evidence to the contrary, it must be assumed that there is a respectable reason for each of these requests—some grounds, for example, to believe that a particular conversation between the President and one or another of his aides has some bearing, one way or another, on the matter at hand. And it is against this background that you have to consider the attitude of the White House and that of the President himself. For what the President is saying is that a line must be drawn somewhere—without ever saying just where. He talks at one nonsensical extreme about backing up trucks and removing everything from the White House, which nobody is suggesting. And he insists, at the other extreme, that he is not claiming confidentiality for *all* of his documents and recordings, which is true enough. But it is also true that he is not acting upon his professed desire to get "the full story out." Rather, he is throughly obfuscating the issue by talking about "weakening of the presidency," as if there is some magic moment when the volume of material turned over to investigators suddenly begins to "weaken" his high office. In his remarks before the Executive Club in Chicago, on March 15, he even argued that he had already passed that point, and went on to say that he had the support in this respect of everyone of his White House predecessors. That, incidentally, is\not so; to the extent that past presidents have been obliged to address the issue at all, they have in fact conceded the essentially unique aspect of an impeachment proceeding which

set it apart from any other investigation which might involve the confidentiality of the office of the presidency.

Still less does it make much sense in this case to talk about breaches of presidential confidentiality in terms of the inhibiting effect upon his advisers of the knowledge that they might somehow be held accountable publicly for having given a President bad advice. "He will be surrounded by a group of eunuchs insofar as their advice is concerned," the President actually argued— this from a President who tape recorded every office conversation he had with his advisers without their knowledge or consent. Quite apart from the solemn charge which is laid upon it by the Constitution and the rights and powers which derive from it, the House is examining impeachable offenses; and if you accept the President's own definition of what that amounts to, this at least gives it a license to search out evidence bearing upon indictable crime. Surely the President's cloak of confidentiality does not extend to discussions in his office with his advisers about their particpation in criminal activity. And equally surely, presidential advisers inhibited from discussing the commission of crimes in the President's presence would not be reduced to "eunuchs insofar as their advice is concerned." In short, the confidentiality argument falls on its face, in the absence of a shred of evidence from the White House that the Rodino Comittee's specific requests are genuinely irrelevant to the matters which the House, under its impeachment powers, is charged with looking into.

An important question remains, and that is whether the President himself ought to be allowed to determine unilaterally, and without producing any evidence, what it is among the material requested, and now subpoenaed, by the Rodino Committee that is or isn't relevant to its proper concerns. To do so, in our view, would make a sham and a shambles of the whole impeachment procedure. For the President, in a very real sense, is in the way of being a defendant in this case and it is hard to imagine how the proceedings now unfolding could conceivably be carried forward in a credible and convincing way if the defendant were to pick and choose the evidence that could be used against him.

Putting it another way, the withholding of even one document, or tape or scrap of conversation or paragraph of a memorandum from the material requested could, at least potentially, rob the rest of the material of any value. For we would have no way of knowing whether the piece that was missing might not be vital to the case. This is in the nature of the process by which a case, for innocence of guilt, is made; it is made by putting pieces together; quite often what makes it an entirely convincing case may be no more than one crucial piece of evidence.

Thus, when the White House offers, as it is currently offering, to turn over some, but not necessarily all, of the material subpoenaed by an overwhelming majority of the House Judiciary Committee, it is not being conciliatory, or reasonable, or flexible or any of these things —this is not a sweetly reasonable compromise to be applauded and encouraged. For what the White House is thereby claiming is the right of the President to determine, in a very real sense, the outcome of an investigation of the President. If the House Committee's subpoena is in fact unenforceable, he may well have the power to do just that. But what he would then be doing ought to be seen for what it is. What he would be doing is to make a farce of the impeachment process.

GOP LOSES MICHIGAN HOUSE SEAT; COMMITTEE GRANTS SUBPOENA DELAY

There were these developments in the Watergate affair during the latter half of April:

■ J. Robert Traxler (D) was elected to Congress in a special election in Michigan's 8th Congressional District April 16. He defeated James M. Sparling Jr. (R), 59,918 (51.4%)–56,575 (48.6%). Traxler had used President Nixon as the major issue in the race. Nixon had visited the district in an effort to help Sparling April 10. It was the first time a Democrat had won the seat since 1932 and the fourth Republican defeat in five recent special Congressional elections.

The President was not "dismayed or disheartened" by the outcome, according to White House Deputy Press Secretary Gerald Warren April 17. He indicated that the results were closer than expected before Nixon's visit to the area. Vice President Gerald R. Ford conceded April 17 that the Republicans had taken "a licking" and that the Watergate issue was at least partially responsible.

■ U.S. District Court Judge John J. Sirica April 18 ordered a subpoena issued on the White House for tapes, transcripts and other documents relating to 64 presidential conversations. Sirica acted at the request of special Watergate prosecutor Leon Jaworski, who had petitioned the court April 16 to issue the subpoena.

Jaworski told the court the material had been requested "as early as" Jan. 9, and despite repeated requests since then, there had been "no definitive response" as to whether the material would be released. In a letter to special presidential counsel James D. St. Clair, dated April 11 and released April 16, Jaworski warned that if the President declined to produce the materials voluntarily, he would be compelled to seek "appropriate judicial process."

■ The House Judiciary Committee met April 25 to hear a report from its legal staff on the scope of the impeachment inquiry and to consider a follow-up in the course of its subpoena to the White House for information. The committee voted 34-4 to extend the deadline for compliance with the subpoena from that day, April 25, to April 30. The extension had been requested April 22 by Nixon's counsel James D. St. Clair.

There had been reports that the White House response to the subpoena would be in the form of edited transcripts of the tapes requested with material deemed irrelevant or impinging on national security deleted. Committee Chairman Peter W. Rodino Jr. had said April 18 that the committee would not accept any procedure in which the White House made "the final determination" of what evidence was relevant to the House inquiry. Furthermore, he said, anything less than full compliance with the subpoena could become in itself part of an impeachment bill.

As for the scope of the inquiry, as outlined in the staff report, the focus was to be narrowed to seven priority areas: the Watergate cover-up attempt; clandestine domestic surveillance; the ITT issue; the dairy industry issue; the $200,000 campaign contribution of Robert L. Vesco; the $100,000 donation from Howard R. Hughes to Nixon's friend, Charles G. Rebozo; and Nixon's personal finances.

The Times-Picayune
New Orleans, La.
April 24, 1974

For an array of reasons — some substantive others just partisan — President Nixon has been variously dubbed a dictator or caricatured as the Sun King, Louis XIV.

But that was before the full repercussions of Watergate and attendant White House weaknesses rolled like shock waves across the nation. In the interim the news media faithfully amplified things.

Now Mr. Nixon would be pictured as the setting Sun King, whose legislating lieutenants on Capitol Hill are being picked off by Democratic sharpshooters out to create a "veto-proof" Congress. In four of the last five congressional races, Democrats have won — if only within 5 per cent victory margins.

Though his peers pounced on him for opening remarks at the Democratic Governors' Conference in Chicago, Georgia Gov. Jimmy Carter sounded a realistic warning: "It is going to be very serious indeed if Nixon remains in office and the Democrats win on the basis of his performance instead of their own. We could win the battle in 1974 and lose the war in 1976.

"The people will vote in 1976 not on Richard M. Nixon, but on the actions of Congress. It appears as though we will be able to elect this year a House and a Senate which is two-thirds Democratic.

"But if we do this and then don't come up with the solutions to the problems of the nation, we are going to be in trouble in 1978. We need a cohesive, unified policy on which we can campaign for the presidency next time."

All of which is Gov. Carter's way of saying what Will Rogers said decades ago: "I am not a member of any organized party — I am a Democrat.

Other governors at the conference were quick to jump on the Georgian for making such impolitic remarks, but Washington pollster Peter Hart likewise cautioned them that talk of an overpowering Democratic majority in Congress, where Republicans are already a debilitated minority, could be "devastating." The reason, said Mr. Hart, is that "the people want to see a continuation of our system of checks and balances."

In short, we don't think the country is willing to swap the fancied dictatorship of a now-weakened Richard Nixon for the dictatorship of an arrogant Democratic Congress. If the 1974 elections show the power pendulum swinging too wildly for Congress, Gov. Carter may be right: his party may "lose the war in 1976."

THE CHRISTIAN SCIENCE MONITOR

Boston, Mass., April 18, 1974

In the test of his **political** strength Tuesday in Michigan's Eighth Congressional District, a test he himself sought, Mr. Nixon found his and his party's political base in the country narrowed considerably.

It would not be wholly accurate to say that the Republican stronghold was lost to the Democrats, for the first time in 40 years, on the Watergate issue alone. Inflation, a 10 percent unemployment rate in the auto-industry-centered cities of Saginaw and Bay City, and even recession worries among farmers gave Democratic candidate J. Robert Traxler an edge. The **Eighth** District vote in part reflected the latest Gallup poll's finding **that** the Democrats nationwide **have** pulled ahead of the Republicans as the party thought most capable of providing prosperity, a point they had trailed on for several years.

What the Eighth District vote showed is that Mr. Nixon's political

cal strength, even with vigorous and emphatic campaigning, may be too weak to make much difference to his party's prospects. Mr. Nixon politically may not be so much an "albatross" for Republicans (as was charged by the Michigan Democratic winner) as an irrelevant political factor for Republicans in the fall. The latest polls show that on the peace issue as well as the prosperity issue, the public now identifies the country's best prospects with the Democrats rather than the Republicans. This further undercuts Mr. Nixon's political usefulness to his party, despite the President's legitimate claims to achievement in foreign affairs.

The Eighth District test was significant in yet another way. With a half-million population, it is not a small district. It has a large ethnic group among its Democrats, who in the last election were staunch Nixon suppor-

ters. It was such voters who had given the President his unique landslide victory in 1972 when they had shunned George McGovern and his, to them, wobbly economic and war positions. Mr. Nixon has apparently been abandoned by these ethnic conservative voters who hold the balance of power in the vital rural-industrial belt in the North.

Of course, Mr. Nixon is himself not running for re-election but is striving to contain the impeachment and court actions hemming him in in Washington. Even so, he can find no comfort in the Michigan outcome. It does nothing to show the House and Senate Republicans, who have stood with their Democratic colleagues against the White House on subpoena and impeachment issues, that the public disapproves of their Watergate steps. The latest Harris survey found that the public indeed supports Congress on

the evidence issue: By 55 to 33 percent a majority believes the House should bring impeachment charges "if President Nixon fails to turn over the information the House Judiciary Committee wants." By a slim margin, 43 to 41 percent, Americans think impeachment should be brought on the basis of what is already known.

What Mr. Nixon achieved by his campaigning last week in Michigan, like his earlier "campaign" before Chicago business executives and Grand Ole Opry fans, was to demonstrate that he can remain active on behalf of himself and his party. But, with Republicans registering an all time low of 24 percent following among the American public, it is Mr. Nixon's effectiveness in behalf of his party that worries the House and Senate faithful. This concern the Tuesday loss in a once "safe" district did nothing to dispel.

The Detroit News

Detroit, Mich., April 18, 1974

Voting in an election which President Nixon, himself, had accepted as a test of his prestige, the citizens of Michigan's 8th Congressional District this week sent a threefold message of gloom to Mr. Nixon and the Republican Party.

One, the political and rhetorical magic by which Richard Nixon has staged so many astonishing comebacks in his remarkable career appears to be failing him at last.

According to the script, he would sweep into the 8th District, rescue Republican James Sparling from defeat, reverse the trend of Democratic victories, and send his own stock soaring. It didn't happen that way. The Democrat, J. Robert Traxler, won.

Two, as Congress perceives a clear expression of public sentiment from a cross-section of America, the harsh possibility of impeachment now grows very real.

Three, it is now clear that the offer of presidential aid in congressional races can be the kiss of death for Republican candidates. Hence, Republicans will tend to draw further away from Mr. Nixon in an effort to establish a distinction between the party and its discredited leader.

You have to feel sorry for candidate Sparling. He became a secondary figure in his own election campaign in a district where ordinarily the Republican candidate would have won.

Logically, the real issue should have been whether Sparling or Traxler would make the best congressman.

That issue was thrust aside not only by Traxler, who called Mr. Nixon "the real candidate," but also by Sparling, who invited Mr. Nixon to the district, assuring, whether Sparling realized it or not, that the election would become a referendum on the President.

If the 8th District election and three out of four previous special elections this year are to be taken as signs of the times, Democratic candidates this year apparently need only to campaign against President Nixon and Watergate to win.

That's obviously absurd and unfair, but people are so fed up with this administration that they will use any means, however illogical, to signify their anger and disenchantment.

At this point, therefore, it looks as if the forthcoming congressional elections will prove disastrous for Republicans, which means that the Democrats will increase their majority and their ability to obstruct. That in turn will mean even deeper conflict between Congress and the White House with discouraging consequences for the President's programs and his ability to lead.

Opponents of resignation or impeachment argue that such drastic steps would plunge the country into a political mess. Yet, it's hard to see how that mess could be any worse than the one America's in right now—a mess which, partly as a result of the presidential referendum in Michigan's 8th District, promises to get a lot worse before it gets better.

The Dallas Morning News

Dallas, Tex., April 19, 1974

"I BELIEVE this will hasten the impeachment process."

Richard Vander Veen talking, the Democrat who grabbed Vice-President Gerald Ford's old House seat in Michigan. Vander Veen was doing an instant commentary on the effect of the second GOP disaster in that state in two months.

It was, of course, a disaster that Nixon himself made personal by going in and campaigning for the loser. He set up the referendum. But not the kind of referendum Vander Veen is making of it.

Well, what kind of referendum was it? Strictly speaking, one on his political standing with his own party (the race was run in a GOP district) and on the power of his presence to help or hurt his own low public standing as President.

BY ORDINARY political standards, the Michigan disaster should be only relative. Commentators would have treated the Democratic victory as a national rejection of Nixon whether he had gone into the state or not. He has only helped them make it more personal.

That is fair enough. Nixon asked for it and thought the chance worth taking. A victory would have meant more for his party's chances in November and for his own morale than anything his detractors could honestly make of what amounted to only one more proof of his low public standing.

You can fault him for foolhardiness in laying his poll-battered name on the line in that way—but what do you say about Vander Veen making impeachment politics out of the loss?

He won't be the only one to do so. The liberal media and the impeachment lobby will join Vander Veen in making the Michigan results an "impeachment referendum" rather than a political one. They will lay their conclusions atop the heap of other evidences (already adduced by them) that Nixon is a goner.

THAT'S THE favorite game nowadays of those politicians and newsmen who are carrying on their own impeachment campaign outside the constitutional process that is supposed to govern and dispose of the question of whether Nixon should be addressed out of office for high crimes and misdemeanors.

Going into Michigan and backing a loser won't be added to the—what is it, 55?—counts the House Judiciary Committee is looking at. Nor is it supposed to affect the committee's judgment, or that of the House or Senate. But the impeachment lobby intends that it shall, if at all possible.

Politics and personal vendettas against Nixon mean most to these people. They are out not just to celebrate a House victory in Michigan but to crow over another milestone in a campaign they hope will be crowned with the political lynching of the President.

Portland Press Herald
Portland, Me., April 16, 1974

It is time for the Congress of the United States to impeach President Nixon or get off his back.

It is time for an end to this infernal bickering and bargaining about tapes. We have no idea, of course, as to the content of the tapes now in dispute. And we don't much care because we're convinced the House Judiciary Committee can make a decision to impeach or not to impeach without those tapes. The conversations on them, or what may be there by the time the commitee staff hears them, probably won't by any more conclusive than all that has gone before.

This is not a brief for Richard Nixon. Whatever the judgment of Congress may be, he has brought dishonor upon one of the great public offices of the world. The people of this country gave him the greatest electoral pledge of confidence any American has ever known. He repaid them with treachery and deception. He has cheated them — or would have if another congressional group hadn't caught up with his income tax returns.

His first vice president has been revealed as a crook. His current vice president has denounced the very machine that carried Mr. Nixon into office for a second term. Confidence in the American President wanes in foreign capitals as his popularity plummets in the domestic polls.

No, this is no brief for Richard Nixon. It is more a plea in behalf of the American people desperately seeking emotional stability. The need is not for a tranquilizer that provides symptomatic relief until the next crisis, but for a level of calm, of security, of leadership that can be trusted — and respected.

It is difficult to believe that the presidency of the United States can regain its customary respectability so long as Richard Nixon remains in office. Nevertheless, the procedure for his removal is specificially set forth in that precious document which, it sometimes seems, is about all we have left of a great and noble ideal.

The charges set forth therein are crimes, not conduct unbecoming a President. If in the judgment of the committee Richard Nixon has committed a crime, let it be alleged, let him be tried in accordance with the prescribed procedure, and subsequently judged.

But in the name of the national sanity, let it be done now. Accuse, try, judge. Or decide not to accuse. But decide! Let the executive, the legislative, the judiciary, and all the many arms of government appended to those bodies, function once again without having to weigh every act and utterance in the light of a possible impeachment.

The nation has been too long on edge. Let those with the power to do so provide some relief.

New York Post
New York, N.Y., April 22, 1974

During a weekend of contemplation at Camp David, President Nixon is reported to have decided to release edited transcripts of some of the tapes sought by the House Judiciary Committee and special prosecutor Leon Jaworski. If he adheres to that course, he will almost surely crystallize what we have long regarded as the crucial issue in the projected impeachment proceeding — calculated, defiant obstruction of justice by the nation's Chief Executive.

His apparent determination to become the arbiter of what material is relevant to the work of both the House inquiry and the man he named as prosecutor—and to deny both access to the original tapes on which the selective transcripts are allegedly based—cannot conceivably be accepted as compliance with the subpenas he confronts. It suggests he is reconciled to the adoption of an impeachment resolution and is staking everything on his ability to rally a conservative alliance of 33-plus-one Senators against his eventual conviction in a Senate trial.

That desperate last-stand strategy is also reflected in seemingly well-founded reports that the Internal Revenue Service has been tenaciously resisting the Senate Watergate committee's investigation of the $100,000 Howard Hughes campaign contribution turned over to Nixon's ubiquitous friend, Charles G. Rebozo. It seems implausible that the IRS, its integrity already under serious challenge, would engage in such maneuvers without White House direction. Its denial of the charge was embarrassingly belated.

Whatever new revelations may ensue, the President's conduct daily strengthens the image of a man frantically seeking to obscure the whole truth—and hamper justice—rather than his self-portrait of a wronged figure who has nothing to hide. He has clearly rejected the counsel of leading Republicans who have implored him to respond fully and freely to the House probers and Jaworski.

* * *

We said many weeks ago that Nixon could serve the national interest best by resignation. But he so far has indicated that he will not step down voluntarily, no matter how many Republican political lives are destroyed by his persistence. If he is indeed prepared to hang on at all cost, he is ironically laying the foundation for the strongest Constitutional case for his removal—his systematic, self-serving obstruction of our judicial processes.

His suppression of vital evidence is hardly the first offense. He was guilty of flagrant transgression when the directorship of the FBI was proffered to the presiding judge in the Ellsberg trial while the case was in progress. His obstinate resistance to full disclosure is his climactic challenge to the rule of law.

ARKANSAS DEMOCRAT
Little Rock, Ark., April 21, 1974

The tortuous and crisis-filled political career of Richard M. Nixon may come to a climax April 25 depending on how he responds to the historic subpoena of the House Judiciary Committee. If Mr. Nixon complies with the demand for all of the Watergate related records, he will buy more time in his defense against impeachment. If he refuses, the suspicion will spread that he is trying to conceal his guilt and this, coupled with a contempt of Congress charge, could no doubt spell his doom.

There is growing reason to suspect that Mr. Nixon may have set a trap for his accusers and that they might fall into it. By ignoring the subpoena, the President will surely bring down on himself the wrath of Congress, even though that body has no power to enforce its demands. Congress' lone recourse then would be to vote a bill of impeachment, and this might be Mr. Nixon's secret desire. If he faces charges on that count alone, he can't lose. Few in Congress feel a President should be impeached on a technicality. But in the unlikely event he should be found guilty on this one, narrow charge, Mr. Nixon could save face and gain fame by going into the history books as the only President ever to be removed from office by fighting to the last ditch to preserve the power and authority of that office.

However, Mr. Nixon may have waited too long to spring his trap. The mood of Congress, and especially the Judiciary Committee, seems to indicate the time for game-playing is past. The President's hope for a quick, one-count impeachment appears futile. What is more likely is for Congress to add the contempt charge to those already being drawn. The Democrats know they have Mr. Nixon on the ropes and they are not about to soften their assault. Besides, they are encouraged by the bipartisan support shown in the subpoena vote. Only three Republicans stood by the President, which was a clear signal to the White House that its hope of dividing the Judiciary Committee had also failed.

Thus the nearly two-year ordeal of Watergate comes down to the wire. If, as he has repeatedly claimed, he has evidence that will clear his name, then the time is certainly at hand for Mr. Nixon to release it. Further delay can only add to the growing suspicion about his guilt and prolong the national agony that such suspicion has inspired.

THE SAGINAW NEWS
Saginaw, Mich., April 18, 1974

J. Bob Traxler becomes the first Democrat in 40 years to represent the 8th Michigan District in Congress because Mr. Nixon and his administration and inflation, unemployment, the price of gasoline and the shortage of nitrogen fertilizer are the overriding issues, as Mr. Traxler insisted throughout his campaign — not the busing issue or the quality or quantity of his legislative ability.

Give or take the weak spots in the latter, and there are some, that was never a serious liability to Mr. Traxler as Tuesday's result indicates. Unfortunately for the opposition, it indulged in overkill on that. Now it is no longer an issue. What happens in Washington will be.

It was stretching it too far to take one of Lansing's busiest legislators with a string of significant legislative accomplishments to his credit and hold him up as one who isn't earning his money — whether you agree with everything he stands for or not. And we do not agree with Mr. Traxler on everything. We won't at all times in the future. But we are confident that this district will have an active, highly articulate representative in Congress — actually quite a student of government as well as a politician.

Yet if there was an overplay of the Lansing record on the part of James M. Sparling Jr. and his campaign managers, Mr. Traxler, too, overplayed it in tieing Mr. Sparling to the great troubles which have beset Mr. Nixon. Mr. Traxler must be careful not to overplay his hand in Washington. He will be of a different dimension there than here.

In many ways the campaign bogged down badly over these issues — but this does not detract from J. Bob Traxler's victory. And there are many reasons for that.

It is a tribute to his stamina, his determination, an engaging personality — and certainly to his ability to exploit those things in Washington which have so many people upset. All of them enabled him to thrive on a tough campaign trail. On the practical side, his victory is owing also to the generous and tireless support he received from those who felt it was time for a change in this district.

This election may well have proved something else, too. It is that the re-shaped 8th District is no longer quite the safe haven for Republicans it once was. That, and changing life styles which have altered even precinct voting patterns, cannot be discounted. There are just too many independents anymore who refuse to be shirt-tailed to either party, particularly when given the issues that were injected into this campaign.

Inescapably, though, the shadow of the President hangs over this campaign. It does because he came here to give his support to Mr. Sparling — and that did turn it into a referendum of some dimension on Mr. Nixon himself.

Generously, Mr. Sparling has said that he lost the election, not Mr. Nixon. That is commendable candor on Mr. Sparling's part. But the fact that can't be washed is that Mr. Nixon's presence, much of it spent in the rural Thumb area, failed to turn the tide in what had been figured as a close race.

It can only be deduced that the President did not rally Republicans in sufficient numbers — nor did he really change many minds. There is a discontent abroad, a lot of it translated into apathy, which Mr. Nixon could not wipe away.

So once again a message has been sent to the White House and its contents are cause enough for concern. The reading is gloomy and that cannot escape Republican party leadership. And that leadership reaches for thin straws when it says that Mr. Sparling would not have done as well without Mr. Nixon.

But the past is now prologue. A new road stretches out ahead for J. Bob Traxler. It is one filled with challenges — and it will challenge the best that is in him. It would be the same were it Mr. Sparling who was heading to Washington.

Mr. Traxler has talked to thousands of persons of diverse interests. He has made a good many hard statements and promises. He has enunciated his position on everything from cross-district busing to federal gun control laws and abortion. He is against all three. More so than are we, it can be added. He's for tougher controls on the oil industry. He's for a government that does more for the people without invading their lives or their pocketbooks excessively.

He has not been adverse to the idea of populism and says he senses that the people are awakening to that movement today.

He candidly admits that he has no instant solutions for inflation but says that if full production doesn't work, some hard steps may have to be taken again in the form of new wage-price controls.

He has shown himself to be keenly aware of the problems which are of particular interest to this district — preservation of rail service in the Thumb, dredging of the Saginaw River for all-season international shipping and water and sewage problems through out the area. And he seems to have a very deep feeling for senior citizens and the economically downtrodden.

We do not expect that in a few months Mr. Traxler can turn miracles. As Mr. Sparling correctly and realistically noted during the campaign, the most freshman of all congressmen can hardly expect to get instant attention.

But Mr. Traxler will have the vote. We expect he'll be using that. Moreover, he has a hardy enthusiasm for legislation and a good way of speaking so that he is heard. We expect him to put those qualities to constructive use.

We congratulate Mr. Traxler on a long and successful campaign that has culminated in victory. We congratulate Mr. Sparling also for his untiring efforts to become elected and the graceful way in which he has accepted the majority wish of the voters.

THE ANN ARBOR NEWS
Ann Arbor, Mich., April 18, 1974

BLAND as it sounds, the most sensible comment we have heard from any politician concerning Tuesday's special election in Michigan's Eighth Congressional District is the one by Gov. Milliken. He simply observed that Democrat Robert Traxler's 51.4 per cent victory cannot be explained solely as a result of Watergate or the Nixon campaign tour of the district's rural counties.

Beyond a doubt, the Nixon administration's efforts to establish a semi-private presidential police force, and Nixon's incredible tax debts, have a great deal to do with voters' feelings toward almost any Republican candidate.

Republican loser James Sparling Jr. carried Huron, Sanalac and Tuscola counties by a margin of only 7,911 compared to the GOP margin of 20,000 in 1972. It is inconceivable that anything Sparling has said or done could account for that much slippage by a party that has held the district since 1934. The GOP was also the traditional winner there before the Depression election of 1932.

Yet, it would be presumptuous for observers outside the Eighth District to assume that the vote there was determined entirely by the Nixon scandals or by any other event beyond the district's boundaries.

The ability of U.S. presidents to influence congressional and senatorial elections by personal campaigning has always been a very debatable matter, even when the presidents involved were in reasonably good standing with the public. President Roosevelt's unsuccessful efforts during the late 1930s to persuade voters to defeat several senators and congressmen who opposed FDR's programs is the classic illustration of this point.

There may be some truth in Sparling's declaration that "it was lost by Jim Sparling," if he means something might be wrong within the county and district-wide GOP organizations of his area. Again, it would be presump-

tuous for an outsider to jump to conclusions, but it is possible for party leaders to become too complaisant after winning easily and often.

A better test of the two parties' organizing and voter-turnout abilities in the Eighth District will come in the next election. It is a certainty that no president will enter that campaign.

Presidents, even popular ones, could enhance the position of Congress and possibly help in efforts to get campaign costs back to some rational level if they would leave campaigning in congressional elections to the candidates.

NIXON RELEASES EDITED TRANSCRIPTS

President Nixon, in a televised address April 29, said he would turn over to the House Judiciary Committee the next day, and also make public, 1,200 pages of edited transcripts of his conversations with key aides concerning Watergate. Asserting he had "nothing to hide," Nixon said the transcripts included "all the relevant portions of all of the subpoenaed conversations that were recorded" and related to Watergate or the cover-up. The transcripts also covered other conversations, he said, which were not subpoenaed by the committee "but which have a significant bearing on the question of Presidential action with regard to Watergate." (The transcripts, which were released April 30, did not cover 11 of the 42 conversations subpoenaed by the committee. Four of them, according to White House counsel J. Fred Buzhardt, occurred on April 15, 1973 and were not recorded because the machine ran out of tape; five occurred on telephones that were not connected to a recorder; and tapes of two others were not found, the implication being that the conversations did not occur.) In essence, the transcripts would show, Nixon said, "that what I have stated from the beginning to be the truth has been the truth, that I personally had no knowledge of the break-in before it occurred, that I had no knowledge of the cover-up" until March 21, 1973, that he never offered clemency and that, after March 21, "my actions were directed toward finding the facts and seeing that justice was done." The panel's Democratic chairman and top Republican would be allowed to verify the transcripts by listening to the actual tapes at the White House, Nixon said.

While asserting the transcripts would clear him and end the Watergate issue, Nixon conceded they would embarrass him and lead to speculation. The transcripts of the President's private conversation were profane and liberally sprinkled with the words "expletive removed." The tone of much of the material also was profane; the subjects covered perjury, "hush money," blocking Congressional probes, tapping grand jury secrecy, fabrication of public and legal positions, and deceiving and manipulating the Watergate prosecutor.

A White House legal brief accompanying the transcripts April 30th asserted President Nixon's innocence in the Watergate matter. The brief, as did the President in his speech, attacked in particular John Dean's credibility.

The House Judiciary Committee split along party lines and voted 20–18 May 1 to inform President Nixon by letter than he had "failed to comply with the committee's subpoena" requesting the White House tapes and documents. The committee's special counsel John M. Doar also informed the panel the White House transcripts were "not accurate." After comparison with some overlapping material obtained previously, some of it from the special prosecutor, the staff's own tape

experts, Doar said, had been able to "pick up parts of conversations" that were marked "unintelligible" in some of the White House transcripts. Doar also said there were sections of the White House transcripts where words had been omitted without any notation that the deletion had been made. Doar stressed that he was not suggesting there had been any "intentional distortion" in the White House version, only that the committee staff could detect, if the actual tapes were available, many of the parts marked "unintelligible" by the White House. Doar advised the committee it would not be "prudent" for the two senior committee members to attempt to verify the accuracy of the transcripts without professional help.

William Randolph Hearst Jr., editor of the Hearst newspapers and a firm Nixon supporter, said in his Sunday column May 5 (published May 3) the transcript conversations revealed Nixon as a man "with a moral blind spot" and made his impeachment inevitable. The *Chicago Tribune,* an influential Republican newspaper, in an editorial in its May 9 edition (published May 8), called for Nixon to leave office for the sake of "the presidency, the country and the free world." Senate Republican Leader Hugh Scott (Pa.) severely criticized and renounced support May 7 for the "immoral" acrivities delineated in the transcripts.

The mounting adverse reaction from Republicans to the revelations of the transcripts led to repeated assertions from the White House that no impeachable offense had been committed and that President Nixon had no intention of resigning. "The President will not quit even if hell freezes over," White House Communication's Director Ken W. Clawson said May 9. Dr. John McLaughlin, a Jesuit priest who was a special assistant to Nixon, held a news conference May 8 to assert that "the President acquitted himself throughout these [transcript] discussions with honor."

The House Judiciary Committee May 9 opened its long-awaited hearings to determine whether to recommend the impeachment of President Nixon. In rules of procedure for the hearings adopted unanimously May 2, the committee had approved television and radio coverage of open sessions and of participation within limits, for presidential counsel James D. St. Clair.

St. Clair announced May 7 that President Nixon would "respectfully" decline "to produce any more Watergate tapes" for use in the House Judiciary Committee's impeachment inquiry, and that Nixon had instructed him to "press forward" with an effort to quash special prosecutor Leon Jaworski's subpoena for tapes of 64 White House conversations. The taped conversations were being sought by the prosecution in preparation for the trial of seven men in the Watergate cover-up conspiracy case and as potential exculpatory evidence for the defendants.

St. Louis Globe-Democrat
St. Louis, Mo., May 1, 1974

By making public more than 1200 pages of transcripts from White House tapes, President Nixon has come out in the open with the Watergate story in a way that should satisfy the American people.

The President's offer to let House Judiciary Chairman Peter W. Rodino, and his ranking Republican colleague, Edward M. Hutchinson, listen to the actual tapes as a check on authenticity of the transcripts is reasonable and should be accepted.

With candor unprecedented in American history, Mr. Nixon conceded Monday night that he is fighting for his life as President.

☆   ☆   ☆

He said, in releasing the transcripts, "blemishes and all — I am placing my trust in the basic fairness of the American people. If read with an open and fair mind, and read together with the record of the action I took, these transcripts will show that what I have stated from the beginning to be the truth has been the truth."

Mr. Nixon's address to the nation may have been the most important political talk an American president has ever delivered. There was no concealing that he was determined to prevent the very real risk of impeachment.

The President was justified in going over the heads of the Judiciary Committee by bringing his case to the American people. The committee has been extreme in its demands.

☆   ☆   ☆

By his action, Mr. Nixon subjects himself to the humiliation of having the spotlight put on confidential sessions with his closest associates. No other President in history has ever been subjected to such treatment. Nor has any President ever volunteered to be so treated.

Instead of appreciating the President's willingness to be reasonable, those who can never bring themselves to say a good word about the man are complaining that he is withholding information.

The President confessed that he expects to be ridiculed and embarrassed by political and journalistic opponents who will attempt to unseat him.

Any sensitive, decent person should understand that statements can be made in a conference session which bear no semblance to the considered judgments a speaker might make after reflection. A person under stress is quite likely to blurt out proposals, even suggestions that he knows to be ill-considered, in a desperate effort to remedy a difficult situation.

☆   ☆   ☆

Having rash thoughts, even out loud, is not a criminal act nor does it amount to a conspiracy. The rough spots in Mr. Nixon's transcripts will have to be assessed as they relate to the whole story.

Political reality dictates that certain persons will never bring themselves to believe Mr. Nixon. They would not believe him under oath. This does not mean they are morally superior to the President.

The House Judiciary Committee can be dissatisfied with the President's proposition if it chooses to be. But it would be advisable for the members to accept Mr. Nixon's materials in good faith at this point, leaving an option open for further evidence if it is thought needed.

The nation does not need a test of strength between the House committee and the President. It needs a chance to evaluate the President's revelations soberly and without malice.

The Birmingham News
Birmingham, Ala., May 1, 1974

The time has come for Rep. Peter Rodino, the House Judiciary Committee and its 100 lawyers to fish or cut bait.

If Rodino and his committee are *really interested* in getting on with their investigation of possible impeachment charges against President Nixon, the way has been fully cleared for them.

President Nixon has now delivered to the committee transcripts on all of the tapes containing conversations relating to Watergate. In the event the transcripts are not in themselves sufficient, Mr. Nixon has agreed to make the actual tapes available to Rodino and his Republican co-chairman, Rep. Edward Hutchinson.

And if these sources are not sufficient in the view of the committee, Mr. Nixon has agreed to answer any additional questions committee members might pose to him either in writing or in person *under oath*.

Fair-minded Americans will consider the President's compromise to be more than adequate when weighed against the sacrifice of confidentiality.

However, within minutes of the President's televised talk, hostile members of the media were saying that the offer of the transcripts was another ploy by the President to evade giving all the facts. Subsequently, the President's known enemies in the Democratic Party have added their monotonous chorus of plaints.

By all logical estimates the transcripts, plus auditing the tapes, plus sworn testimony by the President should be adequate to bring out all the facts relating to Watergate and to White House efforts to discover those facts and to make them known to government prosecutors, the Congress and the public.

If the President were involved in the least in any kind of cover-up, it is inconceivable that such a course could not be readily detected in the 1,200 pages — approximately 200,000 words — of conversations on the transcripts. Even allowing for ambiguities and contradictions, it is virtually impossible that the President's true posture could be hidden, for the transcripts are bound to contain enough outright declarations and statements to confirm the direction, create the sense of what had transpired and was transpiring in the White House during the year since ex-presidential aide John Dean was instructed by the President to get to the bottom of the Watergate matter.

And as Mr. Nixon pointed out in his talk, the transcripts or auditing the tapes can be weighed against the President's actions and orders relating to Watergate subsequent to his order to Dean as a means of corroboration or criticism.

Realizing that his listeners must be confused about the Watergate affair and the whole impeachment process, the President noted that for more than a year "the wildest accusations have been given banner headlines and ready credence. Rumor, gossip, innuendo, accounts from unnamed sources of what a witness might testify to have filled the" newspapers and television and radio newscasts day after day.

In examining a year of supposed media coverage of the Watergate and related events, it is inconceivable that so very little has been provided the public in the way of hard facts. The bulk of the media content has been, as the President said, mostly hearsay, rumor, speculation and allegation. More than a year and a half after Watergate, only John Dean has come forward to testify that the President had any part in the supposed cover-up.

When considering the millions upon millions of words which have been written and spoken about the matter, it is incredible that so few hard facts have been established.

And Rep. Peter Rodino and his House Judiciary Committee must be held responsible, at least in part, for the deplorable lack of progress in getting the matter resolved.

Ever since the committee was empowered to look into impeachment charges more than six months ago, Rodino has complained about the President's unwillingness to cooperate. Yet Rodino has made no move to examine the mountain of evidence the committee's staff of 100 lawyers, which has already cost $1 million, has accumulated.

Only Monday, Rodino said, "If the White House stalls on responding to the committee's requests, I don't see how we can start examining the evidence." He failed to explain why the tapes in the White House kept the committee from examining the material it already had obtained.

Other committee members have complained that Rodino has told them practically nothing about the material already on hand. The members say they cannot understand why they are not examining this material while waiting on new material to be developed.

One committeeman complained that "just sitting on our hands and doing nothing while bellowing for more data is absurd. All that's doing," he said, "is making headlines."

A Texas Democrat, Rep. O. C. Fisher, perhaps, has best summarized the committee's record thus far. Fisher said, "Although in the six months the Judiciary Committee has been considering impeachment charges, it has held no hearings and made no findings. Yet people in and out of Congress are sounding off and jumping at totally unproven conclusions . . . that is being done," he said, "even before there is a consensus as to what constitutes an impeachable offense."

Also criticizing the inaction of the House Judiciary Committee, Rep Dale Milford, D-Texas, said his constituents think "six months is long enough for the Judiciary Committee to consider impeachment charges." The congressman added that disagreement with the President is not an impeachable offense and neither is the fact that he has a feud with the press cause for impeachment.

Milford also pointed out caustically that "nowhere in the Constitution or the law is there a provision for trial (of the President) by public opinion. That is what has been going on, and I'm sick and tired of it," the congressman said.

It is to be hoped that President Nixon's compromise offer will be the weight necessary to break the log-jam in Rodino's mind and put the committee on the road to systematically examining the the mountain of material it has on hand.

If Rodino does not make some effort to bring the full committee into action and to begin whatever hearings are required, the only conclusion the public can draw is that no evidence in the hands of the committee points to the President's complicity, or that Rodino is deliberately stalling in order to build sentiment in the House for a pro-impeachment vote.

Unless Rodino and the Democratic majority want to be indelibly marked with partisan enmity for the President at the expense of the nation's well-being, they had better give immediate and sober attention to the material at hand.

To stall any longer will be to compromise the government's ability to act decisively both at home and abroad and to abrogate sworn responsibilities to the American people.

The nation must have more than rumor, speculation and allegation on which to make judgments about the question of impeachment. Only Rodino and his committee can provide the clarifying facts. For it was with such a purpose that the committee was sanctioned and funded.

No excuses can any longer be tolerated.

The Topeka Daily Capital

Topeka, Kans., May 5, 1974

It's time to hand President Nixon his hat. Having voted twice for the President we confess to a certain heart sickness when we read reports of transcriptions of the tapes.

Since the beginning of Watergate we had hoped the situation would improve with the passing days. Instead, the bad news has snowballed with morality lacking.

The transcript of the tapes dips to sordid depths. They reveal the President threatened to use the Justice department, the F.B.I. and the Internal Revenue Service and other government agencies to seek political revenge. The tapes disclose the gang around the President was prepared to go to any lengths to punish enemies and pursue a course of wanton disrespect for law.

Walls of the White House echoing with conspiracy reminds one that gangland has profaned America's most hallowed halls. The brutal language is not only shocking but it scorns the law it is supposed to uphold.

To recite, what the tapes tell, is that this nation through President Nixon has sunk to a new low in morality and contempt for law. The record is now spread for all to read.

The one bright spot in the record is the President's achievement in foreign affairs through Henry Kissinger.

Fortunately we have Gerald Ford the vice president to step into the breach and carry on. We believe the President should not go through a trial in the Senate but should very quietly resign, pick up his hat and move on. He has had his day and been found wanting.

Even as Vice President Agnew has become the forgotten man, so may President Nixon pass into oblivion and the nation again resume its true posture, one that every American can uphold with pride and dignity. — OSCAR S. STAUFFER.

The New York Times

New York, N.Y., May 2, 1974

A reading of the first installment of the transcripts of the White House tapes as published in The Times supports the contention that President Nixon was aware of a deliberate cover-up of the Watergate scandal. The transcripts also offer a striking insight into the ethical decay that pervaded the Oval Office. The deleted expletives could not have been nearly as appalling as the moral standards which Mr. Nixon and his aides applied to serious problems of politics, law and justice.

Though incomplete and flawed by the long time gaps between some of the recordings, these documents indicate that the President understood the efforts to prevent the facts from becoming known long before the meeting of March 21, 1973, when John Dean confronted him with the sordid details. Six months earlier, on Sept. 15, 1972, Mr. Nixon told Mr. Dean: "But the way you have handled all this seems to me has been very skillful putting your fingers in the leaks that have sprung here and sprung there."

A White House "explanation" that these remarks were made in the context of a political campaign rather than of "a criminal plot to obstruct justice" is hardly relevant. The President knew that a criminal offense had been committed. Motives for the cover-up shift—from winning the election to saving the Nixon Presidency; but the transcripts suggest that the cover-up first drew Mr. Nixon's praise as early as that pre-election month of September.

On March 13, 1973, Mr. Nixon found nothing wrong with Mr. Dean's warning that Hugh Sloan represented a high risk because "he has a compulsion to cleanse his soul by confession" and was therefore being given "a lot of stroking."

Although the notorious March 21 meeting did place Mr. Nixon in the role of the executive intent on having his advisers lay out all the options, that meeting also saw several crucial pieces in the search for truth fall into place. The President learned that perjury had been committed by three persons involved in the case—and took no action. Indeed, his reaction to the perjury charge against Egil Krogh was a consoling: "Perjury is an awful hard rap to prove."

Despite all the pragmatic arguments over the advantages and dangers of paying hush-money to E. Howard Hunt, the transcript shows that Mr. Nixon failed to put a stop to such proposals with his often repeated statement, "But it would be wrong, that's for sure." On the contrary, the President appears to have concluded that "his [Hunt's] price is pretty high, but at least we can buy the time on that. . . ." Shortly thereafter Mr. Nixon added: "Here we have the Hunt problem that ought to be handled now."

Nothing that was subsequently said could be understood to have countermanded that implied order. The $75,000 payment was made later on the same day.

Whether or not Mr. Nixon can make a convincing case that he was misunderstood by those who paid off Mr. Hunt, the fact remains that the President of the United States took no official action against a blackmail threat. Such moral degradation of the Presidency is of a piece with Mr. Nixon's readiness, now clearly documented, to use national security as the ultimate cover-up. (Dean: "I think we could get by on that.")

The shame that emanates from these recorded words ranges from Mr. Nixon's threat to use his power and that of the Department of Justice against "all those who tried to do us in" to the more general assault on integrity in government. The nature of that threat makes it doubly important that the inquiry into the case of Mr. Nixon be carried forward with all the available evidence.

Whatever the most effective political tactics of the moment, the simple fact is that President Nixon has failed to comply with a subpoena duly served by the House Judiciary Committee. Nor, it seems, does he intend to comply with a subpoena served upon him by the special Watergate prosecutor, Leon Jaworski. The subpoenas required the submission of tape recordings, not selective transcripts edited by the person under investigation.

The coming days will be consumed by delicate maneuvering to surmount this potentially grave constitutional problem. Above all in this period, the Judiciary Committee is right to proceed cautiously, to retain the bipartisanship which has proved its greatest strength in the impeachment drama's first acts already passed. A party-line division on a major issue at this stage could destroy much of the credibility and integrity which Chairman Peter W. Rodino and his colleagues have so impressively nurtured.

While the committee considers carefully what step to take next, it would not be remiss for the prosecutor now to assume the initiative in challenging the President's non-compliance. With no constituency to serve except the law, Mr. Jaworski is in a strong position to press the issue at once, engaging the full mechanism of the judicial system.

Compromise arrangements, negotiated verification procedures—these might have had some value earlier in the investigation of suspected criminal activities at the heart of the White House. But once served by a legal summons, the President has no right to decide the extent to which he will obey the law.

The Des Moines Register

Des Moines, Iowa, May 1, 1974

President Nixon's plan to give the House Judiciary Committee transcripts of the "relevant" portions of White House tapes and have the two ranking committee members listen to the tapes is reminiscent of the President's proposal last October when special prosecutor Archibald Cox also sought tapes. The President at that time said Senator John Stennis (Dem., Miss.) should hear the tapes and Cox be given only the White House's version of them. When Cox insisted on direct access to the tapes, he was fired.

President Nixon caved in to pressure and gave the tapes to the special prosecutor. These tapes subsequently were ordered turned over to the House Judiciary Committee. The President did not explain in his televised address Monday night why the two sets of tapes should be treated differently.

Nor should they be. The House committee's subpoena for 42 additional tapes was intended to give the committee physical possession of the evidence. The tapes then could be examined for content and for evidence of tampering.

President Nixon's invitation to Representatives Peter Rodino and Edward Hutchinson "to come to the White House and listen" to the tapes makes no provision for examination of the tapes by technical experts. The President must be aware that committee staff members concerned with gathering evidence are better qualified to determine "relevancy" than the two committee members he named.

The President's offer might have been acceptable had it been made at the outset of the Watergate inquiry as part of a White House policy of cooperation and full disclosure. The offer comes instead after the White House announced that an 18-minute portion of one important recording had been erased and repeated efforts to hide evidence. These shenanigans make it impossible to accept on faith anything from the White House bearing on the Watergate cover-up.

The House committee would be derelict if it backed away from its subpoena and did not insist on the same access to the 42 tapes it obtained to earlier tapes. The special prosecutor would be equally derelict if he did not insist on similar access to the evidence he seeks.

★ ★ ★

The President's plan to make the transcripts public makes it doubly important that the public have confidence in the completeness and authenticity of the transcribed conversations. The public will remain less than convinced it has been given the full story unless the tapes and transcripts are independently examined and verified.

The decision to make the transcripts public is welcome — if long overdue. The public for too long has had to rely on recollections of witnesses and partial quotations from the tapes by the President. If the transcripts are complete, the public will have an opportunity to judge for itself the part played by the President in the Watergate affair.

Though the President reiterated his innocence Monday night and pictured himself as totally dedicated to rooting out misconduct, he admitted that his post-Watergate actions were influenced by other things. He cited his concern about "close advisers, valued friends," "the human impact" on persons "whose lives might be suddenly ruined by something they had done in an excess of loyalty," the "political implications," the effect on those who were "technically indictable but morally innocent." The President also gave "national security" as justification for his behavior.

The President's catalogue of justifications suggests that he was influenced by a lot more than unswerving dedication to uncovering the truth and "getting it out." How much he was influenced by the "political implications" and other factors, and what he did about them, are at the core of the impeachment inquiry. Congress and the American people can be satisfied with nothing less than full disclosure of every shred of evidence bearing on the question.

★ ★ ★

The President spoke Monday night without the usual emotional flourishes, though he did compare himself with Abraham Lincoln again. But this speech was more effective with the public, we feel, than other Nixon statements on Watergate.

The President was trying to convince us that he has gone the extra mile, including transcripts of material not subpoenaed, material that is embarrassing to him and to others and "all the additional evidence needed." In a typical Nixonism, he concluded that "never before in the history of the presidency have records that are so private been made so public."

This performance should not obscure the fact that Nixon still is deciding what is relevant to the impeachment inquiry about himself. All the cuss words and embarrassing personal stuff need not be made public; no one has demanded that. Nor does anyone want to expose what is truly confidential national security material.

Nixon acknowledged for the first time that people think he has not been frank and open in his dealings on the Watergate affair. He as much as conceded that he was being forced to give up the facts to restore confidence in him.

This is true, but he still has not released the evidence the House Judiciary Committee has subpoenaed, and the claims of giving up all should not blind the public to that fact.

ARGUS-LEADER

Sioux Falls, S.D., May 2, 1974

President Richard Nixon has handed over the Watergate transcripts and offered to let Chairman Peter Rodino, D-N.J., and Rep. Edward Hutchinson, R-Mich., the senior Republican on the House Judiciary Committee, listen to the tapes and verify the stenographic record.

His action is late, but it should suffice. Rodino and Hutchinson will be in for a long hot summer if they attempt to verify the transcribing of the White House tapes. If more information is needed beyond this, the committee can ask for it. Meantime, digesting the material which Nixon has handed over deserves the closest look and attention of the committee.

What Americans should do is to suspend judgment on President Nixon and the others involved in the Watergate mess until the House Judiciary Committee, Leon Jaworski, the special prosecutor and the courts have had an opportunity to hear out the case.

The political atmosphere in Washington is so poisonous these days that opponents of the President put the worst possible construction on his every act. In fairness, he deserves his hearing in the several tribunals or agencies where the case is being pursued.

The acquittal of former Atty. Gen. John Mitchell and former Commerce Secretary Maurice Stans by a jury in New York is another sign that judgment before justice has run its course is a hazardous thing. The jury believed them—and found John Dean, the President's main accuser, less believable.

It is useless to wonder how President Nixon, the man who ended the Vietnam War, who achieved detente with Russia and started a dialogue with China, could get himself into such a predicament in the White House with his former staff. His enemies will be satisfied with nothing less than removing him from the White House. But the events starting Sunday, with the jury's acquittal of Mitchell and Stans in New York, and continuing this week with Nixon's response to the Judiciary Committee, indicate the President's enemies may be disappointed. We hope they are.

There are some other pressing problems for this country that run the gamut of everything from inflation to a truce in the Mideast between Syria and Israel. As before, Nixon is doing well on the international scene. Give him the benefit of a doubt—even at this late hour—in the troubles that fell in on him because of the inept people he had around him. It's harder on him than it is on the country. The U.S.A. will survive, regardless of the outcome.

—Transcripts Released

Chicago Tribune

Chicago, Ill., May 9, 1974

We saw the public man in his first administration, and we were impressed. Now in about 300,000 words we have seen the private man, and we are appalled.

What manner of man is the Richard Nixon who emerges from the transcripts of the White House tapes?

We see a man who, in the words of his old friend and defender, Sen. Hugh Scott, took a principal role in a "shabby, immoral and disgusting performance."

The key word here is immoral. It is a lack of concern for morality, a lack of concern for high principles, a lack of commitment to the high ideals of public office that make the transcripts a sickening exposure of the man and his advisers. He is preoccupied with appearance rather than substance. His aim is to find a way to sell the idea that disreputable schemes are actually good or are defensible for some trumped-up cause.

He is humorless to the point of being inhumane. He is devious. He is vacillating. He is profane. He is willing to be led. He displays dismaying gaps in knowledge. He is suspicious of his staff. His loyalty is minimal. His greatest concern is to create a record that will save him and his administration. The high dedication to grand principles that Americans have a right to expect from a President is missing from the transcript record.

Mr. Nixon's strategy backfired when he released the transcripts. It was also a strategic error for him to release the record of his income taxes. Both stripped the man to his essential character, and that character could not stand that kind of scrutiny. Both miscalculations demonstrated an essential Nixon defect—an insensitivity to the standards of ethics and morality that Americans expect of their leaders.

He thought disclosure of the records would help him. He has had a demonstration that his countrymen are not that tolerant.

And it should be noted here that the transcripts and the income tax statement were not the fabrications of his enemies. These were self-created instruments of destruction.

His decision Tuesday to disclose no more information leaves the record as it now stands. And as it stands that record leaves no doubt that he lacks the qualities that could edify and inspire his countrymen with confidence in these difficult times.

The statement of his counsel, James St. Clair, that the President is ready for a confrontation with Congress and his own special prosecutor is ominous.

The balance among the coordinate branches of our government—Executive, Judicial and Legislative—is fragile. It has been established on rather comfortably loose terms by nearly 200 years of experience in practicing the special virtues of American government.

The limits of executive privilege, of congressional power, of judicial authority are not rigidly fixed. We would not relish the prospect of forcing the Supreme Court to make hard decisions in the distorting heat of partisan controversy. This is one confrontation this country does not need and we pray Mr. Nixon will not insist on it.

The President is right in urging a quick end to the Watergate affair. His country needs a swift and merciful termination of this agony.

Two roads are open. One is resignation. The other is impeachment. Both are legitimate and would satisfy the need to observe due process.

Resignation of the President would be quick and simple and a qualified successor stands ready to assume office.

Impeachment is the judicial process prescribed by the Constitution for removing a President. The House can, and probably will, vote a bill of impeachment quickly. A trial in the Senate would be, and indeed should be, long and deliberate. No suggestion of haste or mob justice could be tolerated. The White House could be expected to seize every opportunity for challenge and delay, and the final outcome might be two years in coming.

The objection to resignation that has been raised—and we have raised it ourselves—is that it would not resolve the issues. It would not answer many of the questions about the President's behavior and degree of complicity. It would leave at least a suspicion that the President had been persecuted instead of properly prosecuted out of office. To some he might remain a martyr. To many it would seem a miscarriage of justice, an example of political exorcism.

The transcripts have changed all that. Tho they may clear Mr. Nixon of direct complicity in the Watergate burglary and the early stages of the coverup, nobody of sound mind can read them and continue to think that Mr. Nixon has upheld the standards and dignity of the Presidency which he proclaimed himself as a candidate in 1960. He hoped that, if elected, a mother or father would be able to "look at the man in the White House . . . and say, 'Well, there is a man who maintains the kind of standards personally that I would like my child to follow.'"

We do not share the White House belief that impeachment requires evidence of a specific crime. We believe a President may be removed simply for failing to do his job, or for so discrediting himself that he loses public respect and, with it, his ability to govern effectively.

It is true that this vagueness may tempt opponents to seek to remove a President for political or otherwise inadequate reasons, as they did with Andrew Johnson. But that risk must be accepted. The ultimate arbiter in this matter must be the public, and the public reaction today is clearly one of revulsion. Republican politicians are defecting in droves. The evidence against Mr. Nixon is in his own words, made public at his own direction. There can no longer be a charge that he was railroaded out of office by vengeful Democrats or a hostile press. The fundamental questions have been answered. Filling in the gaps in the transcripts can only make the case against the President stronger.

And so the objections to resignation have largely vanished.

Since the President has rejected this course, we urge the House to act quickly on a bill of impeachment. As the impeachment process progresses, as public opinion becomes clear, and as Mr. Nixon sees support dwindling in the Senate, he will have to reconsider his stand and recognize that resignation will spare the country the ordeal of a trial.

There are three urgent reasons for turning the reins of government over to a new President who can concentrate on his job, and for doing so quickly.

First, without decisive leadership in either foreign or domestic matters, the country will drift along aimlessly during one of the most critical periods of history. In country after country, governments are being toppled and threatened because of popular frustration over inflation, hunger, the energy shortage, and the apparent inability of governments to deal with them. It would be a tragedy for the richest and most powerful country in the world to stagger along, immobile, during such a period.

Second, Mr. Nixon has become a liability to his political party as well as to the Republic. The longer he remains in office as a symbol of Watergate and all it stands for, the more likely it is that the Republican Party will be incapacitated for years to come. The health of our two-party system depends on separating the Republican Party from the evils of Watergate and the character of the President.

Third, it is equally important for the future of the Presidency itself that it be separated from the man who now holds it. We must return to the day when people can shiver with pride instead of shudder with embarrassment when they see the flag or hear "Hail to the Chief." Many of the prerogatives of the Presidency are essential to the country, including secrecy when properly justified for reasons of national security or executive privilege. These principles have been prostituted in order to preserve Mr. Nixon himself and those around him. The longer this goes on, the more likely these prerogatives are to be forfeited — in the public mind if not by act of Congress.

It is saddening and hard to believe that for the first time in our history, it is better that the President leave office than fight to keep it. But things have reached such a state that Mr. Nixon's departure, one way or another, is the best course for the Presidency, the country, and the free world. To perpetuate a state of confrontation between the Executive and Congress—in order to define the limits of power which are probably better undefined — will be tragically costly in the eyes of history and the world.

The Virginian-Pilot

Norfolk, Va., May 6, 1974

It is not a pretty sight to watch the President of the United States twisting and turning in the wind.

But Mr. Nixon now seems to be doomed by his own words.

For no one can read the edited transcript of the White House tapes without being saddened and sickened by them.

The documentation of the moral squalor within the White House is totally unrelieved. The President is revealed on the tapes as no better than his co-conspirators. All are concerned only with keeping on top.

All of the dirty truths of Watergate are unexamined. Blackmail, bribery, burglary, obstruction of justice, perjury — they are but details of the problem to be solved.

And the problem is how to manage the scandal, how to save their own skins, how to keep others from learning the dirty truths. There is no sense of shame, no sense of wrongdoing. It is all a matter of "them" and "us" — and even the apparent good guys, such as former Secretary of State William Rogers, are sucked into the vortex.

Does it matter what John Dean said to the President when both are clearly depicted as devold of ethical sensibilities?

The Oval Office was a moral pigsty. That is the damning truth of the tapes.

Because the edited transcripts are fascinating reading — all the more fascinating perhaps for the unintelligible passages in them — the paperback versions which will be hitting the newsstands and supermarkets soon are bound to be best-sellers.

And because the leading man in the tragedy is also the President of the United States, the transcripts are as cumulatively devastating as they are morally repellent. That is what will bring down Mr. Nixon.

He cannot change the self-portrait in the tapes by flying to Phoenix to make a speech about "what's right about America" or going on to Spokane to open Expo '74.

Patriotism is the last refuge of scoundrels and in the agonies of Mr. Nixon "patriotism" is equated to the Office of the Presidency, with all its dignity and majesty and privileges and trappings.

Mr. Nixon is trying to hide behind the Presidency, as he sought to identify himself with his high office when he ran for re-election. But now he not only stands naked to his enemies, but revealed in the transcripts to all Americans who care to read them.

And the average American who wants to believe the best of the man in the White House must be disappointed by the foul-mouthed, furtive Nixon of the transcripts.

The conservative may feel moved to defend Mr. Nixon, but in his heart he knows he is wrong.

And the loyal Republican is bound to feel betrayed and trapped by Watergate. The fate of the Grand Old Party is tied to the fate of the President, in the White House view. (Dean Burch, for one, says so.) But what will Governor Godwin and Senator Scott and Representative Whitehurst and all the other Republicans in Virginia have to say when they have read the transcripts? What will be the Republican reaction in the rest of the 50 states?

Are we to have three more years of [expletive removed] and [unintelligible] and "Hail to the Thief" and wallowing in Watergate? Has the country come to that?

THE WALL STREET JOURNAL

New York, N.Y., May 7, 1974

In our first comments on the presidential tapes we remarked that it helps to separate two questions: The general propriety of the conversations, and evidence of impeachable offenses. We have tended to emphasize the latter, and will return to it shortly. But today we would like to lay aside impeachment and other legal issues, and simply address what the conversations tell us about Richard Nixon, his administration and American politics.

This is of course what the rest of the press and the nation at large have been discussing all along, and we should perhaps apologize for the quirk of mind that led us to believe the question on the table was whether to impeach the President. In any event, having said so many times over the last year that even without a case for impeachment Watergate will have done enormous harm to the American Republic, we can scarcely disagree with the widespread conclusion that the tapes reveal a flawed mentality

If the case for criminal complicity does fail, for that matter, it will be only on the narrowest of grounds. The President's attorney will be arguing: Yes the President talked about paying blackmail, yes his words say several times he thought paying the money was the only immediate answer, yes someone might construe that as approval, but no that isn't what he meant, and no his words were not directly connected to the actual payoffs. Even if all this is true, what a defense for a President of the United States to offer.

More broadly, the tapes reveal a whole litany of presidential failings: A casual attitude toward lawbreaking by his subordinates. In particular a casual attitude toward perjury, indeed remarks that some lawyers construe as subornation of perjury. A reach for public deception, in particular a willingness to invoke national security and executive privilege for expedient reasons. A disinclination to probe and question his top subordinates on such questions as moving about large monies or "deep sixing" documents. And above all, a general disposition to concentrate almost entirely on the question, what can we get away with? at the expense of the question, what would be right?

Some things can of course be said in exoneration. The President apparently didn't know much before March 21, and part of his reaction was perhaps confusion. The President is not a district attorney, and at least up to a point is entitled to assume that prosecutors will do their job without his help on each fact. There are points, as in sending a message to John Mitchell not to refuse testimony to protect the President, at which he shows a concern with getting the story to law enforcement authorities.

Yet even on a sympathetic reading, the record must be that faced with a mounting crisis, Mr. Nixon reacted deplorably. He was willing to consider patently wrong courses of action. He was willing to trip along, and even conceivably over, the line of outright illegality. He coupled any moves to expose crimes with moves to limit and contain the exposures. And finally, he chose and protected all of the aides whose personalities are so brutally revealed in these conversations.

A preoccupation with image rather than reality, it seems to us, is the characteristic that runs through both the conversations and the faults they reveal. In conversation after conversation, it becomes impossible to tell whether the participants are trying to recall events or concoct a story. One gets the feeling they did not distinguish between the two in their own minds, that to them there was no reality, only the image they could paint.

And always there was a concern not with the meaning of events but with their "PR." When in a conversation with Assistant Attorney General Henry Petersen it became apparent that eventually Mr. Haldeman and Mr. Ehrlichman would have to go, the questions on the President's mind were: Can one go without the other? Should it be before the Magruder testimony or after? Should it be before Dean goes or after?

We come back to a point we have made many times: The inhospitality of the Nixon White House to men of vision, intellect or stature. It is quite impossible to imagine these conversations going on as they did if they had included, to pick two men no longer in the White House at the time, Arthur Burns or Daniel P. Moynihan. To understand why such men were so few there, observe that Leonard Garment, who did see the extent of the danger the moment he learned of it, was treated as an object of faint ridicule.

This is ultimately the President's doing and the President's failing. He has accomplished much and promised more, but he filled his inner world with imaginary men. Empty men committed the type of blunder you would expect of them, and the President himself proved too empty to limit the damage. For this he has paid with his reputation and may yet pay with his job, and to the office and nation he sought to protect and restore, his legacy is further grief and further cynicism.

THE LINCOLN STAR
Lincoln, Neb., May 10, 1974

The desperate gamble to survive that President Nixon took in releasing the transcripts with the claim that he was "telling all" worked at first.

By its sheer bulk, the mass of newly-released evidence heartened his supporters and frustrated his detractors. The release of the transcripts enabled him to achieve a partisan split in the House Judiciary Committee, with all but one of the Republican members voting against a letter telling the President he was not in compliance with the committee's subpoena.

But the strategy is falling apart, transcript by transcript. People have now read them.

The glaring omissions in the edited transcripts of presidential conversations about Watergate generated a new cry for more conclusive evidence from Republicans and Democrats alike. What was **not** omitted — a sordid record of false image-making and sleazy cooked-up schemes to avoid telling the truth — even sickened many of the most resolute Nixon backers. Sadly enough, Nebraska Senators Carl Curtis and Roman Hruska are numbered among those few who have not expressed outrage over what the transcripts reveal about the President and his advisors, even apart from the question of possible criminal activity.

Hugh Scott of Pennsylvania, the Senate minority leader, and Robert Dole of Kansas, a former Republican National Chairman, are but two staunch administration supporters who have been moved to comment on the shabbiness of the moral tone in the White House revealed by the transcripts.

Meanwhile, old Nixon friends in the media and conservative spokesmen for generations, such as the Chicago Tribune and the Omaha World-Herald, have asked that the President go. With each day, Vice President Ford appears to be growing more and more appalled at what went on in the Oval Office and he is sounding more and more like the kind of president this nation needs at this critical point.

New York Times columnist James Reston this week drew a parallel between the careers of Nixon and West German Chancellor Willy Brandt. Both were faced with corruption in their administrations and both publicly acknowledged that it was their responsibility. But Brandt accepted the responsibility by resigning from office to let the people and the parliament decide the issue and in so doing, he showed "class," Reston said. Reston didn't have to say any more.

The Star many months ago joined a number of newspapers across the nation which publicly stated their conviction that President Nixon should resign for the good of the country.

We feel even more strongly now that President Nixon should go, by resignation if he wants to spare the country an ordeal or by impeachment should the Congress decide he has breached the public trust. The grounds are surely there.

The United States should not suffer a law-breaking President — and evidence may prove that he is — and the nation should not have to live the next two years under a leader who has contempt for and abuses its institutions and political processes and who can't approach the moral standard he himself defined for the presidency.

Omaha World-Herald
Omaha, Neb., May 8, 1974

The World-Herald three times indorsed Richard Nixon as a candidate for the presidency. We think still that his administration has a great deal to its credit.

President Nixon brought an honorable end to America's part in a long Asian war.

He has achieved more than any other President in opening relations with Red China and in easing relations with Soviet Russia and with pursuing a settlement in the Middle East.

His handling of the country's domestic affairs has been competent if not spectacularly successful. He has attracted able men such as Henry Kissinger and George Shultz to serve in his administration and he nominated a man of integrity, Gerald Ford, to be Vice-President.

* * *

Important as these accomplishments are, they are overshadowed now by the appallingly low level of political morality in the White House, as indicated in a variety of ways in recent months and confirmed now in damning detail by the White House tapes.

The transcripts have diminished the President's image from that of a moral man surrounded by underlings who had betrayed him to that of an amoral man who compounded his troubles by withholding for more than a year the shocking truth about the mess he and his administration were in.

For many months the question was how much the President knew about the Watergate breakin and coverup and when he learned about them.

In the week since he has released edited transcripts, the question has been, "What did the President **do** when he knew?"

* * *

The tapes reveal that when the President knew, he discussed alternatives which could be construed as obstruction of justice and, while he may not have positively authorized the payment, he was aware of and did not stop a plan to buy the silence of a potential witness.

The tapes also reveal example after example of cynical, self-serving decisions, "scenarios" to put the best "public relations" face on the mess, to make it appear that the White House itself had forced a major break in the case. This latter ploy, if successful, might have been the most biggest deception of all.

Only after it appeared certain that the lid was going to blow completely and that the White House would be deeply involved did the President start looking for scapegoats to sacrifice, to make it appear, in his words, that "as a result of the President's actions, this thing has been broken." (Those words, incidentally, were spoken by the President when he was coaching John Dean as to what Dean should testify.)

* * *

At another point, in another conversation with Dean, this exchange took place:

Dean: So there are dangers, Mr. President. I would be less than candid if I didn't tell you there are. There is a reason for not everyone going up and testifying.

President: I see. Oh no, no, no. I didn't mean to have everyone go up and testify.

Dean: Well, I mean they're just starting to hangout and say here's our story—

President: I mean put the story out PR people, here is the story, the true story about Watergate.

Another Presidential quote:

"What the hell does one disclose that isn't going to blow something?"

This is a picture of a man dedicated to telling the whole truth?

* * *

Some will argue that the President now has acted to put forth the whole story.

It should be remembered that the tapes—edited transcripts of some of the tapes — were produced many months after the investigation started and then only in response to a subpoena from a committee of the House of Representatives.

The President said it was the presidency he was protecting. There was the principle of confidentiality. He must protect it. National security was being breached or threatened. He must protect that.

No doubt some of these matters did involve national security. But were all his actions based on such high ground?

The thrust of the 1,308 pages of the transcript is that the President was trying to save his own skin and would consider almost any option, however, bizarre, if it would help him do that.

* * *

A few examples:

In the March 21 transcript Dean, Haldeman and the President discussed alternatives, including the calling of another grand jury, having the White House witnesses take the Fifth Amendment, or, in Dean's

(continued on next page)

(continued from preceding page)

words, "chancing a very high risk for perjury situation." The President broke in:

"But you can say, I don't remember. You can say, I don't recall. I can't give any answer to that that I can recall."

As for the breakin itself, the President deplored it as stupid and untimely:

"We had just finished the Moscow trip. The Democrats had just nominated McGovern. I mean (expletive deleted) which in the hell were these people doing? I can see their doing it earlier. I can see the pressures, but I don't see why all the pressure was on then."

* * *

No suggestion here that the break-in was immoral or criminal. The only thing that was genuinely reprehensible, it would seem, was the timing.

To keep the President "above and away" from the mess, he and his associates were willing to bend to their uses the Internal Revenue Service, the Federal Bureau of Investigation and the Justice Department's special prosecutor.

The tapes indicate that the President wanted an FBI director who could "play ball" with the administration. As to the Justice Department's special prosecutor in the Watergate case, the President said: "I've got Petersen on a short leash."

The transcripts time and again show that the White House aim was to tell little while appearing to tell all.

* * *

Said the President in the March 13 transcript:

"You've got to do something where it doesn't appear that I am doing this in a, you know, just in a—saying to hell with the Congress and to hell with the people, we are not going to tell anything because of executive privilege. They do not understand.

"But if you say, 'No, we are willing to cooperate,' and you've made a complete statement, but make it very incomplete. See, that is what I mean."

We think we do see what the President means. We believe it sums up the presidential approach to the Watergate coverup—an unwillingness to tell the whole truth and a willingness to condone deplorable means to avoid telling the truth.

Involved here is not a question of Democrat or Republican, liberal or conservative, or of a conspiracy by his enemies to "get" the President. This is a matter of right or wrong, telling the truth or not telling the truth.

* * *

Is the President impeachable? That is for the House to decide. On the narrow issue of criminality, the tapes may be inconclusive so far as the President is concerned. But the issues here are broader than criminality, or presidential credibility against John Dean's credibility.

It is a truism to say — but apparently it needs to be said — that an individual's conduct may be indefensible and reprehensible without being criminal.

We think resignation is a course much to be preferred to impeachment. Impeachment could result in months and months of additional charges and countercharges, accumulating bitterness and, very possibly, an inconclusive decision. (What if, for example, the House votes to impeach and a majority — but not the necessary two-thirds — of the Senate votes to remove the President from office?)

* * *

In the eight days since the publication of the transcripts, we believe there has been an erosion of public confidence in the President and in his ability to govern the country.

We believe that this erosion has reached the point that it will be difficult if not impossible for him to regain the confidence needed to lead the United States effectively.

It is a political tragedy when a President who had so much to his credit and in his favor 18 months ago stands revealed now — by his own words in those damning tapes — as a man incapable of providing the moral leadership which the United States is entitled to expect from its President.

* * *

Some will ask what other presidents would have done under similar circumstances. They will say that "dirty tricks" and Watergate breakins and coverups are "just politics." To which we would reply:

If the revolting picture of conniving and deception revealed by the White House tapes is "just politics" as practiced in the Oval Office of the President of the United States, it is time for the present occupant to vacate that office.

Let a new occupant establish a new level of political morality for the Presidency of the United States.

The President should resign.

THE SACRAMENTO BEE
Sacramento, Calif., May 11, 1974

After having weighed the issue with the most scrupulous concern for the course which would serve the nation's best interest, The Bee now is convinced President Richard Nixon should resign.

The climactic exposures of recent events, particularly the revelations in Nixon's tape transcripts, document a record of presidential misconduct and moral vacuum in the White House which can only be redressed by the President's stepping down from office.

Failing this, it appears the House Judiciary Committee has no alternative but to vote for Nixon's impeachment — a process which surely would prolong the nation's agonizing trauma.

Nixon would and should spare the country this travail by resigning, forthwith.

Calls for this course of action by Republican newspapers across the land, publications which until recent days have supported the President, are reaching avalanche dimensions. Resignation demands or suggestions have come, too, from a swiftly growing number of Nixon's Republican backers in Congress and elsewhere.

What the tape transcripts have revealed of the man, Nixon, and the amoral aura of the White House created by Nixon and his closest henchmen, present no alternative to his immediate departure and a complete new leadership assembled by his successor, Vice President Gerald Ford.

Before the unsavory stench wafted from the tape transcripts now made public, there was ample indication of Nixon's dubious fitness to warrant consideration of his resignation. The Bee drew attention to this on its editorial pages.

Nonetheless, this newspaper had been content to let the due constitutional process of impeachment take its course, to permit the festering boil of Watergate be pricked by way of House indictment and trial by the US Senate.

Now, however, the tape transcripts have provided out of the mouths of Nixon and his aides stark evidence of attempts to obstruct justice, of calculated efforts to cover up Watergate and its unsavory spinoffs, contempt for the American people and no real sign of a sense of right and wrong. This is why Nixon should resign and let the country get on with the binding of its wounds under new, untainted leadership. The Washington Post said succinctly what has become a national outcry: "Mr. Nixon's presidency is beyond recovery."

So says The Bee. It is the tragic truth.

FORT WORTH STAR-TELEGRAM

Fort Worth, Tex., May 12, 1974

It is as if the cry had gone out, "Abandon Ship."

Suddenly Republican politicians — many of whom are national leaders — and newspapers which have supported President Richard Nixon are saying in chorus, "Resign. It is best for you and the country."

The Star-Telegram e n d o r s e d Richard Nixon for the presidency. We supported him in moments when it was unpopular to do so, such as during the days he was trying to extricate us from Vietnam. Generally we have approved of his foreign policy, and more often than not of his domestic policy.

We say these things simply to establish our credentials as being a newspaper which could in no sense be labeled anti-Nixon.

The revelations of the tapes transcripts, however, portray a man whose thought processes sometimes are chilling, who seems unable really to understand the basic philosophy of our democratic system.

The (expletive deleted) portion is rather inconsequential. No doubt those words have been heard in the editorial offices of the Star-Telegram and, indeed, in many other offices and homes of this land.

But what is damning is the discussion of how to use the majesty of the federal government to punish his enemies, the fact that there was no outcry among the top administrators of our land that a wrong had been done and it was time to say so and to punish those who were guilty.

If the law enforcement agencies of this country can be used to punish political enemies, how can we then hold ourselves superior to lands where mere political opposition is a crime? If the simple moral concept of equality before the law is perverted, then on what does our country stand?

It would seem to us that there are now reasons for the House to vote a bill of impeachment.

But, realizing the agony of our land while this process goes on, it still is our feeling that due process should be followed. President Nixon has proclaimed his innocence of impeachable wrongs. Many good citizens of this country see him as a man under attack by political enemies and a biased press.

So long as this is his position, resignation is not the way. The way is to follow out this bitter drama to the end, so that when it is over the system will have worked and everyone will have had his day in court.

And, let us add that the system is working. Many among the highest echelons in our land stand accused in court, or in the Congress, and the process grinds on to the bitter end.

The point is that there is equality before the law — for the President as well as for any other accused person.

Sometimes the principle bends, but it has not yet broken. Surely that is what America is about.

Los Angeles Times

Los Angeles, Calif., May 10, 1974

Nothing short of impeachment by the House of Representatives and trial by the Senate can now resolve the question of President Nixon's fitness to remain in office.

We said in this space last November that there was growing evidence to warrant the President's impeachment. But we did not then believe it was sufficient.

Since then there have been many new and damaging revelations involving Mr. Nixon, including the partial transcripts of presidential conversations issued by the White House on April 30. The evidence is now far more complete, and Mr. Nixon himself has said he is willing to be judged by it.

We now believe the case for his indictment by the House has substantive proportions, and we base this opinion, in large part, on the White House transcripts.

In our judgment, they contain presumptive evidence of at least one impeachable offense—the obstruction of justice—and also cast the gravest doubts on the two major points in Mr. Nixon's year-long defense of his role in the Watergate affair:

—That he was not a party to the coverup.

—That on learning of it he did his best to bring the guilty to justice.

The transcripts do not support either claim. The picture they show is not that of a man determined to expose the truth. Rather, they reveal a man who was trying to conceal or distort the truth for as long as he could to protect himself and his associates.

The transcripts show that on March 21, 1973, the President was told that E. Howard Hunt Jr., then in jail for the Watergate raid, was blackmailing the White House for hush money in exchange for his promise not to implicate high Administration officials in the Watergate scandals.

Later that day, according to grand jury testimony and other evidence, a payment of $75,000 was made to Hunt's attorney.

Although his own words in the transcript suggest otherwise, Mr. Nixon now contends that at no time did he encourage the payment and certainly did not authorize it.

Whether the payment to Hunt was a direct result of the March 21 conference in the Oval Office, and whether the President later put a stop to all such illegal payments, are not the conclusive elements.

The facts speak for themselves. The discussion did take place; the President was a party to it, and at no time did he instruct his advisers to desist from what was patently a conspiracy to obstruct justice.

To the contrary, it was Mr. Nixon himself who frequently brought the conversation back to Hunt; who said the money could be found; who said its payment was urgent, and who said a means of delivery should be found that would escape detection. He said nothing to discourage his aides from rushing to pay the bribe on that same day.

Standing alone, the transcript of March 21, 1973, would appear to justify Mr. Nixon's removal from office under even the narrowest definition of an impeachable offense—the commission of an indictable crime.

Subsequent transcripts expose further actions by the President that had the effect of obstructing a Justice Department investigation into the coverup. Asst. Atty. Gen. Henry E. Petersen was then in charge of the investigation and was in frequent contact with the President concerning the tactics of the prosecutors and their presentation of evidence to the grand jury.

Mr. Nixon, in violation of his pledge to Petersen, gave this secret information to his highest-ranking assistants—John D. Ehrlichman and H. R. Haldeman—although he knew they were facing indictment by that same grand jury and that his leaks of evidence would enable them to anticipate the prosecution case.

The Hunt and Petersen incidents discredit the President's claim that he had no role in the coverup.

Nor do the transcripts bear out Mr. Nixon's contention that his overriding purpose, after learning of the coverup, was to search out the guilty and bring them to trial.

The transcripts show, instead, that his strategy was:

—To "contain" the scandal by limiting the scope, and frustrating the evidentiary rights, of investigations then under way.

—To "buy time" and "reduce our losses" by keeping his associates from testifying under dubious claims of executive privilege and national security.

—To "keep the cap on the bottle" by encouraging his associates to tell no more of the truth than they had to in public statements or in formal testimony.

—To contrive "salable" public relations explanations for his own failure to expose the guilty, even when the evidence of their complicity was known to him.

It is possible to overlook, if not approve, the President's profanities in the transcripts, and the shoddy level of conversations that demean him and the office he holds.

Deviousness, vindictiveness and obscenity may not be impeachable offenses. Obstruction of justice certainly is. We think betrayal of his trust should be.

The transcripts, of course, are incomplete. The White House has taken out the obscenities; fragments of conversations it describes as inaudible or unintelligible, and entire conversations it describes as irrelevant to Watergate.

That may or may not be the case. And the House Judiciary Committee — properly — is demanding the actual tapes to test their authenticity and to restore the gaps. The committee, special prosecutor Leon Jaworski and the Senate Watergate committee are now attempting, through subpoena and other means, to secure additional tapes.

But the President said this week that he would furnish no further Watergate evidence, and the nation now faces another in the long, contentious series of confrontations between him and those who have the constitutional authority—and the public mandate—to investigate his possible malfeasance.

This raises, inevitably, the suspicion that the evidence he is withholding may be even more incriminating than the evidence he has been willing to release.

Justice for the President and for the nation now requires his impeachment.

THE MILWAUKEE JOURNAL
Milwaukee, Wis., May 13, 1974

Last November, when there was a flurry of demands for President Nixon's resignation, The Journal called for his impeachment.

We acknowledged then that resignation was a tempting alternative, for Nixon had disgraced his office, lost the confidence of most of his countrymen and crippled his ability to lead. Certainly, sudden flight from office would avoid the ordeal of impeachment, which involves the bringing of charges by the House and a trial before the Senate.

But, we noted, resignation had a grave flaw. Unless Nixon coupled it with a confession of wrongdoing, the result would be a vacancy without a verdict. The grave allegations against Nixon would be left floating, his defenders bitterly claiming that an innocent man had been unfairly hounded from office. Thus, we concluded that the constitutional remedy of impeachment and trial offered the surest way to resolve charges of presidential misconduct.

* * *

Today, as resignation clamor grows louder, The Journal reiterates that belief. True, release of Nixon's transcripts makes advocacy of resignation less objectionable. For the transcripts are an appalling profile in deception and rascality — a piercing indictment not only of Nixon the man, but, more importantly, of Nixon the elected holder of our highest office.

At a minimum, they demonstrate an impeachable failure to uphold sworn constitutional duties, a failure to "take care that the laws be faithfully executed" and to "preserve, protect and defend the Constitution." The transcripts also come very close to being clinching proof of active presidential participation in obstruction of justice — a felony, clearly impeachable.

Yet, unless Nixon is now willing to admit his soiling of oath and office, resignation is still the wrong route to urge. And, at the moment, he is not budging. Instead, he repeats claims of innocence, argues amazingly that the transcripts can somehow be interpreted in his favor, refuses to produce any more Watergate evidence (even though it means defying lawful subpenas). Given Nixon's attitude, only impeachment will suffice.

Many Americans are understandably apprehensive of the laborious impeachment process. They fear that the nation cannot afford to go much longer with so disabled a president. Yet, while the government is weakened, it still functions. While the customary drum beat of presidential leadership is missing, Congress toils at about an average pace, the bureaucracy chugs along, Kissinger tends to foreign relations. If the nation were actually disintegrating, Nixon's resignation would become imperative, regardless of any question of guilt. Right now, that is not the case.

Thus, impeachment should go forward, fairly, vigorously, with due speed. Most constitutional scholars agree that impeachment covers not only indictable crimes but also gross breaches of high trust and duty. On that basis, The Journal believes that there is cause for impeachment. The chief question is: How many counts?

The immediate task is for the House Judiciary Committee to continue amassing evidence, sift it carefully, narrow charges to those strongly sustainable and then recommend impeachment and trial.

The Charlotte Observer
Charlotte, N.C., May 12, 1974

The entire tenor of the national response to the Nixon scandals has been altered by the increasing defection of his conservative Republican supporters. President Nixon's removal now may come about in a way that will be healing rather than divisive and partisan.

Until the past few days there had been some danger that the impeachment proceedings would break down into party warfare and thus lack the solemn dignity that should characterize such a serious matter.

Curbing Partisanship

To be sure, the Republicans on the House Judiciary Committee in general have refrained from such party partisanship; it was highly significant when almost all of them voted with the Democratic members to pursue impeachment evidence with subpoenas. The Republican committee members also acted with responsibility in choosing for their counsel a man of Albert Jenner's stature.

But there remained the possibility that, on the floor of the House and possibly later in a Senate trial, party partisanship would strongly emerge. That no longer seems a real prospect. One by one, even the congressional Republicans who have most ardently supported President Nixon are coming forward with salient criticism of his conduct and, in many cases, with calls for his removal.

A Different Battle

Impeachment by the House has become virtually a certainty unless resignation intervenes. If impeachment by the House and trial by the Senate are still necessary, at least the battle probably will be largely between Nixon legal strategists and a bipartisan majority in Congress rather than a battle between Republicans and Democrats, or between liberals and conservatives.

Even so, impeachment remains a dreary prospect. We said on Dec. 16 that we had come to the conclusion that Mr. Nixon should be impeached by the House so that the Senate could weigh the evidence against him, with Chief Justice Warren Burger presiding in that trial. Only in that way, we thought, could the air be cleared. We expressed a desire for a careful, judicious approach, not one characterized by haste and partisanship.

The evidence warranting impeachment was ample then. It is more overwhelming now.

Bipartisan Approach

The best outcome for the country would be for Mr. Nixon to resign. But care should be taken by leaders in Congress as they seek to persuade him to do that. A Nixon resignation with no acknowledgment of serious wrongdoing or responsibility for wrongdoing by others — especially a resignation accompanied by an effort on Mr. Nixon's part to portray himself as an innocent man driven from office by political partisans — would further poison the waters of public life in the United States.

His strong supporters of the past should try to see that this does not take place. And by the same token, we think, his strongest political foes should show a willingness to forego pursuing his personal legal responsibility for wrongdoing in the White House if he resigns.

Only a clearly bipartisan approach to the subject by congressional leaders could produce such an outcome. The Republican leadership at last is moving in such a way that the possibility exists. We are closer than ever to a resolution of the matter that would give the country the new leadership it must have without leaving it wounded by bitter strife.

THE BILLINGS GAZETTE
Billings, Mont., May 3, 1974

In the past The Billings Gazette has taken the editorial position that President Nixon should not resign because it would leave such a void in government leadership.

His advisors all gone as a part of the Watergate aftermath, there would be, we reasoned, no one to properly direct the nations course other than President Nixon.

Public reaction to recent oc-currences has changed our thinking. Today we believe the Executive Branch and the Congress are so completely occupied with problems of the presidency that they cannot effectively govern nor legislate.

For this reason, we add our voice to those calling for President Nixon to resign so that the nation may once again set about solving its vital problems.

Richmond Times-Dispatch
Richmond, Va., May 12, 1974

As the Watergate controversy moves into its final, decisive phase, there is a rising, almost hysterical, clamor for President Nixon's resignation. Old Nixon friends are joining old Nixon foes in urging the President to quit now for his own sake and for the sake of his country.

Some argue that impeachment would have a tragic impact upon the nation, inflicting deep wounds from which it would be long in recovering. Others insist that even if Mr. Nixon survived impeachment, he could never regain the nation's confidence. Watergate, some observers are convinced, has destroyed the President's capacity to lead.

It is a tempting argument, this plea for the President's resignation. Surely, it is a possibility that Mr. Nixon has considered in the privacy of his soul, and obviously it is an option that remains constantly available to him. Eventually, the President might indeed decide that the nation would be better off if he turned the White House over to Gerald Ford and disappeared from the official scene.

But we are not prepared to join that growing band of critics and pleaders who seem to think the President has a *moral obligation* or a *patriotic duty* to resign before his case has received the thorough consideration provided for by the Constitution of this great country. Mr. Nixon may deserve to be ejected from office, but the nation has a *moral* as well as a *legal* obligation to guarantee him his constitutional rights. To intimidate and demoralize the President by implying that he is something of a traitor for defending himself is to subject him to the third degree. It *is to* batter him over the head with a psychological rubber hose in an effort to bludgeon him into total submission.

When all the Watergate evidence has been analyzed, Mr. Nixon may be exonerated from criminal blame. Transcripts of White House conversations seem to show con-clusively that the President had no advance knowledge of the Watergate break-in and that he was slow to learn of his aides' participation in that scandalous operation. As for the President's possible involvement in the cover-up of Watergate, the transcripts are more ambiguous. Some who have read them are convinced that the President *was* involved and is therefore guilty of obstructing justice; but others disagree. There is a strong element of doubt, in other words, and it could be strong enough to prevent the President's conviction by the Senate if not his impeachment by the House of Representatives.

Impeachment proceedings, if they are pursued, will be unpleasant for Mr. Nixon and for the nation. About that there is no doubt. But impeachment is the only procedure—the *only* procedure—prescribed by the Constitution for determining a president's guilt or innocence when he has been accused of criminal conduct. No doubt the authors of the Constitution intended for impeachment to be a difficult and painful process, lest Congress be tempted to resort to it routinely and cavalierly. Consider these words from a recent article in *Harper's* by Arthur M. Schlesinger Jr., who certainly is no admirer of Richard Nixon:

"...the President's resignation...would introduce an indigestible parliamentary element into a nonparliamentary system. I hardly think it would be wise in the long run to confer on Congress the power to dismiss presidents without investigation and trial. Think what might have happened, for example, in the fortnight of congressional indignation after President Truman fired General MacArthur, or in the period when John Adams was standing up against congressional agitation for war with France. Yet everyone now agrees that these two doughty Presidents never had finer hours.

"The Founding Fathers were prescient in making impeachment the constitutional remedy. They did not want to make it easy to get rid of Presidents but they were determined to make it possible to do so."

Only through the impeachment process can the agonizing questions about Mr. Nixon's role in Watergate be satisfactorily resolved. Only by following the route prescribed by the Constitution can the nation preserve the integrity of its system of government. Should Mr. Nixon resign now, suspicions about his conduct in the Watergate affair might follow him to his grave and into the pages of history. Should he resign under pressure, he would participate, as Mr. Schlesinger has suggested, in the establishment of a precedent that might seriously enfeeble future chief executives.

So let us go forward with impeachment proceedings, and let us resolve to accept the consequences of our decision to do so. We do not believe that the impeachment and trial of President Nixon would be the horrendous experience that some prophets of doom have predicted. Indeed, the nation might recover from the effects of this constitutional procedure far more quickly than it would from the effects of a forced presidential resignation that left basic issues unresolved.

By arguing in favor of following the constitutional process, we do not mean to pronounce Richard Nixon innocent. Throughout the Watergate controversy, we have defended the President's right to a fair hearing and his right to be *presumed* innocent until proven guilty. His case has now gone to the only tribunal empowered to consider it—the United States Congress—and we are willing to accept its verdict.

Like many others, we are appalled by the tone of those conversations Mr. Nixon had with Counsel John Dean and other creepy White House characters. Mr. Nixon often comes through as a devious schemer who is at least willing to *consider* the possibility of resorting to illegal tactics to pre-vent the complete Watergate story from emerging. We have searched the transcripts in vain for an expression, a *genuine expression*, of presidential outrage at the immoralities of Watergate.

But both charity and realism compel us to say that the portrait of Richard Nixon contained in the Watergate transcripts is not a complete representation of the man. In those conversations, he was reacting as a politician concerned about the political effects of Watergate. It is very well to say that he should have reacted as a responsible elected leader concerned about the legal and moral aspects of the affair, but it is naive to believe that a man who must be a skilled politician to win elective office will forget and abandon his political traits the minute he assumes his official duties.

This observation is not offered as condonation of Mr. Nixon's actions in Watergate. Rather, it is a suggestion that we who sit in moral judgment of Richard Nixon—it is up to Congress to resolve the legal points—should not base our decision entirely upon the transcripts of those private conversations. There is another Richard Nixon—a Richard Nixon who ended the United States' involvement in the demoralizing Vietnam war without abandoning South Vietnam to the brutality of communism, a Richard Nixon who has opened avenues of cooperation to Russia and Red China, a Richard Nixon who has extended America's constructive influence to the Arab world, a Richard Nixon who has worked hard, in our opinion, to improve the quality of life at home.

In the end, the virtues of the public Richard Nixon may not be powerful enough to offset the apparent vices of the private Richard Nixon. In the end, Congress may remove him from office and the public may abandon him. But let us not make it possible for those who write the history of this agonizing period to say that Richard Nixon was the victim of kangaroo justice.

Minneapolis Tribune

Minneapolis, Minn., May 12, 1974

In the wake of the publication of President Nixon's White House tapes, a growing number of his former defenders are calling for his resignation.

Among them is the Chicago Tribune, long a staunchly conservative newspaper and a supporter of Mr. Nixon. Last week it asked for his resignation, as we did somewhat earlier. Similar advice is now coming from other conservative newspapers as well as from members of the president's party in Congress and elsewhere.

If it wasn't clear to Mr. Nixon before, it ought to be clear to him now: It's time for him to leave. And if it wasn't clear to Congress before, it ought to be clear to Congress now: If Mr. Nixon won't go voluntarily, he should be removed by the processes prescribed in the Constitution.

The Evening Bulletin

Philadelphia, Pa., May 10, 1974

When President Nixon went before the American people to say he was making public the edited transcripts of some of his Watergate-related talks with his aides he pleaded that these documents be read with "an open and a fair mind."

That night in his televised address President Nixon also said he was sure that anyone who read the transcripts and kept in mind everything else he had done in connection with what is known as Watergate would be convinced that he had done nothing wrong.

Well, we have read the transcripts—every line of them. And we have gone over what President Nixon and his aides said in these edited and incomplete accounts and compared this with what he did and with what he said in his infrequent press conferences and in his other public utterances.

• • •

The Bulletin does not feel that the 1,254 pages of partial transcripts of the White House tapes clear President Nixon. Quite the contrary. While proof of criminal complicity may not leap from the censored pages, what does come from them is a sickening and distressing view of a great nation's Chief Executive dishonoring the long-revered White House through a pattern of conduct demonstrating that he was interested chiefly in his own political survival—at virtually any cost.

The man who campaigned as the personification of Puritan ethics emerged as a plotter willing to discuss the payment of blackmail if this could be handled. This man who offered himself to the American voters as a clinically cold but skilled government craftsman also emerges as a vague, vacillating and sometimes confused executive whose aides did not hesitate to contradict or interrupt or even dominate him.

Pennsylvania's Republican U. S. Senator Hugh Scott summed it up when he described the transcripts—documents provided by President Nixon himself and not "leaked" or uncovered by another source — as "shabby, disgusting and immoral." And Senator Scott was, for a long time, one of President Nixon's chief defenders and apologists.

In our reading of the transcripts we were appalled at the utter lack of moral indignation over the burglary of Democratic Party headquarters.

Instead, the talk was of handling the messy matter through public relations, of keeping "our losses" to a minimum and of eventually getting back at "the enemy."

• • •

It is difficult to read the transcripts without feeling the moral bankruptcy of Mr. Nixon and his aides, John Ehrlichman, H. R. Haldeman and John Dean 3d — and others who were occasionally involved in the discussions. There seemed to be no real concern shown over the possible effect of the spreading stain of Watergate on the nation and its people. And the man who held aloft the Presidency as his shield in his confrontations with the Congress and the courts did not seem concerned with the irreparable damage his conduct might do to that great office.

Mr. Nixon has contended that once he learned of the seamy scandal called Watergate he was interested only in seeing that justice was done fairly and "according to law." But this is not the way it comes through from the transcripts.

The principals, Mr. Nixon, Ehrlichman, Haldeman and Dean — and occasionally others — come through as cynical schemers intent on a coverup and willing to shift tactics only when threatened with possible criminal involvement in an obstruction of justice.

• • •

Not all will read the transcripts and come away with this judgment. But we suggest that it is difficult to form any other judgment if one carefully reads the entire transcript, and measures the bulky record containing this against Mr. Nixon's other words and deeds. The release of the transcripts has been termed Mr. Nixon's greatest gamble. He obviously felt the action would work to his favor. It has not. The transcripts have mired Mr. Nixon even more deeply in the Watergate mess.

Now Mr. Nixon is refusing to provide the actual tape records on which the transcripts are supposedly based, as well as additional recordings and other documents, to the House Judiciary Committee or to Special Watergate Prosecutor Leon Jaworski.

This is a mistake. The House Judiciary Committee and the American people will certainly believe that Mr. Nixon is afraid to release any additional material because he has something to hide. It is not for Mr. Nixon to say "enough" to the House Judiciary Committee on matters not related to national security.

Many respected individuals have suggested that President Nixon resign. So have several prominent and conservative newspapers.

The Bulletin does not think this would be wise at this point in time. We believe in the constitutional course. We feel that those who are unwavering in their support of and loyalty to Mr. Nixon would be convinced that he was a sacrificial victim, a martyr, and that the nation would be even more divided.

The Bulletin suggests that the material in the transcripts, together with the refusal by the White House to provide any additional data, is all the signal needed by the House Judiciary Committee to proceed just as expeditiously as possible with its inquiry into the possible impeachment of Mr. Nixon. No delays should be permitted.

Representative Peter W. Rodino (D-NJ), the committee chairman, thinks the 38-member committee should be able to finish its awesome and historic assignment by the end of July. Mr. Rodino and the others should try to keep to this target date or make their decision even sooner.

It may be that the public hearings of the House Judiciary Committee will provide new material. The President's case may be strengthened. At this point, and against the background of the transcripts, it might be wise for President Nixon to appear before the committee in open session.

There are, after all, 1,670 parts in the transcript marked as inaudible and in most of these it appears as though President Nixon himself was talking. There are certainly many, many things he can and should tell the members of the House Judiciary Committee — and the American people if he has nothing to hide.

• • •

We hope that the House Judiciary Committee will look fully into the accusations and into the evidence on a nonpartisan basis. The committee should not avoid the knotty question of what constitutes an impeachable offense.

There is no reason, in fact, why the committee proceedings now underway cannot answer some of the historic questions still unresolved concerning the process of presidential impeachment—and the sooner the better.

Washington Star-News

Washington, D.C., May 12, 1974

President Nixon's resignation, the subject of intense speculation this weekend, would absolve the House of Representatives of its onerous duty of ruling on the question of Oval Office culpability in the Watergate scandal. But that is not the point.

Mr. Nixon's precipitous departure from office, as many of his erstwhile supporters have correctly asserted, would be beneficial to the GOP, which faces the possibility of an electoral disaster this November. But that is not the point.

The transferral of the President's responsibilities to Vice President Ford, with a concomitant granting of federal immunity from any possible criminal prosecution, might have some personal attractions for Mr. Nixon. But that is not the point.

Neither the accommodation of Congress, nor the future of the Republican party, nor Mr. Nixon's personal fate is — or ought to be — the primary consideration at this point, as they say, in time. So our readers must excuse us if we decline to participate in the Gadarene rush toward resignation.

This nation, which is to say all of us, finds itself between a rock and hard place. All of us desperately wish this cup would pass. But if Mr. Nixon is to go, the manner of his going is of the utmost importance.

The Constitution prescribes how a president unworthy of his high office is to be dealt with. That process was set in train Thursday when the House Judiciary Committee convened to begin its deliberations on the impeachment issue. We believe that the committee, as Chairman Peter W. Rodino Jr. stated, understands its "high constitutional responsibility." We believe the committee, conscious of the fact that the eyes of history are upon it, will discharge that responsibility fully and fairly.

It is desperately important both that this be done and that it be seen to be done. Because we were born free, because each of us has been nurtured by this land and partakes of its spirit, each of us in effect is called to judge the President and, in so doing, we judge ourselves. And this is a responsibility that cannot be shirked: There can be no plea-bargaining before the bar of history.

The events of the past 18 months have shaken this republic to its foundations, eroded its institutions and shamed its people. We have seen, most recently in the transcripts of presidential conversations, how thoughtless, amoral and ambitious men have sought to pervert the political process. We are not prepared at this point to render final judgment on the President's legal culpability. That, after all, is the responsibility, ultimately, of the Senate. Suffice it to say that we are appalled and sickened by those things done — and left undone — by the man we twice supported for the presidency of the United States.

But we do earnestly believe in those things to which Mr. Nixon gave lip-service. We believe in the Constitution and in due process. We believe that this is a government of laws and not of men. We believe in the resiliency of our institutions, and in the fundamental decency and responsibility of the American people. We do not fear the people's will, for they and we are one.

This being the case, the second impeachment inquiry in the history of this nation holds no fears for us, nor should it be aborted by a presidential resignation. Indeed, we would fear more for this nation if it lacked the courage to grasp this nettle.

As Mr. Nixon noted in his televised speech on April 29, a trial in the Senate, should the House ultimately pass articles of impeachment, would be "a wrenching ordeal." Resignation at such a time, once the House had laid out the case against the President for all the people to see, would be an option worth considering.

But if Mr. Nixon is to leave the White House before the expiration of his second term, it must be clear — beyond the shadow of a reasonable doubt — that he does so as a consequence of the misdeeds of his administration, that he has not been hounded from office for capricious or partisan reasons.

For these reasons, Mr. Nixon's resignation at this time would provide no catharsis and sow bitter seeds of future political discord.

THE SUN

Baltimore, Md., May 12, 1974

In a situation where nobody can predict what new sensations may erupt from day to day, the moment could come when resignation would be the only way out for Richard Nixon and the country; the only way for him to escape from his jungle of troubles and the only way to get him off the country's back. In our opinion that moment is not now. It is better that the process leading to impeachment or non-impeachment, and if to impeachment then to possible conviction, go measuredly forward.

Politically most of the calls for resignation have come from Republicans troubled about their party's future or about their own prospects in this fall's elections. We ourselves are unworried about the fate of the Republican party, which is by no means to say we don't care about the fate of the Republican party. An effective Republican party is necessary for the functioning of our system. But we cannot see that party as dependent upon the personal fortunes of Mr. Nixon, whether those fortunes be fair or ill. To the contrary, one bright spot in the whole mess has been the emergence under its pressures of a notable number of Republicans of wisdom, integrity, intelligence and strength. We would trust these people, along with others simply scared out of their wits, to refrain from nominating in 1976 another Nixon and another Agnew.

Nor are we worried about the supposedly intolerable "wrenching" experience, the so-called "national trauma," that some say an impeachment and a public senatorial trial would visit upon the country. If the country were that fragile, all would be hopeless, anyway. And the country is not that fragile.

Our preference for the impeachment process over resignation is influenced only in slight degree by the argument that if Mr. Nixon resigned he would stand as a "martyr," railroaded from office. Undoubtedly in that case he would try to don a mantle of martyrdom, and undoubtedly the

dwindling but still fervent hard core of his supporters would be duped by the masquerade. But the great majority of the American people has got more common sense than to take any such view of a man already, through his own behavior, thoroughly discredited.

Rather, we hope for impeachment over resignation because we believe that in the nation's interest, present and historical, the record has to be spread in full before the public, and that the constitutional path today being followed is the right path leading to that end. Mr. Nixon's transcripts do not by any stretch of the imagination fulfill the requirement. It is not only that they are edited and doctored, and edited and doctored to Mr. Nixon's advantage. Also, still more important, they seek, as the White House has constantly sought, to narrow the issues to one, the Watergate break-in and coverup, which is a mere part of the story.

If a Nixon resignation left matters where they are now the record would be woefully incomplete, with vast blanks on the subjects of Mr. Nixon's taxes and finances, of domestic surveillance directed by the White House, of any use of federal agencies for political purposes and of the handling of political contributions and funds, including among much else the Rebozo-Hughes money.

The weight of Watergate, plus the overhanging weight of all the rest, may in the event impel Mr. Nixon to leave office voluntarily, at some moment. He says he will not, for what that is worth. We are not privy to his thinking, except as he has made us sketchily privy in the transcripts, which reveal a mind much more impulsive and much less firm and controlled and logical than we had earlier supposed. He is long on "options," and resignation is surely one of his options. We cannot guess what he will do; we can just say that, as of today, it seems to us the interests of constitutional propriety would be best served if he had to undergo the ordeal.

The Oregonian
Portland, Ore., May 9, 1974

President Nixon's decision to release no more tapes or transcripts of private conversations to either the Watergate special prosecutor, Leon Jaworski, or the House Judiciary Committee to help it impeach him, may go to the Supreme Court this time. And the circumstances in each case are different from those before.

Even though he has released 1,300 pages of transcripts of tapes to the Judiciary Committee, in addition to 19 tapes and 700 documents to both the special prosecutor and the committee, the President's legal defense may not be as strong this time.

The 64 recordings of presidential conversations subpoenaed by Jaworski and refused by James D. St. Clair, the President's Watergate counsel, are sought for both the prosecution and defense of White House aides to be tried in September. Last year, after Special Prosecutor Archibald Cox subpoenaed tapes for federal grand juries, the Court of Appeals upheld Judge John Sirica's subpoena and the White House backed down and released the tapes rather than carry the test on to the Supreme Court. This time, St. Clair hinted, the President's defense of executive privilege will be carried all the way.

The indicted White House aides, as well as the prosecution, demand some of the tapes for their defense, and it is unlikely that the appellate court will deny the right to such evidence.

The Senate investigating committee headed by Sen. Sam Ervin subpoenaed tapes last time around and the court did not recognize its authority. This time, however, the House Judiciary Committee is armed with the constitutional authority of the House's power of impeachment. The President has not complied with its subpoena for the actual tapes from which 350,000 words were transcribed. And the committee proposes to subpoena another 141 tapes. The House committee appears to have powers superior to those of a Senate investigating committee, powers which seem to outweigh the privilege of the president it seeks to impeach.

But the legal struggle may not be of paramount importance. The national interest argues against a confrontation between the President and the two other branches of government, the judicial and legislative. The House committee, at least, has massive quantities of information on which to proceed.

President Nixon's offer to permit the chairman and senior Republican member of the committee to audit the tapes and to interrogate him under oath remains valid. The way has been left open for the committee heads to urge expert examination of the edited or inaudible portions, short of delivery of all tapes to the committee—the irrelevant along with the relevant.

The committee should get on with its consideration of evidence now in hand and give the public some certification of what it needs in additional evidence, if any. The people do have a vital stake in the earliest possible determination of the President's guilt or innocence.

MANCHESTER UNION LEADER
Manchester, N.H., May 12, 1974

Abraham Lincoln to publisher Joseph Medill of the Chicago Tribune:

"You, sir, are a coward."

It is an abjuration that might accurately be addressed not only to the present publishers of the Tribune but also to those of other self-proclaimed "conservative" papers who are deserting Richard Nixon because, they allege, President Nixon's use of profanity in taped conversations renders him liable to impeachment.

Indeed, according to these newspapers, it is the only "impeachable offense" brought out in the Presidential tapes. Thus, Mr. Nixon may become the only chief executive in history to be impeached for saying "damn."

As for the Chicago Tribune, its record of treason to the conservative cause, though little known to the public, is historic. Under the late Bertie McCormick it was the Tribune which disclosed that U.S. Navy cryptographers had broken the Japanese naval code, a revelation which is estimated to have lengthened World War II by six months.

Secretary of the Navy Frank Knox at the time advocated McCormick's indictment, but was denied the backing of the Roosevelt Administration.

However, a far worse blow to Americanism was dealt by McCormick when he sold Cissie Patterson's Washington Times-Herald to the leftwing-liberal owners of the Washington Post, thus depriving the nation's capital of its only conservative voice.

In its back-stabbing of Nixon, the Tribune, along with a number of other papers, forfeits any pretext to speak for conservatives. Such papers will find their own influence self-destroyed.

THE ROANOKE TIMES
Roanoke, Va., May 12, 1974

Last November 11 we examined the case for impeaching President Nixon and concluded: "No." The reasoning was that impeachment was too unfamiliar to the people who put Mr. Nixon into office in November, 1972.

Since November the popular understanding of what impeachment is—a charge by the House of Representatives, a trial by the Senate—has advanced considerably. Understanding of the subject is still imperfect, but impeachment is no longer an unknown and therefore terrifying procedure.

Even more important, Gerald R. Ford—a decent, conservative Republican—has become Vice President. Should he replace Richard M. Nixon, the mandate of November, 1972, would not be overruled; it would be reinforced. Vice President Ford appears to be the kind of man Nixon supporters thought they were getting in November, 1972.

On December 9, after Mr. Ford became Vice President, an editorial here examined the impeachment question again and concluded: "Maybe." The time has now come to endorse the impeachment process now in motion, to encourage it and to be grateful that those who wrote the Constitution had the good sense to put the process in.

The factual basis of the November 11 editorial began to erode almost as soon as it was published. The erosion has reached its depth with President Nixon's own, self-edited and self-selected, version of the evidence. These White House tape transcripts show the President of the United States involved in obstruction of justice. Put negatively, they show him observing and not removing the obstructions to justice in the Watergate affair.

They seem to show that the President encouraged or condoned a long list of offenses—bribery to purchase silence from the burglars, subornation of perjury, not very well veiled promises of clemency to felons. The list of possible crimes is long. When compared to President Nixon's public statements on Watergate, the tapes suggest Mr. Nixon was playing loosely with the truth. All of this together may show such a consistent, pattern of misconduct as to warrant removal from office.

But who can determine the exact truth of what these tape transcripts suggest? Who can reach such solemn judgments hinted here? Only those who have the power to obtain all the evidence, including the tapes themselves. The institution which has this power and responsibility is the House of Representatives. It has delegated its responsibility, for the first inquiry and recommendation, to the House Judiciary Committee.

That is where it should be. The national interest requires that this committee act thoroughly and with as little partisanship as is possible in a judicial-political proceeding. It may be that the full House and the full Senate will be called upon to perform their solemn duties. If so, they can rise to the occasion.

We are here endorsing the impeachment process, not impeachment itself; we are willing to leave the first decision to those empowered by the Constitution to make it, under the assumption that Congressmen will rise to the occasion and, despite human frailties, do their best. We have resisted this idea for a long time. We now welcome what we resisted.

Democrat and Chronicle

Rochester, N.Y., May 14, 1974

Profound disenchantment notwithstanding, this newspaper has not yet called, and does not now call, for Mr. Nixon's resignation.

And the reason basically is our reluctance to become party to a posse and thus abort the Constitutional remedy the nation has now embarked upon in the shape of impeachment proceedings.

Having come this far down the road towards the kind of resolution you'd expect from a nation of laws, must we now throw it all away by crying "off with his head" like the Queen in Alice?

Yet even as we say this, it's not only too clear that what started out as an orderly Constitutional process is today in danger of becoming a disorderly rout. Even the faithful among party and press are alike exhorting the President to get out.

Criticism has reached the point in fact where some misgivings are now being expressed.

Columnist Dennis Braithwaite writes in The Toronto Star: "Watergate has gone beyond scandal to the worst kind of hysterical scapegoatism . . . This conversion of a political scandal into a pervasive witchhunt is to me more frightening than anything that has been revealed about dirty tricks and law-breaking by the President's agents."

NOTES WASHINGTON columnist Nicholas von Hoffman: "One senses the decision has been made and that some time in the next year or so, if not sooner, Nixon will be impeached, convicted and thrown out on to the sidewalks of Pennsylvania avenue . . . Beyond all question of guilt or innocence, he must be impeached because Americans — the Super Bowl people — have been promised the show."

And, it must be frankly said, the man who has done the most to set the hounds at his heels has been Mr. Nixon himself.

By the character of the men he surrounded himself with; by his backing and filling on the handing over of White House documents; by the self-indictment of the transcripts; by his insistence that the Judiciary Committee experts not be allowed to check the transcripts against the tapes; by his refusal to give information to his own appointed special prosecutor; by the resort to executive privilege in silencing his staff in matters relating to Howard Hughes and Charles G. (Bebe) Rebozo — by these and other acts, the President has almost invited a search and destroy mission.

What's now being called most into question is Mr. Nixon's judgment.

HOW COULD HE possibly have assumed, for example, that the general release of the transcripts would help his cause? What could possibly offset such damning revelations as Mr. Nixon's urging to get "the most vicious libel lawyer there is" to respond to the charges of Sen. Weicker?

We find it hard to believe with Eric Sevareid that Mr. Nixon, in releasing the tapes, was banking "not on the people's fairness but upon their cynicism."

Yet the fact remains that his judgment was appallingly bad. The contents of the transcripts have almost mortally offended the sensibilities of friends and foes alike.

The President's judgment is also a key factor in the impeachment proceedings. If Mr. Nixon continues to deny the Judiciary Committee the information they feel they need for a full and fair investigation (for example, tapes instead of transcripts), his judgment would once again have to be called into serious question.

We have, as explained, declined to this point to call for Mr. Nixon's resignation because of our preference for an orderly Constitutional resolution. But such a resolution, especially if it were to involve a Senate trial, depends vitally on access to all pertinent information.

There are two tides of opinion flowing against Mr. Nixon.

ONE CONSISTS of the large body of citizens who can no longer point with any pride at all to the occupant of the White House.

The other current of opinion is made up of those members of Congress who want to do what's fair by the President but who are already jittery over their own re-election prospects and whose concern to do the right thing isn't helped when requests for information are rejected.

Although the impeachment process has begun, there's still the chance that the President may be forced out of office without trial.

A momentum has been set up that's almost irresistible. For example, true or false, the most recent charge that the President used ethnic slurs and epithets in his conversations is bound to haunt him and to become one more pressure for ouster.

Mr. Nixon has become a man standing in the path of an avalanche.

He has said he won't resign, but he'll have little choice if the climate continues to build up as it has in the past several months.

Impeachment proceedings will be meaningless if the nation decides that Mr. Nixon has become too heavy a cross to carry, and we're almost at that point now. And because of the shabby conniving revealed by the transcripts, even martyrdom would be denied him in the event of such an outcome.

The Houston Post

Houston, Tex., May 12, 1974

No president before, surely no president ever again, will provide the American public the relentless record of the White House transcripts. Nothing in history is comparable to them. We cannot know what other presidents have said in the private, day-to-day talk in the Oval Office. It will take time to evaluate the 1,308 pages of transcripts turned over to the House Judiciary Committee by the White House. Now we are using the only process we have under the Constitution to make a determination to impeach or not to impeach. The responsibility of the committee is indeed an awesome one, not merely in terms of Mr. Nixon, but of the precedent it will set.

But the most troublesome point in the transcripts for those of us not charged with the political responsibility of the committee is the lack of surprise, indignation and moral outrage reflected in the conversations. They seem to turn more on the question of how this should be handled than on how the integrity of the White House can be reestablished. References were made to the public relations aspects, but no references were made to the morality, ethics or legality of the case. References were made to the effect on the coming election, but no concern was shown for the effect on the body politic.

President Nixon sets a high value on loyalty. He has given generously of that loyalty to his aides, H.R.Haldeman and John Ehrlichman. But there should be a primary loyalty to the law of the land. At inauguration, a president swears under oath that: "I will faithfully execute the office of the President of the United States, and will, to the best of my ability, preserve, protect and defend the Constitution of the United States." White House staff members know what the President has sworn and that it is the solemn obligation of all who work under him to help him uphold his oath.

Many men of average ability thrown suddenly into the presidency have grown and been ennobled by the office. The transcripts give no such portrayal of Richard Nixon.

The House Judiciary Committee and the House of Representatives will have to make a finding on the evidence and determine whether the findings do, or do not, constitute an impeachable offense. But the American people are judging the character, quality and stature of the man in the White House.

MITCHELL, STANS ACQUITTED BY JURY; JOHN DEAN'S CREDIBILITY QUESTIONED

John N. Mitchell and Maurice H. Stans, former Cabinet officials in the Nixon Administration and directors of President Nixon's 1972 re-election campaign, were acquitted by a federal district court jury in New York City April 28 of all charges stemming from a secret cash campaign contribution from Robert L. Vesco, the financier whose mutual funds dealings were under investigation by the Securities and Exchange Commission (SEC). The government had accused Mitchell and Stans of conspiracy, obstruction of justice and perjury for attempting to block the SEC investigation and later lying to a grand jury about their roles.

The verdict was widely seen as a significant boost to Nixon's campaign against impeachment, partly because the Vesco issue would be effectively removed from consideration by the House Judiciary Committee, but more importantly to some observers, because the credibility of former presidential counsel John W. Dean 3rd was brought into question. Dean had been a principal witness against Mitchell and Stans and was one of the President's chief accusers.

Interviewed after the verdict, jurors on the panel of nine men and three women said the basic issue in their 26 hours of deliberations had been the credibility of government witnesses vs. that of the defendants. According to forewoman Sybil Kucharski, a bank teller, the jury turned to the perjury charges after reaching an early impasse on the conspiracy and obstruction of justice counts. Verdicts of not guilty were reached on the perjury counts after lengthy debate, Miss Kucharski said; after that, "the rest was easy." Miss Kucharski said she did not "want to say Mr. Dean was lying, but he was often unbelievable."

According to some jurors and chief prosecutor John R. Wing, another major factor in the case was the absence of Vesco, who had escaped extradition and was a fugitive in Costa Rica.

MANCHESTER NEW HAMPSHIRE UNION LEADER
Manchester, N.H., April 30, 1974

Commenting on last Sunday's historic jury decision declaring former Nixon administration officials John Mitchell and Maurice Stans innocent of all charges of allegedly conspiring to defraud the government by using improper influence in the Robert L. Vesco case, Chief Prosecutor John R. Wing observed: "This is a very different case. It does not have much to do with what's going on in Washington."

That has to be the non sequitur of the century, for the result of the Mitchell-Stans trial cannot help but have a powerful impact on what's going on in Washington, casting doubt not only on the impartiality of the Watergate investigation and the believability of its star witness, John Dean, but also dampening the hopes of those who seek to reverse the 1972 presidential election returns by impeaching the President.

A jury of nine men and three women weighed the testimony of John Dean in the Mitchell-Stans case, the first trial of former Cabinet members since the Harding administration scandals of the 1920s, and obviously found the testimony of the star witness, Mr. Dean, not at all convincing.

Forewoman Sybil A. Kucharski, who delivered the innocent verdicts, diplomatically declined to state specifically that the jury had found Dean not a credible witness, but, referring to Dean, commented, "He admitted guilt, possibly looking for favor."

A major factor in the deliberations, Miss Kucharski acknowledged, was "the credibility of the witnesses and why they were talking now."

"We had a reasonable doubt," the jury forewoman declared, "because of these witnesses and because we didn't feel the evidence was substantiated."

A different set of facts and circumstances may be involved in Watergate, the impeachment process and the Mitchell-Stans trial, but as a matter of practical politics, the impact of the latter on the get-Nixon strategy will prove devastating.

The average citizen can relate more directly to private citizens who are simply serving jury duty than he can to politicians who — as one result of the Watergate controversy — are not held in all that high regard.

THE ARIZONA REPUBLIC
Phoenix, Ariz., March 6, 1974

Judge Lee Gagliardi, sitting in one of the Watergate-related cases in Washington, refused to stop a jury trial of former Attorney General John Mitchell and former Commerce Secretary Maurice Stans. From where we sit the judge appears to have allowed the prosecution too much latitude.

The decision to continue with the first two big fish charged in the Watergate scandal must have wrenched the judge's conscience. It may well become the basis for a reversal if Mitchell and Stans are convicted and appeal.

The point at issue was a statement made by the prosecuting attorney in addressing the jury. Assistant U. S. Attorney James Rayhill charged that the two then cabinet members had agreed "to sell political influence for $200,000 in cash" from a financial wheel named Robert Vesco. (Vesco fled the country so he can't be tried.)

In his statement, Rayhill asked the jury "to consider how essential it is that a jury be given truthful testimony under oath," an obvious attempt to influence the jury against the testimony the defendants would give.

The prosecutor also said the jurors (eight men, four women) should put themselves "in the place of the grand jurors who investigated the case." The grand jurors, as everyone knows, had found there was sufficient reason to try Mitchell and Stans. But a grand jury never rules on the guilt or innocence of a person, and it was highly prejudicial to ask the trial jury to put itself in the shoes of the grand jury.

Judge Gagliardi promptly sustained an objection to the question, and later told the jury, "A grand jury proceeding is in no sense a trial. You and you alone are the judges of the facts."

Over the weekend the judge gave the motion for a mistrial "appropriate consideration and mature contemplation." Then he decided that the trial should go on. Undoubtedly he was influenced by the long delay that would result from stopping the trial now, and the amount of trouble it would take to swear in a new jury.

One can hardly blame Mitchell's and Stans' lawyers for feeling they were being put upon. Such prejudicial statements have no place in a court of law. Unfortunately, they fit into the pattern of Chief Prosecutor Leon Jaworski, who said on a national television show, "We have found no basis for a charge of perjury" against John Dean, whose testimony will be needed to convict at least one of the White House aides now awaiting trial. Jaworski was rebuked by Judge Gerhard Gesell, but that hardly undoes the mischief created by his prejudicial statement.

The judiciary is the backbone of the administration of justice in this country. Much as some federal judges may be worked up over the Watergate cases, they should not depart from the rigid rules of evidence. To allow government prosecutors to get away with such statements as those made by Rayhill and Jaworski will only increase suspicion regarding the political aspects of the Watergate prosecution.

Arkansas Gazette.

Little Rock, Ark., April 30, 1974

A verdict of innocent cannot be appealed, which of course is as it should be, and which is why the drumhead conviction people who so distort the meaning of justice with their shrill, parrot-like, cries of "Law and order! Law and order!" necessarily start with one strike against them. Convictions can be appealed by the defendant, but acquittals cannot be appealed by the prosecution, so in this sense, a defendant has something going for him from the start.

So former Secretary of the Treasury Maurice H. Stans now has been cleared of all criminal charges in connection with the 1972 "Campaign To Re-elect" by a federal trial jury at New York that at the beginning at least was sharply divided on the question of guilt or innocence. Stans's co-defendant, former Attorney General John N. Mitchell, in like manner, has been cleared on all nine counts of criminal conspiracy, perjury and obstruction of justice in the Vesco Case, and, despite his characterization of a reporter's question on this point as "asinine", he obviously has been given a psychological leg up on Phase 2 of his legal difficulties — his trial at Washington in early September on a whole new set of similar charges more directly concerning the central Watergate conspiracy.

By extension, so has President Nixon naturally been given a psychological boost in his stubborn, year-long, campaign to survive in office, if only because the New York jury's sorting out of conflicting testimony in the Vesco Case amounted to the first crack in the credibility of John W. Dean III, perhaps the principal key to Watergate and much of the rest of it. A high-placed White House official who insisted upon anonymity, though shunning use of the word "perjurer", was quick to say that "the jury's verdict by implication makes him [Dean] a liar, which makes one wonder how many other lies he has told [in other cases.].

None of the jurors questioned after the verdict was returned would even use the word "liar", and there was one rather puzzling disclaimer along this line from one of them, an investment banker, who said that "I don't think anybody arrived at a decision on the basis of 'this guy is a liar' or 'this guy told the truth,'" all of which makes you wonder why the jury members aren't still locked up deliberating.

One thing that definitely was blown up by the New York verdict was the notion that Stans and Mitchell could not possibly get a fair trial because of all the "pre-trial publicity", the basis of motions entered by defense counsel for a mistrial. A motion for mistrial is a more-or-less routine defense strategy, of course, and quite proper strategy, it goes without saying. So is the effort to seek a change of venue, as also was done in this case on the ground that not only had the pre-trial publicity made it difficult for the two defendants to get a fair trial but that it had made it especially difficult in supposedly over-communicated-to New York. Considering that the change of venue Mitchell had sought had been to presumably under-communicated-to Aberdeen, Miss., which you have to look for closely upon anything other than an ordnance survey map, it sounded a little odd to hear John Mitchell say, post-verdict, that he had been confident that the New York jury would acquit him all along, that "we've got the jury system [in America] and it always works."

This might make a good theme for Law Day tomorrow, but possibly a better one was provided by one of the jurors, a postman from Ossining, who said that he had come onto the trial jury as one of those drum-head "law-and-order" people we were talking about earlier, convinced that if the prosecutor said something was so it was so:

"I used to believe that when a prosecutor brings a charge they have to be right. I learned an awful lot on this case. When you come in with that view and you go out with a verdict, then the prosecution didn't prove its case."

The education of even one law-and-order man of this type is a distinct "plus" for the feelings and the awareness that the Law Day promoters try to instill in all of us.

As for the juryman's final point — that the prosecutor simply did not prove his case — it is pretty hard to argue with a verdict, even if you were so disposed, when the prosecutor himself somewhat ruefully concedes as much, as the chief government prosecutor, John R. Wing, in effect has done.

Wing did say that the inability to extradite Robert Vesco himself, the pivotal third defendant in the case, necessarily weakened the case against the remaining two, as observers had noted it would before the Stans-Mitchell trial ever began, and it is this recollection that makes most curious indeed one more volunteered thought from the postman-juryman already quoted — that he felt that Vesco had *tried* to put the fix in on the two former Cabinet members, all right, not so much to queer the SEC rap against him as to "get to any top figure [in order] to embarrass the President." The reason this is so curious is that Vesco, safe from the witness stand in his self-exile in the Bahamas, says that he has "evidence" of a plot on the part of others to "get" the President by getting *him*.

DAYTON DAILY NEWS
Dayton, Ohio, April 30, 1974

The acquittal of former Nixon cabinet officers John Mitchell and Maurice Stans extends the skepticism toward government conspiracy charges that juries first displayed in their rejection of the administration's showy trials of political radicals. Mr. Mitchell and Mr. Stans are thus the beneficiaries of a trend that the administration —particularly its then attorney general Mitchell—deplored just a few years ago.

It would be pleasant, in addition, to conclude that the jury's finding in the Mitchell-Stans trial has wiped the slate clean, but a smudgy chalk film remains where the prosecutors outlined their case. The jurors could not conclude, beyond reasonable doubt, that Mr. Mitchell and Mr. Stans took a $200,000 campaign contribution for the President virtually as payment to help the financier Robert Vesco in his troubles with the Securities and Exchange commission.

It remains uncontested, however, that the two, on behalf of the President, accepted the outsized tender, went to extraordinary lengths to keep it secret, knew Mr. Vesco was at least a slightly shadowy character in big-money manipulations, knew he was in probable trouble with federal regulatory agencies, worked desperately to keep the contribution from embarrassing the Nixon re-election campaign, returned the money only when it had become too hot to keep and had proved unneeded.

The picture that remains is not one of an administration operating in easy rectitude but one involved in scurrying dealing, perhaps staying within the law but slipping along its fringes in any case. The Nixon re-election operation took and may have sought funds from a questionable source and, over a period of months, had to exert sometimes frantic effort to spare itself the consequences of the impropriety. It can only be said, even after the jury has reported, that Mr. Mitchell and Mr. Stans did nothing in the matter that was actually illegal.

On that slim branch, the Nixon administration has rushed to hang the conclusion that the jury has exposed former White House counsel John Dean as an implausible witness.

That's not so. Even if the jurors had believed Mr. Dean utterly, it wouldn't have followed that Mr. Mitchell and Mr. Stans necessarily were guilty as charged. The challenge in prosecuting an alleged conspiracy is to establish all the links. Mr. Dean was only one and by no means seemed the weakest in the prosecution case.

In any event, the White House's troubles —that is to say, Mr. Nixon's—will go on. They come less from what Mr. Dean has testified than from logical suspicions about Mr. Nixon's relationship to the known misdeeds of his closest former staff members. Meantime, while their acquittal may have been a great day for justice, and for that hooray, the best that can be said for Mr. Mitchell and Mr. Stans, after all, is that they managed to keep an unethical affair legal.

THE TENNESSEAN

Nashville, Tenn., April 30, 1974

THE ACQUITTAL of Mr. John Mitchell and Mr. Maurice Stans make clear two things: 1. The jury system in America is alive and strong, and 2. pre-trial publicity about a criminal case is not the same as "convicting the defendant in the newspapers."

The New York jury decided the government had not proved its case against the two former Nixon cabinet members on charges of conspiracy, perjury and obstruction of justice in connection with a secret $200,000 campaign contribution to Mr. Nixon's re-election campaign by financier Robert L. Vesco.

★ ★ ★

The verdict shows once again how difficult it is to make a criminal conspiracy charge stand up in court. Juries have shown repeatedly — in recent years, in particular, in the cases of the Chicago 7 and the Berrigans — that they will not convict for conspiracy without hard evidence.

The government did not have a strong conspiracy case against Mr. Mitchell and Mr. Stans. And some may suspect the government did not press its case as hard as it could. But this could not be said about the Chicago 7 and the Berrigans. The government was passionate for conviction in those cases, but the juries would not accept the evidence.

In the perjury counts against Mr. Mitchell and Mr. Stans, the New York jury was up against the proposition of choosing between the word of defendants charged with perjury and that of prosecution witnesses of doubtful veracity.

The jury made the right choice. It is a tenet of the American system of criminal justice that when there is any doubt left about the guilt or innocence of a defendant, the question should be decided in favor of the defendant. This presumption of innocence is due to Mr. Mitchell and Mr. Stans no less than to any other criminal defendant in an American courtroom.

The Mitchell-Stans trial shows above all that defendants in criminal trials in this nation can receive justice in the glare of newspaper and television publicity. Few cases in modern American history have received more publicity than this one. The defense argued that it could not get a fair trial because of the publicity, but it turned out to be wrong. Lawyers have a tendency to underestimate the ability of the American people, when sitting as jurors, to sift the facts in a trial and come up with an objective verdict based on the evidence presented in the courtroom.

Some have said the Mitchell-Stans trial will have the effect of reminding the people that a grand jury indictment does not mean a defendant is guilty. However, this is a way of putting the cart before the horse. The New York jury already knew this.

It is only those of little faith in the jury system and the basic fairness of the American people who claim the people should not be informed on the processes of justice as they unfold.

The acquittal of Mr. Mitchell and Mr. Stans showed — to the great credit of the nation's system of justice — that regardless of the amount of public attention his case may receive, a defendant is not convicted until solid evidence against him is presented to a jury in the courtroom.

WINSTON-SALEM JOURNAL

Winston-Salem, N.C., April 30, 1974

After a year of anguished waiting — a year that included almost seven weeks of trial proceedings — John Mitchell and Maurice Stans walked as free men from the Federal courthouse in New York City on Sunday. They had been accused of conspiracy, perjury and obstruction of justice in a case involving a $200,000 Nixon campaign contribution from fugitive financier Robert Vesco. The details of the suit were intricate, but the jury's decision on the matter could not have been more clearcut: The former attorney general and the former commerce secretary were found not guilty on all counts.

Although not directly linked to the Watergate break-in and cover-up, the Mitchell-Stans case nonetheless fell into the amorphous grouping of charges and countercharges now popularly known as Watergate. The trial itself represented the first prolonged judicial attempt to prosecute and to convict any of the presumed principals in the wide-ranging scandals that have plagued the nation for more than a year. Until this case, only a series of minor Watergate figures had been dealt with at the bar.

Thus Sunday's acquittals suggest several comments about the Mitchell-Stans case in particular, and the Watergate affair in general:

—Despite their self-assurance, the prosecutors in the Mitchell-Stans trial obviously failed to present a satisfactory case in a satisfactory manner. In fact, the chief prosecutor, John Wing, was quoted immediately after the trial as saying, "I guess I wasn't convincing and neither was the evidence."

—It is sickeningly late in the day for a federal prosecutor to discover that neither his performance nor his evidence was "convincing." These trials consume fortunes in both time and money; they undermine the reputations of the accused no matter what the outcome; and w h e n unsuccessful, they raise ominous questions about how an average citizen — someone less wealthy and less well-connected than Mitchell and Stans — could possibly d e f e n d himself adequately against similar federal prosecution.

—Indeed, one must wonder what kind of pressure was brought to bear on such prosecution witnesses as Harry Sears and G. Bradford Cook. Both admitted during the Mitchell-Stans trial that they had committed perjury in the past. How much of their testimony was dictated by the fear that if they did not play the game the prosecution's way, they could easily be standing in the shoes of Mitchell and Stans?

—If Sears and Cook were perhaps draftees, chief prosecution witness John Dean was essentially a volunteer. In his first significant court appearance, Dean continued his by-now famous role as primary accuser of former friends a n d associates. Yet according to the post-trial comments of several jurors, Dean quite simply was not believed.

—If Dean's testimony l a c k e d credibility in the Mitchell-Stans trial, one cannot help but wonder how his testimony will be viewed i n s u b s e q u e n t Watergate and Watergate-related trials. Remember: John Dean is the most significant witness against the President: For Dean to have been found less than believable in a court of law at least raises doubts about the accuracy of his accusations . during all h i s performances before the television cameras.

—If n o t h i n g else, those congressmen and senators heavily inclined toward the impeachment and trial of the President need to review the implications of the Mitchell-Stans trial. The former attorney general and the former commerce secretary can far better withstand a n unsuccessful prosecution than the President and the nation c a n withstand an unsuccessful Senate trial of the President. If a proper case can be made against the President, then it should proceed; but if there are any doubts—any doubts—about the rightness of such a case, then the case must not be permitted to go forward.

Following their a c q u i t t a l s, Mitchell and Stans both stressed their faith in the American judicial system, their belief that the conspiracy case, honestly judged by honest men, could not have turned out any other way. The words may be the words of winners, but considering the year-long ordeal of John Mitchell and Maurice Stans, it is refreshing to see that the two men could react so graciously to their vindication.

THE RICHMOND NEWS LEADER
Richmond, Va., May 14, 1974

Everybody *knew* that Mitchell and Stans were guilty; just knew it — as everybody *knew* that Abbie and Angela and the Catonsville Nine and the Chicago Seven and the Gainsville Whatever and the East Elsewhere Forty-eleven were innocent. They *had* to be, for the myth that has given us The People vs. Amerika has said so, and the myth is always right.

Surprise! John Mitchell, former Attorney General of the United States, and Maurice Stans, former Secretary of Commerce, were found innocent by a jury of New Yorkers. *Innocent?* Mitchell and Stans? Well, jurors sometimes *do* make mistakes.

The New York Times investigated, and this is what they discovered:

> They were nine men and three women who listened to the testimony, considered some of it, admittedly ignored some of it, were admittedly baffled by some of it, and who ultimately relied on their individual backgrounds and experiences to reach a verdict. They were nine men and three women in search of a leader, so awed by their responsibility that one of the men daily battled against going into the courtroom and another spent a day during deliberations vomiting.

This jury — the New York Nine Plus Three — had a certain unity, said *The Times*. Through "sophisticated jury selection" the panel was made to fit a profile that called for "blue collar jurors, primarily Roman Catholic, who earned an average of $8,000 to $10,000 yearly, who read the New York *Daily News*." Marty Herbst, who advised the defense on jury selection, said: "We wanted people who were home oriented, to the Right, more concerned with inflation than Watergate." *The Times* added that Herbst sought jurors who "would associate the dour John Mitchell with John Wayne." Horrors — that was exactly the jury that was chosen.

The exception to the profile was a man named Andrew Choa, a bank vice president, a Hong Kong native, and a man of the world. Originally selected as an alternate, Choa joined the jury when another member became ill. Although a young woman, McGovern-voting Sybil Kucharski ("like ten of the other jurors, Miss Kucharski's education had ended with high school, and this was not a coincidence," said *The Times*) was foreman, Choa soon was leader in fact. And what kind of a man is Choa?

> One acquaintance, who asked to remain anonymous, recalled having served with him on a parents' project at the ...school his children attended, and said that politically Mr. Choa was "to the right of Ivan the Terrible."

So there you have it, a collection of clucks led by a Right-wing nut. No noble populism. No champagne parties. No coaxed quotes, such as "the kids were innocent, the government didn't have a thing on them." No long "I wuz radicalized" statements. Just nine men and three women who did a difficult job under trying circumstances, and did it in the best way they could.

William Buckley has said he would rather be governed by 2,000 persons selected at random from the Boston phone book than by the Harvard faculty. Yes, and it would be far better to be judged by nine men and three women in New York, than by *The New York Times*. The jurors, at least, had not made up their minds *before* the trial.

The Standard-Times
New Bedford, Mass., May 2, 1974

The acquittal of two former Nixon Cabinet members by a jury whose foreman supported George McGovern for president served notice that Watergate critics had best assess some aspects of that situation with more moderation and fairness than has marked much of their comment thus far.

The trial was the first major curtain-opener on alleged Nixon administration coverups and influence peddling. It was an historic event, also, because never before had two Cabinet members been tried together.

The jury, one of unquestioned cross-section membership, found that there had never been a conspiracy involving former Commerce Secretary Maurice Stans and former Attorney General John Mitchell. As for perjury, the jurors apparently decided that any conflict in testimony could be ascribed to the defendants having been "confused" or making "an honest mistake" — mitigations pointed out by the presiding judge — rather than to deliberate lying.

Despite the imposing array of witnesses on the government side and the excellence of the prosecution's handling of the case — an impression the jury shared — we had our doubts that there would be a conviction. Essentially, it is a formidable task to convince the average American that public officials who exert influence in behalf of a cause or a person are necessarily guilty of misuse of power.

"We didn't put them (Mitchell and Stans) above the law," said the 21-year-old foreman, Sybil Kucharaski, referring to the centerpiece of the government's case. "But we felt they were doing things in the course of the normal working day. They weren't sneaking around or anything."

As for the future, it will be interesting to see the consequences of the major setback created by the repudiation of the testimony of John W. Dean 3rd, former White House counselor. Dean has been pictured as far and away the most imposing challenge to President Nixon's claim of having no role in, nor knowledge of a Watergate coverup. The jury found Dean's testimony "incredible" and "unbelievable".

But more, the verdict is a reminder that an indictment is not synonymous with guilt. It is a fair appraisal, we think, to say that pre-trial publicity pictured Stans and Mitchell as ruthless wrong-doers whom a jury would bullseye with dispatch.

Even now, several members of the House Judiciary Committee, which is supposed to be weighing the case for impeachment, are raising funds for impeachment — an offshoot of the frontier justice of hang 'em and then examine the evidence. We have an idea how the Mitchell-Stans jury, or any other, would look upon such misuse of power.

THE KNICKERBOCKER NEWS
··· UNION-STAR ···
Albany, N.Y., May 7, 1974

Former attorney general John N Mitchell and Maurice H. Stans, his co-defendant in a trial for perjury and obstruction of justice, were found innocent by a trial jury . We must believe they are innocent.

It remains proper, however, to observe that they were found innocent on the evidence and that the transcript of the Watergate tapes, released after the conclusion of that trial, reveals that certain evidence that could have been of substantial importance was withheld from the prosecutor. The withholding gives every appearance of having been deliberate.

The crucial portion of the transcript concerns a conversation between John D. Ehrlichman and the President. In that conversation, Mr. Ehrlichman told the President that a quid pro quo (this for that) had been asked by the now fugitive financier Robert Vesco in return for his cash contribution of $200,000 to the Nixon reelection fund. At that time, Mr. Vesco feared the Justice Department was after him for a securities law violation.

After telling the President of the Vesco demand, the transcript shows Mr. Ehrlichman as saying:

" Vesco then got a phone call, allegedly from John Mitchell. Now that's enough to indict."

It must be recalled that before the Mitchell-Stans trial was begun, the U. S. Attorney's Office had asked the White House for copies of every recorded White House conversation in which the Vesco matter had come up. Tapes of four days in which such conversations were held were provided. But the tape of a later date, in which the President and Mr. Ehrlichman discussed the quid pro quo was not supplied.

What effect could this have had on the trial? No one knows. The verdict of innocent might still have been returned. put the opportunity for either the prosecution or the defense to persue the matter was denied them.

Mr. Mitchell and Mr. Stands Stans are innocent. We repeat that quite deliberately.

But the White House stands convicted of deceit in withholding that tape that could have been important and so interfering with the course of justice

It all makes one wonder what other secrets important to the cause of justice the White House is taking such efforts to conceal.

KLEINDIENST PLEADS GUILTY; NIXON FIGHTS SUBPOENAS

President Nixon's release of edited tape transcripts did not cool the controversy surrounding his possible involvement in the Watergate affair.

Events continued to unfold indicating that a full process of impeachment would be needed to resolve the debate over Nixon's guilt or innocence. These were the developments in the case during late May:

■ Press reports emanating from the third closed session of the House Judiciary Committee's impeachment hearings May 15, attributed to a "committee source," said a Sept. 15, 1972 tape heard by the committee contained a threat, not included in the Nixon transcript, by the President to take action against the *Washington Post* and its attorney, Edward Bennett Williams. According to the source, the committee's tape contained a specific reference by Nixon to the *Post's* ownership of a television station and his remarks that, "The main thing is the *Washington Post* is going to have a damnable, damnable thing out of this one" and "I think we're going to fix" Williams. Two groups aligned politically with Nixon later challenged the *Post's* TV licenses in Jacksonville and Miami, Fla.

White House Press Secretary Ronald L. Ziegler criticized the committee later May 15 for the leak. "This is serious business," he said, and the leak of such material was contrary to the committee's stated intent "of a fair and disciplined proceeding." Presidential special counsel James D. St. Clair took the protest against the leak a step further May 16, requesting in a letter to Committee Chairman Peter W. Rodino Jr. (D, N.J.) that all the panel's proceedings be public because the "selective" leaking of information from closed sessions was "prejudicing the basic right of the President to an impartial inquiry on the evidence."

■ Former Attorney General Richard G. Kleindienst pleaded guilty May 16 to a misdemeanor charge that he had refused to testify "accurately and fully" before a Congressional committee investigating the Administration's handling of the controversial International Telephone & Telegraph (ITT) antitrust settlement. The guilty plea was entered in federal district court in Washington. The minor criminal offense related to Kleindienst's testimony in March and April 1972 before the Senate Judiciary Committee, which was considering his nomination to succeed John Mitchell as attorney general.

Kleindienst pleaded guilty to concealing from the committee his communication about ITT with President Nixon and John Mitchell and circumstances surrounding the Justice Department's decision to appeal one of the antitrust cases against ITT to the Supreme Court. In sworn committee testimony, Kleindienst had said, "I was not interfered with by anybody at the White House. I was not importuned. I was not pressured. I was not directed." Later statements issued by Kleindienst and White House documents released recently contradicted this testimony.

■ On May 22 President Nixon informed the House Judiciary Committee that he would not comply with two subpoenas issued May 15 for White House tape recordings and other data to further the committee's impeachment inquiry. Nixon also said that any future subpoenas "allegedly dealing with Watergate" would be rejected. In a letter to Rodino, Nixon reiterated the basic White House argument that production of additional material "would merely prolong the inquiry without yielding significant additional evidence." "More fundamentally," Nixon continued, compliance "with an endless series of demands would fatally weaken this office" in his own Administration and for future presidents. Earlier in the day, St. Clair informed the committee that its requests for additional material on the ITT antitrust controversy and campaign contributions by the dairy industry would not be met.

In a statement issued on behalf of the Judiciary Committee May 22, Rodino said Nixon's response to the subpoenas was "a very grave matter" to which the panel would give "careful consideration" as it determined whether there were grounds for impeachment.

■ The dispute between President Nixon and the and Special Watergate Prosecutor Leon Jaworski charged that the White House had attempted to "undercut" his role as an independent prosecutor. In a situation similar to that which led to the 1973 dismissal of Archibald Cox, the first special prosecutor, the White House said Sirica's order would be appealed.

In a letter to Senate Judiciary Committee Chairman James O. Eastland (D, Miss.), Jaworski said the challenge to the prosecution's right to "take the President to court," was a direct contravention of the conditions under which he had agreed to accept the position of special prosecutor. Meeting in closed session May 21, the committee adopted, 14–1, a resolution stating that Jaworski was "acting within the scope of the authority conferred upon him," and commending him for the "fidelity for the duties imposed upon him."

■ Vice President Gerald Ford acknowledged May 26 he disagreed with President Nixon on the issue of providing relevant information to a House impeachment inquiry. Ford said the difference "was laid out quite candidly" during a meeting with Nixon May 23. The meeting came after Ford had called several times for White House cooperation with the House probe.

CHICAGO DAILY NEWS
Chicago, Ill., May 18, 1974

Of all the bizarre offshoots of Watergate, none is more ironic than this week's conviction of Richard G. Kleindienst on a misdemeanor charge stemming from his testimony in the International Telephone & Telegraph case.

Kleindienst pleaded guilty to the technical charge of refusing to testify before Congress. He thereby became, simultaneously, the first cabinet-level official convicted in the Watergate scandals, the first attorney general ever convicted of misconduct in office, and liable to a $1,000 fine and a prison term of one month to one year.

The irony is that Kleindienst's technical slip came in the midst of a performance that was otherwise gutsy and even, by comparison, rather heroic. Be it remembered that at one point Kleindienst opposed a direct order by President Nixon to drop the appeal from an adverse ruling in the ITT case—and made it stick. Indeed, his co-operation with the prosecution in his own case drew admiring commendation from Special Prosecutor Leon Jaworski.

On the other hand, there is no disputing the fact that the real offense committed by Kleindienst was closer to perjury than to the technical misdemeanor to which he pleaded guilty. For he had told Senate Judiciary Committee members in a memorable statement that in his conduct of the ITT case he "was not interfered with by anybody at the White House" when as a matter of fact he had had the directive from the President, himself. He later explained that he considered the President's communication "privileged and . . . not the focus of the inquiry."

When asked why the perjury charge was not brought, Jaworski more or less danced around the question and said that the misdemeanor charge was "my conception of a fair disposition."

We suspect most Americans will agree, and in fact will be sorry if it turns out that Kleindienst has to go to jail at all for what appears to have been one of the more creditable overall performances in the whole sad Watergate drama.

THE ☁ SUN
Baltimore, Md., May 17, 1974

So now another "first" for the Nixon administration. Richard Kleindienst, the former Attorney General, is the first of the nation's chief law enforcement officers ever to plead guilty to a crime. He admitted he had not told the truth to the Senate Judiciary Committee when he denied there had been White House pressure on him to settle an ITT merger case out of court. Technically he pleaded guilty to a misdemeanor charge of refusing and failing to give proper answers, but to most laymen the difference between that and the more familiar felony-perjury charge—plain old lying under oath—is hard to see. Several senators asked Kleindienst in several different ways about White House pressure. He always said there was none. Yet he later admitted in public and now in court that John Ehrlichman and President Nixon told him to settle the case out of court (on terms Justice Department lawyers thought not in the national interest).

Frankly, it seems to us that Kleindienst has gotten off lightly. After all, consider what happened to Ed Reinecke, lieutenant governor of California. He was called before the Judiciary Committee at the same time Kleindienst was there. He also denied knowledge of certain events in the path toward the ITT settlement. He has now been charged with three felony counts of perjury. Reinecke was there as an outsider of sorts. He had nothing to gain by lying. But Kleindienst was the *subject* of the hearings. His nomination to be promoted from Deputy Attorney General to Attorney General was under consideration. His lies were calculated to bring himself a reward. Even if that reward were not the top law enforcement job in the land, it would be silly to say his false testimony was only a misdemeanor while Reinecke's was felonious. Where's the fairness in that?

Many people will assume the Special Prosecutor made a deal with Kleindienst. Now, presumably, he will testify or otherwise provide evidence against others. What a strange time we live in. A former Attorney General of the United States is treated as a little fish! This development reminds us that the full story of the ITT merger settlement and its relationship if any to a proposed $400,000 contribution to the Republican convention has never been told. It is one of the allegations against the President the House Judiciary Committee is studying, but so far the White House has refused to turn over tapes or conversations concerning it.

WORCESTER TELEGRAM
Worcester, Mass., May 17, 1974

And now to the roll of dishonor add the names of Richard Kleindienst, former attorney general of the United States, and Dwight L. Chapin, former appointments secretary for President Nixon. Kleindienst has pleaded guilty to the charge that he "did refuse and fail to answer accurately" questions on the ITT case during his confirmation hearings before the Senate Judiciary Committee.

He will go to prison unless the sentence is suspended. Chapin has been convicted of lying to the grand jury and has been sentenced to prison for at least 10 months.

They follow others — Hunt, Barker, Dean, McCord, Kalmbach, Liddy, Krogh, Young, Hearing, Magruder, LaRue, Mardian — who have either been convicted or pleaded guilty to various crimes and misdemeanors. And yet to come are others who have been indicted — Mitchell, Stans, Colson, Ehrlichman, Haldeman. Mitchell and Stans have been found innocent in the Vesco case, but face more charges in connection with the Watergate affair and fund raising.

It is almost incredible that the team that won Richard Nixon such a resounding victory less than two years ago should find itself in such an appalling situation. It is disheartening beyond belief that Nixon — at the very least — should have shown such abysmal judgment of men and allowed such criminal activities to take place under his banner.

Whatever happens to Nixon himself at the hands of the House Judiciary Committee and the Congress, and whatever his achievements in foreign and domestic policy, it cannot be denied that this has been a dismal spectacle. The vice president of the United States forced to resign his office and accept a charge of income tax evasion. A former attorney general pleading guilty to a misdemeanor charge and being sentenced to jail like a common felon. Former high officials of the White House and the re-election committee in an unseemly charade of plea-bargaining, indictments, convictions and rationalizations.

It is just too much.

Washington Star-News

Washington, D.C.. May 22, 1974

It appears that the White House is trying to welsh on its promise that Special Watergate Prosecutor Leon Jaworski would have freedom of action, including access to the courts, to pursue the Watergate case wherever it led. That is the only reasonable interpretation that can be put on the argument by President Nixon's lawyer, James St. Clair, that Jaworski can sue the President only when the President says it's okay.

Jaworski, in a memorandum of complaint to the Senate Judiciary Committee, had every right to claim that such a limitation would make a "farce of the special prosecutor's charter." We agree with the observation by one Senate source that it's hard to understand what kind of a game they're playing at the White House "but it's a dumb one."

Nevertheless, there is no reason for the Judiciary Committee to rush into legislative action. There is no justification now, and probably never will be, for completely divorcing the special prosecutor's office from the executive branch and setting it up as an arm of either the Congress or the judiciary.

In the first place, the White House is not going to get away with any such attempt to limit Jaworski, for Judge Sirica has ruled already that it would be illegal. So the issue of whether Mr. Nixon has to turn over the additional tapes subpoenaed by Jaworski in a court action will have to be fought out on grounds other than the spurious claim by the White House that Jaworski had no right to sue the President.

Secondly, there is little foundation for the fear that the President is going to pull another "Saturday night massacre" and fire Jaworski, as he did former Special Prosecutor Archibald Cox. That would bring the wrath of Congress and the nation down around his head again and probably would assure his impeachment. The White House may be dumb but it can't be that dumb.

DAYTON DAILY NEWS

Dayton, Ohio, May 22, 1974

President Nixon really has "fired" his latest special prosecutor, Leon Jaworski. He merely hasn't removed Mr. Jaworski from office.

That is the substance of the special prosecutor's complaint to the Senate Judiciary committee. The President, Mr. Jaworski said, is making a farce of the Watergate investigation by refusing to yield evidence.

That is obviously so, but it is the

Jaworski

President's apparent calculation that, while he probably would be impeached and convicted if he were to come up with the subpoenaed evidence, he is marginally less likely to be removed from office for authorizing a farce. Thus Mr. Nixon's defense, as he keeps putting it, "of the presidency." He can't absolutely be proved guilty of overt crimes without evidence and so he won't relinquish the evidence and so the presidency will be protected as an institution.

It is, of course, a wholly self-serving argument and in fact a horrible abuse of the presidency, and it is additionally a break of faith with the American people. It was to the Senate Judiciary committee, as a representative of the public, that the President promised that Mr. Jaworski, hired to replace fired Special Prosecutor Archibald Cox, would be fully independent and could have any evidence necessary to his investigation.

Now Mr. Nixon says that he, as President, will decide what evidence is germane. That is a privilege every suspect would like, and if it were extended to the population in general, the current pressure on the nation's jails would be ended. Few convictions would occur if suspects could dictate to police, prosecutors and judges what evidence the suspects would permit to be used against them.

Mr. Jaworski has been elaborately patient with Mr. Nixon. He first complained privately to the White House, early this year, of Mr. Nixon's balkiness with evidence. He then permitted only oblique public references to the difficulty he was having in getting evidence. Now he has cycled back through the courts for enforcement of a subpoena, arguing anew the points of law that a federal district court and a federal appellate court settled in the special prosecutor's favor last year.

It is obvious that Mr. Nixon has determined on delaying and obstructionist tactics. In doing so, he is violating his pledge to Mr. Jaworski just as surely as he violated his pledge to Mr. Cox by firing him for seeking evidence. The only difference is of appearances. Mr. Jaworski has not been formally canned, but he has been forbidden from doing his job. The result is the same.

The special prosecutor knows that, and so does the Senate Judiciary committee, but Mr. Nixon knows that there is nothing either Mr. Jaworski or the senators can do about it. Mr. Nixon is guessing that the public will think that the President and the special prosecutor are only arguing about a legal point, rather than catching on that Mr. Nixon, in effect, has fired Mr. Jaworski without bothering to actually remove him from office.

Herald News

Fall River, Mass.
May 22, 1974

Special Watergate prosecutor Leon Jaworski's angry comment that the President is "making a farce" out of his assignment may be the prelude to his exit from the case. Former Attorney General Elliot Richardson remarked that Jaworski's statement sounded as if he were in the same position as his predecessor, Archibald Cox, whose dismissal prompted Richardson's resignation from the cabinet.

Certainly Cox too found his access to evidence he sought blocked by the White House. Now Jaworski, whose probity and ability no one has seriously questioned, is also unable to procure tapes and documents he claims he needs to investigate the Watergate affair thoroughly. The President is apparently deciding for himself what it is desirable for the prosecutor to have. The decision would obviously be out of his hands if he held any other office. He claims the right of executive privilege means that he does not need to hand the documents over either to the prosecutor or to the House Judiciary Committee.

This must be decided finally by the courts, perhaps, if the President stands fast, by the Supreme Court. The issue is really the same where Jaworski and the House Judiciary Committee are concerned, and should Jaworski follow Cox's example and withdraw, it might be as well for the President to end the farce and admit he does not intend a special prosecutor to decide for himself what documents he needs. Let the office of special prosecutor lapse, and let the House Judiciary Committee turn the matter over to the courts to decide.

But it would be nonsense henceforward for the President to claim that he will give any person or agency investigating Watergate full and free access to all the relevant material in his possession.

The Washington Post

Washington, D.C., May 23, 1974

THE PRESIDENT has an odd way of celebrating Watergate anniversaries. Yesterday marked the passage of one full year since Mr. Nixon issued his compendious statement of May 22, 1973, promising to make available all revelant information on the complex of scandals that go by the name of Watergate. He chose to commemorate the occasion by informing the House Judiciary Committee, which is conducting impeachment hearings and which has—if anything—a larger and stronger claim on relevant evidence than the other bodies of inquiry do, that he would decline to produce any further Watergate tapes requested or subpoenaed by it. The full story of Watergate and of his own involvment in it, Mr. Nixon advised the committee, reposes in the White House materials already in the committee's hands.

In more ways than one, that is an interesting assertion. It not only confirms that the President is prepared to defy the committee's requests for material it deems necessary to conducting its inquiry. It also confirms that there is no better documentary case for Mr. Nixon to make concerning his own role in the coverup than that which can be made (if it can) from the highly incriminating documents and tapes now in the committee's possession. May 22, 1974, was a bleak day for those who still held out hope that somewhere, somehow, the President could come forward with persuasive exculpatory evidence. Apparently there is none.

Although we believe that Mr. Nixon's outright defiance of Congress in this matter is as unconstitutional as it is unwise, it does occur to us that he has a point in his assertion that more than enough is now known for the committee to act—never mind that it isn't the point he was seeking to make. For the plain fact is that both the magnitude of the shocks and revelations of the past year and the complicated legal disputes the President has promoted and prolonged with Congress and the courts have combined to distract people from what they already know. They have given the whole sorry affair the aspect of a continuing, if not interminable, Grade B thriller, as distinct from the aspect of a body of confirmed information which is, in itself, more than sufficient to require a public response. The question, in other words, is not so much "what is going to happen next?" or "what will we learn about tomorrow?" but, rather, "what do we already know?"

Think about it: we know plenty.

We know that the President's best defense throughout —and it is a terrible defense—is that he so mismanaged the conduct of his office that he was unaware that his aides were authorizing common burglaries, were forging State Department cables, were perjuring themselves before federal prosecutors and grand juries, were paying blackmail money to criminals to buy silence about the White House's own involvement in their crimes, were systematically seeking to politicize and pervert the allegedly apolitical agencies of government (the CIA, the IRS, the FBI, among others) for the sake of wreaking personal vengeance on institutions and individuals they considered enemies.

We know that the President on the eve of the sentencing of the originally convicted Watergate conspirators, learned that their trial had been skewed by perjured testimony and failed to so inform the judge.

We know that the President has repeatedly and systematically misled the American public in his statements "from the heart" on this matter, telling them things he knew to be untrue.

We know that six of his former aides have been sentenced to terms in federal penitentiaries.

We know that his appointees have conspired to destroy evidence in criminal cases.

We know that the man he twice selected to be his (and our) Vice President has been convicted of a felony, forced to resign office and disbarred from the practice of law.

We know that the President—a great scourge of "welfare cheating"—was found to be almost half a million dollars light on his federal income tax.

We know that indictments are now outstanding and trials awaited for his closest White House associates and one-time most powerful deputies for a series of alleged criminal acts. We know that he has, while claiming all the protections and safeguards accorded an ordinary citizen in trouble with the law, simultaneously and shamelessly utilized the great and unique powers of the presidency not only to argue his own case (falsely) but to protect himself from scrutiny by the Congress or the courts. He declines to honor subpoenas. He fires the Special Prosecutor he has promised to give full rein when that Prosecutor appears to be getting warm. And now he tells us, in the course of telling the House Judiciary Committee, that he is only doing these recalcitrant things to protect "future" presidents. We think the evidence is overwhelming that he is, on the contrary, trying only to protect this one.

Presumably the members of the House Judiciary Committee and those legislators outside the committee who have authorized its inquiry will seek some further action on the materials Mr. Nixon has now declined to furnish. And presumably, too, his defiance of the committee will be added to the list of Constitution-bending offenses for which he, as President, is responsible. But we would hope that the committee would not permit itself to be drawn into a prolonged and diverting dispute over the production of this evidence to the exclusion of its responsibility to continue and conclude its inquiry as quickly and carefully as possible. The American people know plenty—and the members of the Judiciary Committee know even more. A variety of charges against Mr. Agnew were never fully adjudicated because he preferred that they not be, and the same may be true of certain of the charges against Mr. Nixon because he too has now indicated that he will not risk orderly and complete adjudication in a single body that is empowered to consider his case—namely, the United States Congress. Mr. Agnew copped a plea. Mr. Nixon is merely refusing, in the name of his office—or what remains of it—to let the full information come to light.

People have been, in our view, exceptionally patient so far, and that is especially true of the legislators themselves. And they have also been exceptionally judicious and restrained. But it seems to us that by this latest act of evasion and contempt, the President has released everyone from the injunction against drawing inferences from his refusal to produce subpoenaed evidence. And if he will not cooperate—so be it: the House will have to proceed without him on the basis of what it now knows.

The Burlington Free Press

Burlington, Vt., May 23, 1974

WE VIGOROUSLY applaud President Nixon's rejection yesterday of a House Judiciary Committee subpoena for more taped Presidential conversations. The President said his decision also applies to "such further subpoenas as may hereafter be issued," and no more material would be turned over to Special Prosecutor Leon Jaworski.

It has been abundantly clear for a long time that the Judiciary Committee has more material than it can handle, and that it has set out on a vicious, partisan course which makes an utter mockery of its presumed mission.

We always have felt the President made a fundamental mistake in not forcing the issue up to the Supreme Court, if necessary, months ago. Bits and pieces of information contribute only to grotesque distortions, and the programmed "leaks" to favored "newsmen" are an abominable injustice and an unconscionable affront to Constitutional safeguards.

So apparently the "great confrontation" finally has come. We only regret its lateness in coming. — F.B. Smith

THE WALL STREET JOURNAL.

New York, N.Y., May 21, 1974

With the impeachment hearings about to go public, we look in vain for a way out of the current national dilemma. In fact, we are left with the gloomy thought that perhaps the best remaining outcome would be if the Rodino staff comes up with an irrefutable case. That would be tough on Mr. Nixon, but at least the nation could in good conscience unite on an obvious course of action.

Admittedly we come to this gloomy conclusion after wrestling with the personal dilemma of what to say at this stage of the proceedings. We are in no mood to defend Richard Nixon as the man who ought to be President of the United States. But neither do we see any good grounds on which to recommend his impeachment. We suspect that we share this dilemma with a good many citizens, including no few of the lawmakers who will eventually decide the President's future.

The conversations in those Oval Office transcripts reveal a pettiness and narrowness about the President and his closest associates. In an odd way it is a testimony to the system; Madison always told us it was designed to work not because of noble men but despite base men. And in a programmatic sense, Mr. Nixon's presidency has been something of a success despite the approach the tapes reveal.

Still, there is such a thing as moral leadership, Teddy Roosevelt's "bully pulpit." This is what Mr. Nixon has sacrificed for once and all. His problem is not simply having allowed a peek into the private recesses of the White House. If the same tapes had been released a year ago, the nation could have concluded that the President came within an ace of really blowing one, but in the end he did the right thing. Instead, the tapes have been released after a year of Watergate speeches that were perhaps accurate in detail but were smotheringly sanctimonious in tone. It is the contrast between the public and the private, between the seamy conversations and the sanctimonious postures, that have robbed Mr. Nixon of both his moral leadership and his remaining defenders.

There are of course political systems where the loss of moral leadership provides ample grounds for removing a chief executive. Our Founding Fathers insisted instead on "high crimes or misdemeanors," and while the meaning of that phrase can be debated surely it means some offense that is both specific and serious. What's more, the Founding Fathers made impeachment deliberately difficult, fearing that otherwise it might become the instrument of passing passions. So far history seems to have vindicated this fear; the one presidential impeachment has generally been regarded an abuse, and some of the few judicial ones were as well.

Perhaps the Founding Fathers were simply old-fashioned in their fear of passing passions, in their willingness to restrict the democratic principle by forcing it through rigid institutions. Perhaps we should forget such institutions as fixed terms, and simply govern ourselves by submitting all important questions to the Gallup Poll. But the system under which we live has been functioning now for nearly two centuries, longer than any other political system in the world today. Perhaps the Founding Fathers were wise to design institutions that enhanced a stable government.

As we look out over the world today, indeed, it seems to us that stability is a larger problem than ever. In Germany Chancellor Brandt was forced to resign. For the first time in many years Great Britain is ruled by a minority government. France has a new leader with a narrower support than ever. In Canada, all of Prime Minister Trudeau's glamour could not save his government. Israel, Iceland and others have unprecedented leadership crises. And of course, in the United States we are apparently witnessing the destruction of the third President in succession.

It seems that the modern environment is an acid that attacks democratic leaders. The pace of life is so fast, societies are so complex, interdependencies are so wide-ranging, communication is so fast, that any problem or dislocation is likely to divide and inflame the public. In such a hectic and impatient age, political leaders cannot build enduring support; they are bound to fall victim to one passing crisis or another.

It would be a mistake to underestimate this air of perpetual crisis. For the inability of democratic governments to govern creates the greatest danger of authoritarianism in the world today. Already the economic success of the Brazilian junta has attracted notice in the many parts of the world where democracy is not taken as self-evidently the form of government most appropriate to human nature. Or as Alexander Solzhenitsyn warned in his famous Nobel lecture, "As seen from the outside, the amplitude of the tossing of Western society is approaching the point beyond which the system becomes unstable and must fall."

The opposite and more fashionable specter of authoritarianism, we know, is the most frequently used argument for impeachment on expansive grounds. This vision sees a rapacious presidency spreading across the political landscape, finally going beyond legitimate instruments of power and into illegitimate ones. Thus the danger of totalitarianism lies in a proliferation of Gordon Liddys, the argument goes, and even if there are no further grounds we must impeach Richard Nixon to bring the presidency back in line.

It is of course entirely healthy to have an uproar about wiretapping, shady money-raising and the rest. It's quite true that Congress, mostly through its own lack of responsibility, has lost ground to the presidency. Yet a daring leap is made from these truths to impeachment, commonly by men who have devoted their lives to building and celebrating a powerful presidency. In those terms, the argument could scarcely be more profoundly wrong.

It is simply not true, first of all, that the American presidency is exceptionally powerful in comparison with the executives of other democratic governments. The President does of course enjoy the pomp of a head of state, and the protection of a fixed term. It's true that once a Watergate exploded, the heads of most democratic systems would have promptly fallen from office. But would it not have exploded? In few other systems is a Sam Ervin or Archibald Cox even conceivable. Most executives have far greater control, including day-to-day dominance over their legislative branches. The President of the United States cannot get the school milk program out of the federal budget and we hear talk of the need to curb his overweening power.

More specifically about Watergate, in reading those Oval Office conversations we have anything but the impression of men who dominated the political landscape. Surely they did not talk as if they controlled Congress, or the judiciary, or the press, or even the Justice Department or FBI or CIA. Rather, the total impression was of insecure and frightened men, besieged by hostile forces, trying to manage the situation by ekeing out marginal advantages.

When we look to the origin of the Watergate crimes, similarly, we see something nearly opposite to an insatiable greed for presidential power. We see an erosion of the normal social controls that allow governments to function, the erosion of the kind of unenforced authority that would keep government officials from massively leaking official papers, or would keep generally virtuous citizens from thronging the streets trying to take control of foreign policy from duly elected leaders. The origins of the "plumbers," and of much of the White House mentality, lie in an ever more desperate attempt to compensate for this erosion, finally and of course all too easily slipping over the border of the illegitimate. And with that blunder, the Nixon administration gave fatal ammunition to those who had long since tried to discredit it, some of whom even long before Watergate talked of impeaching the President.

Thus the Watergate crisis very much blends in our minds with the general crisis of Western governments, and it is this that creates the impeachment dilemma. On the one hand, impeachment would be a victory, and a most disturbing precedent, for those who thronged the streets seeking to overturn an election, and even worse for the acid spirit that corrodes the stability of the democracies. On the other hand, the President has clearly forfeited his moral leadership, and may have committed more specific offenses against nothing less than the administration of justice.

The only refuge we can find is that of due process, that eternal friend of justice and eternal foe of undue passion. It is entirely conceivable that we may have at hand one of those genuinely exceptional cases when the long-slumbering weapon of impeachment should be invoked. But given the spirit of the age, it seems to us that such a conclusion should be resisted until the whole process has run, until the charge has been framed, the evidence presented, the defense heard, and a constitutional debate held on the meaning of the phrase "high crimes and misdemeanors."

Above all, the process should be free of the taint of changing rules in the middle of the game, of impeaching Mr. Nixon on grounds that would not have been applied to his recent predecessors. For if the rules can be changed for Mr. Nixon they can be changed again when his successors meet their own corrosive crises. Larger things hang in the balance, and whether the President goes or stays is less important than insuring that if he is ultimately impeached and convicted the nation understands precisely why.

The Des Moines Register
Des Moines, Iowa
May 29, 1974

Federal Judge Gerhard Gesell bluntly and unequivocally has served notice that he intends to dismiss charges against John Ehrlichman, Charles Colson and three others indicted for the Ellsberg break-in unless the President produces documents requested by the defense. Judge Gesell declared:

"It seems to me he [the President] is heading this case in the direction of dismissal. . . . The President must know he is acting deliberately . . . [in] aborting this trial."

This is not a case where the prosecution is seeking to implicate the President or his former aides. The defendants want evidence they claim can exculpate them. Nevertheless, the President has been throwing up a smokescreen of executive privilege and national security to prevent access to the requested documents.

Judge Gesell has taken a no-nonsense stand on these secrecy claims. "We are going to proceed with what is relevant in this trial," he said the other day. "There's going to be no executive privilege or national security privilege." The judge ruled that national security cannot be invoked to justify the break-in.

Judge Gesell told the President's attorney the issue is "the President's duty to enforce the criminal laws of this country where his former confederates are under indictment."

But instead of being on the side of the special prosecutor, the President seems to be doing everything he can to aid the defense. The President could perform no greater service for Ehrlichman and Colson than to refuse to give them access to documents and thereby force the court to dismiss charges.

The President's power to frustrate the prosecution extends to every case the special prosecutor brings. H. R. Haldeman, John Mitchell, John Ehrlichman and the four others charged in connection with the Watergate cover-up could have the charges against them dismissed if President Nixon stands fast and refuses to allow access to evidence.

It may be necessary to remove the President from office if only to prevent him from obstructing justice.

The immediate danger of such an obstruction is in connection with the scheduled June 17 trial of Colson. Ehrlichman and three others for the break-in at the office of Daniel Ellsberg's psychiatrist. It seems clear that Judge Gesell is determined to dismiss this case unless the President backs down. If the judge is correct that the President "is acting deliberately . . . [in] aborting this trial," that is an intolerable situation.

The special prosecutor should seek postponement of the trial and take whatever other steps are necessary to prevent such a miscarriage of justice. A postponement could give Congress time to act on impeachment. Ouster of the President would be one way to keep him from suppressing evidence.

President Nixon declared in an address to the American people Apr. 30, 1973:

"I pledge to you tonight from this office that I will do everything in my power to insure that the guilty are brought to justice."

The President is making a mockery of his pledge.

THE KNICKERBOCKER NEWS
••• UNION-STAR •••
Albany, N.Y., May 29, 1974

With his presidency in a shambles, President Nixon apparently has embarked on a strategy to save himself, regardless of the cost to the nation. That strategy now is obvious beyond question.

The key to the Nixon strategy is delay. In a last figurative throw of the dice, the President is attempting to snarl and delay the impeachment inquiry and inevitably to kill it off.

His device is refusal to supply any more information—tape recordings, transcripts, documents or anything else—either to the House Judiciary Committee, which is conducting the impeachment probe, or to Special Watergate Prosecutor Leon Jaworski, who needs the material for his first major Watergate trial.

In pursuing his desperate strategy, Mr Nixon—who has described his regime as a "law and order administration"—has flouted the law (ignoring several subpoenas), defied the courts (refusing to turn over evidence) and reneged on his solemn promise to Congress and the people (that he would not impede the work of Mr. Jaworski).

WHILE THESE arrogant actions may increase the prospect for impeachment, there also is the chance they could have the opposite effect, if Mr. Nixon succeeds in wearing down Congress and getting the people so sick of the whole mess that they'd prefer that it be forgotten and dropped.

As Mr. Nixon and his special Watergate counsel, James St. Clair, know, every time the White House refuses a new request from either the House Judiciary Committee or Special Prosecutor Jaworski, the issue goes to the courts. This means more delay as each side awaits the court's decision and even more delay if the decision is appealed.

We already are close to June. House Judiciary Committee chairman Peter Rodino already is far behind his original timetable calling for a committee decision on impeachment by late July. On that schedule, a vote by the full House had been expected by Aug. 1, if the committee recommended impeachment. If the House voted to impeach, the President would be given 30 days to prepare his defense before trial by the Senate. This would mean the trial would start no earlier than Sept 1.

THE PRESIDENT'S evasive and delaying tactics already have disrupted that timetable. Thus, even if the House voted impeachment by, say, Sept 15 and the trial in the Senate began around Oct. 15,

the election of a new Congress would intervene and a new trial would have to begin in 1975, since there would be a new Senate then.

It doesn't take a mind-reader's ability to conclude that Mr Nixon hopes that by that time, the American people and the Congress will be so weary of the Watergate scandal that they will lose interest in impeachment —and Mr. Nixon will have won with his stalling tactics.

This would be a far graver national tragedy than any possible outcome of the present Watergate investigations and impeachment, for not only would one of our most important constitutional processes have been subverted by the potential defendant himself, but crucial questions about his transgressions would go unresolved.

For instance, by withholding evidence considered essential to the impeachment inquiry and to the trial of seven Watergate defendants, including two of his principal former aides, John Ehrlichman and Charles Colson, the President would be committing a crime: obstructing justice. Morever, he has in effect taken the 5th Amendment, leaving the implication he is refusing to turn over any more evidence because that evidence might incriminate him. This is a valid legal interpretation.

FINALLY, HE HAS been warned by Federal District Judge Gerhard Gesell, who is trying the case of the break-in at the office of Daniel Ellsberg's psychiatrist, that unless he provides the records considered vital by both the prosecution and defense, the judge might have to dismiss the case.

Consider this for a few seconds. If the President stands firm and Judge Gesell dismisses the case, the result, as far as Mr. Nixon's friends, defendants Ehrlichman and Colson, are concerned would be better than had the President granted them clemency, for they would have avoided even a trial.

So by simply "stonewalling it", as he put it so bluntly in his tape-recorded conversations, the President can obstruct justice and grant a better-than-clemency clearance to his pals (squelching any need for them ever to have to testify against him) without any of the major Watergate questions being resolved

That is, if he is allowed to get away with it. The question, which should answer itself, is whether the United States of Washington, Jefferson and Lincoln can afford to allow Richard Nixon to get away with it

JURY NAMED NIXON 'UNINDICTED CO-CONSPIRATOR'

The White House acknowledged June 6 that a Watergate grand jury had voted in February to name President Nixon as an unindicted co-conspirator with his former aides, who were indicted **for the cover-up of the Watergate break-in. The grand jury's vote, reported to be unanimous, had been kept secret under an order by U.S. District Court Judge John J. Sirica.**

Reacting to the public disclosure, special presidential counsel James D. St. Clair said, "It won't be the first time a grand jury was wrong. Grand jury allegations are far from proof and have no legal effect." (An unindicted co-conspirator could not be prosecuted under the indictment in which he was named, but would not be immune from future indictments involving the same alleged offenses.)

According to news reports, the grand jury had at first been inclined to indict Nixon, but had been dissuaded by special Watergate prosecutor Leon Jaworski's contention that such action could not be taken against a President in office.

Attorneys for President Nixon disclosed June 11 that they had petitioned the Supreme Court to decide whether a grand jury had the right "to charge an incumbent President as an unindicted co-conspirator in a criminal proceeding."

Among other Watergate-related developments in late May and early June:

■ The House Judiciary Committee formally notified President Nixon May 30 that his refusal to comply with its subpoenas "might constitute a ground for impeachment" that the committee could take before the House. The committee also approved May 30 issuance of another subpoena (its fourth) for 45 White House tapes and documents and voted to continue its impeachment hearings on evidence in closed sessions.

■ St. Clair said May 30 that President Nixon intended to retain control of evidence purported to be relevant to the defense of two former aides in the so-called Ellsberg break-in trial, even if it resulted in dismissal of the case. The statement was made in a letter to the U.S. District Court Judge Gerhard A. Gesell, who had warned St. Clair May 24 that by withholding documents sought by former aides John D. Ehrlichman and Charles W. Colson, Nixon "must know he is acting deliberately...[in] aborting this trial."

In a May 30 letter to Gesell St. Clair said the President was "not desirous of having...any indictments of former government officials dismissed without a full and fair trial, but he must implement the constitutional responsibilities of his office by not jeopardizing the national security, even if it means...that these cases must ultimately be dismissed."

Gesell ordered Ehrlichman's trial delayed indefinitely June 11, because of what he called Nixon's "resistance to lawful trial subpoenas."

■ In its findings from an investigation of links between an Administration price decision and dairy industry campaign contributions, the staff of the Senate Watergate committee concluded that campaign pledges made by major dairy cooperatives (totaling $2 million) "apparently [were] directly linked to a favorable milk price support decision by the President worth hundreds of millions of dollars to the industry—and costing the same amount to the government and consumers." The staff's draft report, published May 31, also challenged claims by Nixon in a White Paper issued Jan. 8 to justify the 1971 decision increasing federal milk price supports.

In a related development, the Associated Press (AP) reported June 4 that the nation's three largest dairy cooperatives made political contributions ranging from $100 to $11,000 to a minimum of 16 members of the House Judiciary Committee.

■ The Supreme Court May 31 granted Jaworski's plea for prompt consideration of President Nixon's claim of executive privilege over tapes of 64 White House conversations, which Jaworski had said were essential to the trial of seven former Nixon aides accused in the Watergate cover-up.

■ Charles W. Colson, former special counsel to President Nixon, pleaded guilty in Washington federal court June 3 to a felony charge that he "unlawfully ... did ... endeavor to influence, obstruct and impede" the trial of Pentagon Papers defendant Daniel Ellsberg. In return for the plea, the Watergate special prosecutor's office agreed to drop all other charges pending against Colson. As part of his understanding with the prosecutor's office, Colson consented to give it sworn testimony and provide relevant documents in his possession, and in other Watergate-related cases, which observers took to mean the impeachment inquiry against the President.

■ Former Attorney General Richard Kleindienst, who had pleaded guilty to a misdemeanor charge of failing to testify "accurately" before a Senate hearing, received a suspended sentence for his criminal offense June 7. Chief U.S. District Court Judge George L. Hart Jr. imposed the minimum sentence under law—a $100 fine and one month jail term—and suspended both penalties. penalties.

■ President Nixon informed the House Judiciary Committee by letter June 10 that he would refuse to comply with further subpoenas for Watergate evidence. Nixon cited the necessity to protect the presidency from unlimited search and seizure by the legislative branch. He rejected the committee's view that "it should be the sole judge of presidential responsibility." Executive privilege, he contended, was part of the basic doctrine of separation of powers and each branch historically had been "steadfast" in upholding its own independence. The President asserted that his doctrine took precedence even over an impeachment inquiry

The Courier-Journal
Louisville, Ky., June 12, 1974

IT GETS TIRESOME, hearing President Nixon vow to save the presidency by defying congressional subpoenas and court orders for information deemed essential in determining his guilt or innocence of criminal charges But the strength of our system of government, being founded on laws and not men, is that it can surmount this self-serving nonsense and emerge better for having been tested.

In his latest letter to Chairman Rodino of the House Judiciary Committee, Mr. Nixon sounds themes that have become all too familiar. He has given the committee "extensive and unprecedented cooperation." But somebody has to "draw a line" lest the governmental separation of powers get badly out of balance because one branch "attempts to press too hard" on another.

Stretching a doctrine

The Supreme Court should be able to dispense with much of this foolishness when it rules—probably next month—on President Nixon's refusal to supply special prosecutor Jaworski with 64 tapes he says he needs as evidence in the September Watergate cover-up trial. If a President can defy subpoenas and withhold evidence in criminal cases by simply invoking a doctrine—executive privilege—that has justification only as a way to protect confidentiality in discussions of the nation's legitimate business, we might as well fold up shop now.

Moreover, though it has no direct bearing on the case at hand, it's intriguing to hear Mr. Nixon pleading for the integrity of the three branches of government. After his defiance of Congress by impounding funds, and his efforts to load the Supreme Court with pliant mediocrities, this would be merely ironic if it weren't so serious.

As surely everybody can agree, Mr. Nixon is innocent until proven guilty. The same goes for his former aides who still face trial, and for Secretary Kissinger, who rightly resents congressional leaks—based this time on FBI reports read last week to the House Judiciary Committee—that he allegedly initiated wiretap surveillance of subordinates. But the public is entitled to resentment, too, that every detail of those 1969-1971 wiretaps—like everything else that has come to light in the two years since the Watergate burglary—has had to be ferreted out from behind the administration's protective curtain of secrecy.

Innocent until proven guilty, yes. But questions of guilt and innocence can only be decided fairly when all the known evidence that is relevant is made available to those who sit in judgment. This does not mean partial evidence, or edited transcripts, or whatever else Mr. Nixon thinks it's proper or safe to submit. The *accused* man is neither guilty nor innocent in the eyes of the law. But neither, under our system of government, can he be the one to decide which questions can be asked, which evidence he must turn over, which court orders he will obey.

Choosing laws to obey

"Get off his back," cry many of those who admire President Nixon and find little that is disturbing in the series of revelations that have made Watergate a synonym for massive efforts to twist government to political ends. But we didn't elect a king with divine right. We elected an ordinary mortal, and it is the strength of our society and our form of government that no individual has authority to select which laws to abide by and which not.

It's true, as the President says, that somebody has to draw a line. But if Congress and the courts were to knuckle under and let him draw it, despite constitutional provisions for an impeachment process and for the supremacy of the courts in deciding legal questions, they would effectively destroy what Mr. Nixon says he is trying so hard to protect. The only place that line can be drawn is the far side of the truth, and Mr. Nixon's continuing refusal to oblige can only further erode the confidence of that dwindling number of citizens who still think he has nothing to hide.

The Detroit News
Detroit, Mich., June 13, 1974

Considering the House Judiciary Committee's complaints about the difficulty of obtaining information from the White House and getting at the truth about Watergate, you'd think the committee would be delighted when the White House does respond.

That naive supposition ignores the politics of the matter and assumes that the committee actually wants to get Watergate settled rather than drag it out.

After complaining bitterly about the lack of cooperation from the President, after going to court in an effort to obtain tapes and documents, after warning that the President may be opening himself to charges of obstruction of justice—the committee has now rejected a White House effort to give the President's side of the story about the Watergate cover-up.

Mr. Nixon's chief defense lawyer, James D. St. Clair, this week tried to hand the committee the President's response to allegations that he had a hand in that cover-up. Chairman Peter W. Rodino Jr., D-N.J., instructed the committee's chief counsel not to accept the brief because "at this time it is premature."

Premature! The way we get it, explanations are long overdue. If he's genuinely interested in getting at the bottom of Watergate as quickly as possible, Rodino should have grabbed that brief and put it into the record at once, hoping that it would help the committee clarify what happened.

Rodino's rejection of the President's overture will suggest to some that the chairman is less interested in defenses than in allegations, more interested in making political hay than in ending the agony of Watergate. Certainly the rejection makes the next request for a White House response sound less persuasive and less urgent.

THE DAILY OKLAHOMAN
Oklahoma City, Okla., June 11, 1974

HAVING MADE the decision that no further evidence would be released from confidential office records of the White House, President Nixon now seems determined to stick to the decision. His supporters, and many who are not particularly friendly to Nixon but have a concern for the preservation of the office he now holds, have faulted him in the past for announcing some stand-pat position and then abandoning it at the last minute.

The latest demands for more information come close to being the straws that will break the back of the public tolerance camel. The justification for the demands is that the courts and the committees seeking desperately for evidence of crimes committed by the President or with his knowledge have not been able to find such evidence in the thousands of pages of testimony, memoranda, transcripts of conversations, correspondence and other material already provided by the White House and dozens of witnesses.

After two years and thousands upon thousands of man-hours of investigation and analysis, none of those involved in the drawn-out investigation has found evidence that would permit the filing of a charge of wrongdoing against the chief executive. He is convicted, through the convictions and confessions of his aides and associates, of running a sloppy personnel selection system during his first term in office. He is clearly guilty of paying more attention to the duties of his high office than to the political operations of those intent on his re-election. But those are not crimes—they are faults to which all Presidents have been subject.

The whole furor has begun to crystalize into a plainly ideological struggle, complicated by overtones of rivalry among the three branches of our federal government. The battle for supremacy among the executive, the Congress, and the courts is as old as the Republic. In every administration, including those of Washington, Jackson, Lincoln and the two Roosevelts, there have been showdowns of varying degree. The President is required to guard the powers of his office against court orders. The courts have, on many occasions, imposed their authority to invalidate laws that were dear to the hearts of the President and the Congress. Congress has had to fight off encroachments from both the White House and the courts.

But the republic has survived because in each case of a real test of strength, all branches sought refuge in restraint. The President now apparently senses that the day is nearing when the Congress will, while not actually backing down, probably back away from an attempt to oust him from office and revoke the decision of the voters in the 1972 elections. That would be potentially more dangerous to Congress than to the presidency.

The real crisis may come between Nixon and the courts. There are limits the courts should not exceed in issuing orders and demands on the other branches of government.

Meanwhile, Nixon should not be misrepresented as trying to put himself above the law in his decision to stand pat.

The Des Moines Register

Des Moines, Iowa, June 8, 1974

The grand jury that indicted John Mitchell, H. R. Haldeman, John Ehrlichman and four others on Watergate cover-up charges referred to unnamed others in the conspiracy as "persons to the grand jury known and unknown." It now has been revealed that among the persons believed by the grand jury to have been a party to the cover-up was Richard Nixon.

The President's attorney has admitted that the grand jury voted to name President Nixon an unindicted co-conspirator. The vote is reported to have been 19-0. The grand jury withdrew the action, apparently after being advised that responsibility for accusing a president rests with Congress. The grand jury reportedly was dissuaded from indicting the President for the same reason.

No grand jury would lightly consider indicting a president or naming him a co-conspirator. The grand jury's reaction means it must have been persuaded from the evidence it heard that the President was closely linked to the cover-er-up conspiracy. Grand juries indict when they have "probable cause" to believe a suspect committed an offense.

The grand jury's reaction to the evidence makes it imperative that Congress have the opportunity to act on the President's impeachment. The House's function on impeachment is comparable to the grand jury's. The House must screen the evidence to find whether there is sufficient reason to send the matter to the Senate for trial. Conviction by two-thirds vote of the Senate would oust the President from office.

The risk now is that the procedure will become so bogged down there will not be a clear-cut resolution of the case. The large number of allegations is causing the House Judiciary Committee to take months to wade through the evidence. Non-cooperation by the President is contributing to a slow-down.

If both houses of Congress fail to complete action before members elected in November take their seats for the new session beginning in January, there may be legal challenges to the validity of an impeachment and conviction based on inquiry begun in the old Congress. Prolonged legal and procedural snarls could encourage Congress and the public to drop the whole thing.

If that situation threatens, it might be advisable for Congress to consider acting at least on the cover-up issue that concerned the grand jury. It would be demoralizing to the American people if a federal grand jury deferred to Congress to act on a suspected case of criminal conduct and Congress failed to act.

The grand jury's action leaves Congress no choice but to do its constitutional duty and see the distasteful impeachment business through.

Arkansas Gazette.

Little Rock, Ark., June 8, 1974

We know now that the federal Grand Jury at Washington that indicted Ehrlichman, Haldeman and four other persons with connections with the White House wanted to include the biggest and most obvious target as well, only to be dissuaded by Special Prosecutor Leon A. Jaworski on the ground that there was some legal doubt as to whether a sitting President *could* be indicted under the Constitution; that is whether indictment did not have to wait upon a successful impeachment.

This, we imagine, is probably the prevailing view among constitutional lawyers, but it is by no means the unanimous view.

Concurrently with the public confirmation that the 19 Grand Jury members present voted unanimously to indict the President, too, we were treated to a new body of now almost redundant evidence of the lengths to which Mr. Nixon and his chief defense counsel, James D. St. Clair, will go in exploiting the kind of opening that Jaworski thus presented to them. Jaworski's was a legitimate, if still arguable, legal position. But the extensions and distortions of the special nature of the presidency and its temporary occupants, as filtered through the inventive noggins of Nixon's sharp practice lawyers, add up to the royalist notion that the President is simply above all law: just is not susceptible to the laws and rules that govern the lives of all the rest of us, or, as we shall shortly see, susceptible even to the rules of proper public behaviour that Nixon himself sometimes belatedly sets out for people within his own administration.

We refer here to Nixon's one-time view of what ought to be done to persons named by Grand Juries as unindicted co-conspirators, of whom he now is one, so named by all of the same 19 jurors who were restrained by the Special Prosecutor from going all the way with a formal indictment.

When it was thought that John D. Ehrlichman and H. R. Haldeman might only be named as co-conspirators rather than actually indicted, (as, in the events, they were) Nixon indicated a certain esthetic displeasure with the whole unindicted co-conspirator procedure — which he as a lawyer should have known was a quite common proceeding just short of indictment — though possibly only because some of his own top men might be so treated. However, the President's own edited transcript of the once secret White House tapes shows that he told Assistant Attorney General Henry E. Petersen that if any of his people *were* singled out by a Grand jury in any such fashion they would "immediately" be put on leave of absence.

By his own stern test, then, Mr. Nixon, if he did not step out altogether, as he properly ought to do, should temporarily step aside in favor of Vice President Ford under the "compromise" 25th Amendment dodge that Senator Jacob Javits and others have urged upon him. Just how the full truth about his involvement in all these multiple scandals can ever be known if he should temporarily leave office without having yielded up all the evidence, we leave for the 25th Amendment advocates who say that this would provide an opportunity to clear up the whole business. They can try to figure it out for themselves and then they can explain it to the rest of us.

But what has been the official White House reaction to the idea that the President now conform to the rule he laid down for others who might be named unindicted conspirators? Deputy Press Secretary Gerald L. Warren won't even talk about it, or, as he rather elegantly put it, won't "debate" it: "I'm not going to accept questions such as that relating to *the President of the United States.*" It is at this point, we suppose, that we varlets are supposed to drop to our knees and kiss the ermine trim on *"the President's"* robe and, if possible, get in a glancing sweep at Pat's and the Girls' flowing trains in passing. Again, the widening of the Jaworski opening into a tunnel large enough to accommodate the Simplon Orient Express. You could, in brief, "drive a train through it."

James St. Clair, in the nature of the defense lawyer's calling, naturally could not stay mum, like Warren, but said that the whole unindicted co-conspirator business had no legal weight, presumably with regard to non-Presidents, too, a curious enough legal view to be sure. (Representative Wayne Owens of Utah, a Democratic member of the House Judiciary Committee, said the disclosure certainly had weight with him, and he felt would have weight with other Committee members now considering articles of impeachment.)

St. Clair, excess feeding upon excess, could not even be content with that, but had to go on in effect to impugn the whole Grand Jury process, saying that even 19-to-0 Grand Jury findings were frequently wrong, as of course this one was wrong in the case of our wrapped-in-cottonwool President, his client. "He's not a co-conspirator only because a Grand Jury says so."

St. Clair also quoted Nixon as saying when he first learned of the Grand Jury's action that "they just don't have the evidence and they are wrong." This was pretty good, since elsewhere the same day, the same James D. St. Clair appeared in the court of the now weary Federal District Judge Gerhard A. Gesell to argue in a case involving a separate Ehrlichman indictment (the Ellsberg break-in) that the White House, not the court, would continue to be its own best judge, not only of the non-existent national security angle to the subpoenaed tapes but also of their "relevancy."

St. Clair wound up by saying that it was a shame that Mr. Nixon's co-conspirator status was even made public: "I say that it's unfortunate that this was released because this leaves the President with really no way of defending himself — except before the American people." Well, the President *could* waive all his real and claimed immunities and go into court with the evidence he is still withholding and, in sworn testimony, prove his innocence — if in fact he can.

Unfortunate as it all is, St. Clair is not really worried, however, because he does not think the public "is going to draw any inferences based on *part of the evidence.*" (Richer still, in light of all the withheld evidence.)

Unfortunately for James St. Clair, his talkative client once had a word on that point, too, as told by his own edited transcript again. This was April 19, 1973, and, again, the people it was thought might be named as co-conspirators were only Ehrlichman and Haldeman, and the President spaketh thusly:

"It's a hell of a procedure — that co-conspiracy. *It may not kill them legally but it kills them from the standpoint of the public.*"

THE EMPORIA GAZETTE
Emporia, Kans.
June 3, 1974

IN THIS whole Leon Jaworski issue there is something so childishly naive that it would be slapstick comedy if the fate of a national leadership were not at stake.

The President says, in effect, to Jaworski, "Look, pal, I'm innocent. But I want you to conduct a thorough investigation of the Watergate affair, including my alleged participation. You can have any and all the written evidence you request unless you even seem to get too close to involving me. One man got fired for not stopping at that point. The pertinence of certain records and the desirability of making them public is something which I alone shall decide. But of course you understand that you are absolutely independent and you have the power of subpoena."

And Mr. Jaworski, an attorney no less, said, "Sure. I realize from what happened to my predecessor that I am independent except when I am not. So let's get to work."

For public consumption this gives us a virtuous President, sure of his own innocence, and it gives us a brave investigator with unlimited authority. And where is Congress all this time? Well, my dear, Congress approves.

You would have thought that somewhere along the line Congressmen themselves and even Leon Jaworski would have joined our high school students, read the Constitution and discovered that nowhere does it delegate to any President the right to give Leon Jaworski or John Doe or me the power to subpoena the White House.

Why should President Nixon answer Jaworski's subpoena? The Supreme Court probably will back the President. Some constitutional lawyers will tell you that the President doesn't even have to answer a grand jury subpoena, that the office of the chief executive is equal to and separate from any grand jury.

I, for one, am glad the case went to the Supreme Court. For if Jaworski is over-ruled it might prevent some future President from playing to the grandstand by bestowing powers which he has no right to bestow, and has no idea of honoring. And it might prevent some ambitious attorney from accepting these powers and then crying into his soup when he cannot exercise them.

Meanwhile it is difficult to understand why all these long-drawn and expensive special investigations and special prosecutions and Senate hearings are conducted. They have no enforcement power over the President. Only Congress, sitting as a court of impeachment, has that power. So let's get on with the impeachment.

ST. LOUIS POST-DISPATCH
St. Louis, Mo., June 2, 1974

In accepting Special Prosecutor Jaworski's request for an accelerated review of a lower court decision ordering President Richard Nixon to honor a subpena for 64 taped conversations, the Supreme Court has severely undermined the strategy of all-out delay which now characterizes the White House's Watergate defense. The effect of the court's action is to further discredit Mr. Nixon's "stonewalling tactics" by revealing how empty they are of legal substance.

Mr. Nixon had asked the court not to "rush to judgment" on the case but to allow it to proceed through normal appellate channels, a course which might well have made it impossible for prosecutors to properly prepare the case against seven former White House aids and Republican campaign officials charged with covering-up the Watergate burglary. Mr. Jaworski had contended that the tapes are essential to that case, which is scheduled to go to trial Sept. 9.

Although its rejection of Mr. Nixon's initial arguments is no indication of how the high tribunal will rule on the dispute between President and prosecutor, it is difficult to see how the sweeping claims for executive privilege which have been put forth by the White House can be upheld. A small but important body of lower court decisions is unanimous in rejecting such contentions. Indeed, a federal appeals court ruled in a case brought by the first special prosecutor, Archibald Cox, that a president is not immune from judicial orders enforcing subpenas and that executive privilege is not absolute.

As for the court's accelerated review of Judge Sirica's decision, the arguments in favor of it were overwhelming. First there was the fact that the same issues already had been decided by an appellate court. Secondly there were abundant precedents—most conspicuously the Pentagon Papers case and President Truman's seizure of the steel mills—for quick Supreme Court action in cases of paramount public importance. Mr. Jaworski's powerful petition left no question of the importance of this case.

At issue, Mr. Jaworski wrote, is whether "a claim of executive privilege based on the generalized interest in the confidentiality of Government deliberations can block the prosecution's access to evidence material and important to the trial of charges of criminal misconduct by high Government officials who participated in those discussions . . ." Beyond this, Mr. Jaworski posed a profound question that goes to the heart of the entire Watergate investigation. He asked, "Is our constitutional system of government sufficiently resilient to permit the executive branch to establish an independent prosecutor fully capable of investigating and prosecuting allegations of criminal misconduct by officials in the executive office of the President . . .?" If it is not, it means simply that the President is above the law.

In recent weeks, Mr. Nixon's spokesmen have hinted that he may not abide by the Supreme Court's decision should it go against him. Such defiance, however, would be so reckless as to destroy whatever respect Mr. Nixon still commands and it would be further justification for his impeachment.

Whatever the court's decision may be—and presumably it will come shortly after oral arguments are heard July 8—it should have no legal bearing on the impeachment proceedings now underway in the House. The courts are not assigned a role by the Constitution in the impeachment process and the Judiciary Committee has wisely resisted suing Mr. Nixon over his refusal to honor its subpenas. But in terms of public opinion, a decision against Mr. Nixon would greatly strengthen the committee's position in demanding evidence from the White House.

Indeed, the court's rejection of the President's scheme for delay ought to be taken by the committee as a further sign of the urgency with which the Nixon scandals and the future of the Nixon presidency must be resolved.

THE SUN
Baltimore, Md., June 12, 1974

President Nixon has again used extravagant language in spurning the subpoena of the House Judiciary Committee for more evidence in its impeachment inquiry. It is the President, and the President alone, he proclaims, who will draw the line on deciding what Watergate tapes will be made available to the committee. It is Mr. Nixon and Mr. Nixon alone, who will avoid any precedents that would "render the executive branch henceforth and forevermore subservient to the legislative branch, and would thereby destroy the constitutional balance."

There is nothing new in Mr. Nixon's attempt to try his own case on grave constitutional issues rather than on the sordid charges of burglary and obstruction of justice that led to the impeachment inquiry in the first place. When facts are not helpful, it is normal defense strategy to rely on theory. And theory, in Mr. Nixon's case, rests on all the notions of the legislative branch run amuck that can be dredged from history or hypothesis, relevant or not.

The facts are that *this* Congress has not dealt with *this* President in a manner that transgresses the separation of powers. Mr. Nixon would have the country believe the House Judiciary Committee is on a fishing expedition, and willing to dip its hooks in the supposedly forbidden waters of presidential confidentiality. Actually, the committee has been circumspect in seeking evidence directly related to the various transgressions that go under the rubric of Watergate. And in asserting its right to evidence, it has held quite properly that the impeachment process gives Congress—and not the President—the power to determine what evidence is relevant in a case where he is, in effect, the defendant.

What was most disturbing in Mr. Nixon's latest defiance of the House subpoena was his evident intention to deal likewise with the courts, and even the Supreme Court, if necessary. Thus he cited two instances in which the judiciary held that neither the executive nor the legislative branch could encroach on its private deliberations. And without acknowledging the extraordinary aspects of an impeachment, he said "the executive must remain the final arbiter of demands on its confidentiality, just as the legislative and *judicial* [italics ours] branches must remain the final arbiters of demands on their confidentiality."

Before Mr. Nixon carries the doctrine of executive privilege to the extreme of flouting court subpoenas, however, he should heed the warnings of the House Republican leader, John J. Rhodes. Mr. Rhodes has stated that if Mr. Nixon defies the high court as he has already defied the House Judiciary Committee, he could not "survive"—meaning he would be impeached by the House as a whole. Mr. Nixon may well want to make his fight for acquittal in the Senate on such a constitutional issue. But in its other articles of impeachment, we would guess the House would deal with breaking and entering, hush money, violation of election laws and other Watergate-related misdeeds. They just will not go away.

The Chattanooga Times
Chattanooga, Tenn., June 15, 1974

President Nixon's lawyer, James D. St. Clair, said the other day that the main Watergate grand jury was "acting outside its authority" when it named Mr. Nixon as an unindicted co-conspirator at the same time it indicted six former White House or Nixon re-election committee officials for participating in the Watergate cover-up.

Granted, the charge, if it can be called that, is somewhat ambiguous, for unlike an indictment, it gives Mr. Nixon no new clear-cut rights or duties, no right to a trial, no duty to plead to the accusations.

Mr. Nixon appears to be unworried. According to Mr. St. Clair, the President, when informed several weeks ago of the jury's unanimous action, said: "They just don't have the evidence, and they are wrong."

Certainly Mr. St. Clair is correct in saying that "He (Mr. Nixon) is not a co-conspirator only because a grand jury says he is." But it's instructive to consider just what options the grand jurors possessed when they were confronted by the evidence the special prosecutors were able to wrest from the White House.

For months, despite legal contentions to the contrary, the White House lawyers have repeatedly asserted that a President cannot be indicted, and that

he can only be impeached and removed from office for having committed an indictable crime.

How, then, is an investigative body to judge whether a President has committed such a crime? The House Judiciary Committee's impeachment inquiry has run head-on into the White House's refusal to supply tapes and other documents it feels are necessary to its task.

Now, we know, a federal grand jury has unanimously declared it believes the President should be charged with an indictable crime — by submitting its conclusions regarding the cover-up and then by naming Mr. Nixon as a co-conspirator. In effect, the jury was attempting to put on the record its view that the President was "culpable," though not indictable due to legal problems that would ensue because of President Nixon's incumbency.

Despite Mr. Nixon's dismissal of the allegation on the grounds the grand jury didn't have all the evidence — it's worth noting that he has been the chief offender in refusing to release evidence in the Watergate affair — the grand jury's action merely adds to the Judiciary Committee's task in judging the President's conduct in office.

Surely the urgency and importance of their obligation become clearer by the day.

TWIN CITY SENTINEL
Winston-Salem, N.C., June 7, 1974

The news that a federal grand jury named President Nixon as a co-conspirator in the Watergate cover-up sharpens the issue before the country:

Will the American people let Mr. Nixon make a charade of the impeachment inquiry by setting himself up as the sole judge of what evidence the House Judiciary Committee will get to hear?

That is the White House stance today. Already the President has defied two subpoenas issued for his tapes and documents under the constitutional authority of the House of Representatives.

He "complied" with a third by giving not tapes, but edited transcripts riddled with crossed-out material.

And he is fighting other requests for evidence from the special Watergate prosecutor, while hinting again through his mouthpieces that he might defy a Supreme Court ruling to deliver.

The course Mr. Nixon has set could put him in contempt of both Congress and the Supreme Court, should he refuse to make more evidence available.

Now we know, from Mr. Nixon's own lawyer, that a federal grand jury last March named the President as a co-conspirator in a criminal cover-up. Further, according to several accounts, the grand jury would have indicted Mr. Nixon outright, were it not for the Constitution's direction that a president must be impeached and removed from office before he can be tried in court.

The grand jury's judgment, of course, is not a finding of guilt or

innocence. And a co-conspirator is not an indicted man.

But the significance of the grand jury's action is this: The grand jurors are not a band of political partisans after Mr. Nixon's scalp. They are not reporters in search of a story. They are ordinary citizens, a cross-section of the American public, who listened to months of testimony under the direction of a courageous judge and three separate prosecutors, one of whom the White House compromised and another whom Mr. Nixon fired.

James St. Clair, the President's lawyer, argued yesterday that the grand jury made its decision without access to all the evidence.

On that point he is exactly right. The grand jury did not have all the evidence. But the reason is not the jury's fault, but the fault of St. Clair's recalcitrant client, who will not surrender tapes and documents that might settle the question of his guilt or innocence, once and for all.

This matter is now out of the grand jury's hands. It is before the House Judiciary Committee. The committee must decide whether impeachment should proceed.

We believe that question, with all its grave importance, should be decided on the basis of all the evidence. Mr. Nixon does not believe that, or he would cooperate with the committee, as it is his duty to do.

And that is the difference between a President with "nothing to hide," and a President who, like Spiro Agnew before him, has abused the powers of his office to prevent a fair judgment from being made on whether he is fit to continue in that office.

THE ARIZONA REPUBLIC
Phoenix, Ariz., June 8, 1974

A Washington grand jury, in sealed indictments sent the House Judiciary Committee last March, named President Nixon "an unindicted co-conspirator" in the Watergate cover-up. That's a little like being a nonperson in a Communist country.

We don't know just where that puts the President in relation to the seven White House aides who were indicted for conspiracy. One thing is certain, he won't stand trial in a criminal court as a result of this nonindictment. But the information presumably will help the House Judiciary Committee decide whether it should recommend Nixon's impeachment.

The information was first published in the Los Angeles Times. When the action of the grand jury was announced, Judge John Sirica ordered prosecutors, defendants and witnesses not to make any "extrajudicial statements regarding this case."

Obviously, someone leaked the information to the L.A. paper. It's almost enough to make Judge Sirica want to set up a Plumbers Unit to plug the leaks from his court.

Nixon's lawyer, James St. Clair, says Judge Sirica should release the names of any other "unindicted co-conspirators." The judge heard arguments on the matter yesterday, and said the case should go to the Supreme Court.

We hope the judge will see his way to making the names public immediately. We find it increasingly hard to understand why the courts and the congressional committees are claiming the right to get all sorts of confidential material out of the White House while at the same time keeping their own confidential information secret.

It's obvious that the newspaper leak didn't do President Nixon any good. But it is equally obvious that a nonindictment is nothing more than a veiled opinion issued by a grand jury taking its guidelines from a prosecuting attorney.

Even an indictment is no proof of guilt, since the only evidence heard by the grand jury was presented by the prosecutors. The prosecution witnesses haven't been cross-examined by the defense, and the evidence hasn't been scrutinized.

"I've known grand juries to be wrong," said St. Clair.

We'll probably never know whether President Nixon is indeed an unindicted co-conspirator because there is no way to try him on that charge. Sooner or later, we must assume, we'll learn whether he was a conspirator in the Watergate cover-up, because the impeachment proceedings presumably will stand or fall on the merits of the case, if any, against the President.

Unless, of course, the House Judiciary Committee never does get around to taking a vote. And if it doesn't, a newly elected House of Representatives will have to start the entire impeachment business over from scratch next January.

That's a fate worse than any nation should be asked to endure.

KALMBACH, COLSON GET PRISON TERMS; NIXON AIDES HIT COMMITTEE ON LEAKS

President Nixon's personal attorney, Herbert Kalmbach, who had pleaded guilty Feb. 25 to two criminal offenses related to the Watergate investigation, was sentenced June 17 by Judge John Sirica of the U.S. district court in Washington to a jail term of 6–18 months and ordered to pay a $10,000 fine for violating a federal disclosure law governing campaign funds. Kalmbach was ordered to serve a concurrent six-month prison term for promising an ambassadorial appointment in return for a $100,000 contribution to the Nixon campaign, a misdemeanor offense.

Charles W. Colson, former special counsel to President Nixon, was sentenced to one-three years in prison and fined $5,000 by U.S. District Court Judge Gerhard A. Gesell June 21. Colson had pleaded guilty June 3 to a charge that he obstructed justice by disseminating derogatory information in 1971 about Pentagon Papers trial defendant Daniel Ellsberg and one of Ellsberg's lawyers, Leonard Boudin. Before Gesell passed sentence, Colson read a statement reiterating his innocence of the offenses for which he had been indicted, but accepting responsibility for the charge for which he was about to be sentenced: "As to the specific offense charged, the President on numerous occasions urged me to disseminate damaging information about Daniel Ellsberg....I believed what I was doing was right."

Continuing news leaks from the House Judiciary Committee were attacked by White House spokesmen June 18–19. Kenneth W. Clawson, communications director, denounced them June 18 as "a purposeful effort to bring down the President with smoke-filled room operations by a clique of Nixon-hating partisans." According to Clawson, the latest leak, a memo prepared by William P. Dixon, a Democratic staff member and reported that day by the *Washington Post,* indicated that the committee and its chairman "intended to do nothing about this trial by innuendo." The memo quoted Nixon as having told an aide on April 16, 1973 that he was "planning to assume some culpability" in the payment of hush money to a Watergate defendant.

Presidential speechwriter Patrick J. Buchanan denounced the committee's leaks June 19 as "nameless, faceless character assassination" of the President and other officials.

Judiciary Committee Chairman Peter W. Rodino Jr. (D, N.J.) defended the committee later June 19. "We have a job," he said, "and we're going to go forward to do the best we can, despite some unfortunate leaks."

The Judiciary Committee completed its closed evidentiary hearings June 21 and moved June 24 to accelerate its impeachment inquiry in an effort to conclude its work by the latter part of July. A closed committee session June 26 to consider summoning witnesses was marked by sharp partisan discord. The decisions were to call five witnesses, to interview five others as potential witnesses and to conclude the testimonial phase by July 12. Debate over proposed articles of impeachment would follow that. The divisive argument within the committee reached a climax on a motion to call 10 persons as witnesses. It failed by a 19–19 vote. On one side were 19 Democrats. Two Democrats—Reps. Wayne Owens (Utah) and Walter Flowers (Ala.)—joined the 17 Republicans. In other action marked by partisan dispute, the panel decided June 25 to make public the evidence it had gathered.

WORCESTER TELEGRAM.
Worcester, Mass., June 20, 1974

Herbert Kalmbach, President Nixon's former personal lawyer, has been sentenced to six to 18 months in jail amid a rising national controversy about plea bargaining.

Plea bargaining is the process by which a person under indictment agrees to plead guilty to a lesser offense in return for having graver charges against him dropped.

Plea bargaining is defended by some lawyers as essential to the working of the judicial system and condemned by others as so abused as to make a mockery of justice. In a recent article in The New Yorker, Richard Harris writes: "In the end, historians may conclude that the way in which those guilty of crimes in the Watergate affair were brought to justice did more lasting damage to the highest purpose of American law than did the crimes themselves."

But others say that the Watergate mess would never have been unraveled if every defendant had been tried in court on every charge.

The Kalmbach case is a good example. He was allowed to plead guilty to one charge of operating an illegal campaign committee — it raised $4 million and filed no reports — and to another charge of promising an ambassadorship in return for a $100,000 contribution to Nixon's re-election campaign. Obviously, if Kalmbach pleaded guilty to those charges, he probably committed worse crimes that will go unpunished. But if his case had gone to court, he might have appealed it for months and years and eventually have gone free.

An even more striking case was that of a former attorney general, Richard Kleindienst, allowed to plead guilty to a misdemeanor, even though he had told a barefaced lie to the congressional committee studying his nomination to be attorney general. Kleindienst got only 30 days suspended, which certainly seems like a slap on the wrist to someone like James W. McCord Jr., the Watergate burglar who got one to seven years, or even to Jeb Stuart Magruder, who got 10 months to four years for conspiracy to obstruct justice.

But despite these discrepancies, it is hard to argue with those who claim that Watergate would still be bogged down in preliminaries if it were not for plea bargaining. Under ordinary circumstances, delay might be acceptable, but Watergate is a special case in that it points directly to the President of the United States and his possible impeachment. It would be intolerable to let that decision drag on for years. The matter must be resolved as quickly as possible.

The Evening Bulletin
Philadelphia, Pa., June 12, 1974

Former Attorney General Richard G. Kleindienst got off too lightly.

Mr. Kleindienst had cited respect for the criminal justice system as the reason for his guilty plea to the misdemeanor charge of not answering "fully and accurately" questions put to him by the Senate Judiciary Committee about attempted White House influence in an ITT antitrust case.

But Judge George L. Hart has not enhanced respect for the criminal justice system by giving Mr. Kleindienst the lightest possible sentence — a suspended one-month jail term and $100 fine.

This is not to quarrel with the judge's view that Mr. Kleindienst's motives in misleading the senators were loyalty and an attempt to preserve the reputation of another. It was to Mr. Kleindienst's credit that he successfully resisted, as Special Watergate Prosecutor Leon Jaworski had noted, a presidential order to drop an appeal in the ITT case. Mr. Kleindienst's family life is no doubt above reproach, as the judge said.

When, however, Judge Hart termed Mr. Kleindienst's conviction a technical violation of the law, that was to obscure what actually happened. The fact is that the former official testified to senators that the White House hadn't attempted to exert influence when it had. Except for his cooperation and plea bargaining he might have faced a more serious charge.

The circumstances suggested mercy; they did not call for a tap on the wrist, suspended. Judge Hart's praise of Mr. Kleindienst's integrity in this setting seems inappropriate.

If the chief law enforcement officer of the country is to be so excused for failing to do his duty because of "a heart too loyal and considerate of the feelings of others," then how are others to be held accountable for placing personal loyalty above their duty and the requirements of the law?

THE CHRISTIAN SCIENCE MONITOR
Boston, Mass., June 11, 1974

We can heartily endorse Richard Nixon's ringing statement that a strong American presidency is needed to achieve peace in the world. The question Americans must ask themselves is twofold: What constitutes the "strength" of this high office and what uses may that power be put to?

Surely it is beyond any conceivable area of debate that moral integrity as well as intellectual and political competence comprise that strength and that an individual public servant is entitled to the power of office only if he uses it constitutionally. In other words, the office of the presidency does not include the power to misuse that office.

By this definition, Mr. Nixon's statement that he shall "do nothing that will weaken this office" can be deeply challenged. The catalog of abuses and misuses of power in the executive branch of government is already shocking in the extreme and still has to be fully disclosed. Yet Mr. Nixon's concept of not weakening the presidential office now seems to be to resist and defy virtually every constitutional effort of legislative and judicial tribunals to get to the bottom of the Watergate-related scandals and to assure that the cause of integrity in office is served.

To cite one example, federal Judge Gerhard Gesell has sternly suggested that the President may be obstructing justice by going back on his agreement to give Ellsberg defendant John Ehrlichman access to his own personal notes. How can it be reasonably argued that a refusal to honor demands for criminal trial evidence and to honor impeachment inquiry subpoenas "strengthens" the presidency? On the contrary, it only weakens the stature of that office because it suggests the office is being used to prevent the administering of justice.

We would also make the point that there is a distinction between the office of the presidency and the president and that in a certain sense the office has not been weakened by the Watergate developments.

World leaders deal with Mr. Nixon because he represents the presidency and enjoys the powers and perquisites of presidential office. His current journey to the Middle East is ample evidence that, despite Watergate and the threat of impeachment, Mr. Nixon commands the authority due any holder of the office. The gathering storm against him at home did not prevent his Secretary of State from negotiating another major agreement in the Middle East nor inhibit the invitation for a presidential trip.

Hence Mr. Nixon's intimation that attacks on him have weakened the presidency and harmed the prospects for peace does not, in our opinion, have a basis in fact.

DAYTON DAILY NEWS
Dayton, Ohio, June 4, 1974

The guilty plea entered yesterday by former presidential aide Charles Colson rips away the "national security" cover story that President Nixon has used in trying to explain away the break-in at the office of Daniel Ellsberg's psychiatrist. Mr. Colson has put the President even more deeply in trouble with the law than he already was.

Colson

In pleading guilty to a charge of obstructing justice, Mr. Colson concurred in the prosecutor's statement that the break-in was designed to get dirt on Mr. Ellsberg that could be leaked to the press and that the break-in was part of a larger White House plot meant to assure the conviction of Mr. Ellsberg on charges the Nixon administration had brought against him for releasing the Pentagon papers.

In this tawdry matter, Mr. Nixon's White House again has been exposed—this time by an aide who was high in its deliberations and who was an intimate of the President's — as acting against the political and judicial process of this county as if they were enemies.

Unwilling merely to let Mr. Ellsberg be charged and then fairly tried for the offenses of which the government believed him guilty, the Nixon administration resorted to criminal, cynical machinations whose purpose was to defame the defendant and so poison public attitudes against him that he was likely to be convicted regardless of the evidence.

The Nixon White House did not seek justice. It sought revenge—and incidentally hoped, it seems, to wring political advantage from it.

This, then, was the "national security" that President Nixon has so piously talked about. Mr. Colson's verification that the operation was really political is hardly surprising, however.

Testimony to the Senate Watergate committee last summer indicated that the purpose of the break-in was to get information that could be used to smear Mr. Ellsberg. The conversations in Mr. Nixon's transcripts about the case cannot be read convincingly in any other way than to show that the President and his aides were cooking up "national security" strictly as an excuse, long after the break-in and just as it was about to become public knowledge.

Mr. Colson's plea and statement further cheapen the already thin claims by which Mr. Nixon is remaining so precariously in office.

If the President did not know about the break-in at the psychiatrist's office in advance—and so far there is no evidence he did —the conclusion is inescapable that Mr. Nixon knowingly lied when he excused the break-in as a national security necessity. He thus compounded the felony by sending out a smokescreen that was meant to protect his aides, who had planned the operation, from being brought to justice.

Arkansas Gazette.

Little Rock, Ark., June 20, 1974

Richard G. Kleindienst is back in the news again, where his name never should have been allowed to be absent from for even as much time as it has been since his resignation under some outside heat as Attorney General.

Kleindienst appears to have been genuinely put off by some of the more really outrageous (and easily detectable) offenses committed by this administration in the case of the Watergate and related matters, most of them committed under some amorphous conjuring up of the "national security" bogie. But Kleindienst was at heart every bit as much of an ideologue as any of the others, with the exception, perhaps, of the one-and-only G. Gordon Liddy.

We cannot get out of mind Pete Hamill's account of an audience granted by Kleindienst to a group of perfectly moderate, sober, law students from Eastern college campuses during the suppression of the protest demonstrations against the Cambodia. Kleindienst's response to their reasonably stated questions was anything but restrained, so unrestrained in fact that the students came away from the encounter with a feeling almost of shock. Though the plans for *detente* with China (and the Soviet Union) already were progressing in Henry Kissinger's programmed mind, in Richard Kleindienst's view we were in Cambodia, as we were in Vietnam, in order to prevent China's extending its hegemony over the whole of Southeast Asia, through its supposed surrogate, North Vietnam. This was still the official, if by then only implied, line at that time, of course, but Kleindienst, we seem to recall, had the Chinese Communists, or possibly it was only the Russians, also massing on the Channel coast of France.

A zealot, then, but what has brought the former Attorney General's name back to the front pages was not so much an access of zeal, but the *lack* of zeal with which his Justice Department pursued the early Watergate prosecutions, though, since he was a ritually ideological "anti-Communist", as were most of the people found inside the Watergate and the people who directed them there, the two subjects cannot be wholly divorced, not in our own mind at least.

The specific reason for Mr. Kleindienst's recall before the Senate Judiciary Committee is that that panel now is considering President Nixon's nomination of Earl J. Silbert — Kleindienst's chief prosecutor or non-prosecutor in the early Watergate going — to be a United States Attorney for the District of Columbia. Senator Sam J. Ervin,

who by now is all too drearily familiar with the whole Watergate affair, has been especially critical of the roles played by both Silbert and Kleindienst in the early failure to pursue the investigation beyond the ready-made scapegoats who were the men caught, literally, in the act of committing a crime. Kleindienst's memory still is no better than it was in his own confirmation hearing before the same Committee, a performance that ultimately resulted in his pleading guilty to a charge that he had failed to tell the panel the whole truth about all the "deals" and *quid pro quos* involved in the ITT antitrust case fix.

Concurrently with the former Attorney General's reappearance before the Judiciary Committee, his name appeared in an unusual defense by a federal jurist of the light sentence he gave Kleindienst on the guilty plea—a *weightless* sentence, really—and the unusual paean to the pleader's civic-mindedness with which the judge in question, George L. Hart Jr., saw fit to massage away such pain as Kleindienst suffered from the little slap on the wrist he got.

We started to say "unusually light *sentence*", too, and since it was an almost non-existent one (one-month suspended, $100 fine suspended), we suppose that it was, but the spectacle of light sentences for persons of Kleindienst's class and condition as opposed to the lesser breeds within the toils of the law isn't unusual at all, which is why, we suppose, the flood of mail critical of the sentence that prompted Judge Hart's pained rejoinder, which spoke of a public "uninformed" about the precise nature of the case.

Well, the public is not so uninformed as not to know—part of it, at least—that no fewer than three of Special Watergate Prosecutor Leon A. Jaworski's top staff resigned in protest against Jaworski's decision to let Kleindienst cop the first and easiest plea in sight, as Agnew had been allowed to do by other federal prosecutors earlier, instead of pressing forward with the far graver charges that could have been brought against him.

There is a little matter of the ideal of "equal justice under the law" as opposed to the frequent reality of markedly *unequal* application of justice that has offended even some of the rigid law-and-order people (of whom both Agnew and Kleindienst were in the forefront when they were the hunters rather than the hunted), though not enough of them, we are afraid. For the fallen among this administration, amnesty begins at home—and stops there.

BUFFALO EVENING NEWS

Buffalo, N.Y., June 20, 1974

Federal Judge John Sirica lived up to his reputation for severity in imposing a minimum six-month jail sentence and $10,000 fine on Herbert Kalmbach, President Nixon's former personal attorney, for political fund-raising offenses.

Mr. Kalmbach, a middle-level figure in the Watergate-related scandals, has apparently agreed to cooperate with Special Prosecutor Leon Jaworski in other cases. Because he pleaded guilty to a felony, Mr. Kalmbach could also be disbarred, no small penalty to a lawyer.

This contrasts markedly, for example, with the undue leniency of another federal judge, George L. Hart Jr., in the case of Richard Kleindienst, former U. S. attorney general who pleaded guilty to not telling the full truth under oath to a Senate committee. He escaped with a small fine and jail sentence, both suspended.

Any misgivings about the Kalmbach case, however, might better arise, not from the Sirica sentencing, but from the unusual and obscure nature of the offenses to which he pleaded guilty and the long record of virtually no prior enforcement of those laws. One was a technical failure to install proper officers in a 1970 fund-raising committee; the other, the illegal promise of an ambassador's post to a big contributor. As Richard Harris, a legal scholar, wrote recently in the New Yorker magazine, had this law on ambassadorships been "enforced in the past, every President, senator, representative and thousands of their aides would have been fined or sent to prison."

That may be an exaggeration to make a point, but certainly the use of obscure laws, generally unenforced, to penalize one man while not another raises questions about the legal techniques employed to obtain justice. Whether in this case or in any other, we don't think ambassadorships should be up for sale to the highest political contributors. But we also think that, in the long aftermath of the Watergate scandals, the enforcement of such newly-rediscovered laws should be pursued uniformly, and not allowed to lapse into dead-letter status until some other major scandal comes along to revive them.

DAYTON DAILY NEWS
Dayton, Ohio, June 25, 1974

President Nixon and his White House continue to misrepresent impeachment as if it were a case in night court, where the only thing that matters is whether the arresting officer can remember and identify the defendant he collared a few hours earlier. It does not count, the White House says with rising insistence, that Mr. Nixon's presidency has massively, systematically misused the powers of the office.

So the White House has sent its counsel, old pol Len Garment, out to argue that even if President Nixon did order former aide Charles Colson to smear Daniel Ellsberg, as Mr. Colson has testified, well, Mr. Nixon was doing nothing actually illegal.

Legal. Illegal. The distinction, becomes tiresome and is only thinly relevant. Maybe it is not technically criminal for the President of the United States to order a hatchet man to defame a citizen, as long as the President didn't specify that the aide was to do it illegally. But it is wrong, terribly wrong, and everybody knows it.

The government had a potential case against Mr. Ellsberg because of his unauthorized release of the Pentagon Papers, but President Nixon could not be content with prosecution through the courts. He wanted Mr. Ellsberg destroyed. In fact, Mr. Colson says, he demanded it.

Mr. Garment says the President feared that Mr. Ellsberg might become a "hero in the eyes of the American public." In the first place, it is not a president's business to decide for the public who its heroes can or can't be. In the second place, there was no

chance of Mr. Ellsberg being idolized. Anti-war activists cheered his act, but the general public seemed to think Mr. Ellsberg was as marginally wrong in releasing the papers as the government had been in classifying them unnecessarily. That was a sensible view and hardly one from which heroes are mythically born.

The White House is now backed down against the absolute base line, contending that because no one has caught Mr. Nixon doing something provably felonious, the President is exempt from the consequences of his misdeeds, actions, orders, attitudes and mismanagement.

It is not supposed to matter that Mr. Nixon's closest personal aides, acting on his behalf and in ways they believed were acceptable to him, broke more laws than Bonnie and Clyde on a get-away. Neither is it supposed to matter that Mr. Nixon wantonly abused the powers of the presidency. Nor that he is withholding evidence.

The Constitution, making impeachment a deliberative process, promotes stability, and that's good. It is a good, however, that Mr. Nixon and his defense are now typically exploiting and abusing, by claiming—wrongly, in point of fact—that the President has to be caught red-handed, like a nervous junkie on his first gas station stick-up, before Congress can satisfy the Constitution's clear intention of getting misbehaving presidents out of office.

The cover-up continues, intent now on covering up, from a public honestly confused about the issue, what the Constitution means and what impeachment is.

The Cleveland Press
Cleveland, Ohio, June 22, 1974

We don't know which is more bizarre—Charles Colson's surprise charge against President Nixon or the White House's arrogant effort to brush it off.

Colson, who was the President's special counsel and political hatchet man, added to Nixon's troubles yesterday just before he was sentenced to one to three years in prison for obstructing the trial of Daniel Ellsberg.

A former member of Nixon's inner circle, Colson had pleaded guilty to trying to obstruct Ellsberg's trial on charges of stealing the Pentagon Papers by spreading derogatory information about Ellsberg and his lawyers.

Standing before the judge who passed sentence on him, the former White House lawyer said:

"The President on numerous occasions urged me to disseminate damaging information about Daniel Ellsberg, including information about Ellsberg's attorney and others with whom Ellsberg had been in close contact."

Colson said he was convinced that Nixon believed he was acting in the national interest, and that he himself believed he was.

Although Colson is the seventh former White House aide to be sentenced to jail for a Watergate-related offense, he is the first to state that his crime stemmed directly from a Nixon order.

Asked about Colson's serious accusation, the White House replied haughtily through spokesman Gerald L. Warren: "I don't really have any comment on the court procedure this morning."

Really? That's not good enough. If it was a crime for Colson to try to smear Ellsberg while he was under indictment, it was an offense for Nixon to instruct Colson to do so.

The question is: Did he? In what is now year three of Watergate, the country is entitled to a serious reply and truthful answer to a charge made by one of Nixon's former intimates.

It's late in the game for the public to be put off with a nose-in-the-air refusal to discuss public business. That tactic went out with Louis XIV.

The Des Moines Register
Des Moines, Iowa, June 25, 1974

In the atmosphere of intrigue and secrecy that surrounded the Nixon White House, it seems the President was worried about the Central Intelligence Agency (CIA) itself. Charles W. Colson, the former White House aide who was sentenced to prison last week, as told a story of Nixon's fear that CIA was involved in the Watergate affair.

The Washington Post was given the story by a private investigator to whom Colson talked.

According to Colson, Nixon was alarmed about suspected conspirators high in CIA circles and wanted to investigate the intelligence community. He was dissuaded from this on ground that it would result in international and domestic political repercussions.

Colson suspected that CIA was behind the breakins of the office of Daniel Ellsberg's psychiatrist and of the Democratic party headquarters at the Watergate. He said he thought this was to discredit the inner circle around the President.

Last week Colson said Nixon on numerous occasions had urged him to disseminate damaging material about Daniel Ellsberg and about Ellsberg's attorneys. This was the crime to which Colson pleaded guilty and for which he was sentenced. The President viewed the Ellsberg theft of the Pentagon papers as a serious threat to national security. He wanted to discredit Ellsberg to discourage others from doing the same. Thus Colson implicated the President in the crime of obstructing justice.

The tale about Nixon's fears of the CIA, suggests a new possible motivation

for the President's concern. Instead of being fearful about the adequacy of the secrecy system, Nixon may have been worried that CIA officials were playing domestic politics. According to Colson, CIA thought it did not get enough voice in matters of foreign policy and national security.

This adds one more confusing and complicating aspect to the already confusing Watergate affair. Prior to Colson's statement, we had thought Nixon was obsessed with keeping CIA's secret activities from being exposed. He had told the FBI not to investigate the routing of some of his campaign funds through Mexico, because that might expose covert CIA work vital to national security. Now Colson tells us Nixon was suspicious of the CIA and wanted to investigate it.

Colson has dedicated his life to Christ and no doubt is telling the truth as he sees it. But there has been so much lying and deception around the White House we don't know what to believe.

Of one thing we are certain, and have been since long before Watergate. There is danger in any government agency operating as an independent sovereignty, without thorough congressional supervision. CIA is a mountain of mystery, with no control over its activities by the representatives of the people. It spends at a lavish rate with little or no accounting.

No wonder Nixon was scared. We are, too. And Congress ought to do something about it. If CIA did not plot on Watergate, it is surely capable of doing something like that. It needs public exposure.

RAPID CITY JOURNAL—

Rapid City, S.D., June 16, 1974

"The slip of a lip may sink a ship."

That World War II slogan pointed up the danger of loose talk.

Lately there have been a lot of loose lips and some of them threaten the ship of state. It hasn't sunk yet but it has been wallowing.

Much of this loose talk involves opinions of guilt or innocence before all the evidence is in. Culpability is determined before proper judgment has been rendered by the person or body charged with that responsibility.

Now it appears that even the president of the American Bar Association is indulging in a practice which his profession stoutly maintains is not ethical.

The head of the bar association predicts former Atty. Gen. William Kleindienst and former White House aide Charles W. Colson will be found guilty of ethical violations in disciplinary proceedings by local bar associations.

It's true that Kleindienst and Colson have been found guilty of violating the law. The ABA president is entitled to his opinion of their conduct. But in predicting they will be found guilty in further proceedings, he doesn't come off as exactly ethical himself.

A nautical term is also used to describe another prevalent kind of loose talk — leaks. But today's leaks are not mere slips of the lip. In most cases they are planned disclosures, usually slanted to serve the purposes of the leaker or to imply guilt by innuendo or association.

Attempts to plug leaks from the National Security Council led to the wiretaps which have cast a cloud over Henry Kissinger. Leaking of the Pentagon Papers prompted the formation of the plumbers unit which led to the Watergate fiasco.

The investigation of Watergate and the White House involvement in it has been marked by continuous leaks.

Now the House Judiciary Committee which is considering the impeachment of President Nixon appears to have sprung more leaks than a Dutch dike.

For that reason, we think the sessions of that committee should be opened up completely. The public would be best served by being privy to all of the testimony and deliberations rather than being fed bits and pieces through leaks calculated to serve the interests of the leaker.

The Boston Globe

Boston, Mass., June 28, 1974

Lest anyone forget, the inquiry now being conducted by the Judiciary Committee is an investigation by the legislative branch.

It is not a trial. It is not an administrative hearing. It is not a joint effort by the White House and Congress to find out whether an impeachable offense has been committed.

When a prosecutor or a grand jury conducts an investigation, counsel for the potential defendant is not asked for his side of the case. And so it is in the case of impeachment.

But in the interest of fairness, when the Judiciary Committee adopted its rules of procedure for the impeachment inquiry on May 2, the President and his counsel, James D. St. Clair, were granted broad participatory privileges, including the right to request additional evidence and to interrogate committee witnesses. This is consistent with past impeachment practice, although in the only other inquiry involving a President, that of Andrew Johnson, the question of his inclusion or that of his counsel was not considered.

The trouble with these rules is that while they help to insure that the process appears fair, they work against the other two goals, due speed and bipartisanship.

Thus the Committee was caught on Wednesday with what appeared to be a reasonable request from Mr. St. Clair for additional witnesses which, if accepted, would have further jeopardized Chairman Peter W. Rodino's present July 31 deadline for a vote and would have begun to make the process look more like a trial than an inquiry.

Republicans found it comfortable to support Mr. St. Clair's request and enough Democrats agreed with them to make a majority. Mr. Rodino was forced to call a hasty caucus of Democrats and change some minds in order to reverse the vote. The whole performance looked partisan, heavy-handed and unfair.

Having made the decision to allow Mr. St. Clair a broad role in its inquiry, the Judiciary Committee must live with it and respond reasonably to his suggestions. Impeachment is more of a political than a legal process. There is suspicion that a key element of the White House strategy is to undercut the integrity of the Judiciary Committee through leaks and through challenges such as that posed by Mr. St. Clair this week.

A recommendation for impeachment which comes out of a leaky Committee with a partisan vote and a smell of procedural unfairness will be a help to the President in the short run, but disservice to the country. If the price of averting this result is to further delay the vote and to grant Mr. St. Clair more scope than otherwise advisable, it will have to be done.

THE MILWAUKEE JOURNAL

Milwaukee, Wis., June 20, 1974

The leaks that have sprung in the House Judiciary Committee's impeachment inquiry can only be deplored. They are unfair to President Nixon, confusing to the public, damaging to the committee.

For the most part, committee members and staff have maintained confidentiality. But there also have been numerous breaches. Some insiders — usually those inclined most or least toward impeachment — routinely blab selective, often conflicting recollections of what the committee has learned in closed hearings. It's no wonder that recently The New York Times and The Washington Post, carrying stories about the committee's probing of the milk fund, contradicted each other about Nixon's alleged role.

Some leakage also involves documents, such as several memos written for Democratic members by William Dixon, staff attorney and former McGovern campaign aide. Through analysis of discrepancies in White House transcripts, the memos tend to tie Nixon more closely than ever to the Watergate coverup. But they still are only one interpretation, prepared for pondering in private. They should not pop up willy-nilly in the press.

Outraged White House spokesmen, of course, are in a weak position to complain about any attempt to defame or to sway opinion through strategic leaking. Presidential aides often have done precisely that. Nevertheless, the committee has a solemn obligation to be fair, to honor its own rules. Leakers blur the committee's purpose, raising side disputes about motives and tactics. This can seriously erode public confidence in the committee's integrity.

Much of the trouble probably could have been avoided if the committee had shifted to open hearings weeks ago. Now, as the closed phase of the inquiry nears an end, it is important that evidence so far presented be made public soon, as promised, and that all hearings remain open in the future.

Openness can serve several worthy objectives. It can give the president a fairer shake and the public fuller knowledge of what is happening. It can also help assure that ultimately the nature of the evidence will — with as few distractions as possible — determine the fate of Richard Nixon.

Sentinel Star

Orlando, Fla., June 22, 1974

SOME OF THE Watergate defendants are discovering, as Jurgen did in the James Branch Cabell novel of the 1920s, that justice is only a word in the dictionary.

Traveling through mythical regimes in search of perfect justice, the fictional pawnbroker finally met the Master Philologist who led him to it — in the big dictionary standing open before him.

Richard G. Kleindienst got off with a slap on the wrist — a month in jail and a $100 fine, both suspended — while Herbert W. Kalmbach must spend six to 18 months in prison and pay a $10,000 fine.

❀ ❀ ❀

BOTH MEN had held high positions of trust in the Nixon administration, Kleindienst as U.S. attorney general and Kalmbach as Mr. Nixon's personal attorney and an official of his reelection committee.

The offenses were at about the same level of seriousness — Kleindienst's refusing to tell the truth about the ITT case before his Senate confirmation h e a r i n g, Kalmbach's raising illegal political funds and falsely promising the Trinidad ambassador a more prestigious ambassadorship in exchange for a $100,000 campaign gift. Why the big difference?

These cases are extremes, but justice for those convicted of or pleading guilty to Watergate offenses does seem to be strikingly spotty so far.

Some think the full wrath of the law should have been directed at Kleindienst because he was the highest ranking and most responsible official involved.

❀ ❀ ❀

THOSE CAUGHT up in the Watergate prosecution are learning, perhaps to their surprise and dismay, what common criminals have always known, that the rap can depend on the prosecutor's diligence in plea bargaining, on the judge's deeply held beliefs, emotions or prejudices — even on whether His Honor felt good or suffered from a hangover the morning of sentencing.

In Florida, a study showed, youngsters have received terms ranging from 30 days to five years for identical first-offense marijuana infractions.

❀ ❀ ❀

CAN THIS BE excused? Only to the extent of pointing out that justice has never been perfect anywhere. The U. S. Supreme Court recognized this the other day when it ruled a trial doesn't have to be perfect to be valid, only fair. A flawless trial is something we can look forward to when society reaches Utopia.

But we feel that by and large the adversary system evolved from c e n t u r i e s of English-American common and statutory law does happen to be better than the alternative — a rigid, unyielding j u r i s p r u d e n c e used by the autocratic regimes such as the Soviet Union. Before it got to that we'd wager that the Watergate defendant with the rawest deal would rather take his chances before Judge "Maximum John" Sirica.

Richmond Times-Dispatch

Richmond, Va., June 30, 1974

By tentatively deciding not to call all of the witnesses requested by President Nixon's attorney, the House Judiciary Committee has inspired grave new doubts about the fairness of its impeachment inquiry. Many Americans are likely to interpret the decision as conclusive evidence that the committee's Democratic majority already has decided that the President should be impeached and is determined to avert testimony that might help prove otherwise.

James D. St. Clair, the President's lawyer, had requested the appearance of six witnesses: former White House aides John W. Dean III, Frederick C. LaRue and H. R. Haldeman; former Attorney General John Mitchell; Paul O'Brien, formerly a lawyer for Mr. Nixon's reelection committee; and William O. Bittman, attorney for Watergate burglar E. Howard Hunt Jr. But the committee, voting almost entirely along party lines, decided tentatively to hear the testimony of only Mr. Dean and Mr. LaRue. The other four will be called to testify only if committee staff lawyers, who will interview the men, conclude that they possess information essential to the inquiry.

On its face, the committee's decision seems preposterous. Until the Watergate affair forced his resignation, Mr. Haldeman was President Nixon's chief White House aide. For years, Mr. Mitchell was one of the President's closest friends and advisors. If these men do not possess information important to the impeachment investigation, nobody does.

One of the committee's excuses for not calling Messrs. Haldeman, Mitchell, O'Brien and Bittman is that the information they could impart is readily available from other sources. Therefore, their personal appearance does not, at this point, seem to the committee to be necessary. But this is a specious argument. It is entirely possible that the personal testimony of these men could add significantly to the mass of information the committee has compiled, especially if the members of the committee interrogated them intensely.

There is, of course, another compelling reason why the four men should be called to testify. If it is to gain and retain the confidence of the American people, the committee must demonstrate its desire and intention to execute its delicate assignment with the utmost fairness. Already viewed skeptically because of the anti-Nixon leaks that have oozed from its closed meetings, the committee invites new accusations of prejudice by failing to call all of the President's witnesses. For many people, this will constitute proof that the committee is not interested in giving the President ample opportunity to state his case.

It is true, as some members of the committee have noted, that the appearance of the four men would be time-consuming. Certainly the committee is right to be wary of actions that would prolong its mission unnecessarily. But it is more important for the committee to be fair than to be fast. Too much is at stake, for the nation as well as for Mr. Nixon, for the committee to act upon the basis of an inquiry that may be incomplete, or even on the basis of an inquiry that may simply *seem* to be incomplete. Besides, the extension of the committee's investigation by the few extra days that might be required to receive the testimony of the four men surely would be tolerated by the American people, who already have waited more than a year and a half for a resolution of the Watergate controversy.

PORTLAND EVENING EXPRESS

Portland, Me., June 24, 1974

With the sentencing of former presidential special counsel Charles W. Colson yet another close aide or high appointee of President Nixon has been brought to justice. And with each new conviction the chain of evidence seems to move inexorably closer to the involvement of the President.

Colson was convicted of the crime of obstructing justice in the court case involving Daniel Ellsberg for making public the secret Pentagon Papers which detailed the origin and conduct of the Vietnam war.

Prior to being sentenced to at least a year in prison and fined $5,000, Colson told Judge Gerhard A. Gesell that he had attempted to defame Ellsberg and destroy his credibility.

And he did so, Colson told the court, on the repeated urging of the President of the United States.

Said Colson: ". . . the President on numerous occasions urged me to disseminate damaging information about Daniel Ellsberg, including information about Ellsberg's attorney and others with whom Ellsberg had been in close contact."

It has already been established that White House "plumbers" broke into the office in a search for information designed to poison the public's mind against Ellsberg and ensure his conviction.

And it has already been established that President Nixon approached the presiding judge in the Ellsberg case — while a case the government wanted desperately to win was proceeding — and improperly offered him the job as director of the Federal Bureau of Investigation.

Daily, it becomes abundantly clearer that the President of the United States orchestrated the machinations of the most morally reprehensible administration in the history of the nation. And daily the need for an impeachment trial to determine the guilt or innocence of Richard Nixon becomes ever more imperative.

BREAK-IN JURY CONVICTS EHRLICHMAN; WHITE HOUSE TRANSCRIPTS CHALLENGED

John D. Ehrlichman, former domestic affairs adviser to President Nixon, was found guilty July 12 by a federal jury in Washington of conspiring to violate the civil rights of Dr. Lewis J. Fielding, the psychiatrist of Pentagon Papers defendant Daniel Ellsberg. Three other defendants in the trial—G. Gordon Liddy, Bernard L. Barker and Eugenio Martinez—were convicted of the same charge. Ehrlichman was also found guilty of three of four counts of making false statements.

Instructing the jury on the conspiracy charge July 12, U.S. District Court Judge Gerhard A. Gesell said that it need not find Ehrlichman had known in advance of plans for a "covert entry" into Fielding's office files to obtain Ellsberg's psychiatric records. Moreover, Gesell told the jurors, an illegal search need not entail "physical break-in," which only tended to emphasize "lack of permission." In his other instructions, Gesell said, "An individual cannot escape criminal liability simply because he sincerely but incorrectly believes that his acts are justified in the name of patriotism, of national security or the need to create an unfavorable press image or that his superiors had the authority to suspend without a warrant the protections of the Fourth Amendment."

Testifying in his own defense July 8, Ehrlichman denied that he had authorized the break-in. Much of his testimony centered on an Aug. 11, 1971 memorandum, on which Ehrlichman had initialed his approval of a "covert operation" as long as it was "not traceable" to the White House He contended that he thought he was approving "a legal, conventional investigation."

Among other developments concerning the Watergate Affair and related scandals during early July:

■ The Supreme Court July 8 heard oral arguments in the historic cases captioned "The United States vs. Richard M. Nixon" and "Richard M. Nixon vs. the United States." The primary issue had long been central to the Watergate case: the disputed doctrine of executive privilege and access to presidential tapes and documents by the special prosecutor. A second question had arisen more recently: whether a grand jury had the authority to name President Nixon as an unindicted co-conspirator in the Watergate cover-up. In three hours of oral presentation, punctuated with questions from the justices, the two sides re-emphasized positions they had taken in lower court proceedings, special prosecutor Leon Jaworski insisting that there was no constitutional basis for a sweeping claim of privilege—especially when a criminal conspiracy was involved, and special presidential counsel James D. St. Clair maintaining that compliance with Jaworski's subpoena for tapes of 64 White House conversations would irrevocably weaken the presidency.

■ The House Judiciary Committee July 9 made public its own transcripts of a number of taped White House conversations which showed variations from the White House version released April 30. The committee transcripts indicated that President Nixon was more involved in the Watergate cover-up than portrayed in the White House version. On July 11, the committee released 4,133 pages of the evidence it had assembled in its impeachment inquiry dealing with the Watergate break-in and its aftermath.

DAYTON DAILY NEWS
Dayton, Ohio, July 6, 1974

It will be unpoetic injustice if former presidential aide John Ehrlichman is allowed to wiggle out of the blame for approving the break-in at a psychiatrist's office on the grounds that he approved only a "covert operation" and not a "break-in."

If Mr. Ehrlichman's defense succeeds, the Nixon presidency's perversion of language and the resulting distortion of reality will have been accepted as excuses for otherwise inexcusable acts, a closed-loop, self-perpetuating system in which the mere act of misnaming things changes them.

Like the President himself, Mr. Nixon's aides spoke a kind of twilight quasi-language. Fear it as Newspeak, as writer George Orwell did, or merely disdain it as bureaucratic bland, it is an exercise in selective obfuscation. It is meant to delude the public by draining acts of their emotional content, but it no less deludes its users, by inserting an insulating layer of verbal fuzz between what they tell themselves they are doing and what they actually are doing.

Thus "covert operation" for "break-in." It sounds ever so much nicer.

It would have been difficult even for Mr. Ehrlichman to have said yes if one of his operatives had told him that, in order to get dirt with which to smear Mr. Ellsberg for releasing the Pentagon Papers, it would be necessary to break into the psychiatrist's office and steal the confidential medical records. How much easier to approve a covert operation in the interests of national security to secure raw data for the evaluation of Mr. Ellsberg's psychological profile.

But if the operation was to be legitimate, why did Mr. Ehrlichman ask to be assured that it would be untraceable? And since the FBI already had honestly asked to look at the medical records and had been turned down, what means but dishonest ones remained for a covert operation? The White House operatives had to break in and steal the records or to shoplift them during business hours or had to con the psychiatrist out of them by fraud.

It may be something of a genuine surprise to many of Mr. Nixon's aides, indeed to the President himself, that they were not just misbehaving like sly boys but in fact were acting criminally. They stretched language in two directions in order to tell themselves otherwise.

In one direction, they misnamed their political opponents "enemies" and so began to treat them as such and called the release of the Pentagon Papers a national security menace rather calling it what it really was, an annoying but not serious security breach, a perhaps infuriating but a minor political embarrassment. And in the other direction, they rendered their burglaries into covert operations and their acts of political sabotage into mere dirty tricks.

Mr. Nixon and his presidency cannot be exonerated on the basis of their own misapplied language but must be specifically condemned for it. To excuse criminal acts because of their prior distortion would be to establish unreality as the official reality of the nation.

TULSA DAILY WORLD

Tulsa, Okla., July 15, 1974

ONE BY ONE, like trees being chopped down in a forest, the former aides of PRESIDENT NIXON are falling to prosecution axes in Court. The latest is the biggest to date—JOHN EHRLICHMAN, whom the PRESIDENT once called "my right arm."

Convicted with three other men of conspiring to violate the civil liberties of DANIEL ELLSBERG's psychiatrist, EHRLICHMAN will appeal the jury verdict. . . . also three others holding him guilty of lying. But his position obviously has been weakened.

A man like ERLICHMAN does not fall gently; he comes down with a crash. For he was one of the strong ones in the NIXON Administration, one who disdained the apologies and contrition of some of his former colleagues. The memory is clear of his testimony before the Senate Watergate Committee—tough, unyielding, trading blow for blow with his questioners.

In his trial EHRLICHMAN contended he did not authorize the break-in at the office of Dr. LEWIS FIELDING in 1971. But there was evidence that he "approved" a memo approving a "covert" operation to examine medical files in the office. The jury apparently felt this was enough to make him part of the conspiracy.

Judge GERHARD GESELL cut the ground from under EHRLICHMAN's defense when he told the jury any kind of entry, "surreptitious or otherwise," without a search warrant is enough for a search to be illegal.

"When a Government agency invades an area in which there is a legitimate expectation of privacy, to look through such papers without permission, that is a search," the Judge said.

Legal questions will be fought out in the appeal, but as of now the former White House team has been dealt another staggering blow. And it is clear that the justification of almost anything in the name of national security or patriotism will not go far. Meanwhile, a pattern of guilt is being woven in the Court trials, even though the ELLSBERG case is not a direct part of the Watergate cover-up.

One may or may not sympathize with EHRLICHMAN and his objectives, but there is an unmistakable irony in his conviction. While he stands judged guilty of association with an illegal theft, ELLSBERG — whose own disclosure of secret Pentagon papers brought on the break-in — goes free.

Long Island Press

Jamaica, N.Y., July 15, 1974

A District of Columbia jury of six men and six women has struck a significant blow for constitutional government that should have a far-reaching effect on those who think they are above the law.

By convicting John D. Ehrlichman, formerly President Nixon's chief domestic adviser, and three others of conspiracy to violate the civil rights of Dr. Daniel Ellsberg's psychiatrist, the jury reaffirmed the protections of the 4th Amendment.

"The right of the people to be secure in their persons, houses, papers and effects, against unreasonable searches and seizures, shall not be violated . . ." says Article IV of the Bill of Rights. Guided by a thoughtful charge by U.S. District Court Judge Gerhard A. Gesell, the jury took little more than three hours to reach a verdict.

Mr. Ehrlichman's lawyers, and those of his codefendants, did not deny that a "covert operation" was planned in order to see Dr. Lewis J Fielding's files on Dr. Ellsberg. But Mr. Ehrlichman's defense was that he did not specifically authorize a "break-in" or "illegal entry." The defense also tried to claim that national security was at stake, but Judge Gesell refused to allow such an approach, insisting that at issue was a burglary, not national security.

In his charge to the jury, the judge said "a search in the constitutional sense is an intrusion or exploration by government agents of an area which one would normally expect to remain private. A physical break-in is not essential." The jury took it from there, reaching the unavoidable conclusion that Dr. Fielding's rights had been violated.

By its verdict, the jury did more than make Mr. Ehrlichman the sixth former Nixon administration official to be convicted of or plead guilty to a crime. It reinforced that point that unfortunately seems to need repeating all too often: The law must apply to everyone equally or there can be no rule of law.

If those entrusted with enforcing the law break it themselves, then how can there ever be respect for law? That was the point made so forcefully by the Warren Supreme Court, in such decisions as Miranda. It was repeated by the Burger Court in rejecting former Attorney General John Mitchell's circumvention of civil liberties, supposedly in the name of law and order.

Now a jury of his peers has determined that a top presidential aide also must abide by the constitution—and if he doesn't, must be punished. The case will be appealed, particularly Judge Gesell's handling of it, but we would be surprised if the higher courts interpret the Constitution any differently than Judge Gesell did last week.

The Miami Herald

Miami, Fla., July 13, 1974

JUDGE Gerhard Gesell, having charged and sent the jury to its deliberations in the "plumbers case," described John Ehrlichman's defense accurately and succinctly Friday:

". . . his defense has been one of darting and dodging around the various issues in the case, but there is no coherent statement of his defense."

The jury did not hear that, but it knew it, and less than six hours later it returned a verdict of guilty. Conspiracy and perjury, before-and-after consequences of the break-in at Daniel Ellsberg's psychiatrist's office, translate now into a possible prison sentence of 25 years — not as an effort to protect the national security.

Convicted with Ehrlichman were G. Gordon Liddy, the stonewall expert now behind one, and Bernard Barker and Eugenio Martinez, the perhaps sincere but certainly bumbling Miami-based Cubans who even now, knowing what they did not then, have said they would do it all over again in the name of patriotism, or perhaps just imagined anti-communism which is the same thing to them.

Ehrlichman, President Nixon's erstwhile domestic affairs advisor and one of the two "finest public servants" in Mr. Nixon's experience at the time he announced their resignations, served neither the public nor the President in this sordid affair.

Whatever defense efforts he made — surrounded and interspersed by key-point losses of memory, extraneous comment, evasive non-replies and sardonic smiles — hinged on the national security claim.

But, as Judge Gesell pointed out, there were legal means available to stop White House leaks, to investigate possible sources of those leaks, to search offices, even, if a magistrate or judge or constituted authorities were told of the need and authorized the action.

Instead, the job was handled personally. And privately. And illegally.

And after the deed, Ehrlichman lied to the FBI and to a Watergate grand jury about what he knew and when he knew it and some things he said he didn't know but which White House documents proved he did.

After the verdict, Ehrlichman said he had instructed his lawyers to prepare an appeal. He said he had feared that a fair trial would be impossible in the District of Columbia. That he has an abiding faith in the American judicial system. The appeal, the legal protections — they are all his to utilize as he can. It is a civil right.

Breaking into a doctor's office against his will, however, violated a civil right, too. And in this case, violated a nation as well.

THE WALL STREET JOURNAL.
New York, N.Y., July 8, 1974

The Supreme Court today takes up the lawsuit for more presidential tapes. If the case were a straightforward suit from the House Judiciary Committee asking for impeachment evidence, we would have not the least trouble declaring our sympathies with the committee. In fact the suit comes instead from Special Prosecutor Leon Jaworski, and at best we can offer only agonized support.

The Jaworski suit is clouded by several factors that would not trouble a congressional suit. There is, first of all, a jurisdictional problem arising because Mr. Jaworski is in effect suing his superior, asking the courts to referee an intramural dispute in the Executive Branch. Even more importantly, Mr. Jaworski asks for the evidence not for the purposes of impeachment, but more for the purposes of a mere criminal trial—his prosecution of John Mitchell, H. R. Haldeman and others for alleged participation in the Watergate cover-up.

This cloud causes a special problem for those of us who generally believe in the principle of judicial restraint. Indeed, Philip B. Kurland, the University of Chicago's distinguished constitutional lawyer, recently roasted the court for expediting the Jaworski suit. Are we to believe, he asked, that a criminal trial cannot be postponed while the normal course of justice runs? No, the only reason the case was expedited was its relation to impeachment; everyone assumes that the evidence that goes to Mr. Jaworski will also go to the House committee. But, Mr. Kurland reminds us, a court is supposed to decide the case before it, not some other legal case or social controversy.

At the same time, we think the courts are the appropriate agency to decide the limits of executive privilege. We do not think the question of executive confidentiality should be left to the total discretion of the President in any and all cases. Nor do we think the question should be resolved by a unilateral assertion of the congressional power to impeach. Only the courts can draw an ongoing body of standards, that is, a body of law, to balance executive privilege against other necessary principles.

In such a balancing, a congressional impeachment investigation would have an exceedingly powerful claim. It would seem to us even more powerful if the suit were brought by the Senate, after articles of impeachment were framed, for this would define the issue and put limits on any fishing expedition. But even at the House stage, especially with some check from the courts to limit obviously frivolous uses, it would seem to us most difficult to overcome the argument that the President should not be the judge of the relevancy of evidence in his own case.

Technically, Mr. Jaworski's suit is not about the President's case, and thus his claim is far less powerful, even if jurisdictional issues are put aside on the grounds that the controversy is after all a real one. In the first instance, Mr. Jaworski's suit asks for evidence to prosecute criminal cases. In principle the Executive Branch, and thus ultimately the President, clearly has the power to withhold evidence, dropping a case rather than discloing evidence it feels would harm the public interest. The Executive does this routinely in dropping a case rather than revealing a legitimate wiretap or other information source it feels it should protect.

Yet technicalities are not everything, and clearly this is no ordinary criminal case. The President has actually been named as a co-conspirator in the alleged crime. If a precedent is created surely the necessity of convincing a grand jury to cite the President would put a reasonably solid check on frivolous assaults on executive privilege. So a ruling for Mr. Jaworski need not be based simply on large political grounds; there are responsible narrow grounds on which to uphold him without setting a sweeping precedent, though there are also responsible grounds for denying the suit.

We would have no quarrel with and even indeed a certain respect for a ruling that said, take away this case and bring us the one that presents the real issue squarely. For ourselves, though, we think we would uphold Mr. Jaworski, queasy about the general principle of judicial restraint, and aware that under our own legal reasoning there would be a good measure of *ad hoc* desire to do what we can to clarify the current political controversy.

The News American
Baltimore, Md., July 10, 1974

FEW SESSIONS of the United States Supreme Court have been so obviously important as Monday's dramatic hearing on the extent of Presidential power. More than 6,000 advance requests for admission to the 300-seat chamber and its historic legal confrontation had to be rejected, no matter how important the applicant.

Throughout the nation, before and after the event, newspapers and the broadcast media have covered every facet of the great showdown. Anyone who doesn't know what issues are involved simply hasn't been paying attention. No people have ever been so thoroughly informed — and this is no place to repeat those issues.

They are so intricate and of such potential for good and bad on both sides, furthermore, than non-expert opinion here would serve little useful purpose. What seems paramount at the moment is that the issues at last are being considered by the Supreme Court, where they should have been placed long ago. And that's an opinion The Hearst Newspapers have held ever since Congress and President Nixon began arguing his claims of sweeping "executive privilege."

The other basic attitude which must be voiced here today is a disappointment that the issues to be decided have been so legally clouded. President Nixon originally challenged Congress on its right to compel his release of material he considered privileged. This is the clear-cut showdown issue which should be before the Supreme Court. But it is not.

Instead the fundamental dispute is being approached peripherally through the suit for release of 64 White House tapes brought by special Watergate prosecutor Leon Jaworski, a Nixon appointee. This could, possibly, lead to a non-conclusive Supreme Court decision holding that the key issue is beyond its authority since the argument — technically — is one solely within the executive branch.

There are a variety of connective points, to be sure, and no one can predict or even guess what the court will rule. When the ruling comes, however, it is bound to have a major effect on impeachment moves and possibly on the present three-way balance of government authority. Until then the nation has reason to be reassured by the judicial process now approaching its momentous climax.

Anybody who thinks our democratic system of government isn't strong is out of his head. Here, when men joust for ultimate powers, they do so through legal maneuvers. This astonishes many foreign observers. In their countries, equally bitter power disputes long ago would likely have resulted in civic violence and even attempts at revolution.

AKRON BEACON JOURNAL
Akron, Ohio, July 13, 1974

THE ISSUES of law in the historic case of United States of America v. Nixon will be decided by the Supreme Court and that decision will probably be announced within the next two weeks.

But the argument of the President's attorney, James St. Clair, that a decision upholding the subpena for 64 White House tape recordings will "inevitably and inexorably" draw the court into the impeachment process is patently ridiculous.

Anything affecting the President — even letters to the editor, for or against impeachment — could conceivably have an effect on the final decision of one or more congressmen. But the final decision is still up to the House of Representatives.

As established by the Constitution, the only role of the Supreme Court in an impeachment process is for the chief justice to preside at the Senate trial of a President.

It is considered probable that a court decision upholding the subpena would influence some fence-sitters in the House to vote to impeach the President. But the other side of that coin is that a decision supporting the President on executive privilege could influence those same fence-sitters to vote against impeachment.

The White House lost the last round in the legal battle for the tapes, and the case wound up in the lap of the Supreme Court because the White House asked the court to accept it.

Now Mr. St. Clair is arguing that a decision to uphold the lower court would interfere in a proper function of the House of Representatives. He asked the court to involve itself, but he only wants it to "interfere" in his client's favor.

A court decision is not, of course, interference. It in no way binds any member of Congress on any vote. If it influences congressmen, it is only one of many influences on their individual decisions.

To be sure, congressmen will be aware of the court's decision. And if it upholds the order for the tapes, congressmen will be watching the President to see if he obeys the order.

Those properly considering impeachment are concerned with the President, not with the Supreme Court. If the subpena is upheld, the House will first be concerned with whether it is obeyed. Then concern will be directed toward the evidence, if any, contained in the tapes.

Mr. St. Clair cannot be blamed for arguing the case most favorable to his client. But the argument that the court, if it rules against his client, would be involving itself in a process reserved for the House just won't wash.

Minneapolis Tribune

Minneapolis, Minn., July 11, 1974

On April 29, in releasing transcripts of some White House tapes, President Nixon said he wanted "there to be no question remaining about the fact that the president has nothing to hide in this matter." Since those transcripts were damaging to the president, some Americans might have concluded that Mr. Nixon was—to use a phrase from one of the transcripts—finally taking "the hang-out road." This week, the House Judiciary Committee released its transcripts of the same tapes, and this fresh version shows that Mr. Nixon did hide something.

The House version contains additional information damaging to Mr. Nixon. Despite the committee's judicious or political effort to tone down the differences by citing its superior transcribing capabilities, an implication seems clear: The White House — by editing, laundering and omission — misrepresented some important conversations between the president and his aides.

One example:

According to the White House version, John Dean told the president on March 13, 1973: ". . . I think that Chuck (Colson) had knowledge that something was going on over there, but he didn't have any knowledge of the details of the specifics of the whole thing."

According to the Judiciary Committee version, Dean said: ". . . I think that Chuck had knowledge that something was going on over there. A lot of people around here had knowledge that something was going on over there. They didn't have any knowledge of the details of the specifics of, of the whole thing."

Another example:

The president's transcripts for March 22, a day after he claims he first learned of the Watergate cover-up, omitted a lengthy portion of a key conversation. The committee version includes it. In it, Mr. Nixon praises Dean's work in nearly getting the Watergate scandal "nailed down" until past the 1972 election. The president talks about "the plan," "containment" and "the scenario." He says: "I want you all to stonewall it, let them plead the Fifth Amendment, cover up or anything else, if it'll save it—save the plan."

The House transcripts suggest strongly that Mr. Nixon knew of and sanctioned the cover-up. They suggest that the cover-up continues to this day—and that even more damaging evidence against the president may well exist in other tapes that he has refused to give to the special prosecutor and the Judiciary Committee.

Tapes of 64 conversations are one of the Watergate issues now before the U.S. Supreme Court. James St. Clair, the president's attorney, said this week that even if the court rules against Mr. Nixon the president may decide, in the public interest, not to give them up. However, this week's disclosures by the Judiciary Committee suggest that Mr. Nixon's personal interest, not the public interest, is what is at stake in this dispute.

The House transcripts, unlike the president's, show that on March 13, 1973, the president rejected "the hang-out road"—in other words, the idea of telling the American people the whole truth about Watergate. He still does. The committee transcripts portray a president failing to live up to his oath to enforce the nation's laws faithfully.

Right now, Mr. Nixon and his men are engaged in stonewalling the Judiciary Committee, the special prosecutor and the American people. We hope that the Supreme Court knocks down that stone wall. But regardless of any Supreme Court action, we think the duty of the House of Representatives is now clearer than ever. That is to impeach the president and move the case of a president who says he has nothing to hide along to the Senate for trial.

Wisconsin State Journal

Milwaukee, Wis., July 12, 1974

The disclosure by the House Judiciary Committee of differences in the tape recorded conversations within the Oval Office of the White House regarding the alleged coverup of White House participation in the Watergate scandal are among the most shocking to be made so far in an outrageously shocking situation.

According to the Judiciary Committee version of the tapes reluctantly given it by President Nixon, the President encouraged his top aides to continue in the coverup plan.

"I want you all to stonewall it, let them plead the Fifth Amendment, cover up or anything else if it'll save it — save the plan," the President said according to the Committee version of the tapes.

The "plan" in the President's quotation was called "the coverup plan" by Nixon just a few minutes earlier in the same discussion: "But now — what — all that John Mitchell is arguing, then, is that now we, we use flexibility in order to get on with the coverup plan."

Those statements, regardless of the exact context, are about as damaging as anything to emerge so far as regarding the President's complicity in the coverup plan.

One can only wonder what more evidence could be held in the tapes which the President is refusing to give up, choosing rather to risk an unprecedented confrontation with the U.S. Supreme Court which is now deciding whether it feels the President can be legally required to turn over what he considers privileged communications.

Equally disturbing is the President's refusal to commit himself to go along with the Supreme Court decision when it is made.

As columnist Anthony Lewis notes elsewhere on the Page of Opinion today, when Nixon chose Warren E. Burger to be chief justice of the United States more than five years ago, he said:

"Respect for law in a nation is the most priceless asset a free people can have, and the chief justice and his associates are the ultimate custodians and guardians of that priceless asset."

While conceding that legal scholars may differ on just how powerful the Court is, Lewis argues with compelling logic that if the Court cannot decide such questions of evidence, privilege and procedure as raised by the tape case, just what is its legal function?

The Supreme Court must be empowered to resolve jurisdictional disputes or its status as a co-equal branch of government is meaningless.

The President has been much less than candid with Congress and the American people over the Watergate scandal and everything surrounding it.

Justice Lewis F. Powell, one of three Nixon appointees hearing the case, asked a pointed and necessary question of the President's lawyer during the opening argument. The question, which was never answered, was:

"What public interest is there in preserving secrecy about a criminal conspiracy?"

The historic confrontation between the three branches of government which is now being waged will no doubt set the tone of American democracy for years to come.

ERVIN PANEL REPORTS ON FUND ABUSES; CAMPAIGN FUND BILL GAINS IN HOUSE

The final report of the Senate Select Committee on Presidential Campaign Activities was released July 13. The report said the picture presented by its compilation of evidence demonstrated that "campaign practices must be effectively supervised and enforcement of the criminal laws vigorously pursued against all offenders—even those of high estate—if our free institutions are to survive." Accordingly, the report presented 35 recommendations for election campaign reform, including some endorsing legislation already passed by the Senate.

Among the major proposals: An independent and permanent office of "public attorney" with powers similar to those of the existing special prosecutor; A federal elections commission with supervisory and enforcement powers; Limits on cash campaign contributions by individuals, reforms in reporting procedures and restrictions on solicitation of campaign funds by presidential staff; and tightening of laws involving use of federal agencies to aid the election of candidates.

Although the report was adopted unanimously, two Democrats—Daniel K. Inouye (Hawaii) and Joseph M. Montoya (N.M.)—filed a joint statement advocating public campaign financing, a measure opposed by the full report.

Although the report concentrated on a review of the evidence disclosed during the Committee's hearings on the Watergate Affair, it also disclosed several alleged campaign abuses by Democratic presidential candidates. "It should be noted," the report declared, "that improprieties in campaign financing were not limited to any particular candidate or party." Sen. Hubert Humphrey (D, Minn.) was cited for several apparent violations of campaign financing laws, but the committee's investigation was hampered by his refusal to be interviewed by the committee staff, and by his campaign manager's refusal to testify under oath. Humphrey also did not fully comply with the committee's request for campaign records, the report stated. Alleged campaign abuses also occurred in Rep. Wilbur D. Mills' (D, Ark.) brief race for the Democratic presidential nomination. The committee said it was unable to make a complete study of Mills' campaign practices, however, because Mills ignored repeated requests from the committee for an interview and his campaign manager, like Humphrey's, refused to testify, citing his rights against self-incrimination.

The report was critical of Sen. George McGovern's (D, S.D.) resolution of his presidential campaign debt. Evidence was developed, the report stated, that as McGovern's campaign finance committees were making substantial transfers of funds to McGovern Senatorial committees in anticipation of a 1974 contest for his re-election to this Senate seat."

The House Administration Committee tentatively approved July 1 a major campaign spending bill after reversing a decision (made June 28) to eliminate a proposal authorizing the use of limited public funds to help finance Presidential primary elections. The proposed bill was less sweeping than a bill passed by the Senate in April. One of the major differences between the two bills was that the House bill would not provide funds to finance House and Senate campaigns.

Boston Herald American
Boston, Mass., July 1, 1974

Though the stories, perhaps, haven't received as much attention as they deserved, reports last week that Sen. Hubert Humphrey and Rep. Wilbur Mills received big campaign donations from the Milk Lobby as well as illegal corporate contributions during their unsuccessful bids for the presidency in 1972 have raised at least a few eyebrows.

Senator Humphrey denies that there was any wrongdoing involved, and Representative Mills has been unavailable or unwilling to comment.

But whatever the truth of the matter, it does suggest several things. For one, it indicates that President Nixon and the Republicans didn't own a patent on campaign irregularities or shenanigans.

Perhaps the parallel isn't exact, but when you put the latest reports next to some of the things that have been said about the President's indiscretions—and his refusal to help his critics make their case against him—there is an obvious double-standard.

Here we have a case of two very prominent Democratic politicians, both of whom have been sharply critical of Mr. Nixon's handling of the Watergate affair and his refusal to turn over evidence, accused of committing the same kind of indiscretions

And what is their response? Well, for one thing, like the President, they're trying to protect themselves. Their top campaign aides took the Fifth Amendment when they were asked to testify about the matter before the Senate Watergate Committee.

That committee's chairman, Sen. Sam Ervin, sent Representative Mills two letters asking him to supply information concerning the matter—and Mills declined to do so. It is important to note that those letters were sent to Mills last January and February, and it seems both logical and fair to ask why we didn't hear about them 'til June.

Was Sam Ervin so busy complaining about the President's refusal to turn over tapes and documents that he couldn't even lodge one mild complaint against Mills during the last six months?

And that's not all. Senator Humphrey's campaign manager Jack Chestnut now admits that he destroyed all of HHH's early 1972 campaign financial records.

Can you imagine what would have happened if the President or someone else at the White House had burned those tapes? The howls of indignation and outrage were deafening enough when they were turned over one by one or edited and released in transcript form.

What's the difference, really, between Mr. Nixon's—or Senator Humphrey's or Representative Mills'—refusal to cooperate? And how different is either from President Kennedy's refusal to turn over information to a Senate committee in 1962, or the Senate's refusal to comply with a subpoena from a federal court in the same year? They, too, were based on the same doctrine of the separation of powers invoked by President Nixon today.

Unless someone can explain the difference, it strikes us as simply a matter of whose ox has been gored.

ARKANSAS DEMOCRAT

Little Rock, Ark., July 14, 1974

The public's growing impatience with the length of Watergate is matched only by its mounting disgust at the revelations.

If the original Watergate tape transcripts released by the President were not enough to hurry impeachment, those released last week surely are.

The new transcripts, which in the words of one House Judiciary Committee member, show a "coverup of the coverup," clearly point to President Nixon's deep involvement in the scheme and lay a charge of obstruction of justice squarely at his feet. One recording of March 22, 1973, tells it all when the President says, "I want you all to stonewall it, let them plead the Fifth Amendment, coverup or anything else, if it will save it — save the plan."

That ought to do it. It is difficult to imagine anything else that could more clearly show conspiracy and deception. The actual word — "coverup" — is spoken by the President. Then, there's the fact that this particular conversation was itself concealed by the White House in an attempt at more deception, more obstruction.

So why should there be more delay? Why does the Judiciary Committee need more evidence, more hearings, more investigations? Surely it now has all it needs to make up its mind what to report to the full House of Representatives. Does it think the President has done something so serious that it justifies impeachment? Prolonging the agony will not ease the nation's pains but only delay the healing.

In the meantime, America suffers on many fronts and is crying out for relief. Inflation is eating us alive. Business is in the doldrums. Solutions for our energy problems lie dormant. A national health program is on the shelf. Tax reform is hardly being debated. Even the proposal to eliminate campaign expenses — the genesis of Watergate — is bogged down in committee. Everything awaits the end of the impeachment trauma.

But the god of politics must be served. It is apparent that the impeachment timetable has been geared to the fall elections. Both Democrats and Republicans see possible gains in stretching out the process past the first Tuesday in November. Therefore, we witness the strange spectacle of leaders of both parties, for their separate but different reasons, working toward the same questionable end. Once again politics wins, the public loses.

Those in Congress wanting a speedy end to the scandal should take their cue from Mr. Nixon. They should "stonewall" all attempts at further delay. They should insist that enough is enough and demand that the House committee conclude its task.

The Hartford Courant

Hartford, Conn., July 12, 1974

America is getting numb. We are losing our ability and capacity to react. And this is a dangerous condition. Inability to remove one's self from peril, whether through lethargy, exhaustion or sheer fascination, usually is fatal. This holds for sub-zero weather, and certainly chilling Watergate.

The nation and for that matter, the world, are now witnessing what may be the concluding scenario of Watergate, and most viewers are spent. Many find it difficult to summon enough of what it takes to rouse the mind to an awareness of what is really happening, and in this event-drugged tendency to lie down and escape, heritage risks forfeit.

This was predictable. Far too many persons now appear willing, even anxious, to be done with the whole affair on any terms. Far too many persons are now viewing the final act from the back row and as many more have even left the theater. The play has been just too long.

Testimony — both corroborative and conflicting — before the Watergate grand jury, the Ervin committee and the House Judiciary Committee has reached many millions of words, sensation has been piled on sensation, charges and denials have cascaded upon us, days and months have gone by, other affairs of living have pressed upon us until the average person can but falsely pretend a capability for reasonably objective assessment of the Watergate mess.

The news these past few days has completely covered the latest developments in the interminable drama of Watergate. Enough is enough. There has been enough of pre-trial. President Nixon deserves to be impeached and tried; only in this way can the question of his culpability or non-culpability be determined.

In the name of fairness, and for the sake of the people of the United States, let's get on with definitive proceedings, and begin restoring this nation to the world of the living.

The Standard-Times

New Bedford, Mass., July 12, 1974

The House Judiciary Committee's release of eight tapes of President Nixon's Watergate conversations seems likely to have two principal effects:

1. Since the President's conversations differ markedly from the edited transcripts made public by the White House, these differences will damage his case in the impeachment inquiry. Specific among the major discrepancies between the two sets of transcripts are these:

— The committee's version contains several comments by Mr. Nixon that could indicate that he knew of and sanctioned the Watergate coverup before March 21, 1973 — the date he says he first learned the facts of the case.

— The committee's transcripts include additional statements by the President that could also indicate his acquiesence in a payoff to buy the silence of one of the Watergate conspirators.

— The newly released documents contain suggestions by the President that his aides "stonewall" the investigating authorities rather than tell them the truth. In the White House transcript of a March 22, 1973 conversation between Nixon and John W. Dean 3d, his former counsel, the President is quoted as saying, ". . . in order to get off the coverup line." In the committee's transcript, the President says, ". . . in order to get on with the coverup plan."

— The President is depicted in the committee's version as having been pleased with the work of Dean in keeping the cover on the Watergate case through the 1972 election.

Thus the immediate result of the committee's action will almost certainly be a fresh erosion of White House credibility.

2. The second result of making public this new mass of unevaluated evidence — the committee refrained from making any judgment about the obviously important differences between the transcripts — seems likely to be forfeiture in major degree of the role of committee members in deciding what is to happen.

Members of the Judiciary Committee are now saying, in effect, to the public, "Here is the information we have, inconsistencies and all; what do you want us to do with it?" From now on, the committee will be bombarded by public and political pressure in several directions and a decision — whether or not to move in the direction of impeachment — that ought to be made solely on the basis of evidence and law will be pushed, shoved, and eventually shaped by that pressure.

Thus, the irony is that, although the committee members now have more evidence and information than ever, there is a very good chance that whatever decision they make is less likely than ever to be based exclusively on the evidence and information.

In the meantime, assuming that the shocking discrepancies between the White House transcripts and those of the committee stand up — and assuming, as we do, that the President approved the creation of those discrepancies, implicitly or explicitly — we restate our original thesis that he should resign — whether or not he has broken any law.

Mr. Nixon's White House cannot be believed, and an unbelievable leader cannot lead.

THE DALLAS TIMES HERALD

Dallas, Tex., July 4, 1974

WHEN THE U.S. House of Representatives returns from its holiday recess, one of its most important tasks will be approval of a strong and effective campaign finance reform bill.

The measure approved this week by the House Administration Committee has some good points, already in bills passed by the Senate, but there are so many loopholes in the proposal that it falls far short of what the public expects.

In particular, the House committee bill puts Congress itself in charge of supervising campaign finances, a move which means that there would be no more enforcement of any new law than there has been of other campaign finance laws.

The Senate bill creates an independent supervisory commission with its own lawyers and powers of prosecution to enforce the new law. The House version, which faces a floor fight on several issues, leaves prosecution to the Justice Department. That agency has not been noted for diligence in enforcing campaign finance laws; in addition, under the House bill, Congress' own supervisory board would have to request Justice Department action.

There are good sections in the House bill, including limiting cash contributions to $100, ceilings on congressional and presidential campaign spending and better disclosure rules.

But there is no provision for public funds to supplement private donations in congressional races, which implies that Congress is ready to clean up presidential contests but not its own.

We urge the House members to rewrite their committee's bill to bring it more in line with the Senate measure. Genuine campaign finance reform is needed, urgently and now.

The Boston Globe

Boston, Mass., July 4, 1974

The US House of Representatives is about to debate a campaign financing bill drafted by its House Administration Committee and correctly described by Common Cause as a "grossly inadequate" and "loophole-ridden" response to the need for reform.

The bill is the work of Rep. Wayne Hays (D-Ohio), chairman of the committee and vociferous opponent of public financing of campaigns. It is his answer both to the sweeping reform package passed by the Senate and to the urgings of legislators from both parties that a meaningful bill be on the floor before the 1974 elections.

Mr. Hays will try to limit debate so that only certain amendments to his bill can be offered. We see little justification for such restrictions in this case. At the very least, there should be the opportunity for full discussion of those key elements of the Senate bill which were left out of the House version.

First, the House bill includes a weak enforcement mechanism putting Congress in control of the agency that is supposed to oversee campaign financing practices of its own members. Under the Senate bill, as in a new Massachusetts statute, the laws would be policed by an independent elections commission with investigatory and enforcement powers.

The fight for an independent commission has been led in the committee by Rep. William Frenzel (R-Minn.) and he will offer his amendment on the floor of the House.

Second, the House bill makes provision for public financing on a matching basis only for presidential primaries and elections and party presidential nominating conventions.

When the bill reaches the floor, Reps. John Anderson (R-Ill.) and Morris Udall (D-Ill.) will offer amendments to provide public financing on a matching basis for congressional candidates as well.

The bill is not all bad. It places a limit of $100 on cash contributions and proposes a strict limit on the amount of money which can be given by any individual to a candidate. The donation limit should spell the end of the practice of contributions in the six figures buying access, influence and ambassadorships.

But on balance the committee bill is an embarrassment to the Congress in the light of the financial legerdemain of the Nixon campaign and the more recent charges being leveled at Democratic stalwarts such as Sen. Hubert Humphrey (D-Minn.) and Rep. Wilbur Mills (D-Ark.).

What Mr. Hays was unwilling or unable to do in committee it will be up to Democratic leadership, including Majority Leader Thomas P. (Tip) O'Neill Jr. (D-Mass.), to do in the full House.

Failure on campaign financing reform will not only vitiate much of the good that can come out of the revelations of the past year, but will also be a major campaign issue for every congressman in the fall. And we intend to print the rollcall.

San Jose Mercury

San Jose, Calif., July 6, 1974

The House of Representatives finally has taken some positive action on a campaign finance reform bill, with the House Administration Committee clearing a measure it had held captive for several months.

But the bill falls seriously short of the expectations of citizens' groups that have been most active in the campaign finance reform battle. Common Cause, for example, attacks the House version as "loophole-ridden legislation which places members of Congress firmly in control of campaign finance law enforcement."

One of the chief features of California's election reform law, Proposition 9, was the establishment of an independent commission to enforce public disclosure requirements and campaign spending limitations.

Congress hasn't shown any enthusiasm for having its members' campaign activities monitored by an independent agency. Campaign spending records currently are handled by congressional employes. Under the so-called reform bill things would remain essentially unchanged. Instead of a couple of high-ranking congressional employes charged with the job, it would be assigned to a seven-member board comprised of four members of Congress and three congressional aides. That's hardly reform. As Rep. William Frezel (R-Minn.) observes, "If Congress' response to Watergate is to place its own members in charge of federal elections, then it will be hard to blame the public for becoming even more cynical and alienated."

Another serious deficiency campaign finance reform bill is its failure to provide for any form of public financing for congressional elections. The bill includes fairly generous public financing provisions for presidential candidates, but rejects the same for Congress.

If over-reliance on large contributors and special interest groups is destructive to the presidency, it is equally bad in the legislative branch of government.

Congress cannot claim to be conscientiously addressing the campaign finance reform issue until it shapes legislation that provides for an independent enforcement agency and public financing for congressional as well as presidential campaigns.

The San Diego Union

San Diego, Calif., July 8, 1974

We are gratified that the staff of the Senate Watergate Committee took time from its investigation of the financing of President Nixon's 1972 campaign to delve into the books of other candidates. We would be equally gratified if the conscience of Democrats proves to be as sensitive to these findings as it has to the disclosures involing the Committee to Re-Elect the President.

Senate investigators have found that Sen. George McGovern is using $340,416 left over from his 1972 presidential campaign to help finance his current campaign for re-election in South Dakota. The ethical issue of using campaign money for a purpose other than that for which it was solicited is compounded by the fact that the McGovern presidential organization has pleaded poverty to duck payment of some of its 1972 campaign bills. In fact, the Watergate committee found that 37 corporations have settled such accounts for $35,322 less than the full amount—an arrangement open to interpretation as corporate contributions to McGovern's campaign, which would be illegal.

The committee also has discovered that Sen. Hubert Humphrey used a blind trust to conceal the fact he was funnelling $112,000 of his own money into his 1972 presidential campaign, just before a new law took effect making such use of personal assets unlawful. Meanwhile the Justice Department has evidence that a dairy cooperative under fire for its support of the Nixon campaign also made illegal contributions to the presidential campaign of Rep. Wilbur Mills.

We doubt if the public will be satisfied if the Democrat-controlled congress files these disclosures away just because the Watergate committee is now disbanded. They deserve the same thorough examination that Congress and the Justice Department have given to similar money-laundering and other irregularities in the financing of the Nixon campaign.

Campaign ethics have become a political issue in 1974, and a legitimate one. However, if the Democrats try to exploit the issue as a partisan one, we will have the spectacle this fall of a lot of pots calling the kettles black.

Newsday

Long Island, N.Y., July 7, 1974

The Watergate break-in, which was financed with political campaign funds, happened more than two years ago. The milk industry's political slush fund and Robert Vesco's cash-filled attache case made headlines more than a year ago. A dozen top corporations and corporate officers have since been convicted of making illegal campaign contributions, and the misuse of campaign funds is a vital issue in the House's presidential impeachment hearings. But, as syndicated columnist Mary McGrory pointed out recently, "only one issue is proceeding more slowly than impeachment through the House of Representatives. This is the other son of Watergate—campaign reform."

Hardly any member of the House is on record as being *against* campaign reform. After Watergate, that would be like coming out against motherhood. But simply because a congressman isn't against an idea doesn't necessarily mean he's for it. Sometimes the only way to get a true image of a politician's stand is to view it through a mirror.

Only a handful of congressmen have voiced any displeasure over the fact that Administration Committee Chairman Wayne Hays (D-Ohio) spent 18 leisurely months "studying" campaign reform before finally sending a bill to the House floor last week. As long as the reform bill was tied up in Hays' committee, nobody had to vote on the record, and the same old laws that give incumbents a decided edge in raising funds at election time remained on the books.

The bill Hays has let out is only the shell of a much tougher measure already approved by the Senate. Unlike the Senate version, it ignores the question of public financing for congressional elections, although it does provide partial public funding for presidential campaigns—after a last-minute switch in Hays' committee. And perhaps the biggest failing of the House bill is that it doesn't set up adequate machinery to enforce new election laws.

But now the full House has the opportunity to correct these shortcomings—if its members are so inclined. We call the attention of those still on the fence to recent polls showing that the public wants basic campaign reform by a two-to-one margin, and to the recent election in California where the electorate gave many more votes to a campaign reform referendum than to any candidate on the ballot.

The Philadelphia Inquirer

Philadelphia, Pa., July 8, 1974

Congress now is returning from the Fourth of July recess, during which its members have almost unanimously celebrated the joys and traditions of American democracy. Its members — or those in the House anyway—will almost immediately face a challenge which will draw the line between those whose conception of democracy is merely clambake oratory and those who want to make it work democratically.

The issue that will divide them is campaign funding reform.

Few things in the public process are simple, and the financing of politics, its evils and its strengths, is no exception. But it is hard to imagine that two years after the Watergate break-in there can be many right-minded people in the United States who are not appalled by what lay as its root cause: a political financing system that invites big-money perverson.

The Senate has responded well. On April 11 it passed a bill that offers immensely constructive therapy for those ills. It would, most importantly, establish an independent campaign spending enforcement agency and set up long-overdue public funding of election expenses, including matching grant arrangements for Congressional candidates. It would set ceilings on the size of individual contributions and over-all limits on spending by any candidate.

The House meanwhile has stood by its tradition on such reforms — one of delaying when possible and emasculating when delay fails. The House Administration Committee, under the chairmanship of Democratic Sen. Wayne Hays of Ohio, has produced a bill which will go to the House floor this week. It makes mockery of the Senate's efforts and the national needs.

The Hays bill was analyzed by Common Cause, the public interest lobby that has been a pre-eminent campaign-reform force. Its conclusion: ,

"The House Committee's bill is a grossly inadequate response to the money-in-politics scandals that have been the underpinning of the Watergate story. The loophole-ridden proposal virtually ignores the growing public demand for true reform of American political campaign financing."

Those are strong terms. But they could be stronger, for if the committee's bill should be passed, under the guise of a real reform, it could cripple the chances of any actual improvement.

An impressive number of Congressmen are as appalled by the Hays committee's bill as is Common Cause — and ourselves. A number of them have promised efforts to amend into the bill, on the House floor, the main principles and the teeth that the Senate wisely approved.

Those efforts deserve the support of everyone who shares with us the conclusion that American politics is being intolerably corrupted by legislation-through-contribution. Every member of the House this autumn faces re-election or retirement. How each Congressman stands on the campaign-reform issue could very well decide which it is to be for him.

DESERET NEWS

Salt Lake City, Utah, July 5, 1974

When Congress gets back to work early next week after its holiday recess, the moment of truth will be at hand for campaign finance reform.

The truth is that unless the House Administration Committee changes its collective mind, the country could get stuck with an inadequate law.

The proposed law which the committee plans to send to the floor shortly after the Independence Day recess is one which would leave the impression of reform without really getting tough on campaign abuses. Among other weaknesses in the measure, it would:

— Place responsibility for enforcement in the hands of a seven-member board, six of whom would be members of Congress or their direct employees. This arrangement creates a built-in temptation to look the other way when campaign abuses arise.

— Create new loopholes by no longer requiring the disclosure of many campaign expenditures that now must be reported.

— Allow congressional election-law committees to veto rules and regulations proposed by election-law officials.

— Permit the election board controlled by Congress to give "advisory" opinions to candidates about the legality of contemplated campaign financing actions, which for all practical purposes likely would absolve the candidates from legal liability.

— Enable candidates under investigation for violations to keep the investigation secret by refusing to let the election board make it public. Yet one of the most effective ways to enforce campaign reforms is to publicize violations. The very potential of such publicity could, in fact, deter many violations.

No wonder that Common Cause objects to the House bill as a "grossly inadequate response to the money-in-politics scandals that have been the underpinning of the Watergate story. The loophole-ridden proposal virtually ignores the growing public demand for true reform of American political campaign financing."

The shortcomings of the House bill stand out in even sharper contrast when the measure is compared to the Senate's campaign spending reforms. Among the Senate reforms is a more truly independent elections commission to police the campaign law. Members would be nominated by the President from persons recommended by Congress. Appointees would be confirmed by the Senate. Moreover, the commission would have power to issue subpoenas; initiate civil court actions to bring about compliance, and impose fines. In the past 18 months, 16 states have created similar commissions to oversee state campaign finance laws.

Must Americans wait for another major scandal of Watergate proportions before Congress will clean up campaign financing abuses?

HOUSE JUDICIARY GROUP APPROVES THREE ARTICLES OF IMPEACHMENT

The House Judiciary Committee recessed July 30 after approving three articles of impeachment charging President Nixon with obstruction of justice in connection with the Watergate scandal, abuse of presidential powers and attempting to impede the impeachment process by defying committee subpoenas for evidence.

The committee's final deliberations, which were nationally televised, began July 24 with a motion by Rep. Harold D. Donohue (D, Mass.), "I move that the committee report to the House a resolution, together with articles, impeaching the President of the United States, Richard M. Nixon."

The first article, proposed by Paul Sarbanes (D, Md.), was adopted July 27 by a 27–11 vote. Six Republicans joined the panel's 21 Democrats in voting for impeachment. The Sarbanes proposal specifically charged Nixon with failure "to take care that the laws be faithfully executed" by engaging "personally and through his subordinates and agents in a course of conduct or plan designed to delay, impede and obstruct" the investigation into the June 17, 1972 break-in at the headquarters of the Democratic National Committee at the Watergate complex in Washington. The article also accused Nixon of covering up for, concealing and protecting those responsible,

The second article, offered by Rep. William L. Hungate (D, Mo.), was approved July 29 by a 28–10 vote. Rep. Robert McClory (Ill.), second ranking Republican on the committee who opposed Article I, joined six Republican colleagues and 21 Democrats in recommending Nixon's impeachment for abuse of power.

This omnibus charge against Nixon, which McClory called the "crux" of the matter, specifically focused on the following allegations:

Personally and through his subordinates and agents, Nixon attempted to use the Internal Revenue Service to initiate tax audits or obtain confidential tax data for political purposes. He initiated a series of secret wiretaps under the guise of "national security" and misused the results of the tapes. He authorized and permitted to be maintained in the White House a secret, privately financed investigative unit which engaged in "covert and unlawful activities," including the 1971 burglary of the office of the psychiatrist of Pentagon Papers trial defendant, Daniel Ellsberg. He failed to act on the knowledge that "close subordinates" endeavored to impede the Watergate investigation and related matters. He "knowingly misused the executive power by interfering" with the lawful activities of the Federal Bureau of Investigation, the Central Intelligence Agency, the Justice Department, and the Watergate special prosecutor's office.

The third article in the bill of impeachment, approved July 30, charged that the President had sought to impede the impeachment process by refusing to comply with eight committee subpoenas for 147 recorded White House conversations and other evidence. It failed to gain broad bipartisan backing and passed by the narrow margin of 21–17. Rep. Lawrence J. Hogan (R, Md.) joined McClory and 19 Democrats to insure passage. Democrats Walter Flowers (Ala.) and James R. Mann (S.C.) voted to oppose the article.

The New York Times

New York, N.Y., July 19, 1974

Watergate, President Nixon stated in a recent interview, is "the broadest but the thinnest scandal in American history, because what was it about?"

The President was commenting on the comparison with Teapot Dome, pointing out that while in that famous oil-lease scandal of the nineteen-twenties large sums of money were involved (the Secretary of the Interior was convicted of accepting a bribe), none of the high officials accused of criminal conduct in the Nixon Administration had received any financial benefit from their actions.

Even on the assumption that that statement is true, it is revealing that Mr. Nixon evidently conceives of the betrayal of public trust—whether it be Teapot Dome or Watergate—primarily in monetary terms. Irrespective of the money involved, Teapot Dome represented an unconscionable sellout of property belonging to the American people; Watergate, a sellout of their constitutional rights. Of the two, Watergate was incomparably the more serious threat to this Republic.

"What is Watergate about?" asks the President. Is it possible that at this late date he still really does not know? Can he really be so uncomprehending that he considers it, to use his word, a mere "blip"? In his consistent evasion of his responsibilities to Congress, to the courts and to the American electorate—and in his sleazy efforts to escape all personal blame for the degradation of the White House during the last five and a half years, Richard M. Nixon has finally reached the nadir of moral obtuseness in asking this cynical question.

*　*　*　*

What, indeed, is Watergate all about?

Watergate is about a President of the United States who has repeatedly shown contempt for Congress and the courts; who has established a new and imperial doctrine of "executive privilege"; who has subverted the Constitution by his disregard of powers reserved to the Congress; who has flouted the constitutional injunction to "take care that the laws be faithfully executed" and who is deeply suspect of obstruction of justice as well: whose minions dared to trifle both with the electoral process and also with some of the most sensitive agencies of the United States Government; whose close associates and subordinates—for whose actions he is ultimately responsible—have been convicted of crimes against the people of the United States; who himself has already been named as a co-conspirator; who has connived in misuse of campaign funds; who has cut corners on his own income tax returns; whose careful excision of relevant material in supplying transcripts to the public suggests a sense of ethics more fitting to a slippery political fixer than to the President of the United States.

This is what Watergate is all about; and this is why the Judiciary Committee of the House of Representatives now has the clear duty of considering whether articles of impeachment should be presented to the House against Richard M. Nixon—based on the entire spectrum of evidence covering alleged violations of constitutional and statutory law, and, in a broader and more fundamental sense, of the duties and obligations or the Chief Executive to the people of these United States.

Newsday

Garden City, N.Y., July 29, 1974

"Murky, small, unimportant, vicious little things," Richard Nixon said of the charges arising out of the Watergate investigation in its early stages. But in the end they overwhelmed his Presidency. The "vicious little things" continued to grow, until, in the glare of public watchfulness, it was impossible to belittle them. "I cannot, in good conscience, turn away from the evidence of evil that is, to me, so clear and compelling," said Republican Representative Lawrence Hogan, setting the tone for other undecided members of the Judiciary Committee who joined, Saturday evening, in resolving that the President should be impeached. Thus the first shudder of the grand inquest of the nation has passed.

A year ago, a vote for impeachment was still inconceivable; today, for the second time in our history, it is a tragic and irrevocable fact. A year ago, no one outside the White House yet knew of the tapes which proved so pivotal, and finally so damning in the case. Once their existence was revealed, it was inevitable that they would be presumed either to exonerate or incriminate the President.

Nixon's Refusal To Provide the Evidence

But try as his supporters would, they could not persuade him to submit to that test freely. Even now there is no certainty that Congress will get the additional tapes which the Supreme Court ordered Nixon to surrender to the Special Prosecutor, tapes that could supply so many missing pieces in the Watergate puzzle. Toward the last, it was hard to see how there could be anyone still willing to believe that the President was acting in the good faith of innocence. His defense had become caught up in endless contradictions and illogic, and his own voluminous transcripts of White House conversations seemed to confirm the worst suspicions.

Yet many did believe him. His defend-

ers on the Judiciary Committee persisted in the "smoking gun" argument, the need for incontrovertible proof of the President's direct involvement in the Watergate coverup. They frequently borrowed attorney James St. Clair's phrase that the case consisted of "inference piled upon inference," and in the final hours of the impeachment inquiry, they may have succeeded in leaving a sufficient taint of dissension to have some bearing on its future.

The need for consensus reduced the scope of the impeachment articles. There are many who would still argue that the President's use of campaign contributions for personal amenities and his evasion of income taxes were part of the general pattern of abuse of power; and the two young people who were ejected from the committee chamber Friday for protesting the omission of the Cambodia issue no doubt spoke for thousands who view the secret, unauthorized bombing of Cambodia as an impeachable offense.

Why Didn't He Ever Say 'No' to Coverup?

But the agreement on two relatively narrow articles also made it possible for undecided committee members to focus on what was most troubling to them in the President's conduct—his obstruction of justice in the Watergate cover-up and his misuse of Federal agencies to serve his own purposes. What seemed to cut deepest for them was "the absence of any remorse, any regret," as Virginia's Representative H. Caldwell Butler put it, or the absence of any sense of shock over what was being committed in his name.

Representative Hogan, for example, decided the "smoking gun" was not important; it didn't matter to him, he said, whether Nixon had actually authorized the payment of hush money to E. Howard Hunt: "The thing that appalls me is he didn't stand up and say, 'Get out of here, this is the office of the President of the

United States, how can you talk about blackmail payments . . . ' " And it was finally "the whole mosaic of the evidence" that persuaded him to vote for impeachment.

Setting a Limit To Presidents' Power

There must remain in the country substantial numbers of people who will be unconvinced, even embittered, by the Judiciary Committee's decision. In their view, the President's offenses were no worse than those of his predecessors. It was to them that Representative Ray Thornton, an Arkansas Democrat, may have been addressing himself when he said that while earlier Presidents no doubt abused their powers, "I know of no time when it was systematized or carried on in such an organized way."

It was this, especially—the *systematic* nature of the abuses—that set Nixon's Presidency so fatefully apart from those that went before. From the beginning of his term he was like someone trying on, one by one, the perquisites of power as his possession of office dawned on him: First, in child-like dreams of glory—Graustarkian uniforms for the White House guard, a telephone call to the moon, winning plays for football coaches. And then, in increasingly ominous ways—the impoundment of funds voted by Congress, the compiling of enemies lists for Presidential vengeance, the creation of the "plumbers" unit for spying and surveillance—until he no longer seemed able to recognize any limits to his power. Whatever was available to the President was to be used.

Now, by recommending impeachment, the House Judiciary Committee has declared the limits. It had become the overriding necessity of the country's well-being to do so. As Representative Butler suggested at the outset of the final debate, "If we fail to impeach, we have condoned and left unpunished a course of conduct totally inconsistent with the reasonable expectations of the American people."

Chicago today American

Chicago, Ill., July 30, 1974

PRESIDENT NIXON'S loyalists often express the fear that if he is impeached, America's image abroad will be tarnished. In a sampling of international editorial opinion, the Associated Press found that this is hardly true. The consensus seems to be that the move toward the impeachment process is a sign of our government's good health.

The non-Communist Hong Kong newspaper Sing Tao Jih Pao noted that Nixon's problems stem from his preoccupation with "personal success" rather than "upholding the law." The Japanese newspaper Asahi Shimbun was "strongly impressed by the young dynamism of the United States to keep its momentum in time of crisis."

Mainichi Shimbun, a business daily, was "impressed by the soundness of the political consciousness of the American people." The Manchester Guardian said, "America is essentially a moral country, wanting to believe their nation is good . . . respect for the whole political system, including the Congress, can only be recaptured if there is now a moral cleansing."

All this doesn't mean that Mr. Nixon is either innocent or guilty. It means that other peoples will not necessarily confuse the trial of a President with the trial of the Presidency; that the rest of the world out there isn't as dumb as some of us think it is.

Chicago Daily Defender

Chicago, Ill., July 30, 1974

Judging from the **London** Sun, the British reaction to President Nixon's dilemma is not much different from the opinion of a large segment of the American press. In its editorial of July 26, written before the House Judiciary Committee's recommendation to the House of Representatives the impeachment of President Nixon, the Sun says it is time for Mr. Nixon to take a leaf from the book of the late unlamented Greek Colonels. It continues:

"Bad as the junta were, they at least had the grace to quit when the game was up. For President Nixon, the game is up. He should go while he may still draw a shred or two of dignity about him at his going. He can, if he will, legitimately plead medical grounds.

"He should not wait to be thrown ignominiously out. As he surely will be if he clings to the last to an office he has besmirched." Ending in typical British caustic sarcasm, the Sun remarks: "There isn't enough whitewash in the world to make Nixon's White House white again."

If the predictions by those who know the scores are correct, Nixon will be thrown out of the White House before the first snow falls.

THE SAGINAW NEWS

Saginaw, Mich., July 30, 1974

What was only a remote possibility just months ago became reality over the weekend.

The House Judiciary Committee, by a vote of 27-11, recommended to the House of Representatives the impeachment of Richard Nixon for obstruction of justice in the Watergate cover-up.

The size of the majority made it easier for at least one other article of impeachment, for abuse of power, to be approved by the committee and sent to the House.

While it will take months for a final resolution, the past week has given impeachment a kind of inevitability.

As Senate Majority Leader Mike Mansfield observed after the committee's vote, "The line of demarcation has been reached."

That line is the Senate. Clearly the President has lost whatever hopes he may have had of stopping the impeachment process short of that line.

The President's spokesmen have almost conceded as much. For Alexander M. Haig Jr., the White House Chief of Staff, to admit that Mr. Nixon's chances of avoiding House impeachment are "more uncertain" is equivalent to an expectation that the President will, indeed, be impeached.

Haig professed the view that a House floor vote would be "very close." We doubt it. We believe a vote now would result in a sizeable majority for impeachment.

The reason is simple: In the procedural system of Congress, the full House or Senate places great reliance on the recommendations of committees.

The House Judiciary Committee spent seven months considering the masses of material and evidence on the behavior of the President and his subordinates. Its clear conclusion has been that the evidence supports a recommendation of impeachment.

Was this a partisan decision? In many cases, partisanship certainly played a role. It's difficult to believe otherwise in view of the pro-impeachment declarations of some members long before they had even a cursory look at any documentary evidence.

Furthermore, it would be naive to expect the Judiciary members, politicians all, to make their decision without due attention to the impact in their home districts.

The nature of the vote to impeach can be assessed whichever way one chooses. True, it was a bipartisan decision, with six Republicans joining in, while only members of the President's party voted to retain him in office.

On the counterpoint, a reasonable argument would question why all 21 Democrats were persuaded of Mr. Nixon's guilt while only six of the 17 Republicans found the evidence convincing.

Yet, in the end, most of the committee members acquitted themselves well. Whatever the many bases for their decisions, it was apparent that the ultimate votes were cast with a solemnity appropriate to the occasion, a sobriety that not all the members had previously displayed. The moment, it seemed, had caught up with the members, and gave them pause.

The full House will take note that the committee did not act lightly. Nor will it fail to remember that at least six and possibly more Republicans will have supported at least one article.

Had the case for impeachment been fatally weak, this would not have happened. The Judiciary Committee has decided that a case exists.

The lone issue now remaining is whether that case is sufficient to convict and remove the President.

That is up to the Senate, and the House should send it there. In the Senate, unlike the proceedings so far, Mr. Nixon will have a full opportunity to clear himself in accordance with the provisions of the Constitution. The presiding officer of a Senate trial will be Warren E. Burger, Chief Justice of the Supreme Court, not Peter Rodino, New Jersey Democrat. Only in the Senate can the defense receive the full hearing it must have.

For these reasons we support the impeachment of the President and his trial in the Senate.

That support, however, does not include the declaration of the articles of impeachment that the evidence warrants conviction.

While the declaration may be necessary in such an indictment, it is also unfortunate. It is not for the House to decide guilt or innocence, but for the Senate. The role of the House is to either sustain or reject a judgment that the evidence requires a trial.

Not only for the sake of the evidence, but also for the sake of the welfare of the nation, a trial is demanded. This grave issue can be resolved in no other way.

But the Senate, receiving the issue, must abandon forthwith any prejudgment — from the Judiciary Committee, from the House or in its own collective mind — of the final verdict on Mr. Nixon. Otherwise, the President's jury will make a mockery of its awesome duty.

If there is to be a trial, however, the Judiciary Committee and the House must first make sure that trial is on charges of only the most substantial nature. The first impeachment article was defective in that respect because some of its subparagraphs were highly arguable and should have been removed.

Other articles being suggested also would hold little weight in a trial. If the President is to be judged, it must not be on a grab-bag of accusations which, even if proved, would not nearly justify his removal from office. There already are enough charges of the other kind to make the Senate's task a heavy one.

ST. LOUIS POST-DISPATCH
St. Louis, Mo., July 31, 1974

With the passage yesterday of a third article of impeachment by the House Judiciary Committee, President Nixon now faces the most fundamental charge to date of his failure to preserve and protect the Constitution. Approved like its predecessors by a bipartisan majority, Article III accuses Mr. Nixon of attempting to usurp for himself, through defiance of the committee's subpenas, powers which the Constitution entrusts to the House of Representatives alone.

We use the description "most fundamental" because while the first and second articles contain charges of specific ways in which Mr. Nixon has impeded the criminal justice system or abused his vast powers of office, Article III accuses Mr. Nixon of trying to destroy the constitutionally prescribed balance of powers among co-equal branches of government. Thus Article I charges that Mr. Nixon obstructed justice in the Watergate cover-up and Article II is an allegation that he misused the presidency by attempting to pervert federal agencies as well as by creating a private burglary unit within the White House.

Article III, however, turns the nation's attention to this basic question: Shall the President be allowed to exercise powers not given to the Executive Branch in order to nullify the impeachment process? (The question is not unlike the one which faced the Supreme Court last week: Has the President unwritten, unlimited powers to frustrate the judicial process? There the answer was a unanimous No.) By refusing to honor eight subpenas, Article III states, Mr. Nixon "interposed the powers of the Presidency against the lawful subpenas of the House of Representatives, thereby assuming to himself functions and judgments necessary to the exercise of the sole power of impeachment vested by the Constitution in the House of Representatives."

Mr. Nixon is the only president to be served while in office with a subpena from the House, but there is a sizable body of opinion of other presidents on the matter of subpenas and they are unanimous that in cases of impeachment the authority of the House is absolute. Washington, for example, in refusing information about the Jay Treaty, said his papers could not be inspected for any purpose of the House "except that of an impeachment." In cases of impeachment, said Polk, "all archives and papers of the executive departments, public or private, would be subject to the inspection and control of a committee" of the House. Grant stated that the House "may require as a right" information from the Executive Branch pursuant to impeachment.

These presidents fully realized that impeachment was the only protection the people have in the period between elections against an unfit or a criminal Chief Executive. Impeachment, in fact, is the people's way to remove, through the actions of their elected representatives in Congress, a president who fails or refuses to abide by his oath of office. Thus to allow a president to thwart impeachment by refusing to submit evidence to Congress is to remove the public's sole safeguard against executive tyranny. Had the committee failed to pass the article, the entire power of impeachment — as Representative Hogan pointed out — would have been rendered meaningless.

In his letter to Chairman Rodino on May 22, Mr. Nixon argued that to yield to the subpenas "would fatally weaken this office not only in this administration but for future presidencies as well." The committee properly realized that a failure to call Mr. Nixon to reckoning over the subpenas would have "fatally wounded" the Constitution by removing its ultimate check on presidential power.

THE INDIANAPOLIS NEWS
Indianapolis, Ind.
July 30, 1974

It is highly complimentary to America's republican form of government that the word "impeachment" is part of our political vocabulary.

Soviet press reports of President Nixon's troubles have had to borrow the English word "impeachment." The Russian language contains no such word, and the Soviet system provides no such orderly process for removal of high officials. Soviet editors aren't explaining the word, either, leaving readers to guess what it means.

Americans can be grateful they have recourse to legal processes. The only modern precedent Russians have for "impeaching" high officials is the 1917 revolution and the murder of Czar Nicholas I.

CHICAGO DAILY NEWS
Chicago, Ill., July 31, 1974

The second article of impeachment, approved by the House Judiciary Committee by a 28-to-10 vote, contains the heart of the case against President Nixon. A great deal of the evidence amassed against the President has to do with relatively petty matters suggesting avarice or arrogance or vindictiveness in the conduct of the office. There is nothing petty about the abuses of power charged here.

The article charges that he tried to use the Internal Revenue Service both as a source of confidential information to use against foes, and as a bludgeon to harass political enemies. It charges he similarly misused the FBI, Central Intelligence Agency and Secret Service, trying to utilize their investigative skills and equipment for ends wholly contrary to their lawful missions. It charges that he used his power illegally to try to impede lawful investigations and to hide unlawful activities.

It was evidence regarding this particular set of actions that persuaded so staunch a Republican as Illinois' Robert McClory to come over and cast his vote for impeachment — and properly so. These actions meddled perilously with the foundations of government.

For the government of this republic operates on the basis of the faith of the citizens — faith that it will function fairly and honorably to provide equal justice before the law. If the power vested in a government agency can be perverted to a stealthy, vengeful attack on a private citizen, then every American stands in jeopardy of such oppression, and the door is open to the beginning of a police state.

The evidence before the committee indicates that the abuses urged upon the agencies in the President's name and with the President's consent were grave enough to cause the proprietors of those agencies to rise up in dismay and indignation. J. Edgar Hoover simply refused to go along. And a parade of attorneys general filed in and out of the Justice Department's head office as Mr. Nixon kept seeking a man with a conscience flexible enough to do his bidding.

"Power tends to corrupt," wrote Lord Acton; "absolute power corrupts absolutely." He might well have been writing about an administration that has now seen the vice president, four Cabinet members, the President's two top aides and a score of other White House functionaries convicted or indicted for various acts of corruption.

On the basis of all of this the Congress is amply warranted in turning to the man at the top in seeking a common denominator, a central explanation for all that has occurred to the shame of the nation and the detriment of decent, orderly government.

Certainly Richard Nixon is not the proprietor of John Connally's conscience, nor Spiro Agnew's nor John Mitchell's nor even John Ehrlichman's or H.R. Haldeman's. But just as certainly, an ordinary sense of rectitude in the Oval Office would have set a vastly different moral standard for the executive branch. The tragic shortfall of that fundamental quality is the burden of the Judiciary Committee's second article of impeachment.

St. Louis Globe-Democrat

St. Louis, Mo., July 29, 1974

As expected, and even predicted by Richard Nixon himself, the House Judiciary Committee has voted to impeach the President.

The 27 to 11 committee vote, while weighing heavily against the President, does not automatically mean approval by the full House. It can be hoped that sufficient members of the House as a whole will be impressed by the lack of concrete evidence contained in the committee's broadly phrased first article that charges the President "has prevented, obstructed and impeded the administration of justice."

Mr. Nixon, remaining resolute, is not throwing in the towel. After the committee's action, a spokesman said this:

"The President remains confident that the full House will recognize that there simply is not the evidence to support this or any other article of impeachment and will not vote to impeach. He is confident because he knows he has committed no impeachable offense."

The Judiciary Committee now will consider further allegations of abuses by the President. Whether any other articles are adopted or not, the machinery has been geared for a consideration by the full House, where a simple majority approval of the accusations is sufficient to send the President to trial in the Senate. A two-thirds vote is needed in order for the Senate to convict a President and remove him from office.

Thus, a long distance must be traveled before the eventual fate of Mr. Nixon is determined.

☆ ☆ ☆

Viewers of the Judiciary Committee's proceedings have not been deceived by the self-serving, solemn-sounding pronouncements of so many of the participants that they had "an awesome duty" to set in motion the President's removal from office because of the "grave offenses" he has committed.

No rational person would deny that the committee's action has been political. This does not mean that all of those who voted against the President did so with malice, though some of Mr. Nixon's chief accusers made no effort to conceal their venom. At least some of the six Republicans who went against him probably did so because they thought it was to their political advantage to vote for impeachment.

With so many of President Nixon's former top associates in trouble — either indicted or convicted of various offenses — it's difficult to comprehend how the President has "prevented, obstructed and impeded administration of justice." If he wanted to, he certainly didn't succeed at it.

☆ ☆ ☆

Based on the thin charges produced thus far, there is no cause to believe the President can be steamrollered in the Senate, where he would have opportunity to defend himself.

At the worst, Mr. Nixon is accused of a cover-up that didn't work.

If a Democrat were President under the same circumstances as Mr. Nixon, it's a safe bet there would have been a coverup that worked — it would have worked in the Judiciary Committee.

No Democratic-controlled Congress would vote to impeach a Democratic President for the same political offenses charged to Mr. Nixon. If the accused were a member of the majority party, the matter would never get out of committee, if it got that far in the first place.

Democrats are adept at protecting their own. Outnumbered Republicans do not have the same opportunity.

That is the hard truth of impeachment politics.

THE ARIZONA REPUBLIC

Phoenix, Ariz., July 25, 1974

The House Judiciary Committee showed precious little impartiality during the long months it took testimony in the impeachment proceedings against President Nixon.

It held its meetings in secret, but time after time documents injurious to the President were leaked to the press.

For weeks the committee refused to allow the President's lawyer to attend its hearings, presumably because a Republican was acting as assistant counsel to the chief of the committee's paid staff.

Then, in an incredible breach of judicial ethics, it permitted the minority (i.e. pro-Nixon) lawyer, Albert Jenner, to join the majority (i.e. anti-Nixon) lawyer, John Doar, to recommend all-out impeachment of the President.

There isn't a trial judge in the country who would allow a defendant's lawyer to join the prosecution.

According to all the precepts and tenets of American jurisprudence, everyone is entitled to the best legal defense possible. When a lawyer, particularly one of Jenner's stature, turns his back on his own client, he disgraces the entire profession.

The committee showed unbelievable insensitivity when it did not even demote Jenner for his unprofessional conduct, but allowed him to remain under Doar as committee counsel for the impeachment hearings.

President Nixon has his own counsel, headed by James St. Clair, who has about one-third as many lawyers working for him as the Doar-Jenner legal team. And the House committee has had the full advantage of the work done by more than 100 lawyers on the Senate Watergate committee.

The ultimate blow for Nixon would come if he were impeached by the House. He then would have to pay for his own defense lawyers at his trial in the Senate. Already strapped by his income tax settlement with the Internal Revenue Service, the President faces more financial and legal problems than any run-of-the-mill murderer or rapist.

While Sen. Sam Ervin was mixing Southern charm with legal double-talk during the Senate hearings, he used to ask: "Where does the Constitution say the President deserves treatment any different than that accorded every other citizen?"

Someone ought to be asking the House Judiciary Committee that question today.

The Dallas Morning News

Dallas, Tex., July 30, 1974

"IN HIS conduct of the office of the President of the United States, Richard M. Nixon. . .has prevented, obstructed and impeded the administration of justice . . ."

So, at any rate, the House Judiciary Committee formally charges; impeachment, we now know for a certainty, is going to the entire House. Where, one hopes, the debate over whether to oust an incumbent U.S. president will shape up as a just and fair proceeding.

Not that the hope is a bright one. Already the Judiciary Committee has cast doubt on whether Mr. Nixon could receive a fair trial this side of Timbuktu.

That is for three reasons, at the very least:

(1) The outcome of the committee's deliberations was a foregone conclusion. Committeemen like John Conyers and Jerome Waldie could scarcely be restrained from charging Nixon with setting the Great Fire of London. They made it plain that the evidence, so far as they were concerned, already was in. The committee counsel, John Doar, a gentleman who is at political odds with the President (though he is himself a Republican) decided to line up with the impeachment majority. Not very unbiased of the theoretically unbiased Mr. Doar—nor of the Republican counsel Albert Jenner, who seems to have done likewise, for which he was demoted by his employers, the Republican minority.

(2) The vote on the first impeachment article—coverup of the Watergate affair—was mostly partisan. True, the defection of six Republicans from the President's cause has drawn considerable notice. But worthier of emphasis is the unanimity of the committee's Democrats. All 21 went for impeachment.

Now if six Republicans can perceive the President as guilty, surely at least six Democrats can perceive him as innocent. Very well, just one Democrat. Did there not, in the mind of one Democrat, exist the slightest, gnawing doubt as to the President's culpability? It is too much to believe. What is not too much to believe is that impeachment is a party issue. So far, it is all the Democrats vs. most of the Republicans. And woe betide Mr. Nixon—there are far fewer Republicans in Congress than there are Democrats.

(3) The impeachment article is vague and indefinite. Try as they might, Republicans failed to get the committee to single out the precise acts by which Mr. Nixon supposedly covered up Watergate. "He said thus-and-so on such-and-such a day, and this obstructed justice"—the Republicans wanted just such charges made part of the record.

But the committee refused. To get specific, said Doar, "would cause harm. It will just build and build and feed and fester into more and more delay. . ." Whatever he meant by that. Not even when he is asked why he can't be specific is Mr. Doar capable of being specific.

So the President is not to know specifically through what words, what deeds, he is found wanting in the committee's eyes.

Prof. Charles Black Jr. of Yale Law School is accordingly concerned. Black, a leading constitutional lawyer and author of a recent handbook on impeachment, says the wording of the committee's charge "seems to me rather to straddle the question of Mr. Nixon's personal participation or express authorization of any of the particular acts named."

And what, asks Black, is understood by the phrase: "The means used to implement this course of conduct or plan have included one or more of the following"? This he finds "not a very clear way to charge."

It is a clear way to impeach, however, if that is all one really wants to do. And for all the world, it looks as though that is just what the committee is determined on. Given such a will, one should not wonder that the committee has found a way.

Chicago Tribune

Chicago, Ill., July 28, 1974

By a vote of 27 to 11, the House Judiciary Committee has recommended that President Nixon be impeached and tried in the Senate for "high crimes and misdemeanors."

The committee charged that Mr. Nixon violated his oath to defend the Constitution and "take care that the laws be faithfully executed" by obstructing justice and otherwise abusing his powers.

We are confident that this use of the Constitution's impeachment provision would have been supported by the Founding Fathers who wrote it. In The Federalist Papers, Alexander Hamilton defined impeachment offenses as "those offenses which proceed from the misconduct of public men, or in other words from the abuse or violation of some public trust."

The committee properly defeated attempts by some of its Republican members to soften the charges and to help them deal with sharply divided public opinion in their home districts.

The committee also rejected a motion by Rep. Robert McClory to delay the proceedings for 10 days if Mr. Nixon agreed to give the committee promptly the tape recordings and other evidence which the United States Supreme Court has said he must surrender to Special Prosecutor Leon Jaworski.

Mr. McClory was right in thinking that the committee should examine all the evidence obtainable before acting. But we have to grant Chairman Peter Rodino two points: First, the President has consistently refused to cooperate with the committee, and his efforts to withhold the evidence lead to the conclusion that it is detrimental to his case. And second, the evidence will undoubtedly be available in time for any trial in the Senate, if not for the House impeachment debate scheduled to begin Aug. 12.

Tho predictable, it is unfortunate that the committee had to waste so much time with often petty argument when it was obvious that no one on either side was going to be much persuaded by the other. This kind of nitpicking and breast beating might have been dispensed with earler had the committee opened the hearings to the public from the start.

All twenty-one Democrats and six Republicans voted for impeachment. They represented the entire ideological spectrum from liberal to moderate to conservative and every region of the country. The bipartisan character of their action reflected the compelling nature of the evidence and, quite properly, the strength of public opinion —as the Founding Fathers intended. Opinion polls show that most Americans favor impeachment and lack confidence in government. Only 24 per cent approve of Mr. Nixon's conduct of office.

So, saddening as it is to move toward the second Presidential impeachment in our history, we do so in the knowledge that justice is being served, and that the public will is not being frustrated.

The Ottawa Citizen

Ottawa, Ont., July 30, 1974

Despite his continuing show of confidence, Richard Nixon's impeachment by the U.S. House of Representatives is now virtually certain. Still uncertain is the outcome of the subsequent trial in the Senate, where a two-thirds majority is needed to convict. In the House, only a simple majority is needed to impeach.

But with the 27-11 vote in the House judiciary committee (including six Republicans) for the first article of impeachment, the president has almost no hope of surviving the vote by the House.

After that, no matter what happens in the Senate, Nixon's ability to govern will be reduced almost to zero. His influence on domestic policy is now so eroded as to render him quite ineffective at a time when the economy is in difficult straits.

The latest Gallup poll reveals that 51 per cent of the American people believe he should be impeached. He has lost the confidence both of the people, and of the Congress. Even if he survives impeachment, he cannot lead his country into the unpopular decisions that must be made to stabilize the economy.

Conviction would settle the matter. Failing that, Nixon has two alternatives: to mark time for the remainder of his term, or to resign and restore some credibility to the presidency.

Honolulu Star-Bulletin

Honolulu, Hawaii, July 30, 1974

After twice indorsing Richard Nixon for President, this newspaper last Oct. 23 urged him to resign.

The events that brought us to a reaction widely shared throughout America now sometimes go under the name of "Bloody Saturday".

By firing Special Prosecutor Archibald Cox and provoking the resignations of Elliot Richardson and William Ruckelshaus from the top positions in the Justice Department, Mr. Nixon persuaded us and many others that his true interest lay in covering up the mess called Watergate, not cleaning it up.

Today that persuasion is shared by a majority of Americans and documented by mountains of detailed evidence about conduct in the White House during 1972 and 1973.

It has brought the Judiciary Committee of the House of Representatives to vote to bring the first impeachment action in more than a century against a President.

The evidence has driven the President's defenders — a diminishing group — back to two principal and very weak lines of defense:

First, that no one has proved a "smoking gun" was in the President's hands, meaning that no one has proved he actually ordered the many proven crimes committed by his subordinates; second, that impeachment would be damaging to America.

The first argument falls flat on the point of accountability.

Corporate presidents and military commanders-in-chief — and the President is both — stand responsible for what happens under them. The man who can't see or won't clean up an unhealthy situation under him is responsible even if he doesn't have a "smoking gun" in his hand.

In an organization as vast as the government of the United States there always will be some wrong-doing, but when it traces to four former members of the President's Cabinet and two of his closest administrative assistants, there is no need to find a "smoking gun" to know it is time to get a new chief executive.

Where the presidency of the United States is concerned, so much is at stake that the test of accountability ought to apply even more fully than in other situations, and not with the diminished force some of Mr. Nixon's defenders would like.

Having amassed an overwhelming record that the President was interested in cover-up, not clean-up, and documented dozens of crimes committed by his subordinates, it seems to us the worries about the danger of impeachment ought to be reversed.

We are far more worried now about the danger to American faith in government integrity that will result if the President is not impeached, than we are about the pain that lies ahead in the impeachment process.

A resignation is still the President's best course. The sooner the better.

MANCHESTER NEW HAMPSHIRE UNION LEADER

Manchester, N.H., July 30, 1974

As is well known to the readers of this newspaper, we do not think much of President Nixon because of the failure of his domestic policies and what we consider his unfortunate foreign policy. But every man is entitled to fair play, and this is something Mr. Nixon is not getting.

PRESIDENT NIXON

Anyone watching the televised operations of the House Judiciary Committee over the weekend, and coupling this together with previous remarks made by the congressmen about the President, could only be reminded of a group of vultures — in Nevada we call them buzzards — circling around the sky over a wounded animal. A great many of the committee members looked as if they would make the heart of a buzzard appear mild and loving in comparison to theirs.

Unfortunately, the "liberals," and we are not using the word "Democrats," because there is a big distinction, but the "liberals," both Republican and Democratic on the Judiciary Committee give the impression that they see a golden opportunity to reverse the terrible licking their hero, George McGovern, received in the Fall of '72 and to now take control of the nation against the will of the people.

It really is as simple as that. This is a partisan attempt to overturn the decision of the voters two years ago. **But this is NOT the purpose for which the impeachment process was placed in the Constitution by the Founding Fathers.**

Of course, the vultures on the Judiciary Committee have been aided in this process by a united drive by the leftist-dominated communications media — the news magazines, the Washington, New York, and Los Angeles papers, and the TV networks. They have attempted, and in many cases successfully, to so smear the President and create such an atmosphere of hate and hysteria in the country that many people have lost their sense of perspective.

Thus, the Judiciary Committee meets in an atmosphere equivalent to that of the French Revolution, when the mobs shouted for blood, and the leaders of the Revolution obliged.

The members of the Judiciary Committee voting against President Nixon, both Republicans and Democrats, give the impression to this newspaper of having absolutely no sense of fair play or impartiality, but of simply being embarked on a political gutting operation.

What is most repulsive about them is the way they try to obscure their vicious activity with a demonstration of sanctimoniousness and breast-beating that would do credit to the best con men in the nation.

President Nixon is no prize package, as this newspaper has said many times in the past, but, taking one look at his political opposition in Congress and the news media and their tactics in trying to destroy him, one must conclude —

God help us if THEY get their hands on the United States!

The Des Moines Register

Des Moines, Iowa, July 31, 1974

Vice-President Gerald Ford accused Democratic members of the House Judiciary Committee of wanting to undo the 1972 election. He characterized the committee's impeachment vote as "partisan."

Some Democrats — and Republicans — are so anti-Nixon they give the impression that they would vote for impeachment regardless of the evidence. But for the vice-president to dismiss the House committee's votes as a partisan exercise is disappointing — and unfair. Ford is demeaning himself by his attacks on the motives of others.

The Senate vote to create the Ervin Committee to probe Watergate was 77-0. The House vote to fund the Judiciary Committee's impeachment inquiry was 367-51, with Republicans voting overwhelmingly in favor. More than a third of the committee's Republican members have expressed agreement with the committee's Republican counsel that the evidence justifies impeachment.

Ford is himself engaging in partisanship if he can ignore this record and paint the concern over the President's conduct as partisan.

Presidential removal by impeachment of course would undo the results of the election. The Constitution provides for impeachment precisely because some elections should be undone. When evidence comes to light establishing the unfitness of an office-holder, it would be a dereliction of constitutional duty by Congress to refuse to act. President Nixon did not hesitate to "undo" the 1972 election when he forced the resignation of Spiro Agnew for acts of dishonesty.

The voters who installed Nixon by their votes in 1972 also installed the Ninety-third Congress. Voters sent congressmen to Washington knowing they would be armed with the power to impeach and remove the President. Impeachment action by Congress would reflect the "will of the people" today as faithfully as the votes installing Nixon reflected it in 1972.

Impeachment and conviction of Nixon would not undo the victory of the Republican Party. A Republican administration would still control the executive branch, which would be headed by Nixon's chosen successor.

Democrats unquestionably can achieve long-term political advantage by saddling the opposition party with the record of an impeached president. But installing Ford in the White House has the short-run political disadvantage of giving the leading Republican presidential contender a leg up on the 1976 election.

The one way for Democrats to reap long-and short-term political advantage out of impeachment would be for Ford to appear to the public to be a defender and apologist for corruption in the Nixon administration. That is what Ford is accomplishing by his seeming indifference to the evidence showing President Nixon deeply involved in impeachable offenses.

Ford surely must give thought occasionally to the very real probability that he will soon be President. If this occurs, he will be called upon to unite the country and repair shattered confidence in government. He is jeopardizing his own capability of doing this by making partisan comments which have no justification.

The Philadelphia Inquirer

Philadelphia, Pa., July 30, 1974

Vice President Gerald R. Ford is the man who, if the House votes to impeach President Nixon and if the Senate votes to remove him from office, will become President of the United States. If that day comes, the nation's greatest need will be for healing, for drawing together, for rebuilding confidence in its institutions and its leaders.

It is thus dismaying to note some of Mr. Ford's recent comments on the impeachment process.

In Canton, Ohio, on Saturday, Mr. Ford criticized the proceedings of the House Judiciary Committee, which was still in the process of hammering out the first article of impeachment. He said that Mr. Nixon "has been drawn over the coals as much, if not more, than any President I have known," and added, "In my judgment, the President is innocent of any impeachable offense."

"The committee apparently, or a majority of the committee, is not doing in this case what was done in the past in impeachment cases," he said. "I think it's a travesty that they are not."

That evening, after the first article was approved by the votes of all 21 Democrats and six of the 17 Republicans on the committee, Mr. Ford repeated his assertion that Mr. Nixon is innocent of any impeachable offense and asserted that the fact that all Democrats on the committee supported the article, "tends to make it a partisan issue."

The points Mr. Ford made, though perhaps not persuasive, are debatable. They are being debated, largely because they are the precise line of defense coming from Mr. Nixon's staff and lawyers.

Of course, Mr. Nixon is entitled to put forth a defense, and use every persuasion available to him to strengthen it. Mr. Ford, however, owes no debt of loyalty to Mr. Nixon that requires him to parrot that line.

But because he is the potential next President of all the people of the United States, Mr. Ford does owe a responsibility to them, a vital one.

Beyond all other considerations, that responsibility is for Mr. Ford to stand ready, should the Congress and history dictate, to help raise a divided America above the bitterness and strains left by the process that leads to his own Presidency.

Until that day comes, if it does, Mr. Ford would serve the needs of this country best by keeping his own counsel, by remaining silent on the case for or against Mr. Nixon, lest he be drawn into the web of passions and become tarnished by them.

SUPREME COURT UNANIMOUSLY DECIDES PRESIDENT MUST SURRENDER 64 TAPES

The Supreme Court ruled 8–0 July 24 that President Nixon must provide "forthwith" the tapes and documents relating to 64 White House conversations subpoenaed by special Watergate prosecutor Leon Jaworski for the pending Watergate cover-up trial of six former presidential aides. In a statement issued late the same day from San Clemente, Calif., Nixon said he had instructed special counsel James D. St. Clair, who had argued for the President before the court, to "take whatever measures are necessary" to comply with the decision "in all respects."

The decision did not mention presidential impeachment or the current impeachment inquiry in the House, and it defined the limits on presidential privilege on the relatively narrow grounds of the evidentiary needs imposed by Watergate criminal cases. In an opinion written by Chief Justice Warren E. Burger, a Nixon appointee, the court said that a generalized claim of executive privilege, while not explicitly provided by the Constitution, was "constitutionally based." But in the current case, Burger continued, such an assertion of privilege "must yield to the demonstrated, specific need for evidence in a pending criminal trial."

Addressing a secondary issue in a footnote to the opinion, the court left standing a grand jury citation of Nixon as an unindicted co-conspirator in the cover-up case. Calling this issue "unnecessary" to resolution of the privilege question, Burger said the court had "improvidently" granted a White House petition for review of District Court Judge John J. Sirica's refusal to expunge the citation. The court also denied a White House request that the court examine the grand jury's evidence to determine if the citation was justified.

Before dealing with the primary issue of confidentiality of presidential conversations, Burger rejected White House contentions that the tape dispute was an internal issue within the executive branch and should not be considered by the court. A "mere assertion of a claim of 'intra-branch' dispute," Burger wrote, was insufficient. The court noted that regulations establishing the independence of Jaworski's office had the force of law and had not been revoked by the attorney general. Under such conditions, the court said, Jaworski had the standing to pursue specific requests for applicable evidence through the courts, if necessary. Burger also ruled that Jaworski had made sufficient preliminary showing that the potential evidence in the tapes and documents was both relevant and necessary to a criminal proceeding.

Turning to the White House argument that the separation of powers doctrine should preclude judicial review of a claim of presidential privilege, Burger wrote that while one branch's interpretation of its powers "is due great respect from the others," the court must currently reaffirm a principle enunciated by an earlier court (in Marbury vs. Madison, 1803): "It is emphatically the province and duty of the Judicial department to say what the law is." Burger said the powers constitutionally vested in the courts "can no more be shared with the executive branch than the chief executive, for example, can share with the judiciary the veto power, or the Congress share with the judiciary the power to override a presidential veto."

Chicago Tribune

Chicago, Ill., July 25, 1974

The Supreme Court has ruled unanimously against the President in the historic case of the United States v. Richard M. Nixon, and thru his counsel, James St. Clair, the President announced last night that he will comply with the ruling. He will turn the tapes of 64 additional White House conversations dealing with Watergate over to Judge John Sirica's court in response to a subpena from Leon Jaworski, special prosecutor for the Justice Department.

We'd have preferred not to ask the court to define the limits of executive privilege. In matters of as far-reaching significance as this, it is often better to leave the boundaries indefinite, thus imposing some restraint on both sides yet enabling each to press its case when it thinks it is right.

But the issue was thrust before the court and its decision is the best one that could be hoped for at a time when hope, among other things, is in short supply.

In common sense as in law, the correctness of the court's position is indisputable. The unanimity of the vote—and the fact that the decision was written by Chief Justice Burger, perhaps the court's staunchest supporter of the President—should go a long way to eliminate the doubts and contentions that would linger if the decision had been split. The unanimity is also a credit to the court itself; to have differed over so critical a constitutional question would have weakened confidence in it.

What the court ruled was that executive privilege is not absolute and must on occasion yield to the requirements of justice, even where the White House itself is involved. The court wisely avoided any broad statements. It simply held that giving the documents to a court for judgment as to their privileged status would not interfere with the functioning of government or jeopardize the national security.

Even the limited power that the courts have thus been given is not one to be taken lightly. Executive privilege has a real function and an important one. A President's private conversations with members of his staff are of so sensitive a nature that their untimely release could often threaten the orderly functioning of government or the national security. The habit of hiding tape recorders in the Oval Office has, we suspect, come to an unmourned end.

But the important thrust of the court's ruling is that the final decision on executive privilege cannot rest solely with the President. The Watergate case is a striking example of material that has little to do with government policies or national security. If yesterday's decision undermines the power of the Presidency, as Mr. Nixon has contended, then he has nobody to blame but himself.

It would have been better, we repeat, to have avoided this confrontation. There is nothing in executive privilege to stop the President from making anything public voluntarily. A President with a sense of responsibility and good judgment should not need to fear the encroachment of the courts, and we trust that this will be as true with the new ruling as it was without it.

THE DAILY OKLAHOMAN
Oklahoma City, Okla., July 30, 1974

TERMS which are not familiar to most citizens, or which carry a special meaning in the context of an impeachment proceeding, are being used almost daily by Congress and news analysts. Some have special legislative meaning, some are legal terms, and a few have special connotations when used in discussions of the constitution.

One such term is "the symmetry of the law," referred to in many of the discussions of the subpoena question. In common parlance, this is the notion that any law must apply equally to all. What is sauce for the goose is sauce for the gander.

The symmetry of the law lies behind the growing concern that the Supreme Court may have opened the wrong gate with its ruling that the President must surrender certain White House records to Special Prosecutor Jaworski. In that ruling, the high court spelled out the limits on what kinds of working papers and records would be privileged from subpoena, and what kinds it was saying must be surrendered.

It must be remembered that Jaworski occupies a unique role, as the lawyer appointed by the President to find and prosecute wrongdoers within the President's own administration. Thus it can be argued that this ruling does not overturn nearly two centuries of legal precedents. But already, even some members of Congress are confusing this ruling with the subpoena power of the Rodino Committee. They are two different matters.

Privileged papers are not held solely by the executive branch of government. As recently as last May, Congress has refused to surrender its own working papers to a federal court in the District of Columbia for use in a Watergate-related trial. The Supreme Court, throughout its history, has always "stonewalled it" when any demand was made for the records of its own deliberations.

"Executive privilege" is thus misleading as a term for confidentiality of pre-decision records. The doctrine of privilege holds that such records of all branches of government may be held in confidence. That doctrine has been protected as jealously by Congress and the courts as by the long line of presidents who have invoked it.

If the House Judiciary Committee —and the Senate, if Sen. Robert Byrd of West Virginia is a true prophet of Senate intentions—can subpoena White House working papers and records of confidential conversations, then the subpoena power vested in the President and usually delegated to the Attorney General could be used to secure the working papers of committees, courts, and individual members of Congress.

It is easy to see where that might lead, especially in a time when there might be great hostility between a president and Congress. What might Franklin D. Roosevelt have done with the office records of those who opposed his plan to enlarge the Supreme Court—many of whom he tried to "purge" at the next election?

The Rodino Committee's subpoenas have not yet been ruled valid by the Supreme Court; the Jaworski ruling was the only beneficiary of the landmark ruling. But the broad direction of events is toward approval of the committee's subpoena power.

That is why the question of the symmetry of the law is being discussed. And that is why few will predict how far the Supreme Court and Congress will press subpoenas of executive documents and tapes. Neither body is willing to submit its own records to the same vulnerability to exposure. What is in jeopardy is the right of officials to arrive at decisions on the basis of confidential, but complete, information.

THE WALL STREET JOURNAL
New York, N.Y., July 30, 1974

In the performance of assigned constitutional duties each branch of the government must initially interpret the Constitution, and the interpretation of its powers by any branch is due great respect from the others. The President's counsel, as we have noted, reads the Constitution as providing an absolute privilege of confidentiality for all presidential communications. Many decisions of this Court, however, have unequivocally reaffirmed the holding of Marbury v. Madison, 1 Cranch 137 1803, that "it is emphatically the province and duty of the judicial department to say what the law is."

—The United States Supreme Court, The United States v. Richard Nixon, July 24, 1974.

It's eminently reasonable, and a practice settled in the very case on which American constitutional law is built, that the Supreme Court is the ultimate arbiter of the Constitution. The President is not that arbiter, as the court has just reaffirmed. Neither is Congress the arbiter, as at least some members of the House Judiciary Committee are presently asserting.

This is the real issue as the committee debates proposals to offer an article impeaching the President for contempt of Congress in refusing to honor the committee's subpoenas. If it approved such an article, the Congress would in certain important respects be asserting a right to be ultimate arbiter of the Constitution.

The Congress has issued subpoenas for the Oval Office tapes, asserting that its constitutional power to impeach implies a right to all information it in its sole discretion deems relevant. The President has denied these subpoenas, asserting that his constitutional power as Chief Executive implies a right to withhold information when in his sole discretion doing so serves the public interest. The dispute plainly is about what the Constitution says, about what the law is.

In considering what kind of precedent would be created by the use of impeachment to settle such a dispute, the rights and wrongs of a particular case are not especially important. As we have said, the equities of the matter clearly call for the President to surrender more tapes. And now the Supreme Court has clearly ruled that executive privilege is not absolute. We find it for any practical purpose inconceivable that the Supreme Court would fail to support the Congress if the matter were submitted for adjudication.

In terms of precedent, though, the more important thing is not who wins but the methods by which the dispute is settled. There is no reason to believe that the impeachment power was ever designed to settle disputes between the Legislative and Executive about what the Constitution says. The impeachment of Andrew Johnson was in fact over an issue of constitutional powers, later settled in favor of the presidency by the court. The use of the impeachment power over prerogatives is a large reason why the Johnson impeachment has set so badly with history.

If we are to see the nation's first impeachment conviction, it is vitally important to consider what kind of precedent is being created. The primary grounds for impeachment consist of matters in which the facts may be in dispute, but if proven clearly constitute grounds for impeachment. The article on contempt mixes with this a matter in which the facts are undisputed but the issue is whether this is just cause for impeachment. It is moreover a matter with profound implications on the balance of power not only between the Congress and the Executive but between Congress and the court. If it is to be decided it should be fought out on its own merits and not under the rubric of Watergate.

Redress is available to Congress short of impeachment; it only needs to drop its refusal to ask the courts to enforce the subpoenas. If the contempt article is not defeated in the committee or the House, or voted out by the Senate, the Congress will be making a careless decision of most historic consequences.

The Globe and Mail
Toronto, Ont., July 25, 1974

Yesterday's judgment of the Supreme Court of the United States will go a long way to restoring faith in American democracy, which is again proved to have a curious capacity to renew itself.

The Supreme Court, in a vote of 8 to 0, with three justices appointed by President Richard Nixon taking part, ordered that 64 tape recordings be released by President Nixon to Judge John Sirica, who will determine if all or parts of them should in turn be handed over to special prosecutor Leon Jaworski for use in the trial of six defendants in the Watergate cover-up conspiracy case.

The judgment was written by Chief Justice Warren E. Burger, one of the Nixon appointees. It found that the President did not have an absolute right of executive privilege that allowed him to withhold the tapes, which had been subpoenaed by the special prosecutor. If the President were granted "an absolute privilege" to withhold the tapes, said the court, this "would upset the constitutional balance of 'a workable government' and gravely impair the role of the courts."

The court met virtually every argument raised by the President in defending his decision not to hand over the tapes, but it dealt at particular length with the subject of presidential privilege.

"Neither the doctrine of separation of powers, nor the need for confidentiality of high level communications, without more, can sustain an absolute, unqualified presidential privilege of immunity from judicial process under all circumstances," wrote Chief Justice Burger. "The President's need for complete candor and objectivity calls for great deference from the courts. However, when the privilege depends solely on the broad undifferentiated claim of public interest in the confidentiality of such conversations, a confrontation with other values arises.

"Absent a claim of need to protect military, diplomatic or sensitive national security secrets, we find it very difficult to accept the argument that even the very important interest in confidentiality of presidential communications is significantly diminished by production of such material" for private inspection by a federal judge. " . . . The generalized assertion of privilege must yield to the demonstrated, specific need for evidence in a pending criminal trial."

The court's decision demonstrates that the checks and balances that were provided at the time of drafting the United States Constitution can still function. The tripod of Congress, Court and Administration, upon which U.S. liberty was to rest securely, and which a succession of powerful Administrations has thrown out of balance, is back on its three supports, with each, as it must, once again set to keep a careful eye on the other two. On guard against dictatorship.

The judgment does not condemn President Nixon. Indeed, the Chief Justice concluded by cautioning Judge Sirica, who will receive the tapes now that the President has decided to release them, that he "has a very heavy responsibility to see to it that the presidential conversations, which are either not relevant or not admissible, are accorded that high degree of respect due to the President of the United States". If Judge Sirica decides that any of the 64 tapes are neither relevant nor admissible, he would then refuse to turn them over to special prosecutor Jaworski.

But proper evidence will be made available to prosecute a case before the courts, to get down to finding the truth among the millions of words of accusation and counter-accusation that have arisen out of the whole Watergate conglomerate.

The court's decision, unanimous with the exception of one Nixon-appointed judge who withdrew because of previous association with two of the defendants in the cover-up trial, and written by the Nixon-appointed Chief Justice, will reassure the people of the United States that impartiality still exists, that not everything functions on a partisan basis, that Republicans and Democrats can still find it possible to vote by conscience.

The Supreme Court has reaffirmed the principle that nobody—not even the highest official in the land—has the right to withhold evidence, to set himself above and apart from the judicial process.

The court has made it possible for citizens of the United States to sing, with a confidence that has lately been sadly assailed, "My country 'tis of thee, sweet land of liberty!"

BUFFALO EVENING NEWS
Buffalo, N.Y., July 27, 1974

What goes on, we all keep wondering, among the inscrutable Chinese—where one Maoist faction denounces another in big wall posters and the chairman himself has mounted a major attack on the dead Lin Piao and the much longer-dead philosopher Confucius?

But if Red China's curious ways are hard for us to fathom, what agonies must the Politburocrats of Peking be going through in trying to explain OUR quaint customs to their people.

Here is this President Nixon, for example, an American they have decided they can really do business with (in their own cautious way, of course). The most powerful leader in the world, many call him—and how much GNP or nuclear power does Mao control that he should disagree?

So this President Nixon gets sued by some upstart prosecutor, one of his own government's employes, and ordered by a local district judge to produce tapes he thinks are confidential. The President won't be pushed around like that, naturally, so he takes his troubles to the highest court of America—to which he has been busily appointing all his own favorite judges.

And what happens? Well, uh, these judges all tell him — unanimously — that he hasn't a legal leg to stand on and he's got to give up exactly what this upstart prosecutor demanded in the first place.

And what does this most powerful President in the world tell those judges? Well, you're not going to believe this, Comrade, but he merely says that, while he's disappointed by their decision, of course he will comply "in all respects."

No wonder Chairman Mao keeps stirring China's masses against Lin Piao and Confucius. It's so much easier than trying to tell them how things are these days with his new friend Nixon and all those inscrutable Americans!

The Des Moines Register
Des Moines, Iowa
July 26, 1974

Several members of the House Judiciary Committee have said that the committee should suspend its impeachment proceedings until the committee obtains the presidential tapes and documents the Supreme Court ordered released to Judge John Sirica.

Release of additional evidence to the committee could satisfy the doubts some members have about the President's part in the Watergate cover-up. But there is no assurance that the committee ever will see the evidence it wants.

The President's statement that he will comply with the Supreme Court's ruling made no mention of complying with the House committee's subpoenas. The court case concerned the special prosecutor's effort to obtain certain tapes and documents for a criminal trial and did not deal with the right of Congress to obtain evidence for impeachment.

There is no question about the President's obligation to furnish the requested information to Congress, with or without the ruling. Congress can — and should — regard the President's repeated defiance of its requests as an impeachable offense. But the President could choose to give a "strict construction" to the high court ruling and claim it only applies to criminal cases.

Even if the President agrees to give the committee the requested evidence, he could foot-drag interminably. The President has said that the committee has the "whole story." In other words, he claims the evidence sought by the committee is irrelevant.

But this refusal in itself convinces some members that what Nixon holds back is highly relevant. Arguments could go on for months about the relevance to impeachment of portions of tapes and documents.

The unavailability of certain evidence did not prevent the federal grand jury from indicting H.R. Haldeman, John Ehrlichman, John Mitchell and others for obstructing justice and declaring it had probable cause to believe that Richard Nixon "was a member of the conspiracy to defraud the United States and to obstruct justice." The special prosecutor sought the evidence to meet the higher standard of proof needed to convict the President's men.

By the same token, the House committee has ample evidence of the President's involvement in the Watergate cover-up to justify recommending a Senate trial. The President has tried so hard to hide the evidence we may be sure it does not exculpate him. Release of the evidence can only strengthen the case against Nixon.

Congress should make every effort to obtain for the Senate trial or for impeachment action by the full House the evidence it subpoenaed, if it can be obtained in time. But it would be a mistake for the House committee to delay further its eight-month-long proceeding on the iffy chance the President now will deign to give it evidence it has tried for months to get.

St. Louis Globe-Democrat

St. Louis, Mo., July 25, 1974

The Supreme Court's 8 to 0 ruling against President Nixon's claim of executive privilege is evidence that judges will rule in favor of the judiciary in any dispute involving a challenge to their authority.

By failing to rule on the propriety of a grand jury naming President Nixon as an unindicted co-conspirator in the Watergate coverup, the court demonstrated that it was more concerned with its own powers than it was in defining the rights of the President.

It must be understood that the Supreme Court acted on a ruling by District Judge John J. Sirica that Special Prosecutor Leon Jaworski was entitled to tapes he had subpoenaed from the President as evidence against Watergate defendants.

The action is not part of the House Judiciary Committee's impeachment proceedings against the President, though the committee wants the tapes for its own use.

Through his counsel, James St. Clair, Mr. Nixon has contended that the President is subject to the impeachment process only, and is not answerable to the judicial process while still in office.

This view, as it applies to the President himself, is well founded.

The difficulty in the case confronting Mr. Nixon is that others besides himself are involved. And the Supreme Court ruled that the President cannot withhold evidence in a criminal proceeding.

☆ ☆ ☆

In its unanimous opinion written by Chief Justice Warren E. Burger, the court stated:

"A President's acknowledged need for confidentiality in the communications of his office is general in nature whereas the constitutional need for production of relevant evidence in a criminal proceeding is specific and central to the fair adjudication of a particular criminal case in the administration of justice."

The court summarized in these words:

"Neither the doctrine of separation of powers nor the need for confidentiality of high-level communications . . . can sustain an absolute, unqualified presidential privilege of immunity from judicial process under all circumstances."

The court conceded that public interest required that presidential confidentiality be afforded the greatest protection consistent with administering justice. Judge Sirica was instructed to examine the evidence and to guarantee that any material not relevant to criminal prosecution be kept confidential and returned under seal to the White House.

Mr. Nixon was justified in taking the stand that he did. The Constitution vests executive powers in the President and the President alone. He is perfectly entitled to believe that his constitutional role should give him the final say over whether his communications should remain confidential.

The Supreme Court, headed by a Chief Justice appointed by Mr. Nixon, has ruled otherwise. Thus the President cannot claim to be a victim of partisan politics in the court's ruling. The impeachment proceedings are another matter.

☆ ☆ ☆

While a setback to the President's pride and prestige, the court's ruling can be viewed as favoring the public interest.

By complying with the court order, Mr. Nixon can purge himself of any suspicion that he regards himself as being above the law, or that he is not willing or able to faithfully execute his office. The President swore that he would, to the best of his ability, preserve, protect and defend the Constitution of the United States.

Mr. Nixon's obligation is to all the people of the United States, friend and foe alike. If he has had the mistaken notion that he owes a higher loyalty to his former White House associates than he does to the people, he can now stand corrected.

Under the American system of rule by law, Supreme Court interpretations of the Constitution are final and must be respected, even when wrong.

The people are sovereign in the United States of America.

The Supreme Court has ruled that Special Prosecutor Jaworski was right in saying he represents the people.

Richmond Times-Dispatch

Richmond, Va., July 28, 1974

Whatever cataclysmic results may ultimately flow from the Supreme Court's decision on executive privilege, the justices clearly endeavored to avoid potentially disastrous extremes in their evaluation of the comparative powers of the presidency and the judiciary. It was a Solomonic opinion in that it sought to subject the nation's chief executive to the rule of law without rendering him defenseless against unwise and unwarranted intrusions into the confidential affairs of his office. As we noted in an earlier editorial, some of the implications of the decision are disturbing. But under the circumstances, it probably was the wisest the court could have made.

Consider the court's dilemma: A ruling affirming the absolute right of a president to preserve the confidentiality of his records, no matter what they concern, would have constituted authorization for the concealment of information needed for "the fair adjudication of a particular criminal case in the administration of justice." That any president, now or in the future, might have the unquestioned right to withhold evidence relevant to a criminal proceeding is a repugnant thought. Conversely, however, if the court had emphatically rejected the whole concept of executive privilege, the ability of presidents to deal effectively with sensitive matters of state would have been gravely imperiled. Such a ruling would have made every presidential conversation and every presidential document, no matter how confidential it ought to be, subject to potential public exposure.

And so the court compromised. Yes, it said, there is a constitutional basis for executive privilege, for the right of presidents to confidentiality in their "conversations and correspondence." Declared the court:

"A president and those who assist him must be free to explore alternatives in the process of shaping policies and making decisions and to do so in a way many would be unwilling to express except privately."

But executive privilege, the opinion continued, is not absolute. It may be impermissible to breach the confidentiality of the presidency when "military, diplomatic or sensitive national security secrets" are involved, the court wrote; but when there is no presidential claim that such secrets would be exposed, a chief executive may not "withhold evidence that is demonstrably relevant in a criminal trial..."

Contradictory interpretations of the court's opinion obviously are possible. It can be argued that by endowing the principle of executive privilege with constitutional legitimacy for the first time in the nation's history, the court has *strengthened* the presidency. A contrary point of view is that by declaring presidential invocations of executive privilege to be subject to judicial review, by apparently making it possible for a judge to substitute his own assessment for that of the president in determining whether the release of certain information would imperil "military, diplomatic or sensitive national security secrets," the court actually has *weakened* the presidency.

It is impossible, of course, to foresee all of the eventual effects of this momentous decision. However carefully the justices may have tried to limit the impact of their opinion, it could lead ultimately to extensive and undesirable governmental changes. Viewed strictly within the context of conditions that prevail today, the opinion seems reasonable. But seemingly narrow precedents can foster broad new rules of law. Conceivably, this opinion could become the wellspring of an ever-widening legal doctrine that could dangerously impair the effectiveness of the presidency. The nation can only hope that future courts will be as cautious and precise in their application of the opinion as its authors were in formulating it.

The Charleston Gazette

Charleston, W.Va., July 26, 1974

Four of the nine justices of the United States Supreme Court were appointed by President Nixon.

Obviously he didn't personally select them. But they were appointed on the recommendation of Republican party ideologues who hoped desperately to change the character of the court.

"Strict constructionist" was a term in vogue at the time of Mr. Nixon's appointments. That was before the President's lawyer asserted that "executive privilege" is "implicit" in the Constitution even if it actually doesn't appear there.

All four appointments appeared to please the administration and the most vociferous of the critics of the old Warren Court, which was deemed far too liberal.

Relief spread among the rightist ideologues. Things would be different now. No more fuzzy-headed rulings regarding the rights of defendants. No more unsettling decisions to disrupt procedures by which the establishment traditionally dealt with troublemakers. No more embarrassing strictures on constitutional exercise of liberty on the part of dissenters. In short, assuming the cooperation of known middle-of-the-roaders already on the court, the Nixon appointees would safeguard Nixon programs.

On July 24, the court, with three of the four Nixon appointees assenting, held by an 8 to 0 vote that President Nixon must yield White House tapes and documents being withheld from the special Watergate prosecutor. One justice, appointed by Mr. Nixon, abstained because of a previous association with the Justice Department.

It is true that in rulings likely to affect the course of the nation, ordinary majority decisions are joined by dissenters in a show of unity. But the opinion resulting from unanimous decision against Mr. Nixon was written by one of the Nixon appointees, Chief Justice Warren Burger — an indication that he, at least, held with the majority.

If any Supreme Court could be relied upon to affirm the President's position, it is the one presently sitting, popularly called the "Nixon Court." The decision against the President illustrates beautifully the common assertion that high office rids men and women of petty prejudices, forcing them to recognize a duty higher than personal loyalty.

The decision was a stunning victory for the American system, which positions the judiciary as arbiter of executive and legislative actions and assumes that personal considerations will be cast aside in the greater interest of the general welfare.

The court acquitted itself with honor. It now remains to be seen if the legislative branch can similarly discount personal feeling and constituent pressure in an effort to serve the national interest.

Washington Star-News

Washington, D.C., July 25, 1974

The Supreme Court ruling yesterday in the tapes case was historic, definitive and, above all, correct. It held, in essence, that no American, not even the President, is above the law.

That was the issue, really: whether the President could hold himself immune from the system of justice to which every other citizen is subject, whether he could defy the judicial system in its search for the truth.

The matter at hand was President Nixon's use of "executive privilege" in refusing to turn over 64 White House tape recordings subpoenaed by Special Watergate Prosecutor Leon Jaworski. The prosecutor sought them because he believed they were relevant to the Watergate cover-up conspiracy trial scheduled to begin September 9 against six defendants, including former high White House aides. Federal District Judge John Sirica agreed with Jaworski and it was his ruling that the supreme Court upheld.

The President wisely saw there was no logical course other than to comply with the ruling, and he assured last night he would do so. The court decision was unanimous among the eight justices hearing the case, and the opinion was written by the President's own appointee, Chief Justice Burger. There was no way for the President to argue that it is nondefinitive, and for him to have defied it would have courted disaster, for it surely would have assured his impeachment and ouster from office.

The ruling was historic, and monumentally important, because it is the first time the Supreme Court has decided a case directly involving the doctrine of executive privilege. The circumscription of executive authority inherent in the ruling should make for a more careful and cleaner presidency. Over the past several decades, presidents and presidential assistants have tended to arrogate powers unto themselves that the Constitution never intended. They have behaved, as was clearly shown in Watergate, as if they could do anything. The Supreme Court ruling should put some brake on that.

Executive privilege has been a gray area in which guidelines were needed, and now the high court has laid some down. Some legal authorities have argued that executive privilege is a myth, that there is no basis in the Constitution for a president to protect the confidentiality of White House communications under any such doctrine. At the other end, the President's

lawyer, James St. Clair, argued that the president has an "absolute" executive privilege. Jaworski took a middle ground — that an executive privilege does exist but that it is not absolute.

The Supreme Court ruled that protection of the confidentiality of presidential communications does have constitutional underpinnings. For it to have ruled otherwise would have required the President and his advisers to conduct the nation's business in a fishbowl, a situation that would be intolerable and unworkable. But the court said that to extend an absolute privilege to the President "would upset the constitutional balance of 'a workable government' and gravely impair the role of the courts."

Although the case dealt with the specific issue of the 64 tapes and the cover-up trial, the decision goes beyond that. It lays down the unmistakable ruling that presidential executive privilege is subject to check by the courts. It does not mean, however, that the White House is open for wide-scale "fishing expeditions." There is nothing in the decision that indicates, for example, that congressional committees can now begin pawing at will through White House papers.

The ruling would appear to bear significantly, although indirectly, on the impeachment proceedings. If there is justification for requiring the President to turn over the tapes for use in a trial of presidential underlings, it surely follows that the tapes would be material to an impeachment proceeding in which the conduct of the President himself has been called into question.

However, the House Judiciary Committee ought not hold up its proceedings because of the court ruling. From indications at last night's first public debate it will not. Apparently it will be some time before the tapes are processed through Judge Sirica's court to eliminate portions that may be irrelevant or not in the national interest to disclose publicly. The Judiciary Committee has enough material already in hand on which to base its recommendations to the full House. If there is anything on the tapes that would bolster the President's case, he probably would have revealed that by now. Hopefully, by the time the impeachment proceedings reach a vote on the House floor, the relevant portions of the tapes will be available.

The Courier-Journal

Louisville, Ky., July 25, 1974

THOUGH its unanimous ruling on the tapes and papers sought by Special Prosecutor Jaworski, the Supreme Court has done the nation a great service by deflating some of the windy claims of executive privilege that have issued from the White House in recent months. The Court has made clear that the need for confidentiality in White House conversations, while not to be lightly dismissed, cannot prevail over the demands of due process of law in criminal proceedings.

The Court's ruling is historic but hardly unexpected, except perhaps for the unanimity which made President Nixon's announced intention to comply all but inevitable. The relative skill of Mr. Jaworski and presidential lawyer St. Clair may be debated for years. But the basic issues were clear even to the layman.

An 'intolerable' privilege

Mr. Nixon had claimed that he and he alone, as President, can decide what evidence will be turned over to the courts for the September trial of some of his former associates. Mr. Jaworski, to whom authority to prosecute in the Watergate case had been delegated by Mr. Nixon himself, argued that unlimited executive privilege could lead to "intolerable abuse" and that the President shares the obligation of every citizen to come forward with evidence pertinent to a criminal trial.

Mr. Nixon, through Mr. St. Clair, had also claimed that subjecting executive privilege to reversal in the courts would impair "the ability of every President of the United States from this time forward to perform the constitutional duties vested in him." To which Mr. Jaworski had observed, "Surely there will be few occasions where there is probable cause to believe that conversations in the Executive Office of the President occurred during the course of a criminal conspiracy."

And that, of course, is precisely the point. The truly dangerous precedent would have been a Supreme Court ruling upholding Mr. Nixon's extravagant claims of executive privilege or ducking the issue altogether. The Court instead has provided needed support for the argument, accessible to anyone with common sense, that the President is not above the law and that he cannot use claims of confidentiality to excuse a refusal to cooperate with the criminal justice system or, even worse, to subvert the workings of that system when it touches those who have exercised power within the White House.

Despite its inevitable psychological impact, the Court's ruling has no direct bearing on the impeachment proceedings of the House Judiciary Committee. One hopes, however, that this ruling will persuade every member of the committee that there is no valid excuse now for White House refusal to release other materials the committee has unsuccessfully sought. The House, under the Constitution, is vested with the sole power of impeachment. The President has no more right to impede an impeachment inquiry by withholding evidence than he has to impede judicial proceedings with the same tactics. As he now acknowledges in part by his compliance with the Supreme Court ruling, he is not above the law.

RICHARD NIXON RESIGNS PRESIDENCY

Richard Milhous Nixon, 61, resigned as President of the United States Aug. 9, and Vice President Gerald Rudolph Ford, 61, was sworn in as his successor. It was the first time in the history of the nation that the president has resigned.

The resignation was announced Aug. 8, three days after Nixon's disclosures on Monday, Aug. 5 that he had ordered the Federal Bureau of Investigation to halt its probe into the break-in at the Democratic Party's national headquarters in the Watergate building in Washington D.C. Transcripts of three tapes released on Aug. 5 proved that in his conversations with H.R. Haldeman Nixon had known and interfered with the FBI's investigation as early as June 23, 1972, six days after the break-in. Furthermore, Nixon stated, he had kept this part of the record secret from investigating bodies, his own counsel and the public.

The admission Aug. 5 destroyed what remained of Nixon's support in Congress, fading since the House Judiciary Committee had drawn, with substantial bipartisan backing, three articles of impeachment to be considered on the House floor. Within 48 hours of his statement of complicity, which he stated did not in his opinion justify "the extreme step of impeachment," the 10 committee members who had voted against impeachment reversed themselves, on the basis of the new evidence, and announced they would vote for impeachment. This, in effect, made the committee vote for impeachment unanimous.

The development was accompanied by serious defections in the Republican Congressional leadership and acknowledgment from all sides that the vote for impeachment in the House was a foregone conclusion and conviction by the Senate certain.

This assessment was delivered to the President by the senior Republican leaders of the Congress. Shortly afterwards, Nixon made his final decision to resign. He announced his decision the evening of Aug. 8, to a television audience estimated at 110–130 million persons. In his 16-minute address, Nixon conceded he had made "some" wrong judgments. He said he was resigning because he no longer had "a strong enough political base in Congress" to carry out his duties of office. He also reviewed what he hoped would be his legacy of accomplishment in office.

Some of the events of Nixon's last week in office:

■ July 30—The third of the articles on impeachment is approved by the House Judiciary Committee.

■ July 31—Patrick J. Buchanan, special consultant to the President, says that the President had "not ruled out" the plan to bypass the House debate on impeachment and move quickly to the Senate for the impeachment trial. Later that day, the White House drops the plan after Congressional opposition.

■ Aug. 2—Rep. Paul Findley (R, Ill.) proposes that the House consider censure of the President, rather than impeachment. Findley himself abandons the idea in favor of impeachment after the Aug. 5 statement.

■ Aug. 4—Sen. William Proxmire (D, Wisc.) calls on Nixon to transfer presidential powers to Vice President Ford until the impeachment proceedings are completed. Proxmire cites the 25th Amendment's clause on presidential incapacity.

■ Aug. 5—Sen. Robert P. Griffin (Mich.), assistant Senate Republican leader, calls for Nixon's resignation: "I think we've arrived at a point where both the national interest and his own interest would best be served by resigning." Sens. Edward W. Brooke (R, Mass.), James L. Buckley (Cons-R, N.Y.) and Richard S. Schweiker (R. Pa.) also call for the President's resignation. [See pp. 311–321]

■ Aug. 5—Nixon issues his statement on blocking investigation of Watergate break-in.

■ Aug. 6—Nixon tells the Cabinet he will not resign.

■ Aug. 8—Nixon announces his resignation.

Although there was general agreement that Congress did not have the power to grant immunity from prosecution, Sen. Brooke and Rep. John H. Buchanan Jr. (R, Ala.) introduced companion resolutions Aug. 8 expressing the "sense of Congress" that Nixon should not be prosecuted after he left office. Such a measure would not be binding on the prosecution or the courts. Brooke said the next day, however, that he would not press for passage of the resolution because of the lack of contrition or confession in Nixon's televised announcement.

Speculation was widespread both before and after Nixon's resignation as to what legal action, if any, might be taken against him as a private citizen. A key element in the issue was the fact that Nixon had been named as an unindicted co-conspirator in the cover-up case. The grand jury had reportedly wanted to indict Nixon but had been dissuaded by Watergate special prosecutor Leon Jaworski. In a statement released after the resignation announcement Aug. 8, Jaworski said that bargaining regarding possible immunity from prosecution had not played a part in Nixon's decision to leave office. "There has been no agreement or understanding of any sort between the President and his representatives and the special prosecutor relating in any way to the President's resignation," the statement said. Jaworski said his office "was not asked for any such agreement or understanding and offered none."

HOUSTON CHRONICLE

Houston, Tex., August 1, 1974

T h e Chronicle agrees with t h e apparent decision of the White House to discard a suggestion to b y p a s s House of Representatives debate on the impeachment articles by having the President concede impeachment in the House and thus get the matter straight on to the Senate for trial.

To have gone the acccelerated route suggested might possibly have been advantageous to the White House in s o m e respects, and, obviously, it would have taken some of the heat off the House.

But the impeachment proceedings have now come to the point — have been at the point, actually, ever since they began—where it is imperative that due process be strictly followed and that those involved in the proceedings assume fully all of the responsibilities they are charged with.

Rep. Alan Steelman of Dallas put his finger on what would almost inevitably be a consequence, and a dangerous consequence, of skipping the impeachment through the House without full debate, when he said, "If we do, the public would become even more cynical and suspicious than they are now."

There m u s t be no opportunity whatsoever created that would allow a suspicion to develop that anything less than the rules of fairness for all concerned are followed during the proceedings.

Impeachment has been described as a traumatic experience for the American people, and this is probably no overstatement. But if the process is carried o u t cleanly, fairly, w i t h honorable conduct on the part of those involved, and if the country is convinced this is the way it is being carried out, then it is an experience the country can live with.

The Detroit News

Detroit, Mich., August 2, 1974

Any proposal that the House of Representatives take a quick vote without debate, railroading the impeachment issue to the Senate, should be rejected.

Such a scheme would short-circuit an important constitutional process. It would mean the impeachment of a President through the deliberations of a single committee rather than by the full House. Members would be denied their right to discuss, add to or delete articles of impeachment—the most important work ever likely to come before Congress in their political lifetime.

Presidential aides admit that Mr. Nixon has been weighing whether to seek the detour around the House. Presumably, he recognizes that he has no chance of staving off impeachment and wants to save GOP representatives the political embarrassment of impeachment debate on prime time in advance of the elections.

The conduct of the impeachment process should not be influenced by the fact that members of a political party may be embarrassed if the process follows its logical and constitutional course. There has already been too much political manipulation on both sides without adding to it this kind of a "gentlemen's agreement."

Many Republicans indicate that they regard the proposal as demeaning. As a practical matter, the Democratic majority—thinking in hard political terms, as always—is unlikely to let the Republicans off the hook so easily. Certainly the Democrats have no obligation to do so—but they do have an obligation to give every House member, Democrat and Republican, a chance to debate the proposed articles of impeachment.

The fact that the White House even admitted thinking about short-circuiting the House debate shows how badly the President's position has eroded under the flood of recent events, including the Supreme Court decision on executive privilege, the Judiciary Committee's three-fold proposal of impeachment and the conviction and sentencing of former White House aide John Ehrlichman.

Only a few days ago, the President steadfastly insisted that the House would not impeach him. Obviously he now believes that it will. Faced with that hard reality, he might weigh another possible plan—resignation—for saving his party from further embarrassment.

At this point, resignation would also short-circuit impeachment but it would be enormously more effective and acceptable than trying to get the House of Representatives to abdicate its duty.

Herald News

Fall River, Mass., August 5, 1974

The colossal ineptitude of the White House in terms of public relations has been noted almost since President Nixon became the incumbent in January, 1969. Given the stresses and strains of the past two years, however, it would be natural to assume that the White House would have painfully acquired some notion of how to handle the susceptibilities of others without offending them. Such Alas, is not the case.

Patrick Buchanan, a special consultant to the President, last week hinted broadly that Mr. Nixon was considering asking the House to vote unanimously for impeachment so that the issue could move directly to the Senate. Presumably the reason the White House was considering doing so was that it has given up hope of defeating impeachment except in the Senate, where a two-thirds vote will be required to sustain it.

But all the suggestion accomplished was to affront the members of the House still further, and most significantly some Congressmen who have been among the President's relatively few supporters. At this stage of what may well be a losing game, it is vital for the President to retain whatever support he has. To alienate even a single more vote unnecessarily is incredibly foolhardy. Yet this is precisely what this ill-considered suggestion has done.

In terms of ordinary human tact, the present administration is so totally deficient that it now appears that nothing whatever can remedy the lack.

ST. LOUIS POST-DISPATCH

St. Louis, Mo., August 2, 1974

Representative Dennis of Indiana, one of President Nixon's stanchest defenders on the House Judiciary Committee, deserves commendation for denouncing as a "cop-out" a suggestion from a White House aid that the House bypass debate and a roll call vote on impeachment so that the issue can be sent quickly to the Senate for trial. Such a plan is under "active consideration," according to a presidential press spokesman, and its clear — and only—purpose would be to prevent the case against Mr. Nixon from being spelled out in detail in the House. The plan is a clear attempt to disrupt the orderly constitutional impeachment process now underway and deserves to be dropped forthwith. The Watergate coverup has gone on far too long as it is; it scarcely needs to be compounded by a blackout of information in the House.

THE STATES-ITEM

New Orleans, La., August 7, 1974

President Nixon, who has maintained he could be impeached and removed from office only for a serious criminal offense, has now admitted he is guilty of a serious crime — obstruction of justice.

He also has admitted that he lied, not only to the American people on prime-time television, but to his own lawyers, members of his staff and supporters in Congress.

Mr. Nixon has admitted knowing details of the Watergate break-in about nine months before he previously said he had learned of them. Not only did he quickly learn of the break-in details, he authorized the use of the Central Intelligence Agency to thwart a Federal Bureau of Investigation probe of the incident. He did this, not for any reasons of national security, but to save his own skin.

Mr. Nixon has admitted withholding this and other pertinent evidence from Congress, the courts and the American people. It scarcely is any wonder that his strongest supporters are changing their positions.

This is the darkest hour of the Presidency.

Richard Nixon, a man who has talked about respect for the law, has turned out to be its chief violator. He is a criminal who sought but failed to cover his tracks.

This nation has seen bad presidents and weak presidents. But Richard Nixon is our first evil president, a man so corrupt that he has made John Dean, his principal accuser, look good.

There is no other choice now. The nation's best interests can only be served by Richard Nixon's swift impeachment, trial, conviction and removal from office.

The Miami Herald

Miami, Fla., August 7, 1974

BUBBLING with confidence and oozing with the scrubbed-face sincerity that was the hallmark of the Nixon administration's White House advisers, John Ehrlichman said on a public television program Sept. 7, 1972, "And I think after the history of this first term is written and you look back, you're going to see that compared to other administrations or by any standards you'd want to apply, that it has been an extraordinarily clean, corruption-free administration because the President insists on that."

But now there are taped voices within the Oval Office of the White House that tell the country Richard Nixon knew within days of the Watergate burglary that his reelection committee and Republican campaign money were linked directly to the illegal activities of the White House plumbers unit. He knew and he did all possible to cover it up.

If this is not the worst of the case against the President, it is the very confession that his closest political friends and supporters have steadfastly insisted is the only thing that will make them turn their backs on Richard M. Nixon.

Now it is all over. From the mouth of the President comes the admission that he has been lying to the country. He lied to the man he selected as his new vice president. He lied to the brilliant Boston lawyer, James St. Clair, who came to Washington in response to what he thought was a compelling duty to protect the office and honor of the American Presidency.

It turns out there is little honor or defense left for this administration. The House will certainly impeach by an overwhelming margin and there can no longer be any value in counting noses of those senators who will refuse to convict and remove Mr. Nixon from the office he has dishonored. What a tragedy for the nation when only the indicted Sen. Edward Gurney of Florida can be counted the one sure vote for this President.

Think of what President Nixon said April 30, 1973, when he announced the resignations of his four closest aides: "Justice will be pursued fairly, fully and impartially, no matter who was involved." Remember when Mr. Nixon told Sen. Hugh Scott during the same period, "Hugh, I have nothing to hide. The White House has nothing to hide."

Sen. Scott knows now he was betrayed by the President he trusted. So do those Republican congressmen who went on the firing line at the Judiciary Committee hearings and hung in there. Now Rep. Charles Wiggins of California chokes back his tears as he calls on Mr. Nixon to resign and says he will vote to impeach if the President does not quit.

We think the end is near. Not for the Republic which is basically sound and will survive this political and moral tragedy, but for Richard Milhous Nixon. He can be expected to accept resignation after impeachment and thus keep the handsome pension the country gives its former Presidents. That will be the expedient thing to do and Richard Nixon has always done the expedient.

The Globe and Mail

Toronto, Ont., August 6, 1974

On Friday 27 per cent—54 million—of the American people still believed that their President should not be impeached, still believed—must have believed—that guilty as all his associates might be of attempting to cover up the Watergate break-in of Democratic Party headquarters, President Richard Nixon was innocent.

Yesterday he told those 54 million that he had betrayed them.

He did not tell them willingly, of course. Driven into a corner by the tapes which Judge John Sirica had subpoenaed, knowing that the tapes would tell the United States the truth, he rushed in with a written statement to present that truth in the light most favorable to himself. But no light now can make white the black of the President's lies.

He pleads a failure of recollection when he told his nation, on April 29, that "as far as what the President personally knew and did with regard to Watergate and the cover-up is concerned, these materials (the White House tape transcripts he was releasing)—together with those already made available—will tell it all". He says that he later reviewed two tapes of June 23, 1972, and that "although I recognized that these presented potential problems, I did not inform my staff or my counsel of it, or those arguing my case, nor did I amend my submission to the Judiciary Committee in order to include and reflect it".

The June 23 tapes cover conversations with former White House chief of staff H. R. Haldeman, six days after the break-in at Democratic Party headquarters. Mr. Nixon says that he gave instructions designed to protect national security, and then adds, "The June 23 tapes clearly show, however, that at the time I gave those instructions I also discussed the political aspects of the situation, and that I was aware of the advantages this course of action would have with respect to limiting possible public exposure of involvement by persons connected with the re-election committee (the committee for his re-election in 1972)."

So six days after the break-in, however he now puts it, the President was involved in the cover-up in which he has consistently said he had no part.

The agony which this knowledge must have brought to those of his countrymen who trusted him, the humiliation which all America must suffer under this dishonoring of its highest office, can be fully understood only by citizens of the United States. One measure is that the man who led his defence during the House Judiciary Committee consideration of impeachment has called for his resignation.

Yet the U.S. democratic system has proved, after more than two brutal years, that it works. Slowly, surely, the truth has been forced forth. It is ironic that the final clinching piece of evidence of dishonor was built on dishonor itself. If Richard Nixon had not secretly and dishonorably taped his conversations with domestic and foreign visitors, those tapes would not now be at hand to condemn him.

The Philadelphia Inquirer

Philadelphia, Pa., August 7, 1974

"I recognize," said President Nixon in his stunning statement Monday, "that this additional material I am now furnishing may further damage my case."

That is the understatement of the year. It does not just damage his case — it destroys it.

For here we find, in a transcript of conversations in the revered Oval Office of the White House, that the President not only learned of the involvement of his re-election committee in the Watergate break-in less than a week after it happened but personally took a hand at that early date in the cover-up.

Thus, as Republican Rep. Barber Conable of New York says, "I guess we have found the smoking gun, haven't we?

We have indeed.

Beyond that, Mr. Nixon admits that he has withheld this evidence from his own lawyers and from the various investigators to whom he so frequently pledged his full cooperation.

And he further confesses that in previous statements on this sordid affair he has not been truthful to the American people even while assuring them that his only interest was in seeing that the truth was brought out and the guilty brought to justice.

• • •

Up to a point, Mr. Nixon seems to be entering a plea of guilty and throwing himself on the mercy of the Congress and the public. But only up to a point.

He made this statement, it should be remembered, only after losing his fight against giving up these tapes and after it thus became inevitable that his deceptive pose of the last two years would be exposed. And despite an expression of "regret" he shows little sensitivity to the enormous extent to which he has betrayed the trust of his high office.

"I am firmly convinced that the record, in its entirety, does not justify the extreme step of impeachment and removal of a President," he says in conclusion. "I trust that as the constitutional process goes forward, this perspective will prevail."

We cannot believe that it will — **or** that it should.

From the beginning of this tragic chapter in American history, The Inquirer has given Mr. Nixon the benefit of the doubt about his own role in it. On the impeachment question, our position has been that the evidence should be made available and examined and decisions taken, one at a time, in keeping with the constitutional process.

On the strength of the evidence and debate which came from the House Judiciary Committee, we concluded that the President should be impeached by the House and the articles sent to the Senate for trial.

On the strength of the additional information which has now come from the President's own words, we sadly conclude that Richard M. Nixon must be removed from office.

• • •

Mr. Nixon's staff insists that he will not resign. If he holds to that position, it thus falls to the Senate to take the ultimate step — for the first time in the life of the Republic — of unseating a President.

As Mr. Nixon himself concedes, impeachment in the House is now a foregone conclusion. We would hope, therefore, that action there can be speeded up without any violence to due process and that the Senate in turn will move as fast as possible to bring this dreary matter to an end.

The President has lost — indeed, forfeited—the confidence of the American people and his moral authority to lead them. The Federal government is drifting while he spends his time on the scandals which have wrecked his administration. The sooner he can be replaced, the sooner the country can put Watergate behind it and get on with its other business.

The Ottawa Citizen

Ottawa, Ont., August 7, 1974

Now a self-admitted liar in the Watergate cover-up, President Nixon's impeachment in the House of Representatives and conviction in the Senate seem certain.

His confession may have been prompted by one of two motives. Both the House and the Senate, once they had access to the Watergate tapes, would have found out anyway that he knew about a cover-up six days after the burglary — long before he had previously said he knew.

Alternatively, he may hope to make a deal with the Congress. He would resign, and in return receive immunity from criminal charges once he becomes a private citizen. In other words, he may hope to cop a plea, as his vice-president, Spiro Agnew, did when faced with criminal proceedings.

Whatever his motives, and whether he resigns or is convicted in the Senate, his presidency is destroyed. He is not only a self-confessed liar; he has confessed he tried to obstruct justice. In no democratic country can the head of government admit to that and still exercise his office, though he may try to hold office for a short time yet.

The United States remains the strongest country in the non-Communist world. But it is now a country without a head. The sooner it gets a new president, the better for all of us.

MANCHESTER NEW HAMPSHIRE UNION LEADER

Manchester, N.H., August 6, 1974

And now President Nixon has impeached himself.

We use the word impeach here not in its constitutional sense but in its dictionary sense: "to challenge or discredit (a person's honor, reputation, etc.)."

We can see almost no other way to judge the President's latest disclosure when weighed against his repeated previous denials. It reveals his discussing the cover-up with then chief of staff H. R. Haldeman six days after the Watergate breakin. It discloses the President's condoning of use of the CIA to blunt an FBI investigation.

We say "almost" no other way because the President's expressed conviction that "the record, in its entirety, does not justify the extreme step of impeachment and removal" indicates he believes there are other possible interpretations.

We see only two as possible. One is that Nixon is so amoral where partisan and personal politics are concerned that he believes ends justify any means. The other is that he is so callous and so forgetful that he actually forgot the extreme measures he condoned.

Neither amorality nor callous forgetfulness are traits befitting a President of the United States.

Two additional points make the latest White House disclosures all the more damning.

The first is that they were not made public until the President realized their publication by others was inevitably imminent. It was imminent because the Supreme Court over strong presidential objections, forced the release of the accusing tapes. Getting out the facts on his own under those circumstances hardly indicates repentance.

The second is that what the President condoned was use of the CIA to head off an FBI investigation.

That amounts in our view to undermining national security by suborning one of its most vital arms for purely political purposes.

Which brings us to the point that now is the time to get on with impeachment by the House (which even the President now concedes is virtually inevitable) and with trial by the Senate.

As of this writing we can see but one likely verdict in such a trial.

The only alternative is presidential resignation. While we have opposed that in the past, preferring the resolution of the issue by trial as provided in the Constitution, we now admit there could be wisdom in the resignation course.

Either way, what this nation now needs is a change at the top. And soon.

The Greenville News

Greenville, S.C., August 7, 1974

President Nixon's statement and transcripts of White House tapes released Monday come close to admission of obstruction of justice as charged in the first article of impeachment voted by the House Judiciary Committee. Worse still, the new disclosure tends to destroy the President's best defense — that obstruction, if it actually occurred, was necessary in the interest of legitimate national security.

This is devastating. The President's remaining defenders, whom he now says were acting on the basis of incomplete and in some instance erroneous information, are helpless. We are in that position.

We think our readers should know that we had written and scheduled for publication on Tuesday an editorial re-emphasizing the point that the President had not been proved guilty. It discussed the possibility that he might be able to produce solid evidence that his actions were dedicated to the national security and to the protection of American foreign policy. At about 6 p.m. Monday, after reading the President's statement and portions of the transcripts, we were forced to kill that editorial.

The President's statement and the transcripts themselves, taken in context with earlier evidence, indicate that the White House might have used national security as an excuse for the Watergate cover-up.

That changes the whole picture, because the President's defenders were acting upon the presumption that national securi-

ty was the reason — not the excuse — for any cover-up. We had gone so far as to say in the now-dead editorial that national security "covers a multitude of sins."

We believe that, but we are appalled at the idea that a President of the United States would use national security — a most sacred trust of the presidency — as an excuse to cover up political wrong-doing. Unfortunately that implication is clear in the President's own words and actions, as they have been made public so far.

It now is encumbent upon President Nixon to come forward with clear, convincing evidence to the contrary — to prove by White House tapes and documents that national security was indeed the reason for the cover-up. The evidence may be there, because numerous presidential conferences with national security and foreign policy officials have not been made public.

If the evidence of national security is there and is made available, the President still may have a defense. But it is now his obligation to make such evidence available, if it exists. It is disturbing that such evidence itself might breach national security, if made public.

This situation is tragic for the nation. It is heart-breaking for those who have supported the President. For the good of everybody concerned, it is best to get this thing over and done with — one way or another — at the earliest possible moment.

THE PLAIN DEALER

Cleveland, Ohio, August 6, 1974

"If read with an open and a fair mind and read together with the record of the actions I took, these transcripts will show that what I have stated from the beginning to be the truth has been the truth: that I personally had no knowledge of the break-in before it occurred, that I had no knowledge of the coverup until I was informed of it by John Dean on March 21, that I never offered clemency for the defendants, and that after March 21 my actions were directed toward finding the facts and seeing that justice was done, fairly and according to the law."

—From President Nixon's address to the nation announcing his answer to the subpoena from the House Judiciary Committee, April 29, 1974.

". . . In May, I made a preliminary review of some of the 64 taped conversations subpoenaed by the special prosecutor. Among the conversations I listened to at that time were two of those of June 23 (1972). Although I recognized that these presented potential problems, I

did not inform my staff or my counsel of it, or those arguing my case, nor did I amend my submission to the Judiciary Committee in order to include and reflect it.

"At that time, I did not realize the extent of the implications which these conversations might now appear to have. As a result, those arguing my case, as well as those passing judgment on the case, did so with information that was incomplete and in some respects erroneous. This was a serious act of omission for which I take full responsibility and which I deeply regret.

"Since the Supreme Court's decision 12 days ago, I have ordered my counsel to analyze the 64 tapes, and I have listened to a number of them myself. This process has made it clear that portions of the tapes of these June 23 conversations are at variance with certain of my previous statements."

—From President Nixon's statement issued yesterday, Aug. 5, 1974.

Des Moines Tribune

Des Moines, Iowa, August 7, 1974

Richard Nixon appears finally to have decided to come clean on the misdoings in the White House in which he participated. He now admits that he lied to the people, to Congress and to law enforcement agencies about the Watergate cover-up.

This comes after more than a year of delaying tactics, evasions and outright untruths. The ruling of the U.S. Supreme Court that the President can not hold back evidence subpoenaed for a criminal trial on ground of executive privilege may have tipped the scales. Then the careful, massive case built up in the House Judiciary Committee inquiry and the sober, objective presentation of the case in the televised debate showed Nixon he had no chance to prevent impeachment.

In his statement Monday, he acknowledged this. He might well have added that the White House public relations drive for the last year had been rejected by Congress and the people. The story that an innocent Richard Nixon was the victim of "enemies" in politics and the press out to "get him" just would not wash. The Nixon loyalists who have been reciting that line were left hanging on a limb, and they resented it.

Finally, the considerable achievements in foreign relations by the Nixon administration were not seen by many as justification for violations of the laws and the Constitution.

Nixon managed to destroy most of his political capital by deviousness and lack of forthrightness. His ideological backers in both parties have been deserting him as the facts came out on White House involvement in wiretapping, burglary, obstruction of justice. Conservative empathy did not offset dishonesty and playing loose with the law.

This culminated with a crash Monday. Conservative Republicans and Democrats who had long searched for a way to keep in office a man they thought to be on their philosophical side decided he had to go. These included staunch defenders of Nixon in the Judiciary Committee. They had wanted proof of direct complicity of Nixon in the Watergate crimes, and he gave it to them.

We find a hopeful moral lesson in this episode of the Nixon saga. Surely the cynical view that lying and conniving will triumph over truth and straightforwardness has been dealt a blow. It does pay to be honest.

We will not attempt to penetrate the mind of Richard Nixon to find an explanation for his admission of complicity or whatever you want to call it. At this point we will only state that it should help speed up the process of installing a new president, Gerald Ford. That is a service to the nation.

The last few weeks have brought the U.S. government almost to a standstill in dealing with inflation and impending recession. Business and other governments are plagued with uncertainty about what Washington will do. Moving rapidly to settle the transition in the presidency will help restore confidence.

Arkansas ✠ Gazette.
Little Rock, Ark., August 7, 1974

Well, the new tapes did it, or, rather, the Supreme Court, which finally ordered release of the tapes. As was clear then, this was one of the Court's finest hours, but it is scarcely Richard Nixon's finest hour, even given the subject and his record in public office and all the machinations he has been party to in order to get in public office in the first place, going back to the very beginning in 1946.

By his own delayed admission, those who did not already now know that he was not only participant in the Watergate cover-up (and by every indication, in the Ellsberg burglary cover-up, as well) but a prime mover in the cover-up, *the* prime mover from the standpoint of being the one person with the muscle to see to it that the cover-up was kept going.

By his own admission, those who did not already know know now that he lied in saying so many times in such unequivocal terms that all was being done to uncover the malefactors — or already had been done — that could be done by anybody. The somewhat sadly delighted imagination conjures up the image of little clusters of people gathering yesterday on street corners and around cracker barrels the land across to say, as much to themselves as to each other, "I didn't know Richard Nixon would tell a lie, did you?"

If you want to put it that way, the very last defense left to him is a little exercise in a form of logic: How do we know he is not lying now when he acknowledges he is a liar?

Actually, he still *is* lying now when he says that "whatever mistakes I made in the handling of Watergate, the basic truth remains that when all the facts were brought to my attention, I insisted on a full investigation and prosecution of the guilty. I am firmly convinced that the record, in its entirety, does not justify the extreme step of impeachment and removal of a President."

Some "basic truth!"

If he had, in fact, insisted on full investigation and prosecution of the guilty, he would never have fired Archie Cox and the truth would have outed long ago. If he had insisted on full investigaton and prosecution of the guilty, he would never have put the succession of stumbling blocks in the path of Cox's successor, Leon Jaworski, that resulted finally in the air-clearing 8-to-0 "release—or else" ruling by the Supreme Court, which — remember? — came less than two weeks ago.

As it is, the calculated multi-year pattern of cover up, confuse, delay, still must have its effect on the House's impeachment deliberations, though this becomes more academic all the time with people like the die-harder Charles W. Sandman of New Jersey, now saying that he and almost every one else in the House will vote to approve the articles of impeachment that he had defended against with such a decibel assault on the ears of the TV audience during the Judiciary Committee debate.

But the House still will not be operating on the knowledge of all that is in the new tapes if it is to adhere to its schedule for an impeachment vote, because Mr. Nixon has already seen to that. What it will have instead is a set of three transcripts of what Nixon himself says constitutes the full "thrust and purport" of these critically damaging new pieces of evidence, which ought to be enough, to be sure — as the first Nixon transcripts of something resembling the unexpurgated really hot stuff was enough for public opinion — but it is still not the real stuff itself. As we had noted just before the new transcripts and the President's statement were made public, the real stuff could be ready and waiting right now for all who need to see it if Nixon had not waited until *after* the Supreme Court ruling to start putting the material in shape for transmittal to Judge Sirica's Court.

But if the Judiciary Committee could return three articles of impeachment on the basis of what had been made available to it, then the full House, following the Committee's lead, should now be able to register such an overwhelming vote for impeachment that the message cannot help but be received loud and clear by the Senate, as even Mr. Sandman by now seems to anticipate.

Many people have been made fools of, or have made fools of themselves, but the ones put on prominent exhibition most recently are Sandman and the others who defended Nixon so unconditionally, at such length and so loudly on nationwide TV, and who now are peeling off by the numbers. They made embarrassments of themselves, and in so doing, made embarrassments of their "safe" constituencies. The obverse of their uncomfortable revisionist position now is the position of those tortured Republicans and conservative Democrats who, though tortured, voted for one or more of the articles returned on the evidence available to them. They now look like sages, even seers, as well as like the heroes that they so obviously were.

As we said from the beginning, in order for the White House to make out any rational case for Mr. Nixon's defense, it had to prove John W. Dean a perjurer. It could not, and now we know from Nixon himself that he knew of the Watergate cover-up long months before the date that he claimed was the first he heard of it, as Dean said all along Nixon had known. Dean has been sentenced now, as he should have been sentenced (and, incidentally, took it as rather more of a man than the "tough" guy, Ehrlichman), but he was not sentenced as a perjurer. Nixon is not a perjurer because he never could be made to swear to the lies he told, but it is he who is proved now to be the liar.

Finally — and this is important — as we also said all along, we know now that the cover-up was not undertaken out of any considerations for, the national security, but purely for a partisan political reason — "the re-election of the President."

It was all too long coming out, but when it did it was worth the wait. What better time than a matter of months before the celebration of the Bicentennial to be reminded of how far we have come from George Washington's "I will not tell a lie" (an invention on the part of Parson Weems, but an innocent and plausible one) and Richard Nixon's final grudging admission that he has lied on many more than one occason to save his otherwise naked political skin?

The Salt Lake Tribune
Salt Lake City, Utah, August 7, 1974

For better than two years Richard Nixon said he knew nothing about the Watergate breakin and subsequent White House efforts to cover it up until 10 months after the fact. The truth of the matter, by direct admission of the President of the United States, is that within less than a week after the June 12, 1972, burglary, Mr. Nixon okayed a plan by a top aide to use the Central Intelligence Agency to blunt a Federal Bureau of Investigation probe into the crime.

On July 27, the House Judiciary Committee approved the first article of impeachment which accuses Mr. Nixon, in connection with the Watergate unlawful entry, of engaging "in a course of conduct or plan designed to delay, impede, and obstruct the investigation of such unlawful : entry; to cover up, conceal and protect those responsible and to conceal the existence and scope of other unlawful covert activities."

This article is but the first step in what could be the prolonged, but constitutionally proper and historically preferable, impeachment process, involving adoption of the articles of impeachment by the whole House of Representative and trial and conviction by the Senate.

But in consideration of Mr. Nixon's statements Monday, which was accompanied by transcripts of tape recordings made within a week of the Watergate breakin, is it necessary for the nation to go through the agonizing process of impeachment?

Mr. Nixon has, for all practical purposes, confessed his guilt to the Judiciary Committee's first impeachment article. And having admitted that guilt he should immediatley resign.

But Mr. Nixon, following a hastily called meeting of his cabinet Tuesday morning, reiterated that he will not resign.

That being the case, and because of what amounts to Mr. Nixon's confession, there is no reason for delaying full implementation of impeachment.

While Mr. Nixon's confession alone provides ample reason for Congress to proceed with impeachment and trial without delay, two other paramount reasons further demand it act with carefully considered haste.

The nation's economy has taken on all the stablity of a bowl of jelly and this in large measure is directly attributable to the waning lack of confidence the American people have in Mr. Nixon's ability to lead this nation.

Secondly, if Congress fails to dispose of the impeachment issue during the 93rd Congress there is the possiblity the whole matter will have to be reconsidered in its entirety by the 94th Congress. If the impeachment of Richard Nixon is to result in a clear cut, no doubt about it, decision removing him from office, it must be done before the 93rd Congress is forced by the Constitution to adjourn sine die by noon, Jan. 3, 1975. To meet adjournment deadline without resolving Mr. Nixon's political fate will place a cloud over the legality of the ultimate decision by a succeeding Congress.

Mr. Nixon, despite what is tantamount to confession of direct involvement in Watergate cover up, has refused to resign (something permissible under the Constitution). Impeachment and trial is the only course left to the American public. The uncertainity of the economy coupled with the public's lack of confidence in Mr. Nixon's ability to do anything about it, demands it. And the possiblity of a legal cloud hanging over any post-93rd Congress action on impeachment and Mr. Nixon's admission of direct involvement in the Watergate affair leaves the Congress no choice.

The men and women of the House and Senate must proceed, without delay, to impeach, try and if he is found guilty remove Mr. Nixon from office.

Washington Star-News

Washington, D.C., August 6, 1974

Enough. For Richard Nixon, in our estimation, the game is over.

All along, the missing piece in the Watergate puzzle — the proof of Nixon's impeachable guilt — has been some hard evidence tying him to knowledge of cover-up, knowledge he could and should have used to prevent the tragedy that developed in the wake of the break-in at Democratic headquarters. Now we have it. Cornered by a unanimous ruling of the Supreme Court, admitting a "serious act of omission for which I take full responsibility and which I deeply regret," the President has been forced to hand over the smoking pistol demanded by those of us who have insisted he be given the benefit of every doubt.

The relevant portions of the Oval Office tape of June 23, 1972, released yesterday, are devastating to the Nixon case. Here we have H. R. Haldeman, a week after the burglary, pointing out to his chief that it may be awkward if the FBI presses its inquiry too hard. "You seem to think," he says, "the thing to do is to get them to stop?" Nixon's reply is unequivocal. "Right," he says. "Fine." A moment later, he bluntly instructs Haldeman to enlist the CIA in the cover-up effort. "You call them in," he says, " . . . play it tough. That's the way they play it and that's the way we're going to play it."

As the President puts it in his accompanying statement: "At the time I gave those instructions . . . I was aware of the advantage this course of action would have with respect to limiting possible public exposure of involvement by persons connected with the Re-election Committee." That, to understate the point, is a considerable understatement. No rational person, reading these transcripts, can suppose that Nixon and Haldeman were motivated by concern for national security or anything of the sort. Transparently and shamelessly, they were conspiring as to how the rap might be beaten.

It is, we say, enough. The precise denouement still is uncertain. Beyond a doubt, the President must be giving most serious consideration to resigning. We have argued in the past that resignation would leave too many questions unresolved, but that seems no longer a valid objection. People today might well accept a Nixon resignation as a happy way out of his and their afflictions. But this is a stubborn, inward-turning, isolated man, and his reaction to the situation in which he presently finds himself is impossible to predict, even for those who have known him well and long. In any event, it now is virtually inconceivable that Nixon can last out his term. He has betrayed and affronted those loyalists who have bet their political lives on his veracity. If it is not forestalled by his own decision to pull out, the House of Representatives no doubt will impeach him and the Senate, in our view, will convict and remove him from office if it must. And, in our view, if the case goes that far, it must.

These words do not come easily. This newspaper has supported Richard Nixon in all his national campaigns. We have shared many of his domestic aims, and admired his bold initiatives overseas. We have considered, moreover, that any doubt on impeachment should be resolved in the President's favor, because to oust the popularly elected chief executive, in a democracy, is playing with political fire. But to flinch from removing a leader who has dishonored his office and his constitutional role is, clearly, even more dangerous to the national psyche.

The President concluded his statement yesterday with two pleas, both deserving of note. First, he asserted that, regardless of his discussions on July 23, 1972, CIA and FBI officials in fact did right. The truth about the performance of these two agencies is not all that clear, but it is certain that a number of persons in the administration stood their ground in behalf of honesty amid the Watergate debacle. It is fair to say, however, that in so doing they received precious little if any encouragement from Richard Nixon.

Secondly, the President asked that the Watergate evidence be looked at in its entirety, and in perspective. For anyone who has done so conscientiously, the picture that emerges is disgusting. The cumulative record for criminal effrontery, negligence, mendacity, pettiness and stupidity is perhaps without equal in the record of history. Yesterday's final affront to the national sense of decency is simply too much to bear.

ALBUQUERQUE JOURNAL

*Albuquerque, N.M.
August 6, 1974*

President Nixon, finally, has confessed.

But he has not repented. Lacking is the ring of sincere contrition that springs from a deep sense of humility on the part of one who finds himself in error.

The evidence lies in these two incompatible statements:

— " . . . This was a serious act of omission for which I take full responsibility and which I deeply regret."

— " . . . I am firmly convinced that the record, in its entirety, does not justify the extreme step of impeachment and removal of a President. I trust that as the Constitutional process goes forward, this perspective will prevail."

The Albuquerque Journal is one of few American dailies which has not, thus far, called for the impeachment, resignation or removal of the President.

And even now we defer to the constitutionally designated bodies and, once more, call on them to act conscientiously in the light of all the pertinent evidence and with due regard for all extenuating facts.

But the Journal has been persistent in calling on the President for total candor. In this respect he has been found wanting. At this point we can see no reason why he could not have laid all the facts before the American people, either before or after the 1972 election, without betraying a single word of confidence related to national security.

Until the evidence is all in and evaluated, we are disposed to judge the President most harshly for his arrogant contempt toward the great masses of the American people in their compelling concern for the well being of their nation and its government. Constant pleas for reassurance and answers have been met with stony silence or, even worse, evasive replies highly reminiscent of the words of history's first miscreant:

"Am I my brother's keeper?"

Sentinel Star
Orlando, Fla., August 7, 1974

RICHARD Nixon's options have run out. He must promptly resign as President of the United States for the good of his country, of his party — and for his own best interests.

This wretched Watergate mess has dragged on too long as it is. It is senseless now to put the country through the remainder of the impeachment process in the House and the Senate.

For those of us who demanded evidence before joining the crowd determined to drive a President from office, we now have it — in spades.

President Nixon, in releasing, under pressure, the tapes of his conversations with then chief aide H. R. Haldeman on June 23, 1972, has provided the evidence that he knew of and ordered the infamous cover-up of the break-in at Democratic national headquarters. In so doing he admitted that he had lied to the country and even to his own lawyer, and he betrayed the faith of millions of Americans who believed him.

☆ ☆ ☆

WE SUPPOSE some of Mr. Nixon's defenders will continue to excuse the abuses of power that have been revealed to us.

We believe, certainly, that there was a cover-up in the administration and in the Congress during the investigation of the scandals now generally referred to as the Bobby Baker case.

We have personal evidence of heavy-handed political threats against the press in the John F. Kennedy administration.

It is naive to believe that former administrations did not use the Internal Revenue Service and other federal agencies to punish their enemies and reward their friends.

All of that is not necessarily immaterial, but it doesn't excuse the obvious violations of high office by the Nixon administration.

This country cannot tolerate a government turned loose against its own citizens in a vainglorious quest for power.

☆ ☆ ☆

THERE IS no need to further repeat here the charges and the thousands of words that Watergate has generated. We have devoted tons of newsprint to them already.

Perhaps, however, to balance the ledger just a bit we should note some of the accomplishments of the Nixon administration.

The long and costly war in Southeast Asia was brought to an end for American fighting forces during Mr. Nixon's years in office. Because of the President's toughness (the same virtue that got him into impeachment trouble, of course), American POWs came home on acceptable terms.

A generation-long American foreign policy that saw this nation shut off from the most populous country in the world, the People's Republic of China, was reversed in a candid facing up to reality.

American prestige in foreign affairs was raised to a level not enjoyed since the triumphant end of World War II.

☆ ☆ ☆

RICHARD NIXON, on balance, is a loyal, devoted American. He has made some horrible mistakes. Yet, we believe some mercy is due from his countrymen.

Now is not the time for his long-time political enemies to rejoice with their pound of flesh. Nor is it the time for those of us who may have been betrayed in our loyalty to a President of the United States to demand vengeance.

Let Mr. Nixon go as peacefully as possible. He will suffer enough.

The Topeka Daily Capital
Topeka, Kans., August 7, 1974

If there ever was any doubt that President Richard M. Nixon should resign, that doubt has now been removed by his own recorded words.

By releasing a transcript of a tape recording of conversations he had with H. R. Haldeman, his former chief of staff, on June 23, 1972, only six days after the now-notorious Watergate break-in of Democratic National Headquarters, he admits knowledge of the break-in.

The tape transcript reveals incontrovertibly that, while Nixon apparently was not apprised of the break-in or plans for it, he was perfectly willing to participate in the cover-up — hiding the facts from the voters.

To his discredit, the President instantly was willing to use the secret Central Intelligence Agency to halt a Federal Bureau of Investigation search for facts that was moving inexorably toward the White House.

President Nixon, when he released the transcript said that some of the statements were "at variance" with previous ones he had made. In fact they were so much "at variance" that they amounted to pure and unadulterated fabrications.

Now, the President hands out the transcript — after the House Judiciary Committee recommended adoption of articles of impeachment — and says he did not give the information to his staff or his lawyers.

And it is obvious that the President kept the damaging evidence from some of his most ardent defenders on the Judiciary Committee and in the House and Senate generally.

With his belated revelation that he had been told six days after the Watergate break-in of its connections with the Committee to Re-elect the President, he abruptly and calculatedly jerked the rug from under his most loyal and eloquent defenders.

Now, if the President would avoid another miscalculation, he should resign immediately. This would avoid impeachment by the House — now a foregone conclusion — and conviction by the Senate — which grows more probable by the hour.

It would save the nation further embarrassment and trauma, and could result in the President's retention of his pension — something he would lose through conviction by two-thirds of the Senate. The pension would be small payment for his achievements in foreign affairs and for peace and good will.

Readers will recall that on Sunday, May 5 of this year, The Capital-Journal called for the resignation of the President to restore pride and dignity to the highest office in this land. The Capital-Journal then observed:

"Fortunately we have Gerald Ford, the vice president, to step into the breach and carry on. We believe the President should not go through a trial in the Senate but should very quietly resign, pick up his hat and move on. He has had his day and been found wanting.

"Even as Vice President Agnew has become the forgotten man, so may President Nixon pass into oblivion and the nation again resume its true posture, one that every American can uphold with pride and dignity."

And now, it is more imperative than before that President Nixon resign and leave the high office to someone who will hold it in the esteem it deserves and should command.

The Oregonian

Portland, Ore., August 7, 1974

The Nixon presidency came to an inglorious end, for all practical purposes, on Monday afternoon, Aug. 5, when he admitted that he lied to the American people and congressional committees and had joined in a conspiracy to obstruct justice by withholding evidence of the commission of crimes by his subordinates.

He continues to insist that he will not resign. Unless he changes his mind under the pressure of now certain impeachment by the House of Representatives and the revelations of more of the 64 recordings of White House conversations being reviewed by U. S. District Judge John J. Sirica, his scandal-riddled administration will drag on for a time, to the detriment of the nation.

But President Nixon's admission of active participation in the cover-up of the involvement of re-election campaign aides in the break-in and bugging of Democratic National Headquarters, as early as six days after the event in June, 1972, destroys not only the remaining vestiges of his credibility as chief executive. It also makes it almost impossible for his lawyers, whom he also deceived, or for any remaining Nixon loyalists in Congress, to provide for the President a credible defense in a trial in the Senate.

The President is certainly entitled to a fair trial, in common with any citizen accused of crimes and misdemeanors, if he chooses not to give up his office voluntarily. Certainly, there were mitigating circumstances—his determination to be re-elected in 1972, to make more progress toward world peace, to help straighten out the domestic economy, to save himself and his closest advisers from disgrace.

But the deadly transcripts of tapes wrung from his possession by order of the U. S. Supreme Court leave no further doubt of the culpability he has repeatedly denied. The Senate will surely convict him if he attempts to block the use of this material in this trial.

In refusing to resign, as late as his meeting with his Cabinet Tuesday, the President said the constitutional process of impeachment and trial should continue and that the record, in its entirety, "does not justify the extreme step of impeachment and removal of a president." But there is no longer any point in arguing definitions of the constitutional grounds, "high crimes and misdemeanors," for impeachment. President Nixon has confessed his violation of the constitutional requirement that a president must see to the enforcement of the laws. Obstruction of justice is a crime.

The newly released transcripts, above all else, confirm the public recognition of the innate immorality of the Nixon White House. This condition was not ameliorated by the many disclosures that other politicians, members of Congress among them, were elected with funds illegally contributed by special interests, or lied about other matters. It is the President who is on trial. It is the President who did not immediately expose and fire his assistants when he learned of their misdeeds. It is the President who joined in efforts to protect them from exposure and prosecution.

So it should now be conceded by those who have declined to join in lynching Richard M. Nixon and who have insisted that the evidence must be produced for conviction, that he has, himself, provided that evidence, not willingly but by court order. President Nixon is at the end of the road. Inasmuch as he refuses to resign in the national interest of an effective new government, the trial will go on.

But even should the Senate fail to find the charges for impeachment sufficient to remove the President from office, Richard Nixon should resign if acquitted. His ability to govern has been destroyed. He will never again be able to regain the authority he has lost. The nation deserves a new leader.

The Detroit News

Detroit, Mich., August 6, 1974

President Nixon's shocking admission that he had in effect concealed evidence about the Watergate cover-up, coming after Sen. Robert Griffin's call for the President's resignation, has suddenly changed Mr. Nixon's position from precarious to untenable. For his own good and everybody else's, Mr. Nixon should quit.

Impeachment by the full House of Representatives was "virtually a foregone conclusion," as the President himself admitted in his statement. Now his admission of complicity in the cover-up, plus the defection of Sen. Griffin, assistant Senate GOP leader and long a presidential supporter, virtually destroy Mr. Nixon's hopes of successfully defending himself in a trial in the Senate.

The White House had counted on a hard core of 36 friendly senators to save him in the Senate. In recent days, some have become less and less firm in their support. Sen. Griffin's demand for resignation and the President's new admissions will give some of the other "dependables" new excuses for altering their position. It seems almost certain now that Mr. Nixon could not muster the 34 votes he would need for acquittal.

Shortly before asking the President to resign, Sen. Griffin noted the hopeless situation the President would face if he defied the Senate, as he did the House Judiciary Committee, in its quest of tapes of White House conversations. The senator warned that in case of such defiance he would vote for conviction of the President in a Senate trial.

In his new statement, Griffin revealed the question of the tapes has become academic as far as he is concerned and he wants not merely the tapes but the President's departure from office. Even the President's belated decision to turn over to the Senate the tapes of all 64 conversations he is giving U.S. District Judge John J. Sirica is not apt to change Griffin's mind or the positions of the anti-Nixon senators.

In fact, Griffin's view that, "We've arrived at a point where both the national interest and his (the President's) own interest will best be served by resigning," now probably will be shared by an increasing number of senators who previously had stood by the President or had not made their positions known.

Despite his new admissions, which he himself concedes "may further damage" his case, Mr. Nixon makes it clear he is still fighting for his political life and that "the record, in its entirety, does not justify the extreme step of impeachment and removal of a president." The new developments may help him change his mind and give new consideration to resignation, however.

Even before the President made his damaging admissions, there were those who thought that Mr. Nixon soon would see the handwriting on the wall and quit in order to permit new leadership to take over. Sen. Griffin thought so. We hoped so. Now there are additional reasons for thinking the President finally may be considering that course. It would be wise. The agony for the President and for the nation is getting to be too much to bear.

Anchorage Daily Times

Anchorage, Alaska, August 1, 1974

THE BEST INTEREST of the nation calls for a quick retirement of President Nixon from his high office. The work of the nation has been bogged down in Watergate too long and no end is in sight.

The President would serve the nation best by stepping aside and allowing the administration to be reorganized without him.

Too many people throughout the nation have become disenchanted with the President himself and the antics of the people around him. The disenchantment now extends into the halls of Congress where dilatory tactics have been allowed to drag out the investigations and impeachment proceedings over a period of years.

PRESIDENT NIXON has the legal right to a fair trial under the impeachment charges. He will be granted that right insofar as the government agencies have the capability of providing it.

But if he insists on that right it will mean that the nation is tied up for the most of the rest of the year in handling his case.

Right now the prospect is for weeks of proceedings in the House of Representatives before a final vote. Each of the 435 members will have the right to express themselves and most of them will. The speeches will be repetitive and often boring. And they may have little bearing on the outcome of the final vote.

The House action must be followed by a dramatic trial before the Senate in which every one of the 100 senators will play a role. When television is involved, it is a certainty that most of those 100 will have lots to say. For some of them it will be their big claim to national fame and attention.

BY RESIGNING his office the President would be avoiding this drawn-out, agonizing drama before Congress.

It can be expected that his successor would quickly put together a White House team that would lead the way to a return of normal government operations in Washington.

Even if the President was cleared under the Senate proceedings, it is doubtful if he could make himself an effective leader of the nation for the rest of his term. Too many people have lost faith in him. A leader can't lead without followers and we doubt that the President has many left.

AKRON BEACON JOURNAL
Akron, Ohio, August 1, 1974

SCORES OF members of Congress, Republicans and Democrats, senators and representatives, pronounced the verdict: "It's all over."

So it seems to us: Mr. Nixon's voluntary disclosure that he knew about the Watergate coverup only six days after the break-in and nine months before he has previously admitted learning about it, and his further admission that the coverup continued at least until Monday afternoon, makes "everything downhill" from now on, as Sen. Robert Dole of Kansas put it.

Though Mr. Nixon admitted the wrongdoing and said in his statement that it was a "serious act of omission for which I take full responsibility and which I deeply regret," he also argued that what he had done did not "warrant the extreme step of impeachment and removal as President."

This is a defense which, quite obviously, will not carry much impact on Capitol Hill. Even the President's staunchest defenders concede that the President has admitted guilt to one or more of the charges brought against him by the House Judiciary Committee. The disastrous conversations of June 23, 1972, with H.R. Haldeman show without question, even from the President, that Mr. Nixon obstructed justice, abused power and was, at least since the Watergate investigation began, in contempt of Congress.

Thus impeachment by the House is, we believe, a foregone conclusion without the qualifying "virtually" which the President included. It further seems that the Senate will have no choice but to convict on the evidence.

When Robert Griffin, the Senate Republican whip and an administration stalwart, calls upon the President to resign, it means that he has counted the votes and sees no hope for acquittal. Sen. Griffin, who last opposed the White House over the nomination of Clement Haynsworth to the Supreme Court, is not one to take firm positions lightly.

Given this almost inevitable outcome of an American tragedy, we find it difficult to believe that Mr. Nixon will continue to "stonewall" it longer, or to fight, as he seems to be trying to do, a delaying action.

For his own good, resignation makes common sense. Mr. Nixon is a man who has become accustomed to the good life, and resignation — provided he can plea-bargain to avoid criminal prosecution — would permit him to continue. Impeachment and conviction would leave him not only impoverished but subject to the decisions of a federal grand jury which might decide, for example, to look into his tax problems.

Even more important, Mr. Nixon's resignation would make sense for the nation. It is obvious that he is, and has been, unable to lead the country. It is equally obvious that even if the Senate refuses to convict him, a remote possibility, he would be unable to lead for the balance of his term.

The state of the economy, if nothing else, demands firms leadership and undivided attention. Yet the President has twice canceled meetings of his economic advisers in order to devote his time to the Watergate tapes and his defense. The nation cannot continue that way.

Since last November, this newspaper has called for the President's impeachment so all the facts could be brought out and the Senate could decide his guilt or innocence. Now the President has pleaded if not guilt, then at least nolo contendere, which is the response given last Fall by Spiro Agnew when he resigned. So the verdict is in.

Prolonging the trauma and the agony would serve no useful purpose.

LEDGER-STAR
Norfolk, Va., August 6, 1974

Amid the near total shambles of his defenses, President Nixon stands today as a still doggedly protesting but lonely figure. And it is not the kind of loneliness that prompts much sympathy from Americans as they assess, many of them with great disappointment, yesterday's damaging confession of withheld Watergate evidence.

That confession — of cover-up action partly motivated by "political aspects" of the situation, only six days after the Watergate burglary — is painful news to this country no matter how it is turned and examined.

Weighed from the viewpoint of a misled nation, his admission is thoroughly damning to start with. He pleads that in his earlier statements he had relied on memory and other sources in reporting on his actions respecting the CIA and FBI, but that he recognized potential problems just this past May after personally reviewing the tapes of June 23, 1972. This personal review came after his release of transcripts on April 29 of this year, which he labeled as enough "to tell it all."

Well, that is pretty weak, when the obviously crucial nature of the immediate post-Watergate conversations in the White House is considered. It requires a great deal of belief, at a time when belief in this man has worn threadbare, to accept the idea that he had forgotten the motive for trying, through the CIA, to limit the FBI's investigation, and had forgotten, too, his early awareness, revealed in the new tapes, that people high in his administration might have been involved in Watergate.

★ ★ ★ ★

But beyond this there is his own statement that, after he had listened to the June 23 conversations, he did not correct the false disavowals given the American people and did not amend his submission to the House Judiciary Committee.

Can anyone now discount self-protection as the rationale for much of the struggle against releasing this and other tapes? How much is left of the President's case for executive confidentiality?

As to the actual evidence of the early attempt to head off the FBI investigators, the magnitude of the disclosure has been promptly reflected in the sad to embittered words of condemnation from some of his staunchest, most recent supporters.

★ ★ ★ ★

When Mr. Nixon now talks of maintaining perspective on the record in its entirety, arguing that impeachment of a president is not thereby justified, he is talking in terms that had much more validity a month, a week or even a day before the new tape release and the humiliating explanation. Now the issue of impeachment justification has become a very close question to many who were heretofore worried by such a drastic step.

For the shell-shocked country has before it a kind of last-straw situation. That last straw is the concession — atop so much that has been less than candid, or shabby or cynical in the President's approach to the uses of power — that Mr. Nixon has been involved in the Watergate scandal to an extent not communicated even to his lawyers.

Aside from the rapidly changing impeachment outlook, there is now the pivotal matter of the minimum of public trust which the President would need to carry on for the remainder of his term if the apparently assured Senate trial should acquit him. After yesterday's shattering development, there is scarcely a shred of such trust left for now or later.

The Nixon move will not strike the country as any contrite resort to frankness. This latest admission, even more clearly than some of the retreats and evasions of the recent past, was forced from the President by the courts and circumstances he could no longer control.

Despite what has been good and constructive about the Nixon administation, the choices have distressingly narrowed in recent hours. Mr. Nixon, who has himself given up on beating impeachment in the House, faces an almost hopeless task in attempting to repair his credibility and survive. It is time he stopped trying.

He ought to resign.

THE CHRISTIAN SCIENCE MONITOR
Boston, Mass., August 7, 1974

The gravest questions arise in the wake of President Nixon's admission that he was involved in the Watergate cover-up. Can the nation now afford a government that is virtually at a standstill because of the impeachment crisis and would it not be in the national interest if Mr. Nixon resigned?

We feel it would be and once again advocate such a course.

There is no lingering doubt now of the President's deep betrayal of his public trust. Admitting that six days after the Watergate burglary he ordered a halt to the investigation of the break-in and that he withheld evidence from Congress and even from his own staff and lawyer James St. Clair, Mr. Nixon said:

"This was a serious act of omission for which I take full responsibility and which I deeply regret."

Belatedly, the President has finally done what so many Americans have asked him to do — to tell the truth, however damaging. Ironically, had he done so at an early stage he would have won the nation's forgiveness. But the record lamentably makes clear that he sought at every step of the unfolding investigation to "stonewall" attempts to extract the truth. Considerations of person and power overrode concern for moral integrity and loyalty to his oath to uphold the Constitution.

His course of deception is now taking its toll. Even key loyal Republican supporters can no longer in conscience defend his actions and are deserting him. Rep. Charles Wiggins, who so ably defended Mr. Nixon in the Judiciary Committee debate, fought back tears as he poignantly urged the President to resign and said he would vote for impeachment on obstruction of justice.

Without Republican support, it is hard to see how Mr. Nixon can govern. Yet at the moment the nation is in urgent need of direction. The problems of inflation and recession alone call out for vigorous attention in the White House. But economic and other meetings have been canceled because the President is devoting himself to Watergate. And the Congress, preoccupied with the impeachment process, likewise can spare little time for affairs of state.

Impeachment by the House is certain now, as the President himself has conceded, and we ask whether the country need go through it. The purpose of starting the process to begin with was to get at the truth. We needed to know for the country's sake whether or not the laws of the land were being faithfully executed by the President.

Now that so much conclusive evidence has emerged and Mr. Nixon has in effect judged himself, we believe it would be more merciful to him and the country if he removed himself from office. There could then be an orderly transition of power to Vice-President Gerald Ford and the nation could begin the healing process of restoring public confidence in the White House leadership.

The alternative is painful for the country and humiliating to the President. If Mr. Nixon does not resign, the impeachment proceedings will drag on for at least two more months. The government will be further weakened at the very time it needs strength to meet the growing economic dangers that threaten not only the United States but the whole world. Foreign affairs, in which the Nixon administration has so excelled, already are showing signs of strain. There is, for instance, a mounting concern that the gains of detente with the Soviet Union may be undone.

To go ahead with the impeachment and trial would also place the most stringent test on members of the House and Senate who are up for re-election and could well damage their political life in the November elections. Bitterness would be prolonged.

Some may argue that the rule of law and the provisions of the Constitution for impeachment should be carried to their ultimate conclusion, so that present and future generations may have no doubt of the facts of the case. But it seems to us that, because the moral issue has already been settled and the outcome is clear, the national interest dictates a course of resignation.

We would also favor a procedure by which Mr. Nixon would voluntarily resign in return for immunity from prosecution if he cooperated fully with the Justice Department and provided all the evidence required. The objective of the Constitution's provision for impeachment and removal is not to punish a president found guilty of "high crimes and misdemeanors" but to protect the office of the presidency from abuse of power or criminal activity. Now that the President himself has provided proof of his culpability, his resignation would make it possible to shore up and safeguard that office.

At stake at this anguishing time is the concept of government by law and a democratic system in which no ruler stands above the law. The world watches for the restoration of these vital principles.

We therefore call on Richard Nixon to spare his country the ordeal of impeachment and trial and to perform an act of statesmanship by stepping down voluntarily. We do so with deep sadness and in a spirit of compassion but with conviction that a speedy transfer of power will help cleanse the miasma of criminality that has so pervaded the executive branch of government, restore integrity in high office, and thereby strengthen and protect our republic.

WINSTON-SALEM JOURNAL
Winston-Salem, N.C.
August 7, 1974

In a televised address on April 30, 1973, President Nixon told the nation that "as the (Watergate) investigation went forward, I repeatedly asked those conducting the investigation whether there was any reason to believe that members of my administration were in any way involved. I received repeated assurances that they were not." But almost a full year earlier—and only six days after the Watergate burglary attempt—the President had posed this question to H. R. Haldeman: "...Did (Attorney General John) Mitchell know about this break-in conspiracy?" Haldeman had replied: "I think so. I don't think he knew the details, but I think he knew."

There is no softening that discrepancy between the President's public and private postures. Indeed, the just-released transcripts of June 23, 1972 White House conversations make two things painfully apparent: (1) Although the President may not have known of the Watergate burglary in advance, he was almost immediately aware of the complicity of his associates in the break-in and the possible political consequences of a full investigation of Watergate; (2) as a result, he agreed to a plan aimed at turning off the FBI's Watergate investigation through the use of a CIA-supported cover story. No presidential lapse of memory — no known piece of information — can mitigate those facts, or the conclusion that those facts tend to confirm the thrust of two pending articles of impeachment: the first article, involving obstruction of justice, and the second article, involving abuse of power.

Why did the President choose to release such damaging material now? Following the Supreme Court's recent ruling on the tapes controversy, the President realized that he had to surrender the recordings, no matter what they contained. It was too late to say the tapes did not exist, too late to have a fire in the Oval Office wastebasket. So he gave up the tapes, and rather than wait for them to be made public by others, decided to release them himself and to claim again "that the record, in its entirety, does not justify the extreme step of impeachment and removal of a president."

But if that is true, there is only one man in the world who can prove the point: Richard Nixon. Surely Mr. Nixon's case against impeachment and conviction already is known to him — the explanations, the mitigations, the interpretations. He may wait to present that case to the House and the Senate, but he will do so only at the risk of creating a public and congressional stampede in favor of his removal.

The time has plainly arrived for the President to tell everything — to tear down the stone wall and give the nation the full accounting of his actions that he has never offered before.

If, having done that, it is clear that his impeachment and conviction nonetheless cannot be avoided, then Mr. Nixon must resign and spare his country the unspeakable agony of watching an American president disgraced, and the American presidency debilitated, perhaps beyond repair.

The Evening Gazette

Worcester, Mass., August 7, 1974

We have not been among those howling for the scalp of Richard Nixon. He has accomplished much as President. Notably, he brought to an end American participation in the Vietnam war, and he did so through a remarkable mixture of toughness and flexibility.

As a manager of the American economy, he has been a failure. But it is unwise for the country to assume that the economy can be successfully managed out of Washington. Where the President has failed grossly is in his inability to bring federal spending under control.

In the whole Watergate matter, we have been mindful of the fact that many of his early and sharp critics were McGovernites and perennial Nixon-haters. They were licking the wounds of the savage defeat their philosophy suffered at the polls in 1972, and searching for ways to reverse that verdict.

When all this has been said, however, it is now c l e a r that Richard Nixon's ability and right to function as President have been fatally damaged. He should resign and spare his country more of this agony.

If he declines to step down then the impeachment process must proceed as swiftly as is consistent with justice and fair play. The United States is in a weakened state domestically, and in its relations abroad. It is a dangerous period. It will remain so while Richard Nixon clings to the White House.

For some months, we have said that the impeachment process must proceed. We go beyond that now because events of the past few days have been irrevocably damaging to the President and severely damaging to the presidency itself.

The President has told the "full story" of Watergate so often, each t i m e adding details, that no thoughtful citizen can quite know what to believe. Now he gives himself the lie. What he seeks to pass off as "a serious act of omission" was a deliberate and blatant deception. It did not fool his "enemies." to use the White House term. Rather, it most cruelly deceived those who have ached to support him all along and who have hoped against hope that the cloud over the White House would pass.

The nation now knows that the President was involved in the coverup of the Watergate burglary from almost the beginning, despite all the months of denial. In general outline, John Dean told the truth. Richard Nixon lied.

The original episode itself was two-bit stuff, almost trivial, or could have been made to seem so if the President had so spoken honestly from the beginning.

More serious, it seems to us was the administration's attempt to manipulate the work of agencies in whose integrity the citizen should h a v e complete confidence—the Federal Bureau of Investigation, the Internal Revenue Service, the Central Intelligence Agency.

And above all of this is the deception itself, right down to this week. A lot of honest men and women, in the Republican party and in the citizenry at large, were loyal to Richard Nixon under the heaviest of pressure. They went to the wall for him. Indeed, the general attitude of a majority of the public was to give him every benefit of the doubt.

He rewarded that trust by revealing, at long last, a sordid history of duplicity.

The tragedy is personal. Richard Nixon gave enormously of himself to become President. It was the dream of his life. Threaded through it, we believe, was the honest desire to serve the people nobly. In many great matters, he did serve nobly. But in what should have been a tiny matter—Watergate—he was tested and he failed, not once, but again and again. He lacked the moral fiber to do what was right. It is not an uncommon affliction of politicians; we put terrible pressure on those we place in high office. Nevertheless, the people have a right to expect a higher standard of honesty than Nixon's from a person they entrust with the presidency.

It is a sad moment for the Republican party, for he has led and symbolized the revival of a party that seemed at death's door little more than 20 years ago. To many, he was the first real Republican to be elected since Herbert Hoover. The party itself was to be the preeminent force standing for the great American ideals of individual freedom and responsibility. The party will survive, but it did not need this blow.

A few months ago, we felt that whatever happened in the Watergate case t h e country would be deeply split. That is less likely today. The President's revelation of his deception has been the final element in clarifying for the nation which way honesty and morality lie. They do not lie with a continued Nixon presidency.

We do not pretend to know precisely what sort of president Gerald Ford would make, but he has qualities of integrity that are appealing. He has not been corrupted by power. He does not appear blind to his responsibility to the Constitution and to the people.

When Rep. Charles Wiggins of California — long an earnest Nixon man—spoke of the need to bring an end to Nixon's "magnificent public career," his voice broke repeatedly. It is a sad moment, and not just for the past admirers of the President:

But the nation must come first. Richard Nixon has revealed his unfitness to continue in office. He has set a moral standard that would be an appalling precedent for future holders of the nation's highest office if he were allowed to get away with it.

A change must be made.

Tulsa, Okla., August 6, 1974

THE TIME has come for PRESIDENT NIXON to perform the most difficult act of his career—resign his office.

We come to this conclusion painfully. The TULSA DAILY WORLD has supported MR. NIXON through many adversities and we wish there were a brighter alternative for him now. But in all candor we see none.

Sen. ROBERT GRIFFIN, the assistant Republican leader in the Senate, expressed a similar feeling yesterday, with the same reluctance:

"I think we've arrived at the point where both the national and his own interests would best be served by resigning," GRIFFIN said. "It's not just his enemies who feel that way, but many of his friends—and I consider myself one of them—believe now that this would be the most appropriate course."

MR. NIXON is a fighter and the idea of giving up his elected responsibilities is clearly abhorrent to him. But if he doesn't resign, he must dig in and continue the terrible struggle that is already tearing the nation apart. And for what?

IT WOULD TAKE A MIRACLE FOR HIM TO ESCAPE impeachment in the House. Most observers believe it is only a matter of how bad the vote against him will be—the verdict itself is inescapable.

Then comes the Senate trial. The outcome is not so certain, but even MR. NIXON's friends do not believe he has more than a few votes to spare—against the two-thirds vote needed to convict.

Suppose he holds this margin and staves off ouster by a vote of, say 64 for conviction and 36 for acquittal. Is that a *victory*?

Technically it is, for the PRESIDENT would continue in office. But he would be in this position: One House of Congress would have voted to impeach him and the other would have shown nearly two to one in favor of removing him from office. What kind of leadership could he give the country in that situation? He would be, not just a caretaker PRESIDENT but a *discredited* caretaker—one with a vote of no confidence by the Congress.

MEANWHILE, THE COUNTRY WOULD CONTINUE its dispirited, discontented way, mired in a soggy economy and "wallowing in Watergate."

That's about where we are now—torn and tired, a nation marking time, stymied by impotent leadership and something worse—a lack of the zest, hope and uplift that the richest, most powerful, most fortunate country in the world should never lose.

By sticking it out, MR. NIXON will become either the first PRESIDENT turned out of office or a CHIEF EXECUTIVE in name only. By comparison, resignation now would be merciful to both the PRESIDENT and the country, sparing everyone the wrenching impeachment ordeal.

We do not find resignation an easy or happy choice—merely the best one available.

THE KANSAS CITY STAR
Kansas City, Mo., August 7. 1974

Richard M. Nixon now can perform one last great service for his country, for his party and for himself and his family: He can and should resign as President of the United States.

If Mr. Nixon does not resign, then his impeachment must be voted quickly in the House of Representatives. He should then be brought to speedy trial in the Senate. On the basis of his statement Monday—and it amounted to a confession—the Senate should vote for his removal from office.

The quicker the orderly transition of government can begin, the better off the country will be. This is the time for Mr. Ford to take over and for Mr. Nixon to get out. Not soon but *now*.

Mr. Nixon lied repeatedly to the American people. Early this week in releasing the tapes, the President said that he had been guilty of a "serious act of omission" in trying to cover the Watergate trail. He is guilty of much more than that.

Last April 29, with stacks of tape transcripts on view before reporters and TV cameras, the President said:

"If you read with an open mind. . .these transcripts will show. . .that I had no knowledge of the cover-up until I was finally told about it by John Dean on March 21 (1973). . .The entire story is here."

As early as August, 1972, the President told the American people:

"What really hurts in matters of this sort is not the fact that they occur, because overzealous people in campaigns do things that are wrong. What really hurts is if you try to cover it up."

But now Mr. Nixon admits that this is exactly what he tried to do and within a few days after the Watergate burglary of June 17, 1972. This is no mere "act of omission." This is an admission that lie has been piled upon lie and that deception has followed deception.

The immediate panic following the arrest of the men in the Democratic National Headquarters can be understood. The first political urge for self-preservation that resulted in the coverup might even have been forgiven by the people. But not the damning web of lies and deceit that consistently has been spun over the past two years. Even some of the administration's most steadfast supporters are sickened.

The White House says that Mr. Nixon has weighed the option of resigning as an alternative to an impeachment trial but that he would not want to set a precedent "for a President being driven from office."

That forlorn statement is evidence that even now the President does not grasp what has happened. Nobody is "driving" him from office. He has done that himself.

Now it is time for him to go.

RAPID CITY JOURNAL—
Rapid City, S.D., August 7, 1974

Last November this newspaper recommended that the U.S. House of Representatives initiate impeachment proceedings against President Richard Nixon. We felt it was the proper way to investigate and air charges that the President had committed impeachable offenses.

In April, after irregularities in Nixon's income tax returns were revealed, we called for his resignation. At that time we said public confidence in the President had eroded to the point that his ability to lead was irreparably damaged.

Since then, impeachment proceedings were initiated. Votes on articles of impeachment in the House Judiciary Committee crossed party lines and indicated strongly the full House of Representatives would vote impeachment, paving the way for a trial in the Senate.

Until Monday, it appeared a prognostication on the Senate verdict was too close to call.

But we now think the President's disclosure that he did, in fact, participate in the Watergate coverup has removed any doubt that the Senate would vote to remove the President from office.

Allowing the impeachment process to take its course would spread the entire case on the record. We could opt for that if it weren't for the fact that the entire nation is crying for relief from the series of bombshells which have burst in the past 18 months.

The urgency to get the matter settled and move on to the other serious problems facing this country takes precedence over carrying out a procedure the outcome of which is in little doubt.

By his own admission, Richard Nixon is guilty of duplicity. Although he now says he regrets his action, his Monday statement is tantamount to signing a confession that he is guilty of obstructing justice.

What little confidence remained in the President has been further diminished. A decision on his part to "tough it out" would only delay the inevitable and make it more difficult for those who will have to pick up the pieces of a shattered administration. It could even destroy the two-party system so necessary to our way of government.

Richard Nixon has put up a good fight to save himself. It is time for him to give it up and resign his office for the sake of the presidency and the country.

THE PLAIN DEALER
Cleveland, Ohio, August 6, 1974

President Richard M. Nixon should resign from office now.

The President's shocking admission yesterday that he deliberately withheld information and misled Congress and the nation about the Watergate coverup now makes his removal from office a certainty.

To spare the nation the agony of the impeachment process and himself the humiliation of conviction, President Nixon should begin discussions for the orderly transition of power to Vice President Gerald R. Ford.

It is disheartening to advocate this course of action, but The Plain Dealer believes that, in the best interest of the United States, President Nixon should step down.

Even his closest supporters find they are no longer able to defend President Nixon's conduct.

The transcripts of presidential conversations that President Nixon made public yesterday are extremely damaging. But far more damaging is the fact that the President knowingly deceived Congress and the public.

That deception, in itself, was an act of coverup. By acknowledging that deception the President virtually is pleading guilty to the first article of impeachment recommended on July 27 by the House Judiciary Committee. The first article of impeachment accuses the President of obstruction of justice in the Watergate case, including withholding evidence.

On April 29, President Nixon released transcripts of some presidential conversations, saying: "As far as what the President personally knew and did with regard to Watergate and the coverup is concerned, these materials — together with those already made available — will tell it all."

Yesterday the President conceded that he withheld from Congress, the courts and the public — as well as his own lawyer — information about conversations with White House chief of staff H. R. Haldeman on June 23, 1972, just six days after the abortive burglary of Democratic headquarters in the Watergate Apartment complex.

Recordings of those conversations were turned over to U.S. District Judge John Sirica last Friday after the U.S. Supreme Court unanimously rejected a presidential claim of executive privilege.

Nixon admitted the recordings showed he gave instructions on how the Watergate investigation was to be conducted and "was aware of the advantages this course of action would have with respect to limiting possible public exposure of involvement by persons connected with the re-election committee."

On May 10, The Plain Dealer urged the House of Representatives to vote to impeach President Nixon so that he might stand trial by the Senate. We now believe that President Nixon's admission that he withheld information from Congress has predetermined the outcome of that trial. In the interest of the nation it would be best for President Nixon to step down from the office he has misused.

THE DAILY HERALD

Biloxi, Miss., August 7, 1974

President Nixon has advised his cabinet members bluntly that he will not resign in the face of a mounting clamor that he do so.

He should reconsider that decision.

His release of three additional Watergate tapes Monday, revealing in effect that he did indeed obstruct justice and revealing information that conflicts with three of his previous public statements, demands that every American reassess the Presidential situation.

Many influential ones already have. All ten of the Republican members of the House Judiciary Committee who had opposed all proposed articles of impeachment have reconsidered their positions in the light of these new developments and indicated they now support impeachment. Until yesterday, they had been seduced into believing they had fairly considered all of the evidence presented to them during 10 weeks of closed hearings and that evidence failed to convince them to vote in favor of a single impeachment article. Looking at the new evidence quickly brought a change, by all ten of them.

The American people must also reconsider.

The President's actions, in participating in the cover-up of the Watergate burglary, in deceiving the American public about the timing of his knowledge about it, and in publically stating that "everything that is relevant is included" in material released three months ago when he knew it was not, deserve condemnation.

Mr. Nixon underestimates the importance of those recent developments which he characterized as "a serious act of omission for which I take full responsibility."

He must indeed take that responsibility and in so doing, he must consider, above all else, what will be in the best interest of this country.

He has admitted that a House vote of impeachment is "as practical matter, virtually a foregone conclusion and that the issue will therefore go to trial in the Senate."

He has vowed to fight through the Constitutional impeachment process, clinging to the slim hope that this process will vindicate his actions. He has the right to pursue that course of action, but doing so will surely subject this country to several more months of Watergate agony, a period of floundering leadership while serious domestic problems, such as inflation and the economy, continue to be brushed aside.

It is time for President Nixon to return to Camp David and reconsider his decision to remain in office to the bitter end.

It is time for President Nixon to decide to act in the best interests of the United States and its citizens.

It is time for President Nixon to resign.

THE SAGINAW NEWS

Saginaw, Mich., August 7, 1974

Richard M. Nixon's three-tape mea culpa changes his position from precarious to untenable and renders continuance of the impeachment process an exercise in prolonged agony for the country and for a president who is being swept up in a tidal wave of public and congressional shock and dismay.

Last April this newspaper called for Mr. Nixon's resignation considering it the most statesmanlike act he could perform for the nation in what seemed then to be a dwindling presidency. We can only repeat that call today — and with no more joy now than then.

What we are seeing is the final act in one of the great personal political tragedies of our time — and Monday it was Mr. Nixon himself who pushed the button that raised the curtain on that act. The great tragedy is that Mr. Nixon brought this on himself when he opted for scheming over forthrightness. Had he opted the other way he might well have escaped with censure and forgiveness free of court duress.

Sympathy for Mr. Nixon is diminished, however, by what can be considered an equally great tragedy — his studied deceiving of those who have been most loyal to him and willing to give him every last benefit of doubt even when that benefit seemed at times motivated by little more than blind loyalty and apologia for a president's "devine right."

Judging by latest decisions out of the White House it is not likely that Mr. Nixon will heed resignation advice. It is more than likely that a repeat of our earlier call will be received with the same anger by Nixon loyalists.

Moreover, there are legions of Americans including many in the opinion business and not necessarily loyalists at all, who see the full impeachment route and trial by Senate as the only way to purify this situation in the name of justice and Constitutional provisions. Doubtless that is the way it should and will go. But we can no longer subscribe to the theory that this is necessarily preferable to resignation and an orderly transition of the reins of leadership or that it is somehow needed to fully educate the public to the niceties of the Constitutional process.

Were the case against Richard M. Nixon more marginal than it is now revealed, it would be appropriate to fully subscribe to a continuance of the process now under way in the House. Regrettably it is not. The case against Mr. Nixon is now replete with evidence and admission of willful deception on the part of a president who has taken 27 agonizing months to recover his memory and to come to terms with the truth.

Considering the dimension of the hole that he has dug for himself with release to the public of partial contents of three tapes of conversations with H. R. Haldeman just six days after the Watergate burglary, and that more is yet to come if this goes to the Senate, the days can only grow longer and more painful for the President and the nation.

It is obvious that Mr. Nixon has engaged in the great deception to save himself, to sacrifice however many others necessary. Purely on the single article of impeachment dealing with abuse of power, the case against Mr. Nixon is large and his defense lies in shambles.

We repeat, the tragedy here rests not alone with the President's self-destruction. On the low road to getting re-elected and then covering up and stonewalling to hide criminality, he has deceived the nation for more than two years.

He has deceived three of the finest constitutional lawyers in the country who have tried to defend him while he hid from them the full truth.

He has deceived the Congress and some of his best friends on the House Judiciary committee, now making them to feel like dupes and filling their hearts with sadness.

He has deceived those far and wide who have been willing to go down the line with him.

And he has sorely tried just about every level of court in the federal system.

The worst is not this. The worst is that the President and his former lieutenants grossly abused the law of the land and the separation of powers. They played one federal investigative agency against another to thwart due process. They used these and still others to spy upon, harass and burglarize American citizens who by Nixon's lights and those of the Deans, Haldemans and Ehrlichmans fell into the categories of critics, trouble-makers or subversives.

There will be more to fall out, we are sure, in the days ahead if Mr. Nixon insists upon pushing this to a Senate trial. It is a Senate that now will be hard put to find exculpation for what stands as a sleazy record of lies, unbridled abuse of executive power and total disregard for the protections written into the very Constitution before which he now stands to be judged.

Yet even if somehow Mr. Nixon can find political absolution in the Senate, he can never again govern with total credibility. A side tragedy is that he doesn't yet seem to grasp this. Can he ever again stand before a gathering of the DAR or the Boy Scouts and talk about one nation under God and Constitution and law and order and justice?

We do not ask for Mr. Nixon's blood for what he has put this country through the past many months. Though our disdain is high for his perception of the public intelligence, we ask only that he give serious consideration to stepping aside manfully and performing the last gracious act of public service that he can perform — and with full ex-presidential benefits, should Congress consent not to try him in absentia in exchange for full disclosure of all of the facts.

There is no guarantee of the latter, to be sure. But then, this is no "banana republic" as Sen. Carl T. Curtis fears it will become with a Nixon removal or resignation.

This nation deals every day with "banana republics." They are the ones who put leaders on a kingly pedestal and then slit their throats if they fail. We have a constitutional democracy republic which makes laws bigger than men and provides for orderly transition of power of leadership.

This is where our decency, faith and strength is. It is time we put it to use. Mr. Nixon can lead the way by making that hard but now necessary decision.

THE MILWAUKEE JOURNAL
Milwaukee, Wis., August 8, 1974

If there is a consensus about anything in America today it is that Richard Nixon must go — one way or another. Regrettably, the manner of his departure seems almost certainly to be resignation.

The Journal has long argued that the impeachment process offered the best way to resolve the Nixon scandals, to deter future abuses of power by successive presidents and to revitalize our constitutional system of government. Although exposure of Nixon's complicity in the Watergate coverup has sent him into an irreversible tailspin, it is difficult to see great advantage in short-cutting the impeachment process on the eve of judgment.

True, resignation will get him out of power quicker, but it also will tend to make the verdict on his conduct less comprehensive and, in some respects, less clear. Questions of his accountability involve much more than the coverup. They range over a wide assortment of wrongdoing. Moreover, the purpose of impeachment transcends the fate of the accused. The overriding aim has been to reaffirm standards of presidential decency, to send a message to future presidents. It is doubtful that resignation is the ideal way to drive these lessons home.

Nixon, of course, has a different perspective. Without hope of survival, he faces the certain disgrace of Senate conviction. He apparently has little choice but to take his chances on private citizenship, even with its perils of possible criminal prosecution and of being called to testify at the trials of fallen aides. He should not expect — and certainly should not be offered — immunity against criminal liability, for the rule of law must prevail. But if he were ever prosecuted and convicted, he would be a fit subject for mercy. Few Americans wish him in jail.

In the matter of Richard Nixon, the nation has endured much. It is unfortunate that, with the end of the impeachment process in sight, resignation fever has taken hold. Now, it seems, we can only await the president's fateful words of self-removal.

St. Louis Globe-Democrat
St. Louis, Mo., August 7, 1974

Instead of going for a cruise on his yacht, President Nixon would have been wiser to start building an ark if he hopes to ride out the new storm of demands for resignation or impeachment.

The tidal wave of protest following the President's disclosure that he withheld evidence concerning his own role in the Watergate cover-up is ominous because it comes from his friends.

The highly respected Rep. Charles Wiggins, who had defended the President so ably and admirably in the House Judiciary Committee proceedings, was choked with tears when he announced sadly that he would now vote for impeachment based on evidence. In Wiggins' view, President Nixon himself supplied the evidence by admitting he discussed the Watergate cover-up as early as June 23, 1972. Heretofore Mr. Nixon has steadfastly denied knowing about the cover-up until March 21, 1973.

Wiggins' stand is shared by Rep. Charles W. Sandman Jr. of New Jersey, who was the most impassioned of Mr. Nixon's supporters in the Judiciary Committee hearings. Sandman termed the President's new disclosure "devastating" and said he would vote for impeachment for obstruction of justice.

Sandman, a shrewd political analyst, said he doubted if the President had any support left in the House. He went on to say that Mr. Nixon's chances for survival in the Senate had been good prior to Monday, because enough senators would prefer to have Mr. Nixon in office rather than Gerald Ford at the time of the 1976 elections. Now, he said, the senators could not take such a comfortable partisan stance.

☆ ☆ ☆

Despite the new uproar, the President has insisted that he will not resign. He called a special meeting of his cabinet to tell the members face to face he would not be pressured out of office. They in turn pledged him support.

If the President adheres to his position, the stage would appear to be set for a swift trial in the Senate.

There it can be determined in the face of all evidence whether or not Mr. Nixon truly has committed an impeachable offense.

Calls for the President's resignation are so much rhetoric and serve no useful purpose. The country might feel a sudden surge of relief that the Watergate mess had been put behind, but justice would not be served by Mr. Nixon's departure in this manner.

Resignation could be interpreted as a cop-out or an admission of guilt, without proof of either. It would also bear the cynical implication that Mr. Nixon had chosen this course merely to save whatever pension benefits he has accrued, and to spare himself further shame.

☆ ☆ ☆

The preferred course for the nation is to let the Constitutional process run to a conclusion.

Though the outlook for the President is depressingly bleak, a verdict cannot be rendered until the Senate has conducted an impeachment trial.

If the President is tried, convicted and removed from office as a result of deeds he now admits, no one can claim he was persecuted.

The United States of America will survive this ordeal as it has survived wars, depressions and natural disasters.

It's paramount now that all parties to the impeachment proceedings keep cool and conduct themselves with dignity.

As the accused, Richard Nixon is entitled to the benefit of the doubt until a verdict is reached.

No good can come from any lip-licking cries of satisfaction from self-congratulating foes of Richard Nixon.

ARKANSAS DEMOCRAT
Little Rock, Ark., August 7, 1974

In a staggering development, President Nixon has admitted that he deliberately withheld evidence that showed that he participated in the coverup of the Watergate break-in.

From all sides have come cries for him to resign.

As of yesterday, Mr. Nixon was holding firm. He acknowledged that his impeachment by the House was a forgone conclusion, but his position seemed to be that while he had made mistakes, they were not serious enough to justify his removal from office. In other words, he does not think two-thirds of the senators will vote to convict him.

Frankly, it's hard to believe that the President actually thinks this. In effect, he has pleaded guilty, and while many in the Senate would want to be merciful, it is hard for us to believe that 34 of them could afford to support a President who had told as many lies as the evidence and Mr. Nixon's own words reveal. After all, when they vote the senators will have to think of the record they are making for themselves.

And certainly they will. This is why the calls for resignation. No one really wants to vote on the President's guilt or innocence, and in all fairness, the members of Congress fear impeachment and trial would be damaging to the country. Most observers in Washington indicate that they think the President will resign, that he is now merely testing the wind and trying to see what kind of deal he can make.

We hope this is not true. We hope Mr. Nixon sees it through to the bitter end. Resignation, in our opinion, would damage the country more than impeachment and trial, no matter what the outcome.

In the first place, the process is plainly spelled out in the Constitution, and if it is short-circuited, the rumors and doubts will persist for a generation. To many persons he will be a martyr who was hounded out of office. A suggestion to avoid this is for him to make certain admissions before he resigns — a sort of Agnew solution. But this won't eliminate the doubts because Mr. Nixon's alleged misdeeds are not commonly understood ones like bribery. Nothing will clear the air but due process as set out in the Constitution.

After all, this can't be looked at as a temporary problem, or one involving just Richard M. Nixon. What is done here will define the course for future presidents. If the outcome is resignation, then we seem to be saying that if a president is willing to run the risk of being forced to resign, then he is free to do almost anything he wants to. In other words, resignation on a $60,000 annual pension is the worst thing that is ever going to happen to a president.

Then there are the messy details that would go along with resignation. We can be sure that Mr. Nixon will never quit if he is not guaranteed immunity from prosecution. Will this come in a law passed by the Congress as Rep. Wilbur Mills and others have suggested, or will Gerald Ford, as the new president, grant amnesty? Well, it seems to us that the fight over such a bill might be almost as damaging to Congress and the country as an impeachment and trial. And do we think it would restore anyone's faith in government if a new president's first act were to pardon a man who admits to having deceived the people who paid him their highest honor?

What about equity? Fifteen persons already have been convicted of crimes connected with Watergate, and ordered to go to jail. Is it fair for Mr. Nixon to escape even the embarrassment of a trial?

Of course, the decision of whether to resign is Mr. Nixon's. But we will think more of him if he does stick it out, "stonewall it," as he likes to say. It will prove that he at least is not a hypocrite — that he DOES believe in the Constitution and that he DOES think that what he did was justified in order to defend it.

Long Island Press

Jamaica N.Y., August 6, 1974

When the existence of tape recordings of White House conversations became known, President Nixon fought with every device at his command against efforts of investigators to obtain them. The more Mr. Nixon resisted, the more skeptical the public became and the more the suspicion grew that the President had something to hide.

Now we know that suspicion was true and why Mr. Nixon wanted the tapes kept tucked away in the White House. Backed into a corner by the recent unanimous Supreme Court ruling that he must turn over to the courts the tapes Special Watergate Prosecutor Leon Jaworski had subpenaed, Mr. Nixon yesterday made three of them public.

He also made a damning admission that he had lied. Mr. Nixon didn't put it so bluntly. Rather, he said he had withheld from Congress and his own lawyers the contents of the three damaging tapes which contained evidence "at variance with certain of my previous statements."

At variance is putting it mildly. Indeed, Mr. Nixon's latest statement makes many of his public disclaimers of knowledge of the Watergate cover-up, as Ron Ziegler would say, "inoperative."

* * *

The tapes Mr. Nixon made public were recorded on June 23, 1972, only six days after the Watergate burglary. They show Mr. Nixon approved the use of the Central Intelligence Agency in an attempt to block an FBI investigation of the break-in. They also confirm that Mr. Nixon was told by his chief aide, H. R. Haldeman, that John N. Mitchell, the President's campaign manager, may have had prior knowledge of the Watergate burglary and bugging.

As damaging as is the evidence contained on the tapes is the fact that Mr. Nixon withheld the information since May. That is obstruction of justice, by anyone's calculation.

Meanwhile, Mr. Nixon's attorney, James D. St. Clair, Congress and particularly the House Judiciary Committee had the President's word — from his TV address of April 29, the night before he released the original set of White House transcripts — that "as far as what the President personally knew and did with regard to Watergate and the cover-up is concerned, these materials — together with those already made public — will tell it all."

It is clear now that what many suspected was indeed the case. The cover-up that began as soon as the burglars were caught in the Democrats' Watergate offices has never really stopped. Moreover, the cover-up, now by the President's own admission, reached right into the Oval Office.

* * *

Mr. Nixon's announcement struck like a bombshell among his dwindling supporters. Rep. Charles Wiggins, California Republican, who impressed both those who agreed and disagreed with him with his staunch defense of the President in the House Judiciary Committee deliberations, called on Mr. Nixon to resign. If not, Rep. Wiggins said, he would vote to impeach him for obstruction of justice.

Vice President Ford retreated from his constant defense of Mr. Nixon, and other Nixon defenders on the Judiciary Committee also were having second thoughts, as are undoubtedly many in and out of Congress who refused to desert the President without the evidence. Mr. Nixon himself has now made some of the evidence available — though he contends that "the record, in its entirety, does not justify the extreme step of impeachment and removal of a President."

We disagree, and we think a sufficient number of representatives and senators do, too. Mr. Nixon has committed not only the criminal offenses which he insists are the only grounds for impeachment; he has also dishonored the office of the presidency by abusing the public trust.

We believe in the constitutional process, and we are impressed with the manner in which Congress is performing its awesome responsibility. Yet we are disturbed by the effect the length of the proceedings is having on America, and we think Mr. Nixon's resignation would be the best course. As Rep. Wiggins put it so well:

"Under all the circumstances, I believe this is not the time for the President to meet with his attorneys to plan for his defense in the Senate. It is a time for the President, the vice president, the chief justice and the leaders of the House and Senate to gather in the White House to discuss the orderly transition of power from Richard Nixon to Gerald Ford."

The State

Columbia, S.C., August 7, 1974

FOR THE SAKE of the country — and for the preservation of whatever place he has earned in America's political history — Richard M. Nixon should resign as President of the United States.

Resignation is virtually the only initiative left open for the beleagured chief executive, and he should exercise it forthwith. Now that he has himself admitted concealing evidence from his associates and from Congress concerning the sordid Watergate episode, little purpose would be served by playing out the remaining acts of the impeachment drama.

The President's startling disclosures of Monday so eroded his dwindling support in both House and Senate that not only impeachment but conviction now seem to be foregone conclusions. Continuation of the process under present circumstances would simply put the Congress and the country through an additional and unnecessary ordeal.

The State takes no pleasure in reaching the conclusion that Mr. Nixon's resignation is in order. This newspaper supported him in his 1960 bid for the Presidency, lamented his loss to the late John F. Kennedy, and rejoiced in his 1968 and 1972 elections. We felt then, and feel now, that his policies — both foreign and domestic — better bespoke the needs of the nation and of the world than did those of his Democratic opponents.

Furthermore, The State not only concedes but acclaims the notable achievements which President Nixon has scored during his tenure. In passing, we remind our readers that many of his accomplishments — such as terminating the war in Vietnam, ending the draft, striving for economic stability, and others — were goals advanced by political enemies who seldom showed the honesty of acknowledging genuine Nixon accomplishments.

But — unhappily and unfortunately — such positive contributions have become overshadowed by the personal and political excesses stemming from the Watergate incident. The growing accretion of damaging evidence, now capped by the President's own admission of conduct which hardly comports with the stature of the nation's highest officer, portrays Richard Nixon as a man who — for his own protection — has bent both his associates and the law.

Even in the unlikely event that the Senate would reject the House's seemingly inevitable bill of impeachment, the President's usefulness as a respected leader of the United States would be ended. With many of his trusted associates in jail or otherwise stigmatized, with his defenses and his defenders crumbling about him, Mr. Nixon has left to him only the recourse of resignation and the expression of remorse.

There still are many Americans who will find some justification for the President's actions in the Watergate-related developments. And there are millions who cling to the conviction that he was motivated by what he considered to be the best interests of the country — even as he trampled upon procedures and persons which seemed to threaten him.

But Richard Nixon has been found wanting in the exemplary conduct which Americans have a right to expect of the man to whom they entrust the guidance of their nation. History will judge his successes and failures, but he should etch one final entry of his own in the record by stepping down of his own volition at this critical stage in national affairs.

If The State correctly reads the mood of America, there will be widespread acceptance of Vice President Gerald Ford as an interim leader of the nation. No such acceptance is possible for President Nixon.

THE ANN ARBOR NEWS

Ann Arbor, Mich., August 7, 1974

VINDICATED sooner than they expected, members of the House Judiciary Committee can look back on their decision with satisfaction. One of the articles of impeachement passed by Judiciary was titled "obstruction of justice."

Now comes the disclosure that President Nixon deliberately withheld evidence of the Watergate coverup. That would fit "obstruction of justice" in every particular and ease any pangs of conscience Judiciary Committee members still might harbor.

What the nation is seeing now is essentially a countdown. How many more body blows can the President take and still govern effectively? How can his presidency survive the constant battering? How long before the President throws in the towel "for the good of the country" and his own sanity.?

It has been a summer of anguish for many individuals, in and outside of the nation's capital. If the polls are accurate, President Nixon is as good as impeached and convicted in the hearts of his countrymen. If the leaders of Congress know the men and women they serve with, there's more trouble ahead unless President Nixon resigns.

* * *

MR. NIXON'S resignation might satisfy, even delight, a good many people but it would be only a partial solution to the low faith in government that people hold today. The path of resignation would put the honorable Mr. Ford in the presidency, itself a big step on the way back, and it would eliminate Nixon from the scene, but one is convinced that resignation is not what the nation really needs.

It doesn't need shortcuts to justice. It doesn't need resignation under pressure. It DOES need the matter of Richard Nixon's guilt or innocence determined correctly, by the book. It needs a judgment on this matter. by the Congress and the courts.

Perhaps he won't resign, preferring to be impeached by the House (a foregone conclusion by now) and successfully fighting conviction by the Senate. We don't know. How does anyone know what the White House is thinking, given its record of deception, dirty tricks, hostility to the press and lying to the American people.

It's all academic in one sense, because President Nixon is surely the lamest of the lame duck presidents. At this point, events are unfolding so rapidly that what is only wild speculation one day is accepted fact the next. We would only counsel Mr. Gerald Ford to get ready, because it appears as though the man from Grand Rapids who prefers to be called Jerry is going to be the next President of the United States.

The Charlotte Observer

Charlotte, N.C., August 7, 1974

What did the President know and when did he know it? Now, from the mouth of the President himself, the nation knows the answer to that question. At least it knows enough of the answer to be assured that President Richard M. Nixon was a conspirator in the Watergate coverup from the very first.

The transcripts of the President's June 23, 1972, meeting with chief aide H. R. (Bob) Haldeman, six days after the burglary of Democratic national headquarters in the Watergate complex, provide the undeniable proof that investigators had been searching for, the "smoking pistol" that linked the President personally to the crime.

The transcripts confirm the charges made by the House Judiciary Committee in two Articles of Impeachment approved last week: 1) that the President violated his oath of office to enforce the laws by "engaging personally and through his subordinates" in a plan to impede the Watergate investigation and obstruct justice; and 2) that the President abused his high office by "contravening the law of governing agencies of the executive branch and the purpose of those agencies," namely the Federal Bureau of Investigation and the Central Intelligence Agency.

He Betrays Defenders

What else is in the 64 tapes that the Supreme Court ordered the President to turn over to Judge Sirica and Watergate investigators, no one knows as yet. But the President's one conversation with Mr. Haldeman, directing that the CIA be used to divert FBI investigation of the Watergate break-in, is enough to collapse the slim defense the President and his supporters had made before the House Judiciary Committee.

It is obvious why the President neglected to inform his staff or his lawyers about that conversation and why, in a "serious act of omission," he avoided any reference to it in the transcripts that he released to the public and Watergate investigators last April. It removes reasonable doubt about his complicity in the coverup.

But in hiding the legal crime, he committed a grave political one. He allowed his defenders, congressmen like Charles Wiggins of California, Charles Sandman of New Jersey, David Dennis of Indiana, Wiley Mayne of Iowa, Delbert Latta of Ohio and Joseph Maraziti of New Jersey, to put their necks in a political noose by defending him. All of those men, exposed as dupes, risk being defeated for re-election this fall. Congressman Wiggins had cause to weep over Monday's revelations; he had been betrayed.

In that mood, the 435 members of the House are likely to impeach the president by a nearly unanimous vote. Even the need for a two-week, televised debate of the impeachment question now seems like an unnecessary formality. The Congress, like the nation, is impatient for a change in administrations. Pressures on the President to resign are enormous.

A Threat Of Backlash

In that impatience, however, lie grave dangers. Should the President resign or should the impeachment formalities be accelerated to usher in a new president as soon as possible, the nation will be spared some agony and provided with new leadership in a time of deep troubles, but it will not have dealt fully with the awful truths about the Nixon stewardship of the presidency. An ousted President who still proclaimed his innocence would be free to rally his last-ditch supporters by insisting he was hounded out of office by the "liberal press" and left-wing elements in the Congress and the judiciary.

Nothing, of course, could be further from the truth. As the transcripts released Monday again make clear, the most damaging evidence against the President throughout the investigations has come from the President himself. The President is being removed from office by the truth.

Even if he asks to resign, the Congress and the Senate, for the future political health of the nation, ought to make that resignation contingent upon the full disclosure of the President's every act in the whole, shameful Watergate conspiracy, just as the court did when Vice President Agnew was permitted to resign.

The nation can withstand the truth about Richard Nixon. It has been suspecting the worst for almost two years now. Polls taken immediately after the week of televised hearings by the House Judiciary Committee showed an enormous citizen appreciation for what was at stake in the impeachment process. Slowly, viewers all over the country, even in areas where support for Mr. Nixon had been strongest, came to terms with the possibility that this President was about to face the most serious challenge of any chief executive since Andrew Johnson.

The Need For Consent

Removing a president from his duly elected office is the most serious act a nation can perform. It ought not be done, in words of Thomas Jefferson, "for light and transient causes'" or even the appearance of such causes. The nation must fully understand why the act is necessary and must consent to it.

As long as Mr. Nixon insists that he is innocent of an impeachable offense, he should be given every opportunity to answer the charges raised against him. The procedure laid down by the Constitution should be faithfully adhered to. That may require patience, but the nation can afford to take no shortcuts in resolving an issue of such lasting significance.

The San Diego Union
San Diego, Calif., August 6, 1974

Ever since the Watergate break-in began generating suspicion and accusations of misconduct by high government officials, The San Diego Union has taken the position that no effort should be spared in finding out the truth and fixing responsibility where it belongs. We also have not wavered in our conviction that, in fairness to all of the accused and for the sake of the future of our system of government, this search for truth and justice should follow procedures in our Constitution designed to deal with the kind of crisis that Watergate has created.

Nothing has changed our minds. Indeed, our conviction was never greater that the judicial system and the responsibility for impeachment vested in Congress are fully capable of responding to every issue raised by Watergate. Former members of the White House staff and others who were implicated are having their day in court. Some are already in prison. The case against President Nixon has taken the form of three articles of impeachment now before the House of Representatives. Evidence bearing on those articles continues to be assembled, including the belated and most revealing transcripts released by the President yesterday. In short, the case is going forward as the Constitution contemplated.

Mr. Nixon now regards a vote for impeachment in the House as a "foregone conclusion." He is probably right, but this in no way diminishes the responsiblity of House members to review the impeachment evidence as individual, elected representatives of the American people and each of them to decide whether the President should be brought to trial. If Mr. Nixon believes the totality of evidence will help exonerate him, it is in his best interests to get that evidence to the house—late though the hour is—even if it reveals discrepancies of the magnitude which came to the surface yesterday.

Sen. Robert Griffin, the Michigan Republican, is certainly speaking for many of his fellow members of Congress when he says it would be "appropriate" at this time for President Nixon to resign—that such a step would best serve the interests of the nation and Mr. Nixon. We disagree. We view the agonies of a trial in the Senate with the greatest distaste. Yet, a detour around the impeachment process would not be in the best interests of the United States of America and the survival of its political institutions as we know them.

True enough, some members of the House and Senate might like to be relieved of the burden of judging whether President Nixon's conduct in office warrants his impeachment and removal from office. This requires a measure of statesmanship rarely demanded of our elected leaders. However, it is a burden which the Constitution assigns to them, and if it is not accepted and discharged in President Nixon's case the force and meaning of the impeachment clause will be gravely damaged.

Mr. Nixon's statement yesterday can be read as an appeal to the Senate as the body that will finally pass judgment on the impeachment evidence. The Senate may well have to do so, but impeachment remains today an issue before the House and it must receive the deliberation there which such a grave step deserves. The difficult constitutional journey on which Watergate has launched us cannot be made easier by any shortcuts—either through perfunctory treatment of impeachment in the House or by Mr. Nixon's resignation.

The Washington Post
Washington, D.C., August 8, 1974

REPORTS OF Mr. Nixon's decision to resign proliferate. And the belated rush toward impeachment, set off by the President's disclosure of new evidence on Monday, has long since turned into a stampede. Nowhere in any of the sudden ferment, however, is there yet an assurance that either process will produce a result that does justice to the ordeal to which the nation has been put these past two years.

We do not know, of course, what terms may be under negotiation for a prospective resignation by Mr. Nixon, and therefore it is impossible to know whether the conditions of his departure will meet what seems to us to be the minimum requirements and to which we have alluded more than once in this space. These are that a sufficient public record of the reasons for Mr. Nixon's departure be compiled, that it present a compelling case for so extraordinary a step, and that the necessity for this step be accepted by him as well as by a broad and representative majority of the American people. What is alarming, however, is that not even the rush to judgment in Congress, as it is now developing, would insure that these qualifications were met by the processes of impeachment. For what appears to be developing among members of Congress is a kind of Tonkin Gulf mind-set from which could come a resounding but hollow and ultimately dangerous verdict founded upon the simple proposition that the President has committed, and virtually confessed to, a single, identifiable, demonstrable indictable crime—and thus must go.

Even if Mr. Nixon resigns, he will have been propelled into doing so by a sudden, massive defection of hardcore supporters, many of them finding political safety in numbers and clinging fast to a short portion of one presidential transcript which they can claim as evidence sufficiently "clear and convincing" to sustain a charge of obstruction of justice against the President. And to accept this as the sole or even principal basis for removing the President from office, in view of the rest of the case against his conduct of the presidency, would be to destroy the single great benefit the public stands to gain from its ordeal.

We do not mean by this to disparage the difficult decisions made this week by many members of Congress who had previously strongly supported the President. What we mean to do is redirect attention, if we can, to the much more difficult judgments made by a relative handful of Republicans and southern Democrats on the House Judiciary Committee—judgments that went to the heart of the matter so far as we are concerned. We have in mind, among others, Democratic Congressman Walter Flowers of Alabama and Republican Congressman Hamilton Fish of New York whose arguments, reprinted elsewhere on this page today, seem to us to sum up the most important elements in the case for the removal of Mr. Nixon from office. We have also in mind Representatives Thornton, Mann, Railsback, Cohen, McClory, Butler, Hogan and Froehlich, whose votes, together with those of Mr. Fish and Mr. Flowers, gave such significant weight to the margin by which the committee adopted Article II in its resolution of impeachment. It is this article, in turn, which takes the case against the President beyond obstruction of justice (Article I) and defiance of Congress (Article III) to the abuses of presidential powers which do constitute in our view, the heart of the matter.

This is the article which has to do specifically with what Congressman Danielson aptly called "crimes or offenses against the very structure of the state, against the system of government, the system that has brought to the American people the freedoms and liberties which we so cherish." He went on to say: "This is uniquely a presidential offense, Mr. Chairman, and the most important thing that we have in this hearing." We agree with Mr. Danielson's appraisal. For the fact is that the offenses catalogued in Article II—assorted abuses and misuse of the police and tax powers, and of agencies such as the IRS, the CIA and the FBI—go a very long way toward defining the standards of conduct the people demand of the presidency. To be sure, this is a kind of negative definition, a definition of intolerable conduct which in turn sets a standard of expected behavior. But that is precisely why, however Mr. Nixon departs, there must be some direct and specific acknowledgement of these offenses and of their unacceptability. That is why his departure—whether by resignation or impeachment—must not have as either its price or its consequence a dismissal of these grave charges. This purpose could be largely served by the impeachment proceedings in the House and a full trial in the Senate, and this is one argument for letting the impeachment process play out. But we would not preclude the possibility that the same purpose can be served within the framework of whatever transactions may even now be going forward with respect to a presidential resignation.

As we observed the other day, the President has for all practical purposes pleaded guilty to an obstruction of justice in the Watergate cover-up and it is not unreasonable to contemplate some sort of provision of immunity for him from criminal prosecution in matters of this sort after he leaves office. But the President has plainly refused to acknowledge any guilt concerning these larger abuses of specifically presidential powers, and even were he to do so, these are not necessarily crimes in a sense and of a sort which would figure in a negotiated immunity agreement. So their commission must be acknowledged in some other way. And that way, we would submit, requires more than an acknowledgement by the President, as important as that would be. It also requires continuing and thoroughgoing investigation of the damage done. These were offenses to a system of government that does not belong to Mr. Nixon. And we would add that the documentary material concerning his operation of the government does not belong to him either. One condition President Nixon cannot be allowed to impose as part of the terms by which he would resign without a Senate trial is that the three branches of government, and by extension the American public, conspire on his behalf to perpetuate the cover-up.

THE SUN

Baltimore, Md., August 7, 1974

Of the narrowing options still open to Richard Nixon he says again that he will not take the option of resignation. How long this decision will hold there is no way of knowing. After previous assertions to the same effect he has considered resignation, most recently, it seems, during last weekend's emergency huddle at Camp David. Perhaps he is now motivated, as one cabinet member said after yesterday's session of that neglected body, by a genuine conviction that the processes of the Constitution should be "overriding," though it does seem rather late in the day for him to be seized by such a conviction. More probably he still by some involved reasoning seeks to make points out of disaster, as the day before he tried to make points even as he acknowledged having lied largely to the public and to his lawyers, and having obstructed the very process he now espouses by withholding evidence from the House Judiciary Committee.

Let it be remembered that the three tapes he let go of on Monday were bound to become public anyway, since they were among the tapes the Supreme Court ordered released to Judge Sirica, and since Judge Sirica was unlikely to withhold these particular records on grounds of the national security: that is, Mr. Nixon confessed just before he got caught. What is his gambit now? Is it to seem to stand beleaguered and alone against virtually the whole world, and by that posture hope to elicit enough vestigial sympathy to squeeze him, however tarnished, through a Senate trial?

But sympathy, even among his erstwhile supporters, is fast running out. His party wants to get rid of him, as the country wants to get rid of him. If he would only, says the overwhelming consensus, go away. And of course the quickest method of his going away is by resignation. This is one of the several good arguments for resignation, less than good though it may seem to Mr. Nixon. It is said further, and cogently, that under present circumstances he is unable to so much as appear actually to be running the nation; that the populace, after all it has endured at the hands of Richard Nixon, ought to be spared the further agony of a House impeachment and a Senate trial, since Mr. Nixon is a ruined man in any case.

This newspaper inclines rather to think that the additional agony, considering how agonized we already are, would not be that intolerable, and that in fact for the sake of present health and historical record and precedent it had best be endured. There is in the literature of the drama an Aristotelian concept called catharsis, mentioned most often in regard to the Greek tragedies. It is not an abstruse concept at all. It simply means a thorough purging of the emotions, by playing the action out to the bitter inevitable end. That, it seems to us, is the prescription today.

Detroit Free Press

Detroit, Mich., August 6, 1974

THE process of American law and justice even in such a difficult area as presidential impeachment is now working well. This is not the time to begin substituting for that process novel ideas designed to ease the strain on the country, or on the presidency, or on the Congress.

The country is holding up quite well under the constitutional process of impeachment, we think. Millions of Americans are sustaining themselves through these difficult days as it becomes more apparent that the system of law undergirds our complex and sometimes fragile democracy.

Even President Nixon, in releasing some more tape transcripts late Monday, concedes that his impeachment by the House is "virtually a foregone conclusion." The damaging nature of these new transcripts, and Mr. Nixon's admission that he purposely withheld them from his own staff and his lawyer, will certainly further hurt his case. But even as impeachment has become a certainty, some unique if misguided ideas have been thrust forward for changing the process.

One of the president's own aides, Patrick Buchanan, suggests that the House unanimously and without further debate vote to impeach, so that the Senate may get on with the trial. A proposal to censure Mr. Nixon, rather than impeach him, would be introduced in the House. The old notion that the president spare the country agony by resigning is resurrected, and given a new polish by Sen. Robert Griffin, R-Mich., and Rep. Charles Wiggins, R-Calif.

There may be some merit in each of these ideas. But they miss the point, and almost all are now constitutionally unsound.

Now is not the time for shortcuts, or for short-circuiting the provisions wisely included in the Constitution by the Founding Fathers. The country has been holding together precisely because the process of law and justice is being followed in the courts and in the Congress. In a crisis of great historial importance, Congress is showing that it can live up to its responsibilities. The president has been treated fairly by the process so far; indeed, part of the weight of the impeachment recommendations by the House Judiciary Committee lies in the committee's efforts to bend over backwards and let the president's lawyer have every opportunity for rebuttal.

What the country has seen and is seeing is neither a lynch mob nor a whitewash, but a slow and steady application of justice. If we are to come out of this nightmare as a stronger country, a stronger people, we need the process to continue and we need to learn all that was wrong and anything that was right about the administration and the actions of President Nixon.

Sen. Griffin's warning to Mr. Nixon to produce all the evidence in a Senate impeachment trial was good advice. The president is in almost as much trouble now for his failure to tell all the facts to the Congress and to the country as for his misdeeds.

But this is not the time for thwarting the Constitution's due process. The nation needs to get to the bottom, finally, of the mess Mr. Nixon has created. And it needs, equally as much, to see and learn that the law and the Constitution work.

THE DAILY OKLAHOMAN
Oklahoma City, Okla.
August 8, 1974

AS the Nixon presidency wallows deeper in the impeachment waves, with most of the crew having already abandoned ship, there is an understandable urge in Congress for a speedy resolution of the entire sordid episode. Having already constructed the scaffold, there is no desire on the part of many to stay around for the hanging.

Thus the scramble by House and Senate Republicans, obviously engineered by their elected leaders and senior figures, to persuade the President that he should resign.

Despite Nixon's announced intention to suffer through the complete constitutional process of impeachment and trial, GOP leaders believe he can be pressured into changing his mind. The President's conduct of his defense since Watergate broke has been a model of inconsistency, and even White House sources concede that resignation remains a "viable option."

Flowing concurrently with the resignation tide is another congressional movement to accelerate the entire impeachment procedure if Nixon really does stonewall it all the way.

Even some Republicans are suggesting that the House take the Articles of Impeachment so carefully drafted by the Judiciary Committee, ram them through with only a few hours of debate, and be done with it. This would be a mistake with serious potential consequences.

The House may not require as much time as originally planned for its impeachment debate, especially in view of Nixon's latest damaging revelations, but neither should it skip pell mell through the constitutional path. Deliberate, judicious consideration of the impeachment articles for Americans to witness and put into context is more imperative than ever.

Much has been made of Nixon's impending impeachment and Senate trial as a national trauma that could be avoided by his resignation. Even if he should somehow escape conviction by a few votes, so the reasoning goes, the President's ability to govern has been destroyed and the country would flounder for two years.

One suspects that some of these congressional crocodile tears are motivated as much by re-election campaign schedules as by genuine dedication to the national welfare. More important, those who argue that the United States is so weak it cannot survive the application of its Constitution reveal their own lack of faith in this country and its people.

To insist on a rational, dispassionate and fair course through the ordeal of impeachment is not to condone Richard Nixon's personal conduct in the highest office of the land. It is simply the constitutional way to determine whether he should be removed from that office.

Americans should have no fear of that process because this country has always been bigger than one man. After all, that was the message our founding fathers gave to King George.

The News and Courier

Charleston, S.C., August 2, 1974

Throughout the time he has been under pitiless fire as a result of Watergate and other developments connected with his presidency, we have tended to give the benefit of doubt to Richard Nixon.

When Mr. Nixon was accused of tolerating flagrant abuses of authority in the White House, we rejected the thought of personal involvement. When it was said he manipulated agencies of government to achieve personal political aims, we pleaded lack of proof. When wrongdoing was alleged as the result of his refusal to yield information to Congress, we cited a right to executive privacy. When he was charged with ineptness in handling problems elsewhere on the domestic front, we pointed to success in foreign affairs. Finally, when impeachment was called for, we refrained from taking up the cry in our editorial columns. The burden of justifying the President has grown increasingly onerous, however. One after another, charges which seemed frivolous have proven to have substance. One after another, new developments have unfolded to shake our confidence and cause us to reconsider a long-standing position as a Nixon admirer and advocate.

Mr. Nixon's casual acceptance of unjustifiable public expenditures on his private property, his tolerance of violations of the law concerning retention of official gifts, his wheeling and dealing with campaign contributors (of which connections with the milk lobby and his marketing of ambassadorial appointments have been two particularly painful examples), the picture of wretched indecisiveness, brazen manipulation of fellow citizens and unbecoming personal mannerisms exposed by the Watergate tapes — those things and others like them lead us now to endorse the movement to get him out of office.

It is a movement in which we will be more comfortable than we once might have been because it no longer can be identified as the sole possession of those who might be catalogued as Mr. Nixon's enemies, anxious to do him harm. Enlistment in its ranks of such respected people as our Sunday columnist James Jackson Kilpatrick and U.S. Rep. James D. Mann of South Carolina — to mention two outstanding examples — have added depth and respectability. For Mr. Kilpatrick, joining up involved a painful departure — similar to the one we are undertaking here — from a position which once seemed worth defending to the last ditch. For Mr. Mann, the delegate to Congress of a conservative, upcountry district heavily weighted with Republican sentiment, willingness to become — as he put it — the "cutting edge of impeachment" means risking a political career in order to stand for principle.

It would be nice if through some miracle impeachment could be disposed of by a less divisive mechanism than a public trial. But there is no alternative to public trial at hand since Mr. Nixon has not offered to resign.

Is the situation in government really bad enough to warrant the President giving up his responsibilities either by resigning or invoking the 25th Amendment? Yes it is. With the impeachment process barely under way Mr. Nixon already is showing the strains imposed upon him. A recent message on the economy, for example, was a feeble performance uncharacteristic of the vigorous Nixon manner. It reflected the erosion of power Mr. Nixon is experiencing. There are many ways in which the President might slow down the deficit budget-making which is at the root of inflation but all of them require a strong base to operate from. Mr. Nixon's base is diminishing toward the vanishing point.

Mr. Nixon himself has said that a strong President is needed to run the country in these times. Better than anyone else he is in the position to recognize his weakening authority imperils us all. Mr. Nixon can ease the pain for his country — and perhaps even improve his own position — if he will surrender his office. If he refuses to do so, there is but one course to take. That is to press ahead as quickly and decisively as possible with impeachment and try to get the agony over with.

CHICAGO DAILY NEWS

Chicago, Ill., August 7, 1974

On Dec. 7, 1973 — many volumes of history ago — The Daily News said that the impeachment proceedings against President Nixon should progress to a definite finding of guilt or innocence.

That was the way, we said, to get at the truth, to cleanse the nation of a festering sore, to ensure justice and to restore the confidence of the people.

Now the President has made confessions that add up to pleading guilty to the first two articles of impeachment voted by the House Judiciary Committee. In admitting his personal complicity in the Watergate cover-up, he conceded, as charged in Article I, that he prevented, obstructed and impeded the administration of justice, and as charged in Article II that he abused the powers invested in him as President by misusing government agencies for political ends.

Those admissions have desperately weakened Mr. Nixon's position, both legally and in the esteem of many who had remained loyal up to this point.

Inevitably a clamor has arisen for the President to resign. Mr. Nixon said on Tuesday that he would not do so, and one is reminded that Vice President Agnew made the same statement the day before he quit. We presume the President will go on studying his options.

Resignation is a course with many attractions for a nation run haggard by the sickening succession of Watergate disclosures.

The miring of the entire executive branch in the spreading chronicle of corruption has undermined public confidence to the point of imminent disaster. A government absorbed in Watergate has been unable to muster economic leadership or formulate economic policy; inflation runs rampant and the economy drifts out of control. Abroad, both friends and enemies regard the crippled President and downgrade the power of this nation. The two-party system faces its grimmest hour as the November elections loom and the prospect grows for a Congress so lopsidedly Democratic as to be able to overwhelm the executive branch.

Mr. Nixon could give the nation's morale a spectacular boost and set government on a fresh course by simply resigning. While it is by no means certain that he could also preserve his $60,000 pension and other emoluments by so doing, his chances would at least be better than if the Senate finally found him guilty, stripped him of all benefits, and drove him from office.

But this is a decision for the President — and a hard decision it must be, with all that is involved in ignominious retreat, confession of defeat, and disgrace that must inexorably spread to envelop those who have remained close and loyal.

We believe, on balance, that impeachment should continue. The gains in that course, while longer range, more than offset the immediate advantages in resignation. The impeachment process is the way to settle the issue finally and beyond dispute or doubt. It is the way to ensure justice as nearly as human minds can ensure it. And above all it demonstrates to the nation and the world the strength and integrity of this two-centuries-old system. It is a system that is already operating effectively; it was the Supreme Court, performing its role under its mandate, that brought Mr. Nixon to bay by requiring him to produce the tapes that contain proof of guilt.

We would only urge that both houses of Congress get on with the task with all deliberate speed — but we have every confidence they will do so without urging. For Congress is close to the people, and aware that the nation needs a swift end to its ordeal.

The Greenville News

Greenville, S.C., August 8, 1974

The Constitution of the United States is the fundamental rule of law, every day of every year, in all cases, large and small, throughout this nation of states. It is the only real safeguard of our liberties, personal and collective.

For that reason The Greenville News does not join in widespread clamor for President Nixon's resignation — unless the President clearly states that he is guilty of charges of impeachment voted against him by the House Judiciary Committee.

A presidential resignation "for the good of the country" without admission of guilt would subvert if not destroy the Constitution.

It would set a terrible precedent. Henceforth a President could be hounded from office merely because an opposition party in control of Congress disliked him and created a political or ideological furore. That would amount to legislative control of the executive affairs of the nation, in violation of the Constitution.

The destruction of the Constitution's delicate balances of ex-ecutive, legislative and judicial powers at the federal level also would destroy the republican form of government guaranteed by the Constitution to every state. The federal system of states is itself a balance of powers and depends directly upon balanced separation of national power.

Stability of this nation's constitutional government depends upon both separation of power and shielding of power from undue pressure. The Founding Fathers purposely and wisely shielded the presidential power by establishing the Electoral College and giving the President a firmly-fixed term of office.

The impeachment process for removal of a President purposely was made difficult so that a President could not be ousted because of temporary unpopularity with Congress or the public, but only for clearly-proved charges of gross and grave misconduct.

Agonizing though it is, that process has started and must be followed to its constitutional conclusion. Although the nation ob-viously is suffering economically and otherwise because of present upheavals, it must endure until the matter has been resolved constitutionally. Otherwise it will suffer more terribly in the future.

To force President Nixon from office while he still maintains innocence, not only would violate huge sections of the Constitution, it would further polarize this country. It would be wrong constitutionally and politically.

The President may choose to step aside temporarily under the 25th Amendment and allow the vice president to exercise the duties of the presidency until the impeachment process has ended. But resignation without admission of guilt should be out of the question.

Impeachment, having been started, cannot safely be ended until the process has concluded and the President has been either convicted by two-thirds vote of the Senate or exonerated. Any other course subverts the rule of law upon which American liberty and the American system of government rest.

The Courier-Journal

Louisville, Ky., August 8, 1974

There is no longer a question whether Richard Nixon will vacate the presidency. His admission that he has lived a lie for more than two years reduces the issue to when and how he will leave office.

Whether resignation or impeachment would be preferable cannot be judged. There is no precedent to cite in deciding which trauma would be easier to overcome.

But there remain in the nation a cherished Constitution, a basic strength and, as the events of the past months have shown, a stable and orderly process. The Republic will survive the stress, undoubtedly emerging from it stronger, just as the young nation found maturity after a terrible Civil War more than a century ago.

Certainly resignation would be the quicker and less painful. It would spare the nation the ordeal of impeachment, the agony of a drawn-out trial and the speculation over whether a convicted President would voluntarily vacate the White House. But within resignation lie the seeds of a great national division. For even with the overwhelming weight of the evidence spread before them, there are still those who will see Mr. Nixon as the victim of a conspiracy by his political enemies.

Therein lies the advantage of the impeachment process, however long a spectacle. The sight on national television of staunch Republicans and conservative Southern Democrats, the men around whom Mr. Nixon in-tended to forge his new majority, voting against him should convince all but a few die-hards that he had indeed, in his conduct of the presidency, stretched beyond the pale.

Those are votes that will not be lightly cast. The agony undergone by such men as Reps. Charles Wiggins of California and David Dennis of Indiana is evidence of that fact. They used all their legal skills during the House Judiciary Committee's impeachment debate in advocating Mr. Nixon's cause, firm in the belief that the web of circumstance did not warrant a President's removal from office.

All that time the "smoking gun" lay concealed in a White House closet. How they and presidential lawyer James St. Clair must feel betrayed now that the transcript of the June 23, 1972, conversation reveals its existence.

That strips away any remaining doubts of Mr. Nixon's innocence. It would only be idle speculation to try to guess how many votes Mr. Nixon can, as of today, claim in the House and the Senate. There are certainly not enough to keep him in office so, if he chooses to "fight on" as some suggest, the impeachment process must be expedited.

But if it is to be resignation, there must be a clear statement in which Mr. Nixon admits the responsibility for his own downfall.

Whether this is possible in light of the disturbing reports from inside the besieged White House is ques-tionable. Comparisons of the President to The Caine Mutiny's Captain Queeg drifting from within the inner circle can only cause a shiver down the national spine. It is all very well that presidential aides are determined to keep the country running, but who elected Al Haig to public office?

Thus these moments, with history rushing in, have an air of unreality. Even for the hardened Nixon haters, it is not a time to savor. The Republic is suffering and not because it has never seen scandal in the White House before. It has been there, but never before has it reached directly to the President to the extent that he has, by his own admission, been party to the cover-up of a crime.

Rather it is because, unlike his memorable predecessors, Mr. Nixon has shown no capacity to rise to the demands of his office. Instead he has shrunk even while making significant advances in the area of foreign policy. There is a yearning, in company with columnist Garry Wills, for the days of Mr. Nixon and his wife's "respectable Republican cloth coat." As Wills writes in The New York Review of Books:

The days of such respect are gone, not only for Republicans but for the republic. Whatever one said about "Tricky Dick" of the Fifties, at least he did not seem personally venal. Now one wonders if there is anything left for him to be charged with—any code, however low, he still claims to honor; any standard remaining beyond brute survival.

The Dallas Morning News
Dallas, Tex., August 12, 1974

FOREIGNERS stayed up six hours and more past bedtime to hear Nixon's resignation speech. Leaders come and go elsewhere in the world, too—often with shorter shrift than Richard Nixon got —but Nixon, in foreign eyes, was more than merely a national leader: He was a leader for peace in the world.

They heard him say, these hundreds of thousands of people, that he hoped his work for world peace would be his legacy. Doubtless, foreigners and Americans nodded together at that. Nixon's achievements in foreign fields are above the reproaches that shadowed his domestic reign. With the rest of the world, we, too, will probably accord the fallen President his wish.

Americans may differ and will differ over Nixon's domestic record, mainly because our borders are peaceful and what a neighbor does is of little moment compared with what a president is doing in Washington.

But elsewhere nations jostle one another, and in foreign eyes Nixon was not only in Washington — he was in the Mid-East, in Peking, in Moscow, the pressure centers of the world, bringing down the pressures, easing old enmities, in the wake of America's own settlement for peace in Vietnam. To many, he redeemed the "shame" brought on America by that conflict and went on to create a peaceful image, not only for his own country but for the world. To foreigners, Watergate weighed small against all this.

NO WONDER, then, that a thrill of apprehension swept the globe at the news of his impending downfall. What would be the consequences for peace? No wonder that leaders of governments, little concerned with what they considered the political skulduggery of Watergate—but all-concerned with where American foreign policy leads—made the fallen Nixon's achievement for peace his epitaph and crossed their fingers for the future.

The Israelis, especially, feared impeachment. Abba Eban, the brilliant former foreign minister, summed up the resignation as tragedy: "A brilliant period in international relations has ended in domestic collapse." The Arabs showed foreboding, too.

The French, perhaps less moralistic than Americans, wondered why America could cut off such an impressive international achievement on moral grounds. Why judge a leader except by what he does for his country? they asked. The French state television network said, "He restored America to the center of the planet."

PRIVATE press and man-in-the-street commentary were more mixed as to the overall aspects of the resignation—but none belittled the Nixon achievement abroad, however much judgments varied on the justification for the end of the Nixon rule.

History, of course, will shade the portrait of Richard Nixon more wisely and objectively than we can. The lights and shadows of his mixed career we cannot as yet sort. But it would appear that the side of him that sought world peace is already established in full sunlight abroad and that Watergate is unlikely to eclipse it here.

Oklahoma City Times
Oklahoma City, Okla., August 9, 1974

THE TRAGEDY of the inglorious end of the Nixon presidency is that those parts of it that brought indisputably notable achievements will be tainted for posterity.

That Richard Nixon's accomplishments through nearly six years were monumental will be difficult for historians to dispute. In what perspective the misdeeds of the President and his followers are viewed remains for the verdict of history.

When the record of his positive contributions can be examined without the distraction of contemporary hysteria and free of personal bias toward the man, it will be hard to find one to equal it.

GENERATIONS to come may point to the Nixon years as the turning point in the mad race to nuclear extinction. Nixon succeeded in reducing global tensions and inaugurating an era of negotiation in place of confrontation between rival political systems. He opened up contact with Communist China and effected detente with Soviet Russia.

Through the "Nixon doctrine" he maneuvered the United States into a more realistic position in international relations, this nation, rather than serving as a world policeman, would stand ready to help countries who earnestly desired to preserve their own freedom.

Nixon will always have the gratitude of those who felt he pursued the right course in ending U. S. participation in the Vietnam war on honorable terms and in bringing the prisoners of war home. This achievement, plus the ending of the military draft, led to a quieting of the campuses and the cities.

Even while struggling with the Watergate albatross, he and his secretary of state, Henry Kissinger, chipped away at the granite of Israeli-Arab obstinacy and made Middle Eastern peace seem at least possible.

AT HOME, Nixon had less success in dealing with economic woes. But, in an adverse way, he demonstrated the advantage of the free market over wage and price controls.

By his appointments, Nixon moved the Supreme Court into a stance of stricter construction of the Constitution and away from judicial legislating of social programs.

On the debit side, the effort to reverse the tide of federal power, control an almost unmanageable bureaucracy and reduce federal spending has been severely, perhaps fatally, damaged.

When these days are only a painful memory, people may reflect on these things and note, sadly, that Watergate was—among other things—so unnecessary.

THE WALL STREET JOURNAL
New York, N.Y., August 12, 1974

The last speech of Richard M. Nixon's long political career was very likely the best. Under impossible circumstances, he delivered a message that struck to the heart of the matter, that he has been a President with visions for the American future.

Thus in a sense he has managed to confound his critics once more. They clearly expected a message that would vindicate their image of the man, a defensive and spiteful leave-taking. And in their disappointment, it seems to us, lies a warning not to judge too quickly, a warning that emotions perhaps fitting to recent moments may be only partly fitting to final judgments of a man, his life and his future.

Mr. Nixon's plea to the people and to history made two points. With regard to his career, much has been attempted and much accomplished —the end to the Vietnam war, the opening to Russia and China, the hope of building foundations for peace in the future. With regard to Watergate, mistakes have been made, but were made "in what I believed at the time to be the best interests of the nation."

This is by no means an adequate justification for mistakes serious enough in our view to justify the Republic's first successful impeachment. It is always easy for politicians and above all Presidents to believe that the best interests of the nation lie in their own re-election. Yet even after that is said, there is truth in Mr. Nixon's remark that provides a needed relief from the cardboard picture his most bitter critics have erected over the past few months.

For at the center of his critics' composition is a man interested in the mere possession of power, not in the uses to which it can be put. The motives for wiretapping, for burglaries, for covering up crimes, the indictment goes, lay in the blind and indeed insane pursuit of power. In this pursuit, the indictment continues, anything went. We were, in the most extreme versions of the composition, on our way to a police state.

A certain exaggeration is of course a staple of political rhetoric, and perhaps this image was necessary to a task as difficult as unseating a President. Yet it lingers on today, in the lust for prison punishment in those who have always told us prisons had no purpose except to rehabilitate, in the pettiness of a would-be President whose idea in this moment is to revoke Mr. Nixon's pension, and in a milder form in those who deplore his failure to produce a valedictory framed in sackcloth and ashes.

Not feeling guilt in the wake of Watergate may be moral blindness, but confessing it when it is not felt would be the worst sort of hypocritical posturing. Somehow it shows more character to do what Mr. Nixon did, to strike at the heart of the moral charges against him, to defend not his actions but his motives.

One need not accept the defense fully to recognize it as a signal for caution. For our part, we do not know our own minds on the final judgment of Richard M. Nixon, or even on the question of his potential criminal liabilities. But in leaving he reminds us again that it is a complex matter and he is a complex man. Faced with the task of sorting out these complexities, a wise man will plead for a bit of distance and a bit of time.

THE INDIANAPOLIS STAR
Indianapolis, Ind., August 4, 1974

Americans should be acutely conscious that they may be witnessing "the eating of the guts" of their country in the headlong stampede to impeach President Nixon.

Field Marshal Viscount Montgomery coined the phrase to describe the epochal battle of el-Alamein in World War II. It was, he said, "the eating of the guts" of Hitler's famed Afrika Corps which later enabled him to chase the Germans some 1,200 miles across the North African desert and ultimately — with American help — out of Africa.

But "the eating of the guts" is a political as well as a military stratagem. History — including that of Imperial Rome — shows that whole nations have collapsed, or gone down to calamitous defeat in war, because they had been so consumed internally as to become impotent.

Recent history's most glaring example, the fall of France in 1940, resulted directly from the internal weakness contrived by such disloyal yet influential figures as Pierre Laval, a Socialist-inclined demagogue — ultimately shot as a traitor— who twice rose to be premier. Furthered by self-serving politicians and other misguided Frenchmen, unaware they were in fact butchering their country, the machinations of Laval and his accomplices proved to be the incisive instrument for delivering once-great France defeated and helpless to Hitler's invading Nazis.

Stunned, the French people were utterly unable to comprehend what had happened. They could not grasp that "the eating of the guts" of their country had been going on right under their noses, that the France they thought so strong had in fact been reduced to a shell.

Has "the eating of the guts" of America been going on right under the noses of the American people? Is it now reaching a climax in the impeachment proceedings against President Nixon?

Consider that America's latter-day Lavals and their fellow travelers have long been entrenched at almost every significant point of leverage in the nation — government; legal, educational and ecclesiastical establishments; foundations; organized labor; segments of the business community; and news media.

Consider that under prodding of these seldom visible wielders of power — comparatively few in number, but immensely influential — America has taken giant strides away from the open, free-enterprise society that made her great and toward an authoritarian, bureaucratically controlled society of the type that has made other great nations small.

Consider some of their stratagems for laming America, for turning her institutions upside down, for spreading dissatisfaction and discord among her people — contortion of the Constitution, emasculation of the criminal justice system, encouragement of lawlessness in the name of freedom of expression, maneuvering the nation into war as a prelude to screaming bloody murder at those inheriting the carnage, deliberate creation of an octopus-like welfare state, taxation contrived to penalize success, inflationary debauchment of the people's money, and the subjugation of America's separate sovereign states to an ever-growing Federal bureaucracy.

Consider that these insidious schemes were proceeding apace, virtually unchecked until Mr. Nixon, a seeming castaway, arose to be President. His sin has been not Watergate — a stupid political shenanigan blown up and rigged to involve him in scandal and disgrace — but that he has tried to set America's feet back on the road that in the past has led her to peace and prosperity.

Will the American people watch while Mr. Nixon's implacable enemies push on with their avowed purpose to elbow him out of their way by impeachment? If so, they had better be aware they may be witnessing right now "the eating of the guts" of their country.

The Des Moines Register
Des Moines, Iowa, August 10, 1974

Former President Nixon was not bitter or recriminatory in his farewell address. He was not forthright, either, or the least bit apologetic for the agony he inflicted on this nation during the course of what he referred to—only once—as "the Watergate matter."

The address was historic, for no other U.S. president ever resigned the office. But the absence of candor and remorse bars it from greatness.

The national TV appearance was moving, because the hurt of another human being is always moving. Richard Nixon's pain at being the first U.S. president ever forced from office for misconduct was plain beneath his veneer of manful calm.

Mr. Nixon took justifiable pride in his achievements in foreign relations and in his goals for domestic progress. His listeners would agree on these matters.

But rather than face, with the nation, the reality of the events which had brought him to such a moment, Nixon indulged in euphemisms which tended to cloud, in the best public relations fashion, what had happened and why.

He did not acknowledge that there had been a conspiracy to obstruct justice after the Watergate break-in, that he knew about it, and that he lied about that knowledge for months — until the Supreme Court forced him to yield the taped evidence that he knew. He only said, "Some of my judgments were wrong."

He did not acknowledge that one-time supporters on the House Judiciary Committee were persuaded by the evidence to say they would vote for his impeachment. He only said he didn't have a "strong enough political base in the Congress" to continue his effort to complete his term.

It is true that the former president's words had to be guarded on the Watergate crimes, for he may face trial on criminal charges arising from the actions which led to his resignation.

But that would not prevent a frank admission of why he had to resign. Mr. Nixon, in his final words, revealed the same obliviousness to moral questions and the same obsession with "PR" that dismayed so many when the first White House transcripts were released. He seemed to be inviting doubt among his supporters that he really had committed the crimes with which he was charged. He even seemed in doubt himself that he had done anything wrong.

CHICAGO DAILY NEWS
Chicago, Ill., August 10, 1974

Shakespeare had a phrase for it — "hoist by his own petard" — referring to a man destroyed by his own explosive device. Richard Nixon lighted the fuse of his own destruction when he installed the automatic tape machine to record conversations in the Oval Office and other strategic locations in the White House.

The tapes were his undoing. The day their existence became known the fuse began sputtering toward the explosion that came this week. The tapes, meant to provide a historical record of a great and successful Presidency, provided instead the clinching evidence of lawless conspiracy, of a mean, amoral spirit that invaded and finally engulfed the White House, until the only remedy was a thorough cleansing.

Without the record of the tapes, the nature and extent of the Watergate scandal would have remained a matter of conjecture, of suspicion without proof. The long battle to conceal, withhold and in some instances erase the tapes — all in the name of national security or executive privilege — nearly succeeded. But a stubborn judge, some persistent reporters, a stubborn prosecutor (taking over after the first one was fired) and a Supreme Court heavy with Nixon appointees finally broke through the barriers. And the tale of the tapes toppled the President.

Why would a President "bug" himself and everyone he talked with? Recording messages of state, or ensuring the accuracy of oral instructions and decisions — in such cases a tape record becomes understandable. But every spoken word?

Surely Richard Nixon, the astute politician, the consummate statesman with the prodigious memory for detail, would not forget that his every word was being recorded. Yet the words that finally emerged were so self-incriminating that it is hard to believe he remained aware of his own sanctioned eavesdropping.

There may be no logical, reasonable answer to the puzzle of the tapes. One can only speculate that an overpowering ego created the system — in a desire, perhaps, to preserve a private record from which to cull in later years the "definitive" memoir of a President at work. The idea first advanced — that this was to be a public record for historians of the future — can hardly be given credence in the light of the tawdry conversations actually recorded.

But a historic record was certainly made. The ego-massaging tape machine dutifully tucked away all the evidence of corruption, of deception, of a mortally flawed Presidency. And in due course it spewed that evidence forth, and in so doing turned upon its master and destroyed him. Not even Dr. Frankenstein did a more thorough job.

THE ROANOKE TIMES
Roanoke, Va., August 11, 1974

A longer-range view would almost certainly see today and the past several weeks as times that lifted the spirit. A Congress which had been in full retreat for 30 years has reasserted itself. A President who marred his achievement and potential by a gross abuse of power has resigned. The performance of the judiciary has been nothing less than magnificent.

U.S. District Judge John J. Sirica, probably the most important person in shaking loose the scandals and the wrongdoers, is an example of how a seemingly average judge can rise to greatness on the occasion. District Judges Gerhard Gesell and George L. Hart, Jr., are beginning to share judicial responsibilities arising out of the Watergate

scandals and they, too, seem to be honest and learned men.

The United States Supreme Court rendered the vital decision that a President is not above law and that President Nixon had to surrender the Watergate tapes for a criminal trial. The eight unanimous judges included three appointees of Mr. Nixon and proved that they put devotion to law above politics.

Certainly something must be said for special Watergate prosecutor Leon Jaworski. Doubtful eyes were cast upon him when he came on the scene because he replaced Archibald Cox, the original prosecutor whose popularity increased when he was fired by President Nixon. But Mr. Jaworski has done his

duty and may have some more stern duties to perform.

Our previous praise of James D. St. Clair needs extension. In addition to his previous difficulty defending a weak case Mr. St. Clair also had, as was learned last Monday, a client that misled him: Almost the worst thing that can happen to a lawyer in action. Among those who understand the value of adversary proceedings, Mr. St. Clair's reputation has not suffered one whit.

All in all, the previously distorted parts of government are falling back into the place originally intended for them. We invite a reading on this page today of the heart of Federalist Paper No. 51, explaining the separation of powers. It was

written by either a Virginian, James Madison, or New Yorker Alexander Hamilton.

If men were angels, no government would be necessary, No. 51 reads. That is a good closing point for a review of an exciting month. The members of the House Judiciary Committee which recommended impeachment (at a time when it was politically dangerous so to do), did not look like angels. But they looked like good, honest and sincere men—more like the typical Congressman than the cynics would have us believe. When good honest men—in the executive, legislative and judiciary branches—are properly disposed as intended by a good Constitution, surely we are all better off.

THE MILWAUKEE JOURNAL
Milwaukee, Wis., August 9, 1974

There is no joy in the fall of Richard Nixon. He came to the presidency declaring great goals and seeking an honored place in posterity, but the quest ended wretchedly. He will be chiefly remembered as the first president driven from office in disgrace.

For the man, his family, his friends — it is deep human tragedy. And for millions who will no longer call him president it is a melancholy moment. The cold immensity of what has occurred is numbing.

In his somber televised farewell, Nixon was the model of dignity under severe stress, expressing malice toward none, saying he had put the national interest first, urging unity in his wake. The words were touching. Yet the omissions were almost eerie. Aside from vaguely conceding some wrong judgments, there was no recognition of what produced the roar for resignation, no admission of serious misconduct or broken faith. He even lightly implied that "vindication" might have been possible if supporters in Congress had not buckled.

Clearly, resignation is not the ideal way to get rid of a chief executive who has violated his oath, stained his office and cannot bring himself to say so. Impeachment and trial would not have left these loose ends.

Even so, only a partisan zealot can contend that Nixon was hounded from the White House without warrant. His wrongdoing — so often confirmed, directly or circumstantially, by those amazing tapes — placed his incumbency beyond tolerance in a land of law. Clearly visible in Congress

and across the country was a verdict of cumulative unworthiness, a judgment rooted in voluminous proof and ultimately shared by dogged defenders who had given Nixon the benefit of so many doubts.

Some will say that other presidents have abused their authority, that Nixon's tenure climaxed a steady aggrandizement of the presidency, a trend of swelling arrogance and declining accountability. However true, none of this excuses Nixonian excesses, or lessens the need to make his tumble from the top a vivid warning that no successor will be allowed to wipe his shoes on the Constitution. Impeachment and conviction would have scorched the message onto the White House lawn — but the lesson is not lost. And to deny Nixon blanket immunity against the reach of criminal justice in private life would make the point doubly distinct.

As the most durable politician of the post World War II era, Nixon leaves a swirl of memories, a mix of historic feats and tawdry failures. At one point considered washed up, he had, until now, outfought or outlasted all rivals, from John Kennedy to Nelson Rockefeller. Yet he remains largely an enigma, a complex, contradictory man who very few claim to really know.

What was the fatal flaw? Perhaps it was the craving for power, the thirst to prove worth through domination. Perhaps it was the temperament that restricted his reach for openness and diversity, that caused him to snuggle into an Oval Office cocoon, surrounded by narrow counselors and stern

gatekeepers. Perhaps it was the bent of mind that saw life as perpetual war and cast critics as enemies to be destroyed.

In any case, Nixon did not capture the presidency without warning. Foes harped on his reputation as a humorless, ruthless opportunist, lacking deep moral conviction. Yet the worst was discounted, or at least obscured, by his lengthy preparation for lofty office, his impressive grasp of foreign affairs, his plays to prevailing sentiment, his mastery of TV as a campaign weapon.

And his first term was touched with promise. Despite many ominous shortcomings in domestic affairs, he did bring the troops back from Vietnam, draw Red China into the family of nations, lessen tension with Russia. But by the time of his smashing re-election against a feeble foe, clouds of scandals were growing. The second term, envisioned as a crowning achievement, became a nightmare. As the Watergate coverup unraveled and other outrageous activity surfaced, public confidence crumbled.

His pledge that there would be "no whitewash at the White House" proved ludicrous. His initial pleas of aloof purity were eclipsed by tape transcripts that made America cringe. His indignant declaration, "I am no crook," was answered by a grand jury naming him an unindicted co-conspirator. His confident assertion, "I do not expect to be impeached," withered when he finally admitted to living a colossal lie for two years.

Looking back, it's hard to be-

lieve that it all happened — the hammer blows of stubborn Judge Sirica, the piercing accusations of John Dean, the Senate Watergate Committee's astonishing discovery of secret tapes, the firestorm after Archibald Cox was crudely axed as special prosecutor, the parade of top aides bound for prison, the toppling of an errant Agnew, the Supreme Court rebuff of presidential imperialism, the memorable impeachment debates.

Could it have ended differently? Possibly. If Nixon had come clean soon after the Watergate burglary, he would have damaged his re-election bid, but he probably could have won and pressed ahead without mortal wounds. And who is to say what he might have accomplished — from welfare reform to nuclear disarmament?

Yet, it seems plain now that Nixon and his inner circle were afflicted with disastrous fear of the democratic process. It was something to manipulate or subvert, but not trust. Indeed, this Machiavellian mentality, reinforced by the angry challenges of the Vietnam years, spawned the family of obscenities called Watergate — the bugging and burgling, the twisting of government agencies to political ends, the enemy lists and dirty tricks. And, when the pivotal moment came, it was this mentality that made purifying candor impossible.

So it was that Richard Nixon, the extraordinary scrambler who yearned for lasting glory, sealed his doom in layers of falsehood. Now, he may seek personal peace. Sadly, it will be peace with dishonor.

DAYTON DAILY NEWS
Dayton, Ohio, August 11, 1974

It is more to Richard Nixon's informal farewell to his staff then to his formal resignation speech that analysts will look in the future for insights into the former president's character and personality, and count on this: The historians and the psychiatrists of public affairs will spend years mining that small treasure of self-revelation and assaying its meaning.

If less perfectly clear than he so often said he was trying to be, Mr. Nixon was more open in the casual, emotional comments of his East room presidential coda than at any time in his long public career.

There, Mr. Nixon exposed the problem that finally undermined, his long scramble in politics — exposed it even as he testified to its efficacy.

"Adversity." It has had a fatal attraction for Mr. Nixon. He has hinted at that before, and he has demonstrated it often, but this time Mr. Nixon fully revealed his perception. Strength, success, manliness, self-validation, virtue, honor — all are to be had in overcoming adversity.

There is a kind of psychological syllogism at work there. If the rewards of overcoming adversity are so generous, then it follows that adversity is necessary. Follows that, as Mr. Nixon said, it is virtually required that one occasionally descend into dark valleys so that, laboring out of them, the resulting view from the hills will be prettier, more precious, more personally satisfying.

The clues have been handy for years. The major one has been Mr. Nixon's highly public career, marked more by its ups and downs than that of most persons, by peaks and valleys almost as regular as the ones gliding across the screen of an oscilloscope. Revealing, too, was Mr. Nixon's book, "My Six Crises." It dramatized Mr. Nixon's fascination with crises — with their adversity — even to the point of insisting that some merely unpleasant events in which Mr. Nixon was accidentally involved were personal crises.

Thus the attenuation of political opponents into "enemies." The exaggeration of confronted dislike into "hate." The misunderstanding of opposition by "attacks."

Did Mr. Nixon subconsciously contrive or at least indulge the adversity of Watergate so that after his post-re-election high he would be assured of a companion adversity to overcome? That question will excite speculation and argument for years. Most presidencies have been understood by the pattern of their public or at any rate their literal events. It is probable that Mr. Nixon's will come, in time, to be understood instead more by the contours and the patterns that eventually are agreed to have been the events of the inner president.

The Chattanooga Times
Chattanooga, Tenn., August 9, 1974

Besmirched by the scandals that seeped from the Oval Office and finally trapped by his loose regard for the truth, President Richard Milhous Nixon agreed to bring his administration to an end voluntarily. His resignation midway of a second term will go down in history as the first by any American chief executive.

It was a term that began with the greatest endorsement the nation's voters had ever accorded any candidate; his presidency ended after 2,026 days in the bleak certainty of impeachment and removal from office.

The climax came with wrenching suddenness, despite months of probing investigations, of denouncement and denial, of mounting proof and weakening defenses against charges of abuse of power, obstruction of justice and personal rights trampled underfoot.

As late as Wednesday, the word was that Mr. Nixon still intended to "stonewall it," fighting every inch of the way in the House consideration of a bill of impeachment and a Senate trial that lay ahead. As of this writing, we are unsure of what really changed his mind; we may never know for Mr. Nixon has never been one to confide all his knowledge, his intentions, his motivations.

It is a melancholy day for the Union. Let it pass without vengeful partisanship on the one hand, or of unjustified charges of an innocent man being hounded from the place of honor with which he was entrusted.

Indeed there is cause for rejoicing that the system upon which we depend for our governance has shown strength rather than weakness under terrible strain. For, in truth, it was not the nation that failed but a man and his willing coterie whose lust for power was greater than love of country.

There is much for which Richard Nixon is to be praised, particularly in the field of foreign affairs, and no one should find his approval of the President on this score incompatible with harsh judgment on the misdeeds for which he must take ultimate responsibility. A mixture of good and evil is not alien to the human nature or enterprise; sadness occurs when the latter becomes the dominant force.

It was remarked of a British politician: "His conscience is not his guide but his accomplice." As much can be said of Richard Milhous Nixon, and with a heavy heart, the nation accepts the fact of his resignation as the inevitable result of a betrayal, one of the other.

THE SUN
Baltimore, Md., August 9, 1974

The doom Richard M. Nixon so thoroughly invited has now engulfed and destroyed him. Less than two years after standing on a political pinnacle few men have ever attained, the almost undisputed leadership of the most powerful country on earth, he has sunk into an abysm of disgrace as deep as the peak was high. Nothing like it had happened before in our history, and if the dark Nixon episode is taken as a lesson nothing like it will happen again. To see that it doesn't happen again we must understand that Mr. Nixon has not been driven from office. Through his own actions, under the strange compulsions of his own flawed character, he has brought himself to where he is today. No further explanations or excuses or emotional appeals, and no later revisionism, can alter that.

It is impossible not to feel a measure of personal sympathy for anyone brought so low. In recent days, not to say weeks and months, Mr. Nixon must have lived in lonely torture, and for still longer than that his mind must have been burdened by the knowledge that the front he presented to the country and the world was a false facade. So must his family too have suffered, to the extent that they shared his knowledge; or if they did not share it, in observing his tortures. But Richard Nixon was, by his own choice, not a private citizen, and his degradation is not just a personal disaster. The American people he misled are involved in it too, and for his having so unscrupulously misled them there can be no sympathy at all.

Mr. Nixon's fall is not even, in the profounder sense, a tragedy. True tragedy requires as protagonist a person not just of public size but of inner largeness. Such largeness Mr. Nixon lacks. He is, as we have learned through a long process of continued shock, a vindictive and mean-spirited man, drawing misguided loyalty from a dwindling number of people but himself loyal to none; faithful only to the furtherance of his own ambitions.

In pursuit of those ambitions he employed, more than any of his predecessors, the techniques of "public relations," a phrase to which he gave a widened meaning. For Mr. Nixon public relations has been not a way of presenting, to his own advantage, the substance of his policies and programs, but a program in itself. The means became the end, and when the structure started coming apart little remained to be disclosed inside.

There will be time afterwards to examine the worth of Mr. Nixon's actual accomplishments, particularly in foreign affairs. But even there he diminished those accomplishments through misuse, distorting them out of proportion in the interests of his own continuance in a position of dominance. And in those interests he went so far in the direction of absolute power that for this alone he had ceased to deserve the office to which he had been elected.

He now speaks rather of the interests of the country. It is true that those interests are best served by his departure. Of the means available to him he has chosen resignation, over the constitutional processes he said only on Monday he was determined to see through. But in this extremity, the greatest by far of all his crises, he could not face that kind of music, and so he is going, to the nation's immense relief. Our difficult and special system of government, threatened briefly by Richard Nixon, continues.

THE DENVER POST

Denver, Colo., August 9, 1974

The departure of Richard Milhous Nixon from the presidency constitutes an impressive triumph for the American political system at a grave and critical hour in American history.

Without revolution or chaos or any serious disruption of our national life, the awesome powers of the President of the United States have peacefully been transferred from a man who had abused them to one who was confirmed in a spirit of national unity to govern under the Constitution and the laws.

The Constitution set the stage. One hundred and eighty five years ago, in an age of carriages and candlelight, it pointed the way to this peaceful transition, in an age of spaceships and nuclear power by providing for the removal of an offending president during his term of office through the process of impeachment.

The Congress supplied the power. After moving fairly and responsibly along the impeachment course the Constitution had charted, the Congress made it clear to the President that he would be convicted and removed if he did not resign.

The American people provided the decisive impetus. Their growing disenchantment with the President, their unwillingness to tolerate his misdeeds and their quest for a higher standard of honor at the pinnacle of American government left their mark upon the Congress and reinforced its position.

Slowly, irregularly and in a way that strained the patience of Mr. Nixon's critics, the interaction of the three—the Constitution, the Congress and the people—developed the pressures to force the president from office.

A 26-month-old drama that began when a guard found tape on a door in the Watergate office building in Washington has thus come to an end foreseen by the founding fathers. What is to be learned from that drama?

First, the American system works. It falters sometimes, stalls in confusion, creeps at a glacial pace or stumbles in the wrong direction. But, in the end it works. It has wrested massive power from a man who held it with fierce tenacity, and it has separated dishonor from the presidency.

The very slowness of the process has contributed to its effectiveness. When it was time for Mr. Nixon to be forced from office, the country was ready for it; and a bitter polarization has been largely avoided.

Second, the system requires determined vigilance. A series of weak Congresses had allowed the powers of the presidency to develop unchecked to a point where they threatened the balance of the American government.

The new mood of assertiveness on Capital Hill has been long overdue. It ought to express itself in a drive for additional curbs and checks on the activities of the President and in a new willingness in Congress to meet its own responsibilities.

Third, the system needs greater alertness to subterfuge. The worst subterfuge of all has been the chronic invocation by the President of "national security" as an excuse for ignoring the law and exceeding his powers under the Constitution.

The claim of "national security" ought henceforth to be subjected to skeptical scrutiny. Questionable acts in the interest of "national security" ought never to be undertaken by the executive without appropriate consultation with the other branches of government.

An arrangement for such consultation ought to be developed under the leadership of Congress. The abuses committed in the name of "national security" during the Watergate drama demonstrate the need for safeguards.

Fourth, the system ought not to be for sale. The use of massive campaign contributions to buy government favors and swing elections is a threat to democratic government that cries out for attention.

Congress has been too slow and too timid in dealing with this problem, despite the shocking examples of campaign spending abuses brought to light during the hearings of the Senate Watergate Committee and despite convictions of a number of corporate executives.

Big money is an important part of the tragedy of Watergate. Unless Congress acts to keep big money out of future elections, it can anticipate future abuses. The agony of Watergate will be in vain if the most conspicuous lesson in the whole drama is not put into practice.

The significance of Watergate ought not to wait for the dispassionate view of history to interpret. It ought to be interpreted now by every holder of public office and every voter with the responsibility of choosing officials at all levels of government.

What the people would not tolerate in the White House, they ought not to tolerate in the statehouse or in city hall. The demand for higher standards of honor ought to reach through the whole system and raise the quality of government everywhere.

The American people are patient, but their patience is not inexhaustible. Having cleansed the shining shield of the presidency of an ugly stain, they should press on to the larger cleansing job that still awaits them.

Los Angeles Times

Los Angeles, Calif., August 9, 1974

This can only be a moment of sadness for all Americans.

There must be an appreciation that Mr. Nixon has done the right thing in resigning now. To have prolonged the uncertainty of his leadership when there was a certainty of his impeachment and conviction would have served no purpose.

He has, in doing the right thing, somehow not understood the problem, however. His resignation was required not by the loss of support in Congress, as he suggested, but by his admission of impeachable offenses. He clings to the thought that he somehow could have won "personal vindication," while only in passing conceding some wrongdoing, apparently unaware of the seriousness of the things he did.

But his words of Thursday night have set a proper goal and a proper tone for the nation. He has appealed for a healing of wounds, and committed himself to that process. He has affirmed the importance of peace, and justly recalled his contributions in that cause. He has reassured the nation about the quality of the man who today succeeds him.

By his decision to resign, he has made possible now, immediately, that new beginning wanted by so many citizens, needed by the nation.

Gerald Ford goes to the White House, the first man to become Vice President through the procedures of the 25th Amendment, the first man to become President as the result of a presidential resignation.

He goes to the White House as Mr. Nixon's choice as heir, and that confers on him some of the authority that Mr. Nixon received in his remarkable electoral victory less than two years ago.

He speaks on domestic matters for that right-of-center part of the Republican Party with which Mr. Nixon identified and felt most comfortable, and in this way he can reassure those millions who, by their votes for Mr. Nixon, were supporting a program that they thought best for America.

He brings to the Presidency a long experience in and a firm respect for the American political process, the result of his years in Congress. That in itself will help restore a balance in the federal government and improve the working relationship between the executive and the legislative branches.

So, in the 19th month of the second term of the 37th Presidency, Richard Nixon leaves the White House. He was elected in a triumph exceeded in only one other election in the history of the nation. He departs in disgrace, the victim of a thirst for power that was his strength and his frailty. It was a power he used with effectiveness and imagination in many areas, including development of the new relationships for the United States with China and the Soviet Union. But it was a power that corrupted him, leading him to abuse his authority to the point of obstructing justice, encouraging him to justify any means for the end of maintaining himself in office.

The sadness of the nation is with a man and with events. But it cannot be mistaken for despair. On the contrary, we sense through the tragedy a confidence in the nation. We think its institutions have proved themselves both in the exposure of wrongdoing at the highest place of government and in the effective pursuit of justice by the constitutional processes.

Mr. Ford's new beginning comes with a hopefulness built on that confidence, and we are convinced that it will bring a fresh vitality to the political and social fabric of the nation and to its economic structure as well.

The Sun

Vancouver, B.C., August 9, 1974

The people of the United States have emerged at last from a long nightmare but the tragedy of Watergate has proved one thing unmistakably. Despite all the criticism to which it has been subjected, the U.S. Constitution has come through the ordeal with flying colors.

This is one beneficial effect of the tragedy of Richard Nixon, the president w h o s e immoderate craving for power put the constitution in jeopardy. The system of government enshrined in Washington, cumbersome as it seems many times, has worked. It knows how to cleanse itself. Courts and Congress showed their confidence and courage in handling the crisis as the authors of the constitution would have wanted them to do.

As a result of the ordeal of president and nation, the United States proves stronger than many people thought. It needs to be strong because the fall of Mr. Nixon from power could bring with it fresh problems, both domestic and international.

Fortunately, the new president, Gerald Ford, is a man worthy of the confidence of Congress and people. Although he is little known abroad, he is unquestionably a man of honor and integrity. He has seen long service in government and as Republican leader in the House of Representatives he has demonstrated ability to lead and organize. In the long run he should do much to improve political standards — not only at home but, happily, perhaps in other countries as well.

The danger could arise that as a result of the disillusionment of the Nixon catastrophe, the U.S. may turn inward, become isolationist. Basically a conservative, Mr. Ford will set his own course. But he is known to admire the work of State Secretary Henry Kissinger. There is hope in this that the international gains of the Nixon era will not be lost.

In the meantime, the future of Richard Nixon remains overcast with doubt. Despite his resignation he is still open to impeachment and trial in the Senate, and even should he escape this humiliation he is liable to be prosecuted, as many of his former colleagues and advisers already have been, for alleged crimes and misdemeanors.

The world will not soon get over the enormity of the Watergate scandal. Sordid and sensational, it brought a man of undoubted ability and intelligence to unexpected ruin. The leader of the greatest nation on earth, a man at the zenith of powe rand influence, the zenith of power and influence,

so unnecessary, this history of dirty tricks, of espionage and bribery and burglary — and of perjury wholesale.

Like many heroes of Greek tragedy, Richard Nixon was destroyed by his insolent grasp for power. He craved power immoderately and abused it immoderately and with it abused the confidence of the people.

The measure of this amoral man was fixed in his final speech. He spoke, not of remorse but of his lost "power base." He sought no forgiveness, only self-justification. True, he did regret "any injuries" but millions have obviously regretted them more. And then he had the indecency to speak of "a sacred commitment" and to fade out with what, considering the source, must have been one of the blackest benedictions in history. In it, he, of all people, called down

God's grace on a nation sorely in need of it.

The Watergate affair was, as some have said, a bungled burglary, a really minor matter — except that a president connived in the attempt to cover it up, lied about his connivance and withheld vital evidence from the courts and the Congress. And all this nonsense to win an election already won handily — a case of overkill if there ever was one.

The French newspaper France-Soir may have hit it right, saying: "He lived in a country where the words 'morals, work, reliability' still move millions of Americans. The great political and psychological error of President Nixon was to have forgotten these truths in the White House."

Let those who seek the people's confidence, anywhere, remember this.

The New York Times

New York, N.Y., August 11, 1974

Behind the dazzling succession of events of this most extraordinary week in American political history lies one fact of surpassing importance: the long and unmistakable drift toward concentration of power in the hands of one elected official, the President of the United States, has been stopped. Mr. Nixon and his closest associates considered themselves above and beyond the law, unhampered by constitutional limitations, untroubled by moral constraints. Their subtle moves toward subversion of the Government and deception of the people have now been halted, and reversed, by the processes of law and the political system, but most of all by an aroused moral force that has united the nation.

The peaceful transfer of power that has resulted from the convulsion of these last few days has come with a cleansing sense of relief to the American people; and it was accomplished without the slightest trace of disorder and in the most perfect civic tranquility. In the best and most fundamental sense, this nation has proved its commitment to both law and order in political life.

* * *

The resignation of Richard M. Nixon as President of the United States—the first President so to leave office and, we may hope, the last ever to have to do so—was Mr. Nixon's final effort to frustrate the machinery of the law and the processes of the Constitution. With the adoption of three Articles of Impeachment by the Judiciary Committee of the House of Representatives after a long, careful and fair inquiry, it had become clear that the President would surely have to stand trial in the Senate for his alleged "high crimes and misdemeanors;" and the probability was growing daily that he would be convicted—but there lingered a chance that he would not.

What prompted Mr. Nixon at that point suddenly to publish additional information that was sure to damn him is one of the many mysteries surrounding the character, motives and psychology of this darkly complex man. But his explosive action removed the last shred of public doubt of his criminal involvement both in obstruction of justice and misuse of presidential powers.

As Mr. Nixon said, his "political base" in the Congress instantaneously evaporated, and he therefore resigned to forestall impeachment. But what he did not say, and has

not said yet, is that he had acted in any way beyond, outside of, or contrary to the law and the Constitution of the United States. No admission of anything more than misjudgment; no suggestion that he and his closest associates had committed execrable offenses against the American people, the full exposure of which must still be carried to their completion in the interests of justice and of equality under the law. It is true that Mr. Nixon had become unable to govern, as he recognized, but there is no indication that, even today, he really understands why.

This is the tragedy of Mr. Nixon, an articulate, knowledgeable, able political leader with notable accomplishments in the field of foreign policy—but a leader who failed himself, his family, his supporters and the millions of Americans who had faith in him. He defeated himself and, in doing so, he nearly defeated both the American people who had elected him and the institutions of American democracy that had sustained him. But not quite.

* * *

And that is the triumph. With the accession to office of Gerald R. Ford, whom Mr. Nixon himself had chosen Vice President just ten months ago following the ominous disaster of Vice President Agnew, the nation has successfully passed through its traumatic crisis of leadership.

Irrespective of political differences, President Ford has the Congress and the people behind him during these difficult days of transition. While at this time there can be but pity for his shattered predecessor, there is universally warm support for Mr. Ford even among his political adversaries. President Ford's simple, direct approach to people and problems, his unassuming manner, his candor and openness and, we trust, his willingness to accept objective advice from persons in and out of government who are more knowledgeable than he—all these qualities will be of help to him in undertaking the giant task of leadership that now is his.

Mr. Ford has one supreme advantage. He took his solemn oath of office secure in the knowledge that the country stands firm, the structure unshaken, the genius of American democracy renascent. Out of the morass of Watergate, the nation has planted its feet on solid ground once again. Out of the tragedy of Mr. Nixon has evolved the triumph of America.

THE COMMERCIAL APPEAL
Memphis, Tenn., August 9, 1974

THE LONG WATERGATE ordeal that has wrenched the nation is an experience that no one would want to see repeated. It has destroyed a president. But it also has been a strengthening and instructive episode in United States history.

The American people stand strong this morning because their system of government has endured an exceptional test, a trial of its institutions, its instruments of justice, its Constitution.

However one has viewed Richard Nixon, it is a saddening thing to see a president forced from office in deep humiliation. But it is reassuring to see no matter how massive the corruption, or how high the cover-up of misdeeds, the American system has the will and the way to right the wrong, to dig through to the truth, to punish the mighty as it would the least of us — and to overcome even this agonizing trauma.

THERE IS AN ETHIC in the American character, an ethic which runs like a strong thread through the Constitution, which reveres honesty and abhors the liar and the cheat.

Everything about Nixon has run contrary to this ethic. And in the end the court-required revelation of his private conversations with close aides, recorded with his own desire on tapes for posterity, brought his downfall. For in Nixon's own words we saw not only the corruption of high power, the terrible attempts to manipulate the CIA and the FBI and the Internal Revenue Service, but also the deceit, the connivance, the conspiring. And in this lamentable record we saw also the willful and conscious lying to Congress, to the federal courts, to the citizens who by their votes had trusted Richard M. Nixon with the world's most powerful office.

If the tasks of the presidency are awesome, so also is the trust.

At all levels of society's human structures, right down to the family unit, the man and wife, trust is the foundation. The nation asks no more of its elected leader than parents do of their children. Abide by the rules, the laws that have been proved best for the common good, level with us, tell the truth if you make a mistake. That is what we teach our children. And if we expect them to believe that advice, there must be no double standard. We can demand no less of our educators, our business people, our churchmen, our law enforcers, our legislators, our jurists, and our president.

PERHAPS OTHER presidents have abused that trust. But even if they have, that was no justification for Nixon's cynical mauling of the honor, the dignity and the faith of the presidency.

It was Nixon's complaint that too much was made of Watergate for too long. But it was the perseverance of our other institutions — Congress, the courts, and also the free press — that brought an end to Watergate. It was not hastened into the light by the President who preached his concern for the integrity of the executive branch at the same time that his lies built upon lies dragged out the painful search for truth.

Like wars, like assassinations, like some malignant disease, the past two years have been an ugly, depressing time in this nation's life.

But when we teach our children to look to our form of self-government and our Constitution for right and justice, the Watergate experience will be one more proof that this Union can survive in tempest and in fire.

Herald News
Fall River , Mass., August 10, 1974

The role of the information media, especially the newspapers, in the long tragedy beginning with the Watergate break-in will be discussed and debated for many years to come. But no one, even those critical of the way the media handled the affair, will dispute that except for a free press, Watergate would never have come to public attention, and the administration would have succeeded in covering its own tracks.

It is because a free press was essential to the long, painful process of finding out what really happened that in countries with a controlled press, the Watergate affair is regarded as far less sensational in its implications than it seems here or in other nations with similar traditions of free speech. In the Soviet Union, presumably, a burglary such as the one at the Watergate apartments, even if it was bungled, would never become public knowledge and would therefore have no effect on those ultimately responsible.

The Watergate affair is bound to remain for this generation the supreme example of the power of the press to root out the facts in the face of government opposition. Until the President's statement of admission on Monday no one could say for sure that the destruction of the administration was justified. That statement without meaning to be, was the clearest vindication possible of the battle the free press has waged to make sure that the American public knew the facts.

In the midst of the present devastation in Washington no one can be happy about what has taken place. But the facts have been made known. The free press has once again proved its importance to a free people.

The Ottawa Citizen
Ottawa, Ont., August 9, 1974

And so the long inglorious political career of Richard Nixon is over. It is a terrible story, one that the American people and their friends around the world will not wish to dwell on unduly; yet history has no value unless it teaches somebody some lessons.

There has been illness in the American body politic over the past generation, no doubt about it. The moral reign of terror created by Senator Joe McCarthy. The blindly negative foreign policy of Foster Dulles. The assassination of a strong young president. The assassination of black America's most eloquent leader. The assassination of the dead president's brother, himself a potential president. The tragic drift into a hopeless war in Vietnam. And Watergate.

Richard Nixon had nothing to do with any assassination. But he was closely allied with McCarthyism. He was a vocal exponent of the Dulles foreign policy. His kind of thinking led the United States into Vietnam, even though he held no responsibility for the step-by-step decisions that made it happen under Presidents Kennedy and Johnson. Nixon at least ended America's involvement in Vietnam, and Nixon buried the Dulles-Eisenhower Cold War with his approaches to Moscow and Peking. He was ever the opportunist, and his obsession with political victory, perhaps reinforced by bitter setbacks on the road to power, made possible the squalid scandal of Watergate.

To read those devastating transcribed tapes is to shake with shock at the knowledge that this was the man, and these were his closest advisers, who held the topmost office in the world's most powerful nation. It is not that the president used dirty or profane language. It is rather that his whole approach to politics and public affairs was dirty and profane. The question seemed never to be raised in that circle whether a decision was right or wrong, good or bad for the country or the world. The question was always whether they could get away with it, how it would sell, if it would play in Peoria.

There is no use trying to be kind about it. Nixon's has been a disgusting presidency, and the American people are lucky that the president was foolish enough to let the tapes run while he cooked up his crooked schemes.

Well, they are done with him, and we are glad for them. President Gerald Ford, if not exactly cut out for greatness, at least offers the hope of a return to sanity, responsibility and straight thinking in an office where those qualities are desperately needed. He should be able to get the U.S. through the next two years. If he proves inadequate he can be replaced by the electorate at the end of that time. If he is successful he will earn the gratitude of Americans, and of the world in general, and will no doubt then be elected in his own right.

Canadians today join their friends across the border in wishing the new president godspeed and a clean-sweeping broom.

THE LINCOLN STAR
Lincoln, Neb., August 13, 1974

The final question remaining in the case of Richard M. Nixon is that of his criminal liability as a private citizen and it is not an easy question to answer. It is safe to say that those who urge that the full weight of the law be brought to bear against the former President will suffer the accusation of lustful persecution.

The best solution would be that a qualified and objective analysis would show no cause for criminal charges against Mr. Nixon. There is at least serious doubt, however, that such would be the case.

The more prominent thought is that an honest appraisal would mean the indictment of the former President on charges of at least obstruction of justice. The record as we now know it would seem to support such a charge.

But it is argued that it would be inhumane to pursue such a course of action, that Nixon has suffered more than enough for whatever misdeeds are to his credit. We are of the opinion that this would be the majority feeling of the people of the United States.

Such a course of action, however, raises the real and sticky problem of what to do with all the defendants in the Watergate scandal. Having never been as high in public office as Nixon, they have not fallen as far but their disgrace and their personal suffering are no less than his in the area of things beyond the letter of the law.

If Nixon has suffered enough with personal humiliation, what about the dozens of others involved in Watergate? It is not a matter of an eye for an eye or a pound of flesh, but for simple justice and equality.

This observation doesn't put on the side of criminal prosecution of Mr. Nixon. As a matter of fact, we do not favor such prosecution but our difficulty is in finding some legitimate means of avoiding it.

Honolulu Star-Bulletin
Honolulu, Hawaii, August 9, 1974

Even though there is no vindictive mood among most Americans, the question of the judicial handling of former President Richard Nixon's involvement in the Watergate trauma is going to be a vexing one.

The willingness of many to feel that the former president has been punished enough by being forced to leave office comes up against two hard realities:

1—Two dozen of his colleagues, who also were forced to leave office, are facing fines and prison terms as well.

2—Mr. Nixon himself has enunciated a hard line on amnesty for men who avoided service in the Vietnam War by either leaving the country or deserting.

The bid for amnesty for Richard Nixon must face these facts. A column on the opposite page makes a case against forgiveness that is going to seem compelling to many Americans.

The decision does not have to be made at once. But President Ford, the Congress, the courts and the special prosecutor will have to think very hard about the right way to handle the case of the United States of America vs. Richard Nixon.

San Jose Mercury
San Jose, Calif., August 9, 1974

Richard M. Nixon has resigned the presidency of the United States for the good of the nation; it was a necessary act, but it was also one demanding considerable courage.

Two years of Watergate all but tore the country apart; Watergate itself will remain forever a stain in the political annals of the nation. The tragedy is now closed, in the most humane — and just — manner still open to those involved. Mr. Nixon will remove himself from office, allowing President Gerald Ford to carry forward the business of the nation. Surely a sense of relief must permeate the country. It is over now.

Two years ago this newspaper enthusiastically endorsed Richard Nixon for re-election. We did so on the record he compiled in his first administration. It was — and still is — an excellent record.

President Nixon in 1972 had all but ended American participation in the Vietnam war; he was in process of repatriating the prisoners of war. His opening to China persuaded Peking to end 25 years of self-imposed isolation. He furthered detente with the Soviet Union, achieving agreement on the limitation of defensive nuclear weapons systems. At home revenue sharing and other aspects of the "new federalism" were beginning to have their impact on society.

These were Richard Nixon's accomplishments, and he is entitled to full credit for them. Indeed, history may mark him as one of the greatest of American presidents in terms of foreign diplomacy.

Regrettably, these accomplishments do not represent the full Richard Nixon story. For whatever reasons, and they must have seemed compelling to him at the time, Mr. Nixon embraced illegal counterespionage in domestic affairs. When burglars working in his interests if not at his direction were apprehended, he sought to limit the investigation, to keep it away from his political agents in the Committee To Re-Elect the President.

In disclosing this episode to the American people this week, Mr. Nixon said he took full "responsibility" for it. Now, inevitably, he has been held accountable for it as well.

There is little question that had the impeachment process gone forward, Mr. Nixon would have been removed from office. An almost unanimous impeachment vote was being forecast in the House, followed by at least the two-thirds vote needed for conviction in the Senate. The Senators, too, would have been able to listen to the tape of the June 23 conversation between Mr. Nixon and H.R. Haldeman, his then chief of staff, wherein the Watergate cover-up was hatched.

That is now history. Mr. Nixon has resigned. He should be permitted to collect his pension and his annual office allowances and go in peace. Neither should Mrs. Nixon's prospective widow's pension be placed in jeopardy by the threat of criminal prosecution of her husband, now a private citizen. Numerous methods, formal and informal, exist whereby this de facto "immunity" may be conferred, as it should be.

Mr. Nixon's pensions should constitute a just recompense for his many, undeniable services to this country. Deprivation of power and the necessity of living with the shame of Watergate for the rest of his life will be his punishment. It is enough.

The American people are not vindictive, by and large. They are just, generous — and tired. Let Mr. Nixon go in peace, and let the American people get on with the business of living and of governing their country to the best of their ability.

ARKANSAS DEMOCRAT
Little Rock, Ark., August 15, 1974

All of a sudden, many important people are coming up with the suggestion that the country ought to grant blanket amnesty both to Watergaters and to Vietnam draft resisters, on the theory that this would close and heal America's wounds. Frankly, we have a hard time finding either the parallel or the wisdom in the idea.

In the first place, there's the question of precedent. We may never have another Watergate. But there is not much reason to believe that America will never have to go to war again. If we decide that people can evade the draft and get by with it, this country could one day be unable to defend itself or its allies.

Secondly, there are some fundamental differences among the lawbreakers. The Watergaters simply broke laws, willy nilly. The draft-resisters and deserters not only broke them but they insist that the laws be rewritten to say that people have the right to pick and choose the wars that they want to fight in. This goes down pretty hard with Americans (or survivors of Americans) who fought in three other wars and were no more anxious to do so than those people called for service in Vietnam.

Anyway, these are serious offenses, not only against individuals but the nation. The people connected with Watergate committed burglary, perjury, and obstruction of justice. The deserters and draft resisters refused to answer their country's call for help. These crimes should not be excused for any reason — loyalty, national security, or conscience. So in our view there should be no blanket amnesty for either Watergaters or draft resisters.

This brings us, of course, to Richard Nixon. Should there be amnesty for him, when, from his own mouth, he has admitted that he failed to call a constable when he knew a crime had been committed and, in fact, even helped conceal the crimes? We have to say yes.

We do so not because we think he has been punished enough by being pressured into resigning; this is why we were never among those who clamored for his resignation. But because he did sidestep the impeachment process, the record is incomplete. For this reason we favor a so-called Agnew solution — the special prosecutor would grant immunity in return for a precise statement of the extent of his involvement. He should not have immunity from civil suits, however, and if the state of California chooses to disbar him, we would go along with that. But we do not believe that a former President should be subject to criminal prosecution.

Now there will be those who say that this is unfair because all laws should apply equally to all citizens. In the first place, there is only one special law for punishing Presidents, and it was not used. Of course, this was because Nixon resigned, but there's nothing illegal about that. In fact, to a great extent, public pressure was responsible for this, because without it, Nixon would have seen it through to the finish. In the second place, we are being silly if we say that the President is like all other citizens; he's not and never can be because there is only one President. And he doesn't get the office by accident, by inheritance or by being selected by other politicians. The people pick out the man to whom we pay our highest honor. For the people to then turn around and subject him to trial at the hands of any state or federal judge who might be anxious to make a name for himself would be more demeaning to this country than to Richard Nixon.

Therefore, while granting Richard Nixon immunity might be a double standard, not granting it could say that in this country we had no standards at all.

St. Petersburg Times
St. Petersburg, Fla., August 13, 1974

The nightmare of Watergate is over, but one remaining question nags the country.

Will Citizen Richard Nixon, no longer protected by the office of the presidency, be prosecuted in the criminal courts for the obstructions of justice he already has confessed?

We feel strongly that the good of the country demands that this ordeal be put into the past as quickly as possible. For that reason, Nixon should be granted amnesty from prosecution.

It has been argued that to fail to prosecute Nixon would be to place the former president above the law. That is not correct. After all, it was the U.S. Supreme Court, in a unanimous decision, which established that principle beyond any doubt when it forced Nixon to give up the incriminating evidence. That decision by the court checked the power grab of the Nixon presidency, and ultimately brought about his resignation.

THE RULE OF law has been re-established so forcefully by the Supreme Court that it would not be weakened by amnesty for Nixon. Instead, amnesty would be recognized as the natural result of the absence of vindictiveness with which we believe most Americans now think of Nixon.

The man in the middle on amnesty for Nixon is Special Prosecutor Leon Jaworski. His Watergate grand jury wanted to indict Nixon while he was president. Jaworski persuaded the jurors that a sitting president could not be indicated, so they named Nixon an unindicted co-conspirator. For any new indictment to become effective, it must be signed by Jaworski.

Although it has no such legal powers, Congress should help head off any indictment of Nixon by adopting a resolution expressing the hope of its members that no prosecution will be pursued.

IF THE BEST interests of the country require that the man who ordered the coverup be granted amnesty from prosecution, clearly it would not be right to punish those who conspired with him to carry it out.

Justice never can be an absolute. It is a process, not a condition, through which men balance the demands of their consciences. No court ever will find the perfect justice for the Watergate crimes of those who held the public's sacred trust of high office. What is essential is that the nation always try to find that perfect justice.

That pursuit, especially by the Supreme Court, is what brought about the resignation of Richard Nixon. For America, for the Constitution, that was justice.

Tomorrow's justice requires that the wounds begin to heal, that Americans resolve never again to permit such an abuse of power to reach so deeply into the Constitution, and that the people return to their search for national unity under their new President.

LEDGER-STAR
Norfolk, Va., August 9, 1974

On the occasion of President Nixon's departure, one of the questions to be faced is whether action should also be pursued in the courts to impose those criminal penalties which might be possible after he loses his immunity of office.

Well, as wretched as the whole affair appears to the country, it would be most surprising if there should develop any great groundswell of sentiment for trying to put Mr. Nixon in jail. And it is just not a matter, as some of the more dogged of the President's critics seem sure to argue, of putting Mr. Nixon above the law.

There are procedures, among various choices being speculated upon, which could, in good order, hold the President's punishment to that one which is so massively severe in the first place, his step-down under near-total national condemnation.

There have been two urgencies in the crisis which was brought to its anguished climax by President Nixon's admission of complicity in the Watergate cover-up and of an abuse of power in using the CIA and the FBI to that self-serving end. One of the urgencies was to extract the country from the bog Watergate has become and to establish fresh, credible leadership. This is being served by Mr. Nixon's exit from the government.

The other consideration is to see that justice is done. In the case of Mr. Nixon — and, of course, barring some total new revelation as to wrongdoing — it is hard to conceive of a more awesome punishment than that same exit-under-pressure. To have been exposed to the ordeal of shame which has blighted his administration these past months, and then to be forced from office, the first American President to meet such disgrace, more than answers the needs of justice.

New York Post

New York, N.Y., August 12, 1974

Most thoughtful Americans will agree that the nation must ultimately strive to bind up the wounds inflicted during the Nixon presidency; before that, those grievous injuries demand careful treatment to promote healing.

Unfortunately, a predictable reluctance to use strong, if painful, disinfectants seems to be developing in Congress and elsewhere. Asked yesterday to evaluate Congressional sentiment on further legal action against the former President, Senate Minority Leader Scott (R-Pa.), appearing on CBS-TV's "Face the Nation," said he thought the prevailing view was "enough is enough." Former Attorney General Richardson maintains there should be no criminal prosecution "as a matter of discretion" and a special Gallup Poll for Newsweek magazine indicates that 55 per cent of the public agrees

Such feelings may be natural after enervating days of national crisis, but they do not encourage the thorough reckoning that is more essential than ever following a resignation statement in which former President Nixon conspicuously avoided making any forthright response to either the impeachment articles voted by the House Judiciary Committee or other charges.

It remains critical that the House consider the indictment and render an unequivocal opinion, that the Senate be heard from in some fashion and that the special Watergate prosecutor's inquiries go forward independently and impartially—no matter who is involved.

It is manifestly *not* "better for the country" to accept the resignation statement as the final, evasive word. Bygones are not simply bygones in this case; they may amount to precedents. If the whole of the Watergate abomination is at last laid out to public view and those responsible for it duly punished, the lesson will not be lost on future presidents and their associates. If this process is not completed, a formidable deterrent to official abuses will be abandoned.

THE SACRAMENTO BEE

Sacramento, Calif., August 9, 1974

President Richard Nixon's resignation, a decision which affords the nation immense relief, raises several fundamental and salutary considerations.

Chief among these is the prospect for an orderly transition of power to the new President Gerald R. Ford and the healing process of restoring public confidence in White House leadership.

Of equal import is the demonstration this nation remains a system of laws. No man, not even its chief executive, can hold himself above the law with impunity.

A special corollary to this point is that Nixon should not be granted immunity from prosecution of his wrongdoings. Like any other citizen, he must be held accountable for any and all crimes. The Bee flatly rejects proposals from various congressional quarters that Nixon's resignation might warrant waiving prosecution of his arrogant abuse of power and the incredible array of misdeeds brought to light through the Watergate investigation and its halo of related crimes.

———

The President's best moments, in the sorry spectacle of Watergate, came in the way he gave up his office. He left many hard questions about his conduct unanswered, and he failed to talk to the troubling questions of abuse of power which still surround the history of his administration, but he contributed immensely to graceful transition in his appeal to the nation to rally around the new President.

He was correct in his assumption his base of support in Congress had eroded to such a point it would have been impossible for him to govern. He might have gone further: His base of support with the American people had so crumbled, he could have no hope of leading them. The result: Had he not resigned, this land would have groped, vulnerable and divided, so long as he remained as president. There was not time to indulge in this luxury.

In the emotion which surrounds his departure, there still is need for hard and exact appraisal of all of those factors, tangible and intangible, which led to his leaving. Anything less would be faithless to history, and would fail the American institutions. We must be precise in this recollection, and learn from it.

Nixon had subjected the nation to an anguishing trauma. He had only grudgingly admitted, piecemeal, when the admission became unavoidable, that he has lied to the American people, that he has maneuvered desperately to evade exposure, that he has betrayed the sacred trust of his high office.

Even his resignation may not stop Congress from pursuing the impeachment process and trial by the Senate. Beyond that, he faces further possible prosecution by special prosecutor Leon Jaworski.

To permit Nixon to escape inquiry so easily via resignation, to permit him to enjoy a $60,000 annual pension and other benefits, immune from accountability for his wrongs, surely would destroy the people's faith in the equality of justice for all.

———

Now it is Ford's difficult challenge to pick up the pieces left by Nixon's devastated administration and demonstrate the American political system remains viable, that it can and will survive even the agony and disarray precipitated by this failed President.

Ford already has moved commendably to pick up the reins. He has compiled a list of new men to fill key posts. He has indicated some of the better men of the Nixon administration will be retained, such as the able Secretary of State Henry Kissinger.

Overall, however, the prospect is a gradual transition to a largely new administration, a thorough house-cleaning which is manifestly needed if Ford is to succeed in restoring a healthy climate of government leadership.

In this formidable task the new President surely will need and deserves the wholehearted support of the public, the Congress and those he selects to serve him.

Let us begin again.

THE ☼ SUN

Baltimore, Md., August 11, 1974

Much as the country would like to have done forever with Richard Nixon, his departure from office does not spell an end to his brooding presence over the American political scene. Repercussions from his disgrace will last longer, much longer, than his hold on the presidency. Many who served him and ill-served the nation through perjury, obstruction of justice and other crimes still must face court trials and the specter of prison terms. Yet, essentially, those are personal tragedies, and they will become more so now that power has been stripped from the hands of Nixon aides. What remains a national perplexity is what to do with Mr. Nixon himself now that he has lost the special immunities and privileges of the presidency.

So far as his pending impeachment in the Congress is concerned, there seems little sense in pressing this to the literal end. Under the Constitution, to be sure, impeachment in the House and conviction in the Senate need not be confined solely to the ouster of an incumbent; it can be used, too, to preclude his ever again holding an office of public trust. But this would be a spurious pretext for dealing with Mr. Nixon, and it would be seen as such by the nation. A better course would be for the House to find some means of formally accepting and approving the articles of impeachment and the documentation of Watergate evidence prepared by its Judiciary Committee. The Senate may have more difficulty in finding a substitute for its trial procedure under the Constitution. Perhaps a Senate resolution enforcing the findings of the House would be the answer. The important thing for this and future generations is to bring together the evidence in the Watergate case and to demonstrate clearly that it was the will of the Congress that Mr. Nixon should leave office for "high crimes and misdemeanors," particularly obstruction of justice.

The problem of dealing with Mr. Nixon in the courts of law, now that he no longer has presidential immunity, is far more difficult. Many Americans are repelled at the idea of putting an ex-president in prison; many others are affronted by the notion that a person's past high office somehow would place him above the law that every other citizen must face.

Within the past year, two celebrated cases have occurred that may be helpful in finding a way to deal with Mr. Nixon. In the case of Spiro T. Agnew, special prosecutors accepted a no-contest plea on tax fraud and bribery charges only after the former vice president signed what amounted to a confession detailing his misdeeds. In the case of Richard Kleindienst, a former attorney general, a suspended sentence was given after he pleaded guilty to misleading Congress in ITT testimony. Neither the Agnew nor the Kleindienst cases satisfied those who felt these officials should have been sent to prison. But the handling of these cases at least produced the confessions of wrongdoing that so many members of Congress insist the country is due from Mr. Nixon. This, then, may be a way out of the dilemma: neither prison nor immunity, but indictment, confession and a sentence that does not require incarceration.

The end of the Nixon affair will not be easy. In the fantasy he injected in his farewell speech at the White House, Mr. Nixon suggested he might be a latter-day Teddy Roosevelt serving his country as an ex-president, "always in the arena, tempestuous, strong, sometimes wrong, sometimes right." Alas, no such grand denouement awaits Richard Nixon. As an ex-president, he will remain in the national arena all right, but in the inglorious role of a man still awaiting the judgment of a betrayed nation.

FORD GIVES NIXON FULL PARDON FOR ALL OFFENSES AGAINST U.S.

President Ford granted former President Nixon a full pardon Sept. 8 for all federal crimes he "committed or may have committed or taken part in" during his term in office. Nixon issued a statement accepting the pardon and expressing regret that he had been "wrong in not acting more decisively and more forthrightly in dealing with Watergate."

The White House also announced Sept. 8 that the Ford Administration had concluded an agreement with Nixon giving him title to his presidential papers and tape recordings but guaranteeing they would be kept intact and available for court use for at least three years.

The pardon for Nixon was unexpected. Ford made his announcement from the Oval Office on Sunday morning after attending church. After reading a brief statement on his decision before a small pool of reporters and photographers—the event was filmed for broadcast later—Ford signed a proclamation granting Nixon the pardon.

Nixon had not been formally charged with any federal crime, and the granting of a pardon in advance was a reversal of Ford's position on the issue, expressed as recently as his Aug. 28 news conference, when Ford stated that "until any legal process has been undertaken I think it's unwise and untimely for me to make any commitment."

In his statement, Ford said Nixon and his loved ones "have suffered enough, and will continue to suffer no matter what I do." "Theirs is an American tragedy in which we all have played a part," he said. "It can go on and on, or someone must write 'The End' to it. I have concluded that only I can do that. And if I can, I must." There were no historic or legal precedents on the matter, Ford added, "but it is common knowledge that serious allegations and accusations hang like a sword over our former president's head and threaten his health as he tries to reshape his life."

Protest was immediate from Congress against the pardon to Nixon. The White House was flooded with telephone calls and telegrams from the public. A spokesman said Ford was told the evening of Sept. 8, upon inquiry, that the volume of incoming telephone calls was "very heavy and kind of unfavorable." Western Union messages into Washington had reached a volume of 110,000 by Sept. 11.

The Democratic Congressional leadership was outspoken in criticism. Senate Majority Leader Mike Mansfield (Mont.), said that "all men are equal under the law ... and that includes presidents and plumbers." "What about the 40 or 50 already indicted and some of whom have been sent to prison?" he asked. Senate Democratic whip Robert C. Byrd (W. Va.) spoke of "a double standard." However Senate Republican Leader Hugh Scott (Pa.) said Ford acted "with great humanity to bring an end to an American tragedy." House GOP Leader John J. Rhodes (Ariz.) said he believed Nixon had paid "a substantial price" and "anything further would be more overkill than justice."

The Hartford Courant
Hartford, Conn., September 9, 1974

There comes a time — and it has come — when it is necessary to accept the unalterable and make the best of it. President Ford has given Richard M. Nixon a full pardon for whatever offenses he may have committed against the United States during his years as president, and the action is irrevocable.

So the state is not intended to accept the decision with poor grace, but to recognize that now the action has been taken and cannot be changed, the important thing is to move on to waiting tasks and responsibilities which are still within our power to shape and discharge. President Ford has closed the book on Nixon; let us put it away.

National leaders and neighborhood pundits will debate President Ford's reasoning and action for sometime to come, but in the end, what was done yesterday — cleanly and compassionately — will remain for history and posterity truly to evaluate.

This is the certainty. Among the uncertainties are how deeply and seriously and permanently will the nation view and respond to the creation of what appears to be a double standard of justice. The question here is becoming almost trite. Is there one set of laws for the President of the United States and another for its citizens?

No one can deny or ignore the enormity of Mr. Nixon's fall. His potential for suffering is unimagineable. And this, openly, moved President Ford to allow his predecessor some relief from his agony. And even while conceding that many other wrong-doers and sinners have likewise been contrite, repentant and devastated, and yet have been required to accept the formal punishment decreed by an injured society, humaneness prompts us not to continue laying the lash upon a body so pitiably lascerated as that of Mr. Nixon.

It probably is a fair statement that President Ford's brief and unexpected announcement in his Oval Office has brought this nation its second sensation of great relief, the first being the resignation of Mr. Nixon. True, the sense of relief at having a weight lifted is not entirely unmixed, since there are many who would have preferred, or would prefer, the chance to throw it off themselves. But most of us, with the passage of time and with welcome new freedom of movement and choice, learn to come to terms with what is.

It would be easy to say that Watergate and Richard Nixon's role now must remain unresolved, because that is true. It is also true that resolving Watergate and Mr. Nixon's role would not erase either, and that essentially is the impossible dream of most Americans.

Perhaps there are two sentences we should remember from the book of Nixon before we put it away, and both are to be found in the epilogue:

Mr. Ford: My conscience tells me clearly and certainly that I cannot prolong the bad dreams that continue to reopen a chapter that is closed. My conscience tells me that only I as President, have the constitutional power to firmly shut and seal this book.

Mr. Nixon: No words can describe the depths of my regret and pain at the anguish my mistakes over Watergate have caused the nation and the presidency — a nation I so deeply love and an institution I so greatly respect.

Mr. Ford and Mr. Nixon, we accept both statements.

WINSTON-SALEM JOURNAL
Winston-Salem, N.C., September, 9, 1974

In his brief post-inauguration speech, President Gerald Ford expressed the hope that "our former president, who brought peace to millions, (will) find it for himself." Yesterday morning, Mr. Ford acted with all his available power to insure that Richard Nixon will have an opportunity to achieve that peace: He granted a "full, free and absolute pardon" to the former president "for all offenses against the United States which he, Richard Nixon, has committed or may have committed or taken part in" during his presidency.

Just a short while ago, Mr. Ford referred to the pardoning of Nixon as a "last resort" which would have to await the outcome of legal proceedings against the former president. Mr. Ford obviously has spent a great deal of time since then rethinking the problem, and has decided that the judicial process must now be aborted, before "the tranquility to which this nation has been restored . . . (is) irreparably lost" and before a "divisive debate (is created) over the propriety of exposing to further punishment and degradation a man who has already paid the unprecedented penalty of relinquishing the highest elective office in the United States."

As with much of what he has done in the few weeks of his presidency, Mr. Ford's pardoning of Nixon combines compassion and a desire to serve the best interests of the nation. The President believes that Nixon and his family have "suffered enough." Certainly it is difficult to imagine Nixon — having lost his honor, his presidency and his life's work — being able to feel any further punishment, even jail. There comes a point when the lash no longer stings, and surely Nixon has reached it.

But even if he has not, there is no guarantee that the prosecution of Nixon would succeed. "In the end," said Mr. Ford yesterday, "the courts might well hold that Richard Nixon had been denied due process and the verdict of history would be even more inconclusive . . ." What would be guaranteed is more months — even years — of the debilitating distracttions of Watergate, a scandal which has already taken a heavy toll on the nation and the nation's government. America does not need so much as one more day of the agony that has ripped it apart during the past two years.

Indeed, the nation desperately needs the very "peace" that Mr. Ford would have his predecessor achieve. Much must be done to make up for the lost last years of the Nixon administration, and both President Ford and the nation will best be able to move forward freed from preoccupation with the past. As Mr. Ford said yesterday, "it is not the ultimate fate of Richard Nixon that most concerns me, (but) . . . the immediate future of this great country." That future is brighter because of the pardoning of the former president.

The Detroit News
Detroit, Mich., September 10, 1974

If anybody had doubted that President Gerald Ford could make tough decisions, the new President disposed of that doubt by his controversial—and, in our opinion, correct—decision to pardon Richard Nixon.

Mr. Ford knew of course that his action would bring a storm of criticism down upon his head. Against this he weighed the basic rightness and the ultimate benefits of this act of mercy and took the courageous course.

First, Mr. Ford has acted to shut the book on a chapter of conflict and political passion that paralyzed the ability of his predecessor to conduct the affairs of state and could have impaired his own ability to do so.

Looking down the road, he saw endless preoccupation with the question of what to do about Mr. Nixon. "During this long period of delay and potential litigation," Mr. Ford explained in his statement granting pardon, "ugly passions would again be aroused, our people would again be polarized in their opinions and the credibility of government would again be challenged at home and abroad."

Although his decision may not be popular at the moment and may create difficulties for his party in the November elections, it will enable him, after the first roar of protest, to direct public attention toward the constructive business of government. He has acted to produce domestic tranquility—a constitutional duty just as pressing as that of punishing the guilty.

Second, Mr. Ford has acted to prevent the nation from pursuing a broken man in a spirit of vengeance and hatred which, after the passion had subsided, would have left us all with a sense of shame. After all, do you fire a gun at a man who has already been bludgeoned, flayed and ridden out of town on a rail?

We recognize that many persons oppose the pardon on genuine grounds of conscience and in the interest of equal justice. We also recognize that some have a much greater interest in vengeance than in justice.

Both groups ask: Why punish the underlings and let the boss go? We repeat what we said here once before: Mr. Nixon's underlings are suffering a different but not necessarily an inequitable or a more severe punishment. None of them stands to lose as much as the fallen president has already lost or will suffer as much as he has suffered and will continue to suffer.

One who obviously does not share our point of view is Jerald F. terHorst, who resigned as Mr. Ford's press secretary upon hearing of the President's decision. Though terHorst disagreed with Mr. Ford's action, he hastened to assure the public that the President took his position "in good conscience."

TerHorst, former Washington Bureau chief for The Detroit News, described his own resignation as an act of conscience, also. We respect that. But we have here a conflict of consciences. Obviously, the passionate expression of conscience is not in itself a final convincing argument.

Simply holding an opinion strongly does not make one's own opinion right and the opposing opinion wrong. In the present case, we happen to think President Ford has argued the case for his act of conscience most persuasively.

The President asked himself whether further punishment of Richard Nixon is more important than mercy, more important than the restoration of national harmony. He answered: No.

We agree.

Democrat Chronicle
Rochester, N.Y., September 9, 1974

THE NATION and the man have suffered enough.

So saying in effect, President Ford has granted Mr. Nixon a full and free pardon for all offenses he may have committed in the White House.

It is, in our judgment, a wise and humane and proper decision.

Although he seemed cool to such an act in the beginning, the President undoubtedly sensed the prevailing mood of the nation . . .

AMERICANS have never been, and are not now, a vengeful and vindictive people.

They recoil instinctively from putting a former president behind bars.

They understand that no greater punishment could be inflicted on a man than to sack him (for that's what happened in effect) from the most powerful and most prestigious job in the world.

Even if Mr. Ford did not perceive all these things for himself, he also had the evidence of the Gallup Poll to tell him that most Americans are on the side of compassion.

INEVITABLY and understandably, there will be strong and bitter resentments among those who feel that Mr. Nixon has been allowed to slip off the hook and that justice is not blind at all.

But the polarization and the anger and the passions, we have no doubt at all, would be greater if Mr. Nixon were to be put on trial and if all the old wounds were to be kept open and allowed to fester.

Rather than expose the nation to endless agony, Mr. Ford has chosen to try to put an end to the whole ugly sordid mess known as Watergate, and to try to get the nation back to putting first things first.

AS FOR MR. NIXON being let off the hook, surely it's clear that the barb of Watergate will be stuck in his side forever.

Call them errors, or crimes, or misdeeds, or misjudgments, or blindnesses, or betrayals or whatever . . .

. . . Call them what you will, but Mr. Nixon's failure will, as he now says himself, be a burden "I shall bear for every day of life that is left in me."

There could be no greater punishment than that, and the American people know it, and so does Mr. Ford.

This newspaper welcomes his decision.

The Burlington Free Press

Burlington, Vt., September 9, 1974

PRESIDENT FORD has granted a "free, full and absolute" pardon to former President Nixon for any and all offenses allegedly committed while Nixon was President. We trust that this pardon means exactly what it says, and that the former President will be free of the crank lawsuits, the uncivilized mood of vengeance among some of his political enemies, and the nightmare of an uncertain future filled with mindless recrimination.

There are tens of millions of Americans who feel deeply that Richard Nixon was the victim of a massive injustice. The verdict of history will not be evident for many years. What is certain now is that President Ford, in granting the pardon, did the right thing at the right time under the circumstances.

Little has been made of the fact that Richard Nixon was the only President of modern times who could not be helped by the public counsel of a former President. All three former Presidents who were alive when Nixon assumed office — Harry Truman, Dwight Eisenhower and Lyndon Johnson — died prior to the Watergate affair. Only a person who has shouldered the awesome burdens of the Presidency knows the complexity and pitfalls of Presidential leadership.

President Ford, in the job only a month, seems to be learning quickly enough. He understood and he acted, not so much in behalf of a much-maligned former President as in behalf of a confused American public.

The so-called pardon was eminently justified, and we warmly applaud it.

Boston Herald American

Combining the best features of the Herald Traveler and Record American

Boston, Mass., September 10, 1974

President Ford's "full, free and absolute pardon" for former President Nixon was the act of a deeply compassionate man. He reduced his decision to its simplest possible terms when he said:

"Richard Nixon and his loved ones have suffered enough, and will continue to suffer no matter what I do."

We agree with that assessment. No possible punishment could equal the anguish suffered by a proud man in becoming the first Chief Executive of the United States forced to resign his great office under fire.

Richard Nixon, comparing his presidential aspirations with the ultimate tragedy of his shortcomings, furthermore will be a tortured man for the rest of his life.

Critics of Mr. Ford's pardon charge that it was a flagrant violation of a fundamental American principle — the principle of equal justice for all under the law.

They forget there is an ever higher ethic — that justice should be tempered with mercy.

It is according to that higher ethic, as he sees it, that President Ford has acted in trying to ease the suffering of a shattered man and his loyal family.

We commend him for daring to do so, despite the controversy and criticism which he knew were inevitable.

HOUSTON CHRONICLE

Houston, Tex., September 10, 1974

The Chronicle believes President Ford acted in the best interests of the nation in granting a full pardon to former President Nixon.

The act took courage, particularly at this time.

President Ford has shown a great deal of courage since he became president and the pardoning of Nixon shows he is rising above the political quagmire created by Watergate.

The Chronicle believes the President is quite honest and sincere in his conviction that granting Nixon a pardon is best for this country's future.

"My conscience tells me that only I, as president, have the constitutional power to firmly shut and seal this book. My conscience tells me it is my duty, not merely to proclaim domestic tranquility, but to use every means that I have to insure it," Ford said.

President Ford's goal here is an undeniably great one. In our opinion, there are a number of reasons why pardoning Nixon and shutting the book on Watergate are in the best interests of this nation.

We need to get the sordid and tragic scandal of Watergate behind us. We need to restore confidence in government. We need to proceed to deal with the problems now confronting us, of which inflation is number one.

There is also the question of whether Nixon could get a fair trial. Had the constitutional process of impeachment by the House and a finding of guilt by two-thirds of the Senate been followed through to its conclusion, then the Chronicle would have said there had been proper due process of law and that the law had prevailed.

But opponents of Nixon went on so many highly publicized tangents and so much information of a questionable nature was put out against Nixon, it would have been difficult to find a jury of peers in this country that would not have had some strong opinion before walking into the jury box.

Nixon has not escaped punishment for what he now admits were mistakes and misjudgments in the Watergate scandal. "No words can describe the depths of my regret and pain at the anguish my mistakes over Watergate have caused the nation and the presidency," Nixon said. The former president and his family have been through punishment enough.

President Ford's granting of a pardon was not only an act of compassion but above all, a bold act in the best national interest.

Daily Defender

Chicago, Ill., September 9, 1974

President Ford's issuance of complete pardon for former President Richard M. Nixon is a shocking political act that adds one more chapter to the revolting Watergate scandals. It makes mockery of the judicial concept of Equal Justice under the Law, which has been the touchstone of a democratic society, and of which Americans have been boasting since the foundation of this republic.

Mr. Ford's action for which there is no precedent nor moral justification places the trial courts in a great delemma as to the disposition of the cases of the men who are now serving time and those awaiting trial on the Watergate conspiracy in which Mr. Nixon was named by a grand jury as a co-conspirator.

If these men, who are no more guilty than Mr. Nixon, are not pardoned, the notion will be embedded in the public mind that the double standard of justice is the measure by which American justice must be assessed. Translated in common vernacular it means that the law applies only to the poor, the powerless and the blacks. The rich and the powerful are above the law.

Though there had been general suspicion on the impartial application of the law, there never was concrete evidence on which to saddle the suspicion. Mr. Ford's action supplies it in a manner definitive enough to leave an indelible imprint upon the pages of American history long after Watergate will have ceased to flow under the bridge of contemprary politics.

The New York Times

New York, N.Y., September 9, 1974

In giving former President Nixon an inappropriate and premature grant of clemency, President Ford has affronted the Constitution and the American system of justice. It is a profoundly unwise, divisive and unjust act.

Like many lesser public figures who have commented at various stages of the long Watergate controversy, President Ford has sadly confused his responsibilities to the Republic and his understandable sentiments toward one who has inflicted grave damage upon the body politic. Both are valid and compelling but they should be clearly distinguished.

The four reasons that President Ford cites for his decision lay bare this confusion. In summary, he asserts that Mr. Nixon has already suffered enough, an adjudication of his offenses would be divisive; a fair trial would be difficult to achieve; and ultimately, in any event, he — Mr. Ford — would have to decide the matter in the light of his own conscience and sense of compassion.

The adjudication of Mr. Nixon's offenses and the character of the criminal trial in which those offenses would be weighed and argued are one set of concerns. Mr. Nixon's suffering and his claims on President Ford's conscience as a political sponsor, friend and fellow human being are another set of concerns.

President Ford's overriding duty was to his public responsibilities. It is essential that the crimes committed by several of Mr. Nixon's closest associates and apparently by Mr. Nixon himself be determined in a court of law by the same rules of evidence and the same procedures of due process that apply in the American system of justice to every citizen.

Nothing less would satisfy the natural sense of justice of the American people and of a Government founded upon principles of equality and legality. Given the historic significance of Mr. Nixon's offenses that led to his becoming the first President ever to resign, it was essential that the historical record be unmistakably clear.

After the exact nature of the wounds that Mr. Nixon and his associates had inflicted upon the nation had been determined and after the exoneration or conviction of those accused, only then could those wounds begin to heal. Once the processes of justice had run their course, it would be possible and timely for the President and the nation to take into account the personal merits of the offenders and try to mitigate the penalties of law by recourse to the enduring human values of mercy and charity. If clemency had followed conviction rather than preceded it, there would have been wide acceptance of President Ford's exercise of his power to pardon.

* * *

As it is, by recklessly pushing aside special prosecutor Leon Jaworski and the grand jury and the trial jury as well, President Ford has failed in his duty to the Republic, made a mockery of the claim of equal justice before the law, promoted renewed public discord, made possible the clouding of the historical record, and undermined the humane values he sought to invoke.

His duty was to see that the law was enforced and wrongdoers punished. His duty was to see to it that those who have already served in prison for their crimes such as E. Howard Hunt, Donald Segretti and Egil Krogh; those now serving their sentences such as Charles Colson and John W. Dean 3d; and those who stand accused of grave crimes such as H. R. Haldeman, John N. Mitchell and Mr. Nixon himself would all be treated the same.

Instead, he has laid American jurisprudence open to the severe and lingering accusation that there is one kind of justice for the agents and underlings and another for the ex-President in whose name and for whose supposed benefit the misdeeds were committed.

President Ford speaks of compassion. It is tragic that he had no compassion and concern for the Constitution and the Government of law that he has sworn to uphold and defend. He could probably have taken no single act of a non-criminal nature that would have more gravely damaged the credibility of this Government in the eyes of the world and of its own people than this unconscionable act of pardon.

Rather than calm public passions and restore a fundamental sense of national unity, Mr. Ford has ignited fresh controversy. How bitter that controversy is sure to become was shown by the immediate resignation in protest of the President's own press secretary, J. F. terHorst, acting as "a matter of conscience." It might have stirred less public outrage if the President, in what amounted to secret and discreditable plea bargaining with his predecessor, had insisted on a frank and forthright confession of guilt. Instead he settled for an unctuous, guileful statement from Mr. Nixon in which the former President admits nothing specific and skillfully blurs the issues. The Justice Department's deal with former Vice President Agnew last year was seriously questionable; yesterday's arrangement sinks below even that poor precedent.

* * *

Moreover, the arrangement avoids nothing in the way of publicity and public controversy. Presumably, the cover-up trial involving six of Mr. Nixon's former aides is still to be held and he is sure to be called as a witness. He will have to testify at length under oath to all the demeaning details of the cover-up.

Because his pardon has immunized him, he cannot avoid testifying by claiming the Fifth Amendment privilege against self-incrimination inasmuch as he cannot now be prosecuted. If he testifies falsely, he is still open to prosecution for perjury. In short, nothing has changed except that the defendants and the jurors are to be confronted with the savage irony that the man who ordered the cover-up, benefited from it and repeatedly lied to the American people and to his own Congressional defenders about it is now to be a principal witness in the trial of those who did his bidding. They face the possibility of terms in prison while he can look forward to well-paid retirement in his luxurious seaside villa.

Senator Mike Mansfield, the majority leader, and others who urged at the time of Mr. Nixon's resignation that the Congress go forward with the constitutional process of impeachment by the House and trial by the Senate have now been vindicated. Because of the House's refusal to follow through with impeachment and Mr. Ford's preemption of the courts by granting this pardon, neither the political nor the judicial institutions of this country have had an opportunity to weigh all the evidence concerning Mr. Nixon's offenses and reach a clear, final judgment.

In a time when the nation has been repeatedly dismayed by so many acts of corruption, intrigue and deceit, President Ford has signally failed to provide courageous and impartial moral leadership. When asked less than a year ago whether he would do precisely what he has now done, Mr. Ford indicated to Congress that he would not, adding, "I do not think the public would stand for it."

At his first news conference on Aug. 28, President Ford again pledged himself to respect the special prosecutor's obligation to take necessary action against "any and all individuals." Although not ruling out the ultimate exercise of clemency, the President observed: "There have been no charges made. There has been no action by the courts; there has been no action by any jury, and until any legal process has been undertaken I think it's unwise and untimely for me to make any commitment."

Instead of adhering to those wise public pronouncements, Mr. Ford has now moved secretly and suddenly to block the normal workings of justice. It is an act of flagrant favoritism. It can only outrage and dishearten millions of his fellow citizens who thought that at last the laws of this nation would be enforced without fear or favor. This blundering intervention is a body blow to the President's own credibility and to the public's reviving confidence in the integrity of its Government.

Index

This index includes references both to the news digest and the editorial section. Those index entries printed in a roman typeface refer to the news digest. They: (1) Describe the event; (2) Note the date of the event, e.g. 8–9; (3) Indicate the page, the marginal letter parallel to the item on the page, and the column in which the item appears in that order, e.g. 226E1. Index entries referring to editorials are printed in *italic type* after the news digest entries under the **boldface alphabetical headings**. Editorial entries refer only to the page number.

A

ABEL, I. W.
Cmmnts on Ford 8-9, 226E1
ABOUREZK, Sen. James (D, S.D.)
AMPI campaign aid rptd 3-24, 45A1
Cited in Nelson indictment 7-31, 219B2-D3
AMPI fined 8-1, 221C1
Sherman, Valentine plead guilty 8-12, 221B3-D3
ABPLANALP, Robert H.
Nixon-Danner mtg rptd 1-25, 38D3
Nixon reliance rptd 2-1, 23A3
U.S. maintenance of Bahamas home rpd 3-21, 90D3
Rptdly met with Rebozo on Hughes $ 4-8, 129F2-C3
Jaworski rptdly subpoenas tax data 4-11, 132C3
Gives Nixon mortgage extension 7-13, 96G3
ABU Dhabi
Rptdly gave gift to Fulbright 6-12, 96B1
ACREE, Vernon D.
Jud com releases evidence on IRS misuse 7-16, 196G1
ACUFF, Roy
Gives Nixon yo-yo 3-16, 74C2
ADAMS, Sherman
Nixon Watergate tape transcript cites 4-30, 117D1
Cited in panel transcripts 7-9, 181G1
AGNEW, Spiro T.
Md ct panel urges disbarmt 1-14, 37B2-B3
GAO rpts US guard illegal 1-29, 39D1
Magazine to serialize novel 2-6, 41A1
Visits Sinatra 2-13, 40G3
US guard removed 2-17, 40D3
Nixon lauds service 2-25, 31B2, 41G1-B2
Anderson convicted 3-20, 46B2
Nixon Watergate tape transcripts cite 4-30, 126D2
Anderson sntncd to 5 yrs 5-1, 133A2
Barred from Md law practice 5-2, 133B2
Wharton pleads no contest 5-17, 214E1
To repay $1,100 in govt expenses 6-3, 129F3

Rptdly accepted Saudi gifts 6-12, 96B1
GAO cites committee 7-9, 217F2
AGRICULTURE, Department of
Nixon issues milk fund paper 1-8, 35C2; for subsequent developments, see MILK Funds under 'M'
AIKEN, Sen. George D. (R, Vt.)
Opposes campaign reform bill 4-11, 131C3
ALAGIA, D. Paul
Testifies in AMPI suit 5-4, 214C1
ALBERT, Rep. Carl (Bert) (D, Okla.)
On Nixon resignatn 1-21, 16F2
Sees impeachmt vote 1-28, 22C1
On Dem win in Ford district 2-19, 28E2
Assails Nixon on tapes 3-25, 79G3-80C1
Cited in Nixon transcripts 4-30, 104D1
Denies transcript comment on GAO probe 5-1, 138A2-C2
Opposes resignation 5-14, 142B3
Hits Nixon for non-compliance 6-10, 166G3-167A1
Rodino affirms fairness 6-28, 176F2
Backs Rodino on questioning rules 7-1, 177A1
Jud com milk fund evidence cites 7-19, 198B2
Cmmnts on Ford 8-8, 226F2
Meets with Nixon 8-8, 232A3
Cmmnts on Nixon pardon 9-9, 240C3
Opposes more pardons 9-11, 241F2
ALEXANDER, Donald C.
Declines cmmnt on Nixon tax penalty 4-7, 94E3-95B1
Rptdly met with Jaworski on Nixon taxes 4-11, 93B3
Cited in impeachment hearings 6-21, 173G3
Jud com releases evidence on IRS, taxes 7-26, 206F2-E3
ALLEN, James
Pleads guilty on illegal contributions 5-1, 133D1-G1
Resignation rptd 5-10, 214C2
ALLEN, Sen. James B. (D, Ala.)
Senate OKs campaign reform 4-11, 131B3-132F1
Submits pro-Kissinger resolution 6-12, 162B2

ALLEN, Robert H.
Nixon Watergate tape transcripts cite 4-30, 104D1, 106C2
ALLISON, Richard L.
Pleads guilty on illegal contribution 5-6, 135B2-E2
ALL the President's Men (Book)
Film rghts sold 3-6, 60G1
Paperback rghts sold 5-30, 150D3
Published in June 169E2
ALSOP, Joseph
Herschensohn comments on tape theory 3-26, 81D1
AMBASSADORSHIPS
Kalmbach sentenced for selling 6-17, 170C1
'Selling' cited in Ervin panel rpt 7-13, 188G1-D3
'Sale' cited in Jud com rpt 7-16, 196G1-D2
AMERADA Hess Corp.
Ervin panel rpts secret contribution 8-7, 220D2
AMERICAN Airlines
Spater charged with misconduct 4-24, 214B2, D2
Ervin rpt cites illegal contribution 7-13, 187G1
AMERICAN Bar Association
Smith expresses shock on Nixon actions 5-26, 152E3-G3
Resolution urges fair, equal justice 8-15, 235A1-A2
AMERICAN Civil Liberties Union (ACLU)
'Impeach Nixon' drive attacked—259
AMERICAN Conservative Union (ACU)
Parleys with YAF 1-25–1-26, 20E1
Phillips comments on Buckley rsgntn plea 3-20, 77D2
AMERICAN Farm Bureau Federation
Ford addresses 1-15, 14A1
AMERICAN Federation of Labor and Congress of Industrial Organizations (AFL-CIO)
Ford scores anti-Nixon drive 1-15, 14B1
Exec Cncl meets 2-18–2-25; renews impeachmt call 2-18, 28E2-A2, F2
Cope seeks 'veto-proof' Cong 2-20, 28E3
Active in Ohio race 3-5, 56C2
Building trades cheer attack on Nixon 4-1, 82G1-C2

Meany hits Nixon on Moscow trip 6-4, 154D1
Meany urges Nixon quit 8-5, 212B3-D3
Meany cmmnts on Ford 8-9, 226E1
Ford attacks anti-Nixon critics—253
AMERICAN Institute of Public Opinion—See POLLS
AMERICAN Medical Association (AMA)
Rptdly raised $2.9 million for elections 7-10, 217G2
AMERICAN Ship Building Co.
Steinbrenner indicted 4-5, 130D3-131C1
Ervin panel cites illegal contribution 7-13, 187G1-B2
AMERICAN Telephone & Telegraph Co. (AT&T)
To stop providing govt with secret rcds 2-15, 159B3-E3
AMERICANS for Democratic Action (ADA)
Ford scores anti-Nixon drive, ADA rebuts 1-15, 14B1, G1
Reaffirms call for impeachment 5-11, 142F3
'Impeach Nixon' drive attacked—259
AMNESTY Issue
Suggested for Watergaters and draft evaders—383
AMPI—See ASSOCIATED Milk Producers Inc.
ANDERSON, George
Indicted with Gurney 7-10, 217E1
ANDERSON, Jack
Rpts NSC spy scandal 1-11, 157E1-C2
Rptdly got India-Pakistan papers from Radford 1-18, 158G2
Cited in Welander testimony 2-22, 159G3-160C1
Chrgs Nixon studied previous presidents' tax deductions 3-12, 90C2-C3
Nixon Watergate tape transcripts cite 4-30, 125D2
Cited in Baker rpt on CIA 7-2, 178A1
Jud com releases evidence on IRS misuse 7-16, 196A1
Rpts allegations against Rocky 8-17, 235G2-B3
ANDERSON, Rep. John B(ayard) (R, Ill.)
On tape gap rpt 1-15, 15F3

Compromise plan on tapes—245, 247

Nixon rjts subpoena—245, 247

Announces plans to retire—250

Panel votes to continue public hearings—286

Gesell dismisses panel's tape suit—260

Panel rpt notes campaign abuses—338–341

Congress slow in implementing rcmmnd reforms—379

EVANS, Gov. Daniel J. (R, Wash.)
Urges Nixon comply with House subpoenas 6-2, 155B3

EVANS, M. Stanton
Addresses conservatives 1-26, 20F1

EXECUTIVE Privilege (Book)
Book pubd in June 169E2

EXECUTIVE Privilege
Tapes case heard by Supreme Ct 7-8, 178F3–180E1
Supreme Ct decision on tapes limits 7-24, 201D2–206B2
Defined in U.S. vs. Nixon—349–353

EXECUTIVES' Club of Chicago
Nixon addresses 3-15, 73C1–74A2

EXPORT-Import Bank, U.S.—See CASEY, William J.

F

FAISAL, King—See SAUDI Arabia

FAHD, Prince—See SAUDI Arabia

FANNIN, Sen. Paul J. (R, Ariz.)
Attnds Nixon speech in Phoenix 5-3, 138E2

FARAH Manufacturing Co., Inc.
Meany hails accord 2-25, 28F3

FARKAS, Ruth
Nixon releases papers on nomination 5-30, 136B2
Contribution cited in Ervin panel rpt 7-13, 188E2, D3

FEDERAL Bureau of Investigation (FBI)
Enters tape gap probe 1-16, 15G2
Grand jury to probe tape gap 1-18, 17D1
Porter pleads guilty 1-28, 20E3
Attempt to corrupt cited in indictments 3-1, 47E1–F1, 49F1, D2, F3, 50B1, E1, C2, 51C1, E1, E2, 53B1, B3
Gov. Ford charges harassment 3-7, 58B2
Felt testifies at Mitchell, Stans trial 3-15, 65E3
Exprts urge Congressional oversight 3-20, 77F3
Weicker cites release of data on DeAntonio 4-8, 131B2
Porter sentenced for lying to FBI 4-11, 84A3–C3
Cited in Nixon tape transcripts 4-30, 100F1, 103E2, G2, 104B1, 106E2, 107E1, G1, 108G2, 109B1, A2–B2, D3, 117B2–C2, 122G2, D3, 126D2, F2
Sullivan denies Dean rmrks in transcripts 5-7, 138C2
Attempt to involve in cover-up probed 5-15, 144B1
Impeachment panel probes taps 6-4–6-6, 155D3–E3
Role in 'security' wiretaps cited 6-11, 161D3, F3, 162C1, G2–E3
Ruckelshaus backs Kissinger on taps 6-16, 163B1–F1

Cited in Silbert hearings 6-26, 173F2
Cited in Ehrlichman trial 6-28, 174B3, 175F1
Cited in Baker rpt on CIA 7-2, 177G2–F2
Cited in 'plumbers' defense 7-10, 182A2–A3
Ehrlichman convicted for lying 7-12, 184A3
Ervin panel cites campaign abuses 7-13, 187F1, B2, C3, 192B3
Jud com rpts on clandestine activities 7-18, 196D3
Doar's impeachment brief cites 7-19, 200D2–E2
Hogan cites misuse to justify impeachment 7-23, 201B1
Impeachment article cites attempt to misuse 7-30, 208D1, B2–E2, 209G3
Ehrlichman lying charge dismissed 7-31, 212A1
Nixon admits attempt to misuse 8-5–8-9, 223D1, 228B1–230C1
Misuse cited in impeachment rpt 8-20, 236B1, B2
Jaworski's Nixon prosecution memo cites misuse 9-10, 240E1
Misuse cited in impeachment article—342–347
Nixon discloses plan to involve in cover-up—356–374, 376

FEDERAL Communications Commission (FCC)
Plan to pressure Post TV stations leaked 5-15, 144E2–145C1
Staff lawyers aide Nixon defense 5-20, 146B3

FEDERAL Housing Administration (FHA)
2 sentenced in Gurney fund case 2-21, 3-19, 41D1
Priestes released 7-2, 217A1

FEDERAL Power Commission (FPC)
Common Cause suit cites 6-27, 216B2

FEDERAL Trade Commission (FTC)
Cited re AMPI trust suit 3-12, 45F1

FELT, W. Mark
Testifies at Mitchell, Stans trial 3-15, 65E3
Cited in transcripts on Nixon's cover-up role 8-5, 229C2

FIELDING, Fred T.
Quits White House post 1-11, 13A2
Nixon Watergate tape transcript cites 4-30, 104F1, 106E1

FIELDING, Dr. Lewis J.—See PENTAGON Papers Case

FIGUERES, Jose
Vesco connection cited at Mitchell, Stans trial 3-4–3-12, 64G3

FINANCE Committee to Re-elect the President—See also STANS, Maurice
Ends operations, fund put in trust 3-12, 65E1–F1

FINANCIAL Times of London
Cmmnt on Nixon resignation 8-9, 227C2

FINCH, Robert H.
Testifies at Mitchell, Stans trial 4-9, 69E1

FINDLEY, Rep. Paul (R, Ill.)
Abandons censure plan 8-5, 231F3

FIRESTONE, Leonard
Ervin panel rpt cites contribution 7-13, 188D3

FIRST Interoceanic Corp.
Andreas acquitted 7-12, 217C3

FIRST National Bank of East Chicago
Riley pleads no contest on illegal contribution 5-8, 214G1

FIRST Savings and Loan Association (San Angelo, Tex.)
Jacobsen indicted 2-6, 40E2

FISH Jr., Rep. Hamilton (R, N.Y.)
Panel warns Nixon on non-compliance 5-30, 151C1
3 impeachment articles voted 7-30, 208G3

FISHER, Max M.
Testimony barred at Mitchell, Stans trial 4-9, 69B1

FITZSIMMONS, Frank
Hoffa sues to seek office 3-13, 44C1
Cmmnts on Ford 8-9, 226E1

FLANIGAN, Peter M.
Cited in Nixon transcripts 4-30, 115E2
Jud com rpts on ambassadorships 7-16, 196D2
Cited in Nixon transcripts 8-5, 230B2

FLEMING, Peter E.
Defends Mitchell in Vesco case trial 3-4, 63F3

FLORIDA
Nixon heckled in Miami 2-14, 25F3
2 indicted in Gurney fund case 2-21, 3-19, 41B1
Key Biscayne tax write-off rptd 3-12, 90E2
U.S. aid to Nixon estates put at $17 million 3-21, 90C3–91C1
Cong staff rpt says Nixon owes tax on home improvements 4-3, 91B3, 92B2, E2, 93D1, E1, G1, 94A2
Gurney indicted for campaign violations 4-26, 132E3–G3
House unit rpts on Nixon homes 5-14, 95D3
Gurney indictment dismissed 5-17, 135G3–B2
Gurney indicted for bribery 7-10, 217B1–B2
Nixon house improvements questioned by Ervin panel 7-13, 96G2
Ervin panel rpt cites Key Biscayne improvements 7-13, 190B3–C3, 191G2–B3
Doar's impeachment brief cites Key Biscayne 7-19, 200B3
Gurney quits primary 7-23, 218D1
Jud com tax evidence cites Key Biscayne 7-26, 206D3
Impeachment article on Key Biscayne issue loses 7-30, 207D3, 208C3–D3, 210E2–C3

FLOWERS, Rep. Walter (D, Ala.)
Misses opening hearing 5-9, 141D1
Dissents on witness vote 6-24, 174F2
Says probe fair 7-21, 210E3
3 impeachment articles voted 7-30, 208F1, 209F1, B3, 210F1, D2
Cmmnts on Nixon pardon 9-9, 240G3
Votes against 3rd impeachment article—342

FONG, Sen. Hiram (R, Hawaii)
Reinecke found guilty 7-27, 218A2–C2

FORD, Gerald Rudolph
Hints Ervin com tapes compromise 1-6, 11D2
Scores anti-Nixon drive 1-15, 14A1
Cong: viable Nixon successor 1-15, 1-18–1-22, 16A1, C2, F2, D3
'72 campaign gifts rptd 1-31, 39C2
Says secret data clears Nixon 1-22, 18E1–B2
Bars Dean data review 1-25, 22D2
NYC Bar rejcts impeachmt view 1-26, 20B3
Prosecutn backs Dean evidence 1-31, 22F1

Dean evidence dispute continues 2-3–2-7, 24B1
Gallup: preferred to Nixon 2-4, 23F3
Dem wins Pa House seat 2-5, 24D2
On Nixon list for '76 2-6, 23G1
Ct asks Dean dispute curbed; Ford reaffirms chrgs 2-15, 27F2
Dem wins House seat 2-18, reactn 2-19, 28A2
Talks to Nixon loyalists 2-22, 30D1
Aids Ohio Cong candidate 2-20, 30E1
Nixon on seat loss 2-25, 30C3
Says sealed jury rpt should be given to Judiciary Comm. 3-2, 55D3
Doubts any future 'bombshells' 3-8, 56A1
Says evidence doesn't link Nixon to cover-up 3-11, 55F3
Comments on consequences of holding back tapes 3-12, 55E3
Comments on Nixon's role in payoffs 3-12, 57G3–58B1
Defends Nixon 3-15, 78G3
Says GOP must work to avoid disaster 3-23, 78E3
Blasts CREEP 3-30, 81C3–F3
Warns on effect of defiance on impeachment vote 4-2, 82E1
Possible Cabinet decisions rptd 4-13, 86A1–D1
Concedes Watergate effect in elections 4-17, 86C2
Addresses Calif GOP 4-20, 86D3–F3
Backs transcript release 4-29, 103B3
Says Dean's credibility eroded by Mitchell, Stans acquittal 4-29, 71B3
Nixon transcript cites 4-30, 104B2–C2
Backs Nixon despite transcripts 5-3, 5-9, 139F1–A2
Hasty return to DC sparks resignation rumors 5-10, 141A3
Meets privately with Nixon 5-10, 141B1
Speaks at Texas A & M 5-11, 141E1
Urges GOP prevent Dem victory 5-17, 145D1
Urges tape compromise 5-22, 146F2
Differs with Nixon on tapes 5-22–5-26, 148F2–G3
Professes faith in U.S. morals 5-29, 153B2
N.H. paper calls 'jerk' 5-31, 153C2
Defends Nixon in cross-country travels 6-8–6-30, 166D1–B2
Backs Kissinger on wiretap charges 6-12, 162D2
Window shatters on Dallas visit 7-6, 184D3
Says evidence clears Nixon 7-13, 184B3–D3
Discloses hearing tapes 7-18, 201G1–C2
Defends Nixon again 7-25, 7-27, 211F1–B2
Sees trend toward impeachment 8-3, 230F2, 231G3–232A1
Proxmire, Meany say could handle economy better 8-4, 8-5, 212D2–D3
Reacts to new cover-up revelations 8-5, 232D3–233C1
Meets with Nixon 8-6, 232E1
Meets again with Nixon 8-8, 232F2
TerHorst dismisses pardon idea 8-9, 233D2
Becomes President upon Nixon's resignation 8-9–8-10, 223C1–227C3

Doar cites in impeachment brief 7-19, 200D2
Nixon releases transcripts on cover-up role 8-5, 228D1–F3, 229A2–C2, 230A1–D1

GREEN, Judge June
Bars split donation deductions 6-7, 214E3–215A1

GREENE, Judge Harold H.
Nixon bars LA trial role 2-26, 32B2

GREENSBURG (Pa.) Tribune-Review
Urges impeachment 5-14, 143C1

GREGORY, Tom
Ervin panel rpts on campaign abuses 7-13, 192F3

GRIFFIN, Sen. Robert P. (R, Mich)
Attends meeting with St. Clair 3-19, 79F2
Comments on Buckley rsgntn plea 3-20, 77B2
Meets with Burch 4-9, 85B3
Opposes Nixon campaign foray 4-10, 84G2
Calls for Nixon's resignation 8-5, 230G2–B3, 232B1
Cmmnts on Nixon pardon 9-9, 240E3
Calls for Nixon resignation—363, 365, 370, 372

GRIFFIN, William E.
Rptdly returned $ to Hughes agent 4-11, 132D3

GRISWOLD, Erwin N.
Nixon issues ITT paper 1-8; rebuts 1-9, 36F1, F3

GROOT, James L.
Named in Gurney fund suit 3-19, 41E1
Indicted with Gurney 7-10, 217E1

GROSS, Nelson G.
Found guilty of tax fraud, perjury 3-29, 129C3

GUBSER, Rep. Charles S. (R, Calif.)
Not to seek reelectn 1-28, 28A1

GUENTHER, George C.
Ervin rpt cites election impact on job safety 7-13, 186D3–G3

GULF Oil Co.
Nixon campaign gift cited 1-1, 35D1
'72 Cong donatns rptd 1-31, 39B2
Rpts Wild resignatn 3-21, 43G3
Stockholders sue for damages 3-27, 214D2
Ervin panel cites illegal contribution 7-13, 187D2, 190E2

GULF Resources and Chemical Corp.
Ervin panel cites illegal contribution 7-13, 187D3

GURNEY, Sen. Edward J. (R, Fla.)
Vs more Ervin com probes 2-19, 27B3
2 sentenced in fund case 2-21, 3-19, 41B1
Questions cited in cover-up indictments 3-1, 52G3
Indicted for campaign violations 4-26, 132E3–G3
Fla indictment dismissed 5-17, 135G1–B2
Priestes released 7-2, 217A1
Indicted on bribery charges 7-10, 217B1–B2
Opposes permanent special prosecutor 7-13, 185E2
Quits Fla senate primary 7-23, 218D1
Only sure Nixon vote in impeachment trial—356

H

HAIG Jr., Alexander Meigs
Nixon in semi-seclusion 1-9, 13D1

Experts rpt multiple tape erasures 1-15, 14D3; 1-17, 17B3
Rptdly resisted blackmail on NSC scandal 1-25, 158B3
Urges Nixon end ex-aides links 2-1, 23A3
Dean evidence dispute continues 2-4, 24F1
Disputes tape copying rpt 2-17, 27B1
Backs Nixon on transcripts 5-5, 139G3
Rejects resignation rumors 5-10, 141F2
Says Nixon won't be pressured out 5-11, 142B2
Says Nixon in command on foreign policiy 5-23, 154E1
Describes Administration's progress 6-3, 153A3
Kissinger threatens to quit over wiretap charges 6-11, 161C3, 162B3–C3
Role on 'security' taps cited 6-20, 163D2
Jud com evidence on Cox cites 7-20, 198G2–B3
Rptdly complained about Cox probe of San Clemente 7-20, 97B1
Cited in Jud com evidence on tape review 7-20, 198G3–199A1
Says impeachment uncertain 7-28, 210G3
Testifies on Kissinger's wiretap role 7-30, 163F3
Summoned to Camp David 8-4, 232D1
Nixon releases key cover-up transcripts 8-5, 229D1–F1
Rptdly urging resignation 8-7, 232F2
Meets with Ford 8-7, 233A1
Stays on with Ford as Nixon quits 8-9, 225A2
Will stay on 'for duration' 8-14, 234F2
Theory on tape gap—257
Sees impeachment possible—344

HALDEMAN, H(arry) R(obbins) (Bob)
Fielding quits White House post 1-11, 13A2
Experts rpt tape erasures 1-15, 14B3
Malek admits politicizatn progrm 1-15, 37D3
Grand jury to probe tape gap; Bull testifies 1-18, 17F1, B2–C3
Close Nixon links rptd 2-1, 2-4, 23F2, D3
Colson AMPI memo rptd 2-9, 45A2
Tape erasure debated 2-17–2-18, 27E1
Kalmbach pleads guilty 2-25, 41D3
Indicted for cover-up 3-1, 47E1–54D3
Nixon warns against prejudging 3-15, 73E3
Nixon rclls comments on Hunt payoff 3-19, 75B1
Atty argues jury rpt prejudicial 3-21, 76B2, 76A3
LA Times rpts contents of 3-21-73 tape 3-21, 79C2–E2
Proclaims Nixon's innocence 4-2, 82C2–F2
Chapin testifies on okay of dirty tricks, 4-5, 83E3
More tapes of conversations subpoened 4-11, 85B1–C1, 85C3–E3
New subpoena issued for tapes of talks with Nixon 4-18, 86E2
Mentioned in Stans testimony 4-19, 70E3
Colson dscrbs meeting in sworn affadavit 4-29, 88B1

Tape transcripts publshd 4-30, 100D1–126G3
Dean says transcript of meeting has deletions on IRS 5-2, 145C1–EI
Role cited as panel opens hearings 5-10, 141B2
Com studies cover-up evidence 5-21, 5-22, 147D3–E3
Tape on IRS misuse sought 5-28, 149D2, G2–B3
Sirica rjts panel's tape plea 5-30, 152C1
Experts report on gap in tape 6-4, 155C1
Cited re 'responsiveness' plan 6-7, 136B3
Seeks access to White House files 6-12, 167B2
Dixon memo on stonewalling leaked 6-12, 168G1
Rptdly instigated NSC taps 6-20, 163C2
Cited as potential panel witness 6-24, 174D2–F2
Refuses to give panel testimony 7-2, 181D3
Tapes case heard by high ct 7-8, 179D1
Discrepancies in transcripts rptd 7-9, 181D1
Cited in impeachment evidence 7-11, 183A3–184A1
Ervin panel rpt cites campaign abuses 7-13, 189G2, 170D3
Jud com releases evidence on IRS misuse 7-16, 195G3–196D1
Jud com rpts on ambassadorships 7-16, 196A2–D2
St. Clair defense brief cites 7-18, 199D1–G3
Doar cites in impeachment brief 7-19, 200C2
Jud com evidence on tape review cites 7-20, 199A1–C1
Role in White House rptd 7-24, 199E1–A2
Colson testimony cites 7-26, 206G3–207B1
Cited in Reinecke case 7-27, 218E2
Nixon surrenders taped conversations 7-30, 211B3
Cited in transcripts detailing Nixon cover-up role 8-5, 228B1–230D2
Tapes rptd missing 8-9, 233F3
Trial delayed 8-22, 237C1
Pardon request rptd 9-12, 241D3
Sirica rjts delay, dismissal 9-12, 242B2–C3
Panel rpts on tape gap—252-255
Indicted—270–273
Effect on trial of Nixon pardon—388

HALL, Gov. David (D, Okla.)
AMPI campaign aid rptd 3-24, 45A1

HALL, Leonard
Testifies at Mitchell, Stans trial 3-19, 66C1

HALL, Paul
Vs Nixon impeachmt call 2-18, 28F2

HALPERIN, Morton H.
Data on wiretaps leaked from House Judiciary Com 6-4–6-6, 161D2–E2
Impeachment panel probes taps 6-4–6-6, 155E3
Kissinger threatens to quit over wiretap charges 6-11, 161D3–E3
Papers from lawsuit go to Senate panel 6-14, 163F1–B2
Jud com rpts on wirtaps 7-18, 196E3

HAMMOND, Lawrence A.
Rptdly quit Jaworski staff over ITT 5-30, 136B1

HAND, Lloyd
Confirms Maheu on Hughes contribution to Humphrey 4-3, 130B3

HARDIN, Clifford D.
Nixon milk fund paper disputes 1-8, 36F2
Jud com evidence on milk fund cites 7-19, 197G3–198G1

HARLOW, Bryce N.
Notes end to Operatn Candor 1-9, 35F1
Disputes Mills on taxes 3-11, 90F1
Asks tighter relevance in probe 3-12, 61E2
Suggests tape compromise 3-21, 78E2
Plays down fishing expedition chrgs 3-26, 80F2

HARMONY, Sally
Hughes blank checks rptd 1-9, 38B2

HARRINGTON, Rep. Michael (D, Mass.)
Rsltn to probe Mideast alert defeated 4-9, 84D1–F1

HARRIS, Marshall
Gurney indictment dismissed 5-17, 135B2

HARRIS Poll—See POLLS

HARRISON, Marion
Role in campaign $ milk deal rptd 5-2, 133G2

HART, Judge George L.
Succeeds Sirica as chief judge 3-18, 76C3
Denounces leak in Reinecke case 4-3, 130E1
Dismisses Jacobsen indictment 5-3, 134D2–F2
Orders Stans files on contributions surrendered 5-24, 136D1–B2
Extends grand jury term 5-31, 165F2
Gives Kleindienst suspended sentence 6-7, 165F2–E3
Orders Nixon to give up Stans papers 7-25, 206C2–E2
Fines AMPI $35,000 8-1, 220F3–221E1
Jacobsen pleads guilty 8-7, 220B3
Orders Rebozo to surrender rcds 8-22, 236D3–237B1
Suspends Kleindienst sentence—329

HART 3rd, Milledge A.
Cited in Ervin panel probe 8-1, 220–D1

HART, Peter D.
Warns dems on over-optimism 4-22, 87C1

HART, Sen. Philip A. (D, Mich.)
Attacks Nixon on privacy 3-2, 160E3–G3
Criticizes Silbert's role in original Watergate probe 4-23–4-24, 71E3
Questions at Silbert hearings 4-23–4-30, 173A1–C1
Silbert defends Watergate probe 4-24, 132A2
Cmmnts on Nixon pardon 9-8, 240F2
Asks Jaworski for full Nixon rpt 9-11, 242C1–B2

HARTKE, Sen. Vance (D, Ind.)
Riley pleads no contest 5-8, 214A2
Campaign contributions cited by Ervin panel 7-13, 188E1

HARTFORD Fire Insurance Co.—See under INTERNATIONAL Telephone & Telegraph

I

Protests White House obstruction to senate 5-20, 146D1–C2

Richardson compares to Cox 5-20, 146C2–F2

Seeks tape on misuse of IRS 5-28, 149C2–C3

Says no evidence of guilt by ITT execs 5-30, 135E3–136B1

Sup Ct agrees to prompt hearing on tapes 5-31, 152D1–B3

Hart grants grand jury extension 5-31, 165F2

Nixon admits jury named him 6-6, 165C1–D2

Gets access to IRS tape 6-7, 166A1–Cl

Nixon challenges jury citation 6-11, 167E1

Supreme Ct widens case 6-15, 169D1–D2

Defends plea bargaining 6-18, 170F2–F3

Cited in impeachment hearings 6-21, 173G3

Recommends Silbert 6-26, 173G2

Presents tapes case to Supreme Ct 7-8, 178G3–179G1, E3, 180D1

Supreme Ct upholds on tapes 7-24, 201D2–206B2

Won't take part in Connally case 7-29, 219D1

Nixon surrenders 20 tapes to Sirica 7-30, 211C3–F3

Nixon releases transcripts on cover-up role 8-5, 228F1

Says no agreement on Nixon immunity 8-8, 233C1–E1

Tapes rptd missing 8-9, 233D3

No decision on Nixon prosecution 8-13, 234A3–B3

Declines comment on tape custody 8-14, 234F3–235A1

Cover-up trial delayed 8-22, 237C1

Ford cites at press conference 8-28, 237D2

Nixon pardon announced 9-8, 239B2–B3, 240C1

Lacovara quits to protest pardon 9-9, 241G3–242B2

Gesell criticizes for Dean rmk—267

Says needed evidence not forthcoming—266–267

Subpoena issued for 64 tapes—296

Nixon fights tapes subpoenas—320–327

Advised grand jury against Nixon indictment—325, 326

Argues against exec privilege—334–336

Upheld by Supreme Ct—349–353

Nixon post-resignation legal status—377, 382–386

Position after Nixon pardon—388

JENNER Jr., Albert E.

Named House com GOP counsel 1-7, 13A1

Says Nixon accountable for aides 1-13, 13C3

Nixon accountability clarified 1-28, com subpoena power voted 1-31, 21D3, 22B1

Sees St Clair 2-12, briefs com 2-14, 29F2–A3

Impeachmt study issued 2-21, 29A1

Opposes delay in probe 3-6, 55D1

Urges more time for Nixon's response 3-7, 61B1

Position on St. Clair role in hearings 3-21, 78G1

To have direct access to evidence 3-26, 80B3

Rpts on St. Clair role in hearings 4-4, 83F1

Opposes taking case to cts 5-30, 151A2

Says 'cannot accept' transcripts 5-23, 151F2

Backs Doar on impeachment 7-19, 200D1

Burch attacks 7-20, 201G1

Impartiality questioned—346

JENNINGS, W. Patrick

Agrees to end laundering 5-20, 216F2

JEWS

Buzhardt denies Nixon made ethnic slurs 5-12, 143F2–A3

Nixon cmmnts revealed 8-5, 230F3

JOHNSON, Joseph

Ervin panel rpt cites campaign abuses 7-13, 190E2

JOHNSON, Lyndon Baines (1908–73)

Jacobsen indicted 2-21, 40D2

Nixon cites tax advice 2-25, 31E1

AMPI campaign gifts rptd 3-14, 44F1, F2, C3

Milk fund links rptd 5-7, 5-9, 134B1–F1

Home cost put at $5.9 million 5-24, 95E3

Cited in impeachment debate 7-30, 209E1, 210D2

Cited in Ervin probe of fund abuses 8-1, 220B2

JOINT Chiefs of Staff (JCS)—See NATIONAL Security Council

JOINT Committee on Internal Revenue Taxation—See TAXES, INTERNAL Revenue Service

JONES, Henry H.

Cross-examines witnesses for Ehrlichman 7-8, 182F2

JONES, Rep. James R. (D, Okla.)

AMPI rpt cites 3-26, 44C3

Cited in Ervin fund probe 8-1, 220A2–C2

JONES, Kirby

AMPI rpt cites 3-26, 44B3

JONES, Judge Shirley P.

Urges Agnew disbarmt 1-14, 37C2

JONES, Thomas V.

Pleads guilty on illegal contributions 5-1, 133D1–G1

Ervin panel cites illegal contributions 7-13, 187B3–C3

JONES, Judge William B.

Postpones Nader suit on milk 5-14, 214

JORDAN, Rep. Barbara (D, Tex.)

3 impeachment articles voted 7-30, 208F3

JORDAN, Vernon

Cmmnts on Ford 8-9, 226D2

JUDD, Gordon S.

Backs Maheu testimony on Hughes gift to Humphrey 4-3, 130C3

JUDICIARY Committee, U.S. House—See IMPEACHMENT

JUSTICE, U.S. Department of

Saxbe backs trust enforcemt, oil probe 1-3, 12F1

Saxbe sworn atty gen 1-4, 12C1

Nixon issues ITT paper 1-8, 36D1; for subsequent developments, see INTERNATIONAL Telephone & Telegraph under 'I'

Saxbe bars impeachmt role 1-11, 13B3

Judge holds anti-war wiretaps must be disclosed 1-11, 158D1

Demands for secret press phone rcds rptd 2-1, 159C3

Colson AMPI trust suit memo rptd 2-9, 45A2; for subsequent developments, see ASSOCIATED Milk Producers under 'A'

Issues impeachmt study 2-22, 2-27, 33E2

Attempt to corrupt cited in indictments 3-1, 49D2, F3, 50B1, E1, 51E1, 53B1

Gov. Ford charges harassment 3-7, 58B2

Nixon asks campaign reforms 3-8, 43B2

Exprts warn against 'partisan climate' 3-20, 77F3–78A1

Files brief opposing Ervin com tape suit 3-27, 80C3–81A1

Com subpoenas tapes of Petersen, Kleindienst talks with Nixon 4-11, 85B1, 85F3

Chisholm probe closed 4-23, 214F1

Silbert confirmation hearings 4-23–6-26, 172G3–173G2

Cited in Nixon tape transcripts 4-30, 100F1, 103E3, 104B1, 107B1, 109G1, D2, 112B2, 113C3, 114B3, 115B2, 118A1–C1, F1, 122C2

St. Clair rjts request for ITT material 5-22, 147A2

Ervin staff link Hughes, Mitchell 6-25, 215B3–216B1

Weicker urges elected atty general 6-29, 176A1

Ervin panel urges Hatch Act coverage 7-13, 185C2, 189C1, G2, 193G1–A2, E3

Jud com evidence on ITT released 7-19, 197C1–B3

Reinecke found guilty 7-27, 218D2

Misuse cited in impeachment article 7-30, 208D1–E1, E2, 210A1

AMPI accepts consent decree 8-13, 221E3–222A1

Inouye urges independence 8-15, 235D1

K

KALMBACH, Demarco, Knapp & Chillingworth

Kalmbach rpts resignatn 2-26, 41F2

KALMBACH, Herbert W.

Nixon milk fund paper cites 1-8, 36B1

Pleads guilty 2-25, quits law firm 2-26, 31D2, 41B2–42C1

Role in cover-up cited in indictments 3-1, 47D3–E3, 49G1, 50B2, E2, 52F1, 53C3–G3

AMPI secret gifts, trust suit deal rptd 3-6–3-14, 3-26, 44D2, A3, 45D1

Testifies Rebozo gave $ to Nixon aides, family 3-21, 78G2–A3

Disputes Rebozo on Hughes 3-21, 129C1–C3

Mentioned in testimony at Mitchell, Stans trial 3-27, 66G3

Cited by DeMarco in interview on Nixon taxes 4-5, 94C1

Testimony on Rebozo confirmed by Ebner 4-16, 132A3

Nixon Watergate tape transcripts cite 4-30, 105E1–F1, G2, 106G2–C3, 107D2, B3, 108C2, F3, 112H2, 113E2, 120A1, E1, C2, G3, 121B1, 123C3

Jones pleads guilty 5-1, 133G1

Cited in AMPI suit 5-4, 214A1, C1

Testimony on milk fund rptd 5-6, 133D3–F3

Sentenced to 6–18 mths 6-17, 170A1–D1

Panel selects as witness 6-24, 174D2

Common Cause suit cites 6-27, 216C2

Suspended from bar 7-1, 178B1

Rebozo plea against Ervin panel dismissed 7-2, 216G3

Discrepancies in transcripts noted 7-9, 180C3

Cited in impeachment evidence 7-11, 183G3–184A1

Cited in Strachan memo rpt 7-11, 217D2

Nelson cites, pleads guilty 7-31, 219F1

Ervin panel cites campaign abuses 7-13, 187B3, 188G1, C2, B3–C3, 189B2, G2, 190E3, 191F1–G1, 192G3, 194B3

Jud com rpts on ambassadorships 7-16, 196A2–C2

Testifies at impeachment probe 7-17, 196E2–F2

Jud com milk fund evidence cites 7-19, 198E2

Doar cites in impeachment brief 7-19, 200B2

Jud com IRS, tax evidence cites 7-26, 206A3

Fined and sentenced to jail—328, 330

KASTENMEIER, Rep. Robert William (D, Wis.)

Disputes Nixon re impeachmt 2-26, 31D3

3 impeachment articles voted 7-30, 208E3

KAY, Capt. Howard N.

Implicated in NSC spy scandal 1-11, 157G1–C2

KEELER, William K.

Resignation rptd 5-10, 214C2

KEHRLI, Bruce A.

Nixon Watergate tape transcripts cite 4-30, 104G1, 119F2, 120D2

KELLEY, Clarence M.

Testifies on Kissinger's wiretap role 7-15, 163F3

KENNA, E. Douglas

Calls for reconciliation 8-9, 226E1

KENNEDY, Sen. Edward M(oore) (D, Mass.)

Backs campaign pub financing 2-6; vs Nixon plan 3-8, 43D2, F2

Praises campaign reform bill 4-11, 131C3

Court bars defense subpoena in Mitchell, Stans trial 4-16, 69G3

Nixon Watergate tape transcript cites White House Chappaquiddick probe 4-30, 106G2–D3

Dissents on 'weak' resolution backing Jaworski 5-21, 146A1

Jud com releases evidence on IRS misuse 7-16, 196D1

Asks Jaworski for full Nixon rpt 9-11, 242C1–B2

KENNEDY, President John F. (1917–1963)

Memo on plan to link to Diem murder released 7-18, 196G3

Cited in impeachment debate 7-30, 210D2

KERNER, Otto

Supreme ct rjts appeal 6-17, 169G3

KERVICK, John A.

Fined $10,000 6-17, 129E3

KEY Biscayne—See FLORIDA

KILPATRICK, James J.

Interviews Nixon 5-16, 143D1

KISSINGER, Henry A(lfred)

Bars Nixon impeachmt 1-3, 13D1

NSC secrets rptdly passed to Pentagon 1-11, 157C1–158B1

Urges Nixon end ex-aides links 2-1, 23A3

Denies role in probe of NSC scandal 1-22, 158G1–E2

Denies role in probe again 2-6, 159D1–A2

Nixon barred NSC spy ring chrgs 2-23, 30B2

Rptdly exchanged secrets with Kissinger 3-3, 161E1–A2

Senate panel clears on NSC spying 6-26, 163F2

MOORHEAD, Rep. Carlos J. (R, Calif.)

Vs impeachmt probe resolutn 2-6, 25B1

Opposes subpoena for diaries 5-15, 144F1

3 impeachment articles voted 7-30, 208G3

MOOSE, Richard M.

Files and withdraws wiretap suit 6-12, 162G3–163A1

MORGAN, Edward P.

Hughes gift role rptd 1-16, 1-17, 38C1

Rsgns post; Nixon deed under investigation 1-18, 89D3

Study of presidential tax deductions rptd 3-12, 90E2

Cited in Congressional staff rpt on Nixon taxes 4-3, 92A1

Jud com IRS, tax evidence cites 7-26, 206A3

MORGAN, Rep. Thomas E. (D, Pa.)

Gets Kissinger data on Mideast alert 4-9, 84E1

MORRIS, Dwight L.

AMPI trust suit role rptd 3-6–3-14, 45D1

MORTON, Rogers C. B.

Sees breakdown in leadership 5-9, 139E1

On Ford transition team 8-9, 225B2

MOSBACHER, Emil

Rptdly decided Nixons exempt from gift law 5-14, 95B3

MOSS, Rep. John E. (D, Calif.)

GAP rpts Agnew guard illegal 1-29, 39F1

Agnew guard removed 2-17, 40E3

MULCAHY, John

'72 Cong donatns rptd 1-31, 39E2

Testimony barred at Mitchell, Stans trial 4-9, 69B1

MULLEN, Robert R.

Cited in rpt on CIA 7-2, 177E2–F2

MURTHA, Rep. John P. (D, Pa.)

Wins GOP House seat 2-5, 24B2

Declared official winner in Pa. House race 2-28, 56F2

Wins Pa. House seat—260

MUSKIE, Sen. Edmund S(ixtus) (D, Me.)

Rebuts Nixon milk fund paper 1-9, 36B3

Diamond Intl fined 3-7, 42E3, 43A1

Chapin cnvctd in dirty tricks case 4-5, 83F2–D3

Weicker cites Ulasewicz probe 4-8, 131C2

Questions Kissinger on Halperin wiretap 6-7, 161E3

Ervin panel cites campaign abuses 7-13, 187D2, E2, 188E1

Milk contribution cited 7-31, 219B2

Milk fund gift cited 8-1, 221D1

Cmmnts on Nixon pardon 9-8, 240D2

N

NADER, Ralph

Attys dispute Nixon milk fund paper 1-11, 36B3

Ct bars ITT probe bid 1-14, 37EI

Colson milk suit memo rptd 2-9, 45C2

Ct bars ITT merger suit 2-26, 42B3

Rpt hits Mills on dairy $ 4-1, 134B2

Suit delayed 5-14, 214D1

NATIONAL Academy of Public Administration

Panel rpts to Ervin com 3-20, 77F2–78C1

NATIONAL Aeronautics & Space Administration (NASA)

Nixon visits Houston center 3-20, 75B2

NATIONAL Archives

Nixon papers deed rptdly backdated 1-25, 89F2–F3

Nixon papers deed rptdly under Congressional scrutiny 3-8, 90B3

Nixon papers found not tax deductible 4-3, 92B1, 93E1, B3, 94C2

Nixon gift held legally binding 4-12, 95C1

Brown says back-dating on deed 'clear' 6-17, 96G3

DeMarco rsgns notary commission over deed 6-17, 171A3–B3

Jud com releases evidence on Nixon gift 7-26, 206G2–C3

Nixon rptdly deferred access to papers 8-18, 235C2–E2

NATIONAL Association of Broadcasters (NAB)

Nixon speaks at convention 3-19, 74D2–75A2

NATIONAL Citizens' Committee for Fairness to the Presidency—See also **KORFF, Rabbi Baruch**

Nixon hosts supporters 2-22, 30C1

NATIONAL Committee for an Effective Congress

Sees Nixon impeachmt 1-19, 16D3

NATIONAL Education Association

Lobby's fund rpt higher 7-10, 217B3

NATIONAL Governors Conference

Watergate theme of talks 6-5, 155D2–C3

NATIONAL Hispanic Finance Committee

Activities cited in Ervin panel rpt 7-13, 187D3

NATIONAL Institutes of Health (NIH)

Politicizatn chrgd 2-15, 2-16, 40F2–C3

NATIONAL Security Council (NSC)

Secrets rptdly passed to Pentagon 1-11, 157C1–158D1

Moorer denies NSC spy charges 1-18, 158D2–G2

Kissinger denies role in spy probe 1-22, 158G1–D2

Moorer rptdly sought Radford court-martial 2-6, 159B1–B2

Radford says he sent secrets to Moorer 2-8, 159C2–E2

Radford, Welander conflict in testimony 2-21, 22, 159F3–160D2

MacDonald admits rcving secrets 2-22, 160G2–C3

Nixon rptdly barred prosecutions 2-23, 160D2–F2

Nixon barred spy ring chrgs 2-23, 30A2

Jaworski spy ring probe rptd 2-26, 30B2

Buzhardt testifies on spy scandal 3-7, 161A1–E1

Nixon Watergate tape transcript cites 4-30, 117B2

Kissinger threatens to quit over wiretap charges 6-11, 161G2–162E3

Lake, Moose sue Kissinger over wiretaps 6-12, 162G3–163B1

Moorer rptdly cleared by Senate panel 6-26, 163F2

Jud com rpts on wiretaps 7-18, 196E3

NATIONAL Urban League

Jordan cmmnts on Ford 8-9, 226D2

NELSON, Sen. Gaylord (D, Wis.)

Cmmnts on Nixon pardon 9-9, 240F3

NELSON, Harold S.

AMPI trust suit role rptd 3-6–3-14, 45F1

AMPI secret gifts rptd 3-26, pleads not guilty 3-27, 44C2–A3

Role in campaign $ milk deal rptd 5-2, 133G2–134E1

Ervin rpt cites campaign abuses 7-13, 188G3, 189B2

Testimony before Ervin panel rptd 7-17, 219D3–220A1

Pleads guilty 7-31, 219E1–C3

Jones cites 8-1, 220C2

NELSON, Jack

Rpts Rodino cmmnt on Dem votes 6-28, 176D2

NETHERLANDS

Reaction to Nixon resignation 8-9, 227F2

NEW Jersey

Gross found guilty of tax fraud, perjury 3-29, 129C3

NEWMAN, Ralph

Jud com tax evidence cites 7-26, 206A3

NEW Republic (Magazine)

Rpts Ford's Cabinet ideas 4-13, 86AI–D1

NEW York Stock Exchange (NYSE)

ITT trading halted 3-6, 42F2

NEW York Times

IRS returns phone rcds 2-13, 159F2–E3

Rpts Nixon studied previous presidents' tax deductions 3-12, 90C2–C3

Nixon tape transcripts cite 4-30, 105G1, 126E1, F1

Mitchell-Stans trial coverage criticized—316

NEW York Yankees—See **STEINBRENNER, George**

NITZE, Paul H.

Quits, cites Watergate 6-14, 171G3–172D1

NIXON, F. Donald

Hughes gift role cited 1-16, 1-17, 38E1

Surveillance order rptd 2-4, 23G3, 39F2–C3

Vesco links cited at Mitchell, Stans trial 3-4–4-15, 64G1, 64D3, 65A1, 66B1, 67B3, 69G3

Kalmbach testifies on Hughes $ 3-21, 78A3, 129C1–C2

Testifies at Mitchell, Stans trial 4-2, 68F1–F2

Ervin unit to get tax data 4-24, 132B2–D3

Misuse of campaign funds cited 7-13, 191G1, F3

NIXON Jr., Donald F.

Vesco links cited at Mitchell, Stans trial 3-4–4-15, 65A1, 65E2, 66C2, 68G1–B2, 69B3

Weicker cites Ulasewicz probe 4-8, 131C2

NIXON, Edward C.

Payment by foundation probed 1-18, 89E2

Vesco links cited at Mitchell, Stans trial 3-4–3-27, 64G1, 64E2, 66B3

Kalmbach testifies on Hughes $ 3-21, 78A3, 129C1

Testifies at Mitchell, Stans trial 4-5, 68C3–69A1

Misuse of campaign funds cited 7-13, 191G1

NIXON, Mrs. Patricia

Says Pres won't quit 5-10, 141F3

Rcvd gifts from Saudis 5-13, 5-14, 95B2–C3

Attends Nixon rally 6-9, 166G2

Ervin panel says earrings bought with Rebozo funds 7-13, 96G2

Ervin panel rpt cites misuse of campaign funds 7-13, 190B3, 191A2–F2

With husband at Camp David 8-3, 232C1

Rebozo rcds ordered surrendered 8-22, 237A1

NIXON, President Richard Milhous—See also **specific subjects (e.g. IMPEACHMENT)**

January

In semi-seclusn 12-26-73–1-13; celebrates 61st b'day 1-9, 13B1, F3

Calif tax returns to be made public 1-2, 89G1

IRS re-examining returns 1-2, 89C1–G1

Rejects Ervin com tape subpoenas 1-4; compromise hinted 1-6, 1-9, 11B1–F2

Revamps legal team 1-4, 1-8, 11F3

Issues ITT, milk fund papers 1-8, 35E1–36C2

Rcvd Young rpt on military spies in NSC 1-11, 157D1, G2–D3

Physical exam rpt good 1-14, 13G3

Names Cole domestic aide 1-16, 16B1

Hughes aide mtgs rptd 1-16, 1-17, 1-25, 38A1, A3

Asks Ervin tape suit dismissal 1-17, 16G1

Meets 18 GOP reps, vows impeachmt fight 1-22, 19A1

Papers deed rptdly backdated 1-25, 89F2–F3

Names Clawson communicatn dir 1-30, 21E1

Bars resignatn; qualifies Jaworski, House com cooperatn 1-30, 21A2, A3

Addresses Congress on privacy 1-30, 158G3–159B1

At Natl Prayer Breakfast 1-31, 23E1

February

Reliance on ex-aides rptd 2-1, 23F2

Meets GOP, names 4 for '76 2-6, 23F1, 25D1

Explains tape privilege claim 2-6, 24E2

Tape of conversations with Dean obtained for Mitchell, Stans trial 2-8, 63D2

At Lincoln Day rite 2-12, 23A2

At Longworth birthday fete 2-12, 23C2

Physical exam rpt excellent 2-13, 23D2

Appears in Miami 2-14, Ala 2-18, 25F3–26D1

Hosts backers 2-22, 30B1

Rptdly barred NSC prosecutions 2-23, 30A2, 160D2–F2

Annces privacy panel 2-23, 160D3–G3

Sees no impeachmt, reaffirms House com cooperatn 2-25, 30C2, D2, 41G1

Discounts electn issue, bars resignatn 2-25, 30B3

Clarifies Calif tax claims 2-25, 31A1

Lauds Agnew service 2-25, 31B2, 41G1–B2

Declines grand jury testimony 2-25, 30D2, 32E1

Denies amb posts for sale 2-25, 41A3

Issues ITT, milk fund papers—245–251

Impeachment, resignation issue debated—250, 259, 261, 279–281, 284, 289, 300, 302–306

Ford attacks critics—253

Ford, Scott say evidence will clear—254, 257

Subpoenaed for Ehrlichman trial—256

Panel says not responsible for acts of subordinates—259

Panel gets probe go ahead from House—260–261

Panel says crime not necessary for impeachment—263–265

Jaworski says evidence not provided—266–267

Speaks in Huntsville—266

Controversy over 'it would be wrong' statement—270–273

To surrender some tapes, documents—270–273

Grand jury rpts on—273, 323–327

Buckley calls for resignation—279–281

Alleged to block prosecution, House probe—282, 283

St. Clair seeks role in probe—282–284

St. Clair wants definition of offense—282, 283

To pay $465,000 tax debt—285–289

Impeachment panel subpoenas tapes—290–293

Campaigns in Michigan—293

Rptdly misused IRS—292

Jaworski subpoenas 64 items—¹296

Panel extends tape subpoena—296

Releases edited tape transcripts—299–312

Refuses to produce more tapes—311

Allegedly threatened Post—317

Fights tape subpoenas—320, 322, 324–327

Refusal to comply on tapes seen as impeachable—326, 327

Aides attack panel on leaks—332

Jud Com votes 3 impeachment articles—342–347

Plan to speed House vote—354, 355, 372

GOP leaders call for resignation—356, 363, 364, 365, 368, 369, 372

Discloses cover-up role—356–374, 376

Papers urge resignation—361–369

Resigns presidency—361–369, 375–381

Foreign policy successes cited—375, 377–379, 381, 382

Post-resignation legal status—377, 382–385

Ford grants full pardon—385–389

NORTH Atlantic Treaty Organization (NATO)
French rptd wary of Nixon meeting 6-14, 169D3–G3
French leaders shun Nixon 6-26, 173G2–C3

NORTHROP, John B.
Discovers transcript error 5-13, 143D3

NORTHROP Corporation
Execs plead guilty on illegal contributions 5-1, 133D1–G1
Allen rptdly resigned 5-10, 214C2
Ervin panel cites illegal contribution 7-13, 187A3–B3

NORTH Vietnam
Nixon bombing rmrks rptd 6-29, 175G2–D3
Reaction to Nixon resignation 8-9, 227C1

NOVA, Barry
Cites illegal gift to Humphrey 8-2, 220F1

NUNN, Lee
Milk funds rptd laundered 2-15, 40E1

NUNN, Louis
Ervin panel rpt cites campaign abuses 7-13, 191A1–B1

O

O'BRIEN, Lawrence
Dean says transcripts omit plan for IRS audit 5-2, 145D1
Tape on plan to use IRS against sought 5-28, 149C2–C3
Ervin panel rpts on IRS misuse 7-13, 191D3–G3
Jud com releases evidence of use of IRS against 7-16, 196D3–E3
Dems settle civil suit 8-9, 222A2

O'BRIEN, Paul L.
Role in cover-up cited in indictments 3-1, 50F3
Nixon Watergate tape transcripts cite 4-30, 103E2, 104E2, 109F3–G3, 110A1–B1, 119F3
Hunt comments on payoff role 5-10, 143B2
Cited as potential panel witness 6-24, 174E2–F2
Testifies before Rodino panel 7-3, 181E3

OCCIDENTAL Petroleum Co.
Cited in Common Cause suit 6-28, 216B2

O'CONNOR, James
Ervin panel rpt cites campaign abuses 7-13, 191G1

OFFICE of Economic Opportunity (OEO)
Dismantling OEO rptd dropped by impeachment probe 3-23, 79G1

OFFICE of Management and Budget
Malek admits politicizatn 1-15, 14A2, 37C3
Exprts hit concentration of power 3-20, 77D3

OHIO
Ford aids Ohio Cong candidate 2-20, 30E1
Dem wins House seat—274

OKLAHOMA State University
Nixon addresses grads 5-11, 141F3

OLHAUSEN, William G.
Appeals McCord conviction 6-14, 169A1

OLIN Corp.
Olin '72 Cong donatns rptd 1-31, 39D2

OLIN, John M.
'72 Cong donatns rptd 1-31, 39D2

OLIVER, R. Spencer
Civil suit still pending 8-9, 222B2

OLSON, H. Everett
Penalized for GOP gift 3-29, 44A1

OMAHA World-Herald
Urges Nixon resignation 5-7, 139A3

O'NEILL Jr., Rep. Thomas P. (D, Mass.)
On tape gap rpt 1-15, 16A1
Urges Nixon resign 1-21, 16E2
Assails Nixon's attacks on congress 3-20, 80G1
On swing toward impeachment 8-5, 231C1, F3
Opposes further impeachment action 8-7, 233G2
House accepts impeachment rpt 8-20, 235C3

OSBORNE, John
Rpts Ford's Cabinet ideas 4-13, 86A1–D1

OWENS, Rep. Wayne (D, Utah)
Proposes open ITT, milk fund probes 5-30, 151D2
Dissents on witness vote 6-24, 174F2
3 impeachment articles voted 7-30, 208F3, 210G2

P

PACKARD, David
Rptdly upset by Moorer, Kissinger secrets exchange 3-3, 161G1

PACKWOOD, Sen. Robert (R, Ore.)
Cmmnts on Nixon pardon 9-9, 240F3

PAKISTAN—See NATIONAL Security Council

PARDON
TerHorst dismisses idea 8-9, 233D2
Ford comments on topic at press conference 8-28, 237F1–E2
Ford grants Nixon pardon 9-8, 237G3–242B2
Protests continue 9-9, 9-11, 241G3–242B2
Ford considers, rjts other pretrial pardons 9-10, 9-12, 241E1–G3
Ford grants Nixon full pardon—387–389

PARKER, Judge Barrington D.
Plans immediate trial for Reinecke 4-11, 131F2
Reinecke convicted 7-27, 218E2

PARKINSON, Kenneth W.
AMPI seeks Nixon com refund 1-21, 44E3
Indicted in cover-up 3-1, 47E2, 49C3, E3, 50C2, 51C1
Nixon Watergate tape transcript cites 4-30, 104F2, 109F3–G3
Sirica rjts disqualification plea 4-30, 127D1–D2
Seeks Sirica disqualification 7-9, 180F2
Petition on Sirica removal dismissed 7-25, 206C2

PAROLE, U.S. Board of
3 Watergate burglars get parole 1-7, 12B3

PARR, David L.
Pleads guilty 1-11, 37D1
Pretrial dispositn filed 1-21, 45D2
Role in campaign $ milk deal rptd 5-2, 133G2–134A2
Ervin panel rpt cites campaign abuses 7-13, 190D2
Nelson pleads guilty 7-31, 219E2–C3
Jones cites 8-1, 220C2

PASSMAN, Rep. Otto E. (D, La.)
Opposes impeachment 8-6, 231F1 231F1
Votes against impeachment rpt 8-20, 235E3

PASTORE, Sen. John O. (D, R.I.)
Rebuts Nixon campaign fund plan 3-15, 45E2

PATMAN, Rep. Wright
Nixon Watergate tape transcript cites 4-30, 104B2–D2

PAYSON, Joan Whitney
'72 Cong donatns rptd 1-31, 39E2

PEALE, Rev. Norman Vincent
Conducts White House service 3-17, 74D2

PELL, Sen. Claiborne (D, R.I.)
Sen com OKs campaign fund bill 2-6, 43F2

PELSKI, William F.
Sentenced 3-19, 41D1

PENN Colonial Insurance Corp.
Davis '72 Cong donatns rptd 1-31, 39D2

PENNINGTON, Lee R.
Cited in rpt on CIA 7-2, 177E3–178A1

PENNSYLVANIA
Murtha wins GOP House seat 2-5, 24B2
Dem wins House seat—260

PENTAGON Papers Case
Barker: US bugged Sovt emb 1-6, 12D3
AMPI seeks Nixon com refund 1-21, 44F3
Krogh sentenced, denies Nixon role 1-24, 19B1
Nixon to be called in LA trial 1-29, will decline 1-30, 21A1
Ehrlichman-Nixon break denied 2-4, 23E3
Jaworski rptd Nixon evidence bar 2-14, 26B3
Nixon bars LA trial role 2-26, 32B2
Watergate cover-up seen motivated by Fielding break-in 3-3, 56D1–F1
Six indicted for Fielding break-in 3-7, 58F2–60F3
Ellsberg affair cited in testimony on NSC spy scandal 3-7, 161A1–E1
California charges dropped in break-in case 3-13, 62C1–A3
Nixon says break-in 'stupid' and 'illegal' 3-15, 73C3
Colson submits affidavit on leaks 4-29, 88B1–C3
Nixon tape transcripts cite 4-30, 99F3, 106F3–107A1, 107F2, 110E3, 115F3, 126E3
Ehrlichman says Nixon backed break-in 4-30, 127D2–D3
Gesell dismisses DeDiego charges 5-21, 150F2
Gesell bars security defense 5-24, 150F1–E2
Nixon to withhold evidence 5-30, 149D3–150E1
Colson pleads guilty 6-3, 154B1–E3
Panel hears evidence on break-in 6-11, 167C3–D3
Ehrlichman ordered tried with others 6-14, 168C2–G3
Buchanan leak cited in Dixon memo 6-19, 171C1
Krogh released from prison 6-21, 172E1
Colson sentenced 6-21, 172F1–E2
Jud com weighs Colson statements 6-21, 174A1–D1
'Plumbers' trial begins 6-28, 174A3–175G2
Break-in cited in rpt on CIA 7-2, 177D2–D3
'Plumbers' defense rests 7-10, 182B1–183B2
Ehrlichman, others convicted 7-12, 184E1–B3
Ervin panel rpt cites finances for break-in 7-13, 189D2
Jud com rpts on Fielding break-in 7-18, 196F3
Doar's impeachment brief cites break-in 7-19, 200B3
Impeachment article cites break-in 7-30, 208D2, 209G3
Ehrlichman, others sentenced 7-31, 211G3–212C1
Jaworski's Nixon prosecution memo cites break-in 9-10, 240E1
Nixon subpoenaed to testify—256
Nixon's tape stand threatens case dismissal—322
Former Nixon aides found guilty in break-in—334–335

PERCY, Sen. Charles H. (R, Ill.)
Reaffirms '76 pres bid 2-8, 25A3
Comments on Buckley rsgntn plea 3-19, 77F1

Chronology

Sept. 4, 1971: Hunt and Liddy burglarize Ellsberg's psychiatrist's office.

*March 30, 1972: Mitchell, Magruder, Liddy and LaRue meet at Key Biscayne. Mitchell allegedly approves $250,000 plan including entry into DNC offices.

June 17, 1972: Democratic headquarters raided; 5 arrested.

*June 19, 1972: Dean speaks with Colson and Ehrlichman; decision made for Dean to take custody of contents of Hunt's safe.

June 20, 1972: Nixon, Haldeman and Ehrlichman discuss Watergate public relations offensive. Tape of meeting later subpoenaed and turned over to Sirica, but with an 18-minute gap.

*June 21, 1972: Dean meets with Gray regarding FBI's Watergate investigation.

June 22, 1972: Nixon denies White House involvement.

June 23, 1972: Nixon instructs Haldeman to tell the FBI, "Don't go any further into this case period!" Nixon says the rationale for the order could be based on the fear of compromising CIA activity. Haldeman, Ehrlichman, CIA Director Helms and Deputy Director Walters meet. Walters later warns Gray that CIA operations in Mexico might be jeopardized by FBI investigators.

*June 26 & 28, 1972: Dean meets Walters to request CIA money for Watergate conspirators.

*June 28, 1972: Dean meets Mitchell about need for support money to obtain defendants' silence.

*June 29, 1972: Stans meets with Kalmbach on raising and distributing money to Watergate defendants.

June 30, 1972: Nixon, Haldeman and Mitchell meet to discuss Watergate. Tape of conversation subpoenaed and surrendered to Sirica.

July 1, 1972: Mitchell resigns as campaign manager.

July 6, 1972: Gray tells Nixon White House staff was mortally wounding him.

Sept. 15, 1972: Nixon, Dean and Haldeman meet. Nixon compliments Dean on doing a "good job" on Watergate case. Tape subpoenaed and turned over to Sirica.

Sept. 19, 1972: Seven men plead not guilty; released on bond.

Oct. 10, 1972: Washington Post reports break-in part of larger spying and sabotage effort against Democrats.

Jan. 11, 1973: Hunt pleads guilty to all six charges against him; freed on bail.

Jan. 15, 1973: Four Watergate defendants plead guilty; deny pressure from "higher-ups."

Jan. 22, 1973: Hugh Sloan discloses espionage funds paid to Liddy approved by Mitchell and Stans.

Jan. 30, 1973: Liddy, McCord convicted.

Feb. 7, 1973: Senate votes to establish committee to probe Watergate bugging and other espionage.

Feb. 27-28, 1973: Nixon tells Dean to report directly to him on all Watergate matters. Kalmbach's role in payoffs discussed.

March 13, 1973: Dean, Haldeman and Nixon meet and, according to Dean's testimony, discuss the possibility of payoffs to Watergate defendants.

March 21, 1973: Dean meets with Nixon and tells him case may break open and that he would tell the truth to grand jury. Payoffs to Hunt discussed. Haldeman participates in part of the meeting. Later, Nixon meets with Haldeman, Ehrlichman, Ziegler and Dean, to discuss possibility of White House aides testifying before the grand jury.

March 22, 1973: Nixon meets with Haldeman, Ehrlichman, Mitchell and Dean to discuss strategy to deal with Ervin committee. Tape subpoenaed and surrendered to Sirica.

March 26, 1973: McCord asks for private meeting with Judge Sirica in letter. Watergate grand jury reconvenes.

March 27, 1973: Nixon meets with Haldeman, Ehrlichman and Ziegler. They discuss getting Mitchell to take blame for Watergate to take pressure off the White House.

April 5, 1973: Nixon withdraws Gray nomination.

April 6, 1973: Dean secretly meets with federal Watergate prosecutors with information concerning the raid and subsequent developments.

April 15, 1973: Federal investigators learn of break-in at Ellsberg's psychiatrist's office.

April 17, 1973: Nixon announces "major developments" from a "new inquiry" on Watergate; agrees to testimony by his aides with conditions.

April 30, 1973: Haldeman, Ehrlichman, Kleindienst and Dean resign. Nixon accepts responsibility, denies involvement in cover-up.

May 2, 1973: White House aide David Young resigns; Egil Krogh Jr. leaves undersecretary of transportation post. Hunt discloses CIA involved in break-in at Ellsberg's psychiatrist's office.

May 10, 1973: Nixon announces major staff reorganization. Dean charges effort to curb truth.

May 11, 1973: Charges against Ellsberg, Russo dismissed.

May 17, 1973: Senate Select Committee on Presidential Campaign Activities begins hearings.

May 18, 1973: Richardson appoints Archibald Cox special prosecutor for Watergate case.

May 22, 1973: Nixon explains White House role; concedes probable involvement of close aides in cover-up.

May 25, 1973: White House issues statement on San Clemente financing.

June 12, 1973: Sirica grants Dean, Magruder immunity for Senate testimony.

June 21, 1973: GSA reports U.S. spent $1.9 million on Nixon homes.

June 25-29, 1973: Dean implicates Nixon in cover-up during Senate testimony; submits list of "enemies."

July 10-12, 1973: Mitchell tells Ervin panel he withheld Watergate information from Nixon.

July 16, 1973: President's secret tape recording system revealed by former aide during Senate testimony.

July 23, 26, 1973: Nixon defies Ervin and Cox subpoenas on tapes.

July 24-27, 30, 1973: Ehrlichman testifies at Senate hearings; disputes Dean; defends Nixon and Ellsberg break-in.

July 30-August 1, 1973: Haldeman denies cover-up role at Senate hearings; admits refreshing memory by listening to secret tapes.

August 9, 1973: Ervin committee sues for Watergate tapes.

August 22, 1973: Nixon accepts Watergate 'responsibility'; vows not to resign.

August 29, 1973: Sirica orders Nixon to turn over tapes; Nixon refuses.

September 4, 1973: Ehrlichman, 3 others indicted in Ellsberg break-in.

*Asterisks indicate that the event was alleged in testimony and may or may not be true.